Lecture Notes in Computer Science

Edited by G. Goos and J. Hartmanis
Series: GI, Gesellschaft für Informatik e.V.

34

GI – 5. Jahrestagung

Dortmund, 8.–10. Oktober 1975

Herausgegeben im Auftrag der GI von J. Mühlbacher

Springer-Verlag
Berlin · Heidelberg · New York 1975

Editor
Prof. Dr. J. Mühlbacher
Universität Dortmund
4600 Dortmund 50
Postfach 500500
BRD

AMS Subject Classifications (1970): 68-XX, 02B10, 02C99, 02F10, 18B20, 60K30, 60K35, 90B, 94A10, 94A20, 94A25, 94A30
CR Subject Classifications (1974): 2.1, 3.7, 4., 5.2, 5.5, 6., 8.1

ISBN 3-540-07410-4 Springer-Verlag Berlin · Heidelberg · New York
ISBN 0-387-07410-4 Springer-Verlag New York · Heidelberg · Berlin

Offsetdruck: Julius Beltz, Hemsbach/Bergstr.

V o r w o r t

Die 5. Jahrestagung der Gesellschaft für Informatik findet vom 8. bis zum 10. Oktober 1975 an der Universität Dortmund statt. Erfreulicherweise kann man feststellen, daß die Jahrestagung der GI nicht nur im Inland, sondern insbesondere auch im Ausland sehr starke Resonanz gefunden hat. Nicht ganz so plangemäß war der Eingang von Arbeiten über konkrete Anwendungen, so daß für das Gebiet Informatik-Anwendung auch diesmal wieder nicht der an sich gebührende Stellenwert zum Ausdruck kommt. Eine ähnliche Feststellung haben meine "Vorgänger im Amt", die Herren W. Brauer (Hamburg 1973) und D. Siefkes (Berlin 1974) getroffen, so daß man für die Zukunft vielleicht anregen sollte, noch mehr als bisher gesonderte Anstrengungen zu unternehmen, um qualifizierte Arbeiten für den praxisbezogenen Bereich der Informatik vorstellen zu können.

Die Mitglieder des Programmausschusses dieser Tagung sind die Herren

K. Alber, Braunschweig
W. Haacke, Paderborn
P. Mertens, Nürnberg-Erlangen
J. Mühlbacher, Dortmund
C. Petri, Bonn-Birlinghoven
R. Piloty, Darmstadt
P. Reichertz, Hannover
B. Reusch, Dortmund
W. Ruckriegel, Düsseldorf
H. Wiehle, München

Sie haben sich bemüht, aus der Vielzahl der eingegangenen Arbeiten ein möglichst ausgewogenes Spektrum an interessanten Arbeiten auszuwählen.

Besondere Beachtung sollte die unter dem Thema "Brauchen wir für jedes Anwendungsgebiet eine eigene Informatik" angesetzte Podiumsdiskussion finden, die in gewisser Hinsicht die bei der 4. Jahrestagung ausgesprochenen Gedanken zur Informatik-Ausbildung mit geänderter Motivation wieder aufgreift und zum Verhältnis zwischen Theorie und Praxis in der Informatik indirekt Stellung nimmt.

Ich möchte hier den Herren G.Goos, P.Mertens, G.Obelode, M.Paul, W.Steinmüller, H.Wedekind, F.Wingert danken, daß sie sich bereiterklärt haben, an dieser Podiumsdiskussion teilzunehmen. Herr N. Szyperski wird die Leitung dieser Diskussion übernehmen.

Parallel zum wissenschaftlichen Programm werden Hardware-und Softwarehersteller über ihre Produkte referieren, so daß auch die Möglichkeit besteht, sich über kommerzielle Neuentwicklungen informieren zu lassen. Wenngleich die in diesem Rahmen angekündigten Vorträge nicht in dem Sammelband aufgenommen werden, möchte ich doch an dieser Stelle gebührend darauf hinweisen: sie bieten den wissenschaftlich orientierten Informatikern eine gute Gelegenheit, sich weiter in Probleme der Anwender zu vertiefen.

Mein Dank gilt den Vortragenden dieser Tagung und darüber hinaus allen jenen, die zum Zustandekommen dieser Tagung beitragen, insbesondere den Mitgliedern des Programmausssschusses, den Herren des Organisationskomitees mit Herrn V. Claus als Vorsitzenden, und schließlich den Förderern dieser Tagung,

dem Ministerium für Wissenschaft und Forschung
des Landes Nordrhein-Westfalen

der Stadt Dortmund
der Universität Dortmund
der Gesellschaft der Freunde der Universität Dortmund
der Hoesch AG, Dortmund
der IBM Deutschland, Stuttgart
der Siemens AG, München
der OSP Unternehmensberatung, Duisburg
der Signalversicherung, Dortmund
der Union-Brauerei, Dortmund
der Mannesmann Datenverarbeitung

Abschließend habe ich Fräulein R.Kühn und Herrn H.Huwig für ihren idealistischen Einsatz für die Jahrestagung im besonderen zu danken.

Dortmund, im Juli 1975

Jörg Mühlbacher

INHALTSVERZEICHNIS

HAUPTVORTRÄGE 1

Information Systems: A Survey by Examples
P. Lockemann 3

The Problem of Requirements Analysis for Information Systems Applications
R.L. Ashenhurst 35

'Variables considered harmful'
F.L. Bauer ....*)

Speichertechnik und Rechnerarchitektur
H.O. Leilich 49

Mathematische Logik und Informatik
K. Zuse 57

L Systems, sequences and languages
G. Rozenberg 71

Rechnernetzwerke - Möglichkeiten und Grenzen
L. Richter 85

Belästigung der Menschen durch Computer
H.J. Genrich 94

DIALOGSYSTEME 107

Bewertung von Dialogsystemen zum Dokumenten-Retrieval
F. Gebhardt 109

Ein Programmsystem zur Erfassung von Daten aus komplex strukturierten Tabellen
K.H. Dreckmann / G. Hofmann.......... 118

Ein Dialogsystem zur Methodensuche
R. Erbe / G. Walch 133

Die mit *) gekennzeichneten Vorträge wurden zwar gehalten, konnten jedoch nicht mehr in den Tagungsband aufgenommen werden.

TRANSITIONSNETZE 149

Markierte Petrinetze und Σ-Teilsysteme
H.A. Schmid / E. Best 151

Introducing parallelism into sequential programs
E. Riedemann 162

Eine Erweiterung normierter Netze zu asynchronen, parallel arbeitenden Netzen abstrakter Automaten
L. Priese .... *)

GRUNDLAGEN DER PROGRAMMIERUNG 177

Well Formed Programs Optimal with Respect to Structural Complexity
G. de Michelis / C. Simone 179

Merging control-flow and data-flow descriptions of structured systems in a unique notation
G.D. Antoni / M. Maiocchi / R. Polillo 196

The construction of types of abstract machines in SIMAC
C. Daquin / C. Girault 205

DATENBANKMODELLE 219

On the semantics of data bases: the semantics of data definition languages
H. Biller / W. Glatthaar 221

A system to increase data independence in a hierarchical structure
C. Frasson 235

An attribute represented as a data item or databasekey: A basic defect in the CODASYL DDL 1973 and its correction
G.M. Nijssen .... *)

Zugriffssynchronisation in Datenbanksystemen
G. Schlageter 247

Die mit *) gekennzeichneten Vorträge wurden zwar gehalten, konnten jedoch nicht mehr in den Tagungsband aufgenommen werden.

AUTOMATENTHEORIE 259

Problems of the change of operating time of finite automata
J.W. Grzymala-Busse 261

Zur Konstruktion von Decodierautomaten
I. Brückner 269

Zwei-Zähler-Automaten mit gekoppelten Bewegungen
B.v. Braunmühl 280

Darstellung der Kategorie der determinierten Automaten als algebraische Kategorie
D. Wätjen 290

RECHNERVERBUND / EINZELVORTRÄGE 295

Experience of a departmental computer support network
D.R. Innes / S.H. Leong / M.D. Langfield / J.L. Alty 297

Laborautomatisierung und Experimentkontrolle in einem hierarchisch strukturierten Computerverband
H. Hultzsch 310

Schnelle digitale Komponenten für grafische Sichtgeräte
W. Straßer 319

Zur Strukturierung mehrstufiger Mustererkennungssysteme
H. Petersen / N. Vorstädt 333

IMPLEMENTIERUNG VON DATENSTRUKTUREN 349

An Integrated System for Application Programs and Data Base Management
E. Baar / G. Deprez 351

Automatische Analyse und Prüfung von Eingabedaten
P.F. Rennert 366

Implementierung von Zugriffspfaden durch Bitlisten
Th. Härder 379

FORMALE SPRACHEN 395

Kombination von sackgassenfreier Topdown- und Bottomup-Syntaxanalyse
D. Thimm 397

Generierung kontextsensitiver Sprachen durch hyperbeschränkte zweischichtige Grammatiken mit einem Metazeichen
H. Feldmann 409

Allgemeine Σ-Grammatiken
M. Opp 420

BETRIEBSSYSTEME I 429

Dynamische Speicherverwaltung durch Hardware
T. Flik / H. Liebig 431

Neue strukturierte Sprachkonzepte zur Prozeßsynchronisation
P. Kammerer 445

Auswertungsnetze als Hilfsmittel zur Modellbildung - Probleme und deren Lösungen -
L. Stewen 462

ASPEKTE ZU PROGRAMMIERSPRACHEN 475

Eine statistische Analyse der statischen Eigenschaften von PL/I-Programmen
P. Nawrot / P. Rechenberg 477

Pattern Matching and Call by Pattern
G. Levi / F. Sirovich 491

On the Design of Programming Languages including Mini ALGOL 68
L. Ammeraal 500

SCHALTWERKE 505

Asynchrone Schaltwerksimulation mit SSM, einer Simulationssprache für Schaltwerke mittels mehrwertiger Logik
W. Görke 507

Polynomial Separation of Ternary Functions
C. Moraga 523

Eine universelle Klasse O (log(Mx))-testbarer iterativer und sequentieller Schaltungen
W. Coy 534

WARTESCHLANGENMODELLE 545

A model of a time-sharing system with two classes of processes
A. Brandwajn 547

Zur optimalen Steuerung des Multiprogramminggrades in Rechnersystemen mit virtuellem Speicher und Paging
P. Kühn 567

Ein zeitdiskretes Wartesystem mit unterbrechenden Prioritäten
B. Meister 581

COMPUTERGESTÜTZTER UNTERRICHT 593

Ein modernes Netzwerkanalyseprogramm als begleitendes simuliertes Labor zu elektrotechnischen Vorlesungen
H. Nielinger 595

ALTID, eine Sprache für Lehr- und Informationsdialoge
R. Hansen / E.-G. Hoffmann / F. Simon 601

Entwurf und Einsatz eines portablen RGU-Systems für die Lernersteuerung: LEGIS
A. Bode 611

ÜBERSETZERBAU 625

SLS/1: A Translator Writing System
J. Lewi / K. de Vlaminck / J. Huens / P. Mertens 627

An Abstract ALGOL 68 Machine and its Application in a machine independent Compiler
W. Koch / Ch. Oeters.. 642

Verschränkung von Compiler-Moduln
H. Ganzinger / R. Wilhelm 654

LOGISCHE SYSTEME 667

First Order Logic as a Tool to solve and classify Problems
D. Marini / P.A. Miglioli / M. Ornaghi 669

On evaluating recursion
P. Raulefs 680

Analogy Categories, Virtual Machines and Structured Programming
B.R. Gaines 691

BETRIEBSSYSTEME II 701

Kritischer Vergleich von Algorithmen für ein Scheduling-Problem
K. Ecker 703

Performances of "Least Reference Probability" Paging Algorithm under Locality in Program Behavior
Trân-Quôc-Tê.. 715

The Logic of Protection
L. Kohout / B.R. Gaines 736

H A U P T V O R T R Ä G E

INFORMATION SYSTEMS: A SURVEY BY EXAMPLES

Peter C. Lockemann
Fakultaet fuer Informatik, Universitaet Karlsruhe
D-75 Karlsruhe 1

Abstract

Information systems is both a technical term for a particular kind of dynamic systems, and for a comparatively young discipline within informatics. The paper is an introduction to the latter, in particular as computer-assisted information systems are concerned, and an attempt is made to delineate its still somewhat fluid boundaries. A number of topics are introduced and illustrated by examples, and some relevant and pressing problem areas are identified.

1 Introduction

Information systems - or whatever name one chooses for them - have grown into a major discipline in recent years. As an intersection of many seemingly diverse activities they have, at the same time, become many things to many people and evolved into a truly interdisciplinary area of research and development. Today they cover most aspects of computer science because of the multitude of problems in constructing large computer systems; they include concepts from a wide variety of application areas from science to industry to public and business administration, from research to engineering to production; they have captured the interest of the legal and social professions because of their repercussions in everyday life.

Therefore it would prove a futile task to attempt to cover the entire area of information systems or even just all of its major aspects on a few pages or in a one-hour lecture. Instead I shall concentrate on the computer science aspects and, furthermore, limit myself to a few arbitrary but - I believe - typical highlights of work in the area. As such the examples will be neither complete nor unbiased. However, I hope that they will at least provide a feeling of what information systems research is all about in these days.

For many, an information system is any kind of system in which information is exchanged or kept available. Thus, librarians have been among the earliest to lay claim to the term "information system" in connection with libraries and library techniques. On the other hand, computer scientists often take the narrow view of a large central data base supported by one or more computers as the necessary ingredients of an information system. For them information systems are described by technical slogans such as fact-retrieval system, data base management system, question-answering system, document retrieval system, or by application oriented slogans such as inventory control system, airline reservation system, management information system, motor vehicle registration system, accounting system, legislative planning system. Again, I hope that from the examples a clearer understanding will evolve of which activities may conceivably come under the heading of "information systems".

2 Basic concepts

Like all young disciplines the information systems area suffers from the lack of a few, generally accepted and well-understood basic concepts. To name just one example, there is as yet no general agreement on the terms "information" and "data" or the relationship between them. Instead we still observe a state of pre-science in which several schools of thought compete among themselves and frequently resort to philosophical arguments. Fortunately, however, considerable progress has been made in the recent past, and more and more common ground can be detected. Before we present some of the concepts developed so far, a classification scheme is introduced which we shall follow throughout most of the paper.

As a point of departure we choose the notions of dynamic system and organization. A dynamic system is a collection of elements that are related to each other and whose concrete behavior varies with time. An organization in this context is a dynamic system where the elements and relations are determined on a functional basis, that is, they are derived from certain objectives that the system must meet as a whole. Moreover, we shall assume that the functional properties are established once and for all (in practice, if they change they will do so slowly). Therefore, all temporal variations manifest themselves in an exchange of certain quantities among the elements, these quantities being matter, energy or information. Information systems study exclusively the exchange of information, thus emphasizing the aspect of coordination necessary to derive the desired behavior of the total system from the cooperation of its individual elements. The only activities of the system elements that are of interest are those of information processing.

The concepts necessary to describe information systems arise from three levels.

(1) Functions of the individual elements or groups of elements.
The purpose and objectives of the system are considered. Tasks are split into subtasks and assigned to specific elements, or elements are designed to handle specific subtasks; the resources required by the various elements are determined.

(2) Interaction and coordination of the system elements.
Issues on this level have to do with analyzing or planning the proper interplay of the various system elements so that the system objectives determined on level 1 are indeed met. The issues are described by catchwords such as information flow; resource management; deadlocks and bottlenecks; privacy and reliability, sequential, concurrent and alternative processes; interfaces; directives, orders and responses; hierarchical organization.

(3) Information structures.
The concepts on this level investigate the forms of information that are to be exchanged in a particular situation so that the individual elements may function properly with regard to the system objectives. These objectives relate to the world outside the system, that is, what one might call the universe of discourse. Therefore, information structures are the reflection of a universe. Usually, a universe may again be thought of as dynamic, consisting of objects interrelated with each other in more or less complex ways, and within which processes continually take place resulting in the creation of new objects, destruction of old ones, and redefinition of interrelationships.

The three concepts may be tied together by the notion of language. Language is necessary for the system elements to agree among themselves on how to go about meeting the system objectives, that is, how to identify and allocate the subtasks and organize the communication. Likewise, language is necessary to coordinate the actions of the elements in a concrete situation. And finally, language is necessary to pass along knowledge on the state of the universe so that the activities may be guided in a specific way.

It should be noted that none of the concepts mentioned so far imply or demand use of a computer. Indeed, computers are but one out of many possible vehicles for the implementation of system elements, other possibilities being human beings, tabulating machines, conventional libraries, etc. Nevertheless, the remainder of the paper will be devoted to explications of the concepts as they have developed in connection with computers.

In doing so we shall view the concepts from various positions. To begin with, some conceptual and formal approaches to a theoretical foundation of information systems are explored (ch.3), and the integration of the concepts into a linguistic framework will be studied (ch.4). Subsequently we associate the various concepts with some known technical methods and determine how these would have to be expanded (ch.5). In addition, the problem of unifying the concepts and methods into a single approach to system software construction will be touched (ch.6). Finally we investigate the question of how to evaluate whether the efforts that have gone into a system can be justified (ch.7).

3 Models and formal approaches

Information systems are of substantial practical relevance. Consequently, there has been much pressure to develop concepts that are useful in practical applications, and not just chosen because they happen to be amenable to rigid formal treatment. Current efforts seem to fall into three broad categories.

(i) Development of basic concepts for each, functions, coordination and information structures. These concepts must be simple in the sense that they explain any reality of interest in a reasonably straightforward fashion, and they must be logically consistent at least in an intuitive sense. A description of a certain reality by these concepts (i.e. an abstraction) shall be called a model of that reality. Models differ because various sets of concepts emphasize different aspects of reality and treat others lightly. Much of the current effort is directed towards this objective, and a number of proposals have been put forward and are being heatedly discussed. Sections 3.1 through 3.3 will list some of these proposals. Despite of the progress made, this area needs attention for several more years.

(ii) Formal investigation of these concepts. This is an area where developments have been irregular, in part because results in (i) must often be awaited, in part because adequate mathematical tools are sometimes hard to find. On the other hand, the area is of critical importance in order to give precision to the informal notions in (i) and to study the formal properties and the consistency of the concepts. One may expect the area to grow in importance.

(iii) Development of mathematical tools for (ii). The efforts need some guidance as to the requirements of (i) and (ii).

3.1 Functions

Two major topics under this heading are system development in which a given task is divided into a number of subtasks, e.g. for system design or for evaluating and improving system performance, and task standardization in which a stock of building blocks is derived from which a system with given objectives may be constructed.

The classical system development cycle proceeds (usually iteratively) in several steps: system analysis (analysis of the current state), problem definition (statement of objectives), system design and evaluation, system implementation and documentation, system installation. As yet there exists no consistent and uniform formalized approach to system development. Large portions of the cycle are still based on verbal descriptions, check lists, fact sheets, interviews, observations, and estimates resulting in organizational charts, flow diagrams, decision tables, and form sheets which largely preclude the application of formal-deductive methods [Wed 73]. However, in a few limited areas such methods have been or are being developed.

Examples:

(1) Cost/benefit analysis and Net value analysis.
These attempt to formalize system evaluation. Basically in cost/benefit analysis, various designs are examined with respect both to the immediate costs of their implementation and operation and to the costs and benefits to the system environment while they are in operation. A decision rule is defined in order to compare the designs according to their costs and benefits and to select one of them. Net value analysis (Nutzwertanalyse) accounts for the fact that not all costs or benefits may be expressed in terms of monetary values. Instead, a single global objective is successively decomposed into a number of subgoals resulting in a tree with the global objective as its root and the most detailed subgoals as its leaves. Each alternative system design is weighted with respect to each of the leaves, resulting in a matrix (where the weights are not necessarily in terms of monetary values but also, e.g., in terms of priorities). Again a decision rule must be applied. In both cases the decision rules can be translated into mathematical form and hence be treated by standard mathematical techniques [Alt 74].

(2) Optimization techniques.
Linear, nonlinear and dynamic optimizations combine system design and system evaluation insofar as no comparison of designs takes place. A decision function is optimized subject to a number of constraints resulting in precisely one "optimal" solution. Again, the development of appropriate mathematical tools is far advanced [Hen 68]. On the other hand, the approach depends on prior parameterization of the various system aspects by numerical values.

(3) Information system description analysis.
In a process such as system development, where few decisions follow from precise logical rules, documentation is of paramount importance. Teichroew [Tei 74] presents a project in which the characteristics of a "present" system or the requirements of a "proposed" system are expressed in a Problem Statement Language. These expressions are then made the subject of a software package, the Problem Statement Analyzer. In the case of a present system redundancies are exposed, standardizing procedures are suggested, etc. In the case of a proposed system complete documentation is generated which is then intended to be used as input to the design and construction phases of the system.

(4) Abstract machines.

The classical approach to system design - proceeding from a global objective to a number of subgoals or, correspondingly, determining the elements of a system and then in turn treating each element as a subsystem - has an obvious counterpart in the concept of structured programming. This concept has been the subject of formalization in order to prove the correctness of programs. To this end, Dijkstra [Goo 73] introduces the notion of abstract machine for each level in the design process with the following properties. Given a succession of machines $A_0, \ldots, A_n$ where A_n represents the global level, two levels A_i and A_{i+1} are related as follows.

a) The resources and the functions provided by A_i form the complete basis on which to build A_{i+1}. There is no way to use properties of A_{i-1} in building A_{i+1}. Hence every A_i is a complete interface description in the hierarchy.
b) Resources of A_i used in defining new resources of A_{i+1} can no longer be present in A_{i+1} (i.e. they may become resources of A_{i+1} only if they are not part of a definition for another resource of A_{i+1}).

Concerning task standardization, annoyingly little progress has been made so far. This is reflected in the terminological chaos with respect to system types and, on the more practical side, in a complete absence of any standardized information systems software that goes beyond information retrieval.

3.2 Coordination

Of the various formal approaches, marked Petri nets have recently found wide recognition and application [Pet 73]. From the viewpoint of modelling, Petri nets are drastic abstractions of real information systems: Information to be exchanged is represented by mere tokens that are indistinguishable from one another, the communication channels between the system elements degenerate into places that may hold up to a certain number of tokens, and the information processing activities of system elements (transitions) are described by the "firing rule": A transition may fire whenever each one of its input places holds at least one token. As a result, each input place loses one token and each output place gains one token. Thus, the behavior of a particular system may be studied in terms of tokens moving through the places.

Petri nets are usually represented by directed bipartite graphs. N = (P, T, pre, post) where P and T are finite nonempty disjoint sets (places and transitions), and pre, post c PxT are relations connecting places to transitions and vice versa. The dynamic aspects are described by a mapping M:P -> N {0} indicating the number of tokens on each place. The behavior of a system is characterized by the ways in which a marking can be transformed into another marking, e.g.,

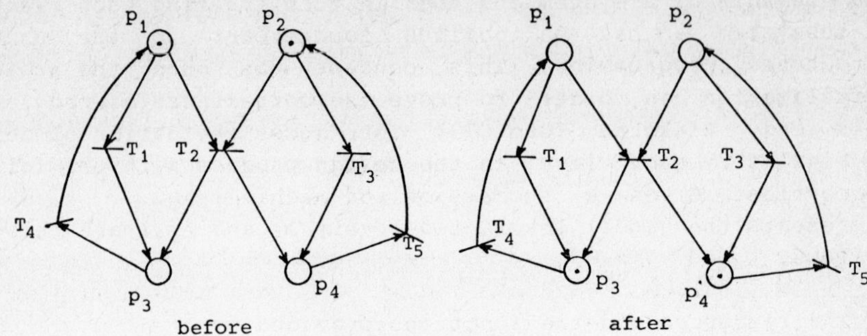

firing of T2

It is essential that, in a case when two or more transitions may fire independently ("concurrently"), no sequential order of their firings is determined. Thus, it is possible to specify the minimal amount of temporal coordination needed for a given task. Furthermore, the behavior of a marked net may be non-deterministic, in the following sense: in a case when two transitions may fire, but share an input place, only one of them can actually fire. (The marking generated in the above example may have resulted as well from a concurrent firing of T1 and T3, but not of T1, T2 and T3). Hence, even in a modest-sized net, it is not feasible to determine, by mere simulation, the important aspects of global behavior, e.g. the absence of deadlocks, absence of place overflows (leading to loss of messages) etc.

One approach to this problem is to determine the properties of a marked net solely on the basis of a given stationary structure N and a given initial marking M. For example, using linear algebra techniques, such properties have been formally derived for certain classes of nets [Lau 74a] and some results have been proven for operating systems [Lau 74b]. A different approach has been to determine easily applicable rules for constructing marked nets which will possess the required properties [Scr 74].

The level of abstraction reflected in the basic definitions of Petri nets is, of course, too drastic to answer a number of practical questions in one step. E.g., the ability of a system element to copy rather than remove a message represented by a token (as in computer storage), the ability to pick up tokens in a certain order (as in a queue) which implies that tokens are distinguishable; the ability to add tokens to selected rather than all output places; the amount of time required for a subtask: all of these are not described at the basic level of transitions. The required extension of the elementary formalism is gained by considering functions defined on nets. Such functions can be chosen either intuitively, on the basis of what is suggested by the intended application, or systematically (by considering maps from nets into nets, [Pet 72]) in order to show how higher-level tasks can be decomposed down to the level of conditions and events. If the choice of functions is intuitive, much of the deductive power of the formal apparatus is lost, and the questions of timing, absence of deadlock and of overflow have to be reconsidered and mostly to be answered by simulation, as for the Evaluation Nets of Noe and Nutt [Noe 73] which allow to detect bottlenecks and not only deadlocks. On the other hand, when simulation is feasible, or when only a precise problem description is needed, the intuitive choice of attributes for net elements is quite appropriate.

Among the formal approaches first results on timed Petri nets have been published recently [Ram 74]; along the same lines, one would also expect contributions from queuing theory. Attempts to list the concepts needed beyond the basic ones of Petri nets, and to formalize them, have only recently been mentioned [May 75]. In particular, first attempts have been made to impose some kind of information structure in place of tokens.

By contrast, the so-called "Scandinavian school" sets out from a detailed analysis of the information structures and proceeds to derive from these a complete system structure. For example, Sølvberg [Søl 74] bases his software system CASCADE/II for the computer-assisted design of automated information systems on three classes of objects: information objects (INF), process objects (PR), and signal objects (SGN). A number of relation types are introduced: input $I \subseteq SGN \times PR$, output $O \subseteq PR \times INF$, maintenance (insertion, deletion, changing, retrieval) $M \subseteq PR \times INF$, entry $N \subseteq SGN \times PR$, exit $X \subseteq PR \times SGN$, component (part relationship) $C \subseteq PR \times PR \cup INF \times INF$, element (set membership) $E \subseteq INF \times INF$. Basically, therefore, the information flowing through the net is differentiated according to its role regarding a particular process. In addition, besides the aspects of coordination the net allows to detail the structures of processes and information hierarchically to any desired level. Example (from [Søl 74]):

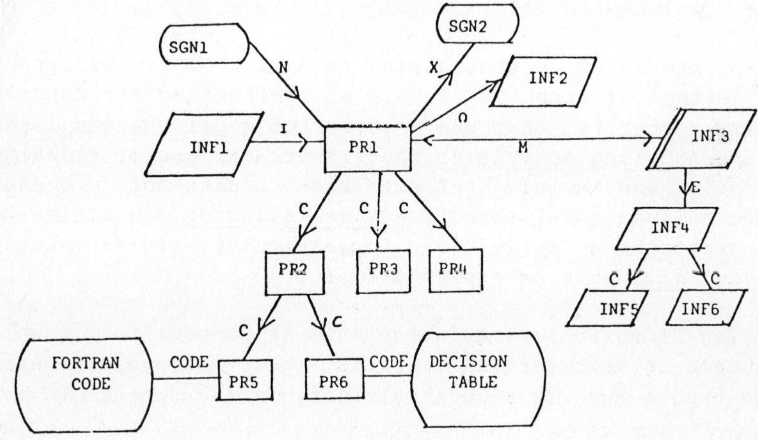

The main objects and main relations of the CASCADE/II model.

3.3 Information structures

It is commonly accepted that data bases are to be considered models of certain realities [Kli 74]. Petri nets have been an excellent illustration of what we meant by a "model" in the beginning of ch.3: They provide the tools by which to abstract from universes made up of information systems. Unfortunately, when one designs the tools with which data bases may form models one faces a dilemma. For economic reasons, data base systems shall serve a wide community of users. The tools must be of wider applicability and hence more general in nature than the ones of, e.g. Petri nets or matrix algebra. On the other hand, completely general tools are also completely useless. Thus a proper balance between generality and specificity must be found. On the next few pages four different approaches to what constitutes a valid set of tools will be discussed.

A number of questions require immediate attention: How can the various approaches be compared? Which of these approaches is the most suitable one for a given problem? Which of the approaches are interdependent, that is, may be defined in terms of one another? The surface has hardly been scratched on these questions.

In order to describe the various approaches, a few concepts have proven extremely useful to the author [Loc 75]. A mode is an abstraction tool. A model is an abstraction of a state of a universe by means of given modes. An elementary mode is an elementary (undefinable) abstraction class (such as "data item", "attribute", "relationship"). A composite mode is a rule of composition which determines how to combine arbitrary models (called components) into new models. An elementary model is an abstraction by means of an elementary mode, a composite model an abstraction by means of a composite mode. A model object is an instance of a model. This implies that the same model may be needed in different contexts (e.g. 35 as the age of a person and as a room number). The value of a model object is the model assigned to it.

Often one is interested in abstracting as well from the processes that take place in the universe. Two levels of abstraction are conceivable: n-ary model operators that map n-tuples of model objects into model objects, and modeling activities that ignore all causal relationships between models and solely reflect the results of processes by manipulating a given model object. A model selector identifies a model object to operators or activities. In particular, if its value is not unique a model name must be assigned to it.

A type is (in first approximation) a rule of composition in which the components have to meet certain criteria. These may again be expressed by types so that a type is recursively defined (as opposed to a mode).

An information structure is a model together with its mode or type. (An information structure must not be confused with a data structure; the latter is an information structure together with a representation [Loc 75].) Usually one calls a language in which types may be described a data definition language, a language in which operations on objects may be expressed a data manipulation language, and the description of a particular type a schema.

Examples.

(1) DBTG [CO 71,CO 73]

Composite modes:

- Records: a collection of pairs of model objects and attributes.
- Areas: disjoint sets of Records.
- Sets: inverse functions (one-to-many relations between Records, called the owner record and member records, respectively.
- Data bases: sets of Areas and Sets.

No activities are defined within records. Within areas records may be stored, deleted, or retrieved. Within sets records may be inserted, removed, modified, and retrieved.

The data definition language is based on the modes and defined in terms of a syntax (expressed in COBOL meta-language) whose application results in the generation of valid data base types. Basically, such a type consists of a number of clauses that determine, among others, the form of particular set, area, and record types, privacy, the identification of particular records, sets, and areas, the interference permitted among users, the ordering of records within sets, the applicability of insert and remove operations.

The DBTG modeling system is often referred to as a "hierarchical" model in contrast to the "relational" model mentioned below. However, classifications such as these should be applied with care since what is meant here is that, by repeatedly forming sets it is possible to arrive at tree-like record arrangements.

(2) Relational model [Cod 70,Wed 74]

Composite modes:

- n-tuples: Data items ordered on a list of attributes.
- relations: Unordered sets of n-tuples with identical attributes Hence the list of attributes effectively becomes part of the relation, and the attributes are called the domains of the relation (the actual definition of "domain" is slightly different).

In contrast to DBTG, the relational model is based on operators instead of activities. Important operators on relations are permutation, projection, join, direct product, restriction. Hierarchies may be formed by including relation names as tuple elements. However, for ease of manipulation and formal treatment it is recommended to eliminate hierarchies by a procedure called normalization. Unfortunately, this procedure is not reversible in the sense that a few accidental hierarchies may be constructed from the normalized relations in addition to the original ones.

Example (from [Cod 70])

<u>supply</u>	(supplier	part	project	quantity)
	1	2	5	17
	1	3	5	23
	2	3	7	9
	2	7	5	4
	4	1	1	12

Advantages of the relational model:

- Ease of formalization. This allows for the introduction of formal methods with which functional dependencies may be declared and relations reorganized with regard to these, and transitive dependencies may be eliminated, both simplifying data base maintenance. Similarly, formal rules have been devised which construct a relational data base from a given set of primitive functional relationships. Furthermore, performance criteria may be introduced.

- Ease of use. In contrast to DBTG, no programming experience is required; all a user has to do is reinterpret his problem in relational terms. Furthermore, a user only has to master a very small number of concepts.

- Disambiguation. Experience shows that in more complex models a given universe may be interpreted in more than one way. Due to its formalization the relational model may provide syntactic criteria for selecting exactly one interpretation.

- Formalization of actions in the data base. In DBTG, the temporal relationships between various model objects may only be established by studying the programs invoking the activities. In the relational model one makes use of the operators to describe the relationships in terms of formal expressions. [Kra 75] demonstrates, for a different modeling system, the opportunities offered by such a formalization.

(3) Data semantics by Abrial [Abr 74]

A more general approach to modeling, and perhaps one that may provide a basis for comparing different modeling systems, is Abrial's Data Semantics: Abrial starts out with very few restrictions:

- Elementary modes: a) (elementary) objects, b) (binary) connections between objects.
- Composite mode: sets of objects together with connections between the objects.

- Elementary types (end of recursion): The set of objects is divided into disjoint sets called categories, i.e. each object is assigned to exactly one category (e.g. John to person).
- Types:
  a) Connections are collected into binary relations defined on categories. Each relation defines two access functions (one in each direction) by which connections may be traversed (e.g. age and personofage on person x number). Note that these don´t have to be functions in the mathematical sense.
  b) Sets of categories together with relations between the categories (categorical structure).
- Operators: cat (category definition), generate (create an instance of a given category), kill (destroy an object), ∋ (connect two objects), ∌ (disconnect), as well as test and access operators.

Example (from [Abr 74]):

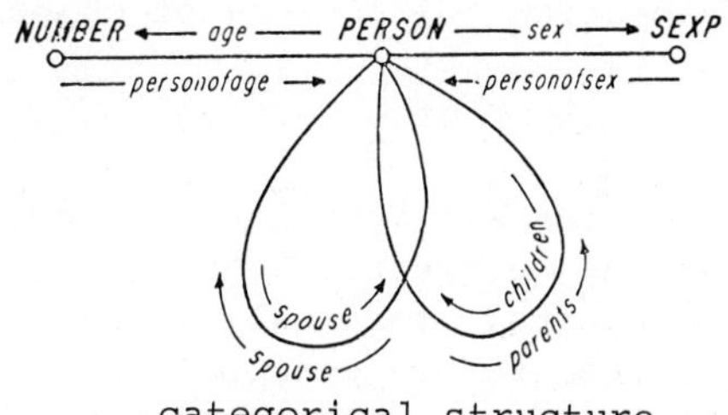

categorical structure

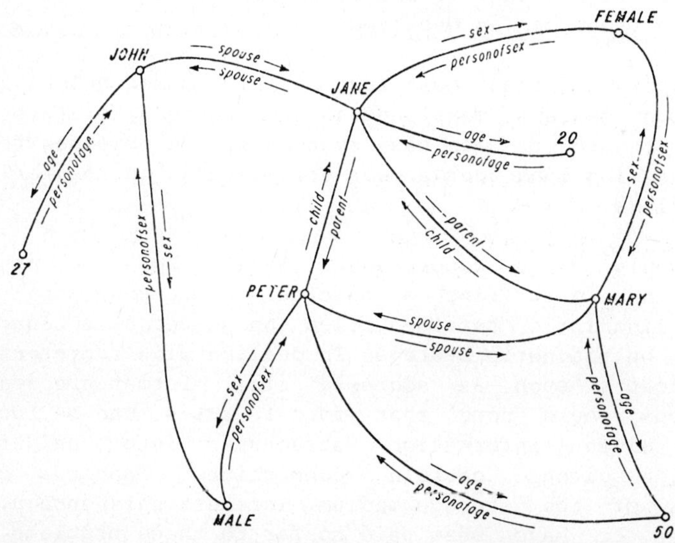

an instance of the categorical structure above

Based on these concepts and a language for expressing further definitions and manipulations, Abrial proceeds to examine the logical information that may be obtained from the model (including deductive capabilities), introduces the notions of program (which, in particular, permits the definition of complex access functions along sequences of connections) and process (for execution of a program), and presents the notion of context in which actions are effective (making it possible to alter a data base temporarily in order to study hypotheses), among others.

(4) Relational level data structures for programming languages [Ear 73].

In parallel to the efforts in data base systems, information structures have received a great deal of attention in higher programming languages. One of these attempts is described by Earley and is interesting insofar as it is based on a relational view of the universe rather than the access path view prevalent in higher programming languages. Modes are

- Tuples: Fixed collections of heterogeneous objects; each object can be referred to by name (called a selector).
- Sets: Unordered non-repeating collections of objects.
- Relations: Sets of tuples.
- Sequences: Ordered collections of objects.

For each of these classes certain operators are defined, e.g. for sets: adding, deleting an element, test for set membership, iterating over the elements, cardinality, and the familiar mathematical set operators; for sequences: access first, last or any desired element, iteration, concatenation, insertion and deletion at first, last or any given place. Tuple, set, relation and sequence types can be declared.

It should be emphasized that these four examples cover only a fraction of the modeling systems mentioned in the recent literature. A good overview with regard to data base systems may be obtained from [Kli 74] while programming languages appear well-covered in the various ACM SIGPLAN proceedings.

Models exist only on a conceptional level. For the purpose of communication they must find a physical representation, e.g. a graphical or linguistic representation on paper or a binary coded representation on magnetic storage. In dealing with representations, additional concepts such as address, size, format are necessary. Furthermore, one would hope that formal rules can be found that translate a given information structure into an efficient representation, given certain constraints imposed by the characteristics of the storage medium. Interestingly enough, little attention seems to have been paid so far to these problems and the whole area of representation still lacks any consistent approach.

4 Languages

As indicated in ch.2, language must deal with all three aspects, functions, coordination, and information, thus providing a vehicle for expressing the concepts introduced in ch.3. Even when restricting it to communication with a computer, the various aspects may impose conflicting demands on language design. As an illustration consider the casual user's confusion of job control languages and higher programming or conversational languages.

A request to a computerized information system usually consists of up to three parts:

(1) Retrieval of certain objects according to some more or less complex selection criteria.
(2) Combination of the objects retrieved.
(3) Modification of the data base on the basis of the results obtained in (2).

Parts 1 and 3 are usually solved by means of the operators mentioned in sec. 3.3. Part 2, however, is much more difficult to systematize due to the lack of standardization of functions (sec. 3.1). As a consequence, one major problem in language design is integrating part 2 with parts 1 and 3. Three approaches are possible:

- Host language systems.
  Part 2 is stated in a conventional programming language such as COBOL, PL/I, ALGOL. Parts 1 and 3 are interfaced with part 2 by means of subroutine or macro calls. In other words, the data manipulation language (DML) is embedded within the programming language used for part 2 (host language). The subroutines, on their part, make use of the schemas which are described by the data definition language (DDL). Contrary to the DML the DDL is usually not embedded but self-contained. The classical example for this kind of approach is DBTG.
- Subroutine packages.
  Sometimes the programs required to perform part 2 already exist. This is especially true in the area of statistical analysis where several extensive subroutine packages have been developed. The problem, then, becomes one of interfacing two software systems, a data base management system and a subroutine package. Strangely enough, no elegant solutions seem to exist; one must still rely on intermediate files and, consequently, turn to job control language on transition between parts.
- Full integration.
  Data base management functions and processing functions have identical status. Experience shows that so far information systems of this kind are highly inflexible with respect to the addition, deletion or modification of functions or types. As a consequence, full integration is usually reserved to systems whose functions are well-understood, well-defined and fixed, e.g. reservation systems or inventory control.

Language design even for parts 1 and 3 turns out to be less and less trivial the more complex the selection criteria are. Suppose that in the relational model several relations are progressively examined (and perhaps intermediate relations constructed), each one providing selection criteria for the next step until the final relation has been reached. Similarly, in Abrial's system one may traverse a large number of connections depending on certain choices at the nodes, that is, execute a long interdependent sequence of access functions, before the desired node is reached. Hence it is not surprising that much effort has been devoted towards the design of retrieval languages for complex data bases. Two extremes can be observed:

- Languages based on mathematical notation, usually some form of predicate logic language. While these languages are difficult to learn by the casual user they allow short and concise statements even of rather complicated situations.
  Example: The language ALPHA for the relational model [Cod 71] where queries have a form such as
  GET W T.LNAME: (∃S) ((T.LNR = S.LNR)∧(S.TNR = B))
  (List the vendor names (LNR) of all vendors that sell a part with part number (TNR) B. S,T are bound and free tuple variables, respectively).
- Natural-language-like query languages. These are supposed to offer the user an interface which is easy to understand and natural to use. Experience shows that many relatively complex situations may be expressed in natural language in a straightforward fashion. However, once the actions desired in the data base exceed a certain degree of complexity, formulations in natural language tend to become lengthy, cumbersome and hence prone to errors by the user. In addition, one can often find circumstances that cannot be expressed in natural language at all although they pose little problems in a mathematical notation.

  After more than a decade of linguistic research, natural-language-like query languages have reached a high degree of perfection. For examples see [Woo 68,Tho 69,Kel 71,Sim 70]. For some critical comments see [Mon 72]. [Kra 75] reports on a system that combines both mathematical and natural language.

When speaking of natural language, a second important area besides query languages should not pass unmentioned. This is the area of documentation systems where results are being sought in order to substitute automatic indexing methods for manual indexing. The linguistic problems are especially severe in morphemically rich languages such as German (see, e.g., [Sco 72]).

5 Technical solutions

Technical solutions have developed independently and often in a somewhat ad-hoc fashion long before comprehensive systematic approaches such as the ones illustrated in ch.3 were attempted. Indeed, the multitude of these technical solutions has been one of the motivations behind some of these attempts. As a consequence, one of the more urgent tasks today is to associate known technical methods with the formal concepts. Once this has been achieved one might hope to define rules that, given a formal description of an information system or some of its aspects, select the most appropriate technical solutions. Conversely, it should be possible to identify areas for which better techniques must still be devised.

In the following sections a few examples of work on technical problems will be presented and related to the concepts previously introduced.

5.1 Functions

If the various aspects of query processing are clearly separated, e.g. by subsystem interfacing (ch.4), the problems of constructing programs for implementing desired functions in information systems are not different from those in other computer applications. However, there is one area that seems to hold particular fascination to information systems people: deductive question-answering.

Deductive question-answering techniques are based on automatic theorem-proving methods on which a wealth of literature exists and which are still the subject of active research, e.g. for purposes of automatic programming. These techniques have been applied to a few experimental question-answering systems, see e.g. [Col 68, Gre 68, Gre 69]. For an introduction to theorem-proving methods, in particular the Robinson resolution technique, see [Nil 71]. Unfortunately, even for extremely small size data bases these methods require vast amounts of processing time so that their practical application so far has been virtually nil.

On the other hand, experience shows that users are often frustrated by a data base system's lack of trivial inferences even though the system may otherwise appear fairly sophisticated. This indicates the desirability of including at least a few limited deductive capabilities in an information system. The question of how far these should go, and how to combine them with standard storage, retrieval and processing techniques appears a highly interesting though completely unsolved problem. An apparent prerequisite is the formal representation of all system activities within the information system. For suggestions, see e.g. [Gre 69, Kra 75].

5.2 Coordination

Two of the celebrated issues of coordination in information systems that arise in connection with large data bases shared by a number of users are data base integrity and privacy. As will be demonstrated below, the known solutions seem to open up as many questions as they answer. Formal approaches so far have touched but isolated aspects, although one may hope to gain further insight through Petri nets or more complicated nets.
Everest [Ev 74] speaks of data base integrity as the completeness, soundness, purity, veracity and confidentiality of data. Data base integrity involves
- protecting the existence of the data base through physical security, backup and recovery measures;
- maintaining the quality of the data base through input validation, diagnostic routines to ensure that the data always conforms to its type, and control of the processes which update the data base;
- maintaining the privacy of the stored data through isolation, access regulation, encryption and monitoring.

For none of these areas there exist completely satisfying solutions. For example, when a process updates a data base concurrently with another update process, the integrity of the data base is threatened. Similarly, the integrity of a reading process is threatened by a concurrent update process. The use of a lockout mechanism is the obvious solution. However, lockout may lead to deadlock situations that have some unique aspects over and above what has been known from operating systems.

Lockout is a process of mutual exclusion; it assigns a part of the data base (which is to be considered a special type of resource, namely a reusable but unconserved one) exclusively to at most one update process at any one time. For a reading process, however, a weaker form of lockout is preferable: Concurrent processes are permitted to look at the corresponding part of the data base but not to change it. The question, of course, arises what is meant by "part of the data base". Many conventional systems define lockout on the file level. This may be too little in one case where several files are manipulated by the same process, and too much in another case where a few records or even just a few items are needed at a time so that a number of processes are locked out unnecessarily or at least unnecessarily long. Unfortunately, lockout on coarse data base units is technically much simpler to handle than lockout on the lowest levels of resolution, both with regard to maintaining lockout information (smaller table sizes) and deadlock prevention (fewer resources).

Since lockout may lead to deadlocks, mechanisms for handling these, i.e. for detecting or preventing them, must be included in an information system. Again, although much is known about the detection and prevention of deadlocks in general, the peculiar situations in data base systems merit additional investigations. Everest discusses four strategies: Presequencing of conflicting processes (unacceptable in an online environment), pre-emption (a process can be forced to release all exclusively controlled resources; unacceptable, however, since data cannot be considered pre-emptible when undergoing modification), pre-ordering of resources (linear ordering of non-preemptible, exclusively controlled resources according to priority; however, data can rarely be linearly ordered in a reasonable fashion), a priori claims (preclaiming exclusive control of all needed resources before using any one of them). The strategy last mentioned is the one universally applied. Unfortunately, a priori knowledge of resources is usually possible only on a coarse level of resolution, thus leading to degradation of performance. On the other hand, lockout is required to be an indivisible operation so that a larger degree of resolution and, consequently, a large number of resources may result in degradation of performance as well.

Problems of privacy are even worse. They arise not only in connection with the unauthorized access to certain data items but also with the unauthorized collection and processing of a large number of items whose individual use may not be dangerous in itself but whose collective use could very well be. The traditional technique of providing locks and keys must now be applied in combination to data and programs and, as a consequence, quickly grows to unmanageable proportions:

- Data to be protected may be assigned an unknown number of locks.
- These locks may have to be further qualified with respect to the operations permitted on the data or, conversely, locks on programs may have to be detailed with regard to the data they may access, modify or destroy.
- While it may sometimes suffice to associate locks with types, assignment of different locks to different instances of a type should not be excluded.
- Again there are questions with regard to the level of resolution. Coarse resolution (e.g. on the file level) may necessitate duplication of data with wider accessibility. Fine resolution (e.g. on the item level) may result in a vast proliferation of locks and, consequently, in large storage overhead as well.

Finally, of course, there remains the problem of keeping the locks and keys themselves confidential. Again, an array of techniques is available ranging from blanking out passwords to alternating passwords between sessions or queries, separating locks from data, jumbling passwords, and elaborate password routines for the calculation of keys.

5.3 Information structures

In view of the large number of technical solutions for implementing information structures that have been developed over the years it is surprising that little is known about how to associate these, in a systematic fashion, with modes or types of modeling systems. It seems that the choice of an appropriate technique cannot only be based on the types themselves but also on the operations planned on the corresponding model objects and in particular, the temporal sequence of these operations. Efficient implementations are still a question of personal experience and expertise. The lack of clear concepts for implementation is manifest, e.g. in the inconsistency of file management system interfaces.

The realization of information structures gives rise to up to three distinct structures in storage:

(a) A storage representation of the value part of an information structure ("encoding").

(b) A storage representation of the mode or type part of an information structure.

(c) Access paths that result from the mapping of the operators on information structures into operators on the corresponding storage structures: Whenever an operator is to be applied to an information structure this structure is to be identified in some way. By the same token, the corresponding storage structure must be identified to the corresponding storage operator. Hence a mapping from information structure identifiers into storage structure identifiers is needed. When speaking of access paths one usually has in mind these identifiers and their mappings.

Structure (a) is often denoted as primary information, structures (b) and (c) as secondary information. In the current section we shall give one example each for work on (a) and (c). Besides the reader is referred to Knuth´s outstanding collection of algorithms [Knu 68, Knu 73] which may almost all find application in information systems as well. This is particularly true for those of sorting and searching.

Concerning (a), one of the more interesting issues is automatic file compression. With evergrowing data base sizes, and with large capacity stores with simple and fast access mechanisms still several years away it is often interesting to reduce the storage requirements for a given information structure even though this will entail higher processor time. As a consequence, some attention has been paid to the use of codes which are specially designed for the purpose of reducing storage. Systems of this kind have three objectives [McC 74]:

(i) analyze the data in order to decide on a coding which reduces the storage requirements,

(ii) compress the data using the codes produced in (i),

(iii) recover the data in its original form by decoding or expanding the compressed representation of it.

Encoding involves the elimination of redundancy from the data. Basically, data contains redundancy if some symbols or groups of symbols in it occur more frequently than would be the case if all the symbols were randomly generated. In formatted files the schema can be considered to describe the deviation from randomness and hence may determine the coding. On the other hand, particularly with non-formatted files automatic methods may be chosen that scan the file to be compressed noting which characters and sequences of characters occur most frequently, and then assign short codes to characters or groups which occur frequently, and longer ones to the others. [McC 74] describes such a system using Huffman variable-length minimum redundancy codes that are defined both on individual characters and on cords (strings of two or more characters) whereby the choice of cords is mechanically optimized.

Other techniques employ variable-length fields, or ignore empty fields. Furthermore, if the universe of entities is well-defined one may assign a unique number to each entity. A set of entities thus corresponds to a set of numbers and may be encoded as a bit string with a 1-bit whenever the corresponding number is an element of the set. These bit strings are subsequently compressed. For a discussion of compression techniques see [Har 74, Byr 73, Hae 74a].

Methods for access paths (c) are primarily selected on the basis of speed but also on space requirements. Mappings may be realized procedurally (e.g. hashing) or by explicit structures (e.g. index). Furthermore, in contrast to the conventional techniques of the sixties one requires that today's methods allow for continual addition and deletion of access paths without serious degradation of performance.

Consider the case of explicit structures ([Bay 74]). Because of additions and deletions the corresponding mapping varies with time:
$\sigma(t) : N(t) \to A$
where $N(t)$ is the set of identifiers which changes with time, and A the set of addresses. $\sigma(t)$ must be realized as a set of pairs $\sigma(t) = \{(n,a)\}_t$

In order to choose one of the methods for organizing σ, these must be compared with respect to the basic operations

(a) given n, find (at a particular time t) the pair $(n,a) \in \sigma$, evaluate σ at n;
(b) insert a new pair into σ if it is not yet there;
(c) delete a pair from σ.

Among the explicit structures balanced trees solve all three addressing problems efficiently, at least under certain circumstances. On balanced trees there has recently been a surge of interest. Some results follow.

(a) True random-access store (e.g. main storage).

For the various balanced trees (e.g. AVL-trees, B-trees, BB-trees) the trade-off must be considered between search time and the amount of effort to be extended on insertion and deletion since these may require rebalancing: Moreover, in each case auxiliary information must be stored with the trees in order to check the balancing criterion. All of these balanced trees render satisfactory results.

(b) Pseudo random-access store (e.g. disks and drums).

The storage structures reflecting the mapping must now be subdivided into blocks. Furthermore, the division must be such that the number of block transfers is close to 1 under all three, search, insertion, and deletion. On the other hand, block size though limited may vary. Among the balanced trees only B-trees meet the requirements and have increasingly found application ([Bay 72]).

These trees are perfectly balanced multiway trees. Each non-leaf (except for the root) has degree g with $k<g<2k+1$, the root itself can have degree g with $2<g<2k+1$ $(k>2)$. All nodes are blocks containing sorted ordered pairs and pointers, as seen from the following example of two B-trees (from [Bay 72]).

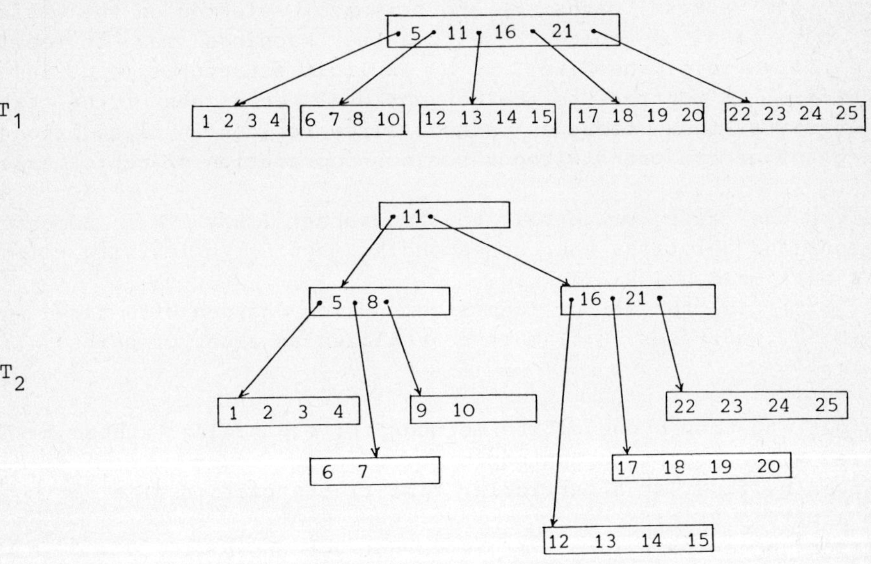

A new pair (n,a) is added to the appropriate node. If this results in overflow, the page is split into two that receive the first or last k pairs and pointers, respectively while the (k+1)st pair is added to the predecessor node (which may also overflow, etc.). For example, the tree T_2 above results from adding '9' to the tree T_1.

(c) Virtual store.

Virtual stores behave like random access store only when addressed objects are in working store. Otherwise they behave more like pseudo random-access store excluding, however, the control that a user may exercise for these (e.g. choice of block size). B-trees seem to adapt rather well to virtual store.

For a more detailed analysis of access time that includes functional and physical characteristics of storage devices see e.g. [Hae 74b]. [Tom 73] reports on an algorithm for evaluating and selecting storage schemata, given certain characteristics of an information structure and the operations performed on them.

6 System construction

Given certain abstract concepts to guide system design, and a set of technical methods for implementing these, they must be combined into a single coherent plan for system construction. Since people are involved this is as much a management problem as it is a technical one. Of course, the problem of a methodological approach to the design and construction of program systems is common to all activities in connection with computers and as such is being widely discussed; the reader is referred to catchwords such as "software engineering" or "structured programming" [SE 73, PM 75]. However, it takes on an added dimension in information systems (though not only for these) because of their sheer size.

In a programming process, two kinds of supporting methods should be distinguished [Hie 75]:

(i) methods supporting the program development process (increasing the transparency, reliability, adaptability and correctness of the system);

(ii) methods and criteria to check the completeness of the results of a programming phase (design and coding errors should be detected as early as possible).

The methods can be further categorized with regard to principles, tools and techniques, and management aspects. Baker [Bak 75] reports on a set of methods that have been employed for several years with the IBM Federal Systems Division.

(a) Principles.

- Top-down development. This refers to the process of concurrent design and development of program systems containing more than a single compilable unit. In top-down development one builds the system in a way which ideally eliminates writing any code whose testing is dependent on other code not yet written, or on data not yet available. Hence development proceeds in a way which minimizes interface problems by integrating and testing modules as soon as they are developed. Furthermore, major portion including the critical parts of the system have been in use long enough by delivery time to ensure high reliability.

  In practice, it has proven difficult to introduce top-down development since it involves changes of approach (top-down development is not just top-down design!). Even at this point in time a number of questions remain unanswered: Management involvement is essential; external constraints abound such as schedule requirements, faulty and late equipment, existing software to interface with; the depth of design must be such that critical problems are recognized and solved while on the other hand programmers should not become bored.

- Structured programming. This refers to practices used in coding individual program modules, and consists primarily of a set of guidelines and coding standards governing control flow, module organization and construction (a formalized description of the standards is presented by Mills [Mil 75]). Since not all programming languages lend themselves easily to structured programming, some of them (e:g: COBOL, FORTRAN, Assembler) had to be augmented and preprocessors had to be implemented for them. In others standard statement sequences are prescribed. The most notable result has been a high degree of programming discipline.

- Formal reviews. Strategies were developed as a formal means for design and code reviews during the development process. The developer or programmer "walks through" his efforts for a group of reviewers which consist of technical managers, other programmers and personnel for program testing.

(b) Tools.

The most important tool is the Development Support Library (DSL) serving as a vehicle for both structured programming and project communication and control. The DSL keeps all machineable data on a project, e.g. source and object codes in their latest version, linkage editor and job control languages, test data. An external library of current status binders is also part of the DSL. Machine and office procedures are provided for library maintenance and clerical tasks, the latter performed by a trained librarian. There is no need for programmers to generate or maintain their own personal libraries, allowing them to fully concentrate on the technical tasks at hand. The use of the DSL, it is claimed, has improved project control and lowered costs; benefits have accrued due to the more concentrated use of programmers and the support of measuring activities.

(c) Management aspects.

To a considerable extent, top-down development is a management problem. Another management innovation has been the introduction of Chief Programmer Teams (CPT). A CPT is a functional programming organization built around a nucleus of experienced professionals: A single highly qualified person, the chief programmer, has complete technical responsibility and will be the manager of the other people. There is an equally qualified backup programmer prepared to assume the role of chief programmer at any time. Both code the top level segments and other critical sections. Other programmers are added to the team only to code specific well-defined functions within a framework established by the chief and backup programmers. Finally, the CPT includes a librarian for the DSL. Although CPT´s have performed well, a few difficulties remain.

7 System evaluation

As part of the system development process various alternative designs, or commercially available solutions must be compared with respect to their effects and characteristics. Likewise, once an information system has been introduced, it requires an ongoing evaluation and monitoring in order to judge whether and to what extent expectations are being met. So far in none of these areas much progress can be detected.

Evaluation requirements fall into two broad categories.
(i) Evaluation with respect to the organizational environment.
(ii) Evaluation with respect to the technical characteristics.

Among the first, questions of interest are:
- Does the system meet the functional specifications, does it accept and generate the appropriate information structures, does it provide means for proper coordination?
- Does the system make provisions for proper communication, e.g. adequate languages, does the user accept the system?
- What effects does the system have on the organization, e.g. does it remove old bottlenecks or create new ones, does it require organization restructuring because of additional and perhaps unexpected capabilities, does it require additional resources that are already in short supply (witness the universally underestimated problem of data acquisition and input)?

Present techniques rarely go beyond checklists and the like. Worse, however, they study an organization before the introduction of the computer system and hence with all the shortcomings that the system is supposed to relieve, thus in effect continuing many of the shortcomings. Likewise, an analysis after introduction does little more than cure a few symptoms of a - perhaps incorrect - decision that cannot be reversed. It is hoped that formal methods such as the ones mentioned in ch. 3 will supply the tools for a rigid systematization of system evaluation.

Surprisingly enough, even on the technical level there do not seem to exist any global strategies for performance evaluation. This is probably due to the fact that the performance of an information system depends not only on the information system software proper, but to a large degree on supporting software such as the operating system, file management systems, message and task handling routines, and last not least on the characteristics of the hardware. As a consequence, from the viewpoint of information systems all performance modeling or measuring techniques are of a local nature. Some examples of these are (for a bibliography see [And 72]):
- Scheduling in multiprocessor, multiprogramming or timesharing systems.
- Scheduling of I/O-requests.

- Device and file management.
- Dynamic memory allocation.
- Console and user behavior.

Some important techniques are [Luc 71]:

- Analytic models: A mathematical representation of a computing system. Models based on queueing theory are particularly numerous. They are frequently employed to provide performance data on one particular component of a system. The major drawbacks of analytical models are oversimplification and exclusion of software performance.

- Benchmarks: One or more existing programs executed in the machine to be evaluated. A comprehensive series of benchmark runs can demonstrate differences in machine and I/O organization as well as in software quality. The difficulty lies in selecting benchmarks that are representative of the current and the expected job mix of the installation, something that is difficult to do for e.g. an interactive system. No adequate benchmarks for information systems have been mentioned so far in the literature.

- Synthetic programs: A program that is coded such that it covers a wide range of activities in the computer. As with benchmarks, evaluation is done by running series of synthetic programs. The difficulty in representing and predicting job mixes is the same as for benchmarks. However, synthetic programs provide more flexibility since they can be designed to include almost any desired measurement parameters. A price must be paid in the form of additional programming manpower required.

- Simulation [McD 70]. There are two basic types, event-oriented simulation that models the actual operations of a computer system, and data-driven simulation that manipulates empirically derived data. A number of simulation packages have been developed and are commercially available. Simulation offers the greatest advantages for projecting performance on proposed systems, however, validation problems are severe. Simulation is also excellent for performance monitoring as it provides a model of the system. Probably the greatest drawback of simulation is the high cost.

- Performance monitoring: A method of collecting data on the performance of an existing system. It is generally used to locate the hardware or software bottlenecks. Two activities are involved: collection of statistics during operations, and analysis of data. For the collection both, hardware and software techniques have been developed. The monitor is primarily oriented towards analyzing the behavior but provides no information on how much improvement can be made.

A further topic of system evaluation not covered by the techniques just mentioned is system reliability including fail-safe and recovery procedures.

8 Conclusion

When I was invited to present an overview on information systems I found it extremely difficult to do so without confining myself to generalities and platitudes. I decided finally on an approach of highlighting what I considered to be the most important topics by a few representative examples. These examples are but a fraction of all the important work going on in the field, and, mostly are research-oriented rather than issues of immediate practical relevance. I apologize to all whose work or whose areas of interest have not been mentioned; omitting them does not reflect in any way on their significance. On the other hand I hope that the paper provides a feeling for the wealth of problems that make information systems such a fascinating field.

Acknowledgement: The author is grateful to P.Deussen, H.Golde, G.Goos, K.-D.Kraegeloh, H.C.Mayr, E.J.Neuhold, C.-A.Petri, H.Visel for careful reading of the paper and helpful suggestions.

Bibliography

[Abr 74] J.R.Abrial, Data Semantics, in [Kli 74], 1-59

[Alt 74] E.Altmann, Einfuehrung in die Planungs- und Entscheidungstheorie, Nutzwertanalyse, Informatik-Kolleg der GMD, 1974

[And 72] H.A.Anderson, R.G.Sargent, Bibliography on Modeling, Evaluation and Performance Measurement of Time-Sharing Computer Systems, Comp.Rev. Vol 13(1972), no.12, 603-608

[Bak 75] F.T.Baker, Organizing for Structured Programming, in [PM 75], 38-86

[Bay 74] R.Bayer, Storage Characteristics and Methods for Searching and Addressing, Information Processing 74, North-Holland Publ.Co.74, 440-444

[Bay 72] R.Bayer, E.M.McCreight, Organization and Maintenance of Large Ordered Indexes, Acta Informatica 1(1972), no.3, 173-189

[Byr 73] S.Byrom, W.T.Hardgrave, Representation of Sets on Mass Storage Devices for Information Retrieval Systems, Proc.AFIPS Natl.Comp.Conf.1973, vol.42, 245-250

[Cod 70] E.F.Codd, A Relational Model of Data for Large Shared Data Banks, Comm. ACM vol 13(1970), no 6, 377-387

[Cod 71] E.F.Codd, A Data Base Sublanguage Founded on the Relational Calculus, ACM SIGFIDET Workshop on Data Description, Access and Control, Nov.1971, 35-68

[Col 68] L.S.Coles, An Online Question-Answering System with Natural Language and Pictorial Input, Proc. 23rd Natl. ACM Conf. (1968), 157-167

[CO 71] CODASYL Data Base Task Group Report, April 1971, available from: IFIP Data Processing Group

[CO 73] CODASYL DDL Journal of Development, June 1973, available from: IFIP Data Processing Group

[Ear 73] J.Earley, Relational Level Data Structures for Programming Languages, Acta Informatica vol 2(1973), 293-309

[Eve 74] G.C.Everest, Concurrent Update Control and Data Integrity, in [Kli 74], 241-268

[Goo 73] G.Goos, Hierarchies, in [SE 73], 29-46

[Gre 68] C.C.Green, B.Raphael, The Use of Theorem-Proving Techniques in Question-Answering Systems, Proc. 23rd Natl. ACM Conf. (1968), 169-181

[Gre 69] C.C.Green, The Application of Theorem Proving to Question-Answering Systems, Tech.Rep. No. CS138, Stanford Univ. 1969

[Hae 74a] Th.Haerder, Die Implementierung von Zugriffspfaden durch Bitlisten, Bericht Nr.DV 74-2, Technische Hochsch. Darmstadt, Fachber. Informatik

[Hae 74b] Th.Haerder, Zugriffszeitverhalten bei der Auswahl von Saetzen aus einer Datenbank, Bericht Nr.DV 74-3, Technische Hochsch. Darmstadt, Fachber. Informatik

[Har 74] W.T.Hardgrave, The Prospects for Large Capacity Set Support Systems Imbedded within Generalized Data Management Systems, Proc.Internatl.Comp.Symp.1973, North-Holland Publ.Co.74, 549-556

[Hen 68] R.Henn, H.P.Kuenzi, Einfuehrung in die Unternehmensforschung, Heidelberger Taschenbuecher Vols 38 and 39, Springer-Verlag 1968

[Hie 75] P.Hiemann, A New Look at the Program Development P in [PM 75], 11-37

[Kel 71] C.H.Kellogg, J.Burger, T.Diller, K.Fogt, The CONVERSE Natural Language Data Management System: Current Status and Plans, Proc. ACM Symp. on Info. Storage and Retrieval, U. of Maryland 1971, 33-46

[Kli 74] J.W.Klimbie, K.L.Koffeman (eds), Data Base Management, North-Holland Publ. Co. 1974

[Knu 68] D.E.Knuth, The Art of Computer Programming, Vol.1, Addison-Wesley Publ.Co. 1968.

[Knu 73] D.E.Knuth, The Art of Computer Programming, Vol.3, Addison-Wesley Publ.Co. 1973

[Kra 75] K.D.Kraegeloh, P.C.Lockemann, Hierarchies of Data Base Languages: An Example, Information Systems (in print)

[Lau 74a] K.Lautenbach, Exakte Bedingungen der Lebendigkeit fuer eine Klasse von Petri-Netzen, Bericht der GMD Nr.82, 1973

[Lau 74b] K.Lautenbach, H.A.Schmid, Use of Petri-nets for proving correctness of concurrent process systems, Information Processing 74, North-Holland Publ. Co 1974, 187-191

[Loc 75] P.C.Lockemann, Information Systems: Concepts, Interfaces, Techniques, in preparation for: Advanced Course on Informatics and Medicine, Hannover 1975

[Luc 71] H.C.Lucas,Jr., Performance Evaluation and Monitoring, ACM Comp. Surv. Vol 3(1971), no. 3, 79-91

[May 75] H.C.Mayr, P.C.Lockemann, Entscheidungs- und Instanzennetze, Bericht der Fak. fuer Informatik, Univ. Karlsruhe 1975

[McC 74] J.P.McCarthy, Automatic File Compression, Proc.Internatl Comp. Symp 1973, North-Holland Publ.Co.74, 511-516

[McD 70] M.H.MacDougall, Computer System Simulation: An Introduction, ACM Comp. Surv. Vol 2(1970), no. 3, 191-209

[Mil 75] H.D.Mills, The New Math of Computer Programming, Comm. ACM Vol 18(1975), no.1, 43-48

[Mon 72] C.A.Montgomery, Is Natural Language an Unnatural Query Language?, Proc. ACM Natl. Conf 1972, 1075-1078

[Nil 71] N.J.Nilsson, Problem-Solving Methods in Artificial Intelligece, McGraw-Hill 1971

[Noe 73] J.D.Noe, G.J.Nutt, Macro E-Nets for representation of parallel systems, IEEE Transact.on Comp., C-22 (1973) Nr.8, pp. 718-727

[Pet 73] C.A.Petri, Concepts of Net Theory, Proc. Math. Foundations of Computer Science 1973, 137-146

[PM 75] C.E.Hackl (ed), Programming Methodology, Lecture Notes in Computer Science, Vol 23, Springer-Verlag 1975

[Ram 74] Ch.Ramchandani, Analysis of Asynchronous Concurrent Systems by Petri Nets, Rep. MAC TR-120, Massachusetts Inst. of Tech., 1974

[Sco 72] G.Schott, Automatic Analysis of Inflectional Morphems in German Nouns. An Algorithm for Indexing, Acta Informatica Vol 1(1971/72), 360-374

[Scr 74] R.Schroff, Vermeidung von totalen Verklemmungen in bewerteten Petri-Netzen, Diss.TU Muenchen, 1974

[Sim 70] R.F.Simmons, Natural Language Question-Answering Systems: 1969, Comm. ACM Vol 13(1970), no. 1, 15-30

[SE 73] F.L.Bauer (ed), Advanced Course on Software Engineering, Lecture Notes in Econ. and Math. Systems, Vol 81, Springer-Verlag 1973

[Søl 74] A.Sølvberg, Computer-Assisted Design of the Automated Information System, Paper presented on GI meeting on "Ansaetze zur Organisationstheorie rechnergestuetzter Informationssysteme", GMD, 1974.

[Tei 74] D.Teichroew, E.A.Hershey, M.J.Bastarache, Information System Description Analysis, An Introduction to PSL/PSA, ISDOS Working Paper no.86, The University of Michigan, 1974

[Tho 69] F.B.Thompson, P.C.Lockemann, B.Dostert, R.S.Deverill, REL: A Rapidly Extensible Language System, Proc. 24th Natl. ACM Conf. (1969), 399-417

[Tom 73] F.W.Tompa, C.C.Gotlieb, Choosing a Storage Schema, Tech.Rep.No.54,May 73, Dept.of Computer Science, U.of Toronto

[Wed 74] H.Wedekind, Datenbanksysteme I, Reihe Informatik, Vol 16, B.I.-Wissenschaftsverlag 1974

[Wed 73] H.Wedekind, Systemanalyse, Carl Hanser Verlag 1973

[Woo 68] W.A.Woods, Procedural Semantics for a Question Answering Machine, Proc.AFIPS Fall Joint Comp.Conf. Vol 33 (1968), 457-471

The Problem of Requirements Analysis for Information Systems Applications

R. L. Ashenhurst
Institute for Computer Research
The University of Chicago
Chicago, Illinois USA

Over the past decade considerable progress has been made in understanding information systems, both their intrinsic nature and the role they play in the functioning of organizations. The impetus for this has of course been the advent of the computer system, the major component of most large information systems which are thereby characterized as "computer-based." The abovementioned understanding has come about as a concomitant of efforts on the very practical problems of developing computer-based information systems to meet stated organizational needs, and of integrating the resulting systems into organizational operations.

The most tangible accomplishments, however, have come in the area which may be termed systems engineering. Technological developments in hardware for implementing processing, file and communication functions have been accompanied by techniques for effectively configuring and estimating performance of this hardware, and by parallel developments in software. Not only have these aspects been put on a reasonably sound technical footing but various methodological aids have thence resulted, many themselves depending on the use of the computer.

This has enabled many organizations, particularly larger corporations, to build their information systems activities into a stable part of organizational functioning, and to evaluate them in terms of cost-effectiveness. Even among such organizations, however, there are occasional costly failures, and the situation with organizations just getting into computerization, or bringing it to a new level, is still far from stable. Despite what has been written about project management for information systems development, there are still many cases of projects which go awry, or result in an unsatisfactory system.

Requirements Analysis

It seems that some, if not the major part, of the cause of these phenomena can be laid at the door of a particular key phase of the system development process, that in which the functioning of the system, in terms of organizational orientation, is specified in detail. Although this phase is usually adequately identified in characterizations of the "system life cycle" [Ref. 2, sect. 4], a methodology for pursuing it, in general terms, is not at all thoroughly worked out.

The phase in question may be termed "requirements analysis." Requirements analysis proceeds from the overall system objectives, as contained in a prospectus or feasibility study, and produces a detailed specification of what information is gathered and processed, and made available in what form to whom and for what purposes. Ideally, no reference is made to particulars of data management systems, communication networks, or the like--the specification is "user-oriented" in terms of organizational functioning, not computer system functioning. Although this ideal may not always be entirely achievable, it is a worthwhile one to have, to mitigate the tendency to introduce the technological particulars too early, thereby losing sight of total system objectives. For purposes of this paper it is desirable to focus on this ideal, and to investigate the extent to which a general methodology for requirements analysis exists.

To put requirements analysis in a little more perspective, the following model of the systems development process is set forth, roughly following that of the ACM Information Systems Curriculum Report [ref. 1, sect. 2.2]. Here information systems development is divided into four main phases: (i) information analysis; (ii) system design; (iii) implementation; and (iv) operation. The first phase is further subdivided into (a) feasibility study and (b) system specification, while the second is subdivided into (c) logical system design and (d) physical system design. The feasibility study plays a vital part in the project but is essentially extraneous to the actual design of the system, being mainly framed in overall terms based on generalizations of the techniques used in succeeding phases. The physical system design consists in a detailed prescription of actual hardware and software, programs and procedures to serve as the basis for implementation. This leaves system identification and logical system design as the vital phases whereby one translates information functions from the organizational point of view into a set of system processes. The latter are concerned with the "content" or "meaning" of the information only incidentally, so all of these aspects must be somehow encompassed in system specification. The Curriculum Report characterized system specification as "analysis of how they [information needs] may be satisfied in terms of requirements on an information system." To emphasize the "system-free" nature of this specification, the term "requirements analysis" is used in this paper.

Roughly similar characterizations are given in other serious studies of the information systems development process, but there are few specifics given concerning how to go about requirements analysis. When such methodology is given, it tends to apply to a more restricted view of information systems than is appropriate--for example, an "input-processing-output" model. Such a model is of limited generality and tends to deemphasize some key aspects which must be paid attention to, such as handling of errors, and the like.

An argument that might be given is that requirements analysis, in the sense used here, is obviously so organization-specific that it would be inappropriate if not impossible to try to develop a general methodology, for either teaching or research purposes. Indeed, representatives of organizations which have "successful" information systems operations might (and do) claim that this should be part of what the information systems practitioner should learn "on the job," and that they have developed effective methods of requirements analysis for the particular type of enterprise (e.g. banking, steel production, or whatever) in which they happen to be engaged. It is still worthwhile, however, to see what can be said in general, abstracting from particular methods where publicly available (and they often are not), and incorporating the results into the body of knowledge concerning information systems which underlies teaching and research in the area. One needs more of an insight into requirements analysis than merely that it is the stage where "one has to think of everything." It may also be expected that such a general characterization might serve to modify the thinking of practitioners in the enterprises for which information systems functioning has already become "cut and dried."

A very simple example may be used to further explicate the notion of requirements analysis, and to show what kind of aspects must enter into a general methodology. Consider a very basic kind of information system, one which performs a single function, that of recording an association between an entity in the real world and an arbitrary (i.e. not predictable from the entity) code. For example, matching a person to social security or other registration number, or a particular thing (machine or article of furniture) to an inventory number. The system is to be given a satisfactory identification of the person or thing and to yield the code, or the information that no code has been assigned. At this stage is is assumed that the only information flowing into the system is queries and updates (new or changed entries, or deletions), and the only information flowing out is responses (to queries) and confirmations (of updates). That is, no summary reports or the like are required. This may be thought of as a basic "database" system, for recording purposes only.

A general requirements analysis for even this simple case could be quite complicated. It would have to be concerned with at least the following aspects. First, the essential _function_: Identification and characterization of _queries_ and _updates_, _responses_ and _confirmations_. What constitutes a valid query? (addressing mainly the problem of "satisfactory identification" of an entity). What constitutes a valid update? (similar considerations). What do valid responses and confirmations consist of? Second, the database: What is the nature of the information recorded, insofar as it is specific to entities and to codes? The word "database" is here used to imply content and interpretation, not merely to characterize the file or retrieval system. Third, anomalies: What are the possibilities for the production of results which do not really reflect the "true" situation and how shall these possibilities be treated? There must be recognition that, since the relationship between entity and code is arbitrary there is always the possibility of an undetectable erroneous update. But the questions of whether inconsistencies or ambiguities in the database will be tolerated, and what kind of verification procedures can be invited by confirmations, offer a range of possibilities.

So far, it seems that "any good systems analyst" would pay attention to these things in a requirements analysis, even if that phase of the systems development process were not specifically identified. In practice, however, it is surprising how often simple hindsight shows vital aspects to have been neglected. Two further sets of considerations are even more likely to be given insufficient attention because they are not on the "main line" of system functioning. One is considerations of confidentiality and security of the system, limiting its accessibility to those authorized, and also the important capabilities of auditing and evaluating. These may generally be grouped under the heading of integrity in the requirements analysis. The other is questions of privacy, and the mode of interaction with users (queriers and updaters) and beneficiaries of the information or other interested parties (who may or may not be the users). Without implying (very much, at least) a value judgement, these may be grouped under the heading of humanity. Of late much attention has been paid to integrity and humanity of information systems [refs. 3, 4], but without much specific as to how they may be satisfactorily incorporated at the requirements analysis stage.

Although for the simple case illustrated it is probable that a general paradigm for requirements analysis could be set up, one that was even logically complete in some sense rather than a group of "check-lists," it is not clear how to extend such a paradigm to cover complicated (much more complicated) cases. The simple example, however, does illustrate the delineation of the requirements analysis area, with no suppositions as to what kind of file and communication systems should be set up to answer the requirements effectively and efficiently.

Systems Characterization

In searching for a way to develop requirements analysis generally, it is clear that the concepts of "systems engineering," such as are applicable to processing, file and communication systems, are not the issue. Even techniques for "data management systems," as the term is usually used, are of limited relevance, although they represent a highly useful vehicle for system design of databases once a requirements analysis has yielded a detailed system specification.

The concept of process has proved useful in technology of computer and operating system design. The relevance of this notion to the general characterization of information systems has been initiated elsewhere [ref. 5]. This notion indeed allows a more general formulation of information systems than either of the classical "input-processing-output" or "file-query-update" models do, separately or in combination. As such, it can play a valuable role in passing from requirements analysis to (logical) system design, especially in permitting integrity to be designed in (multiple simultaneously functioning processes constitute a process) and also humanity (human interaction can be defined in terms of processes). But the notion is only marginally helpful in considering requirements analysis in itself.

The concept of database as a collection of realworld information (in some sense, the definition includes the information and its interpretation) has been mentioned above. The description and documentation of data (or database) management systems are usually formulated in system-functional terms [ref. 6], only tenuously related to this extended interpretation. A data management system in which the files are hierarchically organized is appropriate when the realworld structures represented and the way in which they are to be viewed also have a hierarchical aspect, and it is very inappropriate otherwise. A data management system permitting elements to be organized in "data structure sets" can represent general relationships, and easily lends itself to anomalies which are hard to detect. A data management system with a relational structure is less subject to these anomalies, but suggests very little by way of interpretation.

A notion common to all these types is the "entry-attribute-value" one, which attaches a general interpretation to records in terms of realworld entities, attributes of which are represented by the record format, in which data elements therefore represent specific values of attributes. This is useful as far as it goes, but to say "this says it all," as some writers tend to, is insufficient. From the present point of view, it is now desirable to explore what useful classifications of entities there are, and how properties of information systems involving them can be inferred from observation of their realworld situation.

Returning to the more general problem of information systems, of which the database is only one, albeit crucial, component, it is appropriate to mention some common classifications of aspects which can be used as input to a study of requirements analysis, as contained implicitly or explicitly in treatises on information systems [refs. 7,8,9]:

(a) material-manpower-money decomposition;

(b) space-time decomposition;

(c) organization structure decomposition;

(d) logistical/operational-tactical/strategic decomposition.

Classification (a) implies that an information system can be decomposed into subsystems for managing material--raw material processed to finished goods as well as plant and equipment; manpower--in both line and staff positions;and money --cashflow and general financing. For present purposes it may be noted that these three aspects indeed involve entities which tend to have general properties in common, which are profitably isolated and viewed from the point of view of information systems. A defect in this classification, however, is that intangible entities (other than perhaps accounting ones) such as services (performed as a main function of the enterprise or as auxiliary to it) tend to get obscured, since the classification is so oriented toward tangibles.

Classification (b) indicates that it is often useful to reflect in an information system a partitioning by location (activity sites) and time periods (weeks, months, quarters, etc.), and that this partitioning emphasizes special problems which are associated with spatial or temporal aspects (such as correlating different ways of locating points or locations in the same geographical area, or reconciling weekly with monthly data). Indeed, methods of handling periodic information have been quite well developed, since this is so fundamental to the reckoning of the progress of enterprises, and "geographical" information systems concepts, while not as uniformly applicable, have been recognized as having particular characterizing features (particularly in connection with census data).

Classification (c) implies that the organization structure can be used as a reference framework for structuring information systems which are to be integrated into it. While this may be of some overall help, the fact that the interaction among organizational units is often the essential phenomenon, and that in any case the organization structure only dimly reflects the true activity structure of an organization, limits the usefulness of this way of looking at things.

Classification (d), usually given as a three-component one (logistical/operational not distinguished) has been widely proposed as an appropriate way of looking at "levels" of information system function. Without explicating the distinction between levels here in detail, it may be said that although relevant characterizations of the nature of information handling at each level have been made (e.g. structured to unstructured), the classification has not yielded too much prescription as to how to proceed once the level at which one is working has been determined. One value of the classification, however, is to emphasize that information systems functioning at the higher (tactical/strategic) levels must generally be built upon ones functioning at the lower (logistical/operational) levels, rather than being self-contained. Hence the dreams of "instant MIS" are just that.

A Typology of Information Systems

The remainder of this paper will explore some directions in which useful characterizations may be constructed, making use of the above ideas. This will serve mainly to indicate lines of further study, rather than to set forth in full the foundations of requirements analysis. That task remains to be done, and although it has many aspects, the importance of some general and consistent approach being formulated is the reason for the reference in the paper title to "The Problem of Requirements Analysis."

Product monitoring systems. The first thing to note is that among the more successful information systems applications are those for monitoring the manipulation of tangible entities. The primary example of such are the production and inventory systems of industry. Production processes which proceed from raw materials to finished goods, and the associated inventory activities, are routinely supported by information systems, and the physical procurement and distribution activities on either end of the processes are also included. When the production process is of continuous flow type, such as chemical production or textiles, the quantization of material is different but the essential quality of the support system is similar. Because of the tangible nature of the entities processed, and the understood nature of the processing, the introduction of a model on which to base the information system is straightforward, and the monitoring is thereby rendered effective. The fact that material is only kept track of for the time through the system allows the more common problems with database handling to be avoided.

Such systems will be here termed product monitoring systems, to focus on the intrinsic element which seems to make them more straightforward to design. The methodology of constructing the bill of material and parts explosion, and tracking work-in-progress, all are straightforwardly interpretable and straightforwardly applied. Note that "product" here does not imply the narrow sense of finished or marketable product, but rather any kind of tangible goods involved in the procurement-processing-inventory-distribution cycle.

Indeed, probably the major pitfall associated with such systems is the tendency to design fundamentally different types of systems as if they were product monitoring systems. For example, clinical care support systems that are built on the model that sees patients as "processed through" the system by physicians and other medical personnel, are inappropriate.

The definition can, however, be extended to include two types of "near-tangibles." Systems for processing money, such as banks use in their daily operations, are essentially of this type. Although money as processed does not have tangible form, it does not appear and disappear as it flows through the system, so given proper controls it can be viewed as "product." Another type of entity is information in various tangible forms, such as text and/or pictures. The basic systems employed in the publishing and printing industry, as well as the job-processing functions of a computing center, can be viewed in this light. Here it may be objected that such processing systems do not seem to be so well understood. There is frequent criticism of computing centers as production operations, for example. This can be attributed to the fact that in the early days the design of the corresponding production system itself was not so well understood, and it may be argued that the basic job-oriented facility is now a thing that can be realized effectively, with appropriate monitoring by an operating system. Another seeming counter-example is mailing label production systems, which frequently give demonstrably inferior performance. Here it can be stated that the fault lies in trying to produce mailing labels directly from an essentially different type of system, a database system for keeping track of real or prospective customers, or other sets of individuals.

What is being said here is that once such systems are realized for what they are, the design according to product monitoring principles is reasonably straightforward. Note that "transaction monitoring" has not been the focus in the foregoing characterization. This is because transactions enter into many types of activities, and do not seem to be the important fundamental focus. Indeed, for the next group of systems to be discussed, treating the transaction in the same way as for product monitoring systems can lead to trouble.

Service monitoring systems. The second type to be considered will be called service monitoring systems, although the term is similarly used in a sense extended from that of a marketable service. Services can be internal to an organization or can constitute a major or minor aspect of its external orientation. The point of emphasis is that the fact that service is intangible makes the analysis and design of service systems much more subtle than for product monitoring. Aspects of a service transaction may be separated over time and space, substantial databases representing situations extending over time may be involved, and there may be no straightforward model for how the service is performed in its entirety.

Many service operations in this extended sense can be grouped under two subheadings: registration and fulfilment. These terms are each used in extended senses of the words as ordinarily applied, but comprehend activities which are similar from the information-processing point of view.

Registration systems are in essence the simple record-update-query systems such as appeared in the earlier example. Basically, a registration system is built around a database consisting of records concerning some well-defined set of entities, their attributes and current status. A fourth function may also be included, that of producing extensive or aggregate reports on current status. These may be for the purpose of selecting interesting subgroups of registrants. This category includes systems recording registration in the formal sense, such as license registration, or school enrollment, and also other systems such as catalogues of people or artifacts with certain properties. Many so-called "governmental" applications involve the construction of substantial registries, of land parcels or taxpayers and the like. Problems in maintaining registration systems are as already discussed in the example above. Particular difficulties are encountered when a set of individuals makes up the database who are not enrolled by their own action, such as prospective donors, etc. or have "made the list" by some unrelated voluntary action.

Fulfilment systems are transaction processing systems where there is some idea of commitment to follow up. "Subscription fulfilment" systems are a prime example, where subscribers are enrolled, and pay to receive a sequence of monthly magazine deliveries, or whatever. Besides subscriptions, reservation systems and credit card and charge account systems are of this type, involving transactions directly with the public. The category also includes systems internal to commercial operation,the common accounting systems of accounts receivable, accounts payable and payroll, and the important system complementing the product monitoring system of industry, the order processing system. Calling all these fulfilment systems in an extended sense emphasizes the main problem associated with them, namely maintaining the association among a sequence of transactions and actions separated in time, but logically part of the same record activity. Fulfilment systems frequently have a registration system as a component, such as a file of customers, or employees (in the case of payroll) or equipment, with all the attendant problems.

Both the foregoing types of systems may be discussed as standard types, and if it is realized that the "standard transaction" is subject to anomalies, comprehensively formulated. The main problem seems to be with unanticipated anomalies in the chain of events, and lack of provision for dealing with them.

Professional support systems. Other types of systems which might seem to be in this general category, however, have the further quality that the basic processes supported cannot be completely modelled but depend on "professional expertise." They may therefore be distinguished as professional support systems. Two major subcategories are treatment systems and design systems.

Treatment systems take their name from the clinical care case, where a patient is given medical treatment by a physician, backed up by nursing and other clinical services. The failure in designing such systems has been to recognize the professional component. Not only must the outcome of the treatment depend on this, but the professional must be supported as such, which requires that the system support, not dictate, and be flexible. In the medical case, the concept of the "problem-oriented record" is one which has been developed to give a paradigm for the form support should take. The physicial defines a "problem-list," and prescribes treatment in its context, while the information system integrates test data and prescriptions into that format. Again, the category seems to be a more extensive one than the basic medical treatment one, covering educational systems (teacher-pupil), legal systems (lawyer-client), and others such as social service systems.

Design systems are a related category, somewhat similar in concept. An engineer or system designer, or a product designer, works in a manner determined by professional practice, and needs a system which flexibly supports that mode of operation. Because the design process is not capable of being modelled, much more in the way of information about the designed object must be furnished for the system to be effective. Graphic modes of presentation are important. Sometimes a system is called on to support successive phases of design in an integrated manner, as with information system design itself, or provide a whole framework for design and implementation, as with automated machine tools or laboratory automation.

Both treatment and design systems may have registration and fulfilment systems as ancillaries (billing, etc.), which is another source of problems. The most critical pitfall, however, is not being sufficiently flexible to accommodate professional practice. To paraphrase the riddle about where the gorilla sleeps, it behooves the system analyst to ask, "How does the professional go about his business" and to heed the quick short answer, "Pretty much as he pleases."

Management support systems. As a final category of interest management support systems may be distinguished. Instead of trying to characterize these as systems that work on the tactical/strategic organizational level, the characterization should be based on the functions carried out. Five subcategories which cover most activities of this kind are evaluation, assignment, prediction, planning and control. All of these may function on several levels, with increasing degrees of "sophistication." For example, assignment systems include those which support assignment of workers to duty stations (operational level), construction of budgets (tactical level), and long-term division of production among plants (strategic level). All are "decision-support" systems in some sense, but the nature of the decision activity involved in each case is a crucial part of the analysis. All types may function as interrelated subsystems of a more comprehensive "management information system."

Evaluation systems give an evaluation of some empirical structure or situation, based on a model and an evaluation function. Statistical models are often necessary here. Evaluation can apply at the operational, tactical or strategic level.

Assignment systems support the activities of matching one set of resources to another, to conform to some more or less formally specified objective. Included are systems for allocation (division and distribution of resources), scheduling (matching activities to time slots), and budgeting (matching activities to account categories). In many cases a model exists, often formulated as a mathematical problem, which formally optimizes subject to constraints.

Prediction, or forecasting, is an offshoot of evaluation, where the objective of the evaluation is a prediction of future course. Simulation techniques are a basic tool, while statistical techniques are again heavily used in forecasting.

Planning systems may involve evaluation, assignment and prediction, and prescriptions for what will be done in the future. An important part of plans is contingencies, and planning systems must take alternatives into account.

Control systems incorporate the idea of "feedback" or controlling input. Although the completely automatic control system (e.g. inventory control) is included here, the wider context of "human-mediated control" is what is basically meant. Evaluation, assignment, prediction and planning may be subsystems.

The important thing about the first four of these management systems is to recognize their character, that what they are to do is to aid in producing evaluations, assignments, predictions and plans. These in turn provide a context for control, which may be regarded as the ultimate in function to be achieved, although again at various levels--operational, tactical or strategic.

All of these types of systems have the property that they involve unstructured data, sometimes vague premises, and depend for their validity on complicated realworld systems involving humans. Although these aspects have been identified and appreciated, the system development methodology tends to be more prescribed for the systems which deal with more regular if not regulated phenomena.

A Basis for Requirements Analysis

The relevance of the classification into product monitoring, service monitoring, professional support and management support systems, and the subcategories, can be a starting point for a more systematic approach to requirements analysis. Because the classification is keyed to function, one can proceed from function to information requirements in a relatively straightforward way. For each subcategory, questions of information type (material-manpower-money or time-space, etc.) are appropriately considered. A model of how the system should function may then be developed which does not presuppose specific hardware or software configurations.

In proceeding from the requirements analysis to the logical design, attention must be paid to the capabilities desired other than the "main line" processing. Separate guidelines for integrity and humanity have to be incorporated. Also, a general requirement should be observed of making the system more understandable as its function becomes less specifically keyed to a model. For example, in treatment and design systems, the ability to give the professional a good picture of a current situation or configuration is very important. The latter is often capable of being accurately modelled in observational terms while the professional input is not. For management support systems it is important that the system be able to supply the answers to questions of the type "Did you include..." and "How do you figure..." that managers would ordinarily ask subordinates. In both categories there should be flexibility of the professional or manager to reorient or transform data into a form that seems personally congenial.

Systems analysis techniques have tended to be based on the synthesis of report forms and record forms, as fundamental components in systems structure linking the realworld information to the processing system [ref. 10]. Although these are certainly of prime importance, and can be regarded as having the "system-free" character, they are not the whole story. This traditional emphasis, in fact, often obscures the questions surrounding the handling of exceptions and anomalies which must be an integral part of good requirements analysis.

The essence of what is being proposed is that it is important to specify what a system really "does" in different ways and in more detail than is customary with prelimary documentation. This requires a functional terminology which is not too specific to the application, but not so general as to leave major problems unaddressed. The functions implied by the foregoing systems typology are intended to supply a context in which such terminology may be developed.

Using these ideas as a starting point for requirements analysis may assist in developing a more detailed specification, which can then be subjected to the techniques of logical and physical system design. This can also be a starting point for surveying and evaluating present practice. The problem of having a project not implemented as the specifiers thought it would be should thus be alleviated, since part of the function of a good requirements analysis is to provide a checklist for system features as they are developed in the design. Thus the risks of system projects falling short of expectations should be materially reduced.

It is hoped that by emphasizing a functional approach to requirements analysis, the present ideas can be used as a framework to make that phase of systems development more systematic.

References

1. Ashenhurst, R. L. (ed.) "Curriculum Recommendations for Graduate Professional Programs in Information Systems--A Report of the ACM Curriculum Committee on Computer Education for Management," Communications of the ACM, v. 15, no. 5 (May 1972) pp. 363-98.

2. Benjamin, R. I., Control of the Information System Development Cycle, Wiley-Interscience (1971).

3. Conway, R. W., W. L. Maxwell and H. L. Morgan, "On the Implementation of Security Measures in Information Systems," Communications of the ACM, v. 15, no. 4 (April 1972) pp. 211-20.

4. Sterling, T. C., "Guidelines for Humanizing Computerized Information Systems: A Report from Stanley House," Communications of the ACM, v. 17, no. 11 (November 1974) pp. 609-13.

5. Ashenhurst, R. L., "On the Problem of Characterizing Information Systems," (in Proceedings of the Wharton Conference on Research on Computers in Organizations) Data Base, v. 5, no. 2-4 (Winter 1973), pp. 148-156.

6. Martin, J., Computer Data-Base Organization, Prentice-Hall (1975).

7. Alexander, M. J., Information Systems Analysis, Science Research Associates (1974).

8. Davis, G. B., Management Information Systems, McGraw-Hill (1974).

9. Siegel, P., Strategic Planning of Management Information Systems, Petrocelli Books (1975).

10. Couger, J. D. and R. W. Knapp (Eds.) System Analysis Techniques, Wiley (1974).

Speichertechnik und Rechnerarchitektur

H.-O. Leilich

Institut für Datenverarbeitungsanlagen
Technische Universität Braunschweig

1. Historischer Zusammenhang

Von Anbeginn der mechanisierten Steuer- und Rechentechnik spielte die Art der Speicherung der Befehle und Daten bei der Strukturierung der Geräte eine entscheidende Rolle.

Wenn man an den Jaquard'schen Webstuhl mit der Lochbandsteuerung oder an Babbage's Konzeption des wahlfrei zugreifbaren Speichers (1000 50-stellige Zahlen) denkt, so erkennt man einen Entstehungsvorgang, den man heute mit "TOP-DOWN-DESIGN" beschreibt: nach der (konstruktiven aber noch abstrakten) Idee wurde ein Gerät erdacht. In Babbage's Zeit (1835) konnte der "Random-Access-Speicher" nicht realisiert werden. Konrad Zuse hat den Adreßspeicher mit den technischen Mitteln seiner Zeit gebaut (z.B. 1941: 64 Worte in der Z4). Es ist aber sicher kein historischer Zufall, daß John von Neumann die Brauchbarkeit der Grundfunktion des beschreibbaren adressierbaren Speichers für die effiziente Programmierung von Algorithmen (mithilfe der Sprünge) und die Kennzeichnung der Operanden durch Adreßangaben (samt der Speicherverwaltung durch Adreß-Manipulationen) just in den Jahren erkannte als Williams mit einer Elektronenstrahlröhre einen Speicher baute, der viele Tausend Informationsworte mit elektronischer Geschwindigkeit dem Rechen- und Steuerwerk bereitstellen konnte, und zwar mit wahlfrei adressierbarem Zugriff zum Schreiben und Lesen.

Danach begann die gezielte Erforschung der physikalischen Möglichkeiten zur technischen Herstellbarkeit noch besserer (schnellerer, zuverlässiger, größerer) Geräte für die Realisierung des Adreßspeichers (Cryogenics, Kernspeicher, Filmspeicher) und nach der Erfindung des Kernspeichers (Forrester, 1952) der stürmische Aufschwung der elektronischen Datenverarbeitung.

Gewisse Eigenarten der technischen Geräte mußten inkauf genommen werden und hatten rückwirkend einen wesentlichen Einfluß auf die Architektur der Rechenanlagen:

a) Die feste Wortlänge löste jahrelange Debatten über die optimale Größe und Formatierung der Worte (für Befehle und Daten) aus. Die Art, wie man (mühevoll) "optimal" einen oder mehrere Befehle in ein Wort packte oder mehrere Worte für einen langen Operanden benutzte, bestimmte weitgehend die inneren Rechnerstrukturen.

b) Die Tatsache, daß Arbeitsspeicher nur von einer gewissen Mindestgröße an wirtschaftlich herstellbar waren, führte zum Verharren auf dem Ein-Speicher-Konzept und den großen, zentralen Uniprozessor-Anlagen.

c) Kostengesichtspunkte führten zu automatisch verwalteten Speicher-Hierarchien ("virtuelle Speicher").

d) Die dem Adreßspeicher inhärente Struktur der einseitigen Abbildung eines gegebenen Adreßraumes auf den Inhaltsraum erschwert den Aufbau von allgemeineren Speichersystemen, z.B. von Informationssystemen, bei denen die Informationselemente (Sätze) nicht nach einem bekannten Merkmal, das noch dazu fest an einen teuren Ort gebunden und dicht durchnumeriert ist, sondern nach Relationen zwischen beliebigen Teilen der Inhalte (Felder) und äußeren Anfragen aufgesucht werden sollen. (Man weiß, das Assoziativspeicher die Beschränkung des Namensraumes (=Speicherraum) aufheben und den Zugang zu den Objekten aufgrund von Inhaltskriterien erlauben.)

Die Struktur des Adreßspeichers hat sicherlich Pate gestanden an der Wiege der heute als allgemeingültig gelehrten Definition:

$$\text{Objekt} ::= \langle \text{Name, Wert} \rangle$$

Seit Turing weiß man, daß ein Automat mit einem sequentiellen Bandspeicher alle berechenbaren Funktionen lösen kann, d.h. man könnte damit Universal-Rechenmaschinen bauen. Andererseits ist es bekannt und allgemein üblich, mittels Adreßspeichern sequentielle Speicherstrukturen zu implementieren (z.B. Stacks). Es ist leicht, einen Assoziativspeicher als Adreßspeicher zu benutzen. Möglich, wenn auch langwieriger, ist es aber auch mit einem Adreßspeicher (und einem entsprechenden Programmsystem) die Funktion eines Assoziativspeichers zu simulieren.

Jeder Speichertyp könnte also als (einziger) Speicher eines universellen Automaten eingesetzt werden, es bestehen jedoch gewaltige Unterschiede in ihrer praktischen Brauchbarkeit. Die Art und Größe der Bausteine haben einen grundlegenden Einfluß auf die Architektur und Art und Nützlichkeit der erzielbaren Bauwerke. Die Rechnerarchitektur wird also ganz wesentlich von den physikalischen, technischen und ökonomischen Gegebenheiten der Speichertechnik beeinflußt.

2. Stand und Trend der Speichertechniken

Elektronische bzw. magnetische Speicher mit wahlfreiem Wort-Zugriff im Bereich von bis zu einigen Millionen Bit Kapazität und einigen Mikrosekunden (oder Bruchteilen davon) Zugriffszeit als Arbeitspeicher zur direkten (immer etwas zu langsamen) Zusammenarbeit mit den Rechen- und Steuerwerken sind heute verfügbar (Bild 1 zeigt den heutigen Stand mit dem geschätzen Trend für die nächsten 5-10 Jahre). Seit 1948 gibt es für die Massenspeicherung magnetische Speicher (Bänder, Trommeln, Platten), die durch einen seriellen Datenzugriff mithilfe mechanischer Bewegung des Mediums gekennzeichnet sind. Durch Kombination von kontinuierlich rotatorischer Bewegung, gesteuerter transversaler, mechanischer Bewegung, ausgefeilten Start-Stop-Mechanismen und elektronischer Spurauswahl erlangte man Kapazitäten (pro Einheit) bis zu mehreren Milliarden Bits bei Zugriffszeiten im Bereich von 10 - 100 Millisekunden (Bild 1).

Dazwischen liegt aber der große "Memory-Access-Gap", den sich kein System-Architekt je gewünscht hat! Ingenieure versuchten diese Kluft von beiden Seiten aus zu schließen: durch billige elektronische bzw. magnetische Techniken (Ferrit, Halbleiter) oder schnellere Mechanik (Trommeln etc.). Aufgrund physikalisch-technischer Eigenheiten der verfügbaren Technologien erwies sich der Austausch zwischen Kapazität und Zugriffszeit in diesem Bereich als sehr ineffizient. Neue Technologien wurden erfunden und mit großen Aufwand entwickelt (z.B. magnetische Filme, Ferritplatten und Cryogenics) die sich gegenüber konkurrierenden alten bzw. neuen Techniken nicht durchsetzen konnten. Heute hat man Grund anzunehmen, daß die Kluft sich von der "schnellen" Seite her verengt (CCD, Bubbles, EBEAM).

Zur Ausweitung zu noch höheren Kapazitäten wurden komplizierte mechanische Geräte zum automatischen Nachladen von magnetischen Speichermedien entwickelt (z.B. Magnet-Karten-Speicher). Die neuesten Versionen (IBM 3800, CDC 38000) benutzen kurze Magnetbänder mit sehr hoher Aufzeichungsdichte. Magnetbandmaschinen für den aufwendigen Start-Stop-Betrieb werden langsam durch Magnetplatten verdrängt. Lochkarten und Lochstreifen - als bequem transportable und manipulierbare Speichermedien - haben in Magnetbandkassetten und billigen biegsamen Kunststoffplatten ("Floppy Disks") eine neue Konkurrenz.

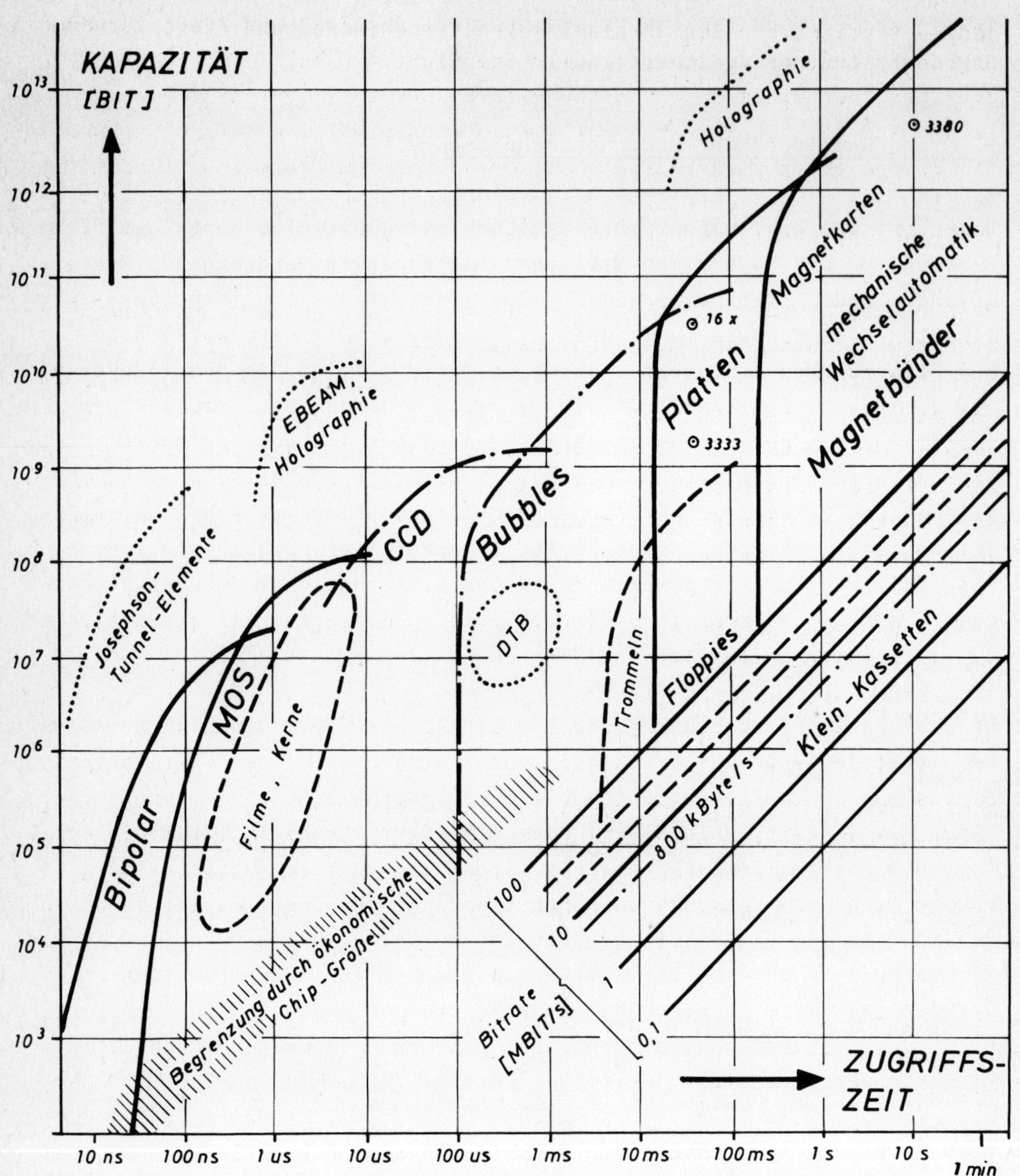

Bild 1 : *Kapazitäts-Zugriffszeit-Diagramm*

Schätzung für 1980 einsetzbare Speichertechnologien

– – – weitgehend überholt

——— sicher einsetzbar

—·— wahrscheinlich einsetzbar

········ experimentell

Aus diesem verfügbaren bzw. sich entwickelndem Spektrum realisierbarer Speichertechniken wurden virtuelle Speicher-Strukturen implementiert, die aus einer Hierarchie von schnelleren und langsameren Speichern bestehen und die mithilfe von Software und speziellen Hardwareeinrichtungen die vom Anwender gewünschten Speichersysteme simulieren. Außer dem virtuellen großen und effektiv schnellen Adreßspeicher gehören hierzu auch Informationssysteme und Datenbanken.

Da die Hardware-Speichereinheiten nicht a priori genügend fehlerfrei arbeiten, benutzt man - meist hardware-unterstützte - Prüf- und Korrekturverfahren zur Implementierung genügend fehlerfreier (virtueller) Speicherstrukturen. Entsprechend dem ingenieurmäßigen Wirtschaftlichkeitsdenken dürften bei immer größeren, dichteren und schnelleren Speichern auch die Korrekturverfahren eine immer größere Rolle spielen, zumal bei der Benutzung moderner Halbleitertechniken der Zusatzaufwand (Hardwarekosten und Zeit) relativ klein, d.h. ökonomisch vertretbar bleibt.

Der technologische Fortschritt bei den verschiedenen Speichertechnologien führte im evolutionären Sinn zu immer schnelleren, billigeren und leistungsfähigeren Rechnern aller bekannten Klassen. Die etwa 1965 auf dem Speichermarkt erschienene Halbleitertechnologie reifte zur Großintegrationstechnik (LSI) aus und verstärkte - seit ca. 1972 über den Kernspeicher dominierend - diesen kontinuierlichen Wachstumstrend. Darüberhinaus wirkt jedoch LSI auf die Rechnerarchitektur revolutionierend. Die Gründe sind nicht ganz neu und wurden schon oft diskutiert - sie sollen aber wegen des Zusammenhangs mit dem Thema dieses Referates im folgenden Abschnitt nochmals zusammengestellt werden.

3. Auswirkungen der Technologie integrierter Schaltungen

Die physikalisch-technischen Eigenarten der großintegrierten Halbleitertechnologie kann man bekanntlich folgendermaßen umreißen:

A Sehr viele (10^3-10^5) Schaltelemente können auf engstem Raum aufgebaut und sehr wirtschaftlich hergestellt werden.

B Daraus können praktisch beliebige Schaltkomplexe zur Verarbeitung und Speicherung von Informationen gebildet werden.

C Die Zahl der äußeren Leitungsanschlüsse für einen Baustein ist wegen technischer Probleme stark beschränkt (12-50).

D Der Entwurf und die Fertigungsvorbereitungen für einen neuen Baustein sind (trotz des Einsatzes von automatischen Entwurfsmethoden, Master-Slice-Techniken etc.) sehr viel teurer als die Massenherstellung eines vorhandenen Bausteins.

Während man also nach A, B und C dahin tendiert, weitgehend in sich abgeschlossene große Schaltungskomplexe mit wenigen Außenanschlüssen zu realisieren, stellt sich - sobald man den ganzen "Computer" nicht mehr "on a chip" realisieren kann - nach D das Problem der großen Typenzahlen bzw. der universellen Benutzbarkeit großer Schaltungskomplexe (Gegensatz: auf der NOR-Baustein-Ebene brauchte man prinzipiell nur einen Typ!). Tatsächlich ist das Angebot von verschiedenen Typen von mittel- und großintegrierten Bausteinen in den letzten Jahren gewaltig angewachsen.

Diese Eigengesetzmäßigkeiten machen die Integrations-Technologien geradezu ideal für die Speichertechnik geeignet, da Speicher schon immer regelmäßige Schaltungsstrukturen mit einer relativ kleinen Anzahl von notwendigen äußeren Verbindungsleitungen darstellten. Kein Wunder, daß nach einem technologischen Reifeprozeß das "integrierte Bit" in Bezug auf Zugriffszeit und schließlich auch auf Preis dem Ferritkern den Rang abgelaufen hat.

Darüberhinaus bietet die Halbleitertechnik die Basis sowohl für die logischen Verknüpfungschaltungen als auch für die Speichertechnik (Punkt B), d.h. die Speicherbausteine sind unmittelbar schaltungsmäßig kompatibel zu denen der Rechen-, Steuer- und Verbindungswerke. Der Fortfall von aufwendigen Anpassungsschaltungen (Leistungs- und Leseverstärker) wirkt sich dahingehend aus, daß auch kleinere Speicherkapazitäten (z.B. einige hundert oder tausend Bit) in praktisch jeder Zugriffsstruktur wirtschaftlich herstellbar sind und dem Rechnerarchitekten zur Verfügung stehen. Der gute alte "zentrale Speicher" ist damit nicht mehr eine technisch-wirtschaftliche Notwendigkeit.

Damit ist es wirtschaftlich vertretbar, jedes beliebige Schaltnetz als Speicher zu realisieren, denn schließlich stellt ja jeder Adreßspeicher (im Lesebetrieb) einen Umordner allgemeiner Art dar, der nämlich jedem Element aus der Menge der Adressen (Eingangsmenge) ein beliebig angebbares Element aus der Menge der möglichen Speicherinhalte (Ausgangsmenge) zuordnet. Ein als ein Bausteintyp hergestellter Adreßspeicher dient also - im Rahmen seiner Adreßkapazität und Wortlänge - als ein Schaltnetz,dessen spezielle Funktionen durch einen letzten Fertigungsschritt ("maskenprogrammierte Festspeicher), durch eine einmalige Vorbehandlung (programmierbare Festspeicher) für den Einsatzzweck festgelegt werden oder gar im

Betrieb elektronisch geändert werden können (EAROM'S oder R/W-Memories). An sehr einfachen Beispielen kann man zwar zeigen, daß (Lese-) Speicher nicht in allen Fällen als Netz-Realisierung praktisch infrage kommen (z.B. ein Übergangsnetz von einem Register zu einem anderen).

Ernsthaft wurde jedoch vorgeschlagen, daß Schaltnetze von einiger Komplexität durch Adreßspeicher sinnvoll ersetzt werden können, um das Problem der Bauteil-Proliferation zu lösen (z.B. die komplette Logik für 3 Bits eines Parallel-Addierers [1]). Da bei Adreßspeichern die Zahl der Worte exponentiell mit der Zahl der Adressenbits steigt, sind Realisierungen von Netzen mit vielen Eingängen als Speicher sehr ineffektiv. Man hat daher vorgeschlagen, assoziative Speicher dafür zu benutzen, deren Wortzahl nicht von der Zahl der Eingangsleitungen abhängt (Functional Memories, Array-Logic [2]. Genauso kann man durch geschickte Kodierung des Speicherinhaltes und evtl. spätere Umsetzung durch weitere Netze (Speicher) die Zahl der Ausgangsleitungen in vernünftigen Grenzen halten.

Das bekannnteste Beispiel für die Verwendung von Speichern an Stelle von Schaltnetzen ist das der Mikro-Programmierung. Wilkes [3] hat die Methodik (und das Wort) 1951 nicht mit der hier behandelten Motivation eingeführt, sondern zur Vereinfachung des Entwurfs von Schaltwerken durch Formatierung der Steuergrößen zu "Mikrobefehlen" und zur Benutzung der von den Maschinensprachen bekannten Programmiertechniken. Neben diesen - heute noch unverändert bedeutsamen und in der Praxis anerkannten - Motiven bietet die Mikroprogrammierung einen Weg zur Lösung des Typenzahl-Problems und ermöglicht die Nutzung der LSI-Technologie für die Herstellung sehr preiswerter Steuerwerke.

Bei der Durchsicht der heute existierenden Rechner zeigt sich, daß sich bei kleineren modernen Anlagen die interne Steuerung durch Mikroprogrammspeicher durchsetzt, bei größeren Rechnern jedoch weitgehend spezialisierte, auf Geschwindigkeit getrimmte Schaltwerke vorherrschen. Die Normierung der Schaltnetze zu Speichern beinhaltet schließlich außer der geringeren Ausnutzung aller inneren Gatterfunktionen auch eine Einbuße an Geschwindigkeit insbesondere durch die notwendige synchrone Arbeitsweise für alle Mikrooperationen. Die neuerdings vielfach angebotenen beschreibbaren Mikrogrammspeicher sind im allgemeinen (bei gleicher Technologie) noch etwas langsamer als die Festwertspeicher.

Die physikalisch-technischen Eigenheiten groß-integrierter Halbleitertechnologie ermöglichen somit nicht nur den Einsatz größerer und schnellerer Speicher zur Steigerung der Leistungsfähigkeit herkömmlicher Rechnerkonzepte. Sie stellt dem Rechnerarchitekten auch kleine und kleinste Speicher zur Verfügung sowie ebenfalls preiswerte Schaltnetze für die Realisierung allgemeiner Verknüpfungs- und Steuerwerke. Seit etwa 1970 bahnte sich daher die Aufgliederung des von-Neumann-Rechners an: in mehrere simultan arbeitende Steuereinheiten eines Großrechners, in Multiprozessor-Systeme, in Satelliten, intelligente Terminals bis hin zu Taschenrechnern und Mikroprozessoren für den Betrieb von Werkzeugen, Geräten und Nachrichtenübertragungssystemen.

Die technologische Basis zu anderen Schaltungskomplexen als Adreßspeicher - z.B. Assoziativ-Speichern und Zellenrechnern - ist vorhanden und eröffnet einen weiten Spielraum für die weitere Entwicklung der Rechnerarchitektur.

Der Bausteinkasten ist größer geworden, die Systeme werden komplexer. Wirtschaftliche Erwägungen bleiben jedoch der Hintergrund aller Strukturplanungen, auch wenn das einzelne Gatter oder Speicherbit so billig geworden ist, daß man es weniger ausnutzen muß. Man wird dafür mehr in Standard-Typenzahlen und Verbindungskanälen denken müssen, immer mehr auch an die Entwicklungszeit, die Dokumentation, die Prüfbarkeit und Wartbarkeit der größer und komplexer werdenden Systeme. Man wird weiterhin Speicherhierarchien und Fehlerkorrektursysteme implementieren müssen; denn keine der modernen - ja keine nur denkbare - Speichertechnologie wird den gesamten Kapazitäts-Zugriffsraum vollständig abdecken können und a priori die Zuverlässigkeit bieten, die vom System verlangt werden.

Literatur

[1] Leininger, J.C.: The Use of Read Only Storage Modules to Perform Complex Logic Functions, Proceedings of the 1970 IEEE International Computer Group Conference, pp. 307-313

[2] Fleisher, H.,: Maissel, L.I. An Introduction to Array Logic, IBM Journal of Research and Development, March 1975 pp. 98-109

[3] Wilkes, M.V.: The best way to design an automatic calculation machine, Manchester University Computer Inaugural Conference Proceedings (1951) p. 16

Professor Konrad ZUSE

Mathematische Logik und Informatik

Die ersten Konstrukteure von Rechenmaschinen wie Schickard, Pascal und Leibniz sahen ihre Aufgabe nur darin, mechanische Hilfsmittel zur Lösung arithmetischer Rechenaufgaben zu entwickeln. Leibniz befaßte sich außerdem mit der Ars combinatoria, einem Vorläufer der heutigen mathematischen Logik. Auch entwickelte er bereits die Möglichkeiten des binären Zahlensystems, das er Dyadik nannte.

Die Lösung der arithmetischen Operationen mit Hilfe von Rechenmaschinen stand dann über 2 Jahrhunderte im Vordergrund. Auch die Idee der Programmsteuerung, wie sie von Babbage konzipiert wurde, diente im wesentlichen noch dieser Aufgabe, wobei allerdings bereits die Grundkonzeption der heutigen Computer vorweggenommen wurde. Aber Babbage muß sich wohl schon weitere Gedanken gemacht haben; denn der bedingte Befehl war ihm bereits bekannt, wenn er ihn auch in seinen konstruktiven Plänen noch nicht benutzte.

Die Lochkartentechnik führte eine Reihe von Rechenmethoden ein, die über den Rahmen der reinen Zahlenrechnung hinausgehen. Auswahl- und Sortierprozesse bereicherten die Möglichkeiten der Rechenmaschinen, wobei man sich allerdings über die Analogien solcher Operationen zur mathematischen Logik noch keine Gedanken machte.

Unabhängig davon wurde die mathematische Logik von Mathematikern weiterentwickelt, womit - beginnend mit Leibniz - eine Reihe berühmter Namen verknüpft ist, wie z.B. Bool, Frege, Schröder, Carnap, Hilbert und andere.

Der Brückenschlag zwischen den Problemen des Rechnens und der mathematischen Logik erfolgte etwa gleichzeitig in den dreissiger Jahren auf verschiedenen Wegen.

Vom Standpunkt der Mathematik aus entwickelte Turing seine inzwischen berühmt gewordene Idee der berechenbaren Funktionen. Wesentlich dabei ist, daß er das gedankliche Modell einer Rechenmaschine nur benutzte, um vom logischen Standpunkt aus den Bereich der beweisbaren Sätze auf die Berechenbarkeit zurückzuführen. Er dachte, jedenfalls zunächst, wohl kaum daran, damit auch die Konstruktion von Rechenmaschinen zu befruchten. Später erkannte man, daß die Idee der Turing Maschine eine gute Basis für theoretische Untersuchungen der Informatik darstellt; jedoch gilt auch heute noch, daß die direkten Auswirkungen dieser Idee auf die konstruktive Entwicklung von Rechenmaschinen unbedeutend sind.

Unabhängig davon bot die inzwischen weiter fortschreitende Entwicklung programmgesteuerter Rechenmaschinen die Möglichkeit, von der anderen Seite, nämlich der praktischen Konstruktion von Rechenmaschinen her, eine Brücke zur mathematischen Logik zu suchen. Programmgesteuerte Rechengeräte führen tausende von aufeinanderfolgenden Rechenoperationen aus, ohne daß dabei der menschliche Benutzer die zahlreichen Zwischenwerte zu Gesicht bekommt. Damit war es möglich, die grundsätzliche Frage nach dem für eine Rechenmaschine günstigsten Zahlensystem zu stellen.

Die traditionelle Rechenmaschinentechnik arbeitete, in Anpassung an den menschlichen Benutzer, mit Ziffernrädchen für 10 Positionen. Die erste große elektronische Rechenanlage, der ENIAC, arbeitete noch mit direkter Simulation solcher aus einer Reihe von Ziffernrädchen aufgebauten Register.

Andere, wie Stibitz und Aiken, benutzten bei ihren ersten Geräten bereits die Relaistechnik, welche konstruktiv das

Arbeiten mit Werten, die nur zwei Möglichkeiten zulassen, also Bits, wie wir heute sagen, bedeutet. Stibitz ging dabei konsequent den Weg, das binäre Zahlensystem zu benutzen. Aiken arbeitete mit durch Bits verschlüsselten Dezimalziffern.

Bei meinen eigenen Entwicklungen in Berlin, die etwa gleichzeitig und unabhängig von Arbeiten in den USA liefen, ging ich, ähnlich wie Stibitz, auch konsequent zum vollen binären System über.

Damit wurde ein neues Gebiet aktuell, das wir heute mit Schaltalgebra bezeichnen. Sie wurde ebenfalls unabhängig an verschiedenen Stellen mit verschiedenartigen Ansätzen entwickelt. Die Idee, die Gesetze für Relaisschaltungen mathematisch zu formulieren, ist allerdings nicht unbedingt an die Entwicklung der Rechenmaschinen gebunden. Hansi Piesch entwickelte Ansätze, die allgemeinen Aufgaben dienten. Shannon dachte zwar schon an die Lösung rechnerischer Aufgaben, aber nur als typisches Anwendungsbeispiel von vielen. Auch Aiken entwickelte einen Formalismus, um Schaltungen und ihre Gesetze zu beschreiben.

Es ist vielleicht bezeichnend, daß all diese Versuche zunächst noch darauf hinausliefen, für Schaltungsprobleme eine eigene formale Sprache zu schaffen.

Auch bei meinen eigenen Bemühungen ging ich ähnliche Wege. Das konsequente Arbeiten mit Relaisschaltungen forderte geradezu dazu heraus, leistungsfähige mathematische Werkzeuge zu schaffen, um damit komplizierte Formulierungen elegant durchführen zu können. Ich entwickelte eine "Bedingungskombinatorik" und erprobte sie an einer Reihe von Schaltungsaufgaben.

Ich schickte diesen meiner Meinung nach neuen Kalkül meinem ehemaligen Mathematiklehrer und hatte das große

Glück, daß er mich auf die Analogien dieser Bedingungskombinatorik zum Aussagenkalkül aufmerksam machte. Damit war der Weg frei, einen bis dahin sehr abstrakten und für rein theoretische Ziele entwickelten Zweig der Mathematik für praktische Aufgaben des Ingenieurs als Werkzeug zu benutzen. Auch an anderer Stelle erkannte man später, daß die Übernahme eines fertig entwickelten Kalküls, nämlich des Aussagenkalküls, große Vorteile bietet. Heute ist uns das völlig selbstverständlich. Die Auflösung von Schaltungen in "Und-" bzw. "Oder-"Glieder ist uns völlig in Fleisch und Blut übergegangen. Nur wenige wissen, daß das ursprünglich nicht selbstverständlich war und z.T. erst auf Umwegen erreicht wurde. Noch Aiken scheute sich, diese einfachen Operationen direkt zu benutzen, und arbeitete anstelle dessen mit - nach unseren heutigen Vorstellungen - umständlichen Formulierungen mit Hilfe der dem Ingenieur geläufigen Operationen der Addition und Multiplikation.

Die Analogien zum Aussagenkalkül erlaubten es nun, die dort geltenden Gesetze sinngemäß auf Schaltungen zu übertragen. So gab mir das Dualitätsprinzip sofort die Möglichkeit, meine Additionsschaltungen gewissermaßen "invers" aufzubauen, was z.T. zu wichtigen Vereinfachungen führte.

Damit war nun auch der Weg vorgegeben, um Schaltungen verschiedener Technologien auf eine gemeinsame Darstellungsform zurückzuführen. Ich entwickelte eine "Abstrakte Schaltglied-Technik", welche wahlweise auf mechanische, elektromechanische und elektronische Schaltungstechnologien übertragen werden konnte. So gelang es auch verhältnismäßig leicht, die gesamte Gleitkomma-Logik im binären Zahlensystem mit all ihren Übersetzungsaufgaben vom Dezimalsystem ins binäre System und umgekehrt nur mit Hilfe von Relais, also logisch gesehen, mit Ja-Nein-Werten aufzubauen. Die z.T. sehr komplizierten Bedingungen waren mit Hilfe aussagenlogischer Formeln leicht und elegant darstellbar. Dabei zeigte sich, daß die Relaistechnik die Möglichkeit bietet, fast direkt von der formalen Darstellung zur konkreten Schaltung überzugehen.

Damit war auch der Übergang zur elektronischen Technologie erheblich erleichtert. Als mein Freund Schreyer mitleidig lächelnd meine mechanischen und elektromechanischen Schaltungen betrachtete, meinte er, das müsse man mit Röhren machen. Durch die Verwendung der mathematischen Logik war nun dieser Übergang zu einer grundsätzlich anderen Technologie sehr erleichtert. Schreyer brauchte nur noch für die logischen Grundschaltungen die Bauelemente zu entwickeln, die dann entsprechend den bereits in anderer Technologie bewährten Modellen zusammengeschaltet zu werden brauchten. Damit ging unsere deutsche Entwicklung elektronischer Rechengeräte auch grundsätzlich andere Wege, als die etwas später einsetzenden in den USA, wo man noch mechanische Zählwerke möglichst direkt simulierte.

Ein solcher Erfolg der mathematischen Logik führte nun zu der Frage, ob nicht auch weitere Kalküle auf dem Gebiete der Computerentwicklung nützlich eingesetzt werden könnten.

Es zeigte sich dann bald, daß der Prädikatenkalkül sehr gut zur Formulierung rechnerischer Probleme geeignet ist. So entstand die Idee des allgemeinen Rechnens, welches wesentlich über das reine Zahlenrechnen hinausgeht.

Damit war der Weg frei für zunächst rein theoretische Untersuchungen. Zwar kannten wir damals noch nicht die Begriffe "Hardware" und "Software". Allerdings konnten nicht alle theoretisch gewonnenen Erkenntnisse sofort praktisch angewandt werden. Wir entwickelten im Kriege Anfang der vierziger Jahre einige Computer im Auftrage der deutschen Luftfahrtindustrie, die jedoch auf klar erreichbare Ziele abgestellt waren.

Diese Arbeiten erfolgten unter sehr beschwerlichen Bedingungen des Krieges, zuletzt während der Bombenangriffe auf Berlin.

Es war im Kriege kaum möglich, Fachkräfte zu bekommen, geschweige denn einen Vollspur-Mathematiker. Da geschah ein Wunder. Die Luftwaffe, die ja an meinen Entwicklungen interessiert war, stellte Fachkräfte von der Front ab,und auf diese Weise erschien eines Tages bei mir Herr Lohmeyer, ein Mathematiker aus der Schule des bekannten Logikers Scholz in Münster. Er traute sich zunächst kaum zuzugeben, daß sein eigentliches Fachgebiet die mathematische Logik wäre und war dann sehr erstaunt zu hören, daß er genau der Mann wäre, den ich gebrauchen könnte.

Mit Begeisterung gingen wir dann daran, die Beziehungen zwischen mathematischer Logik und Rechenmaschinen auszubauen. Wir machten uns meistens nicht erst die Mühe, die erforderlichen Änderungen in den Geräten erst über das Konstruktionsbüro, die Arbeitsvorbereitung usw. laufen zu lassen, sondern nahmen selbst den Lötkolben in die Hand und in wenigen Minuten waren die aussagenlogischen Ansätze vom Papier in die Wirklichkeit übertragen.

Trotz all der Unannehmlichkeiten der letzten Kriegsjahre in Berlin, hatte diese Zeit doch auch ihre Guten Seiten. Das Zusammenspiel zwischen Mathematiker und Ingenieur war sehr harmonisch und wir wuchsen so in das Aufgabengebiet hinein, daß jeder beide Seiten bis zu einem gewissen Grade beherrschte.

Es war auch ein großes Erlebnis für mich, als Herr Lohmeyer eines Tages seinen ehemaligen Lehrer, Herrn Professor Scholz, aus Münster nach Berlin in unsere Werkstatt holte. Ich war zunächst sehr skeptisch und glaubte nicht, bei einem ausgesprochenen Theoretiker Verständnis für derartig "profane"

Aufgaben wie die Konstruktion von Rechenmaschinen erwarten zu dürfen. Zu meiner Überraschung zeigte er jedoch sofort lebhaftes Interesse an den Problemen, was uns ein Ansporn war, unseren einmal eingeschlagenen Weg intensiv weiterzuverfolgen.

Das Jahr 1945 stellte uns dann allerdings zunächst vor sehr reelle Aufgaben. Unsere Diskussionen fanden zunehmend im Luftschutzkeller statt. Zuletzt mussten wir - mitten im Bombenkrieg - das Gerät Z 4 aus Berlin retten. Es wurde schließlich nach abenteuerlicher Reise in einem kleinen Alpendorf, Hinterstein im Allgäu, in einem Schuppen versteckt.

Etwa zur gleichen Zeit, als wir notgedrungenermaßen unsere "Hardware"-Entwicklung von Computern unterbrechen mußten, wurden die Ergebnisse der amerikanischen Entwicklungen weltbekannt. Es lag eine Tragik darin, daß wir nun zusehen mußten, wie an anderer Stelle ähnliche Ideen mit großem materiellem Aufwand verwirklicht werden konnten, während für uns in Deutschland nur rein theoretische Arbeit übrig blieb. Dadurch wird aber auch mancher Unterschied erklärt.

Die bei uns während des Krieges entwickelten Geräte waren auf klar formulierte Ziele abgestellt. Die mathematische Logik wurde dabei voll eingesetzt, um die Schaltungen zu entwickeln. Für die Programmierung bedurften diese Geräte jedoch noch keines besonderen Aufwandes. Für die damals sowohl bei uns als auch in den USA verfügbaren Computer brauchte man noch keine hochentwickelten algorithmischen Sprachen.

Die Einsamkeit des bayerischen Alpendorfes gab mir nun Gelegenheit, meine theoretischen Gedanken zu ordnen. Schon während des Krieges hatte ich an "logischen" Rechengeräten zur "Rechenplan-Fertigung" und anderen Aufgaben gearbeitet. Dabei war es selbstverständlich, daß sämtliche Informationen, also nicht nur Zahlen sondern auch Programme, komplizierte Datenstrukturen usw. in Bitmuster aufgelöst und somit auch gespeichert und der Informationsverarbeitung zugänglich gemacht werden können.

Als einen wesentlichen Punkt bei solchen logistischen Rechenmaschinen erkannte ich die Rückwirkungsmöglichkeit von errechneten Resultaten auf den Ablauf der Rechnung, also das, was wir heute als bedingte Befehle, Umrechnung von Adressen, bedingte Ablaufanweisungen usw. bezeichnen. Man kann diese Möglichkeiten konstruktiv durch einen einzigen Draht symbolisieren, der vom Rechenwerk zum Programmwerk führt. Ich hatte eine ausgesprochene Scheu, diesen Draht konkret zu legen; denn es war mir klar, daß er zu unübersehbaren Konsequenzen in Richtung der Möglichkeiten des Rechnens überhaupt führen würde.

All diese Überlegungen konzentrierte ich nun im ersten Nachkriegsjahr auf die Entwicklung einer algorithmischen Sprache, den Plankalkül. Ich stellte mir die Aufgabe, zunächst einmal einen Formalismus zu entwickeln, mit dem sämtliche überhaupt denkbare Informationsverarbeitungs - prozesse ohne die Wortsprache formuliert werden können. Damit wurden die wesentlichen Charakteristika späterer Entwicklungen algorithmischer Sprachen vorweggenommen.

Einige Jahre später wurde ich dann allerdings wieder durch die auch in Deutschland wieder mögliche Hardware-Entwicklung in Anspruch genommen. Es kam zu der sehr angenehmen Zusammenarbeit mit der Eidgenössischen Technischen Hochschule in Zürich, wo das aus Berlin gerettete Gerät Z 4 für einige Jahre aufgestellt werden konnte.

Auch in Zürich setzte sich zunächst die gute Zusammenarbeit zwischen Mathematiker und Ingenieur fort. Das Zusammenspiel mit den Herren Stiefel, Speiser und Rutishauser war sehr fruchtbar und der Unterschied zwischen Hardware-und Software-Entwicklung begann sich erst allmählich herauszubilden.

Auch die Analogien zwischen Schaltungen und Aussagenlogik wurden uns allen bald zur Selbstverständlichkeit.

Schwieriger war es allerdings, um diese Zeit Verständnis für meine weiteren theoretischen Arbeiten, insbesondere für den Plankalkül, zu finden. Anfang der fünfziger Jahre begannen die elektronischen Rechengeräte sich Schritt für Schritt in Richtung der heutigen Computer zu entwickeln. An anderer Stelle hatte man keinerlei Hemmungen, den entscheidenden Draht der Rückwirkung vom Rechenwerk zum Steuerungswerk zu legen. John v. Neumann konnte als erster ein Gerät mit Programmierspeicherung bauen, bei dem die Möglichkeit der Beeinflussung des Programms selbst durch die Ergebnisse der Rechnung gegeben war. Sein Konzept war sehr allgemein und wurde erst später in seinen Möglichkeiten voll ausgebaut.

Trotzdem bereits damals die Möglichkeit des universellen Rechnens gegeben war, erstreckten sich die Bemühungen der Programmformulierung doch noch auf die gerade vorliegenden Tagesprobleme. Numerische Rechnungen standen noch absolut im Vordergrund. Logische Operationen wurden im wesentlichen nur im Zusammenhang mit bedingten Befehlen eingesetzt.

Dementsprechend waren die damals an verschiedenen Stellen entwickelten algorithmischen Sprachen zunächst auf derartige Probleme beschränkt.

Ich glaubte damals, daß nunmehr die Stunde gekommen sei, meinen Plankalkül ins Spiel zu bringen. Die Entwicklung des Computers war nunmehr auf breiter Basis in Gang gekommen. Was lag da näher, als von vornherein die Weichen richtig zu stellen und alle Möglichkeiten des Einsetzens der mathematischen Logik schon in den Ansätzen zu erfassen.

Es war eine der größten Enttäuschen meines Lebens, daß es bei dieser meiner zweiten Begegnung mit Mathematikern nicht zu einer so harmonischen Zusammenarbeit kam, wie seinerzeit während des Krieges. Hinzu kam, daß ich persönlich durch die Hardware-Entwicklungen und den Aufbau einer Firma voll in Anspruch genommen war und mich daher der Aufgabe der algorithmischen Sprachen nicht mehr widmen konnte.

Rückblickend frage ich mich allerdings, warum es damals nicht zu einer fruchtbaren Zusammenarbeit gekommen ist. Abgesehen davon, daß der Einfluss der amerikanischen Entwicklungen übermäßig stark war, mögen folgende 4 Mißverständnisse dazu beigetragen haben, daß meine Gesprächspartner und ich in den wesentlichen Punkten aneinander vorbeiredeten:

1) Da im Plankalkül von vornherein die volle Variationsbreite aller möglichen Datenstrukturen erfaßt werden sollte, entwickelte ich eine Darstellungsform, die in verschiedenen Zeilen die zu den einzelnen Daten gehörenden Elemente, wie Indizes, Komponentenkennzeichnungen und Datenstrukturen enthalten. Diese Disziplin des preußischen Kasernenhofes gibt zwar ein Maximum an Klarheit, ist aber für den Mathematiker ungewohnt. Es ist nun leider so, daß solche Gewohnheitseffekte für die Einführung neuer Ideen von großer Bedeutung sind.
2) Der Plankalkül arbeitet bewußt mit dem Bit als elementarem Datenelement und baut alle weiteren Strukturen darauf auf. Damit ist u.a. auch die Möglichkeit gegeben, die arithmetischen Operationen in jedem beliebigen Zahlensystem, sei es in Festkomma- oder Gleitkommadarstellung bis in die letzten Bits zu zerlegen.

3) Gerade die damals in den Jahren um 1955 herum interessierenden Programme für numerische Rechnungen wurden im Plankalkül nicht behandelt, weil sie zu trivial erschienen und keine besonderen Schwierigkeiten bei der Entwicklung einer algorithmischen Sprache boten. Das führte wieder zu dem Eindruck einer auf abstrakte Probleme bezogenen Sprache.
4) Im Plankalkül wurde ein verhältnismäßig breiter Raum den logischen Operationen des Prädikatenkalküls überlassen. Insbesondere das Schachspiel zeigte sich als ein hervorragendes Modell, um die Flexibilität einer algorithmischen Sprache zu testen. Dadurch entstand wiederum der Eindruck einer auf logische Operationen spezialisierten Sprache, die man,aus der Sicht von etwa 1955 gesehen, nicht für erforderlich erachtete.

Diese 4 Gründe zeigen, daß die Ablehnung bzw. Ignorierung des Plankalküls in erster Linie psychologische Gründe hatte. Zu wirklich sachlichen Diskussionen ist es damals leider gar nicht erst gekommen.

Die weitere Entwicklung führte bedauerlicherweise zu einer immer weiteren Entfremdung zwischen Mathematiker, Ingenieur und Anwender. Die verschiedenen Aufgaben erforderten bald die Bildung von Spezialgebieten, die nur von Spezialisten beherrscht werden konnten.

Der von John v. Neumann gezeigte Weg wurde in verschiedenen Richtungen konsequent ausgebaut. Van der Poel, Fromme und andere entwickelten sehr flexible Geräte, mit denen sehr komplizierte Informationsverarbeitungsprozesse durchgeführt werden konnten.

An der Entwicklung algorithmischer Sprachen wurde intensiv gearbeitet. Sprachen wie Cobol, Fortran und Algol waren den damals vorliegen Aufgaben gut angepaßt und konnten eine weite Verbreitung finden.

Das alles war jedoch noch stark anwendungsbezogen. Was jedoch nicht ohne weiteres vorauszusehen war, war die Ausbildung eines sehr theoretischen Zaweiges der Informatik, wie wir heute sagen. Die Mathematiker sahen ihre Aufgabe zunächst weniger darin, ihren logischen Scharfsinn auf die Entwicklung einer wirklich universellen algorithmischen Sprache nach Art des Plankalküls zu konzentrieren, sondern eher darin, eine Art Metatheorie zu schaffen, um das Problem der formalen Sprachen, und insbesondere der algorithmischen und Programmiersprachen, zu untersuchen.

Unter dem Motto, algorithmische Sprachen mathematisch klar und eindeutig zu formulieren, sind heute Theorien der Sprachbeschreibung entstanden, die an Abstraktheit den Vergleich mit mancher weltabgewandten mathematischen Theorie ohne weiteres vertragen. Dabei werden neue mathematische Lehrgebäude mit herangezogen bzw. ausgebaut, wie z.B. die Informationstheorie und die Automatentheorie. Ihre Bedeutung für die Computerentwicklung wird z.T. stark überschätzt. Die glückliche Kombination zwischen mathematischer Logik und der Arbeit des Ingenieurs, wie wir sie in den Kriegsjahren begonnen hatten, wurde leider nicht im damaligen Sinne fortgesetzt.

Inzwischen ist es längst klargeworden, daß wir zur Programmierung von Computern Sprachen brauchen, welche den vollen Umfang logischer flexibler Programme abdecken. Wir haben heute denn auch einige Sprachen, wie Algol 68 und PL/1, die diese Bedingung mehr oder weniger erfüllen oder dies zumindestens anstreben.

Um trotz des babylonischen Sprachwirrwarrs zu brauchbaren Ergebnissen zu kommen, hat in letzter Zeit die Idee des strukturierten Programmierens Bedeutung gewonnen. Sie entspringt dem Wunsch des Praktikers nach Klarheit und Übersichtlichkeit. Aber vielleicht ist das nur der halbe Weg.

Die Diskussionen über den Plankalkül, die ich in letzter Zeit führen konnte, haben mir gezeigt, daß dem Begriff der logischen algorithmischen Sprache, die jedoch implementationsnahe ist, besondere Bedeutung zukommt.

Eine logische algorithmische Sprache bietet die Mittel, um rechnerische Abläufe logisch klar zu formulieren, ohne auf Einzelheiten der Implementation, wie Ein- und Ausgabe, Speicherreservierung usw., einzugehen. Sie muß jedoch implementationsnahe sein, um den Übergang zu maschinenfertigen Programmen zu erleichtern.

Eine algorithmische Sprache muß alle Möglichkeiten der mathematischen Logik ausschöpfen, jedoch so formuliert sein, daß sie auch der Praktiker versteht. Es wird heute sehr viel über Sprachtheorien, Dialogsprachen usw. geschrieben. Eine wichtige Aufgabe wird dabei jedoch vernachlässigt: der Dialog zwischen Theoretikern und Praktikern. Man hat manchmal den Eindruck, daß die Theoretiker ihre Ehre darin sehen, ihre Bücher so abstrakt wie möglich zu schreiben. Einen Zusammenhang einfach und klar zu beschreiben, gilt als unfein und unwissenschaftlich. Das führt dazu, daß diese Theoretiker ein Eigenleben führen und daß die Praktiker, hilflos und im Stich gelassen, zusehen müssen, wie sie trotzdem mit den Problemen fertig werden.

Nach rund 40 Jahren intensiver Computerentwicklung sollte das junge Gebiet der Informatik aber langsam aus den Kinderschuhen herauskommen und seiner Reife entgegenwachsen. Die vor uns liegenden Aufgaben sind so groß, daß sie noch gar nicht voll überblickt werden können. Wir werden täglich mit den verschiedenen kritischen Situationen in Politik und Wirtschaft konfrontiert. Die Lösungen dieser Probleme sind nur mit intensivem Einsatz der Computer möglich. In Zukunft werden die Computerfachleute an den Schalthebeln der Weltwirtschaft stehen; und zwar unabhängig von dem jeweiligen Wirtschaftssystem. Fragestellungen, die noch unsere Urgroßväter bewegten, verlieren an Bedeutung.

Sowohl kapitalistische als auch sozialistische Wirtschaftssysteme sind nur so gut, wie das System der Computer, auf welches sie sich abstützen.

Sind wir für diese gewaltigen Aufgaben gerüstet?

Die Beantwortung dieser Frage erfordert eine gründliche Besinnung. Wir brauchen jedenfalls einen neuen Typ von Informatiker, der seine Aufgabe darin sieht, Theorie und Praxis in harmonischer Form zu vereinigen.

L SYSTEMS, SEQUENCES AND LANGUAGES

by

G. Rozenberg

Department of Mathematics
Antwerp University, UIA
Wilrijk, Belgium

and

Institute of Mathematics
Utrecht University
Utrecht, Holland

ABSTRACT

In this paper we provide a short overview of the mathematical theory of L systems. Because of the limitations on the size of this paper the overview is very concise and it treats only the small fragment of the existing theory (the choice of the material covered strongly reflects the personal point of view of the author). Still it is hoped that the reader will get an idea what are the L systems about and may be some of the readers will join the research in this interesting and very promising area.

CONTENTS

0. Introduction
I. Main Definitions
II. L Sequences
III. L Languages
IV. Concluding Remarks
V. References

0. INTRODUCTION

The theory of L systems was originated in 1968 by A. Lindenmayer ([1]). The original motivation of Lindenmayer was the biological one, its aim was to provide mathematical models for the development of simple filamentous organisms. Indeed, the theory turned out to be rather successful with respect to its original aim: it provided a useful theoretical framework within which the nature of cellular behaviour in development can be discussed, computed and compared. Their study has provided a number of biologically interesting results. (See, e.g., [11] , [12] , [15] , [16] , [17].)

Because the essential feature of an L system is string processing (rewriting), the theory of L systems was from its very beginning of interest to formal language theory. As a matter of fact the interest of formal language theorists in the theory of L systems grew constantly with the development of the theory and by today the theory of L systems constitutes perhaps the most vigorously pursued area of formal language theory. The main reason for this success is perhaps the fact that the theory of L systems brought with itself the whole new range of questions and ideas, a lot of which led to quite interesting results and to the development of new mathematical techniques needed in solving the problems. (Consult, e.g., [12] , [24] , [25].)

Because the main research areas of the L systems theory are very closely related to the central topics of (theoretical) Computer Science the interest of (theoretical) computer scientists in the theory of L systems increases steadily. Just to name few cases: the theory of L systems turned out to be of interest in the theory of program schemata (see, e.g. [3]), in the theory of systematic programming (see, e.g., [26]) and in validation of operating systems (see, e.g., [10]).

In this paper we are concerned with the mathematical theory of L systems. We will attempt to acquaint the reader with several main research areas of the theory by presenting typical questions asked and answers obtained so far. For the sake of exposition we will concentrate on the theory of the so called L systems without interactions. (In what follows we will use a generic term "L system" to refer to all kinds of language generating devices one encouters in the L systems theory.)

I. MAIN DEFINITIONS

The main construct in the theory of L systems is defined as follows.

Definition I.1. A TOL system (in words: an L system without interactions and with tables) is a triplet

$G = \langle \Sigma, \mathcal{P}, \omega \rangle$ where

Σ is a finite nonempty alphabet,

ω is an element of Σ^+,

$\mathcal{P}$ is a finite set, $\mathcal{P} = \{P_1, \ldots, P_f\}$ each element P_i of which is a finite binary relation included in $\Sigma \times \Sigma^*$ satisfying the following completeness condition:

$$(\forall a)_\Sigma (\exists \alpha)_{\Sigma^*} (\langle a, \alpha \rangle \in P_i).$$

If $\# \mathcal{P} = 1$ then G is called a OL system.

If, for every P_i we have

$$(\forall a)_\Sigma (\exists ! \alpha)_{\Sigma^*} (\langle a, \alpha \rangle \in P_i)$$

then G is called deterministic.

We use the letter D to denote the deterministic restriction (and so we talk about DTOL or DOL systems). Usually given an element $\langle a, \alpha \rangle$ of P in $\mathcal{P}$ one writes it as $a \to \alpha$ and calls it a production (in P). If G is a OL system with $\mathcal{P} = \{P\}$ then we specify G as $\langle \Sigma, P, \omega \rangle$ rather than $\langle \Sigma, \{P\}, \omega \rangle$.

Definition I.2. Let $G = \langle \Sigma, \mathcal{P}, \omega \rangle$ be a TOL system.

1) Let $x, y \in \Sigma^*$. We write $x \underset{G}{\Rightarrow} y$ if either $x = y = \Lambda$ or $x = a_1 \ldots a_n$ for some $n \geqslant 1$, $a_1, \ldots, a_n$ in Σ and there exists P in $\mathcal{P}$ such that $a_1 \to \alpha_1, \ldots, a_n \to \alpha_n$ are in P and $y = \alpha_1 \ldots \alpha_n$. Thus $\underset{G}{\Rightarrow}$ is a binary re-relation on $\Sigma^* \times \Sigma^*$. Its transitive and reflexive closure is denoted by $\overset{*}{\underset{G}{\Rightarrow}}$.

2) The language of G, denoted as L(G), is defined by $L(G) = \{x \in \Sigma^* : \omega \overset{*}{\underset{G}{\Rightarrow}} x\}$.

By the above definition the language of a TOL system $G = \langle \Sigma, \mathcal{P}, \omega \rangle$ consists of the set of all words that one "generates" in G starting with the "axiom" ω of G. Very often one "excludes" some of the words generated in G and takes as its language the appropriate subset of G. There are various ways of "filtering" languages of L systems (see e.g., [25] or [7]). Here are two examples of such filtering procedures.

Definition I.3. An ETOL system (EOL system), in words: a TOL system with nonterminals (a OL system with nonterminals), is a construct

$H = \langle G, V_T \rangle$ where G is a TOL system (OL system) and V_T is a finite alphabet. The language of H, denoted as L(H), is defined by $L(H) = L(G) \cap V_T^*$.

Definition I.4. A CTOL system (COL system), in words: a TOL system with a coding (a OL system with a coding), is a construct $H = \langle G, f \rangle$ where G is a TOL system (OL system) and f is a letter-to-letter homomorphism of the alphabet of G into some finite alphabet. The language of H, denoted as L(H), is defined by $L(H) = f(L(G))$.

The motivation for the first of these filtering mechanisms is purely mathematical. The use of nonterminal symbols in defining languages of generating devices is a traditional and a very useful device in formal language theory. The motivation for the second of these filtering mechanisms is purely biological. It describes the relationship between the experimental datas and the reality. (For more discussion see, e.g., [13].)

Let us see some examples of (E)TOL systems and languages.

Example I.1.

1) $G = \langle \{a,b\}, \{\{a \to a^2, b \to b^2\}, \{a \to a^3, b \to b^3\}\}, ab \rangle$ is a DTOL system such that $L(G) = \{a^{2^n \cdot 3^m} b^{2^n \cdot 3^m} : n,m \geq 0\}$.

2) $G = \langle\langle \{A,\bar{A},B,\bar{B},C,\bar{C},a,b,c,F\}, P, ABC\rangle, \{a,b,c\}\rangle$ with P consisting of the productions listed below is an EOL system.

$P = \{A \to A\bar{A},\ A \to a,\ \bar{A} \to \bar{A},\ \bar{A} \to a,\ B \to B\bar{B},\ B \to b,\ \bar{B} \to \bar{B},\ \bar{B} \to b,$
$C \to C\bar{C},\ C \to c,\ \bar{C} \to \bar{C},\ \bar{C} \to c,\ a \to F,\ b \to F,\ c \to F,\ F \to F\}.$

We have $L(G) = \{a^n b^n c^n : n \geq 1\}$.

In the sequel, whenever the class of X-type L systems is given we shall use $\mathcal{L}_X$ to denote the class of all languages generated by X-type L systems. Thus, e.g., $\mathcal{L}_{ETOL}$ stands for the class of ETOL languages (languages generated by ETOL systems).

II. L SEQUENCES

From a biological point of view the sequences of words produced by an L system are of primary interest (they correspond to the time order of development). For this reason the theory of L sequences (sequences produced by L systems) originated as a central research area in the theory of L systems. It led to non-trivial and interesting mathematical theory (see, e.g., [18], [21], [27] and [30]). What makes this particular topic even more interesting, is the fact that considering sequences of words is a complete novum in formal language theory which so far was almost exclusively interested in sets of words (languages).

D0L systems form a very natural example of sequence generating devices.

Definition II.1. 1) Let $G = \langle \Sigma, P, \omega \rangle$ be a D0L system. The sequence generated by G, denoted as $\mathcal{E}(G)$, is defined by $\mathcal{E}(G) = \omega_0, \omega_1, \omega_2, \ldots$ where $\omega_i \underset{G}{\Rightarrow} \omega_{i+1}$ for $i \geq 0$.

2) A sequence of words $\tau = x_0, x_1, \ldots$ is called a D0L sequence if there exists a D0L system G such that $\mathcal{E}(G) = \tau$.

II.1. Perhaps the most natural question about L sequences is whether there is anything "regular" about them. For example: is there any kind of periodicity that must occur in every D0L sequence? The positive answer to this question is presented in the following result. (We call an infinite sequence of words doubly infinite if it contains infinitely many different words. If x is a word and k a positive integer then $\mathrm{Pref}_k(x)$ denotes either x itself if $k \geq |x|$ or the word consisting of the first k letters of x if $k < |x|$. Similarly $\mathrm{Suf}_k(x)$ denotes either x itself if $k \geq |x|$ or the word consisting of the last k letters of x if $k < |x|$.)

Theorem II.1. ([21]) For every D0L system G such that $\mathcal{E}(G) = \omega_0, \omega_1, \ldots$ is doubly infinite there exists a constant C_G such that for every integer k the sequence $\mathrm{Pref}_k(\omega_0), \mathrm{Pref}_k(\omega_1), \ldots$ ($\mathrm{Suf}_k(\omega_0), \mathrm{Suf}_k(\omega_1), \ldots$ respectively) is ultimately periodic with period C_G.

II.2. Let us consider the sequence generated by the D0L system

$G = \langle \{a,b\}, \{a \to b, b \to ab\}, a\rangle$. We have $\mathcal{E}(G) = a,b,ab,bab,abbab,\ldots$ and one can easily prove that, in fact, for every $n \geq 2$, $\omega_n = \omega_{n-2}\omega_{n-1}$ where $\mathcal{E}(G) = \omega_0,\omega_1,\ldots$. Thus to obtain a word in the sequence (from the third element on) it suffices to catenate two previous words (in the order they occur). For such sequences one can replace thus the operation of rewriting by that of catenation of limited numbers of previously obtained strings. For this reason such sequences are called locally catenative.

Definition II.1. Let $G = \langle \Sigma,P,\omega\rangle$ be a DOL system with $\mathcal{E}(G) = \omega_0,\omega_1,\ldots$. We say that G is locally catenative if there exist positive integers m, n, $i_1,\ldots,i_n$ with $n \geq 2$ such that, for each $j \geq m$ we have $\omega_j = \omega_{j-i_1}\omega_{j-i_2}\ldots\omega_{j-i_n}$.

One can say that "being locally catenative" is a global property in the sense that it is defined on strings of the DOL sequence independently of a system defining this sequence. It is the most natural to look for a local property (meaning the property of the set of productions) of a DOL system leading to a locally catenative behaviour. Here is a result in this direction.

If $G = \langle \Sigma,P,\omega\rangle$ is a DOL system then the graph of G is the directed graph whose nodes are elements of Σ and for which a directed edge leads from the node a to the node b if and only if $a \to \alpha b\beta$ is in P for some words α,β over Σ.

Theorem II.2. ([23]). Let $G = \langle \Sigma,P,\omega\rangle$ be a DOL system such that $\mathcal{E}(G)$ is doubly infinite, ω is in Σ, P does not contain a production of the form $a \to \Lambda$ and each letter from Σ occurs in a word in $\mathcal{E}(G)$. If there is a σ in Σ such that $\omega \overset{*}{\underset{G}{\Rightarrow}} \sigma$ and each cycle in the graph of G goes through the node σ then G is locally catenative.

II.3. There are various (both physically and mathematically motivated) reasons to investigate only lengths of words occurring in L sequences or languages rather than the words themselves. In case of DOL systems this idea leads to the so called DOL growth functions.

Definition II.2. 1) Let $G = \langle \Sigma,P,\omega\rangle$ be a DOL system. The growth function of G, denoted as f_G, is a function from nonnegative integers into themselves such that $f_G(n) = |\omega_n|$, where $\mathcal{E}(G) = \omega_0,\omega_1,\ldots,\omega_n,\ldots$
2) The function f from nonnegative integers into themselves is called a DOL growth function if there exists a DOL system G such that $f = f_G$.

Among the research topics concerning DOL growth functions one can distinguish the following:

Analysis problem. Given a DOL system determine its growth function.

Synthesis problem. Given a function f determine if possible a DOL system G such that $f_G = f$.

Growth equivalence problem. Given two DOL systems determine whether their growth functions are the same.

Here are some sample results about DOL growth functions.

Let $G = \langle \Sigma, P, \omega \rangle$ be a DOL system with $\Sigma = \{\sigma_2, \ldots, \sigma_k\}$. Let π_G be the k-dimensional row vector such that its i'th component equals the number of occurrences of the letter σ_i in ω, for $i = 1, \ldots, k$. Let η_G be the k-dimensional column vector with all components equal to 1. Let M_G be the k-dimensional square matrix whose (i,j)'th entry equals the number of occurrences of σ_j in the production for σ_i, for $i,j = 1, \ldots, k$.

Theorem II.3. ([18], [29]). The growth function of a DOL system G can be expressed in the form $f_G(n) = \pi_G M_G^n \eta_G$. Consequently the generating function F(x) for the growth function can be expressed in the form $F_G(x) = \pi_G (I - M_G x)^{-1} \eta_G$ where I is the identity matrix.

Theorem II.4. ([29]). The generating function for a DOL growth function is rational. Every DOL growth function satisfies a homogenous difference equation with constant coefficients. The infinite Hankel matrix associated with a DOL growth function is of finite rank.

Theorem II.5. ([18], [29]). The growth equivalence problem for DOL systems is decidable.

III. L LANGUAGES

It is mathematically natural and physically well motivated to consider the sets of words generated by L systems (called L languages). The theory of L languages led already to quite a number of interesting and non-trivial results. (See, e.g., [12], [24], [25]).

III. 1 There is a variety of ways that one can use to define languages by L systems. Some of them come out from biological considerations some of them from purely formal (mathematical) considerations. The first natural step to be done is to compare the generative power of various language defining mechanisms using L systems.

Here is an example of a typical result in this direction.

Theorem III. 1. ([6], [7], [8], [20]).

1) The following diagram holds:

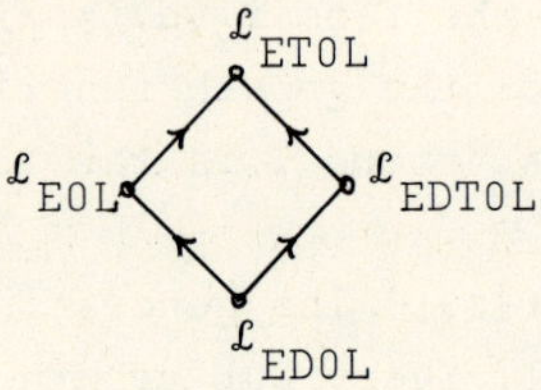

$$\begin{array}{ccccc} & & \mathcal{L}_{ETOL} & & \\ & \nearrow & & \nwarrow & \\ \mathcal{L}_{EOL} & & & & \mathcal{L}_{EDTOL} \\ & \nwarrow & & \nearrow & \\ & & \mathcal{L}_{EDOL} & & \end{array}$$

where a solid line denotes strict inclusion (in the direction indicated) and when two classes K_1 and K_2 are not connected by a path it means that they are incomparable but not disjoint.

2) $\mathcal{L}_{ETOL} = \mathcal{L}_{CTOL}$ and $\mathcal{L}_{EOL} = \mathcal{L}_{COL}$.

One of the pleasant features of dealing with L systems is the fact that the main language classes from the Chomsky hierarchy can be obtained in a simple and elegant way within the main classes of L systems. For example we have the following result.

Let $G = \langle \Sigma, \mathcal{P}, \omega \rangle$ be a 0L system. The adult language of G, denoted as A(G), is defined by

$A(G) = \{x \in \Sigma^* : x \in L(G)$ and if $x \underset{G}{\Rightarrow} y$ then $y = x\}$.

Theorem III. 2. ([31]). A language K is context-free if and only if there exists a 0L system G such that A(G) = K.

III. 2 One of the central aims of the theory of L systems is to understand the structure of a single L language or sequence (in the sense that once we learn that a particular language or sequence K is of a particular L-type we should be able to deduce some properties of K).

Several results in this direction are already available. They are particularily useful in proving that certain languages are not in certain language families (because they do not satisfy certain structural constraints). Let for a nonempty set B of letters and a word x, $\#_B(x)$ denote the total number of occurrences of the letters from B in x. If L is a language over Σ where $B \subseteq \Sigma$ then we define $N(L,B) = \{n : \text{for some } x \text{ in } L, \#_B(x) = n\}$. Now we say that:

1) B is <u>nonfrequent</u> in L iff there exists a constant C(B,L) such that, for every x in L, $\#_B(x) < C(B,L)$.

2) B is called <u>rare</u> in L iff, for every natural number k, there exists a natural number n_k, such that whenever $n > n_k$ and a word x in L contains n occurrences of letters from B, then each two such occurrences lie at a distance $\geq k$ from each other.

3) B is called <u>numerically dispersed in</u> L iff N(L,B) is infinite and, for every natural number k, there exists a natural number n_k such that whenever u_1 and u_2 are in N(L,B) and $u_1 > u_2 > n_k$, then $u_1 - u_2 > k$.

4) B is <u>clustered in</u> L iff N(L,B) is infinite and there exist natural numbers k_1, k_2 both larger than 1 such that whenever a word x in L satisfies $\#_B(x) \geq k_1$, then x contains at least two occurrences of letters from B which lie at a distance $< k_2$ from each other.

<u>Theorem III. 3. ([9]).</u> If L is an ETOL language over an alphabet Σ and B is a nonempty subset of Σ which is rare in L, then B is nonfrequent in L.

<u>Theorem III. 4. ([5]).</u> Let L be an EOL language over Σ and B a nonempty subset of Σ. If B is numerically dispersed in L, then B is clustered in L.

III. 3. One of the central research topics of L systems theory and formal language theory in general is comparison of deterministic and nondeterministic behaviour of language defining systems. Such a research should lead to discovering nontrivial properties which would be inherent to deterministic systems. Some such results are already available in the theory of L systems. (In what follows $\pi_k(L)$ denotes the number of subwords of length k that occur in the words of L).

<u>Theorem III. 5. ([4]).</u> Let Σ be a finite alphabet such that $\#\Sigma = n \geq 2$. If L is a language generated by a DTOL system, $L \subseteq \Sigma^*$, then

$$\lim_{k \to \infty} \frac{\pi_k(L)}{n^k} = 0.$$

The above result is not true for EDT0L languages. However in this case we have another interesting result.

Theorem III. 6. ([8]). Let Σ be a finite alphabet such that $\# \Sigma = n \geq 2$. If L is a language generated by an EDT0L system, $L \subseteq \Sigma^*$ such that $\{m :$ there exists a w in L with $|w| = m\}$ does not contain an arithmetic progression, then

$$\lim_{k \to \infty} \frac{\# \{w \in L : |w| = k\}}{n^k} = 0.$$

IV. CONCLUDING REMARKS

We have tried in this short overview to give the reader a flavour of what is the theory of L systems about. We did not have here a space either to present typical proof techniques or to indicate various applications of the theory.

In the first few years of its existence the theory of L systems turned out to be fruitful and interesting at least in the following areas:

- theoretical biology,
- formal language theory,
- algebra,
- operating systems,
- systematic programming,
- program schemata.

It is the firm belive of this author that we are wittnessing only the beginning of the fruitful development of the theory (and applications) of L systems. In particular, I am firmly convinced that in the near future even more interactions will take place between the theory of L systems and some basic fields of theoretical computer science.

There is a lot of interesting open problems (and problem areas) in the theory. I would like to mention only the following ones.

- For the sake of concise exposition, we have restricted ourselves to disscussing only one-dimensional (string generating) L systems. Obviously such systems form only the first step towards obtaining the more general models for generating multidimensional structures like graphs or maps. There has been a promising "break-through" work done on multidimensional L systems (see, e.g., [1], [2]) and clearly this area should be a major field of research in the near future.
- As it was mentioned, some (partial) results are already available which clarify the structure of L sequences and languages from various classes. (See, e.g., [8]). Clearly much more effort should go in this direction, in particular, as of today, very little is known about the structure of L sequences.
- One can say that L systems constitute a break-through in obtaining models for word generating devices (grammars) parallel in nature. One still has to wait for such models of word accepting devices (machines) parallel in nature. A way of achieving this is to search for classes of acceptors equivalent to various classes of L systems. Although some such models are already available (see, e.g., [14], [22], [28]) still a lot of remains to be done in this direction.

We would like to end this paper with the literature quide for the reader which would like to learn more about the area. For a rather detailed overview of the mathematical theory of L systems the reader may consult [25] and for a surrey of the biological foundation of it we advice to read [16] and [17]. For a more thorough reading we refer the reader either to [12] (more tutorial) or to [24] (more research oriented).

V. REFERENCES

[1]. J. Carlyle, S. Greibach and A. Paz, A two-dimensional generating system modding growth by binary cell division, 15th Annual Symposium on Switching and Automata Theory, 1974.

[2]. K. Culik II and A. Lindenmayer, Parallel rewriting on graphs and multidimensional development, Dept. of Computer Science, University of Waterloo, Canada, Techn. Report No. CS-74-22, 1974.

[3]. P. Downey, Formal languages and recursion schemes, Ph. D. dissertation, Harvard University, 1974.

[4]. A. Ehrenfeucht and G. Rozenberg, A limit theorem for sets of subwords in deterministic TOL languages, Information Processing Letters, 2, 10-73, 1973.

[5]. A. Ehrenfeucht and G. Rozenberg, The number of occurrences of letters versus their distribution in some EOL languages, Information and Control, 26, 256-271, 1974.

[6]. A. Ehrenfeucht and G. Rozenberg, The equality of EOL languages and codings of OL languages, International Journal of Computer Mathematics, 4, 95-104, 1974.

[7]. A. Ehrenfeucht and G. Rozenberg, Nonterminals versus homomorphisms in defining languages for some classes of rewriting systems, Acta Informatica, 3, 265-283, 1974.

[8]. A. Ehrenfeucht and G. Rozenberg, On the (combinatorial) structure of L languages without interactions, 7th Annual ACM Symposium on Theory of Computing, 1975.

[9]. A. Ehrenfeucht and G. Rozenberg, A characterization theorem for a subclass of ETOL languages, Acta Informatica, to appear.

[10]. C. Ellis, The validation of parallel co-operating processes, Dept. of Computer Science, University of Colorado at Boulder, U.S.A., Techn. Rep. No. CU-CS-065-75, 1975.

[11]. G. T. Herman, Simulation of organisms based on L systems, 1974 Conference of Biologically Motivated Automata Theory, 1974.

[12]. G.T. Herman and G. Rozenberg, Developmental systems and languages, North-Holland Publ. Comp., Amsterdam. 1975.

[13]. G.T. Herman, A. Lindenmayer and G. Rozenberg, Description of developmental languages using recurrence systems, Mathematical Systems Theory, 8, 316-341, 1975.

[14]. J. van Leeuwen, Notes on pre-set pushdown automata, in [24], 177- 189, 1974.

[15]. A. Lindenmayer, Mathematical models for cellular interactions in development, Parts I and II, Journal of Theoretical Biology,

18, 280-315, 1968.

[16]. A. Lindenmayer, Developmental systems and languages in their biological context, Chapter 0 in 12 , 1975.

[17]. A. Lindenmayer, L systems in their biological context, Journ. of Theoretical Biology, to appear.

[18]. A. Paz and A. Salomaa, Integral sequential word functions and growth equivalence of Lindenmayer systems, Information and Control, 23, 313-343, 1973.

[19]. G. Rozenberg, TOL systems and languages, Information and Control, 23, 357-381, 1973.

[20]. G. Rozenberg, Extension of tabled OL systems and languages, International Journal of Computer and Information Sciences, 2, 311-336, 1973.

[21]. G. Rozenberg, DOL sequences, Discrete Mathematics, 7, 323-347, 1974.

[22]. G. Rozenberg, On a family of acceptors for some classes of developmental languages, International Journal of Computer Mathematics, 4. 199-228, 1974.

[23]. G. Rozenberg and A. Lindenmayer, Developmental systems with locally catenative formulas, Acta Informatica, 2, 214-248, 1973.

[24]. G. Rozenberg and A. Salomaa (eds), L systems, Lecture Notes in Computer Science, v. 15, Springer-Verlag, 1974.

[25]. G. Rozenberg and A. Salomaa, The mathematical theory of L systems, Progress in Information Processing (edited by J. Tou), to appear.

[26]. C. Roman, R systems, Ph. D. thesis, Moore School of Electr. Engineering, 1975.

[27]. A. Salomaa, On exponential growth in Lindenmayer systems, Indagationes Mathematicae, 35, 23-30, 1973.

[28]. W. Savitch, Some characterizations of Lindenmayer systems in terms of Chomsky-type grammars and stack machines, Information and Control, 27, 37-60, 1975.

[29]. A Szilard, Growth functions of Lindenmayer systems, Dept. of Computer Science, University of Western Ontario, Canada, Techn. Rep. No. 4, 1971.

[30]. P. Vitanyi, Structure of growth in Lindenmayer systems, Indagationes Mathematicae, 35, 247-253, 1973.

[31]. A. Walker, Adult languages of L systems and the Chomsky hierarchy, in [24], 201-216, 1974.

Rechnernetzwerke - Möglichkeiten und Grenzen

Lutz Richter

Einführung

Rechnernetzwerke ist ein Stichwort, unter dem heute eine Vielzahl von verschiedenen Entwicklungstrends im Bereiche der Datenverarbeitung zusammengefaßt wird. Netzwerke offerieren Anwendungsmöglichkeiten, die beim Betrieb von Einzelsystemen nicht zur Verfügung stehen. Andererseits treten bei Netzwerken zusätzliche Probleme auf, die sowohl für den auf diesem Gebiet tätigen Wissenschaftler als auch für den Praktiker Ansatz für reizvolle Aufgaben bieten.

Der Begriff der Rechnernetzwerke soll hier als eine Anzahl $n \geq 2$ von zur selbständigen Abarbeitung von Anweisungen befähigten Prozessoren verstanden werden, die gelegentlich oder überwiegend als autonome Elemente im Netz aufzufassen sind und in unregelmäßiger Folge Information in Form von Nachrichten miteinander austauschen.

Daher finden sich die Probleme, die beim Entwurf von Rechnernetzwerken auftreten auch bereits bei komplexeren Einzelsystemen. Technologische Fragen des Anschlusses gewisser Ein-Ausgabe-Geräte (einschließlich der Geräte der Datenfernverarbeitung) sind häufig vergleichbar mit Aufgaben, die bei der physikalischen Verbindung von Rechnern entstehen. Fragen der Software-Kommunikation von zur Parallelarbeit befähigten Einzelkomponenten und die dabei auftretenden logischen Kommunikationsprobleme haben eine große Ähnlichkeit mit Problemen, die sich beim Nachrichtenaustausch von selbständigen Rechnersystemen untereinander finden. Die Beschäftigung mit Fragestellungen aus dem Gebiet der Rechnernetzwerke ist daher für weite Bereiche der Informatik von Interesse und umgekehrt - Ergebnisse aus zahlreichen anderen Teilgebieten der theoretischen und praktischen Informatik erleichtern die Behandlung der Probleme der Rechnernetzwerke.

Netzwerk-Strukturen

Hinsichtlich der Anordnung der Einzelkomponenten in Rechnernetzwerken zueinander lassen sich verschiedene topologische Strukturen unterscheiden.

Die Vernetzung von n Prozessoren kann vollständig oder auch nur teilweise sein. Ohne Auszeichnung der einzelnen Prozessoren in ihrer Stellung zueinander wird man in jedem Fall von einem *dezentralisierten* Netzwerk sprechen, dessen Kontrolle durch die paarweisen Aktivitäten jeweils zweier kommunizierender Partner im Netz bestimmt ist. Ein Beispiel hierfür wird in [FAR72] beschrieben. Der Grad der Vernetzung bestimmt die Redundanz im Netz und damit auch das Maß der Zuverlässigkeit, mit dem Kommunikationen innerhalb des Netzes vorgenommen werden können. Vollständige dezentralisierte Vernetzung tritt in der Praxis allein deshalb kaum auf, da die Kosten für die $\binom{n}{2}$ physikalischen Verbindungen selten in einem gerechtfertigten Verhältnis zu den Möglichkeiten stehen. Üblicherweise wird Dezentralisierung mit einer Auszeichnung der einzelnen Prozessoren zueinander verbunden, entweder in der Form der Ringstrukturen [FAR75] oder als hierarchische Anordung [ASH75]. Bei beiden Varianten ergeben sich interessante Möglichkeiten der Aufgabenverteilung im Netzwerk. Erfolgt die Konzentration der Kontrolle auf einen einzigen Prozessor, so spricht man von einem *zentralisierten* Netzwerk. Zentralisierung oder auch sternförmiger Verbund finden sich meist bei Anordnungen um mittelpunktsmäßig angeordnete Großrechner, es sei denn, Zentrum eines solchen Netzes ist der nachrichten-vermittelnde Prozessor selbst [RIC74]. In der Praxis finden sich häufig Übergangsanordnungen. Typisches Beispiel für ein partiell dezentralisiertes Verbundsystem ist das mittlerweile kontinentumspannende ARPA-Netzwerk [HEA70,HEA72,KAH70]. Subnetze um einen IMP (Interface Message Processor) stellen den zentralisierten Anteil, das Gesamtnetz selbst ist dezentralisiert.

Neben topologischen Netzstrukturen lassen sich Rechnerverbundsysteme auch nach funktionellen Gesichtspunkten klassifizieren. Werden besondere Dienstleistungen innerhalb des Netzwerkes nur einfach angeboten und bestimmt die Art der Aufgabe das Element, das für eine Leistung benutzt wird, so spricht man von *Funktionsverbund*. Hierbei können sowohl spezifische Dienstleistungen (bestimmte nur lokal verfügbare Programme und Systeme, spezielle Datenbanken etc.) als auch physikalische Betriebsmittel (besondere Ein- oder Ausgabegeräte, Anschlüsse für spezielle Prozessoren etc.) in Anspruch genommen werden. Betrachtet man im Gegensatz dazu die Aufgabe des Netzwerks überwiegend darin, daß Kapazitäten nicht nach Maximalanforderungen bereitgestellt werden müssen, sondern durch andere Elemente im Netzwerk ausgeglichen werden können, so gelangt man zum *Lastverbund*. Hierbei auftretende Probleme sind sowohl pragmatisch [ROB70] als auch analytisch [LAN74] behandelt worden. Es muß angemerkt werden, daß die Grenzen zwischen Last- und Funktionsverbund fließend sind. Daneben wird neuerdings auch noch Datenverbund als zusätzliche funktionelle Klassifikation von Netzwerken erwähnt, obwohl diese Form der Kommunikation unter Funktionsverbund eingeordnet werden kann, da die Verfügbarkeit von Daten an einem bestimmten Knoten im Netz offensichtlich als Funktion dieses Elementes betrachtet werden kann.

Knoten in Netzwerken

Die Prozessoren in Rechnernetzwerken können weitgehend selbständige Einheiten darstellen, die, ausgestattet mit eigener lokaler Konfiguration und autonomem Betriebssystem, ein überwiegendes Eigenleben führen (ARPA-Netz), oder sie können auch innerhalb des Netzes nach einer vorgegebenen Verteilung aufeinander abgestimmte Spezialaufgaben übernehmen. In beiden Fällen unterscheidet man homogene und inhomogene Netze, abhängig davon ob die Knoten identisch oder wenigstens strukturell kompatibel sind oder nicht. Homogene Netzwerke werden häufig benutzt, um den Zugriff zu verteilten Datenbasen zu ermöglichen [MAN74]. Eine identische Architektur der Knoten bietet vor allem erhebliche Vorteile hinsichtlich des Implementierungsaufwandes. Bei inhomogenen Rechnernetzen sind dagegen dezentrale Anpassungen vorzunehmen, deren Aufwand besonders im dezentralen Fall durch die erforderliche Vielfachheit beträchtlich sein kann.

Abhängig von den Anwendungen, für die ein Rechnernetz eingesetzt wird, können die Knoten unterschieden werden nach ihrer Aufgabe im Netz. Neben Prozessoren zur Abwicklung eigener Aufgaben hat man solche, die exklusiv der Netzwerkkontrolle dienen (Multiplexoren, Konzentratoren, Kommunikationsprozessoren).

Die Verbindung der Knoten untereinander zum Zwecke des wechselseitigen Nachrichtenaustauschs erfolgt nach einem der beiden folgenden Prinzipien

- Verbindungsumschaltung (line switching)
- Nachrichtenumschaltung (message switching)

Bei der Verbindungsumschaltung wird die physikalische Kopplung zwischen Sender und Empfänger der Nachricht hergestellt und bleibt für die gesamte Dauer der Transaktion in dieser Form erhalten.
Bei der Nachrichtenumschaltung gelangt die zu übertragende Nachricht ins Netzwerk, bevor der genaue Weg, den die Nachricht zu neh-

men hat, feststeht. Während einer Transaktion kann daher die aktuelle physikalische Verbindung mehrfach wechseln. Nachrichtenumschaltung ist offensichtlich das flexiblere Verfahren, andererseits aber auch mit größerem Verwaltungsaufwand verbunden.

Entwurfsaufgaben

Beim Entwurf eines Rechnernetzwerks müssen eine Reihe von Daten zur Verfügung stehen, damit das aufzubauende Netz auch die gestellten Aufgaben erfüllen kann. Dazu gehören

- Verteilung der Knoten im Netz (geographische Randbedingungen)
- Frequenz und Dichte der zwischen den einzelnen Knoten zu übermittelnden Daten
- Beschränkungen hinsichtlich der geforderten Nachrichtenübertragungszeiten
- Beschränkungen bezüglich der zugelassenen Verfahren für die Übertragung (Übertragungsraten, Kosten etc.)
- Verteilung der erwarteten Maximalanforderungen ans Netz

Selbst wenn diese Daten vollständig zur Verfügung stehen, bleibt dennoch der Entwurf eines Netzwerks eine nicht einfache Aufgabe.

Beim Entwurf der Betriebssoftware für ein Rechnerverbundsystem treten die äquivalenten Fragestellungen auf wie beim Entwurf von Betriebssystemen für Einzel-Prozessoren. Eine Liste der Zielsetzungen ergibt sich nach [ABE73]

- Optimierung der Kommunikationssteuerung
- Maximierung der Möglichkeiten für den Zugriff zu entfernten Datenbasen
- Minimierung der Übertragungskosten
- Maximierung der Adaptierbarkeit des Netzes
- Maximierung der Zuverlässigkeit des Systems
- Maximierung der Effizienz des gesamten Rechnernetzes

Leider stehen mehrere dieser Zielsetzungen von vornherein im Widerspruch, was die Aufgabe für den Entwerfer eines solchen Verbundes nicht leichter macht. Für die Realisierung der einen oder anderen der oben genannten Zielfunktionen gibt es zahlreiche Algorithmen, die beim Entwurf existierender Verbundsysteme auch angewendet wurden [FRA73].

Die Systematisierung des Nachrichtenaustauschs zwischen zwei Partnern in einem Netzwerk kann auf einige Primitivfunktionen zurückgeführt werden, mittels derer die vollständige Abwicklung der Kommunikation möglich ist [WAL72,RIC74].

Von besonderer Bedeutung sind wegen der starken Abhängigkeit der Komponenten von Rechnernetzwerken voneinander Zuverlässigkeitsfragen. Zahlreiche Analyse-Modelle sind entwickelt worden, um die Zuverlässigkeit quantitativ angeben zu können [FRT74,MIT74].

Bestehende Verbundsysteme

Die Anzahl heute eingesetzter Rechnerverbundsysteme ist beträchtlich. Zu den lokale Bedeutung übersteigenden Netzwerken gehören vor allem das ARPA-Netz [KAH70], das MERIT-Verbundsystem [AUP72], das OCTOPUS-Kommunikationsnetz [FLE73] sowie das PRIME-System [FAB73].

Darüberhinaus gibt es zahlreiche Realisierungen, die, obwohl in ihren primären Zielsetzungen ähnlich oder gar identisch, doch zu vollständig verschiedenen Ergebnissen führten [ASH75,FAR75,FRA75]. An dieser Stelle müssen auch Mehrprozessorsysteme genannt werden, die zunächst nicht den Ausgangspunkt Rechnernetzwerke haben, infolge gemeinsamer Teilprobleme aber für Netze wichtige Erfahrungen vermitteln können [WUL75, FRA75].

Neben den Anwenderentwicklungen gewinnen in zunehmendem Maß auch von den Herstellern kommerziell vertriebener Rechner entwickelte Netzsysteme an Bedeutung. Nahezu jeder der heute am Markt tätigen Rechnerhersteller entwickelt sein Konzept des Rechnerverbundes, um der in der Vergangenheit typischen Diversifikation der Aufgaben und der dementsprechend verteilten instrumentellen Ausstattung nachträglich entgegenzuwirken [BLA75,STE74]. Allerdings haben diese Verbundsysteme im Gegensatz zu den im Anwendungsbereich entwickelten Systemen in der Regel den Nachteil, daß die Integration herstellerfremder Komponenten nicht oder nur erschwert möglich ist. Inhomogene Rechnernetzwerke sind daher nahezu ausschließlich die Domäne der Anwender.

Trends

Nach den Diebold-Statistiken [DIE74,DIE75] ist die Absatzentwicklung bei Großrechnern in der Bundesrepublik stagnierend oder teilweise sogar rückläufig. Die Zahl der Neuinstallationen nimmt jedoch noch deutlich im Bereich des Kleinrechnermarktes zu. Obwohl die Diebold-Statistiken keine Aussage über die Vernetzung der installierten Rechner machen, ist nach Kenntnis des Verfassers hier die Entwicklung stark zunehmend. Der Grund hierfür ist einfach in dem Bestreben, die Kostenentwicklung zu begrenzen, zu sehen. Andererseits werden auch in zunehmendem Maß stärker verteilte Aufgaben mit Hilfe von informationsverarbeitenden Systemen in Angriff genommen, die zumindest die jeweils zweiseitige Verbindung von Rechnern erfordern.

Obwohl die Voraussagen der technologischen Entwicklung für die nächsten zehn Jahre noch außerordentlich optimistisch sind hinsichtlich der erwarteten Kapazitätssteigerungen [WITH75], muß jedoch wegen der stark zunehmenden Verflechtung der Aufgaben untereinander mit einem gar nicht hoch genug einzuschätzenden Bedürfnis nach Kommunikation innerhalb der Informationsverarbeitung gerechnet werden. Hierbei werden insbesondere der Trend zu Mini- und Mikroprozessoren in allen Anwendungen nicht unberücksichtigt bleiben. Erste Ergebnisse der Übertragung dieser neuen Konzepte und Technologien auf Rechnernetzwerke liegen bereits vor [COH74].

Infolge seitens der Anwender häufig noch sehr unklar beschriebener Zielerwartungen wird die Einführung befriedigender Verfahren zum Lastausgleich noch einige Zeit auf sich warten lassen. Obwohl es zahlreiche Ansätze für zuteilungstheoretische Modelle gibt [LIU74], scheitern diese häufig noch am Aufwand der Realisierung. Vorerst finden hier überwiegend nur heuristische Verfahren Anwendung.

Bezüglich der topologischen Struktur von Rechnernetzwerken liegt nach Auffassung des Verfassers künftig das Schwergewicht auf dezentralisierten und verteilten Systemen. Diversifikation der Aufgaben und überwiegende Selbständigkeit der Einzelkomponenten für die Primäraufgaben bestätigen diese Auffassung.

"Network structures are already forcing us into new visions of tools and concepts, some of which were reaching religious statute. We will have to learn how to integrate uncertainty and parallelism in our thinking and our languages. Communications are the next challenge in computer structures". [POU73].

Literatur

[ABE73] Abernathy, D.H., Mancino, J.S., Pearson, C.R., Swiger, D.C., Survey of Design Goals for Operating Systems, Operating Systems Review, vol.7, nos.2 and 3, 1973 and vol.8, no.1, 1974

[ASH75] Ashenhurst, R.L. and Vonderohe, R.H., A Hierarchical Network, Datamation, February 1975

[AUP72] Aupperle, E.M. and Becher, W.D., The Communications Computer Hardware of the MERIT Computer Network, IEEE TC, vol. COM-20,3, 1972

[BLA75] Blair, C.R. and Gray, J.P., IBM's Systems Network Architecture, Datamation, April 1975

[COH74] Cohen, D. and Liu, M.T., Emulation of Computer Networks by Microprogrammable Microcomputers, Preprints of the 7th Annual Workshop on Microprogramming, Palo Alto, 1974

[DIE74] Diebold Statistik, Stand 1.7.74, Diebold Management Report, September 1974

[DIE75] Diebold Statistik, Stand 1.1.75, Diebold Management Report, April 1975

[FAB73] Fabry, R.S., and Ruschitzka, M.G., The Prime Message System, COMPCON 1973, pp.125-128

[FAR72] Farber, D.J. and Larson, K., The Structure of a Distributed Computer System, Proc. of the Symposium on Computer Communications Networks and Teletraffic, Brooklyn 1972

[FAR75] Farber, D.J., A Ring Network, Datamation, February 1975

[FLE73] Fletcher, G.J., Octopus Communications Structure, COMPCON 1973, pp.21-23

[FRA73] Fratta, L., Optimal Design of Computer-Communication Networks, Workshop on Computer Networks, Arles, April 1973

[FRA75] Fraser, A.G., A Virtual Channel Network, Datamation, February 1975

[FRT74] Fratta, L. and Montanari, U., Analytical Techniques for Computer Networks Analysis and Design, IRIA Workshop on Computer Architectures and Networks, Aug.12-14, 1974

[HEA70] Heart, F.E. et al, The Interface Message Processor for the ARPA Computer Network, AFIPS SJCC, vol.36, 1970, pp.551-567

[HEA72] Heart, F.E. et al, The Terminal IMP for the ARPA Computer Network, AFIPS SJCC, vol.40, 1972, pp.243-254

[KAH70] Kahn, R.E., Terminal Access to the ARPA Computer Network, Courant Computer Symposium on Computer Networks, Nov. 1970

[LAN74] Landwehr, C.E., Load Sharing in Computer Networks: A Queuing Model, Merit Computer Network, MCN-1174-TR18, 1974

[LIU74] Liu, C.S. and Liu, J.W.S., Performance Analysis of Heterogeneous Multiprocessor Computing Systems, IRIA Workshop on Computer Architectures and Networks, Aug.12-14, 1974

[MAN74] Manning, E., A Homogeneous Network for Data Sharing, IRIA Workshop on Computer Architectures and Networks, Aug.12-14, 1974

[MIT74] Mitrani,I., Networks of Unreliable Computers, IRIA Workshop on Computer Architectures and Networks, Aug.12-14, 1974

[POU73] Pouzin, L., Network Architectures and Components, Workshop on Computer Networks, Arles, April 1973

[RIC74] Richter, L., Kommunikation in Netzwerken, unveröffentl. Manuskript, Dortmund, März 1974

[ROB70] Roberts, L.G., and Wessler, B.D., Computer Network Development to Achieve Resource Sharing, AFIPS SJCC, vol.36, 1970, pp.543-549

[STE74] v. Stelmach, E., Introduction to Minicomputer Networks, Digital Equipment Corp., Maynards, 1974

[WAL72] Walden, D.C., A System for Interprocess Communication in a Resource Sharing Computer Network, CACM, vol.15, no.4, April 1972

[WITH75] Withington, F.G., Beyond 1984: A Technological Forecast, Datamation, January 1975

[WUL75] Wulf, W. and Levin, R., A Local Network, Datamation, February 1975

BELAESTIGUNG DER MENSCHEN DURCH COMPUTER

Hartmann J. Genrich

Institut fuer Informationssystemforschung
Gesellschaft fuer Mathematik und Datenverarbeitung
5205 St. Augustin 1, Schloss Birlinghoven

Vorbemerkung

Der folgende Beitrag zum Thema "Informatik und Gesellschaft" wendet sich in erster Linie an diejenigen Informatiker, die mit dem Autor bereit sind zuzugeben,

- dass der Einsatz von Computern in praktisch allen Bereichen der Gesellschaft auch Gefahren mit sich bringt;
- dass die Abwehr von negativen Auswirkungen einer Entwicklung, von der die Informatik ihre Existenzberechtigung ableitet, nicht nur Juristen oder Soziologen, dem Staat oder dem einzelnen Buerger aufgeladen werden kann;
- dass die Informatiker verpflichtet sind, die Verantwortlichen in Politik, Wirtschaft und Verwaltung immer wieder auch auf die moeglichen negativen Folgen des Computereinsatzes hinzuweisen;
- dass daher die unterschiedlichen Formen moeglicher Belaestigung, Belastung oder Bedrohung durch Computer in der informatischen Theorie und Praxis untersucht, genau verstanden und dann abgebaut werden muessen;
- dass die Informatiker andernfalls in den Ruf verantwortungsloser 'Fachidioten' geraten werden, wenn nicht gar in den Ruf ruecksichtsloser Technokraten.

Wer in keinem dieser Punkte mit dem Autor uebereinstimmen kann, wird auch mit der folgenden Schilderung wenig anzufangen wissen, mag aber immerhin Nutzen aus den Vorschlaegen ziehen, die unten gegeben werden.

1. Formen der Belaestigung

Zweifellos ist die Erfindung der Computer eine der bedeutungsvollsten gesellschaftlichen Leistungen ueberhaupt. Wenn im folgenden vornehmlich die negativen Auswirkungen ihres Einsatzes eroertert werden, so ist das als Appell an alle Verantwortlichen zu verstehen, ueber all den Vorteilen nicht die Nachteile ausser acht zu lassen.

Als erstes sollen an einigen Beispielen die wesentlichen Formen der "Belaestigung der Menschen durch Computer" deutlich gemacht werden: die Belaestigung des Einzelnen, die Belastung sozialer Beziehungen, und die Bedrohung der Gesellschaft.

Eine weitere Form wollen wir ausdruecklich als Nicht-Belaestigung aus der weiteren Betrachtung ausschliessen: die notwendige Umgewoehnung jedes einzelnen an die durch die Existenz der Computer geschaffenen neuen Verhaeltnisse, ohne die eine volle Ausschoepfung der Vorteile und eine erfolgreiche Abwehr der Nachteile nicht moeglich ist. Unsere Aufgabe als Informatiker ist es dabei, die Verhaeltnisse so zu gestalten, dass fuer jeden der Nutzen die Anstrengungen lohnend macht.

Jeder von uns kann von der Belaestigung durch Computer betroffen werden, sei es als Staatsbuerger, als gelegentlicher Benutzer von Computern, oder als 'Computer-Spezialist':

- Man erhaelt eine Mahnung, noch eine Mahnung, und sogar einen Zahlungsbefehl, weil ein Computer 'vergessen' hat, die Zahlung zur Kenntnis zu nehmen.
- Wessen Anschrift einmal von einem Adressen-Vertrieb erfasst wurde, kann den Strom von Werbung hoechstens durch einen Umzug abstellen - oder besser: voruebergehend unterbrechen.
- Ein Versichterter muss unertraeglich lange auf seine Rente warten, weil sein Name wegen eines Schreibfehlers im Computer 'verloren ging'.
- Ein Programm laeuft ploetzlich nicht mehr, weil jemand eine Idee hatte, das System zu 'verbessern'.
- Die Moeglichkeiten, mit einem Computer unverstandene Dinge zu tun, sind unbegrenzt, denn 'intelligente' Compiler finden heraus, was man gemeint haben koennte.

Schwerwiegender als die Belaestigung des Einzelnen, fuer die jeder von uns die Liste von Beispielen aus eigener Erfahrung beliebig verlaengern koennte, ist die Belastung sozialer Beziehungen. Dazu zaehlt vor allem die Tatsache, dass man ueber Computer vielfaeltigen Einfluessen ausgesetzt wird, deren Urheber nicht feststellbar sind. Diese Verschleierung von Interessen und Verantwortung, die durch die Richtung der "kuenstlichen Intelligenz" mit der angestrebten weitestgehenden Verselbstaendigung der Automaten besonders gefoerdert wird, macht fuer den Einzelnen die Verhaeltnisse undurchschaubar.

Eine weitere Belastung drueckt sich in der Erfahrung aus, dass sich die tatsaechlichen oder vermeintlichen Vorteile des Einsatzes von Computern fuer einen bestimmten Zweck in erhebliche Nachteile verkehren koennen, haeufig gerade fuer die Personen, in deren Namen die Veraenderungen vorgenommen werden. So werden durch eine Rationalisierungmassnahme Personen bei ihrer bisherigen Arbeit 'entlastet', nicht um eine hoeher-qualifizierte und menschenwuerdigere Arbeit zu leisten, sondern um dem Computer 'zur Hand zu gehen'.

Sowohl Unkenntnis der Konsequenzen der Computerisierung als auch leicht zu verschleiernder Missbrauch koennen die Ursache hierfuer sein. Moeglich wird dies durch die einseitige Betonung des Vorteils der Einsatzvielfalt der Computer, die durch Hinweise auf riesige verfuegbare Programmbibliotheken noch unterstrichen wird. Das Werkzeug fuer die Herstellung einer garantierten Zweckbestimmung und Zweckbeschraenkung wird nicht mitgeliefert, jedenfalls nicht in annaehernd vergleichbarem Umfang.

- Durch die Einfuehrung der Datenverarbeitung in einer Behoerde erhaelt ein Sachbearbeiter die Moeglichkeit, die Entscheidung ueber einen Antrag eines Buergers mit Unterstuetzung des Computers zu faellen. Da im Computer jedoch nicht seine persoenliche Auffassung ueber seine Taetigkeit und den jeweils verfuegbaren Spielraum niedergelegt ist, sondern die Auffassung eines fuer ihn anonymen Software-Produzenten, kann er haeufig seine Entscheidung gegenueber dem Buerger nur noch unter Berufung auf den 'unfehlbaren' Computer vertreten. Den Verlust an eigener Autoritaet muss der Sachbearbeiter dadurch kompensieren, dass er an der Autoritaet des Computers teilnimmt. Er mystifiziert das Geraet, um als dessen Vertrauter, ja gewissermassen als dessen "Priester", neue gesellschaftliche Bedeutung zu gewinnen. Der Buerger verliert damit jede Moeglichkeit, das Zustandekommen einer Entscheidung zu verstehen und moeglicherweise zu kritisieren; mit dem Computer kann er nicht argumentieren.
- Durch den Computer-gestuetzten Unterricht soll die Lernleistung der Schueler erhoeht und der Lehrer entlastet werden. Die Schueler sitzen am Bildschirm und bestimmen selbst den Fortschritt im Verstaendnis des Stoffes; der Idealfall scheint erreicht zu sein, wenn der Lehrer sich darauf beschraenken kann, bei Schwierigkeiten im Umgang mit dem Geraet

zu helfen. Fuer die am Ende des Schuljahres notwendige Beurteilung eines jeden Schuelers fuehrt der Computer das ganze Jahr ueber jeden Schueler Protokolle.

Wie sollen die Schueler, die die ganze Zeit mit dem Computer als Partner kommuniziert haben, die Rolle des Lehrers verstehen, der aufgrund von "Abhoer-Protokollen" jetzt die Leistungen beurteilt? Wie sollen die Schueler ihre Beziehung zum Lehrer gestalten, wenn sie keine Moeglichkeit mehr besitzen, durch ihr Verhalten in direkt erkennbarer Weise das Urteil des Lehrers ueber sie zu beeinflussen.

- Zum Zwecke der Personalplanung in einem Unternehmen wird eine Personaldatenbank eingerichtet. Fuer jeden Arbeitnehmer wird ein umfangreicher Record zusammengestellt; jedes einzelne Feld dieses Records laesst sich mit einem bestimmten Zweck begruenden, den z.B. auch der Betriebsrat akzeptieren kann. Da es jedoch keine Moeglichkeit gibt, echte Schranken fuer die Verwendung der einzelnen Feldinhalte einzurichten, ist damit der Missbrauch der Daten, d.h. der Gebrauch fuer einen anderen als den von allen Beteiligten akzeptierten Zweck, nicht zu verhindern. Da der Betrieb der Datenbank nicht der Kontrolle des Betriebsrats unterliegt, ist damit eine erhebliche Verschiebung des Kraefteverhaeltnisses zwischen Unternehmensleitung und Arbeitnehmerschaft eingetreten.

Umgekehrt muesste aber auch ein Arbeitnehmer, wenn ihm allein das Einbringen von Daten in seinen persoenlichen Record anheimgestellt waere, bei den heutigen Missbrauchsmoeglichkeiten auch solche Daten zurueckhalten, deren korrekter Gebrauch in seinem wohlverstandenen Interesse liegt, und deren Fehlen eine ordnungsgemaesse Fuehrung eines Betriebs unmoeglich machen wuerde.

Es ist sicher moeglich, bei allen Beteiligten ein Bewusstsein fuer die bisher angedeuteten Formen der Nachteile des Einsatzes von Computern zu schaffen, da es sich um konkret erfahrbare Auswirkungen handelt, die es zu verarbeiten gilt. Die groessten Probleme und Gefahren liegen aber dort, wo die Auswirkungen unseres Handelns erst in der naechsten oder uebernaechsten Generation deutlich werden.

Es bedeutet eine mit der Gefaehrdung unserer Umwelt gleichwertige Bedrohung unserer Gesellschaft, dass heute unmerkbar, ohne ausreichende Einsicht in die Konsequenzen und ohne hinreichende Grundlage Entscheidungen ueber zukuenftige Organisationsformen getroffen werden, die nicht mehr revidiert werden koennen. In Jahrhunderten gewachsene Formen gesellschaftlichen Handelns in Wirtschaft und Verwaltung, im Rechts- und im Bildungswesen, im Melde- und im Nachrichtenwesen, werden so radikal umgestaltet, dass praktisch alle Regelkreise, die eine Gesellschaft im Gleichgewicht halten, gestoert werden oder sogar zerstoert zu werden drohen. Nicht dass die bestehenden Formen nicht revisionsbeduerftig waeren. Die Naivitaet und Kurzsichtigkeit des computer-zentrischen Denkens, das die Plaene von oeffentlichen Stellen, von Hardware- und Softwareherstellern, und nicht zuletzt von vielen Informatikern fuer die Einrichtung von Computer-Netzen, von Informationsbanken, eines automatisierten Meldewesens oder einer bargeldlosen Verteilung von Guetern und Leistungen bestimmt, kann nur erschrecken.

Die ungeheuren direkten Kosten fuer solche Entwicklungen, die wenn ueberhaupt nur einmal aufgebracht werden koennen, machen schon allein einmal getroffene Entscheidungen unrevidierbar. Da aber praktisch alle Bereiche unseres Lebens sich den einmal geschaffenen Verhaeltnissen anpassen muessen, sind die im Lauf der Zeit indirekt investierten Mittel noch um ein vielfaches groesser.

Um uns die Gefahren zu verdeutlichen, sind wir auf Vergleiche, auf Analogien angewiesen:

- Die Verseuchung der Gewaesser ist das Ergebnis einer unbestimmten Fuelle von Einzelentscheidungen staatlicher und privater Instanzen, jede fuer sich wahrscheinlich 'richtig', wenn man den Kontext nur genuegend begrenzt sieht.
- Eine vergleichsweise unerhebliche Entscheidung wie die Wahl zwischen Rechts- und Linksverkehr kann heute von Grossbritannien praktisch nicht mehr revidiert werden, weil die Kosten fuer eine Umstellung, also die Wiederholung einer Jahrzehnte dauernden Entwicklung mit 'unwesentlich' geaenderten Randbedingungen nicht mehr aufgebracht werden koennen.

2. Ursachen der Belaestigung

Die unterschiedlichen Formen der Belaestigung durch Computer ergeben sich natuerlich nicht automatisch, sondern sie sind Ergebnis einer bestimmmten Verwendung von Computern. Um die Belaestigung abzustellen, bedarf es der Lokalisierung ihrer Ursachen. Auch hier kann unsere Untersuchung nur bruchstueckhaft einige Beispiele zur Charakterisierung moeglicher Ursachen enthalten.

Wir beginnen mit einem Komplex von Ursachen, den man unter dem Stichwort 'konsequenter Missbrauch der Sprache' zusammenfassen koennte. Die teils bewusst, teils unbewusst irrefuehrende Verwendung von Ausdruecken der Umgangssprache im Bereich der Datenverarbeitung, und auch die in fast allen relevanten Teilen der Informatik fehlende wissenschaftliche Grundlage fuer die Entwicklung einer praezisen Fachterminologie tragen zu einem erheblichen Teil dazu bei, den Gebrauch von Computern fuer Laien, und fuer Fachleute, undurchschaubar zu machen:

- Wenn einem Laien in einem Atemzug erklaert wird, Computer seien Werkzeuge wie jedes andere Werkzeug auch und sie seien so intelligent, dass man sich mit ihnen unterhalten koenne wie mit einer Person, der man eine bestimmte Aufgabe erlaeutert, dann muss das zwangslaeufig zu Missverstaendnissen fuehren.
- Wenn dem Computer die 'Schuld' fuer eine bestimmte Massnahme gegeben wird, so ist dies eine fahrlaessige oder vorsaetzliche Verwechslung von Schuld und Ursache. Ein Fehler in einem Computer kann eine Ursache fuer eine falsche Massnahme sein; Schuld oder allgemeiner: Verantwortung muessen durch Untersuchung von Kausalzusammenhaengen bei Personen gesucht werden.
- Das Wort 'Queue' dient zur Bezeichnung einer Gruppe von Speicherelementen mit einer 'first in- first out'-Disziplin. Was diese Disziplin bedeutet, laesst sich jedem Laien unmittelbar verstaendlich machen, waehrend es sich die Informatiker erlauben, es manchmal fuer zweckmaessig ('wirtschaftlich') zu halten, eine 'Queue' umzusortieren.
- Die missbraeuchliche Verwendung des Wortes 'wirtschaftlich' ist zwar keine Besonderheit der Informatik. Trotzdem sollten auch Informatiker haeufiger mehr an Zweckentsprechung und Vertraeglichkeit im Grossen anstelle von Wirtschaftlichkeit im Kleinen denken.
- Auch der Missbrauch des Worts 'formal' (und von Formalismen) ist nicht typisch fuer die Informatik, aber die Informatik liefert eine Fuelle von Paradebeispielen dafuer, dass so manche formale Beschreibung weder hinreichend noch notwendig fuer Korrektheit oder wissenschaftliche Strenge ist.

Einen weiteren Komplex von Ursachen fuer Belaestigung sehen wir in den voellig unzureichenden Ausdrucksmitteln fuer den Umgang mit Computern. Wir Informatiker waren, und sind es noch, so fasziniert von der Erfahrung, dass Computer nicht nur Zahlen, sondern auch Symbole manipulieren koennen, dass wir die erheblichen visuellen und taktilen Faehigkeiten des Menschen zur Interaktion mit Geraeten allein zum Lesen und Tippen laengerer oder kuerzerer Zeichenreihen einsetzen. Dabei wuerden graphische Darstellungsmittel fuer strukturelle, vor allem organisatorische Zusammenhaenge, die eine direkte Kopplung zwischen optischer Anzeige und manuellem Eingriff ermoeglichen, die bisherige Form der Benutzung von Computern mittels riesiger Programmpakete weitgehend abloesen koennen.

Schliesslich ist noch der Komplex der mangelnden Zweckgebundenheit des Computereinsatzes zu nennen. Zweifellos ist es einer der ganz besonderen Vorteile der Computer, dass sie programmierbar sind, dass also ihre Funktion innerhalb eines bestimmten organisatorischen Kontexts nicht starr festgelegt ist. Dieser Vorteil der Einsatzvielfalt verkehrt sich jedoch in einen erheblichen Nachteil, wenn es ueberhaupt keine garantierten Schranken fuer den Gebrauch im einzelnen gibt. Wenn Computer so konzipiert sind, dass zunaechst einmal alle Daten von ueberall her gleichmaessig erreichbar und beliebig kopierbar sind, so wird der nachtraegliche Schutz, die Kanalisierung von Datenstroemen, durch rein organisatorische Mittel zu einem praktisch unloesbaren Problem.

Die Informatik hat es bisher versaeumt, dem Begriff der schnell und perfekt kopierbaren Daten den Begriff des einmaligen Datums, des 'Dokuments', entgegenzusetzen. Die Jahrtausende alte organisatorische Praxis menschlicher Gesellschaft enthaelt eine Fuelle von Beispielen dafuer, dass ohne den Dokumentcharakter bestimmter Dinge kein geregeltes Zusammenwirken in einem organisatorischem Ganzen moeglich ist. Ueberall dort, wo Dinge zu Symbolen fuer einzelne Rechte und Pflichten von Personen werden, muss eine Kopie eines solchen Objekts einen voellig anderen Status als das Original besitzen: Sei es die 'Faelschung' einer Banknote, fuer die die Einloesegarantie der Staatsbank nicht gilt, oder sei es ein 'zuviel' abgegebener Stimmzettel bei einer Wahl, der die ganze Wahl ungueltig macht, weil ein einzelnes Stimmrecht nur einmal wahrgenommen werden kann.

3. Vermeidung der Belaestigung

Nach dieser bruchstueckhaften negativen Bestandsaufnahme der Informatik wollen wir im folgenden untersuchen, wie die Informatik zur Vermeidung der von ihr mit zu verantwortenden Nachteile beitragen kann.

Um es ganz deutlich zu machen: Es kann nicht Aufgabe der Informatik allein sein, mit den vielfaeltigen Problemen und Gefahren fertig zu werden, die der Einsatz von Computern mit sich bringt. Eine Informatik jedoch, die diese Probleme und Gefahren negiert, deren Begruendung als Wissenschaft nicht an der durch die Erfindung der Computer geschaffenen Realitaet orientiert ist, verliert ihre Existenzberechtigung.

Unserer Ueberzeugung nach kann eine tragfaehige Grundlage fuer die Informatik nur geschaffen werden, wenn Einigkeit ueber die objektive gesellschaftliche Funktion der Computer besteht, und damit ueber das prinzipiell mit Computern Machbare.

Ohne Zweifel war und ist die subjektive Einschaetzung der Funktion der Computer einer Reihe von Veraenderungen unterworfen; heute kann man jedoch durchaus erkennen, dass und wohin diese Entwicklung konvergiert:

Erfunden wurden die Computer als schnelle Rechenmaschinen, und als solche gewannen sie zunaechst ihre grosse Bedeutung. Durch das v.Neumann'sche Konzept, neben den Zwischenergebnissen einer Rechnung auch den Rechenplan im Zentralspeicher aufzuheben, erhielten diese Maschinen ein solches Mass relativer Selbstaendigkeit gegenueber ihren Benutzern, wie es bis dahin kein Geraet jemals besass. Zusammen mit der Existenz immer groesserer Speicher und der Moeglichkeit, nicht nur Zahlen, sondern beliebige Zeichenreihen zu manipulieren, entstand die Vorstellung eines lernfaehigen, zu selbstaendigem Denken und zur Evolution faehigen technischen "Super-Hirns", entstand die Richtung der 'kuenstlichen Intelligenz'.

Dieser Entwicklung wurde in der Folge durch die Betonung des Werkzeugcharakters der Computer begegnet; jedoch standen jetzt nicht mehr allein die Rechenprozesse im Mittelpunkt der Anwendungen, sondern in Analogie zu den herkoemmlichen, die physischen Faehigkeiten der Menschen verstaerkenden Maschinen wurden die Computer als 'Intelligenzverstaerker', als Werkzeuge zur Unterstuetzung der intellektuellen Faehigkeiten des (einzelnen) Benutzers betrachtet.

Abgesehen davon, dass diese Auffassung nur teilweise zum Verstaendnis der realen, erhofften oder befuerchteten Einsatzmoeglichkeiten der Computer beitraegt, steht sie im direkten Widerspruch zu der Sprechweise - und damit eben auch zur Denkweise! - durch die heute die Benutzung dieser Werkzeuge gekennzeichnet ist. Mit wenigen Ausnahmen dienten naemlich alle Anstrengungen auf dem Gebiet der EDV in den letzten zehn Jahren dem einen Ziel, die Computer zu einem moeglichst vollkommenen Kommunikations-Partner jedes einzelnen Benutzers zu machen.

Beide Auffassungen - die des Werkzeugs und die des Partners - sind nicht falsch, sondern abhaengig von der konkreten Situation manchmal sehr hilfreich, manchmal aber auch unzweckmaessig und sogar irrefuehrend. So ist es ohne eine gewisse den Computer personifizierende Sprechweise schwer moeglich, einem Laien in kurzer Zeit die Vorgaenge in einem Rechenbetrieb zu erlaeutern; schaedlich wirkt sich jedoch diese Personifizierung der Geraete spaetestens dann aus, wenn diese so ernst genommen wird, dass die Verantwortung der dahinter stehenden Personen nicht mehr gesehen wird, oder wenn Computer nur noch danach beurteilt werden, wie gut sie die Partnerrolle wahrzunehmen in der Lage sind.

Daher ist es notwendig, zu einer Auffassung von der Funktion der Computer zu gelangen, die die vorhandenen widerspruechlichen Auffassungen als - moeglicherweise entartete - Spezialfaelle enthaelt, jedoch besser geeignet erscheint, zu einem Verstaendnis der Moeglichkeiten und Gefahren der Computer zu fuehren.

Die praktische Erfahrung zeigt, dass an die Stelle der individuellen Nutzung des Werkzeugs Computer immer mehr die gemeinsame Nutzung durch organisierte Gruppen von Personen tritt. Da aber gesellschaftliche Denkprozesse ihrem Wesen nach Kommunikationsprozesse sind, wird damit die Zweckbestimmung der Computer als die eines Kommunikationsmediums deutlich.

Auch die Auffassung von Computern als Kommunikationsmedien zwischen Personen bedarf noch einer Weiterentwicklung oder Ergaenzung. Betrachtet man z.B. den Einsatz der EDV bei der Erforschung des Universums durch die Radioastronomie oder bei der Steuerung grosser Produktionsanlagen, so laesst sich erkennen, dass wir es insgesamt mit einem allgemeinem Medium fuer einen streng organisierten makroskopischen Informationsfluss zu tun haben.

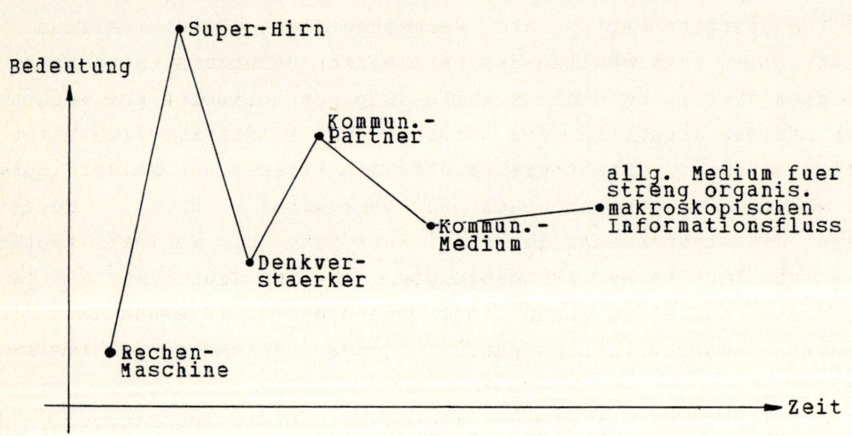

Einschaetzung der Funktion des Computers

Das Besondere und Neuartige an diesem Medium ist zunaechst, dass es alle Funktionen herkoemmlicher Medien in sich vereint: Es leistet die Uebertragung, Speicherung und Vervielfaeltigung von Nachrichten, aber auch deren Verknuepfung, Umformung und gezielte Verteilung; und es leistet dies in zuvor unvorstellbarer Geschwindigkeit, Menge und Praezision.

Darueber hinaus ist jedoch von entscheidender Bedeutung, dass die Funktionsweise dieses Mediums in einem bestimmten organisatorischen Zusammenhang nicht bereits bei seiner Einrichtung genau festgelegt werden muss, sondern dass die angeschlossenen Personen entsprechend ihren Aufgaben und Interessen viele ihrer Taetigkeiten in einer bestimmten Weise an dieses Medium delegieren koennen. Hierzu gehoert insbesondere die Transformation aller Nachrichten auf den individuellen Standpunkt des jeweiligen Empfaengers.

Die Wohlbestimmtheit des Verhaltens dieses Mediums kennzeichnet in besonderem Masse dessen Einsatzmoeglichkeiten; die Vorteile eines 'Mangels' an autonomer Vielfalt koennen fuer die zweckgerichtete Organisation sozio-technischer Systeme gar nicht hoch genug eingeschaetzt werden. Konzentriert man sich auf die Ausnutzung dieser Vorteile, so wird sich die Frage nach 'kuenstlicher Intelligenz', 'simulierter Intuition' oder 'programmierter Kreativitaet' kaum noch stellen.

Ein voellig neues Kommunikationsmedium, dessen Erfindung fuer ebenso bedeutungsvoll angesehen werden muss wie die Erfindung der Schrift, kann nicht ohne Auswirkungen auf das menschliche Bewusstsein und die Organisationsformen menschlicher Gesellschaften bleiben. Kommunikation, Gesellschaft und Bewusstsein sind untrennbar miteinander verbunden und voneinander abhaengig; genau hieraus ergibt sich der unmittelbare Zusammenhang zwischen Informatik und Gesellschaft.

Nimmt man bei der Beurteilung der Computer den zuletzt beschriebenen Standpunkt ein, so erkennt man unmittelbar die Notwendigkeit einer exakten Wissenschaft, deren Gegenstand die Erforschung und Gestaltung streng geregelter und technisierter Kommunikation und Organisation ist. Die Frage, inwieweit die heutige Informatik dieser Notwendigkeit gerecht wird, laesst sich nicht anders als mit 'Kaum!' beantworten.

Die theoretische Informatik (Automatentheorie, Komplexitaetstheorie, Theorie der formalen Sprachen, automatisches Beweisen) bezieht ihre Fragestellungen, wenn ueberhaupt noch aus der Praxis, entweder aus einer seit vielen Jahren ueberholten, die Funktion des Computers erheblich unterschaetzenden Auffassung (Geraet zur schnellen, automatischen Abwicklung von Rechenprozessen, individuelles Werkzeug zur Manipulation von Zeichenfolgen) oder aus einer fruchtlosen Ueberschaetzung (kuenstliche Intelligenz, automatische Kreativitaet, vollstaendige Simulation eines personalen Kommunikationspartners). Sowohl das an der schriftlichen Korrespondenz zwischen Partnern orientierte

Abfassen grosser Programmpakete in Form langer Zeichenreihen, als auch die moeglichst weitgehende Nachahmung der Konversation zwischen Partnern durch immer 'intelligentere' Dialoge mittels kurzer Zeichenreihen beruhen auf dem Missverstaendnis, dass die Interaktion mit einem Medium zum Zweck der Kommunikation dieselbe Qualitaet haben muss wie die auf der Existenz herkoemmlicher Medien beruhenden Formen menschlicher Kommunikation selbst.

Mit einer Begruendung der Informatik als der Lehre vom streng geregelten Informationsfluss wuerde diese nicht nur gleichberechtigt neben die Physik und die Chemie treten, sie koennte sich auch wichtige Erfahrungen in der Entwicklung einer solchen exakten Wissenschaft zunutze machen. Ohne einen Informationsbegriff z.B., der im Fall idealer informationsverarbeitender Prozesse einem Erhaltungssatz genuegt, duerfte es unmoeglich sein, die vielfaeltigen Erscheinungsformen von Information und Informationsfluss zu erforschen. Die Informatik bliebe dann das, als was sie heute erscheint: Eine grosse Sammlung unzusammenhaengender, teilweise grossartiger Einzelergebnisse, die einen gewissen wissenschaftlichen Standard nur dort besitzt, wo sie sich als Teilgebiet der Mathematik etabliert hat, und die ihre praktische Bedeutung aus der Existenz von Einrichtungen ableitet, auf deren Eigenschaften sie bisher keinen sehr wesentlichen positiven Einfluss nehmen konnte.

Zusammenfassung

Die Computer bilden ein neuartiges Medium fuer streng organisierten Informationsfluss, dessen Erfindung in seiner Bedeutung mit der Erfindung des Buchdrucks, vielleicht sogar nur mit der Erfindung der Schrift verglichen werden kann. Computer sind damit nicht die Ursache von Belaestigungen, sondern Instrument und Uebermittler der vielfaeltigen Einfluesse, die die Mitglieder menschlicher Gesellschaften aufeinander ausueben.

Die wirklich grosse Gefahr, die mit dem Einsatz von Computern verbunden ist, ruehrt von der zur Zeit betriebenen radikalen und wegen der fehlenden Einsicht in die Konsequenzen kaum zu verantwortenden Umgestaltung der bestehenden Kommunikationsverhaeltnisse und damit der organisatorischen Grundlage unserer Gesellschaft. Die Abwehr dieser Gefahren kann nur mit Hilfe einer Informatik gelingen, die sich als exakte Wissenschaft der geregelten, technisierten Kommunikation an der durch die Erfindung der Computer geschaffenen Realitaet orientiert.

Unabdingbare Voraussetzung hierfuer ist, dass die Informatik ihr gegenwaertiges Stadium moeglichst schnell ueberwindet. Jedes Handeln mit Daten muss verantwortbar sein und von jemandem verantwortet werden; unser Fachgebiet nimmt jedoch noch kaum Notiz von der einfachen Tatsache, dass seine wissenschaftlichen Gegenstaende, Daten und Maschinen, in ein dicht gewebtes Netz von Rechten und Pflichten, von Nutzen und Schaden eingespannt sind. In dieser Hinsicht befinden wir uns in einem vorwissenschaftlichen Stadium, dem der Alchemie vergleichbar. Wenn wir es ferner hinnehmen, dass die wissenschaftlichen Methoden der computergestuetzten Prognose in Kontexten verwendet werden, in denen nachweislich die Voraussetzungen fuer die Anwendung dieser Methoden fehlen, so muessen wir es uns gefallen lassen, mit Astrologen verglichen zu werden.

Natuerlich ist gesicherte Erkenntnis in die Konsequenzen des Machbaren nicht hinreichend fuer verantwortungsvolles Handeln. Ohne eine solche Einsicht jedoch entbehrt die dringende notwendige Diskussion ueber das gemeinsam Angestrebte jeglicher Grundlage.

<u>Hinweis</u>

Der obige Beitrag gibt die sehr persoenliche Auffassung eines Informatikers zum Thema "Informatik und Gesellschaft" wieder, fuer den die geschilderte Einschaetzung der Moeglichkeiten und Gefahren des Computereinsatzes Richtschnur bei der Schaffung konkreter informatischer Werkzeuge ist. Praktisch alle hier geaeusserten Gedanken entstanden im Verlauf von Gespraechen des Autors mit Kollegen, vor allem mit C.A. Petri, der als erster die Bedeutung der Computer als Kommunikationsmedium erkannte.

D I A L O G S Y S T E M E

BEWERTUNG VON DIALOGSYSTEMEN ZUM DOKUMENTEN-RETRIEVAL

Dr. Friedrich Gebhardt
Gesellschaft für Mathematik
und Datenverarbeitung
Institut für DV im Rechtswesen
Leiter: Prof. Dr. Dr. H. Fiedler
5205 St. Augustin, Postfach 1240

1. Selektionsgüte-Maße bei Stapelverarbeitungssystemen

Zur Beurteilung der Güte eines Dokumentationsssystems (oder einer bestimmten Suchstrategie) werden üblicherweise Selektionsgüte-Maße wie Nachweis- und Relevanzquote herangezogen.

Schon bei Stapelsystemen gibt es gegen diese Maße einige Einwände.

Die Selektionsgüte-Maße beruhen auf dem Postulat, für jedes Dokument gäbe es bezüglich einer Suchfrage einen objektiven Relevanzwert und dieser sei meßbar (im einfachsten Falle: relevant oder nicht relevant). Es ist jedoch stets festgestellt worden, daß mehrere Schiedsrichter häufig stark abweichende Bewertungen vergeben (z.B. [Fraenkel 1968], [Saracevic 1971], [Cuadra 1967]). Das Modell muß also zumindest dahingehend verallgemeinert werden, daß die Relevanz eines Dokuments als Zufallsgröße betrachtet wird [Gebhardt 1973 und 1975b] .

Die Messung der Nachweisquote setzt voraus, daß alle Dokumente der gesamten Datenbasis bewertet werden. Bei größeren Datenbasen ist das eine kaum noch durchzuführende Aufgabe. Vielleicht ist das der Grund, warum viele Untersuchungen auf kleinen Dokumentbeständen (40 bis 300) beruhen. Einer der Haupteinwände gegen die Cranfield II-Experimente (1400 Dokumente, 279 Suchfragen) bestand darin, die Bewertung der Dokumente sei nicht gründlich genug erfolgt [Harter 1971, Swanson 1971].

Zweifellos gibt es Dokumente, die eine Suchfrage nur teilweise beantworten, die also weder wirklich einschlägig noch irrelevant sind. Um diese Fälle zu berücksichtigen, wird den Relevanzbeurteilungen häufig eine mehrstufige Skala zugrunde gelegt. Die üblichen Selektionsgüte-Maße können mehrstufige Bewertungen aber nicht berücksichtigen. Analoge Schwierigkeiten entstehen, wenn das Dokumentationssystem die nachgewiesenen Dokumente gewichtet.

Darüber hinaus ist es zweifelhaft, ob die Maximierung von Relevanz- und Nachweisquote immer das Ziel der Suche ist. Um einen bestimmten Sachverhalt zu erfahren, genügt dem Benutzer der Nachweis eines einzigen einschlägigen Dokuments. Ihm ist also ein relevantes Dokument unter drei nachgewiesenen lieber als vier relevante unter zehn nachgewiesenen, obwohl im letzten Falle sowohl die Relevanz- als auch die Nachweisquote höher ist. Ähnlich argumentiert [Cleverdon 1974] und folgert, daß Relevanz- und Nachweisquote keine angemessenen Maße für eine Benutzer-orientierte Bewertung eines arbeitenden Systems sind. [Farradane 1973] hält die gegenwärtige Situation (Verfahren und Maße zur Beschreibung der Güte von Retrieval-Systemen) für äußerst unbefriedigend und nicht vielversprechend für weitere Fortschritte.

2. Problematik bei Dialog-Systemen

Die Problematik der Selektionsgüte-Maße bleibt bei Dialog-Systemen erhalten oder verschärft sich noch [Fiedler 1975, Kap. 4] .

Da der Benutzer einen viel größeren Spielraum in der Führung des Dialogs hat, werden die Ergebnisse viel stärker streuen. Um also einen Unterschied zwischen zwei Suchstrategien nachzuweisen, braucht man noch größere Mengen von Suchfragen und folglich noch mehr Dokument-Bewertungen.

Noch gravierender ist, daß der Benutzer - hat er nur genügend viel Zeit - die Suchfrage so lange verfeinern kann, bis er fast alle einschlägigen Dokumente und fast keinen Ballast "gefunden" hat, wenn man unter "gefunden" nur diejenigen Dokumente versteht, die sich auf die letzte Version der in den Rechner eingegebenen Suchfrage qualifizieren.

Soll man also die im Verlauf des Dialogs angezeigten Dokumente mitzählen? Das dürfte deshalb unmöglich sein, weil der Übergang von "überblättert" bis "gründlich betrachtet" fließend ist.

Soll man statt dessen die Zeit beschränken, z.B. auf 15 Minuten? Bei manchen Problemen findet man in der ersten Minute das einzige relevante Dokument; die restlichen 14 Minuten sind dann vertan. In anderen Fällen reichen 15 Minuten nicht aus, und derjenige Test-Benutzer erzielt das beste Resultat, der zufällig bereits auf einige einschlägige Dokumente gestoßen ist.

Im übrigen möchte man ja nicht messen, wie schnell ein Benutzer arbeitet (z.B. denkt oder die Schreibmaschinentastatur bedient), sondern wie gut das System als ganzes (mit oder ohne Einschluß des Benutzers) ist. Dafür ist aber die Zeit, die der Benutzer vor der Datenstation verbringt, kein geeignetes Maß und eine Beschränkung dieser Zeit keine geeignete Standardisierung.

Die Unzufriedenheit mit den üblichen Selektionsgüte-Maßen wird sehr deutlich bei [Cooper 1973 a und b] , der eine "naive Methodologie" zur Bewertung von Dialog-Retrievalsystemen auf der Basis einer "utility" der gefundenen Dokumente für den Benutzer entwickelt. Da die "naive Methodologie" nicht praktikabel ist, werden Vereinfachungen vorgenommen, die jedoch wieder auf die Relevanzquote oder ähnliche Maße zurückführen und z.B. weder eine mehrstufige Relevanzbewertung verarbeiten noch unterschiedliche Rollen des Benutzers berücksichtigen.

3. Rolle des Benutzers

Aus den bisherigen Überlegungen ergibt sich, daß für die Beurteilung von Dokumentationssystemen die üblichen Selektionsgüte-Maße nicht befriedigen; während sie bei Stapelverarbeitungssystemen mangels besserer Beurteilungskriterien noch ausreichen mögen, geben sie bei Dialogsystemen höchstens einen Gesichtspunkt unter vielen wieder.

Unbedingt zu berücksichtigen ist die jeweilige Rolle des Benutzers (vgl. [Heine 1974] ; der Einfluß des Zwecks der Suche auf die Relevanz-Bewertung wird z.B. bei [Cuadra 1967] betont). Sein Suchverhalten und seine Antworterwartungen sind ganz anders, wenn er einmal eine möglichst vollständige Bibliographie und ein anderes Mal nur eine kurze Antwort haben möchte.

Bei der Beobachtung von "echten" Benutzern eines Systems muß man wohl dessen Rolle als eine komplexe, zu messende Größe (durch Befragung und Beobachtung) auffassen. Für Experimente zur Bewertung von Systemen ist es einfacher und vermutlich ausreichend und durchführbar, einige Standardrollen zu definieren und dem Testbenutzer jeweils eine dieser Standardrollen zuzuteilen.

Hier sollen die folgenden vier Standardrollen vorgeschlagen werden. Die Erfahrung muß zeigen, ob man damit auskommt.

A. Der Benutzer sucht Auskunft über einen objektiven Tatbestand. Ihm genügt ein einziges Dokument, das diesen Tatbestand darstellt, ersatzweise ein (notfalls mehrere) Dokument, aus dem er die gesuchte Antwort durch Deduktion ableiten kann.

B. Der Benutzer sucht schnell eine Antwort auf eine Frage, bei der verschiedene Autoren verschiedener Meinung sein könnten. Ihn interessiert ein Überblick über die Breite der Meinungsvielfalt ohne Vollständigkeitsambitionen; Schnelligkeit ist dagegen wesentlich. Typischerweise sind das Fragen, die mehr am Rande seines eigentlichen Problems liegen.

C. Der Benutzer sucht einen möglichst vollständigen Überblick über alle wichtigen Arbeiten zu seinem Problem. Dokumente, die sein Problem nur am Rande berühren, sind für ihn Ballast. Der Ballast soll nicht zu hoch sein.

D. Der Benutzer sucht (z.B. für eine Bibliographie) möglichst alle Dokumente, die zentral oder am Rande sein Problem berühren. Da er ohnehin für das Literaturstudium viel Zeit braucht, nimmt er auch einen verhältnismäßig hohen Ballastanteil in Kauf; Vollständigkeit ist wichtiger.

Eine Bewertung eines Dokumentationssystems oder einer Suchstrategie ist dann stets bezüglich einer dieser Rollen vorzunehmen.Das Ergebnis einer Untersuchung könnte dann z.B. die folgende Gestalt haben: "Von den 5 getesteten Suchstrategien eignet sich für einen Benutzer in der Rolle A die zweite am besten."

4. Benutzungshäufigkeit

Ein weiterer Gesichtspunkt könnte in die Rolle des Benutzers einbezogen werden, soll hier aber getrennt werden: Wie intensiv hat sich der Benutzer mit dem Dokumentationssystem beschäftigt, wieviel Übung hat er?

Die meisten bestehenden Systeme scheinen grundsätzlich davon auszugehen, daß sie fast nur von geübten Benutzern bedient werden, so kompliziert ist die Abfragesprache und so dürftig sind die Hilfen. Man muß aber mindestens drei Klassen von Benutzern unterscheiden:

a. Der gelegentliche Benutzer. Er verwendet nur wenige Retrieval-Funktionen und muß sich immer wieder über deren Syntax und Semantik informieren.

b. Der regelmäßige Benutzer. Er kennt Syntax und Semantik aller wichtigen Retrieval-Funktionen auswendig und weiß, welche sonstigen Funktionen existieren. Bei diesen braucht er Hilfe; auch wird er sie nicht immer optimal ausnützen.

c. Der professionelle Benutzer. Er kann mit allen System-Funktionen einwandfrei umgehen und kennt ggf. auch etliche "Tricks".

Ein Retrieval-System oder eine Suchstrategie kann durchaus für eine Benutzerklasse gut und für eine andere schlecht sein.

5. Unterziele der Benutzerbefriedigung

Mit der Einführung der Benutzerrollen ist aber immer noch kein Maß für die Güte eines Systems oder einer Suchstrategie gefunden.

Worauf kommt es an? Letztlich darauf, die rollenmäßigen Wünsche und Erwartungen des Benutzers zu befriedigen (wie bei Bibliotheken und anderen Dienstleistungsunternehmen auch).

"Zufriedenheit" ist aber schlecht faßbar; wir müssen konkrete Unterziele finden. Die folgenden kommen in Betracht.

Ein wichtiges Unterziel ist sicher die Güte der Ergebnisse. Hier kann man teilweise die eingeführten Maße übernehmen:

Bei Benutzerrolle D liegt das Hauptgewicht auf hoher Nachweisquote und ein niedriges Gewicht auf hoher Relevanzquote, bei Rolle C sind die Gewichte ausgeglichener. Jedoch sollten einschlägige Dokumente und solche, die am Rande interessant sind, unterschiedlich bewertet werden.

Ein geeignetes Maß scheint

$$H = \frac{\sum X_i \; Y_i}{\sqrt{\sum X_i} \; \sqrt{\sum Y_i}}$$

zu sein [Gebhardt 1975 b], wobei X_i die Bewertung des i-ten Dokuments durch den Benutzer (oder einen Schiedsrichter), Y_i die Bewertung durch das System ist und über alle Dokumente summiert wird (es ist kein Druckfehler, daß im Nenner keine Quadratsummen stehen!).
Wenn man, um die herkömmlichen Maße benutzen zu können, nur zwischen "relevant" und "nicht relevant" unterscheidet, muß man bei Rolle D mehr Dokumente als relevant einstufen als bei Rolle C.

Bei Rolle A ist dagegen abzuzählen, das wievielte im Verlaufe des Dialogs nachgewiesene Dokument das erste einschlägige ist. Relevanz- und Nachweisquote können in die Irre führen. Bei Rolle B schließlich müßte das abgewandelt werden in "wieviele Dokumente braucht man, um eine gewisse Anzahl (z.B. vier) einschlägige Dokumente zu finden?", oder, wenn man sich nicht auf eine bestimmte Anzahl festlegen will, in eine passende gewichtete Summe. Hierzu muß man jedoch erst genauer festlegen, welche Dokumente mitzuzählen sind, vgl. Abschnitt 2.

Ein weiteres Unterziel ist die Schnelligkeit. Da aber nicht die Schnelligkeit des Benutzers beurteilt werden soll, kommt als Meßgröße die Verweilzeit auf der Rechenanlage (summiert über den ganzen Dialog) in Betracht oder, um eine mögliche ungleichmäßige Belastung der Anlage auszuschalten, eine gewichtete Summe aus CPU-Zeit und Zahl der Sekundärspeicher -Zugriffe.

Zur Schnelligkeit gehören auch kurze Wege zur Datenstation, geringe Wartezeiten infolge Belegung durch andere Benutzer und kurze Einarbeitungszeiten sowohl für den Anfänger als auch für den Benutzer, der das System längere Zeit nicht mehr bedient hat. Diese Zeiten sind jedoch schlecht meßbar und von zu vielen anderen Faktoren abhängig, als daß man sie zur Bewertung des Systems heranziehen könnte.

Als nächstes Unterziel nennen wir die Kosten. Hierbei muß man unterscheiden zwischen dem Arbeitsaufwand des Benutzers (Produkt aus Arbeitszeit und Stundensatz) und den Kosten der Datenverarbeitungsanlage.

Die Arbeitszeit kann von Benutzer zu Benutzer sehr stark schwanken und unterschiedliche Anteile an Denkzeit enthalten, in der der Benutzer nicht sucht, sondern sein Problem (teilweise) löst. Diese Anteile sind kaum festzustellen. Bei der DV-Anlage kommen entweder die tatsächlich in Rechnung gestellten Kosten in Betracht, die jedoch aus abrechnungstechnischen oder marktpolitischen Gründen ein schiefes Bild liefern können, oder solche Maße wie aufgewandte CPU-Zeit, eventuell auch benötigter Hauptspeicherbereich. Andere Kosten, wie etwa die der Datenübertragung, sind zwar für den Benutzer durchaus von Bedeutung, tragen aber nicht zur Beurteilung der Qualität des Systems bei.

6. Hypothesen

Um zu einem eindimensionalen Gesamtmaß zu kommen, müßte man für jedes Unterziel ein Maß aufstellen und diese dann geeignet gewichten und summieren. Die Problematik solcher Gewichtungen ist bekannt.

Für die Bewertung von Retrieval-Systemen oder Suchstrategien reicht es aber aus, die verschiedenen Maße nebeneinander zu stellen. Natürlich kann man dann im allgemeinen nicht mehr sagen, diese oder jene Strategie sei schlechthin die beste; die Vergleiche müssen differenzierter ausfallen.

Die Ergebnisse könnten dann etwa die Form folgender Hypothesen haben.

1. Für einen Benutzer in der Rolle A oder B eignen sich Rangfolgesortierungen besser als Boolesche Verknüpfungen.
2. Metrische Operatoren, vor allem "im gleichen Satz", verbessern insbesondere in den Rollen C und D (evtl. auch in B) die Suchergebnisse beträchtlich (gemessen in den jeweils zuständigen Gütemaßen, Abschnitt 5).
3. Für gelegentliche Benutzer (Klasse a) müssen einfache Standard-Suchstrategien entwickelt werden; ein aussichtsreicher Kandidat ist eine passende Rangfolgesortierung.
4. Ein professioneller Benutzer (Klasse c) und in geringerem Maße ein regelmäßiger Benutzer (Klasse b) erreicht sein Ziel (Rollen A bis D) mit einem leistungsfähigen System vor allem schneller als mit einem einfachen System; dagegen ist die Verbesserung in der Güte der Ergebnisse im allgemeinen wenig ausgeprägt.

Aus Arbeiten des Instituts für DV im Rechtswesen der GMD liegen inzwischen einige noch nicht veröffentlichte Ergebnisse vor, die die Hypothesen 1 bis 3 stützen, vgl. [Fiedler 1975 a].

Literaturverzeichnis

[Cleverdon 1974]
Cleverdon, C. W. User evaluation of information retrieval systems. J. Docum. 30 (1974) 170 - 180.

[Cooper 1973 a]
Cooper, William S. On selecting a measure of retrieval effectiveness. J. Amer. Soc. for Inform. Sc. 24 (1973) 87 - 100.

[Cooper 1973 b]
Cooper, William S. On selceting a measure of retrieval effectiveness, Part II. Implementation of the philosophy. J. Amer. Soc. for Inform. Sc. 24 (1973) 413 - 424.

[Cuadra 1967]
Cuadra, Carlos A.; Katter, Robert V.; Holmes, Emory H.; Wallace, Everett M. Experimental Studies of Relevance Judgments. Final Report. Vol. I - III. TM-3520, System Development Corporation, Santa Monica, Calif., 30.6.1967.

[Farradane 1974]
Farradane, J. The evaluation of information retrieval systems. J. of Documentation 30 (1974) 195 - 209.

[Fiedler 1975]
Fiedler, H.; Gebhardt, F.; Müller, B. S.; Poetsch, J.; Reiner, G.; Stellmacher, I. Methodische Erfordernisse juristischer Informationssysteme. Bemerkungen zur Entwicklung von JURIS. In: [Gebhardt 1975 a], S. 7 - 98.

[Fraenkel 1968]
Fraenkel, Aviezri S. Legal information retrieval. In: Alt, Franz L.; Rubinoff, Morris. Advances in Computers. Vol.9, 1968, 113 - 178.

[Gebhardt 1973]
Gebhardt, Friedrich. Ein wahrscheinlichkeitstheoretisches Modell für den Relevanzgrad von Dokumenten. ACM, German Chapter Lectures I/II-1973, S. 1 - 9.

[Gebhardt 1975 a]
Gebhardt, Friedrich (Hrsg.). Beiträge zur Methodik juristischer Informationssysteme. Beiheft Nr. 5 zur DVR, Schweitzer-Verlag, Berlin 1975, 208 S.

[Gebhardt 1975 b]
Gebhardt, Friedrich. A simple probabilistic model for the relevance assessment of documents. Information Storage and Retrieval (1975) (in Druck).

[Harter 1971]
Harter, Stephen P. The Cranfield II relevance assessments: a critical evaluation. Library Quarterly 41 (1971) 229 - 243.

[Heine 1974]
Heine, M. H. Design equations for retrieval systems based on Swets model. J. Amer. Soc. for Inform. Sc. 25 (1974) 183 - 198.

[Saracevic 1971]
Saracevic, Tefko. Selected results from an inquiry into testing of information retrieval system. J. Amer. Soc. Inform. Sc. 22 (1971) 126 - 139.

[Swanson 1971]
Swanson, Don R. Some unexplained aspects of the Cranfield tests of indexing performance factors.
Library Quarterly 41 (1971) 223 - 228.

Ein Programmsystem zur Erfassung von Daten aus komplex strukturierten Tabellen

K.-H.Dreckmann, G.Hofmann

Zusammenfassung

Es wird ein Programmsystem in Aufbau und Arbeitsweise beschrieben, das entwickelt wurde, um komplex strukturierte Daten im Dialog zu erfassen. Ausgehend von einer speziellen Aufgabe wird gezeigt, wie sich die gefundene Lösung allgemein zur Erfassung von Daten aus Tabellen anwenden läßt.

1. Einleitung

Seit 1969 baut das Betriebsforschungsinstitut (BFI) des Vereins Deutscher Eisenhüttenleute (VDEh) ein Werkstoff-Informationssystem für Eisen- und Stahlwerkstoffe (WIS) auf, das aus den beiden Teilen IST und SOLL besteht. Das Teilsystem IST umfaßt und bearbeitet solche Daten, die gemessene Eigenschaftswerte von Werkstoffen wiedergeben, wie sie z.B. in den Qualitätsstellen der Hüttenwerke im Laufe der Produktion ermittelt werden (Ist-Eigenschaften). Das Teilsystem SOLL ist dagegen auf solche Daten ausgerichtet, die genormte Eigenschaftswerte von Werkstoffen wiedergeben, wie sie z.B. in den DIN-Normen festgelegt sind (Soll-Eigenschaften).

Während das System IST bereits seit längerer Zeit in Betrieb ist, befindet sich das System SOLL in Entwicklung. Wesentliche Teilaufgaben sind die Entwicklung
- eines Datenbanksystems und
- eines Datenerfassungssystems.

Das Datenbanksystem bildet den Kern des Systems SOLL; es befindet sich in der Implementierungsphase. In /1/ wurde über den Entwurf berichtet.

Zur Datenerfassung steht das Programmsystem DACAPO zur Verfügung; die Entwicklung ist abgeschlossen und das System befindet sich seit einiger Zeit in Betrieb.

2. Aufgabenstellung

Die Soll-Eigenschaften von Werkstoffen werden u.a. in DIN-Normen, DIN-Normentwürfen, Stahl-Eisen-Werkstoffblättern des VDEh, ausländischen und internationalen Normen beschrieben; sie werden unter dem einheitlichen Begriff Norm zusammengefaßt. Eine derartige Norm besteht aus
- Texten,
- Tabellen und
- graphischen Darstellungen.

Die Tabellen enthalten dabei die wesentlichen Daten zur Beschreibung der Soll-Eigenschaften der Werkstoffe, während die Texte und graphischen Darstellungen ergänzende Informationen enthalten. Außerdem handelt es sich bei den Tabellen um formatierte Daten im Gegensatz zu Texten und graphischen Darstellungen. Das Datenbanksystem innerhalb des Teilsystems SOLL beschränkt sich daher auf die Speicherung und Verwaltung der Tabellen aus den Normen. In Bild 1 ist als Beispiel für eine Normen-Tabelle Tabelle 6 aus DIN 17 210 dargestellt /2/.

Grundsätzlich muß davon ausgegangen werden, daß jede Tabelle ihr eigenes Format hat, das von dem anderer Tabellen verschieden ist. Übereinstimmung ist jedoch darin gegeben, daß jede Tabelle aus
- einem Kopf,
- einem Rumpf und
- einem Fuß

besteht (Bild 1).

Der Tabellenkopf identifiziert die Tabelle und beschreibt ihr Format. Er gibt die Variablen an (z.B. Streckgrenze) und beschreibt ihre Abhängigkeit von Parametern (z.B. ist die Streckgrenze vom Durchmesser der Probe abhängig). Variable können zu Gruppen zusammengefaßt sein (z.B. mechanische Eigenschaften an blindgehärteten Querschnitten), die auch periodisch auftreten können.

Der Tabellenrumpf enthält die Werte der Variablen. Es kann sich dabei handeln um:
- genau einen Wert,
- mehrere Werte,
- einen Grenzwert (Wert mit Vergleichsoperator),
- einen Wertebereich (Wert 1 - Wert 2),
- einen Irrelevanzanzeiger (-, leer).

Tabelle 6. Gewährleistete mechanische Eigenschaften

Stahlsorte		Härte im Behandlungszustand			Mechanische Eigenschaften an blindgehärteten Querschnitten [8]) von											
					11 mm Durchmesser				30 mm Durchmesser				63 mm Durchmesser			
Kurzname	Werkstoff-nummer	G [1]) [2]) (weichgeglüht) [3])	BF [1]) [2]) (wärmebehandelt auf bestimmte Zugfestigkeit) [4]) [5])	BG [1]) [2]) (wärmebehandelt auf Ferrit-Perlit-Gefüge) [6]) [7])	Streckgrenze	Zugfestigkeit	Bruchdehnung ($L_0 = 5\,d_0$)	Brucheinschnürung	Streckgrenze	Zugfestigkeit	Bruchdehnung ($L_0 = 5\,d_0$)	Brucheinschnürung	Streckgrenze	Zugfestigkeit	Bruchdehnung ($L_0 = 5\,d_0$)	Brucheinschnürung
		HB 30 höchstens	HB 30	HB 30	kg/mm² mindestens	kg/mm²	% mindestens	% mindestens	kg/mm² mindestens	kg/mm²	% mindestens	% mindestens	kg/mm² mindestens	kg/mm²	% mindestens	% mindestens
C 10	1.0301	131	—	90 bis 126	40	65 bis 80	13	35	30	50 bis 65	16	45	—	—	—	—
Ck 10	1.1121	131	—	90 bis 126	40	65 bis 80	13	40	30	50 bis 65	16	50	—	—	—	—
C 15	1.0401	146	—	103 bis 140	45	75 bis 90	12	30	36	60 bis 80	14	40	—	—	—	—
Ck 15	1.1141	146	—	103 bis 140	45	75 bis 90	12	35	36	60 bis 80	14	45	—	—	—	—
Cm 15	1.1140	146	—	103 bis 140	45	75 bis 90	12	35	36	60 bis 80	14	45	—	—	—	—
15 Cr 3	1.7015	174	126 bis 174 [7]) [9])	118 bis 160	52	80 bis 105	10	35	45	70 bis 90	11	40	—	—	—	—
16 MnCr 5	1.7131	207	156 bis 207 [9])	140 bis 187	65	90 bis 120	9	35	60	80 bis 110	10	40	45	65 bis 95	11	40
16 MnCrS 5	1.7139	207	156 bis 207 [9])	140 bis 187	65	90 bis 120	9	35	60	80 bis 110	10	40	45	65 bis 95	11	40
20 MnCr 5	1.7147	217	170 bis 217 [9])	152 bis 201	75	110 bis 140	7	30	70	100 bis 130	8	35	55	80 bis 110	10	35
20 MnCrS 5	1.7149	217	170 bis 217 [9])	152 bis 201	75	110 bis 140	7	30	70	100 bis 130	8	35	55	80 bis 110	10	35
20 MoCr 4	1.7321	207	156 bis 207 [9])	140 bis 187	65	90 bis 120	9	35	60	80 bis 110	10	40	—	—	—	—
20 MoCrS 4	1.7323	207	156 bis 207 [9])	140 bis 187	65	90 bis 120	9	35	60	80 bis 110	10	40	—	—	—	—
25 MoCr 4	1.7325	217	170 bis 217 [9])	152 bis 201	75	110 bis 140	7	30	70	100 bis 130	8	35	—	—	—	—
25 MoCrS 4	1.7326	217	170 bis 217 [9])	152 bis 201	75	110 bis 140	7	30	70	100 bis 130	8	35	—	—	—	—
15 CrNi 6	1.5919	217	170 bis 217 [9])	152 bis 201	70	98 bis 130	8	35	65	90 bis 120	9	40	55	80 bis 110	10	40
18 CrNi 8	1.5920	235	187 bis 235 [9])	170 bis 217	85	125 bis 150	7	30	80	120 bis 145	7	35	70	110 bis 135	8	35
17 CrNiMo 6	1.6587	229	179 bis 229 [9])	159 bis 207	85	120 bis 145	7	30	80	110 bis 135	8	35	70	100 bis 130	8	35

[1]) Siehe Abschnitt 6.1

[2]) Die für diesen Zustand angegebenen Härtewerte gelten nicht für Stahl, der nach der Wärmebehandlung kalt verformt wurde.

[3]) Siehe Abschnitt 9.2

[4]) Siehe Abschnitt 9.3

[5]) Für Durchmesser bis ≈ 150 mm (Ausnahme bei Stahl 15 Cr 3)

[6]) Siehe Abschnitt 9.4

[7]) Für Durchmesser bis ≈ 60 mm

[8]) Beachte Abschnitte 7.5.1 und 8.3.3

[9]) Wenn im Hinblick auf die Zerspanbarkeit eine höhere Festigkeit verlangt wird, kann der Stahl nach Vereinbarung vergütet geliefert werden.

Bild 1. Beispiel für eine Normen-Tabelle

Der Tabellenfuß wird durch Fußnoten gebildet, auf die im Tabellenkopf bzw. -rumpf durch Indizes verwiesen wird (z.B. sind die Fußnoten 1) und 2) u.a. der Variablen G im Tabellenkopf zugeordnet).

Im Rahmen dieser grundsätzlichen Übereinstimmung sind die einzelnen Tabellen sehr unterschiedlich aufgebaut und haben z.T. komplizierte Strukturen und schwierig zu behandelnde Eigenarten. Zur Erfassung der Normen-Tabellen ist daher ein sehr flexibles und anpassungsfähiges Programmsystem erforderlich, wenn die Aufgabe angemessen gelöst werden soll.

3. Lösungsweg

Um zu einer angemessenen Lösung der Aufgabe zu gelangen, wurde vom gegebenen Problem der Erfassung von Normen-Tabellen so weit abstrahiert, daß das Programmsystem allgemein auf Daten angewendet werden kann, die sich folgendermaßen charakterisieren lassen:

- es handelt sich um formatierte Daten und
- die Daten sind in Tabellenform vorhanden oder lassen sich tabellarisch darstellen.

Die Erfassung von in Tabellenform strukturierten Daten, wobei die Strukturen sehr vielfältig und komplex sein können, zerfällt in eine Reihe von Teilaufgaben:

- Die Struktur der Daten muß erfaßt werden.
- Die Daten selbst müssen erfaßt werden.
- Alle erfaßten Daten müssen auf formale und, soweit möglich, auf inhaltliche Fehler geprüft werden.
- Erkannte Fehler müssen korrigiert werden.
- Die Daten müssen in geeigneter Weise gespeichert werden.

Das Programmsystem muß alle Teilaufgaben lösen. Es soll darüber hinaus adaptierbar und portabel sein, damit es zur Bearbeitung verschiedener Probleme auf unterschiedlichen Datenverarbeitungsanlagen eingesetzt werden kann.

Zur Lösung der Aufgabe wurde ein zweistufiges Verfahren entwickelt. Geht man davon aus, daß Tabellen beliebiger Struktur erfaßt werden sollen, so läßt sich die Struktur einer Tabelle (Objekttabelle) wiederum mithilfe einer Tabelle (Strukturtabelle) beschreiben. Eine derartige Beschreibung kann nicht automatisch vorgenommen werden: sie muß unter

Einsatz menschlicher Intelligenz erstellt werden und liefert als Ergebnis ein Formular, in das die Struktureigenschaften der (Objekt-)Tabelle eingetragen sind. Liegt dieses Formular, d.h. diese Strukturtabelle, erst einmal vor, so wird
- in einer ersten Stufe die Strukturtabelle und
- in einer zweiten Stufe die zugehörige Objekttabelle

erfaßt.

Die Erfassung der Tabellen erfolgt auf beiden Stufen nach denselben Prinzipien, so daß zu ihrer Durchführung dasselbe Programmsystem eingesetzt werden kann. Die beiden Stufen der Erfassung müssen für eine individuelle Tabelle nacheinander ablaufen, können jedoch für mehrere verschiedene Tabellen zeitlich überlappt bzw. parallel verlaufen, d.h. es können zunächst für mehrere Objekttabellen die zugehörigen Strukturtabellen im Zusammenhang erfaßt werden (Stufe 1) bevor danach die Objekttabellen selbst gemeinsam erfaßt werden (Stufe 2).

Grundsätzlich ist dieses zweistufige Verfahren als einfache Version eines n-stufigen Verfahrens zu betrachten: Die Struktur der Strukturtabellen läßt sich nämlich wiederum durch Tabellen (Strukturtabellen 2.Stufe) darstellen usf. Auf irgendeiner Stufe muß dieses Vorgehen jedoch abgebrochen werden, und es erscheint zweckmäßig, dies bereits auf der zweiten Stufe zu tun. Das bedeutet, daß die Struktur der Strukturtabellen für eine abgeschlossene Aufgabe fest vorgegeben ist; sie kann dem Programmsystem entweder eingeprägt sein oder jeweils für eine Aufgabe durch einen Initialisierungsvorgang eingegeben werden. Um das Programmsystem flexibel zu gestalten, wurde der zweite Weg eingeschlagen.

Damit läßt sich das Prinzip der Datenerfassung folgendermaßen beschreiben (Bild 2):
- Zur Initialisierung wird einem Generator eine auf die jeweilige Aufgabe zugeschnittene Syntax eingegeben. Diese Syntax beschreibt die Eingabe- und Ausgabedaten des Generators. Im Falle der Initialisierung bestehen die Eingabedaten aus Angaben über die Struktur der Strukturtabellen. Der Generator erzeugt aus den Eingabedaten mithilfe der Syntax Dialog-Ablauf-Regeln zur Erfassung der Strukturtabellen.
- Die Erfassung der Strukturtabellen erfolgt durch ein Dialog-Programm, das auf die Dialog-Ablauf-Regeln für die Erfassung der Strukturtabellendaten zugreift. Die Strukturtabellendaten werden in geeigneter Weise gespeichert.

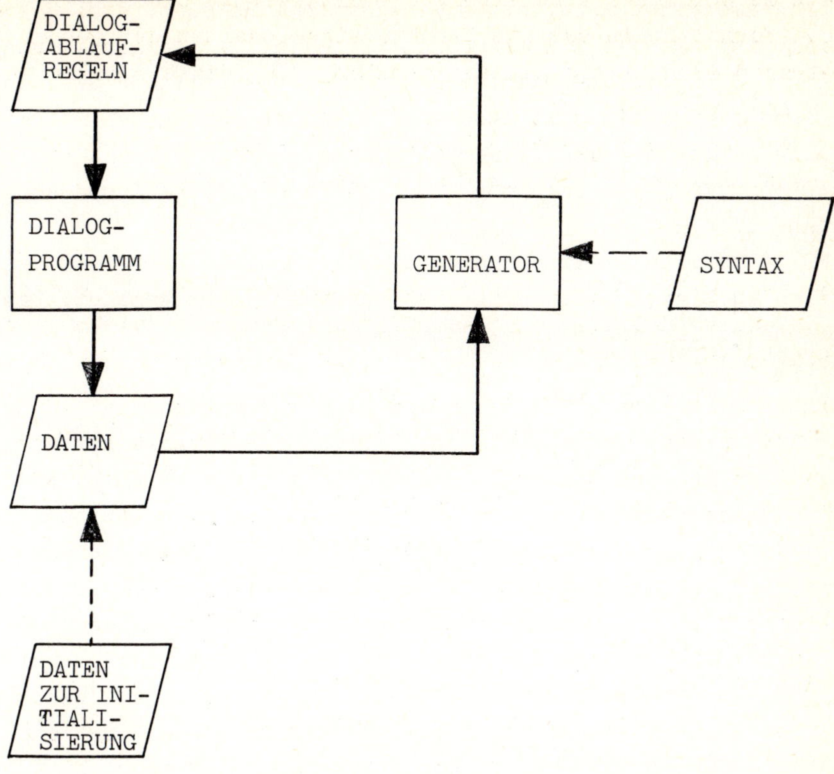

Bild 2. Prinzip der Datenerfassung

- Die gespeicherten Strukturtabellendaten dienen als Eingabe für den Generator, der daraus mithilfe der Syntax Dialog-Ablauf-Regeln zur Erfassung der Objekttabellen erzeugt.
- Die Erfassung der Objekttabellen erfolgt durch das Dialog-Programm, das auf die Dialog-Ablauf-Regeln für die Erfassung der Objekttabellendaten zugreift. Die Objekttabellendaten werden in geeigneter Weise gespeichert.

Das gesamte Programmsystem mit seinen Hauptbestandteilen Generator- und Dialog-Programm wird also zweimal zyklisch durchlaufen (Bild 2), bevor eine Tabelle vollständig erfaßt ist. Neben den Generator- und Dialog-Programmen enthält das Programmsystem weitere Programme, z.B. zur Einrichtung von Dateien und zur Datensicherung, die jedoch nicht zyklisch, sondern nur bei Bedarf eingesetzt werden.

Das Programmsystem arbeitet im Ein-Terminal-Betrieb, d.h. das Dialog-Programm ist auf den Einsatz eines (Bildschirm-) Terminals ausgelegt. Maßgebend für diese Entscheidung waren im wesentlichen zwei Gründe:

- Das Programmsystem soll schon auf einfachen Maschinen mit minimaler Konfiguration eingesetzt werden können.
- Das Programmsystem soll möglichst einfach aufgebaut und kompakt im Umfang sein.

Ein Multi-Terminal-Betrieb hätte demgegenüber das Programmsystem wesentlich komplexer, aufwendiger und umfangreicher gemacht. Das gilt insbesondere für das Dialog-Programm.

Ein Einsatz mehrerer Terminals wird dadurch möglich, daß für jedes Terminal eine eigene und unabhängige Version des Programmsystems, d.h. also im wesentlichen des Dialog-Programms, in einem eigenen Hauptspeicher-Bereich eingesetzt wird. Das setzt voraus, daß der Hauptspeicher der jeweiligen Maschine genügend groß ist, bzw. ein Swap-Mechanismus vorhanden ist, der nicht benötigte Hauptspeicher-Bereiche auf periphere Speicher auslagert, wenn der Hauptspeicher nicht genügend groß ist. Das Programmsystem wird also nicht mit einer eigenen Terminal-Verwaltung und -Koordination belastet; diese Aufgabe wird auf das Betriebssystem der jeweiligen Maschine verlagert, das diese Funktionen in aller Regel mit vorhandenen Prozeduren ausführen kann.

Der Name des Programmsystems ist ein Akronym: DACAPO - Data Acquisition from a Complexly Arranged Pool of Data. Er beschreibt aber auch die Arbeitsweise des Systems:

- Für eine einzelne Tabelle wird das System einmal benutzt, um die Strukturtabellendaten zu erfassen, und in gleicher Weise ein zweites Mal, um die zugehörigen Objekttabellendaten zu erfassen.
- Bei einer größeren Anzahl von Tabellen wird das System für jede einzelne Tabelle immer wieder gleichartig eingesetzt bis zum Ende der Erfassung.

4. Systembeschreibung

4.1 Datenbasis

DACAPO kennt drei Gruppen von Dateien:

- Dateien mit direkter Speicherung (Plattendateien),
- Dateien mit sequentieller Speicherung (Banddateien) und
- Hauptspeicherdateien.

Dabei können die Dateien mit sequentieller Speicherung durchaus auch auf einem Plattenspeicher liegen; es muß sich nicht notwendigerweise um Banddateien handeln (im folgenden ist der Einfachheit halber die Rede von Platten-, Band- bzw. Hauptspeicherdateien).

Es werden drei verschiedene Plattendateien benötigt:
- Eine Datei enthält die vom Generator erzeugten Dialog-Ablauf-Regeln (Dialogdatei).
- Eine weitere Datei enthält die erfaßten Daten, und zwar sowohl Struktur- als auch Objektdaten (Erfassungsdatei). Beide werden im selben Format gespeichert und zur Unterscheidung verschieden gekennzeichnet.
- Eine dritte Datei enthält Daten zur Verwaltung der beiden übrigen Dateien und zur Steuerung des gesamten Erfassungsvorgangs (Verwaltungsdatei).

Weiter gibt es zwei Banddateien mit folgenden Aufgaben:
- Die eine Datei dient zur Sicherung der Daten in den drei Plattendateien (Sicherungsdatei).
- Die andere Datei dient zur Speicherung des Endergebnisses des Erfassungsvorgangs (Ergebnisdatei). Dieses Ergebnis wird aus den Daten der Sicherungsdatei abgeleitet.

Im Hauptspeicher liegen schließlich fünf Dateien (bzw. Datenbereiche):
- Textdatei,
- Formatdatei,
- Bildschirm-Eingabebereich,
- Bildschirm-Ausgabebereich und
- Ausgabepuffer.

Text- und Formatdatei stehen in engem Zusammenhang mit den Dialog-Ablauf-Regeln in der Dialogdatei: diese Dialog-Ablauf-Regeln bestehen u.a. aus:
- Texten, die vom Programmsystem auf den Bildschirm ausgegeben werden und aus
- Formaten, die festlegen, welchen formalen Anforderungen die am Bildschirm einzugebenden Daten genügen müssen.

Zur Abwicklung des Dialogs für eine Gruppe von Tabellen (Struktur- oder Objekttabellen) werden die jeweils relevanten Texte und Formate aus der Dialogdatei in die Text- bzw. Formatdatei geladen.

Die Bildschirm-Eingabe- bzw. -Ausgabebereiche dienen zur Aufnahme von Daten nach der Eingabe am Bildschirm bzw. vor der Ausgabe auf den Bildschirm. Der Ausgabepuffer schließlich wird benötigt, um die erfaßten Daten an die Erfassungsdatei abzuliefern.

4.2 Programme

DACAPO besteht aus fünf Komponenten (Bild 3):

- Das Programm EINRICHTUNG wird zu Beginn eines Datenerfassungsvorgangs oder bei Wiederbeginn nach einem Systemzusammenbruch eingesetzt. Es dient zum Bereitstellen und Initialisieren (zu Beginn) bzw. Rücksichern (bei Wiederbeginn) der Dateien des Programmsystems.
- Der GENERATOR erzeugt aus Eingabedaten, die die Struktur einer Tabelle beschreiben, mithilfe einer vorgegebenen Syntax Dialog-Ablauf-Regeln zur Erfassung des Inhalts der Tabelle. Die Dialog-Ablauf-Regeln umfassen Texte, die auf den Bildschirm ausgegeben werden und die Datenerfassungskraft zur Eingabe von bestimmten Daten veranlassen, Formate, die festlegen, wie diese Eingabedaten auszusehen haben und Angaben über die sachliche und zeitliche Reihefolge von Texten und Formaten.
- Mit dem DIALOG-PROGRAMM wird die eigentliche Erfassung der Daten (Struktur- und Objekttabellendaten) im Dialog durchgeführt. Es stellt den Kern des Programmsystems dar.

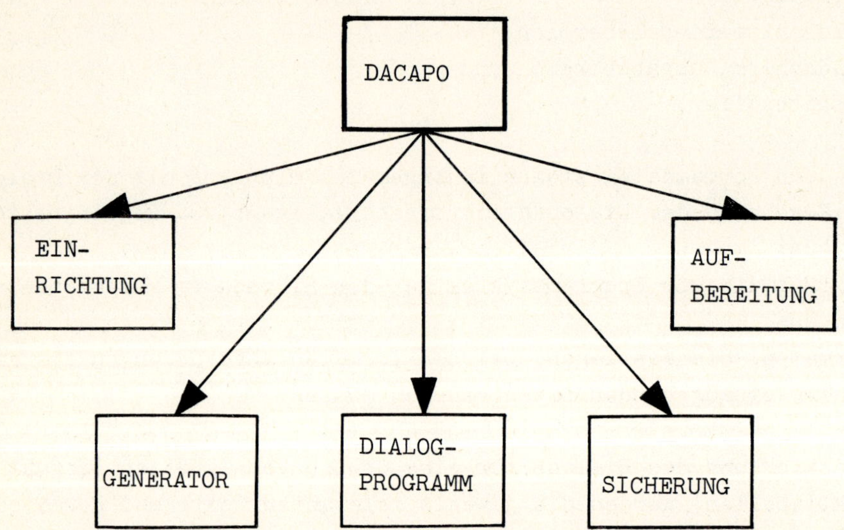

Bild 3. Komponenten des Programmsystems

- Das Programm SICHERUNG dient zur Sicherung der auf Magnetplatte liegenden Dialog-, Erfassungs- und Verwaltungsdateien auf Magnetband.
- Mit dem Programm AUFBEREITUNG wird das auf den Sicherungsbändern gespeicherte Ergebnis eines Datenerfassungsvorgangs so aufbereitet, wie es eine bestimmte Datenverarbeitungsaufgabe erfordert. Dieses Programm muß daher u.U. für jede neue Datenverarbeitungsaufgabe neu erstellt werden.

Die Programme sind modular aufgebaut; sie bestehen jeweils aus einem Steuermodul und mindestens einem weiteren Modul. Der Steuermodul hat dabei die Funktion eines Hauptprogramms, das die übrigen Module als Unterprogramme aufruft. Dieses Prinzip soll am Beispiel des DIALOG-PROGRAMMs näher erläutert werden, während auf die übrigen Programme nicht weiter eingegangen wird.

Das DIALOG-PROGRAMM besteht aus folgenden Modulen (Bild 4):
- Die DIALOG-STEUERUNG steuert den Gesamtablauf des DIALOG-PROGRAMMs. Der Modul wird von der Systemkonsole aus aufgerufen und gestartet. Zur Führung des Dialogs wird zunächst ein Terminal angefordert. Dann wird für die zu erfassenden Tabellen die Art der Erfassung (Struktur- oder Objekttabellendatenerfassung) festgelegt. Zur Durchführung der Erfassung werden die Module LADEN DIALOGE und STEUERN DIALOG-ABLAUF gestartet, in ihrer Arbeitsweise überwacht und gegebenenfalls beendet.
- Durch LADEN DIALOGE werden die für die jeweilige Erfassung relevanten Texte und Formate aus der Dialogdatei (Magnetplatte) in die Text- bzw. Formatdatei des Hauptspeichers geladen.
- STEUERN DIALOG-ABLAUF steuert den eigentlichen Erfassungsdialog. Es werden Module zur Ausgabe von Daten auf den Bildschirm (BEARBEITEN BILDSCHIRM-AUSGABE), zur Bearbeitung von Daten, die am Bildschirm eingegeben wurden (BEARBEITEN BILDSCHIRM-EINGABE) und zum Verkehr mit der Erfassungsdatei (BEARBEITEN AUSGABEPUFFER) gestartet, in ihrer Arbeit überwacht und zu gegebener Zeit beendet.
- Durch BEARBEITEN BILDSCHIRM-AUSGABE wird die dem jeweiligen Stand des Dialogs entsprechende Textzeile aus der Textdatei ausgewählt und in den Bildschirm-Ausgabebereich gebracht. Anschließend wird die Zeile auf dem Bildschirm dargestellt.
- Durch BEARBEITEN BILDSCHIRM-EINGABE wird die dem jeweiligen Stand des Dialogs entsprechende Formatangabe in der Formatdatei ausgewählt. Die am Bildschirm eingegebenen Daten werden in den Bildschirm-Eingabebereich gebracht und mithilfe der ausgewählten Formatangabe auf Gültigkeit geprüft. Sind die Daten gültig, so wird nach bestimmten Regeln

ein Satz aufgebaut und in den Ausgabepuffer übertragen. Sind sie nicht gültig, so wird eine Fehlermeldung erzeugt.

- Durch BEARBEITEN AUSGABEPUFFER wird der Verkehr zwischen dem Ausgabepuffer und der Erfassungsdatei durchgeführt. Arbeitet das DIALOG-PROGRAMM im Erfassungsmodus (Erfassung von Struktur- oder Objektdaten), so wird der im Ausgabepuffer stehende Satz in die Erfassungsdatei geschrieben. Wenn das DIALOG-PROGRAMM jedoch im Prüfmodus (Prüfung bereits erfaßter Daten) arbeitet, wird der früher bereits einmal erfaßte Satz aus der Erfassungsdatei gelesen und in einen zweiten Ausgabepuffer gebracht und danach der Modul VERGLEICHEN ALT/NEU aufgerufen.
- Der Modul VERGLEICHEN ALT/NEU wird zur Prüfung erfaßter Daten eingesetzt. Arbeitet das DIALOG-PROGRAMM im Prüfmodus, so werden die bereits früher im Erfassungsmodus erfaßten und in der Erfassungsdatei gespeicherten Daten ein zweites Mal erfaßt. Die im (ersten) Ausgabepuffer stehenden neuen Sätze werden jedoch nicht in die Erfassungsdatei geschrieben, sondern mit den im zweiten Ausgabepuffer stehenden alten Sätzen verglichen. Ist der Inhalt beider Puffer gleich, erfolgt keine Aktion, ist er jedoch ungleich, wird eine Fehlermeldung erzeugt, und es ist eine neue Eingabe der Daten erforderlich.

Das DIALOG-PROGRAMM arbeitet im Realzeit-Betrieb, während alle anderen Programme im Stapelbetrieb laufen. Wenn das DIALOG-PROGRAMM läuft, kann im Rahmen des selben Erfassungsvorgangs kein anderes Programm laufen, insbesondere nicht der GENERATOR. Das DIALOG-PROGRAMM hat damit absoluten Vorrang vor allen anderen Programmen.

4.3 Arbeitsweise

DACAPO wird eingesetzt, um in einem in sich geschlossenen Erfassungszyklus eine Menge von (Objekt-) Tabellen zu erfassen, die in einem vorgegebenen formalen und inhaltlichen Zusammenhang stehen. Der formale Zusammenhang besteht darin, daß sämtliche zu den betrachteten Objekttabellen gehörenden Strukturtabellen ein- und dieselbe Struktur haben. Es ist also in einem Erfassungszyklus nur ein Initialisierungsvorgang erforderlich. Der inhaltliche Zusammenhang der Objekttabellen ist durch ihre Zugehörigkeit zum selben Sachgebiet gegeben.

Die Menge der Objekttabellen kann in Gruppen eingeteilt werden, die prinzipiell beliebig und auch verschieden groß sein können. Eine Obergrenze für die Größe einer Gruppe ist nur durch den bei einer gegebenen

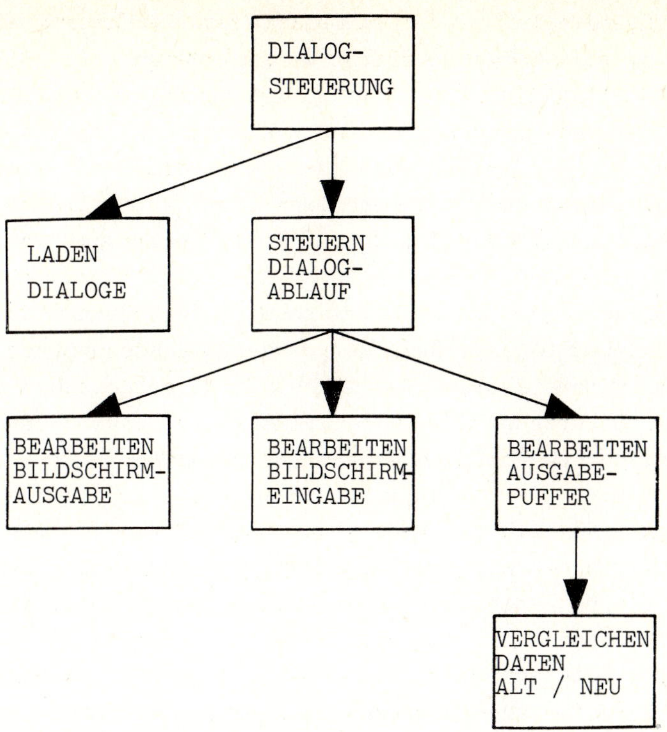

Bild 4. Aufbau des DIALOG-PROGRAMMs

Datenverarbeitungsanlage verfügbaren Speicherplatz auf Magnetplatten für die Dialog-, Erfassungs- und Verwaltungsdateien gegeben.

Jeweils für eine Gruppe von Objekttabellen wird durch eine mit dem betreffenden Sachgebiet vertraute Fachkraft eine Gruppe von zugehörigen Strukturtabellen erzeugt. Dabei kann durchaus der Fall auftreten, daß mehrere Objekttabellen dieselbe Struktur haben: in diesem Fall gibt es für mehrere Objekttabellen auch nur eine Strukturtabelle.

Für die Erzeugung der Strukturtabellen muß deren eigene Struktur bekannt sein. Es kann daher parallel bereits der Initialisierungsvorgang durchgeführt werden: durch das Programm EINRICHTUNG werden die notwendigen Plattendateien eingerichtet und durch einen ersten Lauf des GENERATORs werden aus Angaben über die Struktur der Strukturtabellen Dialog-Ablauf-Regeln zur Erfassung der in den Strukturtabellen enthaltenen Daten erzeugt.

In der Regel wird eine Gruppe von Objekt- bzw. Strukturtabellen nicht in einer Sitzung am Terminal erfaßt werden können (eine Sitzung umfaßt max. einen Arbeitstag), sondern es werden mehrere Sitzungen erforderlich sein. In einer Sitzung können Struktur- oder Objekttabellendaten erfaßt werden; die Erfassung von Objekttabellendaten ist allerdings erst dann möglich, wenn die zugehörigen Strukturtabellendaten bereits erfaßt worden sind und der GENERATOR darauf angewendet worden ist.

Der GENERATOR kann jeweils nach Erfassung (und Prüfung) der Strukturtabellen auf deren Daten angewendet werden, nachdem vorher eine SICHERUNG der Daten, die auf der Magnetplatte gespeichert sind, stattgefunden hat. Er erzeugt für alle Strukturtabellen Dialog-Ablauf-Regeln zur Erfassung der zugehörigen Objekttabellendaten.

Grundsätzlich wird nach dem Ende jeder Sitzung der gesamte Inhalt der Dialog-, Erfassungs- und Verwaltungsdateien durch das Programm SICHERUNG auf Magnetband gesichert. Dabei werden abwechselnd zwei verschiedene Bänder verwendet, so daß sich der Inhalt der beiden Sicherungsbänder dadurch unterscheidet, daß eines der Bänder die Daten der letzten Sitzung enthält, das andere jedoch nicht. Nach dem Ende der letzten Sitzung zur Erfassung der Daten einer bestimmten Gruppe, wenn also alle Objekttabellen der Gruppe (und natürlich auch die zugehörige Gruppe der Strukturtabellen) erfaßt sind, wird der Sicherungslauf zweimal durchgeführt, so daß man zwei Sicherungsbänder mit identischen Inhalten erhält.

Nachdem alle Daten einer Gruppe von Tabellen (im Erfassungsmodus) erfaßt worden sind, können sie (im Prüfmodus) geprüft werden: Sie werden zu diesem Zweck ein zweites Mal erfaßt, jedoch nicht auf die Plattendateien geschrieben, sondern nur mit dem Inhalt der Plattendateien verglichen. Ergibt sich dabei, daß bei der ersten Erfassung ein Fehler gemacht worden ist, so hat das folgende Konsequenzen:

- Ist eine Objekttabelle fehlerhaft, so wird versucht, sie zu korrigieren. Ist das nicht möglich, muß die Objekttabelle neu erfaßt werden.
- Ist eine Strukturtabelle fehlerhaft, so müssen die Strukturtabelle und alle zugehörigen Objekttabellen neu erfaßt werden.

Wird ein Fehler korrigiert, so müssen die beiden betroffenen Sicherungsbänder ebenfalls korrigiert werden.

Die beiden Sicherungsbänder stellen das Ergebnis der Erfassung für die betrachtete Gruppe von Tabellen dar. Die Inhalte der Dateien auf Magnetplatte können nun gelöscht werden, und es kann mit der Erfassung der nächsten Gruppe begonnen werden.

Wenn alle Gruppen von Tabellen eines Erfassungszyklus in dieser Weise bearbeitet worden sind, liegt das Ergebnis der Erfassung bei n Gruppen auf 2*n Sicherungsbändern vor, von denen jeweils ein Paar identische Daten enthält. Jeweils ein Band eines solchen Paares wird dem Programm AUFBEREITUNG zugeführt, um aus seinem Inhalt die für eine bestimmte Datenverarbeitungsaufgabe erforderlichen Daten zu erzeugen (das andere Band des Paares dient weiterhin Sicherungszwecken).

Auf diese Weise erfolgt die Erfassung der Daten unabhängig von einer bestimmten Datenverarbeitungsaufgabe. Das Ergebnis der Erfassung wird in Form von Struktur- und Objekttabellendaten gespeichert, so daß die für eine beliebige Datenverarbeitungsaufgabe erforderlichen Daten und Datenstrukturen daraus jederzeit durch ein entsprechendes AUFBEREITUNGsprogramm erzeugt werden können.

5. Anwendung

Aufgrund der gegebenen Aufgabe wird das System DACAPO angewendet, um Daten aus Normen zu erfassen, die die Soll-Eigenschaften von Eisen- und Stahlwerkstoffen beschreiben. Da diese Daten vom Datenbanksystem des Systems SOLL gespeichert und verwaltet werden, gibt es ein spezielles AUFBEREITUNGsprogramm, das die erfaßten Daten in das Format des Datenbank-Ladeprogramms überführt.

Da jedoch bei der Lösung der Aufgabe bereits weitgehend von dem speziellen Problem der Erfassung von Daten aus Normen-Tabellen abstrahiert wurde, kann das System DACAPO immer dann angewendet werden, wenn Daten in Tabellenform vorliegen (z.B. auf Kartei- oder Formblättern). Die Daten können komplexe und vielfältige, aber auch ganz einfache Strukturen haben. So kann z.B. auch eine konventionelle Datei als eine einfach strukturierte, aber u.U. sehr große Tabelle aufgefaßt und daher mit Hilfe des Systems DACAPO bearbeitet werden.

Dank

Die Entwicklung des Informationssystems für Eisen- und Stahlwerkstoffe wird seit 1971 durch das Institut für Dokumentationswesen mit Mitteln des Bundesministeriums für Forschung und Technologie gefördert.

Literatur

/1/ Dathe, G.; Dreckmann, K.-H.: Entwurf eines Datenbanksystems für normierte Kennwerte von Eisen- und Stahlwerkstoffen. GI-4.Jahrestagung, Berlin, 9.-12.Oktober 1974. Lecture Notes in Computer Science, Vol. 26, S.484-493. Berlin-Heidelberg-New York: Springer (1975)

/2/ Deutscher Normenausschuß (Hrsg.): DIN 17 210 (Einsatzstähle-Gütevorschriften). Berlin: Beuth-Vertrieb (1969).

EIN DIALOGSYSTEM ZUR METHODENSUCHE

R. Erbe
G. Walch
IBM Deutschland
Wiss. Zentrum Heidelberg

Abstract

Die heute verfügbaren Programmbibliotheken bieten im allgemeinen zu wenig Unterstützung, um für ein Problem die Lösungsmethode und das zugehörige Programm aufzufinden und unter gegebenenfalls mehreren einsetzbaren auszuwählen.

Um diese Situation zu verbessern, wurde ein Dialogsystem entwikkelt, das den Benutzer - ausgehend von einer sehr allgemeinen Problembeschreibung - über eine schrittweise Verfeinerung - zur Problemlösung und dem verfügbaren Programm leiten soll. Die der Methodensuche zu Grunde liegende Datenstruktur ist ein Informationsnetzwerk, das durch das Zerlegen von Information über ein Anwendungsgebiet in kleine Teilbereiche entsteht.

Neben der eigentlichen Methodensuche unterstützt das Dialogsystem auch das Aufbauen und Ändern des zu Grunde liegenden Informationsnetzes.

1. Einleitung

Um die in den Rechenzentren von Universitäten und Forschungsinstituten verfügbare Software - sei sie vom Computer-Hersteller, speziellen Softwarefirmen oder von anderen Forschungsinstituten zur Verfügung gestellt oder im Hause selbst entwickelt, - wirkungsvoll nutzen zu können, ist es notwendig, jedem potentiellen Benutzer gute, d.h. vollständige und verständliche, Dokumentation an die Hand zu geben.

Die Benützung dieser Dokumentation ist aber für den weniger Geübten recht mühsam und zeitraubend, oder die Dokumentation ist, vor allem für hauseigene Programme, mangelhaft oder fehlt vollständig, so daß beim Nicht-DV-Spezialisten leicht Resignation eintritt, der Benutzer mit Programmierkenntnissen dagegen verleitet wird, ein eigenes neues Programm zu schreiben.

Auch in verfügbaren Methodenbanken /1/ ist der Aspekt, den Problemlöser von seinem Problem zur adäquaten Lösungsmethode und dem verfügbaren Programm zu führen, nicht genügend berücksichtigt.

Zur Verbesserung dieser Situation schlagen wir ein interaktives System vor, das den Benutzer vom Allgemeinen zum Speziellen führt /2/. Das Allgemeine kann ein sehr weit gefaßtes Anwendungsgebiet sein, z.B. medizinische Forschung, das letzte Spezielle die Dokumentation über ein bestimmtes Programm, z.B. einen statistischen Test.

2. Grundlagen

Um ein solches System zu verwirklichen, ist es notwendig, die bisher eventuell in der Programmdokumentation enthaltene Information über Anwendungsmöglichkeiten und Problembeschreibung von dieser zu trennen, in einzelne Teile zu gliedern, und diese miteinander in Beziehung zu setzen (Bild 1). Das Zusammenfügen mehrerer solcher Ketten, die unter Umständen gleiche Elemente enthalten, führt dann zum Informationsnetz /3,4/ (Bild 2). Wir bezeichnen deshalb die einzelnen Informationsteile als Knoten, die vom Allgemeineren zum Spezielleren führenden Verbindungen als Kanten.

Jeder Knoten kann eine beliebige Zahl von ein- und auslaufenden Kanten haben. Knoten ohne einlaufende Kante sind die allgemeinsten eines Anwendungsgebietes. Knoten ohne auslaufende Kante sind solche mit der Beschreibung einer abstrakten Methode, falls kein Programm vorhanden, oder einer speziellen Programmdokumentation, oder eventuell dem Quellenprogramm selbst.

Mit diesem Konzept ist es möglich, Information über Methoden, d.h. Lösungsverfahren, zu liefern, auch wenn kein ausführbares Programm zur Verfügung steht. Auch kann diese Informationsstruktur bei anderen

Arten der Problemlösung als solche durch Computerprogramme angewendet werden.

Im Prinzip besteht diese Methodensuche in einem schrittweisen durchwandern des Informationnetzes von einem "Problemknoten" zu einem "Methodenknoten". Wird dem Benutzer die Information eines bestimmten Knotens und seiner direkten Folgeknoten angeboten, so hat er zu entscheiden, über welchen der Folgeknoten er seinen Weg durch das Netz fortsetzen will. Dieser Ablauf wiederholt sich, bis ein "Methoden-" oder "Programmknoten" erreicht ist. Abhängig von einer vorliegenden Problemstellung entscheidet also der Benutzer, welcher der durch das Netz vorgegebenen Suchpfade beschritten wird.

Der Startpunkt für eine Methodensuche hängt nun vom Kenntnisstand des Benutzers ab. Hat er keine Kenntnis über den Inhalt der Methodenbank, so kann er zunächst Auskunft über die erfaßten Anwendungsgebiete erhalten. Nachdem er eines davon ausgewählt hat, werden ihm Teilgebiete daraus angeboten.

Falls der Benutzer jedoch schon gewisse Kenntnis über ein Gebiet hat und nur nach detaillierter Information sucht, so kann er direkt das Gebiet oder das Programm angeben, über das er nachfragen will. Jeder Knoten im Netz kann Anfangsknoten einer Suche sein.

Um dieses Vorgehen zu ermöglichen, muß allerdings das Informationsnetz erst aufgebaut werden und zwar von einem intimen Kenner des jeweiligen Anwendungsgebietes. Das Strukturieren der Anwendung ist eine verantwortungsvolle Arbeit, die einerseits dem Experten hilft, sich selbst Klarheit über die Beziehungen der Teilgebiete zu verschaffen, andererseits einer Vielzahl von weniger Kundigen wertvolle Hilfe bietet. Der mehr mechanische Teil dieser Arbeit, das Aufbauen der Netzstruktur und das Einbringen der Information wird weitgehend vom Dialogsystem unterstützt und kann gegebenenfalls von weniger Erfahrenen übernommen werden.

Das Dialogsystem besteht im wesentlichen aus zwei Teilen:

1) dem Konstruktionsteil zum Aufbauen, Ändern und Erweitern des Informationsnetzes,
2) dem Suchteil zum Aufsuchen von Information über Methoden und Programme.

Während die Anwendung des ersten Teils ausgewählten Benutzern mit speziellen Kenntnissen und Verantwortung vorbehalten ist, erlaubt es ein dritter, nicht prinzipiell notwendiger Teil jedem Benutzer, seinen Kommentar einzugeben, seien es Hinweise auf Fehler und Schwächen des Systems oder der dokumentierten Methoden und Programme, seien es Hinweise auf mögliche Erweiterungen, z.B. nicht dokumentierte Anwendungen von dokumentierten Methoden.

3. Experimentier-System

3.1 Allgemeines

Um die Brauchbarkeit dieser Ideen zu überprüfen, wurde ein Experimentiersystem in APL entwickelt. Auf Grund seiner Natur als Dialogsystem und seiner Unterstützung beim Implementieren, Modifizieren, Erweitern und Testen bietet APL große Vorteile für eine rasche Verwirklichung, während der Endbenutzer nicht gewahr wird, überhaupt APL zu benutzen.

In der bis jetzt realisierten Version wurde vom Grundsatz ausgegangen, daß das System ohne Vorkenntnisse benützbar sein soll. Deshalb ist der Dialog vom System geleitet, alle Informationen werden vom System angeboten, der Benutzer hat nur Ja/Nein Entscheidungen zu treffen oder aus einer Liste von mehreren Möglichkeiten (Menu) durch Eingabe ihrer Nummer eine auszuwählen.

Auf Wunsch gibt das System eine Benutzer-Anweisung bei Beginn einer Sitzung. Weitere Informationen können jederzeit durch Eingabe eines '?' und eines Stichworts angefordert werden. Es wurde sorgfältig darauf geachtet, nicht durch fehlerhafte Eingabe in Fallen zu geraten, aus denen man nur mit Kenntnis des Dialogsystems sich befreien kann. Das System muß vielmehr selbst fehlerhafte Eingabe erkennen und eine entsprechende Korrekturaufforderung ausgeben.

Um die Information vor fahrlässiger Zerstörung zu sichern, wurden verschiedene Benutzerklassen eingeführt. Benutzer mit Schreibberechtigung sind in ein Benutzerverzeichnis eingetragen und müssen Name und Passwort eingeben, wenn sie den Konstruktionsteil benützen. Außerdem wird für jeden Knoten der Eigentümer (der Benutzer, der den Knoten definiert hat) registriert und die Änderung nur an eigenen Knoten ermöglicht. Es können mehrere Benutzer je für einen Teil des Netzes verantwortlich sein ohne sich gegenseitig zu stören. Das System erlaubt außerdem gleichzeitiges Lesen und Schreiben mehrer Benutzer.

3.2 Systemfunktionen

Im Dialogsystem stehen die folgenden Funktionsgruppen zur Verfügung (Bild 3):

1) die eigentlichen Suchfunktionen für den Endbenutzer zum Auffinden und Auswählen von Programmen.
2) die Aufbaufunktionen, die dem Anwendungsspezialisten gestatten, ein Netzwerk oder einen Teil davon zu formen und die ensprechende Information zu speichern,
3) die Aenderungsfunktionen zum Aendern von Knotennamen, Netzstruktur und Knotentexten,
4) die Löschfunktionen zum Löschen von Knotentexten und zum vollständigen Löschen von Knoten mit sämtlichen Verknüpfungen und Texten,
5) die Kommentarfunktionen, die allen Benutzern gestatten, Kommentare zu schreiben und zu lesen.

Auf die Möglichkeiten, welche die Suchfunktionen bieten, sei im Folgenden etwas näher eingegangen (Bild 4 und 5).

Bei Beginn einer Methodensuche besteht das ernste Problem, einen Startknoten zu identifizieren. Deshalb wurden zwei Teilmengen von Knoten definiert:

1) die Menge "Anwendungen", welche den allgemeinsten Knoten für jedes Anwendungsgebiet enthält,
2) die Menge "Probleme", die Knoten für allgemeine Problemkreise enthält, die eventuell in verschiedenen Anwendungsgebieten von Bedeutung sein können.

Um die Suche zu beginnen, kann der Benutzer eine Liste aller "Anwendungen" oder aller "Probleme", die dem System bekannt sind, anfordern und von diesen einen bestimmten als Startknoten auswählen. Stattdessen kann ein Benutzer, der schon Kenntnisse über definierte Knoten hat, direkt den Startknoten per Name oder numerischen Code angeben. Falls seine Eingabe keine gültige Kennung ist, wird eine Suche nach ähnlichen Knotennamen ausgeführt, deren Ergebnis ihm zur Bestätigung und Auswahl angeboten wird.

Eine dritte Möglichkeit, einen Startknoten zu finden, ist, eine Ausgabe eines Teilnetzes bis zu einer gewählten Tiefe für eine "Anwendung" oder ein "Problem" zu verlangen, und danach einen der darin enthaltenen Knoten als Startknoten zu bezeichnen.

Wenn nun ein Startpunkt gefunden ist, jetzt als aktueller Knoten bezeichnet, werden alle seine (direkten) Folgeknoten im Informationsnetz aufgesucht. Abhängig von durch den Benutzer gesetzten Parametern wird die Information in einem der drei folgenden Ausführlichkeitsgrade gegeben:

1) kurz: sowohl der aktuelle Knoten als auch die Folgeknoten werden nur per Name angegeben.
2) mittel: der aktuelle Knoten wird mit einem kurzen Text beschrieben, die Folgeknoten per Name angegeben,
3) lang: der aktuelle Knoten wird mit ausführlichem Text beschrieben, für die Folgeknoten werden Kurz-Texte ausgegeben.

In der ersten Form ist ein schneller Gang durch das Netz möglich. In jedem Fall wird die Liste der Folgeknoten zur Auswahl angeboten. Der ausgewählte ist jetzt der aktuelle Knoten und die Suchschleife beginnt von neuem.

Statt dessen kann der Benutzer auch eine der folgenden Alternativen wählen:

1) Erklärung: Sie bietet den ausführlichen Text für die aus den aktuellen und den Folgeknoten ausgewählten Knoten an, besonders nützlich, wenn die Suche in der Kurzform durchgeführt wird.
2) Entscheidungsunterstützung: Sie bietet zusammenfassenden Kurztext für alle Folgeknoten für Suche in kurzer oder mittlerer Form.
3) Ausgabe des bisherigen Suchweges. Danach kann durch direkte Knotenangabe (siehe 6) ein Rücksprung erfolgen.
4) Ausgabe aller möglichen Suchwege, die von einem Wurzelknoten (Knoten ohne Vorgänger) zum aktuellen Knoten führen und den bisherigen Suchweg enthalten. Das ist besonders nützlich, falls die Suche nicht an einem Wurzelknoten begonnen wurde, so daß der Benutzer auf implicite Voraussetzungen prüfen kann, die er andernfalls übersehen hätte.
5) Ausgabe eines Teilnetzes abwärts vom aktuellen Knoten bis zu einer gewissen Tiefe, um Ausschau nach erreichbaren Knoten zu

halten.

6) Direkte Eingabe eines neuen aktuellen Knotens, um auf dem Weg zurückzugehen oder im dargestellten Teilnetz vorwärts zu springen.

7) Abbruch der Suche.

Nach den Alternativen 3), 4) und 5) kann zusätzliche Erklärung von ausgewählten Wegknoten oder Knoten des Teilnetzes angefordert werden oder direkte Knotenangabe gewählt werden. Andernfalls geht die Suche mit der Auswahl eines Folgeknotens weiter.

Ist ein Endknoten (Knoten ohne Folgeknoten) erreicht, so wird dies mitgeteilt. Es bleiben die Alternativen 1) Erklärung, 3) Suchweg, 4) Mögliche Wege, 6) Knotenangabe und 7) Ende der Suche.

3.3 Bemerkungen zur Realisierung

Es gibt drei wesentliche Teile des Informationsnetzes, die gespeichert werden müssen:

1) die Liste der Knotennamen, die eindeutig sein müssen,
2) zu jedem Knoten die zugehörige Knoten-Information in Textform,
3) die Struktur des Netzes, d.h. die Verbindung der Knoten.

Außer durch den Namen können die Knoten durch eine numerische Kennung identifiziert werden. Als Kennung wird einfach der Index des Knotennamens in der Namensliste verwendet. Die Knotenkennung dient gleichzeitig als Record-Adresse in einem direkt adressierten File (Datei), der die Knotentexte enthält.

Die Strukturinformation wird als binäre Relation auf der Menge der Knotenkennungen gespeichert. Namensliste, Binärrelation und Knotentexte werden in Files außerhalb des APL-Workspace gespeichert, um jederzeit mehreren Benutzern Zugriff zum neuesten Zustand des Systems zu gestatten.

Die im Dialog verwendeten Textzeilen sind nicht Bestandteil der einzelnen Programmteile. Sie sind hingegen in einer Dialogliste gesammelt und werden von einer speziellen Funktion verwendet, um dynamisch Menus (Liste von Auswahlmöglichkeiten) aufzubauen. Dieses Vorgehen gestattet auch, wahlweise eine Lang- oder Kurzform des Dialogs oder

Dialog in verschiedenen Sprachen zu verwenden.

Die Verwendung einer Help-Funktion erlaubt es, die Erklärung bestimmter Begriffe - system- oder anwendungsbezogen - nur einmal zu geben und nicht überall, wo der Begriff verwendet wird, wiederholen zu müssen, da der Benutzer sie jederzeit erfragen kann. Außerdem wird bei der Suche nach einem zu erklärenden Stichwort ebenso wie bei der Prüfung eines eingegebenen Knotennamens, falls das Stichwort nicht gefunden wird, nach "ähnlichen" gesucht. Das Ergebnis der Ähnlichkeitssuche wird dem Benutzer zur Entscheidung und Auswahl angeboten.

Zur Suche nach ähnlichen Stichworten /5/ wird jeweils das eingegebene Wort und die Liste der möglichen Worte hinsichtlich der Überdeckung durch gemeinsame Wortelemente untersucht. Hierbei werden unter Wortelementen Zeichenketten mit mindestens zwei Zeichen verstanden. Alle Worte mit maximaler Überdeckung durch gemeinsame Elemente werden als ähnliche Worte betrachtet, vorausgesetzt daß diese Überdeckung 60% des Eingabewortes erreicht. Neben Worten mit Tippfehlern (meist 1 bis 2 Zeichen falsch) werden mit diesem Verfahren u.a. auch Worte mit permutierten Teilketten als ähnlich akzeptiert.

4. Bisherige Erfahrungen

Bis jetzt wurde das entwickelte System nur im eigenen Hause verwendet. Um für den Test eine realistische Anwendung zu haben und eine attraktive Demonstrationsmöglichkeit zu schaffen, wurde für den Problemkreis "Statistik" ein Informationsnetz aufgebaut. Bei seiner Realisierung wurden viele Verbesserungen des ersten Konzepts und des Dialogsystems angeregt. Gleichzeitig wurden im System die Systemfunktionen selbst und ihre gegenseitigen Abhängigkeiten dokumentiert, was sich bei der Implementierung als sehr nützlich erwies, um die eigene Arbeit jederzeit überschaubar zu gestalten.

Außerdem wurde begonnen, ein Informationssystem über die im eigenen Rechenzentrum verfügbare Software aufzubauen. Hier haben Leute, die nicht mit der Entwicklung des Dialogsystems zu tun hatten, mit den System-Internas also nicht vertraut sind, gezeigt, daß es nach nur geringer Anleitung sehr leicht ist, das System zu benutzen. Die selbe Erfahrung wurde in zwei weiteren, mehr speziellen Anwendungen gemacht, wo Studenten die von ihnen geleistete Arbeit, sowohl Programmentwicklung als auch Datenauswertung, mit Hilfe des Dialogsystems dokumentierten, und vermutlich besser und vollständiger als es ohne dieses System geschehen wäre, so daß es nun leichter ist, ihre Arbeit mit anderen Studenten fortzusetzen.

5. Erweiterungen

Die erste Version der Dialogführung durch Auswahl aus Menus war konzipiert unter dem Gesichtspunkt, daß der Benutzer nicht mit dem Lernen von Kommandoworten belastet werden sollte. Das bringt natürlich für den Geübteren eine unnötige Schwerfälligkeit, vor allem solange Schreibmaschinenterminals benutzt werden.

Deshalb wird als Alternative eine vom Benutzer gelenkte Dialogform implementiert, mit der das gewünschte Ziel schneller erreicht werden kann. Dies wird vor allem im Konstruktionsteil von Vorteil sein, wo einerseits eine größere Zahl von Kommandos und ihren Kombinationen angeboten werden müssen als im Suchteil, andererseits weniger Leute relativ oft das System benutzen und sich dadurch Übung und Kenntnisse verschaffen. Bei fehlerhaften Kommandos oder auf Anforderung wird jedoch in die vom System gelenkte Dialogform umgeschaltet.

Ebenso wie der Benutzer durch Systemkenntnis den Dialog effektiver gestalten kann, so kann er durch Kenntnisse aus seinem Anwendungsgebiet die Suche nach der Lösungsmethode beschleunigen. Statt sich nur in kleinen Schritten von einem Knoten zum unmittelbaren Folgeknoten vorzutasten, kann das System auf Grund von Stichwortangaben mögliche Wege auswählen, gegebenenfalls weitere Information anfordern, um die Antwort eindeutig zu machen, und auch auf die vom Benutzer nicht spezifizierten Voraussetzungen aufmerksam machen.

Eine Erweiterung des Methoden-Such-Systems zum Problem-Lösungssystem durch sofortige Ausführbarkeit der gefundenen Programme ist als weiterer Schritt geplant. Das bringt im Falle von APL-Programmen nur die Probleme des Daten-Verkehrs, die mit den verfügbaren Hilfsprozessoren gelöst werden können. Für Programme, die in anderen Programmiersprachen geschrieben sind, erfordert diese Aufgabe eine Kommunikation zwischen APL und Modulen außerhalb APL.

6. Zusammenfassung

Es wurde ein Dialogsystem vorgestellt, das auf der Basis von Informationsnetzwerken den Benutzer bei der Suche nach Problemlösungen und zugehörigen Programmen führen soll. Als Voraussetzung für diese Führung muß das entsprechende Arbeitsgebiet von einem guten Kenner der Materie in die Form des Netzwerkes zerlegt werden. Das Dialogsystem unterstützt ihn beim Aufbau des Netzes und Einbringen der entsprechenden Information.

Außer zum raschen Suchen auf möglichst schmalem Weg kann das System, eventuell mit einigen Modifikationen des Dialogs, zur Wissensvermittlung auf breiterer Basis verwendet und möglicherweise für Computer-Unterstützten-Unterricht eingesetzt werden.

Literatur:

/1/ A. C. Esprester: Datenbank und Methodenbank, data report 9(1974) Heft 3,4.

/2/ R. Erbe, G. Walch: An Interactive Guidance System for Method Libraries, IBM-Deutschland, Wiss. Zentrum Heidelberg, TR 75.o4.oo1 (1975).

/3/ K. Brunnstein, J.W. Schmidt: Structuring and Retrieving Information in Computer Based Learning, Int. J. Computer & Information Sciences, 2(1973)89.

/4/ J.D. Wexler: Information Networks in Generative Computer Aided Instruction, IEEE MMS 11(197o)181.

/5/ R. Erbe, H.-J. Schek: Search with Fuzzy Keywords Applied in a Methods Data Base, IBM-Deutschland, Wiss. Zentrum Heidelberg, TR 75.o5.oo3 (1975).

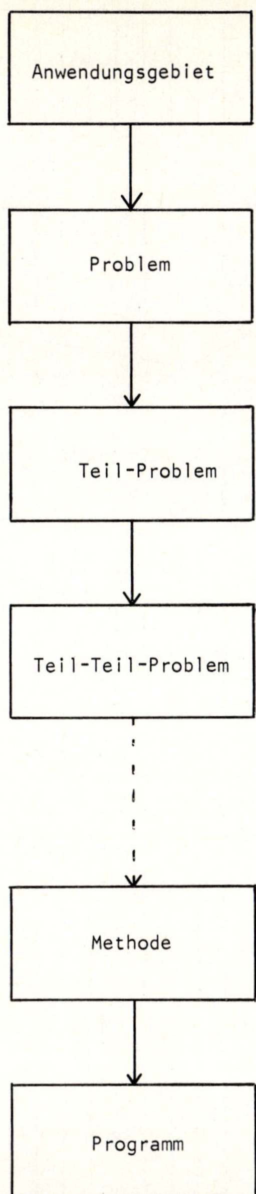

Bild 1: Führung vom Anwendungsgebiet und Problem über mehrere Stufen von Teilproblemen zur Lösungsmethode und zum Programm.

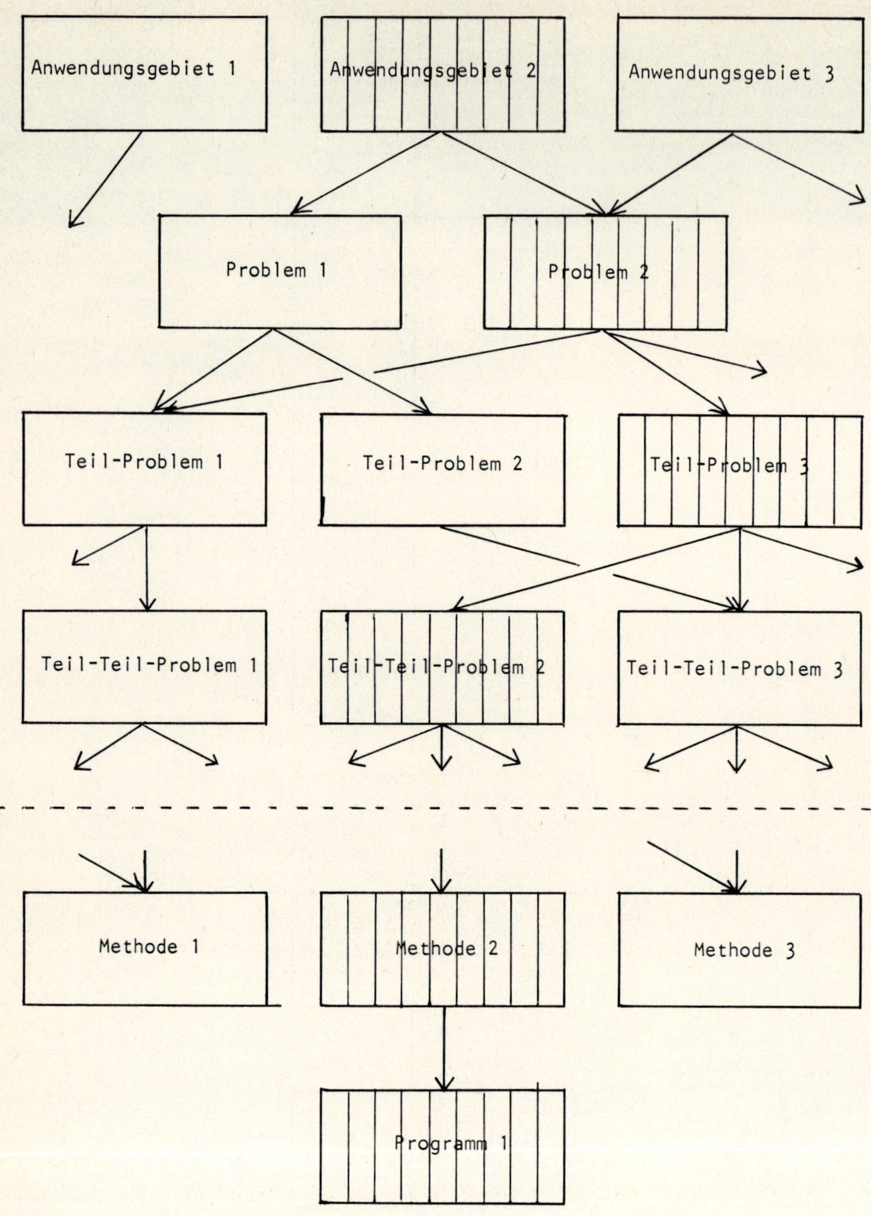

Bild 2: Ausschnitt aus einem allgemeinen Informationsnetz zur Methodensuche (ein möglicher Suchweg schraffiert).

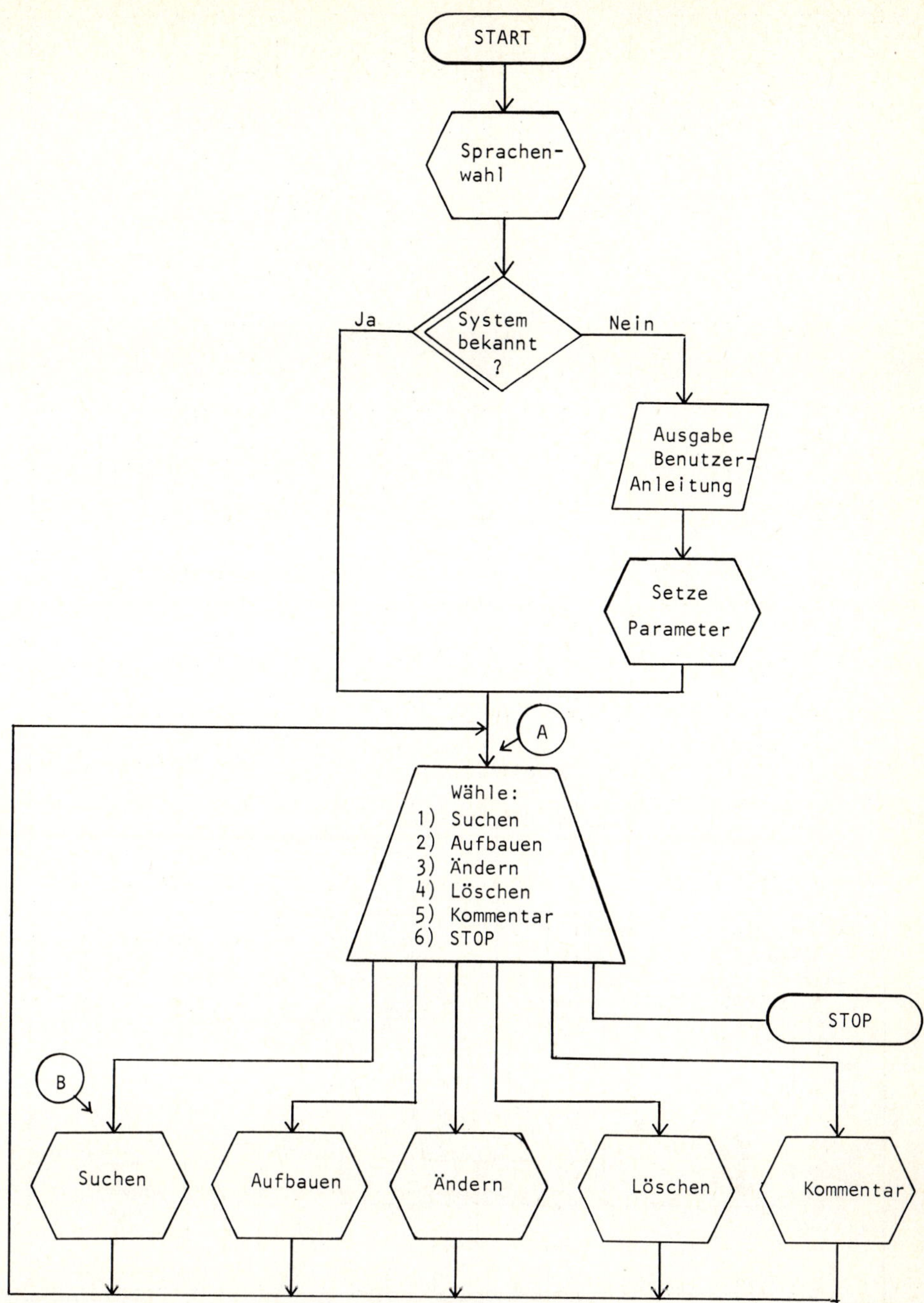

Bild 3: Flußdiagramm des Dialogsystems.

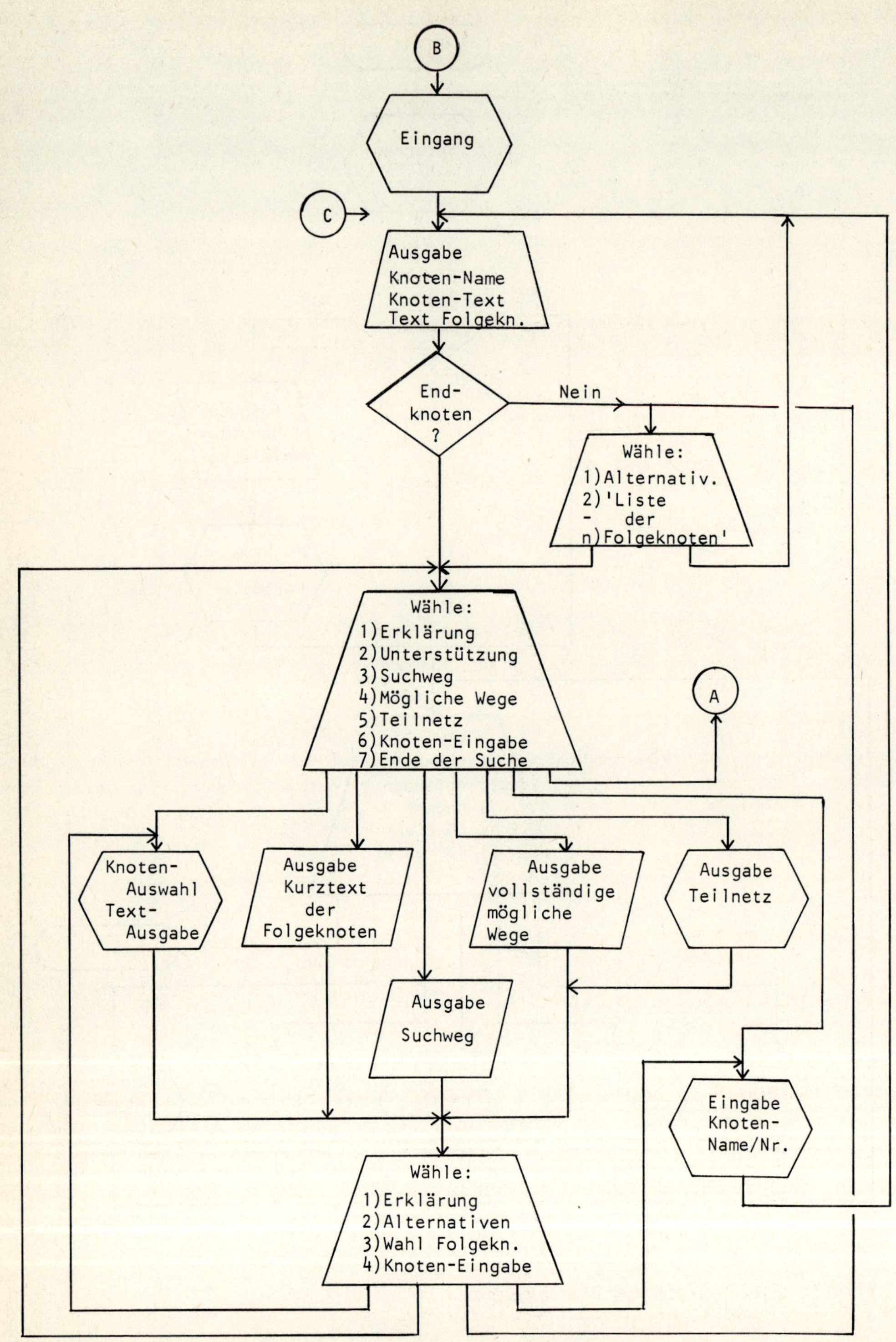

Bild 4: Flußdiagramm des Suchprogramms.

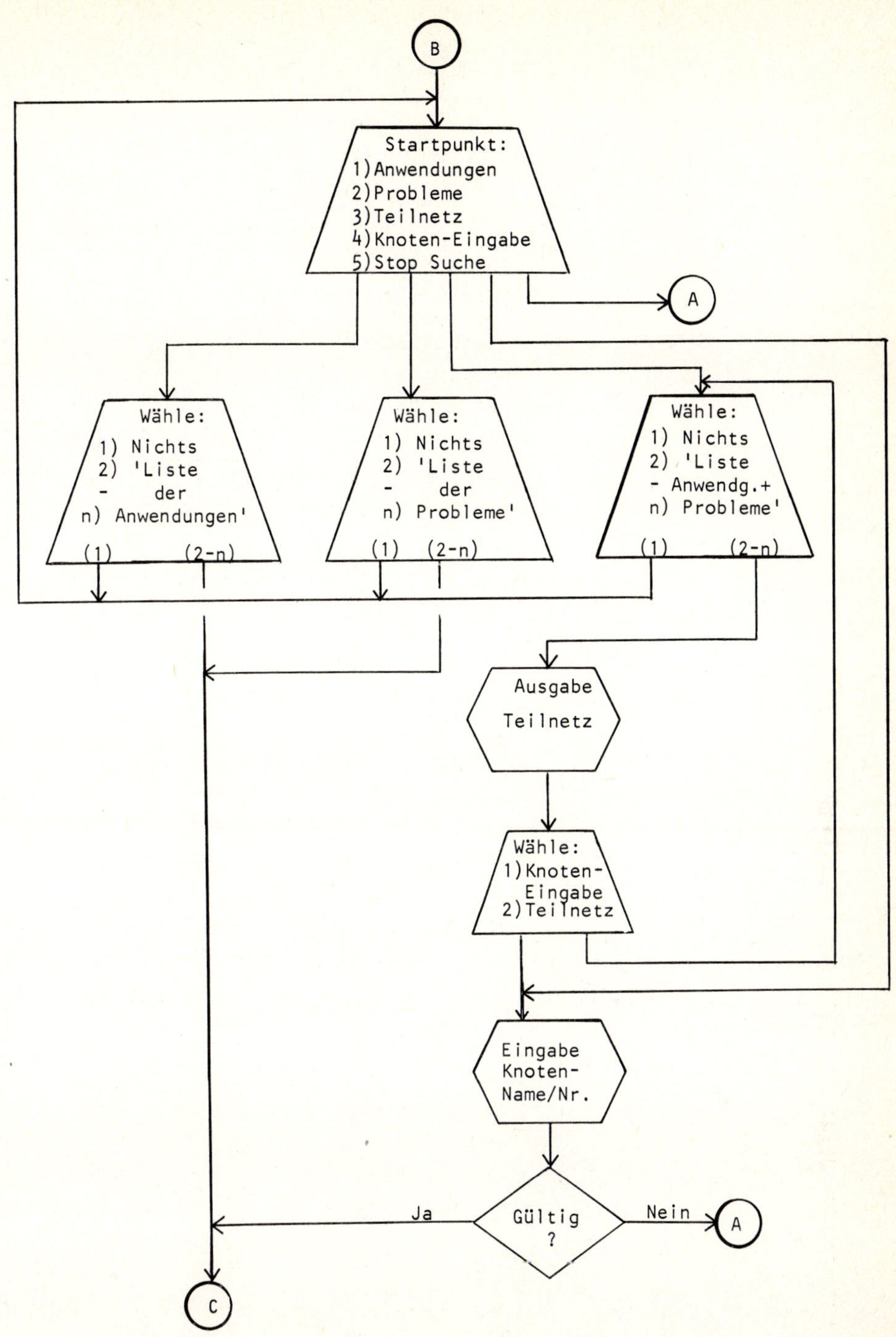

Bild 5: Flußdiagramm des 'Eingang'-Programms.

T R A N S I T I O N S N E T Z E

MARKIERTE PETRINETZE UND Σ - TEILSYSTEME

Eike Best*
5300 Bonn
Lenné Str. 45

Hans Albrecht Schmid*
Department of Computer Science
University of Toronto
Toronto, Canada

1. Einleitung

Abgeschlossenen Systemen werden markierte Netze untergelegt, damit aus Sätzen der Netztheorie auf das Verhalten der Systeme rückgeschlossen werden kann. Insbesondere ist es ein Ziel, aus statischen Eigenschaften der Netze die Dynamik der Systeme kennenzulernen.

In der Praxis treten bei größeren Systemen folgende Fälle auf:

Beispiel 1:

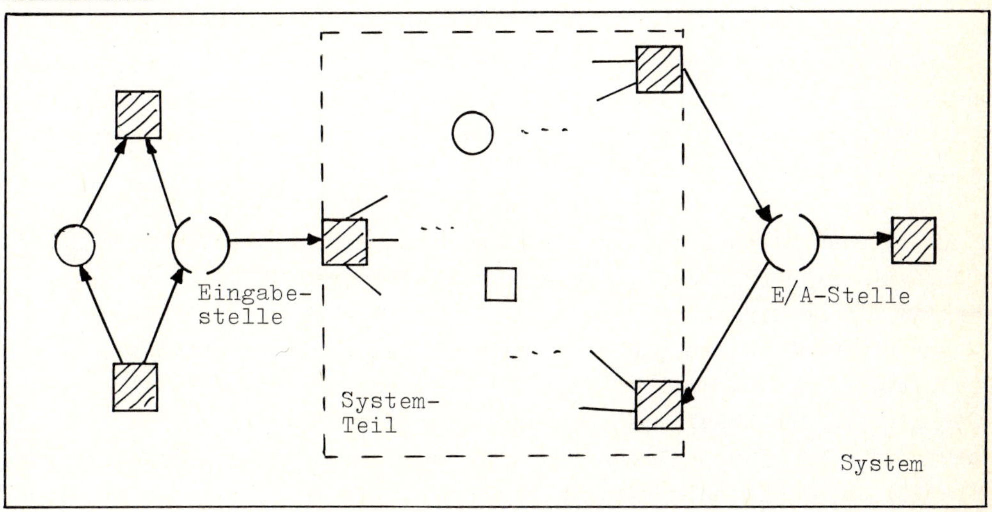

Das Verhalten eines Teils des Systems interessiert nur an gewissen äußeren Stellen. Gibt es für diesen Teil eine übersichtliche Beschreibungsmethode, die sein Verhalten widerspiegelt?

Diese Frage ist auch im nächsten Beispiel von Interesse:

---

* Als diese Arbeit fertig wurde, waren beide Autoren an der Universität Karlsruhe im Institut für Informatik.

Beispiel 2: (s. [LS74])

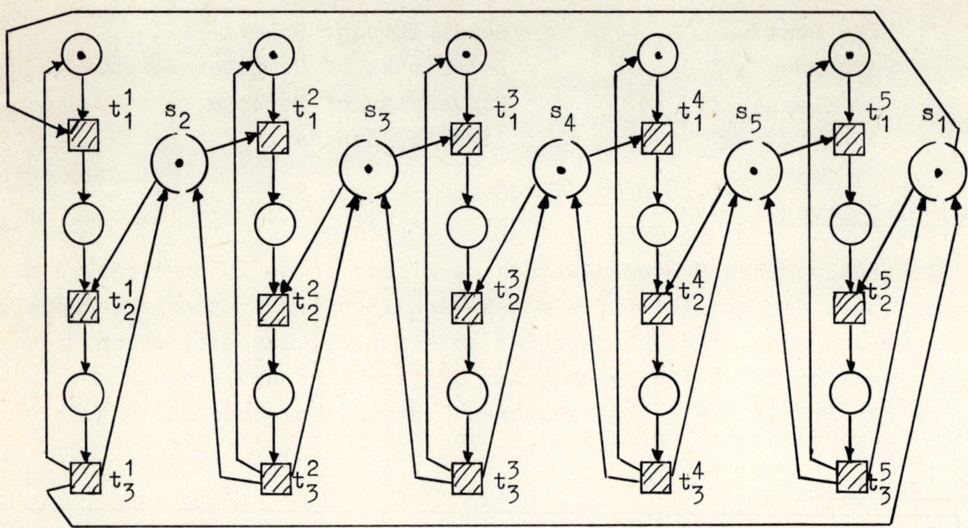

Das Gesamtsystem läßt sich unterteilen in gewisse Teilsysteme, von denen einige gleiches Verhalten zeigen. Gibt es für das Gesamtsystem eine Beschreibung, in der für die verhaltensgleichen Teilsysteme ein einzelner Baustein vorkommt?

In beiden Fällen interessiert eine Beschreibung des Verhaltens eines Teilsystems "nach außen"; dieses und ein anderes mit gleichem Verhalten können dann als gleichartige Bausteine betrachtet werden.

Für eine Präzisierung dieses Problems legen wir zunächst als Schnittstellen von Teilsystemen fest die äußeren oder geteilten Stellen (in den Beispielen als durchbrochene Kreise dargestellt), mitsamt den angrenzenden Transitionen (dargestellt als schraffierte Quadrate). Sodann fordern wir einschränkend, daß in Teilsystemen zwischen Transitionen, die zu Schnittstellen gehören, wohldefinierte Spielräume existieren. Diese zum Bestimmen des Verhaltens wesentliche Eigenschaft schränken wir weiter ein, indem wir nur Teilsysteme betrachten, die "im Innern" Synchronisationsgraphen sind. So gelangen wir zur Definition von σ - Teilsystemen in Abschnitt 4. Vorher definieren wir allgemeine Begriffe (Abschnitt 2) und offene Unterteilungen (Abschnitt 3). Abschnitt 5 untersucht die Klassen verhaltensgleicher σ - Teilsysteme und Abschnitt 6 bringt erste Ergebnisse. Die Frage in Beispiel 2 wird in Abschnitt 7 behandelt.

2. Markierte Netze

Definition 1:

Ein Netz ist ein Quadrupel

$N = (\mathbb{S}, \mathbb{T}, pre, post)$ mit:

- $\mathbb{S}$, $\mathbb{T}$ endliche Mengen (Stellen, dargestellt durch Kreise, Transitionen, dargestellt durch Quadrate)
- $\mathbb{S} \cap \mathbb{T} = \emptyset$
- $pre \subseteq \mathbb{S} \times \mathbb{T}$, $post \subseteq \mathbb{S} \times \mathbb{T}$ (Kanten)
- $\mathbb{S} \cup \mathbb{T} = \text{Feld}(pre \cup post)$

Zu gegebenem Netz N bezeichne $\mathbb{S}(N)$ die Stellen-, $\mathbb{T}(N)$ die Transitionen- und pre(N) bzw. post(N) die Kantenmenge dieses Netzes.

Definition 2:

Sei N Netz.

Sy(N) ("N ist Synchronisationsgraph") : $\Leftrightarrow$
pre(N) und post(N) sind Funktionen $\mathbb{S}(N) \longrightarrow \mathbb{T}(N)$.

Definition 3:

Sei N Netz, $s \in \mathbb{S}(N)$, $t \in \mathbb{T}(N)$.

M heißt Markierung (von N) $:\Leftrightarrow$ $M: \mathbb{S}(N) \longrightarrow \mathbb{N}$

s heißt (bei M) markiert (blank) $:\Leftrightarrow$ $M(s) > 0$ $(M(s) = 0)$

t heißt (bei M) aktiviert $:\Leftrightarrow$ $\forall s \in pre^{-1}(t): M(s) > 0$

Definition 4:

Sei N Netz, $T \subseteq \mathbb{T}(N)$, $M, \tilde{M}$ Markierungen von N.

$$M[T\rangle\tilde{M} \;:\Leftrightarrow\; \forall s \in pre^{-1}(T): M(s) \geq |pre(s) \cap T| \;\wedge$$
$$\wedge\; \forall s \in pre^{-1}(T) \setminus post^{-1}(T): \tilde{M}(s) = M(s) - |pre(s) \cap T|$$
$$\wedge\; \forall s \in post^{-1}(T) \setminus pre^{-1}(T): \tilde{M}(s) = M(s) + |T \cap post(s)|$$
$$\wedge\; \forall s \text{ sonst } \in \mathbb{S}(N): \tilde{M}(s) = M(s)$$

$\tilde{M}$ ist durch (nebenläufiges) Schalten von Transitionen aus T aus M hervorgegangen.

$[M\rangle$: = Die Menge aller Markierungen, die aus M durch eine Schaltung oder durch eine Hintereinanderreihung von Schaltungen hervorgehen.

Definition 5:

Sei N Netz, $t \in \mathbb{T}(N)$, M Markierung von N, $\tilde{M} \in [M]$, wobei $\tilde{M}$ durch eine spezielle Markierungsfolge aus M hervorgegangen sei.

$h_{M \to \tilde{M}}(t)$: = Schalthäufigkeit der Transition t bei der speziellen Markierungsfolge von M nach $\tilde{M}$.

Definition 6:

Sei N Netz, $w_0, w_1 \in \mathbb{S}(N) \cup \mathbb{T}(N)$.

Als Weg von w_0 nach w_1 bezeichnen wir kurz einen einfachen, gerichteten Weg w von w_0 nach w_1; dabei sei Anf(w) := w_0, End(w) := w_1. w heißt Kreis $:\Leftrightarrow$ Anf(w) = End(w).

Sei N Netz, Sy(N), $t, \hat{t} \in \mathbb{T}(N)$, M Markierung von N.

$W_{\hat{t} \to t}(N) := \{ w \mid w \text{ Weg von } \hat{t} \text{ nach } t \}$

$W_{blank \to t}(N) := \{ w \mid w \text{ Weg} \wedge t = \text{End}(w) \wedge \wedge (\text{Anf}(w) \text{ ist Randstelle oder Anf}(w) \text{ liegt auf blankem Kreis}) \}$

Definition 7:

Sei N Netz, $\hat{T}, T \subseteq \mathbb{T}(N)$, $\hat{T} \cap T = \emptyset$, M Markierung von N.

$$sp_M^N(T, \hat{T}) := \max_{\tilde{M} \in [M],\ t \in T} \left\{ h_{M \to \tilde{M}}(t) \mid \forall\, \hat{t} \in \hat{T}: h_{M \to \tilde{M}}(\hat{t}) = 0 \right\}$$

$$mx_M^N(T) := sp_M^N(T, \emptyset)$$

Der Spielraum sp gibt an, wie oft maximal eine Transition aus T schalten kann, ohne daß eine Transition aus $\hat{T}$ schalten muß.

3. Offene Unterteilung eines Netzes

Eine Überdeckung eines vorgegebenen Netzes mit Teilnetzen heißt eine offene Unterteilung dieses Netzes, wenn die Transitionenmenge und die Kantenmenge des Netzes in disjunkte Klassen zerlegt werden, nicht unbedingt aber die Stellenmenge. Diejenigen Stellen, die in mehr als einem Teilnetz liegen, heißen "geteilte", die anderen "innere" Stellen.

Da in der Praxis hauptsächlich Unterteilungen in zusammenhängende Teilnetze vorkommen, definieren wir zunächst:

Definition 8:

Sei N Netz.
$N' = (\mathbb{S}', \mathbb{T}', pre', post')$ heißt zusammenhängendes offenes Teilnetz (von N) : <=>

- $\mathbb{S}' \subseteq \mathbb{S}(N)$, $\mathbb{T}' \subseteq \mathbb{T}(N)$
- $pre' \subseteq pre \cap \mathbb{S}' \times \mathbb{T}'$, $post' \subseteq post \cap \mathbb{S}' \times \mathbb{T}'$
- $\forall t \in \mathbb{T}': \forall s \in pre^{-1}(t) \cup post^{-1}(t): s \in \mathbb{S}'$
- $\forall s \in \mathbb{S}': \exists t \in pre(s) \cup post(s): t \in \mathbb{T}'$

Definition 9:

Sei N Netz, $\{N_i\}_{i=0}^{n}$ Menge von zusammenhängenden offenen Teilnetzen von N.

$$\bigcup_{i=0}^{n} N_i := \left(\bigcup_{i=0}^{n} \mathbb{S}(N_i), \bigcup_{i=0}^{n} \mathbb{T}(N_i), pre \cap \left(\bigcup_{i=0}^{n} \mathbb{S}(N_i) \times \bigcup_{i=0}^{n} \mathbb{T}(N_i) \right), post \cap \left(\bigcup_{i=0}^{n} \mathbb{S}(N_i) \times \bigcup_{i=0}^{n} \mathbb{T}(N_i) \right) \right)$$

Definition 10:

Sei N Netz, $\{N_i\}_{i=0}^{n}$ Menge von zusammenhängenden offenen Teilnetzen von N.
$\{N_i\}_{i=0}^{n}$ heißt offene Unterteilung (von N) : <=>

$\bigcup_{i=0}^{n} N_i = N \wedge$

$\wedge$ für alle $x \in \mathbb{T}(N) \cup pre(N) \cup post(N)$ existiert genau ein $i \in \{0, \ldots, n\}$ mit: $x \in \mathbb{T}(N_i) \cup pre(N_i) \cup post(N_i)$

Definition 11:

Sei N Netz, $s \in \mathbb{S}(N)$, $\{N_i\}_{i=0}^{n}$ offene Unterteilung von N.
s heißt geteilte Stelle : <=> $|\{i \mid s \in \mathbb{S}(N_i)\}| > 1$
s heißt innere Stelle : <=> $|\{i \mid s \in \mathbb{S}(N_i)\}| = 1$

4. σ - Teilsysteme

Im folgenden (bis zum Abschnitt 7) nehmen wir an, daß eine offene Unterteilung eines markierten Netzes vorliegt und richten unser Augenmerk speziell auf ein beliebiges der Teilnetze. Definition 12 erklärt, wann ein solches markiertes Teilnetz σ - Teilsystem heißen soll.

Um das Verhalten von σ - Teilsystemen vergleichen zu können, müssen wir in Definition 13 berücksichtigen, daß dies unabhängig vom jeweiligen Gesamtsystem geschehen soll, in das das σ - Teilsystem eingebettet ist.

Definition 12:

Sei N ein Netz, $S \subsetneq \mathbb{S}(N)$, M Markierung von N.

$$\underline{N_S^{inn}} := (\mathbb{S}(N) \setminus S,\ \mathbb{T}(N),\ pre \cap ((\mathbb{S}(N) \setminus S) \times \mathbb{T}(N)),\ post \cap ((\mathbb{S}(N) \setminus S) \times \mathbb{T}(N)))$$

TS = (N, S, M) heißt $\underline{\sigma \text{ - Teilsystem}}$ $:\Longleftrightarrow$ $Sy\,(N_S^{inn})$

$\underline{S}$ heißt dann die Menge der geteilten Stellen von TS,

$\underline{AT(S)} := \{ t \in \mathbb{T}(N) \mid S \cap (post^{-1}(t) \cup pre^{-1}(t) \neq \emptyset \}$ die Menge der angrenzenden Transitionen.

Beispiel 3:

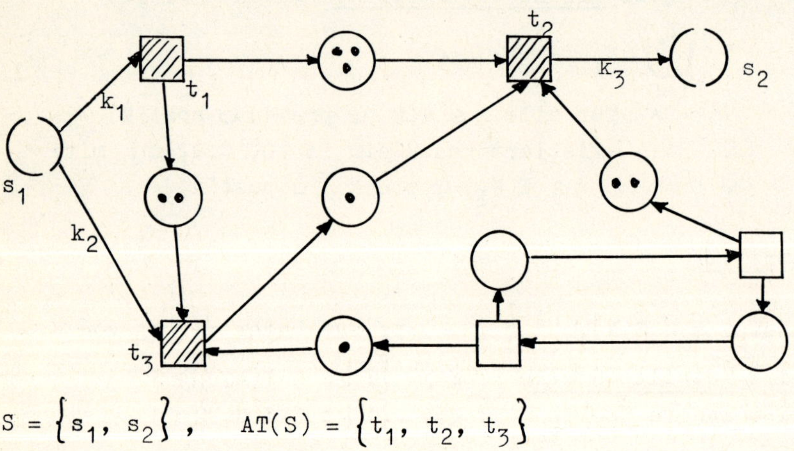

$S = \{ s_1, s_2 \}$, $AT(S) = \{ t_1, t_2, t_3 \}$

nach Streichen von k_1, k_2, k_3 und s_1, s_2 ist das Netz ein Synchronisationsgraph.

Zur nächsten Definition vorweg das

Beispiel 4:

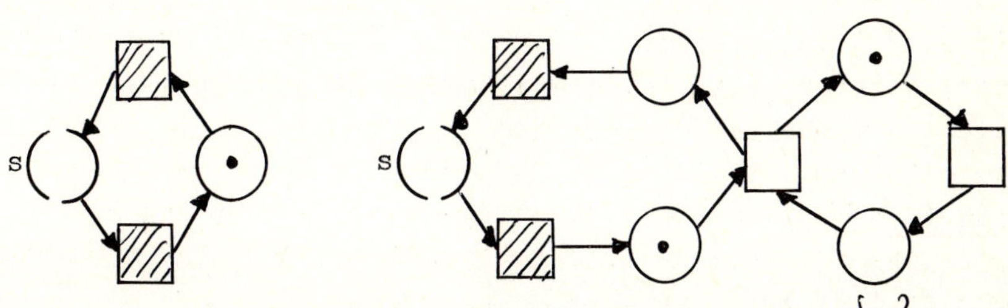

Diese σ - Teilsysteme sind verhaltensgleich auf S = $\{s\}$

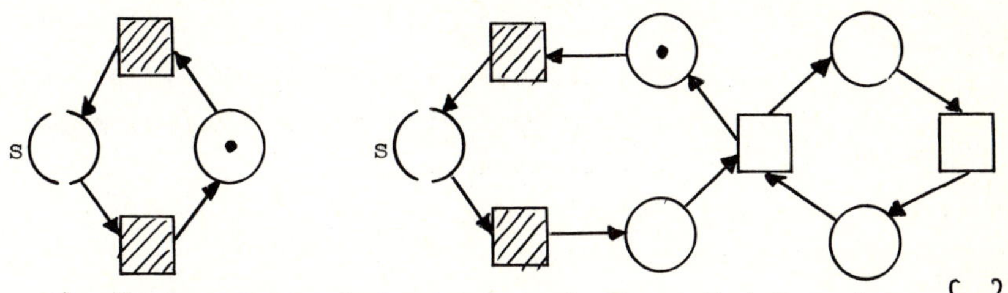

Diese σ - Teilsysteme sind nicht verhaltensgleich auf S = $\{s\}$.

Zwei σ-Teilsysteme TS = (N,S,M) und $\overline{TS} = (\bar{N},\bar{S},\bar{M})$ werden <u>verhaltensgleich</u> genannt ($TS \doteq \overline{TS}$), wenn die Schnittstellen übereinstimmen ($S = \bar{S}$ und $AT(S) = AT(\bar{S})$), und wenn für jedes Gesamtsystem, in das das eine Teilsystem TS eingebettet ist, die möglichen Markierungsbelegungen auf den geteilten Stellen, ausgehend von der anfänglichen Markierung, genau die gleichen sind, wie wenn anstelle von $\overline{TS}$ das σ - Teilsystem TS in das Gesamtsystem eingebettet wäre:

Definition 13:

Seien TS = (N,S,M) und $\overline{TS} = (\bar{N},\bar{S},\bar{M})$ zwei σ - Teilsysteme.

$\underline{TS \doteq \overline{TS}} \quad :\Leftrightarrow \quad S = \bar{S} \wedge AT(S) = AT(\bar{S}) \wedge \langle M \rangle_S = \langle \bar{M} \rangle_{\bar{S}}$

Dabei ist $\langle M \rangle_S$ ($\langle \bar{M} \rangle_{\bar{S}}$) die Menge aller Markierungssequenzen <u>auf S ($\bar{S}$)</u>, ausgehend von M ($\bar{M}$), der folgenden Art:

- es wird entweder in einem Schritt "von außen" auf S etwas verändert (ein anderes benachbartes σ - Teilsystem feuert auf S oder zieht Marken von S ab) und das "Innere" bleibt unverändert,
- oder es wird in einem Schritt beliebig "innen" geschaltet, ohne auf S etwas zu ändern, und dann nebenläufig auf S.

5. Normal- und Minimalformen

Zu einem σ - Teilsystem konstruieren wir nun Normal- und Minimalmatrix, und aus diesen wieder Normal- und Minimalgestalten für das untersuchte σ - Teilsystem.

Abschnitt 6 zeigt dann, daß diese Gestalten ausgezeichnete Elemente in den Klassen verhaltensgleicher σ - Teilsysteme sind.

Definition 14:

Sei TS = (N,S,M) σ - Teilsystem, $\hat{t}, t \in AT(S)$, $\hat{t} \neq t$.

$$\underline{W^{inn}_{\hat{t} \to t}} := \{ w \in W_{\hat{t} \to t}(N^{inn}_S) \mid \text{außer } \hat{t} \text{ und } t \text{ liegen auf } w \text{ keine weiteren Transitionen aus } AT(S) \}$$

$$\underline{W^{inn}_{blank \quad t}} := \{ w \in W_{blank \to t}(N^{inn}_S) \mid \text{außer } t \text{ liegt weder auf } w \text{ eine weitere Transition aus } AT(S), \text{ noch auf dem blanken Kreis, auf dem } Anf(w) \text{ evtl. liegt (s. Definition 6)} \}$$

$$\underline{mx^{inn}_M(t)} := \begin{cases} \min \{ M(w) \mid w \in W^{inn}_{blank \to t} \}, & \text{falls } W^{inn}_{blank \to t} \neq \emptyset, \\ \infty & \text{sonst} \end{cases}$$

$$\underline{sp^{inn}_M(t,t)} := \begin{cases} \min \{ mx^{inn}_M(t), M(w) \mid w \in W^{inn}_{\hat{t} \to t} \}, & \text{falls } mx^{inn}_M(t) < \infty \text{ oder } W^{inn}_{\hat{t} \to t} \neq \emptyset, \\ \infty & \text{sonst} \end{cases}$$

Die Normalmatrix L_{TS} und die Minimalmatrix K_{TS} zu einem σ - Teilsystem werden beide definiert als Funktionen

$$L_{TS}, K_{TS}: AT(S) \times AT(S) \to \mathbb{N} \cup \{\infty\} :$$

Definition 15:

Sei TS = (N,S,M) σ - Teilsystem, $\hat{t}, t \in AT(S)$, $\hat{t} \neq t$.

$$\underline{L_{TS}(t,t)} := mx^{N^{inn}_S}_M(t)$$

$$\underline{L_{TS}(\hat{t},t)} := sp^{N^{inn}_S}_M(t,\hat{t})$$

$$\underline{K_{TS}(t,t)} := \begin{cases} mx_M^{inn}(t), \text{ falls } mx_M^{inn}(t) < \\ \quad < \min \{ M(w) \mid w \in W_{blank \to t}(N_S^{inn}) \setminus \\ \qquad \setminus W_{blank \to t}^{inn} \} \\ \infty \quad \text{sonst} \end{cases}$$

$$\underline{K_{TS}(\hat{t},t)} := \begin{cases} sp_M^{inn}(t,\hat{t}), \text{ falls } sp_M^{inn}(t,\hat{t}) < \\ \quad < \min \{ mx_M^{inn}(t), M(w) \mid \\ \quad \mid w \in W_{\hat{t} \to t}(N_S^{inn}) \setminus W_{\hat{t} \to t}^{inn} \} \\ \infty \quad \text{sonst} \end{cases}$$

Zur Konstruktion der Normalgestalt TS_{norm} bzw. der Minimalgestalt TS_{min} zu einem σ - Teilsystem TS nehmen wir an, daß "X" eine der beiden Matrizen L_{TS} oder K_{TS} bezeichne:

Definition 16:

Sei TS = (N,S,M) ein σ - Teilsystem, X := L_{TS} oder K_{TS}.

$\underline{TS_{norm(min)}}$:= (N_X, S_X, M_X) mit:

- $\mathbb{S}(N_X) := S \cup \{ [\hat{t},t] \mid X(\hat{t},t) < \infty \}$
- $\mathbb{T}(N_X) := AT(S)$
- $pre(N_X) := pre(N) \cap (S \times AT(S)) \cup$
  $\cup \{ ([\hat{t},t], t) \mid [\hat{t},t] \in S_X \}$
- $post(N_X) := post(N) \cap (S \times AT(S)) \cup$
  $\cup \{ ([\hat{t},t], \hat{t}) \mid [\hat{t},t] \in S_X \wedge \hat{t} \neq t \}$
- $S_X := S$
- $M_X(s) := \begin{cases} M(s) & \text{für } s \in S \\ X(\hat{t},t) & \text{für } [\hat{t},t] \in \mathbb{S}(N_X) \setminus S \end{cases}$

Bei dieser Konstruktion wurden Stellen überall dort eingeführt, wo in einer Matrix ein Element $< \infty$ steht. TS_{norm} und TS_{min} sind nach Konstruktion eindeutig bestimmt.

Da in der Definition von K_{TS} alle unnötigen Spielraumberechnungen vermieden wurden (unnötige Spielräume wurden zu ∞ gesetzt), gibt es auch in TS_{min} keine überflüssige Stelle (s. Abschnitt 6).

Das nächste Beispiel verdeutlicht die vorangegangenen Definitionen und Konstruktionen.

Beispiel 5:

Zu dem Teilsystem in Beispiel 3 geben wir K_{TS}, L_{TS}, TS_{min} und TS_{norm} an:

K_{TS} =

	t_1	t_2	t_3
t_1	∞	∞	∞
t_2	∞	∞	∞
t_3	∞	1	1

L_{TS} =

	t_1	t_2	t_3
t_1	∞	3	2
t_2	∞	2	∞
t_3	∞	1	1

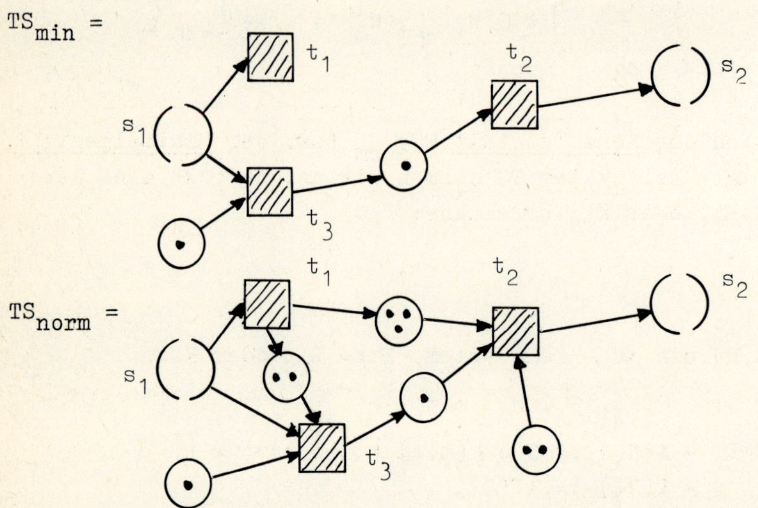

Eine Inspektion zeigt, daß hier TS, TS_{norm} und TS_{min} verhaltensgleich sind.

6. Sätze

a) TS, TS_{norm} und TS_{min} sind verhaltensgleich.

Der Beweis wendet vollständige Induktion an über alle möglichen Markierungsbelegungen der geteilten Stellen.

b) 2 σ -Teilsysteme sind genau dann verhaltensgleich, wenn die Minimalsysteme übereinstimmen.

Beweis:

($\Leftarrow$) klar;

($\Rightarrow$): angenommen, die beiden Minimalsysteme stimmen auf irgendzwei Stellen nicht überein; dann lassen sich auf dem einen σ - Teilsystem Markierungsfolgen mit Belegungsveränderungen auf den geteilten Stellen finden, die auf dem anderen σ - Teilsystem nicht herstellbar sind.

c) Unter verhaltensgleichen σ - Teilsystemen hat das (eindeutig bestimmte) Minimalsystem die kleinste Stellenmenge.

7. Beschreibung eines Gesamtsystems (Beispiel)

Das System aus Beispiel 2 (falsche Lösung des 5-Philosophen-Problems, s [LS74]), kann beschrieben werden durch

- den σ - Teilsystem-Baustein (Matrix, z.B. Minimalmatrix),
- eine Kopplungsmatrix C_i für die Bausteine (Inzidenzmatrix) und
- die Markierung der geteilten Stellen M^* :

K^i_{TS} =

	t^i_1	t^i_2	t^i_3
t^i_1	∞	0	∞
t^i_2	∞	∞	0
t^i_3	1	∞	∞

(Verhalten eines Philosophen)

C_i =

	t^i_1	t^i_2	t^i_3
s_i mod 5	-1	0	+1
s_{i+1} mod 5	0	-1	+1
s_{i+2} mod 5	0	0	0
s_{i+3} mod 5	0	0	0
s_{i+4} mod 5	0	0	0

(Angabe, daß rechter und linker Nachbar die jeweils gleiche Gabel benutzen)

M^* =

s_1	1
s_2	1
s_3	1
s_4	1
s_5	1

(die 5 Gabeln liegen zu Beginn auf dem Tisch)

8. Schluß

Eine Methode wurde angegeben, wie zu Teilsystemen mit spezieller Struktur das Verhalten bestimmt werden kann. Man mußte dazu die Spielräume zwischen den Schnittstellentransitionen kennen.

Diese Methode kann Anwendung finden sowohl bei der Zusammensetzung größerer Systeme aus kleineren Bausteinen, als auch bei der Untergliederung schon vorhandener komplizierterer Systeme.

9. Literatur

[BE74] Best, Eike: Beiträge zur Petrinetz-Theorie, Diplomarbeit Karlsruhe 1974

[GL72] Genrich, H.J., Lautenbach, K.: Synchronisationsgraphen, Acta Informatica 2, 1972

[LS74] Lautenbach, K., Schmid, H.A.: Use of Petri Nets ..., IFIP Congress Stockholm 1974

INTRODUCING PARALLELISM INTO SEQUENTIAL PROGRAMS

Eike Hagen Riedemann
Abteilung Informatik
Universität Dortmund

I. Introduction

In recent years a number of models were developed to describe parallel processes.

Parallel program schemata (Karp/Miller /4/, Keller /5/) have a global control which regulates the execution of the various instructions of a program. Keller demonstrated the existence of a (parallel) closure (an equivalent, maximal parallel program schema) for any repetition-free sequential program (/5/, Theorem 3.6). It is an open problem whether or not the closure is realizable by a finite number of queues (stacks) but it is conjectured. A finite number of counters are not always sufficient to realize the closure (/5/, Theorem 4.7).

Stacks are used by Tjaden/Flynn /12/, Riseman/Foster /9/ and Urschler /14/. Tjaden/Flynn /13/, Baer/Russell /1/, Gonzales/Ramamoorthy /3/ and Reigel /8/ use counters in the form of matrices.

We put up with the limitations of counter realizations and use Petri nets which control the execution of program instructions in a local manner (cf. Shapiro/Saint/11/ and Roucairol /10/). Roucairol analyses programs where a value is assigned to a variable only once in a computation (single assignment) whereas we allow multiple assignment. We analyse and synthesize the data dependency and decision dependency of instructions in a way similar to Shapiro/Saint /11/ but we generalize the analysis of programs with multiple occurrence of the same instruction. Results concerning the correctness and completeness of transformations of parallel program schemata are transmitted to results about our special Petri nets.

Practical goals are considered in the last chapter.

II. Parallel and Sequential Flowcharts

Definition 2.1:

An operation set over V is a finite set OS of operations acting on a countable set V of variables together with the following for each $b \in OS$.

(i) finite ordered subsets OD(b) and OR(b) of V,
OD(b) and OR(b) are called the ordered domain or ordered range of b respectively,
D(b) and R(b) denote the corresponding unordered sets;

(ii) a nonempty finite set of unique symbols $TE(b) = \{b_1, \dots, b_{K(b)}\}$
called terminators or outcomes of b,
b is called decision or decision operation or test if $K(b) > 1$,
b is called data operation and b and b_1 are identified if $K(b) = 1$;

(iii) $b \in OS$ is a test iff $R(b) = \emptyset$.

In addition we define $TE := \bigcup_{b \in OS} TE(b)$ (set of all terminators),

$Op(T') := \{ b \in OS \mid \bigvee_i b_i \in T' \}$ (set of operations of T') if $T' \subset TE$.

The parallel execution of operations is modelled by a Petri net with a special interpretation.

Definition 2.2:

Let OS be an operation set.
A (parallel) flowchart F over OS is a quadruple $F = (N, m_o, M, g)$ where

(i) N is a Petri net $N = (P, TR, pre, post)$ where
P is a finite set of places, TR is a finite set of transitions,
$pre \subset P \times TR, post \subset P \times TR, P \cap TR = \emptyset$,

(ii) $m_o : P \rightarrow \mathbb{N}_o$ is the initial marking of N,

(iii) $M \subset \mathbb{N}_o^P$ is the (forward) marking class of m_o,

(iv) $g: TR \rightarrow TE$ is a partial mapping from TR to the set of all terminators of OS
with the following property for each transition t:
if $g(t) = b_i$ and b is a test
then there exists only one place p with $(p,t) \in pre$ and the set of all transitions t' with $(p,t') \in pre$ is the set of all terminators of b.

In addition we define for any $T' \subset TR$
$g(T') := \{ g(t) \mid t \in T' \}$ called the set of terminators corresponding to T'.

The reader is assumed to be familiar with the following terms:
active (enabled, firable) transition, simultaneously firable set of transitions (at a marking m), next marking obtained by firing a set of transitions, (forward) marking class of a marking m, dead marking, firing sequence, conflict, input place, output place of a transition, number of tokens etc.(/6/ and references of /6/).

Because of condition (iv) of Definition 2.2 there may be a conflict between all transitions which are mapped onto the set of terminators of a decision operation and which share a common input place. In contrast to ordinary Petri nets the transition which can fire if this input place is marked is determined namely by an interpretation of the decision operation and an assignment of the variables (cf. Definition 2.3). With this construction we can simulate test instructions of real programs. The resulting firing sequences determine via mapping g the executed instruction sequences (cf. Definition 2.8).

Definition 2.3:

An interpretation of an operation set OS over a set of variables V is a quadruple

$I = (A, a_0, F, G)$ where

(i) $A = \bigtimes_{v \in V} A(v)$ where A(v) is the set of values assignable to variable v,

(ii) $a_0 \in A$ is called the initial assignment,

(iii) $F = \{F_b \mid b \in OS\}$, $G = \{ G_b \mid b \in OS \}$ and for each $b \in OS$:

$$F_b: A(v_{i_1}) \times \ldots \times A(v_{i_{d(b)}}) \rightarrow A(v_{j_1}) \times \ldots \times A(v_{j_{r(b)}}),$$

$$G_b: A(v_{i_1}) \times \ldots \times A(v_{i_{d(b)}}) \rightarrow T(b) = \{ b_1, \ldots, b_{K(b)}\} ,$$

where $(v_{i_1}, \ldots, v_{i_{d(b)}}) = OD(b)$ and $(v_{j_1}, \ldots, v_{j_{r(b)}}) = OR(b)$;

F_b and G_b are called data (manipulation) function of b and decision function of b respectively.

In addition let Int(OS) denote the class of all interpretations of OS.

Definition 2.4:

Let OS and TR be an operation set and a set of transitions respectively.

(i) $\tilde{C} \subset OS \times OS$ is called conflict relation (over OS) iff

$$\tilde{C} = \{(b,c) \mid (R(b) \cap D(c)) \cup (R(c) \cap D(b)) \neq \emptyset \text{ or } R(b) \cap R(c) \neq \emptyset \text{ and } b \neq c \}.$$

(ii) $C := \tilde{C} \cup \{ (b,b) \mid b \in OS \}$ is called conflict relation too.

(iii) $C \subset TR \times TR$ is called conflict relation (over TR) iff

$$C = \{(u,t) \mid (Op(g(u)) , Op(g(t))) \in C \subset OS \times OS\}.$$

C is called conflict relation because operations b and c with $(b,c) \in C$ in general cause undefined or nondeterminate variable assignments if executed concurrent or in parallel.

Definition 2.5: (cf. Becker/Vogel /2/)

A parallel flowchart is called variable-compatible iff

$$\bigwedge_{m \in M} \bigwedge_{\{u,t\} \subset TR} (\{u,t\} \text{ simultaneously firable at } m \text{ implies } (u,t) \notin C).$$

In the following variable-compatible flowcharts are assumed.

Definition 2.6:

Let F be a parallel flowchart over OS, $I \in Int(OS)$.

(1) (m_o, a_o) is called initial configuration,

(2) $(m', a') = (m,a) \cdot U$ is called next configuration of (m,a) iff

(i) U is a set of transitions simultaneously firable at marking m,

(ii) m' is the next marking of m obtained by firing U,

(iii) for each $b_i \in g(U)$ where b is a test: $G_b(pr_{OD(b)}(a)) = b_i$,

(iv)
$$a'(v) = \begin{cases} a(v) & \text{if } v \notin \bigcup_{b_i \in g(U)} R(b) \\ pr_v(F_b(pr_{OD(b)}(a))) & \text{if } v \in R(b) \text{ for some } b_i \in g(U). \end{cases}$$

(3) Conf(F,I) is the smallest set S such that

(i) $(m_o, a_o) \in S$,

(ii) $(m,a) \in S$ implies $(m,a) \cdot U \in S$ if the latter is defined (cf.(2)).

(4) The partial mapping $\cdot$: $Conf(F,I) \times 2^{TR} \rightarrow Conf(F,I)$ is canonically extended to $Conf(F,I) \times (2^{TR})^*$.

Remark: $pr_{OD(b)}$ and pr_v are the projections of the variable set assignment onto the ordered domain of b and variable v respectively.

Definition 2.7:

A variable-compatible parallel flowchart F is called conflict free iff for each $I \in Int(OS)$ and $(m,b) \in Conf(F,I)$ there exists exactly one maximal set of transitions $U \subset TR$ such that $(m,b) \cdot U$ is defined.

Definition 2.8:

Let A^*, A^∞ denote the sets of strings over A of finite or (countable) infinite length; $A^\wedge := A^* \cup A^\infty$. If $x \in A^*$, $y \in A^\wedge$ let $x \leq y$ iff x is a prefix of y.

Let F be a variable-compatible parallel flowchart over OS, $I \in Int(OS)$.

(1) $t \in (2^{TR})^*$ is called firing sequence (of F at I) iff $(m_o, a_o) \cdot t$ is defined.

(2) $t \in (2^{TR})^\wedge$ is called complete firing sequence (of F at I) iff

(i) $(m_o, a_o) \cdot t = (m', a')$ contains a dead marking m' if t is finite,

(ii) each finite prefix t' of t is a firing sequence and an active transition in t cannot stay active forever without firing ultimately if t is of infinite length (finite delay property, cf. /4/, p. 152).

(3) $x \in (2^{TE})^\wedge$ is called (complete) I-computation for F produced by t iff t is (complete) firing sequence of F at I and $\bar{g}(t) = x$ where $\bar{g}$ is the canonical extension of g to strings over 2TE with $\bar{g}(U) = e =$ empty string if $g(U) = \emptyset$.

Comp(F,I) denotes the set of complete I-computations for F.

III. Introducing Parallelism - Terms, Theorems

Definition 3.1:

A sequential flowchart F over OS is a (parallel) flowchart $F=(N,m_o,M,g)$ over OS where

(1) the Petri net N is a state machine, i.e.

for all $t \in TR$: $|\{p|(p,t)\epsilon pre\}| = |\{p|(p,t)\epsilon post\}| = 1$,

(2) m_o maps exactly one place onto 1 and all other places onto 0,

(3) g: TR → TE is a total function where

for each $p\epsilon P; u,t\epsilon TR$: $(p,t)\epsilon pre$ and $(p,u)\epsilon pre$ imlies $Op(\{g(t)\})=Op(\{g(u)\})$.

To each sequential flowchart F corresponds a labeled directed graph G(F): the vertices are the places of the Petri net, an edge is directed from p to q with label g(t) iff $(p,t) \epsilon$ pre and $(q,t) \epsilon$ post.

Lemma 3.1: Let F be a sequential flowchart over OS, $I\epsilon Int(OS)$. Then $|Comp(F,I)| = 1$.

When we introduce parallelism into a sequential flowchart the resulting parallel flowchart shall execute the "same computations". By this we mean the traces of values stored in each variable during an I-computation (cf. /5/, Definition 2.2).

It is difficult to decide whether the "semantic" relation "equality of traces of values" exists between two I-computations. Therefore we introduce a "syntactic" equivalence relation in which the conflict relation C plays an important role.

Definition 3.2:

Let Comp(OS) be the set of complete I-computations for flowcharts over OS.

(1) Two elements x and y of Comp(OS) are called C-equivalent iff
for each pair (b,c) of data operations $(b,c)\epsilon C$ implies $x|TE(\{b,c\})=y|TE(\{b,c\})$
where $x|U$ denotes the string obtained by deleting all occurrences of elements of $TE\setminus U$ from x.

(2) Two flowcharts F and F' over OS are called C-equivalent iff
for each $I\epsilon Int(OS)$ the sets of C-equivalence classes of complete I-computations for F and F' are equal.

(3) A flowchart F over OS is called C-determinate iff
for each $I \epsilon Int(OS)$ the complete I-computations of F are C-equivalent.

Our definition of C-equivalence is weaker than Kellers E_p-equivalence (cf. /5/, Definition 2.5). Therefore the following Theorem strengthens Theorem 2.1 (1) presented in /5/, p. 522.

Theorem 3.1:

Let F be a C-determinate flowchart over OS. Then for each $I \epsilon Int(OS)$, $v \epsilon V$ the traces of values stored in variable v during different complete I-computations for F are equal.

Proof(idea): Let x and y be I-computations for F which are C-equivalent by hypothesis. There is a one-to-one ordering preserving mapping between corresponding occurrences of a data operation b in x and y and pairs (b,c) of data operations with $R(b) \cap R(c) \neq \emptyset$ in x and y since $(b,b) \in C$ and $(b,c) \in C$. Hence the trace of values stored in a variable during x or y respectively is produced by the same operations.

It remains to demonstrate that the n-th occurrence of a data operation b in x stores the same values in R(b) as the n-th occurrence of data operation b in y.

The assumption of a "least offender" implies a contradiction.

q.e.d.

With the following we may justify the requirement of variable-compatible flowcharts.

Lemma 3.2:

Let F be a flowchart (not necessarily variable-compatible).
If there exists a sequential flowchart F' such that F and F' are C-equivalent then F is C-determinate and variable-compatible.

We conjecture that the converse of Theorem 3.1 (constance of the traces of values implies C-determinacy) is true even if F is only "repetition-free"(cf. /5/, Def. 2.8). The requirement of "losslessness" (i.e. $R(b) \neq \emptyset$ for each $b \in OS$ - for tests too, cf. Keller, /5/, Theorem 2.1 (3)) seems to be unnecessary.

If some variables are used only to store provisional results which do not contribute to the computation of output values we need not require the constance of the traces of values for these variables. Operations which are not "(weak) productive" (cf. Linderman,/7/, Chapter 8) could be deleted in this case. We deal with productive operations only, i.e. each variable can be treated as an output variable.

Definition 3.3:

Let F and F' be flowcharts over OS.

(1) F is called more parallel than F' iff
 (i) F and F' are C-equivalent,
 (ii) for each $I \in Int(OS)$: $Comp(F',I) \subsetneq Comp(F,I)$.

(2) F is called maximal parallel iff
 no flowchart is more parallel than F.

(3) F is called (parallel) closure of F' iff
 (i) F and F' are C-equivalent,
 (ii) F is maximal parallel.

Maximal parallelism and the conflict relation C are associated in a way outlined below (F is assumed to be conflict-free and C-determinate in the following).

Definition 3.4:

Let t be a firing sequence for F at an interpretation I ϵ Int(OS).

(1) Active(t) := Op(g(U))

where U is the maximal set of transitions which are simultaneously firable in F after the firing of t.

(2) Ready(t) := set of operations b ϵ OS $\setminus$ Active(t) such that

for each complete firing sequence z of F at any I' ϵ Int(OS) with prefix t there exists y such that

(i) $t < y \leq z$,

(ii) b ϵ Active(y)

(iii) $\{c \mid (b,c) \in C\} \cap \bigcup_{t<tu<y} \text{Active}(tu) = \emptyset$.

Ready(t) is the set of operations b which are ultimately activated if t is extended to a complete firing sequence z (at any interpretation) and which are not yet activated by t although there is no C-conflict with operations which are firable before b.

Definition 3.5:

A flowchart F is called globally complete iff

for each firing sequence t of F at any I ϵ Int(OS):

Ready(t) = $\emptyset$.

Theorem 3.2:

F is globally complete iff F is maximal parallel.

The proof of this theorem is omitted because it is analogous to that of Keller (/5/, Theorem 3.3).

IV. Introducing Parallelism - Method

The method is simple for a decision-free sequential flowchart F. Such a flowchart defines exactly one complete computation x independent of the interpretation chosen.

In a parallel closure of F all sequences y have to be allowed which are C-equivalent to x, i.e. all sequences in which operations b and c (where $(b,c) \in C$) appear in the same order and equally often as in x.

These orderings are described by C-chains.

Definition 4.1:

Let x and y be elements of $TR^{\wedge}$, $x = x_1x_2 \ldots$, $y = y_1y_2 \ldots$.

(1) x is called division of y iff there exists an indexing $i: \mathbb{N} \rightarrow \mathbb{N}$ where $k < l$ implies $i(k) < i(l)$ and $x_j = y_{i(j)}$, $j = 1,2,\ldots$.

(2) x is called C-chain of y iff
  (i) x is a division of y of length $l(x)$,
  (ii) $(Op(g(x_i)) , Op(g(x_{i+1}))) \in C$, $i = 1,2,\ldots,l(x)-1$,

(3) x is called maximal C-chain of y iff
  (i) x is C-chain of y,
  (ii) for each $x' \in TR^{\wedge}$: x' is C-chain of y and x is division of x' implies $x=x'$.

Construction 4.1:

Let x be the unique complete firing sequence of a decision-free sequential flowchart F over OS.
Define a parallel flowchart F_p over OS with the same set of transitions TR and the same mapping $g: TR \rightarrow TE$. For each pair of transitions u and t where t is a direct successor of u in a maximal C-chain of x there is a place q in F_p with $(q,u) \in post$ and $(q,t) \in pre$.

Theorem 4.1: F_p is the parallel closure of F.

Example 4.1:

G(F): $\bullet \xrightarrow[t_1]{b} \bullet \xrightarrow[t_2]{c} \bullet \xrightarrow[t_3]{d} \bullet \xrightarrow[t_4]{e} \bullet \xrightarrow[t_5]{b} \bullet \xrightarrow[t_6]{f} \bullet \xrightarrow[t_7]{h} \bullet$

$\tilde{C} = \{ (b,d), (e,f), (c,d), (d,b), (f,e), (d,c) \}$ if we assume corresponding intersections of the domains and ranges of the operations.

This implies the following maximal C-chains of F:

$t_1t_3t_5$, $t_2t_3t_5$, t_4t_6, t_7 .

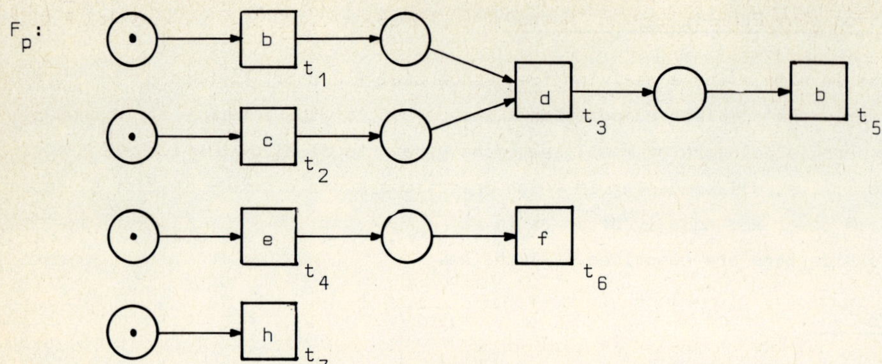

For a specific I-computation of a sequential flowchart <u>with decision operations</u> the order of operations b and c such that (b,c) ϵ C has to be preserved in a more parallel flowchart too.

Therefore we have to consider each possible I-computation, i.e. each sequence of transitions along a path which begins at the starting vertex of G(F), and compute the maximal C-chains (perhaps too many sequences are considered if F is not repetition-free). Besides the ordering relations derived from the maximal C-chains we have to consider the "decision-dependency" of operators, i.e. in general it depends on the outcome of decision operations whether members of C-chains appear in a specific computation.

<u>Construction 4.2</u>:

For each transition t consider all transitions $t_1,\dots,t_k$ which are direct predecessors of t in any maximal C-chain. The reason of the data conflict may be specified more precisely by relations WR_v, RW_v and WW_v which specify whether for a pair (t_i,t) of transitions variable v is read(R) or written upon(W) by $Op(g(t_i))$ or $Op(g(t))$ respectively.

For each t_i where $(t_i,t) \epsilon WR_v$ there has to be a common place p with $(p,t) \epsilon$ pre. If t is fired after t_i in any case without a transition t_j with $(t_j,t) \epsilon WR_v$ being active before then $(p,t_i) \epsilon$ post too. If this is not the case the "minimal sufficient condition" q (see below) is to be determined at which t is active after t_i has fired. t_i and u have to be synchronized with a transition t_s before place p.

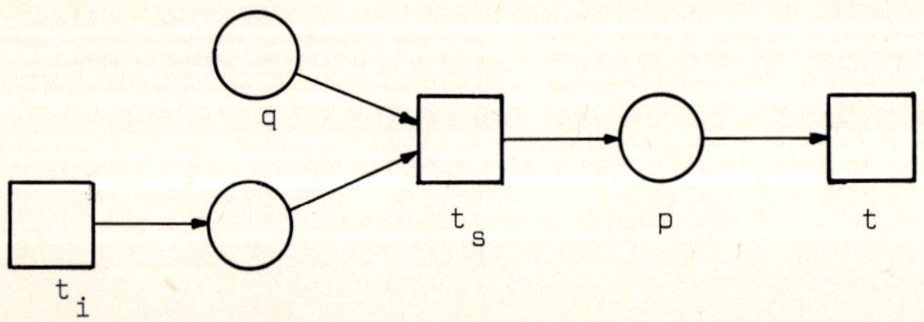

This construction corresponds to the right part of the "variable generation-use" nets of Shapiro/Saint (/11/, p.49).

The other parts of these nets are derived for the transitions in relation RW_v and WW_v respectively.

Since we introduced places whose markings are incremented by 1 if a decision operation b terminates with b_i the possibility of realizing the parallel closure of a sequential flowchart by Petri nets is limited (cf. Chapter I):
If b_i belongs to a loop which contains an operation c not being in C-conflict with any operation of the loop then decision b may take place once more with a different outcome b_j without c being executed. For the parallel closure to work correctly, i.e. produce only C-equivalent computations, the storing of the sequence (ordering) of terminators b_i and b_j is in general necessary. But this is not possible in a Petri net if arbitrary long sequences have to be stored.

Analysis of decision-dependency

Example 4.2: Consider the following sequential flowchart F or G(F) respectively:

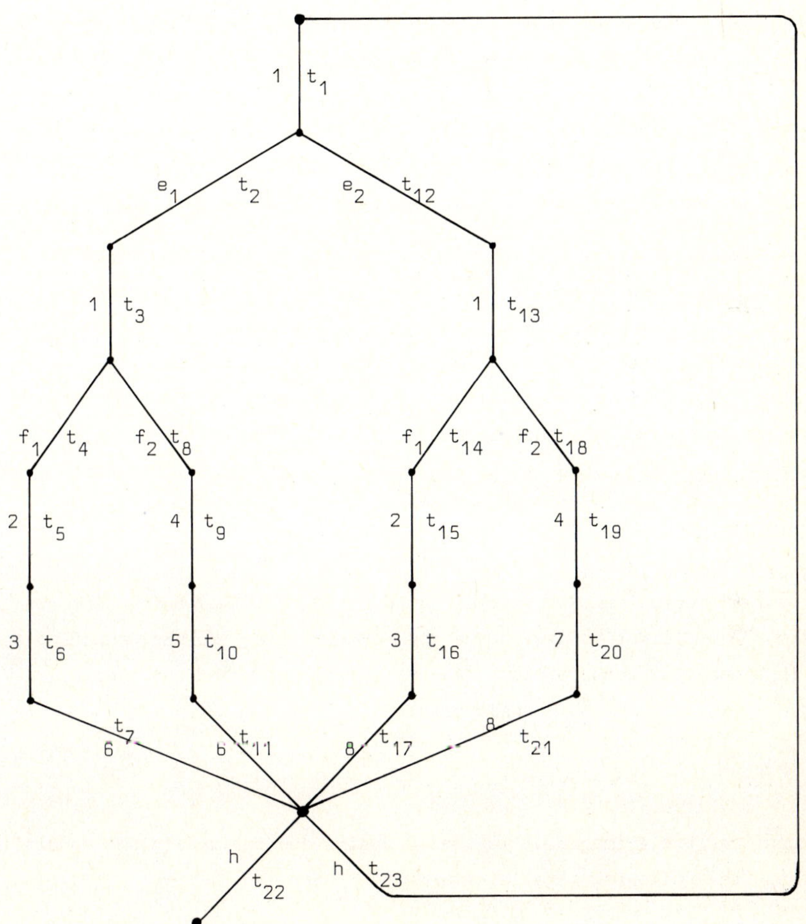

Let $V \supset \{A, B, C\}$, $C = WR_A \cup WR_B \cup WR_C$ where
$WR_A = \{(2, 6), (4, 6), (2, 8), (4, 8)\}$,
$WR_B = \{(3, 6), (5, 6), (3, 8), (7, 8)\}$,
$WR_C = \{(6, h), (8, h)\}$.
The $\bar{g}$-images of maximal C-chains (without cycles relative to TR) are:
26h, 36h, 46h, 56h, 28h, 38h, 48h, 78h, 11.
Sufficient conditions are e.g.:
$\emptyset$ MSC $\{1, e, f, h\}$, $\{e_2, 3\}$ and $\{7\}$ SC $\{8\}$, $\{f_1\}$ MSC $\{2, 3\}$,
$\{h_2\}$ MSCR $\{1, e, f, h\}$, $\{e_1, f_2\}$ MSC $\{5\}$, $\{f_2\}$ MSC $\{4\}$,
$\{e_1, 3\}$ and $\{5\}$ SC $\{6\}$, $\{e_2, f_2\}$ MSC $\{7\}$.

Remarks:

(1) A place p with (initial) marking m(p) is figured by a circle holding m(p) "tokens".

(2) Transition t_7 fires iff t_4 (and not t_8) has fired; t_{11} fires in the inverse case. If t_7 and t_{11} were realized seperately these dependencies have to be preserved. Since operation 6 corresponds to both t_7 and t_{11} it is not dependent on the outcomes of decision f which correspond to t_4 and t_8.

(3) t_{10} fires in any case if t_8 has fired; this is not true for corresponding outcomes 5 and f_2. After f_2 operation 5 is not executed if f_2 was initiated by t_{18}. The distinction is provided by the terminators of e: After e_1 and f_2 operation 5 is always executed. $\{e_1, f_2\}$ is called minimal sufficient condition for the activation of 5 since no subset of $\{e_1, f_2\}$ guarantees the activation of 5. Since e_1 and f_2 can be executed concurrently we have increased the parallelism which would not be achieved if we had treated the transitions seperately.

(4) $\{h_2\}$ is sufficient for the activation of e, the "empty set of conditions" is sufficient too. Nevertheless $\{h_2\}$ is called minimal sufficient condition (namely) for the re-activation of e since after the unconditional first execution of e a further execution of e is only possible if decision h terminates with outcome h_2.

The above introduced terms "sufficient condition", "minimal sufficient condition" and "(minimal) sufficient condition for the re-activation" for an operation to be executed in a parallel computation can be defined as relations over $2^{TR} \times 2^{OS}$ and are denoted by SC, MSC and MSCR respectively.

If we consider the $\bar{g}$-images of maximal C-chains and the sufficient conditions for activations the following parallel flowchart F_p results.

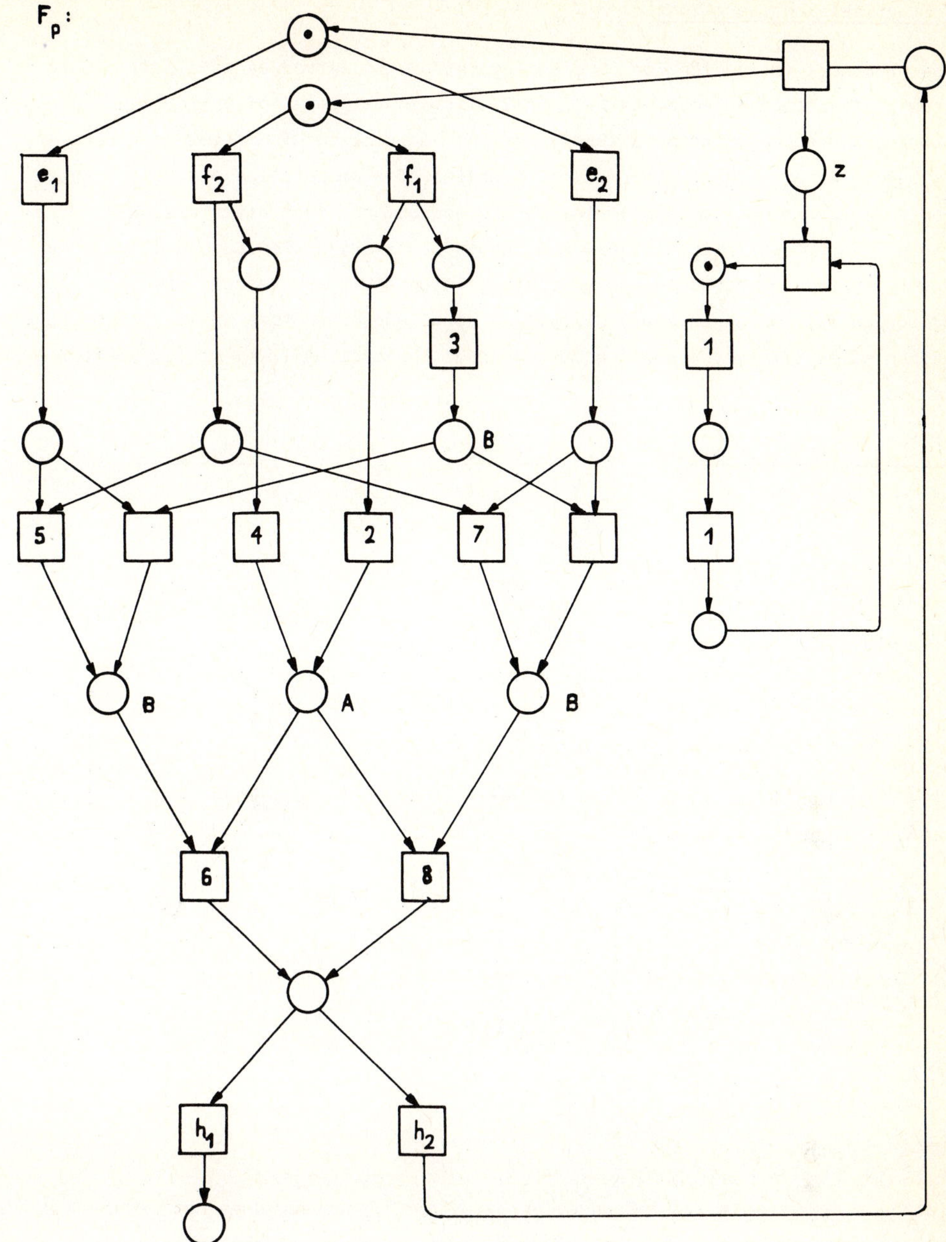

Remarks:

(1) The places which are labeled with A or B signal the availability of the new values of variable A or B respectively.

(2) If operation 1 is very slow the place with label z will hold more than one (arbitrary many!) tokens. The full counter property can be used in this example although the Petri net is not "safe" (cf. /6/).

V. Practical Considerations

The practical motivation for considering methods to introduce parallelism into programs is not to achieve maximal parallelism in the sense of Definition 3.3 but increasing the speed of computations under the restriction of limited resources.

If bcdg, beg and bfg are the maximal C-chains of a computation bcdefg and there are only two processors available to execute operations then after execution of b the three "ready" operations c, e and f cannot be executed simultaneously. If the operating system may schedule the operations in an arbitrary manner then the choice {e,f} would imply an unnecessary delay: the total execution time would be 5 operation execution times (if they are all equal) whereas the choices {c,e} or {c,f} after b would imply 4 time units.

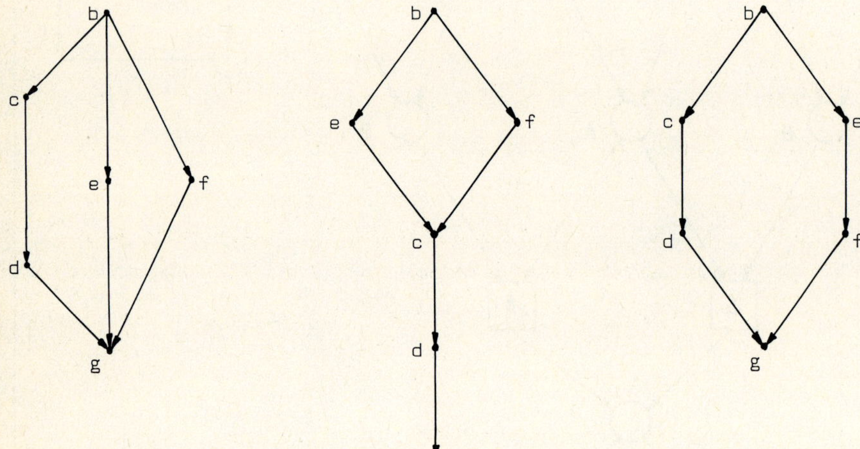

In the above example the introduction of a third processor does not reduce the total execution time of 4 units although the maximal parallel realization cannot be implemented with two processors. In other cases the introduction of an additional processor reduces the total execution time only by a relative small amount. Criteria have to be developed which tell whether the introduction of extra parallelism is advantageous.

"Blocks" of operators of almost equal execution times can then be executed in parallel by a simple FORK/JOIN-synchronizing which reduces the control overhead.

References:

/1/ Baer, J.L. / Russell, E.C.: Preparation and Evaluation of Computer Programs for Parallel Processing Streams, in L.C. Hobbs (Editor): Parallel Processor Systems, Technologies, Application, Spartan, Washington,(1970), 375-415.

/2/ Becker, H.J. / Vogel, H.: E-V-Schemata - Ein Ansatz zur formalen Behandlung paralleler Prozesse, Lecture Notes in Computer Science 26, GI-4.Jahrestagung, Springer, Berlin, (1975), 345-354.

/3/ Gonzalez, M.J. / Ramamoorthy, C.V.: Recognition and Representation of Parallel Processable Streams in Computer Programs, in L.C. Hobbs (cf./1/), 335-373.

/4/ Karp, R.M. / Miller, R.E.: Parallel Program Schemata, J. Computer and System Sciences 3,2 (May 1969), 147-195.

/5/ Keller, R.M.: Parallel Program Schemata and Maximal Parallelism, J.ACM 20 (1973), 514-537, 696-710.

/6/ Lautenbach, K.: Exakte Bedingungen der Lebendigkeit für eine Klasse von Petri-Netzen, Berichte der GMD Nr. 82, Bonn, (1973).

/7/ Linderman, J.P.: Productivity in Parallel Computation Schemata, MIT, Project MAC, Report Nr. MAC TR-111, (Dec. 1973).

/8/ Reigel, E.W.: Parallelism Exposure and Exploitation, in L.C. Hobbs (cf. /1/), 417-438.

/9/ Riseman, E.M. / Foster, C.C.: The Inhibition of Potential Parallelism by Conditional Jumps, IEEE Trans. Computers C-21, 12 (Dec. 1972), 1405-1411.

/10/ Roucairol, G.: Transformation d'un programme sequentiel en programme parallele parfait, Les Actes du colloque sur la programmation, Springer, Paris, (April 1974), 231-234.

/11/ Shapiro, R.M. / Saint, H.: The Representation of Algorithms, Applied Data Research Inc., Final Techn.Report, RADC-TR-69-313, Vol 2 (1969).

/12/ Tjaden, G. / Flynn, M.J.: Detection and Parallel Execution of Independent Instructions, IEEE Trans. Computers C-19, 10 (Oct. 1970), 889-895.

/13/ Tjaden, G. / Flynn, M.J.: Representation of Concurrency with Ordering Matrices, IEEE Trans. Computers C-22, 8 (Aug. 1973), 752-761.

/14/ Urschler, G.: The Transformation of Flow Diagrams into Maximally Parallel Form, Sagamore Computer Conference on Parallel Processing,(1973), 38-46.

G R U N D L A G E N   D E R
P R O G R A M M I E R U N G

WELL FORMED PROGRAMS OPTIMAL WITH RESPECT TO STRUCTURAL COMPLEXITY

Giorgio De Michelis
Carla Simone

Gruppo di Elettronica e Cibernetica, Istituto di Fisica,
Università di Milano, Via Viotti, 5 20133 Milano.

Abstract

A measure of the complicacy of a program can be given considering the minimum number of exits of iterative blocks needed in order to write a program strongly equivalent to the given one.
On the basis of such intuitive notion we introduce in the paper a measure of the "structural complexity" of programs.
This complexity for arbitrary programs can be evaluated by constructing suitable well formed programs. The definition of well formedness is presented and it is shown to be a modification of the one given by Peterson, Kasami and Tokura. On the basis of the above definitions we present an algorithm to construct well formed programs and we prove that the notion of well formedness introduced is well founded.

1) Introduction

The notion of well formed program has been introduced in 1973 by Peterson, Kasami and Tokura [1] . In that paper the authors define as well formed a program in which "loops and if statements are properly nested and can be entered only at their beginning". The importance of such a definition is showed by the theorem that states that every program can be converted by node splitting to a well formed program. Therefore every program by the reduced to a strongly equivalent one which is written with only if, repeat and multilevel exit statements. The reduction algorithm presented by Peterson, Kasami and Tokura is such that the well formed program that they generate is optimal w.r.t. node splitting.
We think that reduction to well formed programs can not have any utility in producing efficient structured programs because it does not involve programming methodology; and because the programs that we obtain by such a reduction algorithm, become less transparent (the example presented in [1] needs repeat-statements which do not play any effective role in computation) also if they gain in structure.
The notion of well formed program, on the contrary, can be an important tool in the analysis of the structure of programs. It can be seen in fact, as a result of the analysis of the structural complexity of a program, if the well formed program that we obtain is built up with the simplest control structures as possible.
In this paper, therefore, we give a classification of control structures by means of their "expressive power", i.e. on the basis of the classes of program schemata that we can build up with them.
We show also that, given any of these classes, it is possible to generate the class of program schemata strongly equivalent to the program schemate of the given class.
Afterwards we give a new definition of "well formed" program, different

from the one proposed by Peterson, Kasami and Tokura: a program is well formed if and only if it uses control structures of the least expressi ve power.
Therefore, given any program, it is possible to build up a well formed program strongly equivalent to it thanks to the constructivness of the above mentioned definitions. The greatest value of the expressive power of control structures used in the well formed program can be assumed as a measure of the "structural complexity" of the original program, i.e. as a measure of the complicacy of the control-flow of the algorithm expressed by the program.
As in [2], the analysis is carried out on the equation system which describes the given program, but the methodology is quite different in that we consider mainly, not the syntactic structure of the system equations, but the calling graph related to it.

2) Expressive power of control structures.

Every iterative statement introduced in existing Programming Languages or proposed in the literature exprimes in a sequential Language a well specified control structure.
As an example the for-statements of Algol 60 (or the equivalent loop statements in Pascal, PL/1 etc.) are different instances of the following control structure

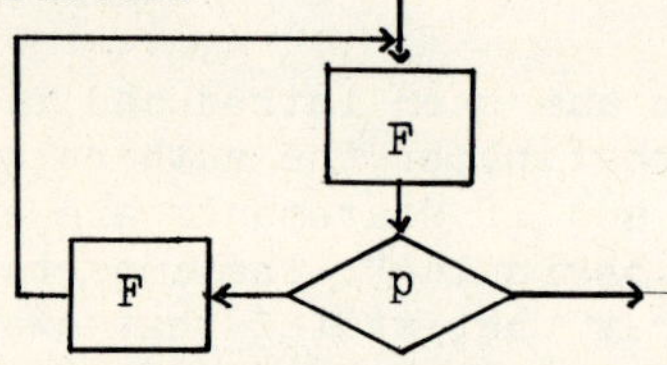

the D-control structure.

Figure 1

In the same way the iterative statement

<label> : repeat.....leave <label> ..... end

proposed in BLISS by Wulf [3] , is an instance of the very much more general RE control structure*, which defines an iterative block with one entry point and a finite and arbitrary number of exit points at different levels.
We can generate a different class of program schemata (flow charts) for each control structure we know.
For example, if we consider the above examples, we have the following two definitions.

Def. 1 D-schemata

1) Every basic function $\rightarrow \boxed{f_i} \rightarrow$ $(1 \leq i \leq n)$ is a D schema.

---

* In a forth coming paper Lanzarone and the authors [4] analyze the differences between control structures which define a precise flow of the control (as the D-control structure) and control environments which indicate only the connections between the blocks (as the RE-control environment).

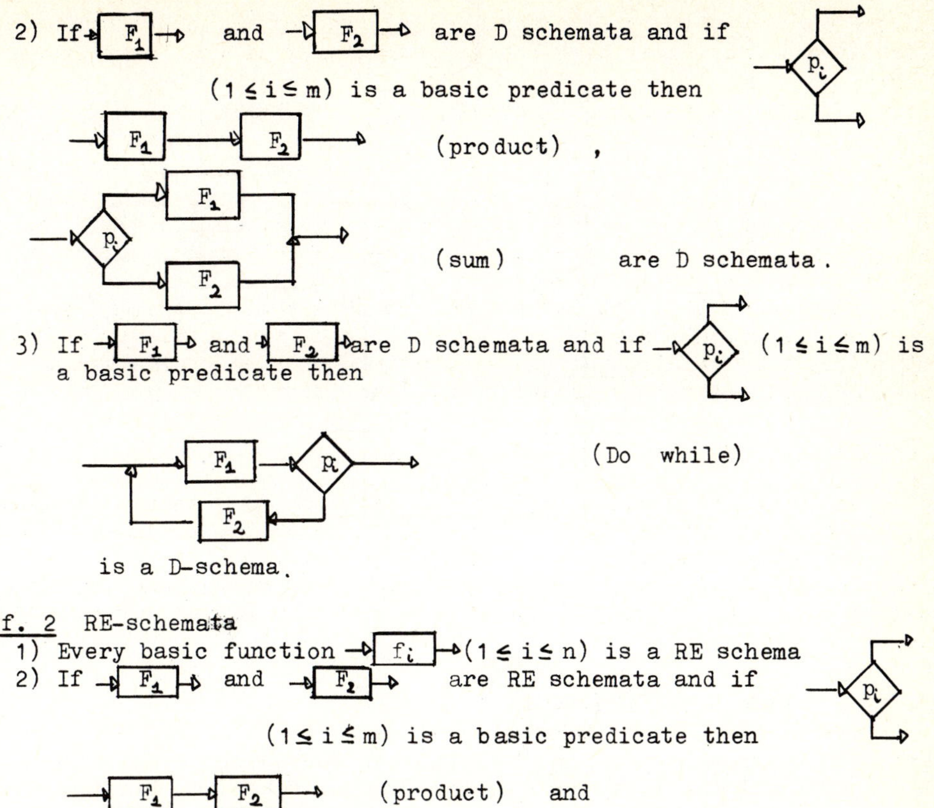

2) If $\to$ F_1 $\to$ and $\to$ F_2 $\to$ are D schemata and if p_i $(1 \leq i \leq m)$ is a basic predicate then

$F_1 \to F_2$ (product) ,

(sum) are D schemata .

3) If $\to$ F_1 $\to$ and $\to$ F_2 $\to$ are D schemata and if p_i $(1 \leq i \leq m)$ is a basic predicate then

(Do while)

is a D-schema.

Def. 2 RE-schemata

1) Every basic function $\to$ f_i $\to$ $(1 \leq i \leq n)$ is a RE schema

2) If $\to$ F_1 $\to$ and $\to$ F_2 $\to$ are RE schemata and if p_i $(1 \leq i \leq m)$ is a basic predicate then

$F_1 \to F_2$ (product) and

(sum) are RE-schemata.

3) Every composition of RE schemata and basic predicates such that all the iterative blocks occurring in it have only one entry point and a finite and arbitrary number of exit points at different levels, is a RE-schema.

It is obvious that for every different control structure we can define such a class of program schemata.

It is also easy to prove that the classes of program schemata generated as above are different.

Let us return to the two above examples. If we call D ps and RE ps the two classes generated respectively by means of the D control structure and of the RE control structure we have

$$Dps \subsetneq REps$$

because the clause 3) of Def. 2 contains as subcase the clause 3) of Def. 1 and because the following program schema:

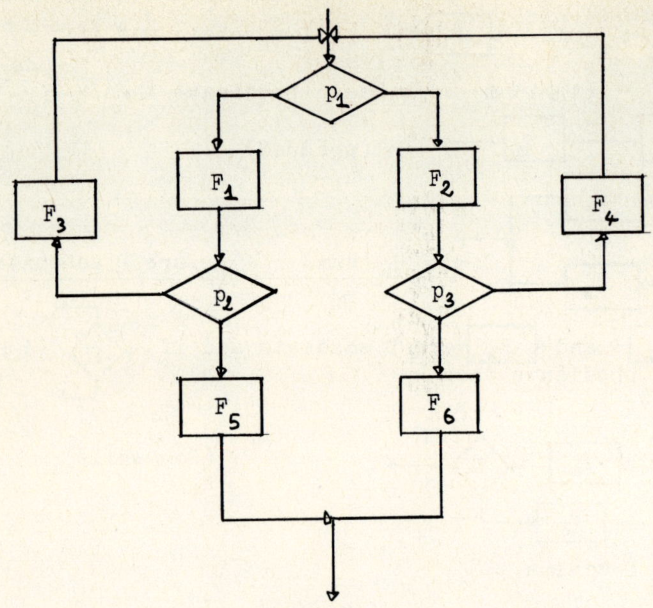

Figure 2

is a RE schema but not a D schema.
We are interested in the set of algorithms that may be written down in a specific Programming Language or, that is the same, by means of a well determined control structure. The Program schemata classes introduced above have to be interpreted as equivalence classes with respect to wider classes of program schemata-: that is, for every class built up by means of a given control structure γ , we can define the class $\mathcal{G}(\gamma)$ of program schemata strongly equivalent to a schema of the given class. It follows that, $\mathcal{G}(\gamma)$ contains the γ schemata class.
Returning to the two examples, we call therefore $\mathcal{G}(D)$ the class of program schemata strongly equivalent to a D program schema, and $\mathcal{G}(RE)$ the class of program schemata strongly equivalent to a RE program schema. The two classes just defined are also different. It is well known (Böhm Jacopini [5]) that the following program schema

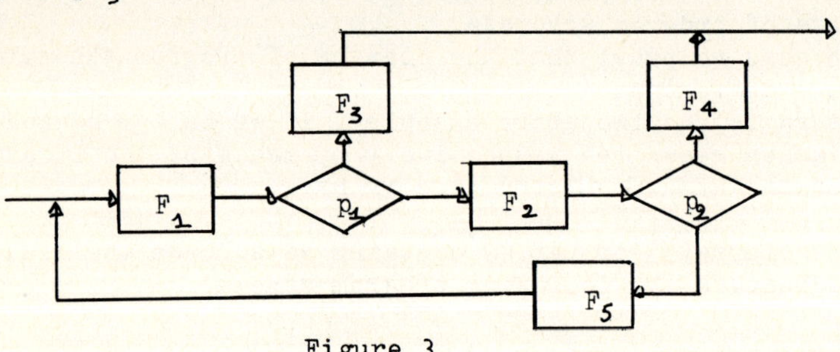

Figure 3

does not belong to the class $\mathcal{G}(D)$ and (Peterson Kasami Tokura [1]) that every program schema belongs to the class $\mathcal{G}(RE)$; therefore the following relation holds

$$\mathcal{G}(D) \subsetneq \mathcal{G}(RE)$$

Given a control structure γ, we can assume as a measure of its expressive power (i.e. its capability of expressing algorithms) a measure of the wideness of the class $\mathcal{G}(\gamma)$. In this way we can give a classification of control structures on the basis of their expressive power, in term of a growing sequence of program schemata classes. In the literature there have been defined two main classes of iterative control structures, which cover all the iterative statements proposed in Programming Languages: the $\{\Omega_n\}$ class and the $\{RE_n\}$ class.
The first one of them, the $\{\Omega_n\}$ class has been introduced by Böhm Jacopini [5] . For every n, the Ω_n control structure is the following:

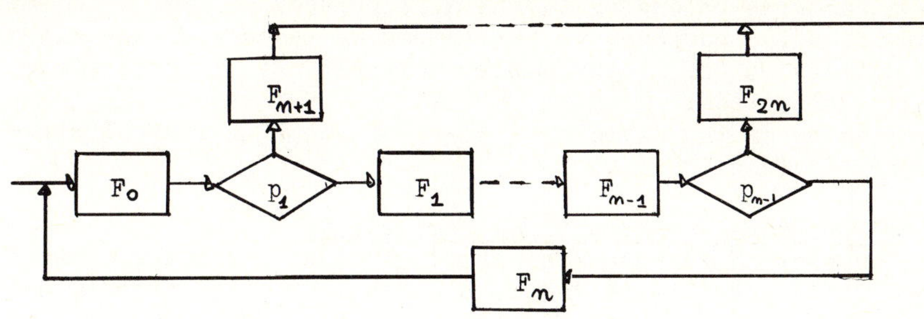

Figure 4

Let us note that the Ω_1 control structure is the above mentioned D control structure, and that the following relation holds (as conjectured by Böhm Jacopini [5] and proved by Kosaraju [6])

$$\mathcal{G}(\Omega_n) \subsetneq \mathcal{G}(\Omega_{n+1})$$

and we do not spend more words about it (For more details about this class see [2]).
The second class of control structures mentioned above, the $\{RE_n\}$ class has been introduced by Kosaraju [6] . For every n, the RE_n control structure is defined as an iterative block with one entry point and n exit points at different levels. The iterative statement introduced by Wirth in his version of Algol W [7]

<u>Repeat</u> .... <u>exit</u> .... <u>end</u>

is, as it is easy to see, an instance of the RE_1 control structure.
If we call BJ_g the limit of the sequence of classes of program schemata $\{\mathcal{G}(\Omega_n)\}$ [2] that is the class of program schemata that we can build up by means of Ω_n control structure (for every n), it is easy to prove that the following relation holds:

$$BJ_g \subsetneq \mathcal{G}(RE_1)$$

In fact the program schema illustrated in Figure 2, is a RE_1 program schema, but we can not solve the two symmetric loops in a single loop with a finite number of convergent exits , without to introduce new variables or new functional blocks, and therefore it does not belong to BJ_g .

Kosaraju [6] proved that for every n

$$\mathcal{G}(RE_n) \subsetneq \mathcal{G}(RE_{n+1})$$

and therefore the class $\{RE_n\}$, as the class $\{\Omega_n\}$ are both ordered with respect to expressive power.

It is easy to see that the limit of the sequence of classes of program schemata $\{\mathcal{G}(RE_n)\}$ is the above mentioned $\mathcal{G}$(RE) class. Therefore the fact that $\mathcal{G}$(RE) is the class of all program schemata guarantees that control structures of the class $\{RE_n\}$ allow to cover all possible algorithms. For this reason we restrict our attention to this second class, that we assume as classification parameter of control structures.

The relation $BJ_g \subsetneq \mathcal{G}(RE_1)$

allows us, if we want it, to introduce further more precise analysis to classify structures belonging to the $\{\Omega_n\}$ class.

For our classification purposes we can assume as measure of the wideness of the classes $\mathcal{G}(RE_n)$ the number n itself. We give therefore the following definition:

Def. 3: The measure of the expressive power of the RE_n control structure (for every n) is n itself.

3) Well formed programs and structural complexity.

In the previous section we have seen that, given an iterative control structure γ it is possible to define a class $\mathcal{G}(\gamma)$ of program schemata strongly equivalent to a schema built up using such a control structure.

Our purpose is now to answer the following question: given a program, which is the minimal n such that the class $\mathcal{G}(RE_n)$ contains the schema relative to the program itself? or, what is the same, how we can characterize the program schemata belonging to the $\mathcal{G}(RE_n)$ class (for every n) ? If we can solve this problem, we make the classes definition fully constructive, since the same problem for the classes $\mathcal{G}(\Omega_n)$ was solved in [2] .

We prove that the problem is decidable, by giving a method to determine such a minimal class.

The method we propose, consists of two parts: firstly, we construct the program schema relative to the given program and the equations system which describes it; secondly, we analyze the calling graph of such a system.

We suppose the program written in a generic programming language. Hence the program may contain in general, declarations, input/output statements, predicates, control and basic statements.

As we have seen in the previous section, the classes $\mathcal{G}(RE_n)$ are defined on the basis of the control structures, used in constructing a program. This fact suggests that the only information we need to solve any problem is contained in the control flow of the program. In other words, we can ignore the interpretation of predicates, basic functions, declarations, etc.. Therefore generating the program schema relative to a given program we ignore declarations and I/O statements, we associate a functional block →[F_i]→ ($i \geq 0$) to every assignment statement, a decisional block →◇P_j ($j \geq 0$) to every predicate and we let correspond to each control statement (like goto, dowhile, if then else etc.) the usual representation in term of flow chart.

As an example to the following Algol program(Knuth [8])

```
          procedure treeprint (t) ; integer t ; value t ;
          begin integer array S [1:n] ; integer k ; k := 0 ;
      L1 :   while t ≠ 0 do
                    k : = k + 1 ; S [k] : = t ;
                    t : = L [t] ; go to L1 ;
      L2 :          t : = S [k] ; k : = k - 1 ;
                    print (A [t] ) ;
                    t : = R [t] ;
             end ;
             if  k ≠ 0 then go to L2 fi ;
             end
```

we associate the following program schema

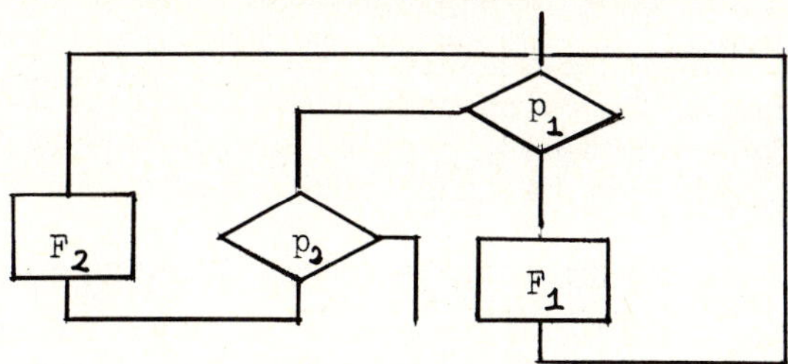

Figure 5

The program schema contains still more information we need, since the functional blocks play role in the control flow analysis. The reason why we need the program schema is that we must be able after our analysis, to build up a new program, strongly equivalent to the original one, and therefore we need to know the matching between blocks and statements.
We further simplify the schema by costructing its skeleton : that is, by ignoring all functional blocks . The skeleton of the previous schema is therefore the following:

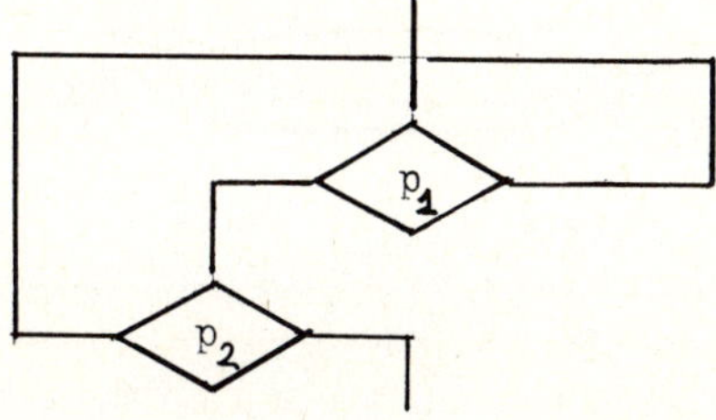

Figure 6

The given program is at this point represented by a simplified flow chart. The equations system, which describes it, can be built up on the basis of the skeleton, using any one of the well known algorithms appeared in the literature. As an example the equations system relative to the above program is the following

$$\begin{cases} d_1 = \underline{\text{if}}\ p_1\ \underline{\text{then}}\ d_1\ \underline{\text{else}}\ (\text{if}\ p_2\ \underline{\text{then}}\ d_2) \\ d_2 = d_1 \end{cases}$$

The analysis of the whole equation system will be carried out on its maximal independent components, so that we must isolate them (by means, for example, of the well known Maggiolo - Strong algorithm [9]).
We call such manipulated system, normalized.
We need now some definitions about equations system.

Def. 4 : Given an equation system

$$\begin{cases} d_1 = f_1\ (d_1,\dots,d_n) \\ \dots \\ d_n = f_n\ (d_1,\dots,d_n) \end{cases}$$

we call d_1 the principal function name and calling graph associated to it the oriented graph, whose nodes are the function names and in which there is an edge from node d_i to node d_j iff the right part of the equation, whose left part is d_i, contains the function name d_j.

Def. 5 : Given an equation system we associate to it a connection tree, whose root is the principal function name, and such that every node is father of all the function names, that occurr in the right part of the equation whose left part is that node itself, and are not its ancestors.

As an example the calling graph associated to the following equation system:

$$\begin{cases} d_1 = f_1\ (d_1,\ d_2,\ d_3,\ d_4,\ I) \\ d_2 = f_2\ (d_1,\ d_2,\ d_3,\ d_4,\ I) \\ d_3 = f_3\ (d_1,\ d_3,\ d_4) \\ d_4 = f_4\ (d_2,\ d_3,\ d_4) \end{cases}$$

is the following:

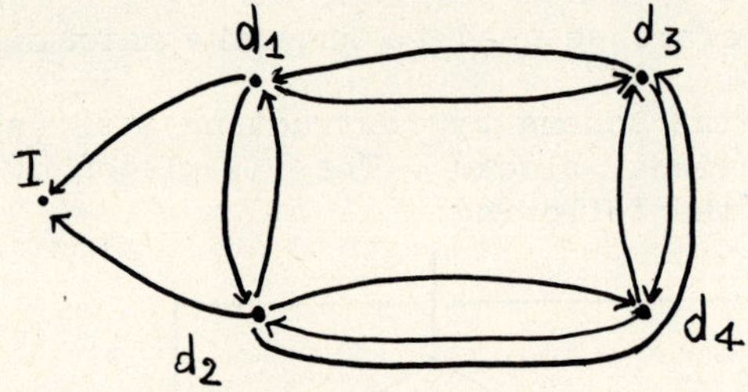

Figure 7

and the connection tree associated to it is the following:

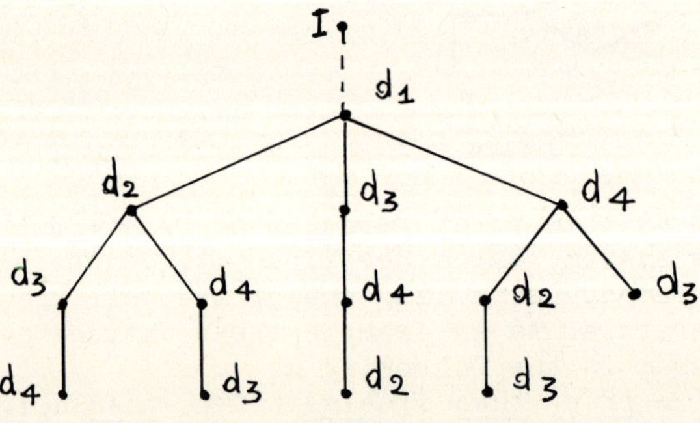

Figure 8

Remark 1: The node I corresponding to the occurrences of the identity function in the equations, has a special behaviour. In fact in the calling graph there are only edges arriving to I and not starting from I, and in the connection tree, it is placed in a particular position, i.e. it is over the root of the tree connected by a special edge.
Such a position is caused by the fact that the identity function corresponds to the end of the computation sequences in the component equations, and therefore it is a node somehow called by the whole component.
Now we can define a family of classes of equations systems, the classes of equations systems of type n (n integer).

Def. 6 : An equation system is of type n, if n is the smallest integer such that all the independent components of the normalized system are of type n.

Remark 2 : For sake of simplicity, in the equations of every component we substitute the identity function for all the occurrences of functions names which are not left part of the component equations. As emphasized in [2] such simplifications do not modify the result of the analysis.

Def. 7 : A component of an equation system is of type n if:

a) it contains at most n equations;
b) it contains $m > n$ equations and its calling graph is of type n;
c) it contains $m > n$ equations and its calling graph can be transformed by espansion into a calling graph of type n.

Def. 8 : A calling graph of an equation system is of type n if we can translate it into a finite tree such that:

1) the identity function I is the root.
2) the root I is connected only with the principal function name d_1 of the equation system.
3) To every node d_i is associated a set of function names $d_{i_1}, \ldots, d_{i_t}$ with $t \leq n$ (memory) every one of which occurring in a path connecting d_i to I. Such a memory is composed of the memories of the sons of d_i (in which the occurrences of d_i are erased) and of function names that occur in the right part of the equation, the left part of which is d_i, and that are not sons of d_i.
4) All function names that occurr in the right part of the equation the left part of which is d_i, and that do not belong to the memory of d_i, have to be sons of d_i.

Def. 9: A calling graph of an equations system is trasformable by expansion, if the right part of one (or more) of these equations, contains a proper subexpression E such that (let the left part of such equations be $d_{i_1} \ldots d_{i_t}$)

a) the function names $d_{j_1}, \ldots, d_{j_k}$ occurring in E do not appear outside the occurrences of E, in the right parts of the equations, the left parts of which are d_{i_h} $(1 \leq h \leq t)$;
b) in the connection tree relative to this calling graph, in the inverse path connecting d_{i_h} $(1 \leq h \leq t)$ to the most immediate predecessor among $d_{j_1}, \ldots, d_{j_k}$, do not occur other function names, left parts of equations, in the right parts of which such a predecessor occurs outside E.

Def. 10: Given a transformable calling graph we can construct by expansion in the subexpression E (we use symbols with the same meaning as in Def. 8) a transformed calling graph such that:

1) its nodes are

   a) all function names not occurring (in the connection tree) in a minimal a path between a node d_{j_ℓ} $(1 \leq \ell \leq k)$ and a node d_{i_h} $(1 \leq h \leq t)$,

   b) all function names $d_{j_1}, \ldots, d_{j_k}$,

   c) different copies of all function names occurring in a minimal path between a node d_{j_ℓ} $(1 \leq \ell \leq k)$ and a node d_{i_h} $(1 \leq h \leq t)$, for every different d_{j_ℓ};

2) every node costructed by clause 1a) is connected to the same nodes as in the primitive graph;

3) every node d_{j_ℓ} $(1 \leq \ell \leq k)$ constructed by clause 1b) is connected to

   a) the function names belonging to the right part of the equation, the left part of which is d_{j_ℓ}, which are ancestors of d_{j_ℓ} in the connection tree,

   b) the function names which are its sons in the connection tree and which are not ancestors of a d_{i_h} (or exactly d_{i_h}) $(1 \leq h \leq t)$,

   c) the appropriate copies of the function names which are its sons in the connection tree and which are ancestors of a d_{i_h} (or exactly d_{i_h}) $(1 \leq h \leq t)$,

   d) the function names occurring in E, to which d_{j_ℓ} is not connected in the primitive calling graph.

4) every copy constructed by clause 1c) is connected to

   a) the appropriate d_{j_ℓ} $(1 \leq \ell \leq k)$,

   b) the function names not occurring in E, which are its ancestors, and are also ancestors of the appropriate d_{j_ℓ} $(1 \leq \ell \leq k)$ occurring in the right part of the equation, whose left part the node under examination is a copy,

   c) the appropriate copies of all other function names not occurring in E, but occurring in the right part of the equation whose left part the node under examination is a copy.

We want to prove now that equations system of type n characterize the program schemata belonging to the $\mathcal{G}(RE_n)$ class. Such a result is achieved by the following two theorems.

Theorem 1. If a program schema P belongs to the $\mathcal{G}(RE_n)$ class then the equations system, which describes it is of type n.

Proof. Since the RE_n class of program schemata is contained in $\mathcal{G}(RE_n)$, and $\mathcal{G}(RE_i) \subsetneq \mathcal{G}(RE_n)$ $(i < n)$ three cases are possible.

case a: $P \in RE_n$ class of program schemata and $\forall i, i < n$ $P \notin RE_i$ class of program schemata.

The hypothesis guaranties that each iterative block of the program contains at most n exit points and that exists at least one iterative block with exactly n exit points. The calling graph corresponding to the related equation system is of type n because we can construct the finite tree, requested by the definition, by putting as memory of each node the set of function names corresponding to the exits of the related iterative block B and as sons the function names related to the iterative blocks contained by B.

case b: $P \in \mathcal{G}(RE_n)$ and $\forall i, i<n\ P \notin \mathcal{G}(RE_i)$
By definition of $\mathcal{G}(RE_n)$ a program P' must exist, such that P' is strongly equivalent to P, and $P' \in RE_n$ class of program schemata. Hence the equations system relative to P' is of type n, because of case a).
As P' is strongly equivalent to P, the computational sequences of the two program schemata are equal; therefore P' can differ from P only in node splitting. But the acceptable duplication of nodes are all considered in the clauses of the definitions of equation system therefore the equation system which describes P must be of type n as the one which describes P'.
case c: $P \in \mathcal{G}(RE_i)$ $(i<n)$
Because of case b of this proof, the equation system which describes P is of type i. But it is immediate that an equation system of type i $(i<n)$ is also of type k with $k>i$, and therefore the equation system which describes P is of type n. □

Theorem 2. If the equation system which describes a program schema P is of type n, P belongs to the $\mathcal{G}(RE_n)$ class.
Proof. The thesis requests the existence of a program schema P', strongly equivalent to P, belonging to the RE_n class of program schemata.
If each component of the equations system which describes P satisfies clause a) of Def. 7, it is easy to see that we can build up a program P', strongly equivalent to P, such that any iterative block occurring in it has at most n different exits (n is the upper bound of the number of equations of every component) and therefore $P \in \mathcal{G}(RE_n)$.
Otherwise, if any component of the equation system, which describes P satisfies clause b or clause c of Def. 7, we can prove that the calling graph relative to this component contains all the informations necessary to build up a segment of program schema S', such that it is strongly equivalent to the segment of program schema S, described by the component itself and such that it belongs to the RE_n class of program schemata. We can analyze such a segment of program schema independently from the other parts of the program because every component of the equation system describes a precise block of the program not entering in any loop. If the component satisfies clause b of Def. 7, starting from its principal function name, we build up the corresponding segment of the program schema S' writing for every node the corresponding iterative block, in which we put a suitable exit point for every occurrence of function names contained in the memory of the node and in which we write explicitly the iterative blocks corresponding to the occurrences of the function names which are the sons of the node itself. Therefore $S' \in RE_n$ class of program schemata.
If the component of the system satisfies the clause c) of Def. 7,

then to prove the theorem it is necessary to verify the equivalence between the segment of program schema relative to the primitive calling graph and the one relative to the transformed calling graph. The segment of program schema relative to the transformed calling graph differs from the one relative to the primitive calling graph in that the instructions inside of the subexpression E are removed from the block relative to the equation, in the right part of which E occurs, and placed in the block relative to the appropriate equation (in the sense mentioned in Def. 10). Such a difference is substantially due to a node splitting and does not modify the computation sequences, therefore the two program schemata segments are strongly equivalent, and the one relative to the transformed calling graph belongs to the RE_n class of program schemata because the transformed calling graph is of type n by definition.
And it is evident that if all segments of the program schema built up following the equation system components belong to the RE_n class of program schemata, and they are strongly equivalent to the segments of the original program schema P, also its composition, P', belongs to the RE_n class of program schemata and it is strongly equivalent to P. Therefore the theorem is proved □

The definition of expressive power of control structures (Def. 3) and the constructive characterization of the program schemata classes, allow us to give a definition of well formed program based on these concepts.

Def. 11. A program P is well formed if it is minimal w.r.t. to the expressive power of the control structures occurring in it.

Remark 3: Our definition of well formed program contains as basic concept the minimality of the number of exits allowed in the iterative blocks. Such a minimality characterizes it w.r.t. the well formed program definition given by Peterson, Kasami and Tokura [1] . As mentioned above these authors build up well formed programs w.r.t. node splitting. Their well formed program notion therefore can be used to give a structure to an existing program only.
Our definition instead is useful to analyze the structure of programs and to study the characteristics of the iterative statements.

Corollary 1: Given a program P we can effectively construct a well formed program P' strongly equivalent to P, by means of the algorithm implicit in the above definitions.

Remark 4: The theorem 2 indicates the fundamental steps of the procedure to construct the subparts of P' corresponding to each component of the equation system related to P.
Such a construction is possible because our definition of equation system of type n is fully constructive. In fact the construction of the calling graph is based on some variants of the algorithm of Maggiolo-Strong [9] . The analysis of the type of the calling graph is effectively the construction of the tree with a finite memory associated to each node.
Further, the transformation by expansion of a calling graph is an easy recognition procedure working on the equation system.
Therefore, as we can not **produce** an infinite sequence of configura-

tions (for the finiteness of the calling graph), every part of our algorithm terminates.
The notion of well formed program is a useful tool in order to give a measure of the complicacy of the control flow of a program. In fact, preserving the algorithm, it allows us to fully individuate the control structures of least expressive power necessary to expresss the algorithm. We can therefore give a measure of such a complexity of a program as follows:

Def. 12 : A program P has structural complexity equal to the greatest expressive power of the control structures occurring in the well formed program strongly equivalent to it.

The notion of structural complexity of programs does not fullfill the characteristics of program structure, which involves also data structure, depth of loops nesting etc., but it is an important tool to give meaningful theoretical properties to the measure of program structure. The requirements proposed by Gileadi and Ledgard [10] for a measure of program structure are the invariance under strong equivalence, and the reflection of the hierarchy of control structures.
Both these requirements are satisfied by the notion of structural complexity which can be a basic attribute for the measure algorithm carried out in [10] . Therefore we think that the study of the relations between the two approaches can lead to a better definition of measure of programs.

4) An example

We illustrate the algorithm to reduce a program to a well formed one implicit inside the definitions and the theorems stated in the previous section, trough an easy example.
Suppose we want to known the structural complexity of the following program, which sorts a file containing N records. The sorting method is the exchange partition one, which is fully explained by Knuth in [11] . We recall here the only formalism we need to understand the program, which is written here in Algol . r, l are the indexes of the first and the least record of the file considered
is the key of the i-th record
is the record relative to the j-th key.
There exists an auxiliary stack, in which are stored pairs of indexes, relative respectively to the first and the least element of a subfile of the given one, to which the algorithm is recursively applied. Further, if the subfile is of lenght less than M, another algorithm, more efficient, is used to sort it. The program is then the following:

```
   begin l:=1; r:=N;
L1:  if r-l< M then begin straight insertion(l,r);
                          if stack=empty then goto L3
                          else begin remove(l',r');l:=l';r:=r';goto L1 end
                     end
                else begin i:=l;j:=r;K:=Kl;R:=Rl;
                          while K< KJ do j:=j-1;
                          if j  1 then  R :=R
```

```
                    else begin R:=R_J;i:=i+1;while K_i< K do i:=i+1;
                          if j≤ i then begin R_J:=R;i:=j end
                                   else begin R_J:=R_i;j:=j-1;goto L2 end
                         end
                    if r-i≥ i-l then begin Insert(i+1,r);r:=i-1 end
                                else begin Insert(l,i-1);l:=i+1 end
                    goto L1
                   end
L3:  stop
   end
```

Remark: We suppose that the three procedures called by the program are somewhere declared.
Straight insertion (m,n) is relative to the sorting algorithm mentioned above. Insert and remove are the usual operations on stacks.
From the control flow point of view we consider them as code portions with one entry and one exit point, like a basic function.
The relative program schema is the following:

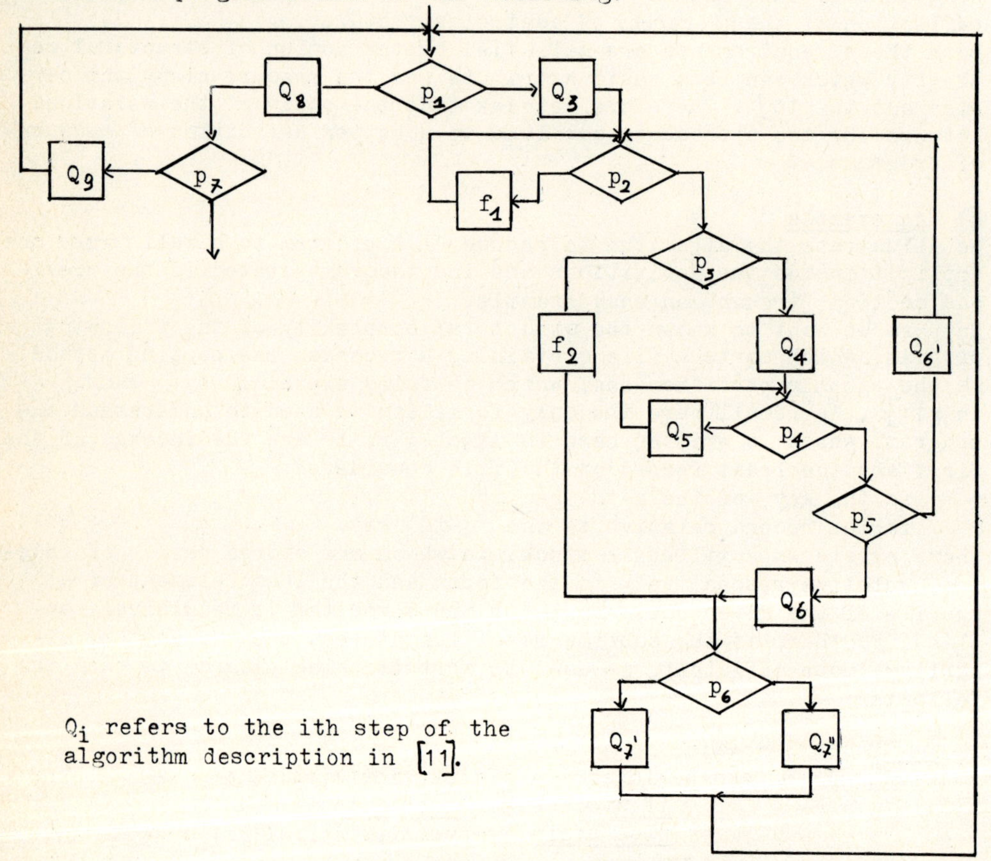

Q_i refers to the ith step of the algorithm description in [11].

Figure 9

The skeleton is the following:

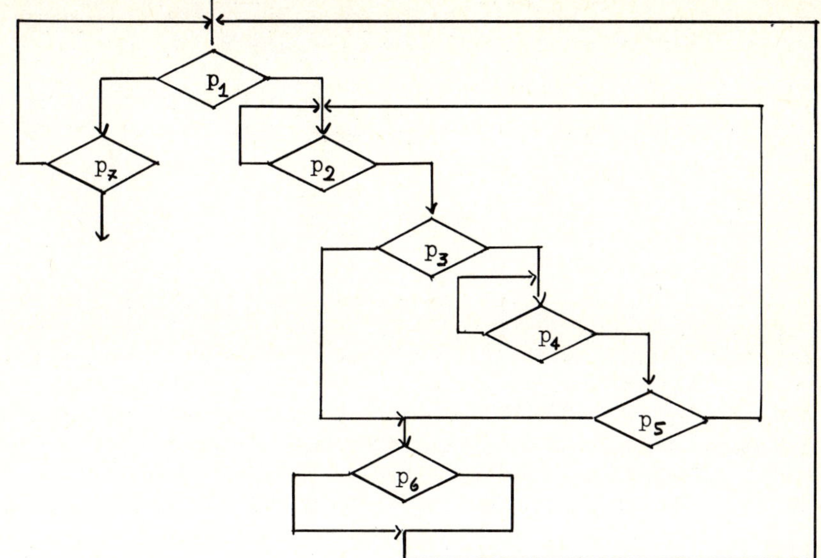

Figure 10

and the normalized equations system is the following:

$$\begin{cases} d_1 = \text{if } p_1 \text{ then (if } p_7 \text{ then } d_1 \text{ else } I) \text{ else } d_2 \\ d_2 = \text{if } p_2 \text{ then } d_2 \text{ else(if } p_3 \text{ then(if } p_6 \text{ then } d_1 \text{ else } d_1 \text{)else } d_4) \\ d_4 = \text{if } p_4 \text{ then } d_4 \text{ else(if } p_5 \text{ then(if } p_6 \text{ then } d_1 \text{ else } d_1 \text{)else } d_2) \end{cases}$$

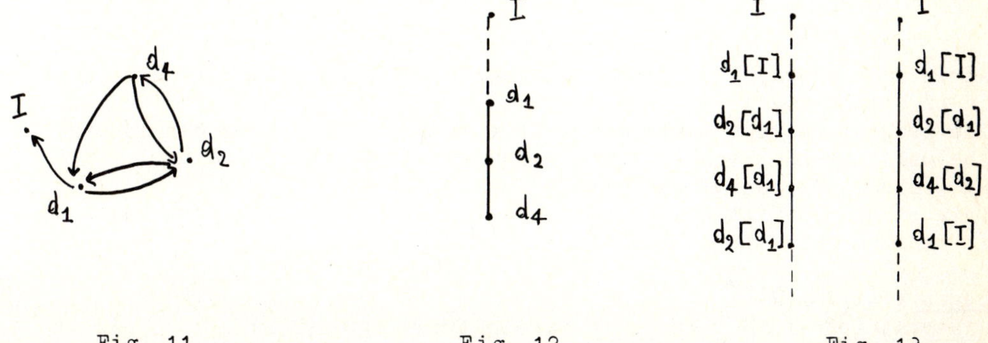

Fig. 11 Fig. 12 Fig. 13

The calling graph is the one sketched in fig. 11.
Following def. 5 we construct the connection tree, which has the form as in fig. 12.
If we try to construct the finite tree with nodes with memory of length 1, we find that it is impossible. In fact, the only trees we can build up, are the ones of fig. 13. Both are infinite trees, since both contain the same node two fold. Hence the trees contain an infinite number of equal subtrees.
We must then try the reduction by expansion of the calling graph.

The equation, whose left part is d , contains a subexpression, satisfying the conditions of def. 7. This expression is the following:

E if p then(if p then d else d) else d

Since d covers d in the connection tree, we substitute for E in the equation the function name d . The new connection tree is the following:

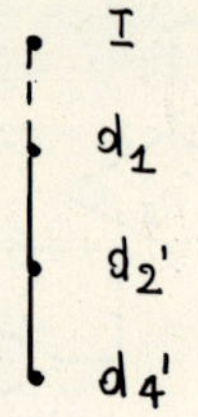

I

d_1

d_2'

d_4'

Figure 14

which is relative to the new equation system.

d_1 = if p_1 then(if p_7 then d_1 else I) else d_2'

d_2' = if p_2 then(if p_3 then(if p_6 then d_1 else d_1)else d_4' ;
(if p_5 then (if p_6 then d_1 else d_1)else d_2') *

d_4' = if p_4 then d_4' else d'_2 .

The finite tree is now the following:

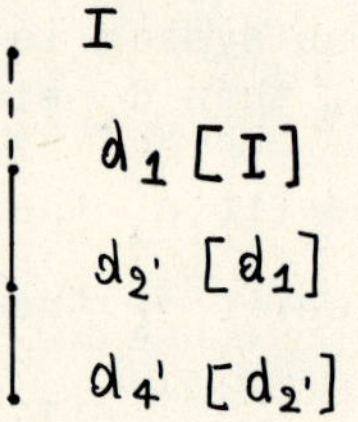

I

d_1 [I]

d_2' [d_1]

d_4' [d_2']

Figure 15

As we have shown, the algorithm succedess: hence the original algorithm is of complexity 1.

The program belongs therefore to the class $\mathcal{G}(RE_1)$: we can construct the well formed program strongly equivalent to it belonging to the RE_1 class of program schemata.

This program, written in Algol with the iterative statement mentioned in section 2 is the following:

```
begin l:=1; r:=N;
  Repeat if r-l < M then begin straight insertion(l,r)
                            if stack=empty then exit
                            else begin remove(l',r');l:=l';r:=r' end
                          end
                     else begin i:=l;j:=r;K:=K_l ;R:=R_l ;
                            Repeat if K< K_j then j:=j-1
```

*) We have introduced in this equation the ";" symbol. Its meaning is simply that, aften the execution of the block, relative to the function name d_4' , we must execute the expression following the semicolon. This is a useful notation in order to construct the program strongly equivalent to the original one.

```
                    else if j≤ i then Ri:=R else
                    begin R:=Rj;i:=i+1;
                      Repeat if Ki< K then i:=i+1 else exit
                      end
                      if j≤ 1 then begin Rj :=R;i:=j end
                      if r -i  i-1 then begin Insert(i+1,r);
                                                R:=i-1
                                              end
                      else begin  insert(l,i-1);l:=i+1 end ;
                      exit
                      else begin Rj:=Ri;j:=j-1 end
                    end
                  end
                end
  end
end
```

5) References

1) W.W.Peterson, T.Kasami and Tokura, "On the capabilities of while, repeat and exit statements", Comm. ACM (1973).

2) G.De Michelis and C.Simone, "Semantic characterization of Flow-diagrams and their decomposability", Proc. 2nd Colloquium on Automata, Languages and Programming, Springer (1974).

3) W.A.Wulf, D.B.Russel and N. Haberman, "BLISS: A language for system programming", Comm. ACM 14 (1971).

4) G.De Michelis, G.A.Lanzarone and C. Simone "Control structures and control environments: a critical assesment"-GEC International report (1975).

5) C.Böhm and G. Jacopini, "Flow-diagrams, Turing machines and languages with only two formation rules", Comm. ACM 9 (May 1966).

6) S.Rao Kosaraju, "Analysis of structured programs", Proc. 5th Annual ACM Symposium Theory of Computing (1973).

7) N. Wirth, "On certain basic concepts of programming languages", STAN-CS-65 (1967).

8) D.E.Knuth, "Structured Programming with GOTO statements", Computing Surveys 6-4 (Dec. 1974).

9) A.Maggiolo Schettini and H.R. Strong, "A Graph-theoretic Algorithm for transforming Recursive Programs", Atti Congresso Informatica Teorica, Pisa (1973).

10) A.N.Gileadi and H.F.Ledgard: "On a proposed Measure of Program Structure" Sigplean Notices 9-5 (1974).

11) D.E.Knuth: "The art of Computer Programming: vol. 3" Addison Wesley (1973).

This research has been sponsored by HISI under project AST and by C N R (Progetto speciale per l'Informatica).

MERGING CONTROL-FLOW AND DATA-FLOW DESCRIPTIONS OF STRUCTURED SYSTEMS IN A UNIQUE NOTATION

M. Maiocchi
R. Polillo

University of Milano, Gruppo di Elettronica e Cibernetica, Via Viotti, 5 - Milano (Italy)

1. Introduction

Modifiability must be considered an essential feature of any large software system. As a matter of fact, one of the fundamental needs in designing a system is to subdivide it into parts (sometimes called 'modules') in such a way that modifications local to a part can be carried on without affecting the remaining ones. A good modularization of a system is a difficult task, the main problem being the difficulty of keeping under control all the 'interconnections' among the various system components, i.e. all the assumptions that each module makes on the behaviour of the environment in which it is plunged. A solution to this problem, at least in principle, is twofold, involving both the design and documentation activities:

- a standard set of possible interconnections must be defined, for the particular system being designed;
- a standard system description language must be used to describe how system components are connected.

Many kind of 'interconnections' can be found in software systems, but two kinds are fundamental from the designer's point of view: those arising from the control-flow among program components and those arising from the data flow. Structured programming has provided a standard set of control connection primitives, as well as a language to describe control structured systems (e.g., BJ-charts or, equivalently, Algol-like linear notation). On the other side, various data connection primitives, as well as various data flow languages, have been introduced (1,2,3). Nevertheless, a structured flow-chart (or a linear representation of it) does not show, in itself, how data flow among the various interconnected components, and viceversa a data-flow chart usually hides the flow of control. Therefore, both kinds of languages reveal unadequate as practical tools for software system design.

In this paper, we propose a very simple language, which allows to describe how software systems must be subdivided into a set of interconnected subsystems. It can be used either as a design and documentation tool (exactly as in the case, e.g., of structured flow-charts) or even as a programming language.

The main goals of the language are:

- to show, at the same time, how <u>control and data</u> flow among the various components;
- to impose a strictly hierarchical structure to the system;
- to allow automatic detection of <u>data conduit effects</u> (4), i.e. those cases in which some data are received as input and transmitted as output from a component, but are never changed within it.

The above features are obtained:

- by imposing a one-entry/one-exit condition not only on control connection primitives, but also on data connection primitives;
- by selecting a set of connection primitives which can be viewed either as control connection primitives and as data connection primitives;
- by imposing that a system description be syntactically well formed if and only if the interface specifications among interconnected components are consistent.

The structure of the language is outlined in the next 2 paragraphs. In the last paragraph, a simple example is given.

2. Outline of the language

Since the purpose of the language is to describe how the elementary functional units are connected to build larger systems, and not to describe their internal structure, the set of functional primitives is left unspecified: a <u>functional primitive</u> will be simply considered a (named) black-box, with a number of distinguishable 'input sockets', and a number of distinguishable 'output sockets', i.e. 'channels' through which data flow to and from the component. Each socket has a label, identifying the set of values which can flow through it, e.g.:

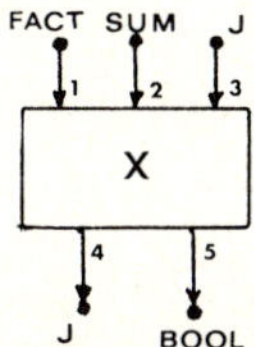

To impose a one-input/one-output condition, we regard the set of the input sockets as a single, indivisible multiple socket, and likewise for the output. Therefore, we can draw a functional primitive box simply as:

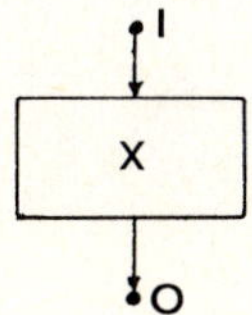

where I and O are, respectively, the name of the input variables set and of the output variables set of X (in the above example, I = {SUM, FACT, J} and O = {J,BOOL}). It is intended that a primitive X can be activated if and only if its input data are present on the input socket and no output data are present on the output socket.

To connect components (of any level) we shall use a set of connection primitives. An n-ary connection primitive is a (named) black-box, with one (multiple) input socket labelled I, one (multiple) output socket O, and n pairs (I_i, O_i) of (multiple) sockets.

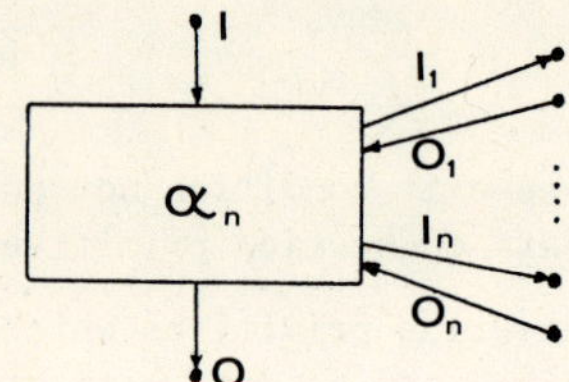

To each connection primitive there will be associated an I/O relation: this is a syntactical condition (i.e. checkable at compile time) which must be satisfied by the sets I, O, I_1, O_1,..., I_n, O_n.

With functional primitives, connection primitives and I/O relations we can construct the schema describing a program. A schema is defined by the following syntax:

1. a functional primitive: 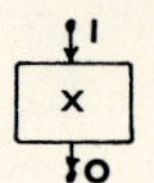

is a schema. We shall write, in linear notation:

X(I,O) = PRIMITIVE

2. if:

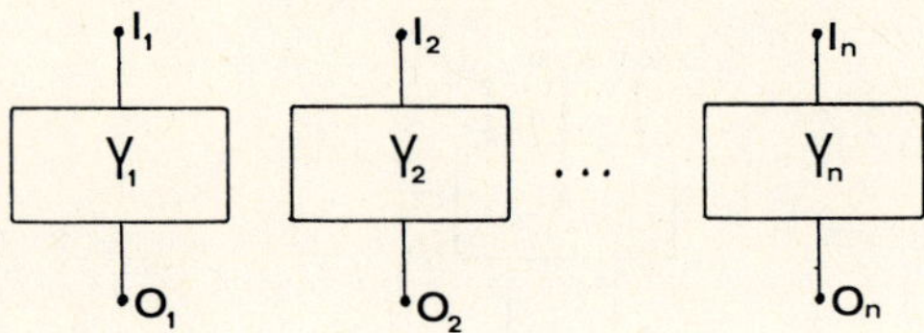

are schemata, then also:

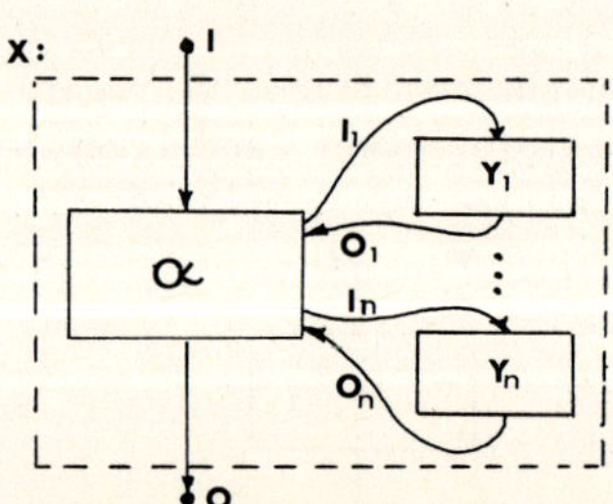

is a schema, provided that I, O, I_1, O_1, ... , I_n, O_n satisfy the I/O relation associated to α. In linear notation, we shall write:

$$X(I,O) = \alpha(Y_1(I_1,O_1), \ldots , Y_n(I_n,O_n))$$

or, when no ambiguity arises (°), simply:

$$X(I,O) = \alpha(Y_1, \ldots ,Y_n)$$

3. nothing else is a schema.

3. Basic connection primitives

We shall briefly describe, in the following, a possible choice of basic connection primitives, which are analogous to the control primitives of structured programming, and the associated I/O relations. These relations have been chosen in such a way as to avoid situations in which a variable:

(a) is required by a component without having been previously produced

(b) is produced by a component without being successively used

(c) is input to a component and, in whatever execution condition, is output by it without being changed.

It is to be noted that, while (a) guarantees that the interconnection of the various components is consistent, (b) and (c) have been introduced to avoid undesirable situations (i.e., useless computation and conduit-effects).

<u>FORK</u>. The choice of imposing a one-entry/one-exit condition to all components requires the introduction of a FORK primitive:

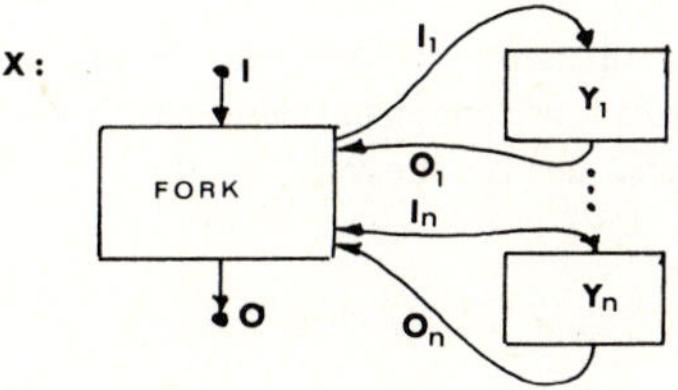

$$X(I,O) = \underline{\text{FORK}}\ (Y_1,\ldots,Y_n)$$

This distributes the variables of its input set I to the input sets $I_1, \ldots, I_n$ of components $Y_1,\ldots,Y_n$ $(n \geq 1)$ and collects their outputs $O_1,\ldots,O_n$ in its output set O.

(°) - The specification of the input and output data sets for a right-hand component name Y_i is mandatory only when they are different from those appearing in the defining relation for Y_i, e.g.:

$$X(A,B) = \alpha(\ldots, Y(C,D), \ldots.)$$
$$Y(N,M) = \ldots\ldots\ldots\ldots\ldots\ldots$$

This situation corresponds to that of a 'subroutine' Y which can be activated with different actual parameters.

The associated I/O relation, which can be easily obtained by case analysis, is:

$$(1) \qquad \boxed{I + O + I' + O' = I\,I'(\overline{O}\,\overline{O'} + O'') + \overline{I}\,\overline{I'}\,O''}$$

where

$$I' = I_1 + I_2 + \dots + I_n \quad ; \quad O' = O_1 + O_2 + \dots + O_n$$

and:

$$O'' = O(O_1\overline{O_2}\,\overline{O_3}\dots\overline{O_n} + \overline{O_1}\,O_2\,\overline{O_3}\dots\overline{O_n} + \dots + \overline{O_1}\dots\overline{O_{n-1}}\,O_n).$$

[If conduit effects within the FORK box are to be allowed, the term $IO\overline{O'}$, containing those output variables which are not supplied by any component Y_i, but are furnished directly from input I, must be added to the second member of (1).]

It is to be noted that no assumption is made on the subcomponents sequence of execution, so that the above schema denotes the whole class of the flow-charts containing the nodes $Y_1,\dots,Y_n$ connected in sequence or through cobegin-coend-like constructs.

SEQUENCE.

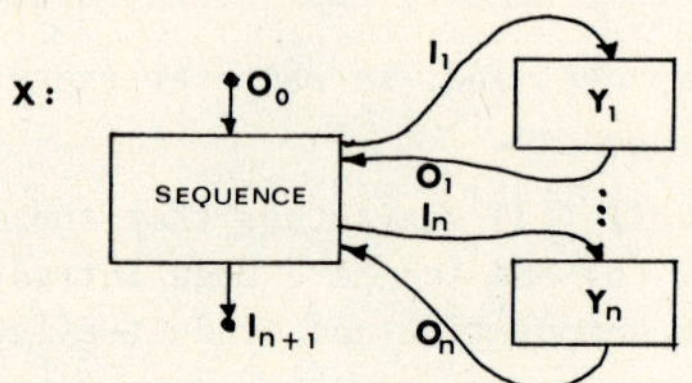

$$X(O_o,\ I_{n+1}) = Y_1;\ \dots\ ;\ Y_n$$

This primitive connects n components ($n \geq 1$) in sequence, i.e. it transfers variables from its input O_o to the first component, then the output O_1 from the first component to the second one, and so on, until the output O_n of the n-th component is transferred in the output I_{n+1}.

The I/O relation is:

$$(2) \qquad \boxed{I' + O' = (\prod_{o}^{n} L_i)(I' + O')}$$

where:

$$I' = I_1 + I_2 + \dots + I_{n+1} \quad ; \quad O' = O_o + O_1 + \dots + O_n \quad ; \quad L_i = (O_i I_{i+1} + \overline{O_i}\,\overline{I_{i+1}}).$$

[To allow conduit-effects, the term $O_o I_{n+1} \overline{O}_n \prod_{1}^{n-1} L_i$ must be added to the second member of (2).]

IFTHENELSE.

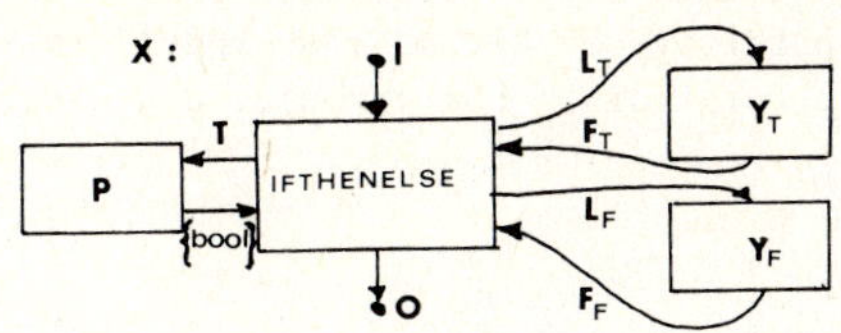

$$X(I,O) = \underline{IF}\ P\ \underline{THEN}\ Y_T\ \underline{ELSE}\ Y_F$$

If P returns TRUE, variables of L_T are passed to Y_T ; if P returns FALSE, variables of L_F are passed to Y_F. The output of the selected component is then passed to O.

The associated I/O relation is:

$$I+O+F'+L'+T = IO(F''' + F''(T+L')) + I\,\bar{O}\,\overline{F'}(T+L') + \bar{I}\,O\,F'''\,\overline{(T+L')} \tag{3}$$

where: $F' = F_T+F_F$; $F'' = F_TF_F$; $L' = L_T+L_F$; $F''' = \overline{F_T}\,F_F + F_T\,\overline{F_F}$.

[To allow conduit effects, the term $IO\overline{F'}$ must be added to the second member of (3).]

IFTHEN. By letting $L_F = F_F = \emptyset$ in (3), we obtain the I/O relation for the IFTHEN primitive.

DOWHILE.

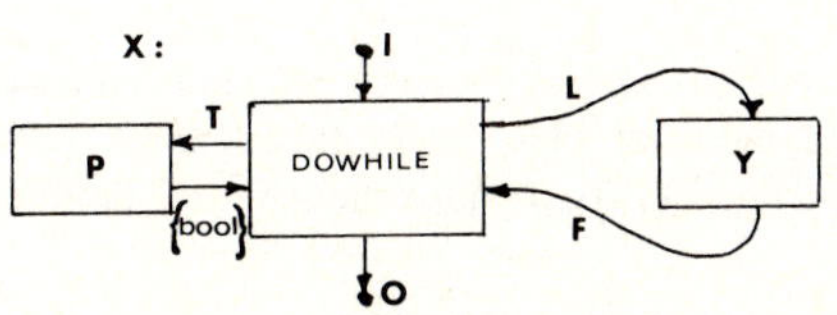

$$X(I,O) = \underline{WHILE}\ P\ \underline{DO}\ Y$$

Variables of T are first passed to P. If the returned value is TRUE, variables of L are passed to Y, which will eventually pass its output F to the connection primitive. The process is then repeated until a FALSE value is returned from P.

The associated I/O relation is:

$$I+O+T+L+F = IOF + I\,\bar{O}(T + L) \tag{4}$$

[If conduit-effects are allowed, the term $IO\bar{F}$ must be added.]

4. Derived connection primitives

The set of connection primitives is, in a sense, open. As a matter of fact, one can define a new connection primitive by giving its 'model' in terms of the basic ones and of the associated I/O relations. For example, a new connection 'DOUNTIL' could be defined as:

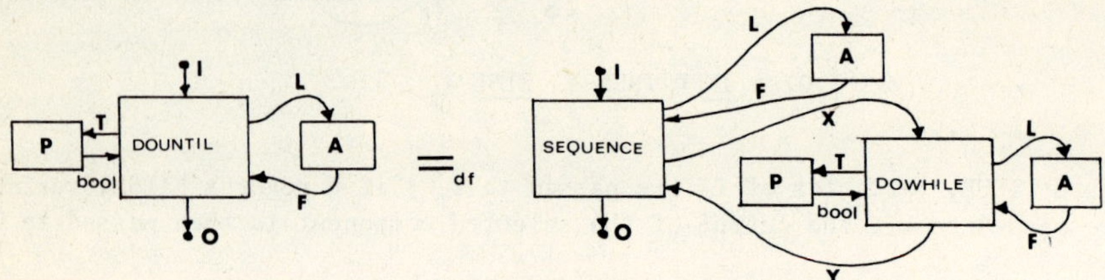

The new I/O relation can be obtained by (2) and (4), by imposing the interface conditions $X = F$ and $Y = O$. The resulting equation is:

$$I+O+T+L+F = ILF + T\bar{L}F(O + \bar{O}\,T).$$

5. An example

A simple example follows, of a program which computes the factorial of N. The example is merely illustrative, and must not be considered as a typical application of the language. As a matter of fact, the language is oriented toward the description of systems in which the elementary components are entire functional units.

In the example, the notation X+Y+...+Z represents the set containing variables X, Y, ..., Z. Note that a description of the function of each <u>PRIMITIVE</u> follows its declaration, and that the input variable F must be initialized to the value '1'.

```
FACTORIAL(N+F,F) = IF GTØ THEN COMPUTE
COMPUTE(N,F) = INITIALIZE; LOOP
INITIALIZE(N,I+F) = FORK (SET(N,I),SET(N,F))
LOOP(I+F,F) = WHILE NE1 DO ONESTEP
ONESTEP(I+F,I+F) = SUB; MUL
SUB(I+F,I+F) = FORK (DECR, )
MUL(I+F,I+F) = FORK (MULTIPLY, )

DECR(I,I) = PRIMITIVE                 {I←I - 1}
MULTIPLY(I+F,F) = PRIMITIVE           {F←F * I}
NE1(I,Boolean) = PRIMITIVE            {I ≠ 1}
GTØ(N,Boolean) = PRIMITIVE            {N > Ø}
SET(X,Y) = PRIMITIVE                  {Y ← X}
```

In graphical notation, the program is represented as:

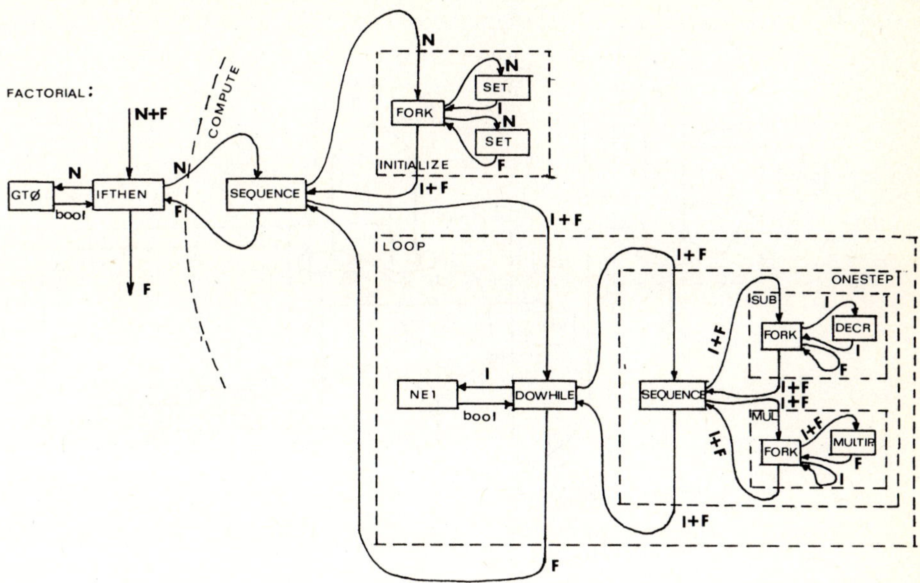

It is important to observe that the above schema (as any schema of the language) <u>can be viewed either as a control-flow-chart or as a data-flow</u> (for the one-input-one-output condition imposed to the connection primitives allows each component to transfer data to - or receive data from - only one component).
As a matter of fact, a schema could be indifferently compiled in a usual programming language, or in a data-flow language. E.g., from the above schema, one could draw the following flow-chart:

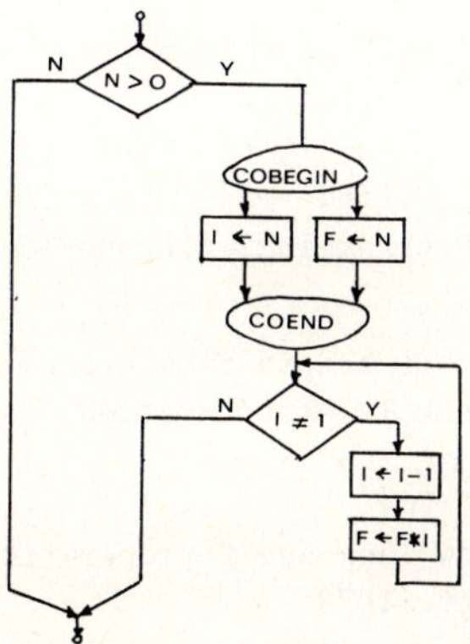

or the following data-flow, written in the language of (2):

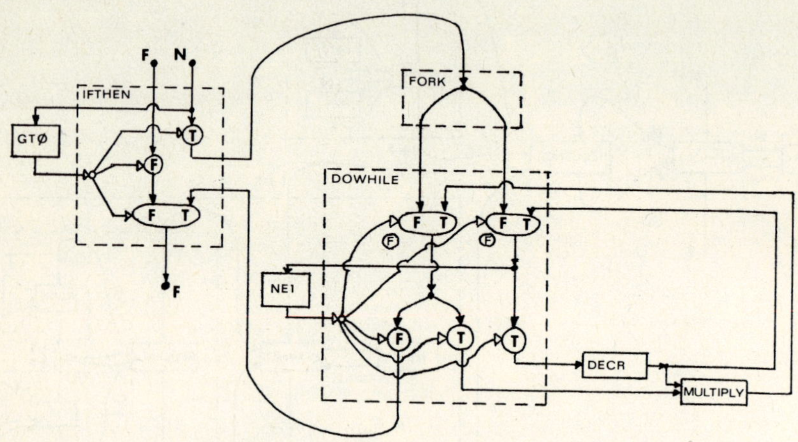

6. Implementation

A prototype version of a compiler for the language described in this paper has been implemented. The target language of the compiler is the same in which elementary components are coded, i.e. PL/I.

7. Acknowledgments

The authors are grateful to prof. G. Degli Antoni, University of Milano, for many helpful comments and suggestions.

8. References

(1) - J.B.Dennis, J.B.Fosseen, J.P.Linderman, "Data flow schemas", International Symposium on Theoretical Programming, A.Ershov and V.A.Nepomniaschy, Springer Verlag, 1974

(2) - J.B.Dennis, "First version of a data flow procedure language", Résumés des communications, Colloque sur la programmation, Paris, April 9-11 1974, 241-271

(3) - P.R. Kosinski, "A data flow language for operating systems programming", SIGPLAN Notices, 8, 9, Sept. 1973

(4) - B.Liskov, "Report of session on structured programming", Proceedings of ACM SIGPLAN-SIGOPS Interface Meeting, SIGPLAN Notices, 8, 9 (Sept. 1973),5-10

The construction of types of abstract machines in SIMAC

C. DAQUIN , C. GIRAULT

1. INTRODUCTION

SIMAC is an extensible system designed to handle ideal machines and automata. Up to now, there does exist a few languages which allow specialized automata description [8], but for each automaton, they require a particular program far too remote from the original formulation. It was for this reason that we realized a first inextensible system, SIMAC.1[3]. It allowed the conversational users to create and activate sets of automata that were directly described by their rules. However, we felt it essential that the users should not be limited to a set of predefined automaton types.

In fact, the type of an automaton is described not only by the form of the automaton's rules but also by a lot of details concerning the control of its execution and computations on elementary structures. Therefore, we have designed a second extensible version, SIMAC.2[4] that allows the users to specify explicitly all operators needed for handling new automata types - even those operators that are usually implicit. In addition, this extensibility enables SIMAC.2 to handle automata as particular cases of more complex systems of abstract machines. Thus, our users will have the possibility of constructing their own control mechanisms (monitors, Petri nets,...) [6,7] and advanced programming languages. Moreover, one of the most important practical advantages of our constructors is that they allow the definition of new types by arranging chosen elements into arbitrary operators. In the first part of this paper, we describe the notions of entities and entity types. Because of its originality, we shall insist upon the creation of new machine types and skim over the classical creation of new structured values [2,9] .

Next, we explain how extensibility is fully used for the system itself, which is a set of machines organized in a hierarchical form. Starting from a *Primitive System* composed of *primitive* elements, we gradually extend it to a *Basic System* provided with an algorithmic language [1] and completed by a *Library*.

Finally, the machine construction mechanisms are very precisely described through an example. It deals with the creation of the machine type of the Basic System and shows how SIMAC.2 can be *self-defined*[5] .

2.PRIMITIVE ENTITIES.

We call *primitive entities* all those that are initially created in the system. They may be neither modified nor destroyed.

The Primitive System $\mathcal{P}$ is composed of :

• primitive types like : *type, model, constructor,...,operator, processor,..,descriptor, grammar,..., integer, boolean, pointer,...*

• primitive constructors like *machine, atom, record, vector,...*

• and primitive machines like *create, destroy, execute,...*

The type τ of an entity e determines, among other things, the structure and initialisation of e. Thus, to create an entity, it is necessary to specify its identifier and its type. The set of all entities makes up the *environnement* $\mathcal{E}$ of every machine.

Constructor calls allow to create new types. The equivalence class of all types created by the same constructor c is called a *model* $\mathcal{M}(c)$. For example all vectors, whatever their components, belong to the same model. In order to define new models, it is possible to create new constructors from several primitive ones.
Primitive machines perform all elementary manipulations of entities and can activate any other machine, whether primitive or not. Hence, they are involved when dealing with any model, type or entity.

3. THE MACHINES.

A machine of a given type includes a set of *rules* defining its actions on the set of entities making up its *context*.

3.1. Type.

The purpose of the constructor *machine* is to create new machines types. By definition each such type belongs to the same model $\mathcal{M}$ *(machine)* and is defined by :

• a set of *computing operators* instructed to handle context entities ;

• a *controlling operator* instructed to analyze the machine rules, to check the state of the machine and to perform additional actions between operators' computations ;

• and a *processor* which links computations and controls.

An operator w is defined by a model M and by a set $\mathcal{U}(w)$ of machines. These machines, called *units* of the operator, are intended to perform all desired manipulations on entities of type $\tau \in$ M . By convention, we shall speak of *computing units* when referring to a computing operator and of *controlling units* when referring to a controlling operator.

3.2. Rules.

The type of a machine determines the language of its rules as follows :

• the *syntax* of the rules is the one which may be parsed by the controlling operator ;

• rules are parsed into *elements* that fall into two classes, *computing* and *controlling elements,* that are respectively associated with computing and controlling operators.

Note that a rule may be restricted to a single element and that there exists primitive syntactic elements (e.g. identifiers, numbers, arithmetic operators,...).
An analysis of the machine's rules modifies the entities of the context through calls of units of the appropriate computing operators. Meanwhile, it determines the logical sequence of computations through calls of units of the controlling operator.

3.3. Creation.

The creation of a machine μ requires the specification of its type τ (optionally, the parser of its calls), its set of parameters P and its set of rules R. With each identifier occurring in P or R, we associate a formal name. The set C_F of these names is called *formal context* of μ as opposed to *real context* C_R. A real context of μ is only defined at execution time. It consists of effective parameters passed during the call, local entities created by μ and global entities picked up from the environnement $\mathcal{E}$.

4. THE PRIMITIVE SYSTEM $\mathcal{P}$.

Primitive machines are procedures that are directly written in an implementation language. They provide $\mathcal{P}$ with :

- an analyzer for *machine calls*,
- a mechanism for recursion,
- a monitor for sequential calls,
- and constructors for the creation of new types.

4.1. The PRIMAC language.

PRIMAC is the language of $\mathcal{P}$. This simple language allows only sequential calls of primitive machines, but is sufficient to define, by way of extensions, all the remainder of SIMAC.

The following productions define the syntax of a *machine call* :

```
<machine call> ::= <machine identifier>|<machine identifier>(<parameter list>)
<parameter list> ::= <primitive list>|<extended list>
<primitive list> ::= <parameter>|<primitive list>,<parameter>
<parameter>::=<identifier>|<identifier>(<specification>).
```

The <parameter list> of all primitive machines, and often of created machines, takes the form of a <primitive list> with an implicit parser. For some machines, it is possible to use the <extended list> form, provided an appropriate parser is specified at their creation.

Additional information about a parameter can be found in its <specification> . This <specification> is parsed according to the type of the parameter.

4.2. Primitive machines.

Some primitive machines used in the following examples are described in appendix 1.

5. THE BASIC SYSTEM $\mathcal{B}$.

The PRIMAC language is sufficient to construct the remainder of the system, but it is much too elementary to be used as such. Therefore, it has been added an extended language, BASMAC, in which we have written the rest of SIMAC. The system supporting BASMAC, and written in PRIMAC, is called the Basic System $\mathcal{B}$

The Basic System comprises :

- a new machine type called BASEMACH,
- machines that define BASEMACH itself,

• and a conversational monitor that accepts users' commands. BASEMACH is, therefore, the first non primitive machine type.

5.1. The BASMAC language.

BASMAC is a programming language without labels and goto ; its syntax is defined by the following productions :

<procedure body>::=<sequence>

<sequence>::=<subsequence>|<sequence>;<subsequence>

<subsequence>::=<iteration>|<statement>

<iteration>::- *begin*<sequence>*end*

<statement>::=<action>|<condition> → <action>|<condition> ↛ <action>|<condition> ↛

Let us give a short and informal description of the semantic :

• all <sub sequence> are executed sequentially ;

• an <action> is a<machine call> as defined by the syntax of PRIMAC ;

• a <condition> is a <machine call> that returns one of the values *true* or *false* ;

• when a <condition> returns the value *true*, it provokes the corresponding <action> of the <statement> ;

• a <sequence> placed between *begin* and *end* is unconditionally iterated until an exit;

• when a <condition> returns the value *false*, a controlling element ↛ causes the exit of the enclosing <iteration> or procedure .

The BASEMACH type is used to create and to activate BASMAC procedures. We shall show in the next paragraphs how this type is described in $\mathcal{B}$. In particular, we shall explain how the <condition> and <action> elements determine the effects of their computing operators, whereas the *begin*, *end*, '→' and '↛' elements determine the effects of the controlling operator. Examples of machines used in this description are given in Appendix 2.

5.2. The BASEPROC processor.

In general, the main part of the definition of a machine type τ is a processor Π . This processor is a program scheme describing the coordination of calls of formal computing units and formal controlling units. The Primitive System $\mathcal{P}$ provides a language SCHEMAC to describe such program schemes. In the case of BASEMACH, the corresponding processor, called BASEPROC, is simply a sequential scheme. Without explicitly defining here the SCHEMAC grammar, let us describe the creation of BASEPROC.

```
* * *
create (processor, BASEPROC(
C1, C2, C3, C4 ; T1, T2 ;
(C1 ;
  (C2 ↛ T1 ;
   C3 → T2 ;
   C4       ))
))
```

* * *

Here, the second line states that parameters C1, C2, C3 and C4 are formal controlling units and that parameters T1 and T2 are formal computing units. The four following lines define the scheme itself ; the corresponding flow-chart is shown in figure 1.

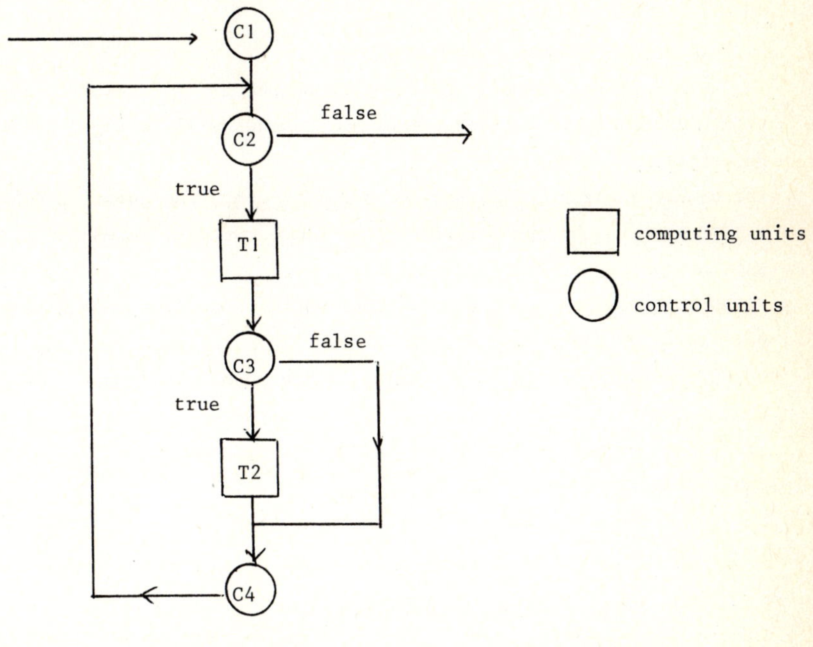

Figure 1

In general, to define a machine type, one must associate with the processor a controlling operator and usually several computing operators. Also, one must specify which real units are to be substituted to formal units. Let us describe below the controlling operator, BASECONT, of BASEMACH together with its two computing operators, CONDITION and ACTION.

5.3. The controlling operator BASECONT.

The grammar below is that which is used by BASECONT. Its description contains first the set of syntactic productions and then the list of the syntactic elements considered as : rules, controlling elements and computing elements.

```
* * *
create(grammar, SEQUENCE(
(SEQUENCE ::= SUBSEQUENCE|SEQUENCE';' SUBSEQUENCE ;
SUBSEQUENCE ::= ITERATION|STATEMENT ;
ITERATION ::= 'BEGIN' SEQUENCE 'END' ;
STATEMENT::=CONDELEM '→' ACTELEM|CONDELEM'↛' ACTELEM|CONDELEM'↛'ACTEMPTY
```

```
                |CONDEMPTY CONTROLEMPTY ACTELEM)
(RULE ::= STATEMENT|'BEGIN'|'END' ;
CONTROLLING ::= 'BEGIN'|'END'|'→'|'↛' CONTROLEMPTY ;
COMPUTING ::= CONDELEM|ACTELEM|CONDEMPTY|ACTEMPTY)
))
```

* * *

The syntax of the computing elements CONDELEM and ACTELEM will state that they are PRIMAC *machine calls*. Other computing elements will be empty. This will complete the description of BASMAC.

Let us now explain the purpose of the four computing units of BASECONT.

• INIT gathers the parameters of the called machine, makes the first rule current and initializes the stack of iterations.

• END controls the iterations, checks whether or not a rule is the last one and if not, makes the condition element current.

• TEST checks the condition result. If the result is *true*, it makes the action element current ; otherwise, if the control element is '↛', it causes the exit of the iteration and makes the END rule current.

• NEXT makes the next rule current.

We are now in a position to define the controlling operator BASECONT :

* * *

create (*operator*, BASECONT(
SEQUENCE ;
M : *model (machine)*, D : *descriptor*, R : *boolean ;*
S = POINTERSTACK ;
(INIT (M, S, D) , END (M, S, D), TEST (M, S, D, R),
NEXT (M))))

* * *

This creation specifies that :

(i) the grammar of the rules is the SEQUENCE grammar ;

(ii) the parameters of BASECONT are : an entity M belonging to model $\mathcal{M}$*(machine)*(cf. §2), a descriptor D and a boolean R ;

(iii) S is a local entity of type POINTERSTACK ; this non primitive type, defined elsewhere, characterizes a usual stack of pointers ;

(iv) the units INIT, END, TEST and NEXT share the entities M, D, R and S ; these units are machines defined in Appendix 2.

5.4. The computing operators CONDITION and ACTION.

Let us define here two computing operators, CONDITION and ACTION, to parse and execute <condition> and <action> in a BASMAC <statement> . Each one parses and treats a current computing element.

```
* * *
create (operator, CONDITION (
machine call ;
D : descriptor ; R : boolean ;
(COND (D, R)))) ;
create (operator, ACTION (
machine call ;
D : descriptor ;
(ACT(D)))) ;
                                   * * *
```

These creations specify that :
(i) the syntax of the computing element parsed is given by the PRIMAC *machine-call* grammar ;
(ii) the parameters are : a descriptor D and a boolean R ;
(iii) there are no local entities ;
(iv) each operator has a single unit : COND or ACT, respectively ; all these units are described in Appendix 2.

5.5. The BASEMACH type.

We can now create a new type, BASEMACH by linking processor BASEPROC with operators BASECONT, CONDITION and ACTION.

```
* * *
create (type, BASEMACH (machine (
M : model (machine), D : descriptor ;
R = boolean ;
BASEPROC (BASECONT (M, D, R) : INIT, END, TEST, NEXT ;
          CONDITION (D,R) : COND, ACTION(D) : ACT)
)))
                                                  * * *
```

This creation specifies that :
(i) the parameters of BASEMACH are : a machine M belonging to model $\mathcal{M}$ *(machine)* and a descriptor D ; constructor *machine* has to construct the executor of M , and D contains the parameter list of a call of M ;
(ii) a local boolean variable R will be allocated whenever a machine M is created;
(iii) to all formal units of BASEPROC, *machine* must substitute the indicated calls of controlling units of BASECONT and computing units of CONDITION and ACTION.
Thus, we get the executor of BASEMACH machines. Its flow chart, shown in figure 2, is one the many interpretations of figure 1.

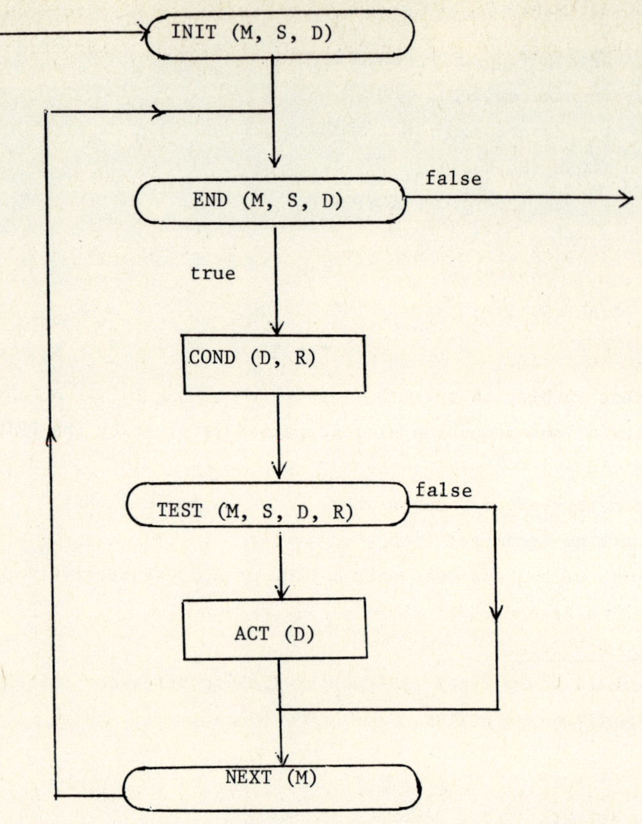

Figure 2.

6. LIBRARY.

To cover common needs, we have provided SIMAC.2 with a library $\mathcal{L}$ described in BASMAC. This library is composed of the most usual types of automata and of all BASEMACH machines needed for handling these types. Thus, the user has at his disposal a variable number of stacks, tapes, variables, etc..., and several control conventions to process the rules of his automata. By combining processors and operators which figure in the Library or are defined by the user, one can considerably diversify the types of machines.

7. CONCLUSION.

In this paper, we have shown how, starting from very elementary tools, one could construct a powerful type of abstract machine with its own language. Machines of this type are pratical enough to construct the remainder of SIMAC.

Through our approach, a machine can be looked upon as a network of other machines (its computing operators) synchronized by the processor and the controlling operator. Of course, this machine can, in turn, be used for further extensions.

To conclude let us point out that the systematic use of extension mechanisms for constructing SIMAC establishes a complete and consistent description of its semantic.

REFERENCES

[1] J. Arsac - Un langage de programmation sans branchements *(RAIRO, B2, Juin 1972).*

[2] T.E. Cheatham - J.A. Fischer and P.Jorrand - On the basis for ELF, an extensible language facility *(FJCC, December 1968).*

[3] C.Daquin, C.Girault - SIMAC, simulateur conversationnel d'automates *(RAIRO,B3, Septembre 1972).*

[4] C.Daquin, C.Girault - SIMAC, an extensible system for abstract machines *(n°I.P. 73.17, novembre 1973).*

[5] C.Daquin - SIMAC, un système extensible de mise en oeuvre de machines abstraites *(thèse de troisième cycle, n°IP, 74-5, Mai 1974)* .

[6] J.B. Dennis - First version of a data flow procedure language *(Colloque sur la programmation, Paris Avril 1974).*

[7] C.A.R. Hoare - An operating system structuring concept *(CACM. october 1974).*

[8] D.E.Knuth - Examples of formal semantics *(Symposium on semantics of algorithmic languages edited by Erwin Engeler, University of Minnesota, Springer lecture notes, 1971).*

[9] B. Liskov, S.Zilles - Programming with abstract data types. *(Proceedings of a symposium on very high level languages March 1974. SIGPLAN NOTICES, Volume 9, number 4, April 1974).*

[10] D.C.Luckam, D.Park, M.S.Paterson - Formalized computer programs *(J.C.S.S. June 1970).*

[11] J.Neuhold - The Formal Description of Programming Languages *(IBM Systems Journal, 1971, vol.10, n°2).*

APPENDIX 1 - PRIMITIVE MACHINES

create : creates an entity of given name and type ;
append : appends rules to a machine (and incidentally creates formal names) ;
assign, return : assigns a value to an entity or to the current machine ;
equal : returns the boolean result of a comparison ;
not : reverses a boolean value ;
increase, decrease : increases or decreases the value of an integer variable ;
first, next : returns the reference of the first or next item of a sub-list ;
item : returns the item referenced by a given pointer ;
value, attribute, entity : returns respectively the value field, attribute field or entity reference field contained in a given descriptor ;
rules, parameters : returns the reference of the first rule or first formal parameter of a given machine ;

current-rule, current-elem : returns the reference of the current rule or element of a a given machine ;
execute : activates the machine corresponding to the heading identifier of a machine call, and transmits it the remaining part of the machine call ;

analyze : either analyzes the parameters of a machine-call and constructs the list of effective parameters, or activates the optional parser.

APPENDIX 2 - BASIC SYSTEM'S MACHINES

1. BASECONT UNITS

```
* * *
  create(BASEMACH, INIT (M, S, D)) ;
  append(INIT
    (create (pointer, PE) ;
     analyze (M, D, PE) ;
     create (pointer, PF) ;
     assign  (PE parameters (M)) ;
  BEGIN
     mot(equal (PF , nil))↛ assign (entity (item (PF)), item (PE)) ;
     assign (PE, next (PE)) ;
     assign (PF, next (PF)) ;
  END ;
  assign (current-rule (M) , rules (M)) ;
  STACKINIT (S))) ;
                                                            * * *
```

Comments

(i) analyze gathers the effective parameters contained in the descriptor D and returns in PE, the reference of the first item of the constructed parameter list ;
(ii) parameters returns the reference of the first formal parameter of M ;
(iii) an *item* of the effective parameter list is a reference of the transmitted entity ;
• an *item* of the formal parameter list is a formal name descriptor ;
• *assign (entity (item (PF)), item (PE))*
assigns the transmitted entity reference tò the *entity field* of the formal name descriptor ;
iv) assign (current-rule (M), rules (M)) makes current the first rule ;
v*i*) STACKINIT is a Basic System machine that initializes the stack S.

* * *

```
create (BASEMACH, END(M, S, D)) ;
append (END)
   (BEGIN
      return (false) ;
      not (equal (current-rule (M) , nil)) ↛ return(true) ;
      assign (current-elem (M) , first (item (current-rule(M)))) ;
      assign (D, item(current-elem (M))) ;
      equal (attribute (D) , controlling) ↛ ;
      equal (value (D), 'BEGIN') → PUSH (S, current-rule (M)) ;
      equal (value (D), 'END') → TOP (S,current-rule (M)) ;
      assign (current-rule (M), next (current-rule (M)))
   END)) ;
```

***

Comments

(i) an *item* of the rule list is itself the head of an element list ;

(ii) in all calls of this machine, D contains the first element of a rule ;

(iii) the occurrence of a 'BEGIN' element causes the stacking of the current rule reference ;

(iv) the occurrence of an 'END' element makes current the rule referenced by the top of the stack S ;

v) in the absence of 'BEGIN' or 'END' the next rule is made current.

* * *

```
create (BASEMACH, TEST (M,S,D,R)) ;
append (TEST
    (return (true) ;
    assign (current-elem (M) , next (current-elem (M))) ;
    equal (R, true) → assign (current-elem (M) , next (current-elem(M))) ;
    assign ( D, item(current-elem (M))) ;
    equal (R, false) ↛ return (false) ;
    equal (value (D), '↛') ↛;
    STACKEMPTY (S) → assign (current-rule (M), nil) ;
    not (STACKEMPTY (S)) ↛ POP (S) ;
    create (integer, LEVEL) ;
    assign (LEVEL , 1) ;
    BEGIN
    not (equal (LEVEL, 0)) ↛ ;
       BEGIN
         BEGIN
           assign (current-rule (M)) , next (current-rule (M)));

           assign (current-elem (M), first (item (current-rule (M)))) ;
```

```
            assign (D, item (current-elem (M))) ;
            equal (attribute (D), computing) ↛
        END ;
            equal (value (D), 'BEGIN') ↛ increase (LEVEL, 1)
        END ;
        decrease (LEVEL, 1)
    END))
```

* * *

Comments

(i) R contains the return value of the tested condition ;

(ii) if R is *true* then TEST takes the value *true* and D is assigned the second computing element of the current-rule ;

(iii) if R is *false* then TEST takes the value *false* and if the current rule contains the '↛' element then it is necessary to search for the last rule of the iteration ;

• LEVEL is a local entity needed to handle nested iterations ;

(iv) STACKEMPTY, POP are Basic System machines that respectively, returns *true* if the stack S is empty, or removes the top of the stack S .

(v) the inner loop looks for a computing element ;

(vi) the surrounding loops wait for the level of iterations to become zero.

***

```
create (BASE MACH, NEXT (M);
append (NEXT
     not (equal (current-rule (M), nil)) → assign (current-rule (M),
                                         next (current-rule (M)))));
```

***

2. CONDITION UNIT

* * *

```
    create (BASEMACH, COND (D,R)) ;
    append (COND
      (assign(R,true) ;
      not (equal (value (D), empty)) ↛ assign (R, false) ;
      execute (D)  → assign (R, true))) ;
```

* * *

Comments

(i) execute activates the machine (if any) referenced in the descriptor D ;

(ii) the value returned in R is *true* if the computing element is empty or if *execute* takes the value *true*.

3. ACTION UNIT

```
* * *
create (BASEMACH, ACT (D)) ;
append (ACT
   (not  (equal (value (D) , empty)) →  execute (D)))
                                                  * * *
```

D A T E N B A N K M O D E L L E

<u>ON THE SEMANTICS OF DATA BASES:</u>
<u>THE SEMANTICS OF DATA DEFINITION LANGUAGES</u>

H. Biller
W. Glatthaar
Institut für Informatik, Universität Stuttgart
D-7000 Stuttgart, Herdweg 51

1. INTRODUCTION

A data base system is a representation of an abstract model of the real world. At any time a state of this model essentially consists of a set of structured objects which is represented in a data base state by means of a set of data structure instances. This representation is called the datalogical level /Sundgren 73/. A schema as introduced for instance in /CODASYL 71/ primarily describes the datalogical level of the data base system, i.e. the data structure instances and their properties which are derivable from the real world model. A schema does not describe a certain data base state but on the one hand it is a description of the set of all data structure instances and on the other hand it is a description of the set of all objects of the model.

To write schemas Data Definition Languages (DDL's) are introduced and a schema can be viewed at as a program of a DDL, which defines data structures and rules how data structure instances can be generated. Accordingly DDL's can be classified by the data structures which they allow to define. For instance network-type DDL's or relational-type DDL's are spoken of. So one meaning of a DDL can be defined to be the set of all abstract objects which it allows to define. This meaning is given by the <u>standard-interpretation</u>, a mapping from the set of DDL-programs to sets of abstract objects.

This understanding of the semantics of a DDL is important if one wants to implement it on a computer system and show the correctness of the implementation. Based on the second definition of the meaning of the DDL as introduced in the foregoing section, namely that a DDL describes the set of data structure instances as well, we define the notion of an <u>implementation concept</u>. With respect to storage implementing a DDL means to be able to realize the data structure instances on the storage medium of a computer.

Therefore we must introduce an abstract model of the storage. In a functional view a state of the storage can be modeled by a partial mapping from structured locations to values (see e.g. /Bekić 71/). Locations can be elementary or composite. In a real implementation the set of elementary locations must be derived from the set of all elementary units of physical storage medium which are available to the system, i.e. we do not differentiate between main storage and secondary storage. Since in a data base the values correspond to the data structure instances we introduce composite values as well as composite locations into which data structure instances can be stored. This induces a close correspondence between the structure of composite locations and the data structure instances.

There is a fundamental difference between a schema and the data declaration part of a programming language like ALGOL68 or PL/I. In ALGOL68 for instance after the generation of a 'name' - or location in our terminology - this 'name' can only exist once in the store, and at any time every variable possesses exactly one location. The structure of the store is only changed by changing the structure of locations /Walk 73/, and therefore on allocating a location one can assign a physical address to it which will remain constant during the runtime of the program. On the other hand for every data structure or type introduced in a schema there may exist a variable number of instances. That is why by a schema only a set of composite locations is defined and the physical addresses can only be assigned to data structure instances during the execution of Data Manipulation Language (DML) statements. Associated with every composite location is a data structure range, that is a set of data structure instances, which can be stored into this location.

Now we are able to define the notion of an implementation concept of a DDL. An implementation concept is a mapping assigning to every schema a partial mapping from the set of locations to the set of data structure ranges. There is a difference to the set of all storage states in a real implementation of a schema which also is a set of mappings from a set of locations to a set of data structure ranges. But in addition the constraint must be satisfied that every set of locations in the domain of this mapping is realizable, that means for instance realizations of locations in a physical storage medium may not overlap. Since both the standard interpretation and the implementation concept are interpretations of the same language interdependencies between them exist which can be used to define the correctness of an implementation concept.

In the following sections we shall give a precise definition of the notions introduced. As an example to illustrate the use of these ideas we take a subset of the CODASYL DDL /CODASYL 73/ for which we define the standard interpretation and an implementation using Scott's and Strachey's theory of semantics of programing languages, which the reader is supposed to be familiar with. It shows the existence of the domains, especially the reflexive ones which will be defined /Scott 70/,/Strachey 73/.

Before we start with the formal description we shortly discuss our considerations for the selection of the used subset of the DDL and the construction of the implementation. It is assumed that the reader is familiar with the CODASYL-proposal and terminology. The CODASYL DDL (henceforth DDL) contains different kinds of information:

1. clauses which describe the logical structuring,
2. clauses which describe implementation features and.
3. clauses which give information needed for the proper execution of DML statements.

The classification of some clauses is not commonly agreed upon. We regard for instance the AREA-entry to be of the second type and therefore it does not appear in the standard interpretation. An example of the third type would be the SET-OCCURRENCE-SELECTION-clause. Except for the AREA-entry the syntax is restricted to the entries and clauses of the first category, i.e. the DDL-constructs which represent properties of the real world model. The other clauses are important for the definition of the semantics of the DML which are not dealt with in this paper. They must be taken into account in the implementation concepts only and so their addition will only lead to a refinement of the implementation mapping. In our abstract implementation we realize AREAs as subsets of the set of locations, SETs as pointer-arrays, i.e. we add to the OWNER-record of a SET-occurence a component which contains an array of pointers to the MEMBER-records. DATA-BASE-KEYs are realized as pointers to locations. To show that the implementation must reflect the semantics of the DML we add to every record instance a component, which contains the name of the record type which the instance belongs to. The reason is, that in the record-selection-expression of the FIND-statement of the COBOL DML /CODASYL 71/ the next record of a certain type within an AREA or SET can be specified.

We start with the formal description of the syntax of the DDL used in the example, then we define the standard interpretation, a realisation of the DDL and finally we define the correctness of an implementation concept and show that our realization is correct.

2. NOTATIONS

1. If $M = \{m_i;\ i \in I\}$ is a set, then the operator B constructs the complete lattice

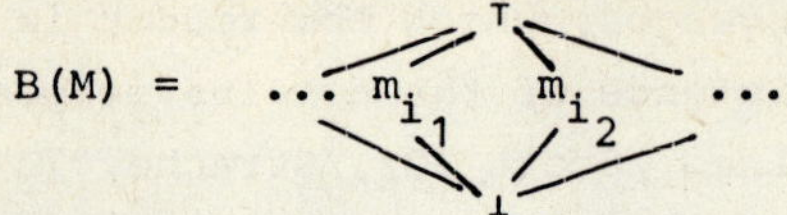

Let be D_i $(1 \le i \le n)$ a finite family of complete lattices. We define compound lattices corresponding to /Scott 70/:

2.a) $\Pi^n_{i=1} D_i$ as the product lattice $D_1 \times \ldots \times D_n$; by a product the concurrent occurrence of several components can be described,

b) if the D_i's are pairwise disjoint, then $\Sigma^n_{i=1} D_i$ denotes the sum $D_1 + D_2 + \ldots + D_n$; by a sum it is described that the elements of the component domains can occur alternatively,

c) $D^n_i = \Pi^n_{k=1} D_i$; $D^*_i = D^1_i + D^2_i + \ldots$,

d) $[D_i \dashrightarrow D_j]$ as the set of continous functions from D_i to D_j.

3. For any compound lattice we have an abstract syntax /Mc Carthy 62/ to decompose it. The names of the predicates and functions are derived from the (unique) names of the described domains as it is done in the Vienna Definition Language /Lucas 70/:
   a) For $\Sigma^n_{i=1} D_i$ the <u>predicate</u> is-D_i(d) is true iff $d \in D_i$.
   b) For $d \in \Pi^n_{i=1} D_i$ the <u>function</u> (selector) s-D_i or the number i extracts the i-th component of d.
   c) For $d \in D_i^*$ the function <u>length</u> is defined as:
      length(d) = n iff $d \in D^n_i$.
   d) Some predicates and functions have self-explanatory names, e.g. first and is-first.
4. Depending on the context |N is used to denote the set of natural numbers or the corresponding lattice constructed by B.
5. By $\supset$ we denote the conditional as it is defined in /Scott 71/.
6. Let be f an element of $[D_i \dashrightarrow D_j]$. Then the <u>domain</u> and <u>range</u> of f are:
   domain(f) = $\{x \in D_i ;\ f(x) \neq \bot\}$,
   range(f) = $\{f(x) ;\ x \in D_i\}$.

3. THE SYNTAX

<u>3.1. The Subset of the CODASYL DDL</u>

We consider the following subset of the DDL taken from /CODASYL 73/:

```
SCHEMA NAME IS schema-name
  {AREA NAME IS area-name}...
  ["record-entry"]...
  [SET NAME IS set-name
    ;OWNER IS record-name
    MEMBER IS record-name-1[,record-name-2]...]...
```

The general format of "record-entry" is:

```
     RECORD NAME IS record-name
       ;WITHIN area-name-1 [{,area-name-2 }...
          AREA-ID IS data-base-data-name ]
     ["data-subentry" ]...
```

area-name, set-name, and record-name must be unique within a schema. data-base-data-name is the name of a special register not defined in the schema. Its value must be an area-name.

The general format of "data-subentry" is:

```
     [level-number ] data-subentry-name

                   ("character-string-picture-specification")
     [;PICTURE IS  {                                         } ]
                   ("numeric-picture-specification"          )

                  (BINARY       )
     [;TYPE IS   { DECIMAL       } ]
                  (DATA-BASE-KEY)

                (integer                )
     [;OCCURS  {                         } TIMES ]
                (data-base-identifier   )
```

level-number is an unsigned integer between 0 and 100. By the level numbers a hierarchical structure is placed on the records.

The data-subentry-name must be unique within a "record-entry". Its format is implementor defined.

"character-string-picture-specification" may be X(n) and "numeric-picture-specification" may be 9(n) where n is any natural number.

We assume that the type-clause has to occur with the specifications BINARY or DECIMAL, if the picture-clause specifies a numeric-picture and vice versa. Therefore no default attributes have to be supplied as it is usual.

The type-clause must not be used within a character-string specification.

If the type-clause is used with the specification DATA-BASE-KEY the picture clause must not be specified.

A data-base-identifier is a reference to a data-item declared in the schema. Its value must be a natural number.

In the following we will refer to this subset. A word of this language will be called a DDL-program or schema.

3.2. The DDL Lattice

Any schema consists of a schema-name, an area-section, a record-section and a set-section. According to the syntax given above we introduce lattices to model the different parts of a schema.

From the sets of all possible schema-names, record-names, area-names, data-base-data-names, and set-names we construct by means of the operator B the corresponding lattices SCHEMA-NAME, RECORD-NAME, AREA-NAME, DATA-NAME, and

SET-NAME.

3.2.1. Record-Section

The whole record-section of a schema is an element of REC-SECT = RE^* where the lattice of record-entries RE is given by

$$RE = REC\text{-}NAME \times AREA\text{-}CL \times DE,$$
$$AREA\text{-}CL = AREA\text{-}NAME^* \times DATA\text{-}NAME, \text{ and}$$
$$DE = DSE^*$$

A single data-subentry is called <u>item</u> if the picture- or type-clause exists but the occurs-clause does not exist, <u>vector</u> if the picture- or type-clause exists together with the occurs-clause, <u>repeating-group</u>, if only the occurs-clause exists and a group with a lower level-number follows.
So the lattice DSE of data-subentries is defined by

$$DSE = ITEM + VEC + REP$$
$$ITEM = PIC \times TYPE$$
$$VEC = PIC \times TYPE \times OCC$$
$$REP = OCC \times DE$$

where any item, vector, and repeating group is an element of the corresponding lattice.
A special item is not identified by a name but by the structure of the lattice of the objects. Therefore a data-base-identifier which refers to any item is represented as an n-tupel of natural numbers from $\mathbb{N}^*$ which are used as selectors as it is defined in 3.c of paragraph 2.
A picture-clause is an element of the lattice

$$PIC = B(\{X(n); n \in \mathbb{N}\} \cup \{9(n); n \in \mathbb{N}\}),$$

a type-clause is an element of

$$TYPE = B(\{\underline{BINARY}, \underline{DECIMAL}, \underline{DATA\text{-}BASE\text{-}KEY}\}),$$

and an occurs-clause of

$$OCC = \mathbb{N} + \mathbb{N}^*.$$

The data-entry part of a record-entry is modeled by DSE^* because there are no hierarchies except within repeating groups.

3.2.2. Set-Section

The <u>set-section</u> SET-SECT consists of several <u>set-entries</u> which are elements of SE, where

$$SE = SET\text{-}NAME \times OWNER \times MEMBER\text{-}CL$$
$$OWNER = REC\text{-}NAME$$
$$MEMBER\text{-}CL = REC\text{-}NAME^*$$

Now we have $SET\text{-}SECT = SE^*$.

3.2.3. Area-Section

The <u>area-section</u> is AREA-SECT = $AREA\text{-}NAME^*$.

3.2.4. The Lattice of Schemas

The lattice of all schemas can now be defined as:

$$DDL = SCHEMA\text{-}NAME \times AREA\text{-}SECT \times REC\text{-}SECT \times SET\text{-}SECT$$

4. STANDARD INTERPRETATION OF DDL

In this paragraph we define the standard interpretation I of DDL. This interpretation determines the semantics of any schema at the infological level /Sundgren 73/ without regard to any restraints which will be imposed by a specific implementation concept. From this point of view the meaning of a schema is the set of all objects of the users abstract world that can be represented in a data base described by the schema.

4.1. The Model of Abstract Worlds

The set of abstract objects contains two kinds of objects:

record-objects occur as meaning of a record-entry in a schema;

set-objects occur as meaning of a set-entry in a schema. Their components are record-occurrences.

The formal definition of the record-objects is based on the elementary objects of the abstract world. They are numbers or strings, i.e. elements of $CHAR^*$ or NR, where

$$CHAR = B(\{A,B,\ldots,Z,0,\ldots,9,\ldots,?\}),$$
$$NR_i = B(\{j \in \mathbb{N};\ 1 \leq j \leq 10^i - 1\}), \text{ and}$$
$$NR = \cup_{i=1}^{\infty} NR_i .$$

A record-object becomes an occurrence by its position in a state of the world. The meaning of a data-base-key is a lattice of all the possible record occurrences which it can identify, i.e. $RO \times \mathbb{N}$.

Then each record object in the real world is an element of

$$RO = (CHAR^* + NR + (RO \times \mathbb{N}) + RO)^*$$

and each set object is an element of

$$SO = (RO \times \mathbb{N}) \times (RO \times \mathbb{N})^* .$$

In a world that can be described by the CODASYL-DDL it is possible that a single object occurs several times. But different occurrences of the same object are distinguished by properties which are not intrinsic to the object. We model them by the position in a n-tuple. Therefore the abstract world is modeled by applying the star operator to RO and SO, and the meaning of any schema given by the interpretation I is a sublattice of $RO^* \times SO^*$. The lattice of all the sublattices of $RO^* \times SO^*$ is called P. P is the model of all possible abstract worlds.

In the following we will define the standard interpretation I as a mapping from DDL to P. Let be s any element of DDL. We define the value of I for s following its syntactical structure.

We use sets = s-SET-SECT(s) and rec = s-REC-SECT(s) as abbreviations.

The meaning of the schema s is given by the meaning of sets and rec:

$$I(s) = I_r(rec) \times I_s(sets)$$

4.2. Interpretation I_r of the Record-Section

We define I_r for the record-section rec

$$I_r(rec) = (\Sigma_{i=1}^{length(rec)} I_r(i(rec)))^*$$

Since i(rec) is an element of RE we continue to define I_r on RE.

We abbreviate de = s-DE∘i(rec) and define

$$I_r(i(rec) = \Pi_{j=1}^{length(de)} I_r(j(de))$$

and extend I_r to record-names by

$$I_r(s\text{-}REC\text{-}NAME \circ i(rec)) = I_r(i(rec)).$$

j(de) is an element of DSE and we complete the definition of I_r for data-subentries using dse as abbreviation for j(de):

$$\begin{aligned} I_r(dse) = \\ &(is\text{-}ITEM(dse) \supset I_i(dse), \\ &\ is\text{-}VEC(dse) \supset I_i(dse)^{v(s\text{-}OCC(dse))}, \\ &\ is\text{-}REP(dse) \supset I_r(s\text{-}DE(dse))^{v(s\text{-}OCC(dse))}, \bot) \end{aligned}$$

where v(s-OCC(dse)) is the natural number denoted by s-OCC(dse) if s-OCC(dse) $\in$ |N, otherwise v(s-OCC(dse)) is the star operator *.

The interpretation I_{PIC} of the picture-clause of an item dse is defined as

$$\begin{aligned} I_{PIC}(s\text{-}PIC(dse)) = \\ &(s\text{-}PIC(dse) = X(i) \supset CHAR^i, \\ &\ s\text{-}PIC(dse) = 9(i) \supset NR_i, \bot) \end{aligned}$$

If dse is an item its meaning is given by

$$\begin{aligned} I_i(dse) = \\ &(is\text{-}\underline{BINARY}(s\text{-}TYPE(dse)) \vee is\text{-}\underline{DECIMAL}(s\text{-}TYPE(dse)) \\ &\qquad\qquad \supset I_{PIC}(s\text{-}PIC(dse)), \\ &\ is\text{-}\underline{DATA\text{-}BASE\text{-}KEY}(s\text{-}TYPE(dse)) \wedge s\text{-}PIC(dse) = \bot \supset RO \times |N, \bot) \end{aligned}$$

4.3. Interpretation I_s of the Set-section

In the CODASYL world it is requested that any record occurrence may appear only once within one set type interpretation, i.e. there may exist at most one set-object of a set type which contains a single record occurrence as owner or member. Therefore we define for the set-section sets of the chosen schema s

$$I_s(sets) = (\Sigma_{i=1}^{n} I_r(s\text{-}OWNER \circ i(sets)) \times |N \times (M_i \times |N)^*)^*, \text{ where}$$

n = length(sets) and

$$\begin{aligned} M_i = &\ I_r(1 \circ s\text{-}MEMBER\text{-}CL \circ i(sets)) + \dots + \\ &\ I_r(length(s\text{-}MEMBER\text{-}CL \circ i(sets)) \circ s\text{-}Member\text{-}CL \circ i(sets)) \end{aligned}$$

and within the elements of the member part no component, i.e. no record-occurrence may occur twice.

5. A REALIZATION OF DDL

We consider implementation concepts as the first step in the development process of a physical data base. Implementation concepts do not deal with the characteristics of a real store. They describe the set of all possible structures which have to be implemented in the real store as a further step not considered in this paper. Our basic elements for an implementation concept are locations already explained in the introduction.

5.1. Locations

The countable set of elementary locations L_e is divided into pairwise disjoint subsets A_i ($i \in I$) to enable us to model the area concept. With the linear structure of a real store in mind we define a linear order on each A_i. To each A_i we add a special greatest and lowest element. Then the set of elementary locations is thought of as the sum of the constructed lattices A_i.

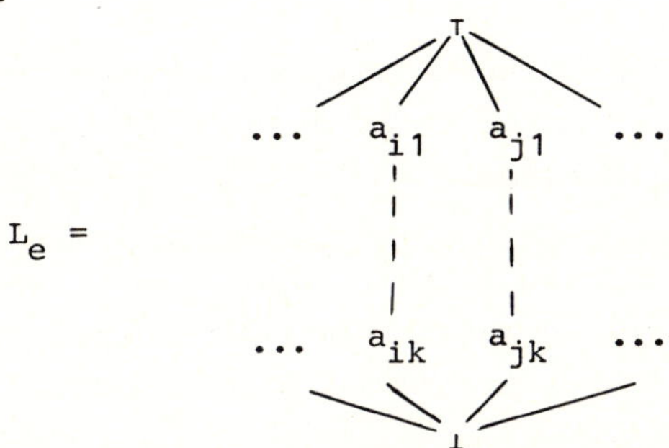

Within each A_i we define composite locations as elements of

$$L_i = A_i + [\,|N \text{ ---> } L_i]$$

The set L of all composite locations is the sum

$$L = \Sigma_{i \in I} L_i$$

Because it is not possible that two different components of a composite location have any components in common, i.e. there is no feature like REDEFINES which is known for example in COBOL, we may only consider an appropriate subset of L as possible structures of a store (cf. /Bekič 71/). We want to model all possible structures of the store which are defined by a schema without determining a special store containing any values. Therefore it is not necessary at this level that different locations are independent. We only require that the components of any location are independent, because it could be possible that this location had to appear in an individual store. Of course the elementary locations have to be independent. To analyse a composite location we have the function:

$\text{comp}: L \times |N \dashrightarrow L,$

$\text{comp}(l,n) = (m \in L_e \supset \bot,$
$\quad l \in [|N \dashrightarrow L_i] \supset l(i), \bot).$

Two locations are called independent if the predicate indep is true. For all $l,m \in L$ indep(l,m) is defined by:

$\text{indep}(l,m) =$

$(l \in \{\bot,\top\} \wedge m \in L_e \supset \text{true},$
$l \in L_e \wedge m \in \{\bot,\top\} \supset \text{true},$
$l,m \in L_e \wedge l \neq m \supset \text{true},$
$l \in L_e \wedge m \in [|N \dashrightarrow L] \wedge \forall i: \text{indep}(l,\text{comp}(m,i)) \supset \text{true},$
$l,m \in [|N \dashrightarrow L] \wedge \forall i: \text{indep}(\text{comp}(l,i),m) \supset \text{true, false})$

The predicate indep is extended to sets of locations in the obvious way. To separate the locations which suffice our requirements we define another predicate for all $l \in L$ by:

good(l) is true iff $\forall i \neq j: \text{indep}(\text{comp}(l,i),\text{comp}(l,j))$.

Now the desired lattice of locations is

$$\underline{L} = \{l \in L;\ \text{good}(l)\}.$$

5.2. Ranges

With any location we associate a range. This is the set of values which can be stored in that location. The lattice of ranges is constructed according to the construction of the locations.

As elementary ranges we have

$\text{DEC}_i = B(\{\text{numbers } n \text{ in decimal representation; } 1 \le n \le 10^i - 1\})$

$\text{BIN}_i = B(\{\text{numbers } n \text{ in binary representation; } 1 \le n \le 10^i - 1\})$

$\text{STRING}_i = B(\text{alphabet}^i)$ where alphabet is the set of characters that can be stored.

The ranges for values of an arbitrary size are elements of one of the following lattices

$\text{DEC} = B(\{\text{DEC}_i;\ i \in |N\})$

$\text{BIN} = B(\{\text{BIN}_i;\ i \in |N\})$

$\text{STRING} = B(\{\text{STRING}_i;\ i \in |N\})$

KEY is the lattice of all possible key values and is not more analysed.

NAME is the lattice of all possible record name values and is not more analysed.

LEN is the lattice of all possible length values of a record and is not more analysed.

Now the lattice C_o of all elementary ranges is

$$C_o = \text{DEC} + \text{BIN} + \text{STRING} + \text{KEY} + \text{NAME} + \text{LEN}$$

Ranges can be combined to form a composite range which belongs to the lattice C given by

$$C = C_o + [|N \dashrightarrow C]$$

5.3. Storage Model

As model of the storages S which are determined by a schema, we use the mappings which define all possible ranges for any possible locations. "Possible" is here to understand with regard to the schema and not to the allocation of the physical store. A range that shall be possible for a location must have the same structure. Therefore we define S as the subset of all structure preserving functions σ in $[\underline{L} \dashrightarrow C]$. These functions σ are defined as limits of the corresponding functions between the projections of the inverse limits $\underline{L}$ and C as it is shown in the diagram (cf. /Scott 71/). $\underline{L}_{i,n}$ are locations of level n within the area A_i and $\underline{L}_{i,o}$ is equal to A_i.

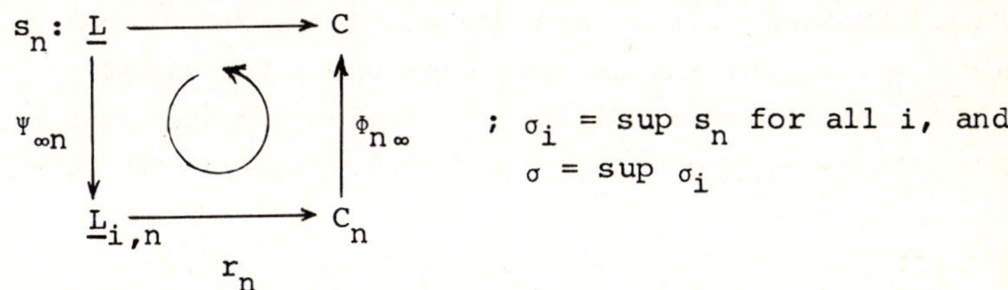

where the r_n's defining one function σ have to satisfy

r_o: $\underline{L}_{i,o} \dashrightarrow C_o$ and

$r_n(l) = (l \in \underline{L}_{i,o} \supset r_o(l), (k \mapsto r_{n-1}(comp(l,k))))$, where $k \in \mathbb{N}$.

Such a function σ is called a location-type-function and we can say now:

S is the lattice of location-type-functions.

5.4 Realization of DDL

A realization or implementation concept of a data definition language DDL is an interpretation of DDL, so that in the range of it, i.e. the semantic universe, any model of storage is used. In this section we define a realization R

$$R: \text{DDL} \dashrightarrow \text{S}.$$

Let be $s \in$ DDL with s = (z,a,rec,sets), hence $z \in$ SCHEMA-NAME, $a \in$ AREA-SECT, $rec \in$ REC-SECT, $sets \in$ SET-SECT.

The interpretation R is constructed by use of the interpretations

R_a for AREA-SECT, R_r for REC-SECT, R_s for SET-SECT,

whereas SCHEMA-NAME is not interpreted.

We define for the area-section:

$R_a(j(a)) = L_i$ for $1 \le j \le length(a)$ and any $i \in I$.

Let be rec = $(\rho_1, \dots, \rho_m)$ and again de = s-DE∘i(rec) with length(de) = n-2. We define for $1 \le i \le m$

$$R_r(\rho_i) =$$

$$\left[\left(\begin{array}{l} 1 \mapsto l_1 \in A_k \\ 2 \mapsto l_2 \in A_k \\ 3 \mapsto l_3 \in \mathrm{domain}(R_r(1 \circ de)) \\ 4 \mapsto l_4 \in \mathrm{domain}(R_r(2 \circ de)) \\ \quad \cdot \\ \quad \cdot \\ n \mapsto l_n \in \mathrm{domain}(R_r((n-2) \circ de)) \\ n+1 \mapsto \bot \\ \quad \vdots \end{array}\right) \mapsto \left(\begin{array}{l} 1 \mapsto \text{s-REC-NAME}(\rho_i) \in NAME \\ 2 \mapsto \mathrm{length}(de) \in LEN \\ 3 \mapsto \mathrm{range}(R_r(1 \circ de)) \\ 4 \mapsto \mathrm{range}(R_r(2 \circ de)) \\ \quad \cdot \\ \quad \cdot \\ n \mapsto \mathrm{range}(R_r((n-2) \circ de)) \\ n+1 \mapsto \bot \\ \quad \vdots \end{array}\right)\right]$$

where the l_i's have to satisfy the condition indep($\{l_h ; 1 \leq h \leq n\}$).

$A_k \leq \Sigma_{j=1}^{m} R_a(j \circ \text{s-AREA-NAME} \circ \text{s-AREA-CL}(\rho_i))$ is the area which is given by the interpretation of the area-clause of the record-entry.

For all $p > 1$ we use the abbreviation $dse = p \circ \text{s-DE}(\rho_i)$.

With the straightforward definition of the interpretation of the picture- and type-clause R_t the meaning of a data-subentry is given by:

$R_r(dse) =$

(is-ITEM(dse) $\supset$ $[A_k \dashrightarrow R_t(\text{s-PIC}(dse), \text{s-TYPE}(dse))]$,

is-VEC(dse) $\supset$

$$\left[\left(\begin{array}{l} 1 \mapsto a_{k_1} \in A_k \\ \quad \cdot \\ j \mapsto a_{k_j} \in A_k \\ j+1 \mapsto \bot \\ \quad \cdot \\ \quad \cdot \end{array}\right) \mapsto \left(\begin{array}{l} 1 \mapsto R_t(\text{s-PIC}(dse), \text{s-TYPE}(dse)) \\ \quad \cdot \\ \\ j+1 \mapsto \bot \\ \quad \cdot \\ \quad \cdot \end{array}\right)\right]$$

is-REP(dse) $\supset$

$$\left[\left(\begin{array}{l} 1 \mapsto l_{p_1} \in \overline{\mathrm{domain}} \\ \quad \cdot \\ \quad \cdot \\ j+1 \mapsto \bot \\ \quad \cdot \\ \quad \cdot \end{array}\right) \mapsto \left(\begin{array}{l} 1 \mapsto \overline{\mathrm{range}} \\ \quad \cdot \\ \quad \cdot \\ j+1 \mapsto \bot \\ \quad \cdot \\ \quad \cdot \end{array}\right)\right]$$

where $\overline{\mathrm{domain}} = \mathrm{domain}(R_r(\text{s-DE}(dse)))$ and $\overline{\mathrm{range}} = \mathrm{range}(R_r(\text{s-DE}(dse)))$ and where $j = v(\text{s-OCC}(dse))$ as defined in section 4.2. if it is a natural number, otherwise there are no restrictions for j,

is-DE(s-DE(dse)) $\supset$

$$\left[\left(\begin{array}{l} 1 \mapsto l_1 \in \underline{\mathrm{domain}} \\ \quad \cdot \\ \quad \cdot \\ k+1 \mapsto \bot \\ \quad \cdot \end{array}\right) \mapsto \left(\begin{array}{l} 1 \mapsto \underline{\mathrm{range}} \\ \quad \cdot \\ \quad \cdot \\ k+1 \mapsto \bot \\ \quad \cdot \end{array}\right)\right] , \bot)$$

where $\underline{\mathrm{domain}} = \mathrm{domain}(R_r(1 \circ \text{s-DE}(\text{s-DE}(dse))))$,

range = range(R_r(1∘s-DE(s-DE(dse)))), and k = length(s-DE(s-DE(dse))).
At last the interpretation R_s for the set-section has to be defined.
For each record-entry ρ of the schema s we define the set O_ρ of the set-entries of which it is the owner:

$$O_\rho = \{k \in |N;\ \text{s-OWNER} \circ k \circ \text{s-SET-SECT}(s) = \text{s-REC-NAME}(\rho)\}$$

λ_ρ is an injective function from card(O_ρ) to O_ρ.
addr: $\underline{L}$ ---> KEY is an injective function assigning each location an unique key.
Now we define for the set-section sets of the schema:

R_s'(sets,ρ) =

$$(O_\rho = \emptyset \supset \{(\perp \dashrightarrow \perp)\},$$

$$\left[\left(\left(\begin{array}{l} 1 \mapsto l_1 \\ \cdot \\ \cdot \\ n \mapsto l_n \\ n+1 \mapsto l_{n+1} \\ \cdot \\ n+k \mapsto l_{n+k} \\ n+k+1 \mapsto \perp \\ \cdot \end{array}\right) \longmapsto \left(\begin{array}{l} \ldots \\ \\ \\ \\ n+1 \mapsto c_1 \\ \cdot \\ n+k \mapsto c_k \\ n+k+1 \mapsto \perp \\ \cdot \end{array}\right)\right)\right] \quad \text{according to } R_r(\rho)$$

where $k = \text{card}(O_\rho)$,
$l_i \in [|N \dashrightarrow L_e]$, and
$c_i \in [|N \dashrightarrow \overline{KEY}_{\lambda_\rho(i)}]$

with $\overline{KEY}_{\lambda_\rho(i)} = \text{addr} \cup \{\text{domain}(R_r(\rho));\exists k: \text{s-REC-NAME}(\rho) = k \circ \text{s-MEMBER-CL} \circ \lambda_\rho(j) \circ \text{s-SET-SECT}(s)\}$

For the interpretation R_s of the set-section sets holds

$$R_s(\text{sets}) = \Sigma_{i=1}^{\text{length(rec)}} R_s'(\text{sets},\rho_i)$$

Now the realization R of the schema s is

$$R(s) = R_r(\text{s-REC-SECT}(s)) + R_s(\text{s-SET-SECT}(s))$$

6. CORRECTNESS OF THE REALIZATION

Given a data definition language with a standard interpretation I. Then a realization R is <u>correct</u>, if there exists a verification function V: S ---> P, so that the following diagram is commutative:

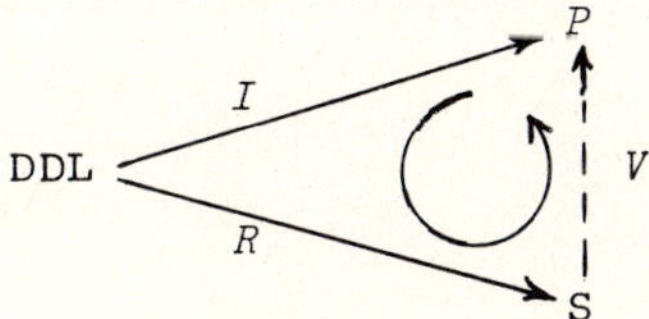

This definition is motivated by the idea that for any set of abstract objects there must exist a suitable structure of the store with regard to the structure of the (composite) locations as well as to the accompanying ranges. If our view of the world goes through the computer representation S nothing is changed.

In our example the following function V proves that the suggested realization is correct.

For $\sigma \epsilon S = [\underline{L} \dashrightarrow C]$ we define V' on the range c of σ:

$c \epsilon DEC_i$: $V'(c) = NR_i$

$c \epsilon BIN_i$: $V'(c) = NR_i$

$c \epsilon STRING_i$: $V'(c) = CHAR^i$

$c \epsilon KEY$: $V'(c) = RO \times |N$

$c \epsilon [|N \dashrightarrow C]$: $V'(c) =$

$$(c(1) \notin NAME \supset V'(c(1)) \times \ldots \times V'(c(def(c))),$$
$$c(c(2)+3) = \bot \supset V'(c(3)) \times \ldots \times V'(c(def(c))),$$
$$\Sigma_{i=c(2)+3}^{def(c)}(((V'(c(3)) \times \ldots \times V'(c(c(2)+2))) \times |N) \times$$
$$(\Sigma_{l_m \epsilon \overline{addr}}(V'(\sigma(l_m)(3) \times \ldots \times V'(\sigma(l_m)(c(2)+2)) \times |N))^*))$$

where $def(c) = n$ iff n minimal, so that $m > n \Rightarrow c(m) = \bot$, and $\overline{addr} = addr^{-1}(range(c(i)))$.

The verification function V is now defined as

$$V(\sigma) = (\Sigma_{\substack{c \epsilon range(\sigma) \\ \wedge\, c(c(2)+3)=\bot}} V'(c))^* \times (\Sigma_{\substack{c \epsilon range(\sigma) \\ \wedge\, c(c(2)+3)\neq\bot}} V'(c))^*$$

7. CONCLUSION

As next step to complete the semantic definition of a data base system we have to consider a storage. This is a function from locations to values and no longer to value ranges. After we have defined so far how all the possible structures can be implemented, it is to be defined by which mechanism the locations are allocated to individual data. It has to be assumed that no location is allocated to different data at one moment, i.e. all allocated data must be independent. All this considerations are affected by the DML. In the framework proposed in this paper this interface between the DDL and DML, the role of the user working area, and their implementation dependencies can be handled in a unique manner which is nevertheless appropriate for each aspect. Thus we can gain an integrated understanding of a data base and its functions.

A SYSTEM TO INCREASE DATA INDEPENDENCE IN A HIERARCHICAL STRUCTURE

C. FRASSON
University of Nice
Parc Valrose
06034 Nice Cedex FRANCE

This paper presents a solution to avoid the problem of data dependence which is inherent to the data base management system whose data model is hierarchical.

From a relational view of the hierarchical structure, it is possible to consider retrievals using a relational query language and a system which builts automatically research programs with optimization techniques.

1- The concept of data independence

It is now widely recognized that data independence is a serious criteria for a data management system to be a good data base management system (DBMS). This important concept has been developed by CODD (3), DATE (6) and BRACCHI (1).

Data independence is generally viewed at two levels : a logical and a physical level. The applications of an enterprise are data dependent if the programs are tightly bound to the way data is physically recorded and the way data is accessed. So, it is not possible to change either without dangerous consequences on the programs. Now, for many reasons (optimization, new hardwares, adding or deleting data or indexes, changing arithmetic representation, ...) such changes are necessary and frequent.

With physical independence a DBMS allows the users to be unaware of the storage structure, i.e. of the physical representation of the data they utilize. So, the application programs are not subjected to the variations of this physical representation. Logical independence acts at the level of the data model definition (the schema) which contains the logical definition of the whole information of the data base.

In fact, the users utilize a subset of this model (a sub-schema) whose definition is logically more adapted to their applications ; from this point of view, we have a logical independence in the sense that all the programs concerned with the data base will remain unchanged if we add new types of data (for new applications) or new fields in a data type.

In addition, and on grounds of expediency, every sub-schema may use particular names or subdivisions regarding the same information of the schema that means each user may reconstruct information contained in the schema for his proper point of view of the applications.

Last, but not least, independence between the schema, the sub-schema and the physical structure is achieved by the interfaces, a logical and a physical mapping model, which realize the correspondancies between on one hand the schema - sub-schema structure and on the other hand the schema and the storage structure.

These are the essential characteristics of a DBMS, but, in fact, the users' conception of the data is more or less dependent of the schema which is presented to them.

The purpose here is to analyze this aspect in a hierarchical data base and to show how a solution can be given using a relational model.

2- The hierarchical structure of IMS

A typical hierarchical DBMS can be represented by IMS (9). The structure of the schema is distinguished by a tree. The data base represented below shows such a structure : in a hospital we have informations associated with each patient and concerning the visits, the diagnosis made by the physician with application of medicine or decision of intervention and, in this case, a complementary diagnosis.

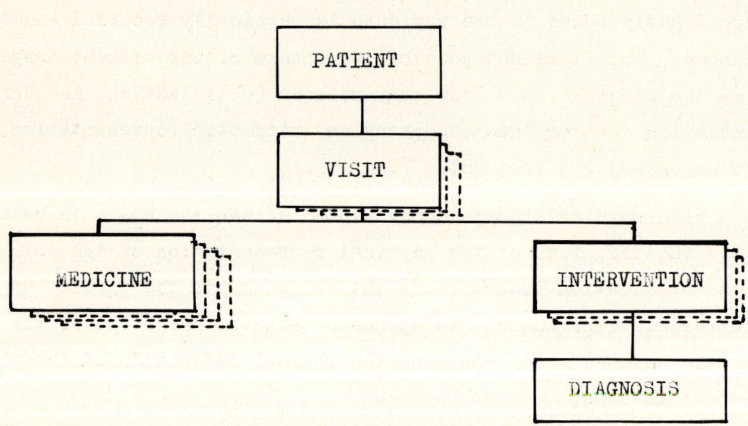

Figure 1 : An IMS data structure

More precisely if we talk about data occurrences and not data type we can distribute the data according to a three-dimensional tree : for one occurrence of the data type "patient" we have several occurrences of the data type "visit" and for each of them we have several occurrences of "medicine" and "intervention" (represented in dotted line).

The problems which arise in such a system are due to the architecture. We can see easily that for example, if we suppress an occurrence of a "visit" we loose information concerning his corresponding "medicine" and "intervention" occurrences.

In this paper, we only shall take an interest in the retrievals problems. In that sense, the user's view of the schema has an impact on the way he conceives and formulates queries. The schema involves for the user to have this logical view of the data in a hierarchy always present in his mind. This constraint associated with a corresponding programming method creates an awkward dependency between the application programs and the data.

Our aim here is not to discuss the utility of reorganizing the repartition methods of the physical records and the data model structure, but rather the possibility to allow a freedom of conception and reasoning necessary from the user's point of view.

If we consider the following hierarchical structure :

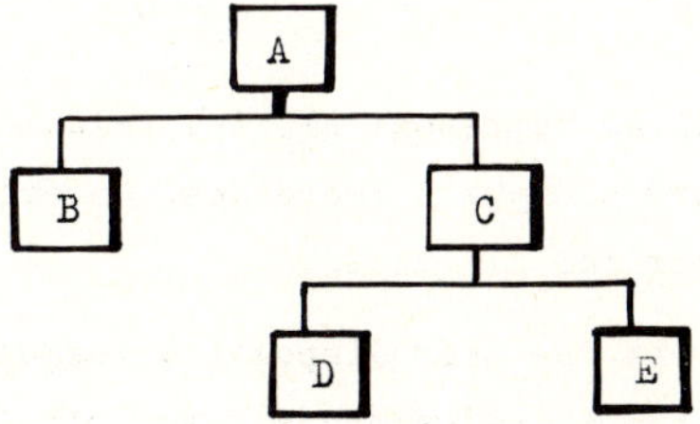

Figure 2 : **General structure HS**

The user will be almost always inclined to inspire the form of the requests from the structure which is presented to him.
For example : requests rather than :

1) what are the D_i such that $A = a_3$ and $B = b_2$?

2) what are the A_i such that $B = b_i$ and $C = c_2$?

We have found, after surveys with some IMS users, that a majority of queries were of the precedent type. More particular queries rather than :

3) what are the B_i such that $D_i = d_3$?

are relatively seldom seen and in addition imply complicated enough programs. It should be observed that programming in IMS is not very easy. The requirements of the IMS data manipulation language, DL/I, necessitate to have a good experience of the system before obtaining efficient application programs.

So, in hierarchical as in network data model access strategies are underlying. These problems are avoided in the relational model (2), (3), (6), (7) for which relations are independent of data and data are independent of any structure.

But if we give to the user a relational structure (RS) formed by a set of data types connected by relations we extend the field of the applications conceivable on the preceding model.

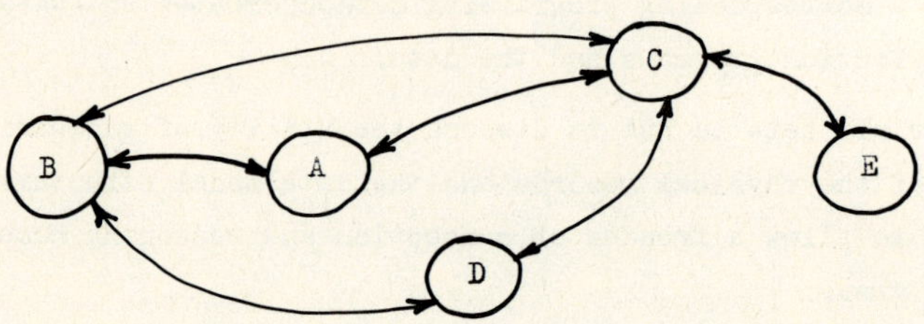

Figure 3 : Relational structure RS

The connections represent all the relations allowed. Then the probability to obtain a query of type 3 increases. However, the difficulty of programming did not disappear for all that.

If we place at the user disposal a language which allows him to formulate requests easily, and if we generate automatically, after interpretation of the language, the application programs which would result in IMS, we extend both the conception power and the exploitation of IMS.

All these characteristics are stored in the system "RIMS" (Relational IMS) (8). The proposed system is, in fact, a translator of a relational machine to a hierarchical machine.

3- General description of the translator

In order to realize a relational exploration of a hierarchical structure we have decomposed our system into three parts :

- first, we have to use a set of relations which assume the hierarchical data base.
- then, each user's request is formulated in a language which implies an interpretor.
- the third part is issued from the precedent ones : using the existing relations and the results of the interpretation, it generates the DL/I instructions necessary to execute the exploration wanted. This last part is associated with optimization techniques in order to produce the most efficient code for the retrieval.

3-1 Relations in IMS

To illustrate our purpose we shall use the example of the hierarchy presented in figure 1. We can distinguish two categories of relations.

- Relations defined on domains which pertain to a same type of data or class.

For example relations :

patient (pnumber, pname, sex, birthdate, address)
visit (vnumber, date, doctor)
medicine (psnumber, diagname, mname)
intervention (icode, gravity, pbody, sname)

where diagname is the diagnosis issued from a visit at the clinic, mname is the name of the drug or medicine prescripted and psnumber the serial number of the prescription; lastly, intervention is qualified by a code of operation, a gravity, the part of the body concerned and the surgeon name. The domain keys are underlined.

- Then we have relations which assume the hierarchy by linking two of the preceding relations according to the hierarchy. These relations are implicit. Their domains are formed by the keys of the two relations plus zero or more domains.

For example : PV (pnumber, vnumber)
PVD (pnumber, vnumber, doctor)
VM (vnumber, date, diagname)

The main difference between those two kinds of relations is due to a semantic concept. In (4) CODD has introduced normalization principles to define relations in first, second and third normal form. Without giving all details about what one can find in (8), the hierarchical relations are in first or in third normal form while the first ones are in third normal form.

We shall consider only hierarchical relations which are in third normal form and, for that, relations whose domains are keys domains (relation PV for example).

From these two basic relations, we can obtain other relations using composition operations.

So, we can have a relation (interesting) between medication and intervention which is illustrated by the query :

"what are the medicines which, for a patient, have involved operation of the vesicle ?"

Note that this relation is specified effectively in the relational structure delivered to the user.

The relational elements of informations result from the DBD (data base description) (12). Each IMS data base generation is indeed joined with a DBD generation which describes the data base entirely and which produces several control blocks.

In our system, all useful information concerning the basic relations is taken out from these blocks and distributed according to tables,matrix,... utilized by the system. This operation is executed once and for all when the user starts to explor the data base.

3_2 The language

Using now a relational structure, we can utilize a relational query language similar to the CODD's α-language (5). Our choice among other systems (11), (12) was determined by the fact this algebraic language is :

- easy to use
- rigorous
- not too difficult to interpret

However the formulation becomes less easy in case of complicated requests. In addition, it is necessary to be aquainted with the relational algebra. For example, let us consider a subset of the relational model that can be applied for figure 1. This model is a little different from our relational structure introduced precedently in the sense that it needs relations which play the part of "join relations" and which allows to have a complete independence (i.e. not only for retrievals but also for insertions, deletions,...)

Regarding the information on "patient" and "medicine" we have three relations : Patient, Medicine, PM

Patient

pno	pname	sex	birthdate	address

PM

pno	psno	physname

Medicine

psno	diagname	mname

Figure 4 : Relations on"patient" and "medicine"

Who are all the patients who have taken Cortisone ?

The expression of this query in α-language is :

RANGE Patient X

RANGE PM Y

RANGE Medicine Z

GET W (patient.pname) : $\exists$ X (patient.pno = X.pno $\wedge$ $\exists$ Y (X.pno = Y.pno $\wedge$

$\exists$ Z (Y.psno = Z.psno $\wedge$ Z.mname = "cortisone")))

In our system the relational structure is the following :

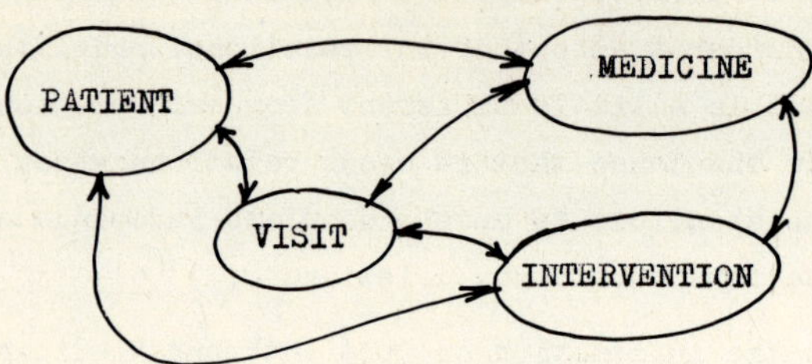

and the corresponding formulation in our query language is now :

GET W (patient.pname) : (medicine.mname) = "cortisone"

The simplification is appreciable. This fact is due to the hierarchical links which form the real structure and which allow unambiguous access to the data.

So, the existential quantifier is implicit and the universal quantifier is replaced by a keyword (ALL) which invoques an internal procedure. This is the principal difference between our query language and the α-language.

And/or operators are allowed so as all the keywords which invoque particular procedures on workspaces used to put the data : MAX, MIN, TOTAL,...

The second part of the translator is then an interpretor of this language. After interpretation and for more convenience with the exigencies of DL/I the request is transformed into a parameter list. This leads up to step three.

3-3 The algorithms

At this point the translator knows exactly

- what data are wanted by the user
- what are the mutual position of those data in the hierarchy.

We have three possibilities and for each one exists a different algorithm to proceed in the data base.

- data are situated under the qualifications as illustrated by queries of type 1. So, exploration proceeds in a top-down manner : we have to reach the qualified occurrences and then the corresponding children.
- the opposite case (queries of type 2) does not imply, however, a symetric process. To avoid exhausting searches, this algorithm uses special methods particular to IMS to retrieve the data directly (bottom-up type algorithm).

- if data are all the same level in the hierarchy an algorithm retrieves the occurrences which are common parents and then consider the corresponding children.
- final and general case : data to be obtained unlike the cases above will be distributed in random manner. The corresponding algorithm is more complex and at times uses a combination of preceding algorithms and at other times special retrieval of the third algorithm and special techniques proper to IMS.

Figure 5 shows the general architecture of the proposed system.

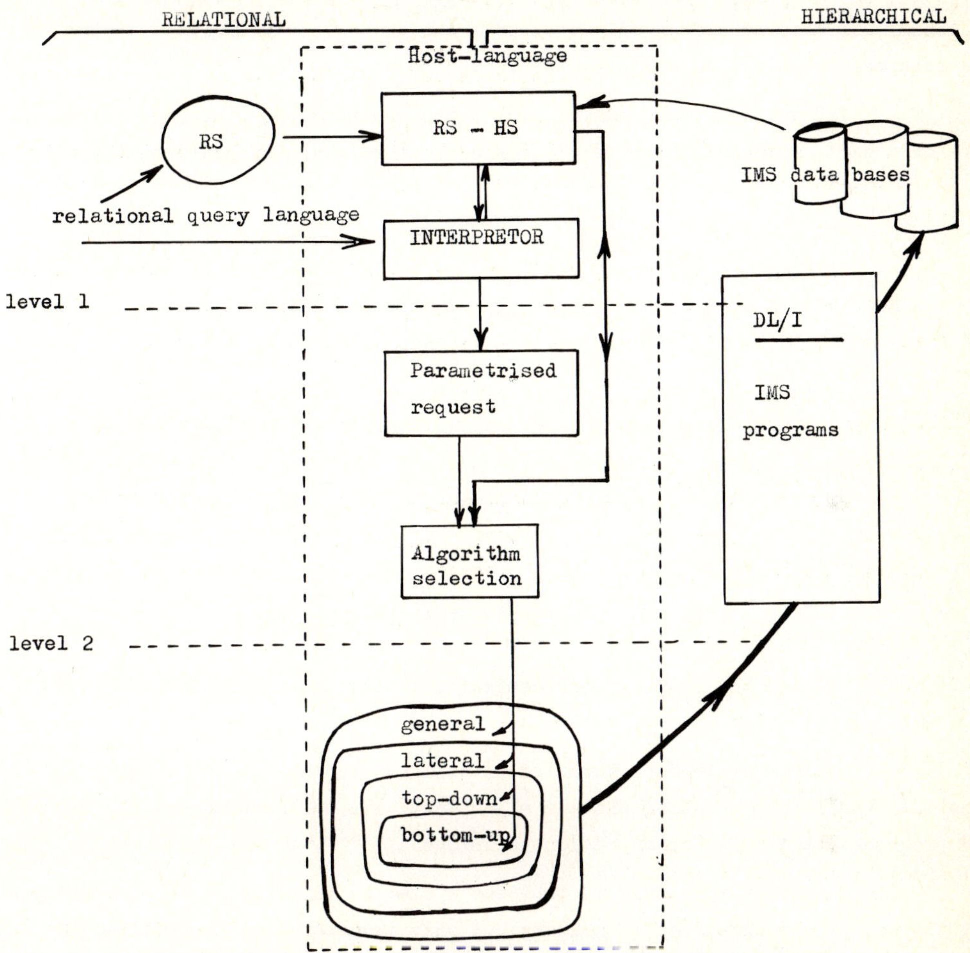

Figure 5 : General aspect of the translator

The translator is programmed in a host language which presently is assembler. The code produced in this case is more efficient but it is possible to use PL/I or COBOL which are also consistent with DL/I.

At level 1, the queries is accepted or rejected and at level 2 the algorithm is choosen using the parameter list issued from the interpretation and the interface RS-HS between the relational and the hierarchical structure.

4- Conclusion

Such a system contributes to solve the important point of data independence. The user specifies only what he wants and no how he has to proceed in the data base. The system executes the last point.

If the data base administrator decides to change the physical structure or a part of the structure the modifications will not affect the user.

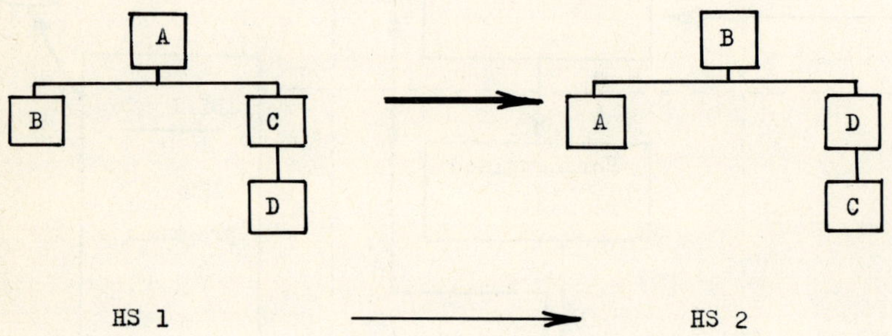

Figure 6 : Reorganization of a data base

In IMS the programs corresponding to the same query for HS 1 and HS 2 will be different.

In our system the formulation will remain the same. At execution time the translator, choosing another algorithm, will build automatically another IMS program always using optimization techniques .

An other advantage is that the system is interactive because we have not to recompile programs at each query but only transfer a parameter list to the translator.

The present interactive system has been implemented under virtual machine (VM-370) but it can be used with also other teleprocessing methods.

Acknowledgement : Many discussions with J.R. ABRIAL of IRIA and Professor J.C. BOUSSARD of University of Nice have been helpful and constructive. I thank them. I thank also all the persons of IBM La Gaude whose contribution has been useful for this project.

REFERENCES

1 BRACCHI G., PAOLINI P., PELAGATTI G. "Data independent description and the specifications", IFIP-TC 2, Special Working Conference, Namur, Belgium, January 1975.

2 CHILDS D.L. "Description of a set theoretic data structure", Proc. FJCC, 33(1), December 1968, 557-564.

3 CODD E.F. "A relational model for large shared data banks", Comm. ACM, 13(6), June 1970, 377-387.

4 CODD E.F. "Normalized data base structure", IBM Research Laboratory, San Jose, November 1971.

5 CODD E.F. "A data base sublanguage founded on the relational calculus", Proc. ACM Sigfidet, Workshop on data base description, access and control, San Diego, 1971.

6 DATE D.J., HOPEWELL P. "File definition and logical data independence", Proc. ACM Sigfidet, Workshop on data base description, access and control, San Diego, 1971.

7 DELOBEL C. "Contributions théoriques à la conception et à l'évaluation d'un système d'informations appliqué à la gestion", Thesis, University of Grenoble, 1973.

8 FRASSON C. "Exploration dynamique en mode relationnel d'une base de données à structure hiérarchique", Thesis, University of Nice, 1974.

9 Information Management System IMS/360, Application description manual (version 2), GH 20-0765-1, IBM, White Plains, New-York, 1971.

10 Information Management System IMS/360, System programming reference manual, SH 20-0911, IBM, White Plains, New-York, 1971.

11 OLLE T.W. "A non procedural language for retrieving information from data bases", IFIP Congress, Edinburg, Noth Holland, Amsterdam, August 1968.

12 SENKO M.E., ALTMAN E.B., ASTRAHAM M., FEDHER P.L. "Data structure and accessing in data systems", IBM System Journal, 12 (1), 1973.

13 STRNAD A.L. "The relational approach to the management of data base", IFIP Congress, Ljubljana, 1971.

ZUGRIFFSSYNCHRONISATION IN DATENBANKSYSTEMEN

G. Schlageter

Institut für Angewandte Informatik und Formale Beschreibungsverfahren der Universität Karlsruhe, D 75 Karlsruhe, Postfach 6380

Zusammenfassung

Synchronisationsprobleme in Datenbanken mit simultanem Zugriff mehrerer Prozesse erweisen sich als außerordentlich komplex, da zur Sicherung der Datenbank-Integrität und zur Vermeidung der Fehlfunktion von Prozessen unterschiedlich große Bereiche gesperrt werden müssen. Es wird zunächst ein sehr einfacher, aber effizienter Lockout-Mechanismus für read locks und write locks entworfen, auf dem aufbauend eine schnelle Deadlock-Analyse möglich ist. Im Anschluß werden allgemeinere Konzepte zur Prozeßsynchronisation in Datenbanksystemen skizziert.

1. Einleitung

Eines der vielen Probleme, die derzeit auf dem Gebiet der Datenbanken nur unbefriedigend gelöst sind, ist das der Prozeßsynchronisation bei simultan auf einer Datenbank arbeitenden Prozessen. Durch Synchronisationsmechanismen muß dafür gesorgt werden, daß diejenigen Prozesse, die auf dieselben Daten zugreifen wollen, sich nicht gegenseitig stören und, sofern mehr als ein schreibender Prozeß beteiligt ist, die Integrität der Datenbank gefährden.

Es genügt in Datenbanksystemen nicht, das jeweils zu ändernde Datenelement für andere Prozesse zu sperren; vielmehr müssen zur wirkungsvollen Synchronisation unterschiedlich große Mengen von Datenelementen als Einheiten betrachtet werden. Der Aufbau eines solchen "geschützten Bereiches" für einen Prozeß muß im allgemeinen sequentiell erfolgen (incremental allocation), wodurch offensichtlich gegenseitige Blockierung von Prozessen möglich wird.

Ein effizientes Synchronisationsverfahren wird skizziert, das sowohl read als auch write locks unterstützt. Auf diesem aufbauend kann ein einfaches Verfahren zur Deadlock-Analyse entwickelt werden. Abschließend werden wünschenswerte Konzepte eines benutzerfreundlicheren und flexibleren Synchronisationsverfahrens diskutiert.

2. Das Problem des parallelen Zugriffs

Wir betrachten eine Datenbank, deren Daten zu Sätzen gruppiert sind. $R = \{R_1, \ldots, R_m\}$ ist die Menge der Sätze, $\Pi = \{P_1, \ldots, P_n\}$ die Menge der im System aktiven Prozesse. Ein Prozeß ist <u>blockiert</u>, wenn er einen Satz verlangt, auf den er gegenwärtig nicht zugreifen darf; ein <u>Deadlock</u> liegt vor, wenn es für einen blockierten Prozeß keine Möglichkeit gibt, ohne abnormalen Eingriff von außen wieder entblockiert zu werden.

Anhand des Beispiels von Bild 1 werden einige Charakteristika des Synchronisationsproblems in Datenbanken aufgezeigt. Item a in Satz A ist funktional abhängig von den Items b_i in allen A zugeordneten Sätzen B (vgl. die RESULT Clause im Codasyl-Report [1,2]).

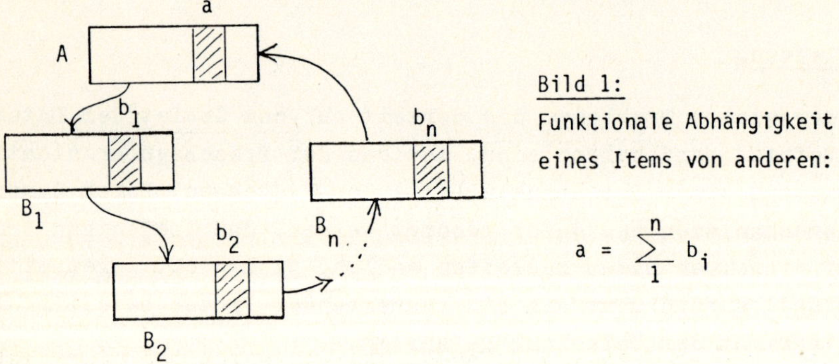

Bild 1:
Funktionale Abhängigkeit eines Items von anderen:

$$a = \sum_1^n b_i$$

Bevor ein Prozeß P ein Element b_i verändert, müssen, um Inkonsistenzen zu vermeiden, sowohl B_i als auch A gegenüber anderen Prozessen gesperrt werden. Geschieht dies nicht, sondern ändert P in folgender Weise

lock B_i
< Änderung B_i >
unlock B_i
lock A
< Änderung A >
unlock A ,

so liefert ein Prozeß, der a und b_i verwendet, u.U. ein inkonsistentes Ergebnis (altes a, neues b_i!).

Setzen wir nun voraus, daß P A und B_i vor der Änderung von b_i sperrt, und betrachten einen zweiten Prozeß Q, der zuerst a ausdruckt und dann die Einzelposten, aus denen a sich zusammensetzt. Hat Q a gelesen vor der Änderung von b_i, erreicht b_i aber erst nach der Änderung durch P, so ist das durch Q gelieferte Ergebnis wiederum inkonsistent. Es gibt verschiedene Lösungen dieses Problems: beispielsweise belegt Q Satz A mit einem read lock, der ändernden Zugriff verbietet; dann kann P wegen

lock B_i
lock A
< Änderung B_i >
< Änderung A >
.
.
.

keine Änderung durchführen, bis Q fertig ist.

Betrachten wir schließlich folgende extreme Situation: der Listprozeß Q hat A gesperrt und A und B_1 und B_2 gelesen. Ein dritter Prozeß S verändert nun die Sortierfolge der B-Sätze, wie in Bild 2 gezeigt.

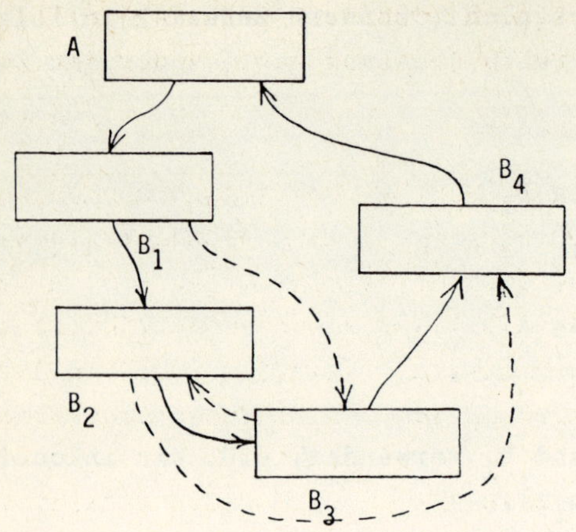

Bild 2:

Beispiel für Fehlfunktion durch Umordnung von Elementen in Listen oder Ketten

Die von Q erstellte Liste sieht dann insgesamt so aus:

$$A \quad B_1 \quad B_2 \quad B_3 \quad B_2 \quad B_4 \quad .$$

Eine solche Fehlfunktion von Q kann etwa dadurch verhindert werden, daß Q alle bereits gelesenen Sätze mit read lock belegt und S einen gesperrten Satz erst dann freigibt, wenn die gesamte Umsortierung beendet ist. Man sieht jedoch, daß wegen der sequentiellen Sperrung vieler Sätze ein überhöhtes Risiko für Blockierung und Deadlock besteht.

3. Ein Lockout-Mechanismus für Read Lock und Write Lock

Zur Prozeßsynchronisation in Datenbanken wurden Lockout-Mechanismen diskutiert, die die exklusive Zuordnung von Sätzen zu Prozessen ermöglichen [5,6,9]. Exklusive Zuordnung ist jedoch im Zusammenhang mit Datenbanken unnötig restriktiv; lesende Prozesse sollten sich gegen Änderungen von Daten schützen können, ohne anderen lesenden Prozessen simultanen Zugriff zu diesen Daten zu verwehren. Diese Forderung erfüllt ein zweistufiger Lock-Mechanismus [3].

<u>lockr</u> x : der Prozeß verlangt, daß Satz x gegen ändernden Zugriff gesperrt wird;

lockw x : der Prozeß zeigt an, daß er x verändern will, und verlangt ebenfalls Sperrung gegen ändernden Zugriff.

Die Wirkung ist die folgende: ist lockr x gesetzt, so können andere lesende Prozesse weitere lockr x absetzen, ohne blockiert zu werden; setzt ein Prozeß lockw x ab, so wird er blockiert. Es können also mehrere lesende Prozesse gleichzeitig auf x zugreifen, jedoch kein schreibender Prozeß. Ist lockw x gesetzt, so führt jedes weitere lockw x oder lockr x zur Blockierung des ausführenden Prozesses.

Für derartige zweistufige Lock-Mechanismen sind bislang keine effizienten Implementierungsmöglichkeiten vorgeschlagen worden, die eine einfache Deadlock-Analyse unterstützen. Das Problem der Deadlock-Analyse ist bei zweistufigen Lock-Mechanismen komplizierter als in einstufigen (exklusiver Fall). Im folgenden wird ein Verfahren skizziert, das Zugriffsynchronisation und Deadlock-Analyse bei zweistufigem Lock-Mechanismus auf sehr einfache Weise ermöglicht. Das Synchronisationsverfahren wird ausführlicher in [6] beschrieben, ohne daß jedoch eine Lösung für die Deadlock-Analyse gegeben wird.

Die Zugriffssynchronisation erfolgt über eine Belegungstabelle, in der alle Sätze eingetragen sind, die augenblicklich mit lockr oder lockw belegt sind. Ein Eintrag in der Tabelle hat die Form

$$\langle i, I(i), P, T(i) \rangle ,$$

wobei i die Nummer des markierten Satzes; I(i) ein 1-Bit Indikator, I(i) = 0, wenn i durch read lock belegt ist; P die Nummer des (ersten) Prozesses, dem i zugeordnet ist; T(i) ein Zeiger zur Prozeßliste, die alle Prozesse enthält, denen gleichzeitig mit P der Satz i zugeordnet ist. P wird nicht ebenfalls in dieser Liste geführt, da i häufig nur durch einen einzigen Prozeß belegt ist. Die Belegungstabelle wird als Hash-Tabelle organisiert.

Bild 3 zeigt eine Belegungstabelle zu einem bestimmten Zeitpunkt. In den Lock-Listen werden für jeden Prozeß die ihm zugewiesenen Sätze geführt (bzw. die Tabellen-Adressen, unter denen der jeweilige Satzeintrag steht).

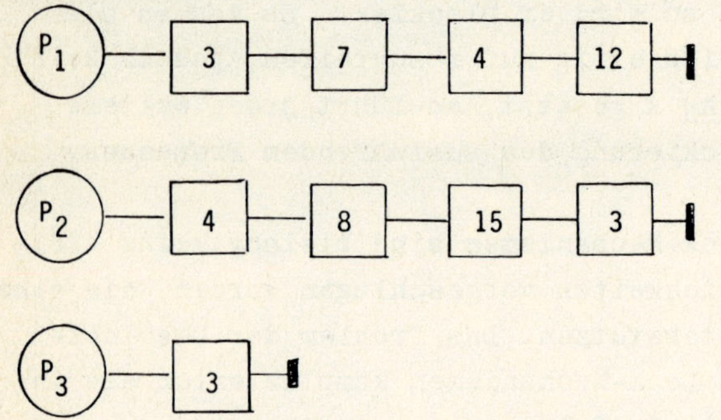

Bild 3:

Locklisten und Belegungstabelle zu einem bestimmten Zeitpunkt

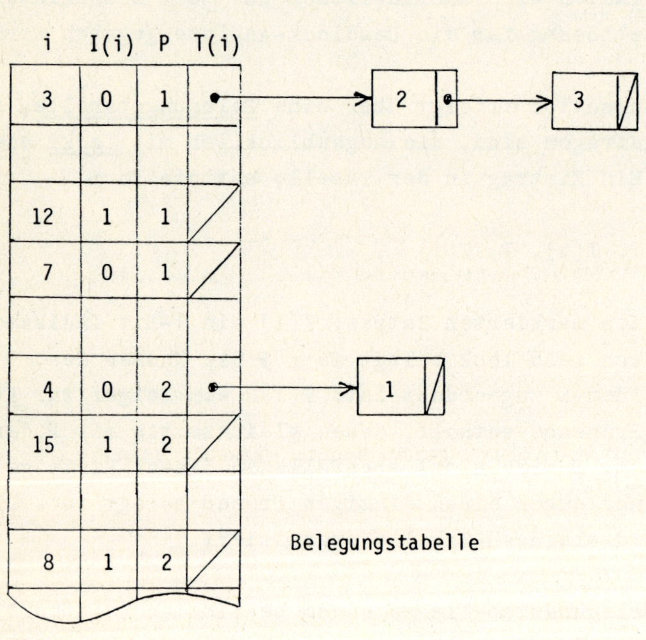

Wir benötigen die bereits eingeführten Operationen lockr(i) und lockw(i), die hier nicht im Detail formuliert werden können. Wenn ein lesender Prozeß P lockr(i) ausführt und es existiert ein Eintrag für Satz i mit I(i) = 0, dann kann P auf i zugreifen und wird in die Prozeßliste von i eingetragen. Ist I(i) = 1, wird P blockiert. Führt P lockw(i) aus, so wird P blockiert, wenn bereits ein Eintrag für i existiert. Führt etwa im Beispiel von Bild 3 Prozeß P_3 ein lockr(12) oder lockw(3) aus, so wird P_3 blockiert.

Dieses einfache Synchronisationsverfahren erlaubt nun eine ebenfalls sehr einfache Deadlock-Analyse.

4. Deadlock-Analyse

In dem zugrundeliegenden System müßte Deadlock-Analyse bei jeder Aktion gestartet werden, die zu einem Deadlock-Zustand führen kann, d.h. offensichtlich, in dem Augenblick, in dem ein Prozeß blockiert wird. Das folgende Analyseverfahren verwendet einen sog. Prozeßgraphen, der, im Unterschied zu Zustandsgraphen von Holt [4] oder access state graphs von King/Collmeyer [5], nur Knoten für Prozesse und nicht für gesperrte Sätze enthält.

Ein Prozeßgraph ist ein gerichteter Graph $G_P = (\Pi, F)$, mit Π = Menge der im System aktiven Prozesse und $F \subseteq \Pi \times \Pi$; ein Pfeil $(P_i, P_j) \in F$ gibt an, daß Prozeß P_i auf die Zuordnung eines Satzes wartet, den P_j gesperrt hat, d.h. P_i ist durch P_j blockiert.

Lemma 1: Ein Deadlock existiert genau dann, wenn G_P einen Zyklus enthält.

Bild 4 zeigt ein Beispiel für G_P; in den Lock-Listen ist gestrichelt angezeigt, welche Sätze von einem blockierten Prozeß verlangt werden. Zu beachten ist, daß ein Prozeß, der lockw(i) ausführt, durch alle Prozesse blockiert wird, die i durch lockr belegt haben.

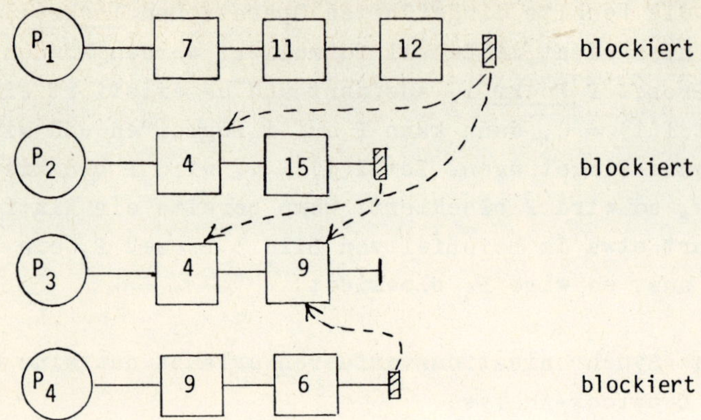

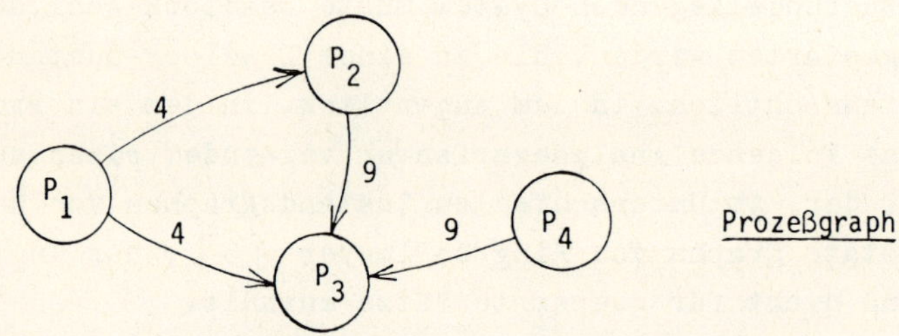

Bild 4:
Locklisten und Prozeßgraph
Die Zahlen an den Pfeilen geben den Satz an, der die Blockierung verursacht.

Deadlock-Analyse bedeutet also Prüfung auf Zyklen bei jeder Blockierung. Wird P_k blockiert, so muß geprüft werden, ob ein Weg existiert, der von P_k ausgehend wieder zu P_k zurückführt. Die Tatsache, daß die Zyklen-Suche sich auf Wege beschränken kann, die den Knoten P_k enthalten, ist offensichtlich sehr vorteilhaft, und wir brauchen nicht auf allgemeine Verfahren zur Feststellung von Zyklen zurückzugreifen. Vielmehr genügt eine systematische Suche von P_k ausgehend, bei der jeweils ein Weg soweit durchlaufen wird, bis er entweder zu einem

Endknoten (Knoten ohne Nachfolger), oder zu P_k zurück, oder zu einem Knoten führt, von dem aus bereits alle Wege verfolgt wurden. Der Algorithmus kann hier nur angedeutet werden, er wird aber am Beispiel von Bild 5 sofort klar. Durchsucht wird folgendermaßen:

1 - 2 - 3 - 4 - 5	kein Erfolg
4 - 8	kein Erfolg
3 - 8	kein Erfolg
1 - 6 - 3	kein Erfolg
1 - 7 - 6	kein Erfolg

Kein Deadlock.

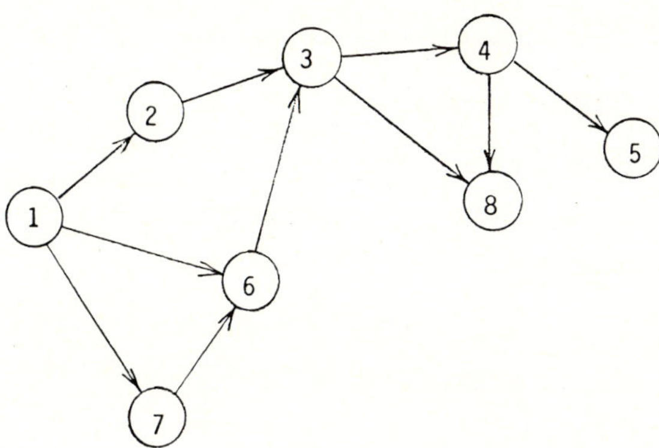

Bild 5: Ein Prozeßgraph

Man sieht, daß jeder Pfeil genau einmal betrachtet wird. Auf diese Weise können sehr effizient auch komplexe Blockierzustände auf Deadlock-Freiheit überprüft werden.

5. Verallgemeinerung der Lock-Operationen

Prinzipiell reicht zur Synchronisation von Prozessen im gegebenen Zusammenhang das skizzierte Synchronisationsverfahren auf Satzebene aus; es weist jedoch folgende Unzulänglichkeiten auf:

1) Die Programmierung kann sehr aufwendig werden.

2) Wegen der sequentiellen Anforderung der Sätze besteht die Tendenz zu unnötigen Sperrungen von Sätzen für blockierte Prozesse.

3) Infolge von 2) besteht eine erhöhte Gefahr von Deadlock.

Wünschenswert wären Verallgemeinerungen der Lock-Operationen, so daß

1) im Schema definierte Bereiche der Datenbank mit einer Lock-Operation gesperrt werden können, ohne daß dem Benutzer die Menge der aktuell zu sperrenden Sätze bekannt sein muß; die zu sperrende Menge ist lediglich typmäßig beschrieben.

Beispiel: (CODASYL Notation)

Definition des kritischen Bereiches im Schema:

```
cr name is KRIT BEREICH;
contains current of A, members of A in set X.
```

Sperrung eines aktuellen kritischen Bereiches vom Typ KRIT BEREICH im Programm:

```
        :
    lock KRIT BEREICH;
        :
```

Es würden der aktuelle Satz vom Typ A (current of A) und alle zugehörigen Members im Set X gesperrt.

Die Sperrung eines solchen schemabezogenen kritischen Bereiches könnte auch automatisch initiiert werden, wenn im Schema eine entsprechende Initiierungsbedingung formuliert ist [7]. Hierzu bietet sich eine analoge Konstruktion zur ON-Klausel des DBTG [1] an. Automatische Sperrung kritischer Bereiche ist vor allem unter dem Gesichtspunkt von großer Wichtigkeit, daß die Verantwortung für die Integrität der Datenbank möglichst weitgehend dem System, und nicht dem Benutzer, übertragen werden sollte.

2) im Benutzerprogramm definierte Bereiche mit einer Lock-Operation gesperrt werden können, z.B.:

Deklarationsteil des Benutzerprogramms:

⋮

<u>cr</u> <u>name</u> <u>is</u> KB1; <u>contains</u> <u>current</u> <u>of</u> B,

<u>owner</u> <u>of</u> B <u>in</u> <u>set</u> X.

⋮

Man beachte, daß auch hier die Definition eines solchen kritischen Bereiches keine genaueren Kenntnisse des angesprochenen Bereiches voraussetzt. Der Benutzer kann dann im Programm die Sperrung eines aktuellen Bereiches veranlassen durch <u>lock</u> KB1.

Die Programmierung mit kritischen Bereichen ist umständlich und unnötig restriktiv, wenn ein Prozeß mehrere kritische Bereiche vom gleichen Typ sperren und zu unterschiedlichen Zeitpunkten wieder freigeben will. Deshalb sollten auch die aktuellen kritischen Bereiche mit Namen belegt werden können, etwa

NAM = <u>lock</u> KB1;

Der mit diesem <u>lock</u> gesperrte Bereich vom Typ KB1 kann zukünftig mit dem Namen NAM angesprochen werden.

Es ist wesentlich, daß mit dem Konzept des kritischen Bereiches der Lock-Mechanismus nicht auf a-priori definierte Grundeinheiten, wie Sätze oder Files, beschränkt ist; vielmehr können in sehr viel geeigneterer Weise die Bedürfnisse einzelner Anwendungen berücksichtigt werden. Probleme bei der Implementierung können sich daraus ergeben, daß mit dem kritischen Bereich nicht mehr notwendig disjunkte Einheiten vorliegen, sondern möglicherweise sich überlappende, wobei aber die Überlappung im allgemeinen erst zur Laufzeit festgestellt werden kann. Einige auf die vorliegende Fragestellung übertragbare Ansätze werden in [8] entwickelt. Man sollte nicht übersehen, daß, sofern simultaner Zugriff mehrerer Prozesse möglich sein soll, in jedem Falle relativ komplexe Schutzmaßnahmen implementiert werden müssen, auch wenn sie sehr teuer sind.

6. Schlußbemerkung

Eine ganze Reihe von Fragen zum Problem der Zugriffssynchronisation in großen Datenbanken ist erst andiskutiert. Erfahrungen mit Implementierungen von Lockout-Mechanismen und Deadlock-Analyse-Verfahren liegen nicht vor. Konzeptmäßige Verallgemeinerungen der klassischen Lock-Operationen müssen weiter untersucht werden, insbesondere im Hinblick auf mögliche Implementierungen. Schließlich sollten Fragen des Restart und Recovery in diesem Zusammenhang nicht übersehen werden.

Literatur

1 CODASYL: Data Base Task Group Report, April 71.

2 CODASYL: DDL Journal of Development, June 73 Report.

3 Everest, G.C.: Concurrent Update Control and Data Base Integrity. In Klimbie, Koffeman (eds.): Data Base Management, Amsterdam, London 1974.

4 Holt, R.C.: Some Deadlock Properties of Computer Systems. Computing Surveys 4 (1972), 179 - 196.

5 King, P.F., Collmeyer, A.J.: Database Sharing - An Efficient Mechanism for Supporting Concurrent Processes. Proc. AFIPS 1973, 271 - 275.

6 Schlageter, G.: Access Synchronization and Deadlock-Analysis in Database Systems: An Implementation-Oriented Approach. Erscheint in Information Systems (1975)

7 Schlageter, G.: Ein Konzept zur Unterstützung konkurrierender Prozesse in Datenbanksystemen. Forschungsbericht 24 des Instituts für Angewandte Informatik und Formale Beschreibungsverfahren der Universität Karlsruhe, Dez. 1974.

8 Schlageter, G.: The Problem of Lock by Value in Large Databases. Forschungsbericht 32 des Instituts für Angewandte Informatik und Formale Beschreibungsverfahren der Universität Karlsruhe, Juni 1975.

9 Shoshani, A., Bernstein, A.J.: Synchronization in a Parallel-Accessed Data Base. CACM 12 (1969), 604 - 607.

A U T O M A T E N T H E O R I E

PROBLEMS OF THE CHANGE OF OPERATING TIME OF FINITE AUTOMATA

Jerzy W. Grzymala-Busse
Institute of Control Engineering
Technical University of Poznan
60-965 Poznan, Poland

ABSTRACT

The necessary and sufficient condition for the finite automata quasicontrollability defined here is presented. For a given set $\mathcal{A}$ of automata the conditions for the existence of an automaton A such that for each member of $\mathcal{A}$ there exists an identical subautomaton of A, associated with the change of operating time of A, are also given.

1. INTRODUCTION

We shall consider two main problems: the problem of quasicontrollability of finite automata and the problem of representability of a given set $\mathcal{A}$ of automata by another automaton A such that for each member of $\mathcal{A}$ there exists an identical subautomaton of A, associated with the change of its operating time (for shorteness, such subautomata are called later simply subautomata).

The notion of quasicontrollability of finite automata is a modified concept of the well-known notion of controllability of finite automata /1, 3, 4/. As we shall see later, there exist quasicontrollable but not controllable automata, and controllable but not quasicontrollable ones.

The later problem considered here has some importance for applications, since results regarding the above mentioned problem of representability of $\mathcal{A}$ has immediate applications - as it has been shown /2/: the set of subautomata associated with the change of operating time of A is obtained from A by way of an additional multichannel clock with different channels frequencies.

Some notions and results of the paper may be also find in /2/.

2. PRELIMINARIES

An automaton is a triple (S, Σ, M) , where S is a finite nonempty state set, Σ is a finite nonempty input set, and M is a transition function of $S \times \Sigma$ into S . The set of all finite sequences of elements from Σ will be denoted by I . The domain of the function M can be extended to $S \times I$ in a normal way: if $M(s,x)$ is defined, then $M(s,x\sigma)=M(M(s,x),\sigma)$, where $s \in S$, $x \in I$, and $\sigma \in \Sigma$.

Here, like in /2/, by a subautomaton A^i of the automaton $A=(S, \Sigma, M)$ we mean a triple (S, Σ^i, M^i) , where $\Sigma^i=\{\sigma_1 \sigma_2 \cdots \sigma_i : \sigma_1, \sigma_2, \ldots, \sigma_i \in \Sigma\}$, M^i is M restricted to $S \times \Sigma^i$, and i is a natural number.

For each $x \in I$ we define a mapping $f_x: S \longrightarrow S$, implied by x , by $f_x(s)=M(s,x)$, where $s \in S$. The set of all mappings, implied by elements of Σ^i , will be denoted by J^i . Each J^i , together with the operation of superposition of mappings, generates a semigroup F^i . Instead of J^1 and F^1 we use also symbols J and F , respectively. For the sequence $J, J^2, J^3, \ldots$ let τ be the smallest non-negative integer and T - the smallest natural number such that $J^{\tau+1}=J^{\tau+T+1}$. We say that A is characterized by numbers τ and T .

Let X and Y be sets of mappings of S into S . By XY we understand the set $\{ff' : f \in X , f' \in Y\}$.

The automaton $A=(S, \Sigma, M)$ is strongly connected if and only if for all $s, s' \in S$ there exists $x \in I$ such that $M(s,x)=s'$.

Let d be a natural number. A strictly periodic automaton V is a triple (S', Σ, M') , where S' is a finite sequence of finite nonempty state sets $S'_0, S'_1, \ldots, S'_{d-1}$, Σ is a finite nonempty input set, M' is a finite sequence of the transition functions $M'_0, M'_1, \ldots, M'_{d-1}$, where $M'_t : S'_t \times \Sigma \longrightarrow S'_{t+1 \pmod d}$ for $t \in \{0,1,\ldots,d-1\}$. The number d will be called a period of V .

A fixed analog V^* of the strictly periodic automaton $V=(S', \Sigma, M')$ is a triple (S^*, Σ, M^*) , where $S^* = \bigcup_{t=0}^{d-1} S'_t$, and $M^*: S^* \times \Sigma \longrightarrow S^*$ is a transition function, defined for each $s \in S'_t$, $\sigma \in \Sigma$, and $t \in \{0,1,\ldots,d-1\}$ as follows: $M^*(s, \sigma) = M'_t(s, \sigma)$.

A strictly periodic representation of the automaton A is a strictly periodic automaton V with period d such that the fixed analog V^* of V and A have the same state sets, input sets, and transition functions.

Among strictly periodic representations of A a strictly periodic representation with the maximal period will be called maximal.

A set Π of nonempty subsets $B_1, B_2, \ldots$ of the set X such that for each different B, B' in Π we have $B \cap B' = \emptyset$ and $X = B_1 \cup B_2 \cup \cdots$, is said to be a partition on X . Sets $B_1, B_2, \ldots$ are called blocks of Π .

3. CONTROLLABILITY AND QUASICONTROLLABILITY

We say that automaton A is controllable if and only if there exists a natural number k such that for all states s, s' of A there exists a sequence $x \in I$ with the length of x equal to k and such that $M(s,x)=s'$.

Obviously, any controllable automaton is strongly connected. The notion of controllability will be modified to release it from the strong connectivity. Namely, automaton A will be called quasicontrollable if and only if there exists a natural number k such that for each member f of the semigroup F there exists a sequence $x \in I$

with the length of x equal to k and such that f is identical with the mapping implied by x, i.e. $f(s)=M(s,x)$ for each state s of A.

A controllable automaton may not be quasicontrollable and a quasicontrollable automaton may not be controllable. As an example for the first assertion, let us consider the automaton $A=(S,\Sigma,M)$, where $S=\{s_0,s_1,s_2\}$, $\Sigma=\{0,1\}$, $M(s_0,0)=M(s_1,0)=s_0$, $M(s_2,0)=s_1$, $M(s_0,1)=M(s_1,1)=M(s_2,1)=s_2$. Mapping f_0 appears only in J, $J\neq J^2$, $J^2=J^3$, and hence A is not quasicontrollable.

Theorem 1. Automaton A is quasicontrollable if and only if $T=1$ and $F^2=FF=F$.

Proof. Let A be quasicontrollable. Then in the set $\{\tau+1,\tau+2,\ldots,\tau+T\}$ there exists a natural number $k=\tau+i+1$ such that $J^k=F$, where $i\in\{0,1,\ldots,T-1\}$. Let T be greater than 1. Then any set among the sets $J^{\tau+1},J^{\tau+2},\ldots,J^{\tau+T}$, except J^k, is different from F, by the definition of T. Let F' be equal to $J^{i+1(\mathrm{mod}\ T)+\tau+1}$. Then $F'\subsetneq F$ and $F'J^{T-1}=F$. Moreover, $FJ^{T-1}=F$, since $F'J^{T-1}=F$, and hence $J^{i-1(\mathrm{mod}\ T)+\tau+1}=F$, a contradiction. Thus $T=1$ and $F^2=F$, since $FJ=F$.

Let $T=1$ and $F^2=F$. Then $J^{\tau+1}=F$, $FJ=F$, and hence for each $f\in F$ there exists a sequence x with the length of x equal to $\tau+1$ such that f is identical with the mapping implied by x, i.e. A is quasicontrollable.

Corollary 1. For the quasicontrollable automaton A a minimal number k such that for each $f\in F$ there exists a sequence x with the length of x equal to k and f is identical with the mapping implied by x, is equal to $\tau+1$.

Note, that A is controllable if and only if it is strongly connected and its maximal strictly periodic representation has period

$D=1$. In other words, this assertion can be found in /3/.

Theorem 2. If the automaton A is strongly connected and quasicontrollable then it is controllable.

Proof. If A is quasicontrollable, then $T=1$, by Theorem 1, and hence the maximal strictly periodic representation of A has period $D=1$.

Let us consider the conditions for $\tau=0$ and $T=1$. We have the following easily proved assertions

Proposition 1. If F is a group and $F=J$, then $\tau=0$ and $T=1$.

Proposition 2. If J , together with the operation of superposition, is a semigroup, then $T=1$.

Theorem 3. If F is a group and the identity permutation id. is in J , then $T=1$.

Proof. Let $T>1$. Then among $F^{\tau+1}, F^{\tau+2}, \ldots, F^{\tau+T}$ there exists a polyadic group G such that G is not a binary group /2/. But id.$\in F^{\tau+1} \cap F^{\tau+2} \cap \cdots \cap F^{\tau+T}$, therefore id.$\in G$, a contradiction.

4. REPRESENTABILITY

Now we shall be considering the problem of representability of the set $\mathcal{A}$ of automata by another automaton A such that for each automaton in $\mathcal{A}$ there exists an identical subautomaton of A . Obviously, the first condition for the existence of such an automaton A for $\mathcal{A}$ is that all automata of the set $\mathcal{A}$ have the same state set S . We formulate our problem in a more convenient way. Let us assume that we have sets $J_1, J_2, \ldots, J_k$ of mappings of the set S into S . Does there exist a set J of mappings of S into S such that for each $i \in \{1,2,\ldots,k\}$ there exists a natural number j such that $J_i = J^j$? J^j denotes $\underbrace{JJ\cdots J}_{j \text{ times}}$. If we omit the structure of sets $J_1,J_2,\dots,J_k$, then we may formulate yet another problem: are $J_1,J_2,\dots,J_k$ elements of a cyclic semigroup ?

In the sequel, for the set X of mappings of the set S into S , by τ_X and T_X we shall denote the smallest non-negative integer and the smallest natural number, respectively, with $X^{\tau_X+1} = X^{\tau_X+T_X+1}$. For the set $J_i \in \{J_1,J_2,\dots,J_k\}$, the set $\bigcup_{a=1}^{\tau_{J_i}+T_{J_i}} J_i^a$ will be denoted by F_i and the set $\bigcup_{a=\tau_{J_i}+1}^{\tau_{J_i}+T_{J_i}} J_i^a$ will be denoted by P_i . By $\mathcal{J}$ we denote the family of all possible sets of the type $J_{i_1}J_{i_2}\cdots J_{i_l}$, where $i_1,i_2,\dots,i_l \in \{1,2,\dots,k\}$, and l is a natural number. Let T be the least common multiple of all $T_{J'}$, where $J' \in \mathcal{J}$.

In general, two cases are possible: the first - when all τ_{J_1}, $\tau_{J_2},\dots,\tau_{J_k}$ are equal to zero, and the second - when there exists at least one $\tau_{J_i}\neq 0$. On the family $\mathcal{J}$ we define a partition Π ; for the first case, the blocks of the partition Π will be denoted by natural numbers from the set $\{T_{J'} : J' \in \mathcal{J}\}$, and for $B_p \in \Pi$ we have $J' \in B_p$ if and only if $T_{J'}=p$; for the second case, the blocks of the partition Π will be denoted by pairs of numbers, the first a non-negative integer, and the second a natural number, from the set $\{(\tau_{J'}, T_{J'}) : J' \in \mathcal{J}\}$ and for $B_{(p,q)} \in \Pi$ we have $J' \in B_{(p,q)}$ if and only if $\tau_{J'}=p$ and $T_{J'}=q$.

For the set X by $|X|$ we denote the cardinality of X .

For the first case we have

<u>Theorem 4</u>. Let $\tau_{J_1}=\tau_{J_2}=\dots=\tau_{J_k}=0$. Then for $J_1,J_2,\dots,J_k$ there exists a set J such that for each $i \in \{1,2,\dots,k\}$ there exists a natural number j with $J_i=J^j$ if and only if for each $B_p \in \Pi$ we

have $|B_p|=\varphi(p)$ and in $\P$ there exists B_T .

$\varphi(p)$ is the Euler function, i.e. the number of natural numbers not greater than the given natural number p , and relatively prime to it.

Proof. Necessity. The family $\mathcal{J}$ can be presented in the form $\{J,J^2,\dots,J^T\}$, where T is some natural number. Let $d_1=1$, d_2 ,..., $d_l=T$ be all divisors of T . Then $\P=\{B_{d_1},B_{d_2},\dots,B_{d_l}\}$. From the definition of $\varphi(p)$ it follows that $|B_p|=\varphi(p)$, where $p\in\{d_1,d_2,\dots,d_l\}$.

Sufficiency. Let J be a member of B_T . Then all sets $J,J^2,\dots,J^T$ are different and they are in $\mathcal{J}$. Let $d_1=1$, d_2 ,..., $d_l=T$ be all divisors of T . In the set $\{J,J^2,\dots,J^T\}$ there are exactly $\varphi(d_i)$ elements J^{i_1} , J^{i_2} ,..., J^{i_l} with $T_{J^{i_1}}=T_{J^{i_2}}=\dots=T_{J^{i_l}}=d_i$, and hence $\mathcal{J}=\{J,J^2,\dots,J^T\}$.

From Theorem 4 we have for the second case

Corollary 2. Let $\P_0=\{B_{(0,q)} : B_{(0,q)}\in\P\}$. Let for $J_1,J_2,\dots,J_k$ there exists a set J such that for each $i\in\{1,2,\dots,k\}$ there exists a natural number j with $J_i=J^j$. Then for each $B_{(0,q)}\in\P_0$ we have $|B_{(0,q)}|=\varphi(q)$ and in $\P_0$ there exists $B_{(0,T)}$.

If for sets $J_1,J_2,\dots,J_k$ there exists a set J such that for each $i\in\{1,2,\dots,k\}$ there exists a natural number j with $J_i=J^j$, then the following conditions are satisfied:

Property 1. For all $i,j\in\{1,2,\dots,k\}$ we have $J_iJ_j=J_jJ_i$.

Property 2. For all $i,j,l\in\{1,2,\dots,k\}$ we have $(J_iJ_j)J_l=J_i(J_jJ_l)$.

Property 3. $\tau_{J_i}=\tau_{J_j}$ and $T_{J_i}=T_{J_j}$ if and only if $F_i=F_j$.

Property 4. T_{J_i} is a proper divisor of T_{J_j} if and only if $P_i \subsetneq P_j$.

Property 5. $J_1^{T_{J_1}} = J_2^{T_{J_2}} = \dots = J_k^{T_{J_k}}$.

Property 6. In $\mathcal{J}$ there exists only one semigroup.

REFERENCES

/1/ COHN, N.: Controllability in linear sequential circuits. IRE Trans. Circuit Theory CT-9, 1(1962), 74-78.

/2/ GRZYMALA-BUSSE, J.W.: Subautomata of finite automata, associated with the change of operating time. Report 46, Technical U. Poznan, 1972 (in Polish).

/3/ HARTMANIS, J., DAVIS, W.A.: Homomorphic images of linear sequential machines. J. Comput. Syst. Sci. 1, 2(1967), 155-165.

/4/ KAMBAYASHI, Y., YAJIMA, S.: Observable sequential machines and controllable sequential machines. Electron. Commun. Japan 52-A, 8(1969), 1-11.

ZUR KONSTRUKTION VON DECODIERAUTOMATEN

Ingrid Brückner

Institut für Angewandte Mathematik, TU Braunschweig
3300 Braunschweig, Pockelsstraße 14

Bevor man eine zu übermittelnde Nachricht in einem Kanal überträgt, wird sie codiert. Die allgemeinste Definition für einen Code lautet dabei:

Definition 1

Gegeben seien zwei Alphabete X und Y, damit ihre Wortmengen W(X) und W(Y). Sei $X' \subset W(X)$ und $Y' \subset W(Y)$. Ein Code ist eine Abbildung f mit

$f : Y' \longrightarrow X'$.

(Man bezeichnet häufig auch die Menge $C = f(Y')$ als Code und die Elemente von C als Codewörter.)

Nach der Übertragung im Kanal muß die codierte Nachricht decodiert werden. Diese Decodierung soll in einem determinierten Mealy-Automaten erfolgen. Als Eingabe erhält der Automat Wörter über dem Alphabet X, als Ausgabe liefert er Wörter über dem Alphabet $Y + \{F\}$, wobei mit $F \notin Y$ eine Fehlermeldung erfolgt. Im folgenden wird ein Verfahren angegeben, zu gewissen vorgegebenen Codes den zugehörigen Decodierautomaten zu konstruieren. Es werden nun einige spezielle Codes betrachtet.

Definition 2

Der Code f heißt Wortcode, wenn $Y' = Y^n$ $(n \geqq 1)$ ist, wobei

$Y^n = \{ y \mid y$ ist Wort über Y mit der Länge $l(y) = n \}$.

Definition 3

Ist der Code f Wortcode mit $f : Y^n \longrightarrow X'$ $(n \geqq 1)$, so kann man die Abbildung f erweitern zu einer Abbildung $f : W(Y^n) \longrightarrow W(X')$ durch die Definition

$f(e) := e$ (leeres Wort),

$f(y'^1 y'^2 \dots y'^k) := f(y'^1) f(y'^2) \dots f(y'^k)$, $k \geqq 1$, wobei

$y'^i \in Y^n$ $(i = 1,\dots,k)$.

Definition 4

Der Code f heißt eindeutig decodierbar (entzifferbar), falls die Erweiterung der Abbildung $f : Y^n \longrightarrow X'$, also die Abbildung $f : W(Y^n) \longrightarrow W(X')$ injektiv ist. Jedes Wort über X ist damit auf höchstens eine Art decodierbar.

Damit ist die Decodierabbildung φ zunächst auf W(C) definiert. Später wird φ auf ganz W(X) erweitert.

Definition 5

Ein Code heißt irreduzibel (Präfix-Code), wenn kein Codewort Anfangsstück eines anderen Codewortes ist.

Satz 1

Jeder irreduzible Code ist eindeutig decodierbar, die Umkehrung gilt nicht.

Es werden jetzt zunächst irreduzible Wortcodes mit $Y' = Y = \{y_1,\dots,y_l\}$ betrachtet. Mit $w_i := f(y_i)$ $(i = 1,\dots,l)$ ist dann $C = \{w_i | i=1,\dots,l\}$ die Menge der Codewörter.

Definition 6

Gegeben sei der irreduzible Code C über dem Alphabet X. Dann wird definiert:

$$C^* := \{ p \mid \text{ex. } w \in C, \text{ ex. } r \in W(X) \text{ mit } w = pr, 0 < l(p) < l(w) \} ,$$

$$S := \{ q \mid q = px \text{ mit } p \in C^* + \{e\}, x \in X \text{ und } q \notin C^* + C \} .$$

Satz 2

Für ein beliebiges Wort $p \in W(X)$ existiert genau eine der folgenden Darstellungen eindeutig:

(1) $p = \bar{w}$,

(2) $p = \bar{w}q$, $q \in C^*$,

(3) $p = \bar{w}sq$, $s \in S$, $q \in W(X)$; es ist jeweils $\bar{w} \in W(C) \subset W(X)$.

Damit läßt sich die Decodierabbildung auf ganz W(X) definieren.

Definition 7

$$\varphi(p) = \varphi(\bar{w})\varphi(r) \text{ mit } \varphi(r) = \begin{cases} e & \text{für } r = e \\ F & \text{sonst} \end{cases} ,$$

wobei $\bar{w}r$ Darstellung von p nach Satz 2 ist.

Die Decodierabbidung φ ist damit eine Wortfunktion über $(X,Y+\{F\})$. Es folgen jetzt zunächst Ergebnisse über den Zusammenhang zwischen Wortfunktionen und Automaten.

Definition 8

$A = (X,Y,Z,\delta,\lambda)$ ist determinierter Mealy-Automat, wenn gilt:

(1) X, Y, Z sind endliche, nichtleere Mengen,

(2) δ ist eine auf $Z \times X$ definierte Funktion mit $\delta : Z \times X \longrightarrow Z$,

(3) λ ist eine auf $Z \times X$ definierte Funktion mit $\lambda : Z \times X \longrightarrow Y$.

Hierbei ist X das Eingabealphabet, Y das Ausgabealphabet und Z die Menge der internen Zustände des Automaten. δ wird Übergangsfunktion (Überführungsfunktion) und λ Ausgabefunktion (Ergebnisfunktion) von A genannt.

Definition 9

Die Erweiterungen $\delta : Z \times W(X) \longrightarrow Z$ und $\lambda : Z \times W(X) \longrightarrow W(Y)$ werden festgelegt durch

$\delta(z,e) := z$,

$\delta(z,px) := \delta(\delta(z,p),x)$ für $p \in W(X)$, $x \in X$,

$\lambda(z,e) := e$,

$\lambda(z,px) := \lambda(z,p)\lambda(\delta(z,p),x)$ für $p \in W(X)$, $x \in X$.

Definition 10

Es sei φ eine Wortfunktion über (X,Y) und $\varepsilon \notin X$. Man nennt φ vom Zustand z des Automaten $A = (X+\{\varepsilon\},W,Z,\delta,\lambda)$ ε-realisiert, falls für alle $p \in W(X)$ gilt:

$\varphi(p) = |\lambda(z,p\varepsilon)|$, wobei $W \subset W(Y)$ und

$|\lambda(z,p\varepsilon)| = \lambda(z,x^1)\lambda(\delta(z,x^1),x^2)\dots\lambda(\delta(z,x^1\dots x^n),\varepsilon)$ mit $p = x^1\dots x^n$.

Definition 11

Es sei φ eine beliebige Wortfunktion über (X,Y). Eine Menge $\mathfrak{Z}^{\varphi}$ mit $\mathfrak{Z}^{\varphi} = \{(\sigma_p,\tau_p) \mid p \in W(X)\}$ nennt man Zustandssystem von φ, wenn die nachfolgenden Bedingungen erfüllt sind:

(1) σ_p, τ_p sind Wortfunktionen über (X,Y) für alle $p \in W(X)$,

(2) $\varphi(pr) = \sigma_e(p)\tau_p(r)$ für alle $p,r \in W(X)$,

(3) $\sigma_e(pr) = \sigma_e(p)\sigma_p(r)$ für alle $p,r \in W(X)$.

Jede Wortfunktion φ besitzt mindestens ein Zustandssystem $\mathfrak{Z}^{\varphi}$, und zwar $\sigma_p(r) = e$, $\tau_p(r) = \varphi(pr)$ für alle $p,r \in W(X)$. Von den möglichen Zustandssystemen von φ wird nun eines ausgezeichnet, das eine gewisse Maximalitätsbedingung erfüllt.

Definition 12

Sei φ eine beliebige Wortfunktion über (X,Y). Das kanonische Zustandssystem von φ

$$\mathfrak{Z}_o^{\varphi} = \{(\sigma_p^o,\tau_p^o) \mid p \in W(X)\}$$

wird folgendermaßen definiert:

$$\sigma_e^o(e) := e \text{ , } \sigma_e^o(p) := q \quad (p \neq e) \text{ ,}$$

falls q für alle $r \in W(X)$ Anfangsstück von $\varphi(pr)$, insbesondere von $\varphi(p)$ ist, ferner $l(q)$ maximal ist. Wegen Definition 11 ist dann für $p \in W(X)$:

$$\sigma_p^o(r) = s \text{ mit } \sigma_e^o(pr) = \sigma_p^o(p)s \text{ ,}$$

$$\tau_p^o(r) = q \text{ mit } \varphi(pr) = \sigma_e^o(p)q \text{ .}$$

Satz 3

Jede Wortfunktion φ über (X,Y) kann in einem determinierten Automaten ε-realisiert werden, der nicht mehr Zustände besitzt, als das kanonische Zustandssystem $\mathfrak{Z}_o^{\varphi}$ von φ Elemente hat, und φ kann in keinem Automaten ε-realisiert werden, der weniger Zustände besitzt, als das minimale Zustandssystem von φ Elemente hat. Dabei hat das kanonische Zustandssystem höchstens einen Zustand mehr als das minimale Zustandssystem.

Satz 4

Eine Wortfunktion φ kann genau dann in einem endlichen Automaten (vgl. Definition 8) ε-realisiert werden, wenn die Menge $\mathfrak{Z}_o^{\varphi}$ endlich ist.

Die in Satz 3 erwähnten Automaten sind allgemeiner als die Automaten nach Definition 8. Die Menge Z der Zustände kann hier auch mehr als endlich viele Elemente enthalten. Beim Beweis von Satz 3 wird jedem Zustandssystem $\mathfrak{Z}^{\varphi}$ von φ ein Automat $A^{\varphi} = (X+\{\varepsilon\},W,\mathfrak{Z}^{\varphi},\delta,\lambda)$ zugeordnet, in dem die Wortfunktion φ durch den Zustand (σ_e,τ_e) ε-realisiert wird. Insbesondere wird dem kanonischen Zustandssystem der Automat A_o^{φ} zugeordnet. Dabei wird definiert:

Definition 13

Gegeben sei eine Wortfunktion φ über (X,Y) mit dem Zustandssystem $\mathfrak{Z}^{\varphi}$. Der zugehörige Automat $A^{\varphi} = (X+\{\varepsilon\},W,\mathfrak{Z}^{\varphi},\delta,\lambda)$ wird festgelegt durch

$$\delta((\sigma_p,\tau_p),x) := (\sigma_{px},\tau_{px}) \text{ , } \quad \delta((\sigma_p,\tau_p),\varepsilon) := (\sigma_e,\tau_e) \text{ ,}$$

$\lambda((\sigma_p,\tau_p),x) := \sigma_p(x)$, $\lambda((\sigma_p,\tau_p),\varepsilon) := \tau_p(e)$

für $(\sigma_p,\tau_p) \in \mathfrak{Z}^\varphi$ und $x \in X$; $W := \{ q \mid q = \sigma_p(x) \text{ oder } q = \tau_p(e)\}$.

Es wird nun das kanonische Zustandssystem (da fast minimal) der in Definition 7 festgelegten Decodierabbildung φ bestimmt.

Satz 5

$(\sigma_{\bar{w}r},\tau_{\bar{w}r}) = (\sigma_r,\tau_r)$, wobei $p = \bar{w}r$ nach Satz 2 .

$(\sigma_{sr},\tau_{sr}) = (\sigma_{s't},\tau_{s't})$ für alle $s,s' \in S$, für alle $r,t \in W(X)$

(Schreibweise (σ_p,τ_p) statt (σ_p^o,τ_p^o) im folgenden).

Für das kanonische Zustandssystem erhält man:

Satz 6

$$\mathfrak{Z}_o^\varphi = \{(\sigma_p,\tau_p) \mid p \in C^*\} + \{(\sigma_e,\tau_e),(\sigma_s,\tau_s)\},\ |\mathfrak{Z}_o^\varphi| = |C^*| + 2 .$$

Zusammen mit Satz 3 und Satz 4, ferner mit Definition 13 ergibt sich:

Satz 7

Die Decodierabbildung φ wird in dem dem kanonischen Zustandssystem $\mathfrak{Z}_o^\varphi$ zugeordneten Automaten $A_o^\varphi = (X+\{\varepsilon\},Y+\{e,F\},\mathfrak{Z}_o^\varphi,\delta,\lambda)$ vom Zustand (σ_e,τ_e) ε-realisiert. Dabei sind δ und λ durch die nachfolgende Automatentafel gegeben:

	x	ε	x	ε
(e)	(x)	(e)	$\sigma_e(x)$	e
(p)	(px)	(e)	$\sigma_p(x)$	F
(s)	(s)	(e)	e	e

Schreibweise: (q) statt (σ_q,τ_q)

mit

$$(qx) = \begin{cases} (qx) & \text{für } qx \in C^* \\ (e) & \text{für } qx \in C \\ (s) & \text{für } qx \in S \end{cases} , \quad \sigma_q(x) = \begin{cases} e & \text{für } qx \in C^* \\ \varphi(w) = y & \text{für } qx = w \in C \\ F & \text{für } qx \in S \end{cases} ,$$

wobei $q \in C^* + \{e\}$, $x \in X$.

Beispiel 1

$X = \{0,1\}$, $Y = \{y_1,y_2,y_3,y_4\}$, $C = \{10,011,110,0101\}$,

$\varphi(10) = y_1$,

$\varphi(011) = y_2$,

$\varphi(110) = y_3$,

$\varphi(0101) = y_4$.

Dann ist $C^* = \{0,1,01,11,010\}$, also

$\mathfrak{Z}_o^\varphi = \{(e),(0),(1),(01),(11),(010),(s)\}$, ferner

$S = \{00,111,0100\}$.

Der dem kanonischen Zustandssystem zugeordnete Automat ist $A_o^\varphi = (\{0,1,\varepsilon\},Y+\{e,F\}, \mathfrak{Z}_o^\varphi,\delta,\lambda)$ mit der Automatentafel

	0	1	ε	0	1	ε
(e)	(0)	(1)	(e)	e	e	e
(0)	(s)	(01)	(e)	F	e	F
(1)	(e)	(11)	(e)	y_1	e	F
(01)	(010)	(e)	(e)	e	y_2	F
(11)	(e)	(s)	(e)	y_3	F	F
(010)	(s)	(e)	(e)	F	y_4	F
(s)	(s)	(s)	(e)	e	e	e

Die Ergebnisse sollen jetzt auf gewisse eindeutig decodierbare Codes verallgemeinert werden. Für die Überprüfung eines gegebenen Codes $\hat{C}$ auf eindeutige Decodierbarkeit ist die Definition 4 ungeeignet. Es läßt sich aber ein Algorithmus angeben, mit dessen Hilfe man diese Frage entscheiden kann. Hierfür werden zunächst Mengen T_j konstruiert.

Definition 14

Gegeben sei die Codewortmenge $\hat{C} = \{ v_i \mid v_i \in W(X),\ i = 1,\dots,m \}$.
Dann wird festgelegt:
$T_o := \hat{C}$,
ferner ist für $j = 1,2,\dots$

$$p \in T_j \;\Leftrightarrow\; \text{ex. } v \in \hat{C}\text{, ex. } q \in T_{j-1} \text{ mit}$$
$$(1)\ v = qp \quad \text{oder}$$
$$(2)\ vp = q\ ,$$
$$\text{wobei } p \in W(X),\ l(p) > 0\ .$$

Mit Hilfe der Mengen T_j kann man jetzt den Test auf eindeutige Decodierbarkeit formulieren.

Satz 8

Ein Code $\hat{C}$ ist eindeutig decodierbar genau dann, wenn keine der Mengen T_j , $j \geq 1$, ein Codewort enthält.

Da nur endliche Decodierautomaten betrachtet werden sollen, werden jetzt nur solche Codes behandelt, die mit beschränkter Verzögerung decodierbar sind.

Definition 15

Der Code $\hat{C}$ heißt eindeutig decodierbar mit beschränkter Verzögerung, wenn $\hat{C}$ eindeutig decodierbar ist und ein $l_o \in \mathbb{N}$ existiert derart, daß für alle $v \in \hat{C}$, für alle p, pr $\in W(X) - \{e\}$ gilt:

$$\left.\begin{array}{l} p = v\bar{v} \text{ mit } v \in \hat{C},\ \bar{v} \in W(\hat{C}) \\ pr = v'\bar{v}' \text{ mit } v' \in \hat{C},\ \bar{v}' \in W(\hat{C}) \end{array}\right\} \Rightarrow v' = v ,$$

wobei $l(p) \geqq l_o \geqq l_{min} = \text{Min}\ \{ l(v) \mid v \in \hat{C} \}$.

Es ist also von einer bestimmten Länge l_o ab möglich, ein Codewort v, das allen Wörtern pr einschließlich p als Anfangsstück gemeinsam ist, abzuspalten und mit der Decodierung zu beginnen.

Satz 9

$\hat{C}$ sei eindeutig decodierbar. Dann ist $\hat{C}$ eindeutig decodierbar mit beschränkter Verzögerung genau dann, wenn es ein $r \leqq N_o + 1$ gibt, so daß $T_r = \emptyset$ ist; dabei ist $N_o := \left| \bigcup_{j=1}^{\infty} T_j \right|$, endlich.

Für die Struktur eines beliebigen Wortes $p \in W(X)$ erhält man:

Satz 10

Für ein beliebiges Wort $p \in W(X)$ existiert mindestens eine Darstellung $p = \bar{v}r$ mit $\bar{v} \in W(\hat{C}) \subset W(X)$. Dabei läßt sich immer erreichen, daß $r \in W(X)$ eine der nachfolgenden Bedingungen erfüllt:

(1) $r = e$,

(2) ex. $v \in \hat{C}$, ex. $q \in W(X)$ mit $v = rq$ und $l(q) > 0$,

(3) ex. $v \in \hat{C}$, ex. $q \in W(X)$ mit $vq = r$ und $l(q) \geqq 0$,

(4) weder (1) noch (2) noch (3) ,

wobei r nicht (3) als einzige Bedingung erfüllt.

Definition 16

Ein Wort r wird fortsetzend genannt, wenn Bedingung (1) oder (2) erfüllt ist, es wird nicht fortsetzend genannt, wenn (4) erfüllt ist (r wie in Satz 10) .

Für die Decodierung von p wird eine der Darstellungen von p ausgezeichnet, wobei die Überlegung mitspielt, daß ein möglicher Fehler möglichst spät aufgetreten sei.

Definition 17

Sei p ein beliebiges Wort aus W(X), Dann läßt sich p darstellen als $p = \bar{v}_p u_p$ mit $\bar{v}_p \in W(\hat{C})$, $u_p \in W(X)$, $l(\bar{v}_p)$ maximal (Wegen der eindeutigen Decodierbarkeit ist $\bar{v}_p$ und damit u_p eindeutig bestimmt) .

Dann wird festgelegt:

$$\varphi(p) := \varphi(\bar{v}_p)\varphi(u_p) \quad \text{mit} \quad \varphi(u_p) := \begin{cases} e & \text{für } u_p = e \\ F & \text{sonst} \end{cases} .$$

Diese Definition ist für die Bestimmung des kanonischen Zustandssystems ziemlich unhandlich. Um einige Ergebnisse für irreduzible Codes verwenden zu können, wird jetzt jedem Code $\hat{C}$ ein irreduzibler Code C zugeordnet. Die Konstruktionsvorschrift hierfür steht in unmittelbarem Zusammenhang mit dem Algorithmus für die Bestimmung der T_j (Definition 14).

Es werden Wörter $p_j = \bar{v}_j = \bar{v}_j{}'u_j$, $u_j \in T_j$, für j = 0,1,...,r-1 konstruiert. Dabei ist r der kleinste Index j mit $T_j = \emptyset$. Der Algorithmus bricht jeweils die Konstruktion ab, wenn das u_j die Eigenschaft hat, nicht fortsetzend zu sein ($j \neq 0$). Für j = 0 bricht die Konstruktion ab, falls $u_j = v$ weder echtes Anfangsstück eines anderen Codewortes ist, noch ein anderes Codewort als echtes Anfangsstück enthält. Sonst wird p_{j+1} aus p_j konstruiert durch:

(1) $p_{j+1} = \bar{v}_{j+1} = \bar{v}_{j+1}{}'u_{j+1}$ mit $\bar{v}_{j+1} = \bar{v}_j{}'v$ und $\bar{v}_{j+1}{}' = \bar{v}_j$,
falls eine Darstellung $v = u_j u_{j+1}$ existiert,

(2) $p_{j+1} = \bar{v}_{j+1} = \bar{v}_{j+1}{}'u_{j+1}$ mit $\bar{v}_{j+1} = \bar{v}_j$ und $\bar{v}_{j+1}{}' = \bar{v}_j{}'v$,
falls eine Darstellung $vu_{j+1} = u_j$ existiert.

Insbesondere wird gesetzt:

$p_o = \bar{v}_o = \bar{v}_o{}'u_o$ mit $\bar{v}_o = u_o$, $\bar{v}_o{}' = e$.

Die Wörter p_j werden in der Menge $\tilde{C}$ zusammengefaßt, die - als Code aufgefaßt - nicht notwendig irreduzibel ist. Man erhält jedoch einen irreduziblen Code C durch $C := \tilde{C} - \tilde{C}^*$ ($\tilde{C}^*$ analog Definition 6 bilden) .

Ein Codewort $w \in C$ hat damit die Eigenschaft

(1) $w = v$, $v \in \hat{C}$ oder

(2) $w = \bar{v} = \bar{v}'r$, r nicht fortsetzend, $\bar{v},\bar{v}' \in W(\hat{C})$.

Es gilt: $\varphi_C(\bar{w}r) = \varphi_C(r)$, wobei φ_C die Decodierabbildung bzgl. C ohne Berücksichtigung von $\hat{C}$ ist (vgl. Definition 7).

Satz 11

$\varphi(\bar{w}r) = \varphi(\bar{w})\varphi(r)$, wobei φ die Decodierabbildung bzgl. $\hat{C}$ ist.

Definition 18

Sei $q \in C^* + S$, es existiere mindestens eine Darstellung $q = \bar{v}u$ mit u fortsetzend. Das längste Wort über $\hat{C}$, das die Darstellung $q = \bar{v}_q u_q$ und die Darstellungen $q = \bar{v}u$, u fortsetzend, als Anfangswort über V gemeinsam haben, wird mit $\bar{v}_q^o$ bezeichnet, das Restwort mit u_q^o.

Es gilt:

$\varphi(qr) = \varphi(\bar{v}_q^o)\varphi(u_q^o r)$ für alle $r \in W(X)$.

Satz 12

$(\sigma_{\bar{w}r}, \tau_{\bar{w}r}) = (\sigma_r, \tau_r)$ für alle $\bar{w} \in W(C)$, für alle $r \in W(X)$ (vgl. Satz 5).

Satz 13

$(\sigma_q, \tau_q) = (\sigma_{u_q^o}, \tau_{u_q^o})$, $q \in C^* + S$. Es ist $u_q^o \in C^*$.

Satz 14

Sei $s \in S$ und existiere keine Darstellung $s = \bar{v}u$ mit u fortsetzend. Analoges gelte für s'. Dann ist:

$(\sigma_s, \tau_s) = (\sigma_{s'}, \tau_{s'})$, ferner $(\sigma_{sr}, \tau_{sr}) = (\sigma_s, \tau_s)$ für alle $r \in W(X)$.

Definition 19

$C_o := \{ p \mid p \in C^*, \bar{v}_p^o = e \}$,

$S_o := \{ s \mid s \in S$, ex. keine Darstellung $s = \bar{v}u$ mit u fortsetzend$\}$.

Für das kanonische Zustandssystem der Decodierabbildung φ (vgl. Definition 17) erhält man:

Satz 15

$\mathfrak{Z}_o^\varphi = \{(\sigma_p, \tau_p) \mid p \in C_o\} + \{(\sigma_e, \tau_e), (\sigma_{s_o}, \tau_{s_o})\}$, $|\mathfrak{Z}_o^\varphi| = |C_o| + 2$.

Zusammen mit Satz 3 und Satz 4, ferner mit Definition 13 ergibt sich:

Satz 16

Die in Definition 17 festgelegte Decodierabbildung φ wird in dem Automaten $A_o^\varphi = (X+\{\varepsilon\}, W, \mathfrak{Z}_o^\varphi, \delta, \lambda)$ vom Zustand (σ_e, τ_e) ε-realisiert. Dabei ist

$W = \{ u \mid u = e$ oder $u = \varphi(p)$ mit $p \in C_o$ oder

$u = \sigma_q(x)$ mit $q \in C_o + \{e\}$, $x \in X \}$.

Die Funktionen δ und λ sind durch die nachfolgende Automatentafel gegeben:

	x	ε	x	ε
(e)	(x)	(e)	$\sigma_e(x)$	e
(p)	(px)	(e)	$\sigma_p(x)$	$\varphi(p)$
(s_o)	(s_o)	(e)	e	e

Schreibweise: (q) statt (σ_q, τ_q) .

mit

$$(qx) = \begin{cases} (qx) & \text{für } qx \in C_o \\ (u^o_{qx}) & \text{für } qx \quad C^* - C_o \\ (s_o) & \text{für } qx \in S_o \\ (u^o_{qx}) & \text{für } qx \in S - S_o \\ (e) & \text{für } qx \in C \end{cases} , \quad \sigma_q(x) = \begin{cases} e & \text{für } qx \in C_o \\ \varphi(\bar{v}^o_{qx}) & \text{für } qx \in C^*-C_o \\ \varphi(\bar{v}^o_{qx})F & \text{für } qx \in S_o \\ \varphi(\bar{v}^o_{qx}) & \text{für } qx \in S-S_o \\ \varphi(w) & \text{für } qx = w \in C \end{cases} ,$$

wobei $q \in C_o + \{e\}$, $x \in X$.

Beispiel 2

$X = \{a,b,c\}$, $Y = \{1,2,3,4,5\}$, $\hat{C} = \{a,ab,bc,abb,bcc\}$.

Der zugeordnete irreduzible Code C ist

$C = \{bcc,abcc,abbcc\}$, d. h.

$C^* = \{a,b,ab,bc,abb,abc,abbc\}$,

$S = \{c,aa,ac,ba,bb,aba,bca,bcb,abba,abbb,abca,abcb,abbca,abbcb\}$.

Man erhält

$C_o = \{a,b,ab,bc,abb\}$, $C^* - C_o = \{abc,abbc\}$,

$S_o = \{c,ac,ba,bb\}$,

$S - S_o = \{aa,aba,bca,bcb,abba,abbb,abca,abcb,abbca,abbcb\}$.

Die Automatentafel lautet

	a	b	c	ε	a	b	c	ε
(e)	(a)	(b)	(s_o)	(e)	e	e	F	e
(a)	(a)	(ab)	(s_o)	(e)	1	e	1F	1
(b)	(s_o)	(s_o)	(bc)	(e)	F	F	e	F
(ab)	(a)	(abb)	(bc)	(e)	2	e	1	2
(bc)	(a)	(b)	(e)	(e)	3	3	5	3
(abb)	(a)	(b)	(bc)	(e)	4	4	2	4
(s_o)	(s_o)	(s_o)	(s_o)	(e)	e	e	e	e

Dabei ist $\varphi(a) = 1$, $\varphi(ab) = 2$, $\varphi(bc) = 3$, $\varphi(abb) = 4$, $\varphi(bcc) = 5$ gesetzt und $W = \{e,F,1,2,3,4,5,1F\}$.

Literaturverzeichnis

[1] BRÜCKNER, I.
Zur Konstruktion von Decodierautomaten
Dissertation, TU Braunschweig, 1975

[2] HENZE, E.; HOMUTH, H. H.
Einführung in die Codierungstheorie
Friedr. Vieweg + Sohn Verlag, Braunschweig 1974

[3] HOMUTH, H. H.
Bemerkungen über automatentheoretische Modelle einfacher Schlüsselverfahren
Angewandte Informatik 5, 244 - 246 (1971)

[4] KAMEDA, T.; WEIHRAUCH, K.
Einführung in die Codierungstheorie I
Bibliographisches Institut, Mannheim/Wien/Zürich 1973

[5] McNAUGHTON, R.
A Decision Procedure for Generalized Sequential Mapability-onto of Regular Sets
ACM, Proc. 3rd ann. ACM Sympos. Theory Computing, Shaker Heights, Ohio 1971, 206 - 218 (1971)

[6] STARKE, P. H.
Abstrakte Automaten
VEB Deutscher Verlag der Wissenschaften, Berlin 1969

ZWEI - ZÄHLER - AUTOMATEN MIT GEKOPPELTEN BEWEGUNGEN

Burchard v. Braunmühl

Gesellschaft für Mathematik und Datenverarbeitung
Bonn - Birlinghoven

Neben den klassischen Automatentypen Turingmaschine, Stackautomat, Pushdownautomat, Counterautomat und finiter Automat gibt es nur noch wenige neuere Modelle, die in die Literatur Eingang gefunden haben. Das Hauptgewicht der Untersuchungen lag bisher nicht so sehr auf den Speicherstrukturen als auf der Speicher- bzw. der Zeit-Komplexität.

Will man in einer systematischen Weise nach Automatenmodellen mit verschiedenem Speicherverhalten suchen, ohne Komplexitätsbetrachtungen zur Hilfe zu nehmen, so kann man einfache und natürliche Bedingungen verwenden, die die Manipulationsmöglichkeiten der Turingmaschine auf ihrem Speicher einschränken. Am unmittelbarsten bieten sich hier Bedingungen an die Maschinentafel und spezieller an die Form der Maschinenbefehle an, Bedingungen, die in den Befehlen der Turingmaschine die Komponenten untereinander oder mit Konstanten gleichsetzen.
Die Befehle einer Turingmaschine mit einem Input- und einem Arbeitsband sind von der Form

$$(q,\ a,\ A,\ q',\ B,\ d_o,\ d),$$

wobei q den augenblicklichen und q' den nachfolgenden Zustand, a das gelesene Inputsymbol, A das gelesene und B das zu druckende Arbeitssymbol, d_o bzw. d die Bewegung des Input- bzw. Arbeitskopfes darstellt. Die Konstanten, die wir zur Verfügung haben, sind der Anfangszustand q_o, das Blank ¤, das die leeren Felder anzeigt, die Bewegungen $1,\ o,\ -1$ und das Kreuz # , das wir als Anfang bzw. Bodenmarke auf das Feld o der Bänder setzen. Unsere Bedingungen setzen sich somit aussagenlogisch zusammen aus folgenden Elementarbedingungen:

$$q = q_o, \quad q = q', \quad q' = q_o$$
$$a = ¤, \quad a = \#$$
$$A = ¤, \quad A = \#, \quad A = B, \quad B = ¤, \quad B = \#$$
$$d_o = 1, \quad d_o = o, \quad d_o = -1, \quad d = 1, \quad d = o, \quad d = -1$$

Daß solche Bedingungen nicht nur formal überzeugend sind, sondern auch die anschaulich gewonnenen klassischen Modelle gut beschreiben, mögen die folgenden Beispiele zeigen.
Wir betrachten Turingmaschinen, deren Befehle folgender # - Bedingung genügen:

(1) $a = \# \Rightarrow d_o \neq -1$

(2) $A = \# \Rightarrow d \neq -1$

(3) $A = \# \Leftrightarrow B = \#$

Durch die # - Bedingung, die schon von der oben beschriebenen Art ist, wird garantiert, daß die Köpfe das Kreuz weder nach links überlaufen, noch gegen ein anderes Symbol austauschen, und daß das Kreuz auf kein Feld größer Null gedruckt wird. Diese Turingmaschinen rechnen also auf Halbbändern.
Einen Zählerautomaten erhalten wir dann mit der Bedingung

$A = ¤ \Rightarrow B = ¤$

Ein Pushdownautomat läßt sich, wie man sich überlegen kann, allein durch die Bedingung

$d = -1 \Rightarrow B = ¤$

definieren und ein Linearbounded-Automat durch

(i) $a = ¤ \Rightarrow d_o \neq 1$

(ii) $d_o = d$

Die Bedingung (i) allein liefert uns eine Turingmaschine mit two-way Inputband, während

$d_o \neq -1$

eine Turingmaschine mit one-way Inputband ergibt.

Von dem Stackautomaten, einem Pushdownautomaten, dessen Arbeitskopf in den Pushdownstack eindringen, dort aber nichts verändern darf, gibt es in der Literatur keine gängige formale Definition, die dem Formalismus der Turingmaschine treu bleibt. Um den Stackautomaten durch Bedingungen unserer Form zu charakterisieren, benützen wir eine Turingmaschine mit 2 Arbeitsbändern, also mit Befehlen der Gestalt $(q, a, A_1, A_2, q', B_1, B_2, d_o, d_1, d_2)$ und der entsprechenden # - Bedingung. Der Stackautomat ist dann durch folgende Bedingung zu bestimmen:

(α) $d_i = -1 \Rightarrow B_i = ¤ \; (i = 1,2)$

d.h. beide Arbeitsbänder sind Pushdownbänder

(β) $A_1 \neq \#, \; A_2 \neq \# \Rightarrow B_1 = A_2, \; B_2 = A_1, \; d_2 = -d_1$

d.h. sind die Pushdownstacks nicht leer, so schaukeln die beiden Köpfe gegenläufig auf den Bändern und tauschen dabei ihre jeweiligen Feldinhalte aus.

(γ) $A_1 = \#, \; A_2 \neq \# \Rightarrow B_2 = A_2, \; d_2 = -d_1.$

Bei leerem ersten Pushdownstack wird nichts verändert. Nur wenn der zweite Pushdownstack leer ist, kann der erste uneingeschränkt arbeiten, also neues drucken oder "wirklich" löschen.

In dieser Arbeit untersuchen wir Turingmaschinen mit zwei Arbeitsbändern, deren Befehle schon den Bedingungen

(4) $d_o \neq -1$

(5) $A_i = \sharp \Rightarrow B_i = \sharp \quad (i = 1,2)$

genügen, also Turingmaschinen mit einem one-way Inputband und zwei Zählerbändern. Wir interessieren uns für Bedingungen der genannten Form, die jedoch nicht die Zustandskomponente und nicht die Inputkomponenten der Befehle betreffen. Es handelt sich also im wesentlichen um Bedingungen, die die Bewegungen der beiden Zählerköpfe miteinander koppeln, in der Art, wie das auch im letzten Beispiel, beim Stackautomaten, geschieht, wenn man von den Forderungen bzgl. der Feldinhalte absieht.
Diese Koppelungsbedingung an die Köpfe tritt nur in Kraft, wenn beide Köpfe über dem # stehen.

Das Ziel ist es, alle Klassen von solchen 2C-Automaten zu bestimmen, die durch eine Bedingung der Form

"für alle Befehle $(q,A_o,A_1,A_2,a',d_o,d_1,d_2)$ aus δ gilt:
$A_1 = A_2 = \sharp \Rightarrow E(d_1,d_2)$"

eingeschränkt sind.
Hierbei sei E irgendeine Eigenschaft des Paares (d_1,d_2). Beispiele sind:

$d_2 = |d_1|$, $d_1 < d_2$, $d_1 \geq -d_2$.

Eine Teilmenge E aus $\{1,o,-1\} \times \{1,o,-1\}$ kann eindeutig beschrieben werden durch eine 3x3 - Matrix $(a_{ij})_{i,j = 1,o,-1}$ über $\{o,1\}$ mit $a_{ij} = 1$ gdw. $E(i,j)$.
So sind die Matrizen für die obigen drei Beispiele:

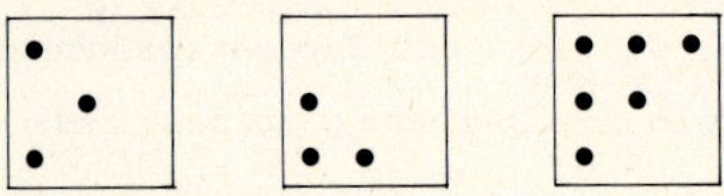

(Punkt steht für 1, Lücke für o)

Wir wollen die Felder der Matrix wie folgt durchnumerieren:

1	4	7
2	5	8
3	6	9

und mit A_t $(t \subseteq \{1,\ldots,9\})$ die Sprachklasse kennzeichnen, die durch die zu der Matrix gehörenden Automatenklasse definiert wird, bei der genau die Felder aus t mit 1 (Punkt) belegt sind. Ist $t = \{i_1,\ldots,i_r\}$, so schreiben wir für A_t auch $A_{i_1 \ldots i_r}$. So definieren die obigen Matrizen die Sprachklassen A_{135}, A_{236} und A_{123457}.

Es gibt $2^9 = 512$ solche Matrizen. Es erhebt sich die Frage: wieviele unter den entsprechenden Typen gibt es, die paarweise verschiedene Sprachklassen definieren, und wie ordnen sich diese Sprachklassen bzgl. der Enthaltenseins-Relation.

Nennen wir zwei Matrizen äquivalent, wenn die durch sie gegebenen Automatenklassen dieselbe Sprachklasse definieren, so kann man sich überlegen, daß alle Matrizen zu einer der 28 auf Bild 1 aufgeführten äquivalent sind.

Bild 1:

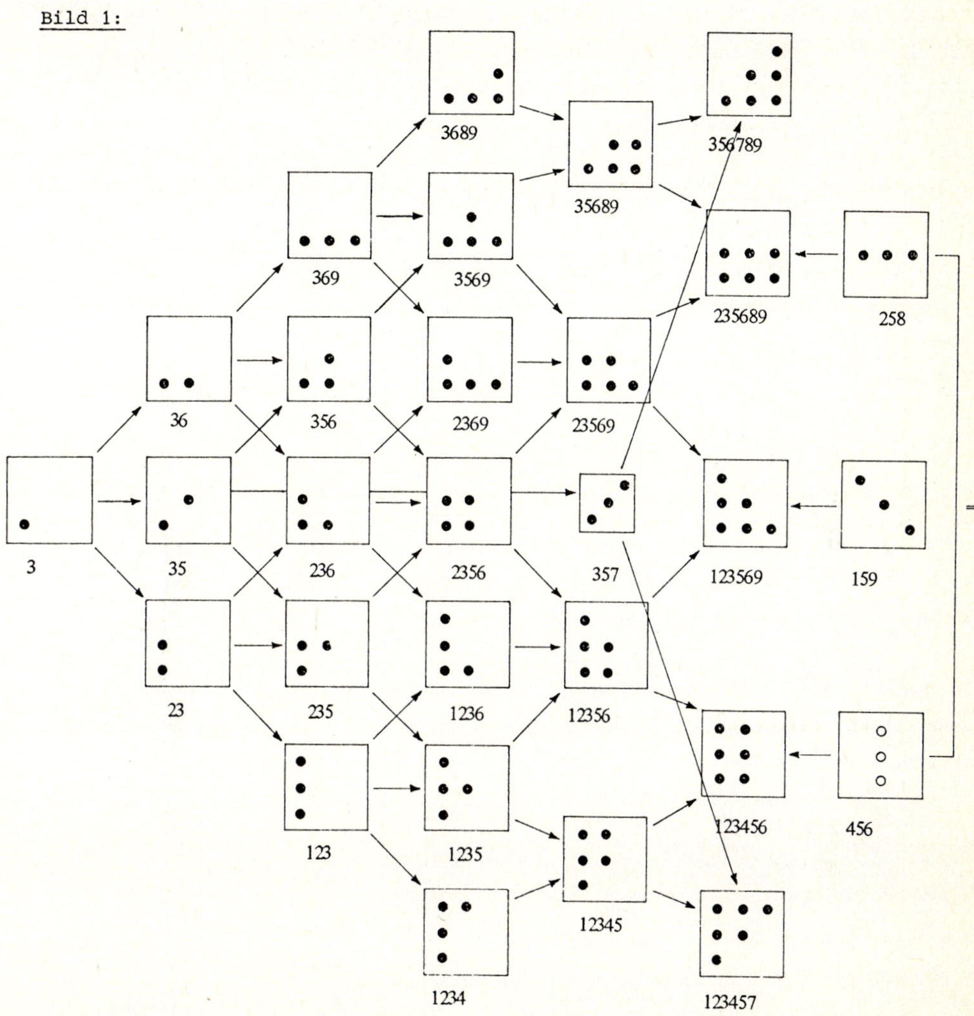

Die Pfeile deuten an, welche "trivialen" Enthaltensein-Beziehungen zwischen den zugehörigen Sprachklassen bestehen.

Die Arbeit beschäftigt sich also genauer mit diesen 28 Typen, weist nach, welche zusammenfallen, und zeigt, daß die übrigen echt verschieden sind. Bis auf eine noch unbewiesene Vermutung wird sich herausstellen, daß die 28 Typen auf 24 zurückgeführt werden können, und daß die im Bild schon angedeutete Halbordnung nur wenig verändert wird.

Nach Bild 1 sind die schwächsten Typen A_3, A_{159} und A_{258}, die minimalen Elemente dieser vorläufigen Halbordnung (der Typ A_{456} ist nur der Symmetrie halber angedeutet. Spiegelung an der Hauptdiagonalen). Bei einem A_3-Automaten können die Köpfe, falls sie beide über dem # stehen, nur eine Bewegung ausführen: K_1 sinkt um ein Feld, K_2 steigt um eines. Steht und verbleibt jedoch einer der Köpfe auf dem #, so ist der andere Kopf frei. Immerhin wird die nicht kontextfreie Sprache $\{a^p b^p a^p \mid p \in \mathbb{N}\}$ von einem A_3-Automaten erkannt.
Damit ist schon klar, daß die A_3-Automaten echt über den Zählerautomaten stehen, ja nicht einmal spezielle Pushdownautomaten sind.
Bei einem A_{159}-Automaten haben die Köpfe schon 3 verschiedene Bewegungen zur Verfügung, falls sie beide über dem Boden stehen. Dennoch ist jede A_{159}-Sprache kontextfrei. Jeder A_{159}-Automat kann nämlich durch einen (determinierten one-way) Pushdown-Automaten (PDA) simuliert werden.
Daß die Klasse der PDA-Sprachen echt über A_{159} liegt und nicht von A_3 umfaßt wird, mit A_3 also unvergleichbar ist, sagt der Satz: Die PDA-Sprache

$$L = \{w\, c\, w^{\tau} \mid w \in \{a,b\}^*\}$$

liegt nicht einmal in A_{123569}, obwohl diese Klasse in unserer vorläufigen und, wie wir später sehen werden, auch in der endgültigen Halbordnung ein maximales Element ist. Das bedeutet, daß keine der Klassen zwischen A_3 und A_{123569} mit der Klasse der PDA-Sprachen vergleichbar ist.

Alle Klassen, die in Bild 1 über A_3 liegen, und A_3 selbst umfassen echt die Klasse der von (determinierten one-way) Zählerautomaten erkannten Sprachen. Noch nicht klar ist, ob die beiden einzigen nicht über A_3 liegenden Typen A_{159} und A_{258} echt über den Zählerautomaten liegen. Für A_{159} zeigt dies der Satz, daß die Sprache

$$L = \{a^p b^q a^q b^p \mid p,q \in \mathbb{N}\}$$

von keinem (determinierten one-way) Zählerautomaten erkannt wird.

Damit liegt die Klasse A_{159} echt zwischen den Klassen der von den Zählerautomaten und der von den Pushdownautomaten erkannten Sprachen.

Den Typ A_{258} diskutieren wir nicht, weil sich später ergeben wird, daß die Klassen A_{159} und A_{258} gleich sind ($A_{159} = A_{258}$).

Es liegt die Frage nahe, wie sich die noch nicht behandelten Automaten zum PDA verhalten. Der Beantwortung dieser Frage dient der nächste Satz. Er besagt, daß auch die A_{235689}-Automaten, die A_{356789}-Automaten und die jeweils darunter liegenden Modelle nicht mit den Pushdownautomaten vergleichbar sind, weil

$$L = \{w\ c\ w^{\tau} \mid w \in \{o,1\}^{*}$$

weder eine A_{235689}-Sprache noch eine A_{356789}-Sprache ist.

Wir werden später sehen, daß wie A_{123569} auch die Klassen A_{235689} und A_{356789} maximal sind und daß dies die einzigen maximalen sind. Das bedeutet, daß außer der Klasse A_{159}, die echt von der Klasse P der von Pushdownautomaten erkannten Sprachen umfaßt wird, alle anderen nichttrivialen Klassen unvergleichbar zu der Klasse der PDA-Automaten sind.

Betrachten wir die unmittelbar über den minimalen Typen liegenden Automatenmodelle. Direkt über A_3 liegen A_{36}, A_{35} und A_{23}.
Dies sind auch die einzigen unmittelbar über A_3 liegenden Typen, da A_{159} und A_{258} spezielle Pushdownautomaten sind, nicht aber A_3.
Die Frage ist: Liegen diese 3 Typen echt über A_3 und wenn ja, sind die entsprechenden Sprachklassen verschieden?
Es ergibt sich nun nicht nur, daß A_{23} nicht in A_{36} oder A_{35} enthalten ist, sondern gleich, daß A_{23} nicht einmal von dem Typ A_{356789} umfaßt wird.
Denn es gilt der Satz

1) $L = \{a^p b^q a^p b^{q+p} \mid p,q \in \mathbb{N}\} \in A_{23}$. $L \notin A_{356789}$

Das bedeutet außerdem, daß A_{23} oder eine A_{23} umfassende Klasse in keiner Klasse enthalten ist, die in Bild 1 unter A_{356789} liegt. Insbesondere ist also A_3 echt kleiner als A_{23}, $A_{23} \nsubseteq A_{35}$ und $A_{23} \nsubseteq A_{36}$.

Ganz analog gilt, daß A_{36} nicht einmal von dem Typ A_{12345} umfaßt wird. Dies ist der umfassendste Typ, der A_{36} nicht schon trivialerweise enthält. Man hat nämlich den Satz

2) $L = \{a^{p+q} b^p a^q b^p \mid p,q \in \mathbb{N}\} \in A_{36}$. $L \notin A_{12345}$

Das heißt, daß A_{36} oder eine über A_{36} stehende Klasse in keiner Klasse enthalten ist, die in Bild 1 unter A_{12345} liegt. Insbesondere ist also A_3 echt kleiner als A_{36}, $A_{36} \nsubseteq A_{23}$ und $A_{36} \nsubseteq A_{35}$.
Der noch verbleibende obere Nachbar von A_3 ist A_{35}. Um festzustellen, daß die drei oberen Nachbarn paarweise unvergleichbar sind und echt über A_3 liegen, müssen wir noch zeigen $A_{35} \nsubseteq A_3$, $A_{35} \nsubseteq A_{36}$ und $A_{35} \nsubseteq A_{23}$.

Dies leistet der Satz

3) $L = \{ a^{p+q}b^{p}a^{r}b^{q}a^{p+q} \mid p,q,r \in \mathbb{N}\} \in A_{35}$.
   $L \notin A_{3689} \cup A_{1234} \cup A_{2369} \cup A_{1236}$

Dieser Satz besagt weiter, daß keine Klasse, die Vorgänger von A_{3689}, A_{2369}, A_{1236} oder A_{3689} ist, die Klasse A_{35} oder einen ihrer Nachfolger umfaßt. Insbesondere ist A_3 echt kleiner als A_{35}, $A_{35} \nsubseteq A_{23}$ und $A_{35} \nsubseteq A_{36}$.

Damit haben wir gezeigt, daß die drei oberen Nachbarn A_{23}, A_{36} und A_{35} von A_3 paarweise unvergleichbar sind und echt über A_3 liegen.

Um festzustellen, daß auch alle oberen Nachbarn der Typen A_{23}, A_{25} und A_{36} paarweise unvergleichbar sind und - was daraus folgt - daß sie alle echt über ihren jeweiligen unteren Nachbarn liegen, genügen außer den Sätzen 1) - 3) folgende vier weitere Sätze:

4) $L = \{a^{p}b^{q}a^{p}b^{p+2q} \mid p,q \in \mathbb{N}\} \in A_{123}$. $L \notin A_{235689}$.

5) $L = \{a^{p+2q}b^{q}a^{q}b^{p} \mid p,q \in \mathbb{N}\} \in A_{369}$. $L \notin A_{123456}$.

6) $L = \{a^{p+q}b^{p}a^{q}b^{p} \mid p,q \in \mathbb{N}\} \in A_{36}$. $L \notin A_{357}$.

7) Alle 1-Symbolsprachen aus A_{235689} sind regulär. Die nichtreguläre Sprache $\{a^{n^2} \mid n \in \mathbb{N}\}$ liegt in A_{357}.

Bisher konnte man den Anschein gewinnen, daß in Bild 1 alle Pfeile echte Inklusionen darstellen und keine Pfeile fehlen. Dies ist jedoch nur beinahe richtig. Schon beim Übergang zur nächsten Schicht von Klassen stoßen wir auf einen fehlenden Pfeil. Bevor wir fortfahren, die Unvergleichbarkeit nicht durch Pfeile verbundener Klassen zu realisieren, wollen wir daher die wenigen fehlenden Pfeile aufzeigen.

Die ersten beiden Sätze installieren die beiden neuen Pfeile. $A_{1234} \rightarrow A_{123}$ und $A_{12345} \rightarrow A_{1235}$. Dies impliziert, daß weder die neuen Pfeile, noch die alten, deren Umkehrung diese sind, echte Inklusionen darstellen.

8) Zu jeder A_{12345}-Turingmaschine M gibt es eine äquivalente A_{1235}-Turingmaschine M'.

9) Zu jeder A_{1234}-Turingmaschine M gibt es eine äquivalente A_{123}-Turingmaschine M'.

Die naheliegende Vermutung, daß auch $A_{12356} = A_{123456}$, erweist sich jedoch als falsch, wie wir in einem späteren Satz sehen werden, nach dem nicht einmal A_{159} von A_{12356} umfaßt wird, obwohl A_{159}, wie der übernächste Satz zeigt, gleich A_{258} $(= A_{456})$ und daher in A_{123456} enthalten ist.

Der nächste Satz zeigt einen Pfeil auf, der nicht zur Gleichheit zweier Klassen führt, sondern eine Inklusion aufweist innerhalb von in Bild 1 noch gleichrangig erscheinenden Typen.

1o) Zu jeder A_{123456}-Turingmaschine M gibt es eine äquivalente A_{123569}-Turingmaschine M'.

Dann führen wir zwei neue Pfeile ein:

11) Zu jeder A_{258}-Turingmaschine gibt es eine äquivalente A_{159}-Turingmaschine. Umgekehrt gibt es zu jeder A_{159}-Turingmaschine auch eine äquivalente A_{258}-Turingmaschine.

Da $A_{258} = A_{456} \subseteq A_{123456}$ folgt daraus sofort, daß $A_{159} \subseteq A_{123456}$.

Der letzte der Simulationssätze schließlich zeigt, daß die A_{123457}-Matrix trivial ist, daß die A_{123457}-Turingmaschine gleichwertig ist zur unbeschränkten Turingmaschine, da wir schon wissen, daß jede Turingmaschine durch einen unbeschränkten 2C-Automaten simuliert werden kann.

12) Zu jedem 2C-Automaten M gibt es eine äquivalente A_{123457}-Turingmaschine M'.

Diese neu eingeführten Pfeile sind auch die einzigen, die hinzukommen. Um dies zu verifizieren, sind nur noch wenige Sätze nötig. Den folgenden Satz formulieren wir als Vermutung, da uns hier der Beweis noch fehlt.

13) Es gibt Sprachen aus A_{3689}, die von keiner A_{123569}-Turingmaschine erkannt wird.

Damit wird klar, daß auch die oberen Nachbarn von A_{123}, A_{235}, A_{236}, A_{356} und A_{369} paarweise unvergleichbar sind und somit echt über ihren jeweiligen unteren Nachbarn liegen, und daß das gleiche auch für deren obere Nachbarn A_{35689}, A_{23569} und A_{12356} gilt.

Wir sagten schon, daß alle 1-Symbol-Sprachen aus A_{235689} und damit auch aus allen Vorgängerklassen regulär sind. Der nächste Satz zeigt dasselbe für A_{123569}.

14) Die 1-Symbol-Sprachen aus A_{123569} sind regulär.

Damit sind also die 1-Symbol-Sprachen aller nichttrivialen Klassen mit Ausnahme von A_{357} und A_{356789} regulär.

In A_{356789} liegt nicht nur die Sprache $\{a^{n^2} \mid n \in \mathbb{N}\}$, die auch in A_{357} enthalten ist, sondern sogar die Sprache $\{a^{2^n} \mid n \in \mathbb{N}\}$.

Mit folgendem Satz über A_{159}

15) $L = \{a^p b^q a^q b^p \mid p,q \in \mathbb{N}\} \in A_{159}$. $L \notin A_{23569} \cup A_{12356} \cup A_{356789}$

haben wir dann alles Material, um uns klarzumachen, daß alle Klassen, die nicht durch Pfeile verbunden sind, unvergleichbar sind, und daß alle Pfeile, zu denen kein inverser explizit angegeben wurde, echte Inklusionen darstellen.

Die neue Halbordnung wird in Bild 2 dargestellt.

Folgende heuristische Betrachtung erleichterte die Verifikation der neuen Halbordnung: Gezeigt ist, daß alle Pfeile echt sind, daß innerhalb einer "Schicht" keine neuen Pfeile hinzukommen und daß weder von noch auf A_{159} und A_{357} neue Pfeile laufen. Von oben nach unten können keine weiteren Pfeile hinzukommen, ohne die Unvergleichbarkeit von Klassen einer Schicht oder die Echtheit der vorhandenen Pfeile zu verletzen. Anhand der Sätze 1)-5) und 13) macht man sich schließlich klar, daß keine weiteren Pfeile von unten nach oben hinzugelangen.

Damit aber haben wir nun die ursprüngliche Zahl der 2C-Klassen auf 24 zurückgeführt und die von ihnen bzgl. der Inklusion gebildete Halbordnung aufgezeigt. Sie hat 2 minimale Elemente, A_3 und A_{159}, und 3 maximale, A_{123569}, A_{235689} und A_{356789}.

Schließlich können wir noch 2 globale Aussagen machen und eine über A_{356789}:

1) Alle Typen sind haltend, d.h. in jeder Klasse gibt es zu jedem Automaten einen äquivalenten, der immer stoppt.

2) Alle nichttrivialen Typen liegen echt unter dem Linear-bounded-Automaten.

3) Die Sprache $L = \{a^{n^3} \mid n \in \mathbb{N}\}$ liegt nicht in A_{356789},
ein Ergebnis des gescheiterten Versuchs, anhand der Sprache L, die von keinem (nichtdeterminierten) one-way Stackautomaten erkannt wird, die Unvergleichbarkeit von A_{356789} mit der Klasse dieser Stackautomaten zu beweisen.

Bild 2

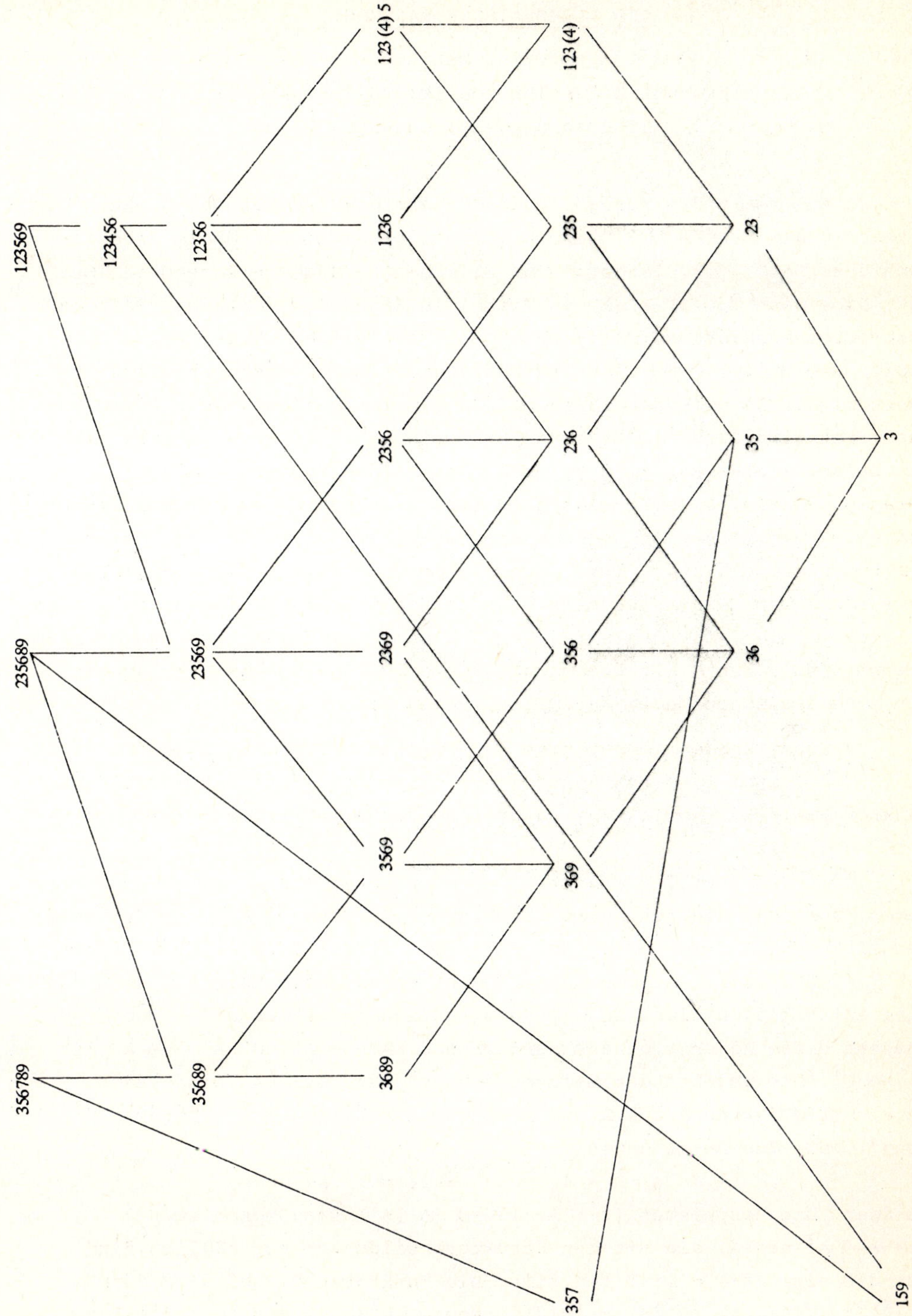
123569
123456
12356
123 (4) 5
1236
2356
123 (4)
235
236
23
35
3
235689
23569
2369
356
36
3569
369
356789
35689
3689
357
159

DARSTELLUNG DER KATEGORIE DER DETERMINIERTEN AUTOMATEN ALS ALGEBRAISCHE KATEGORIE

Dietmar Wätjen
Lehrstuhl C für Informatik, TU Braunschweig
33 Braunschweig, Gaußstr. 28

Es sei Mealy die Kategorie der determinierten Automaten, Set die Kategorie der Mengen. M. Pfender [3] hat gezeigt, daß Mealy algebraisch über $\underline{Set}^3$, d.h. isomorph zur Eilenberg - Moore - Kategorie $(\underline{Set}^3)^{\underline{T}}$ ist. Dabei ist $\underline{T} = (T,\eta,\mu)$ ein Tripel in $\underline{Set}^3$, das durch ein Paar adjungierter Funktoren $V:\underline{Mealy} \longrightarrow \underline{Set}^3$ (vergeßlicher Funktor), $F:\underline{Set}^3 \longrightarrow \underline{Mealy}$, $F \dashv V$ (F linksadjungiert zu V), gegeben wird. Der funktorielle Zusammenhang zwischen Kategorien verschiedener Typen von Automaten wird unter anderem von H. Ehrig [1] untersucht. Dabei wird zum Beispiel ein Paar adjungierter Funktoren $F:\underline{Mdw} \longrightarrow \underline{Mealy}$, $V:\underline{Mealy} \longrightarrow \underline{Mdw}$, $F \dashv V$, angegeben (Mdw: Kategorie der determinierten Medwedew-Automaten). Besonders interessant ist es, wenn einer dieser Funktoren tripelbar ist (was im angegebenen Beispiel nicht der Fall ist), d.h. wenn eine Kategorie algebraisch über der anderen ist. So zeigen wir hier, daß Mealy algebraisch ist über der Kategorie der nichtdeterministischen Mealy-Automaten, ND-Mealy, sowie über der Kategorie der stochastischen Mealy-Automaten, S-Mealy.

Zunächst werden noch einige kategorientheoretische Begriffe erläutert. Ein Tripel $\underline{T} = (T,\eta,\mu)$ in einer Kategorie $\underline{A}$ besteht aus einem Funktor $T:\underline{A} \longrightarrow \underline{A}$ sowie zwei natürlichen Transformationen $\eta:Id \longrightarrow T$, $\mu:T^2 \longrightarrow T$ mit

$$\mu\cdot\eta T = \mu\cdot T\eta = 1_T \quad \text{und} \quad \mu\cdot\mu T = \mu\cdot T\mu \ .$$

Jedes Paar adjungierter Funktoren $F:\underline{A} \longrightarrow \underline{B}$, $G:\underline{B} \longrightarrow \underline{A}$, $F \dashv G$, zusammen mit Einheit $\beta:Id \longrightarrow UF$ und Koeinheit $\alpha:FU \longrightarrow Id$, liefert ein Tripel $\underline{T} = (UF,\beta,U\alpha F)$ in $\underline{A}$. Umgekehrt gibt es zu jedem Tripel $\underline{T}$ in $\underline{A}$ auch eine solche Adjunktion. In der Konstruktion von Eilenberg - Moore [2] besteht diese Adjunktion aus Funktoren $F^T:\underline{A} \longrightarrow \underline{A}^T$, $U^T:\underline{A}^T \longrightarrow \underline{A}$ mit $F^T \dashv U^T$. Die Objekte der Eilenberg-Moore-Kategorie $\underline{A}^T$ sind Paare (A,ϕ) mit Objekten A aus $\underline{A}$ und Morphismen $\phi:T(A) \longrightarrow A$ („Strukturabbildung"), die den Beziehungen

$$\phi\cdot\eta A = 1_A \quad \text{und} \quad \phi\cdot T\phi = \phi\cdot\mu A$$

genügen. Die Morphismen $[f]:(A,\phi) \longrightarrow (A',\phi')$ sind Morphismen $f:A \longrightarrow A'$ aus $\underline{A}$, die mit den Strukturabbildungen verträglich sind, für die also $f\cdot\phi = \phi'\cdot T(f)$ gilt. Die Funktoren F^T, U^T sind durch $F^T(A) = (T(A),\mu A)$, $F^T(f) = [T(f)]$ sowie $U^T(A,\phi) = A$, $U^T([f]) = f$

(vergeßlicher Funktor) gegeben. Ein Funktor $V:\underline{B} \longrightarrow \underline{A}$ heißt nun tripelbar, wenn er einen linksadjungierten $F:\underline{A} \longrightarrow \underline{B}$ besitzt und es einen Funktorisomorphismus $L:\underline{B} \longrightarrow \underline{A}^T$ gibt mit $U^{\underline{T}}L = V$, $LF = F^T$. $\underline{B}$ heißt dann auch algebraisch über $\underline{A}$.

Ist $P:\underline{Set} \longrightarrow \underline{Set}$ der Funktor, der durch $P(M) = \{S \mid S \subset M \wedge S \neq \emptyset\}$ gegeben wird, so sind die Objekte aus $\underline{\text{ND-Mealy}}$ durch 5-tupel (I,O,S,δ,λ) beschreibbar mit Mengen I,O,S und Abbildungen $\delta: I\times S \longrightarrow P(S)$, $\lambda: I\times S \longrightarrow P(O)$. Für einen Morphismus $(f_I,f_O,f_S):(I,O,S,\delta,\lambda) \longrightarrow (I',O',S',\delta',\lambda')$ gilt

$$P(f_S)\cdot\delta = \delta'\cdot(f_I\times f_S) \quad \text{sowie} \quad P(f_O)\cdot\lambda = \lambda'\cdot(f_I\times f_S).$$

Durch die bekannte Zuordnung $V(I,O,S,\delta,\lambda) = (I,O,S,\bar\delta,\bar\lambda)$ mit $\bar\delta(x,s) = \{\delta(x,s)\}$, $\bar\lambda(x,s) = \{\lambda(x,s)\}$ und $V(f_I,f_O,f_S) = (f_I,f_O,f_S)$ wird ein Funktor $V:\underline{\text{Mealy}} \longrightarrow \underline{\text{ND-Mealy}}$ definiert. Es gilt

<u>Satz 1</u>: $V:\underline{\text{Mealy}} \longrightarrow \underline{\text{ND-Mealy}}$ ist tripelbar.

Beweis:
Wir konstruieren zunächst den linksadjungierten Funktor $F:\underline{\text{ND-Mealy}} \longrightarrow \underline{\text{Mealy}}$. Es sei (I,O,S,δ,λ) ein Objekt aus $\underline{\text{ND-Mealy}}$. Mit I^* werde das freie Monoid über I bezeichnet, e sei das leere Wort, I^+ sei die freie Halbgruppe über I. $\delta^*: I^*\times S \longrightarrow P(S)$ und $\lambda^*: I^+\times S \longrightarrow P(O)$ seien die durch $\delta^*(e,s) = \{s\}$, $\delta^*(xw,s) = \bigcup_{s'\in\delta^*(w,s)} \delta(x,s')$

$= \delta(x,\delta^*(w,s))$ $(x\in I,\ w\in I^*,\ s\in S)$ und $\lambda^+(xw,s) = \bigcup_{s'\in\delta^*(w,s)} \lambda(x,s')$

$= \lambda(x,\delta^*(w,s))$ $(x\in I,\ w\in I^*,\ s\in S)$ gegebenen Erweiterungen von δ und λ. Es wird folgende Äquivalenzrelation $\underset{S}{\sim}$ auf S betrachtet:

$s \underset{S}{\sim} s' \iff$ es existieren $n\in\mathbb{N}$, $(w_1,s_1),\dots,(w_n,s_n) \in I^*\times S$ mit
$s \in \delta^*(w_1,s_1)$, $s' \in \delta^*(w_n,s_n)$ und
$\delta^*(w_\nu,s_\nu) \cap \delta^*(w_{\nu+1},s_{\nu+1}) \neq \emptyset$ für $\nu=1,\dots,n-1$.

Ähnlich wird eine Äquivalenzrelation $\underset{O}{\sim}$ auf O definiert:

$y \underset{O}{\sim} y' \iff y=y'$ oder es existieren $n\in\mathbb{N}$, $(w_1,s_1),\dots,(w_n,s_n) \in I^+\times S$
mit $y \in \lambda^+(w_1,s_1)$, $y' \in \lambda^+(w_n,s_n)$ und
$\lambda^+(w_\nu,s_\nu) \cap \lambda^+(w_{\nu+1},s_{\nu+1}) \neq \emptyset$ für $\nu=1,\dots,n-1$.

Man setze $\widehat{S} = S/\underset{S}{\sim}$, $\widehat{O} = O/\underset{O}{\sim}$, wobei die Elemente dieser Mengen durch einen ihrer Repräsentanten bezeichnet werden, z.B. $\overline{s}$, $\overline{y}$. Wir definieren Abbildungen $\widehat\delta: I\times\widehat{S} \longrightarrow \widehat{S}$, $\widehat\lambda: I\times\widehat{S} \longrightarrow \widehat{O}$ durch $\widehat\delta(x,\overline{s}) = \overline{s'}$, $\widehat\lambda(x,\overline{s}) = \overline{y}$ mit beliebigem $s'\in\delta(x,s)$ bzw. $y\in\lambda(x,s)$. Dann ist $F(I,O,S,\delta,\lambda) = (I,\widehat{O},\widehat{S},\widehat\delta,\widehat\lambda)$ ein determinierter Automat. Wir zeigen die Wohldefiniertheit von $\widehat\delta$ (die von $\widehat\lambda$ ergibt sich ähnlich). Seien $s^1,s^2\in S$ mit $s^1 \underset{S}{\sim} s^2$. Dann gilt $\widehat\delta(x,\overline{s^1}) = \overline{s^{1\prime}}$, $\widehat\delta(x,\overline{s^2}) = \overline{s^{2\prime}}$ mit $s^{1\prime}\in\delta(x,s^1)$,

$s^{2\prime} \in \delta(x,s^2)$. Mit den Bezeichnungen der obigen Definition ist $s^1 \in \delta^*(w_1,s_1)$, $s^2 \in \delta^*(w_n,s_n)$, folglich $s^{1\prime} \in \delta^*(xw_1,s_1)$, $s^{2\prime} \in \delta^*(xw_n,s_n)$. Weiter gilt für $\bar{s} \in \delta^*(w_\nu,s_\nu) \cap \delta^*(w_{\nu+1},s_{\nu+1})$

$$\emptyset \neq \delta(x,\bar{s}) \subset \delta^*(xw_\nu,s_\nu) \cap \delta^*(xw_{\nu+1},s_{\nu+1}),$$

insgesamt also $s^{1\prime} \underset{S}{\frown} s^{2\prime}$, d.h. $\overline{s^{1\prime}} = \overline{s^{2\prime}}$.

Für $(f_I,f_O,f_S):(I,O,S,\delta,\lambda) \longrightarrow (I',O',S',\delta',\lambda')$ aus ND-Mealy definieren wir den Morphismus $F(f_I,f_O,f_S) = (f_I,\widetilde{f_O},\widetilde{f_S}):(I,\widetilde{O},\widetilde{S},\widetilde{\delta},\widetilde{\lambda}) \longrightarrow$ $\longrightarrow (I',\widetilde{O'},\widetilde{S'},\widetilde{\delta'},\widetilde{\lambda'})$ aus Mealy durch $\widetilde{f_S}(\bar{s}) = \overline{f_S(s)}$ und $\widetilde{f_O}(\bar{y}) = \overline{f_O(y)}$. F:ND-Mealy $\longrightarrow$ Mealy ist ein Funktor. Wir begnügen uns mit dem Nachweis der Wohldefiniertheit von $\widetilde{f_S}$. Da für $\bar{s} \in \delta^*(w_\nu,s_\nu)$ wegen der Morphismuseigenschaft von (f_I,f_O,f_S)

$$f_S(\bar{s}) \in P(f_S)\delta^*(w_\nu,s_\nu) = \delta'^*(f_I^*(w_\nu),f_S(s_\nu))$$

gilt, folgt aus $s^1 \underset{S}{\frown} s^2$ ähnlich dem obigen $f_S(s^1) \underset{S'}{\frown} f_S(s^2)$.

Zum Nachweis der Adjunktion $F \dashv V$ sei für $(f_I,f_{\widetilde{O}},f_{\widetilde{S}}):F(I,O,S,\delta,\lambda) = (I,\widetilde{O},\widetilde{S},\widetilde{\delta},\widetilde{\lambda}) \longrightarrow (I',O',S',\delta',\lambda')$ aus Mealy der Morphismus

$a(f_I,f_{\widetilde{O}},f_{\widetilde{S}}) = (f_I,f_O,f_S):(I,O,S,\delta,\lambda) \longrightarrow (I',O',S',\overline{\delta'},\overline{\lambda'})$ aus ND-Mealy gegeben durch $f_O(y) = f_{\widetilde{O}}(\bar{y})$, $f_S(s) = f_{\widetilde{S}}(\bar{s})$. Damit erhalten wir den natürlichen Isomorphismus

$$a:\underline{\text{Mealy}}(F(I,O,S,\delta,\lambda),(I',O',S',\delta',\lambda')) \xrightarrow{\sim} \underline{\text{ND-Mealy}}((I,O,S,\delta,\lambda),V(I',O',S',\delta',\lambda')).$$

Unter anderem muß gezeigt werden, daß bei gegebenem (f_I,f_O,f_S) aus ND-Mealy die Abbildung $f_{\widetilde{S}}$ von $a^{-1}(f_I,f_O,f_S) = (f_I,f_{\widetilde{O}},f_{\widetilde{S}})$ durch $f_{\widetilde{S}}(\bar{s}) = f_S(s)$ definiert werden kann (ähnlich: $f_{\widetilde{O}}$). Dies folgt daraus, daß für alle $\bar{s} \in \delta^*(w,s)$ (bei festem $(w,s) \in I^* \times S$) $f_S(\bar{s}) = s_O$ mit gemeinsamen $s_O \in S'$ gilt, was sich durch Induktion über die Länge von w ergibt. Der Induktionsbeginn mit $l(w) = 0$ ist trivial. Für $l(w) = n+1$, d.h. für $w = xw'$ mit $x \in I$, $w' \in I^*$, $l(w') = n \geq 0$ und $P(f_S)(\delta^*(w',s)) = \{s_O'\}$ (Induktionsannahme), ist dann auch

$$\begin{aligned} P(f_S)(\delta^*(xw',s)) &= P(f_S)(\delta(x,\delta^*(w',s))) \\ &= \overline{\delta'}(f_I(x),P(f_S)(\delta^*(w',s))) = \overline{\delta'}(f_I(x),s_O') \\ &= \{\delta'(f_I(x),s_O')\} \end{aligned}$$

einelementig.

Für den Funktor $T = VF$ in ND-Mealy ergibt sich $T(I,O,S,\delta,\lambda) = (I,\widetilde{O},\widetilde{S},\overline{\widetilde{\delta}},\overline{\widetilde{\lambda}})$ und $T(f_I,f_O,f_S) = (f_I,\widetilde{f_O},\widetilde{f_S})$. Es gilt $T^2 = T$. Sei $\eta:Id \longrightarrow T$ die natürliche Transformation mit

$\eta(I,O,S,\delta,\lambda) = (1_I,\eta O,\eta S)$, wobei $(\eta O)(y) = \overline{y}$ und $(\eta S)(s) = \overline{s}$ ist. Dann wird mit den natürlichen Transformationen η und $\mu=1_T:T^2=T \longrightarrow T$ $\underline{T} = (T,\eta,\mu)$ ein Tripel in ND-Mealy. Die Objekte der Eilenberg-Moore-Kategorie $(\text{ND-Mealy})^T$ sind nun Paare $((I,O,S,\delta,\lambda),\phi)$ mit einem Objekt (I,O,S,δ,λ) aus ND-Mealy und einem Morphismus $\phi:(I,\widetilde{O},\widetilde{S},\overline{\overline{\delta}},\overline{\overline{\lambda}}) \longrightarrow (I,O,S,\delta,\lambda)$, für den

$$(1_I,1_O,1_S)=(I,O,S,\delta,\lambda) \xrightarrow{(1_I,\eta O,\eta S)} (I,\widetilde{O},\widetilde{S},\overline{\overline{\delta}},\overline{\overline{\lambda}}) \xrightarrow{(\phi_I,\phi_O,\phi_S)} (I,O,S,\delta,\lambda)$$

gelten muß ($\phi = (\phi_I,\phi_O,\phi_S)$). Ein solches ϕ existiert jedoch nur, falls die durch $\widetilde{O}$ und $\widetilde{S}$ gegebenen Klassen einelementig sind, d.h. $A = (I,O,S,\delta,\lambda) = (I,\widetilde{O},\widetilde{S},\overline{\overline{\delta}},\overline{\overline{\lambda}})$ ein determinierter Automat ist. Dann ist ϕ die Identität und genügt damit auch der Beziehung $\phi\cdot T\phi = \phi\cdot\mu A$. Für die Morphismen aus $(\text{ND-Mealy})^T$ gilt nun $f=T(f)$, d.h. $f = (f_I,f_O,f_S) = (f_I,\widetilde{f_O},\widetilde{f_S})$. Insgesamt ergibt sich schließlich $(\text{ND-Mealy})^T \simeq$ Mealy und daß der Funktor V tripelbar ist.

Wir geben nun an, wie sich gewisse Eigenschaften des nicht-deterministischen Automaten $A = (I,O,S,\delta,\lambda)$ auf den determinierten Automaten $\widetilde{A} = (I,\widetilde{O},\widetilde{S},\widetilde{\delta},\widetilde{\lambda})$ übertragen. Im üblichen Sinn äquivalente Zustände von S ($s \sim s'$) werden durch ηS in äquivalente Zustände von $\widetilde{S}$ ($\overline{s}\sim\overline{s'}$) abgebildet, und für äquivalente nicht-deterministische Automaten A,A' sind auch die determinierten Automaten $\widetilde{A},\widetilde{A'}$ äquivalent. Mit einem initialen Zustand $s_O \in S$ und der Menge der finalen Zustände $F \subset S$ ist die durch A akzeptierte Wortmenge in der durch $\widetilde{A}$ akzeptierten Wortmenge (bezüglich des initialen Zustands $\overline{s_O}$ und der finalen Zustände $\widetilde{F} = \{\overline{s} | s\in F\}$) enthalten, d.h.

$$B(A) = \{w | \delta^*(w,s_O) \cap F \neq \emptyset\} \subset B(\widetilde{A}) = \{w | \widetilde{\delta^*}(w,\overline{s_O}) \cap \widetilde{F} \neq \emptyset\}.$$

Im allgemeinen gilt nicht die Gleichheit. Außerdem geht ein determinierter nicht-deterministischer Automat in den entsprechenden determinierten Automaten über.

Zuletzt wird der Fall der stochastischen Automaten betrachtet. Eine Wahrscheinlichkeit auf der Potenzmenge einer nicht-leeren Menge A, für die $\{a | a\in A, P(\{a\})>O\}$ abzählbar ist, heißt ein diskretes Wahrscheinlichkeitsmaß über A. Mit D(A) werde die Menge der diskreten Wahrscheinlichkeitsmaße P über A bezeichnet. Eine Abbildung $f:A \longrightarrow A'$ induziert eine Abbildung $D(f):D(A) \longrightarrow D(A')$ mit $((D(f))(P))(B') = P(f^{-1}(B'))$ für $B'\subset A'$. Man erhält so einen Funktor D:Set $\longrightarrow$ Set. Ein stochastischer Mealy-Automat (I,O,S,δ,λ) besteht nun aus den Mengen I,O,S sowie Abbildungen $\delta:I\times S \longrightarrow D(S)$,

$\lambda: I\times S \longrightarrow D(O)$. Für einen Morphismus $(f_I,f_O,f_S):(I,O,S,\delta,\lambda) \longrightarrow$
$\longrightarrow (I',O',S',\delta',\lambda')$ gilt

$$D(f_S)\cdot\delta = \delta'\cdot(f_I\times f_S) \quad \text{und} \quad D(f_O)\cdot\lambda = \lambda'\cdot(f_I\times f_S).$$

Der vergeßliche Funktor U:<u>Mealy</u> $\longrightarrow$ <u>S-Mealy</u> ist durch
$U(I,O,S,\delta,\lambda) = (I,O,S,\hat{\delta},\hat{\lambda})$, $U(f_I,f_O,f_S) = (f_I,f_O,f_S)$ gegeben, wobei

$$\hat{\delta}(x,s)(\{s'\}) = \begin{cases} 1 & \text{für } s'=\delta(x,s) \\ 0 & \text{sonst} \end{cases} \quad \text{und} \quad \hat{\lambda}(x,s)(\{y\}) = \begin{cases} 1 & \text{für } y=\lambda(x,s) \\ 0 & \text{sonst} \end{cases}$$

gilt. Man erhält

<u>Satz 2</u>: U:<u>Mealy</u> $\longrightarrow$ <u>S-Mealy</u> ist tripelbar.

Der Beweis erfolgt ähnlich wie bei Satz 1. Für (I,O,S,δ,λ) aus <u>S-Mealy</u> werden die Abbildungen $\delta^*: I^*\times S \longrightarrow D(S)$, $\lambda^+: I^+\times S \longrightarrow D(O)$ durch $\delta^*(e,s)(\{s'\}) = 1$ für $s'=s$ und $=0$ sonst und

$$\delta^*(xw,s)(\{\bar{s}\}) = \sum_{s'\in S} \delta^*(w,s)(\{s'\})\cdot\delta(x,s')(\{\bar{s}\}) \text{ sowie}$$

$$\lambda^+(xw,s)(\{y\}) = \sum_{s'\in S} \delta^*(w,s)(\{s'\})\cdot\lambda(x,s')(\{y\}) \qquad (x\in I,\ w\in I^*,\ s\in S)$$

gegeben. Weiter sei

$$M_{\delta^*(w,s)} = \{s' \mid \delta^*(w,s)(\{s'\})>0\},\quad M_{\lambda^+(w,s)} = \{y \mid \lambda^+(w,s)(\{y\})>0\}.$$

Tritt nun in den Definitionen der Äquivalenzrelationen von Satz 1 an die Stelle von $\delta^*(w,s)$ die Menge $M_{\delta^*(w,s)}$ (entsprechend für λ^+), dann verläuft der weitere Beweis analog.

Auch hier werden wie im Fall der nicht-deterministischen Automaten einige Eigenschaften der stochastischen Automaten auf die zugehörigen determinierten Automaten übertragen.

<u>Literatur</u>

[1] Ehrig,H.: Kategorielle Theorie von Automaten, Überblicke Mathematik, Band 7, 167-218, B.I.-Wissenschaftsverlag, Mannheim(1974).

[2] Eilenberg,S., Moore,J.C.: Adjoint Functors and Triples, Illinois J. of Math. <u>9</u>, 381-398(1965).

[3] Pfender,M.: Kongruenzen, Konstruktion von Limiten und Cokernen und algebraische Kategorien, Dissertation TU Berlin 1971.

RECHNERVERBUND /
EINZELVORTRÄGE

EXPERIENCE OF A DEPARTMENTAL COMPUTER SUPPORT NETWORK

D. R. INNES, S. H. LEONG, M. D. LANGFIELD and J. L. ALTY

Liverpool University Computer Laboratory

P.O. Box 147, Liverpool L69 3BX, ENGLAND.

Summary

A system has been developed which links various mini-computers in departments of Liverpool University to the facilities of the computer centre. This paper explains why the network has been established, describes the hardware and software structure of the system and draws conclusions on its effectiveness. The network is a hierarchy of machines which differs from processor power hierarchies by emphasising shared access to peripherals, filestore and software facilities.

Introduction

The rapid growth of the mini-computer market has been mirrored by a corresponding reduction in cost of the purely logical components. The performance/cost ratio for processors and the cost per bit of core, or equivalent, memory allows distributed systems of mini-computers to be preferred to central mainframe systems in an increasing number of situations.

At the University of Liverpool a variety of departments have purchased mini-computer systems. These machines with only a processor, a small memory and a teletype or VDU, can provide a great deal of local processing power with data collection and operator inter-action at low costs. They are normally dedicated to one application such as controlling an experiment and logging its results. Requirements for data storage, data processing and the output of results vary considerably over the range of applications. An experiment may be long running, generating data at a low rate or it may be performed quickly but with very frequent sampling. Computed results may be required immediately as feedback or the data may be processed as a background activity if interaction is not required. The low cost of a basic mini computer configuration is lost in applications where the usage of such expensive peripheral units as magnetic discs and tapes, card readers, line printers and graph plotters is necessary. The high cost of such peripherals is compounded when several systems are required to provide the dedicated local processing at various sites. The software required to support these facilities will be a further overhead probably requiring additional memory.

The limited financial resources of an individual department together with the narrow application of its mini-computers combine to restrict the enhancement of these systems beyond their initial minimum configuration. The general imbalance of these systems is apparent in their unsuitability for important subsidiary functions, for example program development and accurate computation. In the past information was transferred between the departmental computers and the central computer of the University on paper tape or magnetic tape. Where the central computer is used for accurate computation the delays involved in returning results renders impracticable a range of applications requiring a response on the human scale of a few seconds and makes impossible those experiments which require feedback. In a University environment data acquisition and related applications are an important interest. However, in its use of the central computer it must remain a minority interest. It would not be acceptable to the majority of users of the central computer if its communications system could be saturated by high speed lines, if main storage was reserved for real-time programs or if the processor scheduling algorithm was biased to give a rapid response to users of departmental computers at the expense of batch throughput or multi-access response.

An alternative solution is to have an intermediate support computer connected to departmental computers by a fast data link network. Data links do not represent extra computer power but they enable existing central processors to be made available where they are required, with a definite response time. The support computer is dedicated to the network and is thus a resource common to all the departmental computers. The range of facilities of the support computer and its relationship to the central computer are fully described in the following sections.

Since the Liverpool network was first established a number of similar, but independent, systems have been described. The Bell Telephone peripheral time-sharing network[1] is the most similar in concept particularly in its use of a supporting "midi-computer". The University of Chicago MISS hierarchical network[2], shares the same implementation strategy with remote concentrators and dedicated intermediate computers linking the remote mini-computers to the central service computer. The IBM laboratory automation system[3] exhibits similar characteristics to the others. However, as a laboratory automation facility it has a somewhat restricted scope which appears to make its implementation more rigid. In a university the heterogeneous nature of the application of departmental computers together with a wide range of hardware favours a flexible approach to establishing a network.

Range of Applications

The Departmental Network is supporting a wide variety of applications. This is a more significant design consideration than that imposed by differences in the hardware and configuration of the departmental computers. The applications can be broadly categorised as on-line to experiments or as interactive aids to design.

Examples in the first category are

(a) a dynamic feedback controller to an electric motor set, using a MiniMod computer, in the Department of Electrical Engineering and Electronics,

(b) the control of the stepping motors of a 200 KV electron microscope using another MiniMod computer, in the Department of Metallurgy and Materials Science, and

(c) data collection from automated experiments, using a Nova 820, in the Department of Psychology.

In the first example the response time is so critical that the feedback loop is closed by the local computer while in the second case it can be closed by a remote machine. The Psychology experiments do not require interaction. In this case the data is collected at less than 1000 characters per second for several minutes and stored for later analysis.

Applications in the second category require responses in a human, rather than in a machine, time scale. For example

(a) a Nova 1200 computer is used in the design of bridge structures in the Department of Civil Engineering and

(b) an Alpha is controlling an automatic machine tool as part of a development project in the Department of Mechanical Engineering.

Such a range of applications demand an equally wide range of support facilities including many which are found on medium to large machines in a general computing environment. The requirements are for real-time support, on-line program development, and remote batch processing. Real-time support involves the logging of data, its rapid analysis, and the return of results to the experiment. The computers associated with experiments are in many cases minimum configurations with 8K to 12K of main store. This produces a need for the rapid loading of binary programs and program overlap down the communication lines from a central library. On-line program development requires the availability of a card reader and a line printer, the storage of text with editing facilities, and a compilation system with subroutine library facilities. Remote batch facilities are the secure storage of data, provision of extensive computations including interactive execution, and the printing or graphing of results.

Ease of use, availability and responsiveness are the obstacles to supporting a Departmental Computer Network with a central computer. The solution adopted at Liverpool University is to interpose an intermediate Support Computer between the Departmental computers and the central computer. The role of the support computer is to provide a pool of resources which can be directly accessed by the departmental computers. The support computer can also pass data files to, initiate jobs in, and receive result files from, the central computer. While a guaranteed availability of the support computer and its response time to departmental computers are attainable objectives the turn-around of the central computer depends on the total load of which the departmental network is only a small part. To maintain a stable image while allowing the network to be extended, the support computer needs to have a long service life and is thus a modern machine of proven design with modular hardware facilitating enhancement to meet changing and increasing requirements.

The Network Hardware

The support computer is a Modular One from Computer Technology Ltd. It is a large configuration with 96K bytes of core store, 56 megabytes of disc store, paper tape reader and punch, card reader and line printer, teletypes, graphical display and real time clock. It is a significantly larger system than any of the departmental computers which it supports. Although floating point operations are performed by a software package its basic instruction time of 1.5 microseconds makes it a powerful computer. It is compatiable with a number of the departmental computers facilitating the interchange of software and hardware components.

The flow of messages within the network is effectively between the departmental computers and the filestore of the support computer. A convenient unit for the transmission of these messages is a 512 character block since this is the basic unit of transfer to the disc backing store. With such a large block size the overheads of initiating a message transfer are not significant so that the full transmission rate of the data link is effectively used. Many of the applications require a high transfer rate if only for a short time - to load a program or file the results of an experiment. Serial transmission, synchronous at 9600 baud, was considered to be too slow and maintaining character synchronisation places a heavy processor loading on a Modular One.

The British Standard Interface[4] was chosen as the method for linking computers within the network. This standard was originally developed as a flexible method of attaching source (input) and acceptor (output) devices to computers. It is a byte parallel interface with additional lines for transmission control and parity error detection. Transmission is asynchronous with the rate of transfer controlled by the acceptor device. The interpretation of this standard in the context of computer to computer communication results in a full duplex link with each computer seeing the other as both a source and an acceptor device.

The cost of cable for parallel transmission is a penalty which, because the Liverpool University campus is compact with the longest link being 1000 metres, is not excessive. The maximum transfer rate of the hardware at a megabaud is not reached since in practice the transfer rate is limited to about 0.25 megabaud by the ability of the support computer to handle character interrupt devices. This is only a configuration constraint which, if necessary, can be overcome by adding a second processor specifically to receive and transmit messages. A character is only transferred from a source to an acceptor if both are agreeable. Since the acceptor controls the transfer rate no crisis times are involved for these links. Thus as the support computer becomes increasingly heavily loaded the response time degrades gradually avoiding a conventional overload situation, with complete message retransmission, from occurring.

The computer to experiment links conform to the CAMAC specification[5] and are distinct from the computer to computer communication.

The central computer is an International Computers Ltd. 1906S with 750K bytes of 300 nanosecond main memory and 360 megabytes of drum and disc filestore. It is a conventional large scientific machine with a standard peripheral and communications configuration. It is the most powerful member of the well established 1900 series and has a wide range of application software.

The Communication Protocol

The line control procedures have been designed to fully utilise the duplex links and to reflect the function and topology of the network. The procedures are easy to initiate, robust in operation and have a well defined interface with the higher level functions. There is no master-slave relationship and two-way simultaneous transmission is supported. A Department which wishes to connect more than one computer must use one computer as a concentrator and this single machine will be connected to the Support Computer. The procedures allow a second level of processor addressing and the representation of the procedures at any node of the network can be configured according to the function of that node and its interconnection with other nodes.

All information is transmitted within a message with the following structure:

START SEQUENCE
ADDRESS FIELD
CONTROL FIELD
DATA FIELD
CHECKING SEQUENCE
FINISH SEQUENCE

Messages commence with the two byte sequence DLE STX[6]. A node discards characters until it receives this sequence. A start sequence encountered within a message is an error. Between the start sequence and the finish sequence, transmission is in transparent mode - each occurrence of a DLE pattern is preceded by another DLE which is removed at the receiving node.

The address field is a three byte field with the following structure

Byte 1	Bits 0 - 3	peripheral address at sender
	4 - 7	process address at sender
Byte 2	Bits 0 - 3	peripheral address at receiver
	4 - 7	process address of receiver
Byte 3	Bits 0 - 3	secondary link address (M)
	4 - 7	primary link address (N)

Each address can be set to a value in the range 1 to 15. If it has the value 0 it is not set. If neither M nor N is set the message is destined for a process or peripheral on the sending computer. If N is set and M is not set the message will be sent from computer A on link N to computer B. If both M and N are set the message will be sent from computer B on link M to computer C.

The one byte control field is composed by

Bits	0 - 3	cyclic message count
	4	0/1 = request/response message
	5 - 7	line control function

Each node has a capacity N, where N is 1, 2, 4, 8 or 16, for the storage of requests awaiting acknowledgement. Each such message is queued on its cyclic message count modulo N. Response message counts match request message counts but request messages in opposite directions carry counts from separate sequences. No request or response is accepted if its checking sequence indicates a transmission error. With the exception of STATUS, requests which are received out of sequence are not accepted. The principal request messages are

ACCEPT - the addressed node accepts the request and acknowledges with an ACCEPT response

CONVERSE - the addressed node accepts the message and acknowledges with an ACCEPT response or by sending any request message

RECEIVE - the addressed node accepts the message but only responds if an error is detected

CHANGE - changes the transmission mode in a cyclic manner between ACCEPT, CONVERSE and RECEIVE

RESET - the addressed node resets the status of its line control variables

STATUS - the addressed node constructs a response message containing the current values of all its line control variables

The principal responses are

ACCEPT - the positive acknowledgement of a request message

RESET - the acknowledgement of a RESET request

STATUS - the acknowledgement of a STATUS request

CHECK - the check sequence indicated a transmission error

ADDRESS - the link/process/peripheral is not available

SEQUENCE - the request did not have the expected cyclic count

FAULT - incomplete or overlength message received.

The structure of the data field is determined by the higher level functions but it cannot exceed 1000 characters and may be empty.

The two byte checking sequence is a sum check on the address, control and data field but excluding any DLE characters included to provide transparent mode transmission.

The message terminates with the two byte sequence DLE ETX.

The line level protocol described so far is quite separate from the higher level protocol. The content of the data field of a request varies considerably from function to function. As an example the data field for a function to create a file will contain the function, the user on whose behalf the file is being created the file name, size and protect status. When the file is created or if it fails to create, a high level response, in the form of a low level request, is sent to the originating process.

The Network Software

The support computer runs with the AOF operating system which provides an activity orientated environment with a segmented virtual memory and with peripheral input and output "spooled" in disc files. The network software package in the support computer makes use of all of these facilities. The transmit and receive activities for each link are independent although they share the same code segment and access a common pool of buffers. The segmented virtual memory permits a greater degree of multiprogramming than would be possible in a core based sytem. Only the code, data and buffer segments of active processes are held in core. The spooling of input and output avoids the risk of deadlock which might occur if activities could access real devices. Building the network software on top of this advanced operating system has allowed the problems of processor, core and peripheral scheduling to be delegated to the operating system.

The communications system is a three level structure implemented in the systems programming language CORAL 66. The lowest level is hardware dependent. Its function is to transfer characters from a message buffer to a link or from a link to a message buffer recognising only the start and finish sequences of a message. The middle level handles the communications protocol, the logical complexities of message flow on full duplex links. This line control level is responsible for the structure of messages and the contents of their address and control fields. The highest level is the one at which the user can access the facilities of the system. The system interface is defined at this level in such a way that a user is unaware of any "link", apart perhaps from a somewhat longer response time. The elements of the communications system are implemented as intercommunicating activities and their relationship is illustrated in Figure (a).

Similar software components are present in the departmental computers. However most of these systems are using minimum size core resident executives. Because of the small main memories there is a strong incentive to limit the amount of resident network software they require. If the function level is omitted from a departmental computer its user must interact with the message transmission system rather than with a higher level facility such as the filing system. A departmental computer is unlikely to have very much monitoring or error recovery software. In addition the number and size of message buffers is kept to a minimum.

Software fails when it is used in an original way causing a state to be entered which has always been faulty but has not yet been tested. In the network this faulty state may not be specific to one machine but may be distributed between two or more machines. In this case it is difficult to record its various components. However, the bulk of the software resides in the support computer. Three activities in the support computer handle error recovery, performance monitoring and recording of how the system is used. The error recovery activity is entered whenever a user generated error condition, such as trying to open a non-existent file, is trapped. This activity masks the details of the system operation from the user and protects the system against persistent misuse. The performance monitor is a high priority activity which is regularly entered following an interrupt from the real-time clock. It examines the status of the other system activities to determine if the system or part of it is deadlocked. If it discovers an activity which has waited for an unreasonable length of time it forces the activity to time-out. Since the network runs with a minimum of central operator attention the performance monitor periodically validates the operation of the system and outputs the results to the executive console. The usage of the system is recorded in permanent files on the support computer. This information is necessary to determine the sequence of events immediately prior to subtle system errors, to tune the system to its workload, as well as for statistics on the management of the facilities.

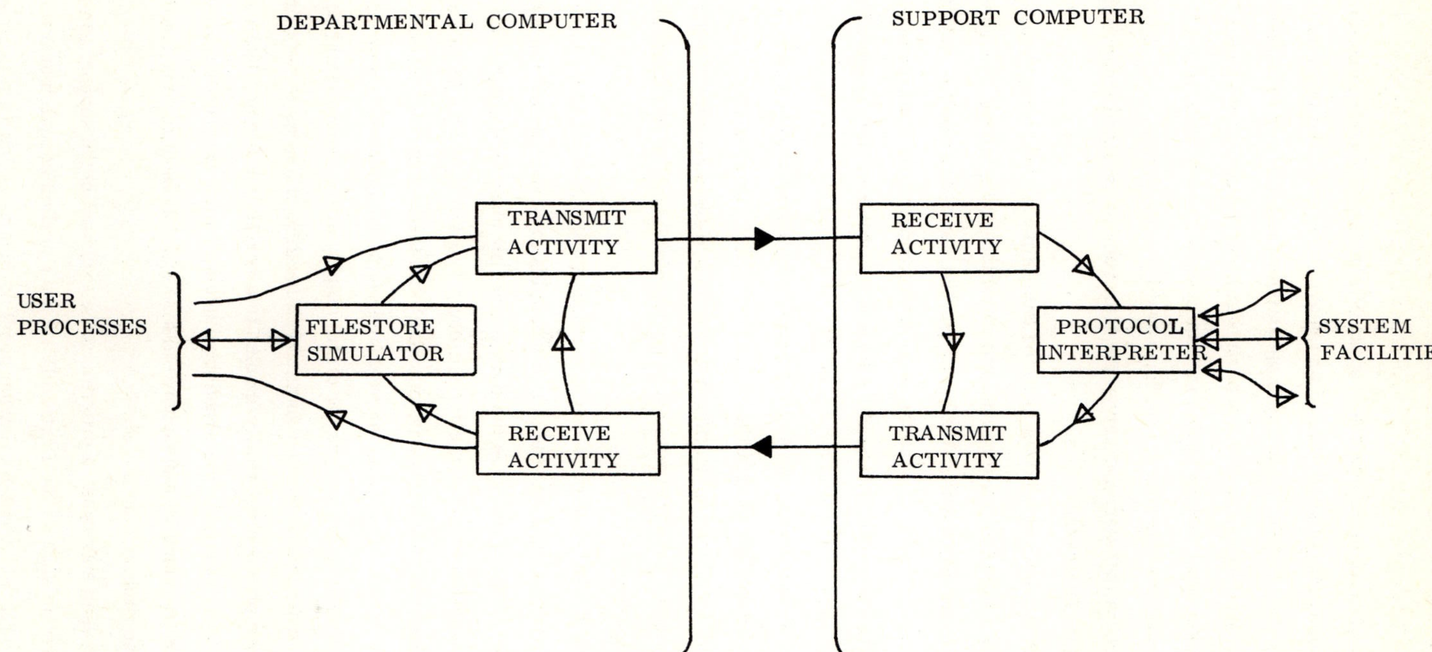

Figure (a): <u>SOFTWARE ORGANISATION OF A LINK</u>

The Network Facilities

The elementary facilities of the support computer are access to the disc filing system and a full complement of peripherals, and provision to execute programs. To a large extent the facilities are part of the basic operating system. The problem has been to provide suitable access to the users of the departmental computers. The solution is to provide a convenient interface through which the facilities of the central computer can be accessed and to schedule the subsequent access to avoid deadlock situations. This same interface provides access one stage further up the hierarchy to the ICL 1906S. Figure (b) illustrates the principal facilities.

There are two primary modes in which data is moved between the departmental computers and the file system of the support computer-block transfer and record transfer. Block transfer gives efficient transmission and is compatible with the unit of disc transfer. It places the cost of buffer space with the departmental computer which must handle the blocking and unblocking of records. A significant feature of this system is that block transfer has been implemented with "clean" access to the files. When a transfer request is received the file is opened if it is not already open, the block is read/written and the file is effectively closed. If the support computer is reinitialised, information already written to a file is secure and subsequent transfers can continue unconscious of the discontinuity. Record transfer is a less secure method but it relieves the departmental computer of holding large buffers and blocking/unblocking records.

There are further specific secondary modes of data transfer which are more directly related to particular applications. Two examples are the transfer of a binary program and the transfer of a line graph. In the first the binary program is being read by a standard loader in the departmental computer as though it was being input from a local peripheral, such as a paper tape reader. It is important that the binary program should be returned in exactly the same format as that produced by the compilation system. There is a similar problem in retrieving line graphs for direct display at the departmental computer.

Access to output peripherals is a natural continuation of access to the filing system. All files output to a peripheral are initially spooled to a serial disc file and later punched, printed or graphed. This feature avoids deadlock since the output devices are allocated to a queue rather than a user. Input on a peripheral is also spooled but it clearly requires more interaction with an operator.

A remote user may cause a program to be executed in the support computer. It may be a system program such as the Fortran IV or the Coral 66 compiler or a text editor. Alternatively it may be a user written program possibly incorporating a system package such

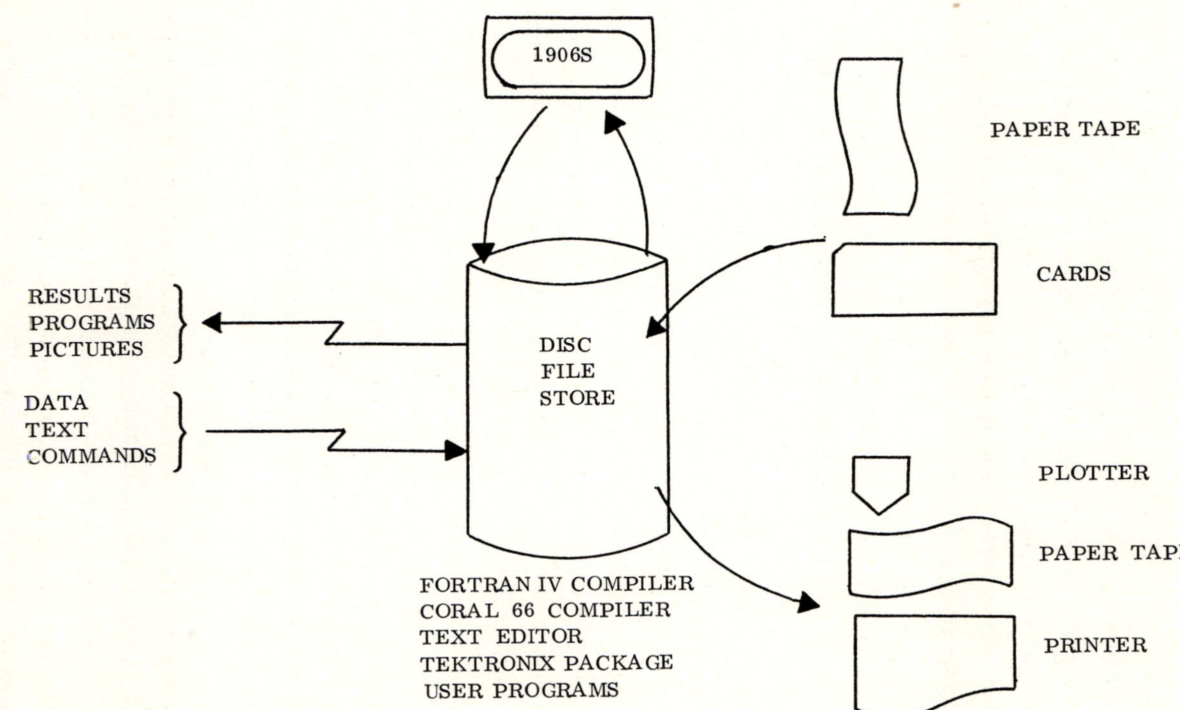

Figure (b): SYSTEM FACILITIES

as the graphics package which produces output suitable for a Tektronik interactive graphical display. The segmented virtual memory feature of the operating system removes much of the responsibility for memory management from the network software. However, although a deadlock situation may not arise, under heavy loading segment thrashing becomes excessive.

Files may be transferred from the support computer to the central computer. From a departmental computer jobs can be initiated in the central computer which will process the data files. Results are returned to named files on the support computer. Software in the support computer makes it look like a standard remote batch entry terminal to the central computer. Transmission is deliberately at the medium speed of 9600 baud on a serial line to govern the effect of the network on the central computer.

Conclusion

To an on-line user the important measure of reliability is the mean time between failures. The characteristics of the reliability of the system must at least match the demands made by its various applications. If, for example, the success of an experiment running for 24 hours depends on the availability of the resources of the support computer then there must be a high probability that this support system will function correctly for this period. A firm foundation has been established by firstly evaluating the reliability of the hardware from both the design and the maintenance aspects. In the design, components from a variety of reputable manufacturers have been linked in a way which avoids crisis times. With equipment from various sources there have arisen the problems of maintenance -assigning responsibility for a fault with one manufacturer and communicating between two or more manufacturers when the source of a fault cannot otherwise be determined. Local testing of sections of the network is carried out with loop back facilities on the transmission lines. Where there are experiments involving high voltage equipment that part of the network is electrically isolated to safeguard the central computer equipment and the other departmental computers.

The economies which have resulted from the development of the network are a secondary aim which assumes user satisfaction with its facilities. This user satisfaction is pursued by providing a wide range of easy to use facilities on a reliable system. The system is made available to the department users when they require it and it is tuned to respond in an adequate tune to their requirements. The system is a fully supported service of the Computer Laboratory. Documentation is produced, courses are given, and there is a member of staff available to provide personal guidance on the use and operation of the system.

There has been a noticeable increase in the interaction between users which has resulted in the sharing of hardware and software expertise. Since very similar equipment is used to link a number of experiments, programs to control the experiment equipment and analyse the data have been developed in a collaborative project. In addition the general level of awareness and technical competence of the user community has been increased by their association on the network. Since the network has been established it has rapidly developed the momentum necessary to ensure its continual growth. Each new participant brings a fresh requirement which stimulates the development of further facilities. This in turn makes the network more attractive to other potential users. When the support computer becomes so overloaded that it cannot maintain the standard of its service, its modular design will allow it to be extended by additional processors. Thus the operational life of the network may well overlap with a number of different central computers providing the guarantee of a stable interface necessary to attract departmental users.

References

1. "A Computer Network for Peripheral Time Sharing" B. J. Barkauskas, R. R. Rezac and C. A. Trlica Seventh Annual IEEE Computer Society International Conference.

2. "A Hierarchical Network" F. L. Ashenhurst and R. H. Vanderohe DATAMATION, February 1975.

3. "System/7 in a Hierarchical Laboratory Automation System" H. Cole IBM System Journal, Number 4, 1974.

4. "A Digital Input/Output Interface for Data Collection Systems" British Standards Institute British Standard 4421 : 1969.

5. "CAMAC. Modular Instrumentation System for Data Handling" Commission of the European Communities FUR 4100 e, August 1974.

6. "A Communications Interface for Computer Networks" D. Karp and S. Seroussi ACM Symposium on Communications 1971.

Laborautomatisierung und Experimentkontrolle in einem hierarchisch strukturierten Computerverbund

H. Hultzsch

Institut für Kernphysik der Johannes Gutenberg-Universität, Mainz, W-Germany

Einleitung

Laborinstrumente werden heute immer stärker von ihrer Verbindung zu Computersystemen beeinflußt. Dies zeigen sowohl die zahlreichen Publikationen über computergesteuerte Experimente als auch jede Ausstellung über Instrumentierung [1]. Für den Experimentator oder Laborfachmann auf der einen Seite wird es deshalb zunehmend von Wichtigkeit, sich mit den neuen Arbeitsmethoden vertraut zu machen; für den Computerfachmann auf der anderen Seite ist eine Auseinandersetzung mit den speziellen Erfordernissen dieses Bereichs notwendig.

In einem Gebiet mit solch weitgestreuten Anwendungen verbindet die Bezeichnung Laborautomatisierung naturgemäß unterschiedliche Vorstellungen je nach Erfahrung der betreffenden Anwendergruppe. Hier wird unter Laborautomatisierung bzw. unter Experimentkontrolle nicht nur die Datenerfassung und die Steuerung einer Apparatur verstanden, sondern alle weiteren Schritte der Datenaufbereitung, die Analyse, Graphik, Dokumentation etc. mit eingeschlossen.

In einem Forschungslaboratorium hat man es meist mit einigen zehn oder im Falle größerer Forschungszentren auch mit einer wesentlich darüber liegenden Zahl verschiedener Anwendungen dieses Bereichs zu tun, und es ist sicherlich ein unökonomisches Verfahren, wenn man für jedes Experiment einen separaten vollständig ausgerüsteten Mini-Computer aufstellt, der dann alle anfallenden Aufgaben erfüllen soll. Im Falle solch umfangreicher Anwendungen müssen die organisatorischen und ökonomischen Probleme beherrscht werden, um optimale Einsatzbedingungen für das installierte Gerät zu erreichen.

Die Verbindung von Instrumenten mit Computerelementen wurde während der zurückliegenden Jahre hauptsächlich durch eine Ankopplung von früher entwickelten Meßgeräten an Kleinrechner verwirklicht. Heute beobachten wir eine wachsende Integration von Prozessoren in die Meßgeräte, wodurch bereits im Gerät selbst eine Datenreduktion und gewisse Überwachungsfunktionen möglich sind. Für den Wissenschaftler ist dies von großem Wert; das hochqualifizierte Instrument liefert ihm bereits fertig präparierte Daten, ohne ihn zu einem Umlernen zu zwingen oder gar ein Verständnis des eingesetzten Datenverarbeitungsgerätes zu verlangen. Normalerweise müssen aber auch die Ausgabedaten solcher Meßgeräte weiter präpariert oder zusammen mit den Daten anderer Apparaturen analysiert werden, bevor die wissenschaftliche Fragestellung beantwortet werden kann. In anderen Bereichen macht der Einsatz von schnellen Prozeßrechnern die erwünschten Untersuchungen erst möglich. Extrem hohe Datenmengen müssen erfaßt und unmittelbar analysiert bzw. weiterverarbeitet werden. Auch dort wird das informationsverarbeitende Gerät deshalb zu einem direkten Bestandteil einer Apparatur, die Daten für globalere Analysen liefert.

Das in dieser Arbeit beschriebene mehrstufige Computernetzwerk demonstriert eine Alternative zu den isolierten stand-alone Implementierungen und es wird gezeigt, wo seine Vorteile insbesondere beim Einsatz in größeren Laboratorien liegen. Wesentlicher Grundgedanke dieses Verbundsystems ist die Integration von Labor-spezifischen, Echtzeit- und Sensor-orientierten Computersystemen mit solchen, die für klassische Rechenzentrumsanwendungen zur Verfügung stehen.

Grundlagen und Konzept

Rechnergeführte Laborgeräte oder Experimente bringen dem Wissenschaftler eine Reihe von Vorteilen insbesondere dann, wenn man den gesamten Zyklus der Datenbehandlung berücksichtigt. In diesem Zusammenhang wird die Produktivität natürlich am häufigsten genannt. Bei Einsatz einer Datenverarbeitungsanlage steigt die bearbeitete Datenmenge leicht auf ein Vielfaches an und die Zahl der durchgeführten Experimente oder Laboruntersuchungen kann, wie in der Literatur gezeigt wird [2)], um Größenordnungen wachsen. Neben all den schon an anderer Stelle genannten Punkten, wie Entlastung von Routinearbeiten, Protokollführung, Geschwindigkeit, Zuverlässigkeit, Eichprozeduren, Datenverwaltung und Dokumentation, graphische Darstellung etc., ist aber besonders die Inspiration des Experimentators oder Laborwissenschaftlers durch die komplexe Analysetechnik zu betonen. Oft entsteht ein Gedanke nur dadurch, daß gemessene Daten in einfacher Weise schnell unter Zugrundelegung unterschiedlicher Modelle analysiert oder betrachtet werden können. Dabei kommt einem hohen Grad an Flexibilität besondere Bedeutung zu.

Für den Arbeitsprozeß im Labor lassen sich unabhängig vom speziellen Anwendungsgebiet charakteristische Strukturen finden (Fig. 1). Dabei sind die Arbeiten, die sich unmittelbar mit der Steuerung der Geräte und der Datenerfassung beschäftigen, meist zeitkritischer Natur, während die weiteren Methoden der Datenaufbereitung im allgemeinen mehr die typischen Merkmale von Teilnehmer- oder Stapel-orientierten Aufgaben tragen.

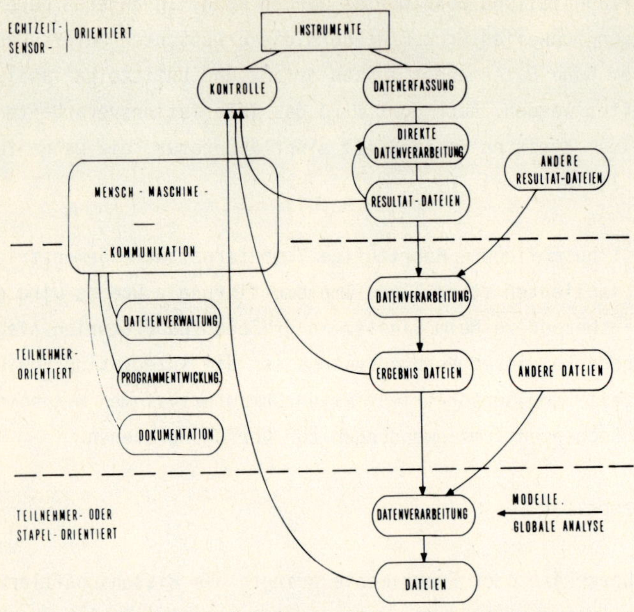

Figur 1: Charakteristische Strukturen der Informationsbearbeitung bei Laborautomatisierung und Experimentkontrolle

Weder eine Ansammlung von speziell zugeschnittenen Installationen noch eine große Zentralanlage ist für die Bearbeitung dieser Aufgaben insgesamt so geeignet wie ein aus mehreren Teilsystemen bestehendes Computernetzwerk.

Sowohl im Echtzeit- als auch im Teilnehmersystem ist die Reaktionszeit einer Anlage nach Auftragsübermittlung ein wichtiger Parameter für die Beurteilung der Leistungsfähigkeit eines Systems (Streeter [3]). So werden Teilnehmersysteme mit einem Nutzungsgrad von etwa 80 % betrieben, um die für den Benutzer zufriedenstellende Reaktionszeit im Bereich von einigen Sekunden zu erreichen (Fig. 2 A).

In der Laborautomatisierung sind zusätzlich die durch den Echtzeitbetrieb bedingten Anforderungen zu erfüllen; die erforderlichen Reaktionszeiten sind dort im allgemeinen um Größenordnungen kleiner und liegen je nach Anwendungsgebiet im Bereich zwischen 10^{-6} und einigen 10^{-1} Sekunden. Der zulässige Nutzungsgrad solcher Computersysteme muß deshalb wesentlich niedriger liegen (Fig. 2 B). Allerdings sind die zur Bearbeitung der Echtzeitprobleme notwendigen Betriebsmittel

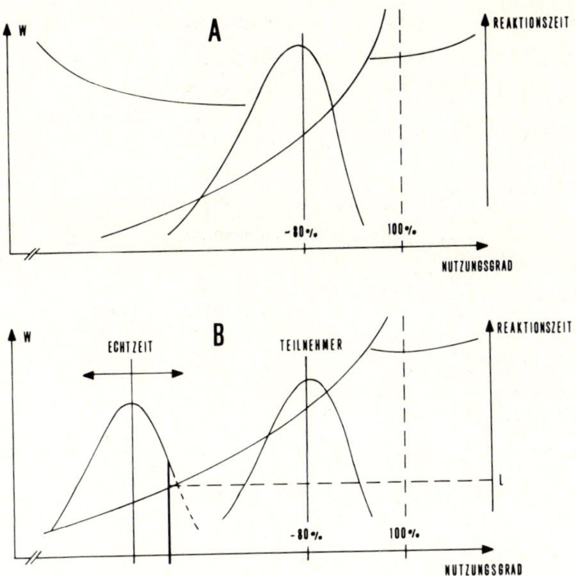

Figur 2: Wert eines Computer-Systems und Reaktionszeit nach Auftragsübermittlung als Funktion des Nutzungsgrades (nach Streeter [3]);

W = Wert des Computersystems für den Benutzer (oder die Aufgabe) bei einer bestimmten Investition;

(A) Teilnehmersystem; die Größe W erreicht einen optimalen Wert bei einem Nutzungsgrad von 70 bis 85 % (nach Streeter);

(B) in der Laborautomatisierung entstehen zwei Maxima; für Echtzeitprobleme muß der Nutzungsgrad niedrig gehalten werden, um die Größe W zu optimieren; überschreitet die Reaktionszeit den Grenzwert L, so fällt die Funktion W auf Null.

meist auch weniger aufwendig und es liegt deshalb nahe, zur Bearbeitung dieser Aufgabenklasse spezielle, in ihrer Ausstattung limitierte Prozessoren einzusetzen. Überdies läßt eine differenzierte Prioritätsstruktur innerhalb der für Laborrechner benutzten Betriebssysteme noch zu, den Parameter Reaktionszeit den Einzelanforderungen anzupassen.

Eine weitere Klassifizierung der Teilaufgaben des Gesamtproblems nach der Zahl der Instruktionen pro Aufgabe läßt die Zusammenstellung der Figur 3 entstehen. Danach lassen sich drei Ebenen mit typischer Aufgabenstruktur und Reaktionszeitanforderung definieren. Jeder dieser Ebenen ordnet man in der diskutierten Hierarchie ein speziell organisiertes Computersystem zu, das jeweils optimale Durchsatzbedingungen für seine Aufgabenklasse anbietet.

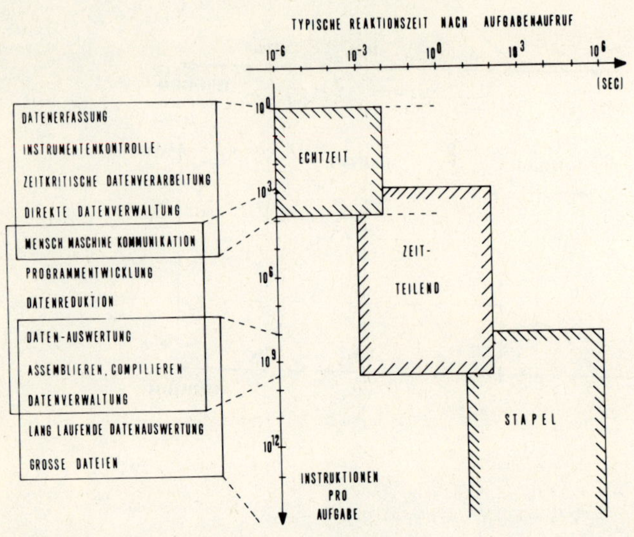

Figur 3: Klassifizierung der Einzelaufgaben nach Benutzerklassen; Klassifizierungsmerkmale sind Maschineninstruktionen pro Aufgabe und erforderliche Reaktionszeit nach Aufgabenabruf

Dabei sind die Ebenen zwei und drei auch für andere als Laboranwendungen zuständig und charakterisieren einen typischen wissenschaftlichen Rechenzentrumsbetrieb mit Teilnehmer- und Stapel-System.

Zwischen den Teilsystemen existiert eine Kommunikationshierarchie mit den Echtzeitsystemen als oberster Stufe. Jede übergeordnete Stufe hat bei voller Berücksichtigung des Datenschutzes Zugriff auf die Betriebsmittel und Dateien untergeordneter Teilsysteme. So ist es den Programmen in der Echtzeitanlage (Stufe 1) möglich, auf die Dateien des untergeordneten Teilnehmersystems zuzugreifen und Aufträge dorthin zu übermitteln, die im Pool mit den übrigen Teilnehmern bearbeitet werden.

Implementierung

Ein System der beschriebenen Art wurde in Computing Systems Department des Thomas J.Watson Research Center, Yorktown Heights implementiert [4] und wird sowohl dort als auch an anderer Stelle seit 1974 für eine größere Zahl von Anwendungen benutzt (Fig. 4). Ebene 1, das Echtzeit- und Sensor-orientierte Teilsystem wird präsentiert durch Laborrechner des Typs IBM System/7 unter LABS, einem Monitor

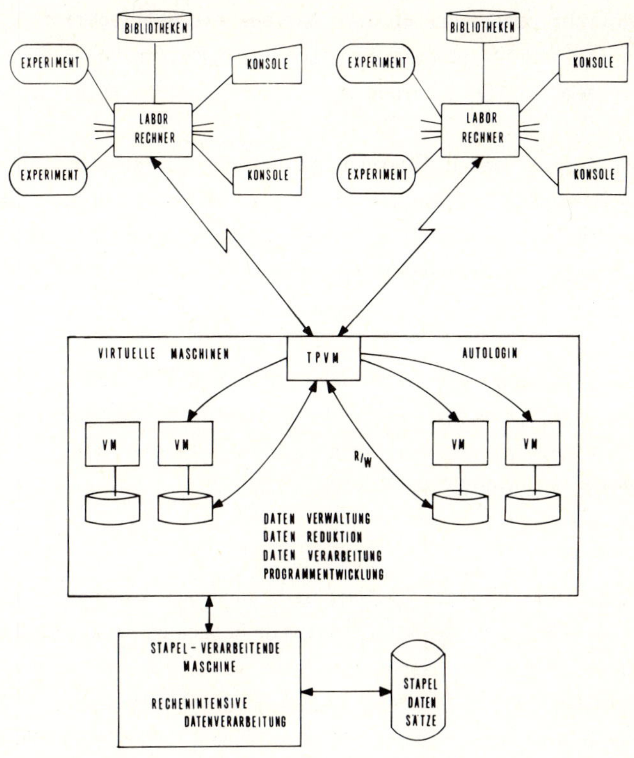

Figur 4: Das implementierte Rechnerverbundsystem

auf Interpreter-Basis mit einer leicht erlernbaren Sprache für Laboranwendungen [5]. Diese Anlagen steuern einzelne, oder wenn dies die Maschinenauslastung zuläßt, auch mehrere Experimente gleichzeitig. Über schnelle Kommunikationsleitungen (277 Kbyte/sec, 50 Kbaud oder 600 baud) sind sie mit der Maschine der Ebene 2, einer IBM 370/145 unter VM/CMS (Virtuelle Maschinen / Conversational Monitor

System) [6] verbunden. Dieses Betriebssystem erlaubt es, eine Reihe von Virtuellen Maschinen unabhängig voneinander zu aktivieren und es war deshalb auch möglich, eine spezielle Virtuelle Maschine (TPVM, Teleprocessing Vitual Machine) nur für die Kommunikationsbearbeitung bereitzustellen. Diese TPVM ist ständig in Bereitschaft, Aufträge von einem der übergeordneten Labor-Computersysteme zu empfangen. Besondere Fähigkeiten verleihen der TPVM die Möglichkeit, unter Beachtung aller Schutzverfahren (Benutzerkennung, Passwort) auf die Dateien anderer zugeordneter Virtueller Maschinen zuzugreifen und über die Autologin-Funktion [7] andere Virtuelle Maschinen zu aktivieren und in einer Master-Slave Beziehung zu dirigieren. Damit ist es möglich, vom Labor-Computer aus auf die Betriebsmittel der leistungsfähigeren Teilnehmersysteme transparent zuzugreifen und die Betriebsmittel des Teilnehmersystems als Erweiterung des Echtzeitsystems zu betrachten.

Für die Implementierung von TPVM werden bedingt durch Eigenschaften des Betriebssystems VM 370 neben dem für jede virtuelle Maschine notwendigen Massenspeicherbereich und dem Kommunikations-Datenspeicher keine anderen Betriebsmittel dauerhaft belegt. Das Verfahren ist damit eine ökonomische Lösung des Problems der Ankopplung von Laborrechnern an Prozeßrechner.

Als Maschine der Ebene drei kann entweder eine CMS-Batch Maschine innerhalb von VM/370 benutzt werden, oder, wie es im obengenannten Rechenzentrum möglich ist, es können Aufträge über ein Hochgeschwindigkeits-Netzwerk (Net [8]), zum Stapelverarbeitenden Teil anderer Anlagen, einer 360/91 oder zwei 370/168 verschickt werden.

Die Transparenz innerhalb dieses Systems wird in Figur 5 deutlich gemacht. Über die Kommandos "TP-READ" und "TP-WRITE" hat ein Programm, wenn ihm Benutzerkode und Passwort einer Virtuellen Maschine bekannt sind, vollständigen Zugriff auf deren Dateien und kann diese als "zum System gehörig" betrachten. "TP-SUBMIT" erlaubt es, über die bereits genannte Fähigkeit von TPVM eine Virtuelle Maschine zu starten und sie zur Bearbeitung von Aufträgen anzustoßen. Auf diese Weise hat ein Programm oder auch der Benutzer an der Konsole eines Prozeßrechners vollständigen Zutriff auf seine virtuelle Maschine. Er kann neben der Kommunikation mit Steuer- und Erfassungsprogrammen komplikationslos den Text-Editor des größeren Rechners benutzen, erstellte Programme übersetzen und zur Ausführung bringen, er kann deren Ergebnisse beobachten und Daten beliebig zwischen den Teilsystemen austauschen. Natürlich ist es ihm auch möglich, so wie bereits beschrieben, Aufträge an die Stapel-verarbeitenden Einrichtungen zu übermitteln und deren Ablauf, wenn erwünscht, über die Kommandos "TP-STATUS" zu verfolgen.

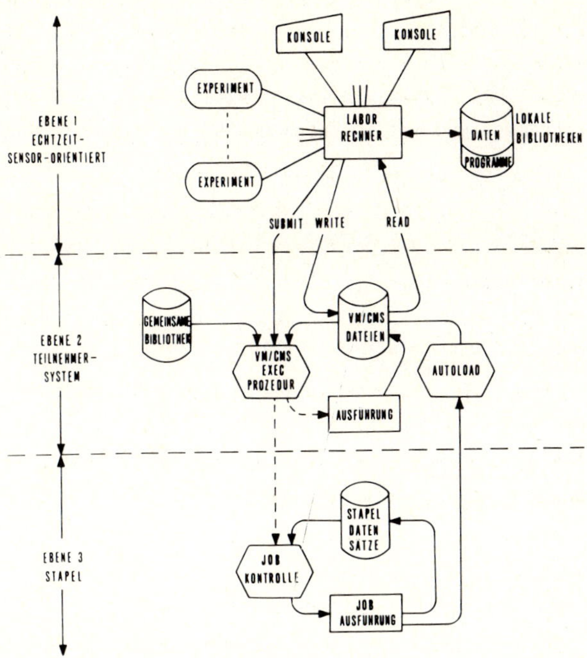

Figur 5: Daten- und Programmhierarchie

Schlußbemerkung

Das beschriebene System bietet als Konzept flexible und ökonomische Lösungsmöglichkeiten für jede Art von Anwendung aus dem Bereich der Laborautomatisierung und Experimentkontrolle. Dabei ist es keinesfalls an die hier genannten Maschinentypen gebunden. Eine Implementierung bei Benutzung anderer Rechenanlagen ist zur Zeit im Institut für Kernphysik der Universität Mainz in der Planungsphase.

In der vorgestellten Implementierung hat sich das Konzept in einer Reihe von zum Teil sehr unterschiedlichen Anwendungsgebieten bewährt. Durch eine Integration von drei Teilsystemen jeweils mit Echtzeit-, Teilnehmer- und Stapel-Orientierung zu einem Gesamtsystem ist es möglich, alle bei Laborautomatisierung und Experimentkontrolle anfallenden Aufgaben in "einem" System zu bearbeiten. Die Verlagerung der Großrechner-spezifischen Arbeiten von Labor- und Experimentbetrieb in zentrale Anlagen vermeidet Vielfach-Installationen und bietet auf diese Weise besonders ökonomische Lösungen an.

Das beschriebene System ist das Ergebnis einer Arbeit im Rahmen des IBM Post Doctoral Fellowship Programms, und ist in Zusammenarbeit mit H.Cole und A.Guido entstanden.

Literatur

1) S.P.Perone:
Computer Applications in the Chemistry Laboratory-A Survey, Analytical Chemistry 43, 1288 (1971)

2) H. Cole:
Growth Path for Computers in Automated Analysis, in Chemical Analysis of the Environment and other Modern Techniques, Plenum Publishing Corporation, N.Y. 1973

H. Cole:
System/7 in a Hierarchial Laboratory Automation System, IBM Systems Journal 13, 307 (1974)

3) D.N.Streeter :
The Scientific Process and the Computer, John Wiley, N.Y. 1974

D.N.Streeter :
Cost/Benefits of Computing Services in a Scientific Environment, in Datenverarbeitung in der Forschung, Jülich-Conf.-7, 179 (1972)

4) H. Hultzsch et al.:
Laboratory Automation in a Novel Computer Hierarchy, IBM Report RC 4714 (1974)

5) R.Alsworth et al. :
LABS/7 Laboratory Automation Basic Supervisor, IBM Report RJ 1185 (1973) und IBM SH20-1363, IBM SH20-1364

6) IBM Virtual Machine Facility/370; Introduction IBM GC20-1800, Command Language User's Guide IBM GC20-1804

7) M.S. Helfer :
Automatic Logon of VM/370 Virtual Machines, IBM Report RC 4662 (1973)

8) S.Hobgood :
Evaluation of an Interactive-Batch System Network, IBM Systems Journal 11, 2 (1972)

J.Meyer and R. Nachbar :
CP/67-OS/360 Network Link, IBM Report RC 4113

SCHNELLE DIGITALE KOMPONENTEN FÜR GRAFISCHE SICHTGERÄTE

W. Straßer

Heinrich-Hertz-Institut Berlin

ZUSAMMENFASSUNG

Die Verfügbarkeit schneller und preiswerter digitaler Bauelemente bietet die Möglichkeit, in grafischen Sichtgeräten Operationen zur Berechnung und Transformation von Bildern hardwaremäßig und damit in Echtzeit auszuführen. Im vorliegenden Aufsatz werden ein Vektorgenerator, Kreisgenerator, Matrizenmultiplizierer/Dividierer und ein Kurven/Flächengenerator vorgestellt, die rein digital arbeiten und in ihrem Aufbau einfach an die Erfordernisse der Anwendung angepaßt werden können.

EINLEITUNG

Grafische Sichtgeräte finden immer mehr Anwendung bei der Simulation dynamischer Vorgänge. Ihre Vorteile hierbei liegen auf der Hand: auf dem Bildschirm können nicht nur die Lösungskurven, sondern das ablaufende Experiment selbst (z.B. fahrendes Auto) dargestellt werden. Voraussetzung für ein flackerfreies, kontinuierliches Bild ist eine Bildwiederholfrequenz von ca. 50 Hz. Die Berechnung aller Veränderungen zwischen zwei aufeinanderfolgenden Bildern und das Zeichnen des Bildes muß dann in 20 ms abgeschlossen sein. Dies ist nur möglich, wenn Vektoren, Kurven und Flächen, sowie die Transformationen (Rotation, Skalierung, Translation, Perspektive) von spezieller Hardware im Display-Prozessor berechnet werden.

DIGITALER VEKTORGENERATOR DVG

Vektorgeneratoren gehören zur Standardausrüstung grafischer Sichtgeräte und sind bisher in Hochleistungsdisplays zur Erreichung hoher Schreibgeschwindigkeiten mit analogen Bauelementen (Integrierern) realisiert worden. Inzwischen gibt es schnelle, digitale Addierer, die eine Lösung nach dem Prinzip des digitalen Integrierers (DDA) nahelegen. Dieser digitale Vektorgenerator (DVG) bietet gegenüber der analogen Version viele Vorteile:

- Konstante Schreibgeschwindigkeit, d.h. keine Intensitätskompensation zur Erzielung gleicher Helligkeit von kurzen und langen Vektoren erforderlich
- Keine Ein- bzw. Ausschwingzeit, d.h. die Schreibzeit ist gleich der Rechenzeit, was besonders bei der Approximation von Kurven durch viele kleine Vektoren von Bedeutung ist
- Durch Änderung von Wortlänge und/oder Taktfrequenz kann der DVG an die Erfordernisse des speziellen Displays oder Plotters angepaßt werden
- Wartungsfrei, d.h. kein Abgleich notwendig

Die Adreßauflösung des DVG wurde entsprechend dem Verhältnis ausnutzbare Bildschirmfläche zu kleinstem Punktdurchmesser und dem Dynamikbereich der Intensitätssteuerung des verwendeten Displays HP 1310 A zu (10 x 10 x 6) bit gewählt. Zur Verbesserung des Tiefeneindrucks bei der Darstellung dreidimensionaler Objekte wurde parallel zur Intensitätssteuerung eine Steuerung der Linienstärke vorgesehen. Diese variable Linienstärke dient außerdem zur Einsparung von Rasterlinien beim Schattieren von Flächen. Die einzelnen Punkte eines Vektors werden durch sukzessive Addition berechnet:

$$Q_{i+1} = Q_i + \Delta P / 2^p \qquad (1)$$

mit

$$Q = [X \; Y \; Z]$$

$$\Delta P = [X_E - X_A, \; Y_E - Y_A, \; Z_E - Z_A] = [\Delta X, \; \Delta Y, \Delta Z]$$

E = Vektorendpunkt, A = Anfangspunkt

2^p gibt die Anzahl der zum Zeichnen des Vektors notwendigen Additionen gemäß Gl. (1) an. Sie wird aus der angenäherten Länge L des Vektors

$$L = \max \left(|\Delta X|, |\Delta Y| \right) \qquad (2)$$

so berechnet, daß der Vektor als geschlossene Linie erscheint. Dazu muß das Inkrement $\Delta P/2^p$ kleiner als eine Rastereinheit sein:

$$|\Delta X| / 2^p < 1 \qquad \text{d.h.: } 2^p > L \qquad (3)$$
$$|\Delta Y| / 2^p < 1$$

Um die Anzahl der Additionen möglichst niedrig zu halten, wird p so berechnet, daß gilt:

$$2^p > L \geq 2^{p-1} \qquad (4)$$

Der Algorithmus des DVG ist in Bild 1 in einem Ablaufdiagramm dargestellt. Man erkennt, daß das Zeichnen eines Vektors und die Berechnung der Inkremente $\Delta P/2^p$ für den nächsten Vektor gleichzeitig geschieht. Dadurch ist gewährleistet, daß die maximale Additionsgeschwindigkeit im Akkumulator ausgenutzt wird und der DVG ohne Unterbrechung zeichnet. Mit dem in Schottky TTL realisierten DVG können unabhängig von der Länge der Einzelvektoren ca. 400 m Vektor flackerfrei bei 50 Hz Bildwiederholfrequenz auf dem Bildschirm dargestellt werden. Das Aussehen der Vektoren zeigt Bild 2. Es läßt sich durch Erweiterung der Wortlänge der Digital-Analog-Umsetzer auf Stellen hinter dem Binärpunkt verbessern, da im DDA die Koordinaten ohnehin mit doppelter Wortlänge, also 20 bit, berechnet werden. Der realisierte DVG enthält eine Skalierung und Wrap-around-Unterdrückung /1/. Bild 3 zeigt einfache Beispiele für die Wirkung von Strichstärkesteuerung und Skalierung. Für sehr hohe Anforderungen, z.B. beim Schattieren von Flächen, reicht die grobe Näherung der Vektorlänge L nach Gl. (2) nicht aus und macht sich durch leichte Helligkeitsunterschiede zwischen den Vektoren störend bemerkbar. Dieser Fehler wird durch Korrekturwerte für die Intensität behoben, die in einem Festwertspeicher zur Verfügung stehen und durch

Auswerten der beiden höchstwertigen Bits von ΔX und ΔY ausgewählt werden.

DIGITALER KREISGENERATOR DKG

Neben dem Vektor ist auch der Kreis ein häufig benötigtes geometrisches Element, dessen Hardware-Realisierung wünschenswert erscheint. In /2/ ist ein Algorithmus zum Zeichnen von Kegelschnitten auf digitalen Plottern beschrieben, der für den Spezialfall des Kreises sehr einfach wird und sich für eine Implementierung in Hardware gut eignet.

Ein digitaler Plotter kann nur acht verschiedene Elementarvektoren zeichnen. Sie werden entsprechend Bild 4 nach ihrer Konstruktion in die beiden Gruppen MOVE1 und MOVE2 eingeteilt.

Die allgemeine Gleichung eines Kegelschnitts lautet /2/

$$\alpha Y^2 + \beta X^2 + 2\gamma XY + 2uY - 2vX = k \qquad (5)$$

Das Flußdiagramm des Algorithmus zur Darstellung der Kegelschnitte als eine Folge von MOVE1 und MOVE2 Vektoren zeigt Bild 5. Hieraus ist zu erkennen, daß die Berechnungszeit für alle Punkte eines Oktanten gleich ist. Diese Eigenschaft bedeutet für einen Kreisgenerator konstante Schreibgeschwindigkeit und damit gleiche Helligkeit für alle darstellbaren Kreise. Bild 6 zeigt bei grober Auflösung, daß - wie auf Grund der Symmetrie des Kreises zu erwarten - die Oktanten durch Spiegelung an den Koordinatenachsen und Winkelhalbierenden auseinander gewonnen werden können. Insbesondere sind zwei benachbarte Oktanten bezüglich ihrer Grenze spiegelsymmetrisch. Weiterhin ist zu erkennen, daß bei diesem Verfahren eine Deformation des Kreises wie z.B. bei Generatoren nach dem DDA-Prinzip /3/ nicht auftreten kann.

Man braucht demnach die Folge der MOVE1 und MOVE2 Vektoren nur für einen Oktanten zu berechnen und beim Zeichnen des ganzen Kreises die Richtung dieser Vektoren entsprechend Bild 4 zu ändern. Es ist deshalb sinnvoll, die Kreisberechnung in einem Oktantenwechsel, z.B. dem Punkt 0, beginnen zu lassen. Der Punkt 0 wird willkürlich in den Ursprung des Bildschirmkoordinatensystems gelegt. Der Kreismittelpunkt liegt dann bei $X_m = R/\sqrt{2}$ und $Y_m = -R/\sqrt{2}$.

Die Kreisgleichung wird damit

$$(X-R/\sqrt{2})^2 + (Y+R/\sqrt{2})^2 = R^2 \quad \text{oder}$$

$$X^2+Y^2+\sqrt{2}R\,(Y-X) = 0 \quad \text{und zur Beseitigung}$$

der Wurzel mit $M = \sqrt{2}\,R$

$$X^2+Y^2+M\,(Y-X) = 0 \qquad (6)$$

Durch Koeffizientenvergleich mit Gl. (5) werden die Anfangswerte im Flußdiagramm für den Kreis:

$$k_1 = k_2 = 2 \quad ; \quad k_3 = 4 \quad , \quad b = M - 1$$
$$a = 1 \quad ; \quad d = \frac{1}{4}(2M-5) \qquad (7)$$

Der Zusammenhang zwischen der Anzahl n der Iterationsschritte für einen Oktanten und dem Kreisradius R ist aus Bild 6 zu erkennen:

$$X_m = n = R/\sqrt{2} = M/2 \qquad (8)$$

Zur Vereinfachung werden neue Parameter so definiert, daß im Kreisalgorithmus nur noch Additionen auszuführen sind. Mit $M = \frac{C}{2}$:

$$\begin{aligned} K &= -8 = -4\,k_1 = 4\,k_2 = -2\,k_3 \\ B &= 4b = 2C-4 \\ A &= -4 \\ D &= 4d = C-5 \end{aligned} \qquad (9)$$

Jetzt müssen noch die neuen Parameter beim Oktantenwechsel berechnet werden. Da als Startpunkt 0 ein DOW gewählt wurde, muß der nächste Oktantenwechsel bei einem QOW stattfinden. Aus dem allgemeinen QOW für die Kegelschnitte /2/ erhält man für den Kreis (die Berechnung wird unterdrückt) folgende Vorschrift zur Parameterbestimmung:

$$\begin{aligned} K &:= -K = 8 \\ B &:= -B = 4 = B + K \\ D &:= -D + A + B \\ A &:= A + 2\,B = A + 8 = A + K \end{aligned} \qquad (10)$$

Nach dem QOW ist der nächste Oktantenwechsel ein DOW. Da der Algorithmus bei einem DOW gestartet wurde, kann auf Grund der Symmetrieeigenschaften dieselbe Parameterinitialisierung wieder verwandt werden. Der Algorithmus beginnt im Punkt 0 mit einem MOVE2. Auch in den anderen Oktantenwechseln ist die Bewegungsrichtung bekannt und unabhängig vom Radius immer gleich. Deshalb kann man die Abfrage auf $D < 0$, d.h. die Entscheidung ob MOVE1 oder MOVE2 folgt, nach einem Oktantenwechsel sparen. Wird dies bei der Initialisierung berücksichtigt, so ergibt sich das in Bild 7 dargestellte Flußdiagramm des Kreisalgorithmus.
Der nach diesem Algorithmus realisierte DKG liefert gute Ergebnisse /4/. Die Kreise sind unabhängig vom Radius gleich hell. Die Schreibdauer t_k ergibt sich aus dem Radius R in Rastereinheiten zu

$$t_k = \frac{18.R + 9,5}{20\ \text{MHz}} \qquad (11)$$

Z.B. für einen Kreis mit einem Radius gleich dem halben Bildschirmdurchmesser $R = 500$: $t_k \approx 450\ \mu s$.
Kreise werden durch Angabe ihres Mittelpunktes, des Radius und des Anfangs- und Endwinkels spezifiziert. Wrap-around wird hardwaremäßig unterdrückt. Die Kreispunkte werden mit einer Wortlänge von 13 bit berechnet. Durch entsprechende Bewertung in den DAU können deshalb ohne wesentliche Qualitätsminderung Kreisbögen gezeichnet werden, deren Radien maximal das Vierfache des Bildschirmdurchmessers betragen. Der kleinste darstellbare Kreis besitzt den"Radius" $R = \sqrt{2}$. Bild 8 zeigt einige mit

dem DKG erzeugte Kreise.

DIGITALER MATRIZENMULTIPLIZIERER/DIVIDIERER

Hochleistungsdisplays besitzen zur Durchführung der linearen Transformationen in Echtzeit einen Matrizenmultiplizierer. Durch die Verwendung von homogenen Koordinaten lassen sich die Rotation, Skalierung, Translation und Perspektive eines Vektors $[x, y, z, w]$ durch Multiplikation mit einer (4x4)-Matrix berechnen

$$[x' \; y' \; z' \; w'] = [xyzw] \cdot \begin{bmatrix} T \\ 4x4 \end{bmatrix} \qquad (12)$$

wobei die Koeffizienten von T folgende Wirkung haben /5/:

Rotation, Scherung, Skalierung (a b c / e f g / i j k); Perspektive (d / h / l); Translation (m n o); Gesamtskalierung (p)

$$\left[\begin{array}{ccc|c} a & b & c & d \\ e & f & g & h \\ i & j & k & l \\ \hline m & n & o & p \end{array}\right]$$

Die Bildschirmkoordinaten erhält man aus den homogenen Koordinaten durch Division:

$$X = \frac{x}{w} \;,\; Y = \frac{y}{w} \;,\; Z = \frac{z}{w} \qquad (13)$$

Zur Durchführung der Transformation nach Gl. (12) sind 16 Multiplikationen und Additionen notwendig, d.h. die Rechenzeit ist etwa proportional einer Multiplikationszeit. Legt man als mittlere Schreibzeit für einen Vektor 5 μs zugrunde, so können die 16 Multiplikationen nacheinander in einem schnellen Multiplizierer ausgeführt werden. Ausgewählt wurde der 2 - Komplement - Multiplizierbaustein AM 25S05, der das Produkt aus zwei 16 bit-Worten in ca. 100 ns liefert. Die Matrizenmultiplikation kann demnach problemlos in der geforderten Geschwindigkeit ausgeführt werden. Zur Berechnung der perspektivischen Projektion und zur Ermittlung der Bildschirmkoordinaten aus den homogenen Koordinaten müssen Divisionen entsprechend Gl. (13) durchgeführt werden. Es ist wünschenswert, daß die Zahl der darstellbaren Vektoren bei einer Echtzeitberechnung der Perspektive nicht wesentlich reduziert wird. Daraus folgt, daß die Rechenzeit für die Division erheblich kleiner sein muß als für die (4x4) Matrix-Transformation. Diese Forderung ist erfüllt, wenn es gelingt, die Divisionszeit in die Größenordnung der Multiplikationszeit zu bringen. Dies wird mit einer iterativen Division erreicht.

$$Q = \frac{X}{Y}$$

Y sei normalisiert: $1 > Y \geq 0{,}5$

Stünde 1/Y mit 16 bit Wortlänge in einem ROM zur Verfügung, so wäre das Problem bereits gelöst. Leider sind Festwertspeicher in dieser Größenordnung bisher nicht vernünftig zu realisieren. Deshalb wird der Reziprokwert I_0 des auf 9 bit gerundeten Nenners Y_R in einem ROM abgespeichert. Durch Erweiterung erhält man

$$Q = \frac{X}{Y} \cdot \frac{I_0}{I_0} = \frac{X_0}{Y_0} = \frac{X_0}{1-z} \qquad (14)$$

mit $1 > Y_0 \geq 1 - 2^{-8}$ bzw. $0 < z \leq 2^{-8}$

Berücksichtigt man die Tatsache, daß das Produkt

$$Y_0 (2 - Y_0) = (1 - z)(1 + z) = 1 - z^2$$

quadratisch gegen 1 geht, so erhält man bereits nach einer Iteration den Quotienten mit einer Genauigkeit von 16 bit:

$$Q = X_0 \cdot (2 - Y_0)$$

$$Q = X \cdot I_0 (2 - Y \cdot I_0) \qquad (15)$$

Die Produkte $X \cdot I_0$ und $Y \cdot I_0$ können, sofern zwei Multiplizierer vorhanden sind, gleichzeitig berechnet werden. Die Division benötigt dann im wesentlichen die Zeit für zwei Multiplikationen. Damit ist unsere Anforderung an die Divisionsgeschwindigkeit erfüllt. Der realisierte Dividierer benötigt 350 ns zur Division zweier 16 bit Worte. Die Genauigkeit ist 14 bit, wobei die beiden identischen Multiplizierer zwei 16 bit Worte in 100 ns auf 1 5 bit genau multiplizieren. Bild 9 zeigt die Schaltung des Dividierers. Damit stehen auch für die Matrizenmultiplikation 2 Multiplizierer zur Verfügung, so daß die gesamte 4x4 Matrix-Transformation einschließlich Division in 4 μs ausgeführt werden kann.

DIGITALER KURVEN/FLÄCHENGENERATOR

Dem Entwurf des Kurven- und Flächengenerators liegt die Parameterdarstellung

$$Q(u, v) = U^T \overline{P} V \qquad (16)$$

zugrunde, mit der alle in Computer Graphics angewandten Kurven und Flächen beschrieben werden können /6/. Dabei ist

$$Q(u, v) = [X(u,v), Y(u,v), Z(u,v)] \qquad (17)$$

der berechnete Flächenpunkt, U und V sind Vektoren der Interpolationspolynome, $\overline{P}$ ist die Hypermatrix der Bestimmungsgrößen und (u,v) sind die Parameter mit $0 \leq u, v \leq 1$.

Flächen werden auf dem Display durch u- und/oder v-Rasterlinien dargestellt. Diese Kurven sind aus obiger Gleichung prinzipiell auf zwei Arten zu gewinnen:

a) Inkremental nach dem Newton'schen Differenzenverfahren

b) Durch Multiplikation mit einem Matrizenmultiplizierer

a) Differenzenverfahren

Die Vorwärtsdifferenz einer Funktion Q (u) ist bei gleichmäßiger Inkrementierung der unabhängigen Variablen u definiert als

$$\Delta Q(u) = Q(u + \delta) - Q(u) \quad , \quad \delta = \frac{1}{N} \qquad (18)$$

$$\Delta(\Delta Q(u)) = \Delta^2 Q = [Q(u+2\delta) - Q(u+\delta) - Q(u+\delta) - Q(u)]$$

$$\Delta^2 Q(u) = Q(u+2\delta) - 2 Q(u+\delta) + Q(u)$$

$$\Delta^3 Q(u) = Q(u+3\delta) - 3\,Q(u+2\delta) + 3\,Q(u+\delta) - Q(u)$$

Durch Umschreiben und Auflösen von Gl. (18) erhält man mit

$$Q(u) \longrightarrow Q_n \quad , \quad Q(u+\delta) \longrightarrow Q_{n+1}$$

$$\begin{aligned} Q_{n+1} &= Q_n + \Delta Q_n \\ \Delta Q_{n+1} &= \Delta Q_n + \Delta^2 Q_n \\ \Delta^2 Q_{n+1} &= \Delta^2 Q_n + \Delta^3 Q_n \\ \Delta^3 Q_{n+1} &= \Delta^3 Q_n = \text{konst} \end{aligned} \qquad (19)$$

Das Polynom ist also durch Angabe von Anfangswerten $Q_0, \Delta Q_0, \Delta^2 Q_0, \Delta^3 Q_0$ völlig bestimmt und iterativ ohne Multiplikation berechenbar. Zur Berechnung eines Punktes sind nur 3 Additionen nötig, die gleichzeitig ausgeführt werden können.

Die Hardware-Realisierung des Differenzenverfahrens besteht aus einem Addierer-Register-Modul, der je nach Grad des zu berechnenden Polynoms entsprechend oft hintereinander geschaltet wird (Bild 10). Die erste Stufe besteht aus dem oben beschriebenen Vektorgenerator, für den die weiteren Stufen die relativen Koordinaten $\Delta P = \Delta Q$ zur Verfügung stellen. Die Praxis hat gezeigt, daß die meisten Kurven bzw. Rasterlinien einer Fläche durch weniger als 100 Vektoren für das Auge völlig glatt wiedergegeben werden. Deshalb wird der DVG zur linearen Interpolation getrennt von den weiteren ARM-Stufen betrieben. Da der DVG alle Vektoren mit gleicher Helligkeit schreibt, treten entlang einer Kurve keine Helligkeitsschwankungen auf Grund der Parametrisierung auf.

Zur Flächendarstellung müssen für jede Rasterlinie neue Anfangswerte geladen werden, die ebenfalls iterativ berechnet werden können /6/. Dies wird parallel zum Schreiben einer Kurve softwaremäßig durchgeführt.

b) Flächenberechnung durch Matrizenmultiplikation

Der digitale Matrizenmultiplizierer DMM berechnet die Transformation (Gl. 12)

$$p' = p \cdot T$$

$$[x', y', z', w'] = [x, y, z, w] \cdot \underset{(4\times4)}{T}$$

Wird p durch U^T und T durch $\overline{P}$ ersetzt, so berechnet der DMM die Kurve

$$Q(u) = U^T\,\overline{P} \qquad (20)$$

Auf diese Weise können höchstens Kurven 3-ten Grades berechnet werden. Die Vektoren U^T werden für das gewählte Interpolations- oder Approximationsverfahren mit einer vorgegebenen Schrittweite für u, $0 \leq u \leq 1$ (z.B. $\delta = 2^{-7}$) in einem ROM zur Verfügung gestellt. Größere Schrittweiten erhält man durch entsprechende ROM-Adressierung. Die Rasterlinien zur Erzeugung der Fläche

$$Q(u, v) = U^T\,\overline{P}\,V \qquad (21)$$

müssen in mehreren Schritten berechnet werden. Zuerst sind die Matrixprodukte $\overline{P}V$ für die v-Rasterlinien bzw. $U^T\,\overline{P}$ für die u-Rasterlinien zu berechnen. Da der

Matrixspeicher des DMM nur 16 Elemente faßt, sind diese Multiplikationen für jede Komponente von $\overline{P}$ getrennt auszuführen und die Ergebnisse in einem zweiten (4x4) Matrixspeicher festzuhalten. Anschließend kann die Rasterlinie berechnet werden. Für das wahlweise Berechnen der u- und/oder v-Rasterlinie wird eine wesentliche Vereinfachung erreicht, wenn U = V ist:

$$Q\,(u,\,v) = U^T\,\overline{P}\,U \tag{22}$$

Man kann dann den Vektor $\overline{P}U$ unter Ausnutzung der Beziehung

$$\overline{P}\,U = (U^T\,\overline{P}^T)^T \tag{23}$$

berechnen. In der Hardware wird dies durch Umkodieren des Adreßzählers für $\overline{P}$ geleistet. Zusätzlich wird ROM-Kapazität eingespart. Trotzdem können in u- und v-Richtung verschiedene Schrittweiten gewählt werden! Bild 11 zeigt 2 Beispiele von Flächen, deren Rasterpunkte hardwaremäßig berechnet wurden. Die Rechenzeit beträgt ca. 2 ms. Durch Verbinden dieser Rasterpunkte und Berücksichtigung der z-Koordinate erhält man die Darstellungen in Bild 12.

LITERATUR

/1/ TEICH, G., "Digitaler Vektorgenerator" Diplomarbeit TU Berlin 1975, Betreuer: Straßer

/2/ PITTEWAY, M.L.V., "Algorithm for drawing ellipses or hyperbolae with a digital plotter", Computer Journal 10 (1968), S. 282-289

/3/ DANIELSSON, P.E., "Incremental curve generation", IEEE Tr. on Computers, Vol. C-19, No. 9, Sept. 1970

/4/ WILHELMI, U., "Digitaler Kreisgenerator", Diplomarbeit TU Berlin 1973, Betreuer: Straßer

/5/ FORREST, A.R., "Co-ordinates, transformations and visualisation techniques", CAD group document No. 33, June 1969, Cambridge, England

/6/ STRASSER, W., "Schnelle Kurven- und Flächenerzeugung auf grafischen Sichtgeräten", Dissertation, TU Berlin 1974

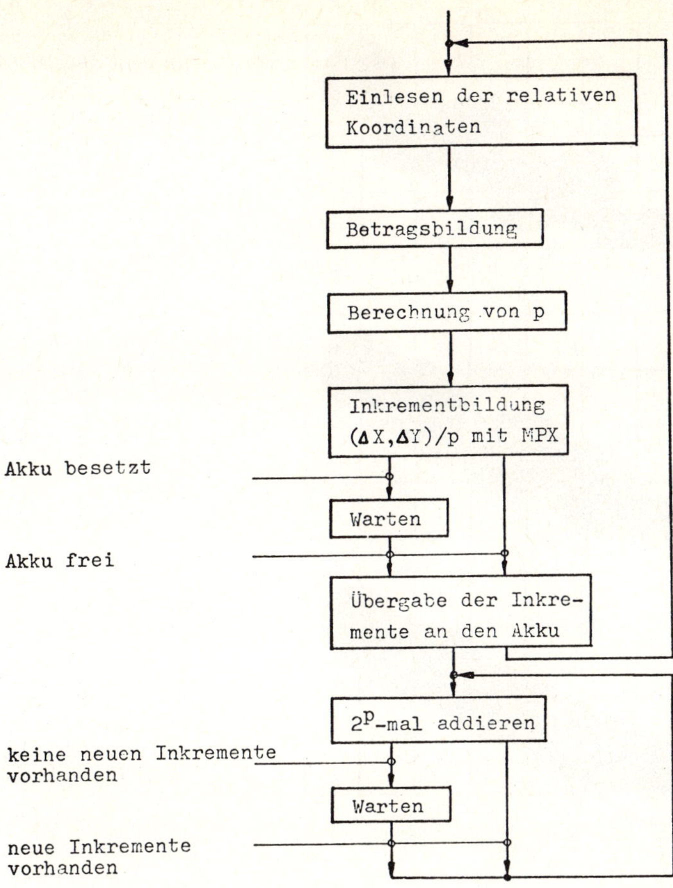

Bild 1 : Ablaufdiagramm des DVG

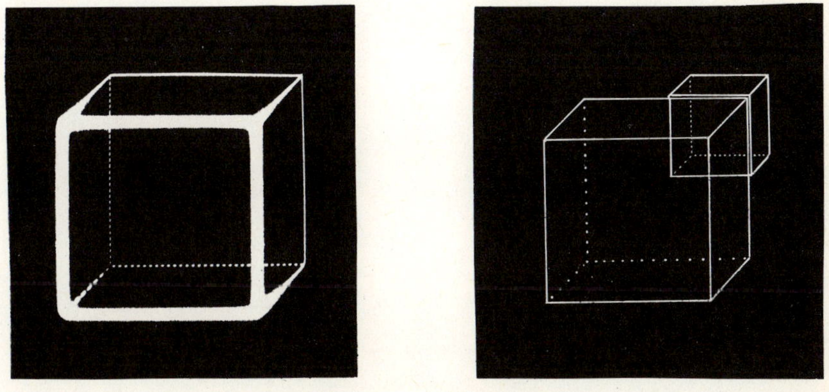

Bild 3 : Strichstärkevariation und Skalierung beim DVG

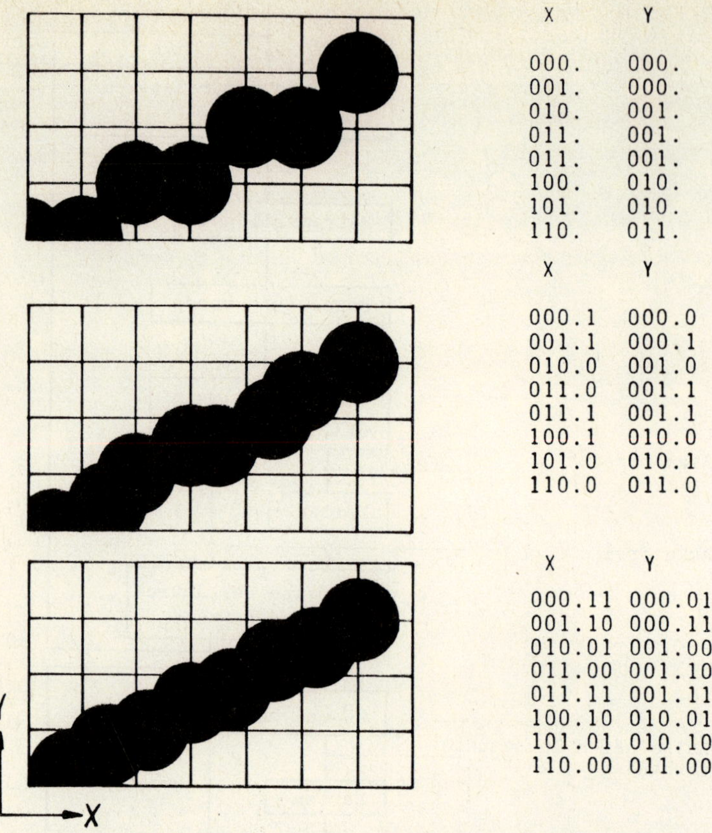

Bild 2 : Aussehen der Vektoren in Abhängigkeit von der Wortlänge

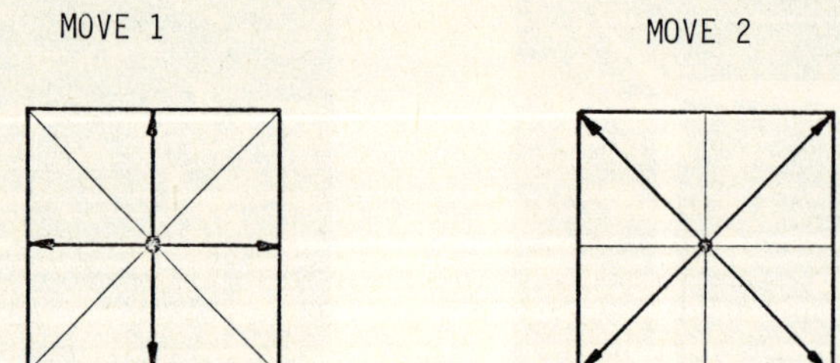

Bild 4 : Einteilung der Elementarvektoren in MOVE1 und MOVE2

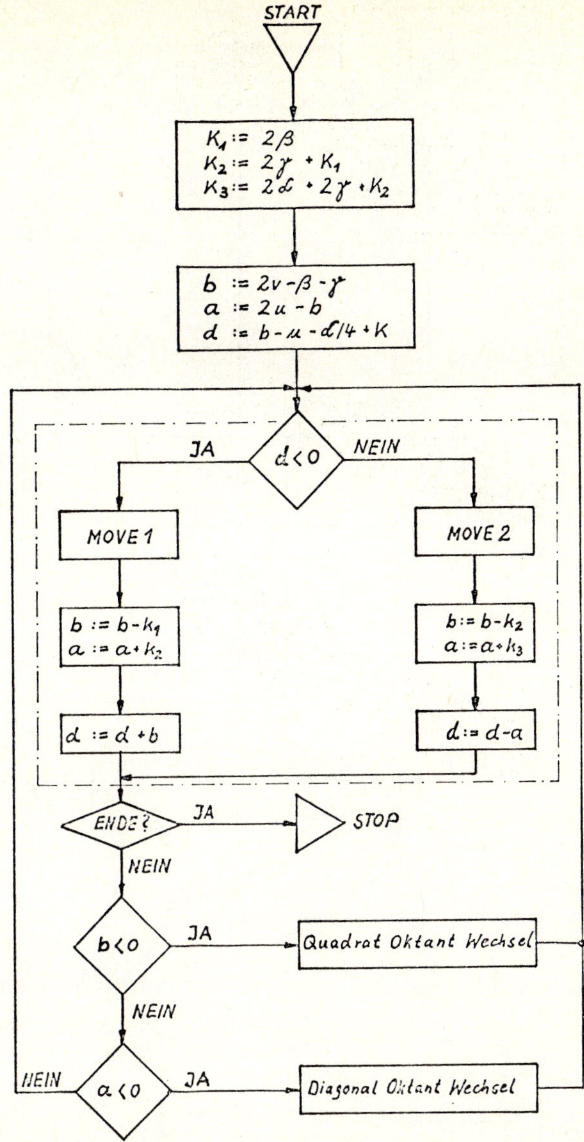

Bild 5 : Flußdiagramm des Kegelschnittalgorithmus /2/

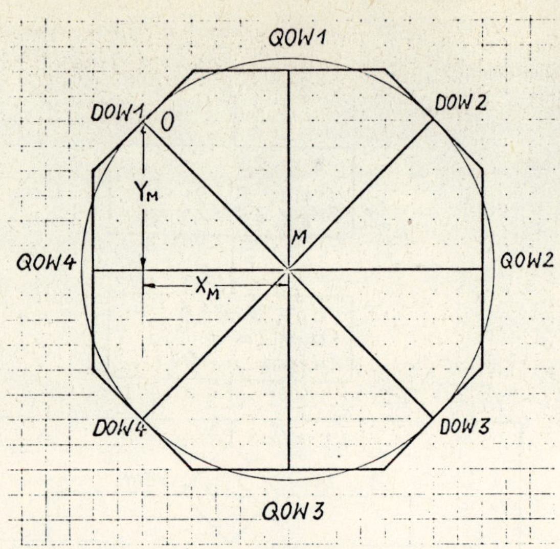

Bild 6 : Kreis aus MOVE1 und MOVE2 Vektoren

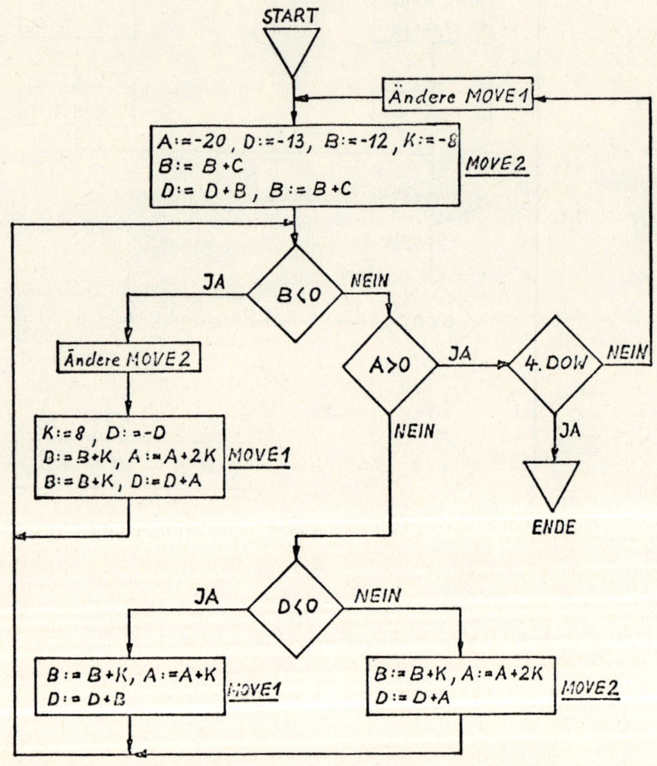

Bild 7 : Flußdiagramm des Kreisalgorithmus

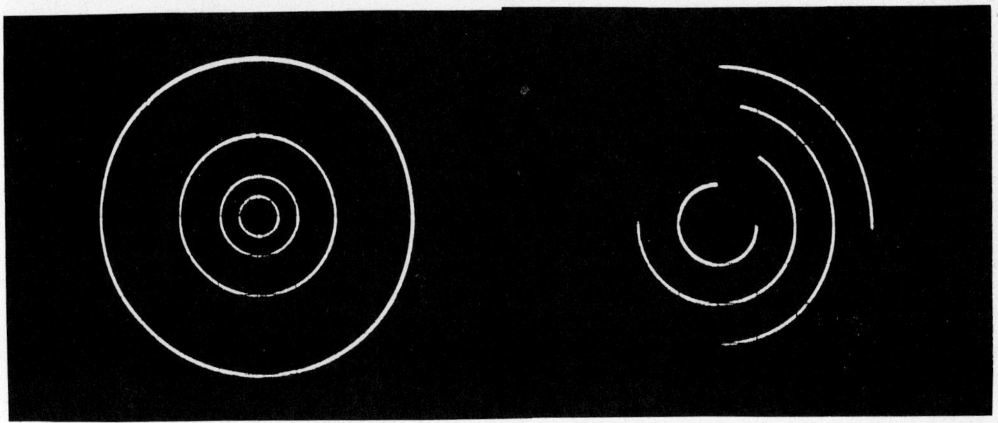

Bild 8 : Beispiele für hardware-generierte Kreise

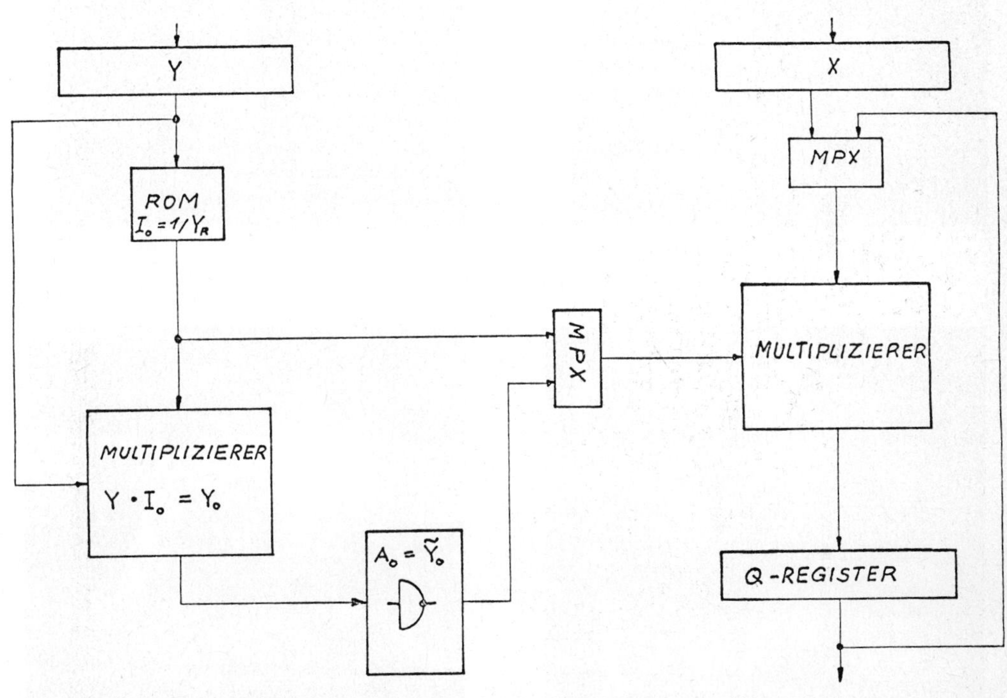

Bild 9 : Blockschaltbild des Dividierers

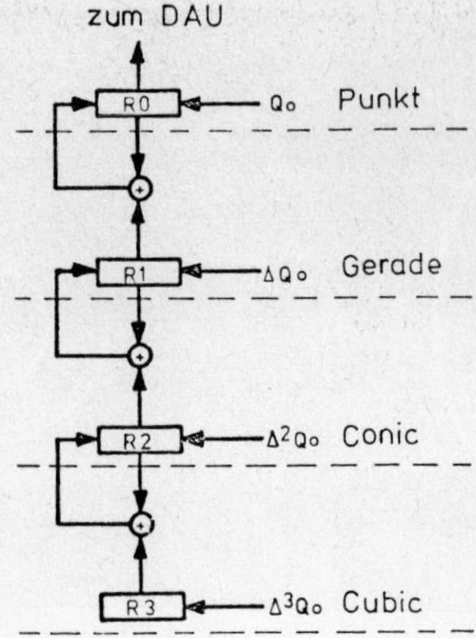

Bild 10 : Addierer-Register-Modul

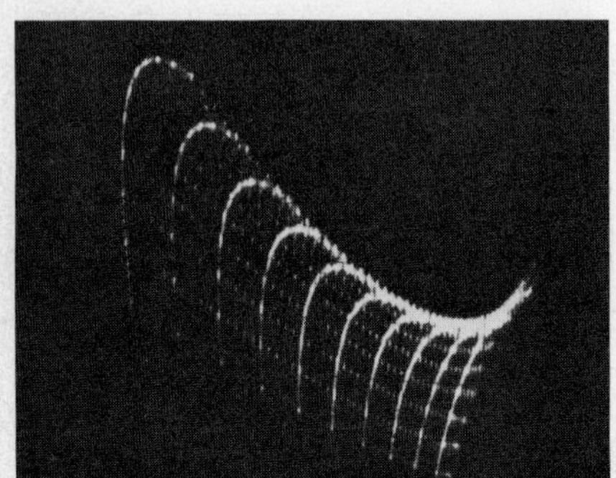

Bild 11 : Rasterpunkte von Flächen

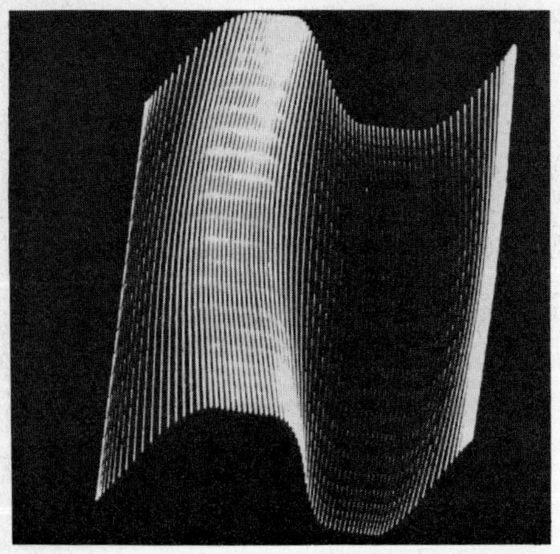

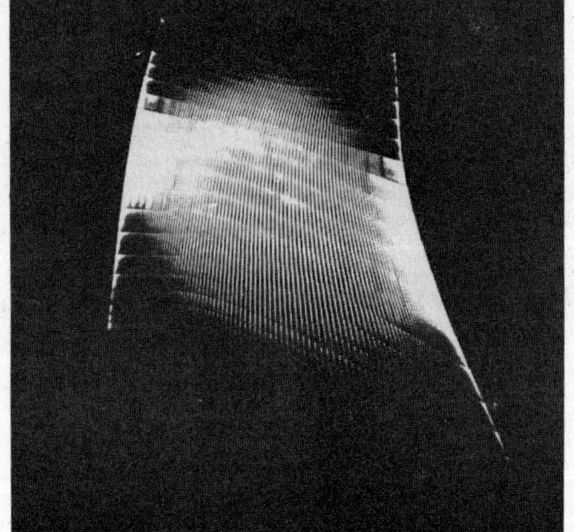

Bild 12 : Rasterpunkte mit Vektorgenerator verbunden; Intensitätssteuerung durch die z-Koordinate

ZUR STRUKTURIERUNG MEHRSTUFIGER MUSTERERKENNUNGSSYSTEME

H. Petersen, N. Vorstädt

Technische Hochschule Aachen,
Informatik-Forschungsgruppe 15

Zusammenfassung:

Die Klassifizierungsleistung mehrstufiger Mustererkennungssysteme ist wesentlich durch die Struktur des Systems und die Art der eingesetzten Verfahren zur Merkmalextraktion bestimmt. Eine Aufgabe besteht bei der Konstruktion mehrstufiger Systeme darin, die zur Verfügung stehenden Extraktionsverfahren und die Systemstruktur aufeinander abzustimmen.

Zu diesem Zweck werden Verfahren beschrieben und miteinander verglichen, welche es gestatten, die Verteilung der Muster im Merkmalraum zu bestimmen und daraus Maße abzuleiten, die Auskunft über die Trennbarkeit der Klassen im Merkmalraum geben. In einem weiteren Schritt können die Trennbarkeiten von Klassenpaaren zur Bestimmung von Gruppentrennbarkeiten und damit zur Strukturierung von mehrstufigen Systemen herangezogen werden.

1. Einleitung

Üblicherweise sind Mustererkennungssysteme im wesentlichen aus einer einzigen Merkmalextraktionsstufe, gefolgt von der eigentlichen Klassifikationsstufe aufgebaut. Die Arbeiten an Verfahren zur on-line Zeichenerkennung, welche in der Forschungsgruppe 15 (Methoden der Informatik für spezielle Anwendungen) an der TH Aachen durchgeführt wurden, haben gezeigt, daß ein wesentlicher Leistungsgewinn durch den Einsatz von mehrstufigen Systemen, insbesondere von Systemen mit Baumstruktur zu erzielen ist. Das wichtigste konstruktive Merkmal eines solchen Systems ist die Zusammenfassung einzelner Musterklassen zu Untermengen der Menge aller in Betracht kommenden Klassen. Als Kriterien für diese Strukturierung können Bewertungsmaße herangezogen werden, welche aus der Verteilung der Musterklassen im Merkmalraum abgeleitet werden.

2. Mehrstufige Mustererkennungssysteme

Mehrstufige Systeme können je nach ihrer Struktur in verschiedene Klassen (parallele, sequentielle usw.) eingeteilt werden. Die hier beschriebenen Überlegungen ergeben sich aus dem Versuch, generelle Gesichtspunkte für die Konstruktion von Systemen mit Baumstruktur abzuleiten.

2.1 Systeme mit Baumstruktur

In derartigen Systemen können sowohl verschiedene Verfahren zur Merkmalextraktion als auch verschiedene Stufen und Verfahren der Zuordnung zu den Merkmalklassen vorkommen. Abb. 1 zeigt den prinzipiellen Aufbau eines Erkennungssystems mit Baumstruktur für 11 Klassen und der Bestimmung von 4 verschiedenen Merkmalvektoren. Aus der Struktur des Systems ist zu erkennen, daß die Klassifizierung in 3 Stufen erfolgt. Jede Stufe kann als vollständiges einstufiges Mustererkennungssystem oder als Zusammenfassung mehrerer Systeme angesehen werden, wobei jedoch nicht die Zugehörigkeit des unbekannten Musters zu einer einzigen aus der Gesamtheit der betrachteten Klassen, sondern u.U. lediglich die Zugehörigkeit zu einer Klasse aus einer Untermenge der betrachteten Klassen bestimmt wird. Außerdem kann die Zuordnung zu einer solchen Untermenge dazu führen, daß in der folgenden Stufe eine andere Art der Merkmalextraktion durchgeführt wird. Grundsätzlich können auf diese Weise beliebige Mustererkennungsverfahren miteinander kombiniert werden. Das Ziel ist dabei, ein optimales Gesamtsystem dadurch zu erhalten, daß die Nachteile eines bestimmten Verfahrens durch die Vorteile eines anderen Verfahrens kompensiert werden.

Der Aufbau eines Systems mit Baumstruktur wird in erster Linie durch die Einordnung der betrachteten Musterklassen in Untermengen aus der Gesamtmenge der Klassen bestimmt sowie die Anordnung dieser Untermengen innerhalb der Struktur des Systems. Sei $K_1 = \{k_1, k_2, \ldots, k_n\}$ die Menge aller n betrachteten Musterklassen, K_i eine beliebige

Untermenge von K_1 und l die Anzahl der Stufen, aus denen ein mehrstufiges System besteht. Dann ist jede Stufe α des Systems ($1<\alpha<l-1$) dadurch gekennzeichnet, daß eine Aufteilung aller Mengen $K_i^\alpha \subset K_1$ mit card $(K_i^\alpha) > 1$ in Untermengen K_j so erfolgt, daß

$$\bigcup_{j=1}^{n_j} K_j^{\alpha+1} = K_i^\alpha \quad \text{und} \quad K_j^{\alpha+1} \bigcap K_k^{\alpha+1} = \emptyset \text{ für alle } 1 < j,\ k < n_j.$$

Dabei ist n_j die Anzahl der Untermengen $K_j^{\alpha+1}$, welche durch die Zerlegung von K_i^α entstehen und - falls card $(K_j^{\alpha+1}) > 1$ - in der Stufe $\alpha+1$ weiter zerlegt werden. Für $l=1$ handelt es sich um ein einstufiges System und es gilt:

$$\bigcup_{j=1}^{n_j} K_j^1 = K_1 \text{ und } n_j = n.$$

Für $l = n-1$ handelt es sich um ein System, bei dem in jeder Stufe α die Klassifizierung in eine Klasse oder in die zu einer Untermenge $K_{\alpha+1}$ zusammengefaßten $n-\alpha$ verbliebenen Klassen erfolgt.

2.2 Strukturierung mit Hilfe von Trennbarkeitsmaßen

Die Zusammenfassung von Klassen zu Untermengen wird man so vornehmen, daß diejenigen Klassen in einer zusätzlichen Systemstufe klassifiziert werden, welche zunächst schlecht oder gar nicht voneinander unterschieden werden konnten. Bei der Konstruktion eines mehrstufigen Systems sind demnach Kenntnisse darüber erforderlich, wie gut oder schlecht die einzelnen Klassen in den verschiedenen Stufen voneinander trennbar sind. Es ist ersichtlich, daß demnach die Struktur eines Systems in der Hauptsache durch die Art der Merkmalextraktion in den einzelnen Stufen bestimmt wird. Aus der Beschreibung eines Verfahrens selbst lassen sich jedoch keine Kriterien für den Systemaufbau ableiten. Andererseits sind Untersuchungen mit Hilfe von vollständigen Klassifizierungssystemen und den notwendigen umfangreichen Versuchsreihen sehr aufwendig und darüber hinaus durch die eigentliche Klassifizierung beeinflußt. Deshalb werden aus der Verteilung von Stichproben im Merkmalraum Maße abgeleitet, welche indirekt Anhaltspunkte für die Trennbarkeit der Klassen ergeben.

3. Trennbarkeitsmaße

3.1 Allgemeines

Zweckmäßigerweise betrachtet man die Trennbarkeit zwischen je zwei Klassen, da sich daraus am besten erkennen läßt, welche Klassen zu einer Oberklasse zusammenzuschließen sind. Aus den Trennbarkeitswerten aller Klassenpaare ergibt sich die sogenannte Trennmatrix, die die Grundlage zur Konstruktion mehrstufiger Systeme bildet.

Zur Bildung der Trennmatrix sind nur die Trennbarkeiten von je zwei Klassen zu bestimmen. Aus diesem Grund können wir uns hier auf die Behandlung von Zwei-Klassen-Problemen beschränken.
Da man bei der Konstruktion mehrstufiger Systeme diejenigen Klassen zusammenfassen will, bei denen die höchste Verwechslungsrate auftritt, wird man also die Trennbarkeit als die maximale Erkennungsrate definieren, die aufgrund der vorliegenden Merkmalverteilung zu erreichen ist. Um die Einflüsse des Klassifikators auf die Erkennungsrate auszuschließen, betrachtet man ein System mit der vorliegenden Merkmalverteilung und einem optimalen Klassifikator. Ein solcher optimaler Klassifikator kann formal folgendermaßen beschrieben werden /3/:

Gegeben seien die beiden Musterklassen k_1, k_2 und die Verteilung des N-dimensionalen Merkmalvektors x. Weiter seien z_1 und z_2 die Mischkoeffizienten der Klassen k_1 und k_2, die als

(3.01) $z_i := P(x \in z_i);\ i=1,\ 2;$

definiert sind. Ein optimaler Klassifikator ist dann eine Abbildung f vom Merkmalraum X auf die Symbolmenge $S := \{s_1, s_2\}$ - der Fall der Rückweisung sei ausgeschlossen - mit folgender Eigenschaft:

(3.02) $f(x) := s_i \iff p(k_i|x) > p(k_j|x);\ i,\ j=1,\ 2;\ j \neq i;$

und dies heißt nach Umformung durch die Regel von Bayes:

(3.03) $f(x) := s_i \iff p(x|k_i)\ z_i > p(x|k_j)\ z_j;\ i,\ j=1,\ 2;\ j \neq i;$

Bei vorgegebenem Merkmalvektor x erhalten wir für die Wahrscheinlichkeit u(x), daß x zur Klasse f(x) gehört:

(3.04) $u(x) := \operatorname{Max}_i p(k_i|x) = \operatorname{Max}_i p(x|k_i)\ z_i \ /\ p(x);\ i=1,\ 2;$

Die gesuchte Trennbarkeit t ist der Erwartungswert von u und demnach

(3.05) $t := E(u) = \sum_{x \in X} u(x)p(x) = \sum_{x \in X} \operatorname{Max}_i p(x|k_i)\ z_i;\ i=1,\ 2;$

oder im nicht diskreten Fall (Abb. 2):

(3.06) $t := E(u) = \int_X u(x)p(x)dx = \int_X \operatorname{Max}_i p(x|k_i)\ z_i\ dx;\ i=1,\ 2;$

Die Schwierigkeit besteht i.A. in der Bestimmung des o.a. Mehrfachintegrals. Bei der Lösung dieses Problems ist es günstig, folgende beiden Schritte zu unterscheiden:
(i) Aus einer gegebenen Stichprobe mit Umfang n von Merkmalvektoren, die Trainingsmenge genannt wird, erstellt man eine Verteilungsbeschreibung. Dabei werden bestimmte

Annahmen über die Art der Verteilung gemacht, deren Parameter aus der Stichprobe ermittelt werden. Ebenfalls ist die Wahrscheinlichkeit zu bestimmen, daß die Verteilungsannahme richtig ist.

(ii) Aus der Verteilungsbeschreibung wird durch numerische Integration oder approximierende Verfahren die Trennbarkeit bestimmt.

Bezeichnet man bei einem Mehrklassenproblem die Trennbarkeit der Klasse k_i zur Klasse k_j mit t_{ij}, so erhält man bei der Berechnung aller gegenseitigen Trennbarkeiten die Trennmatrix (t_{ij}). Da man bei der Bestimmung der Trennbarkeit der Klassen k_i und k_j ein Zweiklassenproblem aus einem Mehrklassenproblem herauslöst, gilt für die Mischkoeffizienten z_i:

$$(3.07) \qquad z_i := \frac{z_i'}{z_i'+z_j'} \; ; \qquad z_j := \frac{z_j'}{z_i'+z_j'}$$

worin z_i' und z_j' die Mischkoeffizienten innerhalb des Mehrklassenproblems sind.

Im folgenden werden einige Verfahren zur Erstellung der Verteilungsbeschreibung und Abschätzung der Trennbarkeit dargestellt.

3.2 Schwerpunktverfahren

Wie der Name des Verfahrens erkennen läßt, wird hierbei als Verteilungsbeschreibung lediglich der Erwartungswert der Klassen bestimmt. Die Schätzung des Erwartungswertes geschieht dabei nach der Formel

$$(3.08) \qquad E(x) = \frac{1}{n} \sum_{i=1}^{n} x^{(i)}$$

oder einer entsprechenden Rekursion.

Aus den Erwartungswerten der beiden Klassen soll jetzt auf ihre Trennbarkeit geschlossen werden. Dazu ist es jedoch nicht allein nötig, Voraussetzungen über die Art der vorliegenden Verteilungen zu machen, sondern auch über deren weitere Parameter, z.B. deren Varianz. Ohne diese Kenntnisse ist eine Abschätzung von t nicht sinnvoll. Unsere Erfahrungen haben gezeigt, daß die Varianz der Merkmalverteilungen aber von Fall zu Fall und von Klasse zu Klasse sehr verschieden sein können, so daß hierüber keine plausiblen Angaben gemacht werden können.

Ein von Schwerdtmann 1973 vorgeschlagenes Verfahren /1/ zur Strukturierung mehrstufiger Systeme verwendet die Erwartungswerte aller Klassen und faßt die Klassen mit geringstem Abstand ihrer Erwartungswerte zusammen. Hierbei verzichtet man also auf die Ermittlung der Trennbarkeit von je zwei Klassen und versucht durch Vergleich der Schwerpunktabstände zu entscheiden, welche Klassen am schlechtesten voneinander zu trennen sind.

Wie unsere Erfahrungen gezeigt haben, und wie sich an einfachen Beispielen demonstrieren läßt, ist dieses Verfahren für die Praxis unzureichend, da auch hier ohne Kenntnisse über die Varianzen der Verteilung keine fundierte Abschätzung der Trennbarkeitsverhältnisse gewonnen werden kann.

3.3 Schwerpunkt-Varianz-Verfahren

In diesem Verfahren werden zur Beurteilung der Merkmalverteilung die Erwartungswerte und Varianzen der Verteilung herangezogen. Die Verteilungsbeschreibung jeder Klasse enthält also den gemäß (3.08) gewonnenen Erwartungswert und die Varianz jeder Komponente des Merkmalvektors, die nach der Formel

$$(3.09)\quad V(x_i) := \frac{1}{n-1} \sum_{i=1}^{n} (x_i^{(j)} - E(x_i))^2;\ i=1, \ldots, N$$

(biasfrei) abgeschätzt wird. Um eine Abschätzung für den Ausdruck in (3.06) und damit für t zu finden, macht man die Annahme, die Merkmalvektoren beider Klassen seien <u>gleichverteilt</u>. Diese Annahme stellt zwar in den meisten Fällen eine nur sehr grobe Annäherung dar, jedoch führt sie zu einer numerisch besonders einfachen Lösung. Zunächst wird die halbe Intervallbreite d jeder Komponente der beiden Verteilungen berechnet:

$$(3.10)\quad d_{ij} := \sqrt{V(x_{ij}) \cdot 3};\quad j=1, 2;\quad i=1, \ldots, N$$

Die Werte der i-ten Komponente liegen also gleichverteilt innerhalb des Intervalls $(E\,(x_{ij})-d_{ij},\ E\,(x_{ij})+d_{ij})$.

Durch Bildung des Schnittes der Intervalle beider Verteilungen in allen Komponenten erhält man das mehrdimensionale Intervall I, in dem sich beide Verteilungen überlappen. Die i-te Komponente dieses mehrdimensionalen Intervalls hat die Grenzen:

$$(3.11)\quad I_i := (\mathrm{Max}\ (E(x_{i1})-d_{i1},\ E(x_{i2})-d_{i2}),\ \mathrm{Min}\ (E(x_{i1})+d_{i1},\ E(x_{i2})+d_{i2})$$

Ist dieses Intervall I leer oder ausgeartet, so folgt aus (3.06) und $z_1+z_2=1$ $t=1$, was eine totale Trennbarkeit der Klassen bedeutet. Ist I nicht leer oder ausgeartet, so gilt:

$$(3.12)\quad t := 1 - \int_i \mathrm{Min}(z_1p_1, z_2p_2)\ dx = 1 - v(I)\ \mathrm{Min}(z_1p_1, z_2p_2)$$

worin p_1 und p_2 die Werte der Dichtefunktionen der Verteilungen in I sind und v für den elementargeometrischen Inhalt eines mehrdimensionalen Intervalls steht. Da wir beide Klassen als gleichverteilt angenommen haben, sind p_1 und p_2 in ganz I konstant und haben den Wert:

$$(3.13)\quad p_j = 2^{-N} \prod_{i=1}^{N} 1/d_{ij};\ j=1,\ 2$$

3.4 Momentenverfahren zweiter Ordnung

Eine noch bessere Anpassung des Beschreibungsmodells an die vorliegende Verteilung erhält man durch die Auswertung aller Momente 1. und 2. Ordnung. Als Verteilungsbeschreibung werden also die Erwartungswerte und Kovarianzmatrizen M_1, M_2 beider Klassen ausgewertet. Diese werden bestimmt nach

$$(3.14)\quad M_{jmn} := E(x_{jm} - \mu_{jm})(x_{jn} - \mu_{jn}) = \frac{1}{n-1} \sum_{i=1}^{n} (x_{jm}^{(i)} - \mu_{jm})(x_{jn}^{(i)} - \mu_{jn});\ j = 1,\ 2;$$

Eine in vielen Fällen weitaus bessere Approximation der vorliegenden Verteilungen als mit einer Gleichverteilung erhält man durch Annahme der Normalverteiltheit der Merkmalvektoren. Eine Überprüfung dieser Annahme ist mit Hilfe eines Signifikanztests mit einfachen Mitteln zu realisieren /2/.
Um aus der Verteilungsbeschreibung unter Annahme einer Normalverteilung die Trennbarkeit der Klassen zu ermitteln, liegt es zunächst nahe, das Integral in (3.06) durch numerische Integration über das Maximum der beiden Dichtefunktionen der Gaussverteilungen zu bestimmen. Dies ist jedoch nur für Merkmalräume mit einer Dimension von bis zu etwa 10 in der Praxis durchführbar. Bei höherdimensionalen Merkmalräumen, wie sie etwa bei der Vektorzerlegung von handgeschriebenen Zeichen vorkommen, ist eine Abschätzung dieses Integrals sinnvoll.
Zu diesem Zwecke betrachtet man die Projektion der Zufallsvariablen x_1 und x_2 auf die Verbindungsgerade der Erwartungswerte beider Klassen:

$$(3.15)\quad D: = (E(x_2)-E(x_1)\ )\ /\ |(E(x_2)-E(x_1)\ )|$$

$$(3.16)\quad w_1: = D\ (x_1-E(x_1)\ );\quad w_2: = D\ (x_2-E(x_1)\ )$$

w_1 und w_2 sind eindimensionale normalverteilte Zufallsvariablen und stellen die Randverteilung von x_1 und x_2 nach einer Translation und Rotation dar, so daß der Erwartungswert von x_1 den neuen Koordinatenursprung bildet und der Erwartungswert von x_2 auf der X-Achse liegt. Eine solche Drehung ist für eine gute Abschätzung durch die Randverteilung erforderlich. w_1 und w_2 haben folgende Parameter, die sich aus (3.15) und (3.16) und der Verteilungsbeschreibung ergeben:

$$(3.17)\quad E(w_1): = o;\quad E(w_2): = |E(x_2)-E(x_1)|\ ;$$

$$(3.18)\quad V(w_1): = \sum_{n,m=1}^{N} D_m D_n M_{imn};\ i=1,\ 2;$$

Da wir jetzt nur noch über das Maximum von zwei Normalverteilungen zu integrieren haben, bietet sich folgende Lösung an: Zunächst bestimmt man die Intervalle, in denen $z_1 p(w_1) > z_2 p(w_2)$ ist und integriert innerhalb dieser Intervalle über $z_1 p(w_1)$. Über den Rest der reellen Achse integriert man dann über $z_2 p(w_2)$. Die Summe ergibt dann die Abschätzung für die Trennbarkeit t.
Die Bestimmung der Intervallgrenzen führt, wie man leicht zeigen kann, auf folgende quadratische Gleichung:

$$(3.19)\quad \frac{1}{2V(w_1)V(w_2)}\left[(V(w_1)-V(w_2))x^2+2(E(w_1)V(w_2)-E(w_2)V(w_1))x - E^2(w_1)V(w_2)+E^2(w_2)V(w_1)\right] + \mathrm{Ln}\left[\frac{z_1}{z_2}\sqrt{\frac{V(w_2)}{V(w_1)}}\right] = 0$$

3.5 Clusterverfahren

Der Fall von normalverteilten Merkmalvektoren ist zwar in der Mustererkennung recht häufig, jedoch sind in bestimmten Fällen die Verteilungen nur unzureichend mit einer Normalverteilung zu approximieren. Keine wesentliche Einschränkung hingegen stellt die Annahme dar, daß die Klassen im Merkmalraum sogenannte Cluster bilden. Trifft dies für bestimmte Klassen nicht zu, so lassen sich diese meistens in clusterförmige Unterklassen zerlegen.
Zur Reduktion des mehrdimensionalen auf ein eindimensionales Problem nimmt man zunächst wieder die Transformation (3.15) (3.16) vor. Aus der Annahme der clusterförmigen Verteilung darf man die Folgerung ziehen, daß sich die mit z_1 bzw. z_2 gewichteten Dichtefunktionen von w_1 und w_2 nur in einem Punkte schneiden. Das heißt, unser optimaler Klassifikator erhält die Form:

$$(3.20)\quad f(x) := \begin{cases} s_1, & \text{falls } w < g \\ s_2 & \text{sonst} \end{cases}$$

wobei w die Transformation von x gemäß (3.15) (3.16) ist. Gesucht ist also zunächst der Wert für g, bei dem f optimal wird. Bezeichnet man die mit z_1 und z_2 gewichteten Verteilungsfunktionen von w_1 und w_2 mit ϕ_1 und ϕ_2

$$(3.21)\quad \phi_i(y) := z_i \int_{-\infty}^{y} p(w_i)\,dw_i;\ i=1,\ 2;$$

so ist f genau dann optimal, wenn $\phi_i + (z_2 - \phi_2)$ maximal wird.

$$(3.22) \quad t: = \underset{g}{\mathrm{Max}} \left[\phi_1(g) + z_2 - \phi_2(g)\right]$$

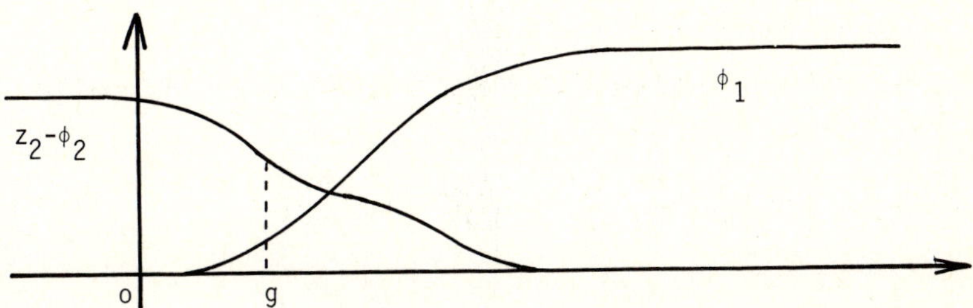

Zur Bestimmung von g werden zunächst aus der nach (3.15) (3.16) transformierten Trainingsmenge die Funktionen ϕ_2 und $(z_2-\phi_2)$ in tabellierter Form erstellt. Diese sind mit der Verteilungsbeschreibung der Verfahren 3.3 und 3.4 zu vergleichen. Die Schrittweite auf der reellen Achse bestimmt dabei die Genauigkeit der Maximierungen von f. Definitionsgemäß ist das Maximum von ϕ_1 + $(z_2-\phi_2)$ die gesuchte Trennbarkeit der beiden Klassen. Als Nebenprodukt fällt g für die Konstruktion eines stückweise linearen Klassifikators ab.

3.6 Rasterverfahren

Will man keinerlei Annahmen über die Art der Merkmalverteilungen machen, so kann man den Merkmalraum mit einem äquidistanten Raster überdecken. Für jedes Rasterfeld bestimmt man die Dichte der beiden Verteilungen. Zur Ermittlung der Trennbarkeit summiert man schließlich über alle Rasterfelder die Maxima der Dichten auf. Der Aufwand des Verfahrens ist abhängig vom gewählten Raster und der Dimension des Merkmalraumes. Schon bei einem 10-dimensionalen Merkmalraum und 10 Stützstellen pro Komponente sind die Speicherplatzprobleme in der Praxis kaum noch zu bewältigen.
Zur Wahl der geeigneten Rasterweite bestimmt man den minimalen euklidischen Abstand zweier Merkmalvektoren der Trainingsmenge, die der gleichen Klasse angehören. Bei genügend großer Trainingsmenge kann man die Rasterweite etwa als das 5- bis 10fache dieser Distanz wählen.
Die Abschätzung der Punktdichten innerhalb eines Rasterfeldes erfolgt nach

$$(3.23) \quad p': = \left[\frac{n'}{\sum_{i=1}^{n'} x^{(i)} - r}\right]^N$$

wobei r der Mittelpunkt des betreffenden Rasterfeldes ist und $x^{(1)} \dots x^{(n')}$ die n' diesem Mittelpunkt am nächsten liegenden Merkmalvektoren der jeweiligen Klasse sind.

Von der Wahl von n' hängt die Stärke der "Verschleifung" der Dichtfunktion ab. n': = 2N+1 dürfte in den meisten Fällen sinnvoll sein. Aus den Punktdichten erhält man gemäß

$$(3.24) \quad p_i := p_i' \,/\, \Sigma\, p_i'$$

die geschätzte Verteilungsdichte, deren Integral über das gesamte Raster ja 1 ergeben muß. Dies wird gerade durch die Normierung (3.24) erreicht.
Der beschriebene Prozeß ist für beide Verteilungen durchzuführen, so daß jedem Rasterfeld zwei Dichtewerte p_1 und p_2 zugeordnet sind. Die Trennbarkeit t ergibt sich dann zu:

$$(3.25) \quad t := \sum_i^{n_r} \operatorname{Max}(z_1 p_{1i}, z_2 p_{2i})$$

worin n_r die Anzahl der Rasterfelder bedeutet.

4. Gegenüberstellung der Verfahren

Bei der Auswahl des günstigsten Verfahrens zur Schätzung von t hat man den benötigten Aufwand und die Genauigkeit gegenüberzustellen.
Das Schwerpunkt-Varianz-Verfahren liefert nur eine sehr grobe Schätzung von t, da die Gleichverteilungsannahme wohl in den meisten Fällen nicht zutreffend ist. Dafür bietet es den Vorteil, fast ohne numerischen Aufwand auszukommen.
Für den Fall, daß zumindest näherungsweise Normalverteilungen vorliegen, bietet das Momentverfahren zweiter Ordnung, von Extremfällen abgesehen, eine recht gute Abschätzung, die der durch das Rasterverfahren gewonnenen an Genauigkeit gleichkommt.
In folgendem Beispiel ist ein solcher Extremfall angegeben, in dem sowohl das Momentverfahren zweiter Ordnung als auch das Clusterverfahren versagt:

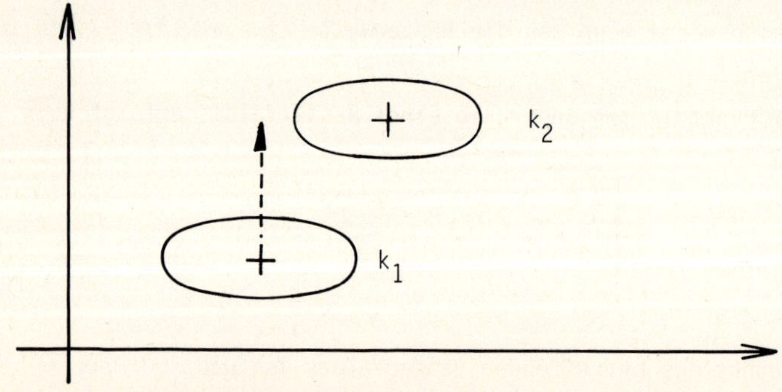

Durch eine Erweiterung sind auch diese Extremfälle mit den in 3.4 und 3.5 beschriebenen Verfahren zu behandeln:
Der Normalenvektor der Projektion in (3.15) wird z.B. nach einem Gradientenverfahren optimal gewählt, was durch die in (3.15) gegebene Wahl nicht immer der Fall ist. Im obigen Beispiel würde sich dann etwa der gestrichelt gezeichnete Normalenvektor zur Projektion ergeben, wodurch die Genauigkeit der Schätzung wesentlich erhöht würde.
Der numerische Aufwand beim Momentverfahren zweiter Ordnung ist nur unwesentlich größer als der beim Schwerpunkt-Varianz-Verfahren, dafür wird jedoch i.A. ein wesentlich besseres Ergebnis erzielt.
Der Aufwand des Clusterverfahrens liegt etwa in der Größenordnung wie der für das Momentverfahren zweiter Ordnung. Dieses Verfahren eignet sich besonders für die Behandlung clusterförmiger nichtnormalverteilter Klassen, während es bei reinen Normalverteilungen der Genauigkeit des Momentverfahrens zweiter Ordnung nachsteht.
Das Rasterverfahren ist auf jede beliebige Verteilung mit hoher Genauigkeit anwendbar. Jedoch sind in der Praxis Grenzen durch die geforderten Speicherkapazitäten gesetzt. Es wird hier ein so hoher numerischer Aufwand getrieben, daß eine Anwendung nur in Spezialfällen, in denen die Verfahren aus 3.4 und 3.5 keinen Erfolg gewährleisten, gerechtfertigt scheint.
Eine Gegenüberstellung verschiedener Trennbarkeitsmaße am Beispiel eines Zweiklassenproblems ist in Abb. 2 angegeben.

5. Verwendung von Trennmatrizen zur Strukturierung mehrstufiger Systeme

Die betrachteten Trennbarkeitsmaße wurden anhand von Zweiklassenproblemen abgeleitet und daraus die Trennmatrix als Charakteristikum eines Extraktionsverfahrens abgeleitet. Bei der Konstruktion mehrstufiger Systeme spielt jedoch, bedingt durch die Baumstruktur, die Trennbarkeit von Untermengen der gesamten Klassenmenge eine besondere Rolle. Der Begriff der Gruppentrennbarkeit läßt sich analog zu den Einzeltrennbarkeiten definieren:

$$(5.01) \qquad t_{G_1/G_2} := \int_X \mathrm{Max}\left(\sum_{m\varepsilon G_1} z_m p(x|k_m), \sum_{m\varepsilon G_2} z_m p(x|k_m) \right)$$

$$\text{mit } G_1 := \{k_{i_1}, k_{i_2}, \ldots, k_{i_j}\} \text{ und } G_2 := \{k_{i_{j+1}}, k_{i_{j+2}}, \ldots, k_{i_l}\}$$

In /4/ wird diese Gruppentrennbarkeit abgeleitet und nachgewiesen, daß aus einer Trennmatrix keine eindeutigen Werte für Gruppentrennbarkeiten folgen. Dies sei an einem Beispiel erläutert:
Beide unten dargestellten Merkmalverteilungen besitzen folgende Mischkoeffizienten und Trennmatrix:

$$z_1 = 0.25 \qquad z_2 = 0.35 \qquad z_3 = 0.40 \qquad T = \begin{bmatrix} 0.50 & 0.85 & 0.80 \\ 0.85 & 0.50 & 0.90 \\ 0.80 & 0.90 & 0.50 \end{bmatrix}$$

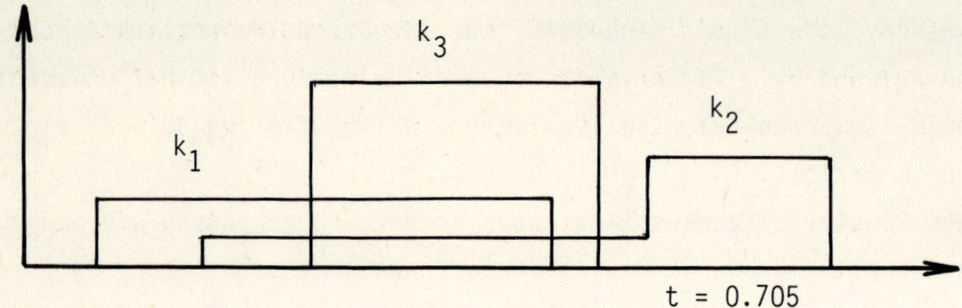

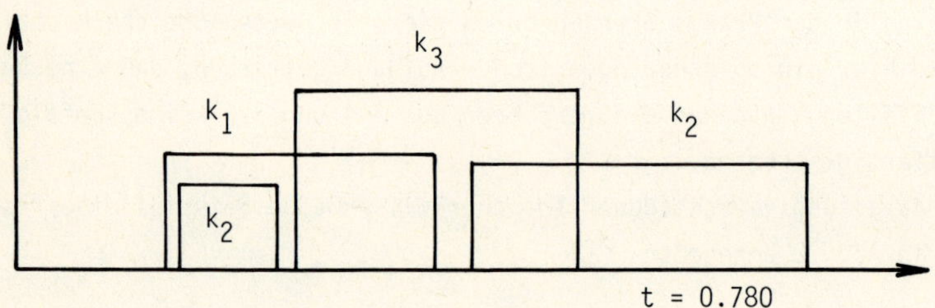

Die obere Merkmalverteilung ergibt gemäß (5.01) eine Gesamttrennbarkeit von 0.705, während die untere eine Gesamttrennbarkeit von 0.780 ergibt.
Aus diesem Grunde werden Verfahren zur Bestimmung von möglichst engen Intervallen angegeben, in denen die Gruppentrennbarkeiten liegen. Diese Abschätzungen können in den Fällen angewandt werden, wo die Ermittlung der Gruppentrennbarkeiten durch entsprechendes Zusammenfassen der Musterklassen und Anwendung der w.o. beschriebenen Verfahren aus Aufwandsgründen nicht möglich ist.

Zur Ermittlung der Struktur eines mehrstufigen Systems werden zunächst die Trennbarkeitsmatrizen der zur Verfügung stehenden Extraktionsverfahren berechnet. Daraus wird die Zusammenfassung der Klassen zu Untermengen in den einzelnen Stufen des Systems sowie die auf diese Untermengen anzuwendenden Extraktionsverfahren bestimmt. Dadurch ergibt sich der Aufbau des Gesamtsystems. Die Trennbarkeit eines mehrstufigen Systems läßt sich als Funktion der Trennbarkeiten in den einzelnen Stufen ableiten. Diese Ableitung wird ebenfalls in /4/ angegeben.
Ein auf diese Weise konstruiertes mehrstufiges System liefert bessere Klassifikationsergebnisse als die einstufigen Systeme, die mit den einzelnen Extraktionsverfahren gebildet werden können, ohne daß der Gesamtaufwand unverhältnismäßig steigt. Unter den möglichen mehrstufigen Systemen ist es jedoch nicht notwendig dasjenige mit der höchsten Trennbarkeitsrate.

6. Schlußfolgerungen

Es hat sich gezeigt, daß Trennbarkeitsmaße abgeleitet werden können, welche mit unterschiedlichem Aufwand mehr oder weniger genaue Ergebnisse liefern. In experimentellen Untersuchungen muß nun weiter festgestellt werden, welche Verfahren mit vertretbarem Aufwand noch brauchbare Hinweise für die Konstruktion von mehrstufigen Mustererkennungssystemen liefern. Darüber hinaus ist damit die Möglichkeit gegeben, Merkmalextraktionsverfahren miteinander zu vergleichen und zu bewerten.

Literatur:

/1/ Werner Schwerdtmann: Ein Vergleich einstufiger und hierarchischer Mustererkennungssysteme.
Dissertation an der Universität Karlsruhe 1973

/2/ Hans Dietrich Höhne: Wahrscheinlichkeitsdichte-Approximation mit Hilfe von Momenten zur Zeichenerkennung und Prozeßbeschreibung.
Technischer Bericht Nr. 163, Heinrich-Hertz-Institut 1973

/3/ Günter Meyer-Brötz, Jürgen Schürmann: Methoden der automatischen Zeichenerkennung.
R. Oldenbourg Verlag München-Wien 1970

/4/ Heinz Petersen, Norbert Vorstädt: Die Verwendung von Trennmatrizen zur Konstruktion mehrstufiger Mustererkennungssysteme.
Zur Veröffentlichung eingereicht.

/5/ J.T. Tou, R.C. Gonzales: Recognition of Handwritten Characters by Tropological Feature Extraction and Multilevel Categorization.
IEEE Trans. on Comp., July 1972, pp. 776-785

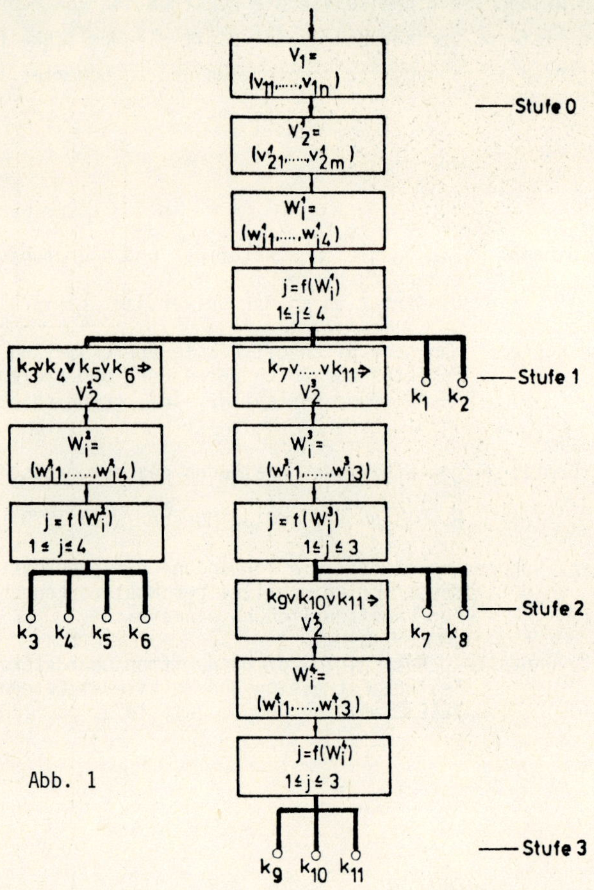

Abb. 1

$K = k_1, \ldots, k_{11}$: Menge der in Betracht kommenden Klassen

V_1 : Diskretisiertes Muster

V^q, W^q : Merkmalvektoren, Gewichtsvektoren nach Verfahren q

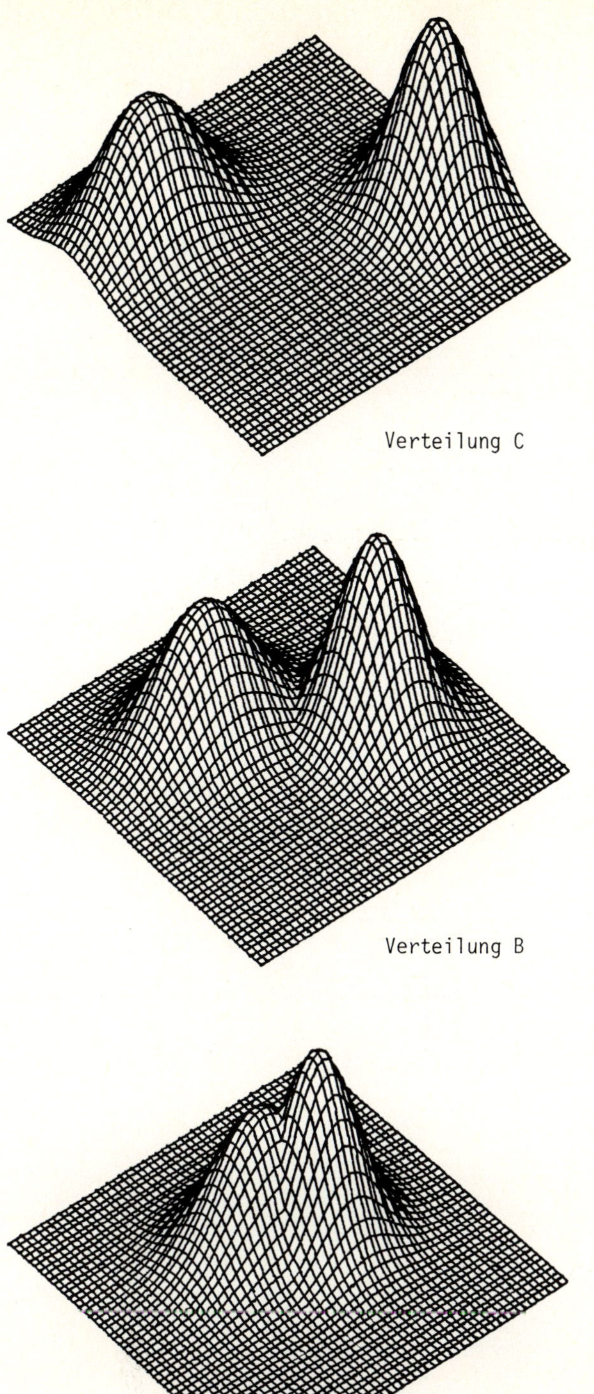

Verteilung C

Verteilung B

Verteilung A

Abb. 2

	Verteilung A	Verteilung B	Verteilung C
Schwerpunkt-Varianz-Verfahren	0.8477	0.9898	1.0000
Momentenverfahren zweiter Ordnung	0.8007	0.9782	0.9994
Cluster-Verfahren	0.8080	0.9870	1.0000
Raster-Verfahren	0.8451	0.9766	0.9919

I M P L E M E N T I E R U N G
V O N D A T E N S T R U K T U R E N

SYSFAP - AN INTEGRATED SYSTEM FOR APPLICATION PROGRAMS AND DATA BASE MANAGEMENT

E. BAAR, Dr. G. DEPREZ

CEPOC : Center for the Promotion of Computer in Civil Engineering
University of Liège
Quai Banning 6
B.- 4000 LIEGE

I. INTRODUCTION :

Data processing systems are organised sets of Functional Elements (programs) capable to perform and to chain the characteristic operations of Data Processing. Such systems have known a considerable development these last years, due to the multiplicity of applications handled by computer.
They have led to a great complexity of the processing of data, mainly because of the fast increase of the volume of the information processed as well as of the number of functional elements involved.

The numerous problems posed by these systems to their users have triggered a great amount of research work, from which two general trends have evolued : one leads to the concept of "integrated system", the other to the concept of "data base management system".

These two concepts are the solution to complementary problems which ought to be globalised inorder to offer a maximum of capabilities. It is to offer such a global solution that the SYSFAP system has been developed at the University of Liège by the CEPOC.

Under development since 1967, SYSFAP became operational in January 1971. A team of several engineers and programmers is currently working to its extension.

II. OBJECTIVES OF SYSFAP :

II. 1. Generalities :

- As mentioned earlier, SYSFAP attempts to meet the objectives proper to both the Data Base and the Integrated System concepts.

- The main purpose of Data Base management systems is to give to the users of the base the ability to manage and use an important volume of interconnected and non redundant informations.

- The main purpose of integrated system is :
  a) to give the users the faculty to process a large range of applications while freeing them of the classical Data Processing constraints(data coding, selection and sequencing of the programs, output data management) ;
  b) to give to the manager of the system the faculty to integrate new or existing programs in order to create and to update a Program Bank.

Several other goals derive from these two fundamental objectives. Many of them are common to both Data Base Management Systems and Integrated Systems, and show the similitude between the two concepts.

Let us review here those goals which led to the realization of SYSFAP.

II. 2. Representativity of the base :

The definition of objects and their connection is achieved in SYSFAP in terms of their Nature and characteristic. This results in a faithful model of reality as it is perceived by the users of the Base.

II. 3. Independence of data regarding processing :

SYSFAP has been build on the basis of this postulate. Particularly, there is a total independence between application programs, the language for consulting and implementing the base.
No additional programming is needed to increase the volume of information in the base. A modification of the nature of information requires programming only if the structure of data is changed.

II. 4. Independence between processing and logical structures :

All functional elements refer to the contents of the base in terms of the nature and characteristics of the object with which the needed data is associated. The elements are therefore not dependant on the relations which may be defined between the different objects represented in the base.

II. 5. The logical structure of the Data Base must be open :

This point concerns the problems of both quantitative and qualitative implementation of the Data Base, and of extension of the logical structures.
In the case of SYSFAP, this implies :
1) that the space reservation on mass storage units be global ;
2) that the global logic is not preestablished, but is built by the system itself from a potential logic.

II. 6. The system must be a support for managing the information contained in the base :

SYSFAP provides an automatical management of the information contained in the base. This covers information storage and retrieval, the establishment of the links between the objects with, as a consequence, the automatic updating of all data depending on some information modified or deleted by the user.

II. 7. Ease of communication between user and system :

In SYSFAP, this is achieved by means of Problem oriented languages, allowing to describe, to point at and to handle objects. These objects are characterised groups of information of the same nature, having as an internal support a language of which the syntax is proper to each nature.

II. 8. Selection and sequencing of the functional elements needed for a processing :

The system uses an application simulator to establish networks of element on the basis of the links they realize between the different objects of the base. These networks, which vary from one application to another depend on the objects existing in the base and on the requests sent by the user. The requests are formulated in terms of demands defining new objects.

II. 9. The bank of functional elements must be open :

When an Element is stored into the Element pool of SYSFAP, it must be made known to the system, to enable it to build new networks according to the links the new Element achieves between the objects in the Data Base. This integration is achieved very simply as it is enough to mention the system the nature of the information which are the direct antecedents (INPUT) and consequences (RESULTS) of the new Element.

II. 10. Protection of information :

In the current version of SYSFAP, the access to information is possible only to the user having the appropriate keys (nature and name of the subject to which the objects of the Data Base are related). This locking does not allow the definition of user classes with corresponding access groups. This problem may be solved by the introduction of virtual Data Bases, corresponding to groups of users.

II. 11. The Data Base should be made of a set of Data Bases reading on different connected computers :

The management of resident volumes is supported by all operating systems. SYSFAP provides an automatic management of mountable volumes within a given installation. It could use Data Bases residing on other connected computers provided the transmission of data between processors is supported.
This general problem is presently examined by computer manufacturers to incorporate it into operating systems. It has therefore seemed better to wait for a global basic solution, in order to avoid probable conflicts between concurrent solutions.

III. SHORT PRESENTATION OF SYSFAP :

The following description is simply intended to show how SYSFAP meets the above requirements. More detail may be found in the references given in the bibliography.

III. 1. SYSFAP generates the numerical model :

SYSFAP is a system which generates numerical models of projects : Data Banks, Building, Highway, Interchanges ... . Each numerical model constitutes a Data Base containing all information pertaining to a given project. The aim of any study beeing the progressive definition of a project to realise, SYSFAP has been considered as a set of processes (functional elements) permitting to progressively define the components of the project (implementation of the base).

III. 2. SYSFAP is a management system for functional elements :

These elements are automatically activated according to a variable sequence, which depends on the user's needs.
SYSFAP selects in the Systems Program Bank those Elements which, using the given or existing information, will generate new information answering the request of the user. Several Elements may be needed and will be automatically chained in the appropriate order.
The system is thus able to build at any moment networks where the nodes are the functional elements establishing the links between existing information and information to be generated in answer to the user's request.
The relations which are established between groups of information by a given Element may be modified by the manager of the system.

III. 3. SYSFAP is a management system for the information contained in the Data Base of a given project :

This management comprises :

III. 3. 1. Information Storage : The storage of all information pertaining to a given project, with for any processing, the selection and automatic association of a base, according to a key supplied by the user at the beginning of the processing.

III. 3. 2. File Management : The management of files on resident or mountable volumes. All information constituting a base need not be physically on the same volume, nor have a common logical or physical structure. The information for a project always contains a general file, which is the root of the Data Base, and possibly, secondary files. Any object associated to a project is represented into the General File by a subset of information describing, among other, the explicit relations with other objects. The information characterising the object are either contained directly in the subset, or in a secondary file which is referred to in the subset by an address (file name + volume identification). The system will handle automatically the mounting requests whenever such a secondary file is needed. From the user's point of view, everything looks as if all information was contained in the General File.

III. 3. 3. Automatic Updating : The updating of the Data Base is automatic on the basis of the relations which are defined between the different objects. This updating includes the deletion by the system of all information which are consequent to any data modified or deleted by the user. The relations between the objects are established by the system, either implicitly from the activation of the functional elements, or explicitly, from information supplied by the user concerning these relations.

IV. SHORT PRESENTATION OF SYSFAP INTERNAL ORGANISATION :

IV. 1. Physical structure of SYSFAP Data Bases :

The several informations associated to a Data Base are recorded in a general file called GENERAL DATA SET OR G.D.S.
The classification of information within the GDS depends of the NATURE of that information and the SUBJECT to which it refers. Each data group of same NATURE referring to the same Subject constitutes an entity which is called SUB-FILE.
In other words, every object associated to a Project (in the sense defined at & III. 1.) will be represented by means of a Sub-File. Each Sub-File will contain :

- either : the information which characterizes the OBJECT with eventually the explicit relations this object has with others ;
- or : the Address of an external file containing the informations which characterizes the object.

IV. 2. External and internal structure of the information processed by SYSFAP :

All the GDS Sub-Files may have two forms :

IV. 2. 1. External Form : Any GDS Sub-File may have an external representation form which will then be called 'ARTICLE'.
All information provided by the user to the system will be transmitted by means of Articles. The general structure of an Article is as follows :

<< KEY WORD FAMILY NAME CHARACTERISTIC
text of the Article .... >>

where :

- KEY WORD : defines the type of Article. The different types of Articles will be analysed at next paragraph (IV. 3.) ;
- FAMILY and CHARACTERISTIC : define the Nature of the article ;
- NAME : defines the Subject name to which the article refers ;
- text : support of information associated to an article.

IV. 2. 2. Internal Form : All GDS Sub-Files have an identical internal structure corresponding to a two dimensional matrix.

The structure was conceived so that access is possible to :
- either all the information contained in the sub-file ;
- or some specific information excluding any other.

The internal address of a sub-file in the GDS is determined by two parameters :
- OBJECT number : associated by the system to the Nature of the sub-file ;
- LABEL number : associated by the system to the Subject name.

The Object number may be :
- either UNIQUE, that is only one number corresponding to a nature. The corresponding article will have an UNIQUE characteristic. Example : FRAME A DEFINITION ....
- or NUMBERED, that is several numbers corresponding to a nature. The corresponding article will have NUMBERED characteristic. Example : FRAME A LOADING CASE 3 ....

Sub-files may only be manipulated by the system programs. There are two manners to generate them into the GDS :

1) They may be given by the user of the base in article form. They will then be transformed from external to internal form. They are called initial or data sub-files ;
2) They may be generated by the calculating programs from informations contained into the data sub-file(s). They are called Consequent or Result sub-files.

From the SYSFAP point of view, there is no difference between data sub-files and results sub-files.

The next figure (1) shows the structure of the two sub-files forms, the passage from one representation form to the other and the relation existing between the article identification and the internal address of the corresponding sub-file.

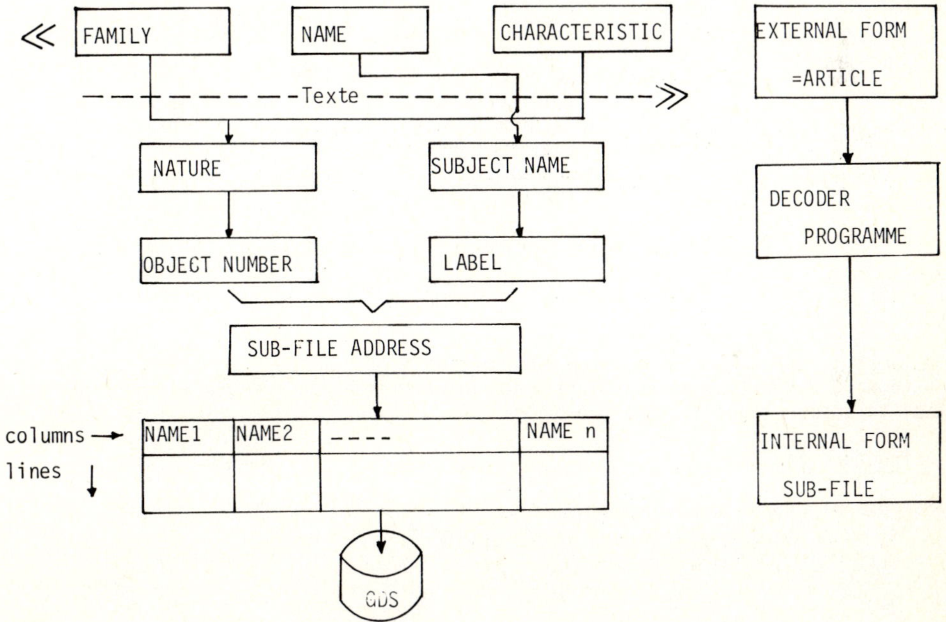

Figure 1.

IV. 3. Types of articles :

There are five types of articles permitting to the manager or the user of the base to communicate with the system providing the Data Base Management.

- 1st type : DATA : This type of article will enable the user to record new informations (new sub-files) into the GDS. This key word is considered as the standard key word and may be omitted.
  Example : << AXIS A DEFINITION
  text ...... >>

- 2nd type : MODIFICATION : This type of article will enable the user to replace informations contained in the corresponding sub-file by the informations given in the accompanying text. The system reacts upon this type of article by performing an automatic updating of the GDS sub-files.
  - GOAL : to eliminate from the GDS every sub-files consequent to the modified sub-file, in order to obtain at any moment a GDS which contains only correct information ;
  - MEANS : in order to realise the GDS updating, the system must have generated informations stipulating the links existing between the system to know which are the sub-files either directly or indirectly consequent or antecedent to any sub-file.
  - RESULT : a modification of a sub-file will lead the system to find all the directly or indirectly consequent sub-files and to delete them from the GDS.
    Example : << MODIFICATION AXIS A DEFINITION
    text .... >>

- 3rd type : SUPPRESSION : This type of article permits to delete an existing sub-file with automatic deletion of all article consequent to the suppressed one.
  Example : << SUPPRESSION AXIS A DEFINITION >>

- 4th type : SUPPLY : This article permits to request the generation of a new sub-file in the GDS, the keys to that new sub-file being defined within the article. The system answers this request by activating one or more calculating programs.
  Example : << SUPPLY AXIS A TABULATED >>
  << SUPPLY FRAME B LOADING CASE 3 >>

- 5th type : SELECTION : This article permits selection of required information.

At the sight of these five types of articles appear two fundamental options of SYSFAP, which are :

- The automatic updating of Data Base information ;
- The automatic activation of calculating programs (which are integrated into the system) to answer requests supplied by the user.

IV. 4. Structure of SYSFAP :

The structure of SYSFAP has been illustrated in figure 2.

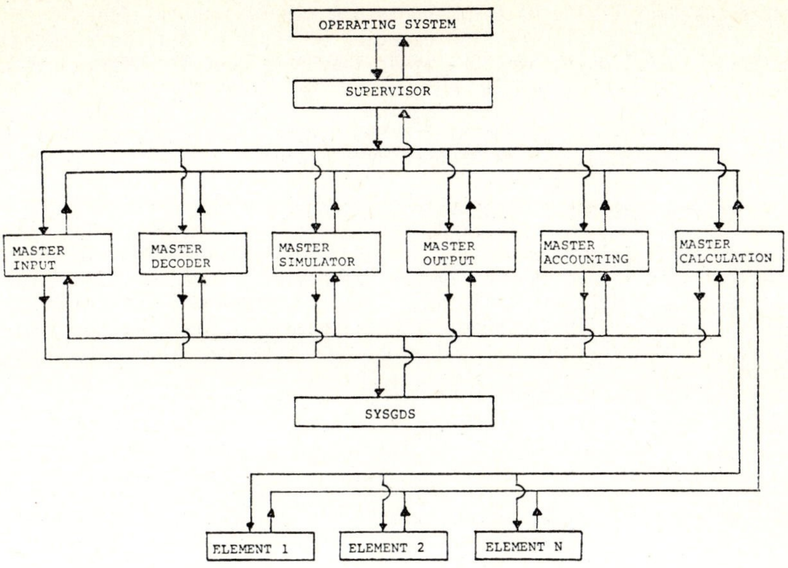

Figure 2.

SYSFAP is essentially constituted by a Supervisor, a Subsystem assuming the GDS management, several Master Programs and Elements.

Supervisor and Master Programs are an integral part of the SYSFAP System, while Elements are calculating programs, that have been integrated into the system and whose organization is completely independant from that of the system. The rules for the integration of calculating programs into SYSFAP are very straightforward so we can say that SYSFAP is really an open system.

IV. 4. 1. Supervisor : The object of the supervisor is to provide general organization and service functions required by SYSFAP which are not provided by the standard operating system of the computer being used. The supervisor will be more or less developed depending on the degree of sophistication of the operating system.
Of all the functions assumed by the supervisor, the most specific to SYSFAP is that which consists in giving control to the Master or Element programs at object time in an essentially variable order including, if necessary, the repetitive use of a given program.

IV. 4. 2. GDS Subsystem Management : This subsystem assumes all operations to be effected on the Data Base (GDS). It contains a set of subroutines making access to the GDS very easy to the programmer who wishes to integrate a new Element into the system.

IV. 4. 3. Master Input : To each new application declared by a user the Master Input associates a new GDS and supplies to the user an access key.
Each time a user resumes an application, he must provide the system with this access key. The Master Input than checks the validity of this key befor associating the corresponding GDS to the current application.
Another function of the Master Input is to read articles provided by the user and to write them in external form in specific sub-files into the GDS.

IV. 4. 4. Master Decoder : The Master Decoder has two fundamental functions. The first is the decoding of "source" Article provided by the user and their insertion in the GDS, after they have been transformed into internal form.

The second function is the activation of the GDS updating procedure in response to articles of the "Modification" or "Suppression" type.

IV. 4. 5. The Adapted Language : The customary language adopted by the user is intimately dependant on the nature of the information to which it is related. This is why each nature of SYSFAP source article has a syntaxic form that is specific to the information it defines. Each specific syntaxic form has a corresponding syntaxic table explaining how the text is to be written. Figure 3 gives an example with an except from a syntaxic table.

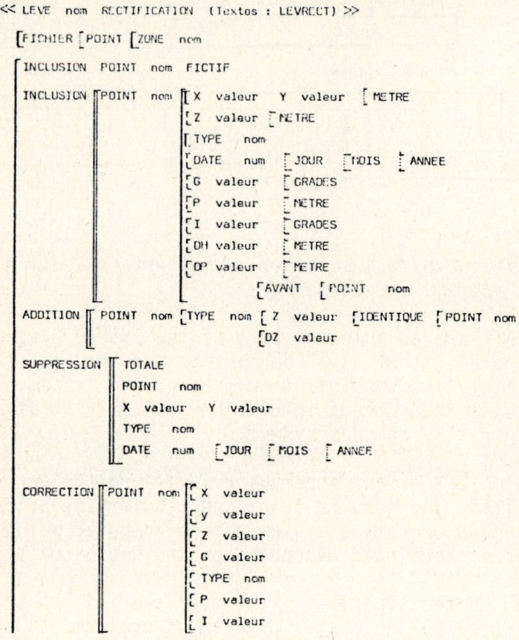

Figure 3.

Preceding the words in this example are different delimiters whose meaning follows :

1) words written behind a [are mandatory ;
2) words written behind a [[are combinable, and any or several of these may be written ;
3) words written behind a [are optional ; if omitted they will be replaced by a standard word or its corresponding value ;
4) words written behind a [are facultative they have no action and are written only with the object of clarifying the text.

The syntaxic table also helps for writing the codes table which is a graph containing the syntaxic logic of a text permitting the decoder program to decode this text. There is in the bank of codes tables one table corresponding to each different nature of article. Manager or user of SYSFAP may write new codes tables and record them in the codes table bank using the system trough the single phrasing of an appropriate SYSFAP article.

IV. 4. 5. Master Simulator : The user of a base must have the possibility to ask some questions (SUPPLY type of article), which are in fact requests for informations. In order to answer those requests one or several elements will have to be activated. The main function of the Master Simulator is to determine the list and sequential order of Elements to be activated.
To accomplish this task, the Master Simulator will rely upon informations which defines the links that an Element establishes between sub-files.

The process of selecting the Element which will be later activated is based on the following principles :

- a user's request is translated into a request for the generation of a sub-file of which the Object and Label numbers are given in the "SUPPLY" article.
- if this sub-file does not already exist into the GDS the Master Simulator creates a sub-list of Elements each able to generate it (usually there will be only one Element in the list but there may be cases where several Elements could generate the same sub-file). The Master Simulator scans this list and selects the Element for which every antecedent sub-files is present in the GDS.
  When one Element is selected, its activation is simulated, i. e. the generated sub-file will be considered as virtually existing in the continuation of the analysis, thus making possible the eventual selection of other Elements by the Master Simulator.
  If no Element of the list could be selected because of some missing antecedent sub-file, the Master Simulator writes into the request list a request for each missing antecedent just as if the user himself had given a "SUPPLY" article for each antecedent. This will drive the Master Simulator to analyse those intermediate requests in order to find one or more Elements which will generate the missing sub-files. The repetitive application of this process allows the system to answer the original user's request. A characteristic of that process is that the user may be completely unaware of the sequence of calculations needed to obtain the results he wants.
  The principles described above concern one request, but, once activated the Master Simulator handles all the requests supplied by the user.
  If at the end of the Master Simulator execution some requests are left unsatified, it means that some sub-files cannot be generated by any Element and can only be given by the user in the form of "DATA" articles. The Master Simulator will then report to the user the following information :

  - a list of the request(s) which cannot be satisfied ;
  - a list of the nature(s) of informations to be supplied to satisfy these requests.

An example of linkage between elements is shown in figure 4.

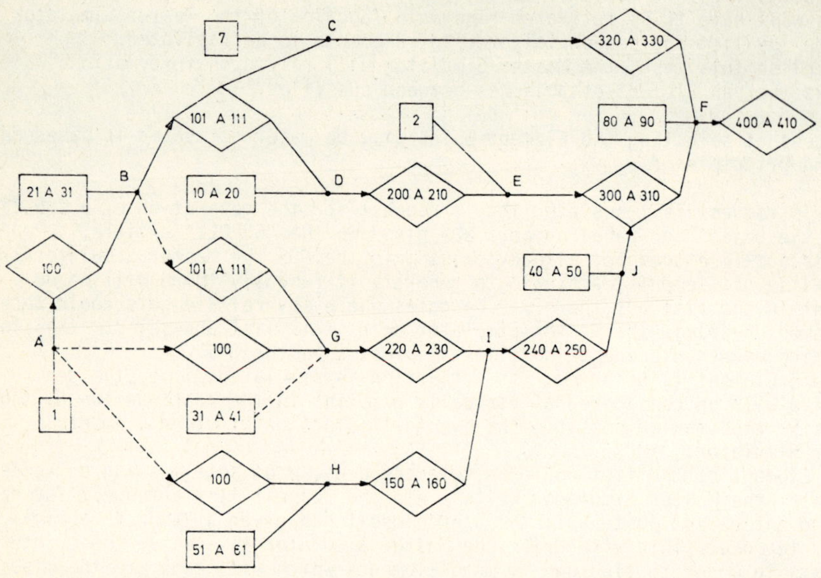

Figure 4.

The letters A, B, C ... represent Elements ; the numerals inside the squares to the left of a letter represent the code numbers of data sub-files needed (and only the user can provide them) to activate the Element. The numerals inside the diamonds represent the code numbers of consequent sub-files generated by the Elements if they are activated. One notices in the figure that the consequent sub-file of one Element may become an antecedent sub-file for another Element (diamonds to the left of a letter).

If, for example, a user had submitted a request translated by a call for sub-file 401, the Master Simulator could generate the following sequence of elements to be activated A-B-C-D-E-F
or , the choice between either possibility depending on the
A-B-C-G-H-I-J-F
information given by the user.

IV. 4. 6. Master Calculator : The main function of the Master Calculator is to establish the links which must exist between the system and the Element at the time of their activation. This procedure has been developped in such a way that Elements belonging to SYSFAP have an organization that is completely independant from that of the system.

Consequently, a calculating program may have been written and test-run outside the system and then be integrated as an Element of SYSFAP in a very straightforwards manner as we will see it next paragraph.

In order not to modify the structure or logic of data and result information of the program included in SYSFAP, it will be enough to write, with the help of routines supplied by the Master Calculator, two small programs which will serve as interfaces ; the first for information located in the sub-file of GDS and required by the program, the other for information given by the program which must be regrouped in sub-file form before being written into the GDS.

In this way, nothing is changed inside the calculating program, except for some items like :

- the unit numbers, which must be compatible with the numbers provided in the system ;
- the formatted read instructions for input data which become unformatted reads ;
- the errors returns which are changed into calls to special routines.

In this way an Element has the three following parts :

- input data interface ;
- data processing program ;
- output data interface.

When the Master Calculator is loaded, it locates the proper input interface program, data processing program, and output interface program and these are activated in that order. When an Element has been executed, the Master Calculator generates new informations stipulating the links existing between the generated sub-files with the other.

Remark : If some errors has occured during execution of an Element, the Master problem will ask the Supervisor to re-active the Master Simulator in order to establish eventually a new chain of Elements keeping in mind that the Element mentionned above must not be activated again.

VI. 4. 6. 1. Required actions to integrate a calculating program as a new Element into SYSFAP :

It is important to remark here that the different actions required to integrate a new Element are performed using the SYSFAP itself.

1) In the Element calls for any new nature of information, this nature must be defined to the SYSFAP. SYSFAP will be used with the following articles as input :
   - an article which defines the table of codes, enabling the system to later decode the articles associated with this new nature ;
   - an article which defines the outline of the sub-file associated to this new nature.

2) The new Element must be logically connected to the system. This will be achieved by means of an article defining the links established by this new Element between the sub-files which are directly antecedent and consequent.

3) The input/output interfaces and the necessary modifications to the calculating program must be written.

4) The three parts of the Element must be recorded into the SYSFAP Element Library, using a special utility program.

IV. 4. 7. Master Output and Accounting : These two masters will bring little if any insight into the logic of SYSFAP. Therefore, we will only say a few words concerning their purpose.

The first,deals with the problem of selecting information in the GDS. The second, deals with accounting problems such as execution times for different runs, the list of Elements being activated during a run, and so one ...

V. PRESENT CAPABILITIES OF SYSFAP :

V. 1. Aids to the programmer and to the user :

SYSFAP contains closed subsystems which may be accessed either by the Elements or by the user, through adapted language. These subsystems permit :

- drawing on automatic plotter ;
- definition of numerical models of surfaces and volumes ;
- use of adapted languages (problem oriented languages) ;
- definition of new adapted languages. The user or manager of the system may define the syntax of new adapted languages ;
- integration of new application programs (functional elements) into SYSFAP ;
- addition of new types of objects into the base.

V. 2. Possibilities to the user :

The functional Elements actually supported by SYSFAP may be classified, according to their function, into the following groups ;

- the analysis of rigid or articulated frames. A graphical output of the frame and drawings of bending moment, shear and axial forces diagrams may be obtained as an additional output (figure 5).
  This subsystem is used for the analysis of buildings as well as for some types of bridges.

- The design of highways including interchanges with, upon request, the automatic drawing of :
  - the numerical model of the naturel terrain ;
  - the perspective representation of the naturel terrain ;
  - the level lines ;
  - the horizontal alignment (figure 6) ;
  - the vertical alignment (figure 7) ;
  - the cross sections with structural details (figure 8) ;
  - the horizontal views of the finished highway (figure 9) ;
  - the perspective views of the finished highway (figure 10) ;

This subsystem is currently applied to the preliminary or final design of motorways and expressways in Belgium.

- The topographic surveys and establishment of Urban Data Base (figure 11). This subsystem is being used for the constitution of an Urban Data Base (above and under the ground) covering different places in Brussel.

This above classification is purely arbitrary as far as the system is concerned. Indeed there is no limitation or preference in the relations between the Elements integrated into SYSFAP.

V. 3. Portability of SYSFAP :

SYSFAP has a modular internal structure. Each module performs a particular task, under control of a Supervisor. All modules are written in a high level language (FORTRAN) and call the Supervisor whenever they need special functions to be performed. The Supervisor complements the Operating System and contains some routines in assembler language.

This structure has been adopted in view of a certain amount of portability. Presently, SYSFAP is operational on IBM computer of the 360/370 series, either in OS or VS. The minimum required configuration is the following :

- 256 K bytes central core memory ;
- at least one disk drive with a 50.10^6 bytes capacity. This include storage for the SYSFAP system modules, the Bank of Elements, and a GDS for one project of average importance ;
- 2 magnetic tape units.

BIBLIOGRAPHY :

- SYSFAP - General description - G. DEPREZ (Colloque International sur les Systèmes Intégrés en Génie Civil. Ed. CEPOC, Université de Liège, Septembre 1972).
- SYSFAP - Internal Organisation - E. BAAR (Colloque International sur les Systèmes Intégrés en Génie Civil. Ed. CEPOC, Université de Liège, Septembre 1972).
- Computer Aided Design Using SYSFAP - R. ANSLIJN (Ed. IFIP. Eindhoven 1973 - International Federation Information Processing).
- SYSFAP - Integrated System in Civil Engineering with Data Base Management - G. DEPREZ (Ed. CEPOC, Université de Liège, 1973).
- Gestion Informatique des projects de bâtiments par un Système de programmes intégrés - G. DEPREZ (Ed. CEPOC, Université de Liège, 1973).
- Optimisation des Etudes de Bâtiment par Utilisation du SYSFAP - G. DEPREZ (Ed. CEPOC, Université de Liège, 1974).
- SYSFAP - The Integration of Road Design Systems with Data Base Management - G. DEPREZ Computer in Highway Design. Proceedings NATO Advanced Study Institut Copenhagen, Septembre 1972 Denmark. (Ed. TURNER, Mars 1973).
- Optimisation des Tracés Routiers - G. DEPREZ et Ch. MASSONNET. (Ed. EYROLLES - Collection UTI, 1974).
- Adaptation du SYSFAP aux Etudes Routières - F. DE SMET et J. BOEMER. Colloque International sur les Systèmes Intégrés en Génie Civil. (Ed. CEPOC, Université de Liège, Septembre 1972).
- SYSFAP - Manuel du Programmeur (Ed. CEPOC, Université de Liège, 1973).
- SYSFAP - Système de Gestion et d'Exploitation de Banques de Données - G. DEPREZ (Ed. SICAB - Bruxelles 1973).
- Perception des volumes et des surfaces par l'Informatique - R. DEROUX (Ed. SICAB - Bruxelles 1973).
- Système SYSFAP - Manuel de l'Utilisateur.
- Sous-Système Route du SYSFAP : Manuel de l'Utilisateur : Chp. 1 - Généralités
Chp. 2 - Planimétrie du Tracé
Chp. 3 - Altimétrie du Tracé
- Sous-Système Modèle Numérique des Surfaces du SYSFAP : Manuel de l'Utilisateur.
- Sous-Système Structure du SYSFAP : Manuel de l'Utilisateur.
- Sous-Système Topographie du SYSFAP : Manuel de l'Utilisateur.
- Utilisation du SYSFAP pour les Etudes Routières : Description succincte.

☆☆

FIGURES DE 5 A 11 :

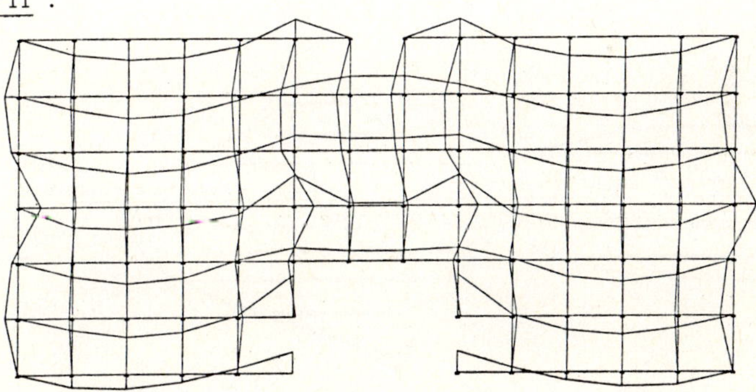

Figure 5.

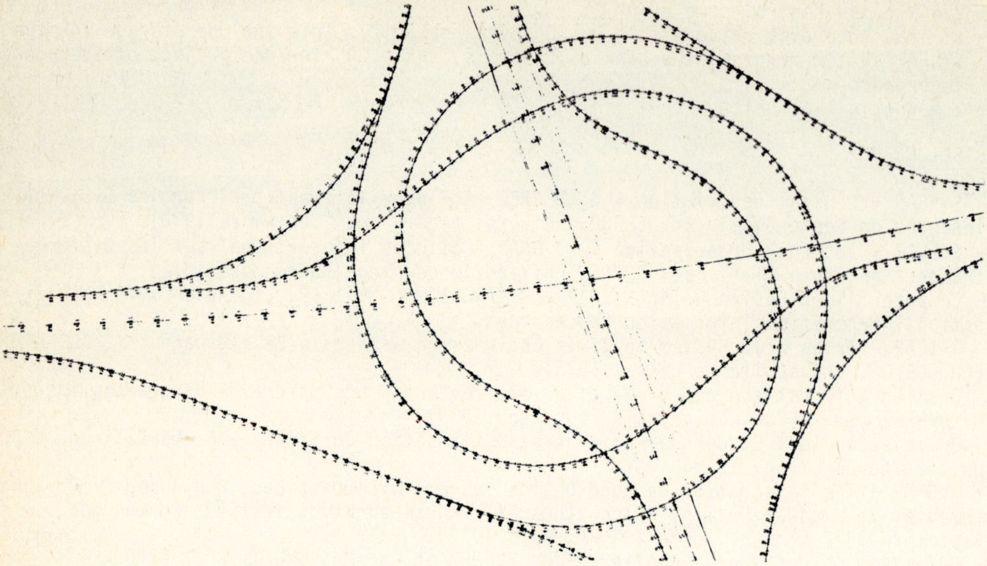

Figure 6.

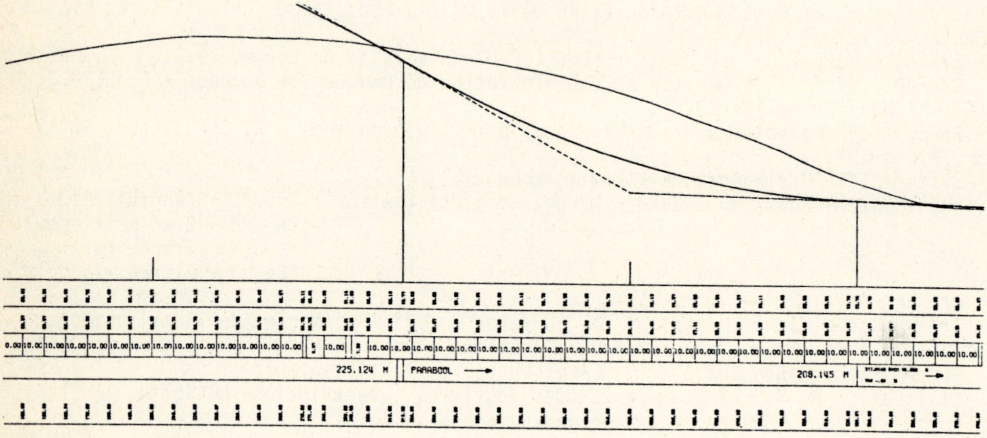

Figure 7.

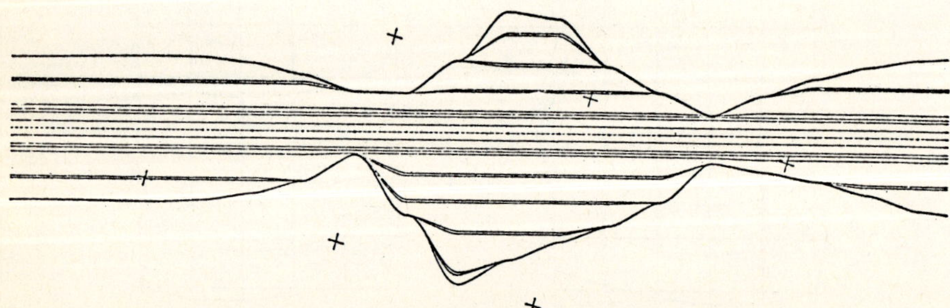

Figure 9.

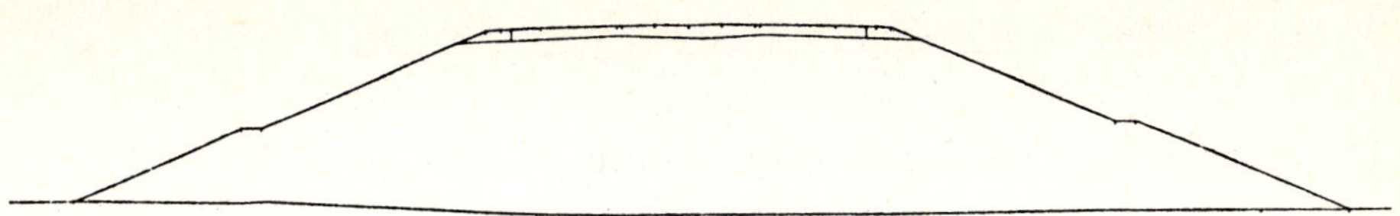

Figure 8.

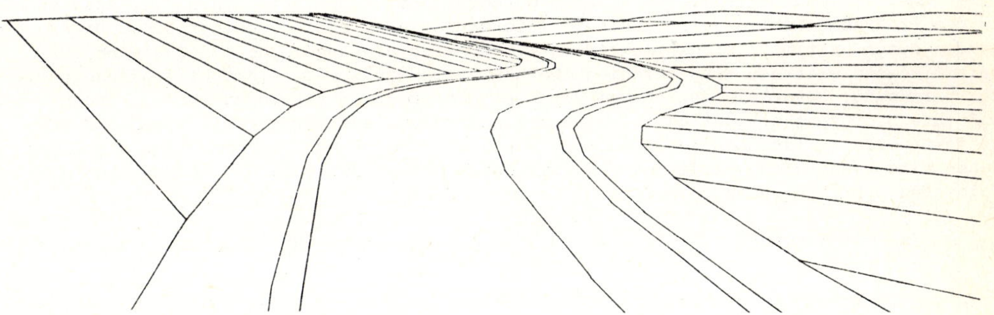

Figure 10.

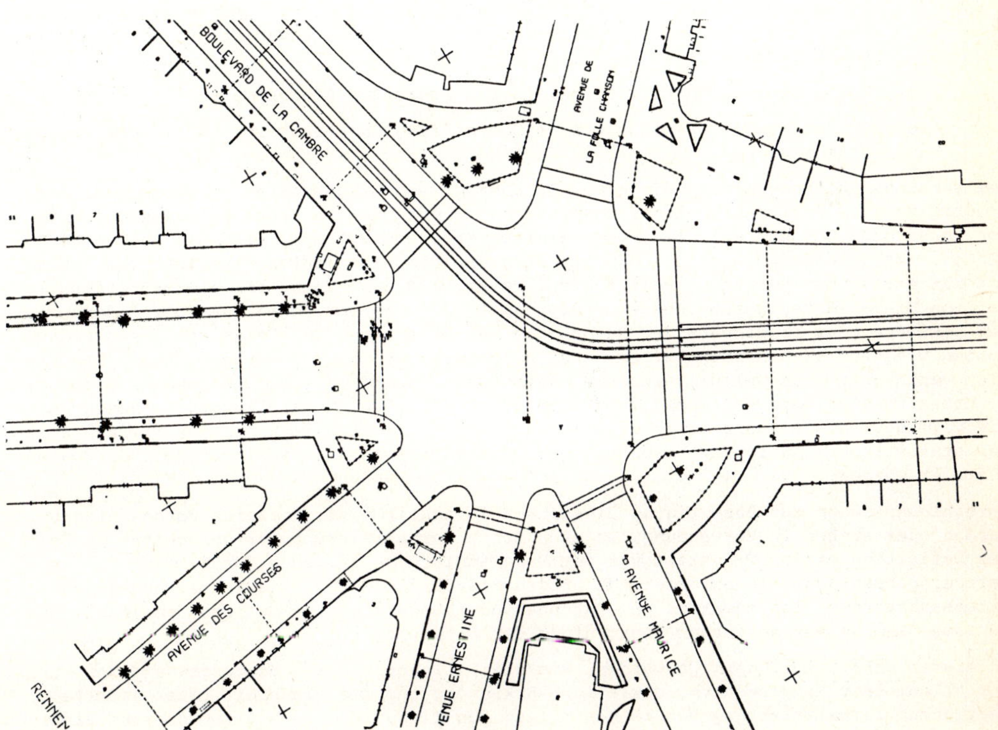

Figure 11.

AUTOMATISCHE ANALYSE UND PRÜFUNG VON EINGABEDATEN

Paul F. Rennert

Hochschule für Sozial- und Wirtschaftswissenschaften
Institut für Informatik
A-4045 Linz-Auhof, Österreich

I. Problemstellung

Programme, die auf Digitalrechenanlagen durchgeführt werden, benötigen i.a. zusätzlich zu den Programmbefehlen selbst weitere Informationen, die Eingabedaten. Diese Daten werden durch bestimmte Programmaktionen ("Lesebefehle") angefordert und stehen auf verschiedenen externen Eingabemedien (Lochkarten, Magnetband, Klarschriftbelege, usw.) zur Verfügung. Bevor sie jedoch vom Verarbeitungsprogramm verwendet werden können, muß ihre Bedeutung erkannt und i.a. auch eine Prüfung auf formale Richtigkeit durchgeführt werden - ist doch schon beim Entwurf von DV-Systemen die Zuverlässigkeit der Daten eine wesentliche Forderung /4/. Zur Durchführung der obigen Vorgänge sind die folgenden Schritte zu durchlaufen:

(a) Prüfung der formalen Richtigkeit der Codierung auf dem jeweiligen Eingabemedium (meist schon hardwaremäßig)

(b) Erkennen der Bedeutung der einzelnen Eingabewerte und Überprüfung der formalen Richtigkeit dieser Werte, je nach ihrer Bedeutung und jeder für sich allein genommen (Plausibilitätskontrolle 1)

(c) Erkennen der Struktur der Daten, also der logischen Zusammenhänge zwischen den Eingabewerten, und Überprüfung der Daten im Zusammenhang (Plausibilitätskontrolle 2)

(d) Zurückweisung der als formal falsch erkannten Eingabedaten

(e) Eventuell weitere inhaltliche Überprüfung im Verarbeitungsteil des Programms selbst.

Bei Verarbeitungsprogrammen, die eine große Menge von Eingabedaten verschiedener Art benötigen, etwa Datenbankspeicherungssystemen, Programmen zur statistischen Auswertung von Versuchsdaten oder größeren kommerziellen Programmsystemen, sind die obigen Prüfungen, insbesondere die formalen Überprüfungen (Plausibilitätskontrollen) (b) und (c), oft nur mit großem Aufwand durchzuführen. Meist wird ein eigens für die betreffende Art von Eingabedaten geschriebenes Prüfprogramm dazu herangezogen, was bei Änderungen der Struktur oder Eingabeart der Daten oder bei Einführung von Daten mit neuen Bedeutungen wiederum zu Schwierigkeiten durch aufwendige Programmänderungen führt. Das Problem verschärft sich weiter, wenn die angebotenen Daten von verschiedenen Programmbenützer stammen, die voneinander abweichende Wünsche und Vorstellungen in Bezug auf die Form der Dateneingabe oder auf die Plausibilitätskontrolle haben, oder wenn (etwa bei statistischen Analysen) besonders hohe Anforderungen an die Richtigkeit der Daten gestellt werden.

Verschiedene Wege zur Beseitigung dieser Schwierigkeiten sind bereits vorgeschlagen worden oder stehen in Verwendung, so etwa durch Formalisierung der Dokumentation bei der Definition eines DV-Systems vor der Programmierung /3/, oder durch Einbettung von Dateneingabesprachen in existierende Programmiersprachen /2/. Die in verschiedenen Datenbanksystemen implementierten Datenbeschreibungstafeln ermöglichen ebenfalls ein gewisses Maß an automatischer Überprüfung der Daten /1/.

In dieser Arbeit soll gezeigt werden, wie die Definition der Bedeutungen und der Struktur allgemeiner Eingabedaten, sowie ihre Erkennung und ihre Plausibilitätskontrolle, weitgehend formalisiert werden können. Diese Funktionen können somit von einem einzigen allgemeinen Datenerkennungs- und -prüfprogramm übernommen werden. Die dadurch erreichte Automatisation der Datenanalyse und -prüfung wirkt sich insbesonders in einer höheren Flexibilität bei der Eingabe und damit einer größeren Benützerfreundlichkeit der Anwendungsprogramme aus.

II. Formalismus zur Analyse und Prüfung von Eingabedaten

II.0 Bezeichnungen

Ein (interner) Eingabestrom (ES) ist eine zeitliche Folge von Mengen von Zeichen in einem maschineninternen Code, die von einem Programm (durch Lesebefehle) angefordert werden. Diese Zeichenmengen stehen auf einem oder mehreren beliebigen externen Eingabemedien zur Verfügung; ihre Darstellung auf dem Eingabemedium wird externer Eingabestrom genannt.

Die einzelnen Zeichen der Zeichenmengen des Eingabestroms können innerhalb der Zeichenmengen numeriert werden. Reiht man die Zeichenmengen nach ihrem zeitlichen Auftreten und die Zeichen innerhalb der Zeichenmengen nach ihren Nummern, so erhält man insgesamt eine Folge von Zeichen. Diese wird Eingabefolge (EF) genannt.

Nach der Programmlogik kann man eventuell den ES aus Teilströmen aufgebaut denken; demnach wird auch von Teilfolgen der Gesamt-EF gesprochen. Im weiteren wird nur eine einzige EF angenommen.

Die Eingabefolge kann nach der engeren logischen Zusammengehörigkeit ihrer Zeichen in Teilfolgen (gleicher oder verschiedener Länge) zerfallen, die als Eingabeeinheiten (EE) bezeichnet werden.

Jede Eingabeeinheit zerfällt wieder in ein oder mehrere Eingabewerte (EW), das sind (meist zusammenhängende) Zeichenfolgen, die einzelne numerische oder alphanumerische Werte darstellen. Diese werden in der vorliegenden Arbeit als die kleinsten logischen Aggregate der Eingabefolge angesehen.

Beispiel:

Die Eingabedaten für ein Programm liegen auf Lochkarten vor, von denen jeweils vier aufeinanderfolgende Lochkarten zusammen gehören. Die definierten Begriffe kommen hier etwa wie folgt vor:

- externer ES: die Inhalte der Lochkarten (als Zeichenmengen) in der Einlesereihenfolge
- ES: die interne Darstellung der Zeichen auf den Lochkarten
- EF: die Folge der Zeichen aller Lochkarteninhalte in der Einlesereihenfolge und innerhalb der Lochkarten gereiht nach Spalten 1 bis 80
- EE: jeweils die Folge der Zeichen der Inhalte der vier zusammengehörigen Lochkarten
- EW: die (internen) Zeichenfolgen, die den einzelnen Eintragungen in die Felder auf den Lochkarten entsprechen.

II.1 Einzelne Datenwerte

II.1.A. Eingabewerte

Für die kleinsten logischen Aggregate in der Eingabefolge, die Eingabewerte, kann man u.a. die folgenden Beispiele anführen:

- logische Werte, durch einzelne Bits dargestellt
- numerische Werte, bereits im internen Code der Rechenanlage codiert, z.B. in ganzzahliger, Fixkomma- oder Gleitkommadarstellung. (Diese könnten etwa von einem Magnetband oder Magnetplatte stammen, auf der sie bereits im internen Format gespeichert sind)
- Zeichenketten, deren einzelne Zeichen im internen Code der Rechenanlage codiert sind, jedoch eine externe (textmäßige) Zeichenkette darstellen. Diese Zeichenkette kann wiederum einen logischen Wert, eine Zahl oder einen alphanumerischen Text darstellen. (Diese Zeichenketten könnten et-

wa von einer Lochkarte, einem Klarschriftbeleg, usw. stammen).
- andere Werte, etwa Bilder oder Bildelemente, die von optischen Lesern erkannt wurden, usw.

Im folgenden werden nur numerische Werte und Zeichenketten als mögliche EW betrachtet, da sie den Großteil der konventionellen Dateneingabe bilden; andere Datendarstellungsformen können auch oft auf diese beiden zurückgeführt werden.

II.1.B. Variablen und Datenwerte

Für die Verwendung eines Eingabewertes genügt es nicht, diesen allein (numerisch oder in Zeichenkettenform) zur Verfügung zu haben. Er muß vielmehr durch Angabe seiner Bedeutung (B) ergänzt werden. Ein solcherart entstehendes Paar (Bedeutung, Eingabewert) wird im folgenden Datenwert (DW) genannt.DW::= (B,EW)

Eine bestimmte Bedeutung kann i.a. nicht jedem beliebigen EW sinnvoll zugeordnet werden, sondern die Menge der erlaubten EW ist gewissen Einschränkungen unterworfen. So etwa wäre es sinnlos, einer alphabetischen Zeichenkette eine Bedeutung "Prozentangabe" zuzuordnen; für andere Bedeutungen müßten die EW etwa innerhalb bekannter Grenzen liegen oder bestimmten Kriterien anderer Art genügen.

Jede mögliche Bedeutung wird gemeinsam mit der Menge m(B) derjenigen Eingabewerte, denen sie sinnvoll zugeordnet werden kann, Variable (V)genannt; eine Variable ist also ein Paar (Bedeutung, Menge von Eingabewerten). V ::= (B,m(B))
Die Elemente der Menge m(B) heißen "die erlaubten Werte der Variable".

Ein formal richtiger DW ist ein Paar (B,EW) mit EW$\in$m(B), ein formal falscher DW ein Paar (B,EW) mit EW$\notin$m(B).

Die Zuordnung der Bedeutung zu einem Eingabewert erfolgt mit Hilfe einer Beschreibung des Eingabewerts. Die für diese Beschreibung notwendigen Informationen können aus verschiedenen Quellen stammen, die in Abschnitt II.2. näher erläutert werden; für das folgende genügt es anzunehmen, daß zu dem gerade betrachteten EW bereits die Bedeutung bekannt ist.

Der Vorgang der Überprüfung eines DW, um festzustellen, ob er formal richtig oder falsch ist (ob also EW$\in$m(B)), heißt Prüfen des Datenwerts oder Plausibilitätskontrolle 1 (PK1).

II.1.C. Definition von Variablen

Um die Zuordnung einer Bedeutung zu einem Eingabewert und anschließend die Plausibilitätskontrolle 1 durchzuführen, müssen bereits vorher die Bedeutung und die Menge der Eingabewerte, denen sie sinnvoll zugeordnet werden kann, bekannt sein: es muß also die Variable definiert sein.

Die Angaben zur Definition einer Variablen fallen in folgende Hauptgruppen:

(a) Identifikation der Variable: ein Code, durch den die Datenwerte in verschiedenen Programmteilen wiedererkannt werden können, im folgenden auch Variablencode genannt.
(b) Bedeutungsangaben, etwa:
  (α) Name im Klartext
  (β) Maß- oder Bezugseinheit
  (γ) Verhältnis zu anderen Variablen
(c) Typ der zu erwartenden Werte, etwa:
  (α) numerisch (=numerisch codiert oder numerische Zeichenkette)
  (β) alphanumerisch
(d) Angaben zur Aufbereitung der Zeichenkette des EW (wenn der EW in Zeichenkettenform vorliegt), z.B.:
  (α) Rechts- oder Linksverschiebung

(β) Ausnullen (Ersetzen von Leerstellen durch Nullen)

(e) Angaben zur Plausibilitätskontrolle 1 der Zeichenkette (wenn der EW in Zeichenkettenform vorliegt), z.B.:
  (α) minimale und maximale Länge
  (β) minimale und maximale Zahl signifikanter Stellen (bei numerischen Angaben im freien Format)
  (γ) andere besondere Prüfungen

(f) Angaben zur Plausibilitätskontrolle 1 des numerischen oder alphanumerischen Werts, den der EW darstellt:
  (α) Unter- und Obergrenze
  (β) Liste der Werte, die die Variable annehmen darf (ibs. bei Werten aus einer Nominal- oder Ordinalskala, "verschlüsselte Werte")
  (γ) andere besondere Prüfungen

(g) Angaben zur Umrechnung des Werts ("Normierung")

(h) Formatangaben zur Druckausgabe bei Ausdruck der Datenwerte

Diese Definition kann
  (a) im Programm selbst
  (b) in derselben oder einer anderen Eingabefolge angegeben sein

II.1.D. Die Variablendatei (eines Datenbank- oder Programmsystems)

Der Begriff einer derart definierten Variablen kann in vielen Komponenten eines Datenbank- oder Programmsystems verwendet werden, da die angeführten Informationen nicht allein für die Plausibilitätskontrolle 1 von Nutzen sind. Bei einer Datenbank etwa können sie auch in den Speicherungs-, Abruf-, Verarbeitungs- und Ausdruckprogrammen Verwendung finden und einen Teil der Funktion der in vielen Datenbanksystemen verwendeten Datenbeschreibungstafeln erfüllen. Es ist auch denkbar, die Variablencodes selbst in der Datenbank als "Selektoren" zu den Datenelementen zu speichern und damit selbstbeschreibende Datenstrukturen erzeugen.

In einer Datenbank ist zu einer bestimmten Zeit jeweils eine Menge von Werten, die zusammen nur endlich viele, bekannte Bedeutungen haben, gespeichert. Die Menge der Variablen mit diesen Bedeutungen kann man als die Variablenmenge der Datenbank bezeichnen. Diese Menge kann durch Speichern von Werten mit neuen Bedeutungen erweitert und durch Löschen aller Werte mit bestimmten Bedeutungen eingeschränkt werden.

Es liegt daher nahe, die Variablenmenge vor dem Aufbau der Datenbank selbst zu definieren und die Definitionen in geeignet verschlüsselter Form in einer Variablendatei zusammenzufassen. Die Variablendatei kann dann je nach Bedarf mit der Zeit erweitert bzw. eingeschränkt werden. Von besonderem Vorteil ist es, daß die Variablendefinitionen nun nicht mehr fix im Programm selbst vorgegeben sein müssen, sondern sich in der Eingabefolge befinden, die durch die aus dieser Datei gelesenen Sätze gebildet wird.

Auch bei Programmen, die nicht an eine Datenbank angeschlossen sind, kann man von der Variablenmenge des Programms sprechen, d.i. die Menge der Variablen mit den Bedeutungen, die den Eingabedaten des Programms zugeordnet sind. Auch hier kann eine Variablendatei angelegt und verwendet werden.

II.1.E. Ablauf des Erkennens und Prüfens eines einzelnen Datenwerts

Der Algorithmus, nach dem ein Datenwert erkannt und geprüft wird, ist im folgenden Diagramm veranschaulicht:

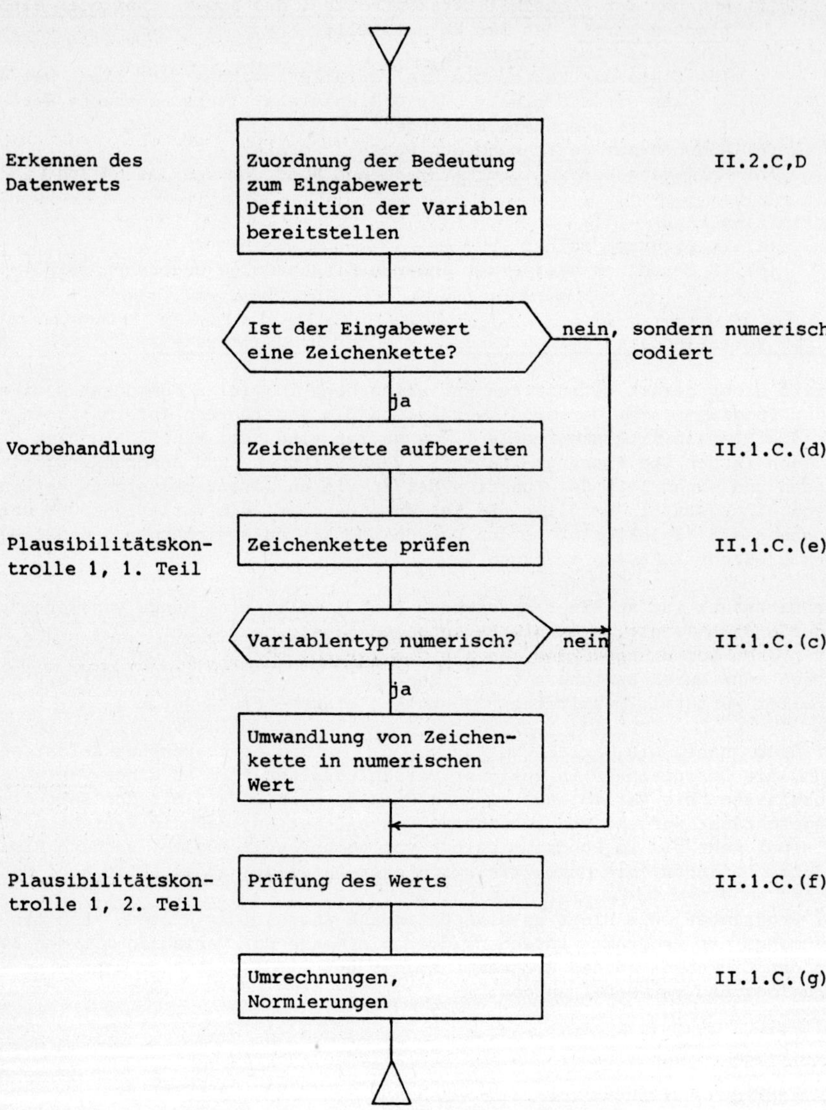
Erkennen des
Datenwerts
Zuordnung der Bedeutung
zum Eingabewert
Definition der Variablen
bereitstellen
II.2.C,D
Ist der Eingabewert
eine Zeichenkette?
nein, sondern numerisch
codiert
ja
Vorbehandlung
Zeichenkette aufbereiten
II.1.C.(d)
Plausibilitätskon-
trolle 1, 1. Teil
Zeichenkette prüfen
II.1.C.(e)
Variablentyp numerisch?
nein
II.1.C.(c)
ja
Umwandlung von Zeichen-
kette in numerischen
Wert
Plausibilitätskon-
trolle 1, 2. Teil
Prüfung des Werts
II.1.C.(f)
Umrechnungen,
Normierungen
II.1.C.(g)

II.2. Datenwerte im Zusammenhang

II.2.A. Eingabeeinheiten und ihre Definition

Eine Eingabeeinheit (EE) ist eine Teilfolge der Eingabefolge, deren Elemente Eingabewerte (EW) bilden, die logisch zusammengehören. Die einzelnen EW der EE werden auch Eintragungen genannt, wenn sie in Zeichenkettenform vorliegen.

Zum Verständnis des folgenden ist es günstig, sich als Beispiel einer Eingabeeinheit den Inhalt einer Lochkarte mit mehreren vordefinierten Feldern, in die Eintragungen gelocht werden können, vorzustellen.

Ist eine EE gegeben, so sind auf ihren Inhalt verschiedene Funktionen auszuüben:

(a) Erkennen der DW und Prüfen der einzelnen enthaltenen EW (s. II.1.)
(b) Feststellung und Überprüfung eventueller Zusammenhänge zwischen den DW (Analyse der Struktur und Plausibilitätskontrolle 2)
(c) eventuell die Errechnung neuer Werte aus den DW
(d) Weitergabe der geprüften Eingabeeinheit (oder ihres Inhalts in geänderter Darstellung) an das Verarbeitungsprogramm, bzw.
(e) Zurückweisung der Eingabeeinheit, falls sie den Prüfkriterien nicht entspricht.

In den folgenden Abschnitten werden diese Teilfunktionen erläutert.

Je nach Herkunft und Bestimmung der EE werden i.a. die Bedeutung, die Überprüfungsvorschriften und die Verarbeitungsart ihres Inhalts verschieden sein. EE, bei denen diese Merkmale übereinstimmen - sodaß höchstens ihre Eingabewerte verschieden sind - heißen von der gleichen Art.Um sie zu erkennen und von EE anderer Art zu unterscheiden, ist es notwendig, jeder Art von EE eine Identifikation zuzuweisen.

Diese Identifikation sowie alle Angaben, die zur Durchführung der in den folgenden Abschnitten beschriebenen Aktionen notwendig sind, also Angaben über die Bedeutung des Inhalts, die Struktur sowie die Überprüfungsmöglichkeiten für alle EE einer gewissen Art, werden in der Definition der Eingabeeinheit angegeben. Diese kann, wie schon die Variablendefinitionen, entweder im Programm selbst fix vorgegeben sein oder sich in derselben oder einer anderen Eingabefolge befinden. Jedenfalls müssen die Angaben der EE - Definition bereits bekannt sein, um den Inhalt einer EE der beschriebenen Art analysieren und prüfen zu können.

Als besonders vorteilhaft für die Automatisation der Datenanalyse und Plausibilitätskontrolle erweist es sich, die Definitionen aller in einem bestimmten Datenbank- oder Programmsystem verwendeten EE-Arten in einer Eingabeeinheitsdatei zu speichern und in Verbindung mit der bereits erwähnten Variablendatei zu verwenden.Hierdurch sind Änderungen und Erweiterungen in der Datenerfassung wesentlich leichter durchzuführen und nicht mit Programmänderungen verbunden.

II.2.B. Erkennen der Eingabeeinheit

Das Feststellen der Identifikation einer vorliegenden EE wird Erkennen der EE genannt. Die Identifikation kann auf drei Arten bekanntgegeben werden:

(a) durch fixe Zuordnung im Programm
(b) durch Angabe an einer vorbestimmten Stelle in der EE selbst
(c) außerhalb der EE an einer anderen Stelle derselben oder einer anderen Eingabefolge.

II.2.C. Die Eingabewerte der Eingabeeinheit

Die EE ist als Teilfolge der EF definiert, sie ist also eine Folge von (intern codierten) Zeichen. Die Auftrennung dieser Zeichenfolge in die Teilfolgen,die den einzelnen Eingabewerten entsprechen, muß eindeutig vollziehbar sein; die Informationen dazu können aus verschiedenen Quellen stammen; sie gehören zur Beschreibung der EE-Art.

Im wesentlichen kann man zwei verschiedene Arten von Eingabewerten unterscheiden:

- Eingabewerte mit fixem Feld: der EW besteht aus einer bereits vor der Eingabe in Ort und Ausdehnung festgelegten Teilfolge der EE (etwa in Spalten a_1 bis a_2 einer Lochkarte)
- Eingabewerte mit variablem Feld: der EW liegt in beliebiger Form und Länge vor, ist aber vom vorhergehenden und nachfolgenden auf eine vorgegebene Weise getrennt, bzw. Ort und Ausdehnung der Zeichenfolge des EW wird vorher in der EF selbst angegeben.

Man kann in beiden Fällen einen bestimmten EW durch seine Ordnungszahl in der Reihenfolge der EW der vorliegenden EE identifizieren.

Es ist oft sinnvoll, bestimmte numerische und Zeichenkettenwerte (z.B. Leerstellen) vorzugeben, deren Auftreten als Eingabewert bedeutet, daß der EW, der eigentlich an der entsprechenden Stelle hätte stehen sollen, unbekannt ist und daher fehlt. In diesem Fall soll von einem fehlenden Eingabewert gesprochen werden.

II.2.D. Zuordnung der Bedeutungen zu den Eingabewerten

Den EW einer EE können die Bedeutungen auf vier verschiedene Weisen zugeordnet werden:

(a) Festlegung im Programm:das Programm nimmt von sich aus an, daß ein bestimmter EW ein Wert zu einer vorgegebenen Variable ist. Diese Art der Zuordnung wird am besten vermieden, da sie starr ist und Änderungen erschwert.

(b) Festlegung in der Definition der EE-Art:in allen EE der gegebenen Art ist ein bestimmter EW ein Wert zu einer vorgegebenen Variable.

(c) Angabe in der EE selbst:an einer anderen Stelle in der EE ist ein EW, der eine Variable kennzeichnet, zu der ein bestimmter EW gehört. Der Eingabewert, der die Variable kennzeichnet, wird Codeangabe genannt, weil er meist den Variablencode darstellt. Die Bedeutung "Variablencode" der Codeeintragung kann ihm wieder auf eine der beschriebenen Arten zugeordnet werden.

(d) Angabe an anderer Stelle in der Eingabe: also eine Codeangabe in einer anderen EE derselben oder einer anderen EF.

Für jeden Eingabewert einer EE muß gewährleistet werden, daß ihm auf eine der oben erwähnten Arten eine Bedeutung zugewiesen wird; auf diese Weise wird die EE in eine Folge von Datenwerten umgewandelt.

II.2.E. Die Eingabestruktur

Die DW, die aus den EW einer EE erkannt werden, stehen i.a. in einem bekannten logischen Zusammenhang. Die Zusammenhänge zwischen den einzelnen EW können verschiedener Art sein:

(a) rein bedeutungsmäßige Über- und Unterordnung der enthaltenen Information

(b) bestimmte logische Relationen müssen für die betreffenden Eingabewerte sein

Ein Sonderfall der bedeutungsmäßigen Abhängigkeit zweier Eingabewerte liegt dann vor, wenn die Bedeutung des einen von dem Wert des anderen abhängt. Dies ist z.B. bei einer Codeeintragung der Fall. Zur einfachen Behandlung solcher variabler Bedeutungsangaben wird die folgende Annahme über die Eindeutigkeit der Beschreibung einer EE getroffen:

Stellt man die Menge der Eingabewerte einer EE als Knoten eines gerichteten Graphen dar, wobei genau dann von EW_i zu EW_j eine gerichtete Kante führt, wenn die Bedeutung von EW_j von EW_i direkt abhängt, so sollen in diesem Graphen keine gerichteten Kreise existieren (d.h. die Bedeutung eines EW hängt nie direkt oder indirekt vom EW selbst ab).

Bei der Überprüfung der EW in der EE kann es vorkommen, daß gewisse EW als falsch erkannt und zurückgewiesen werden, oder daß erwartete EW fehlen. Trotz solcher Fehler und Unvollständigkeiten ist es oft möglich, einen Teil der restlichen Daten der EE, der davon nicht betroffen wird, zur Verarbeitung weiterzugeben. Nach ihrer Wichtigkeit für die Akzeptierung des Inhalts der EE kann man die EW in drei Gruppen teilen:

(a) EW, deren Vorhandensein und formale Richtigkeit für die Akzeptierung der gesamten EE unerläßlich sind ("notwendige Eingabewerte");
(b) EW, deren Vorhandensein und formale Richtigkeit für die Akzeptierung eines bestimmten Teils des Inhalts der EE notwendig sind;
(c) EW, deren Fehlen oder Unrichtigkeit auf die Akzeptierung der anderen EW keinen direkten Einfluß haben.

Auch die aufzustellenden logischen Relationen zwischen DW können bei Nichterfüllung oder bei Unmöglichkeit der Überprüfung (wenn ein in sie eingehender DW fehlt oder falsch ist) verschiedenen Einfluß haben:

(a) die Nichterfüllung der Relation führt zur Zurückweisung der gesamten EE
(b) die Nichterfüllung der Relation führt zur Zurückweisung eines oder mehrerer DW

Die beschriebenen Zusammenhänge und Relationen zwischen den DW aus der EE einer bestimmten Art führen also in der Folge der DW eine Struktur ein, die im folgenden mit Eingabestruktur (ES) bezeichnet wird.

II.2.F. Plausibilitätskontrolle der Eingabestruktur

Die Überprüfung der Relationen, die in der Eingabestruktur gelten müssen, wird Plausibilitätskontrolle 2 (erster Teil) genannt.

Es liege eine EE vor. Das Erkennen der Datenwerte (also die Zuordnung der Bedeutungen zu den EW und die Plausibilitätskontrolle 1 einerseits sowie das Erkennen der Eingabestruktur und die Plausibilitätskontrolle 2 andererseits können nicht unabhängig voneinander durchgeführt werden. So muß z.B. eine Codeangabe stets vor dem Erkennen des in der Bedeutung abhängigen DW erkannt und geprüft werden. Unter der Annahme der Eindeutigkeit (II.2.E) ist es möglich, das Erkennen der DW und die PK1 in folgender Weise vorzunehmen:

Schritt (a): Allen EW, denen die Bedeutungen aus Angaben in der Definition der EE-Art, im Programm oder in anderen EE zugeordnet werden können, werden diese Bedeutungen zugeordnet.

Schritt (b): Die erkannten Datenwerte werden behandelt und der PK1 unterzogen.

Schritt (c): Denjenigen noch nicht behandelten EW, deren Bedeutungen aus den in Schritt (a) und (b) zuletzt überprüften DW hervorgehen, werden die Bedeutungen zugeordnet; wurden diejenigen DW, die die Bedeutun eines EW bestimmen, überprüft, aber als falsch (oder fehlend) zurückgewiesen, so wird auch der neue EW als falsch zurückgewiesen.

Schritt (d): Schritte (b) und (c) sind so lange zu wiederholen bis all DW entweder erkannt und geprüft oder zurückgewiesen sind.

Die Plausibilitätskontrolle 2, also die Überprüfung der Relationen, die zwizwischen den Datenwerten gelten müssen, wird folgendermaßen durchgeführt:

(a) Eine Relation nach der anderen wird geprüft.
(b) Ist die Relation nicht erfüllt oder kann sie wegen Fehlens bzw. Unrichtigkeit der verwendeten Datenwerte nicht gebildet werden, so wird - je nach Angabe in der Definition der EE-Art - die gesamte EE oder eine Untermenge der Datenwerte der EE als falsch markiert.
(c) Im ersten Fall kann der Ablauf abgebrochen und die EE zurückgewiesen werden.
(d) Im zweiten Fall kann es sein, daß die als falsch markierten Datenwerte direkt oder indirekt die Bedeutungen gewisser anderer noch nicht als falsch markierter EW bestimmten. Dann werden die entsprechenden DW als falsch markiert.

(e) Wurden die neu als falsch markierten DW in früher überprüften Relationen verwendet, so geht man zur ersten solchen Relation zurück und setzt bei (a) fort.
Sonst setzt man mit der nächsten Relation bei (a) fort.

Dabei wird die Annahme getroffen, daß die logischen Relationen derart sind, daß ihre Auswertung nach dem obigen Algorithmus bei jeder möglichen Kombination von EW durchführbar ist. (Es dürfen also keine Endlosschleifen auftreten.)

Nach diesen Überprüfungen hat man eines der folgenden Ergebnisse:

- die EE ist als falsch markiert
- die Eingabestruktur ist bekannt und die enthaltenen DW sind formal geprüft, wobei allerdings gewisse Teile als falsch oder fehlend markiert sein können.

II.2.G. Die Ausgabestruktur

Die im vorhergehenden Abschnitt dargelegte Bildung und Prüfung der Eingabestruktur möge von einem allgemeinen Datenanalyse- und -prüfprogramm durchgeführt werden. Die dem eigentlichen Verarbeitungsprogramm schließlich übergebene Struktur kann vom Datenprüfprogramm aus als "Ausgabe" angesehen werden und wird deshalb Ausgabestruktur (AS) genannt.

Oft ist es der Fall, daß die AS gleich der ES ist. Manchmal ist es jedoch erwünscht, aus den Datenwerten der ES neue Datenwerte zu erzeugen oder die DW umzuordnen und in neue Beziehungen zueinander zu bringen. Auch diese Funktion kann vom Datenanalyseprogramm übernommen werden. Es ist also sinnvoll, zwischen ES und AS eine klare Unterscheidung zu machen und für jede Art von EE die Regeln zu definieren, nach welchen aus der ES die AS gebildet werden soll.

Diese Angaben gliedern sich in drei Teile:

(a) Bildung neuer DW aus den DW der ES oder aus bereits vorher gebildeten neuen DW, durch Berechnung oder sonstige Verfahren. Nicht nur der Wert, sondern ggf. auch die Bedeutung eines neuen Datenwerts könnte aus der ES bestimmt werden.
(b) Zusammensetzung der AS aus den DW der ES sowie den neuen DW.
(c) Logische Relation, die für die neuen DW im Zusammenhang miteinander sowie mit den DW der ES erfüllt sein müssen.

II.2.H. Plausibilitätskontrolle der Ausgabestruktur

Die aus der ES neu berechneten DW können ihrem Wesen nach genauso wie die DW der ES behandelt werden, außer daß ihre Werte nicht als Eingabewerte vorliegen. Auch die neu definierten logischen Relationen sind im wesentlichen nicht verschieden von den logischen Relationen zwischen den DW der ES.

Für sie gilt also alles, was im Abschnitt II.2.E. ausgeführt wurde und man kann die Plausibilitätskontrolle der AS genauso durchführen, wie sie in II.2.F. für die ES beschrieben wurde.

Es werden also nach der Prüfung der ES zuerst die neuen DW berechnet bzw. gebildet. Aus ihnen und den DW der ES wird die AS gebildet und dann wie die ES in II.2.F. überprüft. Diese Überprüfung heißt Plausibilitätskontrolle 2 (2. Teil).

Das Endergebnis ist eines der folgenden:

- die EE wird als falsch verworfen
- die AS ist bekannt und geprüft und wird zur Verarbeitung weitergegeben; eventuell fehlen gewisse Teile oder sind als falsch markiert.

II.2.I. Ablauf des Erkennens, der Analyse und der Plausibilitätskontrolle der Daten einer Eingabeeinheit

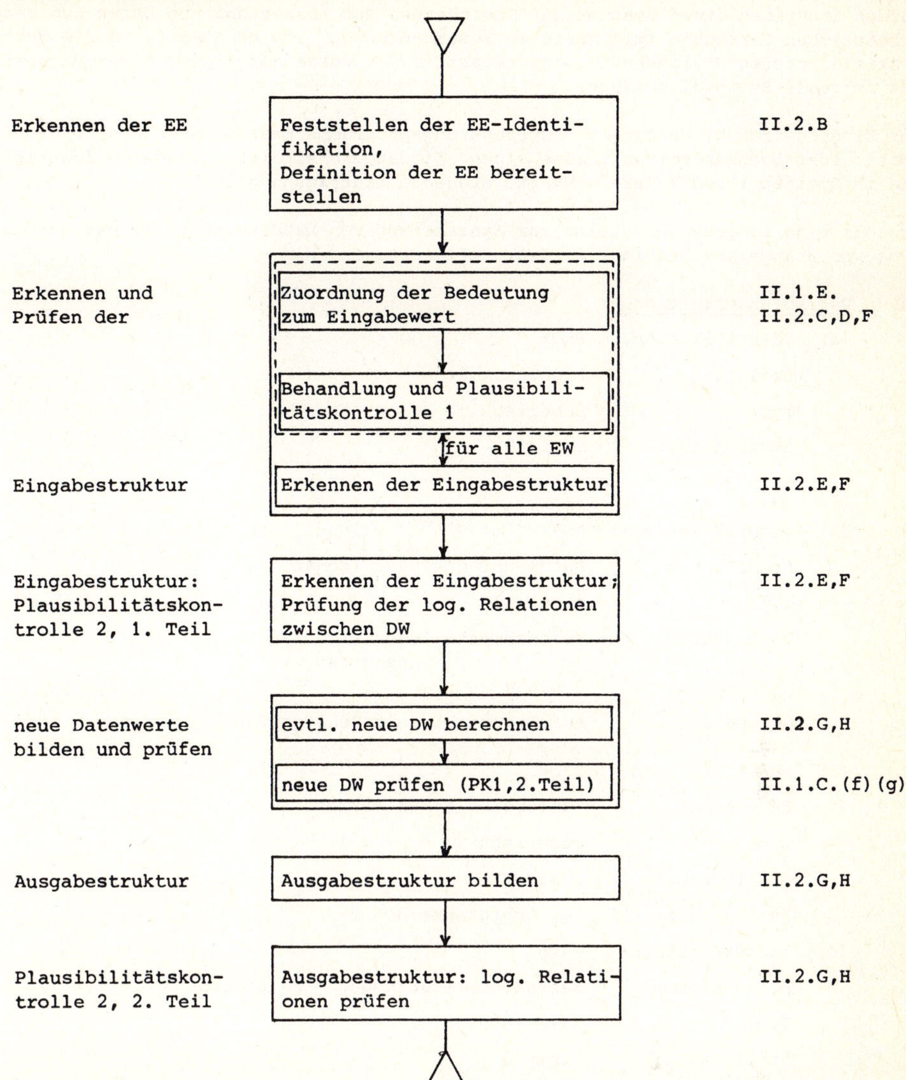

III. Beispiel

Die beschriebenen Verfahren zur Analyse und Plausibilitätskontrolle von Eingabedaten wurden im Rahmen eines Systems zur Speicherung und Auswertung von Daten aus landwirtschaftlichen Versuchen (mit gewissen Beschränkungen) implementiert. Um die für die Praxis gebotenen Möglichkeiten zu demonstrieren, wurde aus diesem Anwendungsbereich das folgende Beispiel gewählt.

Der Eingabestrom eines Datenbankspeicherungsprogramms bestehe aus Lochkarteninhalten, wobei jeder Lochkarteninhalt eine eigene Eingabeeinheit ist, als deren Identifikation die in Spalten 1 und 2 der Lochkarte stehende Eintragung gilt.

Es soll eine Eingabeeinheitsart zur Speicherung von Laborwerten, die bei der Malzanalyse von Braugerste bestimmt werden, definiert werden.

(1) Variablendefinitionen:

(a) Identifikation: PROB
Bedeutung: Probennummer
Typ: numerisch
Stellenzahl: 1 bis 5
Untergrenze: O

(b) Identifikation: ADAT
Bedeutung: Datum der Analyse (Monat, Tag)
Typ: numerisch
Vorbehandlung der Zeichenkette: nach rechts verschieben und ausnullen
Stellenzahl: 3 bis 4
Umrechnung: auf Tageszahl seit Jahresanfang

(c) Identifikation: H2OM
Bedeutung: Wassergehalt des Malzes (in Prozent)
Typ: numerisch
Stellenzahl: 2 bis 4
Untergrenze: 10; Obergrenze:30

(d) Identifikation: RFFS
Bedeutung: Refraktometerablesung - Feinschrot
Typ: numerisch
Stellenzahl: 2 bis 4
Untergrenze: 40; Obergrenze:60

(e) Identifikation: RFGS
Bedeutung: Refraktometerablesung - Grobschrot
Sonst wie RFFS

(f) Identifikation: EXFS
Bedeutung: Malzextraktwert - Feinschrot
Typ: numerisch
Stellenzahl: 2 bis 4
Untergrenze: 60; Obergrenze:80

(g) Identifikation: EXGS

Bedeutung: Malzextraktwert - Grobschrot

Typ: numerisch

Stellenzahl: 2 bis 4

Untergrenze: 40; Obergrenze:70

(2) Definition der Eingabeeinheit:

Die Eingabeeinheit ist ein Lochkarteninhalt, die Eintragungen sollen in fixen Feldern der Lochkarte vorgenommen werden. Man kann sie daher durch Anfangsspalte und Länge eindeutig kennzeichnen, ihre Bedeutungen werden durch den Variablencode und eventueller Dezimalstellenanzahl angegeben:

Eintragung	Spalte	Länge	Bedeutung	für die Akzeptierung der EE
-	1	2	Identifikation = 12	notwendig
1	3	4	ADAT	nicht notwendig
2	7	5	PROB	notwendig
3	12	3	H2OM, mit einer Dezimalstelle,	notwendig
4	15	4	RFFS, mit zwei Dezimalstellen,	notwendig
55	19	4	RFGS mit zwei Dezimalstellen	notwendig

(Der Rest des Lochkarteninhalts wird hier nicht beachtet).

Die Eingabestruktur ist (verbal beschrieben) folgendermaßen:

Eintragung 2 ist die Probenummer zu den Ablese- und Meßwerten 3,4, und 5.
Eintragung 1, wenn vorhanden, ist das Analysendatum zu den Werten 3,4 und 5.

Die Plausibilitätskontrolle 1 ist nach den Variablendefinitionen vorzunehmen.

Aus den angegebenen Meßwerten sind neue Datenwerte zu bilden, nach den folgenden Formeln (in denen die Variablencodes an Stelle der Datenwerte verwendet werden!):

Bedeutung	Formeln
EXFS	$\frac{(800+H2OM).p.100}{(100-p).(100-H2OM)}$ mit $p=\frac{RFFS-15}{4-0,005.(58-RFFS)}.0,99549$
EXGS	$\frac{(800+H2OM).q.100}{(100-q).(100-H2OM)}$ mit $q=\frac{RFGS-15}{4-0,005.(58-RFGS)}.0,99549$

Als Plausibilitätskontrolle 2 soll die folgende logische Relation überprüft werden:

$$0,5 \leq \text{Extraktdifferenz} \leq 10$$
mit Extraktdifferenz = EXFS-EXGS

Sie muß erfüllt sein, um die EE akzeptieren zu können.

Die neuen Datenwerte sollen statt der alten Ablesewerte weiterverwendet werden; die Ausgabestruktur besteht also aus den Datenwerten mit den Bedeutungen, die durch die Variablencodes ADAT, PROB, H2OM, EXFS und EXGS gekennzeichnet werden; (die Struktuierung bleibt jedoch gleich, außer daß EXFS an die Stelle von RFFS und EXGS an die Stelle von RFGS tritt).

Die EE wird zurückgewiesen, wenn eine oder mehrere der folgenden Fälle eintreten:

(a) Eintragungen 2,3,4 oder 5 werden von der Plausibilitätskontrolle 1 als falsch erkannt

(b) Eintragungen 2,3,4 oder 5 fehlen

(c) die EE-Identifikation fehlt

(d) die neuen Datenwerte werden von der Plausibilitätskontrolle 1 (2. Teil) als falsch erkannt

(e) die in der Plausibilitätskontrolle 2 zu prüfende logische Relation ist nicht erfüllt.

Zusammenfassung

Es wird eine Methode zur Formalisierung der Definition von Struktur und Bedeutungen der Eingabedaten zu EDV-Programmen vorgestellt. Hierdurch kann die Erkennung und Plausibilitätskontrolle verschiedenartiger Daten weitgehend automatisiert werden, sodaß diese Funktionen von einem einzigen allgemeinen Datenerkennungs- und Prüfprogramm übernommen werden können, mit dem Ziel, eine höhere Flexibilität bei der Eingabe größerer Datenmengen zu erreichen.

Summary

A method is introduced which allows the formalization of the definition of EDP program input data structure and meaning. Thus it is feasible to automatize a large part of the recognition and plausibility checking of many different kinds of data, allowing these functions to be performed by a single general data recognition and checking program - the goal being a higher flexibility in the input of large amounts of data.

Literaturhinweise

/1/ CODASYL SYSTEMS COMMITTEE: Feature Analysis of Generalized Data Base Management Systems, May 1971 (erhältlich bei IFIP Data Processing Group, Stadhouderskade 6, Amsterdam)

/2/ GORNY, P.: An Effective Data Language System Attachable to Existing Programs, in: Angewandte Informatik, Heft 2/75, S.75-77

/3/ LYNCH, H.J.: ADS:A Technique in Systems Documentation, in: Database, Vol.1, No.1, Spring 1969, S.6-18

/4/ WEDEKIND, H.: Systemanalyse. München: Carl Hanser Verlag 1973

IMPLEMENTIERUNG VON ZUGRIFFSPFADEN DURCH BITLISTEN

Theo Härder, Technische Hochschule Darmstadt

1. Einleitung

Eine vollständige Modellbildung eines datenunabhängigen Datenbanksystems wurde von M.E. Senko et al. [Se 73] durchgeführt. Dieser Entwurf resultiert in den vier hierarchisch angeordneten Ebenen:

- logische Datenstrukturen (Entity Set Model)
- logische Zugriffspfade (String Model)
- Speicherungsstrukturen (Encoding Model)
- Speicherzuordnungsstrukturen (Physical Device Model)

Wir gehen davon aus, daß die Ebene der logischen Datenstrukturen durch normalisierte n-stellige Relationen [Co70] vollständig beschrieben wird und durch Zugriffspfade keine zusätzlichen Informationen zur Ergänzung des logischen Datenmodells abgeleitet werden können. Zugriffspfade sind immer nur Hilfsmittel, um eine bestimmte, durch eine Frage qualifizierte Untermenge der Datensätze ohne sequentielle Suche in der ganzen Datenbank zur Verfügung stellen zu können. Während auf der Ebene der logischen Zugriffspfadstrukturen nur eine detaillierte Beschreibung der ausgewählten Zugriffspfade erfolgt, ohne Einzelheiten der Implementierung festzulegen, werden diese Strukturen auf die Ebene der Speicherungsstrukturen, die sich als unbegrenzter linearer Adreßraum auffassen läßt, in bestimmter physischer Ausprägung abgebildet. Zur tatsächlichen Abspeicherung müssen diese Strukturen in Speicherzuordnungsstrukturen auf realen Speichermedien, bei denen Parameter wie Blockungsfaktor, Belegungsfaktor, Lage der Überlauf- und Indexbereiche etc. zu berücksichtigen sind, dargestellt werden.

Die Vorteile deskriptiver Datenbanksprachen für relationale Datenbanksysteme [Ch74] , die Datensätze auf Grund ihres Inhaltes und nicht auf Grund ihrer relativen Position innerhalb einer Speicherungsstruktur qualifizieren und somit ein hohes Auswahlvermögen besitzen, sollten durch geeignete Implementierungstechniken für die Zugriffspfade gewahrt werden. Durch Trennung von Zugriffspfaden und Primärdaten ist die Teilmengenbildung der durch eine Frage qualifizierten Sätze allein in den Sekundärdaten möglich. Das System kann dann den günstigsten Weg auswählen, die gesuchten Sätze durch Zugriffe zu den Primärdaten bereitzustellen. Bei Vermischung von Primär- und Sekundärdaten hat das System nur geringe Möglichkeiten, die Auswertung von Fragen zu optimieren, da die Zugriffsfolge durch die Speicherungsstruktur vorgeschrieben wird.

2. Klassifizierung der möglichen Implementierungstechniken

Zur Organisation und Verwaltung von Sekundärdaten für große Datenbestände gibt es zwei grundsätzlich verschiedene Philosophien, nämlich entweder Sekundärdaten von den Primärdaten strikt zu trennen oder diese teilweise zu vermischen und einzubetten. So haben sich zwei verschiedene Verweistechniken herausgebildet [Sc72] :

- die Methode der Invertierung (inverted file method)
- die Methode der Adreßverkettung (address chaining)

Diese Methoden zur Darstellung von Zugriffspfaden für Sekundärschlüssel oder allgemeiner für Schlüssel, die auf mehr als einen Datensatz führen, sollen klassifiziert werden:

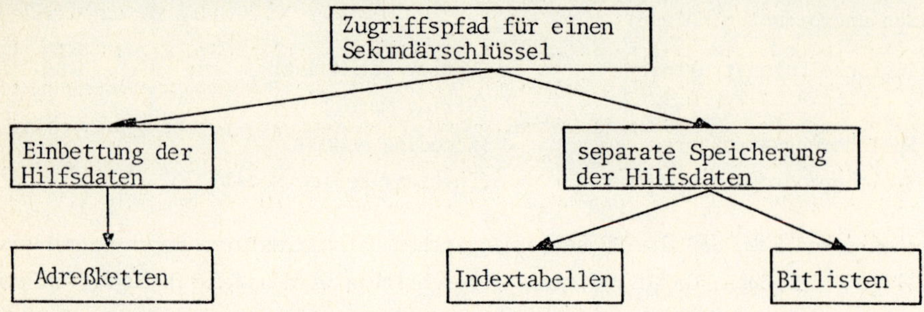

Bild 1: Gliederung der verschiedenen Implementierungstechniken für Sekundärschlüsselzugriff

Folgende aus der Literatur (z.B. [Ma69]) bekannte Implementierungstechniken sind als Mischformen von Adreßketten und Indextabellen anzusehen:

- Adreßketten mit kontrollierter Kettenlänge (gleiche Kettenlängen, multi-list file organization with controlled list length)
- Adreßketten mit beschränkter Kettenlänge (durch die Speichereinteilung eingeschränkte Kettenlängen, cellular multi-list file organization)
- Indexierte serielle Organisation (cellular serial file organization)

Diese drei Verfahren können in der angegebenen Reihenfolge als schrittweise Modifikation der Adreßkettenmethode hin zur Indextabellenmethode verstanden werden. In der praktischen Anwendung haben diese Verfahren keine Bedeutung erlangt. Der Nachteil solcher Mischformen besteht darin, daß bei ihrer Implementierung einem Datenverwaltungssystem Algorithmen für die Behandlung zweier grundsätzlich verschiedener Methoden zur Verfügung stehen müssen, was bei der Vielzahl der Such- und Pflegeoperationen zu einer beträchtlichen Komplexität in ihrer Anwendung führt.

Die Methode der Invertierung ist zur Erfüllung der Forderung geeignet, einen Systementwurf in verschiedenen, möglichst unabhängigen Ebenen im Sinne von DIAM [Se73] durchzuführen. Nach diesem Verfahren implementierte Zugriffspfade können unabhängig von den Primärdaten verwaltet, organisiert und geändert werden, während bei der Adreßkettungsmethode durch die Einbettung von Verweisadressen eine starke physische Bindung der Hilfsdaten an die Primärdaten erzielt wird. Die auf Grund eines vorgegebenen Kriteriums zusammengehörigen Datensätze werden bei der Adreßkettungsmethode durch eine

Satzkette dargestellt, wobei ausgehend von einer Ankeradresse außerhalb des Primärdatenbestandes Adreßzeiger (Satzadressen) die einzelnen Sätze in einer bestimmten Reihenfolge verbinden. Beim Indextabellenverfahren wird dieser Zusammenhang in getrennt abgespeicherten, variabel langen Ziellisten (Satzadreßlisten, Satznummernlisten) hergestellt. Inhalt dieser Ziellisten können physische Satzadressen oder, um eine zu starke Bindung an die Primärdaten zu vermeiden, logische Satzadressen oder Primärschlüssel sein. Eine zweite Verweistechnik, die Sekundär- und Primärdaten strikt trennt und grundsätzlich mit dem Indextabellenverfahren verglichen werden kann, ist die Invertierung mit Hilfe einer Bit-Pattern-Matrix. Dabei werden zusammengehörige Sätze nicht explizit mit ihren Schlüsseln oder Adressen aufgelistet, sondern relativ zu einer vorgegebenen Reihenfolge aller Sätze mit Hilfe von Bitlisten markiert, in denen für jeden Satz des Datenbestandes ein Bit geführt wird und gesetzte Bits (Einsen) die Auswahl von Sätzen anzeigen.

Der Zugriff zu den Bitlisten oder zu den Ziellisten des Indextabellenverfahrens oder zu den Ankeradressen bei Adreßkettungssystemen kann in allen Fällen durch eine zweistufige Hierarchie - die erste Stufe für Deskriptoren (Attribute), die zweite Stufe für Deskriptorwerte (Attributwerte, freie Deskriptoren) - organisiert werden. Bezieht man den Katalog für sämtliche Relationen mit in die Betrachtung ein, so entspricht diese Realisierung einer dreistufigen Hierarchie.

Die Darstellung in Bild 2 zeigt nur schematisch den Zugriffspfad. Unabhängig voneinander und unabhängig von der gewählten Implementierung der Verweistechnik können alle Hierarchiestufen durch Tabellen sequentiell oder index-sequentiell, durch B-Bäume oder B*-Bäume realisiert und für sich optimiert werden [We74] . Der gleiche Aufbau

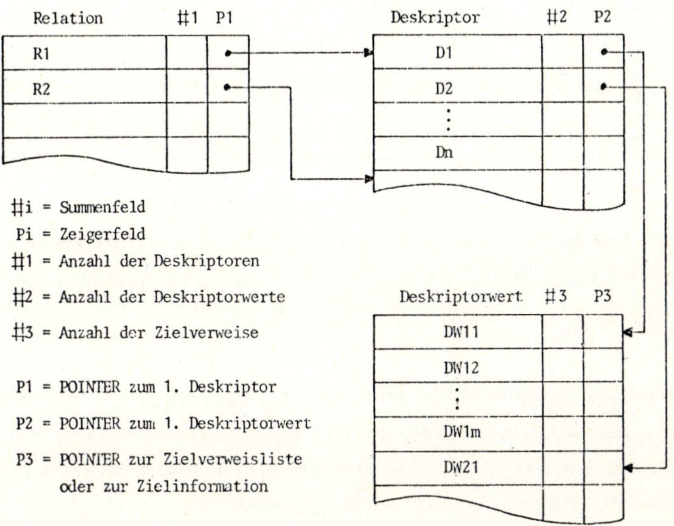

Bild 2: Schematischer Aufbau des Kataloges für Sekundärschlüssel

der Elemente (Knoten) auf allen Hierarchiestufen und die gleiche Behandlung des Zugriffs für alle Sekundärschlüssel (freie und gebundene Deskriptoren) und Primärschlüssel unterstützt das Bestreben, die Zugriffspfade zu normieren. Das Mitführen der Anzahl der jeweils zugehörigen untergeordneten Elemente auf allen Hierarchiestufen durch Summenfelder gestattet die Durchführung von Kontrollen und die Beantwortung bestimmter Anfragen (statistische Fragen), ohne auf die Primärdaten zugreifen zu müssen.

3. Bitlisten fester Anordnung (Bit-Pattern-Matrix)

Eine Bit-Pattern-Matrix hat unabhängig davon, ob eine Speicher- oder Satzmarkierung durchgeführt wird, den in Bild 3 skizzierten Aufbau.

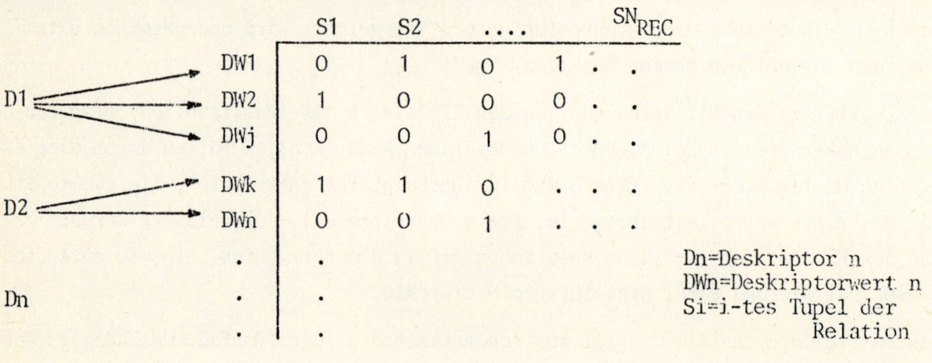

Bild 3: Aufbau einer Bit-Pattern-Matrix

Für jeden Deskriptorwert muß eine Bitliste der Länge N_{REC} Bits angelegt werden. Das Auftreten eines bestimmten, an einen Deskriptor gebundenen Deskriptorenwertes wird in der dazugehörigen Bitliste entsprechend der vorhandenen oder vorgegebenen Satzfolge markiert. Bei einer normalisierten Relation der Mächtigkeit N_{REC} sind für alle Deskriptorwerte eines Deskriptors zusammen genau N_{REC} Markierungen notwendig, falls in allen Sätzen (Tupeln) für diesen Deskriptor (Bereich) definierte Werte vorhanden sind.

Formal kann man einen Auflösungsfaktor R, der die durchschnittliche Häufigkeit eines Deskriptorwertes in einem Datenbestand bestimmt, einführen. Sind für einen Deskriptor j Deskriptorwerte vorhanden, so ergibt sich

$$R = \frac{N_{REC}}{j} \quad \text{. Resolution nach C.P. Wang [Wa73]}$$

Je geringer der Auflösungsfaktor für einen Deskriptor wird, d.h. je mehr Deskriptorwerte vorhanden sind, umso ungünstiger wird das Speicherplatzverhalten der Bitlisten konstanter Länge, weil ja nicht nur die Anwesenheit, sondern auch die Abwesenheit eines Deskriptorwertes (durch Null-Bits) dargestellt wird.
Werden in einer Bit-Pattern-Matrix Datensätze relativ zu einer vorgegebenen Ordnung markiert, so ergibt sich eine Abhängigkeit aller vorhandenen Bitlisten von Einfüge-

und Löschoperationen, unabhängig davon, ob bestimmte Deskriptorwerte von diesen Operationen betroffen sind.
Im Falle der Markierung vorformatierter Speichermedien wird die Abhängigkeit der Bitlisten vom Änderungsdienst aufgehoben. Dafür wird aber eine starke Bindung der Zugriffspfade an ein bestimmtes Speichermedium eingeführt, so daß eine dynamische Reorganisation der Datensätze unmöglich wird.
Die Eignung von Bitmatrizen fester Anordnung für die Invertierung ist nur bei einer relativ dichten durchschnittlichen Verteilung der Deskriptorwerte gegeben. Es soll hergeleitet werden, bis zu welcher Größe des Auflösungsfaktors R Bitlisten für einen Deskriptor speicherplatzgünstiger sind als Ziellisten (Listen mit Satzadressen oder Satznummern).
In einer normalisierten Relation gibt es für einen Deskriptor unabhängig von der Anzahl der Deskriptorwerte j insgesamt höchstens N_{REC} Zielverweise, die als variabel lange Ziellisten nach dem folgenden Schema implementiert werden:

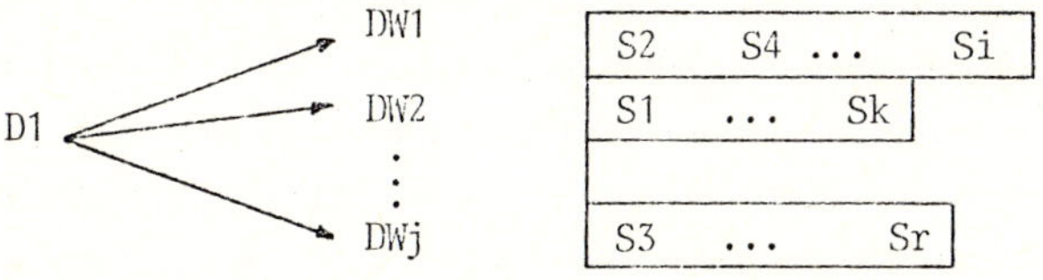

Bild 4: Schematischer Aufbau von variabel langen Ziellisten

Wenn in einem Datenverwaltungssystem S_M Bits (S_M = 8,16,24,32..; in byteorientierten Systemen wegen der Ausrichtung auf Bytegrenzen) zur Darstellung einer Adresse benötigt werden, so können die Ziellisten für einen Deskriptor unabhängig von seinem Auflösungsfaktor durch $N_{REC} \cdot S_M$ Bits abgespeichert werden. Eine Bitmatrix ist dann vorzuziehen, wenn

$$N_{REC} \cdot j < N_{REC} \cdot S_M \qquad \text{oder} \qquad j < S_M \quad \text{ist.}$$

4. Bitlisten variabler Länge

Die Anzahl der Deskriptorwerte pro Deskriptor ist jedoch in realen Datenbeständen wesentlich höher, so daß bei der vorgegebenen Markierungstechnik relativ wenige Einsen und lange Nullfolgen in Bitlisten erscheinen. Durch geeignete Komprimierungstechniken lassen sich Bitlisten als Strings variabler Länge abspeichern; auf diese Weise ist ein erheblicher Anteil an Speicherplatz einzusparen.

Dies geht natürlich zu Lasten der CPU-Zeit, die bei jedem Zugriff auf einen Deskriptor durch die algorithmische Rekonstruktion der "logischen Bitliste" aufgewendet werden muß. Da aber bei diesem Verfahren nur die komprimierte Bitliste vom Sekundärspeicher in den Hauptspeicher zu übertragen ist, wird andererseits im Verhältnis der Komprimierung E/A-Zeit eingespart. Der Vergleich von variabel langen Bitlisten beim Retrieval (Matchen) - durch effiziente Assemblerprogrammierung unterstützt - kann recht zeitgünstig erfolgen [Kr74] . Der Änderungsdienst in solchen Bitlisten ist jedoch dann sehr zeitaufwendig, wenn beim Einfügen oder Löschen alle vorhandenen Bitlisten erweitert oder verdichtet werden müssen. Daraus kann gefolgert werden, daß das Konzept der variabel langen Bitlisten keine geeignete Lösung für die Implementierung von Zugriffspfaden bei Systemen mit starkem Änderungsdienst ist, wenn auf Grund der Markierungstechnik Einfüge- und Löschoperationen nur umständlich zu handhaben sind.

Im folgenden werden geeignete Codierungen für die Komprimierung der Bitlisten und der daraus resultierende Speicherplatzbedarf untersucht.

Das Ziel der Komprimierung ist es, Nullfolgen großer Länge, die nur die Abwesenheit eines Deskriptorwertes beschreiben, aus der Bitliste zu eliminieren, um Speicherplatz einzusparen, ohne dabei Information zu verlieren. Wenn die Bitliste der Länge N_{REC} in Blöcke gleicher Länge k_1 eingeteilt wird, dann können alle Blöcke ausgelassen werden, die nur Nullbits enthalten, in dem man die Auslassungen durch einen gesonderten Bitstring B_1 (Directory) der Länge N_{REC}/k_1 kennzeichnet. Dieser Bitstring kann bei vielen Deskriptorwertverteilungen wiederum große Nullfolgen besitzen, die durch Anwendung des gleichen Schemas zu eliminieren sind. Der Bitstring B_1 wird in Blöcke der Länge k_2 eingeteilt, so daß solche Blöcke nach Kennzeichnung in einem weiteren Bitstring B_2 der Länge $N_{REC}/(k_1 \cdot k_2)$ weggelassen werden können. Dieses Prinzip läßt sich rekursiv anwenden, bis sich im Bitstring B_h der höchsten Hierarchiestufe h die Eliminierung von Nullfolgen nicht mehr lohnt.
In Bild 5 ist dieses Komprimierungsverfahren schematisch dargestellt. Dabei werden die gestrichelt gekennzeichneten Blöcke nicht gespeichert. Die logische Bitliste ist jedoch leicht rekonstruierbar. In den Blöcken der Stufe B_o sind die tatsächlichen Markierungen aus der ursprünglichen Bitliste gespeichert. Die Blöcke auf den Stufen B_1 bis B_h, die Markierungen beinhalten, enthalten alle notwendigen Informationen zur Rekonstruktion.

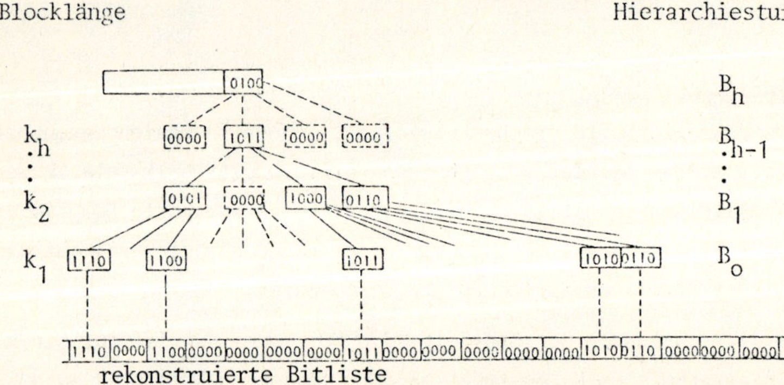

Bild 5: Schematische Darstellung der Komprimierung durch eine Hierarchie von Bitstrings [Ba74, S. 151]

Für die Abschätzung des Speicherplatzbedarfs pro Markierung betrachten wir den Fall, bei dem die Deskriptorwerte eines Deskriptors so über den gesamten Datenbestand verteilt sind, daß in der dazugehörigen Bitliste die Markierungen äquidistant nach jeweils j-1 Nullfolgestellen vorkommen. Im Hinblick auf die angestrebte Verdichtung der Bitlisten entspricht dieser Fall dem "worst case".

Solange $j \leqslant k_1$ unter Annahme der Äquidistanz ist, kann auf der untersten Ebene der Hierarchie kein Speicherplatz eingespart werden. Wir erhalten:

$$S_M = \frac{N_{REC} + \frac{N_{REC}}{k_1} + \frac{N_{REC}}{k_1 \cdot k_2} + \ldots + \frac{N_{REC}}{k_1 \cdot k_2 \ldots k_h}}{R} = (1 + \frac{1}{k_1} + \frac{1}{k_1 \cdot k_2} + \ldots + \frac{1}{k_1 \cdot k_2 \ldots k_h}) \cdot j$$

Für $j > k_1$ ist zur Darstellung einer Markierung im "worst case" Falle auf der untersten Hierarchiestufe genau ein Block mit k_1 Bits notwendig, während ein von j abhängiger Speicherplatzanteil auf allen anderen Stufen hinzukommt:

$$S_M = k_1 + (\frac{1}{k_1} + \frac{1}{k_1 \cdot k_2} + \ldots + \frac{1}{k_1 \cdot k_2 \ldots k_h}) \cdot j \qquad \text{für} \qquad k_1 < j \leqslant k_1 \cdot k_2$$

Auf jeder Stufe der Hierarchie wächst mit steigendem j der relative Speicherplatzanteil pro Markierung, bis jeweils genau eine Markierung in einem Block der entsprechenden Hierarchiestufe auftritt.

Daraus resultiert folgender Speicherplatzbedarf pro Markierung:

$$S_M \leqslant \begin{cases} (1 + \frac{1}{k_1} + \frac{1}{k_1 \cdot k_2} + \ldots + \frac{1}{k_1 \cdot k_2 \ldots k_h}) \cdot j & \text{für} \quad j \leqslant k_1 \\ k_1 + (\frac{1}{k_1} + \frac{1}{k_1 \cdot k_2} + \ldots + \frac{1}{k_1 \cdot k_2 \ldots k_h}) \cdot j & \text{für} \quad k_1 < j \leqslant k_1 \cdot k_2 \\ k_1 + k_2 + (\frac{1}{k_1 \cdot k_2} + \ldots + \frac{1}{k_1 \cdot k_2 \ldots k_h}) \cdot j & \text{für} \quad k_1 \cdot k_2 < j \leqslant k_1 \cdot k_2 \cdot k_3 \\ \vdots & \\ k_1 + k_2 + k_3 + \ldots k_h + \frac{1}{k_1 \cdot k_2 \ldots k_h} \cdot j & \text{für} \quad k_1 \cdot k_2 \ldots k_h < j \end{cases}$$

Für diese Speicherbedarfsfunktion sind die Blocklängen k_i und die Anzahl der Hierarchiestufen h so zu wählen, daß bei einem gegebenen Auflösungsfaktor R möglichst wenig Speicherplatz zur Darstellung einer hierarchischen Bitliste benötigt wird. Wir nehmen zunächst an, daß alle Variablen k_i Elemente aus der Menge der reellen Zahlen sind.
Es muß die Funktion

$$S_M = k_1 + k_2 + \ldots + k_h + \frac{j}{k_1 \cdot k_2 \ldots k_h}$$

für den Bereich $j > k_1 \cdot k_2 \ldots k_h$ minimiert werden.
Es kann gezeigt werden, daß ein relatives Minimum nur für

$$k_1 = k_2 = \ldots = k_h = k \qquad \text{existieren kann.}$$

Folglich geht die zu minimierende Funktion über in

$$S_M = k \cdot h + \frac{j}{k^h} \quad .$$

Formal erhält man ein relatives Minimum für

$$k = e$$
$$h = \ln j - 1$$
$$\ln j > 1 \quad ,$$

so daß sich die Minimalwerte der Speicherbedarfsfunktion zu

$$S_M = e \cdot \ln j$$

ergeben. Da die Variablen k und h nur positive ganzzahlige Werte annehmen können, stellt die Funktion eine untere Schranke für die Speicherbedarfsfunktion dar. Für k = 3 kann die beste Nachbildung der Minimalwerte der Speicherbedarfsfunktion erreicht werden. Die Anzahl der Hierarchiestufen h wird dabei so gewählt, daß bei einem minimalen h

$$S_M^{(h)} = k \cdot h + \frac{j_g}{k^h} \leq S_M^{(h+1)} = k \cdot (h+1) + \frac{j_g}{k^{h+1}}$$

für ein vorgegebenes j_g bleibt. Daraus resultiert die folgende Bedingung

$$\frac{k-1}{k} \cdot j_g \leq k^{h+1}$$

zur Bestimmung von h.
Wählt man zu große Blöcke k zur Darstellung der Markierungen in den einzelnen Hierarchiestufen, so hat das beträchtliche Folgen für den Speicherplatzbedarf. Es ist beispielsweise ein nicht vertretbarer Vorschlag, $k = 2^{11}$ zu wählen [By73] . In diesem Fall ist für $j > 2^{11}$ ein $S_M > 2^{11}$ Bits = 2^8 Bytes zu erwarten.

Eine weitere Möglichkeit, eine Bitliste zu verdichten, besteht darin, Folgen gleichartiger Bits durch eine Binärzahl zu codieren und Folgen ungleich gesetzter Bits als "Bitmuster" zu übernehmen.

Wenn in den einzelnen Codierfolgen (Taktfolgen) einer komprimierten Bitliste zu je k Bits nur zwei verschiedenartige Zustände unterschieden werden sollen, so braucht zur Kennzeichnung der Folge nur ein Bit reserviert werden. Das folgende Bild zeigt das Schema einer solchen Taktfolge:

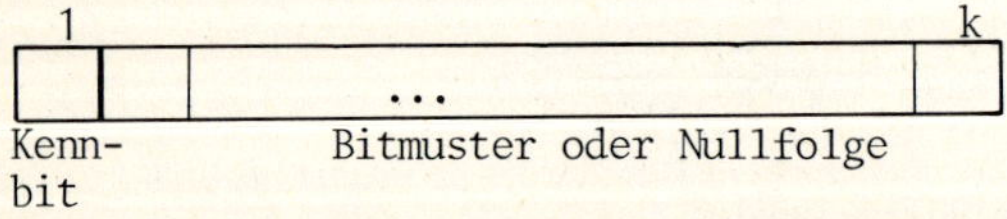

Die beiden möglichen Zustände des Kennbits geben an, ob ein Bitmuster oder eine Nullfolge codiert ist.

Durch die Codierungsstrategie der Bitliste werden, falls eine oder mehrere Markierungen auftreten, k-1 aufeinanderfolgende Bits als Bitmuster ohne Komprimierung übernommen. Anschließend wird die verbleibende Nullfolge bis zu nächsten Markierung überprüft. Wenn mehr als k-1 Nullfolgestellen darzustellen sind, wird eine Nullfolge codiert. Dabei können bis zu $2^{k-1}-1$ aufeinanderfolgende Nullen als Binärzahl ausgedrückt werden. Wenn eine sehr große Anzahl von Nullfolgestellen nicht durch eine Taktfolge codiert werden kann, schließen sich weitere Takte mit Nullfolgen an, bis wiederum eine Markierung auftritt.
Wenn Nullfolgen großer Länge durch mehrere gleiche Taktfolgen derselben Kapazität codiert werden müssen, wächst der Speicherplatzbedarf in jeweils konstanten Bereichen von j additiv, wie in [Hä74] gezeigt wurde.
Dieses Verhalten vermindert besonders bei kleinem Auflösungsfaktor die Wirksamkeit der Komprimierung. Es sollte deshalb für die Codierung eine Kennung vorgesehen werden, die die Darstellung von Nullfolgen erlaubt, die nicht durch die Länge einer Taktfolge beschränkt sind. Durch die Zusammenfassung von zwei Taktfolgen mit Hilfe von Kennbits wächst das Darstellungsvermögen von Binärzahlen exponentiell zur Basis 2 von $2^{k-1}-1$ auf $2^{2k-2}-1$. Somit können wesentlich längere Nullfolgen durch eine doppelte Taktfolge codiert werden. Für Einsfolgen ist diese Codierungsmaßnahme nicht notwendig, da es in realen Datenbeständen kaum Deskriptorwerte geben wird, die lange geschlossene Einsfolgen in der Bitliste bilden werden. Sollen in einer Codiereinheit mehr als zwei unterschiedliche Folgen erkannt werden können, so ist die Zahl der Kennbits zu erhöhen. Für eine Taktfolge der Länge k werden zwei Kennbits eingeführt.

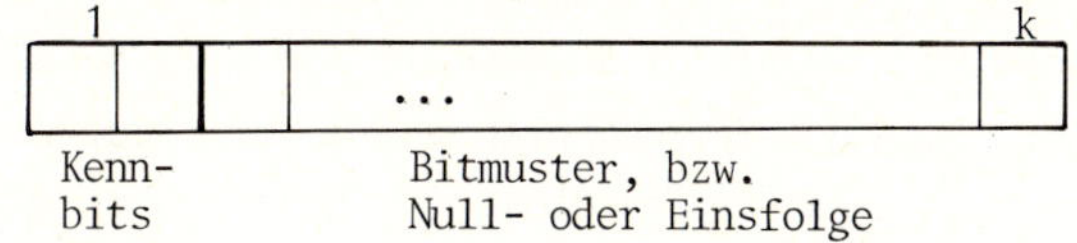

Die ersten beiden Bits jeder Taktfolge bestimmen ihren Inhalt.
Es wird folgende Codierung für die Kennbits vorgeschlagen:

KENNBITS =	11	Bitmuster
	10	Einsfolge (Taktfolge = k Bits)
	01	Nullfolge (Taktfolge = k Bits)
	00	Nullfolge (Taktfolge = 2k Bits)

Ist die Anzahl der hintereinanderfolgenden Nullen oder Einsen kleiner als 2^{k-2}, so wird sie durch eine Taktfolge verschlüsselt. Mit der Codierung einer doppelten Taktfolge sind Nullfolgen der Länge $2^{2k-2}-1$ zu erfassen. Dies ist dann vorteilhaft, wenn in einem großen Datenbestand ein Deskriptorwert selten auftritt. Durch Einführung der zusätzlichen Regel, daß zwischen zwei aufeinanderfolgende Nullfolgen immer eine implizite Eins angenommen wird, lassen sich bei kleinem Resolutionsfaktor Bitlisten codieren, in denen unter Umständen keine expliziten Eins-Markierungen vorkommen. Folgende Codierungsstrategie wird gewählt. Wenn in der "logischen Bitliste" nach dem

Codieren einer Nullfolge eine Markierung auftritt, wird die Anzahl der Nullfolgestellen d bestimmt. Falls $d < k-2$ ist, wird die Markierung explizit in einem Bitmuster übernommen. Ist $d \geq k-2$, wird wiederum eine Nullfolge codiert und so die Markierung implizit dargestellt. Ist $d \geq 2^{k-2}$, so wird zur Codierung eine doppelte Taktfolge herangezogen. Für $d \geq 2^{2k-2}$ scheitert dieses Verfahren, wenn nicht zusätzliche Regeln zur Komprimierung von Nullfolgen verwendet werden.

Mit der Annahme äquidistanter Abstände zwischen den Markierungen kann der Speicherplatzbedarf folgendermaßen abgeschätzt werden:

$$S_M = \begin{cases} \frac{k}{k-2} \cdot j & \text{für} \quad j \leq k-2 \\ k & \text{für} \quad k-2 < j \leq 2^{k-2} \\ 2k & \text{für} \quad 2^{k-2} < j \leq 2^{2k-2} \end{cases}$$

Da in der eben untersuchten Codierung mit 2 Kennbits schon alle sinnvoll zu komprimierenden Folgen erfaßt werden konnten, wird auf die Behandlung einer Codierung mit 3 oder mehr Bits verzichtet, da Kennbits nur notwendiger, minimaler Verwaltungsaufwand sein sollten.

Als Einheit der Codierung bietet sich in großen Datenbeständen $k = 16$ (Byteausrichtung) an. Bei äquidistanter Verteilung der Deskriptorwerte führt die Verdichtung durch den vorgeschlagenen Codierungsalgorithmus im allgemeinen zu einem geringeren Speicherplatzbedarf als durch die hierarchische Darstellung. Wenn für die Blocklängen Byteausrichtung gefordert wird, ist der Speicherplatzbedarf bei hierarchischer Darstellung in relevanten Bereichen von j sogar um den Faktor 2 größer. Bei Clusterbildung der Markierungen vermindert sich der Speicherplatzbedarf für beide Verdichtungsprinzipien erheblich. In Sonderfällen kann jedes dieser beiden Verfahren das günstigere sein, je nachdem, wie gut die vorliegende Verteilung des Deskriptorwerte dem Verdichtungsprinzip angepaßt ist.
Bei Indextabellensystemen wird statt einer Markierung die Adresse oder der Primärschlüssel in der Zielliste explizit aufgeführt. Für die Darstellung einer Adresse in einem hinreichend großen Datenbestand kann davon ausgegangen werden, daß mindestens 3 Bytes erforderlich sind.

Bitlisten variabler Länge sind den Ziellisten der Indextabellensysteme in weiten Bereichen von j schon im ungünstigsten Fall um 50 % bezüglich des Speicherplatzbedarfs überlegen. In Sonderfällen reduziert sich der Platzbedarf um den Faktor 30 und mehr. Es ist ein $S_M \ll 1$ möglich.

Es ist festzuhalten, daß auch die Bitlisten variabler Länge die Vorteile der Indextabellensysteme, implizit die Pointer FIRST, PRIOR, NEXT und LAST zu enthalten, besitzen. In Adreßkettungssystemen (Chain-Mode in DBTG [CODA]) müssen alle diese Pointer, falls sie deklariert sind und deren Wirksamkeit vorteilhaft eingesetzt werden soll, explizit durch 3 oder 4 Byte Adressen dargestellt werden, was zu einem hohen Speicherplatzbedarf führt und wegen der Unübersichtlichkeit und Vielfalt der Adreßketten den Änderungsdienst sehr erschwert.

5. Trennung von Zugriffspfadebene und physischer Geräteebene

Die eben diskutierten Vorteile der Bitlisten variabler Länge werden stark eingeschränkt, wenn nicht Datensätze, sondern physische Bereiche eines Speichermediums (Speicherplatzmarkierung) markiert werden. Gravierend ist dabei die starke Bindung der Zugriffspfade an ganz bestimmte physische Speichermedien. Im Sinne des Entwurfs von Datenverwaltungssystemen nach DIAM liegt hier eine eklatante Verletzung der Forderung eines möglichst unabhängigen Entwurfs der einzelnen hierarchischen Systemebenen vor, da auf der Zugriffspfadebene (access path level) unter Umgehung des Betriebssystems, unter dessen Kontrolle das Datenverwaltungssystem laufen soll, Annahmen (Adreßberechnungen) über den physischen Bereich der Geräteebene (physical device level) getroffen werden. Die Trennung der Zugriffspfadebene von der Geräteebene wird bei Indextabellen dadurch gewährleistet, daß in den Ziellisten der Sekundärschlüssel Primärschlüssel geführt werden. Bei jedem Zugriff zur Zielinformation muß dann der Zugriffspfad des Primärschlüssels, auf dessen Optimierung besonders zu achten ist, verfolgt werden. In allen Fällen ist bei jeder beliebigen physischen Reorganisation nur ein Zugriffspfad zu ändern.

Bei Adreßkettungssystemen ist diese strikte Trennung von Zugriffspfad und Daten nicht möglich, da die in die Datensätze eingebetteten Adreßzeiger nicht durch logische Schlüssel ersetzt werden können, ohne daß damit dann der Grundgedanke dieser Organisationsform (multi-chaining) aufgegeben wird.

In einer Bitliste werden weder Primärschlüssel noch Satzadressen eingetragen. Es lassen sich nur relative Positionen in einer vorgegebenen Ordnung markieren. Das Kriterium oder die Folge, nach der die Markierung der Datensätze durchgeführt werden kann, ist von entscheidender Bedeutung für den Speicherplatzbedarf und den Änderungsdienst der gesamten Sekundärdaten beim Bitlistenverfahren. Der günstigste Fall liegt dann vor, wenn der Primärschlüsselbereich aus der Menge der natürlichen Zahlen genommen wird. Durch die Komprimierungstechnik besteht keine Notwendigkeit, fortlaufende Schlüsselnummern zu vergeben. Die vorhandenen Schlüssel einer Relation lassen sich als Zahlengerade auffassen, auf der beliebig viele Lücken vorkommen können. Die Bitlisten werden durch eine dünne Besetzung der Zahlengeraden nicht wesentlich ausgedehnt, da ohnehin bei vielen Werteverteilungen nur Nullfolgen abgespeichert werden. Die Idee, auch Lücken im Wertebereich des Schlüssels mitzuverwalten, bringt vor allem für den Änderungsdienst große Vorteile. Beim Einfügen oder Löschen eines Satzes in der Sortierreihenfolge sind nur die durch den Inhalt des Satzes betroffenen Bitlisten zu ändern. Beim Zugriff über einen sekundären Index lassen sich die Schlüssel der ausgewählten Sätze aus den Bitlisten direkt ermitteln, so daß die Datensätze über den Zugriffspfad des Primärschlüssels bereitgestellt werden können.

In vielen Anwendungsfällen, beispielsweise bei Dokumenten, Büchern in einem Bibliotheksdatenbestand, Aufträgen, Rechnungen und Buchungen (time-stamped relations), werden häufig laufende Nummern vergeben, so daß die beschriebene Markierungstechnik direkt anzuwenden ist.

Liegt ein numerischer Primärschlüssel vor und soll eine Markierung bezüglich der absoluten Adressen eines physischen Speichermediums aus den diskutierten Gründen vermieden werden, so kann die Markierung relativ zu einer Zuordnungstabelle, die Primärschlüssel und Satzadresse enthält, erfolgen. Aus der Bitposition in der Bitliste läßt sich der zugeordnete Tabelleneintrag bestimmen. Schematisch ist dies in Bild 6 veranschaulicht.

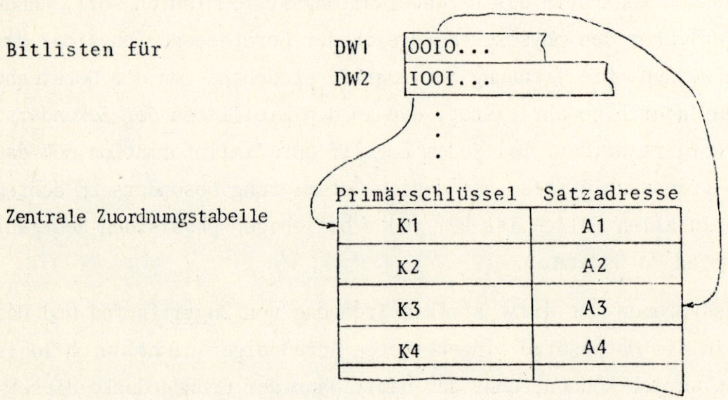

Bild 6: Direkte Zuordnung der Bitlisten

Die Zuordnungstabelle kann als Zugriffspfad für den Primärschlüssel aufgefaßt werden. Für die physische Reorganisation wird bei einem solchen Verfahren eine absolute Trennung von Primär- und Sekundärdaten erreicht, da in der Zuordnungstabelle die Satzadressen beliebig geändert werden können, ohne daß irgendwelche Rückwirkungen auf die Zugriffspfade auftreten. Die Schwerfälligkeit des Änderungsdienstes ist aber damit noch nicht aufgehoben. Bei jedem Einfügen oder Löschen eines Satzes sind sämtliche Bitlisten zu erweitern oder zu verdichten, wenn eine vorgegebene Ordnung (Sortierfolge) beibehalten werden soll. Die Änderungen beschränken sich nicht nur auf die Listen der angesprochenen Deskriptorwerte, wie das bei Indextabellensystemen der Fall ist.

Ein sinnvolles Verfahren für den Änderungsdienst besteht darin, neu einzufügende Sätze am Ende der Zuordnungstabelle einzutragen und zu löschende Sätze in den Tabelleneinträgen zu markieren. Dafür ist allerdings eine periodische Reorganisation von Bitlisten und Zuordnungstabelle erforderlich.

Besteht jedoch die Forderung, mit vertretbarem Aufwand unter Beibehaltung einer bestimmten Ordnung einfügen und löschen zu können, so muß der mögliche Wertebereich des Primärschlüssels vom Zeitpunkt der Dateigenerierung an durch die Bitlisten abgedeckt sein. In vielen Fällen hat eine solche Maßnahme wegen der Komprimierungstechnik nur geringe Auswirkungen auf die Längen der Bitlisten. Die Zuordnungstabelle nach Bild 6 würde jedoch sehr viele Leereinträge besitzen. Sinnvollerweise wird sie deshalb durch eine "indirekte Zuordnungstabelle" ersetzt, so daß nur die vorhandenen Tabelleneinträge mitgeführt werden müssen. Die Verwaltung dieser Tabelle und die Zugriffe auf bestimmte Einträge erfolgen wiederum über eine Bitliste variabler Länge.

Schematisch kann diese indirekte Zuordnung der Markierungen in den Bitlisten zu den Tabelleneinträgen folgendermaßen dargestellt werden:

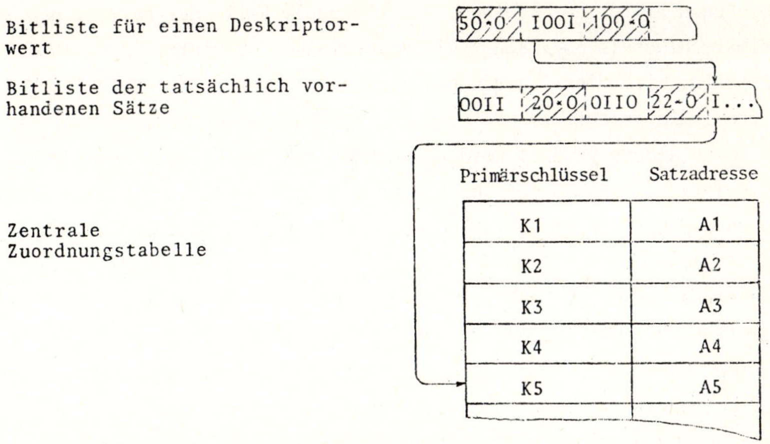

Bitliste für einen Deskriptorwert: 50·0 | 1001 | 100·0

Bitliste der tatsächlich vorhandenen Sätze: 0011 | 20·0 | 0110 | 22·0 | I...

Zentrale Zuordnungstabelle

Primärschlüssel	Satzadresse
K1	A1
K2	A2
K3	A3
K4	A4
K5	A5

Bild 7: Indirekte Zuordnung der Bitlisten

Komprimierte Nullfolgen sind in den Bitlisten schraffiert eingezeichnet. Der Zugriff zu einem Satz, der in der Bitliste eines Deskriptorwertes markiert ist, erfolgt über die Bitliste der tatsächlich vorhandenen Sätze. Aus dieser Liste wird durch Summieren der gesetzten Bits die Verschiebeadresse für den Eintrag in der zentralen Zuordnungstabelle errechnet. Nach dem Lesen des entsprechenden Tabelleneintrages ist es möglich, direkt zur physischen Position des gesuchten Satzes zuzugreifen. Soll im Falle eines numerischen Primärschlüssels der Zugriff über eine solche Zuordnungstabelle durchgeführt werden, so läßt sich die Zuordnungstabelle in Bild 7 auf einen Adreßvektor reduzieren. Aus der Bitliste der vorhandenen Sätze wird dann die Verschiebeadresse oder das Vektorelement ermittelt.

6. Tauglichkeit der Bitlisten bei der Implementierung und Konstruktion von Zugriffspfadtypen

In einem Datenbanksystem sollten folgende Typen von Zugriffspfaden realisiert werden können:

- eine geordnete Folge aller Tupeln in einer Relation
- ein sekundärer Index auf einem Nicht-Schlüssel-Bereich

- eine hierarchische Struktur, die Tupeln zweier verschiedener Relationen verbindet
- eine komplexe Netzwerkstruktur, die Tupeln zweier Relationen mit Tupeln einer dritten Relation verbindet
- beliebige Kombinationen der obigen Typen.

Zum Abschluß soll geprüft werden, welche der aufgezählten Zugriffspfadtypen durch Bitlisten implementiert und welche aus diesen dann abgeleitet werden können.
Im allgemeinen Fall kann bei einer Bitlisteninvertierung keine bestimmte Ordnungsrelation der Datensätze erzwungen werden. Die Markierungen in der Bitliste müssen nach einem vorgegebenen Kriterium erfolgen. Das können im Falle der natürlichen Zahlen der Wert des Primärschlüssels oder sonst die Reihenfolge der Eintragungen in der Zuordnungstabelle sein. Wird diese Zuordnungstabelle in einer Sortierfolge nach einem bestimmten Kriterium angelegt, so bleibt diese Folge in allen Bitlisten erhalten. Es kann jedoch keine andere gewählt werden. Deshalb läßt sich die geordnete Folge aller Tupel einer Relation selbst nicht durch eine Bitliste darstellen. Dieser Zugriffspfadtyp wird durch die Datenorganisationsform für den Primärschlüssel oder durch eine Zuordnungstabelle realisiert.
Die Bitliste selbst wurde im Hinblick auf die Invertierung von Nicht-Schlüssel-Bereichen entworfen. Bei der Implementierung dieses Zugriffspfadtyps ist sie allen anderen Verfahren beträchtlich überlegen. Dies gilt sowohl aus Speicherplatzgründen als auch für die zeitgünstige Auswertung von Fragen an eine Datenbank.
Nach dem hier beschriebenen Verfahren lassen sich Bereiche einer Relation direkt invertieren. Als Deskriptorwerte sind nicht unbedingt diskrete Attributwerte (Entity-Namen) notwendig. Es können beispielsweise auch Wertebereiche, die durch die Vergleichsoperatoren Θ ($\Theta = \{<, \leq, =, \geq, >, \neq\}$), oder durch boolesche Operatoren $\vee, \wedge, \neg$ zu bilden sind, herangezogen werden. Sind nur einfache Bereiche vorhanden, d.h. ist die zu invertierende Relation normalisiert, so sind allerdings nur die booleschen Operatoren $\vee$ und $\neg$ sinnvoll anzuwenden.
Auf diese Weise lassen sich für bestimmte Fragen oder Teilfragen direkte Zugriffspfade implementieren. Solche direkten Zugriffspfade sind auf Benutzerfragen (Queries) zugeschnitten, so daß die qualifizierten Sätze ohne zusätzliche Such- oder Vergleichsoperationen ausgewählt werden können. Ein Zugriffspfad für eine hierarchische Struktur ist ebenfalls durch eine Bitlistenimplementierung zu realisieren. Die hierarchische Beziehung muß nicht unbedingt über zwei verschiedene Relationen definiert sein, sondern sie kann auch für einen Bereich einer Relation gelten.
Charakteristikum einer hierarchischen Struktur ist die funktionale Beziehung zwischen MEMBER-Satztyp und OWNER-Satztyp [CODA] ; ein oder mehrere MEMBER-Sätze sind mit genau einem OWNER-Satz verbunden. Zur Implementierung dieses Zugriffspfadtyps läßt sich im Katalog ein Schema nach Bild 8 heranziehen. Besteht zwischen zwei Relationen oder genauer deren Schlüsselbereichen eine n:m Beziehung, so muß diese wiederum durch eine Relation explizit ausgedrückt werden, d.h., man muß ein neues Entity einführen, damit

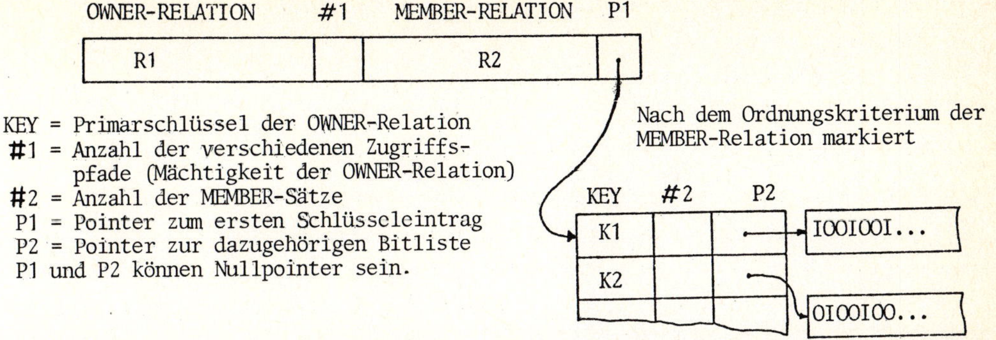

Bild 8: Schematische Darstellung der Einträge für einen hierarchischen Zugriffspfadtyp

die gesamte Information auf der Ebene der logischen Datenstruktur darstellbar ist. Dadurch wird die n:m Beziehung aufgelöst in zwei funktionale Beziehungen, wobei die neu eingeführte Relation als MEMBER der beiden ursprünglichen OWNER-Relationen zu betrachten ist. Das Problem der Zugriffspfadbildung ist damit prinzipiell auf jeweils zwei Ausprägungen vom hierarchischen Zugriffspfadtyp zurückgeführt. Somit kann der hierarchische Zugriffspfadtyp als Baustein für die Realisierung komplexer Zugriffsnetzwerke angesehen werden.

Literaturverzeichnis

[Ba74] Bachmann, C.W.: Implementation Techniques for Data Structure Sets, in: Data Base Management Systems, D.A. Jardine (ed.),North-Holland Publishing Company, 1974, oo. 147-157.

[By73] Byrom, S.T., Hardgrave, W.T.: Representation of Sets on Mass Storage Devices for Information Retrieval Systems, in: AFIPS, Proc. National Computer Conference, 1973, pp. 245-250.

[Ch74] Chamberlin, D.D., Boyce, R.F.: SEQUEL: A Structured English Query Language, in: Proc. of 1974 ACM SIGFIDET Workshop, Ann Arbor, Michigan, April 1974.

[CODA] CODASYL DATA BASE TASK GROUP, (DBTG) REPORT, April 1971, erhältlich bei IFIP Data Processing Group, Stadhouderskade, Amsterdam (IAG).

[Co70] Codd, E.F.: A relational Model of Data for Large Shared Data Banks, in: CACM, Vol. 13, No. 6, 1970, pp. 377-387.

[Hä74] Härder, T.: Implementierung von Zugriffspfaden durch Bitlisten, Forschungsbericht DV 74-2, FG Datenverwaltungssysteme, TH Darmstadt, 1974.

[Kr74] Krägeloh, K.-D., Lockemann, P.C.: Schichten von Datenmodellen und Datenbanksprachen, Sommer-Seminar 1974, GMD, Seminarunterlagen.

[Ma69] Martin, L.D.: A Model for File Structure Determination for Large On-Line Data Files, in: File Organization, Selected Papers from File 68, IAG Conference, Swets u. Zeitlinger, N.V.-Amsterdam, 1969, pp. 223-245.

[Sc72] Schröder, K.: Vergleich der Verweistechniken in Datenbanksystemen: Adreßkettung contra Indextabellen, in: Angewandte Informatik,Heft 4/1972,S.145-153.

[Se73] Senko, M.E. et al.: Data structures and accessing in data base systems, in: IBM Systems Journal, Vol. 12, 1973, No. 1, pp. 30-93.

[Wa73] Wang, C.P.: Parametrization of information system application, IBM Research Report, RJ 1199, April 11, 1973.

[We74] Wedekind, H.: On the selection of access paths in a data base system, in: Data Base Management, North-Holland Publ. Comp., 1974, S. 385-397.

F O R M A L E S P R A C H E N

KOMBINATION VON SACKGASSENFREIER TOPDOWN- UND BOTTOMUP-SYNTAXANALYSE

D. Thimm
Technische Universität Berlin

Zusammenfassung:

Die Kombination der Syntaxanalyseverfahren wird vorgenommen, um Konstruktionen einer gegebenen Grammatik, die durch eine Topdown-Syntaxanalyse nicht erkennbar sind, durch eine Bottomup-Analyse zu erkennen. Es wird ein Algorithmus angegeben, der bei Vorliegen bestimmter Bedingungen die Zerlegung einer gegebenen Grammatik in eine Pseudo-LL(k)-Grammatik (verwandt mit den LL(k)-Grammatiken) und mindestens eine SLR(k)-Grammatik automatisch durchführt. Ein syntaxorientierter PLL(k)/SLR(k)-Parser, der mit einer baumartigen Datenstruktur arbeitet, wird ebenfalls angegeben.

1. Einleitung

Unter den sackgassenfreien Syntaxanalyseverfahren haben die Methoden, die einen zu analysierenden Satz von links nach rechts durch Vorgriff um höchstens k Zeichen bearbeiten, eine besondere Bedeutung erlangt. Die beiden bekannten auf diese Methoden bezogenen Grammatikklassen sind die der LL(k)-Grammatiken (für die Topdown-Analyse) und die der LR(k)-Grammatiken (für die Bottomup-Analyse).
Neben den LL(k)-Grammatiken gibt es die von RECHENBERG /8/ angegebenen sogenannten *Pseudo-LL(k)-Grammatiken* (abgekürzt: PLL(k)-Grammatiken), die gegenüber den LL(k)-Grammatiken insbesondere den Vorteil haben, daß sie direkt linksrekursive Regeln und Alternativen einer Regel, die mit dem gleichen Symbol anfangen, enthalten können.
In den Grammatiken von Programmiersprachen gibt es aber auch Konstruktionen, die nicht durch eine PLL(k)-Analyse für beliebig großes k erkennbar sind. Insbesondere können dies Konstruktionen sein, die überhaupt nicht topdown erkannt werden können. Ist eine Grammatik mit solchen Konstruktionen LR(k), liegt es zunächst nahe, die Grammatik einer Bottomup-Analyse zu unterziehen. Bezüglich der Übersetzung ist jedoch die (sackgassenfreie) Topdown-Analyse vorteilhafter, da hier bekannt ist, welche Regel angewendet werden muß, bevor die aus der linken Seite dieser Regel ableitbaren Terminalsymbole gelesen wurden. Da außerdem die Tabellen für die PLL(k)-Analyse i.a. weniger Speicherplatz beanspruchen als die Tabellen, die z.B. zur SLR(k)-Analyse (und erst recht zur LR(k)-Analyse) notwendig sind, scheint die Kombination der PLL(k)-Analyse mit einem sackgassenfreien Bottomup-Analyseverfahren eine geeignete Syntaxanalysemethode darzustellen.
Um eine Kombination von Topdown- und Bottomup-Analyse durchführen zu können, kontruieren wir aus der gegebenen Grammatik eine Kombination von Topdown- und Bottomup-Analysetabellen. Der Prozeß vollzieht sich in folgenden Schritten:

- Zerlegung der gegebenen Grammatik in eine *Topdown-Teilgrammatik* und in eine oder mehrere *Bottomup-Teilgrammatiken*
- Konstruktion von Analysetabellen in Form *baumartiger Datenstrukturen*

- Ermittlung und Speicherung der zur Analyse erforderlichen Vorgriffsmengen

2. Automatische Zerlegung einer gegebenen Grammatik in Teilgrammatiken

Bevor wir auf das Zerlegungsverfahren eingehen, sollen die Definitionen der Grammatikklassen angegeben werden, auf die später Bezug genommen wird.
Als Topdown-Teilgrammatik wählen wir wegen der bereits genannten Vorteile die PLL(k)-Grammatiken. Die Bottomup-Teilgrammatiken sollen der Klasse der von De REMER /3/ eingeführten *Simple-LR(k)-Grammatiken* (SLR(k)-Grammatiken) angehören. Durch eine Modifikation des Verfahrens können jedoch auch andere Grammatikklassen herangezogen werden.

2.1 Im Zerlegungsalgorithmus benutzte Definitionen

Die im folgenden angegebene Definition der PLL(k)-Grammatiken weicht von der in /8/ angegebenen Definition dahingehend ab, daß die Vorschriften zur Berechnung der terminalen Start- und Nachfolgerketten modifiziert wurden. Da die *modifizierten PLL(k)-Bedingungen* die Berechnung weniger restriktiver Vorgriffsmengen gestatten, wird durch die unter Zugrundelegung dieser Bedingungen definierten PLL(k)-Grammatiken eine grössere Sprachklasse abgedeckt. Bei der Definition der PLL(k)-Grammatiken wird vorausgesetzt, daß diese in der *Topdown-Form* (TDF) dargestellt sind /8/. Die für die Definition der PLL(k)-Grammatiken benötigten Vorgriffsmengen $\underline{L}_k(\alpha)$ und $\underline{N}_k(X)$ lassen sich aus den unten angegebenen modifizierten PLL(k)-Bedingungen berechnen. Wir benutzen hierzu Hilfsmengen $\underline{L}'_k$ und $\underline{N}'_k$ und ordnen für jedes Auftreten eines Nonterminalsymbols X in einer Alternative der Grammatik dem Symbol X eine Nummer $j \geqslant 0$ zu, was durch X_j symbolisiert wird. Der Wert j=0 nimmt eine Sonderstellung ein, indem $X_0=X$ definiert wird mit der Bedeutung, daß jede Alternative der Grammatik, die Symbol X enthält, zur Berechnung der Vorgriffsmengen heranzuziehen ist. Vor Beginn der Berechnung von $\underline{L}_k(\alpha)$ oder $\underline{N}_k(X)$ wird für jedes Symbol $A \in \underline{V}_N$ definiert: $A=A_0$. Zur Darstellung der Mengen aller terminalen Ketten der Länge k, die sich aus der Verkettung der Terminalsymbole $y_1 \dots y_m$ und aller Elemente von $\underline{L}'_{k-m}(X_j)$ ergibt, wird folgende Notation verwendet: $y_1 \dots y_m || \underline{L}'_{k-m}(X_j)$. Die modifizierten PLL(k)-Bedingungen lauten:

Definition 2.1

Seien A,X,Y Nonterminalsymbole, S das Satzsymbol der Grammatik, $x_1 \dots x_m, y_1 \dots y_m$ mit $0 \leq m \leq k$ Terminalsymbole, ρ, ρ_1, ρ_2 Restalternativen, $\alpha, \alpha_1, \dots \alpha_n$ Alternativen und $\omega, \omega_1, \omega_2 \in \underline{V}^*$ beliebige Zeichenketten. Es sei ferner $\underline{L}_o(X)=\underline{L}_o(\rho)=\underline{L}_o(\alpha)=\underline{N}_o(X)=\underline{L}'_o(X_j)=\underline{L}'_o(\rho)=\underline{L}'_o(\alpha)=\underline{N}'_o(X_j)$ $=\{\varepsilon\}$ mit $j \geqslant 0$. Die Mengen $\underline{L}_k(\alpha)$ und $\underline{N}_k(X)$ sind wie folgt definiert:

Nr.	Vorschrift	Bedingung
1	$\underline{L}_k(\alpha)=x_1 \dots x_m || \underline{N}_{k-m}(X)$	$\alpha=x_1 \dots x_m$ der Regel $X \to \rho_1$
2	$\underline{L}_k(\alpha)=x_1 \dots x_m || (\underline{N}_{k-m}(X) \vee \underline{L}'_{k-m}(\rho_2))$	$\alpha=x_1 \dots x_m$ der Regel $X \to \rho_1[\rho_2]^*$
3	$\underline{L}_k(\alpha)=x_1 \dots x_m || \underline{L}'_{k-m}(X_j)$	$\alpha=x_1 \dots x_m X\omega$, j=0 für m=0, j>0 für m>0
4	$\underline{L}_k(\alpha)=x_1 \dots x_m || \underline{L}'_{k-m}(\rho)$	$\alpha=x_1 \dots x_m\{\rho\}$

Nr.	Vorschrift	Bedingung
5	$\underline{L}'_k(X_j)=\underline{L}'_k(\rho_1)$	$X \to \rho_1$ oder $X \to \rho_1[\rho_2]^*$, $j\geq 0$
6	$\underline{L}'_k(\rho)=\bigcup_{i=1}^{n}\underline{L}'_k(\alpha_i)$	$\rho=\alpha_1\|\alpha_2\|\ldots\|\alpha_n$, $\alpha_1\ldots\alpha_{n-1}\in\underline{V}^+$, $\alpha_n\in\underline{V}^*$
7	$\underline{L}'_k(\alpha)=y_1\ldots y_m\|\|\underline{N}'_{k-m}(A_j)$	$\alpha=y_1\ldots y_m$ der Regel $A \to \rho_1$, $j\geq 0$
8	$\underline{L}'_k(\alpha)=y_1\ldots y_m\|\|(\underline{N}'_{k-m}(A_j)\cup\underline{L}'_{k-m}(\rho_2))$	$\alpha=y_1\ldots y_m$ der Regel $A \to \rho_1[\rho_2]^*$, $j\geq 0$
9	$\underline{L}'_k(\alpha)=y_1\ldots y_m\|\|\underline{L}'_{k-m}(Y_1)$	$\alpha=y_1\ldots y_m Y_1\omega$, $l>0$
10	$\underline{L}'_k(\alpha)=y_1\ldots y_m\|\|\underline{L}'_{k-m}(\rho)$	$\alpha=y_1\ldots y_m\{\rho\}$
11	$\underline{N}_k(X)=\underline{N}'_k(X_j)$	$j=0$
12	$y_1\ldots y_m\|\|\underline{N}'_{k-m}(A_i)\subseteq\underline{N}'_k(X_j)$	$\alpha=\omega_1 X_j y_1\ldots y_m$, $i,j\geq 0$
13	$y_1\ldots y_m\|\|(\underline{N}'_{k-m}(A_i)\cup\underline{L}'_{k-m}(\rho_2))\subseteq\underline{N}'_k(X_j)$	$\alpha=\omega_1 X_j y_1\ldots y_m$, $i,j\geq 0$
14	$y_1\ldots y_m\|\|\underline{L}'_{k-m}(Y_1)\subseteq\underline{N}'_k(X_j)$	$\alpha=\omega_1 X_j y_1\ldots y_m Y_1\omega_2$, $j\geq 0, l>0$
15	$y_1\ldots y_m\|\|\underline{L}'_{k-m}(\rho)\subseteq\underline{N}'_k(X_j)$	$\alpha=\omega_1 X_j y_1\ldots y_m\{\rho\}$, $j\geq 0$
16	$\varepsilon\in\underline{N}'_k(S_j)$	$j=0$

Für die PLL(k)-Grammatiken gilt nun (wie in /8/) folgende Definition:

Definition 2.2

Eine (kontextfreie) Grammatik heißt PLL(k) für $k \geq 1$, wenn bei ihrer Darstellung in Topdown-Form für jede ihrer Restalternativen $\rho=\alpha_1|\alpha_2|\ldots|\alpha_n$ mit $n>0$, $\alpha_1\ldots\alpha_{n-1}\in\underline{V}^+$, $\alpha_n\in\underline{V}^*$ folgendes gilt:

1. $\underline{L}_k(\alpha_i)\cap\underline{L}_k(\alpha_j)=\emptyset$ mit $1\leq i\neq j\leq n$ und
   $\underline{L}_k(\alpha_i)\cap\underline{N}_k(X)=\emptyset$ mit $1\leq i\leq n$
   für $\rho=\rho_2$ einer Regel der Form $X \to \rho_1[\rho_2]^*$
2. $\underline{L}_k(\alpha_i)\cap\underline{L}_k(\alpha_j)=\emptyset$ mit $1\leq i\neq j\leq n$ für alle übrigen ρ.

Die SLR(k)-Grammatiken lassen sich bekanntlich auf der Grundlage von *LR(0)-Konfigurationsmengen* definieren, wobei eine LR(0)-Konfiguration für eine Regel $X \to \omega_1\omega_2$ mit $\omega_1,\omega_2\in\underline{V}^*$ einer CFG in der (nichtarithmetisierten) Form $[X \to \omega_1.\omega_2]$ dargestellt werden soll. (Bevor die Prüfung, ob eine CFG SLR(k) ist, durchgeführt werden kann, müssen die LR(0)-Konfigurationsmengen aus den Regeln der Grammatik konstruiert werden.)

Definition 2.3

Eine CFG G heißt *Simple-LR(k)-Grammatik* (abgekürzt SLR(k)-Grammatik), wenn für jede aus G konstruierte Konfigurationsmenge $\underline{S}$ folgendes gilt (s. auch /1/): Seien $[X \to \alpha.\beta]$ und $[Y \to \Gamma.\delta]$ zwei verschiedene Konfigurationen aus $\underline{S}$, so muß (in Abhängigkeit von β und δ) eine der folgenden Bedingungen erfüllt sein:

1. $\beta\neq\varepsilon$, $\delta=\varepsilon$: $\quad FOLLOW_k^G(Y)\cap EFF_k^G(\beta\ FOLLOW_{k-1}^G(X))=\emptyset$

2. $\beta=\varepsilon,\ \delta\neq\varepsilon$: $FOLLOW_k^G(X) \cap EFF_k^G(\delta FOLLOW_{k-1}^G(Y))=\emptyset$

3. $\beta=\delta=\varepsilon$: $FOLLOW_k^G(X) \cap FOLLOW_k^G(Y)=\emptyset$.

Hierbei ist

$EFF_k^G(\alpha)=\{\omega\in \underline{V}_T^{*k} \mid \exists\ \alpha \Rightarrow_r^* \omega\beta$ mit $|\omega|=k$ oder $|\omega|<k$ und $\beta=\varepsilon$,
im letzten Schritt in $\alpha\Rightarrow_r^*\omega\beta$ wird keine
Regel der Form $A \rightarrow \varepsilon$ herangezogen$\}$,

$FOLLOW_k^G(X)=\{\omega\in \underline{V}_T^{*k} \mid \exists\ S \Rightarrow_r^* \alpha X\beta$ und $\beta\Rightarrow_1^*\omega\gamma$ mit $|\omega|=k$ oder
$\beta\Rightarrow^*\omega$ mit $|\omega|<k\}$.

(Die Heranziehung der Funktion EFF gestattet die korrekte Reduktion von Regeln der Form $X \rightarrow \varepsilon$ bei der SLR(k)-Analyse.)

Eine Konfigurationsmenge mit Konfigurationen der oben angegebenen Form wird nach De REMER /3/ *inadäquat* genannt. Die Definitionen der bereits erwähnten Topdown- und Bottomup-Teilgrammatiken sind wie folgt:

Definition 2.4

Gegeben ist eine CFG $G=(\underline{V}_N,\underline{V}_T,\underline{P},S)$ in TDF.
Eine Topdown-Teilgrammatik G_T ist definiert durch $G_T=(\underline{V}_{NT},\underline{V}_{TT},\underline{P}_T,S)$. Hierbei ist $\underline{V}_{NT}\subseteq \underline{V}_N$, $\underline{V}_{TT}\subseteq \underline{V}_T$, $\underline{P}_T\subseteq \underline{P}$ mit $\underline{P}_T=\{X \rightarrow \rho_1\in\underline{P}$ oder $X \rightarrow \rho_1[\rho_2]^*\in\underline{P} \mid$ Die Regel für X ist PLL(k)$\}$

Die Topdown-Teilgrammatik ergibt sich also aus der gegebenen Grammatik in Topdown-Form dadurch, daß sie keine Regeln enthält, die die PLL(k)-Bedingungen verletzen.

Definition 2.5

Gegeben ist eine CFG $G=(\underline{V}_N,\underline{V}_T,\underline{P},S)$ (wobei jede Regel in P von der Form $X \rightarrow \omega$ mit $\omega\in\underline{V}^*$ ist). Eine Bottomup-Teilgrammatik G_B ist definiert durch $G_B=(\underline{V}_{NB},\underline{V}_{TB},\underline{P}_B,A)$. Hierbei ist $\underline{V}_{NB}\subseteq \underline{V}_N$, $\underline{V}_{TB}\subseteq \underline{V}_T$, $\underline{P}_B\subseteq \underline{P}$ mit $\underline{P}_B=\{X \rightarrow \omega\in\underline{P} \mid S \Rightarrow^* \alpha A\beta \Rightarrow^* \gamma X\delta$ in G mit $\omega,\alpha,\beta,\gamma,\delta\in\underline{V}^*\}$

In der Grammatik G_B sind also alle Regeln enthalten, die zur Ableitung einer Terminalkette aus dem Nonterminalsymbol A herangezogen werden müssen.

In dem Zerlegungsprozeß werden alle Regeln der Form $X \rightarrow \rho_1$ oder $X \rightarrow \rho_1[\rho_2]^*$, die mindestens eine PLL(k)-Verletzung enthalten, aus der gegebenen Grammatik in TDF entfernt. Danach ist die so entstandene Topdown-Teilgrammatik nicht reduziert, da sie z.B. Nonterminalsymbole enthält, die sich nicht aus S ableiten lassen. Die Regeln für diese Nonterminalsymbole werden daher aus der Topdown-Teilgrammatik entfernt.

Jedes Nonterminalsymbol A, das auf der rechten Seite einer Regel in G_T vorkommt, für das aber keine Regel in G_T existiert, soll durch eine SLR(k)-Analyse erkannt werden: Symbol A ist das Satzsymbol einer Bottomup-Teilgrammatik. Für jedes dieser Nonterminalsymbole A muß die zu der jeweiligen Teilgrammatik G_B gehörigen Regelmenge P_B (nach Def. 2.5) gefunden werden.

Damit bei der Syntaxanalyse die Erkennung des Satzsymbols einer Bottomup-Teilgrammatik eindeutig möglich ist, darf es nicht auf der rechten Seite einer Regel dieser Teilgrammatik auftreten. Ist dies der Fall, so muß die Bottomup-Teilgrammatik mit dem (bisherigen) Satzsymbol A durch eine Regel der Form $A' \rightarrow A$ *erweitert* werden. Eine erweiterte Bottomup-Teilgrammatik G_B' ist also wie folgt definiert:

Definition 2.6

Sei $G_B=(\underline{V}_{NB},\underline{V}_{TB},\underline{P}_B,A)$ eine Bottomup-Teilgrammatik. Eine *erweiterte* Bottomup-Teilgrammatik G_B' ist dann gegeben durch

$$G_B'=(\underline{V}_{NB}\cup\{A'\},\underline{V}_{TB},\underline{P}_B\cup\{A'\rightarrow A\},A') \text{ mit } A'\notin\underline{V}_N.$$

Nach Auffindung der Regelmengen für alle (ggf. erweiterten) Bottomup-Teilgrammatiken wird aus ihnen eine sog. *integrierte Kollektion* von LR(0)-Konfigurationsmengen konstruiert. Anschließend wird die integrierte Kollektion dem SLR(k)-Test gem. Def. 2.3 unterzogen. Wird der Test bestanden, so wurde eine geeignete Zerlegung gefunden. Ist die Kollektion nicht SLR(k), so läßt sie sich bezüglich der Art ihrer SLR(k)-Verletzungen einer der folgenden zwei Gruppen zuordnen:

Gruppe 1

Die SLR(k)-Verletzungen, die ausschließlich von solchen Paaren von Konfigurationen verursacht werden, bei denen die eine Konfiguration von der Form $[A'\rightarrow A.]$ und die andere von der Form $[X\rightarrow\alpha.\beta]$ mit $\beta\in(\underline{V}_{NB}\cup\underline{V}_{TB})^+$, $X\in\underline{V}_{NB}$ ist, sind folgender Art:

$$FOLLOW_k(A')\cap EFF_k(\beta FOLLOW_{k-1}(X))\neq\emptyset \text{ mit } A'\neq S',\ S \text{ ist Satzsymbol von } G.$$

SLR(k)-Konflikte dieser Art lassen sich ggf. eleminieren, indem wir jedes Nonterminalsymbol $Z\in\underline{V}_{NT}$ zum Satzsymbol einer weiteren Bottomup-Teilgrammatik erklären, für das gilt, daß auf der rechten Seite der Regel $Z\rightarrow\rho_1$ bzw. $Z\rightarrow\rho_1[\rho_2]^*$ in der Topdown-Teilgrammatik das Symbol A mindestens einmal auftritt. Sind alle auf diese Weise hinzugekommenen Bottomup-Teilgrammatiken SLR(k), so kann Symbol A im Zuge der Bottomup-Erkennung eines der Symbole Z bottomup erkannt werden. (Die Regeln $Z\rightarrow\rho_1$ bzw. $Z\rightarrow\rho_1[\rho_2]^*$ aus G_T sowie die Bottomup-Teilgrammatik mit dem Satzsymbol A' werden entfernt.)

Gruppe 2

Die SLR(k)-Verletzungen werden von solchen Paaren von Konfigurationen verursacht, bei denen die eine Konfiguration von der Form $[X\rightarrow\alpha.\beta]$ und andere von der Form $[Y\rightarrow\gamma.]$ mit $\alpha,\beta,\gamma\in(\underline{V}_{NB}\cup\underline{V}_{TB})^*$ sowie $X,Y\in\underline{V}_{NB}$ oder $X,Y\in\underline{V}_{NB}\cup\{A'\}$ (falls die Teilgrammatik erweitert wurde), wobei nicht gleichzeitig $Y=A'$ und $\beta\neq\varepsilon$ gelten soll. In diesem Fall ist eine Beseitigung der SLR(k)-Verletzung $FOLLOW_k(Y)\cap EFF_k(\beta FOLLOW_{k-1}(X))\neq\emptyset$ durch die Bottomup-Erkennung weiterer Nonterminalsymbole nicht möglich.

2.2 Algorithmus zur automatischen Zerlegung in Teilgrammatiken

Eine gegebene kontextfreie Grammatik $G=(\underline{V}_N,\underline{V}_T,\underline{P},S)$ ist - wenn möglich - in eine Topdown-Teilgrammatik G_T und in eine oder mehrere Bottomup-Teilgrammatiken G_{Bj} zu zerlegen, falls G nicht PLL(k) ist. Die Grammatik G_T soll PLL(k) und die Grammatiken G_{Bj} sollen sämtlich SLR(k) sein.

Es wird vorausgesetzt, daß die Grammatik G dem Algorithmus in zwei unterschiedlichen Darstellungsformen zur Verfügung steht:

a) in Topdown-Form

b) jede Regel ist von der Form $X \rightarrow \omega$ mit $\omega \in \underline{V}^*$

Durch Entfernung der Nicht-PLL(k)-Regeln aus der Grammatik G gemäß a) erhalten wir die PLL(k)-Grammatik G_T. Aus den Regeln der Grammatik G gemäß b) lassen sich die Bottomup-Teilgrammatiken G_{Bj} und aus diesen die integrierte Kollektion von LR(0)-Konfigurationsmengen gewinnen. (Es ist aber auch möglich, bei Vorgabe der bottomup zu erkennenden Nonterminalsymbole die LR(0)-Konfigurationsmengen der integrierten Kollektion direkt aus den Regeln von G gemäß b) zu konstruieren, d.h. ohne vorher die Regelmengen $\underline{P}_{Bj}$ explizit zu ermitteln. Die Mengen $\underline{P}_{Bj}$ ergeben sich also dynamisch während der Erzeugung der LR(0)-Konfigurationsmengen.)

Die Konfigurationsmengen werden von einem hier nicht spezifizierten Algorithmus konstruiert, welcher außerdem die Übergangsfunktion GOTO berechnet. Dieser Algorithmus ergibt sich durch eine Modifikation des in /5/ angegebenen Algorithmus (KNUTH's 2. Methode). Die Funktion GOTO wird wie folgt definiert:

Definition 2.7

Seien $\underline{S}_i$ und $\underline{S}_n$ zwei einer Bottomup-Teilgrammatik G_B zugeordnete LR(0)-Konfigurationsmengen derart, daß gilt $[Z \rightarrow \alpha.X\beta] \in \underline{S}_i$ und $[Z \rightarrow \alpha X.\beta] \in \underline{S}_n$ mit $\alpha, \beta \in (\underline{V}_{NB} \cup \underline{V}_{TB})^*$, $X \in (\underline{V}_{NB} \cup \underline{V}_{TB})$, so definieren wir die Funktion GOTO auf den Konfigurationsmengen für G_B wie folgt: $\mathrm{GOTO}(\underline{S}_i, X) = \underline{S}_n$.

Der Algorithmus zur Grammatikzerlegung läßt sich etwa wie folgt formulieren:

1. Wenn G PLL(k) ist (nach Definition 2.2), ist der Algorithmus bereits beendet. Sonst markiere jedes Nonterminalsymbol, das sich auf der linken Seite einer Regel (in TDF) befindet, die mindestens eine PLL(k)-Verletzung enthält. Die Topdown-Teilgrammatik G_T ist anfänglich mit G äquivalent.

2. Entferne alle Regeln aus G_T, deren linke Seiten markiert wurden. Enthält G_T danach Regeln, deren linke Seiten nicht aus dem Satzsymbol von G_T ableitbar sind, so entferne diese Regeln ebenfalls aus G_T.
   Erzeuge anschließend für jedes markierte Nonterminalsymbol A_i, das aus dem Satzsymbol von G_T ableitbar ist, die zugehörige Bottomup-Teilgrammatik G_{Bi} gemäß Definition 2.5. Enthält G_{Bi} eine Regel der Form $X \rightarrow \omega_1 A_i \omega_2$, wobei A_i das Satzsymbol von G_{Bi} ist, führe folgendes aus:

   2.1 Ersetze G_{Bi} durch die erweiterte Grammatik G'_{Bi} gemäß Definition 2.6.
   2.2 Ersetze in G_T das Satzsymbol A_i durch A'_i an jeder Stelle, an der es auftritt.

3. Berechne die integrierte Kollektion von LR(0)-Konfigurationsmengen sowie die Funktion GOTO (Definition 2.7) aus den Regeln der Bottomup-Teilgrammatiken. Hierzu wird jedem Satzsymbol einer Bottomup-Teilgrammatik eine separate anfängliche Basiskonfigurationsmenge zugeordnet, die aus den Regeln für dieses Satzsymbol konstruiert wird.
   Prüfe anschließend für jede inadäquate Konfigurationsmenge, ob die in Definition

2.3 angegebenen SLR(k)-Bedingungen erfüllt sind. Hierbei sind drei Fälle zu unterscheiden:

3.1 Die Konfigurationsmenge enthält keine SLR(k)-Verletzungen.

3.2 Die Konfigurationsmenge enthält nur SLR(k)-Verletzungen gemäß Gruppe 1. Dann markiere jedes Nonterminalsymbol aus G_T, für das gilt:
$\exists$ eine Regel $X \rightarrow \rho_1 \in \underline{P}_T$ oder $X \rightarrow \rho_1 [\rho_2]^* \in \underline{P}_T$ mit mindestens einer Alternative $\alpha = \omega_1 A' \omega_2$ mit $\omega_1, \omega_2 \in (\underline{V}_{NT} \cup \underline{V}_{TT})^*$. (Die neu markierten Nonterminalsymbole sind ebenfalls bottomup zu erkennen.)

3.3 Die Konfigurationsmenge enthält mindestens eine SLR(k)-Verletzung gemäß Gruppe 2.

4. Testauswertung:

Sind alle Konfigurationsmengen SLR(k), ist der Algorithmus erfolgreich beendet. (Es wurde eine geeignete Zerlegung von G in eine Topdown- und mindestens eine Bottomup-Teilgrammatik gefunden, die für die SLR(k)-Parsertabellen benötigten LR(0)-Konfigurationsmengen konstruiert und alle benötigten Vorgriffsmengen berechnet.)
Gibt es nur SLR(k)-Verletzungen gemäß 3.2, so gehe zurück nach Schritt 2. (Erzeuge neue Zerlegung von G.)
Gibt es mindestens eine SLR(k)-Verletzung gemäß 3.3, so ist der Algorithmus erfolglos beendet. (Es wurde keine geeignete Zerlegung gefunden.)

Für den Fall, daß nach Ausführung des Algorithmus keine Zerlegung von G in eine PLL(k)- und mindestens eine SLR(k)-Grammatik gefunden wurde, muß entweder der Wert für k erhöht oder die Grammatik G geeignet transformiert werden. Mit der transformierten Grammatik kann anschließend die Grammatikzerlegung durch erneute Ausführung des Algorithmus wiederholt werden.

3. Baumartige Datenstruktur zur Syntaxanalyse von Bottomup-Teilgrammatiken

Wurde in dem oben angegebenen Algorithmus eine Zerlegung der gegebenen Grammatik in eine PLL(k)- und mindestens eine SLR(k)-Teilgrammatik gefunden, so können die dort berechneten LR(0)-Konfigurationsmengen sowie die Funktion GOTO in eine baumartige Datenstruktur transformiert werden, die von einem syntaxgesteuerten Analysealgorithmus benutzt werden kann. Ein Element dieser Datenstruktur ist das (ebenfalls in /13/ benutzte) Tripel VAL,LP,RP, das entweder eine Konfiguration der Form $[A \rightarrow \omega.]$ oder die Funktion GOTO($\underline{S}_i$,X) repräsentiert:

1. Repräsentation von $[A \rightarrow \omega.]$ (*Reduzierkomponente*):

VAL: Negativer Wert der laufenden Nummer von A in einer Symbolliste.

LP: Zeiger auf ein Baumelement, das derselben Konfigurationsmenge zugeordnet ist wie das gerade betrachtete Element. Der Linkszeiger des letzten Baumelements einer Konfigurationsmenge ist 0.

RP: Anzahl der bei der Reduktion zu A auszukellernden Elemente, also $|\omega|$.

2. Repräsentation von $GOTO(S_i,X)=S_n$ (*Lesekomponente*):

VAL: Wert von X, wobei $X \in (V_{NB} \cup V_{TB})$ das Symbol ist, durch das der Übergang von S_i nach S_n veranlaßt wird, nachdem X gelesen worden ist.

LP: wie unter 1.

RP: Zeiger auf das erste der Konfigurationsmenge S_n zugeordnete Baumelement.

Ferner führen wir noch eine sog. *Startkomponente* ein:

VAL: Nummer des Satzsymbols der entsprechenden Bottomup-Teilgrammatik.
LP: Der Wert des Linkszeigers der Startkomponente ist stets 0.
RP: Zeiger auf das erste der anfänglichen Konfigurationsmenge der betreffenden Bottomup-Teilgrammatik zugeordnete Baumelement.

Auf die Angabe eines Algorithmus zur Erzeugung der baumartigen Datenstruktur für die SLR(k)-Analyse muß hier verzichtet werden. Stattdessen wollen wir die Zerlegung einer gegebenen Grammatik G und die anschließende Transformation der Teilgrammatiken in die zur Syntaxanalyse benötigten Datenstruktur an einer Beispielgrammatik demonstrieren (Die Topdown-Teilgrammatik wird auf die in /8/ angegebene Weise gespeichert.):

Gegeben sei eine CFG G mit

$P=\{S \to cAe,\ S \to Bf,\ A \to Ba,\ A \to a,\ B \to Ab,\ B \to a\}$, wobei die Regeln für A und B nicht PLL(1) sind. Zur Bottomup-Erkennung von A und B lassen sich aus G folgende erweiterte Bottomup-Teilgrammatiken ableiten: $G'_{B_1}=(V'_{NB_1},V_{TB_1},P'_{B_1},A')$, $G'_{B_2}=(V'_{NB_2},V_{TB_2},P'_{B_2},B')$ mit

$P'_{B_1}=\{A' \to A, A \to Ba, A \to a, B \to Ab, B \to a\}$, $V'_{NB_1}=\{A',A,B\}$, $V_{TB_1}=\{a,b\}$

$P'_{B_2}=\{B' \to B, B \to Ab, B \to a, A \to Ba, A \to a\}$, $V'_{NB_2}=\{B',A,B\}$, $V_{TB_2}=\{a,b\}=V_{TB_1}$

Die anfänglichen Basiskonfigurationsmengen für G'_{B_1} und G'_{B_2} zur Konstruktion der integrierten Kollektion von Konfigurationsmengen sind:

$S_1=[\,A' \to .A\,]$ und $S_2=[\,B' \to .B\,]$.

Nach Erzeugung der integrierten Kollektion (sie ist SLR(1)) konstruieren wir aus ihr und der Funktion GOTO die im untenstehenden Bild mit Bottomup-Struktur bezeichnete baumartige Datenstruktur:

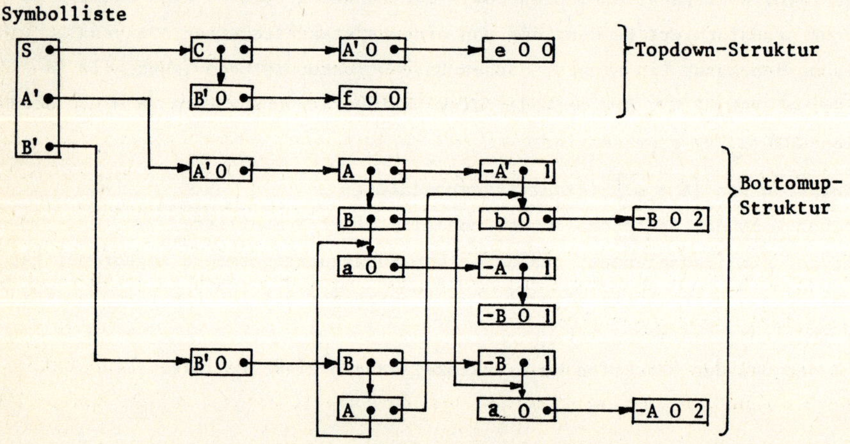

Die Verwendung dieser Datenstruktur hat folgende Vorzüge:

1. Topdown- und Bottomup-Analyse verwenden die gleiche Art von Baumelementen. Hierdurch sind Optimierungen relativ günstig durchführbar (z.B. können während der Phase der Bottomup-Analyse Nonterminalsymbole bei Erfülltsein bestimmter Bedingungen topdown erkannt werden).
2. Konfigurationen der Form $[X \rightarrow \omega.]$, die in mehreren Konfigurationsmengen enthalten sind, können gegebenenfalls durch nur ein Baumelement repräsentiert werden.

Die Berechnung der Vorgriffsmengen gemäß Def. 2.1 für die PLL(k)-Grammatiken läßt sich durch rekursives Durchwandern der Topdown-Baumstruktur durchführen /8/. Die für den SLR(k)-Test benötigten Vorgriffsmengen lassen sich nach den in /1/ angegebenen Methoden berechnen. Es ist aber auch möglich, die Vorgriffsmengen für den SLR(k)-Test rekursiv zu definieren (ähnlich wie in Def. 2.1) und diese Vorgriffsmengen durch rekursives Durchwandern der Bottomup-Baumstruktur zu berechnen. Auf nähere Einzelheiten kann hier jedoch nicht eingegangen werden.

4. Algorithmus zur Syntaxanalyse einer Kombination von PLL(k)- und SLR(k)-Grammatik

Nach Konstruktion der Topdown- und Bottomup-Datenstrukturen und Berechnung der Vorgriffsmengen $\underline{L}_k$ und $FOLLOW_k$ aus einer gegebenen CFG G können mit dem unten angegebenen rekursiven Algorithmus PARSE(loc) Zeichenketten ω daraufhin analysiert werden, ob $\omega \in L(G)$ ist. Der Parameter loc zeigt entweder auf den Anfang der rechten Seite der Regel eines topdown zu erkennenden Nonterminalsymbols oder auf die dem bottomup zu erkennenden Nonterminalsymbol zugeordnete Startkomponente der Bottomup-Datenstruktur.

Der Algorithmus läßt sich in folgender Weise formulieren:
Gegeben ist eine Topdown-Teilgrammatik in der in /8/ spezifizierten baumartigen Datenstruktur und eine aus den Bottomup-Teilgrammatiken konstruierte Datenstruktur gemäß Abschnitt 3. Die Anzahl der Nonterminalsymbole ist n und die der Terminalsymbole ist t. Eine Symbolliste ANF(1:n) hat folgende Funktionen:
ANF(j) zeigt entweder auf den Anfang der rechten Seite der Regel für das Nonterminalsymbol mit der laufenden Nummer j in der Topdown-Baumstruktur, auf die dem bottomup zu erkennenden Nonterminalsymbol j zugeordnete Startkomponente oder ANF(j) ist 0.
Die Zeichenkette $\omega = z_1 z_2 \ldots z_m$ mit $z_i \in \underline{V}_T$, $1 \leq i \leq m$ stellt den zu analysierenden Satz dar, wobei die globale Variable i der Index des ersten noch nicht bearbeiteten Zeichens der Kette ist (anfänglich gilt also i=1). Wir benutzen ferner die globalen binären Variablen w und td, wobei w den Erfolg (w=1) oder Mißerfolg (w=0) der Analyse angibt und td entscheidet, welche Analyseart durchzuführen ist (td=1: Topdown-Analyse, td=0: Bottomup-Analyse). Eine Variable s dient als Zwischenspeicher der Nummern aller während der Bottomup-Analyse zu erkennenden Symbole.

Von einem übergeordneten Programm wird der Algorithmus PARSE mit den Anfangswerten loc, i, td $\leftarrow$ 1 aufgerufen. Ist nach seiner Ausführung w=1, so ist $\omega \in L(G)$, sonst nicht.

PARSE(loc)

1. Initialisiere locl mit loc (locl ist der Startindex der zu bearbeitenden Alternative). Wenn td=0 ist, initialisiere s mit VAL(loc). (VAL(loc) ist in diesem Fall die Nummer des zu erkennenden Satzsymbols einer Bottomup-Teilgrammatik.)

2. Erkenne ein Nonterminalsymbol. Solange locl>0 ist, führe folgendes aus:

2.1 Setze x ← VAL(locl) (td=1: x ist Startsymbol der laufenden Alternative, td=0: x ist positiver oder negativer Wert der Nummer des bottomup zu erkennenden Symbols.)

2.2 Topdown-Analyse durchführen? Wenn td=1, führe einen der folgenden beiden Schritte aus:

2.2.1 Terminal. Wenn x>n, prüfe, ob z_i gleich dem Terminalsymbol x-n ist. Wenn ja, erhöhe i um 1 (lies nächstes Zeichen) und setze w ← 1. Wenn nein, setze w ← 0.

2.2.2 Übrige Fälle. Wenn 0≤x≤n ist, prüfe, ob gilt: $z_i \ldots z_{i+k-1} \in L_k(\alpha)$ (α bezeichnet die aktuelle Alternative). Wenn ja, sind zwei Fälle zu unterscheiden:

2.2.2.1 Nonterminal. Wenn x>0 ist, führe folgendes aus: Wenn VAL(ANF(x))=x, setze td=0. (x soll bottomup erkannt werden.) Führe PARSE(ANF(x)) aus (erkenne x). Wenn anschließend w=0 ist, ist der Algorithmus beendet (Mißerfolg).

2.2.2.2 ε. Wenn x=0 ist, setze w ← 1 (eine leere Komponente wird immer erkannt).

Wenn nein, setze w ← 0 (es ist nicht die richtige Alternative).

2.3 Bottomup-Analyse durchführen? Wenn td=0 ist, führe einen der folgenden beiden Schritte aus:

2.3.1 Lesekomponente. Wenn x>0, prüfe, ob x=s ist. (Ist Komponente gleich dem zu erkennenden Symbol?) Wenn ja, führe folgendes aus: kellere Komponentennummer locl ein, für x>n erhöhe i um 1 (wenn x eine Terminalkomponente ist, lies nächstes Eingangszeichen), setze s ← z_i (als nächste Komponente ist möglicherweise eine Terminalkomponente mit dem Wert z_i zu lesen) und setze w ← 1 (die Komponente wurde erkannt). Wenn nein, setze w ← 0 (es war nicht die richtige Alternative).

2.3.2 Reduzierkomponente. Wenn x<0 ist, prüfe, ob gilt: $z_i \ldots z_{i+k-1} \in \mathrm{FOLLOW}_k(X)$, wobei Symbol X die Nummer -x hat. Wenn ja, führe folgendes aus:

2.3.2.1 Kellere RP(locl) Komponentennummern aus und setze w ← 1 (Reduktion ausgeführt). Wenn x=-VAL(loc), setze td ← 1 und der Algorithmus ist beendet (Satzsymbol VAL(loc) der Bottomup-Teilgrammatik erkannt), sonst setze s ← -x (als nächste Komponente ist die Nonterminalkomponente mit dem Wert -x zu lesen).

2.3.2.2 Setze locl auf den Wert des obersten Kellerelements. (Setze Analyse bei Komponente locl fort.)

Wenn nein, setze w ← 0.

2.4 Analyse bei nächster Komponente oder Alternative fortsetzen. Wenn w=1 ist, setze locl ← RP(locl), sonst setze locl ← LP(locl) (bei erfolgreicher Erkennung der Komponente locl versuche die nächste Komponente, bei Mißerfolg die nächste Alternative zu erkennen).

3. Gegebenenfalls Umschaltung auf Topdown-Analyse und Ende. Wenn td=0 ist, setze td ← 1 (Satzsymbol der Bottomup-Teilgrammatik wurde nicht erkannt). Wenn w=1 ist, wurde das mit loc beginnende Nonterminalsymbol topdown erkannt, sonst nicht.

5. Abschließende Bemerkungen

Bei Anwendung des beschriebenen Zerlegungsverfahrens auf Grammatiken von Programmiersprachen ergeben sich in vielen Fällen wenige, dafür jedoch große Bottomup-Teilgrammatiken, was zu einer entsprechend großen integrierten Kollektion von LR(0)-Konfigurationsmengen führt. Dies liegt neben dem strukturellen Aufbau der Grammatiken daran, daß die Wahrscheinlichkeit des Auftretens einer PLL(k)-Verletzung in einer Regel mit der Größe der mit ihren Alternativen assoziierten Vorgriffsmengen ansteigt. Zur Ableitung eines Nonterminalsymbols, dem eine große Menge von terminalen Startketten zugeordnet ist, müssen im allgemeinen aber viele Regeln herangezogen werden, d.h. es entstehen große Bottomup-Teilgrammatiken.

Ein weiterer Grund dafür, daß kleine Bottomup-Teilgrammatiken seltener sind, ist der, daß topdown nicht erkennbare Nonterminalsymbole meist nicht aus dem Satzsymbol der Topdown-Teilgrammatik ableitbar sind, wenn zur Ableitung dieser Nonterminalsymbole in Terminalketten nur wenige Regeln benutzt werden müssen. Diese Nonterminalsymbole werden dann im Zuge der Bottomup-Erkennung anderer Nonterminalsymbole automatisch bottomup erkannt.

Oftmals können nun während der Phase der Bottomup-Analyse einige Nonterminalsymbole topdown erkannt werden, so daß sich dadurch die Anzahl der Konfigurationsmengen gegebenenfalls stark reduzieren läßt, insbesondere dann, wenn zur Erkennung dieser Nonterminalsymbole sehr viele Regeln benutzt werden müssen. Außerdem können dadurch die Vorteile der Topdown-Analyse bezüglich der Fehlererkennung und Übersetzung für einen größeren Teil des zu analysierenden Satzes ausgenutzt werden.

Literatur

/1/ AHO,ULLMAN: The Theory of Parsing, Translation and Compiling, Vol.1, Parsing, Vol.2, Compiling, Prentice-Hall, Englewood Cliffs, N.J., 1972.

/2/ COHEN, GOTLIEB: A list structure form of grammars for Syntactic Analysis, Computing Surveys 2(1970), 1, 65-82.

/3/ DE REMER: Practical Translators for LR(k) Languages, Project MAC Report MAC TR-65, MIT, Cambridge, Mass., 1969.

/4/ GRIFFITHS, PETRICK: Top-Down versus Bottom-Up Analysis, Information Processing 68, North-Holland Publishing Comp., Amsterdam (1969)

/5/ KNUTH: On the Translation of Languages from Left to Right, Information and Control 8, 6(1965), 607-639.

/6/ KNUTH: Top-Down Syntax Analysis, Acta Informatica 1, 2(1971), 97-110.

/7/ KORENJAK: A Practical Method for Constructing LR(k) Processors, Comm. ACM 12, 11(1969), 613-623.

/8/ RECHENBERG: Sackgassenfreie Syntaxanalyse, Elektronische Rechenanlagen, 15(1973), 3, 119-125, 170-176.

GENERIERUNG KONTEXTSENSITIVER SPRACHEN DURCH HYPERBESCHRÄNKTE ZWEISCHICHTIGE GRAMMATIKEN MIT EINEM METAZEICHEN

von

Harry Feldmann

Universität Hamburg

Computing Reviews Category: 5.23

Key words and phrases:

Two-level grammar, nonhypercontracting, hyperbounded, Turing-Generator, noncontracting, Automaton, linear bounded, language, context sensitive.

Summary:

It is shown that every context-sensitive language can be generated by a hyperbounded two-level grammar with only one metanotion. Two-level grammars (and such with only one metanotion) were introduced by A.van Wijngaarden [1,5] . "Hyperbounded two-level grammar"s were defined by J. L. Baker [3] who denoted them "context-sensitive Van Wijngaarden grammar"s.

Zusammenfassung:

Es wird gezeigt, daß jede kontextsensitive Sprache generiert werden kann durch eine hyperbeschränkte zweischichtige Grammatik mit nur einem Metazeichen. Zweischichtige Grammatiken (und solche mit nur einem Metazeichen) wurden eingeführt von A.van Wijngaarden [1,5]. "Hyperbeschränkte zweischichtige Grammatiken" wurden eingeführt von J. L. Baker [3] unter der Bezeichnung "context-sensitive Van Wijngaarden grammar"s.

0) Einleitung

Da die klassischen Chomsky-Grammatiken im kontextfreien Fall gut, im nicht-kontextfreien Fall aber kaum praktisch anwendbar sind, konstruierte A.van Wijngaarden [1] aus zwei Schichten kontextfreier Grammatiken "zweischichtige Grammatiken", die gerade im nicht-kontextfreien Fall gut anwendbar sind.

Mit der zweischichtigen Grammatik für die Programmiersprache Revised-ALGOL 68 [7] werden z. B. nicht-kontextfreie Spracheigenschaften wie "Zusammenhang von Vereinbarung und Aufruf" (definition-application) adäquat dargestellt (siehe auch [4]).

M. Sintzoff [2] und J. L. Baker [3] ordneten die zweischichtigen Grammatiken in die Chomsky-Hierarchie ein, und A. van Wijngaarden [5] beantwortete die Zusatzfrage, wieviele Metazeichen der zweischichtigen Grammatik zur Generierung von Typ 0-Sprachen höchstens erforderlich sind: "One (metanotion) is enough".

Satz 3 beantwortet die entsprechende Zusatzfrage für hyperbeschränkte zweischichtige Grammatiken und Generierung von Typ 1-Sprachen: "Ein Metazeichen genügt".

Eine Übersicht zur Chomsky-Typisierung zweischichtiger Grammatiken, auch solcher mit nur einem Metazeichen, gibt die Zusammenfassung 5.

Einige Grundbegriffe wie die Definition zweischichtiger Grammatiken [1,2,3,7] (ausführlich in [6]), die Definition der Chomsky-Sprachklassen und insbesondere die Äquivalenz kontextsensitiver Chomsky-Grammatiken mit linear beschränkten Automaten (etwa mit Wortbegrenzer) müssen der Kürze halber als bekannt vorausgesetzt werden.

Um bei der Simulierung linear beschränkter Automaten durch hyperbeschränkte zweischichtige Grammatiken mit nur einem Metazeichen in Satz 3 nicht invers vorgehen zu müssen, werden an Stelle linear beschränkter Automaten mit Wortbegrenzer, d.h. nichtexpandierender Turing-Akzeptoren mit Wortbegrenzer, von vornherein die invers arbeitenden nichtkontrahierenden Turing-Generatoren mit Wortbegrenzer (siehe Definition 2) betrachtet.

Die Typisierung zweischichtiger Grammatiken kann entweder nach der von ihr generierten Sprache (strict language) L, "der Menge aller darstellbaren Symbolworte, die nach den Regeln (entstanden aus Hyper- und Metaregeln) aus der Startvokabel herleitbar sind", oder nach der von ihr generierten Darstellungssprache (representation language) L', "der Menge aller dargestellten Symbolworte, die nach den Regeln (entstanden aus Hyper- und Metaregeln) aus der Startvokabel herleitbar sind", erfolgen (ausführlich in [6]).

In beiden Fällen ist eine Darstellung(stabelle) D erforderlich; für die Sprache L allerdings nur die linke Tabellenseite von D mit der Auflistung aller darstellbaren Symbolvokabeln.

Während J. L. Baker [3]auch nichtbijektive Darstellungen D betrachtet und damit auch Sprachen L und L' von i.a. verschiedenem Chomsky-Typ, setzen wir von vornherein D bijektiv voraus. Ohne Änderung der Sprache L' kann jede nichtbijektive Darstellung D, z. B. D(a1 symb) = D (a2 symb) = A, durch Hinzunahme weiterer Hyperregeln, hier al:a symb. a2:a symb. , und Austausch von Darstellungen, hier D(al symb) = D(a2 symb) = A gegen D(a symb) = A , in eine bijektive Darstellung überführt werden.

1) Definition (hyperbeschränkte zweischichtige Grammatik):

Eine zweischichtige Grammatik

G=(Metazeichmg, Zeichmg, Startvok, Metaregmg, Hyperregmg, Darst)
=(Xm , X , S , Rm , Rh , D)

heißt (nach unten) hyperbeschränkt (nichthyperkontrahierend) ("context-sensitive" Baker [3]) genau dann, wenn

für alle vh:wh. aus Rh gilt:

$|vh| \leq |Ke(wh)|$ ^

für alle nichtleeren xm aus Xm gilt:

$|vh|[xm] \leq |Ke(wh)|[xm]$ ^

für alle auchleeren xm aus Xm gilt:

$|vh|[xm] = |Ke(wh)|[xm]$

" Jede Hyperregel aus Rh hat links
nicht mehr Hyperzeichen xh als rechts
und von jedem nichtleeren Metazeichen xm
links nicht mehr als rechts
und von jedem auchleeren Metazeichen xm
links genau so viel wie rechts" .

Dabei gelten die folgenden Bezeichnungen:
Hyperwortmenge $Wh=Vh^*(Ko\ Vh^*)^*$, Hypervokabelmenge $Vh=(X+ Xm)^*$, Kommamenge Ko={ , } und Kommaelimination Ke.

Ein Metazeichen xm aus Xm heißt "auchleer", wenn aus ihm mit den Metaregeln aus Rm das leere Wort produziert werden kann (siehe z.B. WORTER in Satz 3), und sonst "nichtleer" (entscheidbar, da die Metaregeln kontextfrei sind).

| Ke(wh)| gibt die Anzahl aller Hyperzeichen xh aus Xh in Ke(wh) aus Xh^* an.

| Ke(wh)|[xm] gibt die Anzahl (Häufigkeit) eines bestimmten Metazeichens xm aus Xm in Ke(wh) aus (X+ Xm) an.

2) Definition (nichtkontrahierender Turing-Generator):

Ein i. a. nichtdeterministischer Turing-Generator T kann ohne Beschränkung der Allgemeinheit definiert werden als

T=(Zustmg Z , Zeichmg {# }+ X, Anfzust, Haltzust, Leerz, Progr)
=({!,-1,···,m},{#,(0),···, (n)},-1 bzw 1, ! , # , P)

mit natürlichen Zahlen m,n aus {1,2,3,···} .

Dabei wird das Turing-Programm P als Tabelle von Tripeln (q)vs bzw. (q)v! aus Folgezeichen (q) , Verschiebung v=L,M,R der Arbeitsstelle um eine Stelle nach links L bzw. nach rechts R bzw. keine Verschiebung (Mitte) M und Folgezustand s in Abhängigkeit vom Zustand r und vom Zeichen (p) bzw. # notiert.

Zur Abkürzung wird vereinbart, daß (q) entfällt, falls p=q, daß s entfällt, falls r=s, und daß v entfällt, falls v=M (p,q aus 0 bis n und r,s aus -1 bis m) .

P	#	(0)	(1)	···	(n)	
-1	{ ! / 1 }					
0	R!	L	L	···	L	
1	(0)	beliebige Tripel				
·	·	(q)vs bzw. (q)M0				
·	·	nichtdeterministisch				← P'
·	·	q aus 0 bis n				
m	(0)	s aus 1 bis m				

In Klammern { } nichtdeterministische Vielfachheiten.

Je nach Wahl des Anfangszustands -1 bzw. 1 für T ist das leere Wort in der von T generierten Sprache enthalten bzw. nicht enthalten.

T besteht aus einem "lokalen Turing-Generator"

T'=(Zustmg Z', Zeichmg{(0)}+ X', Anfzust, Haltzust, Leerz, Progr)
=({0,···,m}, {(0),···,(n)} , 1 , 0 , (0) , P')

mit "lokalem Leerzeichen" (0), "lokalem Haltzustand" 0 und frei programmierbarem Programm P' (Teil der Tabelle von P zwischen Zustand 1 bis m und Zeichen (0) bis (n)) sowie einem festen Programmteil, in dem das "globale" Leerzeichen # auf dem Teil des Bandes, den die Maschine erreicht, "automatisch" durch das "lokale Leerzeichen" (0) ersetzt wird (Wortexpansion) und die Arbeitsstelle nach dem Halt 0 von T' auf das erste Zeichen rechts vom linken Wortbegrenzer # gesetzt wird.

Damit ist jedes von T generierte Wort w aus X* eindeutig bestimmt (insbesondere ist die Wortlänge von w berechenbar).

Da das Programm P keine Wortbegrenzer # schreiben, d.h. keine Wortkontraktion ausführen kann, ist T ein nichtkontrahierender Turing-Generator.

3) Satz (Nichtkontrh. Generat.als nichthyperkontrh.zweisch. Gramm.)

" Jeder nichtkontrahierende Turing-Generator ist durch eine nichthyperkontrahierende zweischichtige Grammatik mit nur einem Metazeichen simulierbar "

Beweis : Gegeben ist ein i.a. nichtdeterministischer nichtkontrahierender Turing-Generator

T=(Zustmg Z , Zeichmg{#}+ X, Anfzust, Haltzust, Leerz, Progr)
=({!,-1,···,m},{#,(0),···,(n)},-1 bzw 1, ! , # , P)

mit natürlichen Zahlen m,n aus {1,2,3,···} .

Dabei sei das Turingprogramm P und der Teil P' von der in Definition 2 angegebenen Form.

Simuliert wird T durch die im folgenden konstruierte hyperbeschränkte (nichthyperkontrahierende) zweischichtige Grammatik mit nur einem Metazeichen WORTER

G=(Metazeichmg, Zeichmg, Startvok, Metaregmg, Hyperregmg, Darst)
=({ WORTER } , Xg , (/) bzw (0/1) , Rm , Rh , D) .

Zeichenmenge : Xg={0|···|max(m,n)|a|···|z|(|)|/ }
(als Zahl)

Der " Wortbegrenzer" # kommt in der zweischichtigen Grammatik nicht vor. Den linken Wortbegrenzer simuliert die Hyperregel 2 und den rechten Wortbegrenzer die Hyperregel 5 .

Metaregelmenge_Rm :

WORTER ::;(0);···;···;(n);(0) WORTER ;···;(n) WORTER . (n als Zahl)

Hyperregelmenge_Rh:

```
0            (/)           :      leere Wort symb;(0/1).
```

Zu jedem im Programm P' vorhandenen Quintupel r(p)(q)vs bzw. r(p)(q) MO (p,q aus 0 bis n und r,s aus 1 bis m) werden endlich viele Hyperregeln wie folgt eingeführt:

```
1.0 WORTER1 (0)(p/r) WORTER2 : WORTER1 (0/s)(q) WORTER2 . )
1.1              .                          .             |
1.2              .                          .             |
1..              .                          .             }r(p)(q)Ls
1.n WORTER1 (n)(p/r) WORTER2 : WORTER1 (n/s)(q) WORTER2 . |
                                                          |
2              (p/r) WORTER  :         (0/s)(q) WORTER  . )

3   WORTER1  (p/r)   WORTER2 : WORTER1  (q/s)   WORTER2 . }r(p)(q)Ms

4.0 WORTER1 (p/r)(0) WORTER2 : WORTER1 (q)(0/s) WORTER2 . )
4.1                 .                         .           |
4.2                 .                         .           |
4..                 .                         .           }r(p)(q)Rs
4.n WORTER1 (p/r)(n) WORTER2 : WORTER1 (q)(n/s) WORTER2 . |
                                                          |
5   WORTER  (p/r)            : WORTER  (q)(0/s)         . )

6   WORTER1 (p/r)    WORTER2 : WORTER1 (q)   WORTER2 /0 . }r(p)(q)MO
```

Je nach Wahl des Anfangszustands -1 bzw. 1 von T wird (/) bzw. (0/1) als Startvokabel von G gewählt und je nachdem ist das "leere wort symb" in der von G generierten Sprache enthalten oder nicht enthalten.

Im "lokalen Haltzustand" 0 wird ein "WORTER/0" generiert, das keinen ("Situations") Teil "(p/r)" mehr enthält und daher auch nicht mit den (dem Turingprogramm P' entsprechenden) Hyperregeln 0-6 weiter abgeleitet werden kann.

symb - Einsetzung in WORTER (spezielle Hyperregeln):

7.0 WORTER (0)/0: WORTER , 0 symb.
7.1 . .
7.2 . .
7.. . .
7.n WORTER (n)/0: WORTER , n symb.

8.0 WORTER (0) : WORTER , 0 symb.
8.1 . .
8.2 . .
8.. . .
8.n WORTER (n) : WORTER , n symb.

Darstellung D :

0 symb ... n symb (n als Zahl)   (0) ... (n)   (n als Zahl)
leere wort symb   ^

Die folgende Ablauf - Übersicht erläutert die Simulation des nicht-kontrahierenden Turing-Generators T durch die hyperbeschränkte zweischichtige Grammatik G :

Arbeitsweise Turing- Gener. T	Arbeitsweise zweisch. Grammatik G
Anfangssituation0: ···#··· ↑ -1 (falls -1 Anfzust)	:(/).
d.h. T beginnt im Zustand -1 irgendwo auf dem leeren Band, geht dann entweder in den Haltzustand ! über und generiert damit das leere Wort, ···#··· ↑ !	:leere wort symb. Darstellung: ∧
oder geht in den Zustand 1 über.	
Anfangssituation1: ···#··· ↑ 1	:(/).
d.h. T beginnt im Zustand 1 irgendwo auf dem leeren Band.	
Anfangssituation2: ···#(O)#··· ↑ 1	:(O/1).
d.h. T bleibt im Zustand 1 und setzt (O) für # .	
Situation: ···#w1(p)w2#··· ↑	: WORTER1 (p/r) WORTER2 .
w1,w2 aus X*, p aus O bis n , r aus 1 bis m	
Haltsituation: ···#$\overline{w}$#··· ↑ O (falls vorhanden)	: WORTER /O .
d.h.falls T' im Haltzustand O irgendwo auf $\overline{w}$ hält, dann generiert T' das Wort $\overline{w}$ aus X+ ; z. B. $\overline{w}$ = (1)(1)(2)(2)(3)(3) .	z. B.:(1)(1)(2)(2)(3)(3)/O.
Anschließend läuft T nach links und hält im Haltzustand ! auf dem ersten Zeichen rechts vom linken Wortbegrenzer # (und generiert ebenfalls das Wort $\overline{w}$ aus X+).	Darstellung: z. B. (1)(1)(2)(2)(3)(3)

q.e.d.

4) Beispiel (a hoch n b hoch n c hoch n ,n nichtneg.ganz)

Der nichtkontrahierende Turing- Generator T sei gegeben durch:

P'	0 (0)	a (1)	b (2)	c (3)	B (4)	
1	(4)				{ R / 2 }	(B hoch n)
2	(1) 3	L	L		L	(links ein a)
3	(3) 0	R	R	R	(2) 4	(rechts statt B ein b)
4	(3) 5		R	R	R	(rechts ein c)
5		0	L	L	(2) 2	(links statt B ein b)

In Klammern { } nichtdeterministische Vielfachheiten.

-1 sei Anfangszustand von T, d.h. das leere Wort ist in der von T generierten Sprache enthalten.

Die Simulation von T durch die nach Satz 3 gegebene nichthyperkontrahierende zweischichtige Grammatik G wird an einer speziellen Produktion (entspricht a hoch 2 b hoch 2 c hoch 2) erläutert:

	:			(/)				.
⊢0--	:			(0/1)				.
⊢35-	:			(4)	(4/2)			.
⊢12-	:		(1/3)	(4)	(4)			.
⊢34-	:		(1)	(2/4)	(4)			.
⊢45-	:		(1)	(2)	(4)	(3/5)		.
⊢13-	:		(1)	(2)	(2/2)	(3)		.
⊢12-	:	(1/3)	(1)	(2)	(2)	(3)		.
⊢45-	:	(1)	(1)	(2)	(2)	(3)	(3/0)	.
⊢678	:	,1 symb	,1 symb	,2 symb	,2 symb	,3 symb	,3 symb	.
⊢-D-	:	(1)	(1)	(2)	(2)	(3)	(3)	

Um nicht den Eindruck entstehen zu lassen, daß zweischichtige Grammatiken in der Anwendung so unhandlich seien wie Turing-Generatoren, geben wir noch ohne Simulation direkt eine kürzere hyperbeschränkte zweischichtige Grammatik mit nur einem Metazeichen N für obiges Beispiel an:

Metaregelmenge Rm: N::1;N1.
X::a;b;c.(durch Einsetzen eliminierbar)

```
Hyperregelmenge Rh:      start:leere wort symb;aNbNcN.
                           XN1:XN,X symb.
                            X1:X symb.

Darstellung D:       a symb                  a
                     b symb                  b
                     c symb                  c
                     leere wort symb         ^
```

5) Zusammenfassende Typisierung zweischichtiger Grammatiken

Aus einem Satz von A. van Wijngaarden [5] und der Turing'schen These folgt die Chomsky 0 - Typisierung:

> " Die Menge der von zweischichtigen Grammatiken generierten Sprachen ist genau
>
> die Menge der von zweischichtigen Grammatiken mit nur einem Metazeichen generierten Sprachen und diese ist genau
>
> die Menge der Sprachen vom Chomsky- Typ 0 "

Aus einem Satz von J. L. Baker [3] und Satz 3 folgt die Chomsky 1-Typisierung :

> " Die Menge der von hyperbeschränkten zweischichtigen Grammatiken generierten Sprachen ist genau
>
> die Menge der von hyperbeschränkten zweischichtigen Grammatiken mit nur einem Metazeichen generierten Sprachen und diese ist genau
>
> die Menge der Sprachen vom Chomsky- Typ 1 d.h. die Menge der kontextsensitiven Sprachen "

Die Voraussetzung "hyperbeschränkt" kann noch auf "beschränkt" erweitert werden, indem man nicht die Hyperregeln aus Rh, sondern die (i.a. unendlich vielen) Regeln (entstanden aus Hyper- und Metaregeln) aus R betrachtet und voraussetzt [6]:

" Jede Regel aus R hat links nicht mehr Zeichen x als rechts" .

Man kann zeigen [6], daß der Übergang von "hyperbeschränkt" auf "beschränkt" die Sprachklasse nicht verändert.

Eine weitere Einschränkung zweischichtiger Grammatiken auf die Chomsky- Typen 2,3 ist trivialerweise durch Wahl der leeren Menge als Metaregelmenge (und restriktive Einschränkung der Hyperregelmenge entsprechend Chomsky - Typ 2 bzw.3) möglich.

6) Literatur

[1] A.van Wijngaarden: " Orthogonal design and description of a formal language", MR 76, Math. Centrum, Amsterdam, 1965.

[2] M. Sintzoff: " Existence of a Van Wijngaarden syntax for every recursively enumerable set" , Extr. Ann. Soc. Sci. Bruxelles, T81, II, pp 115-118, 1967.

[3] J. L. Baker: " Grammars with structured Vocabulary: a Model for the ALGOL-68 Definition", Inf. and Contr. 20, pp 351-359,1972

[4] H. Feldmann: " Grammatische Darstellung von Vereinbarung und Aufruf am Beispiel einer Sprache für Melodien", Meeting "Automatentheorie und formale Sprachen", Oberwolfach, Oktober 1972, published in Mitt.d. Gesellschaft f. Math. u.Datenverarb., Bonn, Nr.27 (1974),pp 38-43, editors Hotz, Kopp, Langmaack.

[5] A.van Wijngaarden: " One is enough (The generative power of two-level grammars)", Lecture held in Winnipeg, June 1974.

[6] H. Feldmann: " Einführung in ALGOL 68", Lecture script, University of Hamburg, July 1974, complete edition to appear 1975.

[7] A.van Wijngaarden et al.: " Revised Report on the Algorithmic Language ALGOL 68" , to appear in Acta Informatica.

ALLGEMEINE Σ-GRAMMATIKEN

Manfred Opp
Inst. f. Informatik, Universität Hamburg

Seit einigen Jahren beschäftigen sich viele algebraische Untersuchungen mit der Lage der Chomsky-Sprachklassen in speziellen algebraischen Strukturen.

Besonders wichtige und abgerundete Ergebnisse sind für absolut freie Algebren (Termalgebren) T_Σ über endlichen Operatorbereichen Σ erzielt worden. Hier ist von Mezei,Wright[3], Brainerd[1], Shepard[4] nachgewiesen worden, daß die Klassen der erkennbaren, contextfreien (gleichungsdefinierten) und TO-Sprachen übereinstimmen.

Wir wollen nun einen Grammatiktyp auf T_Σ definieren, der die oben erwähnten Grammatiken als Spezialfälle enthält (die linken Seiten der Regeln sind beliebige, d.h. nicht notwendig endliche) Termmengen) und zeigen, daß die Menge der von diesen Grammatiken erzeugten Sprachen gerade wieder genau die Menge der erkennbaren Sprachen ist.

Die schwierige Inklusionsrichtung der Ergebnisse von Brainerd und Shepard ergibt sich also als direkte Folgerung unseres Satzes, der auch beweistechnisch eine erhebliche Vereinfachung liefert.

Es ergibt sich jedoch, daß man bei der Erzeugung erkennbarer Teilmengen mit allgemeinen Σ-Grammatiken i.a. mit einem Axiom nicht auskommt (es stehen keine Hilfszeichen zur Verfügung).

Wir stellen jetzt die wesentlichen Grundbegriffe zusammen.

(Σ,a) (oder kurz Σ) sei im folgenden der zugrundegelegte Operatorbereich mit der Stelligkeitsabbildung $a \in \mathrm{Abb}(\Sigma,\mathbb{N}_0)$; $a^{-1}(n)$ werde mit Σ_n bezeichnet ($a^{-1}(0)$ sei stets ungleich leer vorausgesetzt).

Die Termalgebra $(T_\Sigma(X),\Sigma)$ ist die freie Σ-Algebra in der Klasse aller Σ-Algebren über dem Erzeugendensystem X (für $(T_\Sigma(\emptyset),\Sigma)$ schreiben wir (T_Σ,Σ)). Die Trägermenge $T_\Sigma(X)$ ist damit die Menge aller wohlgeformten Σ-Bäume:

(1) $\Sigma_o \cup X \subset T_\Sigma(X)$.

(2) $\omega \in \Sigma_n,\ t_1,..,t_n \in T_\Sigma(X) \Longrightarrow \omega(t_1,..,t_n) \in T_\Sigma(X)$.

(3) Genau die in endlich vielen Schritten aus (1) und (2) ableitbaren Terme liegen in $T_\Sigma(X)$.

(Die von $\omega \in \Sigma_n$ auf $T_\Sigma(X)$ induzierte Operation f_ω arbeitet in natürlicher Weise: $f_\omega(t_1,..,t_n) = \omega(t_1,..,t_n)$.)

Die Formalisierung des Subterm- und Substitutionsbegriffes übernehmen wir von Brainerd [1].

(1.0) Def.: $(\mathbb{N}^*, \cdot, 0)$ sei das von $\mathbb{N}$ erzeugte freie Monoid (mit Einselement 0). Wir definieren für $a,b \in \mathbb{N}$: $a \leq b \Longleftrightarrow \exists x \in \mathbb{N}^*$: $a \cdot x = b$. (a ist also kleiner als b, wenn a linkes Anfangsstück von b ist.)

(1.1) Def.: Eine endliche Menge $D \subset \mathbb{N}^*$ heißt Baumnumerierung, falls :

(1) $b \in D \wedge a \leq b \Longrightarrow a \in D$.

(2) $a \cdot j \in D \wedge i \leq j \Longrightarrow a \cdot i \in D$.

In natürlicher Weise können wir nun Terme $t \in T_\Sigma$ mit einer eindeutig bestimmten Baumnumerierung versehen :

(a) $t = f(t_1,..,t_n)$, so wird f mit 0 numeriert.

(b) Ist $t' = g(t_1',..,t_m') \in T_\Sigma$ eine in t vorkommende Zeichenfolge und ist g mit $a \in \mathbb{N}^*$ numeriert, so werden die 'Spitzen' von $t_1',..,t_m'$ mit $a \cdot 1,..,a \cdot m$ numeriert.

Beispiel:

$$
\begin{array}{ccc} & f & \\ g & & \lambda \\ \lambda \; \delta \; \lambda & & \end{array}
\longrightarrow
\begin{array}{ccc} & (f,0) & \\ (g,1) & & (\lambda,2) \\ (\lambda,1\cdot1) \; (\delta,1\cdot2) \; (\lambda,1\cdot3) & & \end{array}
$$

Der $t \in T_\Sigma$ auf diese Weise zugeordnete Baum werde mit $\overline{D}(t)$ bezeichnet. Die zu t gehörige Baumnumerierung $D(t)$ ist nun durch $pr_2(\overline{D}(t))$ definiert (hier ist $\overline{D}(t)$ aufgefaßt als Menge von Paaren aus $\Sigma \times \mathbb{N}^*$).

Für das folgende denken wir uns von vorneherein Bäume durchnumeriert, d.h. Knoten und Blätter sind durch Paare aus $\Sigma \times \mathbb{N}^*$ bezeichnet Bäume können deswegen auch einfach als Menge dieser Paare aufgefaßt werden). Dies ist notwendig beim genauen Lokalisieren auszutauschender Subterme, die ja als reine Terme an verschiedenen Stellen auftreten können.

(1.2) Def.: Sei $t \in T_\Sigma$, $t_1,..,t_n \in T_\Sigma$. $a_1,..,a_n \in \mathbb{N}^*$ seien paarweise unvergleichbare Elemente aus $D(t)$. Dann sei $Subst(t; a_1,..,a_n; t_1,..,t_n) := \{(x,b) \in \overline{D}(t) \;/\; b \not\geq a_1,..,a_n\} \cup \bigcup_{i=1}^{n} a_i \cdot \overline{D}(t_i)$. $(a_i \cdot \overline{D}(t_i)$ ist in folgendem Sinne als Komplexschreibweise zu verstehen : z.B.

$$
a_i \cdot \left(\begin{array}{ccc} & (f,0) & \\ (\lambda,1) & & (\delta,2) \end{array} \right) = \begin{array}{ccc} & (f,a_i) & \\ (\lambda,a_i\cdot1) & & (\delta,a_i\cdot2) \end{array} \Bigg) .
$$

Der obige Substitutionsoperator ersetzt damit im Baum t die an den Stellen $a_1,..,a_n$ wurzelnden Teilbäume durch die neuen Bäume $t_1,..,t_n$. Hierzu noch ein Beispiel: $a_1 = 1$, $a_2 = 2\cdot 2$;

t = (Baum: f mit Söhnen g und f; g mit Söhnen g und δ; g mit Söhnen λ und δ; f mit Söhnen δ und δ)

$t_1 = \delta$

t_2 = (Baum: g mit Söhnen λ und λ)

$$Subst(t;\ a_1, a_2;\ t_1, t_2) = \{(f,0), (f,2), (\delta, 2\cdot 1)\} \cup \{(\delta, 1)\} \cup \{(g, 2\cdot 2), (\lambda, 2\cdot 2\cdot 1), (\lambda, 2\cdot 2\cdot 2)\}.$$

Subst(t; 1,2·2; t_1,t_2) stellt also den Baum (Baum: f mit Söhnen δ und f; f mit Söhnen δ und g; g mit Söhnen λ und λ) dar.

(1.3) Def.: Seien $t,t' \in T_\Sigma(X)$. t' heißt Subterm von t an der Stelle a, falls $a\cdot\bar{D}(t') \subset \bar{D}(t)$. Wir schreiben dann $t' \preccurlyeq t$.

Es kann für $t,t' \in T_\Sigma(X)$ durchaus verschiedene Elemente $a,a' \in \mathbb{N}^*$ geben, so daß $a\cdot\bar{D}(t') \subset \bar{D}(t)$ und $a'\cdot\bar{D}(t') \subset \bar{D}(t)$ gilt.

Sprechen wir in Zukunft von dem Subterm t' von t (bzw. dem fixierten Subterm), so meinen wir den ganz genau in t positionierten Subterm (d.h. eigentlich ist nicht nur t' gegeben, sondern das Paar (t',a), wobei $a\cdot\bar{D}(t') \subset \bar{D}(t)$). Für $Subst(t;a_1,..,a_n;\ t_1,..,t_n)$ werden wir aufgrund dieser Sprachregelung auch $Subst(t;\ t'_1,..,t'_n;\ t_1,..,t_n)$ schreiben, falls die t'_i gerade die bei a_i wurzelnden Subterme von t sind, und umgekehrt ist bei der Schreibweise $Subst(t;\ t'_1,..,t'_n;\ t_1,.t_n)$ eben nicht außer Acht zu lassen, daß die t'_i als fixierte Subterme von t zu betrachten sind.

Wir definieren nun die erkennbaren, contextfreien und TO-Sprachen für Termalgebren T_Σ und stellen die bekannten Zusammenhänge zwischen diesen Sprachklassen dar.

(1.4) Def.: Die Menge der erkennbaren Teilmengen von T_Σ ist definiert durch $Erk(T_\Sigma) := \{U \subset T_\Sigma \ /\ \exists$ Kongruenz $\mathcal{K} = \{K_1,..,K_r\}$ mit endlichem Index auf T_Σ mit $U = \bigcup_{K_i \cap U \neq \emptyset} K_i\}$.

(1.5) Def.: Eine Σ-Grammatik über T_Σ ist ein Tupel $G = (T_\Sigma,X,P,A)$, wobei : (1) X eine endliche Menge von Nonterminalzeichen ist.

(2) $P \subset T_\Sigma(X) \times T_\Sigma(X)$ eine endliche Regelmenge ist.

(3) $A \subset T_\Sigma(X)$ eine endliche Axiomenmenge ist.

G heißt contextfrei, falls $P \subset X \times T_\Sigma(X)$ und $A \subset X$, $card(A) = 1$ (die zweite Forderung besitzt jedoch keinerlei prinzipielle Bedeutung).

Die durch $G = (T_\Sigma, X, P, A)$ definierte Ableitungsrelation $\mathcal{R}_G \subset T_\Sigma(X) \times T_\Sigma(X)$ ist :
$(t,t') \in \mathcal{R}_G \Longleftrightarrow \exists (t_1,t_2) \in P$: $Subst(t; t_1; t_2) = t'$.
Wie üblich schreiben wir für $(t,t') \in \mathcal{R}_G$ auch $t \longrightarrow t'$ und $t \xrightarrow{*} t'$, falls das Paar (t,t') in der reflexiven, transitiven Hülle von $\mathcal{R}_G$ liegt. Die durch G definierte Sprache ist dann $L(G) = \{ t \in T_\Sigma \,/\, \exists a \in A: a \xrightarrow{*} t \}$, das ist also die Menge der aus Axiomen ableitbaren Worte t, die keine Variablen als Blätter besitzen.

Teilmengen von T_Σ heißen contextfrei (bzw. TO), falls sie von dem dazugehörigen Grammatiktyp erzeugt werden.

(1.6) Satz (Mezei, Wright [3]): Die contextfreien Teilmengen von T_Σ sind genau die erkennbaren .

(1.7) Satz (Brainerd [1], Shepard [4]): Σ-Grammatiken über Termalgebren T_Σ erzeugen genau die erkennbaren Teilmengen von T_Σ .

Brainerd hat darüberhinaus gezeigt, daß die erkennbaren Teilmengen von T_Σ sich bereits erzeugen lassen durch Σ-Grammatiken der Form $G = (T_\Sigma, \emptyset, P, A)$, d.h. ohne Nonterminalzeichen. (Für $(T_\Sigma, \emptyset, P, A)$ schreiben wir (T_Σ, P, A).)

Die wesentliche Aussage '$G = (T_\Sigma, X, P, A)$ Σ-Grammatik $\Longrightarrow L(G)$ erkennbar in T_Σ', ist bereits bewiesen, falls die Aussage '$G = (T_\Sigma, P, A)$ Σ-Grammatik ohne Nonterminalzeichen $\Longrightarrow L(G)$ erkennbar in T_Σ' für beliebige Operatorbereiche Σ gültig ist, denn:

Für eine gegebene Σ-Grammatik $G = (T_\Sigma, X, P, A)$ definiere $\Sigma' := \Sigma \cup X$, (die Elemente von X werden als zusätzliche nullstellige Operatoren in Σ' betrachtet). Jeder Baum aus $T_\Sigma(X)$ kann damit als Baum aus $T_{\Sigma'}$ aufgefaßt werden. Wendet man diese Identifizierung auf P und A an, so erhält man eine Σ-Grammatik $G' = (T_{\Sigma'}, P, A)$ ohne Nonterminalzeichen mit $L(G') \cap T_\Sigma = L(G)$. Unter der Voraussetzung, daß $L(G')$ in $T_{\Sigma'}$ erkennbar ist, ist dann ebenso $L(G)$ in T_Σ erkennbar.

Aus diesem Grunde führen wir den Typ der 'allgemeinen Σ-Grammatik' bereits gleich als Grammatik ohne Nonterminalzeichen ein

(1.8) Def.: Σ sei ein Operatorbereich. Eine allgemeine Σ-Grammatik ist ein Tripel $G = (T_\Sigma, P, A)$ mit der endlichen Axiomenmenge $A \subset T_\Sigma$ und der endlichen Regelmenge $P \subset \mathcal{P}(T_\Sigma) \times T_\Sigma$.

Die Regeln (K,w), $K \subset T_\Sigma$, $w \in T$, sollen auch in der Form $K \longrightarrow w$ geschrieben werden. Es sei noch einmal betont, daß die linken Seiten der Regeln keinen (!) Beschränkungen unterliegen.

In Analogie zum Ableitungsbegriff bei Chomsky-Grammatiken definieren wir:

(1.9) Def.: (a) Die von einer allgemeinen Σ-Grammatik $G = (T_\Sigma, P, A)$ erzeugte 2-stellige Ableitungsrelation $R_G \subset T_\Sigma \times T_\Sigma$ ist definiert durch: $(u,v) \in R_G \Longleftrightarrow \exists u' \preccurlyeq u \ \exists (K,w) \in P: (u' \in K \wedge v = \mathrm{Subst}(u; u'; w)$. (Schreibweise: $u \xrightarrow[G]{(K,w)} v$ oder $u \xrightarrow{(K,w)} v$). Die transitive reflexive Hülle von R_G bezeichnen wir mit $TRH(R_G)$. (Schreibweise: $(u,v) \in TRH(R_G) \Longleftrightarrow u \xrightarrow[G]{*} v$ oder $u \xrightarrow{*} v$.)

(b) Die von einer allgemeinen Σ-Grammatik $G = (T_\Sigma, P, A)$ erzeugte Sprache ist definiert durch $L(G) = \{ w \in T_\Sigma \ / \ \exists u \in A: u \xrightarrow{*} w \}$.

Eine Regel einer allgemeinen Σ-Grammatik besitzt also die Ableitungskapazität von card(K)-vielen TO-Regeln (die betrachtete Regel sei (K,w)) einer Σ-Grammatik mit einheitlicher rechter Seite.

Für die Durchführung des Beweises von Satz (1.11) benötigen wir noch folgende Definition:

(1.10) Def.: Gegeben sei eine allgemeine Σ-Grammatik $G = (T_\Sigma, P, A)$, $P = \{R_1, .., R_n\}$. Dann definieren wir zu $\Sigma' = \Sigma \cup \{\lambda_1, .., \lambda_n\}$ die Abbildung

$$W_G: \begin{cases} T_\Sigma \longrightarrow \mathcal{P}(T_{\Sigma'}) \\ w \longrightarrow \{ w' \in T_{\Sigma'} \ / \ \exists k \in \mathbb{N}_0 \ \exists v_1, .., v_k \end{cases}$$

$\preccurlyeq$ w disjunkte Subterme von w $\exists n_1, .., n_k \in \{1, .., n\} \ \exists \tilde{v}_1, .., \tilde{v}_k$, $\tilde{v}_i \in K_{n_i}$: $w' = \mathrm{Subst}(w; v_1, .., v_k; \lambda_{n_1}, .., \lambda_{n_k})$ und $v_i \xrightarrow[G]{*} \tilde{v}_i$ für $i=1, .., k \}$. (Wir haben hier $R_i = (K_i, w_i)$ angenommen.)

W_G wird in der üblichen Weise additiv auf $\mathcal{P}(T_\Sigma)$ fortgesetzt. $W_G(w)$ enthält also diejenigen Worte aus $T_{\Sigma'}$, die durch Austauschen von Subtermen $v_i \preccurlyeq w$ durch λ_{n_i} entstehen, falls die v_i in irgendein Wort aus K_{n_i} ableitbar sind. Diese Definition ist also apriori nicht konstruktiv. Der mithilfe dieser Definition geführte Beweis zu Satz (1.11) unterscheidet sich daher auch von den Beweisen, die von Brainerd [1] bzw. Shepard [4] für Spezialfälle erbracht wurden.

(1.11) Satz: Zu jeder allgemeinen Σ-Grammatik $G = (T_\Sigma, P, A)$ gibt es eine allgemeine Σ'-Grammatik $\tilde{G} = (T_{\Sigma'}, \tilde{P}, \tilde{A})$ $(\Sigma' = \Sigma \cup \{\lambda_1,..,\lambda_n\})$ mit $\tilde{P} \subset \{\lambda_1,..,\lambda_n\} \times T_{\Sigma'}$, die $L(G) = L(\tilde{G}) \cap T_\Sigma$ erfüllt.

($\tilde{G}$ ist damit in der einleitend gebrauchten Sprechweise eine contextfreie Σ-Grammatik mit den Nonterminalzeichen $\lambda_1,..,\lambda_n$.)

Beweis: Es sei $P = \{R_1,..,R_n\}$. Dann konstruieren wir $\tilde{G}$ wie folgt: $\tilde{A} = W_G(A)$, zu $R_i = (K_i, w_i)$ sei $\tilde{R}_i = \{(\lambda_i, \tilde{w}_i) \,/\, \tilde{w}_i \in W_G(w_i)\}$. Jeder Regel R_i wird also eine Menge von Regeln bzgl. $\tilde{G}$ zugeordnet. $\tilde{P}$ wird dann als $\bigcup_{i=1}^{n} \tilde{R}_i$ definiert.

(1) Wir zeigen: $W_G(L_k(G)) \subset L(\tilde{G})$ ($L_k(G)$ ist die Menge der in höchstens k Schritten ableitbaren Worte).

k=0 : $L_o(G) = A$ und $W_G(A) = \tilde{A} \subset L(\tilde{G})$. Die Behauptung sei für k bewiesen. Sei $v \in W_G(L_{k+1}(G))$, d.h. für ein $\tilde{v} \in L_{k+1}(G)$ sei $v = \mathrm{Subst}(\tilde{v}; v_1,..,v_m; \lambda_{n_1},..,\lambda_{n_m})$ gemäß (1.10) ($v_i \xrightarrow[G]{*} \tilde{v}_i$ für gewisse $\tilde{v}_i \in K_{n_i}$). Da $\tilde{v}$ in k+1 Schritten ableitbar ist, gibt es $\tilde{v} = \mathrm{Subst}(\tilde{\tilde{v}}; u; w_i)$ für $u \in K_i$ und $\tilde{\tilde{v}} \in L_k(G)$. Abhängig von der Lage der $v_1,..,v_m$ innerhalb $\tilde{v}$ müssen wir nun verschiedene Fälle betrachten:

Fall 1: Keins der $v_1,..,v_m$ ist ein echter Oberterm von w_i: Seien ohne Einschränkung der Allgemeinheit $v_1,..,v_{\tilde{m}} \leq w_i$, $v_{\tilde{m}+1},..,v_m \not\leq w_i$. Dann ist $\mathrm{Subst}(w_i; v_1,..,v_{\tilde{m}}; \lambda_{n_1},..,\lambda_{n_{\tilde{m}}})$ in $\tilde{G}$ von λ_i ableitbar, da die Regel (K_i, w_i) in $\tilde{G}$ die Regeln $\{\lambda_i\} \times W_G(w_i)$ induziert und der obige Substitutionsausdruck ein Element aus $W_G(w_i)$ ist.

Weiter ist $\mathrm{Subst}(\tilde{\tilde{v}}; u, v_{\tilde{m}+1},..,v_m; \lambda_i, \lambda_{n_{\tilde{m}+1}},..,\lambda_{n_m})$ als Element von $W_G(L_k(G))$ nach Induktionannahme in $\tilde{G}$ ableitbar (u darf durch λ_i ersetzt werden, da $u \in K_i$ trivialerweise nach K_i ableitbar ist).

Dann ist auch $v \in L(\tilde{G})$, da v erhalten wird durch Einsetzen von $\mathrm{Subst}(w_i; v_1,..,v_{\tilde{m}}; \lambda_{n_1},..,\lambda_{n_{\tilde{m}}})$ in den nullstelligen Operator λ_i des Terms $\mathrm{Subst}(\tilde{\tilde{v}}; u, v_{\tilde{m}+1},..,v_m; \lambda_i, \lambda_{n_{\tilde{m}+1}},..,\lambda_{n_m})$.

Fall 2: Eins der $v_1,..,v_m$ ist ein echter Oberterm von w_i: Ohne Einschränkung der Allgemeinheit sei dies v_1. Da (K_i, w_i) eine Regel aud G und $u \in K_i$ ist, gilt $\mathrm{Subst}(v_1; w_i; u) \xrightarrow[G]{(K_i,w_i)} v_1$.

Nach Voraussetzung gilt $v_i \xrightarrow[G]{*'} \tilde{v}_i \in K_{n_i}$, also Subst($v_1$; w_i; u) $\xrightarrow[G]{*} \tilde{v}_i \in K_{n_i}$. Anwendung der Induktionsannahme auf $\tilde{\tilde{v}}$ liefert v = Subst($\tilde{v}$; $v_1,..,v_m$; $\lambda_{n_1},..,\lambda_{n_m}$) = Subst($\tilde{\tilde{v}}$; Subst($v_1$;$w_i$; u), $v_2,..,v_m$; $\lambda_{n_1},..,\lambda_{n_m}$) $\in W_G(\tilde{\tilde{v}}) \subset L(\tilde{G})$.

(2) Wegen $L(G) \subset W_G(L(G))$ folgt aus (1): $L(G) \subset L(\tilde{G}) \cap T_\Sigma$.

(3) Wir zeigen $L(\tilde{G}) \subset W_G(L(G))$.

Dies wird durch $L_k(\tilde{G}) \subset W_G(L(G))$ über vollständige Induktion gezeigt. k=0: $\tilde{A} = W_G(A) \subset W_G(L(G))$. Sei die Behauptung für k bewiesen. Sei weiter $v \in L_{k+1}(\tilde{G})$, d.h. v = Subst($\tilde{v}$; λ_i; u), wobei $\tilde{v} \in L_k(\tilde{G})$, $u \in W_G(w_i)$ (es wurde zuletzt also eine der von (K_i,w_i) induzierten Regeln aus $\tilde{G}$ angewendet).

$\tilde{v}$ ist nach Induktionsannahme aus $W_G(L(G))$, d.h. $\tilde{v}$ = Subst(w; $\tilde{v}_1,..,\tilde{v}_m$; $\lambda_{n_1},..,\lambda_{n_m}$), wobei $w \in L(G)$ und die $\tilde{v}_i$ nach K_{n_i} ableitbar sind. Sei $\lambda_{n_{\tilde{m}}}$ der in $\tilde{v}$ durch u ausgetauschte nullstellige Operator. Subst(w; $\tilde{v}_{\tilde{m}}$; w_i) $\in L(G)$, da $\tilde{v}_{\tilde{m}} \xrightarrow[G]{*} \tilde{\tilde{v}}_{\tilde{m}} \in K_{n_{\tilde{m}}}$ $(=K_i)$, $\tilde{\tilde{v}}_{\tilde{m}} \xrightarrow[G]{(K_i,w_i)} w_i$.

Damit ist $v \in W_G(L(G))$, denn v entsteht aus Subst(w; $\tilde{v}_{\tilde{m}}$; w_i) durch Austauschen der $\tilde{v}_1,..,\tilde{v}_{\tilde{m}-1},\tilde{v}_{\tilde{m}+1},..,\tilde{v}_m$ durch $\lambda_{n_1},..,\lambda_{n_{\tilde{m}-1}},\lambda_{n_{\tilde{m}+1}}$, $..,\lambda_{n_m}$ und Austauschen der passenden Subterme aus w_i durch nullstellige Operationen (wegen $u \in W_G(w_i)$).

(4) Wir zeigen $L(\tilde{G}) \cap T_\Sigma \subset L(G)$.

Aufgrund von Teilbehauptung (3) gilt $L(\tilde{G}) \cap T_\Sigma \subset W_G(L(G)) \cap T_\Sigma$. $W_G(L(G)) \cap T_\Sigma$ ist gerade diejenige Menge, die aus L(G) durch Austauschen keines Subterms durch $\lambda_i \in \Sigma' \setminus \Sigma$ entsteht, das ist aber gerade L(G) selbst: $W_G(L(G)) \cap T_\Sigma = L(G)$.

<u>(1.12) Korollar:</u> Jede von einer allgemeinen Σ-Grammatik $G = (T_\Sigma,P,A)$ erzeugte Sprache L(G) ist eine erkannte Teilmenge von T_Σ $(L(G) \in Erk(T_\Sigma))$.

Beweis: Betrachtet man G als eine contextfreie Σ-Grammatik mit den Nonterminalzeichen $\{\lambda_1,..,\lambda_n\} = \Sigma' \setminus \Sigma$, so ist die erzeugte Sprache über dem Terminalzeichenalphabet Σ ja $L(\tilde{G}) \cap T_\Sigma$. Diese Menge ist nach

Mezei, Wright [3] erkannte Teilmenge von T_Σ. Zusammen mit dem Satz (1.11) ist dann alles gezeigt.

Die von allgemeinen Σ-Grammatiken erzeugten Sprachen aus T_Σ sind damit Elemente von $Erk(T_\Sigma)$. Umgekehrt sind natürlich auch alle erkannten Teilmengen von T_Σ von allgemeinen Σ-Grammatiken erzeugbar, da nach Brainerd bereits die Σ-Grammatiken ohne Nonterminalzeichen diese Kapazität besitzen. Der Satz (1.14) zeigt, daß wir im allgemeinen jedoch nicht mit einer einelementigen Axiomenmenge auskommen. Die Nichtexistenz eines endlichen Gegenbeispiels sieht man leicht an der folgenden Behauptung.

<u>(1.13) Beh.</u>: Jede endliche Teilmenge von T_Σ wird von einer allgemeinen Σ-Grammatik mit einem Axiom erzeugt.

Beweis: Sei $E = \{t_1,..,t_m\} \subset T_\Sigma$. Für ein bzgl. der Subtermordnung ' $\leqslant$ ' maximales Element $t_{n_0} \in E$ definieren wir G durch $A = \{t_{n_0}\}$ und $P = \{t_{n_0} \longrightarrow t \; / \; t \in E\}$. Wegen der Maximalität von t_{n_0} ist offensichtlich, daß $L(G) = E$ gilt.

<u>(1.14) Satz:</u> Es gibt erkennbare Teilmengen von T_Σ, die nicht von allgemeinen Σ-Grammatiken mit nur einem Axiom erzeugbar sind.

Beweis: Wir geben folgendes Gegenbeispiel an:
Sei $\Sigma = \{f,g,\lambda\}$ mit $a(f) = a(g) = 1$ und $a(\lambda) = 0$. Dann ist $E = E_1 \cup E_2$ mit $E_1 = \{f(gf)^n(\lambda) \; / \; n \geqslant 0\}$, $E_2 = \{g(fg)^n(\lambda) \; / \; n \geqslant 0\}$ eine erkannte Teilmenge von T_Σ, die z.B. von $G = (T_\Sigma, P, A)$ mit $A = \{f(\lambda), g(\lambda)\}$, $P = \{g(\lambda) \longrightarrow gfg(\lambda),\; f(\lambda) \longrightarrow fgf(\lambda)\}$ erzeugt wird.
Es gibt jedoch keine allgemeine Σ-Grammatik $G' = (T_\Sigma, P', A')$ mit $L(G') = E$ und $card(A') = 1$. Wir nehmen nun an, daß $A' = \{f(gf)^m(\lambda)\} \subset E_1$, $m \in \mathbb{N}_0$ (dies bedeutet keine Einschränkung, da der andere Fall $A' \subset E_2$ sich wegen der Symmetrie des Problems auf analoge Weise behandeln läßt).

Wäre nun $L(G') = E$, so müßte es Terme $t \in E_2$, $\tilde{t} \in E_1$ geben mit $\tilde{t} \xrightarrow[G']{R_i'} t$. Sei also $t = g(fg)^k(\lambda)$, $\tilde{t} = f(gf)^{k'}(\lambda)$, $R_i' = (K_i \longrightarrow w)$.
Da die Wurzeln von t und $\tilde{t}$ unterschiedlich sind, muss notwendig durch R_i' der ganze Term ausgetauscht worden sein, d.h. $\tilde{t} \in K_i$, $w = t$.
Das führt aber wegen $f(gf)^{k'+1}(\lambda) = fg(f(gf)^{k'}(\lambda) \in E_1$ und $fg(g(fg)^k)(\lambda) \notin E$ auf einen Widerspruch.

LITERATUR

[1] Brainerd, W.S.: Tree Generating Regular Systems. Inf. a. Contr. 14 (1969).

[2] Costich, O.L.: A Medvedev Characterisation of Sets Recognized by Generalised Finite Automata. Math.Syst.Th. Vol. 6, No 3 (1972).

[3] Mezei, J. Wright, J.B.: Algebraic Automata and Contextfree Sets. Inf. a. Contr. 11 (1967).

[4] Shepard, C.D.: Languages in General Algebra. Doct. Dissertation, Univ. of Illinois, (1969).

[5] Thatcher, J.W., Wright, J.B. Generalised Finite Automata Theory with an Application to a Decision Problem of Second-order Logic. IBM Research Paper, RC-1713.

B E T R I E B S S Y S T E M E I

DYNAMISCHE SPEICHERVERWALTUNG DURCH HARDWARE

T. Flik, H. Liebig
Institut für Technische Informatik
Technische Universität Berlin

Kurzfassung

Es wird eine hierarchische Speicherstruktur vorgestellt, die der begrifflichen Trennung von Operanden, Adressen und Verweisungen auf Adressen entspricht. In drei Ebenen sind mehrere technisch getrennte Speichermoduln vorgesehen: ein Operandenspeicher, ein Adreßspeicher und ein sogenannter Organisationsspeicher. Die Organisation in den ersten beiden Ebenen erlaubt die dynamische Vereinbarung von Feldern durch Hardware. Durch die zusätzliche Speicherebene für die Verweisungen auf Adressen wird eine übersichtliche Verwaltung der Daten- und Adreßbereiche für einfache und geschachtelte BEGIN-END-Blöcke und für einfache, geschachtelte und rekursive Prozeduren ermöglicht. Die Blockorganisation, der Prozeduraufruf, die Parameterübergabe und die Prozedurrückkehr erfolgen durch spezielle Maschinenbefehle.

Zukünftige Untersuchungen an diesem Modell sollen zeigen, inwieweit sich diese Rechnerstruktur für die Implementierung höherer Programmiersprachen eignet und inwieweit eine Realisierung dieser Struktur in LSI-Technik wirtschaftliche Lösungen erwarten läßt.

1. Einleitung

Höhere Programmiersprachen wie z.B. PL/1 oder ALGOL implizieren eine dynamische Speicherverwaltung für die Datenbereiche von Programmblökken und Prozeduren. Da im allgemeinen die Rechnerhardware keine direkte Unterstützung hierfür vorsieht, erfolgt diese Verwaltung durch Software in einem meist umfangreichen Runtime-System. Die Ineffizienz dieser Softwarelösung legt es nahe, einen Rechner zu entwerfen, der die dynamische Speicherverwaltung durch Hardware unterstützt.

Ein solches Rechnerkonzept wurde von der Firma Burroughs mit der Rechnerserie B-5000/6000 realisiert /1,2/. In Anlehnung an die "Basic Language Machine" von Iliffe /3/ und den "Rice Research Computer R-2" /4/ wurde dabei von der linearen Speicheradressierung abgewichen und eine baumstrukturierte Speichersegmentierung eingeführt. Die Strukturinformation wird in sog. Kontrollwörtern zusammen mit den Operanden eines Jobs im Primärspeicher gespeichert. Trotz eines zusätzlichen Registerspeichers (Display-Register) zur Aufnahme von Datenbasisadressen des Primärspeichers wirkt sich beim Operandenzugriff der zum Teil mehrfache durch Kontrollwörter gesteuerte indirekte Zugriff auf den Primärspeicher als Nachteil aus.

In dem hier vorgeschlagenen Modell wird im Gegensatz zu den Burroughs-Rechnern die Strukturinformation von den Operanden getrennt und darüber hinaus nur eine einfache indirekte Adressierung vorgesehen. Dazu werden zusätzlich zum herkömmlichen Randomspeicher zwei weitere Speicherebenen eingeführt. Der erhöhte Hardwareaufwand an Speichern verringert den erforderlichen Steueraufwand für den Operandenzugriff. Dieser Zugriff läuft innerhalb der verschiedenen Speicherebenen asynchron ab, womit bei einer Realisierung mit Halbleiterspeichern eine relativ günstige Zugriffszeit für den Gesamtspeicher erreicht wird. Die folgenden Betrachtungen zu unserem Modell beziehen sich ausschließlich auf die Maschinen- und Assemblerebene.

Ausgangspunkt soll eine Primärspeicherstruktur sein, bei der symbolische Adressen nicht durch den Assembler, sondern durch die Maschine verarbeitet werden, wodurch eine dynamische Speicherorganisation ermöglicht wird. In einem ersten Modell bietet sich dafür als Primärspeicher ein Assoziativspeicher an, in dessen Adreßteil die symbolischen Adressen in codierter Form eingetragen werden (Bild 1a). Die dynamische Platzreservierung erfolgt durch einen Maschinenbefehl RES

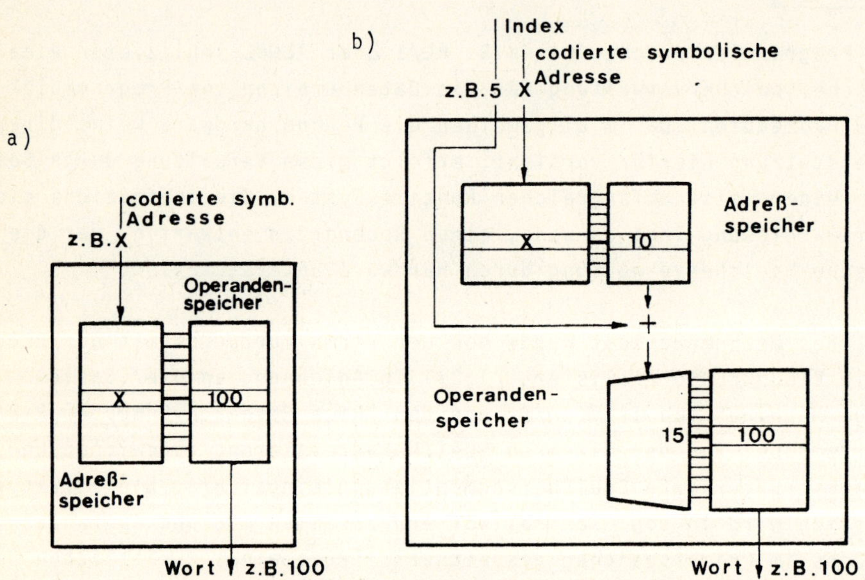

Bild 1. Primärspeicherstruktur: a) Assoziativspeicher, b) Randomspeicher mit vorgeschaltetem Assoziativspeicher

(reserviere), der die symbolische Adresse des zu reservierenden Wortes in den Adreßteil der ersten freien Speicherzelle schreibt und den Zeiger auf die erste freie Zelle um 1 erhöht. Nachteilig hierbei ist, daß sich mit einem RES-Befehl nicht mehrere Speicherzellen reservieren lassen, daß keine indizierte oder relative Adressierung möglich ist und daß sich Adressen nicht mehrfach bezeichnen lassen.

Wir betrachten deshalb ein zweites Modell mit einer hierarchischen Speicherstruktur, bei dem ein Assoziativspeicher einem Randomspeicher über ein Addierschaltnetz vorgeschaltet ist (Bild 1b). Dadurch werden die oben genannten Nachteile vermieden. Darüber hinaus erhält man eine klare räumliche Trennung der verschiedenen gespeicherten Informationen. Im oberen Speicher stehen nur Adressen (Adreßspeicher), zu denen ein Index addiert werden kann; im unteren Speicher stehen die Operanden (Operandenspeicher). Auf die Befehlsspeicherung und die Programmorganisation wird später eingegangen.

Ein weniger aufwendiges, drittes Modell ergibt sich, wenn man den Assoziativspeicher des zweiten Modells durch einen Randomspeicher ersetzt (Bild 2). Das bedeutet, daß der Übersetzer (Assembler) die symbolischen

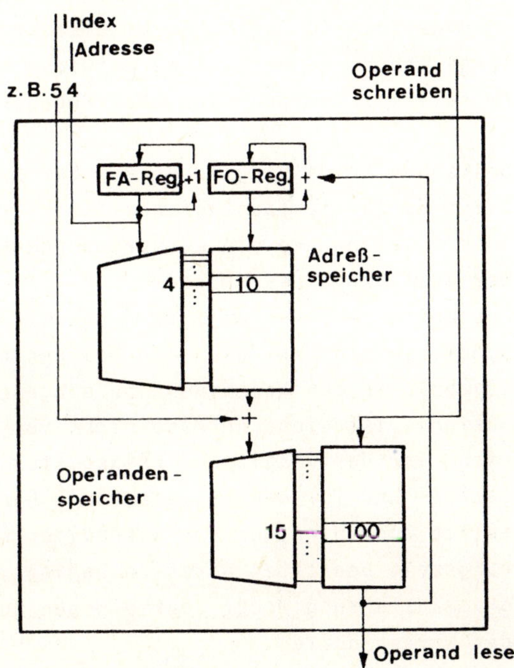

Bild 2. Primärspeicherstruktur: Randomspeicher mit vorgeschaltetem Randomspeicher.

Adressen in numerische umwandeln muß, indem er sie in der Reihenfolge ihres Auftretens durchnumeriert. Dieses dritte Modell liegt den weiteren Betrachtungen zugrunde.

2. Speicherverwaltung für Felder variabler Länge

Bild 2 zeigt das dritte Modell mit den zur Verwaltung des Adreß- und des Operandenspeichers notwendigen Registern FA und FO. Das FA-Register ist als Zähler ausgeführt und enthält die Adresse des ersten freien Speicherplatzes im Adreßspeicher während der Laufzeit eines Programms. Das FO-Register enthält die Adresse des ersten freien Speicherplatzes im Operandenspeicher. Dieser Zeiger kann im Adreßspeicher abgelegt werden. Der Inhalt von FO wird jeweils um die Anzahl der im Operandenspeicher reservierten Zellen erhöht. Zur dynamischen Platzreservierung sehen wir den Maschinenbefehl RES vor.

RES s N   Reserviere (N) Speicherzellen[1)]
RES reserviert zur Ausführungszeit ein Feld im Operandenspeicher mit der unter der Adresse N angegebenen Anzahl an Feldelementen. Dazu wird zunächst der Inhalt des FO-Registers im Adreßspeicher unter der im FA-Register gespeicherten Adresse abgelegt. Anschließend wird der Inhalt des FA-Registers um 1 und der des FO-Registers um die durch den Inhalt von N angegebene Feldlänge erhöht. N bezeichnet entweder einen Direktoperanden oder die Adresse eines Operanden des Operandenspeichers.

Die Zuordnung der symbolischen Feldanfangsadresse s zur jeweils belegten Adreßspeicherzelle ist durch die fortlaufende Numerierung der Adreßsymbole bei der Assemblierung und die entsprechende Fortschaltung des FA-Registers bei der Ausführung des Programms hergestellt. Das Symbol s ist nur zur Assemblierzeit von Bedeutung und wird zur Festlegung einer numerischen Adresse benutzt, die dann bei den nachfolgenden Befehlen anstelle des Symbols in den Maschinencode eingesetzt wird. Im Maschinencode des RES-Befehls ist diese Adresse nicht vorhanden; zur Ausführungszeit entspricht ihr der Inhalt des FA-Registers. RES ist für den Assembler ein Zweiadreß- und für den Prozessor ein Einadreßbefehl. Diese implizit hergestellte Zuordnung der zur Assemblierzeit ermittelten zu den zur Ausführungszeit benutzten Adressen bedingt, daß RES-Befehle während der Programmausführung weder übersprungen noch in Programmschleifen verwendet werden dürfen.

---

1) (...) bedeutet "Inhalt von".

3. Speicherverwaltung für Blöcke

Mit der Einführung des RES-Befehls können wir Speicherplatz dynamisch reservieren, ohne daß wir die Möglichkeit vorgesehen haben, Speicherplatz dynamisch wieder freigeben zu können. Zu diesem Zweck strukturieren wir ein Assemblerprogramm durch Blöcke in der Weise, daß das gesamte Programm den äußeren Block bildet, in den nebeneinander oder ineinander weitere Blöcke eingebettet sind (vgl. ALGOL 60). Das dynamische Reservieren von Speicherplatz erfolgt durch RES-Befehle innerhalb der Blöcke; beim Verlassen eines Blockes wird der im Block reservierte Speicherplatz wieder freigegeben. Das bedingt eine Speicherorganisation, bei der beim Eintritt in einen Block die Adresse des ersten freien Speicherplatzes als Basisadresse gespeichert und beim Verlassen eines Blockes wieder gelöscht wird. Innerhalb eines Blockes wird die Adresse des ersten freien Speicherplatzes mit jedem RES-Befehl hochgezählt. Man erhält so eine pulsierende Speicherbelegung für Adressen und Operanden.

Für unser Speichermodell bedeutet die Datenverwaltung in Form von Blöcken die Hinzunahme einer weiteren Speicherebene zur Aufnahme der Basisadressen. Mit der Datenblockung ändert sich auch die Datenadressierung. Ein Operand wird jetzt durch ein Adreßpaar (BT,RA) adressiert. Die statische Blockschachtelungstiefe BT, die durch die Blockstruktur des Programms bestimmt wird, wählt die Datenbasisadresse aus, zu der die Relativadresse RA des Operanden addiert wird. Bei Feldern werden die Feldelemente durch einen zusätzlichen Index adressiert. Die entsprechend modifizierte Speicherstruktur, die jetzt auch die Programmorganisation einschließt, zeigt Bild 3. Die neu hinzugekommene Speicherebene wird im folgenden als Organisationsspeicher bezeichnet.

Datenorganisation. Die Erweiterung der Datenorganisation sieht einen Adreßbasisspeicher und einen Operandenbasisspeicher vor, die beide über einen gemeinsamen Dekodierer adressiert werden. Das Zählregister FB gibt den jeweils ersten freien Speicherplatz beider Basisspeicher an. Zur Verwaltung der Datenbereiche von Programmblöcken führen wir zwei weitere Maschinenbefehle ein.

BEGIN Blockeintritt

BEGIN eröffnet jeweils einen neuen Speicherbereich im Adreßspeicher und im Operandenspeicher. Dazu werden die Inhalte der Register FA und FO (Basisadressen) im Adreßbasisspeicher bzw. im Operandenbasisspeicher unter der im FB-Register stehenden Adresse gespeichert. Anschließend wird der Inhalt des FB-Registers um 1 erhöht.

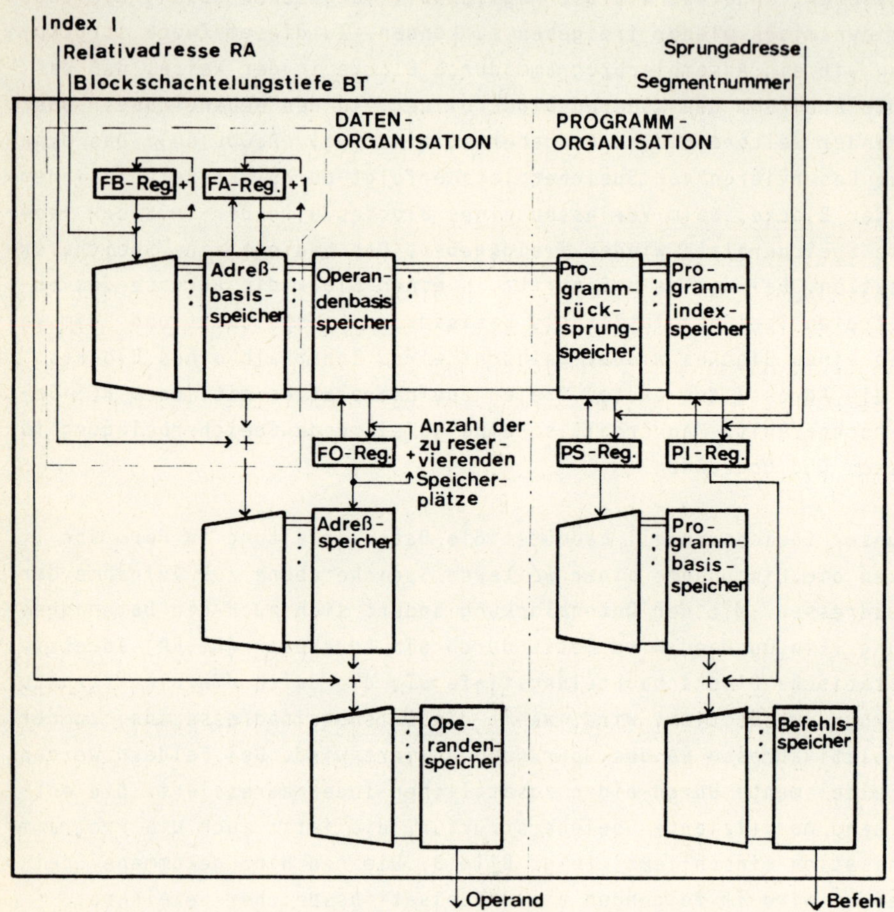

Bild 3. Primärspeicherstruktur für die Daten- und Programmorganisation bei Blöcken. Bei Hinzunahme von Prozeduren wird der gestrichelt gezeichnete Teil durch Bild 4 ersetzt.

END Blockende

END gibt die durch den zugehörigen Programmblock belegten Speicherbereiche im Adreßspeicher und Operandenspeicher frei. Dazu wird zunächst der Inhalt des Registers FB um 1 vermindert. Anschließend werden der Adreßbasisspeicher und der Operandenbasisspeicher mit der im FB-Register stehenden Adresse adressiert und die dort gespeicherten Basisadressen in die Register FA bzw. FO geladen.

Der Operandenbasisspeicher wird allein für die Speicherplatzfreigabe im

Operandenspeicher benötigt. Der Adreßbasisspeicher hingegen wird für die Speicherplatzfreigabe im Adreßspeicher und für die laufende Adressierung der Operanden eingesetzt. Während der Programmausführung sind sämtliche Basisadressen über die Adreßleitung für die Blockschachtelungstiefe zugänglich. Daten, deren Basisadresse über die Blockschachtelungstiefe des momentan aktiven Programmblocks adressiert wird, sind dessen lokale Daten; Daten, deren Basisadresse über eine kleinere Blockschachtelungstiefe adressiert wird, sind dessen globale Daten.

Programmorganisation. Der Programmcode wird entsprechend den Blöcken und Prozeduren in Segmente unterteilt, die unabhängig voneinander in den Befehlsspeicher geladen werden. Die Adressierung eines Befehls ist nur über den Programmbasisspeicher, in dem die Programmbasisadressen der Segmente stehen, möglich (Bild 3). Dazu wird jedem Programmsegment eine Segmentnummer zugeordnet, die vor der Ausführung des Segments in das Programmsegmentregister PS geladen wird und so den Programmbasisspeicher adressiert. Zur Programmbasisadresse wird ein Programmindex addiert, der im Programmindexregister PI steht. Das PI-Register entspricht dem Befehlszähler; sein Inhalt wird zu Beginn der Ausführung eines Segments auf 0 gesetzt.

Mit jedem Blockeintritt werden die Inhalte der Register PS und PI als Rücksprunginformation in den Programmrücksprung- bzw. den Programmindexspeicher, die mit der neuen Blockschachtelungstiefe adressiert werden, gerettet. Sie werden beim Blockende wieder in die Register PS und PI geladen.

4. Speicherverwaltung für Prozeduren

Die Verwaltung von Prozeduren, die intern vereinbart werden, ähnelt der Verwaltung von Blöcken. Ein wesentlicher Unterschied ergibt sich jedoch durch die Datenorganisation bei der Parameterübergabe. Für die Parameterübergabe benutzen wir die beiden auch allgemein verwendbaren Maschinenbefehle DATA und EQU.

DATA s|& N   Initialisiere Variable s mit (N)
DATA reserviert zur Ausführungszeit eine Zelle im Operandenspeicher und lädt sie mit dem durch die Adresse N bezeichneten Operanden. Dieser kann entweder ein Direktoperand oder der Inhalt einer Zelle des Operandenspeichers sein. Die Reservierung und Belegung der zum neuen Operanden s gehörenden Adreßspeicherzelle über die beiden Register FA und FO und die Zuordnung der Adresse s zu dieser Zelle erfolgt analog zum RES-Be-

fehl. Der Inhalt des FO-Registers wird dabei jedoch nur um 1 erhöht. Wird DATA als Parametertransportbefehl benutzt (call by value), so ist s durch das Platzhaltesymbol & zu ersetzen.

EQU s|& N Setze s gleich N
EQU reserviert zur Ausführungszeit eine Zelle im Adreßspeicher und lädt sie mit der zur symbolischen Adresse N gehörenden numerischen Operandenspeicheradresse. Diese kann entweder ein Direktwert oder der Inhalt einer Adreßspeicherzelle sein. Die Reservierung der zum neuen Operanden s gehörenden Adreßspeicherzelle und deren Zuordnung zur Adresse s erfolgt analog zum RES-Befehl. Der Inhalt des FO-Registers bleibt jedoch unverändert. Wird EQU als Parametertransportbefehl benutzt (call by reference), so ist s durch das Platzhaltesymbol & zu ersetzen.

Der DATA- und der EQU-Befehl dürfen wie der RES-Befehl bei der Programmausführung weder übersprungen noch in Programmschleifen verwendet werden.

Prozeduraufruf und Parameterübergabe. Der Aufruf einer Prozedur erfolgt mit dem Maschinenbefehl CALL, die Parameterübergabe mit den Maschinenbefehlen DATA und EQU.

```
Prozeduraufruf        CALL  Name  Parameterzahl
                      EQU   &     adr1
                      EQU   &     adr2
                      DATA  &     adr3
                       :
```

Mit dem Befehl CALL wird der Aufruf eingeleitet. "Name" bezeichnet den Prozedurnamen; er wird im Maschinencode durch die Segmentnummer ersetzt. "Parameterzahl" gibt die Anzahl der auf CALL folgenden Parametertransportbefehle an. Durch CALL werden zunächst die neuen Datenbasisadressen (Inhalte von FO und FA) und die bisherige Segmentnummer (Inhalt von PS) in den Organisationsspeicher gerettet, der dazu mit der Blockschachtelungstiefe der aufgerufenen Prozedur adressiert wird. Da der Aufruf einer Prozedur in unterschiedlichen Blockschachtelungstiefen erfolgen kann, muß zusätzlich die Blockschachtelungstiefe des aufrufenden Segmentes als Rücksprunginformation für die Datenorganisation gerettet werden. Dazu kann z.B. der Programmrücksprungspeicher mitbenutzt werden. Anschließend werden in der bisherigen Blockschachtelungstiefe die Parametertransportbefehle ausgeführt. Während der Parameterübergabe, die unter der Steuerung des aufrufenden Segmentes erfolgt, sind mit dessen Datenumgebung auch die aktuellen Parameter zugänglich[1]. Die transportierten Parameter

1) Siehe dazu nachfolgenden Absatz:"Verdeckung von Datenbereichen".

belegen jedoch Zellen, die nach abgeschlossenem Prozeduraufruf in der lokalen Datenumgebung der Prozedur liegen. Die symbolischen Zieladressen der Transportbefehle sind durch das Platzhaltesymbol & ersetzt, da sie zum lokalen Datenbereich der Prozedur gehören und deshalb auch in ihr vereinbart werden müssen.

Nach Abschluß der Parameterübergabe wird der Programmindex (Inhalt von PI) in den Organisationsspeicher, der mit der Blockschachtelungstiefe der aufgerufenen Prozedur adressiert wird, gerettet. Der Programmsprung zur Prozedur erfolgt, indem das PS-Register mit der neuen Segmentnummer geladen und das PI-Register auf Null gesetzt wird. Diese abschließenden Ausführungsschritte sind Bestandteile des CALL-Befehls, der durch den Parametertransport in seiner Ausführung unterbrochen wurde.

Die Vereinbarung der formalen Parameter in der Prozedur wird durch die Assemblerdirektive proc mit dem Namen der Prozedur im Namensfeld und den formalen Parametern im Adreßfeld vorgenommen.

```
Prozedurdefinition          Name  proc  par1, par2, par3,...
                                    :
                                  RETURN
```

Der Assembler ordnet den formalen Parametern par1, par2, par3,... die numerischen Adressen 0,1,2,... zu, die der Speicherplatzzuordnung bei der Parameterübergabe entsprechen. Die Wiederherstellung der vor dem Prozeduraufruf gültigen Daten- und Programmumgebung erfolgt durch den Maschinenbefehl RETURN unter Auswertung der im Organisationsspeicher abgelegten Rücksprunginformation.

Verdeckung von Datenbereichen. Durch den Aufruf einer Prozedur in einer Blockschachtelungstiefe, die nicht mit der der Prozedurvereinbarung identisch ist (z.B. auch bei rekursivem Aufruf einer Prozedur),ergeben sich Programmzustände, in denen bestimmte Datenbereiche gegenüber einem Zugriff verdeckt sind (vgl. ALGOL 60). Das bedeutet, daß die Basisadressen dieser Datenbereiche im Adreßbasisspeicher für die Zeit der Verdekkung nicht adressierbar sein dürfen. Sie müssen jedoch zu einem späteren Zeitpunkt nach Aufhebung der Verdeckung wieder aktiviert werden können. Eine anschauliche Organisationsform erhält man durch einen dreidimensionalen Organisationsspeicher, der in der Vertikalen als Randomspeicher und in der Horizontalen als LIFO-Speicher adressiert wird[1]. Dabei ent-

1) Eine ähnliche Speicherorganisation wird in dem Rechnerkonzept HYDRA /5/ zur Organisation des Befehlspuffers für die blockstrukturierte Programmiersprache TPL (The Programming Language) vorgeschlagen.

sprechen die vertikalen Adressen den Blockschachtelungstiefen; die horizontalen Adressen geben die Verdeckungstiefe in einer Blockschachtelungstiefe an. So spiegelt z.B. die vorderste Speicherebene des Adreßbasisspeichers gerade die aktuelle Adreßumgebung wider. Für diesen Speicher muß in der dritten Dimension für jede Blockschachtelungstiefe genügend Speicherkapazität vorgesehen werden, da ein Überlauf innerhalb einer Blockschachtelungstiefe nicht in einer anderen Blockschachtelungstiefe aufgefangen werden kann. Dadurch kommt es zu einer sehr ineffektiven Speicherbelegung. Deshalb schlagen wir für den Organisationsspeicher eine Assoziativspeicherorganisation entsprechend Bild 4 vor.

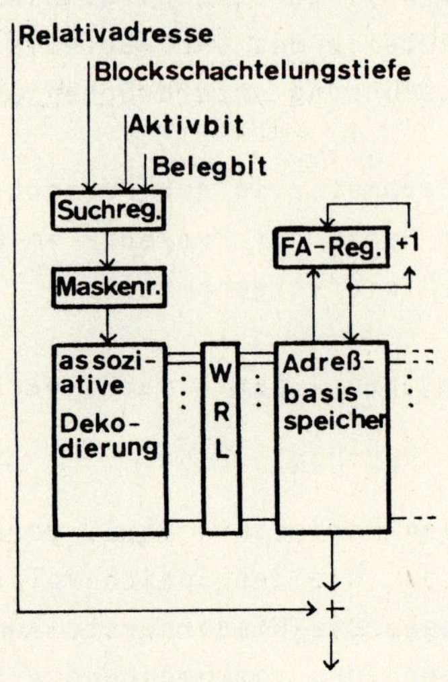

Bild 4. Organisationsspeicher mit assoziativer Dekodierung zur Verwaltung verdeckter Datenbereiche. Ersetzt den gestrichelten Teil in Bild 3.

Bild 4 zeigt den Ausschnitt des assoziativen Organisationsspeichers, der den in Bild 3 gestrichelt umrandeten Teil ersetzt. Die Adressierung des Speichers erfolgt jetzt über eine assoziative Dekodierung, die über ein Suchregister und ein Maskenregister angesteuert wird. Das Suchregister nimmt zusätzlich zur Blockschachtelungstiefe ein Bit zur Unterscheidung von freien und belegten Speicherzellen (Belegbit) und ein Bit zur Unterscheidung der Basisadressen unverdeckter und verdeckter Datenbereiche (Aktivbit) auf. Das Maskenregister ermöglicht eine Ausblendung der eigentlichen Suchinformation. Da bei einem assoziativen Suchvorgang mehrere Adressen gleichzeitig assoziiert werden können, ist eine Wortrandlogik (WRL) erforderlich, deren Hauptbestandteil eine Prioritätenschaltkette ist. Diese Schaltkette wählt die erste assoziierte Adresse aus und ersetzt damit das FB-Register in Bild 3 bei der Lokalisierung des ersten freien Speicherplatzes. Durch unterschiedliche Masken lassen sich sämtliche Funktionen wie Blockeintritt, Prozedureintritt, rekursiver Prozedureintritt, Blockrückkehr, Prozedurrückkehr usw. ausführen.

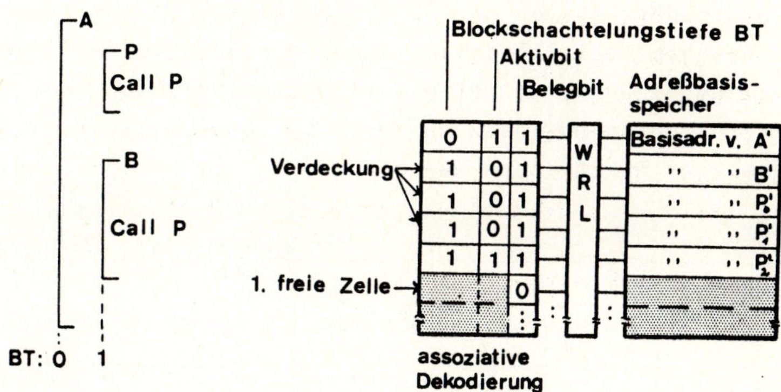

Bild 5. Programmbeispiel mit rekursiver Prozedur und Belegung der assoziativen Dekodierung und des Adreßbasisspeichers nach dem zweiten rekursiven Prozeduraufruf.

Bild 5 zeigt die Belegung des assoziativen Dekodierers und des Adreßbasisspeichers am Beispiel von zwei ineinander geschachtelten Blöcken A und B, wobei im inneren Block B eine im äußeren Block A vereinbarte rekursive Prozedur P aufgerufen wird. Die zu A,B und P gehörenden Datenbereiche sind mit A',B' und P' bezeichnet; der Index bei P' gibt die Verdeckungstiefe bei rekursiven Prozeduraufrufen an. Das Bild zeigt die Speicherbelegung nach dem dritten Aufruf der Prozedur, d.h. nach dem zweiten rekursiven Aufruf.

6. Ein Programmbeispiel

Die Funktionsweise des beschriebenen Speichermodells soll anhand eines Programmes, das in Bild 6 in Assemblerschreibweise angegeben ist, verdeutlicht werden. Es führt die Addition dreier Vektoren $\mathbf{x}$,$\mathbf{y}$ und $\mathbf{z}$ aus, die im Speicher als Felder X,Y und Z der Länge N dargestellt werden. Die Operation $\mathbf{x}:=\mathbf{x}+\mathbf{y}+\mathbf{z}$ wird in die beiden Einzeloperationen $\mathbf{x}:=\mathbf{x}+\mathbf{y}$ und $\mathbf{x}:=\mathbf{x}+\mathbf{z}$ zerlegt, die nacheinander von einer Prozedur zur Vektoraddition (VADD) ausgeführt werden.

Die Größen X und N werden im äußeren Block der Blockschachtelungstiefe 0 vereinbart, so daß sie während der gesamten Programmausführung zur Verfügung stehen. Die Ausführung der beiden Einzeloperationen erfolgt durch zweimaligen Aufruf der Prozedur VADD, die im äußeren Block vereinbart ist und somit ihren lokalen Datenbereich in der Blockschachtelungstiefe 1 hat. Die beiden Aufrufe finden in zwei inneren Blöcken derselben Blockschachtelungstiefe statt, wodurch sich eine Verdeckung der Basisadressen der zu den Blöcken gehörenden Datenbereiche ergibt. Da diese Datenbereiche gerade die Felder Y und Z umfassen, müssen die Feldanfangsadressen als Parameter in den lokalen Adreßspeicherbereich der Prozedur übergeben werden. Die Übergabe der Feldanfangsadresse X und die Feldlänge N als Parameter ist nicht unbedingt erforderlich, da beide Größen global bezüglich der Prozedur sind. Dazu müßte jedoch die Prozedur mit nur einem formalen Parameter geschrieben werden.

```
START  BEGIN                          Beginn des äußeren Blocks (BT=0)
       RES    N         '1            Reserviere 1 Speicherzelle für N
       READ   N         '1            Lies 1 Wort nach N
       RES    X          N            Reserviere (N) Speicherzellen für X
       READ   X          N            Lies (N) Worte nach X
       VADD   proc        M , A , B   Prozedurvereinbarung, formale Parameter M,A,B
              LOAD        I     '0    Lade Indexregister I mit 0
       L      ADD         A,I   B,I   Addiere Vektorkomponenten A,I ← (A,I)+(B,I)
              ADD         I     '1    Inkrementiere Indexregister um 1
              CMP         I     M     Vergleiche (I) mit (M)
              GOTO        L           Gehe nach L, wenn (I) < (M)
              RETURN                  Prozedurrückkehr , wenn (I)=(M)
              BEGIN                   Beginn des ersten inneren Blocks (BT=1)
              RES         Y     N     Reserviere (N) Speicherzellen für Y
              READ        Y     N     Lies (N) Worte nach Y
              CALL        VADD  '3    Prozeduraufruf mit 3 Parametern
              DATA        &     N     Parameterübergabe (call by value)
              EQU         &     X            "          (call by reference)
              EQU         &     Y            "          (call by reference)
              END                     Speicherplatzfreigabe für Y
              BEGIN                   Beginn des zweiten inneren Blocks (BT=1)
              RES         Z     N     Reserviere (N) Speicherzellen für Z
              READ        Z     N     Lies (N) Worte nach Z
              CALL        VADD  '3    Prozeduraufruf mit 3 Parametern
              DATA        &     N     Parameterübergabe (call by value)
              EQU         &     X            "          (call by reference)
              EQU         &     Z            "          (call by reference)
              END                     Speicherplatzfreigabe für Z
       :
       :
       END    START                   Speicherplatzfreigabe für X,N,...
```

Bild 6. Programmbeispiel: Vektoraddition $\mathbf{x}:=\mathbf{x}+\mathbf{y}+\mathbf{z}$

Beim Verlassen des ersten inneren Blockes wird mit END der Speicherbereich Y freigegeben, so daß er für den zweiten inneren Block zur Verfügung steht. Hier werden die Y-Werte durch die Z-Werte überschrieben. Nach Verlassen des zweiten inneren Blockes wird auch der Speicherbereich Z wieder freigegeben, so daß dann nur noch die Größen X und N des äußeren Blockes existieren. Durch die Blockstruktur wird also jeweils nur so viel Speicherplatz belegt, wie momentan benötigt wird.

Bild 7 zeigt die Speicherbelegung und die Inhalte der Register FO, FA und des Suchregisters nach dem ersten Prozeduraufruf bei abgeschlossener Parameterübergabe. Als eingelesener Wert für N wurde 100 gewählt. Die gestrichelten Pfeile im Adreßspeicher geben die Parameterübergabe

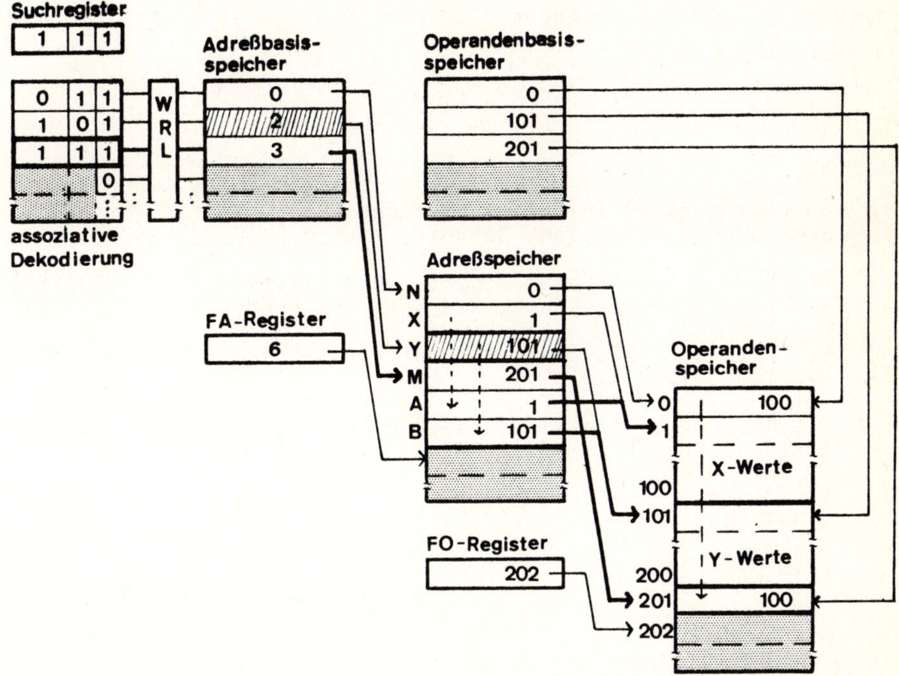

Bild 7. Speicherbelegung nach dem ersten Prozeduraufruf im Programmbeispiel von Bild 6.

"call by reference", der gestrichelte Pfeil im Operandenspeicher die Parameterübergabe "call by value" an. Die schraffierten Bereiche im Adreßbasisspeicher und im Adreßspeicher kennzeichnen die Verdeckung des Datenbereichs des ersten inneren Blocks, die durch das zugehörige Aktivbit in der assoziativen Dekodierung festgeschrieben ist. Mit dem Inhalt des Suchregisters wird der lokale Datenbereich der Prozedur aktiviert. Die Adressierung des Adreßspeichers durch die Relativadresse und des Operandenspeichers durch den Index (vgl. Bild 3) ist hier der Übersichtlichkeit halber weggelassen.

Bei der Übersetzung des symbolischen Programms löst der Assembler die beiden inneren Blöcke und die Prozedur aus dem äußeren Block heraus und behandelt sie als eigenständige Programmsegmente, deren Datenbereiche eine definierte Blockschachtelungstiefe haben und die von einander unabhängig in den Befehlsspeicher geladen werden. Lediglich die BEGIN-Befehle bleiben im umgebenden Block stehen, da sie neben der Datenbereichsorganisation auch den Sprung zum zugehörigen Block bewirken. Dazu wird jedem Programmsegment eine Segmentnummer als Kennzeichen zugeordnet. Die Programmausführung beginnt mit jenem Befehl, der das im letzten END-Befehl angegebene Startsymbol - hier START - im Namensfeld enthält.

Literatur

/1/ Burroughs B6700 Information Processing Systems Reference Manual, Burroughs Corporation, Detroit, Michigan 48232, 1972.

/2/ ORGANICK,E.I.: "Computer System Organization, The B5700/6700 Series", Academic Press, New York and London, 1973.

/3/ ILIFFE,J.K.: "Basic Machine Principles", American Elsevier Inc., New York, 1972.

/4/ FEUSTEL,E.A.: "The Rice Research Computer - A tagged architecture", SJCC, 1972, 369 - 377.

/5/ McFARLAND,C.: "A language-oriented computer design", FJCC, 1970, 629 - 640.

NEUE STRUKTURIERTE SPRACHKONZEPTE ZUR PROZESSYNCHRONISATION

Peter Kammerer
Fakultaet fuer Informatik, Universitaet Karlsruhe
D-75 Karlsruhe 1

Abstract

We assume that parallel programs can be started repeatedly without earlier runs of the same program having finished. This leads to the notions of process classes and classes of critical passages. To formulate synchronisation between such classes in a higher level language, new structured notations are proposed, which are extensions of the concepts "conditional critical regions" and "monitor". These new notations have two major advantages. Firstly they allow not only to express mutual exclusion but also single exclusion, an exclusion relation which often occurs in application problems (e.g. the second problem of readers and writers). Secondly because they deal with classes instead of single processes, the usual counting mechanisms to count several runs of the same program coexisting in time become invisible to the programmer. For instance, this makes unnecessary the use of "readercount" and "writercount" in the second problem of readers and writers.

1. Einleitung

In letzter Zeit wurden verschiedene strukturierte Sprachkonzepte zur Formulierung der Synchronisation von Prozessen diskutiert. Hoare [Ho74] und Brinch-Hansen [BH73, BH74] schlugen das Konzept der bedingten kritischen Abschnitte (conditial critical regions) und das Monitor-Konzept vor. Mit Hilfe dieser Konzepte lassen sich die Synchronisationsbeziehungen zwischen Prozessen klar und uebersichtlich auf Benutzerebene formulieren. Sie leisten insofern einen wesentlichen Beitrag zur Konstruktion korrekter Programme.

Die oben erwaehnten Sprachkonzepte besitzen jedoch gewisse einschraenkende Eigenschaften:

1. Sie erlauben dem Programmierer nur den Ausdruck der Synchronisationsbeziehung des gegenseitigen Ausschlusses (mutual exclusion), nicht aber der des einfachen Ausschlusses. Es gibt jedoch wichtige Anwendungsfaelle in denen diese Beziehung des einfachen Ausschlusses auftritt.

2. Sie unterstuetzen nur die Formulierung von Synchronisationsbeziehungen zwischen <u>einzelnen</u> Prozessen. Wie wir unten sehen werden, hat man es jedoch haeufig mit der Synchronisation ganzer Gruppen von Prozessen zu tun. Dieses ist genau dann der Fall, wenn man fuer Programme fordert, dass sie mehrmals nacheinander gestartet werden koennen, unabhaengig davon, ob ein etwa frueher begonnener Programmlauf bereits beendet ist. Diese Forderung ist zum Beispiel fuer Systemprogramme ueblich.

In dieser Arbeit sollen anstelle der oben erwaehnten Sprachkonzepte neue erweiterte Konzepte vorgeschlagen werden, die nicht mehr die obigen Einschraenkungen besitzen. Ferner wird zur uebersichtlichen Darstellung der Synchronisationsbeziehungen eine weiterentwickelte Version der Ausschlussgraphen (exclusion graphs [BW73]) vorgestellt. Fuer diese Graphen werden einige Regeln angegeben, insbesondere eine zu deren Reduktion. Diese Graphen sind eine nuetzliche Hilfe beim Entwurf von Prozessystemen, da sie eine einfache und uebersichtliche Darstellung von Synchronisationsbeziehungen gestatten und somit zur Vermeidung von Synchronisationsfehlern beitragen.

2. Kritischer Abschnitt und kritischer Ablauf

Zwischen zwei kritischen Abschnitten A und B eines oder verschiedener Programme kann folgende Relation bestehen: "A schliesst B aus". Diese Relation nennen wir Ausschlussrelation. Sie macht folgende Aussage ueber die zeitlichen Ablaufmoeglichkeiten der kritischen Abschnitte A und B: wenn der kritische Abschnitt A begonnen wurde, dann kann nicht zugleich der kritische Abschnitt Abschnitt B begonnen werden, sondern dessen Beginn muss verzoegert werden, bis der kritische Abschnitt A beendet ist. Diese Ausschlussrelation ist weder transitiv noch symmetrisch. Gilt zwischen zwei kritischen Abschnitten eine solche Ausschlussrelation, jedoch nicht deren Umkehrung, dann reden wir von einfachem Anschluss. Gilt jedoch auch die Umkehrung oder schliesst sich ein kritischer Abschnitt selbst aus, dann besteht die Beziehung des gegenseitigen Ausschlusses. Diese Faelle treten in Anwendungsproblemen haeufig auf und sind bekannt als Problem des gegenseitigen Ausschlusses (mutual exclusion problem).

2.1 Ausschlussgraphen

Die Darstellung der Ausschlussrelation erfolgt zweckmaessigerweise als gerichteter Graph in einer erweiterten Form der Ausschlussgraphen (exclusion) graphs) [BW73]. Hierbei werden die kritischen Abschnitte (k.A.) als Knoten und die Relationen als gerichtete Kanten dargestellt. Betrachten wir als Beispiel das erste Leser-Schreiber Problem im [CHP71], so haben wir folgende Ausschlussbeziehungen zwischen den kritischen Abschnitten (k. A.) "Lesen"und "Schreiben":

- Solange ein Schreiber schreibt, darf kein weiterer Schreiber zu schreiben beginnen.

- Solange ein Leser liest, darf kein Schreiber beginnen zu schreiben und umgekehrt, d.h. die kritischen Abschnitte Lesen und Schreiben schliessen sich gegenseitig aus.

Dieser Sachverhalt laesst sich einfach darstellen in dem folgenden Ausschlussgraphen:

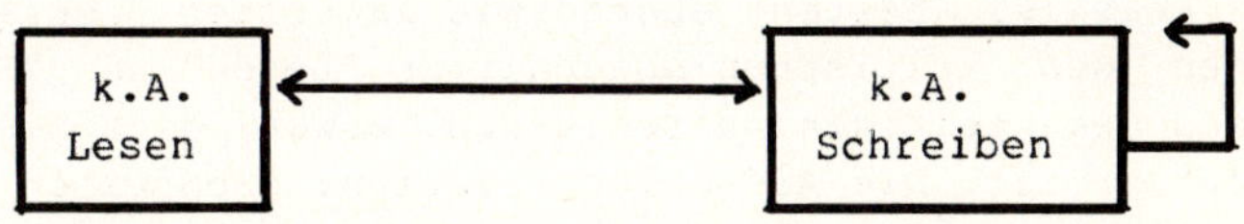

Abb. 2.1 Ausschlussgraph fuer das erste Leser-Schreiber Problem

Eine Besonderheit dieser Ausschlussgraphen ist, dass hier auch geschachtelte Knoten, d.h. Knoten die andere Knoten enthalten, auftreten koennen. Dadurch wird der Tatsache Rechnung getragen, dass in Programmen kritische Abschnitte geschachtelt auftreten koennen.

Fuer solche geschachtelte Knoten werden die folgenden Eigenschaften definiert:

Regel 1: Schliesst ein geschachtelter Knoten einen anderen Knoten aus, so gilt das auch fuer alle inneren Knoten, d.h. fuer die Knoten die in ihm enthalten sind.

Regel 2: Wird ein geschachtelter Knoten von einem anderen Knoten ausgeschlossen, so werden auch alle inneren Knoten ausgeschlossen.

Untersuchen wir als Beispiel das zweite Leser-Schreiber Problem [CHP71], so ist dieses aufzufassen als eine Erweiterung des ersten Leser-Schreiber Problems. Zu den beiden kritischen Abschnitten "Lesen" und "Schreiben" tritt noch der Dritte: "Anmeldung zum Schreiben" hinzu. Die oben angefuehrten Ausschlussbeziehungen sind zu erweitern um die Bedingung:

- wenn sich ein Schreiber zum Schreiben anmeldet, darf kein (weiterer) Leser beginnen zu lesen.

Fuer diesen Sachverhalt erhalten wir folgenden Ausschlussgraphen:

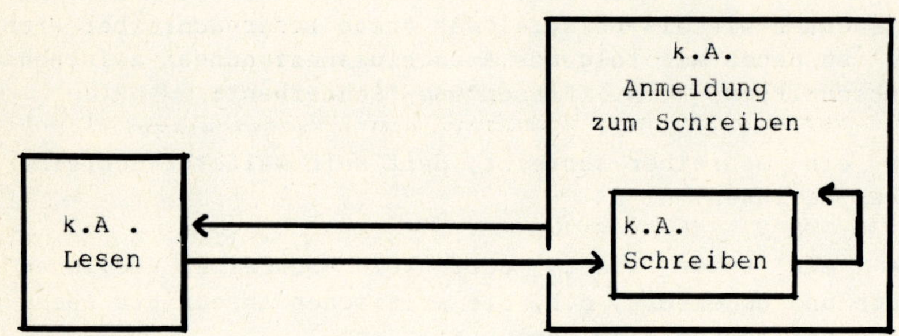

Abb. 2.2 Ausschlussgraph fuer das zweite Leser-Schreiber Problem

Bei diesem Beispiel besteht ebenso wie im ersten Leser-Schreiber Problem zwischen den kritischen Abschnitten "Lesen" und "Schreiben" die Beziehung des gegenseitigen Ausschlusses, obwohl dies nicht direkt im Graphen sichtbar ist. Die Ausschlussrelation: "Schreiben schliesst Lesen aus", wird durch die obige Regel 1 impliziert. An diesem Beispiel ist ferner hervorzuheben, dass neben der haeufig zu findenden Beziehung des gegenseitigen Ausschlusses auch die des einfachen Ausschusses auftritt. Der kritische Abschnitt "Anmeldung zum Schreiben" schliesst den kritischen Abschnitt "Lesen" aus, jedoch nicht umgekehrt.

Wie diese Beispiele zeigen, erlauben Ausschlussgraphen eine einfache und uebersichtliche Darstellung der Synchronisationsbeziehungen in einem System von Programmen. Ihre Bedeutung ist aber weniger in ihrer Verwendung als Dokumentationshilfsmittel zu sehen, sondern in ihrer Anwendung beim Entwurf von Programmsystemen. Sie bieten ein Hilfsmittel zur Entdeckung von Vereinfachungsmoeglichkeiten in der Synchronisation durch die im folgenden zu besprechende Moeglichkeit der Reduktion von Ausschlussgraphen. Dazu sollen zuvor noch einige Begriffsbildungen eingefuehrt werden.

Ein Knoten A kann von mehreren anderen Knoten $B_1 \ldots B_n$ ausgeschlossen werden. Wir nennen dann die Menge derjenigen Knoten $\{B_1 \ldots B_n\}$ die A ausschliessen die ausschliessende Menge von A.

Ein Knoten A kann mehrere andere Knoten $C_1 \ldots C_m$ ausschliessen. Dann nennen wir die Menge der ausgeschlossenen Knoten $\{C_1 \ldots C_m\}$ die ausgeschlossene Menge von A.

Haben zwei Knoten R und S dieselbe ausschliessende Menge und dieselbe ausgeschlossene Menge, so sagen wir die Knoten haben dieselbe Aussenbeziehung. Treten solche Knoten in einem Ausschlussgraphen auf, so ist er reduzierbar. Er wird reduziert, indem man solche Knoten zu einem neuen zusammenfasst. Dabei spielt es keine Rolle, ob die durch die Knoten dargestellten kritischen Abschnitte in einem oder in verschiedenen Programmen liegen. Uns interessiert nur ihre Synchronisationsbeziehung, nicht jedoch die Funktion innerhalb des, oder der Programme. Kritische Abschnitte mit gleichen Synchronisationsbeziehungen werden also im reduzierten Graphen durch einen Knoten dargestellt. Die Kodierung ihrer Synchronisationsmassnahmen ist gleich.

2.2 Klassen kritischer Ablaeufe

Bei unseren weiteren Betrachtungen gehen wir davon aus, dass folgende Forderung erfuellt ist:

> Ein Ablauf eines Programmes kann jederzeit gestartet werden, unabhaengig davon, ob ein etwa frueher gestarteter Ablauf desselben Programmes bereits beendet ist.

Dann koennen also zu einem Programm mehrere Programmablaeufe existieren. Jedem dieser Ablaeufe ist ein Adressraum zugeordnet. Einen solchen Programmablauf im zugeordneten Adressraum nennen wir Prozess. Mehrere zeitlich zugleich existierende Prozesse desselben Programmes bezeichnen wir als Prozessklasse.

Wir nehmen an, dass Programme einen oder mehrere kritische Abschnitte enthalten. Den Ablauf eines solchen kritischen Abschnittes bezeichnen wir als kritischen Ablauf. Ebenso wie zu einem Programm eine Prozessklasse existieren kann, koennen zu einem kritischen Abschnitt mehrere kritische Ablaeufe zeitlich zugleich existieren. Wir reden dann von einer Klasse kritischer Ablaeufe. Eine solche Klasse, sei es eine Prozessklasse oder eine Klasse kritischer Ablaeufe, nennen wir zu einem bestimmten Zeitpunkt existent, falls zu diesem Zeitpunkt auch nur ein Prozess beziehungsweise kritischer Ablauf begonnen und noch nicht beendet wurde. Die Existenz einer Klasse kritischer Ablaeufe impliziert stets die Existenz einer Prozessklasse, jedoch nicht umgekehrt. Von einem Programm, das einen kritischen Abschnitt enthaelt, kann zu einem Zeitpunkt eine Prozessklasse existieren und keine Klasse kritischer Ablaeufe existent sein. Dies ist dann der Fall, wenn sich saemtliche Prozesse der Prozessklasse in der Abarbeitung des Programms ausserhalb eines kritischen Abschnitts befinden.

Die oben eingefuehrten Begriffsbildungen sollen anhand eines Beispiels verdeutlicht werden. Wir waehlen dazu das bekannte erste Leser-Schreiber Problem[CHP71]. Bei diesem Problem ist der Synchronisationsalgorithmus fuer zwei Programme LESER und SCHREIBER zu entwickeln, die jeweils einen kritischen Abschnitt LESEN beziehungsweise SCHREIBEN enthalten. Die Ausschlussbeziehungen der kritischen Abschnitte wurden bereits im vorangehenden Abschnitt 2.1 formuliert und mittels Ausschlussgraphen dargestellt. Jedes der beiden Programme soll gemaess unserer eingangs zugrundegelegten Forderung mehrmals nacheinander gestartet werden koennen, unabhaengig davon, ob ein etwa frueher gestarteter Ablauf desselben Programmes bereits beendet ist. Es koennen somit zu den Programmen LESER beziehungsweise SCHREIBER jeweils Prozessklassen existent sein. Ebenso koennen zu den kritischen Abschnitten LESEN und SCHREIBEN Klassen kritischer Ablaeufe auftreten. Betrachten wir die Ausschlussbeziehungen, so stellen wir zunaechst fest, dass die Klasse kritischer Ablaeufe zum Abschnitt SCHREIBEN hoechstens einen kritischen Ablauf enthalten kann, da sich der kritische Abschnitt SCHREIBEN selbst ausschliesst. Dagegen kann die

Klasse kritischer Ablaeufe zum Abschnitt LESEN mehrere kritische Ablaeufe umfassen. Dies ist zu beachten bei der Programmierung der Ausschlussbedingung: "Solange ein LESER liest, darf kein SCHREIBER beginnen zu schreiben". Mit den oben eingefuehrten Begriffen kann diese Bedingung umformuliert werden in: "Solange die Klasse kritischer Ablaeufe des Abschnittes LESEN existent ist, darf kein SCHREIBER in seinen kritischen Abschnitt SCHREIBEN eintreten". Bei der Programmierung dieser Ausschlussbedingung muss man also durch eine geeignete Methode die Existenz der Klasse kritischer Ablaeufe zum Abschnitt LESEN feststellen. Dies geschieht programmtechnisch ueblicherweise durch einen Zaehlmechanismus, bei dem bei Eintritt in den kritischen Abschnitt eine diesem Abschnitt zugeordnete Zaehlvariable um eins erhoeht beziehungsweise bei Austritt um eins erniedrigt wird. Diese Zaehlvariable - im untenstehenden Programm rr - wird bei Systemstart initialisiert (z.B. mit null) und vor Eintritt in den kritischen Abschnitt SCHREIBEN abgeprueft. Da auf diese Zaehlvariable von beiden Programmen zugegriffen wird, darf dies nur unter gegenseitigem Anschluss, das heisst innerhalb der Programmkonstruktion kritischer Abschnitt (critical region) geschehen. Wir erhalten so als Loesung des ersten Leser-Schreiber Problems, formuliert mittels bedingten kritischen Abschnitten in einer PASCAL-aehnlichen Schreibweise:

```
var v : shared record rr : integer end;
rr := 0; % Initialisierung der Zaehlvariablen rr

cobegin
    begin % LESER                        begin % SCHREIBER
        region v do rr:= rr+1;             region v do
                                             begin await rr=0;
        LESEN                                SCHREIBEN
        region v do rr:= rr-1              end
    end;                                 end
                                         coend
```

Betrachten wir nochmals die eben durchgefuehrte Entwicklung der obigen Loesung, so lassen sich daraus einige allgemeingueltige Schluesse ziehen. Die eingangs gestellte Forderung hat das Auftreten von Prozessklassen und Klassen kritischer Ablaeufe zur Folge. Bei der Formulierung der Ausschlussbeziehung hat man es dann nicht mehr mit einem einzigen Ablauf zu tun, sondern prinzipiell mit einer Klasse von kritischen Ablaeufen. Eine Ausschlussrelation (im obigen Beispiel etwa "LESEN schliesst SCHREIBEN aus") gilt fuer alle Ablaeufe des ausschliessenden kritischen Abschnittes. Deshalb ist es zweckmaessig, diese zu Klassen zusammenzufassen und so vom einzelnen Ablauf zur Klasse kritischer Ablaeufe zu abstrahieren. Wir gelangen damit zu einer Neuformulierung der Anschlussrelation.

> "A schliesst B aus" bedeutet: solange die Klasse kritischer Ablaeufe von A existent ist, kann kein kritischer Ablauf von B beginnen.

Will man diese Ausschlussrelation programmieren, so steht man stets vor der Aufgabe, vor Eintritt in den kritischen Abschnitt B abzupruefen, ob die Klasse kritischer Ablaeufe existiert. Diese Aufgabe tritt stets im Zusammenhang mit der programmtechnischen Formulierung der Ausschlussrelation auf, wenn wir fuer unsere Programme die eingangs gestellte Forderung zugrundelegen. Es liegt daher nahe, diese Aufgabe als Bestandteil der Implementierung in neue strukturierte Sprachkonzepte zur Synchronisation einzugliedern, so dass sie auf Benutzerebene nicht mehr auftritt. Dazu sollen im folgenden Abschnitt einige Vorschlaege gemacht werden.

3. Strukturierte Sprachelemente zur Synchronisation von Klassen kritischer Ablaeufe

In juengster Zeit wurden verschiedene strukturierte Sprachelemente zur Synchronisation vorgeschlagen. Die zwei wesentlichen Konzepte sind:

- bedingte kritische Abschnitte (conditional critical regions) [BH73].

- Monitor [BH74, Ho74]

Beide Konzepte sollen im folgenden so erweitert werden, dass sie dazu geeignet sind:

- Klassen kritischer Ablaeufe zu behandeln und

- neben der Synchronisationsbeziehung des gegenseitigen Anschlusses, die des einfachen Ausschlusses zu formulieren.

Es soll nicht Aufgabe der folgenden Abschnitte sein, eine neue Sprache zu entwerfen oder zu definieren, vielmehr sollen Konzepte vorgestellt werden, die in der einen oder anderen Form in nichtsequentiellen Programmiersprachen Verwendung finden koennen.

3.1 Erweiterte bedingte kritische Abschnitte

Zur Formulierung von kritischen Abschnitten (k.A.) wird in Anlehnung an [BH73] das folgende strukturierte Sprachelement vorgeschlagen.

```
region <Bezeichnung des k.A.>
    exclude <Liste von Bezeichnungen k.A.>
    exclude mutually <Liste von Bezeichnungen k.A.>

            -Anweisungen des kritischen Abschnitts-

endregion
```

Hierbei wird jedem kritischen Abschnitt in einem Programmsystem, d.h. jedem Knoten im reduzierten Ausschlussgraphen eine Bezeichnung zugeordnet. Diese steht hinter dem Wortsymbol <u>region</u>. Nach <u>exclude</u> und <u>exclude mutually</u> erscheinen die Bezeichnungen jener kritischen Abschnitte, die ausgeschlossen werden, beziehungsweise die im gegenseitigen Ausschluss mit dem betrachteten kritischen Abschnitt stehen. Die Schreibweise <u>exclude mutually</u> soll lediglich eine zusaetzliche Moeglichkeit zur Ueberpruefung der Konsistenz der Programme bieten. Der kritische Abschnitt beginnt mit dem Wortsymbol <u>region</u> und und endet mit <u>endregion</u>. Er besitzt ein Einleitungselement (region...exclude mutually...) und ein Endeelement (endregion). Die Semantik beider Sprachelemente kann definiert werden mit Hilfe der von Belpaire und Wilmotte [BW73] eingefuehrten d-Operationen. Diese sind unteilbare Elementaroperationen zur Synchronisation , was unten durch die Klammern [ ] angedeutet werden soll. Diese Operationen koennen aufgefasst werden als eine Verallgemeinerung der Semaphoreoperationen P und V. Das Einleitungselement ist definiert durch

[test $S_i \ldots S_k$; down S_a].

und das Endeelement durch

[up S_a]

Hierbei bezeichnet S die Semaphorevariablen. Diese sind globale Systemvariable. Sie werden bei Start des Systems mit Null initialisiert. Fuer jede Bezeichnung eines kritischen Abschnitts, d.h. fuer jeden Knoten im Ausschlussgraphen, wird eine Semaphorevariable S_a eingefuehrt, die diesem Abschnitt bzw. Knoten zugeordnet ist. Der ausschliessenden Menge dieses Knotens sind die Semaphorevariablen $S_i \ldots S_k$ zugeordnet. Die Semaphoreoperation test prueft die Werte aller Semaphorevariablen der nachfolgenden Liste. Solange einer dieser Werte negativ ist, wird die begonnene unteilbare Elementaroperation durch Abbruch beendet und muss wiederholt werden. Das bedeutet, dass die Ausfuehrung der Operation down und die des kritischen Abschnitts verzoegert wird. Die Operation down erniedrigt die Werte aller in der nachfolgenden Liste folgenden Semaphorevariablen um eins.

Mit der eingefuehrten Sprachkonstruktion koennen bis jetzt zwar Ausschlussprobleme (exclusion problems) jedoch keine Benachrichtigungsprobleme (synchronisation problems) formuliert werden. Deshalb fuehren wir eine sogenannte inspect-Anweisung ein:

```
<inspect-Anweisung>::=
   inspect <Variablenbezeichnung> do
              <zusammengesetzte Anweisung>
              await <Boole´scher Ausdruck> endinspect.
```

Diese Anweisung kann als Anweisung eines kritischen Abschnittes auftreten. Sie bezieht sich aehnlich wie die critical regions bei [BH73] auf eine bestimmte Variable (Verbund). Zwei inspect- Anweisungen, die sich auf dieselbe Bezeichnung beziehen, koennen nur unter gegenseitigem Ausschluss ablaufen. Innerhalb der inspect-Anweisung kann nur auf Verbundkomponenten der angefuehrten Bezeichnung zugegriffen werden. Um die Ausdrucksmoeglichkeiten des vorgeschlagenen Sprachkonzeptes zu zeigen, seien im folgenden zwei Beispiele angegeben.

3.1.1. Zweites Leser-Schreiber Problem mit erweiterten bedingten kritischen Abschnitten

Wir formulieren als erstes das bereits unter dem Abschnitt 2.1 behandelte zweite Leser-Schreiber Problem. Entsprechend dem dort aufgestellten Ausschlussgraphen treten drei kritische Abschnitte auf:

L Lesen
AS Anmeldung zum Schreiben
S Schreiben.

Die Programme fuer die Leser- und Schreiber Prozesse lauten (in einer PASCAL aehnlichen Sprache):

```
LESER: repeat                 SCHREIBER: repeat
                              region AS exclude L
region L exclude S            region S exclude mutually S
.......lesen........          .......schreiben.......
endregion                     endregion
                              endregion
forever                       forever
```

Bei dieser Loesung ist hervorzuheben, dass hier keine Zaehlvariablen (readcount und writecount) auftreten, wie etwa in der in [BH73] angegebenen Loesung. Diese Variablen sind fuer den Programmierer unsichtbar geworden.

3.1.2 Ein Erzeuger-Verbraucher Problem mit erweiterten bedingten kritischen Abschnitten

Als zweites Anwendungsbeispiel wollen wir das erste Leser-Schreiber Problem behandeln. Auch dieses Problem wurde bereits in Abschnitt 2.1 (Ausschlussgraphen) untersucht. Wie wir sahen, ist es ein reines Ausschlussproblem. Es soll daher erweitert werden zu einem Benachrichtigungsproblem durch folgende Spezifikationen:

- ein Schreiber erzeugt jeweils einen ganzen Pufferinhalt und ein Leser liest jeweils einen ganzen Pufferinhalt;

- gelesen werden kann nur, wenn ein Pufferinhalt erzeugt wurde;

- geschrieben werden kann nur, wenn ein Pufferinhalt mindestens einmal gelesen wurde.

Damit hat sich an den Ausschlussbeziehungen nichts geaendert. Diese bleiben nach wie vor die des ersten Leser-Schreiber Problems. Entsprechend der in 2.1 aufgestellten Ausschlussgraphen haben wir zwei kritische Abschnitte: Lesen (L) und Schreiben (S). Damit koennen wir die Programme fuer die Leser- und Schreiber-Prozesse in einer PASCAL aehnlichen Sprache formulieren:

```
                shared variable FULL:boolean

LESER:repeat                           SCHREIBER:repeat
region L exclude mutually S            region S exclude  mutually S,L
     inspect FULL do                        inspect FULL do
       await FULL                             await not FULL
     endinspect;                            endinspect;
     ..lesen......                          ..schreiben.....
     inspect FULL do                        inspect FULL do
             FULL := false                          FULL := true
     endinspect                             endinspect
endregion                              endregion
forever                                forever
```

Bei dieser Loesung ist der Vergleich mit bisher ueblichen Loesungen des ersten Leser-Schreiber Problems [BH73] interessant. Erstens faellt auf, dass die bei den bisherigen Sprachkonstruktionen uebliche Zaehlvariable fehlt. Zweitens scheint die Formulierung der Programme komplizierter geworden zu sein. Dies ruehrt natuerlich daher, dass wir das erste Leser-Schreiber Problem durch zusaetzliche Bedingungen erschwert haben. Bei dem betrachteten Beispiel sind zwei Probleme ueberlagert, naemlich das Ausschlussproblem und das Benachrichtigungsproblem. Die Loesung des einen sollte ohne Beachtung der Loesung des anderen moeglich sein. Das bedeutet aber, dass diese Trennung auch klar im Programm hervortreten muss. Deshalb erscheinen klar getrennte Programmierkonzepte vorteilhaft, die den beiden verschiedenen Synchronisationsproblemen angepasst sind, so dass diese Trennung auch klar in der Formulierung der Loesungen zum Ausdruck kommt. Die Warteoperation await tritt dann nur noch bei der Formulierung von Benachrichtigungsproblemen auf.

3.2 Erweitertes Monitorkonzept

Zur klareren Strukturierung von nichtsequentiellen Programmsystemen (z.B. Betriebssystemen) wurde von Hoare [Ho73] und Brinch-Hansen [BH74] das Monitorkonzept eingefuehrt. Hierzu wird folgende erweiterte Form in einer PASCAL aehnlichen Schreibweise vorgeschlagen:

```
var M: monitor
        var V1 : T1 ;...VM : TM ;
        shared var S1 : TS1;....SM : TSM ;
        proc entry P1 (...)
               exclude <Liste von Prozedurbezeichnungen>
                   exclude mutually <Liste von Prozedur-
                                     bezeichnungen>;
               begin
                ---Prozedurrumpf---
               end;
              .
              .
              .
        begin <Anweisungen zur Initialisierung> end;
```

Diese Formulierung vereinbart einen Monitor mit der Bezeichnung M. Er ist eine Verallgemeinerung des in [BH74a] angegebenen Monitors. Die Erweiterungen bestehen in den folgenden Punkten:

- Es wurde ein exclude-Element eingefuehrt, dessen Bedeutung dem in Abschnitt 3.1 behandelten entspricht. Ebenso entspricht die semantische Definition des Prozedurkopfes mit exclude der des Einleitungselementes und die des Prozedur - end´s der des Endeelements.

- Innerhalb des Prozedurrumpfes einer Prozedur kann eine inspect-Anweisung auftreten.

  <inspect-Anweisung> ::= inspect <Variablenbezeichnung> do <Anweisungsteil> endinspect

  Die Definition dieser Anweisung erfolgt analog zu der im 3.1 eingefuehrten inspect-Anweisung. Die Variablenbezeichnung muss die einer mit dem Zusatz shared vereinbarten Groesse sein. Nur innerhalb des Anweisungsteils der inspect-Anweisung koennen die im [BH74a] definierten Warteschlangenoperationen delay(q) und continue(q) ausgefuehrt werd

Im uebrigen entspricht die Definition des Monitors, der Warteschlangen usw. dem in [BH74a] eingefuehrten Konzept.

3.2.1 Zweites Leser-Schreiber Problem mit erweitertem Monitorkonzept

Die Aufgabenstellung dieses Problems wurde bereits in den Abschnitten 2.1 und 3.1.1 behandelt, so dass wir uns hier auf die Formulierung der Loesung beschraenken koennen. Das Programm fuer die Leser - beziehungsweise die Schreiber - Prozesse lautet:

```
var BL : block;
LESER : repeat
        READ (BL)
        forever
```

```
var BS : block;
SCHREIBER  : repeat
             AWRITE (BS)
             forever
```

mit dem Monitor:

```
monitor
var P : buffer; ...

proc entry READ (B : block) exclude WRITE;
begin - lese aus Puffer P - end;

proc entry AWRITE (B:block) exclude READ;
begin WRITE(B) end;

proc WRITE (B:block) exclude WRITE;
begin - schreibe in Puffer P - end;

begin -initialisierung- end
```

3.2.2 Ein Erzeuger-Verbraucher Problem mit dem erweiterten Monitorkonzept

Die Aufgabenstellung ist dieselbe wie in Abschnitt 3.1.2. Wir koennen uns daher auf die Formulierung der Loesung beschraenken. Das Programm fuer die Erzeuger-(Schreiber-) beziehungsweise Verbraucher-(Leser-) Prozesse lautet:

```
var BV:block;
VERBRAUCHER:repeat

            READ(BV)

            forever
```

```
var BE:block;
ERZEUGER:repeat

         WRITE(BE)

         forever
```

mit dem Monitor

```
monitor
var P:buffer ;
shared var FULL:boolean ;
var READERS, WRITERS:queue;

proc entry READ (B:block) exclude mutually WRITE;
begin inspect FULL do
        if not FULL then delay (READERS)
      endinspect;
      - lese aus Puffer P -
      inspect FULL do
              FULL:=false; continue (WRITERS)
      endinspect
end READ;

proc entry WRITE (B:block) exclude mutually WRITE, READ;
begin inspect FULL do
        if FULL then delay (WRITERS)
      endinspect;
      - schreibe in Puffer P -
      inspect FULL do
              FULL:=true; continue (READERS)
  endinspect
end WRITE;

begin -Initialisierungen- end;
```

Man beachte bei dieser Loesung, dass mehrere Verbraucher zugleich im Puffer lesen koennen. Trotzdem wird keine Zaehlvariable benoetigt, um festzustellen, ob noch ein Verbraucher liest, wenn ein Erzeuger schreiben will.

4. Zusammenfassung

Die Ausschlussbeziehungen zwischen kritischen Abschnitten lassen sich sehr uebersichtlich an Hand von Ausschlussgraphen darstellen. Dazu wird eine erweiterte Version der Ausschlussgraphen von [BW73] entwickelt. Die Analyse verschiedener Anwendungsbeispiele mit Hilfe dieser Graphen, etwa die des zweiten Leser-Schreiber Problems, zeigt, dass neben der Ausschlussbeziehung des gegenseitigen Ausschlusses auch noch die des einfachen Ausschlusses auftritt.

In dieser Arbeit stellen wir an Programme die Forderung, dass ein Programm jederzeit gestartet werden kann, unabhaengig davon, ob ein frueher gestarteter Programmablauf bereits beendet ist. Dies fuehrt zur Einfuehrung neuer Begriffe, dem Begriff Prozessklasse und - sofern das Programm kritische Abschnitte enthaelt - dem Begriff der Klasse kritischer Ablauefe. Bei der Aufgabe, die Synchronisation von Programmen zu formulieren, die der obigen Forderung genuegen, hat man es stets mit der Teilaufgabe zu tun, kritische Ablauefe zu zaehlen. Dieser Tatsache sollten Sprachkonzepte zur Synchronisation in hoeheren Programmiersprachen Rechnung tragen und zwar dadurch, dass sie diese Teilaufgabe als Einzelheit der Implementierung enthalten. Es ist unzweckmaessig, einen immer wieder auftretenden Zaehlmechanismus auf der Ebene hoeherer Programmiersprachen formulieren zu muessen, wie das bei den zur Zeit gebraeuchlichen Sprachkonzepten wie z.B. "conditional critical regions" [BH72] und "monitors" [BH74, Ho74] notwendig ist. Es werden deshalb neue strukturierte Sprachkonzepte vorgeschlagen, die die oben erwaehnten Konzepte als Sonderfaelle enthalten, darueberhinaus aber die folgenden Vorteile bieten:

- Sie erlauben eine einfache Umsetzung der mit Hilfe der Ausschlussgraphen gefundenen Synchronisationsbeziehungen in Programme.

- Sie erlauben neben der Beziehung des gegenseitigen Ausschlusses auch die Formulierung des einseitigen Ausschlusses.

- Sie erlauben eine getrennte Entwicklung und Darstellung der Loesung des Ausschlussproblems und des Benachrichtigungsproblems.

- Die mit diesen Sprachkonzepten formulierten Programme koennen mehrfach nacheinander gestartet werden, unabhaengig davon, ob ein etwa frueher gestarteter Programmlauf bereits beendet ist. Auf Benutzerebene muessen keine Zaehlmechanismen mehr programmiert werden. Die Programme werden so von unnoetigem Ballast befreit und damit uebersichtlicher.

Literatur

[BW73] Belpaire G. and Wilmotte P.
A semantic approach to the theory of parallel processes. in A.Guenther et al. (eds.), International Computing Symposium 1973 (Davos).

[CHP71] Courtois P.J., Heymans F., and Parnas D.L.;
Concurrent control with readers and writers. CACM 14,10 (October 1971).

[BH73] Brinch-Hansen P.;
Operating System Principles. Prentice-Hall, Englewood Cliffs, N.J., 1973.

[BH74] Brinch-Hansen P.;
A programming methodology for operating system design. Lecture Notes of the IFIP Congress 1974.

[Ho74] Hoare C.A.R.:
Monitors: an operating system structuring concept. CACM 17, (October 1974).

[BH74a] Brinch-Hansen, P.;
Concurrent Pascal - a programming language for operating system design. Technical Institute of Technology, Pasadena California.

AUSWERTUNGSNETZE ALS HILFSMITTEL ZUR MODELLBILDUNG

- PROBLEME UND DEREN LÖSUNGEN -

L. Stewen
Philips Forschungslaboratorium Hamburg GmbH,
2 Hamburg 54, Vogt-Kölln-Straße 30

ZUSAMMENFASSUNG

Für die Beschreibung von Modellen auf dem Gebiet der Rechensysteme stehen, je nach Aufgabenstellung, eine Reihe unterschiedlicher Modellbeschreibungsverfahren zur Verfügung. Auswertungsnetze eignen sich besonders gut zur Beschreibung von Modellen, die zur Ermittlung von Leistungsparametern mit Hilfe der Simulation dienen, da sich hiermit parallele Prozesse, Verzögerungszeiten und Datenflüsse gut darstellen lassen.

Grundbegriffe und Anwendung der Auswertungsnetze werden an Beispielen erläutert. Bei der Anwendung auftretende Probleme und Vorschläge für deren Lösung werden diskutiert.

Die diesem Bericht zugrunde liegenden Arbeiten wurden mit Mitteln des Bundesministers für Forschung und Technologie (Kennzeichen: DV 2.008) gefördert.

EINLEITUNG

Modelle sind Bilder der Wirklichkeit, bei denen jeweils das Wesentliche dargestellt und das Unwesentliche weggelassen wird. Was wesentlich und was unwesentlich ist, wird in einem Abstraktionsprozeß durch den Modellbildner bestimmt und hängt von der zugrunde liegenden Aufgabenstellung ab.

Ein Modell kann erstellt werden:

- als Darstellungshilfsmittel zur Erläuterung von Funktionsabläufen und der darin enthaltenen logischen Zusammenhänge,
- zur Überprüfung komplizierter Vorgänge auf Fehlerfreiheit,
- zur Ermittlung von Leistungsparametern mit Hilfe der Simulation.

In diesem Bericht soll der zuletzt genannte Aspekt, die Ermittlung von Leistungsparametern, im Vordergrund stehen.

Der Vorgang der Modellbildung ist im allgemeinen äußerst kompliziert, da dem Modellbildner in der Regel keine eindeutigen Verfahren zur Umsetzung des Originals in das Modell zur Verfügung stehen und er deswegen weitgehend auf seine Intuition und seine Erfahrung angewiesen ist. Dabei kann ein geeignetes Modellbeschreibungsverfahren die Modellbildung wesentlich unterstützen.

Bekannte Beschreibungsverfahren sind z.B. Programmablaufpläne, Zustandsdiagramme und Petri-Netze, von denen jedes für sich meist einem speziellen Anwendungsgebiet zuzuordnen ist.

Programmablaufpläne werden häufig als Vorstufe zur Programmierung eingesetzt. Man stellt hiermit den logischen Ablauf eines Programms dar, das in der Regel seriell abgearbeitet wird.

Zustandsdiagramme [1] werden häufig beim Entwurf von Schaltwerken verwendet. Sie stellen in übersichtlicher Form die Übergangsbedingungen von einem Zustand in den folgenden Zustand dar. Das Schaltwerk kann zu jeder Zeit immer nur einen Zustand einnehmen.

Petri-Netze [1,2,3,4,5] wurden eingeführt, um Konkurrenzprobleme zwischen Operationen innerhalb eines Systems beschreiben zu können. Mit ihrer Hilfe werden z.B. Deadlock-Probleme in Rechensystemen untersucht. Petri-Netze eignen sich, im Gegensatz zu den Programmablauf-plänen und Zustandsdiagrammen, auch zur Darstellung paralleler Prozesse.

Das in letzter Zeit aus einigen Veröffentlichungen bekanntgewordene Beschreibungsverfahren Auswertungsnetze [6,7,8] baut auf den Petri-Netzen auf. Es benutzt eine ähnliche graphische Darstellung, erlaubt ebenfalls die Beschreibung paralleler Prozesse, läßt aber zusätzlich noch weitere Parameter zu, so daß mit Hilfe der Auswertungsnetze eine Beschreibung von Datenflüssen und Verzögerungszeiten möglich wird. Als wesentliches Beschreibungselement enthalten die Auswertungsnetze neben der graphischen Darstellung noch eine formale Beschreibung, die bei den Petri-Netzen nicht erforderlich ist. Wegen ihrer zusätzlichen Eigenschaften eignen sich die Auswertungsnetze besonders zur Beschreibung von Modellen, mit deren Hilfe über die Simulation auf einem Rechner Leistungsparameter ermittelt werden sollen.

Im folgenden wird das Beschreibungsmittel Auswertungsnetze an einigen einfachen Beispielen dargestellt. Es werden Probleme bei der Beschreibung mit Auswertungsnetzen aufgezeigt und Möglichkeiten zu deren Lösung angegeben.

AUSWERTUNGSNETZE

Ein einfaches Anwendungsbeispiel ist in Bild 1 als Blockschaltbild dargestellt. Über ein Eingabegerät, z.B. einen Kartenleser, werden einem Rechner Aufträge zur Bearbeitung zugeführt. Der Rechner übernimmt immer dann einen anliegenden Auftrag, wenn er den letzten Auftrag abgeschlossen und das Ergebnis ausgegeben hat.

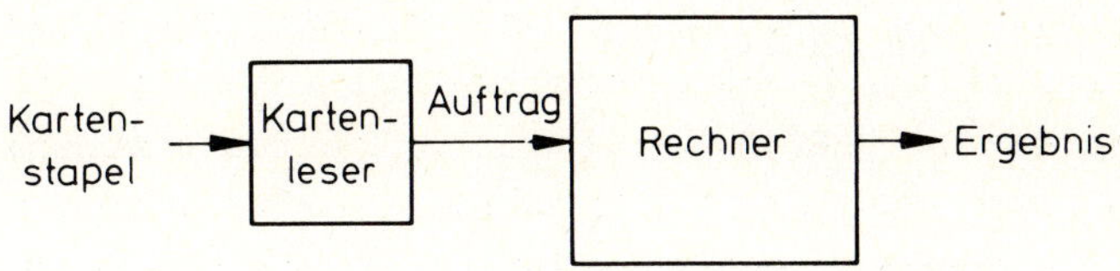

Bild 1: Teil eines Rechensystems

Bild 2 zeigt ein entsprechendes Modell in den verschiedenen Phasen der Auftragsbearbeitung. Die Kreise werden als Stellen b, die Balken als Übergänge a und die schwarzen Punkte als Kerne K bezeichnet. Das Modell enthält drei verschiedene Übergangstypen. Der Übergang a1 stellt einen T-Übergang, a2 einen J-Übergang (join) und a3 einen F-Übergang (fork) dar. Diese 3 Übergangstypen sind neben zwei weiteren, die später erläutert werden, die Grundelemente der Auswertungsnetze.

Zu Beginn seien die Stellen b1 und b3 besetzt, d.h. es befindet sich ein Kern in jeder der beiden Stellen (Bild 2a). Ein Kern in b1 bedeutet, daß ein Kartenstapel in den Kartenleser eingelegt wurde. Ein Kern in b3 gibt an, daß der Prozessor frei ist.

In Bild 2b hat der Kartenleser gerade die Karten gelesen und ihren Inhalt im Hauptspeicher abgelegt. Der Kern aus b1 ist dabei über den T-Übergang a1 nach b2 gewandert. Man sagt hier auch, der Übergang a1 hat gefeuert. Ein T-, J- oder F-Übergang feuert immer dann, wenn seine Ausgangsstellen leer und seine Eingangsstellen besetzt sind. Das wird durch das Schema eines Übergangs ausgedrückt.

Schema des T-Übergangs:

$$T(b1,b2): \quad (1,0) \longrightarrow (0,1)$$

Im Schema wird nur der Fall dargestellt, in dem der Übergang feuert. Die 1 steht für eine besetzte Stelle, die 0 steht für eine leere Stelle. Die linke Seite des Schemas gibt den Zustand vor dem Feuern, die rechte Seite gibt den Zustand nach dem Feuern an.

Für das Feuern eines Übergangs wird eine Zeit, die Übergangszeit, benötigt. In dem Beispiel stellt die Übergangszeit von a1 die Zeit dar, die der Kartenleser zum Lesen des Kartenstapels braucht. Die Übergangszeit kann, wie in diesem Fall, eine Funktion von Parametern sein, die als Attribute eines Kerns durch das Netz wandern und bei jedem Übergang durch die sogenannte Übergangsprozedur modifiziert, hinzugefügt oder gelöscht werden können. In dem Beispiel habe der Kern nur ein Attribut K(1), das die Kartenanzahl angibt. Die Übergangszeit von a1 wird damit die Form

$t(a1) = l_1 \cdot K(1)$ $\quad$ l_1 = Konstante annehmen.

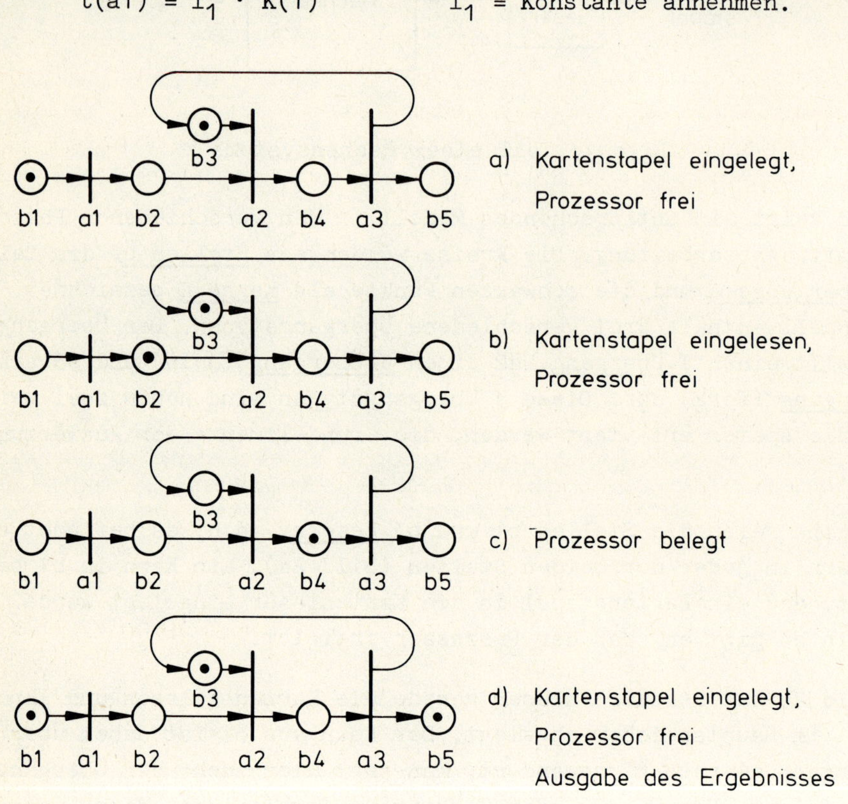

Bild 2: Modell des Rechensystems in den verschiedenen Phasen der Auftragsbearbeitung

Da die gleiche Kartenanzahl Attribut des Kerns in b2 sein soll, entfällt hier die Angabe der Übergangsprozedur q(a1). Sie wird später in der formalen Beschreibung dieses Modells durch einen Strich gekennzeichnet.

Aus Bild 2b ist zu ersehen, daß das Schema für den J-Übergang a2 erfüllt ist, da sowohl b2 (Kartenstapel eingelesen) als auch b3 (Prozessor frei) besetzt sind. Der Übergang feuert, so daß anschließend durch einen Kern in b4 (Bild 2c) der Prozessor belegt wird. Ist die Bearbeitungszeit für den Auftrag, die dem F-Übergang a3 zugeordnet ist, abgelaufen, so feuert a3. Das Ergebnis, das zum Beispiel in einer bestimmten Zahl von Ausgabezeichen bestehen kann, wird über einen Kern nach b5 übermittelt. Gleichzeitig wird der Prozessor durch einen Kern nach b3 für neue Aufträge, die zu beliebigen Zeiten in b1 eintreffen können, freigegeben (Bild 2d).

Da sowohl Übergangszeiten als auch Übergangsprozeduren nicht mit in der graphischen Darstellung angegeben werden können, benötigt man bei den Auswertungsnetzen noch eine formale Beschreibung. Eine solche Beschreibung wird hier beispielhaft und leicht vereinfacht für das Modell in Bild 2 angeführt.

Übergang	Typ	Eingangsstelle		Ausgangsstelle	Übergangszeit	Übergangsprozedur
↓	↓	↓		↓	↓	↓
a1 =	(T	(b1,		b2),	50 · b1(1),	——)
a2 =	(J	(b2,	b3,	b4),	0 ,	b4(1):=b2(1))
a3 =	(F	(b4,	b3,	b5),	17 · b4(1),	(b5(1):=35 · b4(1),b3:=1))

Das folgende Beispiel, das Modell eines Terminalsystems mit Zeitscheibenzuteilung, enthält die beiden noch fehlenden Übergangstypen, den X- und den Y-Übergang. Es soll zeigen, daß man relativ komplexe Probleme auf einfache und übersichtliche Weise mit Hilfe der Auswertungsnetze darstellen kann. Dabei wurden hier schon neue Elemente eingefügt, die nicht in den fünf Grundelementen enthalten sind.

In Bild 3 ist ein Terminalsystem bestehend aus einem zentralen Rechner und N Terminals im Blockschaltbild dargestellt. Es handelt sich um ein Abfragesystem, bei dem jedes Terminal jeweils einen Auftrag an den Rechner erteilen kann. Der Rechner vergibt seine Rechenzeit in Zeitscheiben. Die angeschlossenen Terminals werden zyklisch abgefragt. Eine Anfrage eines Terminals wird gegebenenfalls in mehreren Zeitscheiben durch den Rechner bearbeitet. Eine Fertigmeldung des Rechners an das Terminal löst nach einer Reaktionsverzögerung durch den Bediener eine neue Anfrage aus.

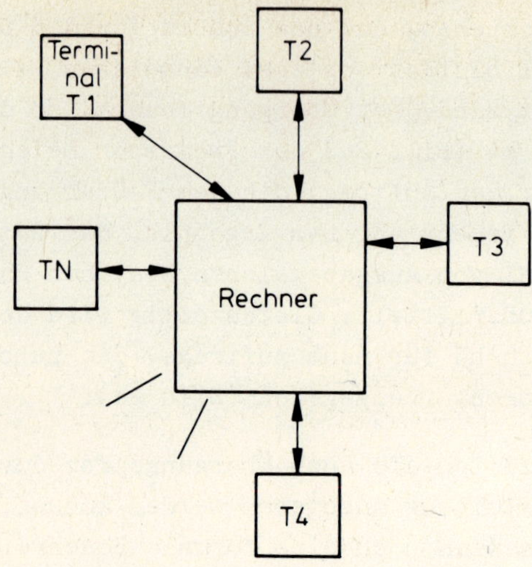

Bild 3: Terminalsystem mit N Terminals

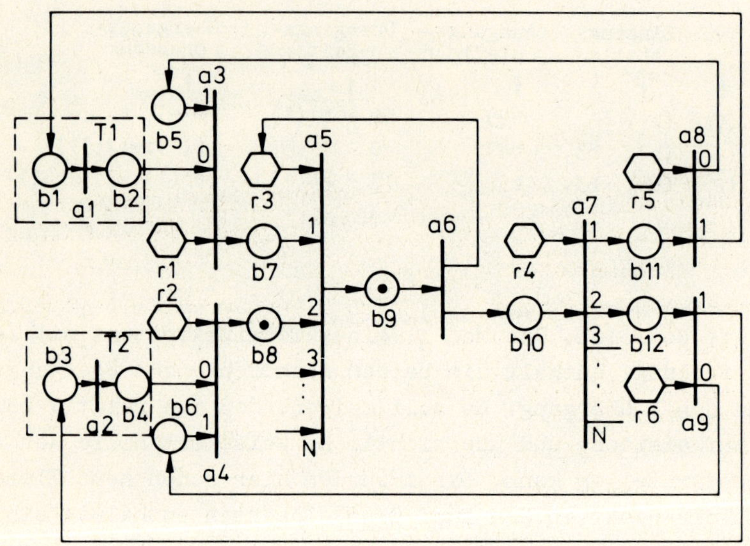

Bild 4: Modell des Terminalsystems

a1, a2:	Reaktion des Bedienens von T1 bzw. T2	a6 :	Auftragsbearbeitung (max. 1 Zeitscheibe)
a3, a4:	neuer Auftrag oder Fortsetzung des alten Auftrags von T1 bzw. T2	a7 :	Ermittlung des Auftraggebers (Terminalnr.)
a5 :	Zeitscheibenzuteilung	a8, a9:	Antwort an Terminal bzw. Warten auf nächste Zeitscheibe

Bild 4 zeigt das Modell des Terminalsystems. Der Übersichtlichkeit halber sind nur zwei Terminals T1 und T2 eingezeichnet. Die Erweiterung auf N Terminals ist angedeutet. Die Terminals T1 bzw. T2 sind durch die Übergänge a1 bzw. a2 dargestellt. Die Übergangszeit dieser beiden Übergänge kann z.B. durch eine statistische Verteilung als Näherung für das Bedienerverhalten in der formalen Beschreibung angegeben werden.

Die mit r bezeichneten Stellen (Sechsecke) in Bild 4 werden Entscheidungsstellen genannt. Der Inhalt einer Entscheidungsstelle entscheidet jeweils darüber, welcher Eingang des zugehörigen Übergangs feuern darf, wenn mehrere Eingänge miteinander konkurrieren, bzw. in welchen Ausgang gefeuert wird, wenn mehrere Ausgänge alternativ in Frage kommen. In dem Modell stellen die Übergänge a3 und a4 mit den Entscheidungsstellen r1 und r2 sogenannte Y-Übergänge, die Übergänge a8 und a9 stellen sogenannte X-Übergänge dar. Ist die Entscheidungsstelle eines X-Übergangs bzw. eines Y-Übergangs definiert, so verhält sich der Übergang wie ein T-Übergang, bei dem die durch r bezeichnete Eingangsstelle (Ausgangsstelle) als Eingangsstelle (Ausgangsstelle) eines T-Übergangs aufgefaßt werden kann. Die Entscheidungsstelle r kann dabei nur frei, besetzt oder undefiniert sein und dementsprechend die Werte 0, 1 oder Φ annehmen.

Jeder Entscheidungsstelle wird eine Entscheidungsprozedur zugeordnet, die die Entscheidung bestimmt. Diese Prozedur wird immer dann angewendet, wenn der Übergang bei irgendeinem definierten Wert der Entscheidungsstelle feuern kann. Da sich diese Prozedur gegebenenfalls auch auf Attribute von Kernen in beliebigen Stellen bezieht, kann eine Entscheidungsstelle undefiniert sein, wenn z.B. bei ihrer Auswertung kein Kern in der betreffenden Stelle existiert. In diesem Fall feuert der Übergang nicht.

Die Übergänge a5 und a7 sind in der ursprünglichen Menge von Grundelementen nicht enthalten. Sie werden in Anlehnung an Y- bzw. X-Übergang mit MY-Übergang bzw. MX-Übergang bezeichnet (M für Makro) und als zusätzliche Elemente aufgenommen, da sie erfahrungsgemäß sehr oft benötigt werden. Im Gegensatz zu den X- und Y-Grundtypen muß den Entscheidungsstellen der MX- bzw. MY-Übergänge ein Attribut zugeordnet werden, über das eine beliebige Ausgangs- bzw. Eingangsstelle ausgewählt werden kann. Während der MX-Übergang gegenüber dem X-Übergang sonst keine Besonderheit aufweist, sind beim MY-Übergang besondere Vereinbarungen zu treffen, da diese nicht selbstverständlich aus dem Y-Grundtyp hervorgehen. Bezieht sich die Entscheidungsstelle eines MY-Übergangs auf eine leere Eingangsstelle, so feuert die zyklisch nächste besetzte Stelle dieses Übergangs.

Durch den Kern in b9 (Bild 4) ist der Prozessor mit der Bearbeitung eines Auftrags des Terminals 1 beschäftigt. Der Kern in b8 stellt einen Auftrag von Terminal 2 dar, der auf Zeitscheibenzuteilung wartet. Nach Ablauf der Zeitscheibe feuert der F-Übergang a6, der als Übergangszeit jeweils das Minimum aus Zeitscheibenlänge und Rechenzeitbedarf der Abfrage zugewiesen bekommt. Als Folge davon gelangt ein Kern nach r3 und ein Kern nach b10. Der nach r3 wandernde Kern trägt als Attribut die um 1 modulo N erhöhte Terminalkennzahl, so daβ nach der Zeitscheibenzuteilung für Terminal 1 dem Terminal 2 eine Zeitscheibe zugeteilt wird. Benötigt Terminal 2 diese Zeitscheibe, was in diesem Beispiel wegen des Kerns in b8 zutrifft, so feuert als nächstes der Übergang a5, so daβ der Prozessor im Übergang a6 die nächste Zeitscheibe an Terminal 2 vergeben kann. Benötigte Terminal 2 diese Zeitscheibe nicht, so würde sie dem zyklisch nächsten Terminal, das einen Auftrag erteilt hat, zugewiesen.

Im Übergang a7 wird der Ursprung des vom Prozessor bearbeiteten Auftrags ermittelt. Der Auftrag aus Terminal 1 wird nach b11 weitergegeben. Im Übergang a8 entscheidet dann die Entscheidungsstelle, ob der Auftrag fertiggestellt ist. Bei Fertigstellung des Auftrags feuert der Übergang den Kern nach b1, was einer Antwort an das Terminal gleichkommt. Ist der Auftrag noch nicht vollständig abgearbeitet, so müssen ihm noch weitere Zeitscheiben zugeordnet werden. Das wird im Modell dadurch dargestellt, daβ jetzt der Kern nach b5 wandert, von wo aus er direkt über a3 an b7 weitergeleitet wird. Entsprechend werden auch die Aufträge der anderen Terminals behandelt. Auf eine formale Beschreibung dieses zweiten Modells soll hier verzichtet werden.

PROBLEME BEI DER MODELLBESCHREIBUNG MIT AUSWERTUNGSNETZEN

Bei der Anwendung von Auswertungsnetzen zur Beschreibung simulationsfähiger Modelle können unter anderem folgende Probleme auftreten:

- Modellierung von Interrupt und Time Out
- Modellierung hierarchisch strukturierter Systeme
- Effektivitätsverlust durch komplizierte Darstellung einfacher Funktionen.

Modellierung von Interrupt und Time Out[1)]

Die Übergangszeit eines feuernden Übergangs läßt sich nicht beeinflussen. Sie wird direkt zu Beginn des Feuerns ermittelt und läuft bis zum Ende ab. Damit wird z.B. die Darstellung eines Time Out[1)], das auf eine bestimmte Zeit gesetzt und im Normalfall vor Ablauf der Zeit wieder gelöscht wird, praktisch unmöglich. Eine einmal gestartete Aktivität läßt sich zwischenzeitlich nicht stoppen. Theoretisch wäre zwar eine Aufteilung des Vorgangs in beliebig fein unterteilte Zeitschritte bei entsprechender Darstellung im Modell denkbar. Das würde jedoch zu unübersichtlichen Modelldarstellungen und zu unzumutbaren Simulationszeiten führen. Eine mögliche Lösung besteht in der Erweiterung der Grundelemente um einen zusätzlichen Übergang, der hier TI-Übergang genannt wird. Darunter ist ein T-Übergang mit Interruptmöglichkeit zu verstehen.

Der TI-Übergang ist mit seinem Übergangsschema in Bild 5 angegeben. In dem Schema stellen die Blitze anstelle der sonst üblichen Pfeile den Interruptvorgang dar. Ist die linke Seite einer einen Blitz enthaltenden Zeile des Übergangsschemas erfüllt, so feuert der Übergang

---

1) Ein Time Out dient in der Regel zur Absicherung gegen Fehler. Es wird z.B. dann gesetzt, wenn ein Prozessor P_A einem zweiten Prozessor P_B einen Auftrag erteilt und auf Antwort wartet. Für den Fall, daß aus irgendwelchen Gründen die Antwort ausbleibt, z.B., weil die Übertragung fehlerhaft war oder weil P_B ausgefallen ist, würde P_A beliebig lange warten und damit blockiert. Um das zu verhindern, setzt P_A mit Erteilen des Auftrags eine maximale Wartezeit, das Time Out, bis zu der er auf Antwort wartet. Ist die Zeit abgelaufen, ohne daß eine Antwort erfolgte, so kann P_A nach vorprogrammierten Prozeduren auf den Fehler reagieren. Im Normalfall kommt die Antwort von P_B jedoch vorher. Dann muß das vorher gesetzte Time Out sofort gelöscht werden.

dem Übergangsschema entsprechend sofort mit der Zeit t = 0, unabhängig davon, ob gerade eine Übergangszeit in dem betreffenden Übergang abläuft.

Über die Übergangsprozedur kann dem Kern in der Ausgangsstelle im Falle eines Interrupts eine Information darüber mitgegeben werden, zu welchem Prozentsatz der betreffende Prozeß bearbeitet worden ist bzw. welche Restzeit für eine endgültige Bearbeitung noch erforderlich wird, so daß in einem späteren Prozeßschritt die bereits geleistete Arbeit berücksichtigt werden kann.

Ist die Stelle b2 (Bild 5) frei, so verhält sich der Übergang wie ein T-Übergang. Wird b2 besetzt, so wird ein eventuell in b1 vorhandener Kern, unabhängig von einer noch verbleibenden Übergangszeit, an b3 weitergegeben. Der Kern aus b2 verschwindet. Er verschwindet auch dann sofort, wenn sich kein Kern in b1 befindet, d.h., wenn kein Vorgang zu unterbrechen ist. Durch dieses Grundelement lassen sich sowohl Time Out als auch Interrupt ohne großen Aufwand in die Modelle einbauen. Mit dem TI-Übergang kann ein unterbrechbarer Prozessor modelliert werden.

(1, 0, 0,) → (0, 0, 1) Prozeß ohne Unterbrechung

(0, 1, 0) ↯→ (0, 0, 0) Unterbrechungsmeldung ohne Prozeß

(1, 1, 0) ↯→ (0, 0, 1) Prozeß mit Unterbrechung

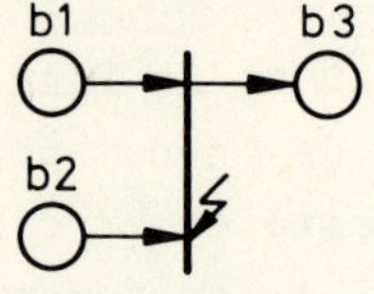

Bild 5: TI-Übergang mit Übergangsschema

Modellierung hierarchisch strukturierter Systeme

Bei hierarchisch strukturierten Systemen kann jedes Element einer bestimmten Ebene auf jedes Element der niedrigeren Ebene zugreifen. Eine solche hierarchische Struktur liegt z.B. in einem Rechensystem in Form von Betriebssystem und Hardware vor. Jede Operation im Betriebssystem läuft auf der Hardware ab. Das Problem, das sich hier stellt, ist vor allem ein Darstellungsproblem. Man will einmal die Funktionen der verschiedenen Ebenen (Betriebssystem und Hardware) getrennt voneinander und in sich geschlossen darstellen. Zum anderen möchte man das Zusammenspiel der beiden Ebenen beschreiben. Ein Beispiel für eine mögliche Darstellung zeigt Bild 6. Die Doppelpfeile in der übergeordneten Ebene sind ein Hilfsmittel zur Darstellung der Verkopplung beider Ebenen. Ihr Äquivalent ist in Bild 7 angegeben.

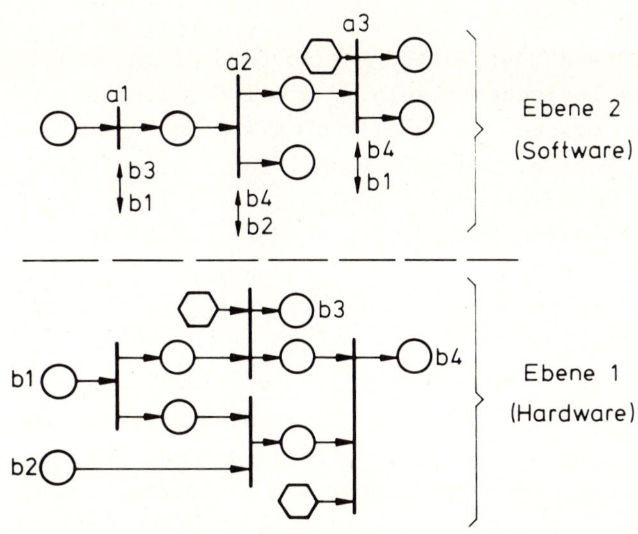

Bild 6: Ausschnitt aus dem Modell eines hierarchisch strukturierten Systems

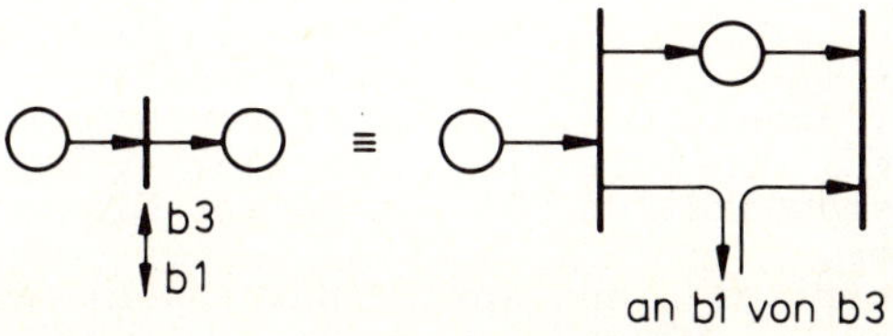

Bild 7: Vereinfachte Darstellung bei hierarchisch strukturierten Systemen

Die Bezeichnung b1 an dem in Richtung Hardwaremodell (Ebene 1) weisenden Pfeil bedeutet, daß die Stelle b1 der Ebene 1 Ausgangsstelle des Übergangs in der Ebene 1 ist. Entsprechend weist die Bezeichnung b3 an dem Pfeil in Richtung Ebene 2 darauf hin, daß die Stelle b3 der

Ebene 1 Eingangsstelle des Übergangs in der Ebene 2 ist. Damit wird die Ablaufzeit in der übergeordneten Ebene jeweils um die Ablaufzeit in der niedrigeren Ebene verlängert. Im Prinzip läßt sich so wieder ein allerdings sehr unübersichtliches, jedoch zusammenhängendes Auswertungsnetz darstellen.

Effektivitätsverlust durch komplizierte Darstellung einfacher Funktionen

Die Grundelemente der Auswertungsnetze beinhalten bereits jedes für sich eine Reihe logischer Regeln, die bei der Simulation jeweils bearbeitet werden müssen, die häufig aber von der Anwendung her gar nicht benötigt werden. Ein T-Übergang kann z.B. nur feuern, wenn die Eingangsstelle besetzt und die Ausgangsstelle leer ist. Bei der Simulation sind alle diese Bedingungen zu überprüfen, obwohl vom Modell her schon häufig bestimmte Situationen ausgeschlossen werden und daher auch nicht überprüft zu werden brauchten. Die Stelle b4 im Bild 2 kann z.B. nie besetzt sein, wenn b2 und b3 besetzt sind. Die damit verbundenen überflüssigen Abfragen in der Simulation bedeuten Redundanz und damit längere Laufzeit. Diesen Nachteil wird man wohl kaum ganz vermeiden können. Es ist der Preis, den man für den durch die wenigen standardisierten Übergangstypen gegebenen Komfort zu zahlen hat.

LITERATUR

[1] Peterson, J.L., Bredt, T.H.: A comparison of models of parallel computation. IFIP Congress Stockholm (1974), Nr. 3, S. 466-470.

[2] Petri, C.A.: Kommunikation mit Automaten. Dissertation, Universität Bonn, 1962.

[3] Misunas, D.: Petri nets and speed independent design. Comm. ACM, 16 (1973), Nr. 8, S. 474-479.

[4] Miller, R.E.: A comparison of some theoretical models of parallel computation. IEEE Tr. on Comp., C-22 (1973), Nr. 8, S. 710-716.

[5] Tsichrikis, D.C., Bernstein, P.A.: Operating Systems. Academic Press Inc., 1973, S. 249-261.

[6] Nutt, G.J.: The formulation and application of evaluation nets. Ph. D. dissertation, University of Washington, Computer Science, 1972.

[7] Nutt, G.J.: Evaluation nets for computer system performance analysis. Fall Joint Comp. Conf. 1972, AFIPS Conf. Proc., 41 (1972), S. 279-286.

[8] Noe, J.D., Nutt, G.J.: Macro E-Nets for representation of parallel systems. IEEE Tr. on Comp., C-22 (1973) Nr. 8, S. 718-727.

A S P E K T E Z U
P R O G R A M M I E R S P R A C H E N

EINE STATISTISCHE ANALYSE DER STATISCHEN EIGENSCHAFTEN VON PL/I-PROGRAMMEN

P. Nawrot und P. Rechenberg

Johannes-Kepler-Hochschule Linz

Die statistische Untersuchung der statischen Häufigkeit von Statements in PL/I-Programmen zeigt bereits nach der Untersuchung von rund 22 000 Quellkarten deutliche Schwerpunkte bei der Anwendung dieser Sprache in technisch-wissenschaftlichen und in kommerziell-administrativen Bereichen.

Die Ergebnisse und ihr Vergleich mit denen ähnlicher Untersuchungen geben Hinweise für das Schreiben von Compilern, für die Entwicklung neuer Programmiersprachen, für die Entwicklung von Syntaxanalyseverfahren und für den Aufbau von Lehrveranstaltungen über Programmierungstechniken.

1. Einleitung

Angeregt durch die Arbeit von Knuth "An empirical study of Fortran programs" [1], in der er Fortran-Programme hinsichtlich ihrer statischen und dynamischen Eigenschaften analysierte, haben wir in ähnlicher Weise PL/I-Programme analysiert. Unsere Untersuchung bezieht sich nur auf die statischen Eigenschaften von PL/I, analysiert diese dafür aber genauer als Knuth.

Zweck und praktischer Nutzen der Untersuchung bestehen in der Beantwortung einer Reihe von Fragen, die sowohl für den Compilerbauer als auch für den Entwerfer von Programmiersprachen Bedeutung haben. Wir wollen hier die wohl wichtigsten vier Fragen formulieren:

1. Welche Sprachkonstruktionen treten in praktischen Programmen besonders häufig auf? Die Analyse ergibt Aussagen über eine Reihe von Merkmalen, die den Compilerbauer besonders interessieren, wie die Länge von Ausdrücken, die Schachtelungstiefe von IF-Statements, von Unterprogrammen, von Deklarationsattributen, die Größe von Konstanten und ähnlichem.

2. Werden die Möglichkeiten von PL/I ausgenutzt? Sehr interessant ist die Beantwortung der Frage, inwieweit die Fülle von PL/I-Möglichkeiten in der Praxis überhaupt benutzt wird, ob das Anwendungsspektrum tatsächlich so groß ist, daß fast alle von der Sprache gebotenen Möglichkeiten auch Verwendung finden oder ob sich die Programmierer zum größten Teil mit einer kleinen Teilmenge (à la Fortran) zufrieden geben.

3. Sind bestimmte statistische Merkmale unabhängig von der untersuchten Quellsprache? Die allgemeine Aussagekraft von empirischen Untersuchungen der vorliegenden Art wird immer dadurch geschmälert, daß sie nur für eine bestimmte Sprache durchgeführt werden und daß die untersuchten Quellprogramme hinsichtlich ihres Umfangs und ihrer Auswahl nicht unbedingt repräsentativ genug sind, um allgemeine Aussagen zu ermöglichen. Es ist deshalb interessant, nachzuprüfen, ob gewisse Ergebnisse mit denen aus der Untersuchung anderer Sprachen mit ganz anderem Ausgangsmaterial übereinstimmen. Wenn das der Fall wäre, könnte man daraus schließen, daß die be-

treffenden Meßwerte mehr oder weniger sprachunabhängig sind, und daß es auf die Auswahl der betrachteten Programme gar nicht so sehr ankommt.

4. Gibt es Unterschiede im statischen Aufbau von technisch-wissenschaftlichen und kommerziellen Programmen, die sich in den statistischen Untersuchungen deutlich niederschlagen? Es wird zwar allgemein postuliert, daß ein Unterschied zwischen technisch-wissenschaftlichen und kommerziellen Programmen besteht, und man hat gewisse gefühlsmäßige Vorstellungen von diesen Unterschieden. Es ist aber sicherlich interessant zu untersuchen, ob diese Unterschiede bei einer statistischen Untersuchung sich tatsächlich zeigen oder ob sie objektiv so wenig ausgeprägt sind, daß die übliche Ansicht darüber einer Revision bedarf. Es wäre weiterhin interessant nachzuprüfen, ob man diese beiden Gebiete noch feiner unterteilen und die Grenzen zwischen den Gebieten anders legen sollte. Die Untersuchungen könnten zum Beispiel ein bestimmtes "Programmprofil" für technisch-wissenschaftliche und ein anderes für kommerzielle Programme ergeben, und man könnte dann die Zugehörigkeit eines vorgelegten einzelnen Programms zu einem dieser Teilgebiete feststellen, ohne dessen Semantik zu kennen.

Ähnliche Untersuchungen wie die von Knuth [1] sind bisher von Alexander [2] und Nußbaumer [3] gemacht worden. Diese werden von uns zur Beantwortung der dritten Frage mit herangezogen. Die vier vorliegenden Untersuchungen (unsere eingeschlossen) unterscheiden sich in der untersuchten Sprache,in dem Umfang und in dem Inhalt des untersuchten Materials. Sie unterscheiden sich darüber hinaus auch noch in der Art und Weise der Untersuchung und damit in der Fülle und Differenziertheit der Ergebnisse. Knuth und Nußbaumer haben nur lexikalische Eigenschaften analysiert, also die Häufigkeit von Schlüsselwörtern und ähnliche Dinge. Alexander hat den XPL-Compiler selbst zur Analyse benutzt, indem er ihn durch Zusätze, die die Zählungen ausführen, erweiterte. Wir haben einen Syntax-Checker für eine sehr große Untermenge von PL/I geschrieben, in dem die Zählmechanismen zur Analyse eingebaut sind. Eine tabellarische Zusammenstellung der verschiedenen Untersuchungen und ihrer Eigenschaften zeigt Bild 1.

Autor	Quell-sprache	Anzahl der Quellkarten	Charakter der Untersuchung	Untersuchungs-methode
Knuth	FORTRAN	220.000	techn.-wiss. Programme Systemprogramme Programmbibliothek	Lexikalischer Analysator
Alexander	XPL	40.000	techn.-wiss. Programme zum Schreiben von Compilern	Erweiterung des XPL-Compilers zur Analyse
Nussbaumer	PL/I	6.000	techn.-wiss. Progr., ca 40% admin.-komm. Progr., ca 60%	Lexikalischer Analysator
Nawrot, Rechenberg	PL/I	22.000	techn.-wiss. Progr. (Comp.) ca 30% kommerziell-admin. Progr. (medizin.Progr., Progr.zur Hochschulverwaltung) ca 70%	Syntaxanalysator mit Zähleinrichtungen

Bild 1 Merkmale der bisherigen empirischen Untersuchungen

Unsere Programme sind sämtlich selbst in PL/I geschrieben worden und dienten zugleich als Teil des Untersuchungsmaterials. Die Arbeit wurde durch die Firma Philips in Eiserfeld finanziell unterstützt, wofür wir ihr hiermit unseren Dank aussprechen möchten.

2. Vorgehensweise

In diesem Abschnitt beschreiben wir kurz das von uns untersuchte Material an Quellprogrammen und das von uns benutzte Analyseverfahren und geben eine tabellarische Zusammenstellung aller analysierten Eigenschaften der Quellprogramme.

Untersuchtes Material. Die Quellprogramme aus insgesamt 22.000 Karten stammen zu etwa 30 % aus dem technisch-wissenschaftlichen Bereich, zu etwa 70 % aus dem kommerziell-administrativen Bereich. Die technische Gruppe enthält vor allem die von uns geschriebenen Programme zur Software-Produktion (verschiedene Syntaxanalyse-Programme und Compiler) und das Programmsystem zur statistischen Zählung selbst. Eigentliche Anwendungsprogramme aus Mathematik, Physik und anderen technischen Bereichen sind nicht darin enthalten, weshalb man die Programme nur bedingt mit "technisch-wissenschaftlich" bezeichnen kann. Es wäre wohl angemessener, für sie eine eigene Kategorie "Software-Programme" oder "Informatik-Programme" einzuführen. Die kommerzielle Gruppe setzt sich aus einigen großen Programmsystemen zur Hochschulverwaltung und zur statistischen Auswertung von medizinischen Daten zusammen.

Zählverfahren. Zur statistischen Analyse können mehrere Verfahren angewendet werden. Erstaunlich viel Information liefert bereits die Analyse des lexikalischen Aufbaus der Quellprogramme. Dazu braucht nur jede Zeile des Quellprogramms gelesen und auf Schlüsselwörter und Statementtypen hin untersucht zu werden. Grammatische Zusammenhänge werden dabei aber nicht oder nur bei Betrachtung umfangreichen Kontextes erkannt. Dennoch lassen sich bereits viele statistische Kenngrößen mit dieser Methode auffinden. Ihr Vorteil liegt daran, daß sie sich leicht auf die verschiedensten Sprachen anwenden läßt. Die zweite Möglichkeit ist der Einbau von Zählern in einen Interpretierer oder Compiler. Damit kann eindeutig jedes Statement und jede Konstruktion innerhalb eines Statements schnell und genau analysiert werden. Sie setzt natürlich voraus, daß man an dem betreffenden Compiler Änderungen vornehmen kann.

Da in der vorliegenden Untersuchung eine Änderung des PL/I-Compilers nicht in Frage kam, das lexikalische Verfahren wegen seiner zu wenigen Ergebnisse aber auch nicht benutzt werden sollte, wurde ein Mittelweg eingeschlagen. Es wurde ein lexikalischer Analysator und ein Syntaxanalysator für PL/I geschrieben, der nach dem Prinzip der Pseudo-LL(1)-Technik arbeitet [4]. Bei der Anwendung dieser Analysetechnik ist es leicht, nach der Erkennung einer jeden syntaktischen Konstruktion eine Routine aufzurufen, die die betreffende Konstruktion zählt. Wegen des großen Umfangs von PL/I und der überaus seltenen Benutzung mancher seiner Teile wurde nur eine Untermenge (etwa 66 % der ECMA-Beschreibung) ausgewählt, die sich auch als ausreichend erwies. Die Untermenge entspricht etwa der in [5] angegebenen Untermenge von PL/I.

Da unser Syntaxanalysator nur eine Untermenge von PL/I erfaßt, mußte berücksichtigt werden, daß Quellprogramme, die andere PL/I-Konstruktionen enthalten, zu Syntaxfehlern führen. In diesem Fall wird der Fehler gekennzeichnet und ein kurzes Stück Quelltext überlesen. Die vom Analysator als Fehler angesehenen seltenen PL/I-Konstruktionen wurden dann mit der Hand ausgewertet.

Untersuchte Eigenschaften. Bild 2 enthält eine tabellarische Zusammenstellung aller auf diese Weise untersuchten Spracheigenschaften. Wir besprechen in den nächsten Abschnitten nur die wichtigeren unter ihnen.

3. Äußere Form der Programme

Die durchschnittliche kommerzielle Prozedur besteht aus etwa hundert Quellkarten und 71 Statements; die technisch-wissenschaftliche aus 60 Quellkarten und 47 Statements. Die Einzelwerte schwanken stark, so daß der Mittelwert nicht sehr aussagekräftig ist. Er liegt für technisch-wissenschaftliche Programme aber nicht viel höher als der von Alexander mit 34 Statements ermittelte. 75 % der Hauptprogramme enthielten weniger als 50, 88 % der Unterprogramme weniger als 30 Statements. Der früher öfter zu beobachtende Hang zu wenigen und langen Programmen scheint also nicht mehr vorhanden zu sein.

1. Äußere Form
   1.1 Anzahl gelesener Karten
   1.2 Anzahl der Kommentare
   1.3 Anzahl von Kommentarzeilen
   1.4 Anzahl von Leerzeilen
   1.5 Mittlere Anzahl von Kommentarzeichen je Karte
   1.6 Mittlere Anzahl von Leerzeichen je Karte
   1.7 Mittlere Anzahl von führenden Leerzeichen je Karte
2. Lexikalische Analyse
   2.1 Häufigkeit der Schlüsselwörter
   2.2 Häufigkeit der Sonderzeichen
   2.3 Verteilung von Konstanten und Variablen
   2.4 Anzahl der argumentierten und strukturierten Variablen
   2.5 Längen von Variablennamen
   2.6 Variablen pro externe Prozedur
   2.7 Anzahl von Statements und Variablen
   2.8 Größen von Integer-Konstanten
3. Ausdrücke
   3.1 Anzahl von Ausdrücken je Statement
   3.2 Anzahl von Operatoren in Ausdrücken
   3.3 Verteilung der Operations- und Relationszeichen
   3.4 Analyse der Operationen (Additionen von 1, Subtraktionen von 1, Multiplikationen mit 2, Divisionen durch 2, Exponentiationen mit 2)
   3.5 Anzahl von Operanden in Ausdrücken
   3.6 Klammertiefen in Ausdrücken
4. Deklarationen
   4.1 Anzahl explizit deklarierter Variablen
   4.2 Verteilung der Deklarations-Attribute (Festkomma-Variablen, PICTURE-Variablen, Bitketten, Zeichenketten, Gleitkomma-Variablen)
   4.3 Häufigkeit und Länge von Feldern
   4.4 Häufigkeit von Feldern variabler Länge
   4.5 Anzahl der Feldindizes
   4.6 Häufigkeit und Tiefe von Strukturen
5. Statements
   5.1 Häufigkeit der Statements
   5.2 Analyse der DO-Statements (Art der DO-Statements, Schachtelungstiefen, Anzahl von Statements in DO-Gruppen, Analyse von Startwerten, Endwerten und Inkrementen)
   5.3 Analyse der BEGIN-Statements (Schachtelungstiefen der BEGIN-Blöcke, Anzahl von Statements in BEGIN-Blöcken)
   5.4 Analyse der IF-Statements (IF-Statements mit ELSE-Anteil, Schachtelungstiefen, Folgestatements nach THEN und ELSE)
   5.5 Analyse der Assignment-Statements (Häufigkeit von gleichen Links- und Rechtsvariablen, Zuweisungen von 0 und 1, Häufigkeit von Mehrfachzuweisungen, Anzahl von Operanden je Assignment-Statement)
6. Sonstige Analysen
   6.1 Ein- und Ausgabe (I/O-Statements, Häufigkeit der verschiedenen Formate)
   6.2 Markenhäufigkeiten je Prozedur
   6.3 Art der OPEN-Statements
   6.4 Anzahl von Unterprogrammparametern
   6.5 Builtin-Functions
7. Prozeduren
   7.1 Anzahl externer und interner Prozeduren
   7.2 Anzahl von Statements in Prozeduren
   7.3 Schachtelungstiefen von Prozeduren

Bild 2 Zusammenstellung der untersuchten Eigenschaften

Ein Fünftel bis ein Sechstel aller Statements ist kommentiert (bei Knuth ein Sechstel). Der Kommentar ist durchschnittlich 36 Spalten, also eine halbe Lochkarte lang. Jede Quellkarte enthält im Mittel 40 bis 50 Leerzeichen (bei Knuth 48). Insgesamt sind etwa 75 % aller gelesenen Zeichen bedeutungslos, d.h., drei Viertel aller Zeichen müssen vom lexikalischen Analysator möglichst schnell überlesen werden.

Interne Prozeduren werden kaum tiefer als zweifach geschachtelt, d.h., ein internes Unterprogramm enthält selten mehr als ein weiteres internes Unterprogramm. Es wurden etwa doppelt so viele interne wie externe Unterprogramme benutzt; die Möglichkeit von PL/I, interne Unterprogramme zu schreiben, ist also gegenüber Fortran eine häufig ausgenutzte Bereicherung. Auf ein kommerzielles Hauptprogramm kommen 3.7, auf ein technisch-wissenschaftliches 8, also gut doppelt so viele interne und externe Unterprogramme.

4. Lexikalische Konstruktionen

Bild 3 zeigt die Verteilung der häufigsten Schlüsselwörter.

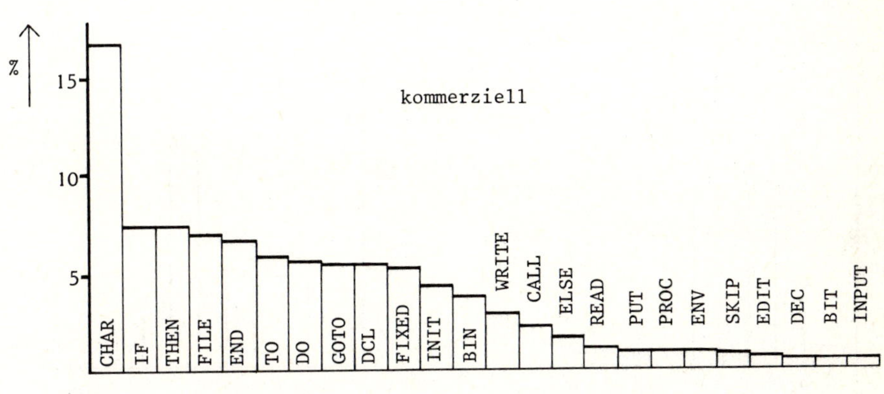

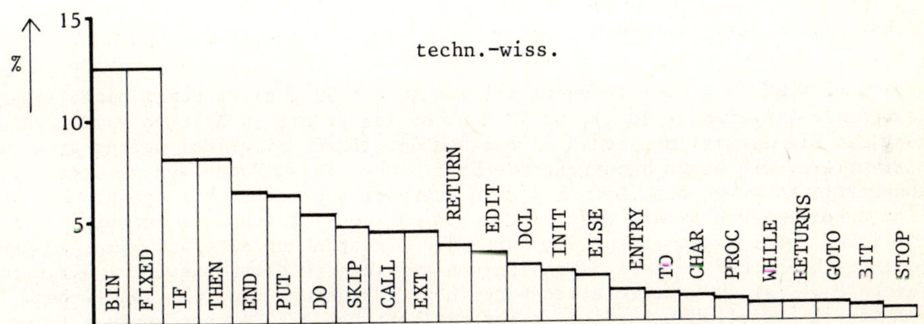

Bild 3 Verteilung der häufigsten Schlüsselwörter

Interessant ist daran zunächst, daß nicht die Namen von Statements am häufigsten auftreten, sondern Attribute, die nur in Deklarationen vorkommen. Dies erklärt sich daraus, daß zur Zählung die Faktorisierung von Attributen rückgängig gemacht wurde. Wenn also drei Zeichenketten gleicher Länge einmal mit dem Attribut CHAR deklariert wurden, ist das Attribut CHAR dreimal gezählt worden. Wie zu erwarten war, zeigen die Bilder, daß kommerzielle Programmierer mehr mit Zeichenkettenvariablen, technisch-wissenschaftliche mehr mit ganzzahligen Variablen arbeiten. Auf die Unterschiede der einzelnen Statementarten soll später in Abschnitt 6 näher eingegangen werden.

Die Verteilung der Sonderzeichen wurde gemessen, zeigt aber keine bemerkenswerten Eigenschaften, außer vielleicht der, daß nicht das Semikolon als Statementende das am häufigsten vorkommende Sonderzeichen ist, sondern Klammern und Komma.

Variablen und Konstanten traten ungefähr mit gleicher Häufigkeit auf. Zu den Variablen wurden dabei auch Aufrufe von Funktionen und Subroutinen gerechnet, also alle Namen, denen eine eingeklammerte Argumentliste folgt. Etwa ein Viertel aller im Quelltext stehenden Variablen (und Prozeduraufrufe) waren indiziert (oder besaßen Argumente), von ihnen hatten drei Viertel nur einen Index (ein Argument). Nur ein Zehntel aller mit Argumenten versehenen Namen hatte mehr als zwei Argumente. Ungefähr vier Fünftel aller Konstanten waren ganzzahlig, der Rest waren Zeichen- und Bitkettenkonstanten. Gleitkommakonstanten traten so gut wie überhaupt nicht auf.

Bild 4 zeigt die Längen von Variablennamen.

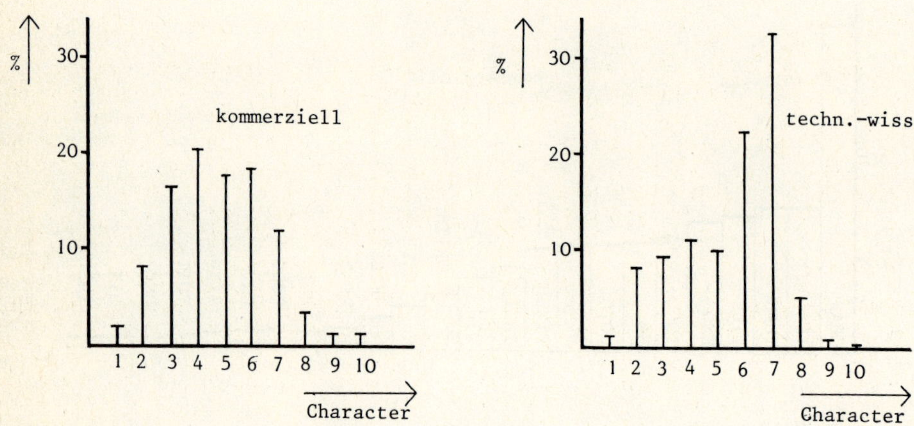

Bild 4 Längen von Variablennamen

Übereinstimmend sind in beiden Anwendungsbereichen gut 93 % aller Namen nicht länger als 7 Zeichen (bei Alexander 80 %). Da 99 % nicht länger als 10 Zeichen waren, kann man sagen, daß die maximal möglichen 31 Zeichen der IBM-Compiler bei weitem nicht ausgenutzt werden. Die öfter anzutreffende Empfehlung, lange Namen wegen ihres Dokumentationswertes zu verwenden, hat sich also entweder noch nicht herumgesprochen oder sie ist zu unbequem. Das scharf ausgeprägte Maximum von 7 Zeichen im technisch-wissenschaftlichen Bereich ist sicherlich durch die Beschränkung externer Namen zu erklären, die sich vermutlich auch psychologisch auf interne Namen auswirkt. Der durchschnittliche Name ist im kommerziellen Bereich am kürzesten, nämlich 4.6 Zeichen. Im technisch-wissenschaftlichen Bereich stimmt der Wert von 5.5 Zeichen genau mit dem Wert aus der Untersuchung von Alexander überein.

Kommerzielle externe Prozeduren enthalten im Durchschnitt 130, technisch-wissenschaftliche 41 verschiedene Variablen. In einem der kommerziellen Programme waren über 400 Variablen deklariert worden. Der Unterschied ist beträchtlich und wird auch nicht viel kleiner, wenn man die Anzahl der Variablen pro Statement berechnet (0.6

bei kommerziellen, 0.34 bei technisch-wissenschaftlichen). Es wäre interessant festzustellen, ob andere Messungen ähnliches ergeben.

Bild 5 gibt einen Einblick in die Größenverteilung von ganzzahligen Konstanten. Danach ist rund ein Drittel aller Konstanten Null oder Eins und 16 Bit genügen für die Darstellung von mehr als 99 % aller Konstanten. Die Werte stimmen mit den von Alexander gemessenen wieder gut überein.

Länge in Bit	kommerz.	t.-w.	Alexander
1	28.6	30.3	33.0
4	81.0	65.0	56.0
8	97.5	94.5	94.0
12	99.7	99.5	98.0
16	99.8	99.97	99.0

Bild 5 Längen von Konstanten

5. Ausdrücke

Die Hauptaussagen, die über Ausdrücke gemacht werden können, sind, daß Ausdrücke überaus häufig auftreten (jedes Statement enthält durchschnittlich 1.1 Ausdruck) und daß sie zum allergrößten Teil sehr einfach aufgebaut sind (nur ein Drittel bis ein Viertel aller Ausdrücke enthält Operatoren). Beide Aussagen bekräftigen, daß man bei der Syntaxanalyse den Ausdrücken besondere Aufmerksamkeit schenken und sie so analysieren soll, daß zur Erkennung eines Ausdrucks, der eine einfache Variable oder Konstante ist, nicht sämtliche Zwischenstufen von Ausdrücken durchlaufen werden, wie es bei den heute üblichen systematischen Topdown- und Bottomup-Analyseverfahren meist geschieht.

Von den Operationen in Ausdrücken machen Relationen und Additionen zusammen über 70 % aus. Multiplikation und Division stellen zusammen nur etwa 10 % (ähnlich bei Knuth und Alexander). Wie arithmetische Ausdrücke sind auch logische Ausdrücke meist sehr einfach aufgebaut. Die Operatoren $\neg<$ und $\neg>$ treten so gut wie nicht auf. Über die (wohl psychologischen) Gründe dafür ließe sich nachdenken.

Es ergab sich weiter, daß bei Additionen zu 50 bis 60 % eine 1 addiert wurde; und daß beinahe in der Hälfte aller Subtraktionen eine 1 subtrahiert wurde. Bild 6 zeigt die Summenhäufigkeit der Anzahl von Operanden in Ausdrücken. Danach bestehen Ausdrücke zu beinahe drei Vierteln aus einer einzigen Variablen oder Konstanten (Knuth fand das gleiche Ergebnis).

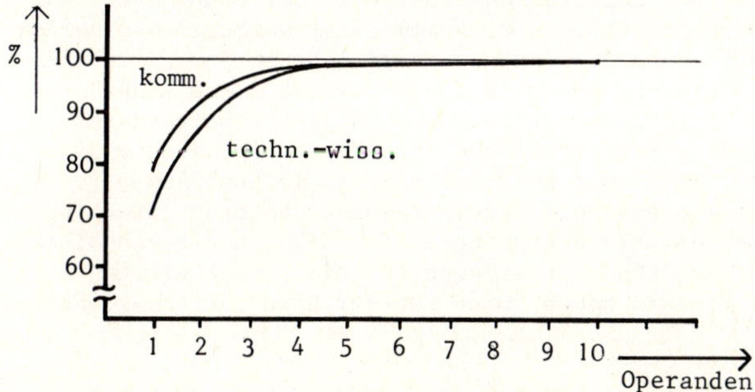

Bild 6 Anzahl von Operanden in Ausdrücken

Bei der Untersuchung von Klammerungstiefen ergab sich, daß beinahe 90 % der Ausdrücke, die Klammern enthalten, in den äußeren Klammern keine weiteren Klammern enthalten.

6. Statements

Statementarten. Bild 7 zeigt die Verteilung der häufigsten Statementarten.

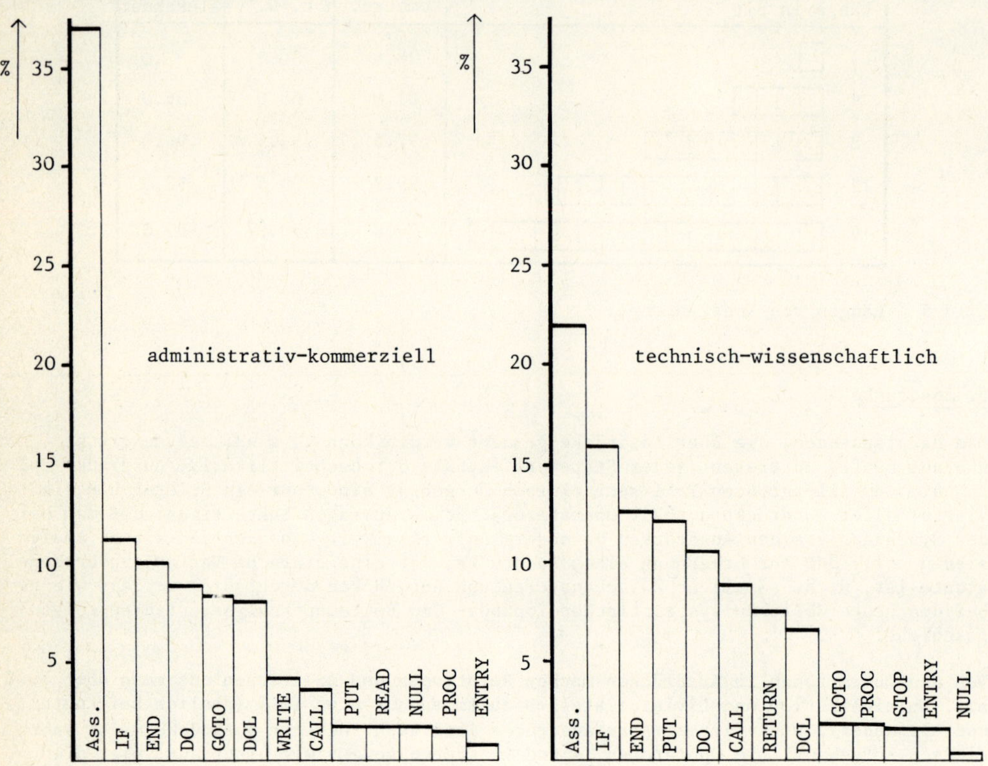

Bild 7 Verteilung der häufigsten Statements

Das weitaus häufigste Statement ist das Assignment-Statement. In kommerziellen Programmen sind mehr als ein Drittel, in technisch-wissenschaftlichen mehr als ein Fünftel aller Statements Assignment-Statements. Es folgen - ziemlich übereinstimmend bei beiden Anwendungsarten - das If-, das Do- und das End-Statement. Der hohe Anteil von Put-Statements in den technisch-wissenschaftlichen Programmen ist vermutlich eine Besonderheit des untersuchten Materials, denn die von uns geschriebenen Programme enthalten eine Fülle von Ausgabe-Statements zum Ausprüfen, die auch nach dem Ausprüfen als "verborgene Hilfsdrucke" in den Programmen verbleiben. Ein großer Unterschied zwischen kommerziellen und technisch-wissenschaftlichen Anwendern zeigt sich beim Goto- und beim Call-Statement. Stop-, Null- und Entry-Statements werden kaum, Rewrite-, Allocate-, Fetch- und Signal-Statements werden beinahe überhaupt nicht verwendet. Interessant für die Liebhaber der Blockstruktur dürfte sein, daß Begin-Blöcke so gut wie gar nicht benutzt werden. Man könnte überlegen, ob sie in zukünftigen Programmiersprachen überhaupt noch ihren Platz haben, wenn man zur Strukturierung interne Prozeduren besitzt.

Bild 8 zeigt zum Vergleich die Ergebnisse der anderen drei Untersuchungen. Sie stimmen im wesentlichen gut überein. Daß Fortran-Programmierer so wenig Do-Statements benutzen, liegt daran, daß in Fortran das Do nur zur Schleifenbildung, nicht aber zur Gruppenbildung benutzt wird. Hinsichtlich des Goto- und Call-Statements zeigen die Messungen von Nußbaumer nicht so deutliche Unterschiede wie unsere.

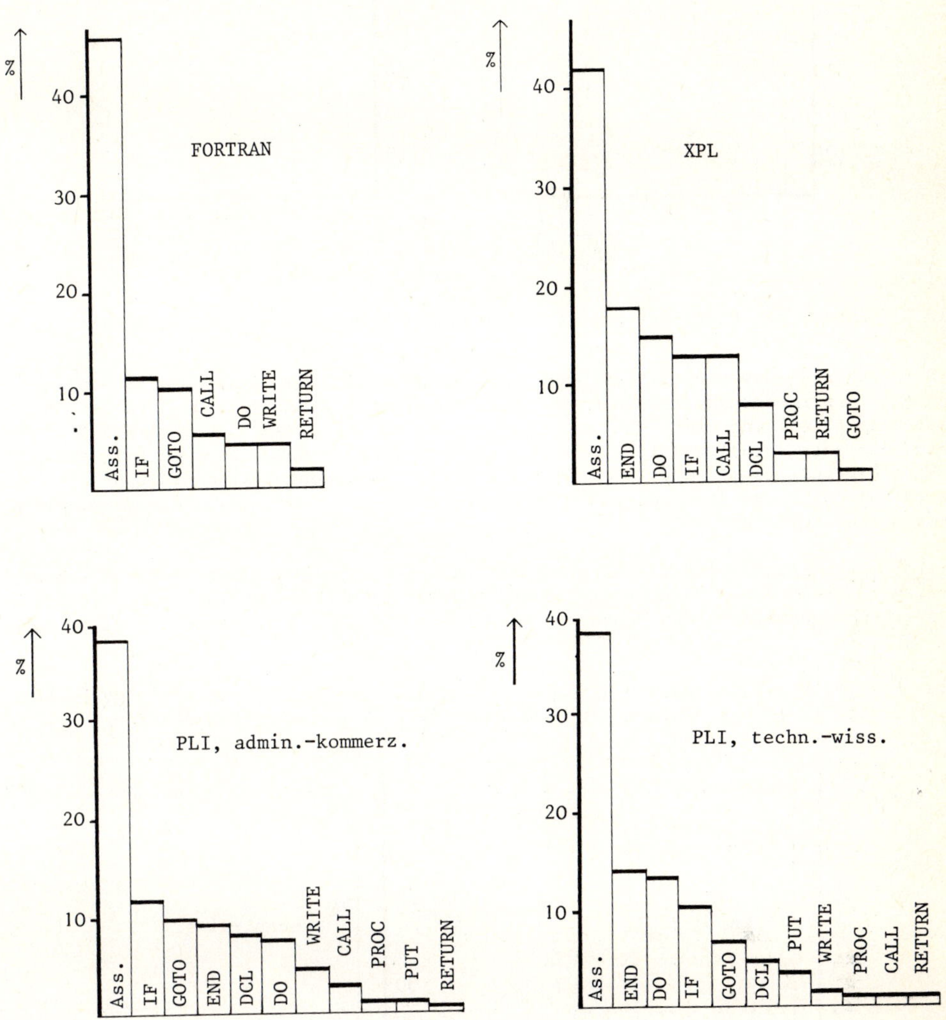

Bild 8 Statementverteilung der anderen Untersuchungen

Die vier häufigsten Statementarten, Assignment-, If-, Do- und End-Statement machen zusammen mit den Deklarations-Statements etwa 75 % aller Statements aus. Es ist deshalb gerechtfertigt, wenn wir ihnen nähere Aufmerksamkeit widmen.

Assignment-Statement. 10 % der Assignment-Statements haben die Form v = 0, etwa 6 % die Form v = 1. 10 % aller Assignment-Statements in kommerziellen und 20 % in technisch-wissenschaftlichen Programmen lauten v = v ... (der Ausdruck beginnt mit der

Variablen der linken Seite). Knuth fand hier einen Anteil von etwa 12 %. Bild 9 zeigt die Anzahl von Operanden rechts vom Gleichheitszeichen.

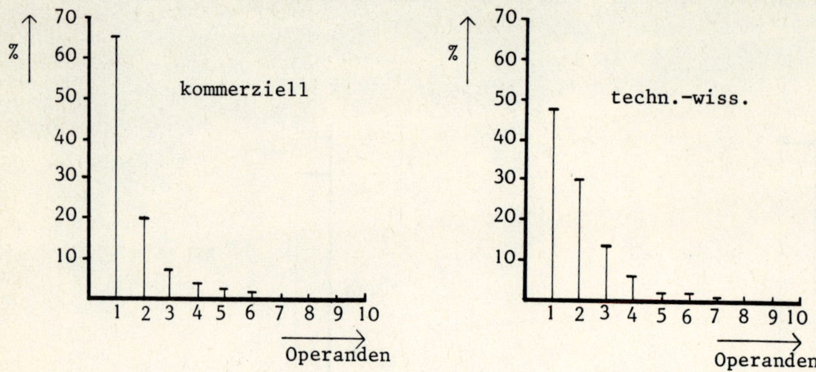

Bild 9 Anzahl der Operanden auf der rechten Seite von Assignment-Statements

50 % (technisch-wissenschaftlich) und 66 % (kommerziell) der Assignment-Statements sind nur Umspeicherungen der Form $v_1 = v_2$. Dabei ist v_2 noch zu etwa 40 % (technisch-wissenschaftlich) oder 20 % (kommerziell) Null oder Eins. Mehr als 90 % der Assignment-Statements enthalten nicht mehr als drei Operanden (wobei eine doppelt indizierte Variable bereits mit drei Operanden eingeht). Assignment-Statements sind also kurz. Sie enthalten zu gut 75 % nur zwei Operanden, d.h. nur einen Operator oder nur eine einfach indizierte Variable.

If-Statement. Etwa 25 % der If-Statements (ohne große Unterschiede zwischen kommerziellen und technisch-wissenschaftlichen Programmen) hat einen Else-Teil. Dies steht in starkem Gegensatz zu den Messungen Alexanders, der bei 60 % einen Else-Teil gefunden hat.

Bild 10 enthält die Schachtelungstiefen von If-Statements und zeigt, wie geringfügig geschachtelt wird. Das Maximum lag aber immerhin bei 10-facher Schachtelung.

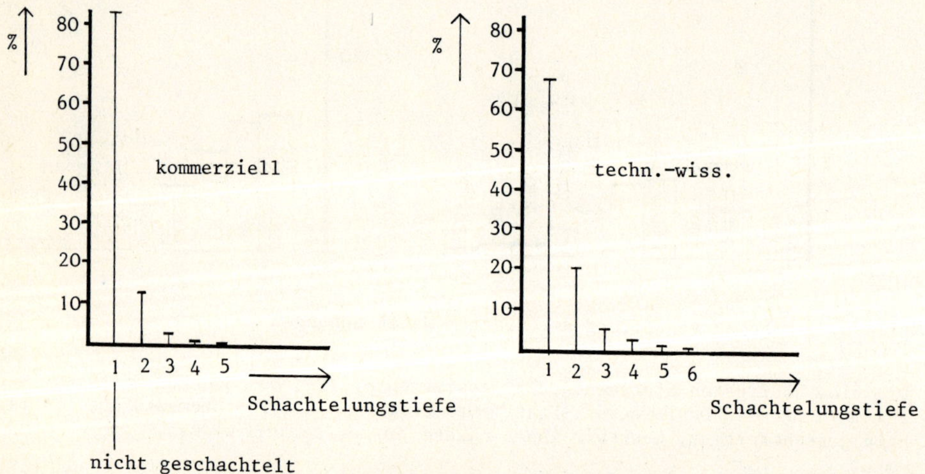

Bild 10 Schachtelungstiefen von IF-Statements

Gemessen wurde auch die Verteilung der Statementarten, die auf das THEN oder ELSE folgen. Am häufigsten (mit etwa 33 %) folgen Do-Statements zur Gruppenbildung und danach Assignment- und Goto- (kommerziell) und Assignment-, If-, Call- und Return-Statement (technisch-wissenschaftlich). Bei Knuth waren 71 % der Folgestatements Goto-Statements, was auf die Struktur von Fortran zurückzuführen ist.

Do-Statement. Hier muß unterschieden werden zwischen Do-Gruppen und Do-Schleifen. Das Schlüsselwort "Do" wird zu 60 % für Gruppen und zu 40 % für Schleifen benutzt. Interessanter ist die Frage, mit welchen Häufigkeiten die acht verschiedenen Schleifenspezifikationen, die PL/I anbietet, ausgenutzt werden. Die folgende Tabelle gibt Aufschluß darüber:

DO TO	76.2 %
DO TO WHILE	13.8 %
DO WHILE	5.2 %
DO TO BY	2.1 %
DO TO BY WHILE	1.9 %
RESTLICHE FÄLLE	0.8 %

Die Tabelle zeigt (wie sich auch bei Alexander und Nußbaumer bestätigt), daß über drei Viertel aller Schleifen einfache induktive Schleifen mit dem Inkrement 1 sind. Die mit 13.8 % immer noch recht häufigen kombiniert-induktiv-iterativen Schleifen dürften darauf zurückzuführen sein, daß unsere technisch-wissenschaftlichen Programme dieses Stilmerkmal besonders oft enthalten. Würde man mehr Quellprogramme untersuchen, ergäbe sich hier sicherlich eine Verschiebung zugunsten der rein iterativen Schleife.

In Bild 11 sind die Schachtelungstiefen von Do-Schleifen dargestellt (für kommerzielle und technisch-wissenschaftliche Programme zusammengefaßt, weil keine großen Unterschiede zwischen ihnen bestehen). Bei der Betrachtung der Startwerte und Inkremente zeigte sich, daß etwa 75 % der Schleifen den Startwert 1 besitzen und über 90 % in Schritten von +1 aufwärts zählen (Knuth: 90 %). Das negative Inkrement -1 ist nur im technischen Bereich üblich.

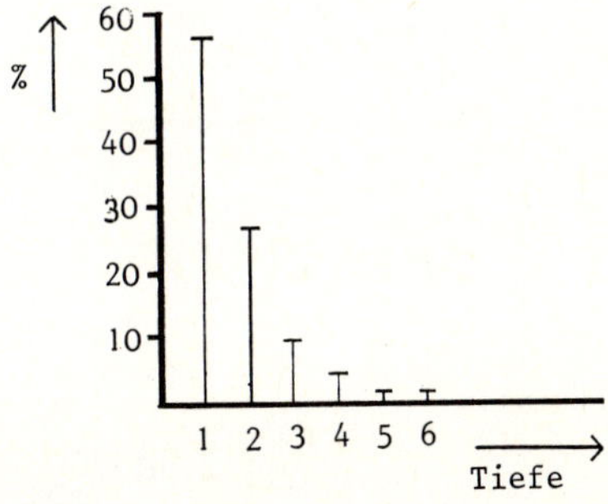

Bild 11 Schachtelungstiefen von DO-Schleifen

7. Sonstiges

Eingebaute Funktionen. Bild 12 zeigt die Verteilung der eingebauten Funktionen. Zwischen kommerziellen und technisch-wissenschaftlichen Programmen ergeben sich dabei gewisse Unterschiede. Daß UNSPEC bei den technisch-wissenschaftlichen die erste Stelle einnimmt, zeigt an, daß es sich hier vorwiegend um "Informatik-Programme" handelt, bei denen häufig Typkonvertierungen ohne Änderung der zu Grunde liegenden Bitmuster stattfinden. Die große Häufigkeit der MOD-Funktion zeigt an, daß es sich hauptsächlich um ganzzahlige Rechnungen handelt. Abgesehen von MOD und SQRT fehlen mathematische Funktionen ganz. Daß vom PL/I-F-Compiler über 90 eingebaute Funktionen angeboten werden und davon weniger als 10 % benutzt werden, stimmt nachdenklich.

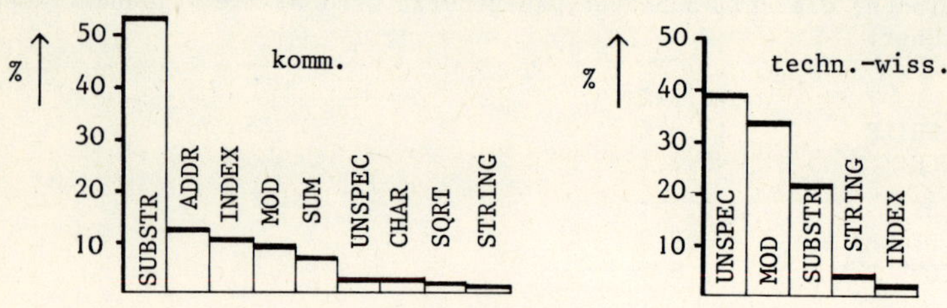

Bild 12 Verteilung der eingebauten Funktionen

Deklarationen. 80 bis 90 % aller Variablen werden explizit deklariert. Bild 13 zeigt die Verteilung der Deklarationsattribute.

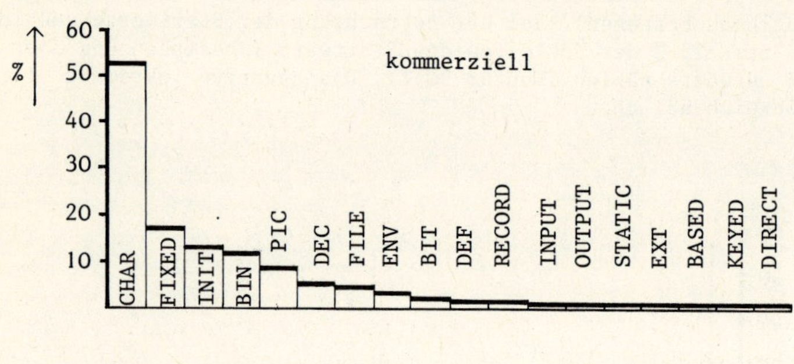

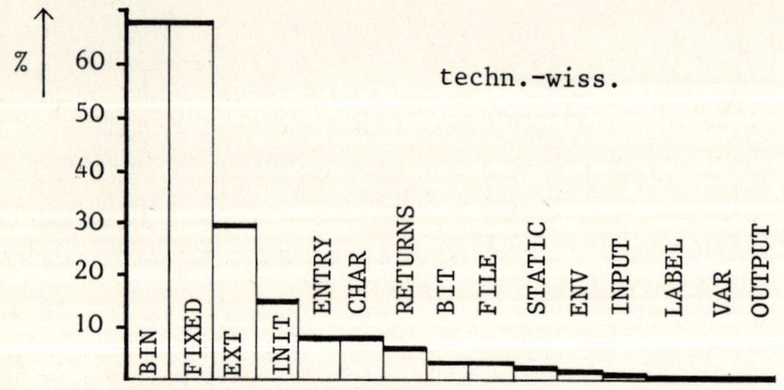

Bild 13 Verteilung der Deklarationsattribute

Kommerzielle Programmierer bevorzugen neben Zeichenkettenvariablen dezimale Festkomma- und Picture-Variablen, technisch-wissenschaftliche benutzen weitaus häufiger binäre Festkomma-Variablen (70 % der Länge 31 Bit, 30 % der Länge 15 Bit). Gleitkommavariablen fehlen ganz. Felddeklarationen sind mit 10 bis 20 %, Bitvariablen nur mit 2 bis 3 % vertreten. Bei der Untersuchung der Bitketten zeigte sich ein deutlicher Schwerpunkt (kommerziell 65 %, technisch 99 %) bei Ketten der Länge 1. Ketten, die nicht ein ganzes Vielfaches der Länge 8 sind, fehlen fast ganz.

Initialisiert werden etwa 15 % der deklarierten Variablen. Ein Drittel aller Zeichenketten hat die Länge 1. Länger als 80 Zeichen waren nur 3 % der Ketten.

95 % aller Felder sind eindimensional, die restlichen 5 % zweidimensional. Felder mit variabler oder zur Übersetzungszeit nicht spezifizierter Länge sind selten (etwa 5 %).

Ein/Ausgabe. Bei der Ein/Ausgabe herrscht die EDIT-gesteuerte Ausgabe vor. Das A-Format für Zeichenkettenvariablen steht dabei an der Spitze. B- und E-Formate für Bitketten und Gleitkommavariablen fehlen fast völlig.

Marken. Der unterschiedlichen Anzahl von Goto-Statements entspricht auch die dreimal so große Anzahl von Marken in kommerziellen gegenüber den technisch-wissenschaftlichen Programmen.

8. Beurteilung der Ergebnisse

Die Untersuchung hat gezeigt, daß die Meßergebnisse zum großen Teil so ausfallen, wie man sie bei Kenntnis der Dinge etwa erwarten würde. Insbesondere ist die Übereinstimmung mit anderen Meßergebnissen in vielen Fällen deutlich. Es hat sich aber auch ergeben, daß die untersuchten 22.000 Karten zu wenig und zu einseitig ausgewählt sind. So müssen einige unerwartete Meßwerte (die großen Häufigkeiten von Put-Statements, von kombiniert-induktiv-iterativen Schleifen und der Funktion UNSPEC, sowie das völlige Fehlen der mathematischen Funktionen) auf stilistische Eigentümlichkeiten und ein zu einseitiges Anwendungsgebiet der Programme zurückgeführt werden. Weitere Untersuchungen müssen darum besonders Anwendungsprogramme aus der Physik, Mathematik und den Ingenieurwissenschaften einschließen.

Die in der Einleitung formulierten vier Fragen erhalten durch die Untersuchungen etwa folgende Teilantworten:

1. Besonders häufige Konstruktionen sind Ausdrücke, unter ihnen speziell die sehr einfach gebauten, aus einer Variablen oder Konstanten bestehenden, und unter den verschiedenen Schleifenformen die induktiven Do-Statements, speziell die mit dem Inkrement +1. Überaus selten (und darum bemerkenswert) traten in unseren Programmen Begin-Blöcke und Gleitkommazahlen auf.

2. Die Möglichkeiten, die PL/I bietet, werden bei weitem nicht ausgenutzt. Die Speicherklasse CONTROLLED kommt selten vor, Pointer-Variablen und Multitasting fehlen so gut wie ganz. Von den vielen Schleifenformen werden nur wenige ausgenutzt, Zeichen- und Bitketten variabler Länge kommen selten vor, und die Möglichkeiten zur Erzeugung von Überlagerungsstrukturen werden auch nicht verwendet. Im großen und ganzen begnügt man sich mit den Konstruktionen, die Fortran und Algol bieten, womit jedoch nicht gesagt sein soll, daß man die vorliegenden Programme in diesen Sprachen hätte ebenso gut schreiben können, denn an einigen Stellen werden eben doch weitergehende Konstruktionen benutzt.

3. Es gibt eine ganze Reihe von statistischen Merkmalen, die unabhängig von der untersuchten Quellsprache zu sein scheinen. Die mittlere Länge der Namen beträgt in allen Untersuchungen 4 bis 6 Zeichen, etwa ein Drittel aller Konstanten ist Null oder Eins, und mehr als 99 % aller Konstanten sind kleiner als 2^{15}. Der durchschnittlich sehr einfache Aufbau der Ausdrücke ist sprachunabhängig, und das im Vergleich zur Addition und Subtraktion sehr viel seltenere Auftreten von Multiplikation und Division ebenfalls. Gleiches gilt für die Häufigkeit der verschie-

denen Statementarten und für den Aufbau von Assignment-Statements.

4. Zwischen technisch-wissenschaftlichen und kommerziellen Programmen gibt es einige deutliche Unterschiede. Technisch-wissenschaftliche Programme arbeiten fast ausschließlich mit ganzen Dualzahlen, benutzen wenig unbedingte Sprünge, rufen dafür öfter Unterprogramme auf, zeigen eine größere Schachtelungstiefe bei If-Statements und benutzen unter den eingebauten Funktionen am meisten die Mod-Funktion. Kommerzielle Programme dagegen arbeiten vorwiegend mit Zeichenketten und dezimalen Festkommazahlen, sie verwenden viel unbedingte Sprünge und weisen kleinere Schachtelungstiefen im If-Statement auf. Die am weitaus meisten benutzte eingebaute Funktion bei ihnen ist SUBSTR. Im Mittel enthalten technisch-wissenschaftliche Programme weniger, aber dafür längere Assignment-Statements als kommerzielle Programme und mehr und tiefer geschachtelte Unterprogramme als kommerzielle.

L i t e r a t u r

[1] ECMA-Beschreibung der Sprache PL1

[2] Rechenberg, P.
Programmieren für Informatiker mit PL1.
R. Oldenbourg, 1974

[3] Rechenberg, P.
Methoden der Syntaxanalyse.
Vorlesungsskript, Technische Universität Berlin, 1972

[4] Alexander, W.G.
How a programming language is used.
Computer Systems Research Group, 1972

[5] Knuth, D.E.
An empirical study of FORTRAN programs.
Software-Practice and Experience, 1971

[6] Nussbaumer, P.
Eine empirische Untersuchung von PL1-Programmen.
Semesterarbeit bei Prof. K. Bauknecht, Zürich, 1974

PATTERN MATCHING AND CALL BY PATTERN

G. Levi F. Sirovich
Istituto di Elaborazione della Informazione
Consiglio Nazionale delle Ricerche

Pisa, Italy

Abstract. The paper describes SNARK, a new pattern matching language which was specifically designed with the aim of extending programming languages with a new and effective control mechanism (pattern directed procedure call). SNARK features a powerful and extensible pattern language and an efficient pattern retrieval mechanism. SNARK pattern language interpreter is based on a technique called symbolic evaluation, which is currently of great interest in connection with program verification.

1. Pattern matching in programming languages.

Pattern matching languages have been originally developed for string and formula manipulation (from COMIT [1] to SNOBOL4 [2], and to LISP70 [3]) and have later found wide application in the field of Artificial Intelligence (AI). Programs in pattern matching languages are generally defined as sets of rewriting rules. The left-hand side component of a rewriting rule specifies a decomposition of the input stream (or of a part of it), while the right-hand side specifies the prescribed modification of the matched input stream. The problem of pattern matching is typical of AI where a pattern matching procedure is a basic component for example of theorem proving, problem solving, natural language processing systems. Inference rules, state transformation operators, and reduction operators are in fact examples of rewriting rules.

More recently, pattern matching is taking up a wider role because of the introduction of procedural representation of knowledge for AI systems [4,5]. In these systems, a pattern is associated to each procedure and describes the class of goals which might be achieved by the procedure. Instead of being called by name, a procedure is called by pattern when the current goal matches the procedure pattern.

Pattern matching primitives are important components of all languages for AI [6-10]. The paper describes the pattern matching language SNARK (from the name of a chimerical animal of undefinable characteristics and potentialities). SNARK was actually primarily designed as a component of a goal oriented language being built on top of MAGMA-LISP [11,12], an extended LISP system for complex control structures programming.

Call by pattern is an intrinsically non-deterministic control mechanism which, besides being fundamental to the implementation of knowledge representation by procedures, can be profitably embedded into standard programming languages. Several procedure features, besides the goal class can be taken into account by the procedure pattern. An important procedure feature which could be described in the pattern is the set of the applicability conditions that define the domain of the function computed by the procedure.

The pattern specification of applicability conditions has the effect of removing from the procedure body those portions which are concerned only with procedure selection thus obtaining a procedure body which is neatly reduced to its essential. Therefore, the pattern language must allow to specify user-defined data types (by means of abstract constructors and decomposers) and user-defined n-ary predicates over the procedure formal arguments.

Typically, call by pattern is useful whenever several procedures are available to compute a function. The pattern of each procedure can specify the domain subset the procedure is the most appropriate for. As a toy example, we will consider a simple recursive program for computing the greatest common divisor in an ALGOL-like language extended with call by pattern. The program consists of three procedures. Each procedure applies to a specific case (x=y, x > y or x < y), which is selected by the procedure pattern.

```
'FUNCTION' G1
  'PATTERN' (GCD, X, Y), ['INTEGER' X,Y; X=Y];
  G1 ← X;
'END';
'FUNCTION' G2
  'PATTERN' (GCD,X,Y), ['INTEGER' X,Y; X>Y];
  'COMMENT' NOTE THE CALL BY PATTERN BELOW;
  G2 ← (GCD  X-Y Y);
'END';
'FUNCTION' G3
  'PATTERN' (GCD,X,Y), ['INTEGER' X,Y; X<Y];
  G3 ← (GCD  X Y-X);
'END';
```

Patterns are here expressed in a humpty-dumpty notation. In the next section we will show the actual patterns expressed in SNARK.

Call by pattern not only amounts to a flexible, problem-oriented programming style, but also leads to a new system design philosophy oriented towards non-hierarchical module systems, in the direction pointed out by Hewitt's actors [13] and Kay's classes [14]. In fact, call by pattern allows a system to be organized as a collection of objects (modules) which interact only be means of messages (patterns) in a multiprocessing environment whose loci of control are the objects themselves.

All the above mentioned applications need a powerful and flexible pattern language, and an efficient mechanism for associatively retrieving patterns. In the next section we will introduce the pattern language SNARK while the pattern retrieval mechanism will be described in section 4.

2. The Pattern language SNARK.

In most AI languages (Micro-planner [6], QA4 [7], Conniver [8]) patterns are a list structure representation of first order logic atomic formulas. Namely, patterns are built up from constant symbols, uninterpreted function symbols, and variable symbols. Consequently, matching is coincident with first order logic unification, where variables can consistently be bound to (be matched by) any term (list structure). In addition, fragment variables are allowed, which can be matched by any (possibly empty) sequence of contiguous terms.

SNARK language extends the above mentioned pattern languages with respect to the following aspects.

a) Several basic primitive data types are built-in (e.g. atoms, integers, characters).

b) A collection of primitive pattern functions is available. Primitive pattern functions are executed within the matching process. Several primitive data structures besides lists are available. Examples are list fragments, and sets and multisets (borrowed from QA4 [7]). Primitive data structures are implemented by primitive pattern functions.

c) The pattern matching system includes an interpreter for non--primitive pattern functions, which makes some ideas suggested by Hewitt [4] effective.

d) Variables are handled through the "assignment" primitive pattern function which allows to specify restrictions on variables (e. g. data type) and looks akin to the conditional variable assignment in SNOBOL 4 [2].

SNARK system has two standard operation modes. In the search mode an input pattern is given to the system which will return either one of, or all of, the patterns which are associated to procedures in the system data base and which match the input pattern. In the match mode two patterns are given to the system which will return either failure or the unified pattern. Side effects may also occur through variable assignements in a substitution list (s-list). We will describe the search mode in section 4 and be concerned here with the procedure MATCH.

The arguments of MATCH are patterns, i.e. list structures whose elements are either constants or pattern function applications. MATCH traverses the list structure of the patterns by recurring on the substructures, unless one of the following situations occurs.

a) If one of the arguments is a non-primitive pattern function application φ, the interpreter is called on φ and returns with an updated call of MATCH (see the description of the interpreter in the next section).

b) If one of the arguments is a primitive pattern function application, the corresponding code is executed. The execution may result in a failure, or return a unified pattern, possibly by a recursive call on MATCH.

c) If one of the arguments is a constant, MATCH returns successfully only if the arguments are equal.

The behavior of the primitive pattern functions is described in the following.

a) <u>Data structures</u> (e.g. <FRAGMENT $a_1 \ldots a_n$> , <SET $a_1 \ldots a_n$>, <MULTISET $a_1 \ldots a_n$> are pattern functions which embody the matching semantics of the corresponding data structures.

b) <u>Free data</u> (e.g. <*ATOM>,<*INTEGER>,<*CHARACTER>) and <u>free data structures</u> (e.g.<*TERM>,<*FRAGMENT>,<*SET>, <*MULTISET>) are used in connection with variables and match any object of their type.

c) <ALLOF $p_1 \ldots p_n$> matches a pattern p if each pattern $p_1, \ldots, p_n$ matches p. <ONEOF $p_1 \ldots p_n$> matches a pattern p if at least one of the patterns $p_1, \ldots, p_n$ matches p. <COMPLEMENT p> matches a pattern g if p does not match **g**.

d) The variable assignment<► v r>,where v is a variable name and r is a (restriction) pattern, behaves in the following way when matched against a pattern p.

i) If variable v is bound to pattern t in the s-list, then t is matched against r. Let u' be the unified pattern returned by MATCH in case of success. u' is matched against p. If matching is successful, variable v is bound to the resulting pattern u" in the s-list.

ii) If variable v is free, pattern r is matched against p and v is bound to the resulting pattern u in case of success.

The variable assignment function allows to cope in a uniform way with free and bound variables, and it is the basis for the symbolic evaluation capability of the system.

We can now show the form of the procedure patterns taken as examples in Section 1. The pattern for G1 is (GCD <►X<*INTEGER>> <►X<*INTEGER>>). G2 and G3 patterns are respectively

(GCD<► X <*INTEGER>><► Y<LESSTHAN <► X <*INTEGER >> > >) and

(GCD<► X <*INTEGER>> <► Y<GREATERTHAN<►X <*INTEGER>>>>)

where LESSTHAN and GREATHERTHAN must be appropriately defined.

Before turning to the non-primitive pattern function interpretation, we will show an example of two patterns which do not contain non-primitive pattern functions.

p_1= ((A <SET B D>)<SET B C<►Y <*TERM>>><► Z <*FRAGMENT>> D)

p_2= ((A <► X <*SET>>) <SET B D B C> C C <ONEOF A<► Y <*TERM>>>)

Matching p_1 and p_2 results in the following unified pattern

((A <SET B D> <SET B C D> C C D)

and the corresponding s-list

```
X =<SET B D>
Y = D
Z =<FRAGMENT C C>
```

3. Pattern function interpretation.

Non-primitive pattern function definitions are lists of pairs of the following form.

('function formal pattern' 'function body')

All formal patterns of a given function have the only restriction that their first element is the function name itself.All the variable names that occur in the formal patterns act as function formal arguments. The function body is a pattern and may contain a recursive application of the function.

Let us consider as an example the pattern function times on a list structure representation of the natural numbers.

```
(((TIMES 0 <► X <*NATURAL>> ) 0)
 ((TIMES (S 0)<► X<*NATURAL>>)<► X <*NATURAL>>)
 ((TIMES (S(S <► X <*NATURAL>>)) <► Y <*NATURAL>>)
      <PLUS <► Y <*NATURAL>><TIMES (S <► X<*NATURAL>>)<► Y<*NATURAL>>>>)
```

Note that PLUS and *NATURAL are non-primitive pattern functions. Specifically, *NATURAL defines the data structure for the natural numbers and has the following definition.

```
(((*NATURAL) <ONEOF 0 (S <*NATURAL>) > ))
```

SNARK interpreter receives an application φ of a pattern function f. Formal argument binding is obtained by matching φ against one formal pattern of f which adds the resulting variable bindings to the s-list. Actual argument evaluation takes place within this matching. The function body corresponding to the matched formal pattern is finally substituted for the application.

The interpreter is non-deterministic because a given application of a function f can match several formal patterns of f. Non-determinism, which is also caused by the primitive pattern functions ONEOF and *FRAGMENT, is handled by using the powerful primitives for non-deterministic programming provided by MAGMA-LISP [12].

The matching system is able to perform symbolic evaluation [15], i.e. to evaluate open function applications, where some of the function arguments contain free variables. Such a characteristics basically depends on the use of the s-list (where variables can be bound to patterns containing variables), on the semantics of the assignment pattern function, and on the interpreter evaluation mechanism (in which argument binding is carried out by pattern matching). Of course, the matching system is able to perform the standard evaluation. For example, (MATCH <TIMES (S(S 0)) (S(S(S 0)))> <*TERM>) evaluates to

(S(S(S(S(S(S 0)))))). An example of symbolic evaluation is the following (MATCH <TIMES (S(S 0)) <- X <*TERM>>>(S(S(S(S 0))))), which returns the value (S(S 0)) for X in the s-list.

Because of its symbolic evaluation capability, SNARK has proved to be a useful tool in program verification [16]. In fact, the semantics of a "well-structured" programming language can easily be defined in terms of a set of pattern function definitions, thus letting the SNARK interpreter act as a symbolic interpreter of the programming language. If specific rules for handling induction are provided, the system can prove properties of programs. The system has actually been specialized and used as a LISP symbolic interpreter [15], while its application to restricted PASCAL is now in progress [17].

4. The pattern retrieval system.

The system is required to efficiently retrieve in the permanent data base those patterns which match a given input pattern. The above requirement is achieved by indexing patterns through binary discrimination trees, which are similar to the net used by QA4 [6] for indexing "constant" patterns, i.e. patterns containing constant symbols and uninterpreted function symbols only. Since in our case, the indexed patterns may contain pattern functions and variables the discrimination must be based on the matching semantics of the patterns.

It is worth noting that non primitive pattern functions are called by pattern. We will thus discuss the pattern retrieval system with respect to pattern function definitions. The same technique applies to the retrieval of patterns associated to procedures. All the formal patterns of a given pattern function f share the first element, i.e. the function name f. Hence, for each function f the permanent data base contains a discrimination tree which indexes all the formal patterns of f and which is accessed by hash-coding the function name itself.

Each node of a tree requires matching a pattern associated to the node (node pattern) against an input pattern element selected by a function associated to the node (node selector). Each node has two outcoming branches labelled "success" and "fail". As an example consider the discrimination tree of the function TIMES which is shown in Figure 1.

The input pattern is referred to by the variable ip. The only selector needed in this examples is the function 1st which gets the first element of a list of naturals and could be defined as follows

```
(((1st <- x <*NATURAL>> <*FRAGMENT>) <- X <*NATURAL>>))
```

The search procedure is the following. Variable ip is initialized to the list of the actual arguments of the function application. Starting from the root, the tree is traversed by branching below each node according to the result of node matching operation. In case of success, if the unified pattern returned by MATCH is different from (is a restriction of) the second argument, then both outcoming branches

and the old one. The two node patterns associated to the new terminal nodes are the pattern being inserted and the unified pattern returned by MATCH. The latter terminal made will point to all function bodies pointed by the other two terminal nodes. Therefore, any function body may generally occur in several lists which correspond to different access paths. On the other hand two function bodies occur in the same list when the corresponding formal patterns match, and therefore they share a part of the domain.

When intermediate non-terminal nodes have to be inserted, the matching procedure provides information about the matching failure state and about instantiated variables. This information can be exploited for interactively defining the node pattern and selector. A tree editor is provided to ennable the user to modify the discrimination trees, for example to balance them.

5. Concluding remarks.

The pattern matching system we have described in the paper was originally developed as a building component for Artificial Intelligence systems, and as such stems on one side from earlier pattern matching languages developed for string and formula manipulation, and on the other side from recent work in AI.

Knowledge representation by procedures emphasizes the role of pattern matching dramatically. Pattern matching is first of all required to be a flexible and powerful symbol manipulation system by itself. SNARK embodies some very suggestive ideas that have been proposed in the literature along this line. The close connection that thus turns out with symbolic evaluation is very interesting (and should hardly be surprising). The use of symbolic evaluation in proving properties of programs is one of the most promising approaches currently being investigated in the field of computer-aided software development.

Procedural knowledge representation assigns to pattern matching a basic role also as an innovative control mechanism. Pattern directed procedure call leads to a heterarchical system organization, where control is distributed in a collection of active entities which interact by exchanging messages in a multiprocessor environment instead of by "passing control". Such a system design philosophy has been proven very effective in building large and complex AI systems, and seems to be of great interest also to other fields, expecially if recent trends in computer system architecture are considered.

References.

1. Yngve, V.H., COMIT Programmer's Reference Manual. MIT Press, Cambridge Mass., 1962.

2. Griswold, R.E., J.F. Poage and I.P. Polonsky, The SNOBOL4 Programming Language. Prentice Hall, Englewood Cliffs, N.J.,1969.

3. Tesler, L.G. et al. The LISP70 pattern matching system. Proc. Third Intl. Conf. on Artificial Intelligence, Stanford, USA, August 20-23,

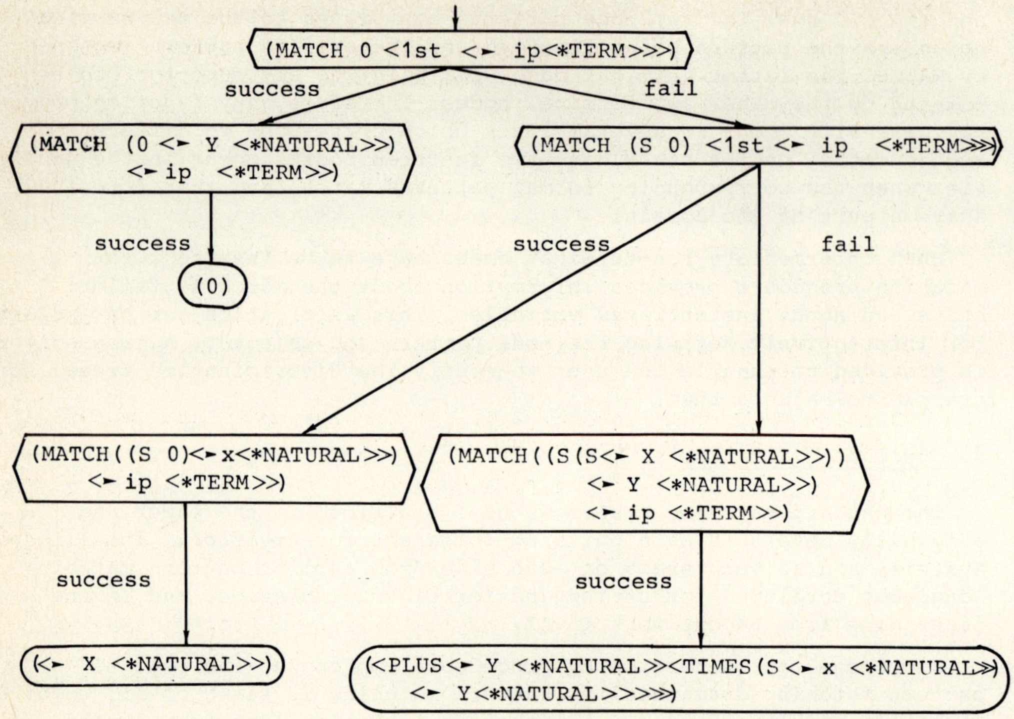

Figure 1. The discrimination tree of the function TIMES.

have to be taken. This typically occurs when the input pattern contains a free variable which can take values for which the node matching would fail.

Terminal nodes, where the whole input pattern is matched against a function formal pattern, are passed through upon success only, and give access to the list of exactly those function bodies whose corresponding formal patterns match the input pattern.

The above described search procedure is also a substantial part of the procedure for creating the discrimination trees. When a new function pattern has to be inserted into a tree, the tree is traversed and the body corresponding to the new pattern is added to the list associated to all passed terminal nodes. However, two situations may occur that need specific operations.

If a failure on a terminal node occurs, a new non-terminal node must be inserted whose outcoming success branch points to the terminal node. A new terminal node is appended to the fail branch, where ip is matched against the pattern being inserted.

If a success occurs on a terminal node, and at least one variable needs to be instantianted, then a cascade of two non-terminal nodes must be inserted in order to discriminate among two new terminal nodes

1973, 671-685.

4. Hewitt, C., Description and theoretical analysis (using schemata) of PLANNER : A language for proving theorems and manipulating models in a robot.AI Memo No. 251. MIT Project MAC (April 1972).

5. Winograd, T., Procedures as a representation for data in a computer program for understanding natural language. Ph. D. Th., MIT, Cambridge, Mass. (January 1971).

6. Sussman, G.J. and Winograd, T. Micro-planner reference manual. AI Memo No. 203, MIT Project MAC (July 1970).

7. Rulifson, J.F., Derksen, J.A. and Waldinger, R.J. QA4, a procedural calculus for intuitive reasoning.SRI AI Center Technical Note 73 (November 1972).

8. McDermott, D.V. and Sussman, G.J. The Conniver reference manual. AI Memo No. 259, MIT Project MAC (May 1972).

9. Davies, D.J.M. POPLER 1.5 Reference Manual. Univ. of Edinburgh. TPU Report No. 1 (May 1973).

10. Swinehart, D. and Sproull, B. SAIL. Stanford AI Project Operating Note No. 57.2 (January 1971).

11. Montangero, C., Pacini, G. and Turini, F. MAGMA-LISP: A Machine language for artificial intelligence. Proc. Fourth Intl. Joint Conf. on Artificial Intelligence, Tbilisi, USSR, September 3-8, 1975.

12. Montangero, C., Pacini, G. and Turini, F. Two-level control structure for non-deterministic programming. IEI Internal Report B74-31. Pisa, Italy (October 1974).

13. Hewitt, C. et al. Behavioral semantics of non-recursive control structures. Proc. Programming Symposium, Paris, France, April 9-11 1974, 385-407.

14. Kay, A. Personal computing. Meeting on 20 Years of Computer Science, Pisa, Italy, June 16-18, 1975.

15. Levi G. and Sirovich, F. Valutazione simbolica e unificazione. Proc. Symposium on Theoretical Computer Science, Mantova, Italy, November 21-23, 1974, 97-116.

16. Levi G. and Sirovich, F. Proving program properties, logical procedural semantics and symbolic evaluation. Proc. Mathematical Foundation of Computer Science 1975, Marianske Lazne, Tchechoslovakia, September 1-5, 1975.

17. Levi, G. and Sirovich, F. Un sistema per la produzione e la verifica di programmi strutturati, XXII Intl. Conf. on Electronics, Roma, Italy, March 12-15, 1975, 181-188.

ON THE DESIGN OF PROGRAMMING LANGUAGES INCLUDING MINI ALGOL 68

L. Ammeraal
Mathematical Centre
Amsterdam, Netherlands

ABSTRACT

Some general characteristics of ALGOL-like programming languages are introduced. It is discussed what kind of language concepts are useful enough for most users to justify their presence in new languages. As an illustration, Mini ALGOL 68 is proposed as a modest successor of ALGOL 60.

SOME REMARKS ON THE INTRODUCTION OF NEW LANGUAGE CONCEPTS

When a new programming language is presented, most of us are only interested in the question whether the set of new language concepts contains the things that we consider useful in a language. If the language also offers a number of features that we do not need ourselves, we, as "humble programmers", usually assume that they will be useful to others. Sometimes we even learn those new features eagerly and then teach them to others without knowing their merits from our own practical experience. The following three considerations justify a less tolerant attitude towards new languages.

First, unnecessary language elements are undesirable from an educational point of view. The subject-matter for students should consist of useful and interesting things. Special care should be taken to avoid teaching the wrong programming habits as a consequence of inappropriate tools in a language.

Secondly, a language should be well implementable and its availability should not be limited to users of large computers. As a companion to the definition of the language, a fast and reliable compiler is much more wanted than a clever doctoral thesis on some advanced implementation topic.

The third argument has to do with style. Useless things should be absent in a programming language, even if they do not harm anybody. Their presence shows the same bad taste as a number of unused buttons for air-conditioning in a motor-car whose driver always prefers to open the window a little bit for fresh air.

SOME CHARACTERISTICS TO CLASSIFY LANGUAGES

The idea of choosing only a small number of mutually independent elementary language concepts, which can be used to build more complex constructs, was introduced by VAN WIJNGAARDEN and called *orthogonal design* [1]. There is a strong relationship between this idea and the introduction of the terms *width* for the number of elementary language concepts, and *depth* (or *profundity*) for the amount of more complex consequences that are immediately implied by them. A classical example of a profound language aspect is the use of recursive procedures. Profound language properties are easily overlooked at first sight because they are hardly mentioned in the language definition and may even be discovered later on. A language element that looks very simple may have such profound implications that is seems wise to abolish it. A well-known example of such a "harmful" element is the "goto statement" [2]. In connection with this, it makes sense to mention a third characteristic of language concepts, viz. the *level*: the more a language concept is suited as a tool for our process of abstract thinking, the "higher" is its level. We call the level low if the concept is closely related to the construction of a machine. The adjectives high and low are frequently used for a language as a whole, e.g. to compare ALGOL-like languages with assembler languages. However, high-level languages may contain low-level elements. These elements may have been included on purpose, as an attempt to give the programmer a better grip of the facilities offered by the machine. Typical low-level elements are the DEFINED-attribute in PL/I and bits and bytes structures in ALGOL 68. In environments where more attention is paid to the design of general, reliable and machine-independent algorithms than to the exploitation of a particular piece of hardware, low-level language elements are not popular. Low-level elements may also exist in new languages for historical and conservative reasons, as a consequence of the designers' lack of courage to reject such an inheritance from preceding languages. Descended from a branch instruction in machine language, the goto statement is such a typical low-level element, which has been maintained even in ALGOL 68.

Inspired by Dijkstra's critical arguments against the goto statement, WULF proposed to consider the global variable harmful [3]. In this case, however, it should be kept in mind that not all tools that are dangerous should be considered harmful. A butcher will not follow the advice to replace a sharp knife by a blunt one, although he will admit that the latter is less dangerous. Similarly, global variables and, in particular, functions with side-effects, though dangerous, can be used as very powerful tools and should not be abolished as long as no satisfactory other means are given to replace them.

How wide and how deep a language should be depends on the kind of people and of machines that will work with it. It is not unreasonable to require that a high-level computer scientist should be familiar with a language as wide as PL/I or as profound as ALGOL 68. In most professions experts have to study several years and there is no reason why a computer scientist must be taught a programming language in only a week. On the other hand, only a small fraction of all computer users are computer scientists. There are a great many people who are working in completely different fields, such as e.g. chemical engineering, and who write computer programs from time to time, to solve their problems. They need a much simpler language than ALGOL 68 or PL/I. Theoretically, they could be taught only a well-chosen subset of such an extensive language and use the compiler for the full language. This philosophy, however, requires a compiler for the full language as well as a good teacher who is able to restrict himself. Such a compiler is more than most users need and there is a consequent danger that they will pay for things they do not use.

Mini ALGOL 68: A MODEST SUCCESSOR OF ALGOL 60

ALGOL 60 is a high-level language of moderate width. Most complaints from its users concern their implementations, and not the language itself. At those places where a good ALGOL 60 compiler is available, the language has proved to be very useful and convenient for a great variety of applications. Yet, fifteen years after the definition of this language, it is well-known from experience that, on the one hand, the language badly lacks a few simple extensions and that, on the other, some elements of the language are seldom used and can be considered superfluous. String and character handling facilities, e.g., would have made the language more appropriate for commercial applications. The <u>own</u> and <u>switch</u> concepts are examples of language elements that have not proved their right to exist. A very useful thing in ALGOL 60 is the conditional expression. This is a typical high-level language concept. It allows us to express ourselves in much the same way as we think and it enables us to write things much more briefly, i.e. without repetitions of pieces of program text, than with only conditional statements. The following example shows this.

Suppose that we want to output the value of $p * i$ if $a[i] = x$, with the additional restriction that this test can only be made if $i \leq n$ and should be considered to fail if $i > n$. Otherwise we want to output the value of $(p+1) * q$. In ALGOL 60 this may be achieved by

output (<u>*if*</u> (<u>*if*</u> $i \leq n$ <u>*then*</u> $a[i] = x$ <u>*else*</u> <u>*false*</u>)
<u>*then*</u> $p * i$ <u>*else*</u> $(p+1) * q$).

But for conditional expressions this could only be programmed in a considerably more laborious way. It is curious that some newer programming languages such as PL/I and PASCAL lack conditional expressions. Using our terminology it can be said that these languages lack something in the depth dimension, which is available in ALGOL 60. ALGOL 68, on the other hand, has something more than ALGOL 60 in this direction (and so has Mini ALGOL 68), e.g. "unitary clauses" as an elegant generalization of "statements" and "expressions". If we do not recognize a fundamental distinction between statements and expressions any longer, many things become much simpler. Inside "expressions" flow-of-control facilities become available in a quite natural way. Constructions that were formerly called "statements" may now occur in syntactic positions where only "expressions" used to be allowed. An example of such a syntactic position is the text between <u>*while*</u> and <u>*do*</u>. Suppose that we want to construct a loop with the test for termination placed neither at the beginning nor at the end, but somewhere in the middle, say between *part A* and *part B*. In the old days this was programmed as, e.g.,

```
again:  part A;
        if i > n then goto ready;
        part B;
        goto again;
ready: .
```

In ALGOL 68 this can be written as

while part A; i ≤ n do part B od.

It should be noticed that *part A* or *part B* may be empty. These possibilities yield the PASCAL while and repeat statements as special cases of this construction.

The need for this more general form of a loop is discussed in detail by KNUTH [4]. Referring to personal communication with Dijkstra and Wirth, KNUTH calls it the n + ½ problem. He discusses some proposals for language extensions to solve this problem. In (Mini) ALGOL 68, however, this problem is solved very easily, as we have seen, or, in other words, there is no n + ½ problem at all. This example illustrates my statement that profound language properties are easily overlooked. It is clear that KNUTH would have mentioned this ALGOL 68 facility in his comprehensive paper [4] if he had been aware of it.

We may conclude that, of all well-known languages, ALGOL 68 is probably the best candidate for programming without goto statements. However, ALGOL 68 is not only a language with fine profound properties, but it is also extremely wide, in our terminology. It offers too many facilities to be the optimum choice for everybody. A modest sublanguage of ALGOL 68 seems to be a better successor of ALGOL 60 in a number of situations. A proposal for such a sublanguage is Mini ALGOL 68. It has about the width of ALGOL 60 but is considerably more profound. The low-level concepts bits, bytes and gotos are not included in the language. The absence of structured values, united modes, heap generators, operator declarations, mode declarations, casts, flexible bounds, formats, completers and semaphores will probably disappoint those who are familiar with ALGOL 68. It would be a mistake, however, to conclude that Mini ALGOL 68 would hardly offer anything more than ALGOL 60. In addition to many useful ALGOL 60 elements, it offers the general concept of a unitary clause as mentioned before, the loop clause as an improvement of the for-statement, the case clause, variables to assign values of the modes char and string to, the improved parameter mechanism for procedures, the routine text as a special case of a unit and many other specific ALGOL 68 concepts. The following Mini ALGOL 68 program shows some possibilities concerning data types that exist neither in ALGOL 60, nor in PASCAL, SIMULA 67 and PL/I.

```
begin proc ([ ]int) [ ] int p;
      real pi 3 = pi/3;
      p := ([ ]int a) [ ] int:
           ([1:upb a] int b;
           for i to upb a do b[i]:=-a[i] od;b);
      # now a routine has been assigned to the variable p #
      [1:3] int x := (10,20,30);
      [1:3] int y := p(x); # yields (-10,-20,-30) #
      [1:3] proc (real) real q := (cos,sin,exp);
      print (q[1](pi3));
      # .5 (=cos(pi/3)) is now written #
      q[1] := sqrt;
      print (q[1](25))
      # 5 (=sqrt(25)) is now written #
end
```

In most languages neither can a function yield an array, nor can elements of arrays be functions. In the program above these things happen to the "function" *p* and the "array" *q*, respectively. Further details about Mini ALGOL 68 can be found in the User's Guide [5]. A compiler [6] and a run-time-system for Mini ALGOL 68 were written by the author of this paper in about eight months, which indicates that implementing this language is an order of magnitude simpler than building an ALGOL 68 compiler.

A few choices with respect to the inclusion of certain concepts in Mini ALGOL 68 were made somewhat arbitrarily. E.g., the question can be raised whether it was right to include modes beginning with an arbitrary number of refs. It was, however, not the intention of this paper to claim that Mini ALGOL 68 is better than any other sublanguage of ALGOL 68. Its main goal was to emphasize that we should think about the question what tools are useful in programming.

REFERENCES

[1] WIJNGAARDEN, A. VAN, *Orthogonal Design and Description of a Formal Language*, Mathematical Centre MR 76, Amsterdam (1965).

[2] DIJKSTRA, E.W., *Goto Statement Considered Harmful*, CACM 11 (1968), 147-148.

[3] WULF, W. & M. SHAW, *Global Variable Considered Harmful*, SIGPLAN Notices (1973), 28-34.

[4] KNUTH, D.E., *Structured Programming with go to Statements*, ACM Computing Surveys 6 (1974), 261-301 (278,279 in particular).

[5] AMMERAAL, L., *Mini ALGOL 68 User's Guide*, Mathematical Centre IW 32/75, Amsterdam (1975).

[6] AMMERAAL, L., *An Implementation of an ALGOL 68 Sublanguage*, Proceedings of the International Computing Symposium 1975, North-Holland Publishing Company, Amsterdam (1975), 49-53.

S C H A L T W E R K E

ASYNCHRONE SCHALTWERKSIMULATION MIT SSM, EINER SIMULATIONSSPRACHE FÜR SCHALTWERKE MITTELS MEHRWERTIGER LOGIK

von W. Görke
Institut für Informatik IV,
Universität Karlsruhe

1. Einleitung

Beim Entwurf asynchroner Schaltwerke bilden die Laufzeiteffekte realer Bauelemente eine Einflußgröße, die zu Fehlfunktionen führen kann, wenn sie nicht beim Entwurf hinreichend berücksichtigt wird. Neben den Zeitintervallen, die in realen logischen Gattern zur Ausführung der Funktion benötigt werden, sich folglich als Verzögerung zwischen der Ausgangsgröße in Bezug auf ihre Eingangssignale äußern, sind vor allem Toleranzen in Lage oder Steilheit der Signalwechsel sowie Signalverzerrungen von Bedeutung. Letztere können zur Absorption kurzer Impulse führen, während Laufzeitverzögerungen allgemein zu Signalwettläufen führen, die sich in unbestimmten Ausgangssignalen bei gewissen Eingangswerten äußern. Die Möglichkeit zu unbestimmten, mithin evtl. fehlerhaften Ausgangssignalen bezeichnet man als Hasard.

Will man sich bei einer Entwurfsüberprüfung durch Simulation nicht auf die reine logische Funktion beschränken, sondern auch eine Erkennung von Laufzeiteffekten berücksichtigen, sind digitale Schaltungsbeschreibungssprachen erforderlich, die sich nicht nur auf synchrone Vorgänge beschränken, sondern Verzögerungen einbeziehen. Obwohl mehrere Sprachen dieser Art bekannt geworden und auch implementiert worden sind /1, 2/, wurde eine neue Sprache dieser Art entworfen und mit Hilfe von Burroughs extended ALGOL auf der Rechenanlage B 6700 implementiert /3, 4/. Die Sprache wurde SSM - Simulationssprache für Schaltwerke unter Verwendung von mehrwertiger Logik - genannt. Ihr Compiler/Simulator ist seit einigen Monaten betriebsbereit.

Da im Rahmen dieser Arbeit nicht ausführlich auf die Sprache eingegangen werden kann, seien im folgenden Abschnitt lediglich einige wichtige Eigenschaften erläutert. Anschließend wird auf die Möglichkeiten der Simulation mit Hilfe von Beispielen eingegangen, wobei die oben erwähnten Laufzeiteffekte in digitalen Schaltungen im Vordergrund stehen sollen.

2. Einige Eigenschaften der Sprache SSM

Die Syntaxbeschreibung der Sprache SSM ist im Anhang beigefügt, ein Teil ihrer Konstruktionen wird in den folgenden Beispielen auch in Bezug auf den semantischen Inhalt deutlich.

Grundsätzlich verfügt sie über eine Blockstruktur ähnlich den höheren Programmiersprachen, wobei sich die Elementtypen jedoch an digitale Bauelemente anlehnen. Jeder Block verfügt über einen Definitions-, Deklarations-, Verbindungs- und Simulationsbereich, die jeweils auch leer sein können. Dabei werden durch Definitionsanweisungen neue Elementtypen vom Benutzer definiert,sofern nicht die 7 Grundelemente AND,OR,NAND,

NOR (mit je 2 Eingängen), DELAY, REGISTER (mit einem Eingang) oder FUNCTION (Signalgenerator ohne Eingang) verwendet werden. Alle verwendeten Elemente müssen deklariert werden, wobei einfache Namen oder ein- bis dreidimensionale Felder mit indizierten Namen die deklarierten Elemente beschreiben. Verbindungen lassen sich bedingt und unbedingt angeben, wobei neben der direkten Bausteinverbindung auch Boolesche Ausdrücke aus Signalvariablen bzw. Vektorausdrücke möglich sind. Schließlich erlauben die Simulationsanweisungen eine Signalinitialisierung, die evtl. bedingte Ausgabe bestimmter Signale in fortranähnlichem Druckformat sowie die Angabe der auszuführenden Simulationsschritte bzw. des Simulationsmodus.

SSM-Programme lassen sich in freiem Format darstellen, wobei das Sonderzeichen % Kommentar bis zum Zeilenende einleitet, während $ auf Compileranweisungen hinweist.

Alle Signale sind Elemente der 5-wertigen Logik 0,E,U,A,1. Dabei haben 0 und 1 die bekannte zweiwertige Bedeutung, während die übrigen Werte Signalübergänge darstellen, nämlich E (ein) Übergang von 0 nach 1, A (aus) von 1 nach 0, U unbestimmter Signalwert. Gerade diese 5-wertige Signaldarstellung erlaubt die Hasardsimulation, da nämlich Folgen von E- bzw. A-Werten nur einen Übergang beschreiben, der mit Zeittoleranz versehen früher oder später innerhalb der Folge auftreten kann, jedoch einen mehrfachen Signalwechsel ausschließt. OUU1 dagegen erlaubt 4 Interpretationen mit einem oder drei Signalwechseln.

Als Zeitbasis ist eine Gatterlaufzeit der Grundelemente AND, OR, NAND, NOR vorgesehen. Das Verzögerungselement DELAY erlaubt ebenfalls diesen Wert, eine beliebige Vervielfachung oder die Angabe einer toleranzbehafteten Verzögerung, deren Auswirkung in den Beispielen erläutert wird. REGISTER entsprechen lediglich benannten Signalpunkten in der Schaltung. Vielleicht ist diese Typbezeichnung etwas irreführend gewählt, da bei ihnen eine Signalzuweisung sofort, also ohne Verzögerung, erfolgen kann. Da jeder Block auch EXECUTE-Anweisungen enthalten kann, lassen sich beliebige Kombinationen aus Fein- und Grobzeitintervallen für die Simulation beschreiben, wobei die Simulation eines Elementes abgebrochen wird, wenn alle Eingangssignale stabile Werte erreicht haben. Der Simulationsmodus braucht nicht gesondert gewählt zu werden, da normal die zweiwertige Betriebsart BINARY impliziert wird. Befinden sich Verzögerungselemente in der Schaltung, wird automatisch zu SINGLE (dreiwertige Simulation mit 0,U,1) oder RACE (5-wertige Simulation) übergegangen. Der Modus HAZARD ist noch nicht implementiert, ebenso Konstantenverkettungen; allerdings wird dadurch die im folgenden beschriebene Hasardsimulation nicht beeinträchtigt.

Die soweit kurz umrissene Syntax der Sprache SSM erlaubt vor allem die folgenden Simulationsmöglichkeiten:

1. Darstellung gatterbedingter symmetrischer Verzögerungen,
2. Darstellung beliebiger, auch asymmetrischer Verzögerungen sowie toleranzbehafteter Übergänge,
3. Definition beliebiger Bausteintypen durch den Benutzer,

4. Direkte Dateneinausgabe mit Hilfe einer speziellen extern zu vereinbarenden Dialogroutine,
5. Externer Anschluß anderer Simulationsroutinen,
6. Vorübersetzung von Simulationsprogrammen.

Einige Simulationsbeispiele in SSM sind bereits an anderer Stelle veröffentlicht worden /5/, wobei vor allem auf die Simulation der logischen Funktion einer Schaltung unabhängig von deren Implementierung eingegangen wurde (Register-Transfer-Ebene). Hier sollen dagegen vor allem Vorgänge untersucht werden, die von den Laufzeiteffekten der Bauelemente beeinflußt werden.

3. Verzögerungen bei Beschränkung auf binäre Signale

Der einfachste Verzögerungseinfluß logischer Gatter ist die Gatterverzögerung, also die Zeitdifferenz zwischen einer Eingangssignaländerung und deren Auswirkung am Gatterausgang. Grundsätzlich beträgt dieser Zeitraum bei den Grundelementen NAND, NOR, AND, OR die Einheit eines Simulationsschritts. Auch DELAY ohne weitere Spezifikation verzögert um diese Einheit. Da die Grundelemente NAND, NOR, AND, OR keine weitere Spezifikation der Gatterlaufzeit erlauben, erfordert die Darstellung aller anderen Verzögerungseffekte besonders spezifizierte DELAY-Glieder oder anders zusammengesetzte Elementtypen.

In /5/ wird gezeigt, daß zwei rückgekoppelte NAND-Gatter die wohlbekannte asynchrone Realisierung eines RS-Fangflipflops erlauben. Jedoch zeigt die Simulation dieser Schaltung bei sonst idealen NAND-Verknüpfungen mit einer Einheitsverzögerung Schwingverhalten, falls der kritische Signalübergang 00 nach 11 dargestellt werden soll. Obwohl solche Schwingungen bei üblichen Bauelementen nachgewiesen werden konnten /6/, führen diese in der Praxis stets nach wenigen Übergängen zu einem stabilen Zustand. Auch bei der Simulation dieser Schaltung erreicht man eine Stabilisierung, wenn die Gatter nicht gleich und symmetrisch, sondern verschieden spezifiziert werden, wobei es nicht auf eine unterschiedliche Gatterverzögerung sondern auf unsymmetrische Übergänge der Ausgangsgröße ankommt.

Bild 1 zeigt diese Schaltung als Einführung in die Simulationsbeschreibung mit SSM, Bild 2 die zugehörige Simulation. Das mit V bezeichnete Gatter ist nach Bild 1 b realisiert, wobei erreicht werden soll, daß ein Ausgang 1 nach vorangehendem 0-Ausgang sich sofort am ODER-Gatter G2 bemerkbar macht, während ein 0-Ausgang nach vorangehender 1 wegen der Gatterverzögerung am ODER-Gatter Q erst bei dessen Wiederholung am Ausgang erscheint. Natürlich soll Bild 1 b nur die verzögerte Reaktion des in Bild 1 a mit V bezeichneten Gatters bewirken, nicht etwa 2 oder 3 Gatterlaufzeiten dafür erzwingen. Deshalb wird von Feinschritten Gebrauch gemacht.

Die Beschreibung in SSM (Bild 2) läßt 2 neue Elementdefinitionen, nämlich des unsymmetrisch verzögernden Gatters NA10V sowie des Flipflops FANG erkennen. Anschliessend wird ein solches Flipflop mit dem Namen RS deklariert, die Eingangssignale A und B durch FUNCTION spezifiziert, darauf A und B mit den Flipflopeingängen verbunden.

WRITE (INITIAL,...) sorgt für den Ausdruck des Tabellenkopfes, die anschließende Anweisung druckt am Ende jedes der 15 Simulationsschritte die Flipflopein- und ausgangsgrößen aus, entsprechend viele Eingänge wurden als FUNCTION spezifiziert.

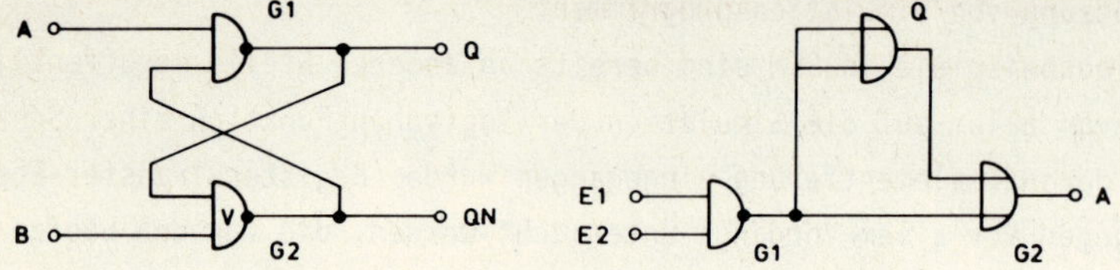

Bild 1 a) Fangflipflop aus ungleichen NAND - Gattern

b) NAND - Gatter mit verzögertem 1 → 0 - Übergang

2 weitere EXECUTE-Anweisungen tauchen bei den Typdefinitionen auf, die ihrerseits abgeschlossene Blöcke sind, jedoch keine weiteren Definitionen enthalten. NA10V deklariert zunächst die Gatter von Bild 1 b, beschreibt darauf die Verbindungen, wobei E1 und E2 der Bausteinparameter als Eingänge aufgefaßt werden, da aus ihnen die NAND-Funktion G1 gebildet wird, während umgekehrt A auf der linken Seite erscheint, also Ausgang sein muß. Die Reihenfolge der Parameter oder ihr Name spielt keine Rolle, nur ihr Auftreten rechts oder links einer Zuweisung wird für ihre Interpretation ausgewertet. WRITE erlaubt hier die Ausgabe von Zwischenwerten zur Erleichterung der Programmierung, diese Zeile kann später entfallen. EXECUTE 2 sorgt dafür, daß die Ausgangsverzögerung innerhalb des Typs NA10V ausgewertet wird, innerhalb des Flipflops dagegen beide Gatter gleich schnell reagieren.

Der gleiche Unterschied zwischen äußerer und innerer Betrachtung gilt bezüglich der EXECUTE 5-Anweisung für das Element FANG. Jede äußere Signaländerung an A und B erlaubt hier 5 Feinschritte, evtl. weniger, falls alle Signale stabile Werte erreicht haben. Erfahrungsgemäß war dieser Wert ausreichend, jeder größere Wert würde am Verhalten der Schaltung nichts ändern.

Da keine Initialisierung der Signale angegeben wurde, sind zu Beginn alle Variablen, also auch A,B,Q und QN des Flipflops 0. Der erste Simulationsschritt mit dem Eingang AB = 11 zeigt also bereits die Stabilisierung des Flipflops auf den Wert Q = 0, QN = 1, wobei kurzzeitig der unerwünschte Ausgang Q,QN = 1,1 auftrat. Der verzögerte 10-Übergang ist im 3. Simulationsschritt der Gesamtschaltung zu erkennen, in dem der Eingang AB von 11 nach 01 verändert wird. Aus Platzgründen zeigt Bild 2 nur einen Teil des Protokolls.

Im SSM-Programm von Bild 2 fällt auf, daß das ODER-Gatter Q von Bild 1 b lediglich eine Verzögerungsfunktion ausführt. Man hätte infolgedessen statt OR Q in Bild 2 auch DELAY Q deklarieren können; das Simulationsprotokoll wird durch diese Änderung nicht beeinflußt.

Wird DELAY mit einem größeren, aber festen Wert deklariert, z.B. als DELAY (3) D1, so erscheint am Ausgang von D1 der Eingang um 3 Simulationsschritte verzögert, wobei

```
$COMPILE,          RUN
BEGIN                                                          % SIM/EING/FANG
DEFINE  NA1OV(E1,E2,A);
   BEGIN                    NAND  G1; OR G2, Q;
   G1:=E1,E2;   Q:=2(G1);   G2:=Q,G1;   A:=G2;
  WRITE(<X43,4(B1,X2)>,E1,E2,Q,A);
   EXECUTE 2;
   END  NA1OV;
DEFINE FANG(A,B,Q,QN);
   BEGIN NAND G1; NA1OV  G2;
   G1:=A,G2;   G2:=B,G1;  Q:=G1;   QN:=G2;  % A,B INPUT; Q,QN OUTPUT
   EXECUTE 5;
  WRITE(<X23,4(X1,B1)>,A,B,Q,QN);
   END  FANG;
 FANG RS;
 FUNCTION  A=(1,1,0,0,3(1),0,1,1,0,0,1,0,1)
         ,B=(3(1),0,1,1,3(0),2(1,0,1));
   RS.A,RS.B:=A,B;
 WRITE(INITIAL,<X2,'RS: A B Q QN',X4,'FANG: A B Q QN'
                    X4,'NA1OV: E1 E2 Q  A'>);
 WRITE(<X5,4(X1,B1)>,RS.A,RS.B,RS.Q,RS.QN);
  EXECUTE 15;
END;
* END OF COMPILATION:      0  ERROR(S) FOUND
```

```
  0000   RS: A B Q QN    FANG: A B Q QN    NA1OV: E1 E2 Q  A
  0001                                             1  0  0  0
  0002                                             1  0  1  1
  0001                         1 1 1 1
  0001                                             1  1  1  1
  0002                                             1  1  0  1
  0002                         1 1 0 1
1 0001                                             1  0  0  0
  0002                                             1  0  1  1
  0003                         1 1 0 1
  0001                                             1  0  1  1
  0002                                             1  0  1  1
  0004                         1 1 0 1
  0005                         1 1 0 1
  0001       1 1 0 1
2 0002       1 1 0 1
  0001                         0 1 1 1
  0001                                             1  1  1  1
  0002                                             1  1  0  1
  0002                         0 1 1 1
  0001                                             1  1  0  0
3 0002                                             1  1  0  0
  0003                         0 1 1 0
  0004                         0 1 1 0
  0005                         0 1 1 0
  0003       0 1 1 0
  0001                                             0  1  0  0
  0002                                             0  1  1  1
  0001                         0 0 1 1
  0001                                             0  1  1  1
4 0002                                             0  1  1  1
  0002                         0 0 1 1
  0003                         0 0 1 1
  0004       0 0 1 1
  0001                                             1  1  1  1
  0002                                             1  1  0  1
  0001                         1 1 0 1
```

Bild 2: SSM-Programm eines NAND-Fang-Flipflop

selbstverständlich der Eingang genau nachgebildet wird, also insbesondere isolierte 0- oder 1-Werte ebenfalls verzögert am Ausgang erscheinen. Unter Umständen möchte man aber die Absorption von Kurzimpulsen bei der Simulation nachbilden, bei der z.B. eine bestimmte Signalverzögerung mit der Nebenbedingung erreicht werden soll, daß nur ein mindestens 2 Schritte nacheinander gleicher Eingang sich am Ausgang auswirken soll, während kürzere Eingangswerte verschluckt werden. Anschaulich läßt sich dieser Effekt durch die folgende logische Beziehung beschreiben, die offenbar Schaltwerkcharakter hat:

$$A^t = E^{t-1}E^{t-2} \vee (E^t \vee E^{t-1})A^{t-1}$$

Man kann sich mit Hilfe einer Wertetabelle leicht davon überzeugen, daß diese Gleichung die erläuterte Verzögerungsfunktion im Hinblick auf die Eingangs-(grob)-Schritte beschreibt, wobei der Eingang um 2 Schritte verzögert am Ausgang erscheint.

Natürlich gibt es mehrere Realisierungsmöglichkeiten dieser Funktion; eine ist in Bild 3 dargestellt /7/, während Bild 4 das zugehörige SSM-Programm zeigt. Wie man sieht, erfordert die 3-stufige Implementierung des definierten Typs DEL 2 die Ausführung von 3 Feinschritten, damit sich überhaupt eine Eingangsänderung auswirken kann. Entsprechend wird das vorangehende Eingangssignal durch eine feste Verzögerung DELAY (3) erzeugt. Die in Bild 4 simulierte Eingangssignalfolge macht deutlich, daß isoliert auftretende 0- und 1-Werte unterdrückt werden, erst ein doppelt auftretendes Eingangssignal kann den Ausgang beeinflussen.

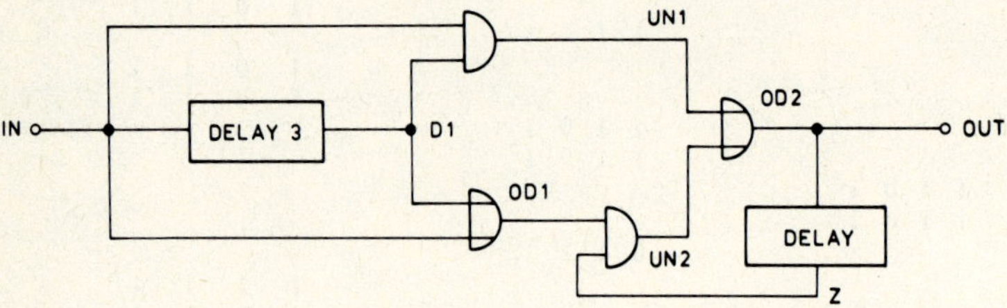

Bild 3 Verzögerungselement mit Absorption von Kurzimpulsen

Erwähnt werden soll, daß das oben beschriebene Element NA10V unsymmetrisch Kurzimpulse unterdrückt, nämlich nur isolierte 0-Ausgangswerte. Mithin sind durch entsprechende Kombination beliebige andere feste Verzögerungselemente mit oder ohne Absorptionseigenschaft möglich, so daß beliebige Bausteintypen definiert werden können.

Auch die Simulation von Totzeitmodellen /8/, durch die der Entwurf asynchroner Schaltungen erleichtert werden kann, ist ohne weiteres möglich und so einfach darstellbar, daß sich eine ausführliche Behandlung hier erübrigt. In SSM ist lediglich zu beachten, daß ideale Gatter noch über eine Einheitsverzögerung verfügen, so daß die Verzögerungszeiten der Totzeitelemente entsprechend zu korrigieren sind. In /7/ sind die in /8/ angeführten Beispiele ausführlich simuliert.

```
$COMPILE
BEGIN
%                 *** PROGRAMM 1.6 ***
                                                    % DATEI DEL5
% DELAY-GLIED MIT VERZOEGERUNG 2 UND ABSORPTION
% VON KURZIMPULSEN.

DEFINE DEL2 (IN,OUT);
BEGIN DELAY Z; DELAY(3) D1; AND UN1,UN2; OR OD1,OD2;
    D1:=IN; UN1,OD1:=2(D1,IN); UN2:=Z,OD1;
    OD2:=UN1.UN2; Z:=OD2;
    OUT:=OD2;
    EXECUTE 3;
END  DEL2;

DEL2 VZ;
FUNCTION X = (3(0),3(1),0,3(1),0,0,3(1),
                  3(0),1,3(0),1,1,3(0),3(1));
VZ:=X;
WRITE(INITIAL,<'  IN   OUT'>);
WRITE(<2(X3,B1)>,VZ.IN,VZ.OUT);
EXECUTE 30;
END;
* END OF COMPILATION:      0  ERROR(S) FOUND
  COMPILE TIME    4.35 SEC

$RUN

0000    IN  OUT
0001     0   0
0002     0   0
0003     0   0
0004     1   0
0005     1   1
0006     1   1
0007     0   1
0008     1   1
0009     1   1
0010     1   1
0011     0   1
0012     0   0
0013     1   0
0014     1   1
0015     1   1
0016     0   1
0017     0   0
0018     0   0
0019     1   0
0020     0   0
0021     0   0
0022     0   0
0023     1   0
0024     1   1
0025     0   1
0026     0   0
0027     0   0
0028     1   0
0029     1   1
0030     1   1

END OF SIMULATION, MAX NUMBER OF CYCLES EXECUTED
  RUN TIME    0.76 SEC
```

Bild 4: SSM-Programm einer Verzögerung mit Absorption

4. Verzögerungen mit toleranzbehafteten DELAY-Elementen

Im vorangehenden Abschnitt wurde gezeigt, daß SSM eine Beschreibung komplexerer Verzögerungseffekte mit Hilfe geeignet gewählter Gatter mit Einheitsverzögerung erlaubt. Der Simulationsmodus bleibt dabei binär, die mehrwertige Signaldarstellung kommt nicht zur Auswirkung. Erst durch eine Verwendung des DELAY-Grundelements mit toleranzbehafteter Verzögerung werden die mehrwertigen Spracheigenschaften ausgenutzt und der entsprechende Simulationsmodus impliziert.

Bild 5 zeigt das Verhalten derartiger DELAY-Elemente im Detail, wobei als Eingang eine Folge von 0-1-Signalen spezifiziert wurde /7/. Drei Elemente mit den Verzögerungen (1), (1-2) und (1-3), sind deklariert, allen wird der gleiche Eingang EIN zugewiesen. Wie man sieht, reproduziert die feste Verzögerung V1 lediglich das Eingangssignal, wobei zwischen Eingang und Ausgang in der gleichen Zeile ein Simulationsschritt zur Auswirkung kommt. Die toleranzbehaftete Verzögerung V1-2 verwandelt die Eingangsfolge 011 in den Ausgang 0E1, 100 dagegen in 1A0. Dabei bedeutet E, daß der Ausgangswert noch 0 oder schon 1 sein kann, entsprechend den Toleranzgrenzen. Deutlicher wird dieser Effekt bei der Verzögerung V1-3, wo aus den Eingangsfolgen 0111 bzw. 1000 der Ausgang 0EE1 bzw. 1AA0 entsteht. Auch hier bedeutet EE, daß nur ein Übergang möglich ist, so daß 0EE1 die Möglichkeiten 0001, 0011 und 0111 beschreibt, jedoch nicht 0101.

Natürlich ergibt sich sofort die Frage, was passiert, wenn der verzögerte Übergang durch eine erneute Signaländerung beeinflußt wird. Während isolierte 1- oder 0-Eingänge bei V1-2 zur Folge EA bzw. AE führen, zeigt die Spalte für V1-3, daß hierbei undefinierte Signalwerte entstehen. Ein Eingang 0100 überlagert hier die Ein- und Ausschaltwerte, so daß 0EUA entsteht. Doch für nachfolgende Schaltelemente ist im Grunde die Folge EA ebenfalls undefiniert, erlaubt sie doch die Interpretation 01, 10, 00 und 11, wobei aber auch bei 00 ein Übergang in beiden Richtungen erfolgt sein soll. Das ist nur durch die Vorstellung eines kurzen Fehlimpulses zwischen beiden Signalen möglich, der sich im verlängerten Toleranzbereich als U äußert. Da für die komplementäre Signalfolge diese Interpretation umgekehrt einen Einbruch im Ausgangswert 1 ermöglicht, ergibt sich mit Hilfe der 5-wertigen Signaldarstellung eine einfache Simulation von Hasard- und Wettlaufeffekten, wobei das Auftreten des Wertes U die Möglichkeit eines Hasardfehlers anzeigt.

5. Simulation statischer Hasards

Unter Hasards versteht man die Fehlermöglichkeit einer Schaltung durch unterschiedliche Signalverzögerungen bei einem Eingangssignalwechsel (Übergang). Ein statischer Hasard bezieht sich dabei auf Übergänge, die den gleichen Funktionswert erzeugen /9/. Demnach kann sich ein Hasardfehler als ungewollter Impuls oder Signaleinbruch äußern, wobei das Auftreten des Fehlers in der implementierten Schaltung von den realen Verzögerungen abhängt, die sich beim Entwurf kaum vorhersagen lassen. Da solche Fehler in komplexeren Schaltungen weitere Schaltvorgänge auslösen können, besteht

```
$COMPILE, RUN
BEGIN
%                   *** PROGRAMM 1.1 ***
                                                   % DATEI DEL1

% PROGRAMM ZUM AUSTESTEN DER DELAY-GLIEDER
% MIT FESTER VERZOEGERUNG 1 UND DEN VARIABLEN
% VERZOEGERUNGEN 1-2 UND 1-3.

DELAY DEL1;  DELAY(1-2) DEL12;  DELAY(1-3) DEL13;
FUNCTION EIN = (3(1),3(0),1,3(0),2(1),3(0),3(1),0,3(1),2(0),3(1));
DEL1 := EIN;  DEL12 := EIN;  DEL13 := EIN;
WRITE(INITIAL,<' EIN   V1 V1-2 V1-3'>);
WRITE(<X2,B1,X5,B1,2(X3,B1)>,EIN,DEL1,DEL12,DEL13);
EXECUTE 27;
END;
* END OF COMPILATION:      0  ERROR(S) FOUND
  COMPILE TIME   3.16 SEC

0000  EIN   V1 V1-2 V1-3
0001   1     1   E   E
0002   1     1   1   E
0003   1     1   1   1
0004   0     0   A   A
0005   0     0   0   A
0006   0     0   0   0
0007   1     1   E   E
0008   0     0   A   U
0009   0     0   0   A
0010   0     0   0   0
0011   1     1   E   E
0012   1     1   1   E
0013   0     0   A   A
0014   0     0   0   A
0015   0     0   0   0
0016   1     1   E   E
0017   1     1   1   E
0018   1     1   1   1
0019   0     0   A   A
0020   1     1   E   U
0021   1     1   1   E
0022   1     1   1   1
0023   0     0   A   A
0024   0     0   0   A
0025   1     1   E   E
0026   1     1   1   E
0027   1     1   1   1

END OF SIMULATION, MAX NUMBER OF CYCLES EXECUTED
  RUN TIME   0.30 SEC
```

Bild 5: Simulation fester und toleranzbehafteter Verzögerungen

die Aufgabe im Entwurf hasardfreier Schaltungen. Ihre Möglichkeiten sind ausgedehnt untersucht worden /9/, wobei theoretische Methoden zur Hasarderkennung angestrebt wurden. Hier soll gezeigt werden, daß eine Simulation in SSM ebenfalls eine Hasarderkennung erlaubt, wobei lediglich das Verhalten der Schaltung unter dem Einfluß von Verzögerungstoleranzen nachzubilden ist.

Das Prinzip wird durch die Betrachtung eines UND- bzw. ODER-Gatters mit 2 Eingängen deutlich. Hier verursacht der Eingangssignalübergang 01 nach 10 oder umgekehrt einen Hasard, da der Ausgang kurzzeitig 1 bzw. 0 werden kann, wenn beide Eingänge zu unterschiedlichen Zeitpunkten, also toleranzbehaftet, ihren Wert ändern.

Bild 6 zeigt die Entstehung statischer Hasardfehler, wobei die Verknüpfung in der 5-wertigen Logik ausgewertet wird /1, 3, 10/, nachdem DELAY-Elemente mit der Verzögerung (1-2) aus den binären Eingängen E- und A-Werte erzeugt haben. Wie man sieht, führt das Auftreten des Eingangswechsels 01 nach 10 bzw. umgekehrt zum Eingang EA bzw. AE am Gatter G, das daraufhin U an seinem Ausgang erzeugt. Tatsächlich sind dies die kritischen Übergänge, bei denen ein Hasardfehler entstehen kann, wenn die Signalwechsel nicht genau gleichzeitig, sondern toleranzbehaftet auftreten. U ist folglich auch hier als Möglichkeit für einen Hasardfehler zu interpretieren, also kurzer Fehlimpuls oder Signaleinbruch.

Will man sich auf solche Hasards beschränken, wären 3-wertige Simulationsergebnisse anzustreben, bei denen neben den festen logischen Werten nur U für jeden Hasard auftreten soll. Man muß also dafür sorgen, daß die Werte E und A wieder auf 1 und 0 reduziert werden, so daß die fortlaufende Ausgangssignalfolge toleranzfreie logische Werte enthält, aber die hasardbehafteten Übergänge anzeigt. Bild 7 zeigt, daß das sehr leicht durch einen zusätzlichen Feinschritt möglich ist, wobei mittels bedingter Zuweisung der um einen Feinschritt verzögerte Gatterausgang zum Bausteinausgang wird, falls dieser Wert U ist. Hier ist das REGISTER-Element als fiktive Zwischengröße erforderlich, die diese bedingte Signalzuweisung an den Ausgang weiterleitet.

Während dieser Weg einer Hasardanzeige über Feinschritte und Verzögerungselemente die Entstehung solcher Hasards anschaulich darstellt, ist mit Hilfe des REGISTER-Elements und einer geeigneten logischen Beziehung eine solche Simulation auch in einem Schritt abstrakt möglich, nämlich durch

```
DEFINE    HASARDUND (E1, E2, A);
  BEGIN   REGISTER   R, S1, S2;
   R:= (E1 * E2 + (E1*E2'*S1'*S2 + E1'*E2*S1*S2') * U);
   S1:= E1;        S2:= E2;       A:= R;
  END;
```

Offenbar wird hier der vorangehende Eingang als S1 und S2 gespeichert und neben der normalen UND-Funktion der Ausgang auf U gesetzt, falls gerade die hasardbehafteten Übergänge auftreten. Dies erfordert natürlich weniger Simulationszeit als Bild 7, hat

```
$COMPILE,RUN
BEGIN                                                    % SIM/HASUND
 DEFINE  HAND(E1,E2,A);
  BEGIN   AND  G;  DELAY(1-2)  D1,D2;                    % DELAY(1-2)
   D1:=E1;  D2:=E2;  G:=D1,D2;   A:=G;
   WRITE(<X20,3(X2,B1)>,D1,D2,G);
    EXECUTE 2;
  END;

  HAND  H;                                               % HASARD-UND
  FUNCTION  A=(2(0),2(1,0),0,1,2(1,0),4(1)),
            B=(0,1,3(0),2(1,0),3(1),0,0,1,1);

  H:=A,B;

  WRITE(<2(X2,B1),X4,B1>,A,B,H);
  WRITE(INITIAL,<'  A  B    H           D1 D2  G'>);
  EXECUTE  16;
END;
* END OF COMPILATION:      0  ERROR(S) FOUND
  COMPILE TIME    4.41 SEC

0000   A  B    H         D1 D2  G
0001                      0  0  0
0001   0  0    0
0001                      0  E  0
0002                      0  1  0
0002   0  1    0
0001                      E  A  0
0002                      1  0  U
0003   1  0    U
0001                      A  0  0
0002                      0  0  0
0004   0  0    0
0001                      E  0  0
0002                      1  0  0
0005   1  0    0
0001                      A  E  0
0002                      0  1  U
0006   0  1    U
0001                      0  A  0
0002                      0  0  0
0007   0  0    0
0001                      E  E  0
0002                      1  1  E
0008   1  1    E
0001                      1  A  1
0002                      1  0  A
0009   1  0    A
0001                      A  E  0
0002                      0  1  U
0010   0  1    U
0001                      E  1  0
0002                      1  1  E
0011   1  1    E
0001                      A  1  1
0002                      0  1  A
0012   0  1    A
0001                      E  A  0
0002                      1  0  U
0013   1  0    U
0001                      1  0  0
0002                      1  0  0
```

Bild 6: Simulation eines UND-Gatters mit Hasarderkennung

```
$COMPILE,RUN
BEGIN                                                     % SIM/HASUND1
 DEFINE  HASUND(E1,E2,A);
  BEGIN   AND  G;  DELAY(1-2)  D1,D2;
   DELAY  D; REGISTER  R;
   D1:=E1;  D2:=E2;  G:=D1,D2;  D:=G;  R:=G;
   ON  (D=U)  DO  R:=D;     A:=R;
   EXECUTE 4;
  END;

  HASUND  H;                                              % HASARD-UND
  FUNCTION  A=(2(0),2(1,0),0,1,2(1,0),4(1)),
            B=(0,1,3(0),2(1,0),3(1),0,0,1,1);

  H:=A,B;

  WRITE(<2(X2,B1),X4,B1>,A,B,H);
  WRITE(INITIAL,<'  A  B    H '>);
  WRITE((H=U),<X30,'HASARD'>);
  EXECUTE  16;
END;
* END OF COMPILATION:      0  ERROR(S) FOUND
  COMPILE TIME   5.07 SEC

0000   A  B    H
0001   0  0    0
0002   0  1    0
0003   1  0    U
0003                               HASARD
0004   0  0    0
0005   1  0    0
0006   0  1    U
0006                               HASARD
0007   0  0    0
0008   1  1    1
0009   1  0    0
0010   0  1    U
0010                               HASARD
0011   1  1    1
0012   0  1    0
0013   1  0    U
0013                               HASARD
0014   1  0    0
0015   1  1    1
0016   1  1    1

END OF SIMULATION, MAX NUMBER OF CYCLES EXECUTED
  RUN TIME   0.63 SEC
```

Bild 7: Hasarderkennung bei sonst zweiwertigen Signalen.

dafür den Nachteil, daß das entsprechende Element HASARDODER einen komplexen anderen logischen Ausdruck erfordert, während in Bild 7 lediglich das Gatter G in OR abgewandelt zu werden braucht. Das gleiche gilt für hasardbehaftete NAND- bzw. NOR-Gatter.

Sofern das Auftreten von U am Eingang entsprechend berücksichtigt wird, lassen sich offensichtlich auf entsprechende Weise auch dynamische Hasards simulieren. Diese beziehen sich auf Übergänge mit Signalwechsel, wobei kurzzeitig ein Zusatzfehlimpuls auftreten kann, wenn die Signalverzögerungen ungünstig zusammenwirken.

6. Zusammenfassung und Vergleich

In den vorangehenden Beispielen wurde gezeigt, daß die aus asynchronen Schaltungen bekannten Laufzeiteffekte und ihr Einfluß auf das Schaltungsverhalten durch speziell entwickelte Bausteintypen einigermaßen bequem vom Benutzer definiert und in beliebige SSM-Simulationsprogramme einbezogen werden können. Natürlich sollten derartige Bausteine in Form einer Bibliothek zur Verfügung stehen, so daß zukünftige Benutzer von SSM darauf zurückgreifen können und sich nicht erneut die Feinfunktion zu überlegen brauchen.

Da auch andere Sprachen im Hinblick auf solche Simulationsmöglichkeiten entworfen sind, sollen kurz einige Punkte berührt werden, die sich bisher als wesentlich erwiesen haben und die bei einem Vergleich der Simulationsmöglichkeiten sorgfältig zu betrachten sind.

1. Lassen sich neue Bausteintypen definieren und leicht in zukünftige Simulationsprogramme eingliedern?
2. Lassen sich die in dieser Arbeit betrachteten Laufzeiteffekte nachbilden, so daß "reale" Verknüpfungselemente dargestellt werden können?
3. Erlaubt die Beschreibung über die zweiwertige logische Funktion hinaus eine Signalauswertung im Hinblick auf Hasards, Zustandswettläufe, Signalverzerrungen usw.? (Offenbar ist dies nur bei mehr als zweiwertiger Signaldarstellung möglich /10/.)
4. Läßt sich die Ausgabe ergebnisbezogen steuern, so daß eine Ausgabe nur erfolgt, wenn bestimmte Signalwerte erreicht sind?
5. Ist interaktiver Simulationsbetrieb möglich?
6. Lassen sich simulierte Ausgabesignale als Eingabe für weitere Simulationsprogramme verwenden?
7. Läßt sich die Simulation ergebnisbezogen abbrechen?
8. Ist die Implementierung anlagenunabhängig?
9. Welche Bausteine stehen zur Simulation zur Verfügung?

Ohne hier auf weitere derartige Kriterien einzugehen, läßt sich bisher feststellen, daß die Punkte 1 bis 5 von SSM unmittelbar erfüllt werden. Dagegen treffen 6 bis 8 nur unter erheblichen Einschränkungen auf SSM zu. Punkt 9. ist an den Aufbau einer auf die vorliegenden Simulationsprobleme bezogenen Bausteinbibliothek geknüpft und wird Gegenstand weiterer Untersuchungen sein. Zwar setzt das voraus, daß der Simulator die Erwartungen erfüllt, die vor allem im Hinblick auf die notwendige Rechenzeit zur Simulation komplexerer Probleme aufgestellt werden müssen, doch scheint das nach den bisherigen Erfahrungen erreichbar zu sein.

Herrn cand. inform. Hans-Jürgen Hoffmann möchte ich an dieser Stelle für zahlreiche Diskussionen und Anregungen danken; die Implementierung von Compiler und Simulator ist nur durch seinen unermüdlichen Einsatz möglich geworden.

7. Literaturverzeichnis

/1/ Jentsch, W.: Simulation binärer Schaltwerke, Nachrichtentechn. Fachberichte 49, 1974, S. 44 - 58.

/2/ ACM German Chapter Lectures W-1974 (Workshop on Computer Hardware Description Languages).

/3/ Hoffmann, H.J.: Simulation digitaler Schaltwerke unter Berücksichtigung von Laufzeiteffekten - Vergleiche und Konzeptentwurf, Diplomarbeit 1974, Fakultät für Informatik, Universität Karlsruhe.

/4/ Hoffmann, H.J.: SSM-Simulationssprache für Schaltwerke unter Verwendung von mehrwertiger Logik - Benutzeranleitung, Interner Bericht 18/1974, Fakultät für Informatik, Universität Karlsruhe.

/5/ Görke, W., Hoffmann, H.J.: Simulation of switching circuits by SSM - a new hardware simulation language, Workshop on Computer Hardware Description Languages, New York, 1975.

/6/ Chaney, T.J., Molnar, C.E.: Anomalous behavior of synchronizer and arbiter circuits, IEEE Trans. C-22, 1973, p. 421 - 422.

/7/ Banzhaf, G.: Simulation von Zeitverhalten mit SSM, Studienarbeit 1975, Institut für Informatik IV, Universität Karlsruhe.

/8/ Beister, J.: Ein Totzeitmodell für asynchrone Schaltwerke, Nachrichtentechn. Zeitung 28, 1975, S. 13 - 17.

/9/ Beister, J.: Beiträge zur Theorie der Hasards in Schaltnetzen, Dissertation 1973, Universität Karlsruhe.

/10/ Muth, P.: Ein Verfahren zur Erkennung statischer und dynamischer Hasards in Schaltnetzen, Elektron. Rechenanl. 16, 1974, S. 188 - 192.

ANHANG: Syntax der Sprache SSM

Konvention:

```
<X - LIST> ::= <X> , <X - LIST>  ! <X>
<X - ROW>  ::= <X>   <X - ROW>   ! <EMPTY>

1.
<PROGRAM>             ::=<PROG.BLOCK> <COMMENT> ;
<PROG.BLOCK>          ::=BEGIN
                         <DEFINE-ROW>
                         <DECLARE-ROW>
                         <TRANSFER-ROW>
                         <SIM.STATEMENT-ROW>
                         END
<COMMENT>             ::=<POSSIBLY EMPTY STRING WITHOUT ; OR END>

2.
<DEFINE>              ::=DEFINE <IDENTIFIER> ( <DECL.SEGMENT-LIST> ) ;
                         <DEFINE BODY>
<DECL.SEGMENT>        ::=<IDENTIFIER-LIST> <INDEXPART> ! <IDENTIFIER-LIST>
<INDEXPART>           ::=[ <INDEX-LIST> ]
<INDEX>               ::=<INTEGER GREATER O>
<DEFINE BODY>         ::=<PROG.BLOCK> <COMMENT> ; !
                         EXTERNAL  ' <FILENAME> ' ;

3.
<DECLARE>             ::=<TYP> <DECL.SEGMENT-LIST> ! <DELAY DECLARE>
                         <FUNCTION DECLARE> ! <BLOCK DECLARE>
<TYPE>                ::=<TRIVIAL TYPE> ! <IDENTIFIER>
<TRIVIAL TYPE>        ::= AND ! OR ! NAND ! NOR ! REGISTER

3.1
<DELAY DECLARE>       ::=DELAY <DELAY SPECIFIER> <DECL.SEGMENT-LIST>;
<DELAY SPECIFIER>     ::= ( <MINDELAY> - <MAXDELAY> ) !
                         ( <MIN/MAXDELAY> ) ! <EMPTY>
<MINDELAY>,<MAXDELAY>,<MIN/MAXDELAY>::=<INTEGER GREATER O>

3.2
<FUNCTION-DECLARE>    ::=FUNCTION <FUNCTION BODY-LIST>;
<FUNCTION BODY>       ::=<IDENTIFIER> = ( <CONST.SEGMENT-LIST> )
<CONST.SEGMENT>       ::=<CONSTANT> ! <FACTOR> ( <CONST.SEGMENT-LIST> ) !
                         <CONST.STRING>
<CONSTANT>            ::= O ! 1 ! U ! E ! A
<CONST.STRING>        ::=<CODE> ' <STRING> '
<CODE>                ::= B ! O ! H ! I ! <EMPTY>
<STRING>              ::=<ANY SEQUENCE OF CHARACTERS EXCEPT '>

3.3
<BLOCK DECLARE>       ::=BLOCK <IDENTIFIER> ( <DECL.SEGMENT-LIST> ) ;
                         <DEFINE BODY>
4.
<TRANSFER>            ::=<CONDITION PART> <TRANSFER BODY>
<CONDITION PART>      ::= ON <SINGLE POINT> DO ! ON <CONSTANT> DO !
                         ON ( <BOOLEAN EXPRESSION> ) DO ! <EMPTY>
<TRANSFER BODY>       ::= <POINTINTERVALL-LIST> := <RIGHT SIDE> ; !
                         BEGIN <TRANSFER> <TRANSFER-ROW> END <COMMENT> ;
<RIGHT SIDE>          ::=<RIGHT PRIM-LIST> ! V ( <VECTOR EXPRESSION> )
<RIGHT PRIM>          ::=<POINTINTERVALL> ! <CONSTANT> ! <CONST.STRING>
                         <FACTOR> ( <RIGHT PRIM-LIST> ) !
                         ( <BOOLEAN EXPRESSION> )
```

```
4.1
<SINGLE POINT>         ::=<ELEMENT> . <SINGLE POINT> ! <ELEMENT>
<ELEMENT>              ::=<IDENTIFIER> <INDEXPART> ! <IDENTIFIER>
<POINTINTERVALL>       ::=<ELEMENTINTERVALL> . <POINTINTERVALL> !
                          <ELEMENTINTERVALL>
<ELEMENTINTERVALL>     ::=<IDENTIFIER> <BOUND PART> ! <IDENTIFIER>
<BOUND PART>           ::= [ <BOUND-LIST> ]
<BOUND>                ::=<FROM INDEX> - <UNTIL INDEX>  !  <INDEX>
<FROM INDEX>,<UNTIL INDEX>::=<INTEGER GREATER 0>

4.2
<BOOLEAN EXPRESSION>::=<EQUIVALENCE> ! <BOOLEAN ASSIGNMENT>
<BOOLEAN ASSIGNMENT>::=<SINGLE POINT> := <BOOLEAN EXPRESSION>
<EQUIVALENCE>          ::=<SUM> = <EQUIVALENCE> ! <SUM>
<SUM>                  ::=<PRODUCT> + <SUM> ! <PRODUCT>
<PRODUCT>              ::=<FACTOR> * <PRODUCT> ! <FACTOR>
<FACTOR>               ::=<BOOLEAN PRIMARY> ! <BOOLEAN PRIMARY> '
<BOOLEAN PRIMARY>      ::=<SINGLE POINT> ! <CONSTANT> !
                          ( <BOOLEAN EXPRESSION> ) !
                          * <VECTOR PRIMARY> ! + <VECTOR PRIMARY>
4.3
<VECTOR EXPRESSION> ::= <CONCATENATION> ! <VECTOR ASSIGNMENT>
<VECTOR ASSIGNMENT> ::=<POINTINTERVALL-LIST> := <VECTOR EXPRESSION>
<CONCATENATION>        ::=<V.EQUIVALENCE-LIST>
<V.EQUIVALENCE>        ::=<VSUM> = <V.EQUIVALENCE> ! <VSUM>
<VSUM>                 ::=<VPRODUKT> + <VSUM> ! <VPRODUKT>
<VPRODUKT>             ::=<VFACTOR> * <VPRODUKT> ! <VFACTOR>
<VFACTOR>              ::=<VECTOR PRIMARY> ! <VECTOR PRIMARY> '
<VECTOR PRIMARY>       ::= ( <VECTOR EXPRESSION> ) !
                          * <VECTOR PRIMARY> ! + <VECTOR PRIMARY> !
                          <POINTINTERVALL> ! <CONSTANT> ! <CONST.STRING>

5.
<SIM.STATEMENT>        ::=<INITIAL STATEMENT> ! <WRITE STATEMENT> !
                          <EXEC. STATEMENT> ! <SIM. MODUS>
5.1
<INITIAL STATEMENT> ::=INITIAL <POINTINTERVALL-LIST>:=<RIGHT SIDE>; !
                          INITIAL <CONSTANT> ;
5.2
<WRITE STATEMENT>      ::=WRITE ( <WRITE CONDITION> <FORMAT> <DATA> ) ;
<WRITE CONDITION>      ::= INITIAL , ! <SINGLE POINT> , ! <CONSTANT> , !
                          ( <BOOLEAN EXPRESSION> ) , ! <EMPTY>
5.3
<FORMAT>               ::= / ! <<FORMAT SEGMENT-LIST>>
<FORMAT SEGMENT>       ::=<FACTOR> <FORMAT CHARACTER> <FIELDWIDTH> !
                          <FORMAT CHARACTER> <FIELDWIDTH> !
                          <FACTOR> ( <FORMAT SEGMENT-LIST> ) !
                          /<FORMAT SEGMENT> ! / ! ' <STRING> '
<FORMAT CHARACTER>     ::= B ! O ! H ! I ! X
<FIELDWIDTH>           ::=<INTEGER GREATER 0>

5.4
<DATA>                 ::= , <DATA SEGMENT-LIST> ! <EMPTY>
<DATA SEGMENT>         ::=<POINTINTERVALL> ! ( <VECTOR EXPRESSION> ) !
                          <CONSTANT> ! <CONST.STRING>
5.5
<EXEC. STATEMENT>      ::= EXECUTE <MINEX> , <MAXEX> ; !
                          EXECUTE <MAXEX> ;
<MINEX>,<MAXEX>        ::=<INTEGER GREATER 0>

5.6
<SIM.MODUS>            ::=BINARY ; ! SINGLE ; ! HAZARD ; ! RACE ;
```

POLYNOMIAL SEPARATION OF TERNARY FUNCTIONS

Claudio Moraga [§]

Abstract: It is shown that quasi-threshold realization of a set of ternary functions is possible, when separating surfaces in the hypercube of a ternary function are allowed to be of second degree. Only one constraint is required to obtain simple physical realizations of these "Polynomial Separable" functions, which considerably outnumber the Linear Separable functions. It is shown that monotonic-transformability is a necessary condition for a ternary function to be polynomial separable. There are 2967 2-place and over 1.5 million 3-place ternary polynomial separable functions. Identifiers and realization parameters have been listed for the 2-place case and for a subset of the 3-place case.

0. Historical background:

One of the reasons for the development of binary digital systems was the existence of reliable two-state devices. Today, with the advances in semiconductor integration technology and synthesis of active circuits, multi-stable circuits ready for integration have been designed and laboratory-tested. Moreover, this same IC, MSI, LSI technology, which allows a great density of hardware in a minimum chip, also presents a new problem to the digital engineer: interconnections between LSIs become a bulky net of wires or a complex set of printed circuits, which somehow impair the beauty of a design at the subsystem's level. If density of information per terminal could be improved, the interconnection problem could be lightend. Multiple-valued Logic appears to be one of the possible alternatives to provide a good solution.

Since increasing information density is desired, the study of multi-valued threshold logic seems to be a natural choice. A good number of contributions on this subject may be found in the literature (1).

Refering to ternary threshold logic, it has been shown that there are 471 2-place and 85,629 3-place ternary threshold functions (2,3,4). Tables have been published for realization of 2- and 3-place functions (4,5,6). Since the relative number of threshold functions is low, ex-

§ Alexander von Humboldt Research Fellow at the Universität Dortmund, Abteilung Informatik; on leave from: Dept. of Computer Science, University Santa María, Valparaîso, Chile.

tensions on ternary threshold logic have been looked for, to provide quasi-threshold realization of non-threshold ternary functions. Among these extensions, Bilineal Separability (7,8), Multithreshold Periodic Ternary Logic (9,10), Spectral Logic (11), the present and former papers on Polynomial Separation (12,13) may be mentioned.

1. Notation and Definitions:

Def. 1: Let V=(0,1,2) be the set of possible values for a ternary variable. Let the space vector V^n be the set of vectors $\underline{v}_i=(v_{i1},v_{i2},\ldots,v_{in})$, $(i=1,2,\ldots,3^n)$, which represent all the possible state assignments to the variables $X_1,X_2,\ldots,X_n$. A ternary function $F(\underline{X}) = F(X_1,X_2,\ldots,X_n)$ is a mapping of the space vector V^n into V and sets a partition defining three blocks: F_0, F_1 and F_2 which are mapped onto 0, 1 and 2 respectively.

Def. 2: A ternary function has High Order Separability (HS), iff there exists in V^n a set of parallel hypersurfaces -not necessarily planes- such that they separate F_0 from F_1 and F_1 from F_2 in that order. i.e.: A ternary function has HS iff there exists a set $(\underline{g},\underline{w},B)$ such that:

$$\begin{array}{lllll} L > S & & \Leftrightarrow & F(\underline{X}) = 0 \\ H > S \geq L & & \Leftrightarrow & F(\underline{X}) = 1 \\ S \geq L & & \Leftrightarrow & F(\underline{X}) = 2 \end{array} \quad (1)$$

where: $B=(H,L)$, $H \geq L \in \mathbb{R}$, thresholds,

$\underline{w}=(w_1,w_2,\ldots,w_n)$, weight vector; $\underline{w} \in \mathbb{Z}^n$

and $S=\sum_i g_i(\underline{X})\cdot w_i$

Def. 3: When $F(\underline{X})$ satisfies the requirements of Def. 2 and

$$\forall i \quad w_i g_i(\underline{X}) = w_i g_i(X_i) \in V \quad (2)$$

then $F(\underline{X})$ is said to be Polynomial Separable (PS). When $F(\underline{X})$ is PS, it will be written $F(\underline{X}):(\underline{g},\underline{w},B)$.

Def. 4: Vectorial representation of a function.

$$F(\underline{X}) := rst\ldots z \Leftrightarrow r=F(00\ldots0),\ s=F(00\ldots01),\ t=F(00\ldots02),\ldots,\ z=F(22\ldots22) \quad (3)$$

Def. 5: $F(\underline{X}) < G(\underline{X}) \Leftrightarrow$ the vector representation of $F(\underline{X})$ is smaller than the vector representation of $G(\underline{X})$, both representations considered as integers.

Def. 6: $\forall X \in V$, let $\overline{X} = 2-X$, be the complement of X.

Def. 7: $\beta F(\underline{X}) = \overline{F}(\overline{\underline{X}})$ is the dual function of $F(\underline{X})$, where $\overline{\underline{X}}=(\overline{X}_1,\overline{X}_2,\ldots,\overline{X}_n)$. If $\beta F(\underline{X}) = F(\underline{X})$, the function is called self-dual.

Def. 8: $F(\underline{X})$ is said to be monotonic increasing with respect to X_i, if for each combination of the values of the variables $X_1, X_2, \ldots, X_{i-1}, X_{i+1}, \ldots, X_n$: $F_{i2} \geq F_{i1} \geq F_{i0}$, where $\forall k \in V$, $F_{ik} = F(X_1, X_2, \ldots, X_{i-1}, k, X_{i+1}, \ldots, X_n)$.

Def. 9: If $F(\underline{X})$ is monotonic increasing with respect to every variable X_i $(i=1,2,\ldots,n)$, $F(\underline{X})$ is said to be a monotonic increasing function.

Def. 10: If $F(\underline{X})$ becomes a monotonic increasing function under permutation of the values of its variables, $F(\underline{X})$ is said to be a monotonic-transformable function.

Def. 11: Let $(\underline{w}\cdot\underline{X})'$ be máx.$(\underline{w}\cdot\underline{X})$ such that $F(\underline{X})=0$ and let $(\underline{w}\cdot\underline{X})''$ be min.$(\underline{w}\cdot\underline{X})$ such that $F(\underline{X})=1$. Then,

$$L = 0.5((\underline{w}\cdot\underline{X})' + (\underline{w}\cdot\underline{X})'') \tag{4}$$

is said to be a balanced (low) threshold. Similarly for a balanced (high) threshold.

Def. 12: $Y \in! (a,b,c)$ means that Y takes values exactly from the full set and not only from a proper subset.

2. Theorems:

(Note: proof of a Theorem will be left to the reader, whenever it follows from simple application of the above given definitions.)

T1: Every Threshold function is also a PS function.

T2:
$$F(\ldots X_i \ldots X_k \ldots):(\ldots g_i(X_i)\ldots g_k(X_k)\ldots w_i \ldots w_k \ldots, H, L) \iff$$
$$F(\ldots X_k \ldots X_i \ldots):(\ldots g_k(X_k)\ldots g_i(X_i)\ldots w_k \ldots w_i \ldots, H, L) \tag{5}$$

T3: Let $F(\underline{X})$ be PS, such that exist $g_i(X_i) \in (0,1)$, then,

$$F(\underline{X}):(g_1(X_1)\ldots g_i(X_i)\ldots g_n(X_n), w_1,\ldots w_i \ldots w_n, H, L) \iff$$
$$F(\underline{X}):(g_1(X_1)\ldots g_i'(X_i)\ldots g_n(X_n), w_1\ldots w_i'\ldots w_n, H', L') \tag{6}$$

where:

$g_i'(X_i)$	w_i'	H'	L'
$1 + g_i(X_i)$	w_i	$H + w_i$	$L + w_i$
$2g_i(X_i)$	$0.5w_i$	H	L

(7)

T4:
$$F(X_1 \ldots X_n):(g_1(X_1)\ldots g_n(X_n), \underline{w}, B) \iff$$
$$F(X_1^{p_1} \ldots X_n^{p_n}):(g_1'(X_1) \ldots g_n'(X_n), \underline{w}, B) \tag{8}$$

where: $X_i^{p_i} := X_i \xrightarrow{\theta} V$, i.e.: $p_i \in \mathbb{P}_3$

$$g_i'(X_i) = g(X_i^{p_i}) \in V \tag{9}$$

Proof: Since $\mathbb{P}_3$ is a Group, $p_i \Rightarrow p_i^{-1}$; (here: p_i').

let:

$$(X_1^{p'_1}) = X_\alpha \quad \ldots\ldots \quad (X_n^{p'_n}) = X_\nu$$

then, $F(X_1 \ldots X_n) = F(X_\alpha^{p_1} \ldots X_\nu^{p_n}) : (g_1(X_\alpha^{p_1}) \ \ldots \ g_n(X_\nu^{p_n}), \ \underline{w}, \ B)$

now let $X_\alpha = X_1 \ \ldots\ldots \ X_\nu = X_n$

then, $F(X_1^{p_1} \ldots X_n^{p_n}) : (g_1(X_1^{p_1}) \ \ldots \ g_n(X_n^{p_n}), \ \underline{w}, \ B)$ ∇∇∇

T5: $F(\underline{X}) : (\underline{g}, \ \underline{w}, \ B) \iff \overline{F}(\underline{X}) : (\overline{\underline{g}}, \ \underline{w}, \ B')$ (10)

where: $\overline{\underline{g}} = \{\overline{g}_i(X_i)\}$ and $B' = (2\sum_i w_i - L \ , \ 2\sum_i w_i - H)$

Proof: Let $S = \sum_i w_i g_i(X_i)$, $S' = \sum_i w_i \overline{g}_i(X_i)$ and $k = 2\sum_i w_i$

Following Defs. 2 and 6:

$$\begin{array}{lclcl} H \leq S & \iff & F(\underline{X}) = 2 & \iff & \overline{F}(\underline{X}) = 0 \\ L \leq S < H & \iff & F(\underline{X}) = 1 & \iff & \overline{F}(\underline{X}) = 1 \\ S < L & \iff & F(\underline{X}) = 0 & \iff & \overline{F}(\underline{X}) = 2 \end{array}$$

i.e.:

$$\begin{array}{lcl} -S > -L & \iff & \overline{F}(\underline{X}) = 2 \\ -L \geq -S > -H & \iff & \overline{F}(\underline{X}) = 1 \\ -H \geq -S & \iff & \overline{F}(\underline{X}) = 0 \end{array}$$

then,

$$\begin{array}{lcl} S' > (k-L) & \iff & \overline{F}(\underline{X}) = 2 \\ (k-L) \geq S' > (k-H) & \iff & \overline{F}(\underline{X}) = 1 \\ (k-H) \geq S' & \iff & \overline{F}(\underline{X}) = 0 \end{array}$$

$$\rightarrow \quad \overline{F}(\underline{X}) : (\overline{\underline{g}}, \ \underline{w}, \ (2\sum_i w_i - L, \ 2\sum_i w_i - H))$$ ∇∇∇

<u>Lemma 6</u>: $F(\underline{X}) : (\underline{g}, \ \underline{w}, \ B) \iff \beta F(\underline{X}) : (\{\overline{g}_i(\overline{X}_i)\}, \ \underline{w}, \ B')$ (11)

<u>T7</u>: $\forall F(\underline{X}) \ \varepsilon! (0,1)$, $F(\underline{X}) : (\underline{g}, \underline{w}, B) \iff F'(\underline{X}) : (\underline{g}, \underline{w}.B')$ (12)

where:

$$\begin{array}{llll} F'(\underline{X}) : & 2F(\underline{X}) & 1+F(\underline{X}) \\ B' \quad : & (L,L) & (L,-0.5) \end{array} \qquad (13)$$

<u>T8</u>: $\forall F(\underline{X}) \ \varepsilon! (0,1)$, $F(\underline{X}) : (\underline{g}, \underline{w}, B) \iff F'(\underline{X}) : (\underline{g}', \underline{w}, B')$ (14)

where $F'(\underline{X})$ and $\underline{g}'$are duals of $F(\underline{X})$ and $\underline{g}$ respectively, within their own interval of definition, and

$$B' = (H', L') = (H, \ H-L-0.5) \qquad (15)$$

Proof: To simplify the notation, let $g_i := g_i(X_i)$ and let g''_i denote the complement of g_i within its interval of definition.

Following T2, there is no loss of generality letting:

$g_1, g_2, \ldots, g_k \;\; \varepsilon! \; (0,1,2)$ and $g_{k+1}, \ldots, g_n \;\; \varepsilon! \; (0,1)$

i) From Def. 2, $H > \max \sum_i w_i g_i$. Let $H = 0.5 + \max \sum_i w_i g_i$, then,

$H = 0.5 + 2 \sum_{i=1}^{k} w_i + \sum_{i=k+1}^{n} w_i$, and, from the definitions of $F'(\underline{X})$ and $\underline{g}', H' = H$.

ii) Since $F(\underline{X}) \; \varepsilon! (0,1)$, $F'(\underline{X}) = \text{ß}F(\underline{X})-1$.

Here,

$$S > L \iff F(\underline{X}) = 1 \iff \overline{F}(\underline{X})-1 = 0$$
$$L > S \iff F(\underline{X}) = 0 \iff \overline{F}(\underline{X})-1 = 1$$

$$-S > -L \iff \overline{F}(\underline{X})-1 = 1$$
$$-L > -S \iff \overline{F}(\underline{X})-1 = 0$$

but:

$$2 \sum_{i=1}^{k} w_i + \sum_{i=k+1}^{n} w_i - S = 2 \sum_{i=1}^{k} w_i + \sum_{i=k+1}^{n} w_i - \sum_i w_i g_i =$$

$$= \sum_{i=1}^{k} (2-g_i) w_i + \sum_{i=k+1}^{n} (1-g_i) w_i = \sum_i g_i'' w_i$$

and $\quad 2 \sum_{i=1}^{k} w_i + \sum_{i=k+1}^{n} w_i - L = H-L-0.5$

Following T4, case: complementation of all variables,

$\rightarrow \; F'(\underline{X}) : (\underline{g}', \; \underline{w}, \; H, \; (H-L-0.5))$ ∇∇∇

Up to this point, Theorems 2 through 8 allow a first partition on the set of PS functions, reducing the set of input functions $\{g_i(X_i)\}$ to:

$$G = (012, \; 001, \; 011) \tag{16}$$

(Constant inputs have not been considered, as in this case $F(\underline{X})$ would be independent of the corresponding input variable.)

<u>T9</u>: Let $G' = (001, 011)$, $g_i \; \varepsilon \; G$, $g_i' \; \varepsilon \; G'$, $w_1 \leq w_2 \leq \ldots \leq w_n$

$$F(\underline{X}) : (g_1', g_2 \ldots g_n, w_1, w_2 \ldots w_n, \; B) \quad \Rightarrow$$
$$F(\underline{X}) : (012, g_2 \ldots g_n, w_1, 2w_2, \ldots 2w_n, B') \tag{17}$$

Analysis: For 2-place functions, the set of possibilities may be reduced to one of both indicated in Fig. 1. By direct inspection it is possible to see that any separation of cells on the left side maps, may be accomplished on the right side maps.

For functions of more than two variables, Fig. 1 may be considered to depict the possible situation at every set of planes $X_1 X_i$ (i=2,3...n). All planes $X_i X_j$ ($i \neq j$; i,j=2,3...n) would not be affected, since scaling of weights, with a suitable scaling of thresholds, preserves mapping.

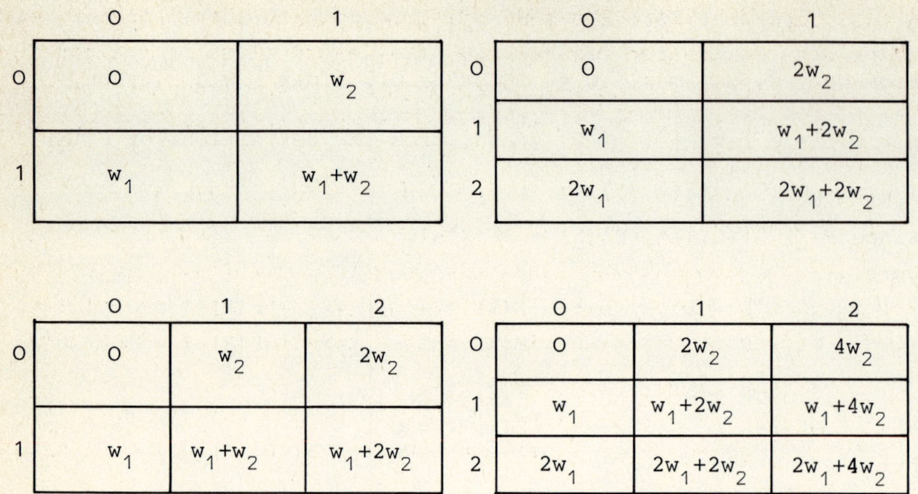

Fig. 1: Map representation of the weighed summation, according to possible input combinations. (T9)

It may be shown, that when H and L are balanced thresholds, one possible option for B' is (2H ± 0.5 ; 2L ± 0.5) according to whether g_1' is 001 or 011.

∇∇∇

T10: Monotonic transformability is a necessary but not sufficient condition for a ternary function to be PS.

Proof: Since without loss of generality the input set may be reduced to G = (012,001,011), then $\forall i\ g_i(0) \leq g_i(1) \leq g_i(2)$.

But, $g_1(X_1)w_1+\ldots+g_i(X_i)w_i+\ldots+g_n(X_n)w_n \overset{?}{\gtrless} (H,L) \iff F(\underline{X})=0/1/2$

then, $F(X_1\ldots X_{i-1},0,X_{i+1}\ldots X_n) \leq F(X_1\ldots X_{i-1},1,X_{i+1}\ldots X_n) \leq$

$\leq F(X_1\ldots X_{i-1},2,X_{i+1}\ldots X_n)$

i.e.: $F(\underline{X})$ is monotonic increasing. The inverse is not necessarily true. (For instance, a MIN function is monotonic increasing, but it is not a PS function.) Then, monotonicity - and following T4 - monotonic-transformability is a necessary but not sufficient condition for a given $F(\underline{X})$ to be PS.

3. Listing and counting PS ternary functions:

Using theorems 2 through 9, it is possible to define a partition on the set of PS functions, which is defined both in the range of identification and realization parameters. If at every class in the partition the number of functions may be counted or calculated, the cardinality of the set of PS functions of a given number of inputs may be obtained.

A table for 2-place functions and a partial table for 3-place functions have been produced via computer work. These tables list one function of each class, corresponding, but not necessarily unique input set; minimum integer weighs, balanced thresholds, symmetry parameters and number of functions in the class. The representative function of a class satisfies the following conditions:

+ It is the monotonic increasing function which has the smallest vector representation of the class and together with a monotonic increasing weight vector.

+ Its input functions belong to G.

+ $\underline{0} \leq F(\underline{X}) < \underline{1}$

+ $F(\underline{X}) \in (0,1)$ or $F(\underline{X}) \in! V$

By means of these tables, it has been proven that there are 2,967 2-place ternary functions and over 1.5 million 3-place PS functions. (These figures show an interesting improvement over the 471 and 85,629 ternary threshold functions of 2 and 3 variables respectively.)

4. Testing and Realization of PS functions:

The following procedure is suggested to test PS realizability of a ternary function with aid of a table:

i) Test whether $F(\underline{X})$ is monotonic transformable. If it is, the corresponding set of permutations over the individual variables should be remembered. If it is not transformable, $F(\underline{X})$ is not PS.

ii) If $F(\underline{X})$ is binary, map it onto (0,1), following T7.

iii) Let the transformed function be $H(\underline{X})$ and let $H'(\underline{X})$ denote the dual of $H(\underline{X})$ within its interval of existence.

Select min. $(H(\underline{X}), H'(\underline{X}))$ consistent with an increasing monotonicity dominance in X_n over $X_{n-1}, \ldots,$ in X_2 over X_1. This may be accomplished through apropriate permutation on the set of variables. This guarantees that $\underline{w}$ may also be monotonic increasing.

iv) Enter the Table. If the function is not listed, $F(\underline{X})$ is not PS. If it is listed, read input functions, weight vector and thresholds.

v) Execute the corresponding inverse permutations from those required at step iii). (T2,L6).

vi) Every input function should be preceded by the corresponding permutation detected in step i).

vii) Reduce all possible two-steps unary functions obtained after step vi).

viii) Make the threshold corrections required if a mapping was made at step ii).

<u>Example</u>: Test PS realizability of $F(\underline{X})$ shown in Fig 2a.

(a) $F(\underline{X})$

X_1 \ X_2	0	1	2
0	0	0	0
1	2	2	1
2	2	2	0

(b) $F(X_1^o, \overline{X}_2)$

X_1^o \ $\overline{X}_2$	2	1	0
0	0	0	0
2	0	2	2
1	1	2	2

Fig. 2a: Karnaugh map of the given function.
2b: Karnaugh map of the transformed function.

i) It is possible to see that $F(X_1^o, \overline{X}_2)$ is monotonic increasing, with $X^o := 2X \bmod 3$,(See Fig. 2b). Let $F(X_1^o, \overline{X}_2) = H(\underline{X})$.

iii) $H(\underline{X}) < H'(\underline{X})$, with the required monotonicity dominance.

iv) From the table: G =012, G =011, $\underline{w}=(2,3)$, B=(4.5 , 3.5)

v) and vi) lead to the logic diagram shown in Fig. 3a.

vii) Leads to the reduced diagram of Fig. 3b.

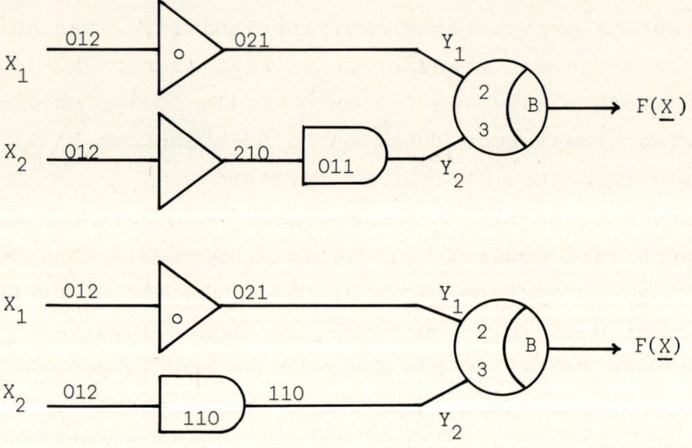

Fig. 3: Logic realization of $F(\underline{X})$. (a) After steps v) and vi).
(b) After step vii).

Full truth table shown in Fig. 4, provides a final check.

X_1 X_2 Y_1 Y_2	$2Y_1 + 3Y_2$	$F(\underline{X})$
0 0 0 1	3	0
0 1 0 1	3	0
0 2 0 0	0	0
1 0 2 1	7	2
1 1 2 1	7	2
1 2 2 0	4	1
2 0 1 1	5	2
2 1 1 1	5	2
2 2 1 0	2	0

Fig. 4: Truth Table of PS realization of $F(\underline{X})$

5. Conclusions:

A new type of quasi-threshold logic has been disclosed, which allows compact realization of a large number of non linear separable functions. Best realization parameters have been listed. 2,967 2-place and over 1.5 million 3-place ternary PS functions have been computed. Faster and more efficient algorithms are being looked for, in order to enable exploring the whole set of ternary 3-place functions. This would allow the computation of the number of PS ternary 3-place functions, as well as listing a full identification-realization table.

From the theoretical point of view, it may be regretable that a necessary and sufficient condition for a ternary function to be PS has not yet been found, other than belonging to one of the classes listed in a table. From the operational point of view, though, check-table methods have proven to be quite convenient. As a matter of fact, it is known that full monotonicity is a sufficient condition for a 3-place function to be threshold (4), yet it is much simpler to test threshold realizability by means of a table (6), which beyond saying whether a given $F(\underline{X})$ is or not a threshold function, gives all the required data for the best realization.

It should finally be recalled, that physical implementation of the gates used in a PS logic design are already available, as reliable (integrable) electronic circuits. (See references in (14).)

Table of PS Ternary 2-place Functions.

g_1 = 012

n	Function			w_1	w_2	g_2	H	L	Total
1	000	000	000	1	1	012	4.5	4.5	3
				1	1	011	3.5	3.5	
				1	1	001	3.5	3.5	
2	000	000	001	1	1	012	4.5	3.5	54
				1	1	001	3.5	2.5	
3	000	000	011	1	1	011	3.5	2.5	108
4	000	001	002	1	2	012	5.5	4.5	72
				1	2	001	3.5	2.5	
5	000	001	011	1	1	012	4.5	2.5	216
6	000	001	012	1	1	012	3.5	2.5	72
7	000	001	111	1	1	001	3.5	1.5	216
8	000	001	112	1	1	001	2.5	1.5	72
9	000	002	012	2	3	012	7.5	6.5	144
10	000	002	112	2	3	001	4.5	3.5	72
11	000	011	o11	1	2	011	4.5	2.5	54
12	000	011	022	1	2	011	3.5	2.5	72
13	000	011	122	1	1	011	2.5	1.5	72
14	000	022	122	2	3	011	4.5	3.5	72
15	001	001	001	1	3	012	8.5	5.5	36
				1	3	001	5.5	2.5	
16	001	001	002	1	3	012	7.5	5.5	36
				1	3	001	4.5	2.5	
17	001	001	112	1	2	001	3.5	1.5	18
18	001	002	002	1	3	012	6.5	5.5	36
				1	3	001	3.5	2.5	
19	001	002	012	1	2	012	4.5	3.5	144
20	001	002	022	2	3	012	6.5	5.5	144
21	001	002	112	1	2	001	2.5	1.5	72
22	001	011	012	1	2	012	5.5	2.5	144
23	001	011	112	1	1	012	3.5	1.5	72
24	001	012	022	2	3	012	6.5	4.5	144
25	001	012	112	2	3	012	7.5	3.5	144
26	001	012	122	1	1	012	2.5	1.5	36
27	001	111	112	1	1	001	2.5	0.5	72
28	001	112	112	1	2	001	2.5	0.5	18
29	002	002	012	1	3	012	5.5	4.5	72
30	002	002	112	1	3	001	2.5	1.5	36
31	002	012	012	1	3	012	5.5	3.5	72
32	002	012	022	1	2	012	3.5	2.5	72
33	002	112	112	1	3	001	2.5	0.5	36
34	011	011	012	1	3	012	7.5	2.5	72
35	011	012	012	1	3	012	6.5	2.5	72
36	011	012	112	1	2	012	4.5	1.5	72
37	011	111	112	1	1	012	3.5	0.5	36
38	012	012	012	1	3	012	5.5	2.5	12

Number of PS functions: 2967

6. References:

(1) Moraga C.: "Mehrwertige Schaltalgebra", Class-notes, Special Vorlesung, Universität Dortmund WS 74/75,(Refs. chapter 6).

(2) Merrill R.D.: "Ternary Threshold Logic" in: Research on Automatic Computer Electronics, Lockheed Missiles and Space Co. Palo Alto, Calif., Rpt. Nr RTD-TDR-4173, Vol II, pp B-187-230, (Oct.1963)

(3) Moraga C.: "Ternary Threshold Functions: 2-place case", Report EOSD 7105, Universidad Santa María, Chile, (1971)

(4) Aibara T. and Akagi M.: "Enumeration of Ternary Threshold Functions of Three Variables", IEEE Tr. C-21, 402-407, (1971)

(5) Nazarala J. "A study on Ternary Threshold Logic", E.E. Thesis, Universidad de Chile, (1973)

(6) Nazarala J. and Moraga C.: "Minimal Realization of Ternary Threshold Functions", Proc. 1974 Internat. Symposium on Multi-valued Logic, W.Va., USA, 347-358, (May 1974)

(7) Nazarala J. and Moraga C.: "Bilineal Separation of Ternary Functions", 1st Chilean Symposium on E.E., Santiago, Chile, (Aug. 1974)

(8) Nazarala J. and Moraga C.: "Bilineal Separability of Ternary Functions", 1975 Internat. Symposium on Multi-valued Logic, Indiana, USA, (May 1975)

(9) Gutiérrez J.: "Realization of Ternary Functions by means of Multithreshold Periodic Threshold gates", E.E. Thesis, Universidad Santa María, Chile ,(1972)

(10) Gutiérrez J. and Moraga C.: "Multithreshold Periodic Ternary Threshold Logic", Proc. 1974 Internat. Symposium on Multi-Valued Logic, W.Va., USA, 413-422, (may 1974)

(11) Moraga C.: Research in progress.

(12) Moraga C.: "Ternary Threshold Logic with Polynomial Separability" Report EOSD 7104, Universidad Santa María, Chile, (1971)

(13) Moraga C.: "Non-Linear Ternary Threshold Logic",Proc. 1972 Internat. Symposium on the Theory and Applications of Multiple-valued Logic Design, NY, USA, 65-74, (May 1972)

(14) Vranesic Z. and Smith K.C.: "Engineering Aspects of Multiple-Valued Logic Systems", IEEE CS Computer, 7, (9), 34-41, (Sept. 1971)

UNIVERSELLE KLASSEN O(log(MxN))-TESTBARER ITERATIVER UND SEQUENTIELLER SCHALTUNGEN

Wolfgang Coy
Technische Hochschule Darmstadt

0. EINLEITUNG

Die vollständige Überprüfung der logischen Übertragungseigenschaften eines Schaltkreises mit n Eingängen erfordert 2^n Testvorgänge. Dieses Verfahren ist also nur bei sehr kleinen Schaltkreisen praktisch durchführbar. Bei Schaltungen mit Verzögerungsgliedern und Rückkoppelungen ergeben sich weitere Schwierigkeiten. In der Praxis ist deshalb ein Fehler-Modell entwickelt worden, das eine große Anzahl tatsächlich auftretender logischer Übertragungsfehler erfasst. Diesem Leitungsfehler-Modell (engl. stuck-at fault model) liegen drei Annahmen zugrunde:

- jeder Übertragungsfehler ist (während des Testvorgangs) permanent;
- jeder Übertragungsfehler verändert das logische Verhalten des Schaltkreises so, als nehme eine Leitung a den konstanten Wert 0 oder 1 an;
- der Fehler wirkt sich so aus, als nehme genau eine Leitung einen konstanten Wert an.

Im folgenden sollen funktional vollständige (kurz: universelle) Klassen kombinatorischer, iterativer und sequentieller Schaltungen angegeben werden, die mit Hilfe geringfügiger Modifikationen eine Überprüfung aller möglichen Leitungsfehler in kurzer Zeit erlauben.

1. KOMBINATORISCHE SCHALTUNGEN

Die Ergebnisse dieses Abschnitts dienen der Vorbereitung der beiden folgenden Abschnitte; Beweise der einzelnen Ergebnisse findet man, sofern dies nicht besonders vermerkt wird, in |4|.

Wir betrachten Schaltkreise S, die aus n-stelligen Konjunktionsgattern $\underline{K}^n$, n-stelligen Disjunktionsgattern $\underline{D}^n$, einstelligen Invertern $\underline{N}$ und den Leitungselementen $\underline{I}$ (Leitungsstück), $\underline{Y}^k$ (k-fache Verzweigung) und der Vertauschung $\underline{X}$ mit Hilfe der sequentiellen Verknüpfung $S_1 o S_2$ (die Eingänge von S_1 werden mit den Ausgängen von S_2 belegt) und der parallelen Verknüpfung $S_1 x S_2$ aufgebaut werden. Wie in |1| sei mit Q(S) die Zahl der Eingänge von S und mit Z(S) die Zahl der Ausgänge bezeichnet. $S_1 o S_2$ ist nur dann definiert, wenn $Q(S_1) = Z(S_2)$ gilt.

Wir wiederholen einige aus der Literatur (vgl. |2|, |3|,|4|) bekannte Definitionen und Ergebnisse.

Definition 1

i) Ein logischer Übertragungsfehler, der dadurch beschrieben werden kann, daß eine einzelne Leitung a des Schaltkreises S fehlerhaft einen konstanten Wert 0 oder 1 annimmt, heißt Leitungsfehler; geschrieben wird a-0 bzw. a-1.

ii) Der vom Leitungsfehler F befallene Schaltkreis S realisiere statt der korrekten Übertragungsfunktion $f(S):B^n \to B^m$ die fehlerhafte Funktion $f_F(S):B^n \to B^m$. Jedes Wort $t \in B^n$ mit $f(S)(t) \neq f_F(S)(t)$ heißt Test $t(F)$ des Fehlers F in S.

iii) Eine Menge $T \subseteq B^n$ heißt vollständige Testmenge aller Leitungsfehler des n-stelligen Schaltkreises S gdw jeder Leitungsfehler F in S von mindestens einem $t \in T$ entdeckt wird; T heißt minimal wenn es kein T' mit $|T'| < |T|$ gibt. Die Kardinalität minimaler, vollständiger Testmengen T(S) heißt Test-Komplexität $\phi(S)$.

iv) Eine Testmenge T(K) heißt universell bezüglich der Klasse K von Schaltkreisen gdw jeder Schaltkreis $S \in K$ von T(K) vollständig (aber nicht notwendig minimal) getestet wird.[1)]

Aus der Literatur ist das folgende Lemma bekannt:

Lemma 1

Jedes n-stellige Konjunktionsgatter $\underline{K}^n$ besitzt die eindeutig bestimmte, minimale und vollständige Testmenge $T(\underline{K}^n)$, die aus den n+1 Belegungen der Eingänge $x_1,\ldots,x_n$:

$$t_i = \langle x_1=1,\ldots,x_{i-1}=1,x_i=0,x_{i+1}=1,\ldots,x_n=1\rangle$$

für $1 \leq i \leq n$ und

$$t_{n+1} = \langle x_1=1,\ldots,x_n=1\rangle$$

besteht.

Für zweistellige EXOR-Gatter sei eine beliebige interne Leitungsstruktur zugelassen (wobei auch die internen Leitungen fehlerhaft sein mögen); mehrstellige EXOR-Gatter seien als Kaskaden zweistelliger Gatter aufgebaut. Für die zweitelligen Gatter $\underline{E}^2$ genügt die Testmenge $\langle 0,0\rangle,\langle 0,1\rangle,\langle 1,0\rangle,\langle 1,1\rangle$. Für $\underline{E}^n = \underline{E}^2 o(\underline{E}^{n-1} x \underline{I})$ gilt:

---

1) Der Begriff universell wird hier nicht im Sinne von AKERS |10| verwendet.

Lemma 2

Eine n-stellige Kaskade $\underline{E}^n$ wird durch die vier Tests

$t_1 = \langle x_1=0,\ldots,x_n=0\rangle$, $t_2 = \langle x_1=1,\ldots,x_n=1\rangle$,
$t_3 = \langle x_1=0,x_2=1,\ldots,x_n=1\rangle$ und $t_4 = \langle x_1=1,x_2=0,\ldots,x_n=0\rangle$

vollständig bezüglich aller Leitungsfehler getestet.

Die konstante Testkomplexität der n-stelligen EXOR-Gatter legt es nahe, beim Entwurf testarmer Schaltkreise diese Eigenschaft auszunutzen, zumal die Realisierung von EXOR-Gattern heute technologisch keine Schwierigkeiten mehr bereitet.

Definition 2

i) Die Darstellung einer Funktion $f:B^n \to B$ in der Form

$$f(x_1,\ldots,x_n) = c_o \oplus (c_1 x_1) \oplus \ldots \oplus (c_{n+1} x_1 x_2) \oplus \ldots$$
$$\ldots \oplus (c_{n(n+1)/2}\, x_{n-1} x_n) \oplus \ldots \oplus (c_{2^n-1}\, x_1 \ldots x_n)$$

mit geeignet gewählten $c_i \in \{0,1\}$ heißt polynomiale Normalform von f.

ii) Wird die Funktion $f:B^n \to B^m$ in die Funktionen $f_1:B^n \to B, \ldots f_m:B^n \to B$ zerlegt und wird jede Funktion f_i in der entsprechenden polynomialen Normalform $P(f_i)$ dargestellt, so soll die Menge $\{P(f_1),\ldots,P(f_m)\}$ polynomiale Normalform P(f) heißen.

Bei der technischen Realisierung polynomialer Normalformen als Schaltkreise können die Terme mit der Konstanten $c_i=0$ (wegen $a \wedge 0=0$) wegfallen; die Terme mit $c_i=1$ müssen wegen $a \wedge 1=a$ die Konstante c_i nicht explizit realisieren. Die Konstante c_o soll aber zu Testzwecken explizit realisiert werden; die Begründung für diese Vereinbarung wird im nächsten Satz ersichtlich werden.

Definition 3

Werden in der polynomialen Normalform P(f) einer Funktion $f:B^n \to B^m$ die Konjunktionen mit der Konstanten $c_i=0$ $(1 \leq i \leq 2^n-1)$ weggelassen und in den anderen Konjunktionen die Konstanten $c_i=1$ weggelassen, so heißt der entstehende Ausdruck reduzierte polynomiale Normalform R(f).

Es ist leicht zu sehen, daß jeder reduzierten polynomialen Normalform P ein Schaltkreis S zugeordnet werden kann.

Definition 4

i) Ein Schaltkreis $C(f) = \underline{E}^{n+m} \circ (\underline{I}_1 x \ldots x \underline{I}_k x \underline{K}_1 x \ldots x \underline{K}_m)$ heißt Kern des Polynomial-Schaltkreises der Funktion $f:B^n \to B$ gdw der Konstanten c_o die Leitung $\underline{I}_1$ und jedem einstelligen Konjunktionsterm genau eine

eine Leitung $\underline{I}_j$ $(2\leq j\leq k)$ und jeder Konjunktion genau ein Konjunktionsgatter $\underline{K}_h$ $(1\leq h\leq m)$ zugeordnet wird.

ii) $C(f) = C(f_1)x\ldots xC(f_m)$ heißt Kern des polynomialen Schaltkreises der Funktion $f:B^n\rightarrow B^m$ mit der reduzierten polynomialen Normalform $R(f) = \{R(f_1),\ldots,R(f_m)\}$.

iii) Eine Verdrahtung V ist eine beliebige Parallel- und Serienschaltung von Leitungsstücken $\underline{I}$ und Vertauschungen $\underline{X}$.

iv) C(f) sei Kern des Polynomial-Schaltkreises der Funktion f. Mit $Y = h_1x\ldots xh_{n+1}$ sei eine Parallelschaltung von Leitungen $\underline{I}$ und k-fachen Verzweigungen $\underline{Y}^k$ gemeint $(h_i\in\{\underline{I}\}\cup\{\underline{Y}^k|k\geq 2\})$. Ist V eine geeignete Verdrahtung mit $Q(V)=Z(Y)$ und $Z(V)=Q(C(f))$, so daß $S(f) = C(f) \circ V \circ Y$ die Funktion f realisiert, dann heißt S(f) Polynomial-Schaltkreis zur Darstellung der Funktion f.

In |4| wird gezeigt, daß jeder Polynomial-Schaltkreis S mit $f(S):B^n\rightarrow B^m$ durch eine n+4-elementige Testmenge T(S) bezüglich aller Leitungsfehler, die nicht die Eingangsleitungen von S befallen, vollständig testbar ist. Wir verallgemeinern dieses Resultat mit Hilfe der folgenden Definition:

Definition 5

Ein Polynomial-Schaltkreis S, der an mindestens einem Ausgang die Funktion $c_o\oplus x_1\oplus\ldots\oplus x_n$ oder $c_o\oplus(x_1\wedge\ldots\wedge x_n)$ erzeugt, heißt modifizierter Polynomial-Schaltkreis.

Mit dieser Definition gilt:

Satz 1

Die Klasse der modifizierten Polynomial-Schaltkreise S(f) mit maximal n Eingängen ist mit der universellen, n+4-elementigen Testmenge T(S), die aus den Tests

$t_i = \langle x_o=c_o, x_1=1,\ldots,x_{i-1}=1, x_i=0, x_{i+1}=1,\ldots,x_n=1\rangle$ für $1\leq i\leq n$,
$t_{n+1} = \langle x_o=c_o, x_1=1,\ldots,x_n=1\rangle$,
$t_{n+2} = \langle x_o=\underline{c_o}, x_1=0,\ldots,x_n=0\rangle$,
$t_{n+3} = \langle x_o=\overline{c_o}, x_1=1,\ldots,x_n=1\rangle$ und
$t_{n+4} = \langle x_o=\overline{c_o}, x_1=0,\ldots,x_n=0\rangle$

besteht, bezüglich aller Leitungsfehler vollständig testbar.

2. ITERATIVE SYSTEME

Iterative Systeme kombinatorischer Zellen sind partielle Darstellungen endlicher Automaten, wobei die Arbeitsweise aber nicht sequentiell, sondern parallel ist. Das zunehmende Interesse an iterativen Systemen mag ursächlich mit den technologischen Möglichkeiten der Groß-Integration von Schaltkreisen zusammenhängen. Hier sollen nur eindimensionale Systeme betrachtet werden; die Ergebnisse sind bei geeigneter Erweiterung der Definitionen ohne Schwierigkeiten auf mehrdimensionale Systeme übertragbar.

Unter einem <u>eindimensionalen iterativen System</u> $\underline{S}$ verstehen wir eine Kaskade aus r gleichen, kombinatorischen Zellen $S_1,\ldots,S_r$ mit $r \in \mathbb{N}$. Jede Zelle S_i besitzt m (externe) Eingangsleitungen $x_1^i,\ldots,x_m^i$ und n interne Eingangsleitungen $z_1^i,\ldots,z_n^i$, die für $2 \leq i \leq r$ Ausgangsleitungen der Zelle S_{i-1} sind. Für S_1 sind die Leitungen $z_1^1,\ldots,z_n^1$ extern belegbar; die Leitungen $z_1^{r+1},\ldots,z_n^{r+1}$ sind extern beobachtbar. Bei Systemen mit externen Ausgängen besitzt jede Zelle S_i die Ausgangsleitungen $y_1^i,\ldots,y_k^i$, die extern beobachtbar sind. Ein eindimensionales iteratives System $\underline{S}$ besteht also aus r Zellen S, die alle die gleiche Funktion $f:B^{n+m} \rightarrow B^n$ bzw. $f:B^{n+m} \rightarrow B^{n+k}$ darstellen. Die Zellen sind iterativ verknüpft. Mit $\underline{S}^i$ sei ein System aus i Zellen beschrieben; dann gilt:

$$\begin{cases} \underline{S}^1 = S \\ \underline{S}^i = S \circ (\underline{S}^{i-1} \times \underline{I}_1 \times \ldots \times \underline{I}_m). \end{cases}$$

Abbildung 1 zeigt zwei eindimensionale, iterative Systeme (mit bzw. ohne extern beobachtbare Ausgangsleitungen).

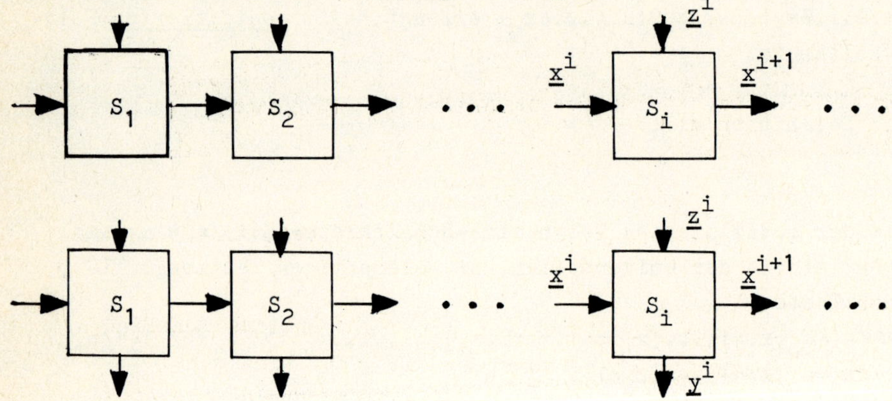

Abbildung 1. Eindimensionale, iterative Systeme.

Wir vereinbaren die folgende Redeweise: die Belegung $x_1^i,\ldots,x_m^i$ der Eingänge von S_i heißt Eingabewort $\underline{x}^i$, die Belegung der Eingänge $z_1^i,\ldots z_n^i$ heißt Zustand $\underline{z}^i$, die Ausgabe $z_1^{r+1},\ldots,z_n^{r+1}$ der Zelle S_r heißt Ausgabe-Zustand $\hat{\underline{z}}^r$ von S_r. Trotz der Bezeichnung Zustand arbeitet ein iteratives System (idealisiert) ohne Zeitverzögerung; es handelt sich um einen speziellen kombinatorischen Schaltkreis. Wir definieren nun eine Unter-Klasse der eindimensionalen, iterativen Systeme:

Definition 6

S heißt modifiziertes, eindimensionales, iteratives System gdw die folgenden Einschränkungen gelten:

i) die r Zellen $S_1,\ldots,S_r$ sind Polynomial-Schaltkreise;

ii) die Konstanten c_o werden für alle Zellen S_i mittels einer einzigen, extern belegbaren Leitung geschaltet;

iii) die von den Zellen S_i realisierte Funktion $f:B^{n+m} \to B^n$ wird in in der folgenden Weise eingeschränkt (für das Wort $w = \langle ß_1,\ldots,ß_m \rangle$ wird W_b geschrieben, wenn b die Dezimal-Darstellung der Binärzahl $ß_1\ldots ß_m$ ist):

$$f(Z_o,X_o) = Z_{2^n-1}, \quad f(Z_{2^n-1},X_{2^m-1}) = Z_o,$$

$$f(Z_{2^n-1},X_k) = Z_{2^n-1} \text{ wenn } X_k \text{ genau m-1 Einsen enthält,}$$

$$f(Z_k,X_{2^m-1}) = Z_k \text{ für alle } Z_k \neq Z_{2^n-1}$$

und die Zustände Z_o und Z_{2^n-1} sind sonst nicht erreichbar.

Die Restriktionen der Zellenfunktion sind in der folgenden Abbildung eines Zustands-Graphes dargestellt; es werden also nur zwei Zustände und ein Eingabewort für Testzwecke reserviert (wobei eine feste Kodierung dieser Zustände und des Eingabewortes verlangt wird).

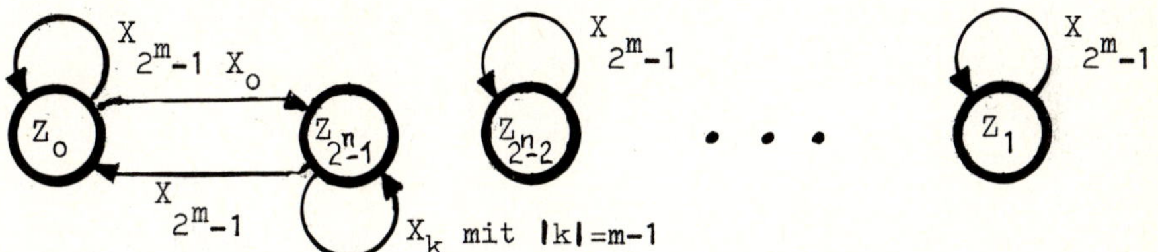

Abbildung 2. Der eingeschränkte Teil eines Zustandsgraphen.

Offensichtlich ist jede Schaltfunktion $g:B^{n+m} \to B^n$ in eine Funktion $f:B^{n+m+2} \to B^{n+1}$ homomorph einbettbar, so daß jedes eindimensionale iterative System auch als modifiziertes eindimensionales iteratives System realisierbar ist, wobei bei geeigneter Um-Kodierung maximal zwei Zustände und ein Eingabewort ergänzt werden müssen. Mit dieser Definition gilt nun die folgende Erweiterung von Satz 1:

Satz 2

Es gibt eine universelle Testmenge T(S) aller modifizierten eindimensionalen iterativen Systeme S, die aus r Zellen S_i mit der Zellen-Funktion $f:B^{n+m} \to B^{n+k}$ $(n,m \geq 1,\ k \geq 0)$ bestehen und T(S) hat die Test-Komplexität

$$\Phi(S) \leq n+m+4.$$

<u>Beweis-Skizze</u>

Satz 2 ist in [9] ausführlich bewiesen. Wir skizzieren die Konstruktion die im wesentlichen eine Rechtfertigung der Definition 6 ist.
Wird an alle Zellen S_i das Eingabewort $X_{2m-1}=\langle 1,\ldots,1\rangle$ angelegt, so kann an jeder Zelle die Testmenge $(\underline{z};\underline{x}) = (1,\ldots,1,0,1,\ldots,1;1,\ldots,1)$ im fehlerfreien Fall angelegt werden; wird die Zelle S_1 mit dem Anfangszustand $Z_{2n-1} =\langle 1,\ldots,1\rangle$ belegt, so lassen sich mit den entsprechenden Zellen-Eingabeworten X_k die Tests $(\underline{z};\underline{x}) = (1,\ldots,1;1,\ldots,1,0,1,\ldots,1)$ durchführen. Diese Testmengen entsprechen den Tests $t_1,\ldots,t_n$ aus Satz 1 und es kann gezeigt werden, daß ein Einzelfehler einer Zelle stets am Ausgang $\underline{\hat{z}}^r$ der letzten Zelle beobachtbar ist.
Die Tests $t_{n+1} = (c_o,0,\ldots,0)$ und $t_{n+2} = (c_o,1,\ldots,1)$ lassen sich abwechselnd an der Zelle S_i und S_{i+1} erzeugen, indem die Zelle mit dem Zustand Z_{2n-1} mit dem Eingabewort X_{2m-1} und die Zelle mit dem Zustand Z_o mit dem Eingabewort X_o belegt wird. Entsprechend lässt sich die Testmenge $t_{n+3} = (\overline{c_o},0,\ldots,0)$ und $t_{n+4} = (\overline{c_o},1,\ldots,1)$ für die Zellen S_i und S_{i+1} abwechselnd erzeugen. Auch in diesen Fällen ist ein einzelner Zellenfehler stets am Ausgang $\underline{\hat{z}}^r$ beobachtbar.
Damit ist Satz 2 auf Satz 1 zurückgeführt.

Bemerkenswert an diesem Ergebnis ist die Unabhängigkeit der Test-Komplexität von der Anzahl der Zellen; dies ist im allgemeinen Fall nichtmodifizierter Systeme nicht zu erwarten ([6]).

4. SEQUENTIELLE SCHALTUNGEN

Bei der Fehler-Diagnose von Schaltwerken wird in der Literatur meist das Leitungsfehler-Modell zugunsten einer Untersuchung mit diagnostischen Experimenten, wie sie schon in den Arbeiten von MOORE, v.NEUMANN und anderen in der Mitte der fünfziger Jahre in Angriff genommen wurden, aufgegeben. Dies führt dann zu den bekannten Schwierigkeiten, daß der zugrunde liegende Automat nur unter starken Einschränkungen "einfach" testbar ist, wobei trotz allem Testfolgen mit einer exponentiellen Länge (relativ zur Zahl der Rückkoppelungen und/oder der Eingangsleitungen) zu erwarten sind. Wird dagegen, wie in [8] das Leitungsfehler-Modell benutzt, so wird zum Test ein "Auftrennen" der Rückkoppelungen verlangt, was bei m Rückkoppelungen technisch gleichbedeutend mit der Einfügung von m zusätzlichen Ausgangsleitungen ist. Beide Verfahren sind in der Praxis nur für sehr kleine Schaltwerke akzeptabel. Wir wollen, ausgehend von Satz 1 und 2, zeigen, daß bei geigneter Wahl der Realisierung sequentielle Schaltungen mit sehr niedriger Test-Komplexität konstruiert werden können, sofern das Leitungsfehler-Modell mit der Einzelfehler-

Annahme vorrausgesetzt wird.

Definition 7

Eine (binär kodierte) sequentielle Schaltfunktion $\Sigma=(\underline{X},\underline{Y},\underline{Z},\delta,\lambda)$ wird beschrieben durch

eine Menge $\underline{X}$ der benutzten Eingabeworte $(x_1,\ldots,x_m)\in B^m$,
eine Menge $\underline{Y}$ der benutzten Eingabeworte $(y_1,\ldots,y_k)\in B^k$,
eine Menge $\underline{Z}$ der internen Zustände $(z_1,\ldots,z_n)\in B^n$

und durch die beiden Funktionen

δ: $\underline{X} \times \underline{Z} \rightarrow \underline{Z}$ (der Folge-Zustands-Funktion) und
λ: $\underline{X} \times \underline{Z} \rightarrow \underline{Y}$ (der Ausgabe-Funktion).

Mit S_δ und S_λ seien Schaltkreise bezeichnet, deren Übertragungsfunktionen $f(S_\delta)$ und $f(S_\lambda)$ die Funktionen δ und λ überdecken.

Definition 8

$S = (B^m,B^k,B^n,S_\delta,S_\lambda)$ heißt modifiziertes Polynomial-Schaltwerk zur Darstellung der sequentiellen Schaltfunktion $\Sigma=(\underline{X},\underline{Y},\underline{Z},\delta,\lambda)$ gdw

i) die Schaltkreise S_δ und S_λ Polynomial-Schaltkreise sind;

ii) die externe Eingabe-Variable x_m (über eine geeignete Verzweigung von Leitungen und Invertern) zur Belegung aller Konstanten c_o in S_δ und S_λ dient;

iii) die Folge-Zustandsfunktion δ den folgenden Einschränkungen unterliegt ($LS(Z_k)$ bezeichne den zyklischen Links-Shift der Binärzahl k):

$$\delta(Z_o,X_o) = Z_o \quad \text{und} \quad \delta(Z_o,X_1) = Z_{2^n-1}$$

$$\delta(Z_k,X_{2^m-1}) = \begin{cases} Z_o & \text{wenn } |k| < m-1 \\ Z_{2^n-1} & \text{wenn } k = 2^{n-1} \\ LS(Z_k) & \text{wenn } |k| = n-1 \text{ und } k \neq 2^{n-1} \end{cases}$$

$$\delta(Z_{2^n-1},X_k) = \begin{cases} Z_{2^{n-1}} & \text{wenn } k=2^{m-1} \\ Z_{2^n-1} & \text{wenn } |k| = m-1 \text{ und } k \neq 2^{m-1} \end{cases}$$

und Z_o und Z_{2^n-1} sonst keine Folgezustände sind.

iv) die Ausgabefunktion λ den folgenden Einschränkungen unterliegt:

$\lambda(Z_o,X_o) = \alpha$, $\lambda(Z_{2^n-1},X_k) = \beta$ für $|k|=m-1$,

$\lambda(Z_k,X_{2^m-1}) = Y_i$ für $|k|=n-1$ mit beliebigem, aber festen $Y_i\in\underline{Y}$

und $\lambda(Z_k,X_{2^m-1}) \neq Y_i$ für $|k|\neq n-1$;

dabei seien α und β Ausgabeworte aus B^k, die ausschließlich in diesen Transitionen vereinbart sind.

In der folgenden Abbildung ist der Zustandsgraph eines modifizierten

Polynomial-Schaltwerks partiell dargestellt:

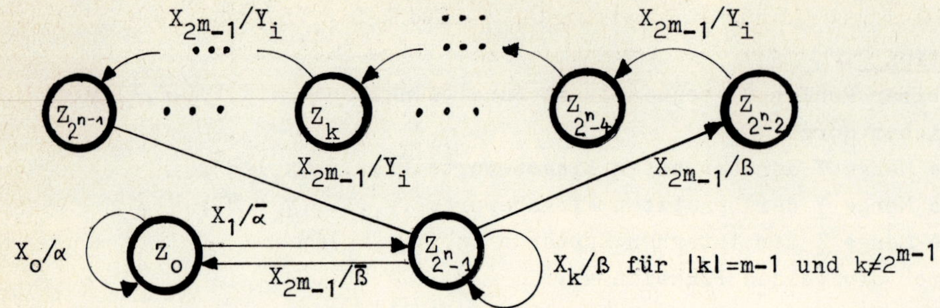

Abbildung 3. Die Restriktionen im Zustandsgraph von S.

Der Begriff des modifizierten Polynomial-Schaltwerks ist in gewissem Sinn funktional vollständig:

Lemma 3

Jede sequentielle Schaltfunktion $\Sigma=(\underline{X},\underline{Y},\underline{Z},\delta,\lambda)$ mit $\underline{X} \subseteq B^m, \underline{Y} \subseteq B^k, \underline{Z} \subseteq B^m$ lässt sich durch ein Polynomial-Schaltwerk $S = (B^{m+2}, B^{k+1}, B^{n+1}, S_\delta, S_\lambda)$ darstellen.

Auf Grund der sequentiellen Arbeitsweise von Schaltwerken lässt sich der Begriff der Test-Komplexität nicht mehr als Kardinalzahl, sondern nur als Länge einer Testfolge auffassen. Bevor wir nun eine Aussage über die Test-Komplexität modifizierter Polynomial-Schaltwerke treffen, sollen die folgenden Schreibweisen vereinbart werden: mit $\{X_{|m-1|}\}$ sei die Menge aller Eingabeworte X_i, welche m-1 Einsen enthalten, bezeichnet; mit $\langle X_{|m-1|}\rangle$ sei eine Folge minimaler Länge der Worte aus $\{X_{|m-1|}\}$ bezeichnet wobei $\langle X_{|m-1|}\rangle$ mit dem Wort $X_{2^{m-1}}$ ende. $(X_i)^k$ bezeichne die k-fache Wiederholung des Wortes X_i.

Lemma 4

Jedes modifizierte Polynomial-Schaltwerk $S = (B^m, B^k, B^n, S_\delta, S_\lambda)$ besitzt im fehlerfreien Fall die Synchronisierungsfolge $T_o(S) = (X_{2^m-1})^{n+2}$ für den Zustand Z_o. Wird dieser Zustand wegen eines Leitungsfehlers in S nicht erreicht, so wird nach der folgenden Eingabe von X_o die Ausgabe α nicht erzeugt.

Den Beweis dieses Lemmas findet man ebenso wie den Beweis des folgenden Lemmas in [9]. Es ist im wesentlichen eine Rechtfertigung von Definition 8.

Lemma 5

Für jedes modifizierte Polynomial-Schaltwerk $S = (B^m, B^k, B^n, S_\delta, S_\lambda)$ gilt: wird auf S nach der Synchronisierungs- Folge $T_0(S)$ eine Folge

$$T_1(S) = (X_0)(X_1)\langle X_{|m-1|}\rangle(X_{2^m-1})^{n+2},$$

angewendet, so ist S genau dann frei von Leitungsfehlern wenn die Ausgabefolge

$$T_2(S) = (\alpha)(\bar{\alpha})(\beta)^m(Y_i)^{n+1}(\bar{\beta})$$

erzeugt wird.

Es folgt:

Satz 3

Die Klasse $\underline{S}$ der Polynomial-Schaltwerke $S = (B^m, B^k, B^n, S_\delta, S_\lambda)$ besitzt eine universelle Testfolge

$$T(\underline{S}) = (X_{2^m-1})^{n+2}(X_0)(X_1)\langle X_{|m-1|}\rangle(X_{2^m-1})^{n+2}$$

der Länge n+m+6, die alle Leitungsfehler in einem Schaltwerk $S \in \underline{S}$ entdeckt $(n,m,k \geq 2)$.

In der Literatur wird die Länge der Testfolgen häufig auf die Zahl M der Eingabeworte und die Zahl N der Zustände bezogen; mit dieser Vereinbarung ergibt sich als

Korollar zu Satz 3

Jede sequentielle Schaltfunktion $\Sigma = (\underline{X}, \underline{Y}, \underline{Z}, \delta, \lambda)$ mit $\underline{X} \subseteq B^m, \underline{Y} \subseteq B^k, \underline{Z} \subseteq B^n$ und $M = |\underline{X}|$, $N = |\underline{Z}|$ ist als modifiziertes Polynomial-Schaltwerk $S = (B^{m+2}, B^{k+1}, B^{n+1}, S_\delta, S_\lambda)$ mit der Test-Komplexität

$$\Phi(S) \leq 2 \cdot \log_2(N) + \log_2(M) + 10$$

darstellbar.

5. LITERATUR

|1| G. Hotz, Schaltkreistheorie, Berlin, 1974.

|2| A.D. Friedman/P.R. Menon, Fault Detection in Digital Systems, Englewood Cliffs, 1971.

|3| W.Görke, Fehlerdiagnose digitaler Schaltungen, Stuttgart, 1973.

|4| W.Coy, On the realization of arbitrary switching functions with a linear number of tests, in J.Rosenfeld (Hrsg.), Information Processing 74, Amsterdam, 1974.

|5| W.Coy, Zur Konstruktion einfach testbarer Schaltkreise, (erscheint in Elektronische Informationsverarbeitung und Kybernetik).

|6| A.D. Friedman, Easily testable iterative systems, IEEE Trans. Comp., Vol. C-22, pp. 1061-1064, Dez. 1973.

|7| R.W. Landgraff/ S.S. Yau, Design of diagnosable iterative arrays, IEEE Trans. Comp., Vol. C-21, pp. 1183-1188, Nov. 1972.

|8| J.M.Galey/R.E.Norby/J.P.Roth, Techniques for the diagnosis of switching circuit failures, IEEE Trans. Comm. Elec., Vol. 83, pp. 509-514, Sept. 1964.

|9| W.Coy, Testkomplexität als Entwurfskriterium, Berichte der Informatik-Forschungsgruppen Nr. AFS-16, Technische Hochschule Darmstadt, Darmstadt, 1975.

|10| S.B. Akers, Universal test sets for logic networks, IEEE Trans. Comp. Vol. C-22, No. 9, pp. 835-839, Sept. 1973.

W A R T E S C H L A N G E N M O D E L L E

A MODEL OF A TIME-SHARING SYSTEM WITH TWO CLASSES OF PROCESSES

Alexandre Brandwajn
IRIA-LABORIA
Domaine de Voluceau
Rocquencourt
F-78150-Le Chesnay
France

Abstract

We present a model of a multiprogrammed, virtual memory interactive system, in which the processes are assumed to form two different classes as regards characteristics such as total compute time, input-output rate and program locality. The effect of memory sharing among processes is explicitly taken into account via life-time functions. We use our model to examine the efficiency of two policies of controlling the admission of processes into real core in order to avoid thrashing with two fixed-partition memory allocation schemes. An approximate analytical solution for our model is obtained owing to an equivalence and decomposition approach.

1. Introduction

In the past few years, a considerable amount of work has been done in computer systems modelling [1 - 6].

The overwhelming majority of the queuing models proposed assume that all the processes present in the system are statistically identical. This seems to be partly motivated by the fact that, in the case of one class of customers, not only an analytical solution to fairly general networks of interconnected queues is known since several years [7], but also efficient computational methods have been developped for it [8]. An analytical solution for queueing networks with different classes of customers has been given relatively recently [9] and, unfortunately, it does not apply to the often encountered First-Come-First-Served queueing discipline. A direct application of numerical methods seems practically impossible because of the very important state-space size resulting from even a modest model ; this is due to the fact that a very detailed state description is needed in order to be able to write the balance equations with several classes of customers.

On the other hand, as the queueing systems, even with only one class of customers, for which an exact analytical solution was known did not take into account some complex dependencies important in computer systems, there has been a trend to look for approximate solutions [10 - 14]. Some of the methods used appear to apply to networks of queues with different classes of customers [15]. Our approach in this paper is an extension of the equivalence and decomposition method used in [14], and is close in spirit, but not identical, to the parametric analysis method of [15].

We consider a model of a time-sharing, multiprogrammed, virtual memory computer system with two different classes of processes. The effect of memory sharing among processes as well as different program locality, total compute time and I/O rates for each class, are explicitly taken into account. The model is used to study the efficiency of two policies of controlling the admission of processes into real core in order to prevent thrashing, and, in conjunction with them, of two "fixed-partition" (see [16]) memory management schemes.

The model is described in Section 2 ; an approximate explicit solution is found in Section 3, and the next section is devoted to numerical results which illustrate the influence of system parameters and of admission control and memory allocation schemes on system performance measures such as mean response times and throughput. In Section 5, finally, we mention possible extensions of the model to more than two classes of processes and to the influence of batch jobs in our system.

The present paper is based on the author's doctoral dissertation [23].

2. The model.

The model of the time-sharing virtual memory system under consideration is represented in Figure 1. The system consists of a set of terminals from which active users generate commands, an admisssion control mechanism (AC), a CPU, a secondary memory paging device (SM) and a filing disk (FD). The latter three devices, each having an associated queue of requests, constitute the processing part of the system (R). The generation of a command by a user (who will then remain inactive until the system provides the proper response) is represented by a process entering the admission control before joining, sooner or later, according to system state, the CPU queue. The completion of a command is represented symbolically by a departure of a process from the CPU to the terminals. The behavior of a user at a terminal is characterized by his think time, i.e. the time elapsed between a system response and the next command the user generates. We shall assume that all the users are statistically identical and independent as regards their think time and that the latter is exponentially distributed with mean $1/\lambda$. We shall also assume that there are two different classes of commands (processes) in the system, the probability that a generated command is of class 1 (respectively, 2) being p_1 (respectively, $p_2 = 1 - p_1$).

The behavior of processes of either class is represented by a compute time followed by either a page fault (the process then enters the SM queue) or an explicit file request, in which case the process joins the FD queue.

Denote by N the total number of terminals, by n_c the number of active terminals, k_1 and N_1 (respectively, k_2 and N_2) the numbers of class 1 (respectively, class 2) processes waiting for admission in AC and executing in R. At any instant of time we have

$$N = n_c + k_1 + k_2 + N_1 + N_2 \ , \tag{2.1}$$

and

$$N_1 = n_{o1} + n_{11} + n_{21} \ ,$$
$$N_2 = n_{o2} + n_{12} + n_{22} \ , \tag{2.2}$$

where n_{oi}, n_{1i} and n_{2i} are the numbers of class i processes (i=1,2) at the CPU, the SM and the FD, respectively.

It is assumed that real memory is shared among processes in R which are at the CPU and the SM (i.e., processes requesting a file access lose their memory allocation), so that, when a class i, i=1,2, process is executing on the CPU at time t, a command completion, a page fault or an I/O request will occur during a small interval of time $(t,t+\delta t]$ with probability

$$\delta t/c_i + o(\delta t),$$
$$\delta t/q_i(n_1,n_2) + o(\delta t), \tag{2.3}$$
or
$$\delta t/r_i + o(\delta t) \ ,$$

respectively,
where

$o(\delta t)$ denotes any function of δt such that

$$\lim_{\delta t \to 0} \frac{o(\delta t)}{\delta t} = 0 \ , \tag{2.4}$$

and

$$n_i = n_{oi} + n_{1i} \quad , \qquad i = 1,2. \tag{2.5}$$

This is equivalent to assuming that the service time during a single pass through the CPU is exponentially distributed with a state dependent parameter

$$u_{oi}(n_1,n_2) = 1/c_i + 1/q_i(n_1,n_2) + 1/r_i , \qquad i = 1,2 \qquad (2.6)$$

where c_i, $q_i(n_1,n_2)$, r_i may be regarded as the mean total compute time, the mean virtual (i.e., execution) time between two succesive page faults when there are n_1 class 1 and n_2 class 2 processes at the CPU and at the SM, and the mean virtual time between two successive file requests, respectively, for a class i process.

As we would like to use our model to study the efficiency of the admission control mechanism in conjunction with certain memory allocation policies, we need a model relating $q_i(n_1,n_2)$ to the amount of space allocated to each process. We shall choose the life-time function [17] (which gives the mean CPU time between page faults, q, for a process executing in memory space m) and, more precisely, its two-parameter fit proposed by Chamberlin, Fuller and Liu [18] :

$$q = \frac{2b}{1+(\frac{d}{m})^2} , \qquad (2.7)$$

where d is "a relative measure of page frames needed to enable the process to be executed efficiently" and b is the expected execution time between page faults when the process is allocated d page frames. Two examples of life-time functions are shown in Figure 2. The curves labelled 1 and 2 correspond to the parameter values :

$$\begin{array}{l} b = b_1 = 20 \text{ ms} \\ d = d_1 = 60 \text{ pages} \end{array} , \quad \text{and} \quad \begin{array}{l} b = b_2 = 25 \text{ ms} \\ d = d_2 = 50 \text{ pages} \end{array} ,$$

respectively. These values, taken from [18], will be used throughout this paper.

We shall assume that the random variables representing the service times of the SM and the FD devices are exponentially distributed with mean $1/u_1$ and $1/u_2$, respectively, and that the queueing disciplines in R are First-Come-First-Served.

We still have to specify how works the admission control mechanism. The control schemes we shall consider will be of the following type : to each pair $(l_1=k_1+N_1 , l_2=k_2+N_2)$ corresponds <u>only one</u> possible pair (N_1,N_2) ; in order to achieve this, it may be necessary to remove processes from the processing part (the "removal" loop in Figure 1). It is assumed that admission and removal of processes take place in <u>zero time</u>. Examples of admission controls of this type would be : no control at all (free admission), or up to m_1 class 1 and m_2 class 2 processes in R, etc.

We would like to obtain mean response times for each class and system throughput (average number of commands processed per unit time) as measures of system performance.

Using a detailed state description one could write the system balance equations. Note, however, that the analytical solution of our system is not known (essentially, because of the state-dependent service rate and the FCFS discipline at the CPU). Note also that a direct numerical solution of the system equations seems practically impossible for two reasons : first, the transition rate matrix is ill-conditioned (it contains terms corresponding to the user's think time of order of 10 s and to page faults of order of 10 ms); second, the rather formidable size of the state space. Thus we shall use an equivalence and decomposition approach.

3. <u>The solution method</u>.

We shall proceed in three major steps. First, we shall state a theorem showing that our system is equivalent in a given sense to a much simpler queueing network with only one class of customers. Using a decomposition argument, one can show that the service rates in this equivalent network may be approximately computed by analysing a simple subnetwork. This analysis will constitute our second step. Finally, we shall be concerned with the solution of the equivalent network.

Let us begin by a definition of equivalence.

Definition 3.1

Two queueing systems are equivalent from the point of view of a given state description if the probability distributions of the chosen state vectors are identical in both systems.

Consider the following state description for our model

$$\bar{s} = (n_c, l_1, l_2) \quad , \tag{3.1}$$

where

$$l_1 = k_1 + n_{o1} + n_{11} + n_{21} \quad ;$$

$$l_2 = k_2 + n_{o2} + n_{12} + n_{22} \quad ;$$

$$n_c = N - l_1 - l_2 \; .$$

Theorem 3.1

The model described in Section 2 is equivalent from the point of view of the state description $\bar{s}$ (3.1), in the sense of Definition 3.1, at the stationary state, if it exists, to the queueing network represented in Figure 3. This equivalent network is composed of three servers, labelled 1 to 3, with service rates

$$v_1'(l_1, l_2) = A_1^*(l_1, l_2)/c_1 \; , \tag{3.2}$$

$$v_2(l_1, l_2) = A_2^*(l_1, l_2)/c_2 \; , \tag{3.3}$$

$$v_3(n_c) = n_c\lambda \quad , \tag{3.4}$$

respectively,
where

$A_1^*(l_1, l_2)$ is the stationary conditional probability of the CPU being active executing a class 1 process given that the system state is $\bar{s} = (n_c, l_1, l_2) = (N - l_1 - l_2, l_1, l_2)$, i.e.,

$$A_1^*(l_1,l_2) = \text{Prob}\ \{\text{ CPU executing a class 1 process} \,|\, (l_1,l_2)\}, \tag{3.5}$$

similarly

$$A_2^*(l_1,l_2) = \text{Prob}\ \{\text{ CPU executing a class 2 process} \,|\, (l_1,l_2)\}. \tag{3.6}$$

A total of $N = n_c + l_1 + l_2$ statistically identical customers circulate in the network, and the probability that a customer leaving server 3 will direct himself to server 1 (respectively, to server 2) is p_1 (respectively, p_2).

The proof of this theorem is similar to other equivalence proofs, i.e., it consists, essentially, in writing down balance equations for the chosen state vector in both the original and the equivalent systems (see, for example, [14]), and we shall not present it.

Owing to the exponential assumptions, our model is a finite-state Markov chain, and it can be shown that the stationary state exists.

Consider again the original system of Figure 1. Internal transitions in R, corresponding to page faults and I/O requests, take place, typically, at a time scale of tens of ms, while the time scale of transitions corresponding to generations and completions of commands (i.e., to changes in (l_1,l_2)) is of order of seconds. Thus, it is intuitively clear that, on the average, the processing part of the system should reach its steady state relatively rapidly between two successive changes in (l_1,l_2). Therefore, $A_1^*(l_1,l_2)$(respectively, $A_2^*(l_1,l_2)$) should not be much different from $A_1(N_1,N_2)$(respectively, $A_2(N_1,N_2)$), the probability of the CPU being active executing class 1 (respectively, class 2) processes in the closed network obtained by cutting off the links between R and the "external world" (see Figure 4) with a total of N_1 class 1 and N_2 class 2 processes in it, where (N_1,N_2) is the unique pair corresponding to a given (l_1,l_2), i.e.

$$\begin{aligned} A_1^*(l_1,l_2) &\approx A_1(N_1,N_2) \\ A_2^*(l_1,l_2) &\approx A_2(N_1,N_2) . \end{aligned} \tag{3.7}$$

To this intuitive decomposition argument can be substituted a rigorous proof of the so-called near-complete-decomposability property [19], [20], [10], and one can show that a sufficient (but not necessary) condition in order for (3.7) to hold is

$$\alpha(n_{11}+n_{12})u_1+\alpha(n_{21}+n_{22})u_2+\alpha(n_{oi})\alpha(n_{o1}+n_{o2})[1/q_i(n_1,n_2)+1/r_i]<<n_c\lambda+\alpha(n_{oi})\alpha(n_{o1}+n_{o2})/c_i,$$
$$i=1,2 , \tag{3.8}$$

where

$$\alpha(x) = \begin{cases} 0, & \text{if } x = 0 \\ 1, & \text{otherwise ;} \end{cases} \tag{3.9}$$

and, if $n_{oi} = 0$ for a given class i but $n_{o1}+n_{o2} \neq 0$, (3.8) should be evaluated for the other class.

The proof of this statement will be omitted.

It is not difficult to see that inequality (3.8) is satisfied for most values of system parameters which are of interest. Thus, our second major step will be the analysis of the system represented in Figure 4 (transitions changing (N_1,N_2) being neglected, the CPU service rate becomes $u_{oi}(n_1,n_2) = 1/q_i(n_1,n_2) + 1/r_i$, for a class i process).

We apply again the equivalence and decomposition method. Suppose that there are N_1 class 1 and N_2 class 2 processes in the queueing network of Figure 4, and consider the following state description

$$\bar{s}_a = (n_{21},n_{22}). \tag{3.10}$$

We have

<u>Theorem 3.2</u>

The system considered is equivalent at the steady state, in the sense of definition 3.1, from the point of view of $\bar{s}_a$, to a single exponential server (see Figure 5) with two classes of customers served in a FCFS order. The service rate for either class is u_2 and the arrival rate for class i (i=1,2) customers is

$$\lambda_i(n_{21},n_{22}) = a_i^*(N_1 - n_{21}, N_2 - n_{22})/r_i , \tag{3.11}$$

where

$$a_i^*(N_1-n_{21},N_2-n_{22})=\text{Prob}\{\text{CPU active executing class i process}|\text{state}(n_{21},n_{22})\}. \tag{3.12}$$

The proof of this theorem will be omitted.

Again, a decomposition argument can be used, and $a_i^*(n_1,n_2)$ may be approximately computed as being equal to $a_i(n_1,n_2)$, the stationary probability of the CPU being busy executing class i processes in a two-server network obtained by isolating the subnetwork B, and, consequently, setting the CPU class i service rate to $1/q_i(n_1,n_2)$ (see Figure 6), where n_1 and n_2 are the total numbers of class 1 and class 2 processes in this simple system.

There is no particular difficulty in obtaining a computationally efficient numerical solution for such a network (see [24]).

It remains, once we have computed $a_i(n_1,n_2) \approx a_i^*(n_1,n_2)$, to solve the equivalent queue of Figure 5. An approximate explicit solution can be found by applying once more the equivalence approach :

Theorem 3.3

The two-class single server FCFS queue of Figure 5 is equivalent at the stationary state, in the sense of Definition 3.1, from the point of view of the state variable n_{21}, to a single M/M/1 queue with arrival rate

$$\lambda_a(n_{21}) = \sum_{n_{22}=0}^{N_2} \text{Prob}\{n_{22}|n_{21}\} \, \lambda_1(n_{21},n_{22}) \,, \quad n_{21} = 0,\ldots,N_1-1 \quad (3.13)$$

and with service rate

$$\mu_a(n_{21}) = u_2 \sum_{n_{22}=0}^{N_2} \text{Prob}\{n_{22}|n_{21}\} \, w_1(n_{21},n_{22}), \quad n_{21} = 1,\ldots,N_1 \quad (3.14)$$

where

$\text{Prob}\{n_{22}|n_{21}\}$ is the stationary conditional probability of having n_{22} class 2 processes in the queue (including the one in service) given that there are n_{21} class 1 processes ;

$$w_i(n_{21},n_{22}) = \text{Prob}\{\text{class } i \text{ process in service}|(n_{21},n_{22})\} \,, \quad i=1,2 \,. \quad (3.15)$$

The proof of this theorem will be omitted.

Formally, we have for the probability that there are n_{21} class 1 processes

$$p_a(n_{21}) = \frac{1}{G_a} \prod_{i=1}^{n_{21}} \frac{\lambda_a(i-1)}{\mu_a(i)} \,, \quad n_{21} = 0,1,\ldots,N_1 \,;$$

$$G_a = \sum_{n_{21}=0}^{N_1} \prod_{i=1}^{n_{21}} \frac{\lambda_a(i-1)}{\mu_a(i)} \,, \quad (3.16)$$

a well-known and computionally efficient solution form .

Suppose we know $w_i(n_{21},n_{22})$. Although there may be no time scale discrepancy, the system of Figure 5 may be shown to enjoy the near-complete-decomposability property as regards the variables n_{21} and n_{22}, so that $\text{Prob}\{n_{22}|n_{21}\}$ may be approximately computed by considering, for a given n_{21}, all the transitions which do not change n_{21}. This yields, for $n_{21} = 0,\ldots,N_1$,

$$\text{Prob}\{n_{22}|n_{21}\} \approx \frac{1}{H_a(n_{21})} \prod_{j=1}^{n_{22}} \frac{\lambda_2(n_{21},j-1)}{u_2 \, w_2(n_{21},j)}, \quad n_{22}=0,\ldots,N_2 \,;$$

$$H_a(n_{21}) = \sum_{n_{22}=0}^{N_2} \prod_{j=1}^{n_{22}} \frac{\lambda_2(n_{21},j-1)}{u_2 \, w_2(n_{21},j)} \,. \quad (3.17)$$

Now, as checked by a set of direct numerical solutions, with a fair approximation we have

$$w_i(n_{21},n_{22}) \approx \frac{n_{2i}}{n_{21}+n_{22}} \quad , \qquad i=1,2 \; . \tag{3.18}$$

Using (3.18) in (3.13), (3.14) and (3.17), we obtain an approximate explicit solution for the stationary probability of having n_{21} class 1 and n_{22} class 2 processes at the FD in the queueing network of Figure 4 :

$$p_a(n_{21},n_{22}) = p_a(n_{21})\text{Prob}\{n_{22}|n_{21}\} \; , \tag{3.19}$$

where $p_a(n_{21})$ is given by (3.16) and $\text{Prob}\{n_{22}|n_{21}\}$ is given by (3.17).

It seems worth noting that when the two classes of processes have the same page-faulting behaviour (and thus $\lambda_1(n_1,n_2)/r_2 = \lambda_2(n_2,n_1)/r_1$), (3.19) appears to be the exact solution for the equivalent network of Figure 5.

Using (3.19) we compute the stationary probability of the CPU being busy executing class i processes in the queueing network of Figure 4 with a total of N_1 class 1 and N_2 class 2 processes

$$A_i(N_1,N_2) = \sum_{n_{21}=0}^{N_1} \sum_{n_{22}=0}^{N_2} a_i^*(N_1-n_{21},N_2-n_{22})p_a(n_{21},n_{22}), \tag{3.20}$$

with

$$a_i^*(n_1,n_2) \approx a_i(n_1,n_2), \qquad i=1,2 \; ; \tag{3.21}$$

which completes our second major step.

At this point of the solution procedure we have approximately computed the unknown parameters $A_i^*(l_1,l_2)$ of the three-server network equivalent to our original model of Section 2. The last major step is thus to solve the queueing network of Figure 3.

It would be nice, if an exact analytical solution was known for this network. Unfortunately, as far as the author knows, this is not the case, and we shall apply yet another time the equivalence and decomposition approach in order to obtain a computationally efficient approximate explicit solution.

Theorem 3.4

The queueing network under consideration is equivalent at the stationary state, in the sense of Definition 3.1, from the point of view of the state variable l_1, to a single M/M/1 queue with arrival rate

$$\lambda_b(l_1) = \lambda p_1 \sum_{l_2=0}^{N-l_1} \text{Prob}\{l_2|l_1\}\,(N-l_1-l_2) \; , \qquad l_1=0,..,N-1 \; ; \tag{3.22}$$

and service rate

$$\begin{aligned} \mu_b(l_1) &= \sum_{l_2=0}^{N-l_1} \text{Prob}\{l_2|l_1\}\; v_1(l_1,l_2) = \\ &= \frac{1}{c_1} \sum_{l_2=0}^{N-l_1} \text{Prob}\{l_2|l_1\}\; A_1^*(l_1,l_2), \quad l_1 = 1,\dots,N \; . \end{aligned} \tag{3.23}$$

We shall not present the proof of this theorem.

It results from Theorem 3.4 that the stationary probability distribution of l_1 in the network of Figure 3 is given by

$$p_b(l_1) = \frac{1}{G_b} \prod_{i=1}^{l_1} \frac{\lambda_b(i-1)}{\mu_b(i)}, \quad l_1=0,\ldots,N,$$

with (3.24)

$$G_b = \sum_{l_1=0}^{N} \prod_{i=1}^{l_1} \cdot \frac{\lambda_b(i-1)}{\mu_b(i)} .$$

This solution contains one unknown parameter which appears in the expressions for $\lambda_b(i)$ and $\mu_b(i)$ ((3.22) and (3.23)) : $\mathrm{Prob}\{l_2|l_1\}$, i.e., the stationary conditional probability of having l_2 customers at server 2 given that there are l_1 customers at server 1. Again, the system may be shown to be nearly completely decomposable as regards the state variables l_1, l_2, so that we compute approximately $\mathrm{Prob}\{l_2|l_1\}$ by considering, for a given l_1, all the transitions which do not change this variable. This yields

$$\mathrm{Prob}\{l_2|l_1\} \approx \frac{1}{H_b(l_1)} \prod_{j=1}^{l_2} \frac{(N-l_1-j+1)\lambda p_2}{v_2(l_1,j)}, \quad l_2=0,\ldots,N-l_1; \; l_1=0,\ldots,N;$$

$$H_b(l_1) = \sum_{l_2=0}^{N-l_1} (\lambda c_2 p_2)^{l_2} \cdot \prod_{j=1}^{l_2} \frac{(N-l_1-j+1)}{A_2^*(l_1,j)} . \qquad (3.25)$$

Hence, we obtain, using (3.25) in and together with (3.24), an approximate expression for the stationary joint probability distribution of l_1 and l_2

$$p(l_1,l_2) \simeq p_b(l_1)\,\mathrm{Prob}\{l_2|l_1\}, \qquad (3.26)$$

and we can now easily compute the performance measures we are interested in. Before doing so, let us note first that, in general, there is no reason for assuming that l_1 varies more slowly than l_2, i.e., there is no reason for particularizing this variable. Indeed, we have observed that, in some cases when the variables l_1 and l_2 are symmetric, (3.26) doesn't reproduce exactly this symmetry. Therefore, we compute two solutions : as previously

$$p_1(l_1,l_2) = p_b(l_1)\mathrm{Prob}\{l_2|l_1\},$$

and, similarly, choosing l_2 as the reference variable,

$$p_2(l_1,l_2) = p_b(l_2)\mathrm{Prob}\{l_1|l_2\}, \qquad (3.27)$$

and we let

$$p(l_1,l_2) \approx (p_1(l_1,l_2) + p_2(l_1,l_2))/2, \qquad (3.28)$$

which seems to be a good approximation (see [24]).

Let us note also that we have reduced the solution of our model to three major steps. The systems appearing at each of those steps are sufficiently simple to be solved numerically ; eventually, a simulation could be used. We have preferred, however, to further apply the equivalence and decomposition approach, so as to end up with a computationally efficient approximate solution. An interesting feature is that, in the case when an exact analytical solution has a product form, our approach yields the exact probability distribution.

Denote by W_1, W_2 and W the mean response time (i.e. the average time elapsed between the moment a command enters the system and the moment it leaves it) for a command of class 1, of class 2 and of any class, respectively. Let $\bar{l}_1$ and $\bar{l}_2$ be the mean numbers of class 1 and class 2 processes in the system. Using Little's formula [21], we have

$$W_i = \frac{\bar{l}_i}{(N-\bar{l}_1-\bar{l}_2)\lambda p_i} \quad , \quad i=1,2 \; ; \tag{3.29}$$

and

$$W = \frac{\bar{l}_1+\bar{l}_2}{(N-\bar{l}_1-\bar{l}_2)\lambda} \; . \tag{3.30}$$

It is not difficult to see that for $\bar{l}_1 + \bar{l}_2$ close to N, a small relative error in the mean numbers of processes can produce an important relative error in the response times which will then not be reliable.

We have

$$\bar{l}_i = \sum_{l_1=0}^{N} \sum_{l_2=0}^{N-l_1} l_i \, p(l_1,l_2) \; , \quad i=1,2 \; . \tag{3.31}$$

System throughput, θ, is given by

$$\theta = B_1/c_1 + B_2/c_2 \; , \tag{3.32}$$

where B_i, i=1,2, is the stationary probability of the CPU being busy executing class i processes, i.e.,

$$B_i = \sum_{l_1=0}^{N} \sum_{l_2=0}^{N-l_1} A_i^*(l_1,l_2)p(l_1,l_2). \tag{3.33}$$

Under equilibrium, a simple flow conservation argument suffices to obtain the following relation

$$B_1/B_2 = p_1c_1/(p_2c_2) \quad , \tag{3.34}$$

so that we have

$$\theta = B_1/(c_1p_1) = B_2/(c_2p_2).$$

Note that in the case when $c_1 = c_2 = c$, system throughput is directly proportional to total CPU utilization $B = B_1 + B_2$.

In the next section we shall present the control and allocation schemes studied, and the numerical results obtained.

4. Numerical results

Let us consider the admission control represented in Figure 7. There is a control switch (CS) with a waiting line for processes of either class. The position of a control switch (open or closed) is a function of the system state. We shall first assume that either control switch works so as to prevent the total number of processes of the corresponding class from exceeding a fixed value, say m_1 and m_2 ($m_1,m_2 > 0$) for CS_1 and CS_2, respectively.

The "removal" loop is not used, and, as already indicated, it is assumed that CS position changes and introduction of processes from the AC into R take place in zero time. We shall start by considering the case when real memory is equally shared among processes at the CPU and the SM, i.e., M being total memory available, we shall first assume that each process is allocated an amount of memory m

$$m = \frac{M}{n_1+n_2} \quad , \tag{4.1}$$

where n_i, i=1,2, is given by (2.5), so that we have

$$q_i(n_1,n_2) = \frac{2b_i}{1+\left[\frac{d_i(n_1+n_2)}{M}\right]^2} \quad , \quad i=1,2 \; . \tag{4.2}$$

Memory equipartition we are considering now, has been shown to be inefficient from the point of view of page faulting (see [16]). Our goal is to evaluate its influence on the overall system performance in conjuntion with the admission control described above, so as to use it as a comparison basis for other admission and allocation schemes.

Since we are primarily interested in the memory sharing control effect, we shall first neglect the I/O behaviour by letting $r_1 = r_2 = \infty$; consequently, in the solution procedure we have to take

$$A_i^*(l_1,l_2) \approx a_i(N_1,N_2), \quad i=1,2 \; ; \tag{4.3}$$

where $a_i(N_1,N_2)$ is the stationary probability that the CPU is busy executing class i processes in the two-server network of Figure 6 with a total of N_1 class 1 and N_2 class 2 processes.

In Figure 8 we have represented the mean response times W_1,W_2,W and the total CPU utilization B versus N, the total number of terminals, for a set of system parameters with m_1 (the maximum number of class 1 processes admitted into R) set to 1 and m_2 (the maximum number of class 2 processes in R) equal to 1,2, and 3. The same curves are drawn in Figures 9 and 10 for m_1 set to 2 and 3, respectively. Note that, as we have $c_1 = c_2$, total CPU utilization is directly proportional to system throughput. The mean service time of the secondary memory paging device $t_{SM} = 1/u_1$ is kept constant throughout Figures 8 to 10 at 5 ms. We observe that there exists a pair (m_1,m_2) for which system throughput is maximum and, at the same time, the mean system response time is minimum. It is not surprising that maximum system throughput corresponds to minimum mean response time. Indeed, under equilibrium, we obtain from a flow conservation argument

$$(N - \bar{I}_1 - \bar{I}_2)\, \lambda = B_1/c_1 + B_2/c_2 = B/c \; ,$$

i.e.,

$$\bar{I}_1 + \bar{I}_2 = N - B/(\lambda c). \tag{4.4}$$

We see from (4.4) that the mean number of processes in the system is minimum when system throughput is maximum, and hence, using (3.30), that also the mean system response time is then minimum. Similar curves with $t_{SM} = 10$ ms are drawn in Figures 11 and 12. We notice that not only system throughput decreases while the response times increase, but also the "optimum" pair $(m_1,m_2)^*$ changes. It seems to correspond now to a lower value of m_2; this, however, contradicts our intuition, since class 2 processes have a better locality than class 1 processes. On the other hand, the relative difference in B between the cases $m_1 = 1$, $m_2 = 1$ and $m_1 = 1$, $m_2 = 2$ is less than 1% which is very likely to be below the precision of the approximation method. The results of a direct numerical solution of the equivalent queueing network of Figure 3 confirm those obtained with our approximation method.

---

* Note that the pair (m_1,m_2) which corresponds, the other system parameters (memory size, mean drum service time,...) being kept constant, to maximum system throughput seems also to ensure a relative balance between the response times W_1 and W_2.

In Figure 13 we have represented the probabilities of the CPU being busy executing class 1, class 2 processes, the total CPU utilization $(a_1(n_1,n_2), a_2(n_1,n_2), a(n_1,n_2) = \sum_{i=1}^{2} a_i(n_1,n_2))$ and the mean execution times between two successive page faults in the two-server network of Figure 6, as a function of the numbers of processes of either class present in the network, for the set of system parameters used in Figures 8 to 10.

Chamberlin, Fuller and Liu indicate in [18] that pages should be allocated to nonidentical processes in such a way that their mean execution intervals between page faults are the same. Figures 14 to 16 and 17, 18 show the results obtained with such an allocation policy in conjunction with the admission control considered, for a set of system parameters with t_{SM} equal to 5 ms and 10 ms, respectively. Again, we observe the existence of optimum pairs as regards system throughput, but it is somewhat surprising to see not only that there is little improvement in the maximum CPU utilizations, but also that, for some values of (m_1,m_2), system throughput is lower than in the case of equipartition, and the difference may be of about 10% ,i.e. presumably greater than the precision of the approximation method. The results of a direct numerical solution of the equivalent queueing system of Figure 3 seem to confirm our remark.

An advantage of this allocation scheme (if it is to be regarded as an advantage) is that it equalizes the average class response times W_1 and W_2.

In Figure 19 we have represented the CPU utilizations in the two-server subnetwork $(a_i(n_1,n_2)$, $i=1,2$, $a(n_1,n_2) = \sum_{i=1}^{2} a_i(n_1,n_2))$, the numbers of pages allocated to a process of either class and the resulting mean execution intervals between page faults for the set of system parameters used in Figures 14 to 16.

The influence of the I/O behavior is illustrated in Figures 20 and 22 which correspond to the same admission and allocation scheme as in Figures 17, 18 and to a set of system parameters with r_2 (the mean execution time between two file requests) equal to 40 ms and 80 ms, respectively. The corresponding CPU utilizations in the three-server subnetwork of Figure 4 $(A_i(N_1,N_2)$, $i=1,2$, $A(N_1,N_2) = \sum_{i=1}^{2} A_i(N_1,N_2))$ as a function of the numbers of processes present, are represented in Figures 21 and 23.

We have seen that maximum system throughput corresponds to minimum mean response time and relatively balanced mean class response times W_1, W_2. This suggests the following admission control. We assume that the control switches of Figure 7 are used together with the "removal" loop in such a way that at every instant of time the pair (N_1,N_2) corresponding to a given (l_1,l_2) ensures the highest system throughput (in our case, the highest total CPU utilization B). Note that Formula (3.25) of the third major step of our solution procedure may not be applicable, because it may well happen that to a non zero l_i corresponds now a $N_i = 0$. Thus, the curves represented in Figure 24 have been obtained by a simulation of the equivalent network of Figure 3. We observe that system performance seems better than with the admission control scheme of Figures 8 to 10 (balanced memory allocation is used in both cases).

5. A few extensions

Due to the space limitation, herein we shall merely mention the extensions of our model which are discussed in detail in [24]. The first extension is a model of a time-sharing-oriented system in which, in addition to an interactive part, there is a batch processing facility including independent primary memory space and secondary storage device. A batch process may be given the CPU only if the interactive part is idle. In the second extension, batch and interactive processes share primary and secondary memory, and are given CPU control on a FCFS basis. As a final point, we discuss the generalization of the model of Section 2 to more than two classes. It is shown that the major steps extend easily. Problems arise while solving the models appearing at those steps, since each additional class of processes requires an additional application of the equivalence and decomposition method which, presumably, increases the approximation errors.

References

[1] Scherr, A.L. : An analysis of time-shared computer systems. Cambridge (Mass.): M.I.T. Press 1967.

[2] Arora, S.R., Gallo, A. : The optimal organization of multiprogrammed multilevel memory. Proc. ACM-SIGOPS Workshop on System Performance Evaluation, Harvard University, April 1971, p. 104-141.

[3] Buzen, J. : Queueing network models of multiprogramming. Harvard University, Ph. D. Thesis, 1971.

[4] Moore, C.G. : Network models for large scale time-sharing systems. University of Michigan, Ph. D. Thesis, 1971.

[5] Sekino, A. : Throughput analysis of multiprogrammed virtual-memory computer systems. 1st Annual SICME Symposium on Measurement and Evaluation, Palo Alto, 1973, p. 47-53.

[6] Brandwajn, A., Buzen, J., Gelenbe, E., Potier, D. : A model of performance for virtual memory systems. Proc. 1974 SIGMETRICS Symposium, October 1974.

[7] Jackson, J.R. : Jobshop-like queueing systems. Management Science 10, 131-142 (1963).

[8] Buzen, J.P. : Computational algorithms for closed queueing networks with exponential servers. Comm. ACM 16, 527-531 (1973).

[9] Muntz, R.R., Baskett, F. : Open, closed and mixed networks of queues with different classes of customers. Stanford Electronic Laboratories, Technical Report No. 33, August 1972.

[10] Courtois, P. : On the near-complete-decomposability of networks of queues and of stochastic models of multiprogramming computing systems. Carnegie Melon University, November, 1971.

[11] Avi-Itzhak, B., Heyman, D.F. : Approximate queueing models for multiprogramming computer systems. Operations Research 21, 1212-1230 (1973).

[12] Mitrani, I. : Nonpriority multiprogramming systems under heavy demand conditions - customers' viewpoint. Journal ACM 19, 445-452 (1972).

[13] Chandy, K.M., Herzog, U., Woo, L. : Approximate analysis of general queueing networks. IBM Research Report RC 4931, July 1974.

[14] Brandwajn, A. : A model of a time-sharing virtual memory system solved using equivalence and decomposition methods. Acta Informatica 4, 11-47 (1974).

[15] Sauer, C.H., Chandy, K.M. : Approximate analysis of central server models with non-exponential service distributions, different classes of customers and priority queueing disciplines. University of Texas at Austin Report TR-45 (1974).

[16] Denning, P.J., Graham, G.S. : Multiprogrammed memory management. To appear in IEEE Proceeding on Interactive Computer Systems, June 1975.

[17] Belady, L., Kuehner, C.J. : Dynamic space sharing in computer systems. Comm. ACM 12, 282-288 (1969).

[18] Chamberlin, D., Fuller, S., Liu, L. : An analysis of page allocation stategies for multiprogramming systems with virtual memory. IBM J.R and D, September 1973.

[19] Simon, H. Ando, A. : Aggregation of variables in dynamic systems. Econometrica 20, 111-138 (1961).

[20] Ando, A., Fisher, F.M. : Near-decomposability, partition and aggregation, and the relevance of stability discussions. International Economic Review 4, 53-67 (1963).

[21] Little, J.D. : A proof of the queueing formula L = λW. Operations Research 9, 383-387 (1961).

[22] Jordan, C. : Calculus of finite differences. New York : Chelsea Publishing Company 1965.

[23] Brandwajn, A. : Equivalence et décomposition dans les modèles à files d'attente et leur application à l'évaluation des performances de systèmes d'exploitation. Thèse d'Etat, University of Paris VI, January 1975.

[24] Brandwajn, A. : A model of an interactive system with two classes of processes. To appear.

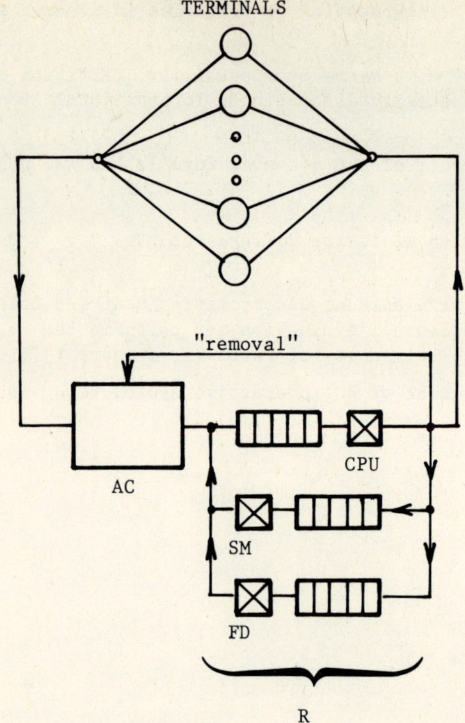

Figure 1

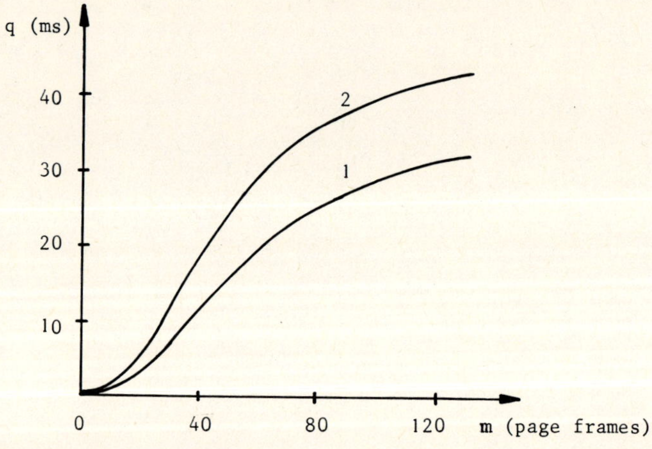

Figure 2

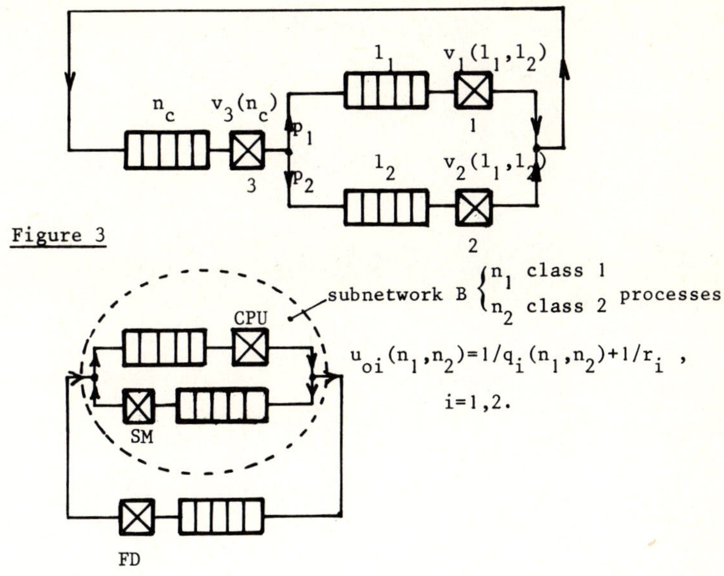

Figure 3

Figure 4

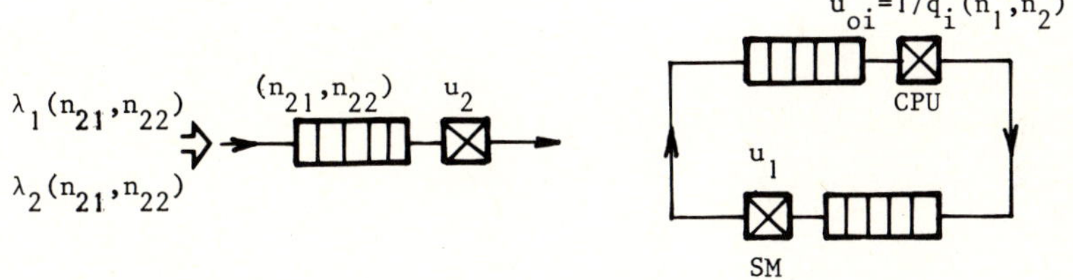

Figure 5

Figure 6

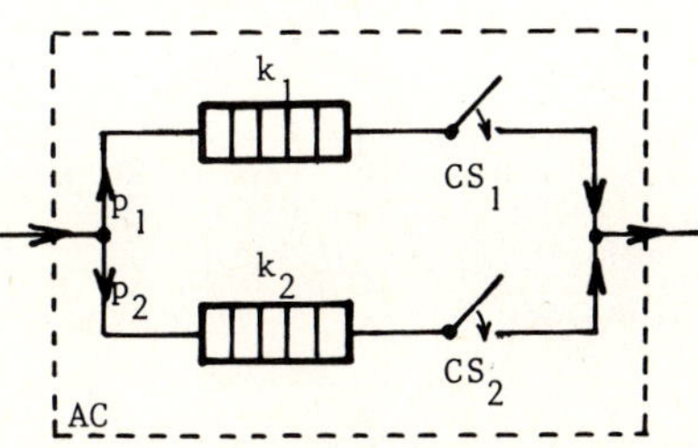

Figure 7

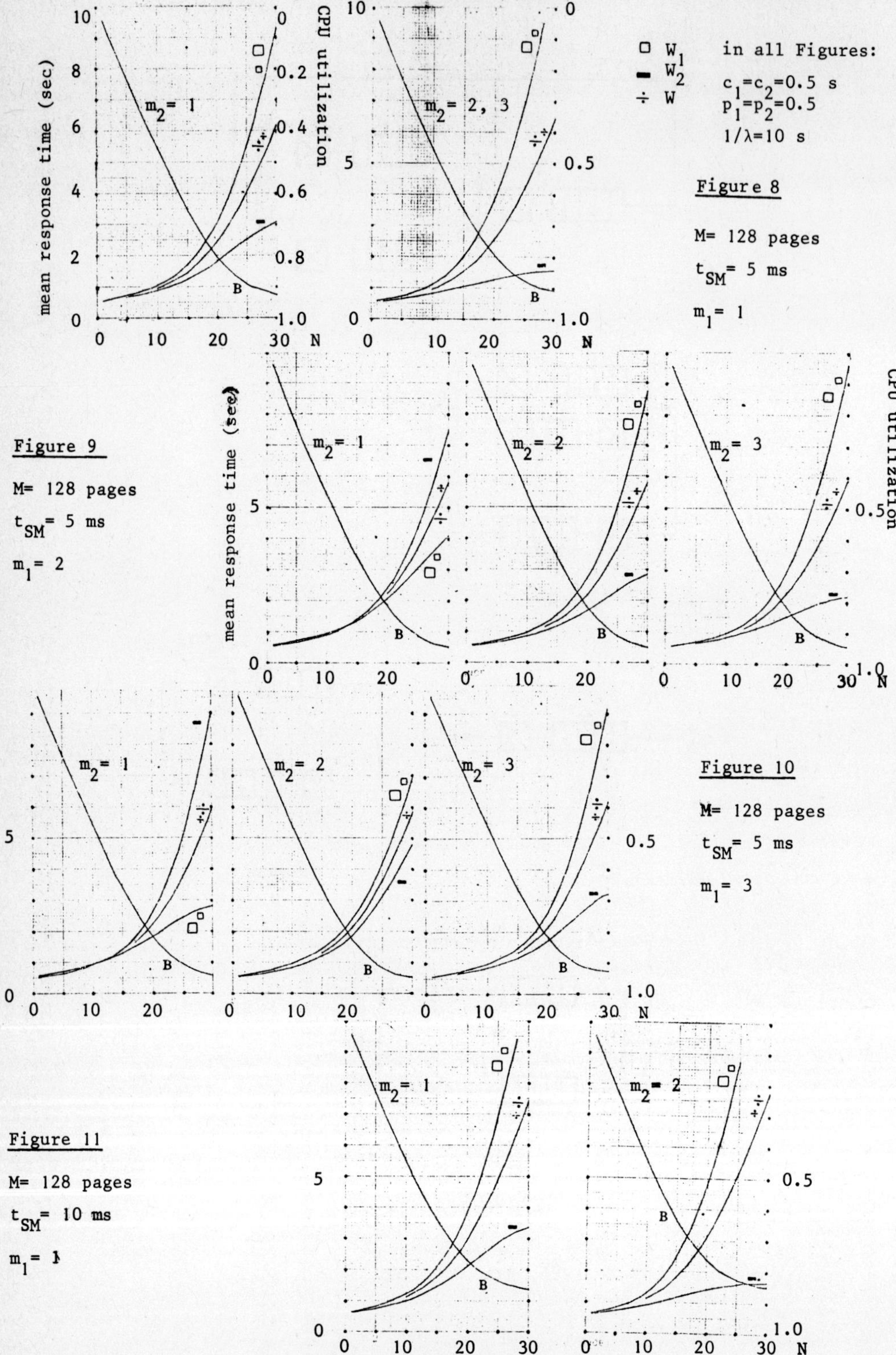

Figure 8

M= 128 pages

t_{SM}= 5 ms

m_1= 1

Figure 9

M= 128 pages

t_{SM}= 5 ms

m_1= 2

Figure 10

M= 128 pages

t_{SM}= 5 ms

m_1= 3

Figure 11

M= 128 pages

t_{SM}= 10 ms

m_1= 1

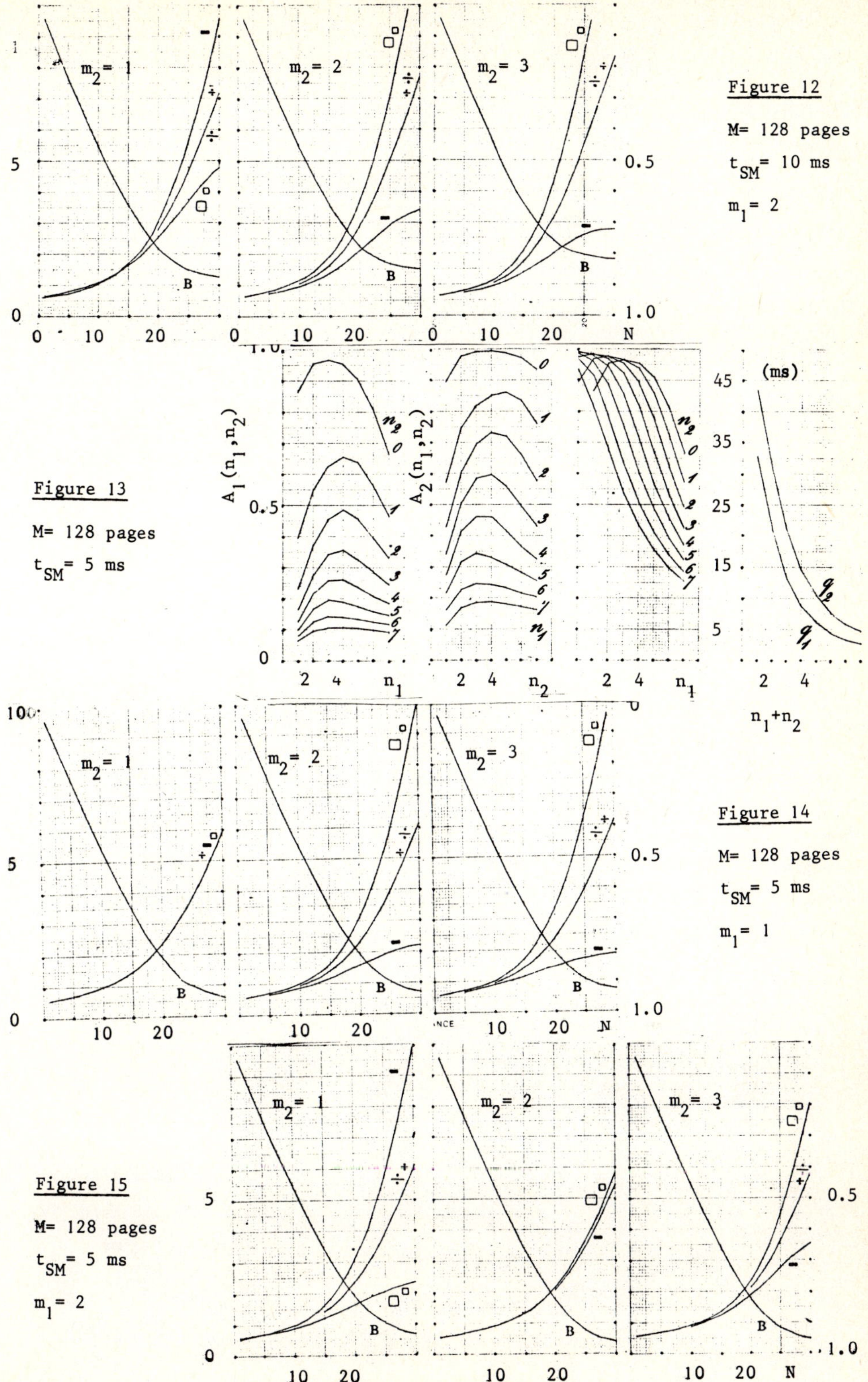

Figure 12

M= 128 pages

t_{SM}= 10 ms

m_1= 2

Figure 13

M= 128 pages

t_{SM}= 5 ms

Figure 14

M= 128 pages

t_{SM}= 5 ms

m_1= 1

Figure 15

M= 128 pages

t_{SM}= 5 ms

m_1= 2

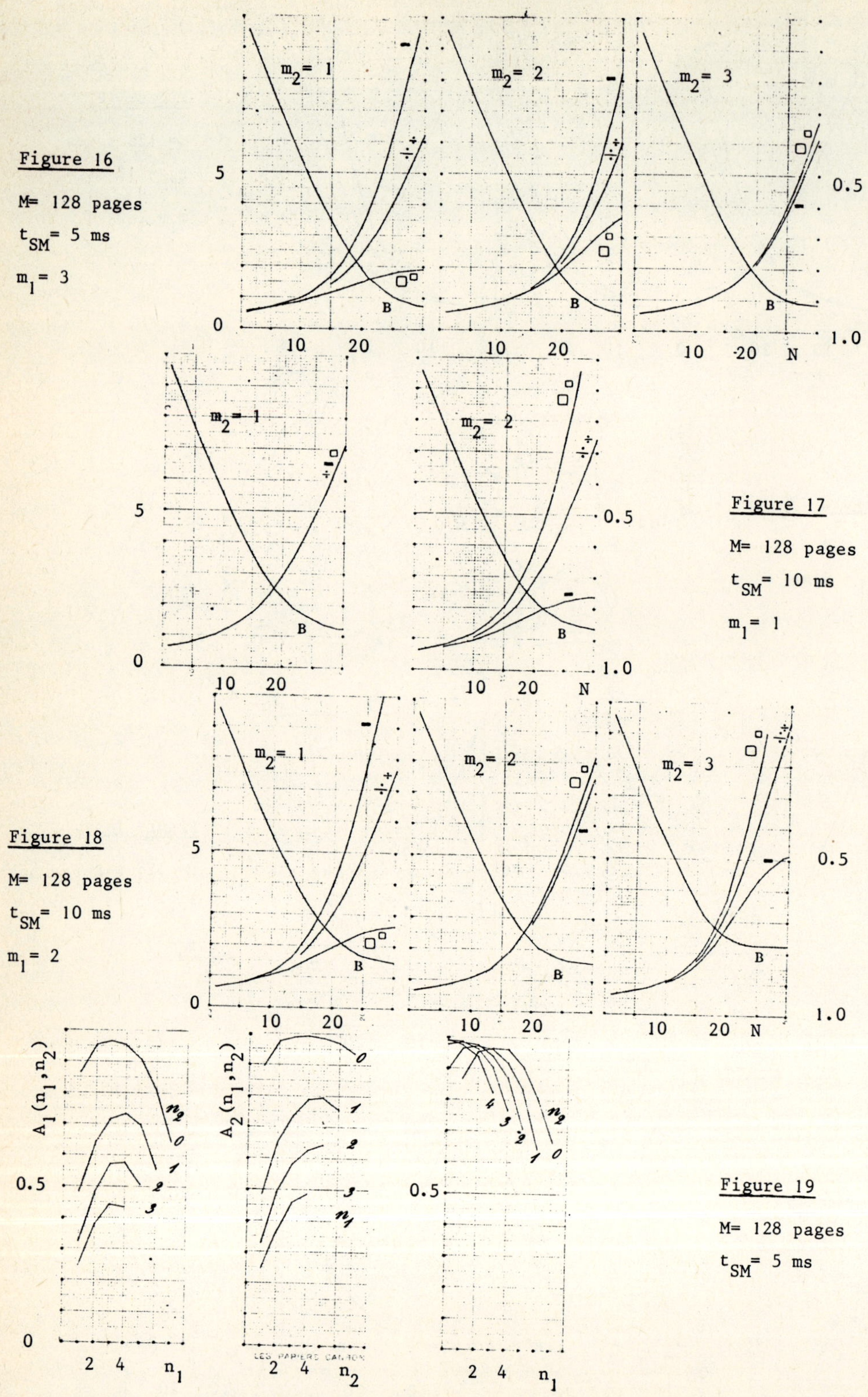

Figure 16

M= 128 pages

t_{SM}= 5 ms

m_1= 3

Figure 17

M= 128 pages

t_{SM}= 10 ms

m_1= 1

Figure 18

M= 128 pages

t_{SM}= 10 ms

m_1= 2

Figure 19

M= 128 pages

t_{SM}= 5 ms

n_1	1	1	1	1	1	1	2	2	2	2	2	3	3	3	3
n_2	1	2	3	4	5	6	1	2	3	4	5	1	2	3	4
np_1	78	53	41	32	27	24	46	37	30	26	22	34	28	24	21
np_2	50	37	29	24	20	17	33	27	22	19	17	25	20	18	16
q_1	25.1	17.5	12.7	8.9	6.7	5.5	14.8	11.0	8.0	6.3	4.7	9.7	7.2	5.5	4.4
q_2	25.0	17.7	12.6	9.4	6.9	5.2	15.2	11.3	8.1	6.3	5.2	10.0	6.9	5.7	4.6

n_{pi} : number of memory pages allocated to a class i process, i=1,2 .

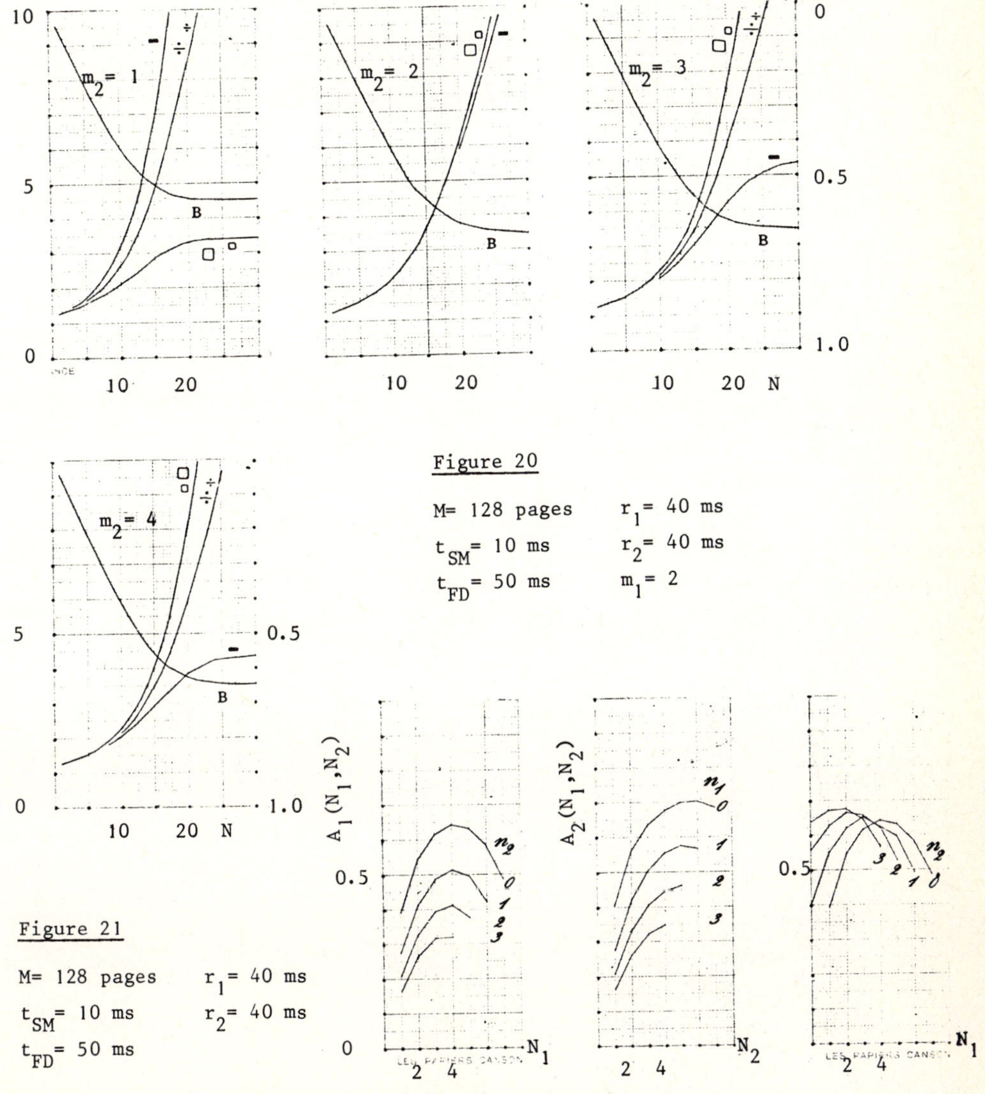

Figure 20

M= 128 pages r_1= 40 ms

t_{SM}= 10 ms r_2= 40 ms

t_{FD}= 50 ms m_1= 2

Figure 21

M= 128 pages r_1= 40 ms

t_{SM}= 10 ms r_2= 40 ms

t_{FD}= 50 ms

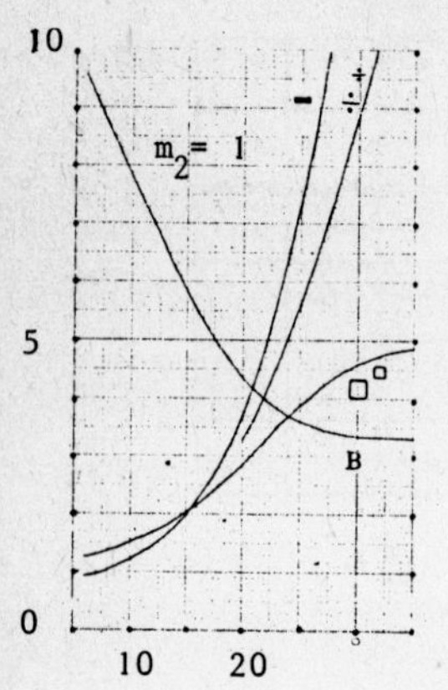

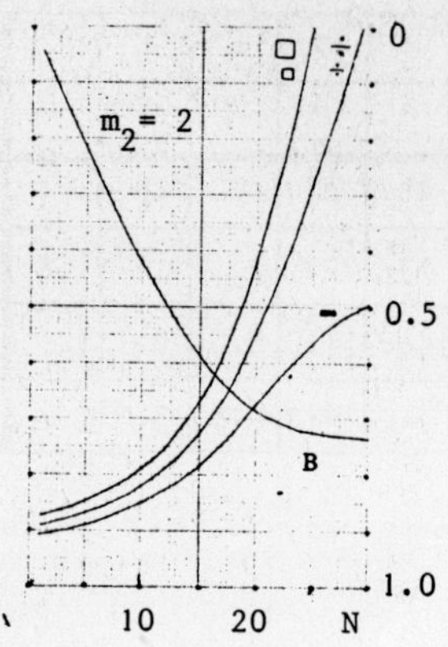

Figure 22

M= 128 pages

t_{SM}= 10 ms

t_{FD}= 50 ms

r_1= 40 ms

r_2= 80 ms

m_1= 2

Figure 23

M= 128 pages

t_{SM}= 10 ms

t_{FD}= 50 ms

r_1= 40 ms

r_2= 80 ms

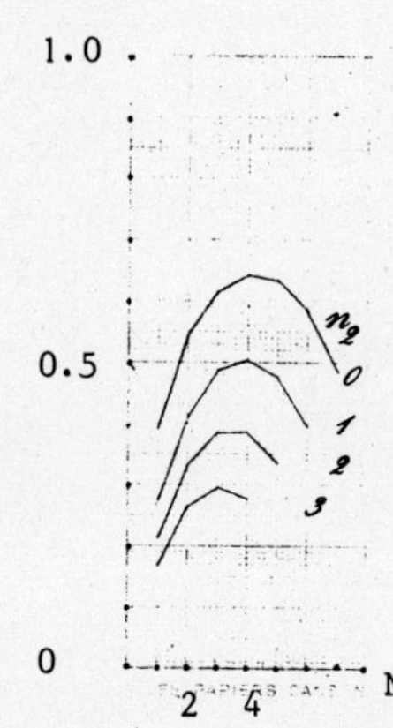

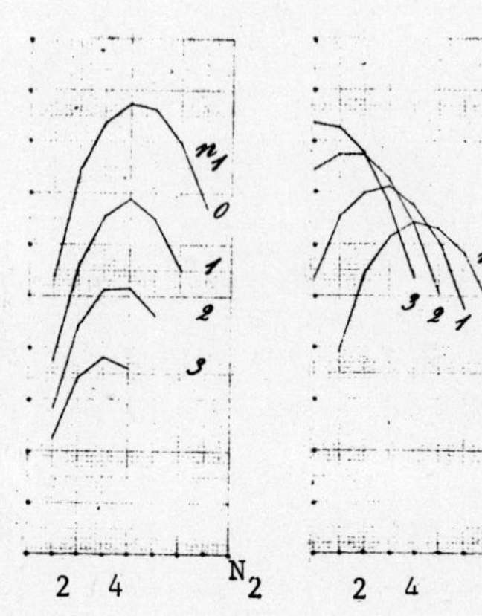

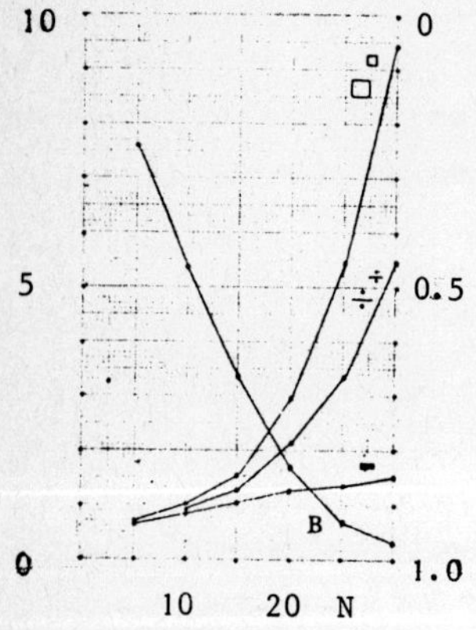

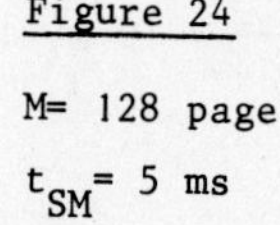

Figure 24

M= 128 pages

t_{SM}= 5 ms

ZUR OPTIMALEN STEUERUNG DES MULTIPROGRAMMINGGRADES IN RECHNERSYSTEMEN MIT VIRTUELLEM SPEICHER UND PAGING

Paul Kühn
Institut für Nachrichtenvermittlung und Datenverarbeitung
Universität Stuttgart

1. PROBLEMSTELLUNG

Heutige Großrechnersysteme für den technisch-wissenschaftlichen wie auch für den kommerziellen Einsatz sind durch den Aufbau einer Speicherhierarchie gekennzeichnet. Hierbei werden in der untersten Ebene schnelle, in ihrer Kapazität jedoch begrenzte Speichermedien eingesetzt, welche an die Verarbeitungsgeschwindigkeit schneller Prozessoren angepaßt sind. Massendaten werden dagegen in darüberliegenden Ebenen aus Speichern größerer Kapazität, aber geringerer Zugriffsgeschwindigkeit gehalten. Diese Konfiguration verbindet kleine Zugriffszeiten mit großer Speicherkapazität in wirtschaftlicher Weise, hat aber andererseits einen umfangreichen Datenaustausch zwischen verschiedenen Ebenen der Speicherhierarchie zur Folge, welcher u.U. zu Engpässen führen kann.

Durch die Virtualisierung des Speichers wird jedem Benutzerprogramm ein zusammenhängender Adressraum zur Verfügung gestellt, welcher i.a.wesentlich größer ist als der reale Adressraum des Arbeitsspeichers. Zum Ablauf der einzelnen Programme müssen daher nacheinander Teile der Programme in den Arbeitsspeicher geladen werden. Dies erfolgt i.a. nach dem sog. Paging-Verfahren, bei welchem der Datenaustausch nur in Blöcken gleicher Größe erfolgt; hierzu wird der virtuelle Adressraum in Seiten (pages) und dementsprechend auch der Arbeitsspeicher in Rahmen (page frames) unterteilt, wobei ein Seitenrahmen genau eine Seite aufnehmen kann. Um einen sinnvollen Ablauf der Programme zu gewährleisten, sollte stets eine arbeitsfähige Menge von Seiten eines Programmes im Arbeitsspeicher verfügbar sein. Bei Auftreten einer Seitenreferenz bezüglich einer momentan nicht im Arbeitsspeicher befindlichen Seite (page fault) erfolgt eine Unterbrechung, und der Ablauf des unterbrochenen Programmes kann frühestens erst dann fortgesetzt werden, wenn die fällige Seitennachladung erfolgt ist.

Um die Verarbeitungsgeschwindigkeit schneller Prozessoren besser auszunutzen, wird das Prinzip der Parallelarbeit von Prozessoren und Kanälen angewendet. Es werden hierbei mehrere Programme in den Arbeitsspeicher geladen. Infolge beschränkter Speicherkapazität ist es i.a. erforderlich, diese Programme nur teilweise zu laden. Auf diese Weise kann sich der Prozessor nach dem Auftreten einer Programmunterbrechung infolge eines page faults der Ausführung eines anderen (ablaufbereiten) Programmes widmen, während parallel dazu die Seitennachladung des soeben unterbrochenen Programmes ausgeführt wird (Multiprogramming).

Das Ablaufgeschehen innerhalb von Rechnersystemen mit virtuellem Speicherprinzip hängt u.a. von folgenden Einflußgrößen ab [1,2,3]:

1. Parameter der Rechnerstruktur
   - Arbeitsspeicher-Größe
   - Verarbeitungsgeschwindigkeit von Prozessoren
   - Zugriffszeiten zu Speichern
2. Betriebssystem-Strategien
   - Multiprogramminggrad
   - Speicherplatzverwaltung
   - Seitenholstrategie
   - Seitenersetzungsstrategie
3. Programmeigenschaften
   - Größe der Programme (Seitenzahl)
   - Ausführungsdauer der Programme (Prozessorzeit)
   - Lokalitätseigenschaften der Seitenreferenzen.

Um einen möglichst großen Durchsatz des Systems zu erzielen, müssen die Betriebsmittel des Rechnersystems ausgewogen dimensioniert und verwaltet werden. Insbesondere ist durch die Betriebsmittel-Verwaltung der Effekt des "Seitenflatterns" (thrashing) zu vermeiden, bei welchem der Prozessor infolge uneffektiv laufender Programme entweder unterbeschäftigt ist oder, durch häufige Unterbrechungen bedingt, nützliche Rechenkapazität für Systemprogrammzeiten verbraucht (system overhead).

Ziel der Untersuchungen ist es, Bedingungen für eine Durchsatz-optimale Steuerung des Multiprogramminggrades anzugeben, wobei die wesentlichsten Einflußgrößen berücksichtigt werden. Dies erfolgt anhand einer exakten Analyse eines geschlossenen Warteschlangenmodells, in welches neben realistischen "Bedienungszeiten" wesentliche Merkmale realer Programme und Betriebssysteme einbezogen werden. Als Ergebnisse werden gewonnen:

- Auslastungen des Prozessors durch Benutzer- bzw. Systemprogramme
- Durchsatz
- Auslastungen von Kanälen
- Mittlere Warteschlangenlängen und mittlere Wartezeiten
- Mittlere Durchlaufzeiten der Programme.

Insbesondere wird aus den Ergebnissen dieser Untersuchung der Zusammenhang zwischen Systemauslastung und Multiprogramminggrad für Programmtypen mit sehr unterschiedlichem Lokalitätsverhalten deutlich.

2. VORAUSSETZUNGEN UND MODELLIERUNG

2.1 Rechnerstruktur

Die Grundkonfiguration des Rechnersystems umfaßt einen Rechnerkern CPU (central processing unit) und eine zweistufige Speicherhierarchie bestehend aus einem Arbeitsspeicher ASP und einem Hintergrundspeicher HSP, vergl. Bild 1.

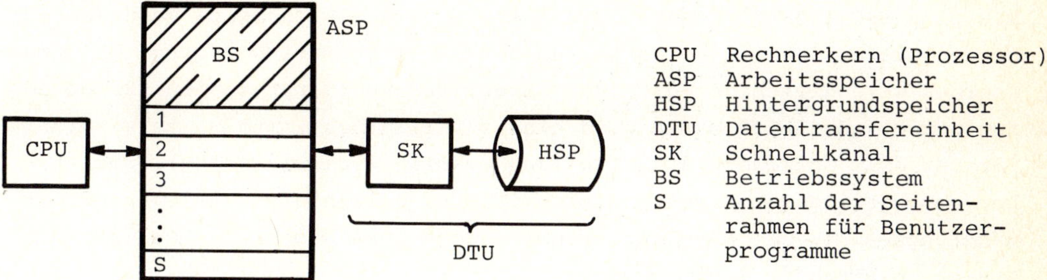

Bild 1. Systemkonfiguration eines Rechnersystems mit zweistufiger Speicherhierarchie

Der Arbeitsspeicher enthält neben den residenten Systemprogrammteilen des Betriebssystems S gleichgroße Seitenrahmen für Benutzerprogramme. Der Hintergrundspeicher HSP (Trommel, Platte) ist über einen Schnellkanal SK mit dem Arbeitsspeicher verbunden. Schnellkanal und Hintergrundspeicher werden im folgenden zur DTU (data transfer unit) zusammengefaßt. Der Ein-/Ausgabeverkehr erfolge über einen E/A-Prozessor und wird im folgenden nicht weiter betrachtet. Es wird davon ausgegangen, daß alle Benutzerprogramme vor und nach ihrer Bearbeitung auf dem Hintergrundspeicher stehen.

2.2 Betriebssystem-Strategien

a) Multiprogramminggrad

Es wird bei den Untersuchungen von einem beliebigen, doch jeweils konstanten Multiprogramminggrad M ausgegangen.

b) Speicherplatzverwaltung (memory management policy)

Die Platzaufteilung des Arbeitsspeichers unter die am Multiprogramming beteiligten Programme sei fest (fixed partitioning), d.h. jedes aktivierte Programm erhält einen festen Teil des Arbeitsspeichers für sich. Darüberhinaus wird vereinfachend angenommen, daß alle Programme denselben ASP-Anteil S/M erhalten (balanced partitioning).

c) Seitenholstrategie (page fetch strategy)

Als Seitenholstrategie wird demand paging vorausgesetzt, d.h. es wird eine Seitennachladung nur nach dem Auftreten eines page faults initiiert.

d) Seitenersetzungsstrategie (page replacement strategy)

Die Seitenersetzungsstrategie bestimmt diejenige Seite, welche bei Seitennachladung aus dem ASP verdrängt wird, falls kein freier Seitenrahmen verfügbar ist. Es werden nur lokal wirkende Strategien zugrundegelegt, welche sich nur auf Seiten des betreffenden Programmes beziehen. Ferner wird vorausgesetzt, daß für die Untersuchungen nur Ersetzungsstrategien für feste Speicherplatzaufteilung zugelassen werden sollen wie z.B. LRU (least recently used: es wird diejenige Seite verdrängt, deren letzter Zugriff am weitesten zurück liegt), FIFO (first-in, first-out: es wird diejenige Seite verdrängt, welche zuerst in den ASP geladen wurde) oder RANDOM (es wird eine zufällig bestimmte Seite verdrängt). Für variable Speicherplatzaufteilung (variable partitioning), wie etwa bei dem Working Set-Ersetzungsalgorithmus, gelten die Überlegungen nur näherungsweise. Die Näherung stimmt jedoch umso besser, je weniger die Speicherplatzaufteilung schwankt.

2.3 Programmeigenschaften

a) Größe der Programme

Benutzerprogramme haben i.a. eine beliebige Anzahl L von Seiten. Vereinfachend wird jedoch angenommen, daß alle am Multiprogramming beteiligten Programme gleich groß sind (konstante Programmgröße).

b) Ausführungsdauern

Die Gesamt-Ausführungsdauern der Programme durch die CPU, d.h. alle CPU-Rechenphasen der Programme jeweils zusammengenommen, seien hyperexponentiell verteilt. Die Verteilungsfunktion (VF) ist festlegbar durch den Mittelwert der CPU-Gesamt-Ausführungsdauer h_{GR} und den Variationskoeffizienten c_{GR}. Diese Voraussetzung bedeutet allerdings keine wesentliche Einschränkung, da die VF der CPU-Gesamt-Ausführungsdauern wegen des konstant angenommenen Multiprogramminggrades und der in 2.3.c angenommenen gleichen Lokalitätseigenschaften der Programme praktisch keinen Einfluß auf den Durchsatz hat.

Im Gegensatz dazu hat jedoch die VF der einzelnen Phasen für die CPU-Rechenzeit zwischen zwei page faults einen entscheidenden Einfluß. Sie wird, in Übereinstimmung mit Messungen an realen Systemen, ebenfalls hyperexponentiell angenommen mit Mittelwert h_{1R} und Variationskoeffizient c_{1R}. Die mittlere Ausführungsdauer der CPU bezüglich einer Seitenreferenz sei h_{1Ref}; sie setzt sich im wesentlichen aus Zugriffszeiten zum Arbeitsspeicher und Befehlsausführungsdauern zusammen.

Die mittlere Gesamt-Ausführungsdauer eines Programmes durch das System (mittlere Durchlaufzeit) t_F setzt sich aus den einzelnen CPU- und DTU-Phasen bzw. -Wartezeiten zusammen; sie ist eine Ergebnisgröße.

c) Lokalitätseigenschaften der Seitenreferenzen

Programme weisen eine mehr oder weniger stark ausgeprägte "Lokalität" bezüglich der zeitlichen Häufung ihrer Zugriffe zu einzelnen Seiten auf. Dieses Lokalitätsverhalten kann meßtechnisch ermittelt werden in Form spezieller Charakteristiken wie

- Working Set-Charakteristik [4]

  Relative Häufigkeit der Zugriffe auf Seiten außerhalb des momentanen Working Set in Abhängigkeit einer "Fensterbreite" τ. Der Working Set ist die Menge derjenigen Seiten, auf welche während der letzten τ Seitenreferenzen zugegriffen wurde.
- Fehlseiten-Charakteristik (page fault rate function) [1]

  Relative Häufigkeit f von page faults in Abhängigkeit des relativen Anteils x von ASP-Seiten eines Programmes bezogen auf dessen Gesamt-Programmgröße L sowie der Seitenersetzungsstrategie.

Für die Untersuchungen werden gemessene Fehlseiten-Charakteristiken zugrundegelegt, welche für verschiedene Programmtypen relativ gut bekannt sind. Bild 2 zeigt sechs Beispiele für verschiedene technisch-wissenschaftliche und kommerzielle Programmtypen [5,6]. Zur Untersuchung wird vereinfachend angenommen, daß alle Programme jeweils dieselbe Fehlseiten-Charakteristik besitzen.

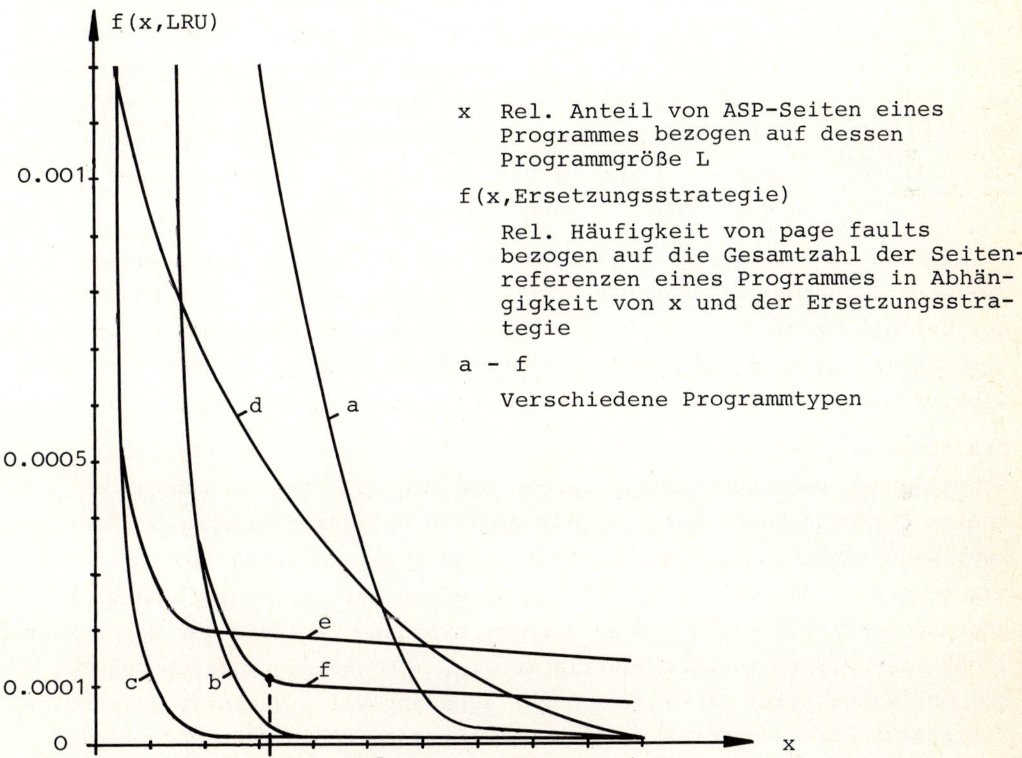

Bild 2. Fehlseiten-Charakteristiken verschiedener Programmtypen

2.4 Warteschlangenmodell

Die analytische Beschreibung des Ablaufgeschehens erfolgt mit Hilfe eines geschlossenen Warteschlangenmodells [3], vergl. Bild 3.

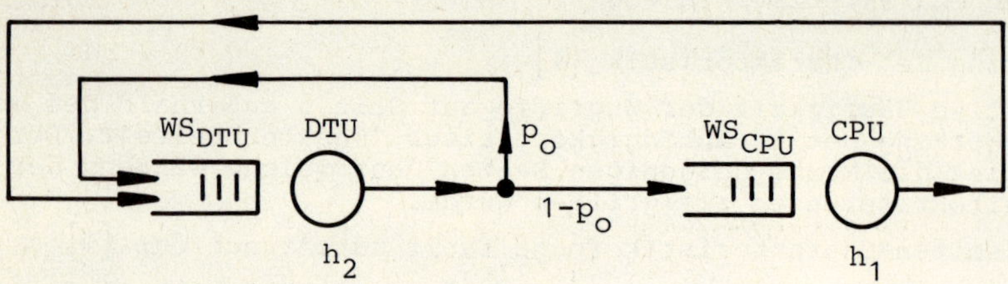

Bild 3. Geschlossenes Warteschlangenmodell

Das Warteschlangenmodell nach Bild 3 besitzt zwei Bedienungseinheiten CPU und DTU, welche die Ausführungsdauern eines laufenden Programmes bis zum nächsten page fault bzw. die Belegungsdauern je Seitennachladung charakterisieren. Die Warteschlangen WS_{CPU} bzw. WS_{DTU} enthalten Anforderungen ablaufbereiter Programme an die CPU bzw. Anforderungen unterbrochener Programme an die DTU zwecks Seitennachladung. Die Verzweigung nach der DTU mit Wahrscheinlichkeit p_o charakterisiert das Bearbeitungsende eines Programmes. In dem geschlossenen Modell, in welchem eine konstante Anzahl M von Anforderungen zirkuliert entsprechend einem konstanten Multiprogramminggrad M, charakterisiert die mit p_o abgezweigte Rückkopplung nach der DTU, daß nach dem Bearbeitungsende eines Programmes momentan ein neues Programm aktiviert wird.

Die Bearbeitungsfolge eines Programmes kann mit den in Bild 4 dargestellten Programmzuständen beschrieben werden. In Bild 4 ist bereits der Zustand berücksichtigt worden, in welchem nach Auftreten einer Unterbrechung infolge page faults die CPU durch Systemprogramme für eine bestimmte Systemverwaltungszeit (system overhead) belegt ist.

Das Ablaufgeschehen wird nicht unwesentlich durch die statistisch schwankenden Bedienungszeiten in CPU und DTU bestimmt. Messungen an realen Systemen haben gezeigt, daß die CPU-Belegungszeiten zwischen zwei page faults (Benutzerprogramme) zu hyperexponentiellem Charakter neigen. Demgegenüber sind Zugriffszeiten auf rotierende Speicher hypoexponentieller Natur. Bild 5 zeigt typische Verläufe der Wahrscheinlichkeits-VF für die Zufallsvariablen T_{H1} (CPU-Belegungszeit) und T_{H2} (DTU-Belegungszeit) im Vergleich zur exponentiellen Verteilungsfunktion. Die starke Streuung der CPU-Belegungszeiten zwischen zwei page faults rührt von dem Lokalitätsverhalten der Programme her: es treten bevorzugt sehr kurze Zeiten (bei Lokalitätswechsel) und sehr lange Zeiten (Verweildauer innerhalb einer Lokalität) auf. Die schwache Streuung der DTU-Belegungszeiten hat ihre Ursachen in einer konstanten Übertragungszeit pro Seite und einer nahezu linearen Speicherzugriffszeit (Positionierzeit bei rotierenden Speichern); die VF wird ferner beeinflußt durch Strategien, welche die Reihenfolge der Abfertigung wartender DTU-Anforderungen entsprechend der momentanen Position der Leseköpfe verändern.

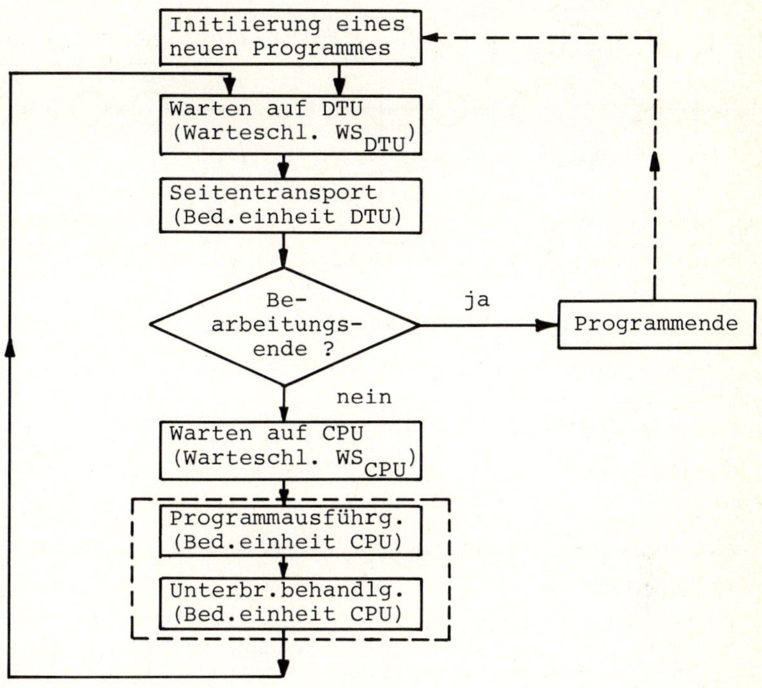

Bild 4. Zustandsfolge eines Programmes entsprechend Bild 3

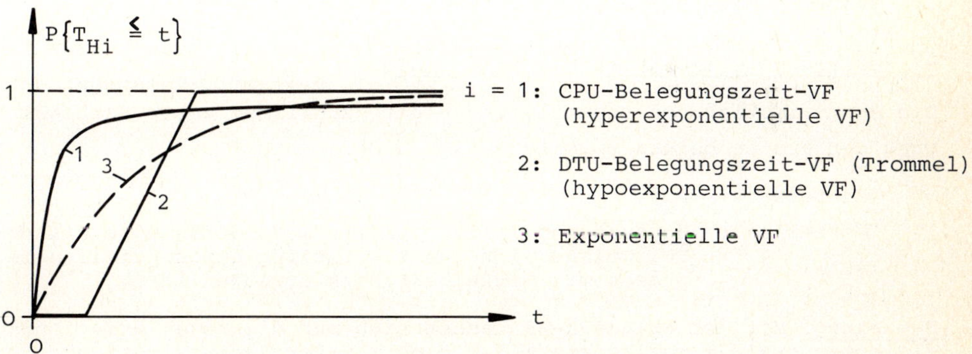

Bild 5. Belegungszeit-Verteilungsfunktionen für CPU und DTU

Zur analytischen Untersuchung werden Bedienungszeit-VF zugrundegelegt, welche in den ersten beiden Momenten (Mittelwert und Varianz) realistisch sind. Um das Warteschlangenmodell noch analytisch exakt analysieren zu können, werden die durch zwei Momente festgelegten Charakteristiken durch Zusammenschaltung aus fiktiven exponentiellen Teilphasen wie folgt erzeugt, vergl. Bild 6:

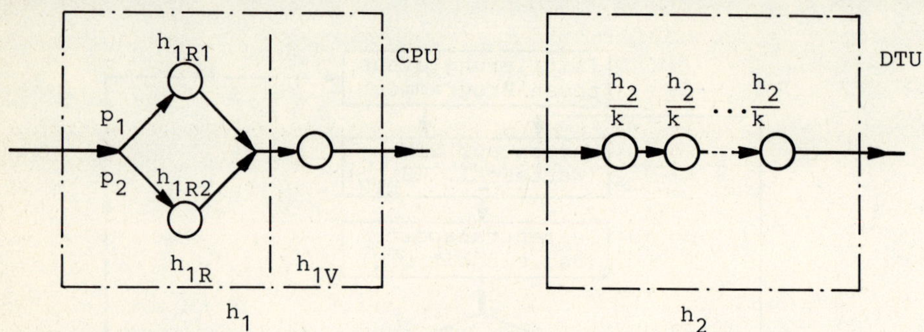

Bild 6. Ersatz-Darstellungen der Bedienungszeit-Charakteristiken für CPU und DTU

a) Bedienungszeit-Charakteristik der CPU

Jede CPU-Bedienungsphase (Mittelwert h_1) setzt sich aus zwei Teilen zusammen:

1. CPU-Bedienung für Benutzerprogramm-Bearbeitung
   Mittelwert: h_{1R}
   Verteilung: Hyperexponentiell; repräsentiert durch 2 alternative exponentielle Teilphasen mit Mittelwerten h_{1R1}, h_{1R2} und Alternativwahrscheinlichkeiten $p_1, p_2=1-p_1$ entspr. vorgegebenem Variationskoeffizienten c_{1R}.
2. CPU-Bedienung für Unterbrechungsbehandlung (Systemprogramme)
   Mittelwert: h_{1V}
   Verteilung: Exponentiell.

b) Bedienungszeit-Charakteristik der DTU

Die Approximation von Trommel- und Plattenzugriffen unter Berücksichtigung der ersten beiden Momente ergibt [10]:

Mittelwert: h_2
Verteilung: Hypoexponentiell, repräsentiert durch eine Erlang-k-VF, welche sich aus k seriellen exponentiellen Teilphasen mit Mittelwert h_2/k erzeugen läßt.

Bemerkung: Mit der Erlang-k-VF lassen sich nur diskrete Variationskoeffizienten $c_2=1/\sqrt{k}$ realisieren; ist eine genauere Approximation erforderlich, so kann mit einer seriellen Anordnung aus Erlang-k-VF und einer weiteren exponentiellen VF jeder beliebige Variationskoeffizient $1/\sqrt{k} \geq c_2 \geq 1/\sqrt{k+1}$ eingestellt werden, k = 1,2,...

3. MODELLANALYSE

Die Analyse des Warteschlangenmodells nach 2.4 erfolgt im Zusammenhang mit den übrigen Voraussetzungen über Betriebssystem-Strategien (2.2) und Programmeigenschaften (2.3).

3.1 Parameterfestlegung

In dem Warteschlangenmodell nach Bild 3 und Bild 6 sind folgende Parameter festzulegen:

M	Multiprogramminggrad
h_{1R}	Mittelwert der CPU-Benutzerprogramm-Bearbeitungsphasen
h_{1R1}, h_{1R2} p_1, p_2	Parameter der hyperexponentiellen Ersatz-Darstellung der CPU-Benutzerprogramm-Bearbeitungsphasen. Festlegung durch h_{1R} und den Variationskoeffizienten c_{1R}
h_{1V}	Mittelwert der CPU-Systemprogrammphasen
h_2	Mittelwert der DTU-Bedienung
k	Phasenzahl der Erlang-k-VF für DTU-Bedienungszeiten
p_o	Verzweigungswahrscheinlichkeit

Die Parameter werden wie folgt festgelegt:

a) Aus der Vorgabe von Multiprogramminggrad M, Arbeitsspeichergröße S, Programmgröße L sowie der Ersetzungsstrategie und dem Programmtyp folgt zunächst $x = S/(ML)$ und damit aus Bild 2 die Fehlseitenrate f.

b) Mit der weiteren Vorgabe der mittleren CPU-Gesamt-Ausführungsdauer h_{GR} lassen sich folgende Bilanzen aufstellen, wobei der Wert $1/p_o-1$ die aus Bild 3 folgende mittlere Anzahl von CPU-Bearbeitungsphasen eines Programmes darstellt:

$$h_{GR} = \left(\frac{1}{p_o} - 1 \right) \cdot h_{1R} \tag{1}$$

$$h_{1Ref} = f \cdot h_{1R} \quad , \tag{2}$$

woraus folgt

$$h_{1R} = \frac{h_{1Ref}}{f} \tag{3}$$

$$p_o = \frac{1}{1 + f \cdot \frac{h_{GR}}{h_{1Ref}}} \quad . \tag{4}$$

c) Aus h_{1R} nach (3) und c_{1R} aus bekannten Messungen folgen

$$h_{1R\,1,2} = \frac{h_{1R}}{1 \pm \sqrt{1-2/(1+c_{1R}^2)}} \tag{5}$$

$$p_{1,2} = \frac{h_{1R}}{2 \cdot h_{1R1,2}} \quad . \tag{6}$$

d) Die Parameter h_{1V} und h_2 sind durch das Rechnersystem selbst festgelegt. Für k wurden die Werte 3 (Trommel- bzw. Festkopfplattenzugriffe) bzw. 5 (Plattenzugriffe) ermittelt.

3.2 Analyse des Warteschlangenmodells

a) Bekannte Lösungen

Eine allgemeine Lösung für geschlossene Warteschlangennetze existiert nur im Falle exponentieller Bedienungsdauern [7]. Unter allgemeineren Voraussetzungen lassen sich i.a. nur Näherungslösungen ableiten [8]. Ein ähnliches Modell mit einer entartet negativ-exponentiellen CPU-Bedienungszeit-Charakteristik, exponentiell verteilten DTU-Bedienungszeiten und einer Durchsatz-optimalen CPU-Zuteilungsstrategie hat Walke [9] analysiert, wobei ebenfalls gemessene Fehlseiten-Charakteristiken zugrundegelegt wurden. Es werden dort Aussagen über den optimalen Multiprogramminggrad gemacht, welche hier prinzipiell bestätigt werden. Die Analyse in [9] macht in Erweiterung dazu noch Aussagen über den Einfluß streuender Programmgröße.

b) Analyse durch Phasenmethode

Da die Bedienungszeiten der CPU- und DTU-Stufe nach Bild 6 aus fiktiven exponentiellen Phasen zusammengesetzt wurden, kann eine exakte Analyse mit Hilfe eines geeignet definierten mehrdimensionalen Markoff-Prozesses erfolgen nach der sog. Phasenmethode [10,11]. Als Systemzustand wird definiert:

$$(x_1, x_{1P}, x_{2P})$$

wobei

x_1 = Anzahl der Anforderungen in CPU und WS_{CPU}, $x_1 = 0,1,\ldots,M$

x_{1P} = Phasenzustand der CPU-bedienten Anforderung, wobei

$$x_{1P} = \begin{cases} 1 & \text{Benutzerprogrammphase mit Mittelwert } h_{1R1} \\ 2 & \text{Benutzerprogrammphase mit Mittelwert } h_{1R2} \\ 3 & \text{Systemprogrammphase mit Mittelwert } h_{1V} \end{cases}$$

x_{2P} = Phasenzustand der DTU-bedienten Anforderung, $x_{2P} = 1,2,\ldots,k$.

Die Zustände $x_{1P} = 0$ bzw. $x_{2P} = 0$ bedeuten, daß die Bedienungseinheiten CPU bzw. DTU nicht belegt sind.

Das Zustandsgleichungssystem wird mit Hilfe eines iterativen Verfahrens (sukzessive Überrelaxation) aufgelöst. Aus den Zustandswahrscheinlichkeiten werden u.a. folgende Kenngrößen gewonnen:

$Y_{CPU,R}$	Auslastung der CPU durch Benutzerprogramme
$Y_{CPU,V}$	Auslastung der CPU durch Systemprogramme
D	Durchsatz (Anzahl fertig bearbeiteter Programme je Zeiteinh.)
Y_{DTU}	Auslastung der DTU
Ω_{CPU}	Mittlere Warteschlangenlänge von bearbeitbaren Programmen
Ω_{DTU}	Mittlere Warteschlangenlänge von Programmen, welche auf Seitennachladung warten
t_F	Mittlere Durchlaufzeit eines Programms.

4. ERGEBNISSE

4.1 Voraussetzungen zu den numerischen Ergebnissen

Das Warteschlangenmodell nach Bild 3 und Bild 6 wurde für die sechs verschiedenen Programmtypen nach Bild 2 untersucht, wobei gewählt wurde:

S	= 50	c_{1R}	= 2
L	= 50, 100	h_{1V}	= 10 msec
h_{GR}	= 100 sec	h_2	= 25 msec
h_{1Ref}	= 10 μsec	k	= 3 (Trommel)

4.2 Optimale CPU-Auslastung und mittlere Durchlaufzeiten

In Bild 7 bzw. Bild 8 sind die CPU-Auslastungen $Y_{CPU,R}$ in Abhängigkeit des Multiprogramminggrades M für die sechs Programmtypen nach Bild 2 unter den Annahmen L = S bzw. L = 2S aufgetragen. Man erkennt, daß die Programmtypen a und d, welche eine schlechte Lokalität besitzen oder deren Seiten durch Fixierung an den Arbeitsspeicher gebunden werden, für $M > 1$ nicht geeignet sind. Dagegen weisen die Typen b,c,e und f Eigenschaften auf, welche die Wahl eines Durchsatz-optimalen Multiprogramminggrades $M \geq 1$ nahelegen.

Wie z.B. für den Programmtyp f deutlich wird, existiert ein optimaler Multiprogramminggrad M = 3 bzw. M = 2; unterhalb dieser Werte sinkt die CPU-Auslastung infolge Unterbeschäftigung der CPU (DTU ist Engpaß),oberhalb davon sinkt die CPU-Auslastung infolge thrashing, welches einen stark ansteigenden Anteil der CPU-Auslastung infolge Systemverwaltungszeiten, $Y_{CPU,V}$, bedingt (vergl. Bild 7 und Bild 8).

Ein Vergleich der Bilder 7 und 8 mit Bild 2 hinsichtlich der Lage des Durchsatz-Optimums läßt folgenden Schluß zu, daß der optimale Multiprogramminggrad offenbar mit der Existenz und Lage eines ausgeprägten "Knickes" in der Fehlseiten-Charakteristik zusammenhängt ("Paracore"x_o). Der Kehrwert $1/x_o$ bestimmt den optimalen Multiprogramminggrad

$$M_{opt} \cong \frac{S}{L \cdot x_o} \quad . \qquad (7)$$

Diese Ergebnisse können dazu dienen, um mit Hilfe von dynamisch gemessenen Fehlseiten-Charakteristiken eine optimale Steuerung des Multiprogramming durchzuführen. Ferner können solche Untersuchungen dazu genutzt werden, neue Systeme richtig auszulegen bzw. Engpässe an bestehenden Systemen gezielt zu beseitigen wie bei Fragen der Arbeitsspeicher-Erweiterung oder der Kanal-Erweiterung.

In Bild 9 schließlich ist die mittlere Durchlaufzeit t_F eines Programmes in Abhängigkeit des Multiprogramminggrades M angegeben. Allgemein steigt t_F mindestens linear mit M; man bemerkt jedoch, daß die Zunahme von t_F umso geringer ist, je flacher das Maximum der CPU-Auslastung ausfällt.

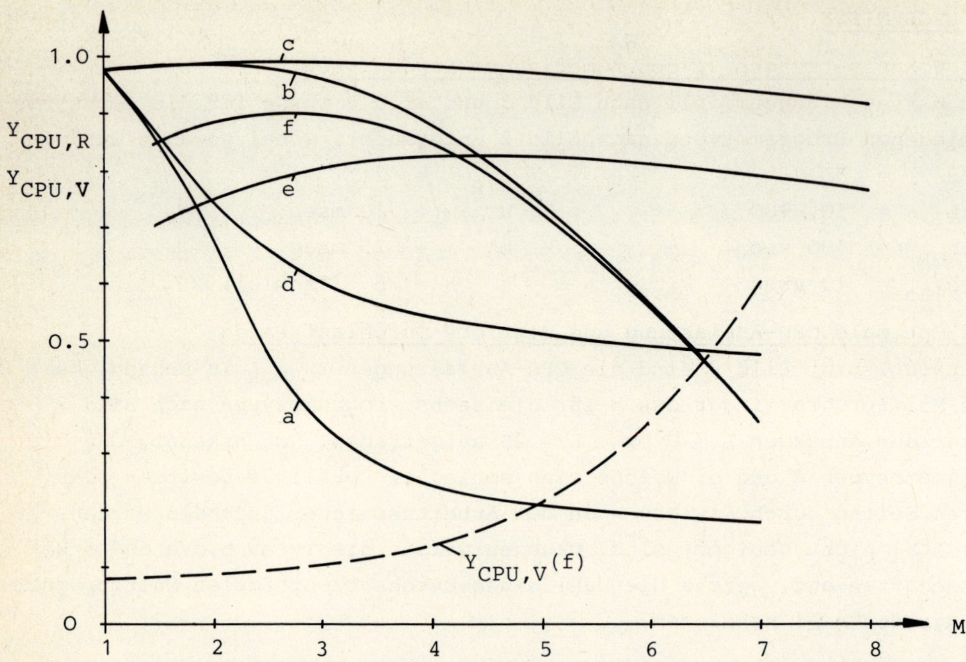

Bild 7. Auslastung der CPU in Abhängigkeit des Multiprogramminggrades
Parameter: L = S = 50.

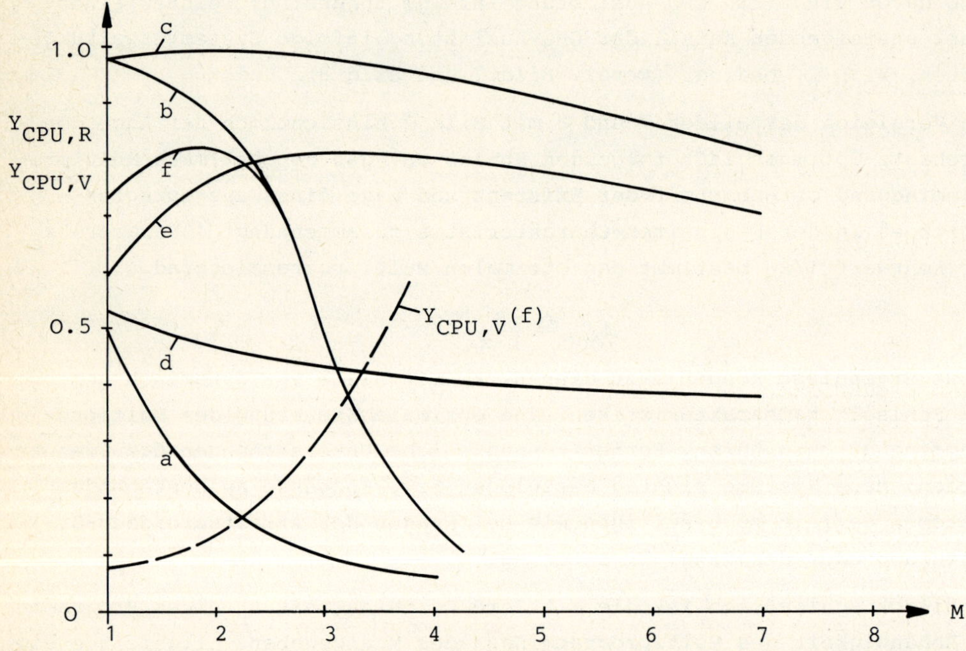

Bild 8. Auslastung der CPU in Abhängigkeit des Multiprogramminggrades
Parameter: L = 2S = 100.

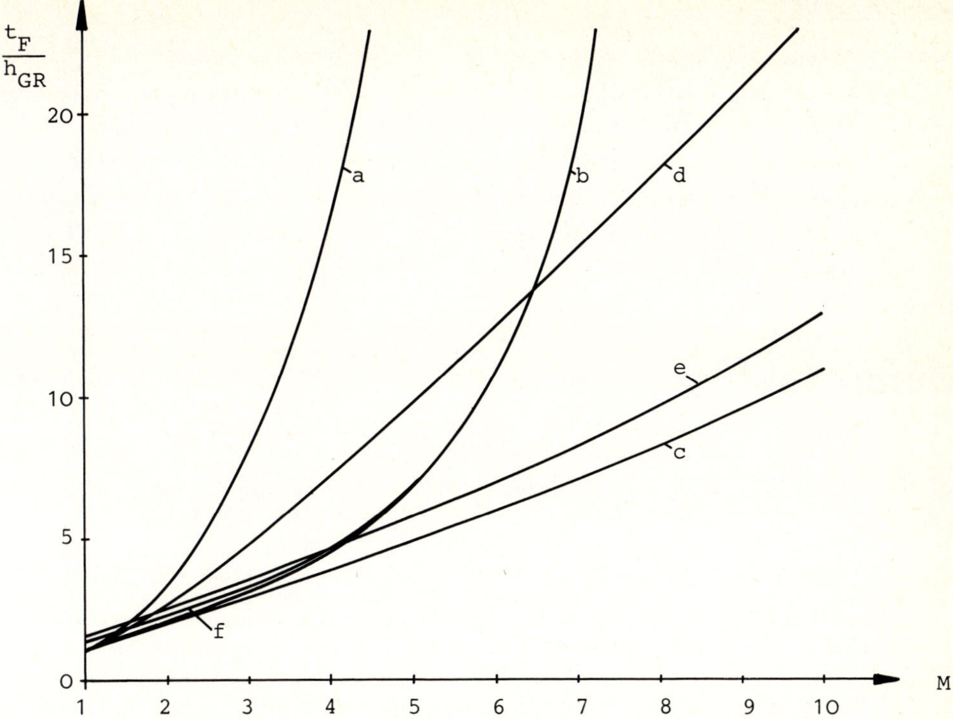

Bild 9. Bezogene mittlere Durchlaufzeit eines Programmes in Abhängigkeit des Multiprogramminggrades Parameter: L = S = 50.

5. ERWEITERUNGEN

Aufbauend auf diesen und früheren Untersuchungen [3] wurde eine Modellhierarchie entworfen, welche u.a. den Ein-/Ausgabeverkehr von größeren Datenmengen (file I/O) über eigene Kanäle berücksichtigt. Die Untersuchungen werden auf zwei Ebenen durchgeführt:

a) Simulation

Die Simulation erfolgt für wesentlich detailliertere Modelle unter Berücksichtigung von

- mehreren DTU für page I/O
- mehreren DTU für file I/O
- künstlich erzeugten Seitenreferenzketten
- ASP-Verwaltung für die Seiten der einzelnen Programme
- Seitenersetzungsstrategien (LRU, Working Set)
- Suspendierung ineffektiv laufender Programme
- konstantem sowie variablem Multiprogramminggrad
- Systemverwaltungszeiten.

b) Mathematische Analyse

Hierfür wurden komplexere Warteschlangenmodelle entworfen, welche nach einem approximativen Verfahren analysiert werden [11,12].

ZUSAMMENFASSUNG

In der vorliegenden Untersuchung wurde ein Warteschlangenmodell für Rechnersysteme mit zweistufiger Speicherhierarchie, virtuellem Speicherprinzip und Paging unter Einbeziehung realer Programmeigenschaften und Betriebssystem-Strategien exakt analysiert. Es wurde unter vereinfachenden Voraussetzungen gezeigt, daß der Durchsatz-optimale Multiprogramminggrad mit Hilfe solcher Untersuchungen bestimmt werden kann in Abhängigkeit von Lokalitätseigenschaft realer Benutzerprogramme und Systemparametern.

SCHRIFTTUMSVERZEICHNIS

[1] Coffman,E.G., Denning,P.J.: Operating Systems Theory. Prentice-Hall, Inc., Englewood Cliffs, New Jersey, 1973.

[2] Denning,P.J., Graham,G.S.: Multiprogrammed Memory Management. IEEE Proc. on Interactive Computer Systems (to appear).

[3] Herzog,U., Krämer,W., Kühn,P., Wizgall,M.: Analyse von Betriebssystem-Modellen für Rechnersysteme mit Multiprogramming und Paging. GI-NTG Fachtagung "Struktur und Betrieb von Rechensystemen", Braunschweig, 20.-22.3.1974. Lecture Notes in Computer Science, Springer-Verlag, Berlin/Heidelberg/New York 1974, S.266-288.

[4] Oliver,N., Chu,W.W., Opderbeck,H.: Measurement Data on the Working Set Replacement Algorithm and their Applications. Proc. Symp. on Computer-Communications Networks and Teletraffic, Brooklyn, 4.-6.4.1972. Polytechnic Press of the PIB, S.113-124.

[5] Hatfield, D.J.: Experiments on Page Size, Program Access Patterns, and Virtual Memory Performance. IBM J. Res. and Develop. 16 (1972), S. 58 - 66.

[6] Wolf,P.: Eine Methode zur Untersuchung von Programmen bezüglich eines Betriebssystems mit virtuellem Speicher - Anwendung zur Vorhersage des Programmverhaltens. GI-NTG Fachtagung "Struktur und Betrieb von Rechensystemen", Braunschweig, 20.-22.3.1974. Lecture Notes in Computer Science, Springer-Verlag, Berlin/Heidelberg/New York 1974, S. 289 - 300.

[7] Gordon,W.J., Newell,G.F.: Closed Queuing Systems with Exponential Servers. Opns. Res. 15 (1967), S. 254 - 265.

[8] Chandy,K.M., Herzog,U., Woo,L.: Approximate Analysis of General Queuing Networks. IBM J. Res. and Develop.19(1975), S. 43 - 49.

[9] Walke,B.: Durchsatzberechnung für Rechenanlagen bei wählbarer Aufteilung des Arbeitsspeichers unter mehrere Programme unterschiedlichen Platzbedarfs. Dissertation Univ. Stuttgart, 1975.

[10] Cox,D.R.: A Use of Complex Probabilities in the Theory of Stochastic Processes. Proc. Camb. Phil. Soc. 51(1955), S. 313 - 319.

[11] Ertelt,R., Kühn,P.: Analyse komplexer Warteschlangennetze für Rechnersysteme. Monographie Institut für Nachrichtenvermittlung und Datenverarbeitung, Univ. Stuttgart, 1975.

[12] Kühn,P.: Analysis of Complex Queuing Networks by Decomposition (Veröffentlichung in Vorbereitung).

EIN ZEITDISKRETES WARTESYSTEM MIT UNTERBRECHENDEN PRIORITAETEN

Bernd Meister

IBM Forschungslaboratorium Zürich
8803 Rüschlikon, Schweiz

1. Einführung

Ein besonders wichtiger Parameter bei der Betriebsmittelzuteilung ist die Verweilzeit einer Aufgabe in Bezug auf ein Betriebsmittel. Darunter ist die Zeit zu verstehen, die eine Aufgabe auf die Zuteilung eines angeforderten Betriebsmittels warten muss, zusammen mit der Bedienungszeit, also der Zeit, während der das Betriebsmittel von der Aufgabe belegt wird. Die Verweilzeiten werden in dieser Arbeit als zufällige Grössen aufgefasst, deren Momente bestimmt werden sollen.

Bei der Zuteilung von Betriebsmitteln in Rechnersystemen muss man häufig verschiedene Prioritätsklassen einführen. Insbesondere in Echtzeitsystemen sind diese Prioritäten oft unterbrechend, d.h. die Verarbeitung einer Aufgabe wird unterbrochen, wenn Aufgaben mit höherer Priorität eintreffen. Diese werden zuerst abgearbeitet, ehe die Verarbeitung der unterbrochenen Aufgabe wieder fortgesetzt wird ([1],[2]).

Warteschlangenmodelle spielen eine wesentliche Rolle beim Entwurf und der Analyse von Betriebsmittelzuteilungsalgorithmen. Die meisten derartigen Modelle setzen allerdings Poissonprozesse als Eingangsprozesse voraus. Obwohl diese Annahme bei vielen Anwendungen brauchbare Resultate liefert, so gibt es doch andere Systeme, deren Eingangsprozesse nicht durch Poissonprozesse approximiert werden können ([3] - [6]).

Wenn die Varianzen der Eingangsprozesse kleiner sind als die Mittelwerte, liefern Poissoneingangsprozesse zu pessimistische Resultate für die Verweilzeiten, falls die Varianzen grösser als die Mittelwerte sind, erhält man zu optimistische Ergebnisse. Der zweite Fall ist dabei meist der kritischere Fall.

Ein weiterer Nachteil der meisten Warteschlangenmodelle besteht darin, dass eine analytische Beschreibung des gesamten Eingangsprozesses, also etwa ein analytischer Ausdruck für die Zeit zwischen zwei Ankünften bekannt sein muss. Dadurch wird es sehr umständlich, aus Messungen des Eingangsprozesses gute Abschätzungen für die Verweilzeiten zu erhalten. Es ist ja im allgemeinen sehr viel leichter, einige

Momente einer Verteilung mit brauchbarer Genauigkeit zu messen, als die ganze Verteilung selbst zu bestimmen [5].

Daher wird im folgenden ein Warteschlangenmodell analysiert, wie es insbesondere bei der Modellierung von Echtzeitsystemen und Systemen mit Teilnehmerbetrieb Verwendung findet und das mit geringeren Voraussetzungen bezüglich der Eingangsprozesse auskommt. Das Modell ist ein zeitdiskretes Wartesystem mit N Prioritätsklassen und unterbrechenden Prioritäten. Es werden die ersten zwei Momente der Verweilzeit einer Aufgabe berechnet, wobei nur die ersten drei Momente der Bedienungszeiten und der Eingangsprozesse bekannt sein müssen.

2. Beschreibung des Modells

Wir betrachten N Klassen von Anforderungen (Aufgaben), die von einer gemeinsamen Bedienungsstation P (einem Prozessor) bedient werden (Abb. 1). Die Anforderungen der i-ten Klasse, $i = 1, \ldots, N$, deren Ankünfte durch einen zufälligen Prozess X_i beschrieben werden, warten in einer Warteschlange W_i auf ihre Bedienung. Die Warteräume werden als unbeschränkt vorausgesetzt. Den Anforderungen der Klasse i sei die Priorität i zugeordnet, wobei die Prioritäten mit aufsteigender Klassennummer abnehmen, die Klasse 1 hat also die höchste Priorität. Innerhalb einer Klasse werden die Anforderungen in der Reihenfolge ihrer Ankünfte bedient (first come-first served). Die Bedienungszeit für die Anforderungen aus der Klasse i sei durch eine nicht-negative, ganzzahlige Zufallsvariable S_i gegeben. Es wird also angenommen, dass alle Bedienungszeiten ganzzahlige Vielfache eines Zeitquantums sind, dessen Länge auf eins normiert ist.

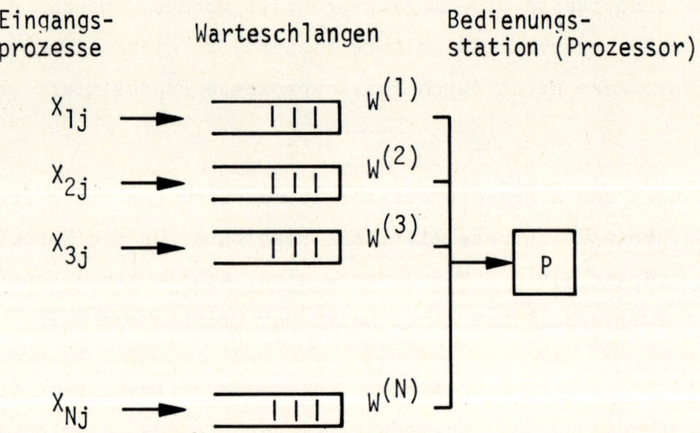

Abb. 1: Das Warteschlangenmodell.

Die Bedienung erfolgt jeweils zu den diskreten Zeiten $j = 1, 2, \ldots$, der Abstand zwischen zwei Bedienungszeitpunkten beträgt ebenfalls ein Zeitquantum. In jedem dieser Bedienungspunkte wird der Anforderung mit der momentan höchsten Priorität ein Zeitquantum (normiert auf die Länge 1) Bedienungszeit zur Verfügung gestellt, es wird also die Anforderung am Anfang der Warteschlange W_i mit $i = \min_j (W_j \neq \emptyset)$ bedient. Zum darauffolgenden Bedienungszeitpunkt wird die Anforderung mit der momentan höchsten Priorität gesucht und in der gleichen Weise behandelt. Die Bedienung der ersten Anforderung in W_i erfolgt also nur zu solchen Zeiten j, für die Warteschlangen $W_1, \ldots, W_{i-1}$ alle leer sind. Die Prioritäten sind unterbrechend, wenn während der Bedienung einer Anforderung A_i aus W_i in einer der Schlangen $W_1, \ldots, W_{i-1}$ Anforderungen eingetroffen sind, so werden diese erst in der Reihenfolge ihrer Prioritäten abgearbeitet, ehe die Verarbeitung von A_i fortgesetzt wird. Nur Anforderungen, die genau ein Zeitquantum Bedienungszeit benötigen, werden immer ohne Unterbrechung bedient.

Wenn $I_{j-0}(W_i)$ die gesamte für die Abarbeitung des momentanen Inhalts der Warteschlange W_i zum Zeitpunkt $j - 0$, also unmittelbar vor dem j-ten Bedienungszeitpunkt, benötigte Zeit darstellt, so gilt zum Zeitpunkt $j + 0$, also nach der Bedienung:

$$I_{j+0}(W_1) = \max \left[I_{j-0}(W_1) - 1,\ 0 \right] \tag{2.1}$$

und

$$I_{j+0}(W_i) = \max \left[I_{j-0}(W_i) - \chi_{I_{j-0}(W_1 + \ldots + W_{i-1}) = 0},\ 0 \right] \tag{2.2}$$

wobei $\chi_A = 1$ wenn das Ereignis A eintritt und $\chi_A = 0$ sonst.

Bezüglich der Eingangsprozesse und Bedienungszeiten treffen wir die folgenden Voraussetzungen:
Die $\mathfrak{X}_i$ sind unabhängige stationäre Prozesse mit unabhängigen Zuwächsen:

$$\mathfrak{X}_i = \left\{ X_{ij},\ 1 \leq i \leq N,\ 1 \leq j < \infty \right\} \quad , \tag{2.3}$$

dabei beschreibt X_{ij} die Anzahl der Anforderungen der Klasse i, die im Zeitintervall $[\,j - 1, j)$ im System eintreffen.

Die Wahrscheinlichkeiten

$$\Pr \left\{ X_{ij} = k \right\} = p_{ik} \tag{2.4}$$

sind unabhängig von j.

Die Bedienungszeiten S_i sind untereinander und von den $\mathfrak{X}_i$ unabhängige Zufallsvariable, die nur ganze nicht-negative Werte annehmen können und die bekannten Verteilungen

$$\Pr\left\{S_i = k\right\} = q_{ik} \quad , \tag{2.5}$$

$$1 \leq i \leq N, \quad 0 \leq k < \infty$$

besitzen.

Die zugehörigen erzeugenden Funktionen seien

$$P_i(z) = E(z^{X_{ij}}) = \sum_{k=0}^{\infty} p_{ik}\, z^k \tag{2.6}$$

und

$$Q_i(z) = E(z^{S_i}) = \sum_{k=0}^{\infty} q_{ik}\, z^k \quad . \tag{2.7}$$

Dabei bedeutet E den Erwartungswert.

Damit das System stabil ist und der Erwartungswert für die Verweilzeit einer beliebigen Anforderung endlich ist, muss noch vorausgesetzt werden:

$$\sum_{k=1}^{N} E(S_k)\, E(X_{kj}) < 1 \tag{2.8}$$

und

$$\mathrm{Var}\,(S_k) < \infty, \quad \mathrm{Var}\,(X_{kj}) < \infty, \quad 1 \leq k \leq N \quad . \tag{2.9}$$

Var bedeutet hier die Varianz.

Die Verweilzeiten haben genau dann endliche Varianzen, wenn zusätzlich gilt:

$$E\left[X_{kj} - E(X_{kj})\right]^3 < \infty \tag{2.10}$$

und

$$E\left[S_k - E(S_k)\right]^3 < \infty , \quad 1 \leq k \leq N \quad . \tag{2.11}$$

3. Lösungsmethode

Zur Berechnung der Verteilung der Verweilzeit einer Anforderung der Prioritätsklasse i betrachten wir das folgende äquivalente Ringsystem (Abb. 2). N Eingangsstationen $U^{(1)} \ldots U^{(N)}$ und eine Ausgangsstation 0 sind durch eine gemeinsame Ringleitung verbunden. An den Eingangsstationen, die mit einem unendlich grossen Speicher ausgerüstet sind, treffen Datenstapel ein, deren Ankünfte durch die Prozesse $\mathcal{X}_1, \ldots, \mathcal{X}_N$ beschrieben sind. Die Stapelgrössen, d.h., die Anzahl von Datenelementen pro

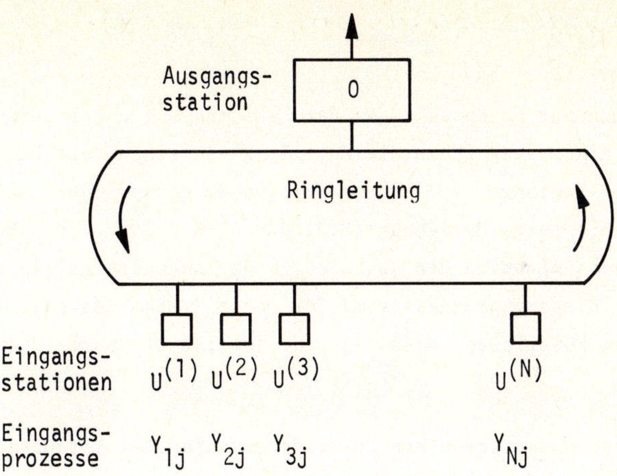

Abb. 2: Das äquivalente Ringsystem.

Stapel, werden durch die Zufallsvariablen S_i beschrieben. Unter einem Datenelement kann man hier eine beliebige Einheit verstehen wie etwa ein Wort fester Länge. Die Datenstapel warten in den Speichern der entsprechenden Einheiten auf die Uebertragung zur Ausgangsstation. Die Ringleitung überträgt pro Zeiteinheit (ebenfalls normiert auf die Länge 1) ein Datenelement zur Ausgangsstation. Diese Uebertragung erfolgt jeweils zu den Zeiten $j = 1, 2, \ldots$.

Sei $\tilde{W}_{ij}$ die Anzahl der Datenelemente, die zur Zeit $j - 0$ im Speicher von $U^{(i)}$ warten. Dann gelte für das Ringsystem:

$$\sum_{k=1}^{i} \tilde{W}_{kj} = \max\left(\sum_{k=1}^{i} \tilde{W}_{kj-1} - 1, 0\right) + \sum_{k=1}^{i} Y_{kj} \tag{3.1}$$

Y_{kj} sei der zufällige Prozess mit der zusammengesetzten erzeugenden Funktion

$$E\left(z^{Y_{kj}}\right) = R_k(z) = P_k\left[Q_k(z)\right] \quad . \tag{3.2}$$

Dann gilt der folgende Zusammenhang zwischen unserem Wartesystem und dem eben beschriebenen Ringsystem:

$$\sum_{k=1}^{i} \tilde{W}_{kj} = I_{j-0}\left(\sum_{k=1}^{i} W_k\right) \tag{3.3}$$

$$1 \leq i \leq N, \qquad 1 \leq j < \infty \qquad ,$$

falls die Anfangsinhalte beider Systeme gleich sind,

$$\tilde{W}_{k0} = I_0(W_k), \quad 1 \leq k \leq N \quad . \tag{3.4}$$

Zum Beweis muss man nur beachten, dass der Uebertragung eines Datenelements von der i-ten Station im Ringsystem genau die Zuteilung von einem Zeitquantum an die erste Anforderung in der Schlange W_i in unserem System entspricht. Bei gleichen Anfangswerten gilt dann die obige Beziehung (3.3) für alle Zeiten. Die Bedienung im Ringsystem muss übrigens nicht in der Reihenfolge der Ankünfte erfolgen, wenn nur (3.1) erfüllt ist. Die Eingangsprozesse sind für unser System und das Ringsystem gleich, da die erzeugenden Funktionen $R_k(z)$ gerade jeweils die Summe über S_k Datenelemente darstellen.

Aus [7] folgt, dass das untersuchte Wartesystem unter der Voraussetzung (2.8) einen stationären Zustand besitzt und die Verteilungen der Grössen

$$I_{j-0}\left(\sum_{k=1}^{i} W_k\right)$$

für $j \to \infty$ gegen Grenzverteilungen konvergieren, deren erzeugende Funktionen durch

$$H_i^*(z) = \left[1 - \sum_{k=1}^{i} E(Y_{kj})\right] \frac{(z-1)\prod_{k=1}^{i} R_k(z)}{z - \prod_{k=1}^{i} R_k(z)} \tag{3.5}$$

gegeben sind.

Wir kommen nun zur Bestimmung der Verteilungen von Verweilzeiten. Wir nehmen an, unser System befindet sich bereits im stationären Zustand und an der Warteschlange W_i trifft unmittelbar vor einem Bedienungszeitpunkt eine Testaufgabe oder Testanforderung ein, deren Verarbeitungszeit eine Zufallsvariable m ist mit der erzeugenden Funktion

$$E(z^m) = M(z) \quad . \tag{3.6}$$

In vielen praktischen Fällen wird man annehmen, dass m die gleiche Verteilung für die Verarbeitungszeit besitzt, wie die Anforderungen der i-ten Klasse. Wir wollen hier aber auch andere Fälle zulassen. m sei unabhängig von allen Eingangsprozessen $\mathcal{X}_i$ und Bedienungszeiten S_i. Die Zeit bis zur vollständigen Verarbeitung dieser virtuellen oder Testanforderung ist eine Zufallsvariable, die wir mit $d_i(m)$ bezeichnen und eine virtuelle Verweilzeit oder auch einfach eine Verweilzeit nennen.

Wir wollen jetzt die zugehörige erzeugende Funktion

$$E\left[z^{d_i(m)}\right] = D_{i,m}(z) \tag{3.7}$$

bestimmen.

Zunächst ist die erzeugende Funktion für die Gesamtverarbeitungszeit des Inhalts der ersten i Warteschlangen einschliesslich der Testanforderung gegeben durch:

$$H_i^*(z)\ M(z) \quad . \tag{3.8}$$

Nun treffen während der Verarbeitung der ersten i Warteschlangen an den Warteschlangen $W_1, \ldots, W_{i-1}$ Anforderungen mit höherer und unterbrechender Priorität ein. Damit ist die Zeit $d_i(m)$ gerade die Zeit, die benötigt wird um eine Aufgabe mit der Bedienungszeitverteilung $H_i^*(z)\ M(z)$ zu verarbeiten, wenn während dieser Verarbeitung noch Aufgaben entsprechend den Prozessen $\chi_1, \ldots, \chi_{i-1}$ mit den Verarbeitungszeiten $S_1, \ldots, S_{i-1}$ ankommen, die eine höhere Priorität besitzen. Ein analoges Problem wurde in [8] gelöst und ergibt für unseren Fall:

$$D_{i,m}(w) = H_i^*\left[\theta_i(w)\right] \quad M\left[\theta_i(w)\right] \tag{3.9}$$

$$i = 1, \ldots, N \quad ,$$

wobei die erzeugende Funktion $\theta_i(w)$ für $i > 1$ Lösung der Gleichung

$$\theta_i(w) = w \prod_{k=1}^{i-1} R_k\left[\theta_i(w)\right] \tag{3.10}$$

und $\theta_1(w) = w$ ist.

Bisher haben wir eine Testanforderung betrachtet, die unmittelbar vor einem Bedienungszeitpunkt eintrifft. Der andere Grenzfall ist das Eintreffen unmittelbar nach einem solchen Zeitpunkt und kann leicht aus den bisherigen Ergebnissen erhalten werden.

Wir bezeichnen analog zu vorher die Verweilzeit einer Testanforderung, die unmittelbar nach einem Bedienungszeitpunkt an der Schlange W_i eintrifft, mit $t_i(m)$.

Die zugehörige erzeugende Funktion sei

$$E\left[w^{t_i(m)}\right] = T_{i,m}(w) \quad . \tag{3.11}$$

Wir erhalten:

$$T_{i,m}(w) = D_{i,m}(w) \frac{w}{R_i\left[\theta_i(w)\right]} , \qquad (3.12)$$

da in diesem Fall die Testanforderung mindestens eine Zeiteinheit warten muss, ehe die Bearbeitung beginnt (Multiplikation mit w), aber Ankünfte nach der Testanforderung nicht mehr berücksichtigt werden dürfen $\left(\text{Division durch } R_i\left[\theta_i(w)\right]\right)$.

Es wird später gezeigt, dass $d_i(m)$ gerade den günstigsten Fall und $t_i(m)$ den ungünstigsten Fall darstellt. Aus beiden Grössen erhält man Schranken für den Erwartungswert der Verweilzeit einer Testanforderung, die zu einem beliebigen Zeitpunkt eintrifft.

Wenn wir die Verweilzeit einer Testanforderung, die zu einem beliebigen Zeitpunkt eintrifft, exakt ermitteln wollen, müssen zusätzliche Voraussetzungen über die Eingangsprozesse getroffen werden. Es genügt dann nicht mehr vorzuschreiben, wieviele Anforderungen während eines Zeitquantums eintreffen, sondern die Zeitpunkte der Ankünfte müssten auch vorgegeben werden. Da aber jede zusätzliche Voraussetzung die Anwendbarkeit des Modells einschränkt, haben wir hier darauf verzichtet. Für alle praktischen Anwendungen ist die Betrachtung der beiden von uns untersuchten Grenzfälle völlig ausreichend.

Im Prinzip kann man aus (3.9) und (3.12) die gesamte Verteilung der entsprechenden Verweilzeiten bestimmen, wenn die Funktionen $\theta_i(w)$ bekannt sind. Für einen zusammengesetzten Poissonprozess lassen sich die θ_i tatsächlich explizit angeben [9]. In [10] ist auch ein Algorithmus zur Bestimmung der Verteilung beschrieben.

Wir wollen im folgenden die ersten zwei Momente für die Verweilzeiten im günstigsten und im ungünstigsten Fall berechnen. Die dazu notwendigen Momente für die θ_i kann man direkt durch Differenzieren der Gleichung (3.10) gewinnen, so dass keine expliziten Ausdrücke für die θ_i bekannt sein müssen.

4. Momente der Verweilzeit

Wir werden jetzt explizite Ausdrücke für die ersten zwei Momente, also für den Erwartungswert und für die Varianz der Verweilzeiten angeben. Die entsprechenden Testanforderungen treffen an einer beliebigen Warteschlange W_i an und haben die Zufallsvariable m als Verarbeitungszeit. Wir werden die beiden definierten Grenzfälle betrachten, also eine Testanforderung, die umittelbar vor einem Bedienungszeitpunkt eintrifft mit der Verweilzeit $d_i(m)$ und eine unmittelbar nach einem Bedienungszeitpunkt eintreffende Testanforderung mit der Verweilzeit $t_i(m)$.

Im folgenden machen wir keinen Unterschied zwischen den Momenten einer Zufallsvariablen und den Momenten der zugehörigen erzeugenden Funktion, wir setzen z.B.

$$E\left[M(z)\right] = E(m) \quad .$$

Mit dieser Bezeichnungsweise erhalten wir

$$E\left[d_i(m)\right] = E\left(H_i^*\left[\theta_i(w)\right]\right) + E\left(M\left[\theta_i(w)\right]\right) \tag{4.1}$$

und

$$E\left[t_i(m)\right] = E\left[d_i(m)\right] + 1 - E\left(R_i\left[\theta_i(w)\right]\right) \quad . \tag{4.2}$$

Ebenso gilt

$$\mathrm{Var}\left[d_i(m)\right] = \mathrm{Var}\left(H_i^*\left[\theta_i(w)\right]\right) + \mathrm{Var}\left(M\left[\theta_i(w)\right]\right) \tag{4.3}$$

und

$$\mathrm{Var}\left[t_i(m)\right] = \mathrm{Var}\left[d_i(m)\right] - \mathrm{Var}\left(R_i\left[\theta_i(w)\right]\right) \quad . \tag{4.4}$$

Weiterhin gilt für eine zusammengesetzte erzeugende Funktion $F\left[G(w)\right]$:

$$E\left[F\left(G(w)\right)\right] = E(F)E(G) \tag{4.5}$$

und

$$\mathrm{Var}\left[F\left(G(w)\right)\right] = \mathrm{Var}\,(F)\left[E(G)\right]^2 + E(F)\,\mathrm{Var}\,(G) \tag{4.6}$$

und für die 3. zentrierten Momente

$$\left(\mu_3(X) = E\left[X - E(X)\right]^3\right) \quad :$$

$$\mu_3\left(F\left[G(w)\right]\right) = \mu_3(F)\left[E(G)\right]^3 + 3\,\mathrm{Var}\,(F)\,E(G)\,\mathrm{Var}\,(G) + E(F)\mu_3(G) \quad . \tag{4.7}$$

Damit erhalten wir aus (3.9) und (3.10):

Die Erwartungswerte der Verweilzeiten $d_i(m)$ und $t_i(m)$ sind gegeben durch:

$$E\left[d_i(m)\right] = \frac{1}{2}\,\frac{\dfrac{\sum_{k=1}^{i} \operatorname{Var}\left[R_k(z)\right]}{1 - \sum_{k=1}^{i} E\left[R_k(z)\right]} + \sum_{k=1}^{i} E\left[R_k(z)\right] + 2\,E(m)}{1 - \sum_{k=1}^{i-1} E\left[R_k(z)\right]} \tag{4.8}$$

und

$$E\left[t_i(m)\right] = E\left[d_i(m)\right] + \frac{1 - \sum_{k=1}^{i} E\left[R_k(z)\right]}{1 - \sum_{k=1}^{i-1} E\left[R_k(z)\right]} \tag{4.9}$$

mit

$$E\left[R_k(z)\right] = E(X_{kj})\,E(S_k) \tag{4.10}$$

und

$$\operatorname{Var}\left[R_k(z)\right] = \operatorname{Var}(X_{kj})\,\left[E(S_k)\right]^2 + E(X_{kj})\,\operatorname{Var}(S_k) \quad . \tag{4.11}$$

Für die Verweilzeit einer Anforderung, die zu einem beliebigen Zeitpunkt an der Warteschlange W_i eintrifft, $\delta_i(m)$, gilt:

$$E\left[d_i(m)\right] \leq E\left[\delta_i(m)\right] \leq E\left[t_i(m)\right] \quad , \tag{4.12a}$$

falls die Ankünfte über die Intervalle $[\,j-1,\,j)$ gleichverteilt sind. Im allgemeinsten Fall gilt:

$$E\left[t_i(m)\right] - 1 \leq E\left[\delta_i(m)\right] \leq E\left[d_i(m)\right] + 1 \quad . \tag{4.12b}$$

Für die zweiten Momente erhält man:

$$\operatorname{Var}\left[d_i(m)\right] = \left[\operatorname{Var}(H_i^*) + \operatorname{Var}(M)\right]\left[E(\theta_i)\right]^2 + \left[E(H_i^*) + E(M)\right]\operatorname{Var}(\theta_i) \tag{4.13}$$

mit

$$\mathrm{Var}\,(H_i^*) = \frac{\sum\limits_{k=1}^{i} \mu_3(R_k)}{3\left[1 - \sum\limits_{k=1}^{i} E(R_k)\right]} +$$

$$+ \frac{1}{4} \left[\frac{\sum\limits_{k=1}^{i} \mathrm{Var}\,(R_k)}{1 - \sum\limits_{k=1}^{i} E(R_k)} + 1 - \sum_{k=1}^{i} E(R_k) \right]^2$$

$$- \frac{1}{12} \left[2 \sum_{k=1}^{i} E(R_k) - 1\right] \left[2 \sum_{k=1}^{i} E(R_k) - 3\right] \tag{4.14}$$

$$\mu_3(R_k) = \mu_3(X_{kj}) \left[E(S_k)\right]^3 +$$

$$3\,\mathrm{Var}\,(X_{kj})\; E(S_k)\; \mathrm{Var}\,(S_k) + E(X_{kj})\, \mu_3(S_k) \tag{4.15}$$

$$E(H_i^*) = \frac{1}{2} \left[\frac{\sum\limits_{k=1}^{i} \mathrm{Var}\,(R_k)}{1 - \sum\limits_{k=1}^{i} E(R_k)} + \sum_{k=1}^{i} E(R_k) \right] \tag{4.16}$$

$$E(\theta_i) = \frac{1}{1 - \sum\limits_{k=1}^{i-1} E(R_k)} \tag{4.17}$$

und

$$\mathrm{Var}\,(\theta_i) = \frac{\sum\limits_{k=1}^{i-1} \mathrm{Var}\,(R_k)}{\left[1 - \sum\limits_{k=1}^{i-1} E(R_k)\right]^3} . \tag{4.18}$$

Die Varianz von $t_i(m)$ ergibt sich aus (4.4) mit

$$\mathrm{Var}\left[R_i(\theta_i)\right] = \mathrm{Var}\,(R_i)\left[E(\theta_i)\right]^2 + E(R_i)\,\mathrm{Var}\,(\theta_i) \quad . \tag{4.19}$$

Aus (4.4) sieht man, dass die Varianz der Verweilzeit im ungünstigsten Fall $t_i(m)$ kleiner ist als die Varianz von $d_i(m)$. Es wird daher immer zweckmässig sein, die Momente für beide der betrachteten Grenzfälle zu berechnen.

5. Literatur

[1] E. G. COFFMANN und P. J. DENNING, *Operating Systems Theory*, Prentice-Hall, Englewood Cliffs, N.J., 1973.

[2] U. HERZOG, Preemption - distance priorities in real time computer systems, *Nachrichtentechn. Z.* Jahrg. 25 (1972), 201-203.

[3] F. BASKETT, *Mathematical Models of Multiprogrammed Computer Systems*, Ph.D. Thesis, Computation Center, University of Texas at Austin, January 1971.

[4] K. KUEMMERLE, A model for the I/O-channel traffic in computer systems, *Nachrichtentechn. Z.* Jahrg. 25 (1972), 137-141.

[5] C. M. HARRIS, Some New Results in the Statistical Analysis of Queues, Mathematical Methods in Queueing Theory, Proceedings of a Conference at Western Michigan University, Lecture Notes in Economics and Mathematics, Springer-Verlag, Berlin-Heidelberg-New York, 1973.

[6] A. L. DUDICK, E. FUCHS und P. E. JACKSON, Data Traffic Measurements for Inquiry-Response Computer Communication Systems, Proceedings of the IFIP Congress, Ljubljana, 1971, TA-4-79-83.

[7] A. G. KONHEIM und B. MEISTER, Service in a loop system, *J. Assoc. Comput. Mach.* 19 (1972), 92-108.

[8] A. G. KONHEIM und B. MEISTER, Waiting lines and times in a system with polling, *J. Assoc. Comput. Mach.* 21 (1974), 470-490.

[9] A. G. KONHEIM, Service Epochs in a Loop System, 22nd Intern. Symp. on Computer Communication Networks and Teletraffic, Polytechn. Inst. Brooklyn, N.Y., April 1972.

[10] A. G. KONHEIM und B. MEISTER, Distributions of queue lengths and waiting times in a loop with two-way traffic, *J. of Comp. System Sci.* 7 (1973), 506-521.

C O M P U T E R G E S T Ü T Z T E R
U N T E R R I C H T

EIN MODERNES NETZWERKANALYSEPROGRAMM ALS BEGLEITENDES SIMULIERTES LABOR ZU ELEKTROTECHNISCHEN VORLESUNGEN

Dr. H. Nielinger
CUU-Forschungsgruppe
Fachhochschule Furtwangen

1. Das Labor - notwendiger Bestandteil der Ingenieurausbildung

Unbestritten gehört das Labor zur parxisorientierten Ingenieurausbildung. Im Idealfall ergänzt es die in der Vorlesung vorgetragene Theorie, zeigt die Gültigkeit der mathematischen Modelle, aber auch deren Grenzen. Insbesondere bei Schaltungen mit nichtlinearen Bauelementen (Transistoren, Dioden usw.) ist es häufig sinnvoll, die technische Aufgabenstellung zu linearisieren, um überhaupt eine leichtfassliche theoretische Behandlung durchführen zu können. Der damit notwendig verbundene Informationsverlust über weitere wichtige Eigenschaften der Schaltung kann durch sinnvolles Experimentieren in einem Labor ausgeglichen werden. Hier besteht die Chance, praktische Erfahrungen zu sammeln und ingenieurmäßiges Wissen zu erwerben unter bewußtem Verzicht auf eine exzessive Mathematisierung auch des letzten störenden Effekts.

2. Kritische Bemerkungen zur Effizienz des klassischen Labors.

Leider ist in der Ausbildungspraxis eine unmittelbare Verzahnung der Vorlesung und der praktischen Laborarbeit nur in den seltensten Fällen möglich. Meistens findet das Labor ein bis zwei Semester nach der betreffenden Vorlesung statt, zu einer Zeit also, in der der Student sich schon wieder theoretisch mit anderen Problemen beschäftigt und sich häufig nur unvollkommen in den früher einmal gelernten Vorlesungsstoff einarbeitet. Hinzu kommt, daß oft die Zusammenhänge zwischen Theorie und Praxis durch die Tücken der verwendeten Meßgeräte und Leitungen verdeckt werden. Sicher gehört das Kennenlernen der verschiedenen Geräte und der meßtechnischen Probleme auch zu den wichtigen Aufgaben der Laborarbeit; festzustellen ist aber, daß viele Studenten in der für das Labor vorgesehenen Zeit gerade mit Mühe das Ziel "Meßkurve auf dem Millimeterpapier" erreichen. Eine kritische Diskussion der Meßergebnisse unterbleibt dann häufig, da der Student bei bis zu 30 Wochenstunden Belastung das Gefühl hat, überdurchschnittlich viel für dieses Fach gearbeitet zu haben und sich mit der Beschreibung der Äußerlichkeiten und des Meßergebnisses zufrieden gibt.
Ein weiterer Nachteil des klassischen Labors ist die Starrheit des Versuchsaufbaus. Um in der begrenzten Laborzeit möglichst viele Erkenntnisse zu vermitteln, müssen bestimmte typische Messungen vorgeschrieben

werden. Man hat sich für die Spannung am Transistor zu interessieren und nicht für den Stromverlauf, der in vielen Fällen viel erhellender wäre, aber da schwerer meßbar, nicht zum Bestandteil der Untersuchung gemacht wird. Diesen Abschnitt zusammenfassend, läßt sich wohl sagen, daß eine sinnvolle Ergänzung der theoretischen Ausbildung durch ein Labor schwierig ist und daß häufig trotz hohen Einsatzes von menschlicher Arbeitskraft und nicht unbeträchtlicher Summen für Meßgeräte das Ergebnis ausgesprochen mager ist.

3. Ein simuliertes Labor unter Verwendung eines modernen Netzwerkanalyseprogramms

Ein modernes universelles Netzwerkanalyseprogramm bietet heute die Möglichkeit, viele unterschiedliche Schaltungen mit den verschiedensten Bauelementen kostengünstig zu analysieren. Damit liegt die Verwendung eines solchen Programms als begleitendes simuliertes Labor für die verschiedensten elektrotechnischen Vorlesungen nahe.

3.1 Batch-Betrieb oder Dialog-Betrieb?

Im Gegensatz zur industriellen Verwendung solcher Programme, wo Schaltungen häufig bei laufenden Parameteränderungen untersucht werden und deshalb ein Dialogbetrieb am Terminal wünschenswert ist, genügt im Ausbildungsbereich eigentlich der kostengünstige und effektvolle Batch-Betrieb eines solchen Programms. Die klassische Laboraufgabe ist die Analyse einer gegebenen Schaltung, nicht die Synthese einer Schaltung mit bestimmten vorgeschriebenen Eigenschaften durch Trial und Error, eine Methode, die nur von einem erfahrenen Entwickler angewendet, Erfolg verspricht. Erhält der Student dagegen ein fehlerhaftes Analyseprotokoll in der Batch-Ausgabe, so ist es ein beachtlicher Vorteil dieses Betriebs, daß er nicht unter dem Zwang der begrenzten Terminalzeit seine Fehler korrigieren muß, sondern sich in Ruhe bis zur nächsten Batch-Eingabe überlegen kann, was er falsch gemacht hat. Das spart in der Summe Belegungszeit, Rechenzeit und Papierkosten.

3.2 Laufende Kontrolle und Ergänzung des Vorlesungsstoffs durch begleitende simulierte Experimente

Moderne Netzwerkanalyseprogramme erlauben, mit einem Minimum an Aufwand eine weitgehend realistische Aussage über das Verhalten von elektronischen Schaltungen in einer befriedigenden, ingenieurmäßigen Form (Print-Plot-Kurven als Schnelldruckerprotokolle) zu erhalten. Durch die Integration eines solchen Programms in den Unterricht ist die Realisierung eines idealen didaktischen Konzepts für die Ingenieurausbildung möglich: Einfache theoretische Ansätze, Hauptschwerpunkt: Effekte erster

Ordnung, Diskussion mathematisch schwer faßbarer Probleme am Ergebnis des simulierten Experiments.

3.3 Motivationssteigerung durch frei wählbaren "Versuchsaufbau"

Während zu Beginn der Vermittlung eines neuen Gebiets der Dozent die Durchführung des simulierten Experiments mehr oder weniger genau vorschreiben sollte, kann bei fortschreitendem Wissensstand dem Studenten die Freiheit gewährt werden, die Möglichkeiten des Netzwerkanalyseprogramms mehr und mehr auszunutzen. Er kann die Schaltungen, die er zur Übung entwerfen soll, auch ausprobieren, kann sich mit einem Minimum an Aufwand Klarheit verschaffen über Frequenzgang, Impulsverhalten, Temperaturverhalten, kann sich beliebige Ströme und Spannungen in ihrem zeitlichen Verlauf anschauen und gewinnt dabei eine Fülle von wichtigen ingenieurmäßigen Erkenntnissen. Dieses Erfolgserlebnis, selbst aktiv mit der Theorie arbeiten zu können, steigert seine Motivation, sich mit dem Vorlesungsstoff auseinanderzusetzen, und führt letztlich zu einer Leistungssteigerung. Noch ein wesentlicher Unterschied zum klassischen Labor: Da es praktisch kaum Mühe macht, die Meßkurven zu ermitteln, beginnt die Arbeit hier, wo sie dort häufig aufgehört hat, nämlich bei der Auswertung der Meßkurven. Die Geduld und Kraft ist nicht durch Äusserlichkeiten verbraucht worden, bevor die wesentliche Verknüpfung von Theorie und Praxis geleistet werden soll.

3.4 Sensitivity-Analyse zur Beurteilung von Parameterstreuungen und als Hilfsmittel zur Schaltungsoptimierung

Besondere Erwähnung verdient die Möglichkeit moderner Netzwerkanalyseprogramme, das totale Differential einer gesuchten Ausgangsgröße zu berechnen. Technisch ausgedrückt handelt es sich dabei um die Berechnung der Abhängigkeit der Ausgangsgröße von den Änderungen der Bauelemente der Schaltung. Bei dieser sog. Sensitivity-Analyse bekommt der Student also Informationen, welcher Parameter besonders stark auf die Ausgangsgröße eingeht, und er kann gegebenenfalls diese Größe gezielt ändern, um ein gewünschtes Ergebnis zu erhalten. Eine Möglichkeit, die beim klassischen Labor undenkbar wäre, denn man kann nicht jeden Widerstand in einer Versuchsschaltung als Potentiometer ausführen und dann vom Studenten verlangen, den Einfluß aller Widerstandsänderungen meßtechnisch zu erfassen. Damit liefert das klassische Labor wichtige Informationen nicht, die Aussagen über die Stabilität und Reproduzierbarkeit von Schaltungen erlauben, Gesichtspunkte, die im Zeitalter von Massenfertigungen nicht vernachlässigt werden dürfen.

4. Netzwerkanalyseprogramme an der Fachhochschule Furtwangen

An der Fachhochschule Furtwangen hat sich eine gewisse Tradition in der Arbeit mit Netzwerkanalyseprogrammen gebildet. Schon im Sommersemester 1971 wurde ein regelmäßiger Übungsbetrieb mit dem Programm ECAP eingerichtet. /1/. Im Jahre 1973 gelang es, eine IBM-360-Version des Programm SPICE (Simulation Program with Integrated Circuit Emphasis) von der Univeristy of California, Berkeley zu bekommen. SPICE ist eine moderne Version des Programms CANCER /2/ und wurde an der University of California, Berkeley, entwickelt. Das Programm umfaßt etwa 8000 FORTRAN-Statements und benötigt einen Kernspeicherplatz von etwa 50 k Worten. Durch die sog. Sparse-Matrix-Technik, in der Rücksicht auf die außerordentlich dünne Besetzung der Matrizen bei elektronischen Problemen genommen wird, ist dieses Programm unvergleichlich leistungsfähiger als das erwähnte ECAP. Es gestattet, das Gleichstrom-, Wechselstrom- und Impuls-Verhalten von Schaltungen mit bis zu 400 Knoten zu 100 Halbleiterbauelementen zu berechnen. Die frei-formatige Eingabesprache ist bemerkenswert leicht zu lernen, für die wichtigsten Halbleiter hat das Programm eingebaute Modelle, wobei bei fehlender Parametereingabe durch den Benutzer vom Programm automatisch "vernünftige" sog. Default-Parameter gesetzt werden. Unternetzwerke, die mehrmals in einer größeren Schaltung vorkommen, können vom Benutzer als Modell (ähnlich einem Unterprogramm) definiert und immer wieder aufgerufen werden. Zum Schluß sei noch die hervorragende Fehlerdiagnostik erwähnt, die es auch EDV-Laien sehr bald ermöglicht, fehlerfrei und effektvoll mit SPICE zu arbeiten.

Im Rahmen einer Ingenieur-Abschlußarbeit wurde dieses Programm auf der Rechenanlage DEC-1040 der Fachhochschule Furtwangen im WS 73/74 implementiert. Seit dem SS 74 findet eine Vorlesung "SPICE" statt, in der anhand von vielen Beispielen aus allen Gebieten der Elektronik die einfache Eingabesprache gelehrt wird. Gleichzeitig wurde im Rechenzentrum ein nächtlicher unbeaufsichtigter Batch-Betrieb für das Programm "SPICE" eingerichtet, so daß ein Student, der abends seine Lochkarten mit den wenigen Eingabe-Statements abgibt, am anderen Morgen seine Simulationsexperiment-Ergebnisse erhält. Die Erfahrung, daß diese Möglichkeit mit wachsender Begeisterung von den Studenten wahrgenommen wird, legte den Gedanken nahe zu untersuchen, ob Netzwerkanalyseprogramme in die Ausbildung einer Fachhochschule integriert werden können. Deshalb wird im Rahmen des CUU-Forschungsprojekts der Fachhochschule Furtwangen (das vom BMFT gefördert wird) unter dem Gesamtthema "CUU an Fachhochschulen" das Teilprojekt: "Integration eines Netzwerkanalyseprogramms (hier als Beispiel SPICE) in elektrotechnischen Vorlesungen als begleitendes simuliertes Labor" bearbeitet.

5. Ergebnisse aus der CUU-Forschungsarbeit

In /3/ wird der Einsatz von SPICE als begleitendes simuliertes Labor zu einer Vorlesung "Analoge Grundschaltungen" beschrieben. Anhand der Behandlung des einstufigen Emitterverstärkers mit Gegenkopplung wird gezeigt, daß sich insbesondere die mathematisch etwas schwer faßbaren nichtlinearen Effekte mit Hilfe der Simulation technisch befriedigend darstellen lassen.
In /4/ wird auf die Gewinnung realistischer Modellparameter für die wichtigsten Halbleiterbauelemente eingegangen. Die Glaubwürdigkeit der Simulation steht und fällt mit der möglichst realistischen Abbildung der in der technischen Praxis verwendeten nichtlinearen Halbleiterbauelemente. Für die Ingenieurausbildung gilt es einen Kompromiß zu finden zwischen einer Beschreibung, die auch den letzten störenden Effekt berücksichtigt und die eine umständliche Messung vieler Parameter des zu simulierenden Halbleiterbauelementes erfordert, und einer zu stark linearisierten Darstellung der Bauelemente, die dann die bei der praktischen Messung auftretenden Grenzen nicht erfaßt.
In /5/ wird der Einsatz von SPICE bei der Behandlung von integrierten Schaltungen gezeigt. Während in /3/ die Computer-Simulation lediglich eine Steigerung der Effektivität gegenüber dem klassischen Labor und eine Vertiefung des Lehrstoffs durch begleitende simulierte Experimente bewirkte, ist der Einsatz von modernen Netzwerkanalyseprogrammen bei der Behandlung von grundlegenden Techniken bei der Integration von elektronischen Schaltungen besonders gerechtfertigt. Die experimentelle Ermessung von Kennlinien und Parameter von integrierten Schaltungen aus der Industrie ist ein recht unvollkommener Weg, die komplizierten Schaltungen und Abhängigkeiten zu verstehen. Die rein theoretische Darstellung der Zusammenhänge zwischen den technologischen und elektrischen Parametern scheitert häufig am hohen mathematischen Aufwand oder einfach an der begrenzten Zeit, die für den Stoff zur Verfügung steht. Hier hilft die Simulation, die komplexen nichtlinearen Schaltungen in einer technisch befriedigenden Form darzustellen.
Den Abschluß der Forschungsarbeit im Rahmen des genannten CUU-Teilprojekts bildete die Erweiterung des Programms SPICE auf Leitungsschaltungen im Rahmen einer Ingenieurabschlußarbeit. Da die eigentlichen Schaltungen heute fast ausnahmslos als integrierte Schaltungen fertig geliefert werden, treten die eigentlichen Entwicklungsprobleme bei der Verdrahtung von integrierten Schaltungen auf. In einer modernen Ingenieurausbildung müssen deshalb die komplexen dynamischen Vorgänge, die sich auf den Leitungen zwischen integrierten Schaltungen abspielen, unbedingt

berücksichtigt werden.

6. Zusammenfassung und Schluß

Die breite Nutzung eines modernen Netzwerkanalyseprogramms in der Ingenieurausbildung zur quasi-experimentellen Untersuchung komplizierter technischer Zusammenhänge bietet beachtliche Vorteile gegenüber der üblichen klassischen Laborarbeit. Diese sind:

1. Laufende Kontrolle und Ergänzung des Vorlesungsstoffs durch begleitende simulierte Experimente.
2. Motivationssteigerung durch frei wählbaren "Versuchsaufbau".
3. Sensitivity-Analyse zur Beurteilung von Parameterstreuungen und als Hilfsmittel zur Schaltungsoptimierung.

Selbstverständlich ist das klassische Labor durch ein Computersimuliertes Labor nicht völlig zu ersetzen. Im Vordergrund der Laborarbeit sollte aber dann mehr das Kennenlernen der Meßgeräte und die Problematik des praktischen Messens stehen. Ideal wäre, wenn alle Experimente des klassischen Labors vorher simuliert worden wären, die theoretischen Bezüge der Studenten dadurch völlig klar wären und im Labor anhand einiger weniger Kontrollmessungen das Simulationsergebnis bestätigt und dabei die Meßmethode und das Gerät kennengelernt werden könnte.

LITERATUR

/1/ G. Krauß, H. Nielinger, J. Strube:
Digitalrechner simuliert Schaltungen in der Ingenieurausbildung
Elektronik 1973, Heft 5, S. 185 - 190

/2/ L. Nagel, R. Rohrer:
Computer Analysis of Nonlinear Circuits Excluding Radiation (CANCER)
IEEE Journal of Solid-State Circuits
Vol. SC-6, No. 4, August 1971

/3/ H. Nielinger: Netzwerkanalyse im simulierten Labor
NTZ 1975, Heft 8 (voraussichtlich)

/4/ H. Nielinger: Modellparameter aus Datenblattangaben zur Simulation des Schaltverhaltens von Diode und Transistor
erscheint demnächst in der Zeitschrift "Elektronik"

/5/ H. Nielinger, W. Schneider:
Der Einsatz eines modernen Netzwerkanalyseprogramms bei der Behandlung von integrierten MOSFET-Invertern.

A L T I D , EINE SPRACHE

FÜR LEHR- UND INFORMATIONSDIALOGE

R.Hansen, E.-G.Hoffmann, F.Simon

Institut für Informatik und Praktische Mathematik
der Universität Kiel

Abstract: This paper presents ALTID (Algorithmic Language for Teach and Information Dialogs). ALTID is an ALGOL-like language which includes appropriate data types and syntactic constructions to allow different strategies of "Computer Assisted Instruction" (tutorial, learner control, simulation, problem solving).

1. Einleitung

Rechner werden seit langem als Medien im Ausbildungsbereich eingesetzt, sowohl als Lerngegenstand selbst, als auch zur Vermittlung von Wissen im computerunterstützten Unterricht (CUU) in der Form von Lehrprogrammen. Ausgehend von behavioristischen Lernmodellen (Skinner und Crowder siehe [1]) und den Erfahrungen mit programmierter Instruktion übertrug man zunächst lineare Lernprogramme auf den Rechner. Bei dieser Lehrform beschränkt man sich auf das Anbieten und Abfragen von Fakten in einer fest vorgegebenen Sequenz, wobei der Lernerfolg durch eine genügend große Dichte detaillierter Lernschritte gesichert wird.

Eine wesentliche Erweiterung in der Lehrform stellen die heute vor allem benutzten tutoriellen Lehrprogramme dar, bei denen Antworten des Adressaten auf Fragen im Programm zur Auswahl des nächsten Lernschrittes mit herangezogen werden. Als Beispiel sei die Technik von 'multiple choice'-Fragen erwähnt, bei der dem Adressaten eine Auswahl möglicher Antworten geboten wird und dann je nach der von ihm markierten Antwort auf die nächste Einheit des Lehrprogramms verzweigt wird. Man kritisiert an der tutoriellen Lehrform, daß der Dialog zwischen Lehrendem (dem Programm) und dem Lernenden sich in dem sehr engen Rahmen der vom Lehrprogramm-Autor antizipierten Antworten bewegen muß.

Dem vollständig vom Autor organisierten Lernprozeß steht die Selbstorganisation des Lernens durch den Adressaten (learner control) gegenüber, d.h. der Adressat arbeitet mit einem Lehrprogramm, das ihm die Freizügigkeit gewährt, seine eigenen Lernprozesse selbst zu steuern. Während diese Art des Lernens in der klassischen Pädagogik kaum eine Rolle spielt, läßt sie sich im CUU sehr gut einsetzen.

Nach einer anfänglich euphorischen Einschätzung von linearen bzw. tutoriellen Lehrformen entzündete sich zunehmend Kritik an diesen Lehrstrategien (Freibichler [2]), die vor allem in der Forderung nach mehr Möglichkeiten für Schüleraktivitäten mündete. Die zunächst entwickelten CUU-Autorensprachen weisen wegen ihrer Fixierung auf diese Lehrformen in Hinblick auf ihre Anwendbarkeit für schülerzentrierte dialogische Lehrformen erhebliche Mängel auf (Bode, Dütting [3]).

2. Zielsetzung

Beim Entwurf der Sprache ALTID wurde bewußt darauf verzichtet, dem Konzept eine bestimmte Lehrform des CUU zugrunde zu legen. Es wurde vielmehr versucht, Sprachmittel für Dialoge aus dem gesamten Bereich zwischen tutorieller Lehrform und Problemlösen zur Verfügung zu stellen. Als Konsequenz ergibt sich daraus zwar, daß ein Autor bei der Realisierung seines Lehrprogrammes kaum auf vorgegebene Moduln der Sprache als Grundschema einer Unterrichtseinheit zurückgreifen kann, höher zu bewerten sind jedoch die wesentlich größeren Möglichkeiten in der Programmierung verschiedener Lehrformen.

Schülerzentrierte dialogische Lehrformen lassen sich grob wie folgt klassifizieren (siehe [2],[3]):

- Lehrdialoge (in der Form von tutoriellen Lehrprogrammen mit Eingriffsmöglichkeiten für den Adressaten)
- Simulation, Spiel
- Informationssysteme (z.B. Lexika, semantische Netze)
- Problemlösen

Jede Autorensprache sollte die Arbeit an der Entwicklung eines Lehrprogrammes unterstützen, insbesondere

- die Formulierung von Algorithmen,
- die Umsetzung von Didaktogrammen,
- die Fehlersuche,
- die Verifikation des Lehrprogrammes und
- die Modifikation des Lehrprogrammes.

Beim Entwurf der Sprache ALTID wurde versucht, die hier nur knapp skizzierte Palette von Anforderungen mit geeigneten Konzepten abzudecken.

3. Wesentliche Sprachelemente

Bei der Darstellung der Sprachelemente entschied man sich für einen ALGOL-ähnlichen Stil, wobei auf die zur Fehlererkennung notwendige Redundanz Wert gelegt wurde.

a) Programmaufbau

Ein Programm setzt sich aus globalen Deklarationen und zwei syntaktisch gleichen Teilen, diagram und dialog, zusammen. Die Struktur beider Teile ist bestimmt durch die Didaktogrammstruktur tutorieller Lehrprogramme. Diese Didaktogramme bestehen aus weitgehend in sich abgeschlossenen Lehreinheiten, die durch ein netzartiges Ablaufschema verbunden sind, das die Menge der möglichen Wege des Schülers durch das Lehrprogramm angibt. Die Didaktogramme werden realisiert durch eine Menge von benannten Blöcken und eine davon getrennt angelegte, gerichtete Netzstruktur mit den Bezeichnungen der Blöcke als Knoten. Der Autor kann den Weg des Schülers durch das Netz z.B. anhand von Schülerantworten steuern. Der diagram-Teil wurde primär für die Umsetzung tutorieller Lehrprogramme vorgesehen, während der dialog-Teil für die Reaktionen auf spontane Schüleranfragen bestimmt ist. Für Lehrformen, bei denen die Netzstruktur ohne Bedeutung ist, erlaubt das Blockkonzept der Sprache zusammen mit den Prozeduren eine adäquate Programmstruktur.

Zusammen mit der Möglichkeit, Blöcke als gemeinsam (common) für diagram und dialog global zu vereinbaren, erweist sich dieses Konzept auch als geeignet, die schülerzentrierte Seite des dialog darzustellen. Spontane Anfragen unterbrechen den diagram-Teil an vom Autor dafür vorgesehenen Stellen bzw. bei I/O-Kontakten mit dem Terminal und bewirken den Start des dialog-Teils.

Dieser modulare Programmaufbau reflektiert nicht nur die Didaktogrammstruktur und erleichtert die Modifikation der Programme durch Änderungen in der Netzstruktur, sondern er erlaubt auch eine problemgegebene Segmentierung der übersetzten Programme und trägt damit zur Reduktion des Speicherbedarfs zur Laufzeit bei.

Jeder Block besteht aus einem evtl. leeren Deklarationsteil für lokale Variable und Prozeduren, gefolgt von einem lokalen Netz oder einzelnen Anweisungen mit einer einfachen Möglichkeit zur Blockschachtelung.

Die Tendenz, den Benutzer von ALTID zum Schreiben gut strukturierter Programme zu motivieren, bestimmte auch die Konstruktion der if-, cond-, for-, while- und case-Anweisungen.

Zu erwähnen ist schließlich noch, daß bei Prozeduren die Parameterübergabe auf die Übergabe des Wertes (call by value) bzw. der Bezeichnung eingeschränkt ist und daß eine Prozedur nur über einen Notausgang (escape) oder ein return bzw. das Prozedurende verlassen werden kann.

b) Datentypen

Es gehört zu den Merkmalen höherer Programmiersprachen, für die Programmierung der Algorithmen spezifische Datentypen bereitzustellen. ALTID kennt die elementaren Datentypen boolean, integer, real, character, reference und position; aus ihnen können Arrays aufgebaut werden. Zur Speicherung der Lehrtexte gibt es den Typ string, zum Aufbau von Bildern der Typ picture und, um z.B. den Anforderungen der Antwortanalyse gerecht zu werden, den Typ list. Das Arbeiten mit den Typen list, string und picture erfordert dabei neben dem üblichen 'stack' die Benutzung eines 'heap' und ein 'garbage collecting'.

c) Dialog am Terminal

Die Qualität eines Dialoges wird wesentlich durch den Aufwand bestimmt, den der Autor treibt. Wie "frei" ein solcher Dialog ist, hängt einerseits ab von den Intentionen des Autors und andererseits von den Möglichkeiten, die ihm das System dabei zur Realisierung seiner Dialoge bietet. Der Umfang der Sprache kann voll ausgenutzt werden, wenn ein Display mit der Fähigkeit zu graphischem Input/Output zur Verfügung steht. Über den Bildschirm werden Texte und Bilder angeboten, zu denen zusätzliche Informationen, z.B. über spontane Anfragen, eingeholt werden können, ohne die ausgegebene Bildinformation zu überschreiben. Die symbolorientierte Ein- und Ausgabe erfolgt im allgemeinen über FORTRAN IV-ähnliche Formate.

Der Text einer Mitteilung des Adressaten wird durch die Input-Anweisung scan anhand von frei wählbaren separate- und layout-Symbolen in Teilstrings zerlegt, um eine Antwortanalyse vorzubereiten. Das Sprachkonzept erscheint für Versuche zur Analyse natürlicher Sprache umfangreich genug zu sein.

Die graphische Darstellung von Informationen stellt eine wünschenswerte Bereicherung der Kommunikation mit dem Adressaten dar. In ALTID lassen sich Bilder mit Hilfe des Datentyps picture und geeigneter Operatoren aus den elementaren geometrischen Objekten point, line, area und target aufbauen. So erzeugte Bilder können entweder direkt oder in aufbereiteter Form von Files her auf dem Terminal ausgegeben werden. Zur graphischen Eingabe ist ein 'lightpen' od.ä. vorgesehen, mit dessen Hilfe Punkte des Bildschirms bzw. im Bild definierte Zielpunkte (targets) markiert werden können.

d) Informationssysteme

Die Forderung nach einem komfortablen Konzept für die Filemanipulation ist nicht nur aufgrund der Notwendigkeit zur bequemen Handhabung der im CUU anfallenden umfangreichen Lehrtexte gegeben, sondern auch die Erstellung von einfachen Informationssystemen, z.B. Lexika, verlangt Files als Datenstrukturen. Es gibt in ALTID sequentielle und indexsequentielle Files zur Speicherung von binärer oder symbolischer Information. Der Zugriff auf einen indexsequentiellen File kann auch über einen mit dem File assoziierten Hash-Algorithmus erfolgen. Z.B. hat man dadurch eine einfache Möglichkeit, in Abhängigkeit von einem Stichwort auf ein Lexikon zuzugreifen.

Realisiert man ein Informationssystem als semantisches Netz (Simmons[4], Brunnstein [5]), so bieten sich die binären Listen von ALTID als adäquate Datenstruktur an, um Relationen anzugeben, die zwischen den Objekten des Netzes bestehen. Dynamische Veränderungen der Größe des Netzes im Rahmen eines Dialoges sind bei der Benutzung von Listen unkritisch.

4. Beispiel

Die vorgestellten Sprachelemente sollen an einem Beispiel zu einem Teilgebiet der Mechanik im Physikunterricht erläutert werden. Es vermittelt dem Adressaten das Verständnis der Übersetzungsmechanismen von Räderwerken, bestehend aus Rädern, Wellen und Treibriemen. Dieser Unterrichtsgegenstand wurde von Spada, Fischer und Heyner [6] zur Validierung eines statistischen Lernmodelles benutzt.

Mit der Vorstellung dieses Beispiels soll weder ein vollständiges Lehrprogramm präsentiert werden noch geht es um die Verwirklichung eines didaktischen Konzeptes sondern ausschließlich um die exemplarische Darstellung von Sprachelementen.

<u>global</u>	<u>Globale Deklarationen</u>
<u>in</u> <u>bin</u> <u>hash</u> <u>file</u> <u>array</u> raederwerksbegriffe <u>size</u> 1oo = "dskc:radwb[1ooo,1oo12]";	File zur Speicherung der Bildschirminhalte für die Informationen zu den einzelnen Begriffen; Zugriff über ein Hash-Schlüsselwort.
<u>in</u> <u>bin</u> <u>file</u> <u>array</u> begriffsgruppen <u>size</u> 5 = "dskc:radwbg[1ooo,1oo12]";	Indexsequentieller File zur Speicherung der zu den tutoriellen Blöcken gehörigen Begriffe.

```
diagram
 frame f1 = motivation(f2),
       f2 = auswahl(f3,f4,f5,exit),
       f3 = drehsinn(f2),
       f4 = drehzahl(f2),
       f5 = drehmoment(f2);
```

Diagrammteil
Didaktogramm: Darstellung der Ablaufstruktur. Bei Eintritt in den frame f_i wird der zugehörige Block durchlaufen, also bei f3 der Block 'drehsinn'; in Klammern stehen die möglichen Nachfolger.

```
 motivation:block
               :
            endblock;
 auswahl:block
            :
         endblock;
```

Ablauf-
struktur

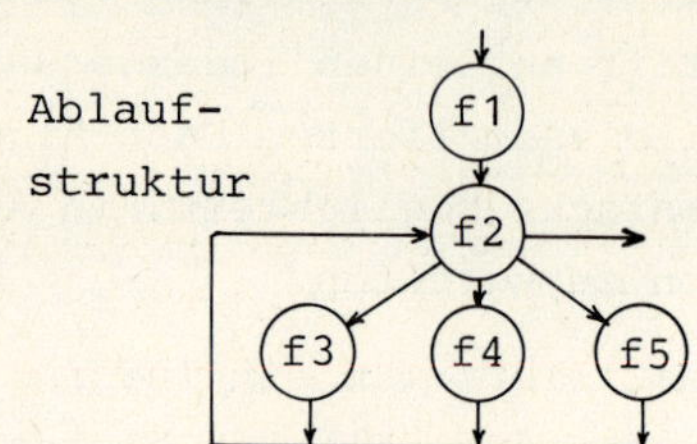


```
drehsinn:block
 int i, anzahl; string begriff;
 proc information(string begriff);
  begin int i,teilbildzahl;
        string weiter; picture bild;
    read raederwerksbegriffe
       key begriff: bild;
    for i until teilbildzahl do
     write from raederwerksbegriffe
          key begriff: bild;
     !"weiter?";
     ?weiter @a1@;
    od
  end;
```

Block
'drehsinn'
Die Prozedur 'information' gibt die zu 'begriff' gehörigen Bildinformationen nacheinander auf dem Terminal aus und wartet jeweils auf eine Reaktion des Schülers zur Fortsetzung der Ausgabe. Die Ausgabe erfolgt direkt vom File 'raederwerksbegriffe'.

Es wird ein Symbol eingelesen.

```
 proc aufgabe(string begriff);
  begin
    :
  end;
```

Die Prozedur 'aufgabe' sollte das für Präsentation und Analyse von Aufgaben zu einem Begriff notwendige Programmstück enthalten.

```
  read begriffsgruppen index 3:anzahl;
  for i until anzahl do
    read begriffsgruppen index 3:
      begriff;
    information(begriff); clear;
    aufgabe(begriff); clear;
  od; next 1;
endblock;
```

Zu jedem Begriff für 'drehsinn' werden Informationen angeboten und Aufgaben bearbeitet. clear löscht jeweils den Bildschirm. Über next i erfolgt der Übergang zum nächsten Frame, und zwar dem i-ten in der Liste der möglichen Nachfolger von f3.

```
drehzahl: block
            :
       endblock;

drehmoment: block
              :
         endblock;
```

```
dialog                                          Dialogteil
block list anfrage;                             Im File 'lexikon' sind die Kurz-
  in bin hash file array lexikon                informationen zu allen Begriffen
   size 1oo="dskc:radwlx[1ooo,1oo12]";          gespeichert.
  proc analyse(list satz);                      Die Prozedur 'analyse' sucht in
    begin string begriff,s; char f;             der Liste 'satz' von Worten das
      while not empty satz do                   letzte Wort, das nicht nur aus ei-
        if not f:=head satz                     nem Symbol (Satzzeichen) besteht
          then begriff:=head satz; fi;          und gibt den zu diesem Begriff ge-
          satz ← tail satz;                     speicherten Text aus.
        od;
      !from lexikon key begriff: s;             Die Anweisung scan x zerlegt eine
    end;                                        Schülerantwort in Worte und lie-
  scan anfrage; analyse(anfrage);               fert sie in der Variablen x vom
endblock;                                       Typ list ab.
```

Um auch graphische Sprachelemente vorzustellen, soll ein Programmstück zum Zeichnen von Räderwerken auf dem Bildschirm angegeben werden, wie es z.B. für die Bearbeitung von Aufgaben oder bei der Simulation erforderlich ist.

Die Darstellung eines Räderwerkes sei durch die Initialisierung folgender Arrays gegeben:

```
  real array yw size aw;                   yw = y-Koordinaten der Wellen
  real array xr,rr size aw*marw            xr = x-Koordinaten der Räder
                    index matrix           rr = Radius der Räder
  real array klg size aw*marw*2            klg= Angaben über die Kopplungen
                  index mat3;                   der Räder
  int array arw size aw;                   arw- Anzahl der Räder pro Welle
  ref array tr size aw*marw                tr = Beschriftungen für die Räder
                 index matrix;             aw = Anzahl der Wellen
                                           marw = maximale Anzahl
```

```
int i,j;
real rd=2.o,d,r,r2,xo,x,y,sin,cos;
string t; picture rad,bild;
```

Weitere Variablen für den Algorithmus

```
for i until aw do xo←o.o;
 for j until arw [i] do
  x←xr[i,j]; y←yw[i,j];
  r←rr[i,j];
  bild←bild +
        rad at{x,y} scale{r,r}+
        line{xo,y} to{x-r,y};
  xo←x; t:=.tr[i,j];
  bild←bild + text t at{x+r,y+r};
  if (d←klg[1,j,1]) ne o then
   r2←klg[i,j,2]; sin←(r2-r)/d1;
   cos←sqrt(1-sin↑2);
   bild←bild +
         line{x+r*cos,y+r*sin}
           to{x+r2*cos,y-d+r2*sin}+
         line{x-r*cos,y+r*sin}
           to{x-r2*cos,y-d+r2*sin};
  fi
 od;
 bild←bild + line{xo,y} to{rd,y};
od;
write bild scale{a,a/2};
```

Der Algorithmus baut das Räderwerk Welle für Welle und Rad für Rad in der Variablen 'bild' auf. Dabei wird vorausgesetzt, daß in der Variablen 'rad' ein Kreis in normierter Größe gespeichert ist. Bei anschließender Ausgabe mit geeigneter Gesamtskalierung kann so z.B. folgendes Bild entstehen:

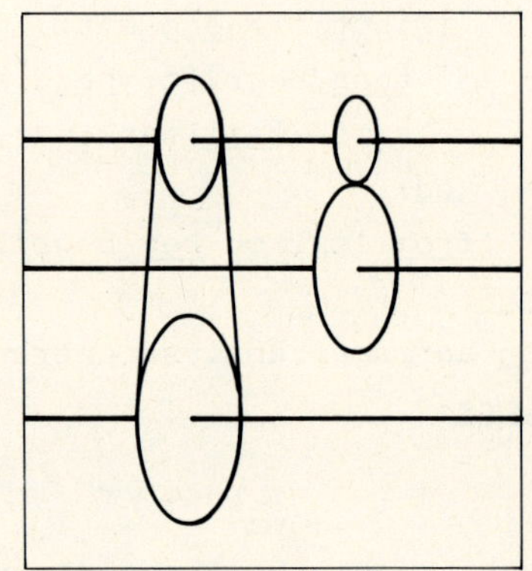

An drei einfachen Beispielen soll gezeigt werden, wie Prozeduren zur Antwortanalyse in ALTID formuliert werden können.
Die Unterscheidung der Datentypen string zur Speicherung von Symbolen in gepackter Form und character array für den indizierten Zugriff bei der Symbolmanipulation ist im Programm explizit zu berücksichtigen und geschieht nicht implizit in fest vorgegebenen Standardprozeduren.

```
bool proc member(val string s,
                 val list a);
begin string s1;
 s1:=head a;
 return if empty a then false
        else if s eq s1 then true
        else member(s,tail a) fi fi;
end;
```

Die Prozedur 'member' prüft, ob der String s unter den Strings der Liste a auftritt ($s \in a$).

```
bool proc listmember(val list s,a);
return if empty a then true
       else if member(head a,s)
            then listmember(s,tail a)
            else false fi
       fi;
```

Die Prozedur 'listmember' liefert den Wert true, wenn die Elemente von a in s enthalten sind ($a \subset s$).

```
bool proc cont (val string s,
                val list a);
begin
 int l=length s, j1=1,j,k;
 char array cs=spell s;
 string s1,s2="";

 while not empty a do
  s1:=head a; a←tail a; k←length s;
  for j from j1
      while (j1←j+k-1) le l
            and s1 ne s2
      do s2:=cs[j:j1] od;
  if s1 ne s2 then return false;
 od;
 return true;
end;
```

Die Prozedur 'cont' prüft, ob die Elemente der Liste a in der gleichen Reihenfolge als Substrings des Strings s auftreten.
s wird in ein char array entpackt.
s1, s2 werden durch den leeren String initiiert.
Der Zugriff auf Listen erfolgt über head bzw. tail; empty fragt auf die leere Liste ab.
loop-Anweisung

Packen eines Teilarrays in eine Stringvariable.
Die Prozedur wird mit return η verlassen. Der Ausdruck η definiert den Wert der Prozedur.

5. Schlußbemerkungen

Es gibt Autorensprachen, in denen die Erstellung von Lehrprogrammen komfortabler ist. Man kann sich jedoch leicht durch entsprechende ALTID-Programme mehr Komfort verschaffen: Die Fixierung auf eine bestimmte Lehrform ermöglicht eine verkürzte, schematische Erzeugung von Lehrprogrammen, und für Standardaufgaben wie Antwortanalyse und graphische Programmierung können Prozedurbibliotheken erarbeitet werden.

ALTID wird zur Zeit an einer PDP1o auf der Basis von CDL (Koster [7]) portabel implementiert.

Literatur

[1] Markle, S.M. Good frames and bad
New York, 1969

[2] Freibichler , H. Tendenzen in der Entwicklung und im Einsatz von Systemen für den Computer-unterstützten Unterricht: Eine kritische Bestandsaufnahme
Zeitschrift für Datenverarbeitung, 1972

[3] Bode, A. und Dütting, M.
Computer-Unterstützter Unterricht: Probleme, Autorensprachen, Systemvergleiche
Diplomarbeit, Universität Karlsruhe, 1972

[4] Simmons, R.F. Mapping English Strings into Meanings
Technical Report NL1o
Department of Computer Science and CAI Laboratory
University of Texas, Austin/Texas, 1973

Simmons, R.F. Process Models for Natural Language Meanings ...
in: International summer seminar of concepts of automatic processing of natural languages
Stuttgart, 1974

[5] Brunnstein, K. Structuring and Retrieving Information in Computer-Based Learning
Vortrag, 4. International Symposium on Computer and Information Sciences, COINS-72
Miami Beach/Florida, 1972

Brunnstein, K. Datenstrukturen im CUU
in: GI, Fachausschuß 5
Fachgespräch: Problemgegebene Datenstrukturen
St. Augustin, 1973

[6] Spada, H., Fischer, G.H. und Heyner, W.
Denkoperationen und Lernprozesse bei der Lösung von Problemstellungen aus der Mechanik
in: Kongreß der Gesellschaft für Psychologie
Bericht 28, Saarbrücken, 1972

[7] Koster, C.H.A. Using the CDL Compiler Compiler,
Lecture Notes of an Advanced Cource on Compiler Construction
München, 1974

[8] Hansen, R., Hoffmann, E.-G. und Simon, F.
ALTID, eine Sprache für Lehr- und Informationsdialoge - Sprachkonzept -
Bericht 1/75 des Instituts für Informatik und Praktische Mathematik der Universität Kiel

Entwurf und Einsatz eines portablen RGU-Systems fuer die Lernersteuerung: LEGIS

Arndt Bode
Universität Karlsruhe
Institut für Informatik I

0. Zusammenfassung

LEGIS ist ein spezielles Informationssystem für Unterrichtszwecke. Es besteht aus einem Dialogteil (Prozessor) zur Führung des Lehrdialogs und einem Autorenteil (Übersetzer) für die Eingabe von Lehrprogrammen. Eingebettet in beide Teile ist die Stringmanipulationssprache SMAL für die Programmierung von Tests und Simulationsteilen. Die mit LEGIS realisierbare Lehrform "Lernersteuerung" fußt auf der kognitiven Lerntheorie. Weitere Einsatzmöglichkeiten für LEGIS ergeben sich - bedingt durch die Editiermöglichkeiten - für die Dokumentation von rasch veraltenden Informationen (z.B. Softwaredokumentation). Geschildert wird der Entwurf und die portable Implementierung von LEGIS sowie erste, bei der Erprobung erzielte Ergebnisse über die Lernersteuerung.

1. Zielsetzung

1.1 Entwicklung eines Systems für die Lernersteuerung im RGU

Der Rechner-Gestützte Unterricht (RGU) war bis vor wenigen Jahren weitgehend durch das Vorbild des programmierten Unterrichts geprägt. Diese ausschließliche Orientierung an belehrenden Lehrformen trat erst in letzter Zeit zugunsten der Entwicklung von RGU-Systemen für lerneraktive Unterrichtssituationen in den Hintergrund.

Seit etwa 1971 entstanden zunächst Arbeiten in den zwei folgenden Bereichen der Anwendung dialogischer Unterrichtsformen für das Lernen mit dem Rechner:

- Simulationen und Spiele (Realisierung durch Programmiersprachen mit flexiblen Datenstrukturen und der Möglichkeit zur graphischen Informationsdarstellung: z.B. LEKTOR, APL)
- Problemlösen und interaktives Programmieren (mit Dialogprogrammiersprachen wie LOGO, BASIC oder APL).

Mit der Entwicklung des LErner Gesteuerten Informations-Systems LEGIS sollte die Lernersteuerung als eine weitere Variante, das entdeckende Lernen, für den RGU erschlossen werden.

Dem Prinzip der Lernersteuerung liegt eine heute weitgehend akzeptierte Auffassung von Lernvorgängen zugrunde: Lernen wird verstanden als der schrittweise Erwerb kognitiver Strukturen, die die Umwelt im Lernenden in Form eines "inneren Modells" wiederspiegeln. Lernmotivation (als primäre Motivation) entsteht durch den Wunsch des einzelnen, Ungleichgewichtszustände zwischen dem inneren Modell und der realen Umwelt zu beseitigen. Da die kognitiven Strukturen - bedingt durch unterschiedliche Vorbildung und Erfahrungen - insbesondere bei Erwachsenen stark differieren, müssen von außen gesteuerte, belehrende Lehrformen vor allem im tertiären Bildungsbereich (Universitäts- und Erwachsenenbildung) an der Motivation der Lernenden vorbeigehen (übliche Lehrformen greifen daher zu sekundären Effekten zurück: Erzeugung von Lernmotivation durch Prüfungsdruck, Belohnung durch sachfremde "Verstärker" oder Strafandrohung). Da die kognitive Lerntheorie (PIAGET, GALPERIN, AEBLI) zudem zeigt, daß der Erwerb kognitiver Strukturen nur durch aktiven Vollzug von Lernschritten gefördert wird, bietet sich die Lernersteuerung als eine Lehrform an, bei der der einzelne bei vorgegebenen Lernzielen seinen Lernweg selbst bestimmt, den Unterricht damit aktiv gestaltet und das Vorgehen gemäß seines eigenen inneren Modells festlegt.

1.2 Einsatz von LEGIS zu Dokumentations- und Forschungszwecken

Neben der Anwendung für die Lernersteuerung sollte mit LEGIS auch ein System geschaffen werden, das sich zur Dokumentation von kurzlebigen Informationsmengen eignet, auf die häufig selektiv zugegriffen werden muß. Die einfache Änderung (Editieren) der Information spricht ja allgemein für die Verwendung von Informationssystemen, die der gedruckten Darstellung, die meist während ihrer Verteilung veraltet, überlegen ist. Ein besonderer Vorteil von LEGIS besteht darin, daß die Daten nicht nur einfach gespeichert und editiert werden, sondern auch in didaktisch ansprechender Form an Informationssuchende ausgegeben werden (Übersichten, Informationspfade, automatisch erstellte Querverweise, Tests zur Überprüfung des Wissens). Eine typische Anwendung wäre die Dokumentation von Software und Hardware einer Rechenanlage.

HAEFNER, 1974 [5] sieht für lernerorientierte Informationssysteme weiterhin Einsatzmöglichkeiten in der Forschung, wobei dann die didaktische Funktion wie bei der Anwendung zu Dokumentationszwecken durch eine Auskunftsfunktion ersetzt würde.

Im folgenden soll im wesentlichen auf den Einsatz von LEGIS für die Lehre im tertiären Bildungsbereich eingegangen werden.

2. Kurze Beschreibung von LEGIS

2.1 Der Lehrdialog mit LEGIS

Der Zugriff auf die einzelnen Lehrelemente in LEGIS geschieht durch eine Lernerkommandosprache. Sie umfaßt Kommandos für folgende Aufgaben:

1. Auswahl von Lehrinformation und Übersichten
2. Zugriff auf Lehrinformation
3. Definition eines individuellen Lernweges
4. Aufruf der Lehrstoffstruktur
5. Sonstige (Hilfsinformation, Tischrechnermodus, Kommentare, Protokollerstellung).

(Für die einzelnen Befehle vergleiche Tabelle 1).

Wichtigstes Prinzip der Kommandosprache ist es, daß jedes Kommando an jeder beliebigen Dialogstelle eingegeben werden darf. Es gibt also weder systembedingte noch stofflich begründete Einschränkungen in der Lernersteuerung, sämtliche Orientierungshilfen (vgl. unten) sind nur als Empfehlungen für den Lernenden gedacht.

Jede Lehrinformation gliedert sich in die folgenden drei Grundelemente:
- Die eingentlichen Lehrinhalte, die in textueller, graphischer oder simulativer Form dargeboten werden.
- Die zugehörige Lehrstoffstruktur (stellt als eigenständiges Lehrstoffelement die Zusammenhänge zwischen den Lehreinheiten dar).
- Die Testeinheiten zur Selbstüberprüfung des Wissens (die Antworten des Lerners werden durch das System beurteilt, dienen aber nicht zur Bewertung der Lernleistung oder zu Verzweigungsentscheidungen wie in tutorialen Lehrprogrammen). Es werden adressatenbezogene und lernzielbezogene Tests unterschieden: erstere wählt das System auf Anfrage des Lerners gemäß dessen Lernweg individuell aus, während die lernzielbezogenen Tests statisch auf die von außen gesetzten Lernziele bezogen sind.

Die Lehreinheiten in LEGIS werden Frames genannt, die zu Gruppen und Regionen zusammengefaßt werden (für eine detailliertere Beschreibung vgl. BODE, 1974 [1] und 1975 [2]).

Um dem Lernenden die Übersicht über den Lehrstoff zu erleichtern, stellt LEGIS eine größere Anzahl von Orientierungsmöglichkeiten zur Verfügung:
- Angabe der Lernziele zu jeder Gruppe in einem speziellen Frame
- Didaktische Zusatzinformationen (Beispiele, Anwendungen, alternative Darstellungen je nach Programmierung des Lehrprogrammautors) in den Subframes
- Vom System automatisch gesetzte lexikalische Querverweise auf alle innerhalb einer Region vorhandenen Frames
- Lehrerempfehlungen zur Weiterarbeit in den Frames und den Testsequenzen
- Die Autorensequenz als ein vom Lehrer vorgegebener Musterlernweg (Programmsteuerung für den Lerner, falls er die Übersicht verloren hat)
- Erklärung der Systemfunktion im Help-Frame und weitgehende Fehlermeldungen bei falschen Schülereingaben.

Als Beispiel für eine Lehreinheit in LEGIS vgl. Bild 1!

```
→   :F SACKGASSE
    ***FRAME SACKGASSE
    Gegeben eine =Chomsky-2-Grammatik= G=(V,T,P,Z).
    Sei y ex NB(Z) (=Nachbereich= von Z) und
        x nicht ex NB(Z).
    Dann heißt die =Reduktion= X⇒ Y eine =Sackgasse=.

    Folgende Zusatzinformaiton existiert noch:
    ANWENDUNG
    BEISPIEL
    ABGRENZUNG
    Wollen Sie eine Liste der weiterführenden Frames? (JA)
→   JA
    Weiterführende Frames
    :F SACKGASSENFREI
    :F LRK-GRAMMATIK
    :F LLK-GRAMMATIK
     :
     :
```

Bild 1: Darstellung eines Lehrdialogs in LEGIS. Eingaben des Lerners durch "→" gekennzeichnet. Der Lerner wählt das Frame "Sackgasse" der Gruppe "Formale Sprachen" zur Region "Übersetzerbau" an. Im Lehrtext lexikalische Querverweise auf die Frames "Chomsky-2-Grammatik", "Nachbereich", "Vorbereich" und "Reduktion".

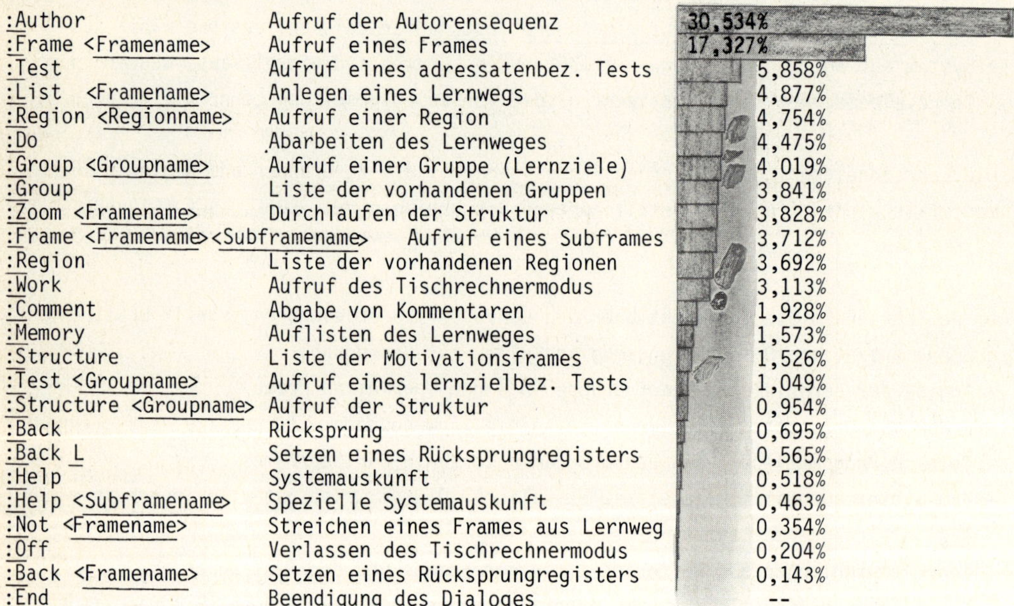

Kommando	Bedeutung	Anteil
:Author	Aufruf der Autorensequenz	30,534%
:Frame <Framename>	Aufruf eines Frames	17,327%
:Test	Aufruf eines adressatenbez. Tests	5,858%
:List <Framename>	Anlegen eines Lernwegs	4,877%
:Region <Regionname>	Aufruf einer Region	4,754%
:Do	Abarbeiten des Lernweges	4,475%
:Group <Groupname>	Aufruf einer Gruppe (Lernziele)	4,019%
:Group	Liste der vorhandenen Gruppen	3,841%
:Zoom <Framename>	Durchlaufen der Struktur	3,828%
:Frame <Framename><Subframename>	Aufruf eines Subframes	3,712%
:Region	Liste der vorhandenen Regionen	3,692%
:Work	Aufruf des Tischrechnermodus	3,113%
:Comment	Abgabe von Kommentaren	1,928%
:Memory	Auflisten des Lernweges	1,573%
:Structure	Liste der Motivationsframes	1,526%
:Test <Groupname>	Aufruf eines lernzielbez. Tests	1,049%
:Structure <Groupname>	Aufruf der Struktur	0,954%
:Back	Rücksprung	0,695%
:Back L	Setzen eines Rücksprungregisters	0,565%
:Help	Systemauskunft	0,518%
:Help <Subframename>	Spezielle Systemauskunft	0,463%
:Not <Framename>	Streichen eines Frames aus Lernweg	0,354%
:Off	Verlassen des Tischrechnermodus	0,204%
:Back <Framename>	Setzen eines Rücksprungregisters	0,143%
:End	Beendigung des Dialoges	--

Tabelle 1: Die LEGIS-Lernerkommandos, aufgelistet in der Reihenfolge ihrer Benutzung im Beobachtungszeitraum vom 1. 7. - 31. 12. 74. Bemessungsgrundlage: 14682 Kommandos (100%). Die Aufstellung umfaßt sämtliche Einsatzformen von LEGIS, also auch die informelle Benutzung durch Neugierige.

2.2 Die Programmerstellung in LEGIS

Dem Lehrprogrammautor steht eine größere Anzahl von Befehlen zur Erstellung, Eingabe, Manipulation und zum Editieren von Lehrprogrammen zur Verfügung (vgl. Tabelle 2).

1. Befehle zur Strukturierung der Lehrprogramme

Befehl	Bedeutung
!Region <Regionname>	Aufbau einer Region
!Group <Groupname>	Aufbau einer Gruppe
!Frame <Framename>,<Testframenumber>	Aufbau bzw. Überschreiben eines Frames
:Test	Frageteil
:Match	Beginn eines SMAL-Programms
:Subframe <Subframename>	Subframe
:Next {<Framename>}	Weiterführende Frames
:Halt	Ausgabe anhalten
:Page	Bildschirm löschen
!Testframe <Testframenumber>	Aufbau eines Testframes
:Test	Frageteil
:Match	Beginn eines SMAL-Programms
!Testframe <Groupname>	Beginn des Gruppenabschlußtests
:Test	Frageteil
:Match	Beginn eines SMAL-Programs

2. Befehle zur Eingabe und Manipulation von Lehrprogrammen

Befehl	Bedeutung
!Input Frames/Structure	Eingabe von Frames oder Struktur
!Stop	Eingabe beendet
!Jump	Eingabe überspringen bis
!Mark	Marke
!Delete <Regionname>	Region löschen
!Update	Querverweise setzen
!Check	Region überprüfen
!Edit <Regionname>	Region editieren
:Garbage-Collection	Speicherbereinigung
:Okay	Lehrprogrammfreigabe
:Okay Author	s.o. mit Autorensequenz
:Save	Thesaurus retten
!Output Frames/Groups/Regions/Structure/Thesaurus/Printer	Druckerprotokoll von Lehrprogrammen, Lehrprogrammteilen, Struktur, Thesaurus, Speicherabzug etc....

Tabelle 2: Die LEGIS-Lehrerbefehle, im Dialog- oder Stapelbetrieb zu verwenden.

Mit Hilfe der in LEGIS eingebetteten SMOBOL-4-ähnlichen Stringmanipulationssprache SMAL, die aufgrund ihres Prozedurkonzepts (lokale-, Bibliotheks- und intrinsische Prozeduren) leicht erweiterbar ist, werden die Simulations- und Testteile der Lehrprogramme erstellt. Gegenüber den konventionellen Autorensprachen ergibt sich dabei der Vorteil, daß die Antwortauswertung wahlweise entweder vom Lehrprogrammautor Zeichen für Zeichen völlig frei programmiert werden kann, oder durch bereitgestellte Bibliotheksprozeduren (Antwortauswerteroutinen) übernommen wird.

3. Die Implementierung von LEGIS

LEGIS besteht aus zwei voneinander getrennten Hauptteilen: dem Übersetzer für die Eingabe und Aufbereitung der Lehrstoffe und dem Prozessor zur Führung des Lehrdialogs. Der SMAL-Übersetzer und das Laufzeitsystem sind in die entsprechenden Teile eingebettet.

Bei der Implementierung von LEGIS mußten im wesentlichen die folgenden Forderungen erfüllt werden:

- Zuverlässige Verwaltung von großen Datenmengen.
- Einfachste Handhabung des Systems durch den Lerner bei größtmöglicher Flexibilität der Abfragemöglichkeiten und minimalen Antwortzeiten.
- Portabilität des Gesamtsystems.
- Weitgehende Möglichkeiten zur Erhebung von Lernerdaten (Recordingsystem, Schnittstelle zu externen Datenauswerteprogrammen).

Die erste Forderung wurde durch die Trennung der drei Arten von anfallenden Daten in jeweils permanente Dateien erreicht (vgl. auch Bild 2):

- globale Systeminformation auf der Systemdatei
- Lehrstoffspezifische Informationen auf getrennten Lehrstoffdateien
- Dialogdaten auf der Recording-Datei.

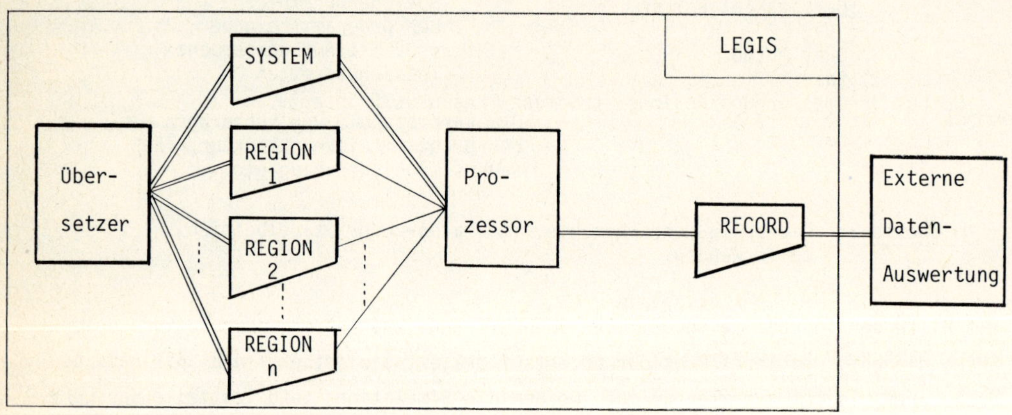

Bild 2: Dateiorganisation von LEGIS; Kommunikation mit Dateien:

═══ Schreiben, Lesen
——— Lesen

SYSTEM: Systemdatei
REGION 1..n: Lehrstoffdateien
RECORD: Datei zur Aufzeichnung von Dialogdaten

Ferner wurden für LEGIS Algorithmen zur automatischen Lösung von Dateizugriffskonflikten und von Wiederaufrufproblemen bei Systemzusammenbrüchen entwickelt, um eine hohe Systemzuverlässigkeit zu erreichen.

Die einfache Handhabung des Systems wurde durch die Lernerkommandosprache angestrebt, die im wesentlichen auf die Thesauri zugreift. Diese bilden das Kernstück von LEGIS und enthalten sämtliche Verwaltungsinformation für Frames, Testframes und deren Zusammenhänge.

Aus Effektivitätsgründen wurde dabei auf das Hash-Index-Tabellenverfahren zurückgegriffen (vgl. auch Bild 3). Zur Berechnung des Schlüssels wurde ein kombiniertes Verfahren angewandt, das eine sehr günstige Abbildungsfunktion darstellt.

Die Kernspeicherverwaltung beim Prozessor von LEGIS sollte so ökonomisch wie möglich vorgenommen werden, um rasche Antwortzeiten zu garantieren. Es wurde daher

1. die Freispeichertabelle des Thesaurus nur blockweise im Kernspeicher gehalten
2. der entsprechende Datenbereich wechselseitig von der Thesaurusverwaltung und den SMAL-Laufzeitdaten belegt.

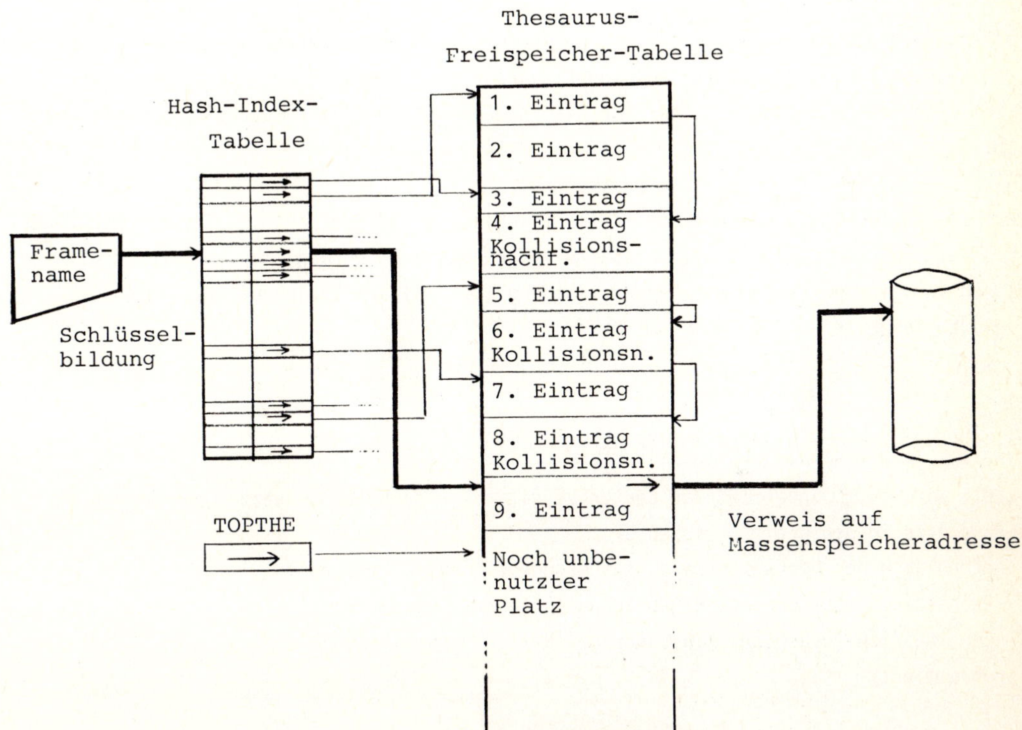

Bild 3: Aufbau des Thesaurus von LEGIS: Trennung in Hash-Index-Tabelle und Freispeichertabelle mit Einträgen variabler Länge und Kollisionsauflösung

Durch das Verbleiben des gesamten Thesaurus im Kernspeicher zur Übersetzzeit war es jedoch möglich, die Wiederaufrufprobleme bei Systemzusammenbrüchen eindeutig zu lösen.

Die Portabilität von LEGIS, die durch Übertragungen des Systems von der Rechenanlage Burroughs 6700 auf die UNIVAC 1108 und die PDP 10 demonstriert wurde, konnte durch eine Reihe von Maßnahmen erreicht werden:

- Implementierung in gereinigtem FORTRAN IV
- Verwendung einer vom jeweiligen Gastrechner unabhängigen eigenen Zeichencodierung mit variablem Zeichensatz
- Beschränkung der Wortgröße auf 32 bit (da alle größeren Rechenanlagen mindestens diese Wortlänge umfassen)
- Definition und Abprüfen eines eigenen Zahlenbereiches
- Zugriff auf Massenspeicher durch eine einzige standardisierte Routine
- interne Lösung von Dateizugriffsproblemen
- Selbstdiagnose des Systems und verschiedene Testausdrucke
- modulare Programmerstellung
- klare Programmierung ohne Verwendung von "Tricks"; programminterne Dokumentation.

Die Aufzeichnung der Dialogdaten wurde gefordert, um erste Erhebungen über das Lernerverhalten in einer Lernersteuerungssituation zu ermöglichen. Der Prozessor von LEGIS legt diese Daten auf einer für externe Auswerteprogramme zugänglichen Datei ab.

Auf die Realisierung von SMAL als Kellermaschine, die einen eintrittsinvarianten Code erzeugt, kann an dieser Stelle nicht weiter eingegangen werden, da sie nicht spezifisch für ein RGU-System mit Lernersteuerung ist (weitere Implementierungsdetails vgl. bei BODE 1975 [2]).

4. Untersuchungen beim Einsatz von LEGIS

LEGIS wird seit Januar 1974 an der Universität Karlsruhe eingesetzt. Dazu wurden Lehrstoffe in den drei Bereichen :
- Grundlagen des Übersetzerbaus (insbesondere Formale Sprachen)
- Rechnerorganisation (Grundausbildung in technischer Informatik)
- Lerntheorien (Lehrbereich Rechner-Gestützter-Unterricht)

programmiert.

Die etwa 300 bis Ende 1974 registrierten Benutzer von LEGIS wurden je nach Versuchsanordnung mit verschiedensten Erhebungsinstrumenten beobachtet:

- automatisches Lerndatenrecording
- Fragebogen zur Motiveinstellung
- Lernleistungstests
- Gespräche.

So konnten erste Ergebnisse gewonnen werden, die (bei aller Vorsicht mit empirischen Daten im Bildungsbereich) als Anregungen für detailliertere Untersuchungen im Bereich der Lernersteuerung dienen mögen:

1. Die Lernersteuerung im Sinne von LEGIS wird von den Benutzern akzeptiert und verwendet (vgl. dazu die Benutzerstatistik in Tabelle 1 sowie Tabelle 3). Der relativ hohe Anteil an Zugriffen auf Lehrinformation durch Programmsteuerung (Kommando :A) zeigt jedoch auch, daß Autorensequenzen als vorgegebene "Ideallernwege" für die Orientierung des Lerners auch in einem Informations-System notwendig sind.

Einsatzform	Anzahl der beobachteten Framezugriffe	Durchschnittlicher Grad der Lernersteuerung
Gesamt	10 079	55,52 %
Mit Einführung	4 029	62,075 %
Ohne Einführung	6 050	51,157 %

Tabelle 3: Durchschnittlicher Grad der Lernersteuerung bei kontrollierten Versuchsreihen (mit Einführung in die Benutzung von LEGIS) und bei informeller Benutzung des Systems (ohne Einführung). Der durchschnittliche Grad der Lernersteuerung ergibt sich aus der Anzahl der Zugriffe auf Frames durch Lernersteuerung bezogen auf die Gesamtzahl der Framezugriffe.

2. Der spezifische Grad der Lernersteuerung variiert mit dem Strukturierungsgrad der Lehrstoffe (vgl. Tabelle 4), d.h. bei stark hierarchisch aufgebauten Lehrstoffen (im Gegensatz zu mehr lexikalisch-unstrukturierten Stoffen) benötigt der Lerner mehr Lenkungshilfen.

Lehrstoff (Strukturierung)	Anzahl der beobachteten Framezugriffe	Durchschnittlicher Grad der Lernersteuerung
Formale Sprachen (stark)	1 367	42,356 %
Rechnerorganisation (schwach)	2 199	62,392 %
Lerntheorien (schwach)	1 451	56,168 %

Tabelle 4: Durchschnittlicher Grad der Lernersteuerung für verschieden stark strukturierte Lehrstoffe.

3. Die Lernleistung einer Versuchsgruppe mit Lernersteuerung ist kurzfristig leicht-, langfristig signifikant besser als die Leistung einer Vorlesungsgruppe, die mit gleichem Aufwand lernt (vgl. Tabelle 5).

	Vortest		Nachtest				Spättest			
	Vpn	L_{vor}	Vpn	L_{vor}	L_{nach}	ΔL	Vpn	L_{vor}	$L_{spät}$	ΔL
Vorlesung	26	6,14	14	6,14	26,19	20,05	13	4,61	21,92	17,30
LEGIS	27	6,55	14	6,50	27,79	21,29	13	5,15	25,31	20,15

Tabelle 5: Darstellung der Lernleistung (Reproduktion von Faktenwissen) im Vortest (L_{vor}), Nachtest (L_{nach}) und im Spättest ($L_{spät}$), ferner der Lernleistungsdifferenz (L), gemessen direkt nach dem Unterrichtseinsatz (Nachtest) sowie 2 Monate später (Spättest). Signifikanz bei Parallelstichproben: etwa 2 % Niveau im Spättest. (Vpn = Anzahl der Versuchspersonen)

Die Versuchsteilnehmer wurden dabei durch Losentscheid in zwei Gruppen (LEGIS/Vorlesung) eingeteilt und wurden etwa 1 Monat lang getrennt unterrichtet.

4. Der Versuch, verschiedene Lernertypen zu ermitteln, deren Fähigkeit, lernergesteuert Lehrstoffe zu erarbeiten, eindeutig zu unterscheiden ist, muß bisher als gescheitert betrachtet werden (vgl. Tabelle 6).

5. Die Lernersteuerung wirkt motivierend, die Einstellung der Teilnehmer zum Lernen mit LEGIS ist weitgehend positiv (z.B. würden ca. 90 % der Befragten bei entsprechendem Angebot wieder mit LEGIS arbeiten).

	MOTIVE		
	Intrinsische Anschluß Kombinationen	Leistung Macht Kausal	Motivkonflikt erster Art
Beobachtete Vpn	18	20	15
Framezugriffe	1 024	1 135	1 518
Durchschnittlicher Grad der Lernersteuerung	63,78 %	65,64 %	53,89 %

Tabelle 6: Durchschnittlicher Grad der Lernersteuerung für verschiedene Motivausprägungen (Lernergruppen). Die Arbeitshypothese, daß Intrinsisch- und Anschlußmotivierte mehr lernergesteuert arbeiten als andere Lernergruppen mußte verworfen werden. Lediglich Versuchspersonen mit Motivkonflikten erster Art haben einen geringeren Lernersteuerungsgrad.

6. Die Lernwege der einzelnen Teilnehmer differieren stark, gleiche Lernwege treten praktisch nicht auf, die Sitzungszeiten schwanken zwischen wenigen Minuten und bis zu 3 Stunden.

5. Ausblick

Die Erfahrungen mit LEGIS zeigen, daß mehr lerneraktive Lernformen für den RGU mit Recht gefordert werden. Offensichtlich sind die Lernenden auf Universitätsniveau tatsächlich in der Lage, auf sinnvolle Weise eigene Lernwege zu bestimmen. Weitere detaillierte Untersuchungen müssen nunmehr zeigen, welche Lernergruppen besonders für die Lernersteuerung geeignet sind und welche zusätzliche Orientierungshilfen den übrigen Adressaten für einen optimalen Lernerfolg angeboten werden müssen.

Für die weitere Entwicklung des RGU wird man von dem in der Versuchssituation angebrachten "puristischen" Ansatz (reines Lernersteuerungssystem) abgehen und versuchen, die Fähigkeiten von LEGIS mit einer flexiblen Autorensprache wie LEKTOR (vgl. SCHMITT, WRIGHTSON, 1974 [6]) anstelle von SMAL zu verbinden, um gleichzeitig auch andere Lehrstrategien (Simulationen, Übungsaufgaben, Graphik in größerem Ausmaß) anbieten zu können. Ein solches "RGU-Supersystem" würde die heute bereits in getrennten Ansätzen realisierten Vorteile der einzelnen RGU-Sprachen für das menschliche Lernen vereinigen.

Eine qualitative Erweiterung des Gedankens der Lernersteuerung gegenüber LEGIS wird jedoch erst dann erreicht, wenn der Dialog mit dem Rechner nicht über eine Kommandosprache und Stichworte, sondern in natürlicher Sprache (bzw. Untermengen) abgewickelt wird. In einem solchen Frage-Antwort-System müßte dann mit generativen Methoden auf der Basis eines semantischen Netzwerks gearbeitet werden. Erste, momentan allerdings pädagogisch nicht befriedigende Ergebnisse liegen hierzu aus dem Bereich der Künstlichen Intelligenz vor (vgl. etwa CARBONELL, COLLINS 1973 [4]). So lange die hier auftretenden Probleme (Antwortzeiten, Informationseingabe) nicht gelöst sind, werden LEGIS-ähnliche Systeme in größerem Maße eingesetzt werden, was auch durch die Entwicklungen an anderer Stelle(LGU auf der Basis GOLEM-Informationssystem, vgl. STAHL, 1974 [7] oder TICCIT, vgl. BUNDERSON, SCHNEIDER, 1974 [3]) dokumentiert wird.

6. Literatur

[1] BODE, A.
Lernersteuerung im RGU: erste Erfahrungen mit LEGIS.
In: GOOS, HARTMANIS (Hrsgb.); Lecture Notes in Computer Science,
Vol. 17, pp. 329 - 337
Springer, Berlin-Heidelberg-New York 1974

[2] BODE, A.
Lernersteuerung im Rechner-Gestützten Unterricht: Entwicklung und Erprobung des Systems LEGIS.
Eingereichte Dissertation, Karlsruhe 1975

[3] BUNDERSON, V.C., SCHNEIDER, E.
Design Strategy for Learner Controlled Courseware.
In: GOOS, HARTMANIS (Hrsgb.) a.a.O. pp. 308 - 322 1974

[4] CARBONELL, I.R., COLLINS, A.
Natural Semantics in Artificial Intelligence.
In: Proceedings of 3rd IJCAI, pp. 344 - 351 1973

[5] HAEFNER, K.
Struktur fachsystematischer Netze als Komponente von Infotheken.
In: GOOS, HARTMANIS (Hrsgb.) a.a.O. pp. 338 - 346 1974

[6] SCHMITT, A., WRIGHTSON, G.
Basisbeschreibung des LEKTOR-Programmiersystems.
Fakultät für Informatik, Universität Karlsruhe 1974

[7] STAHL, V.
Lernergesteuerter Unterricht auf der Grundlage eines Datenbanksystems.
In: Perspektiven Nr. 1 (SIEMENS AG)
München 1974

Ü B E R S E T Z E R B A U

SLS/1 : A TRANSLATOR WRITING SYSTEM

J. Lewi, K. De Vlaminck, J. Huens, P. Mertens

KATHOLIEKE UNIVERSITEIT LEUVEN
Applied Mathematics and Programming Division
B-3030 Heverlee, Belgium

CONTENTS

1. INTRODUCTION
2. BRIEF DESCRIPTION OF THE TRANSLATOR WRITING SYSTEM
3. THE LEXICAL ANALYSER GENERATOR
4. THE SYNTAX ANALYSER GENERATOR
5. THE SEMANTICAL ANALYSER GENERATOR
6. CONCLUSION
REFERENCES

1. INTRODUCTION

The idea of automating parts of compilers dates from the compiler-compiler of Brooker and Morris [1], [2], [3]. Since then, numerous systems have been developed. In Feldman and Gries [4] the development of translator writing systems is thoroughly viewed representing the state of the art up to 1967.

The stimulus for automating the (context-free) syntax part of compilers is given by the development of Algol 60 [5] using the context-free formalism for describing most of its syntax. Since then, a great variety of syntax analyser generators (often misusing the term 'translator writing system', 'compiler-compiler') came into existence.

The idea of treating the semantic as well as the syntactic part of the compiler was first born in the article of Irons [6]. The idea consists in associating semantic routines with the context-free rules, introducing a high level of flexibility and modularity in compiler writing.

The only new idea added to this came from Knuth [7], introducing a nice and systematic way to control static information, called attributes, within a program. This control mechanism was already used by Samelson and Bauer [8] but in a very restricted form. In fact, any compiler computes static information in order to generate the appropriate code, but Knuth introduces a very systematic way to do it, augmenting the reliability of compilers.

In constructing a translator writing system, it is the semantic part that is the most difficult one and it is in that part that most systems fundamentally differ.
In our system, the emphasis is laid on the semantic part.

2. BRIEF DESCRIPTION OF THE TRANSLATOR WRITING SYSTEM

The main concepts of the translator writing system stems from a study on compiler methodology. This study was made by a compiler group at MBLE of which one of the authors took part. The basic principles resulting from this study have been applied on the construction of an Algol 68 compiler [9], [10], [11], [12], [13] and [14].

The translator writing system is simple in its use and allows efficient compilers to be produced in a flexible and modular way. The system is therefore an excellent tool for writing compilers for languages which are in their definition or experimental stage. It applies on a wide class of applications and can be used in a very general way. It provides the user with a great number of debugging aids and with a flexible file management.

There are two versions of the system : a didactic version to be used for a compiler course and an operational one. The only difference between the two versions is the way the syntactic structure, output of the syntax analyser, is stored : in the form of a tree (didactic version) or in a linear form using prefix and postfix markers (operational version).

The general schema of the translator writing system can be illustrated as follows :

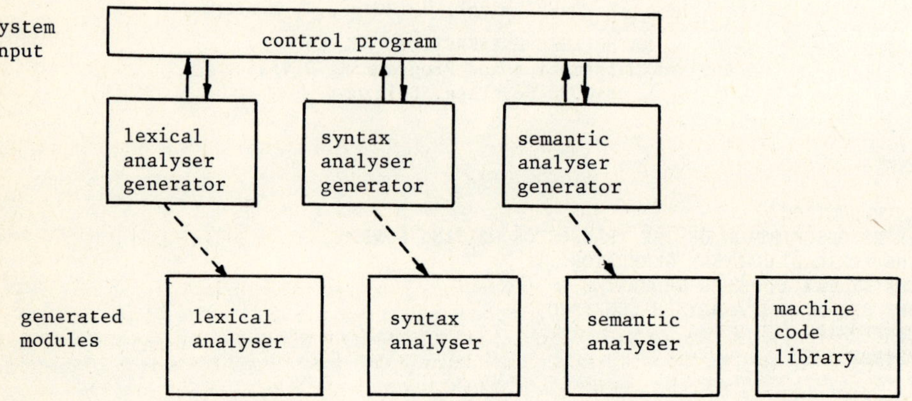

The control program treats the system input. This input consists of the definitions of the parameters of the programs to be generated and of the calls for the generators. The parameters are divided into 2 classes : global parameters that are shared by two or three generators and the local parameters for each generator in particular.

Our system consists of three generators : the lexical analyser generator, the (context-free) syntax analyser generator and the semantic analyser generator. The analysers, constructed by these generators, can be used independently. They also can be linked together to form a compiler. Therefore, a standard interface between the analysers and a standard method for passing information between each analyser is defined by the system. This is described further in this paper.

The machine code library is the only machine-dependent part of the system. For each type of an intermediate instruction (instructions are parametrized), there is an object routine in the library, producing machine code from this intermediate instruction.

The whole translator writing system is written in PL/I. Also the modules generated by the system are PL/I programs. The semantic routines are PL/I procedures. Each module is now described in more detail and is applied on a non-trivial example 'PICO-ALGOL'. In order to reduce the lenght occupied by the example, a PL/I-like notation is used to describe the system input and the semantic routines.

3. THE LEXICAL ANALYSER GENERATOR

The user input of the lexical analyser generator consists of

(1) the alphabet of (most elementary) tokens of the language to be lexically analysed
(2) a regular expression describing the syntactic features of the lexical analysis
(3) a number of semantic routines describing the (semantic) actions to be performed during lexical analysis. These semantic routines are incorporated in the regular expression as will be explained further
(4) a number of global variables and global routines which are accessible from any semantic routine. In this manner communication between the semantic routines is possible. The variables can be simple or composed such as structures and tables
(5) a number of print routines allowing the compiler builder to print out all kinds of results (e.g. tables, variables) at any stage of the lexical analysis process. This seems to be a valuable debugging aid for the system user
(6) a number of commands concerning file organization to handle data such as tables. Tables can be put on files and then passed on to another generated module.

There exists also system defined variables and routines. E.g. 'in' is a character variable containing the current symbol read from the input string. It is initialized with the first symbol of the string.
The action of the routine call 'read(in)' consists in reading the next symbol from the input string in 'in'.
If the lexically analyzed program, output of the lexical analyser, is to be used as input of the next module (which is the syntax analyser), the output must be of a given standard format.
Namely, the output elements must be structures with two fields : a class field and a specification field. The description is :

```
DCL 1 OUTPUTELEM,
      2 CLASS CHAR(1),
      2 SPEC BIN FIXED;
```

In our example of PICO-ALGOL the set of classes, called vocabulary VT, is
{<u>iden</u>,<u>intct</u>,<u>begin</u>,<u>end</u>,<u>int</u>,<u>bool</u>,<u>true</u>,<u>false</u>,<u>print</u>,+,-,★,/,=,(,),;,:=}
The specification fields will be indexes of SYMBTAB in the case of <u>iden</u> and integer values in the case of <u>intct</u>. In all other cases the specification field contains 0. Note that VT will play the role of terminal vocabulary in the syntax analysis.

<u>THE LEXICAL ANALYSER FOR PICO-ALGOL</u>

<u>The alphabet of tokens</u>

A = {a,b,c,d,e,...,z,
0,1,2,3,4,5,6,7,8,9,
+,-,★,/,=,
.,;,,(,),'}

<u>Definition of sets of tokens</u>

let = {a,b,c,...,z}
dig = {0,1,...,9}
nonletdig = A-let-dig
nondig = A-dig
op = {+,-,★,/,=,(,)}

<u>Regular expression with calls of semantic routines (ρ)</u>

$$(\; ' \; \rho_0 \; (\text{ let } \rho_1 \;)^\star \; ' \; \rho_2 \; |$$
$$\text{let } \rho_1 \; (\text{ let } \rho_1 \; | \text{ dig } \rho_1 \;)^\star \text{ nonletdig } \rho_3 \; |$$
$$\text{dig } \rho_4 \; (\text{ dig } \rho_5 \;)^\star \text{ nondig } \rho_6 \; |$$
$$\text{op } \rho_7 \; |$$
$$. \; \rho_0 \; (= \rho_8 \; | \; , \; \rho_9 \;) \;)^\star$$

The finite-state transducer represented by the regular expression

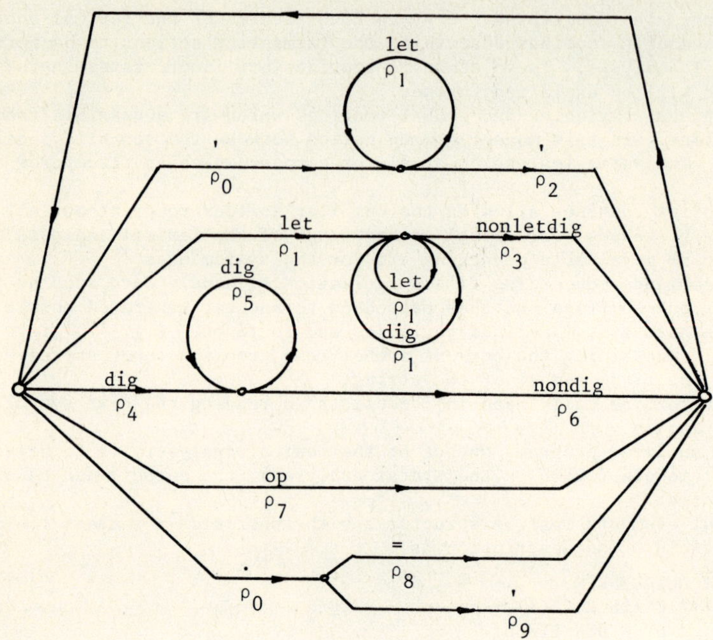

The class symbols (terminal symbols of the context-free syntax, input of the syntax analyser generator)

VT = {iden,intct,begin,end,int,bool,true,false,print, +,-,★,/,=,(,),;,:=}

The lexical analysis consists of two main tasks :

(1) - It groups tokens of the vocabulary A into keywords giving the classes : begin, end, int, bool, true, false and print. This action is performed by the routines ρ_0, ρ_1 and ρ_2 using the global variables 'KEYTAB' and 'auxstring'.

- It groups tokens of A into identifiers resulting in the class iden. This action is performed by the routines ρ_1 and ρ_3 using 'SYMBTAB' and 'auxstring'.

- It groups tokens of A into integer constants resulting into the class intct. This is done by the routines ρ_4, ρ_5 and ρ_6 using the variable 'integer'.

- It groups tokens of A into operators and separators giving the classes : +, -, ★, /, =, (,), ; and :=. This is done by the routines ρ_0, ρ_7, ρ_8 and ρ_9 using the variable 'OPTAB'.

(2) It constructs a symbol table SYMBTAB having an entry for each identifier. Each entry of the table consists of three fields : type and access field, to be used during the semantic analysis, and alpha field, filled in during lexical analysis. SYMBTAB is a global input parameter of the system. It is transmitted from the lexical analyser to the semantic analyser where the type and access fields will be treated.

Global variables and routines

```
DCL 1 KEYTAB(1:11),
      2 KEYWORD CHAR(8) INIT('BEGIN','END','INIT','BOOL','TRUE','FALSE','PRINT',
                                                     'IF','THEN','ELSE','FI'),
      2 CODE BIN FIXED INIT(begin,end,int,bool,true,false,print,if,then,else,fi);
      /* underlined words are used as symbolic codes to augment the readability */
DCL 1 OPTAB(1:7),
      2 OPERATOR CHAR(1) INIT('+','-','*','/','=','(',')'),
      2 CODE BIN FIXED INIT(+,-,*,/,=,(,));
      /* +,-,*,/ etc. are symbolic codes.  This augments the readability of the
         routines in the sequel */
DCL 1 SYMBTAB(1:N),
      2 TYPE CHAR(1),
      2 ACCESS,
        3 CLASS CHAR(1)
        3 LEVEL BIN FIXED,
        3 ADDRESS BIN FIXED,
      2 ALPHA CHAR(8);
DCL AUXSTRING CHAR(8) VARYING INIT('');
DCL INTEGER BIN FIXED INIT(0);
DCL J BIN FIXED;
LOOKUPKEYTAB:PROC (CHAR(8)) RETURNS (BIN FIXED);
  /* This routine searches KEYTAB for an entry with index j such that KEYTAB field
     of that entry is equal to the argument of the routine call.  If such an entry
     does not exist, then j becomes 0 */
LOOKUPOPTAB:PROC (CHAR(1)) RETURNS (BIN FIXED);
  /* This routine searches OPTAB for an entry with index j such that the OPERATOR
     field of that entry is equal to the argument */
LOOKUPSYMBTAB:PROC (CHAR(8)) RETURNS (BIN FIXED);
  /* This routine searches SYMBTAB for an entry with index j such that the ALPHA
     field of that entry is equal to the string argument of the routine call.  If
     such an entry does not exist, a new entry is added to SYMBTAB.  The ALPHA field
     is filled with the argument.  A table overflow test is provided in this
     routine */
ERROR:PROC;
  /* An error is found : the process halts.  Error diagnostics are produced */
READ:PROC (CHAR(1));
  /* This routine reads the next token of the input string in the variable IN */
```

Definition of the semantic routines

```
ρ0:PROC;
  CALL READ(IN);
  END;
ρ1:PROC;
  IF LENGTH(AUXSTRING)=8
     THEN CALL ERROR;
  AUXSTRING=AUXSTRING||IN;
  CALL READ(IN);
  END;
ρ2:PROC;
  LOOKUPKEYTAB(AUXSTRING);
  IF j=0
     THEN CALL ERROR;
     ELSE CALL OUT
          (KEYTAB.CODE(J),0);
  AUXSTRING='';
  CALL READ(IN);
  END;
ρ3:PROC;
  CALL LOOKUPSYMBTAB(AUXSTRING);
  CALL OUT(iden,J);
  AUXSTRING='';
  END;
ρ4:PROC;
  INTEGER=IN;CALL READ(IN);
  END;
ρ5:PROC;
  INTEGER=INTEGER*10+IN;CALL READ(IN);
  END;
ρ6:PROC;
  CALL OUT(intct,INTEGER);INTEGER=0;
  END;
ρ7:PROC;
  CALL LOOKUPTAB(IN);
  IF J=0
     THEN ERROR;
     ELSE CALL OUT
          (OPTAB.CODE(J),0);
  CALL READ(IN);
  END;
ρ8:PROC;
  CALL OUT(:=,0);CALL READ(IN);
  END;
ρ9:PROC;
  CALL OUT(;,0);CALL READ(IN);
  END;
```

An example of the output of the lexical analyser for PICO-ALGOL

The inputstring is :

```
'begin''int'a=3.,'int'b.,'bool'c.,'if'c'then'b.=a'else'b.=2'fi'.,'print'b'end'
```

```
begin,0
int,0
iden,1 /* identifier a */
=,0
intct,3
;,0
int,0
iden,2 /* identifier b */
;,0
bool,0
iden,3 /* identifier c */
;,0
if,0
iden,3 /* identifier c */
then,0
iden,2 /* identifier b */
:=,0
iden,1 /* identifier a */
else,0
iden,2 /* identifier b */
:=,0
intct,2
fi,0
;,0
print,0
iden,2 /* identifier b */
end,0
```

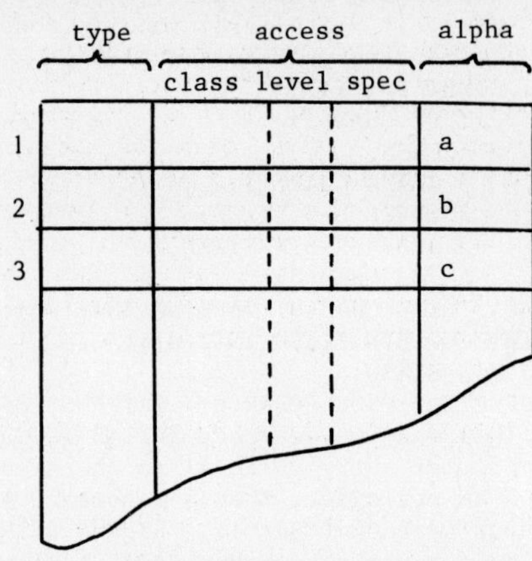

4. THE SYNTAX (CONTEXT-FREE) ANALYSER GENERATOR

The user input of the syntax analyser generator consists of

(1) the vocabulary of terminal symbols;
(2) a number of context-free rules;
(3) resynchronisation information in the case errors are detected during syntax analysis.

The syntax analyser generator is of the LALR(1) type of Lalonde [15]. This choice is made because it covers a wide class of context-free grammars and because the generation of the syntax analysers is still efficient.

The user is able to specify symbols upon which resynchronisation will be built in the generated module. This specification has the form of triples of symbols : two terminals (called begin and end symbol) and one non-terminal, e.g. (,) and E. If during syntax analysis an error occurs, the smallest string of terminals enclosed between a pair of begin and end symbols is skipped and parsing is resumed by reducing this string by the corresponding non-terminal. This process is recursive.

In the didactic version of the system, the output of the syntax analyser is a tree. In the operational version of the system, the output is a linear form of the tree using prefix and postfix phrase markers. The latter version will consume less time and space.

THE CONTEXT-FREE DESCRIPTION FOR PICO-ALGOL

```
<program> → begin <declarationlist> ; <statementlist> end
<declarationlist> → <declarationlist> ; <declaration> | <declaration>
<declaration> → int iden | bool iden | int iden := E | bool iden := E |
                int iden = E | bool iden = E
<statementlist> → <statementlist> ; <statement> | <statement>
<statement> → <assignment> | <printstatement> | <conditionalstatement>
<assignment> → iden := E
<printstatement> → print E
<conditionalstatement> → if E then <statement> else <statement> fi
 E → E + T |
     E - T |
     T

 T → T ★ F |
     T / F |
     F

 F → iden |
     intct |
     true |
     false
     ( E )
```

<u>An example of the output of the syntactic analyser for PICO-ALGOL</u> (the source program is not meaningful; it is kept simple only for practical reasons of space economy)

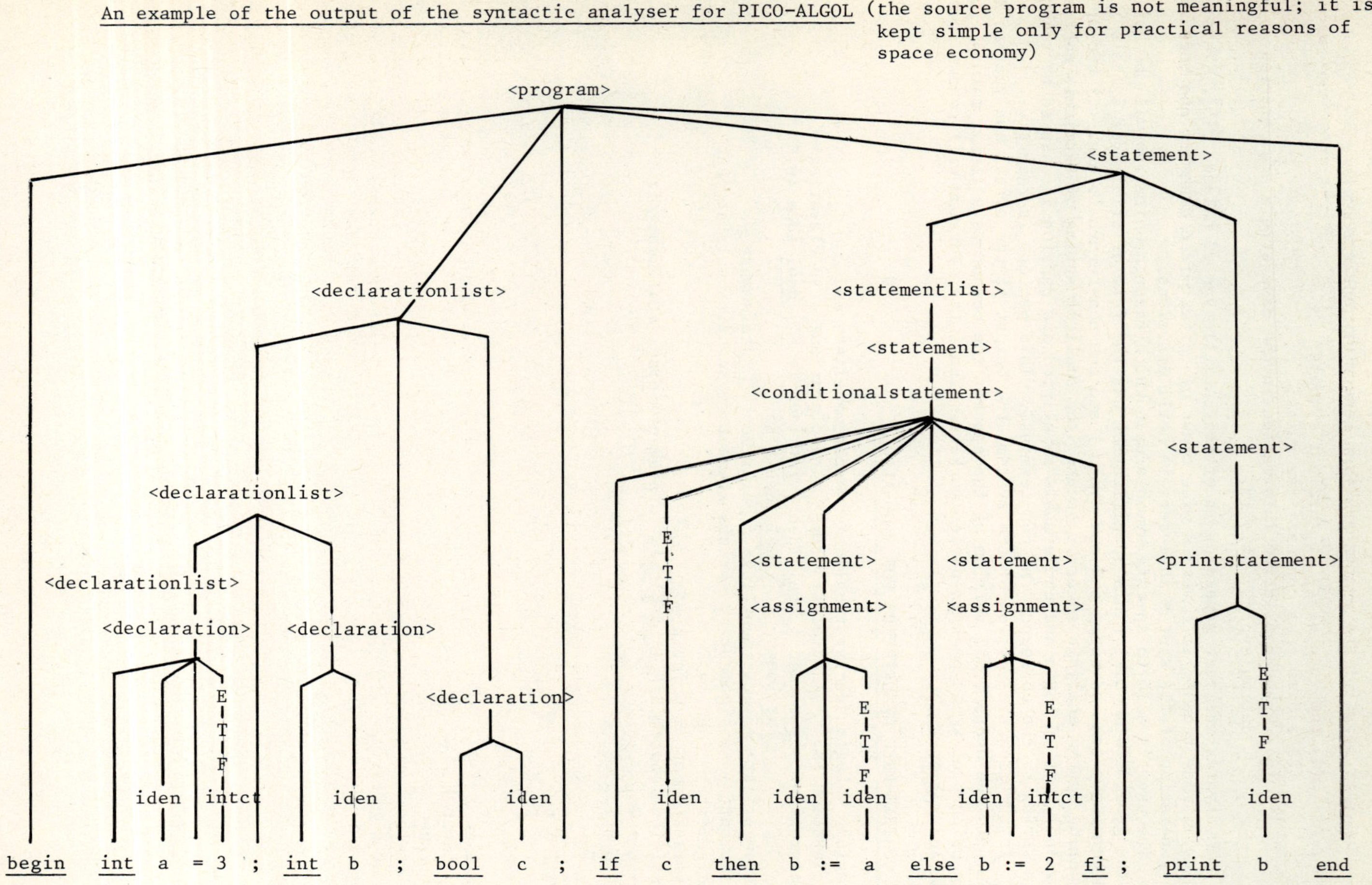

5. THE SEMANTIC ANALYSER GENERATOR

The user input of the semantic analyser generator consists of

(1) a number of context-free rules with calls of semantic routines associated with them;
(2) a number of semantic routine definitions describing the (semantic) actions to be performed during semantic analysis;
(3) a number of global variables and global routines which are accessible from any semantic routine;
(4) a description (declaration) of the attributes to be controlled by the semantic analyser;
(5) a number of print statements for debugging aids;
(6) a number of file organisation commands.

The input of the semantic analyser is the syntax tree, output from the syntax analyser. This tree is passed through in a so-called prefix-infix-postfix mode. Each node A of the rule

$$A \rightarrow A_1\ A_2\ \ldots\ A_n$$

is passed through exactly n+1 times, once in prefix, n-1 times in infix and once in postfix. At each pass a corresponding semantic routine, if it exists, is called :

$$A \rightarrow \rho_{prefix}\ A_1\ \rho_{infix_1}\ A_2\ \rho_{infix_2}\ \ldots\ \rho_{infix_{n-1}}\ A_n\ \rho_{postfix}$$

The scanning of a node A is illustrated as follows :

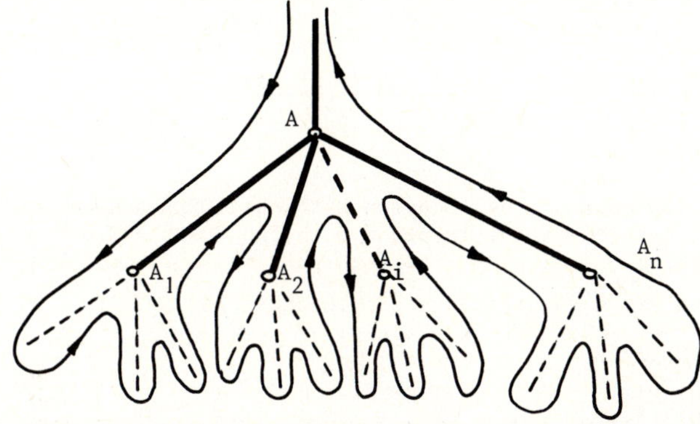

This tree scanning mode together with the control mechanism of attributes, explained below, constitute the kernel of the semantic analyser generator. The translation of actions of the source language (code generation) occurs in the nodes of the tree of a particular program of that language and is performed by the call of semantic routines. However, code generation in a node (e.g. <assignment>) is only possible if enough information is available at that node (in our example, 'type' and 'access' of left and right part of the assignment). This needs a calculation and control of a number of information items, called attributes, all over the tree. This process is often called static elaboration or static control of the source program. It is the system user who specifies the attributes he wants to control. The system allocates with each node an attribute space. The semantic routines in a given rule : $A \rightarrow A_1\ A_2\ \ldots\ A_n$ have direct access of any attribute space of any node A, A_1, A_2, ..., A_n. This is an important semantic mechanism built-in in the system. In our example, the user description of the attributes for PICO-ALGOL is :

```
DCL 1 ATT BASED,
      2 TYPE CHAR(1),
      2 ACCESS,
        3 CLASS CHAR(1),
        3 LEVEL BIN FIXED,
        3 SPEC BIN FIXED,
      2 LABEL BIN FIXED;
```

In the semantic routine ρ_8 of the rule '<assignment> → iden := E ρ_8' one may speak about E→ATT.TYPE,E→ATT.ACCESS.LEVEL etc... . The information associated with terminal symbols can be accessed using the name of that terminal symbol followed by '→SPEC' e.g. IDEN→SPEC. Intermediate code can be generated by a special built-in function 'GENERATE' with any string of characters as actual parameter.

THE SEMANTIC DESCRIPTION FOR PICO-ALGOL

Run-time organization

There are two run-time spaces, IDEN% (1) and WORK%.
The identifier space IDEN% treats locations associated during identifier declarations.
The current table index used for filling up IDEN% is IDENP (compile-time variable).
The working space WORK% treats locations of intermediate results in expressions.
The current table index of WORK% is WORKP.

The attribute description (input of the generator)

```
DCL 1 ATT BASED,
      2 TYPE CHAR(1),
      2 ACCESS,
        3 CLASS CHAR(1),
        3 LEVEL BIN FIXED,
        3 SPEC BIN FIXED,
      2 LABEL BIN FIXED;
```

The different types: <u>ref</u> <u>int</u>, <u>ref</u> <u>bool</u>, <u>int</u>, <u>bool</u> and <u>void</u>

/* these type representations are considered to be one single character */

The accesses	The value characterized by the access
(literal,0,a)	the integer a : Integers are supposed to hold in the spec field of an access.
(idenspace,0,a)	the IDEN% address a.
(idenspace,1,a)	the contents of the location with the IDEN% address a.
(workspace,1,a)	the contents of the location with the WORK% address a.
(nihil,0,0)	no value.

All classes of accesses are considered one single character.

Global variables and routines

```
DCL IDENP BIN FIXED INIT(1),
    WORKP BIN FIXED INIT(1),
    LABEL BIN FIXED INIT(0);
```

For SYMBTAB, the declaration made for the lexical analyser generator is taken.

```
SIZE:PROC (CHAR(1)) RETURNS (BIN FIXED);
  /* This routine calculates the number of memory cells data of a given type
     (argument of the call) occupies */
ERROR:PROC;
  /* An error is found, the process halts.
     Error diagnostics are produced */
```

The intermediate code instructions

operation field	parameters(s) field
(assign	type of the left part, access of left part, access of right part)
(plus	type of left operand, type of right operand, access of left operand, access of right operand, access of result)

---

(1) % is used for run-time devices and variables.

idem for minus, times, divide

```
(print                    type of the value to be printed,
                          access of the value to be printed)
(jump false               access of the value of the boolean condition
                          label)
(labeldef                 label)
(jump                     label)
```

The operation fields are considered to be one single character.

The semantic routines

<declaration> → int iden ρ_1

```
ρ1:PROC;
   SYMBTAB(IDEN→SPEC).TYPE=ref int;
   SYMBTAB(IDEN→SPEC).ACCESS=(idenspace,0,IDENP);
   IDENP=IDENP+SIZE(int);
   END;
```

<declaration> → int iden = E ρ_3

```
ρ3:PROC;
   IF E→ATT.TYPE=int|E→ATT.TYPE=ref int
      THEN SYMBTAB(IDEN→SPEC).TYPE=int;
      ELSE CALL ERROR;
   IF E→ATT.ACCESS.CLASS=workspace
      THEN DO;
           SYMBTAB(IDEN→SPEC).ACCESS=(idenspace,1,IDENP);
           CALL GENERATE(assign,ref int,
                                (idenspace,0,IDENP),
                                E→ATT.ACCESS);
           IDENP=IDENP+SIZE(int);
           WORKP=E→ATT.ACCESS.SPEC;
           END;
      ELSE IF E→ATT.ACCESS.CLASS=idenspace &
              E→ATT.ACCESS.LEVEL=0
              THEN DO;
                   SYMBTAB(IDEN→SPEC).ACCESS=idenspace,1,IDENP);
                   CALL GENERATE(assign,ref int,
                                        (idenspace,0,IDENP),
                                        (idenspace,1,
                                        E→ATT.ACCESS.SPEC));
                   IDENP=IDENP+SIZE(int);
                   END;
              ELSE SYMBTAB(IDEN→SPEC).ACCESS=E→ATT.ACCESS;
   END;
```

<assignment> → iden := E ρ_5

```
ρ5:PROC;
   IF E→ATT.TYPE=ref int|E→ATT.TYPE=ref bool
      THEN DO;
           E→ATT.TYPE=DELETEREF(E→ATT.TYPE);
           E→ATT.ACCESS.LEVEL=1;
           END;
   IF SYMBTAB(IDEN→SPEC).TYPE=ref int
      THEN DO;
           IF E→ATT.TYPE¬=int
              THEN CALL ERROR;
           END;
      ELSE IF SYMBTAB(IDEN→SPEC).TYPE=ref bool
              THEN IF E→ATT.TYPE¬=bool
                      THEN CALL ERROR;
```

```
    CALL GENERATE(assign,SYMBTAB(IDEN→SPEC),TYPE,
                         SYMBTAB(IDEN→SPEC).ACCESS,
                         E→ATT.ACCESS);
    IF E→ATT.ACCESS.CLASS=workspace
       THEN WORKP=E→ATT.ACCESS.SPEC;
    <assignment>→ATT.TYPE=void;
    <assignment>→ATT.ACCESS=(nihil,0,0);
    END;

<printstatement> → print E ρ6

ρ6:PROC;
    IF E→ATT.TYPE=ref int|E→ATT.TYPE=ref bool
       THEN DO;
            E→ATT.TYPE=DELETEREF(E→ATT.TYPE);
            E→ATT.ACCESS.LEVEL=1;
            END;
    CALL GENERATE(print,E→ATT.TYPE,
                        E→ATT.ACCESS);
    <printstatement>→ATT.TYPE=void;
    <printstatement>→ATT.ACCESS=(nihil,0,0);
    END;

<conditionalstatement> → if E ρ7 then <statement>1 ρ8
                                  else <statement>2 ρ9 fi

ρ7:PROC;
    IF E→ATT.TYPE=ref bool
       THEN DO;
            E→ATT.TYPE=bool;
            E→ATT.ACCESS.LEVEL=1;
            END;
       ELSE IF E→ATT.TYPE ¬=bool
               THEN CALL ERROR;
    <conditionalstatement>→ATT.TYPE=void;
    CALL GENERATE(jumpfalse,E→ATT.ACCESS,LABEL);
    E→ATT.LABEL=LABEL;
    LABEL=LABEL+1;
    IF E→ATT.ACCESS.CLASS=workspace
       THEN WORKP=E→ATT.ACCESS.SPEC;
    END;

ρ8:PROC;
    CALL GENERATE(jump,LABEL);
    <statement>_1→ATT.LABEL=LABEL;
    LABEL=LABEL+1;
    CALL GENERATE(labeldef,E→ATT.LABEL);
    END;

ρ9:PROC;
    CALL GENERATE(labeldef,<statement>_1→ATT.LABEL);
    <conditionalstatement>→ATT.ACCESS=(nihil,0,0);
    END;

E1 → E2 + T ρ10

ρ10:PROC;
     IF E_2→ATT.TYPE=ref int &
        E_2→ATT.ACCESS.CLASS=idenspace &
        E_2→ATT.ACCESS.LEVEL=0
        THEN DO;
             E_2→ATT.TYPE=int;
             E_2→ATT.ACCESS.LEVEL=1;
             END;
```

```
        ELSE IF T→ATT.TYPE=ref int & T→ATT.ACCESS.CLASS=idenspace &
                T→ATT.ACCESS.LEVEL=0
                THEN DO;
                     T→ATT.TYPE=int;
                     T→ATT.ACCESS.LEVEL=1;
                     END;
                ELSE IF E_2→ATT.TYPE=int & T→ATT.TYPE=int
                        THEN E_1→ATT.TYPE=int;
                        ELSE CALL ERROR;
    IF E_2→ATT.ACCESS.CLASS=workspace
       THEN DO;
            E_1→ATT.ACCESS=(workspace,1,E_2→ATT.ACCESS.SPEC);
            WORKP=E_2→ATT.ACCESS.SPEC+SIZE(int);
            END;
       ELSE IF T→ATT.ACCESS.CLASS=workspace
               THEN DO;
                    E_1→ATT.ACCESS=(workspace,1,T→ATT.ACCESS.SPEC);
                    WORKP=T→ATT.ACCESS.SPEC+SIZE(int);
                    END;
               ELSE DO;
                    E_1→ATT.ACCESS=(workspace,1,WORKP);
                    WORKP=WORKP+SIZE(int);
                    END;
    CALL GENERATE(plus,int,
                       int,
                       E_2→ATT.ACCESS,
                       T→ATT.ACCESS,
                       E_1→ATT.ACCESS);
    END;
```

$E \rightarrow T\ \rho_{12}$

```
ρ12:PROC;
    E→ATT.TYPE=T→ATT.TYPE;
    E→ATT.ACCESS=T→ATT.ACCESS;
    END;
```

$F \rightarrow$ iden ρ_{16}

```
ρ16:PROC;
    F→ATT.TYPE=SYMBTAB(IDEN→SPEC).TYPE;
    F→ATT.ACCESS=SYMBTAB(IDEN→SPEC).ACCESS;
    END;
```

$F \rightarrow$ intct ρ_{17}

```
ρ17:PROC;
    F→ATT.TYPE=int;
    F→ATT.ACCESS=(literal,0,INTCT→SPEC);
    END;
```

$F \rightarrow$ true ρ_{18}

```
ρ18:PROC;
    F→ATT.TYPE=bool;
    F→ATT.ACCESS=(literal,0,true);
    END;
```

$F \rightarrow$ false ρ_{19}

```
ρ19:PROC;
    F→ATT.TYPE=bool;
    F→ATT.ACCESS=(literal,0,false);
    END;
```

Since the few semantic routines that remain are analogous, they are not given here.

An example of intermediate code generation for PICO-ALGOL

intermediate code

```
   jumpfalse,(idenspace,1,2)
                  l0
   assign, ref int,
           (idenspace,0,1)
           (literal,0,3)
   jump l1
l0:
   assign, ref int
           (idenspace,0,1)
           (literal,0,2)
l1:
   print int,
         (idenspace,1,1)
```

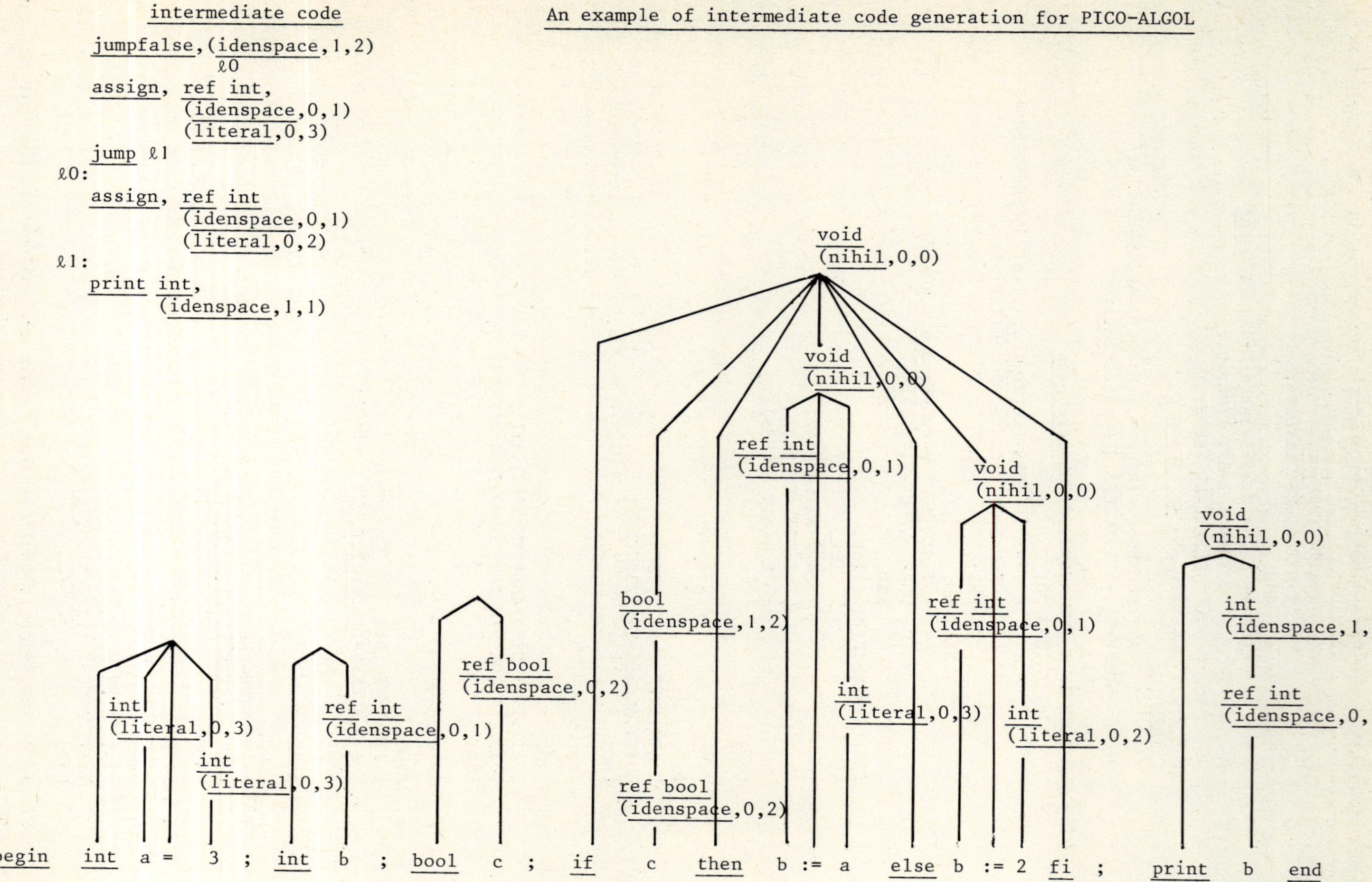

CONCLUSION

The translator writing system in its didactic version is an ideal tool upon which a course on compiler construction can be based. The student can treat non-trivial examples in a flexible and modular way within a reasonable limit of time [16]. This version is implemented in PL/I on the IBM 370 model 158 under OS.

The didactic version can easily be transformed into an operational version, where the syntax tree, built by the syntax analyser, is stored in a linear form and treated by the semantic analyser by means of two semantic stacks, see [10]. The syntax analyser generated by the operational version will consume less space and time.

It is this transformation that will be the next step in our implementation.

REFERENCES

[1] Brooker, R. and Morris, D., A general translation program for phrase structure languages. Journal ACM, Jan. 1962.

[2] Brooker, R., The compiler compiler. Annual Review of Automatic Programming III, 1963.

[3] Rosen, S., A compiler-building system developed by Brooker and Morris. C. ACM, vol. 7, no. 7, July 1964.

[4] Feldman, J.A. and Gries, D., Translator writing system. C. ACM, vol. 11, no. 2, Febr. 1968.

[5] Naur, P. (ed.), Revised report on the algorithmic language Algol 60. C. ACM, vol. 6, no. 1, Jan. 1963.

[6] Irons, E.T., The structure and use of the syntax directed compiler. Annual Review of Automatic Programming III, 1963.

[7] Knuth, D.E., Semantics of context-free languages. Mathematical Systems Theory, vol. 2, no. 2, Febr. 1968.

[8] Samelson, K. and Bauer, F.L., Sequential formula translation. C. ACM, vol. 3, no. 2, Febr. 1960.

[9] Branquart, P., Lewi, J., A scheme of storage allocation and garbage collection for ALGOL 68. Report R133, MBLE Res. Lab., April 1970, (presented at "Working Conference (IFIP) on Algol 68 Implementation, Münich 1970). "Proceedings of Working Conference on ALGOL 68 Implementation", North-Holland Publ. Comp., Amsterdam.

[10] Branquart, P., Cardinael, J.P., Lewi, J., An optimized translation process and its application to ALGOL 68. Part I : General principles, Report R204, Sept. 1972. Presented at the "International Computing Symposium 1973" The European Chapters of the ACM, Davos, Switzerland, 4-7, September 1973.

[11] Branquart, P., Cardinael, J.P., Lewi, J., Delescaille, J.P. and Van Begin, M., An optimized Translation Process and its Application to ALGOL 68, Part II : Block Constructions, Report R204 II, MBLE Research Lab., February 1974.

[12] Branquart, P., Cardinael, J.P., Lewi, J., Delescaille, J.P. and Van Begin, M., An optimized Translation Process and its Application to ALGOL 68, Part III : Other Constructions, Report R204 III, MBLE Research Lab., February 1974.

[13] Branquart, P., Cardinael, J.P., Lewi, J., Delescaille, J.P. and Van Begin, M., An optimized Translation Process and its Application to ALGOL 68, Part IV : Machine Code Generation, Report R204 IV, MBLE Research Lab., May 1974.

[14] Branquart, P., Cardinael, J.P., Lewi, J., Delescaille, J.P. and Van Begin, M., Data Structure handling in ALGOL 68 Compilation, Report R254, MBLE Research Lab., May 1974.

[15] Lalonde, W.R., An efficient LALR parser generator. CSRG-2, Computer Systems Research Group, University of Toronto, Febr. 1971.

[16] Lewi, J., De Vlaminck, K., Huens, J., Mertens, P., Examples worked out with the SLS/1 Translator Writing System, Report K.U.L., Applied Mathematics and Programming Division. In preparation.

An Abstract ALGOL 68 Machine and its Application in a machine independent Compiler

Wilfried Koch / Christoph Oeters

Informatik-Forschungsgruppe Programmiersprachen und Compiler 2

Technische Universität Berlin

0. Summary

An intermediate language for the machine independent compilation of ALGOL 68 is described. It makes very few assumptions on the target machine but provides a strong descriptive mechanism for abstract machine objects by which they can easily be mapped on target machine objects.

1. The Berlin ALGOL 68 Compiler

At the Technical University of Berlin a portable ALGOL 68 compiler is under construction. The compiler is designed to eventually implement full ALGOL 68 apart from parallel processes. It will include the possibility of separate compilation. The compiler consists of three parts:

- building up a syntax tree in three full passes and one intermediate pass (planting, growing, budding, blooming pass)
- generation of a macro program by the picking pass, i.e. mapping the syntax tree on a sequence of instructions for the abstract machine
- expansion of the macros to the object code of a concrete machine

There will be a special linker for separately compiled segments.

The compiler is implemented in CDL 2 (by Koster), a language supporting machine independent programming. The macro language is also machine independent. It is going to be expanded first on an IBM 370/158.

2. The Runtime System

We assume there is a linear random access store which can be divided into two separate areas: stack and heap. For operations, the stack is preferred over the heap, but in some cases, data is placed on the heap. The stack contains one dynamic storage area (DSA) per routine call.

Every object has a static and a possibly empty dynamic part (row elements). According to this a DSA consists of a static and dynamic part. The static part consists of three parts:

- administrative area
- identifier stack (static parts of declared objects)
- working stack (static parts of intermediate results)

There is no separate dynamic working stack. Dynamic parts of intermediate results are placed in the dynamic area which is freed on range exit or they are placed on the heap.

3. Design Criteria for the Macro Language

One of the main goals of our compiler is machine independence. This means not only the front end of the compiler must be portable but also the programs in the macro language. Therefore, the macro language does not contain any properties of a particular machine which could be used for macro generation. In particular, the compiler's machine independent part does not know anything about the presence of registers or even about their number or kind; it does not have knowledge about the addressing mechanism of the target machine or the amount of space occupied by objects; and it does not know the instruction set of the target machine.

On the other hand, the operations of the abstract machine should be so primitive that their translations are essentially fixed pieces of code. The modifications on the translation of a macro should depend only on the kind of the parameters and the way they are accessed, e.g. whether a parameter originates from a denoter or a variable. There should be no modifications due to different semantics of one source language construct like different complexities of generators; they are treated by the picking pass who produces the appropriate macro sequences.

Since the macro expander has to be rewritten for every machine the macros should be easy to expand. Their operational kernel should be as small as is possible with regard to the other aims. The expander writer should not have to know much about ALGOL 68, especially not about the dark corners in the semantics of ALGOL 68; these problems should be solved in terms of abstract machine instructions, e.g. by explicitly putting the dope vector arising from a ref-slice on the heap.

The macro expander should have to maintain only few globals. The implicit use of globals may force the expander to stack and unstack them on encountering certain macros and thus considerably increase its complexity. Therefore all objects including intermediate results which are used in more than one macro are designated by "tokens". The information associated with them is kept in tables and can be accessed by use of a token as a macro parameter.

Ease of expansion also means that the expander should not have to implicitly build up all kinds of information but should rather be explicitly told what it has to do (e.g. allocate working space for an intermediate result). Thus the picking pass can be considered to control the expander. In order to make the control as simple as possible, macros manipulating tables (descriptive macros) are separated from macros producing code (code macros).

The macro language should be so flexible that it supports machine independent optimizations, e.g. minimizing copying operations. On the other hand the macro expander should have enough information for machine dependent optimizations, e.g. on the lifetime of intermediate results to support register allocation.

4. Features of the Macro Language

4.1. General Remarks on the Macros

Macros are instructions for the expander either to build up information which is later accessible via tables or to generate code. They are ordered in such a way that code can be generated in 1 1/2 passes. The first part of the macro program is a descriptive section where information globally needed is built up but no code is produced. The second part is a code section. Among the macros for which code is produced there are descriptive macros for objects temporarily needed. In both sections the static nesting of routine texts is turned into a linear sequence such that the code produced by the expander need not be reordered; the range nesting is preserved.

The macros are mostly parametrized by tokens. These are numbers used as designators giving access to expander tables containing information about data and other objects. They are designed such that one can easily see to which table they refer and map them onto an index for that table. Other macro parameters may be numbers (dimensionality of a row), codes (to identify standard prelude routines), or representations (of constants). The number of parameters is not fixed but depends on the macro. Generally, the first parameter is either specified (in a descriptive macro) or destination of an operation.

The context dependence of the macros is rather small. For storage administration the expander maintains the current and maximal storage requirements of the routine it is processing, and in the descriptive section it knows which routine and range it is processing. All other information is kept in tables and explicitly entered or obtained.

4.2. Descriptive Macros

The aim of a specification is to introduce a new token to the expander; a description moreover defines properties of it. The specification of a token should always precede all its applications so that the expander can rely on the fact that when a token is applied at least some basic information about it has already been established.

In the descriptive section, objects which may be globally needed are specified:

- modes: A full mode table is built up in the form of a linked list. For each mode, it contains the amount of space occupied by its static part, and for structures, it contains the offsets of the fields. The mode table is used for storage allocation and later passed to the linker for mode check between separately compiled segments and to the garbage collector.
- routines, ranges, identifiers: For each routine, its ranges are described in their original nesting, and within each range, space is allocated to its identifiers. So at the end of the descriptive section the expander knows the compile time address of every identifier and the bottom of the working stack of every routine.
- labels may be specified either in the descriptive section (user labels) or in the code section (compiler labels).
- denoters: The expander is given the source language representation of each denoter since the conversion of denoters depends on the target machine.
- external objects are described by means of a representation and their mode; a list of them is passed to the linker to perform mode check and fill in their addresses.
- standard prelude objects are described by a code which the expander knows; they are either substituted (enquiries) or passed to the linker (routines).

In the code section, objects only temporarily needed are specified:

- compiler labels, case switch bars, translation tables for union descriptors.
- working stack objects: These are not only intermediate results of ALGOL 68 constructs like the result of a formula, but also temporaries needed for the elaboration of complex operations like an element address in a row-of-row-of-amode-generator.

For data objects, always a compile time address is kept in the corresponding table. Their mode is not supposed to be kept in expander tables but explicitly provided when it is needed: for space allocation, copying, and for building up garbage collector tables.

The description of a (data) object consists of three parts: attaching an address, allocation of space, and determination of lifetime with respect to the garbage collector. An address is normally attached together with space, but it may also be derived from a given address, e.g. by selection. In such a case, space must not be attached again since allowing this would complicate the expander's storage administration scheme. However, selected objects may be described as relevant for the garbage collector. Space for identifiers is allocated and freed on range entry and exit, thus an identifier stack is automatically implemented. Space for working stack objects has to be allocated and freed on a lifo basis in order to simplify the expander's work. Allocation of space is separated from determination of garbage collector lifetime since the construction of a complicated object (structure) which consists of more than one operation may involve a garbage collector call when the object has only been partially built up but already fully allocated.

4.3. Code Macros

The code macros are in principle designed such that they support the algorithms described in the Revised ALGOL 68 Report. There is one macro for each standard prelude operator, the number of longs is a parameter of the macro. The complex actions like generation and assignation have been split up into copying static parts of values, getting and putting elements out of or into dope vectors, incrementing counters and addresses, and jumping on simple end conditions.

The macros are parametrized explicitly with operands and result; so the expander need not to know what kind of source program construct is just being processed. The addresses may be direct or indirect - this may save copying operations.

For some frequently occurring special cases macros have been provided to allow the picking pass to pass its machine independent optimizations to the expander. Such cases are:

- call: routines may be called by descriptor or directly by their address.
- copying loops are differently complicated depending e.g. on whether the row may be sliced or not.
- do loops may or may not have a to-part.

For examples of macros the reader is referred to the program example; a full description of the macros will be published.

5. A Program Example

5.1. Source Program

```
begin  co range main co
real x, y;
ref real xx;
[1:10] real r;
print (xx := if x+y > 0 then x else r [3] fi)
end
```

5.2. Form of the Macro Program

Normally, all macros as well as all parameters are coded by numbers which might be on a binary file; thus the expander need not lexically analyse them. In our example, the macros and parameters are named for readability. Tokens of different kind are distinguished by prefixes (ws means working stack, the others should be self-explaining). The superscript i indicates indirect addressing. Numbers are interpreted as such and quoted strings stand for themselves.

5.3. Translation of the Program Example

begin

1. Descriptive Section	The following macros do not produce any code, they just create tables for the code section
1.1. Description of Modes	A mode table is created which contains the space occupied by the static part of each mode; the table will be passed to the linker and the garbage collector.
plain mode (mode int, int code, 0)	mode int is specified as int with 0 longs
plain mode (mode real, real code, 0)	
plain mode (mode void, void code, 0)	
plain mode (mode file, file code, 0)	The mode file is considered primitive.
plain mode (mode scope indicator, scope indicator code, 0)	Scope indicators are used for scope check e.g. of routine results.
ref mode (mode ref file, mode file)	
ref mode (mode ref real, mode real)	The following structure is built up:
ref mode (mode ref ref real, mode ref real)	
row mode (mode row of real, non flex code, 1, mode real)	nonflexible row with 1 dimension
mode list element (mode parameter 2, mode real, 0)	mode table entries for the parameter list
mode list element (mode parameter 1, mode ref file, mode parameter 2)	which is considered to be a structure
struct mode (mode parameter list, mode parameter 1)	
mode list element (mode plan, mode void, mode parameter list)	
proc mode (mode proc, mode plan)	mode of put real: proc (ref file, real) void (the call of print is mapped on a call of put real)

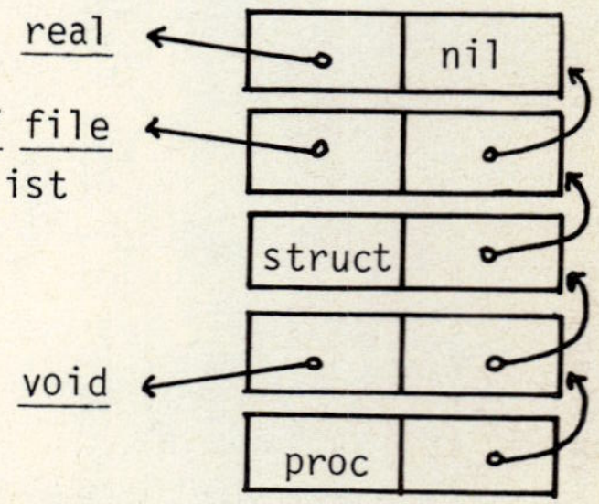

real | nil
ref file
struct
void
proc

1.2. Description of Routines, Ranges and declared Objects	Create tables for routines, ranges and identifiers and allocate space to identifiers
spec routine entry (routine main, 0, range routine main, identifier destination address, identifier destination scope, identifier actual parameter list)	routine nest is 0; the range containing the formal parameters (range routine main) is also specified hereby; the last 3 parameters are only useful for user-defined routines.
spec range entry (range main)	
idf (identifier x, mode real) *idf (identifier y, mode real)* *idf (identifier xx, mode ref real)* *idf (identifier r mode row of real)*	Identifiers declared by variable declarations are specified with their modes dereferenced.
spec range exit (range routine main)	We are in range routine main again
spec routine exit	

1.3. Description of Constants	
const (const 1, mode int, "1") *const (const 10, mode int, "10")* *const (const 0, mode int, "0")* *const (const 3, mode int, "3")*	Constants are given to the expander in their source language representations.

1.4. Specification of standard prelude Objects	Standard prelude objects are supposed to be known by the expander and precompiled if they are routines.
apply standard prelude routine (routine put real, put real code, 0)	0 longs
standard prelude const (const stand out, mode ref file, stand out code)	
standard prelude const (const dummy, mode void, dummy code)	

2. Code Section

begin execution (routine main)	linkage from the operating system
enter routine (routine main, 0)	routine nest 0
enter range (range main, range routine main)	copy free local area pointer from old range into new range
initialize (identifier xx, mode ref real)	On range entry, critical declared objects are initialized (e.g. names)
init build dope (identifier r, 1)	Build dope vector for r. The constant 1 denotes either the dope vector's dimensionality or the dimension currently being dealt with.
set innermost stride (identifier r, 1, mode real)	
attach lwb address (ws lower bound, identifier r, 1)	
copy static part (ws lower bound, const 1, mode int)	
attach upb address (ws upper bound, identifier r, 1)	
copy static part (ws upper bound, const 10, mode int)	
finish build dope (identifier r, 1)	
reserve row elements (identifier r, 1, local code, range main)	Get space in the local area of range main.
attach address and space (ws parameter list, mode parameter list)	Start building the parameter list for put real.
attach selected address (ws parameter 1, ws parameter list, mode parameter 1)	Select 1st parameter's address; do not attach space.
copy static part (ws parameter 1, const stand out, mode ref file)	
attach mode (ws parameter 1)	begin of relevance for the garbage collector
attach selected address (ws parameter 2, ws parameter list, mode parameter 2)	ws parameter 2: target address for the elaboration of the 2nd parameter
attach address and space (ws result plus, mode real)	
plus real (ws result plus, indentifier x, identifier y, 0)	length (0 for this instance) is a parameter of all arithmetic operators.

detach space (ws result plus)	ws result plus will not get lost before the next operation.
attach address and space (ws result relation, mode bool)	
greater real (ws result relation, ws result plus, const 0, 0)	
detach space (ws result relation)	
spec label (label else)	Create table entry for label else - definition will occur later.
jump on false (ws result relation, label else)	
attach address and space (ws result cond clause, mode ref real)	ws result cond clause is passed as target address to the then and else parts.
create name (ws result cond clause, identifier x, routine main, range main)	A name is built for x whose scope is determined by routine main and range main.
spec label (label fi)	
jump local (label fi)	jump within a routine
define label (lcbel else)	
push first element address (ws result cond clause, identifier r, 1)	} ref-slice
subscribe (ws result cond clause, identifier r, 1, const 3)	} ref-slice
set scope field (ws result cond clause, routine main, range main)	take the scope of r } ref-slice
attach mode (ws result cond clause)	
define label (label fi)	
attach address and space (ws scope xx, mode scope indicator)	
create scope indicator (ws scope xx, routine main, range main)	For a scope check involving xx, its scope is built up.

check scope (ws scope xx, mode scope indicator, ws result cond clause, mode ref real)	
detach space (ws scope xx)	
copy static part (identifier xx, ws result cond clause, mode ref real)	assignation to xx
detach space (ws result cond clause)	
detach mode (ws result cond clause)	
check nil (identifier xx)	2nd dereferencing of xx - the 1st did not produce macros due to the special treatment of variables
copy static part (ws parameter 2, (identifier xx)^i, mode real)	
attach mode (ws parameter 2)	
call by address (routine put real, ws parameter list, const dummy, const dummy, range main)	The two dummies denote target address and scope of the result; range main contains the free local area pointer needed for opening a new dynamic storage area.
detach mode (ws parameter 2)	} releasing the parameter list.
detach mode (ws parameter 1)	}
detach space (ws parameter list)	}
range exit (range main)	
routine exit (routine main)	
end execution	
end	

6. References

van Wijngaarden, A. (editor):	Revised Report on the Algorithmic Language ALGOL 68, (to be published)
Peck, J.E.L. (editor):	ALGOL 68 Implementation, North-Holland, 1971
Tanenbaum, A.:	Design and implementation of an ALGOL 68 virtual machine, Mathematisch Centrum, Amsterdam, 1973
Bourne, S.:	ZCODE - a simple machine, Cambridge (UK), 1974
Lane, H.J.:	An ALGOL 68 Machine and Translator, UCLA, 1973
Gries, D.:	Compiler Construction for Digital Computers, Wiley, 1971
Koster, C.H.A.:	Towards a machine independent ALGOL 68 translator, MR 129, Mathematisch Centrum, Amsterdam, 1972
Koster, C.H.A.:	A Compiler Compiler, MR 127, ibidem, 1971

VERSCHRÄNKUNG VON COMPILER-MODULN*

Harald Ganzinger und Reinhard Wilhelm
Institut für Informatik
der Technischen Universität
8 München 2, Arcisstr. 21

0. EINLEITUNG

In (2) und (3) propagieren McKeeman und DeRemer die Idee der "rückkopplungsfreien Modularisierung von Compilern". Darunter verstehen sie die Aufspaltung von Compilern in Moduln entsprechend einer funktionsgerechten Aufteilung des Übersetzungsprozesses in Teilaufgaben wie lexikalische, syntaktische und semantische Analyse, sprachabhängige und maschinenabhängige Codeoptimierung und Codeerzeugung, sowie eine klare Beschreibung der Schnittstellen zwischen solchen Moduln.

Besondere Wichtigkeit erlangt die Compiler-Modularisierung für die automatische Erzeugung von Übersetzern für Programmiersprachen, da sie eine getrennte Beschreibung der einzelnen Übersetzer-Teilaufgaben mit den für sie jeweils geeigneten formalen Methoden erlaubt und damit auch eine formal-sprachliche Beschreibung der Schnittstellen.

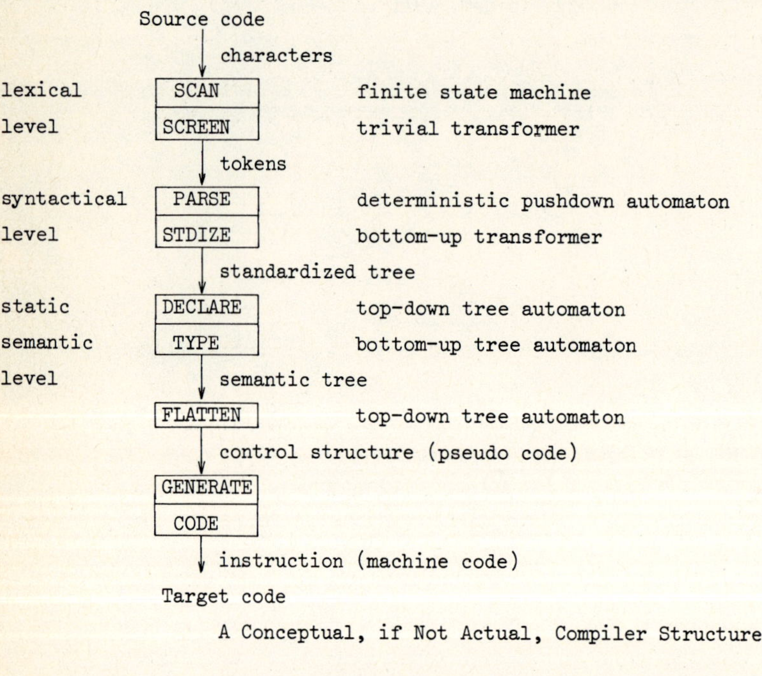

A Conceptual, if Not Actual, Compiler Structure

Fig. 1 übernommen aus (4)

*Diese Arbeit ist im Sonderforschungsbereich 49 -Informatik- an der TU München entstanden.

Wie in Fig. 1 wird der Übersetzungsprozess *konzeptionell* in eine Reihe sequentieller Teilprozesse aufgeteilt samt Angabe der formalen Methoden, die zu ihrer Beschreibung dienen und einer Beschreibung der Zwischenformen von zu übersetzenden Quellprogrammen.

Diese *konzeptionell sequentielle* Compiler-Struktur entspricht im allgemeinen nicht der Struktur implementierter oder generierter Compiler; denn abhängig von der Komplexität der vorliegenden Programmiersprache, den vom Compiler verlangten Aufgaben und den für die Übersetzer-Teilaufgaben ausgewählten Verfahren lassen sich verschieden viele der Moduln verschränken, d.h. unter Unterdrückung von Zwischenformen des Quellprogramms kurzschließen. Unter günstigen Voraussetzungen – einfache, geschickt beschriebene Programmiersprache, Verwendung geeigneter Verfahren zur Realisierung der Teilaufgaben – läßt sich auch aus einer solchen sequentiellen Beschreibung ein 1-Lauf-Compiler erzeugen.

Im folgenden werden Betrachtungen angestellt und Bedingungen angegeben, wann sich Compiler-Moduln aus einer solchen konzeptionellen sequentiellen Beschreibung in der Realisierung auf dem Rechner verschränken lassen.

In diesen Bedingungen spielen die Aufruf- und die Informationsfluß-Beziehung zwischen Moduln eine starke Rolle. Deshalb wird für jede Kombination dieser Beziehungen ein Beispiel angegeben, nämlich die Verschränkung Scanner mit Parser und Parser mit der Auswertung semantischer Attribute.

1. KLASSE, KONTROLLPROGRAMM, MODUL

Im folgenden wird eine zweistufige Definition eines *Moduls* gegeben. Die obere Stufe, das *Kontrollprogramm*, ist ein endlicher Automat, dessen Operationen durch Sequenzen von Operationen aus bestimmten *Klassen*, die sich auf der unteren Ebene befinden, realisiert werden. Eine Klasse ist eine Abstraktion der SIMULA-class (7) insofern, als die internen Zustände einer Klasse nur durch Operationen dieser Klasse geändert werden können und nach dem Rücksprung in das Kontrollprogramm bis zum nächsten Aufruf einer Klassenoperation erhalten bleiben. Kommunikation mit der Umgebung ist nur mithilfe von Parametern möglich.

<u>Definition 1</u> (Parametrisierte Operation).
Gegeben sei eine endliche Menge O von *Operationssymbolen*. Ein Tripel $(o, P_I(o), P_O(o))$ mit $o \in O$ und den o zugeordneten Mengen $P_I(o)$ (Inputparameterwertebereich) $P_O(o)$ (Outputparameterwertebereich)

heißt eine *parametrisierte Operation.*

Nachfolgend sei eine param. Operation durch das Operationssymbol eindeutig gegeben. Ein Funktionsaufruf werde durch $o(p_1,p_2)$ mit $p_1 \in P_I(o)$, $p_2 \in P_O(o)$ dargestellt. Außerdem sei $P_I := \bigcup_{o \in O} P_I(o)$, $P_O := \bigcup_{o \in O} P_O(o)$.

Definition 2 (Klasse).
Eine *Klasse* K ist ein Tupel $K = (S_K, S_K^o, S_K^e, \delta_K, O_K)$, wobei S_K eine (nicht notwendig endl.) Menge der *Konfiguration,* $S_K^o, S_K^e \subset S_K$ die Menge der Anfangs- bzw. Endkonfigurationen, O_K eine endl. Menge param. Operationen und $\delta_K : (S_K - S_K^e) \times O_K \times P_I \rightarrow S_K \times P_O$ eine partielle Abbildung ist. Für δ_K gelte dabei: Ist $\delta_K(s,o,p_1) = (s',p_2)$, so ist $p_1 \in P_I(o)$ und $p_2 \in P_O(o)$.

Anschaulich bedeutet $\delta_K(s,o,p_1) = (s',p_2)$, daß die Ausführung der Operation o mit dem Eingabeparameter p_1 in der Klassenkonfiguration s definiert ist, bei Ausführung die Klasse in die Konfiguration s' überführt und dabei p_2 als Ausgabeparameter liefert.

Definition 3 (Folgekonfiguration).
Sei K eine Klasse, $n \in \mathbb{N}_0$ und $w = o_1(p_1^1,p_1^2)o_2(p_2^1,p_2^2)\ldots o_n(p_n^1,p_n^2)$ mit $o_i \in O_K$. $s' \in S_K$ heißt dann *w-Folgekonfiguration* von $s \in S_K$ (i.Z. $s \underset{w}{\rightarrow} s'$), falls es $s_1, s_2, \ldots, s_{n+1}$ aus S_K gibt mit $s_1 = s$, $s_{n+1} = s'$ und $\delta_K(s_j,o_j,p_j^1) = (s_{j+1},p_j^2)$, für $1 \leq j \leq n$.

Definition 4 (Vereinigung von Klassen).

Seien K_i, $1 \leq i \leq n$, $n \geq 1$ Klassen mit paarweise disjunkten O_{K_i}.

Dann sei die *Vereinigung* $K := \bigcup_{i=1}^{n} K_i$ folgendermaßen definiert:

$S_K = \prod_{i=1}^{n} S_{K_i}$, $S_K^o = \prod_{i=1}^{n} S_{K_i}^o$, $S_K^e = \prod_{i=1}^{n} S_{K_i}^e$, $O_K = \bigcup_{i=1}^{n} O_{K_i}$,

$\delta_K(s,o,p_1) = (s',p_2)$, falls $s = (s_1, \ldots, s_n)$ $s' = (s_1', \ldots, s_n')$ und es gibt ein j, so daß $o \in O_{K_j}$ und $\delta_{K_j}(s_j,o,p_1) = (s_j',p_2)$ und $s_i = s_i'$ für $i \neq j$.

Definition 5 (Kontrollprogramm).
Ein Tupel $C = (S_c,s_c^o,S_c^e,O_c,o_c^o,\delta_c)$ heißt ein *Kontrollprogramm,* falls S_c eine endl. Menge (Zustandsmenge), $s_c^o \in S_c$ (Anfangszustand), $S_c^e \subset S_c$ (Endzustandsmenge), O_c endl. Menge von param. Operationen (Kontrolloperationen), $o_c^o \in O_c$ mit $|P_I(o_c^o)| = 1$ (Initialisierungsoperation) und $\delta_c : (S_c - S_c^e) \times O_c \times P_O \rightarrow S_c \times O_c \times P_I$ eine partielle Abb. ist, wobei aus $\delta_c(s_1,o_1,p_1) = (s_2,o_2,p_2)$ folgt: $p_1 \in P_O(o_1)$

Sprechweisen:
$w_0 w_1 \ldots w_n$ heiße *Arbeitssequenz* von M bei Eingabe von s , i.Z. $as_M(s)$. Nachfolgend entstehe $as_M^E(s)$ bzw. $as_M^A(s)$ aus $as_M(s)$ durch Streichen aller $o(p_1,p_2)$ mit $o \notin O_E$ bzw. $o \notin O_A$ und heiße *Eingabesequenz* bzw. *Ausgabesequenz*.

Bed. 1) fordert, daß ein Aufruf einer Kontrolloperation o mit Input p_1 im Klassenzustand s höchstens eine im Sinne einer existierenden Klassen-Folgekonfiguration wohldefinierte Sequenz w von Aufrufen von Klassenoperationen liefert. Ein $o(p_1,p_2)$ ist damit als Prozeduraufruf aufzufassen, wobei o EUFUA-Operationen als primitive Statements besitzt.

Bed. 2) stellt sicher, daß jede Eingabe in M (in Form einer Anfangskonfiguration s aus S_E) eine deterministische Arbeitsweise des Moduls bestimmt, die mit der Erstellung der Übersetzung m(s) von s als Ausgabe (in Form einer Endkonfiguration aus S_A) endet.

Bed. 3) besagt: Liefert der Aufruf einer Kontrolloperation o mit Input p in zwei verschiedenen Klassenzuständen verschiedene Realisierungssequenzen w und w' , so unterscheiden sich w und w' erstmals im Output einer Operation aus derjenigen Klasse, deren Ausgangskonfigurationen sich beim Aufruf von o unterschieden.

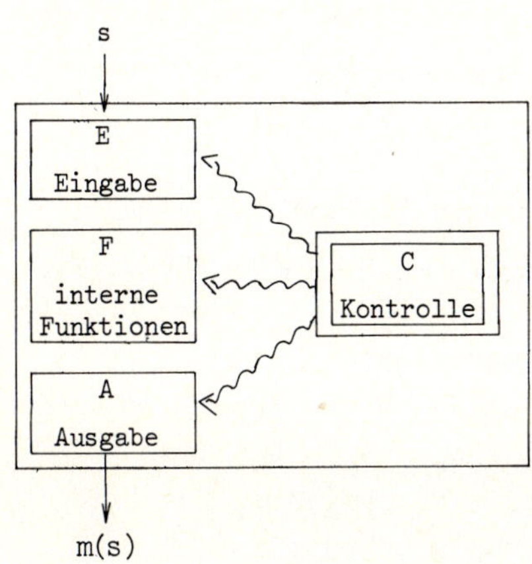

⇝ deutet die Realisierung von Kontrolloperationen an.

Fig. 2 Modul

Beispiel 1
Die formale Beschreibung der Syntax wird i. allg. durch eine CF-Grammatik $G = (V_N, V_T, \pi, Z)$ definiert. Jede Realisierung der Syntaxanalyse durch Auswahl einer speziellen Strategie ergibt einen Modul, der von dieser und der Grammatik abhängt.

und $p_2 \in P_I(o_2)$.

Hierbei besage $\delta_c(s_1,o_1,p_1) = (s_2,o_2,p_2)$: Hat die Ausführung der Operation o_1 im Zustand s_1 den Outputparameter p_1 geliefert, so geht C in den Zustand s_2 über und führt als nächstes die Operation o_2 mit dem Inputparameter p_2 aus.

Definition 6 (Modul).

Ein *Modul* M ist ein Tupel $M = (E,F,A,C,m,\rho)$, wobei

- E,F und A Klassen (*Eingabeklasse, Klasse der internen Funktionen* und *Ausgabeklasse*) mit $S_F^o = \{s_F^o\}$ und $S_A^o = \{s_A^o\}$
- $m : S_E^o \rightarrow S_A^e$ eine Abbildung (*durch* M *realisierte Übersetzung*)
- C ein Kontrollprogramm.
- $\rho : S_{EUFUA} \times O_C \times P_I \rightarrow W^+ \times P_O$ eine partielle Abbildung (*Realisierungsfunktion*), wobei W die Menge aller Funktionsaufrufe aus O_{EUFUA} sei. ρ erfülle die folgenden Bedingungen:
  1) -- Ausführbarkeit der Realisierung von Kontrolloperationen --
     Ist $\rho(s,o,p_1) = (w,p_2)$ mit $w = o_1(p_1^1,p_1^2)o_2(p_2^1,p_2^2)\ldots o_n(p_n^1,p_n^2)$, so ist $p_1^1 = p_1$, $p_{i+1}^1 = p_i^2$ für $1 \le i < n$, $p_2 = p_n^2$ und es gibt ein $s' \in S_{EUFUA}$, so daß $s \xrightarrow[w]{} s'$.
  2) -- Realisierbarkeit der Übersetzung --
     Für jedes $s \in S_E^o$ gibt es eine Sequenz
     $s_0o_0(p_0^1,p_0^2)s_1o_1(p_1^1,p_1^2)s_2 \ldots s_no_n(p_n^1,p_n^2)s_{n+1}$ mit folgenden Eigenschaften
     a) $s_0 = s_c^o$, $o_0 = o_c^o$, $\{p_0\} = P_I(o_0)$, $s_{n+1} \in S_c^e$.
     b) $(s_{i+1}, o_{i+1}, p_{i+1}^1) = \delta_c(s_i,o_i,p_i^2)$ für $1 \le i < n$ (Hierbei sind o_{n+1} und p_{n+1}^1 irrelevant.)
     c) Es gibt $w_i \in W^+$ und $\bar{s}_i \in S_{EUFUA}$, mit $\bar{s}_0 = (s,s_F^o,s_A^o)$, $(w_i,p_i^2) = \rho(\bar{s}_i,o_i,p_i^1)$ und $\bar{s}_i \xrightarrow[w_i]{} \bar{s}_{i+1}$, $0 \le i \le n$ und $\bar{s}_{n+1} = (s^1,s^2,m(s))$ mit $s^1 \in S_E^e$, $s^2 \in S_F^e$.
  3) -- Verbot von Seiteneffekten zwischen den Klassen --
     Seien $s' = (s_1',s_2',s_3')$ und $s = (s_1,s_2,s_3)$ aus S_{EUFUA}, $o \in O_c$ und $p \in P_I$. Weiter sei $s_1' \neq s_1$, $s_2' = s_2$, $s_3' = s_3$ (bzw. $s_1' = s_1$, $s_2' \neq s_2$, $s_3' = s_3$, bzw. $s_1' = s_1$, $s_2' = s_2$, $s_3' \neq s_3$). Ist dann $\rho(s,o,p) = (w,\bar{p}) \neq \rho(s',o,p) = (w',\bar{p}')$, mit $w = o_1(p_1,p_2)o_2(p_2,p_3) \ldots o_n(p_n,p_{n+1})$
     $w' = o_1'(p_1',p_2')o_2'(p_2',p_3') \ldots o_m'(p_m',p_{m+1}')$,
     so existiert ein j mit $1 \le j \le \min(n,m)$, so daß $o_i(p_i,p_{i+1}) = o_i'(p_i',p_{i+1}')$ für $1 \le i < j$, $o_j = o_j' \in O_E$ (bzw. O_F, bzw. O_A) und $p_{j+1} \neq p_{j+1}'$.

Wir wählen als Beispiel einen LL(1)-Parser und beschreiben grob den entstehenden Modul (E,F,A,C,m,ρ) .

Einleseklasse E:
S_E: restliche Symbol-Eingabefolge, O_E = {read_symbol}

Ausgabeklasse A:
S_A: bereits ausgegebene Produktionsnummernfolge,
O_A: {write_production, write_reduction}

Interne Funktionen-Klasse F:
S_F: Keller, π; O_F = {push, pop, choose_alternative,...}

Kontrollprogramm C:
Sei $nr: \pi \to \mathbb{N}$ eine konsekutive Numerierung der Produktionen aus π.
$S_c = \{(nr(p),j) \mid p \in \pi,\ 0 \le j \le \text{Länge}(p)\}$
O_c = {produce_nonterminal, start_production, continue_production}

Die CF-Grammatik geht folgendermaßen in den Modul ein:
$V_N = P_I$ (produce_nonterminal), $V_T = P_O$(read_symbol),
$nr(\pi) = P_O$ (write_production), $-nr(\pi) = P_O$ (write_reduction)
aus π ergibt sich δ_c und die Wirkung von choose_alternative (s.u.).
Der ausgewählte Algorithmus hat Einfluß auf O_c, O_F, O_A und die Realisierungsfunktion ρ.

Seien z.B. die Produktionen
factor : var; const; '(',expr,')'. mit der Numerierung
n n+1 n+2
gegeben. factor trete in der Produktion der Nummer m auf der Position i auf. Dann ist

```
ρ(-,produce_nonterminal,"factor") =
      (read_symbol("factor",("factor",symb))
       push(("factor",symb),("factor",symb))
       choose_alternative (("factor",symb),prodr),prodnr)
```

wobei
choose_alternative(("factor",symb), $\left\{\begin{array}{ll} n, & \text{falls symb = id} \\ n+1, & \text{falls symb = const} \\ n+2, & \text{falls symb = (} \end{array}\right\}$)
und var $\to$ id gelte.

Weiter ist
δ_c((m,i),produce_nonterminal,prodnr) =

$$\left\{\begin{array}{ll} ((n,1),\text{produce\_nonterminal},\text{"var"}), & \text{falls prodnr} = n \\ ((m,i+1),\ \text{continue\_production},-), & \text{falls prodnr} = n+1 \\ ((n+2,1),\ \text{produce\_nonterminal},\text{"expr"}), & \text{falls prodnr} = n+2 \end{array}\right.$$

Aus einem Modul $M = (E,F,A,c,m,\rho)$ kann durch Abspaltung der Kontrollfunktion δ_c eine Klasse $K_{M,O}$ folgendermaßen erzeugt werden: $K_{M,O} \overline{\overline{df}} (S,S^o,S^e,\delta,O)$, mit $S = S_{EUFUA}$, $S^o = S^o_{EUFUA}$, $S^e = S^e_{EUFUA}$, $O \subset O_c$ und $\delta(s_1,o,p_1) = (s_2,p_2)$, falls $\rho(s_1,o,p_1) = (w,p_2)$ und $s_1 \underset{w}{\rightarrow} s_2$ gilt. Auf diese Weise kann man sich eine Klasse aus einem Modul entstanden denken.

2. ÄQUIVALENZ UND VERSCHRÄNKBARKEIT VON COMPILER-MODULN

Betrachtet man zwei Moduln, die dieselbe Übersetzungs-Teilaufgabe mit verschiedenen Verfahren realisieren, so stellt sich die Frage, ob ein Austausch der Moduln die konzeptionelle bzw. realisierte Compiler-Struktur unverändert läßt. Die folgenden Äquivalenzbegriffe erlauben es, Bedingungen für solchen Invarianzen zu formulieren.

Definition 7 (Äquivalenz von Moduln).
Zwei Moduln M_1 und M_2 heißen *schwach äquivalent* falls $m_1 = m_2$ gilt.
M_1 und M_2 heißen *eingabeseitig äquivalent*, falls
a) $m_1 = m_2$ und $E_1 = E_2$
b) $\forall s \in S^o_E : as^E_{M_1}(s) = as^E_{M_2}(s)$

M_1 und M_2 heißen *ausgabeseitig äquivalent*, falls
a) $m_1 = m_2$ und $A_1 = A_2$
b) $\forall s \in S^o_E : as^A_{M_1}(s) = as^A_{M_2}(s)$

M_1 und M_2 heißen *stark äquivalent*, falls sie sowohl eingabeseitig als auch ausgabeseitig äquivalent sind.

Die schwache Äquivalenz zweier Moduln läßt die konzeptionelle Compiler-Struktur unverändert. Ein sequentieller Anschluß beider Moduln ist möglich. Ein Beispiel für die schwache Äquivalenz zweier Moduln wäre eine Links-Rechts- und eine Rechts-Links-Syntaxanalyse zur selben kontextfreien Grammatik.

Die starke Äquivalenz zweier Moduln erlaubt den Austausch dieser Moduln, ohne die im folgenden definierte verschränkte Compiler-Struktur zu berühren. Zum Beispiel sind alle kanonischen Links-Rechts-bottom up-Syntaxanalyse-Verfahren stark äquivalent.

Die Richtung des Informationsflusses zwischen Compiler-Moduln läßt sich aus der konzeptionellen Struktur des Compilers entnehmen. Bei einer sequentiellen Realisierung dieser Struktur verfügt jeder Modul über sein eigenes Kontrollprogramm. Sollen jedoch Moduln verschränkt arbeiten, so zeigt sich, daß die inhärente Aufrufbeziehung zwischen den Moduln sowohl gleich- als auch entgegengerichtet zum Informationsfluß sein kann. Die Aufrufbeziehung zwischen Scanner und Parser geht notwendig vom Parser zum Scanner, falls eine kontext-freie, nicht-reguläre Sprache analysiert werden soll, und der Scanner nur die Realisierung einer einseitig linearen Grammatik ist. In diesem Fall geben wir Bedingungen an für die Verschränkbarkeit von Scanner und Parser auf der Eingabeseite des Parsers (Fig. 3a).

Soll die Auswertung der semantischen Attribute (5),(6) parallel zur Syntaxanalyse erfolgen, so laufen Informationsfluß und Aufrufbeziehung gleichgerichtet vom Parser zur Attributbehandlung. Hier geben wir Bedingungen an für die Verschränkbarkeit der beiden Moduln auf der Ausgabeseite des Parsers als des steuernden Moduls (Fig. 3b).

Jetzt zeigt sich, weshalb eine zweistufige Definition eines Moduls zweckmäßig für die Beschreibung der Verschränkung ist. Der an der Eingabeseite eines steuernden Moduls verschränkbare Modul wird durch Abspaltung seiner Kontrollfunktion zu einer Klasse gemacht und für die Eingabeklasse des steuernden Moduls eingesetzt. Analog wird im zweiten Fall, bei der Verschränkung an der Ausgabeseite des steuernden Moduls, der gesteuerte Modul nach Abspaltung seiner Kontrollfunktion als Ausgabeklasse des steuernden Moduls verwendet (siehe Fig. 3).

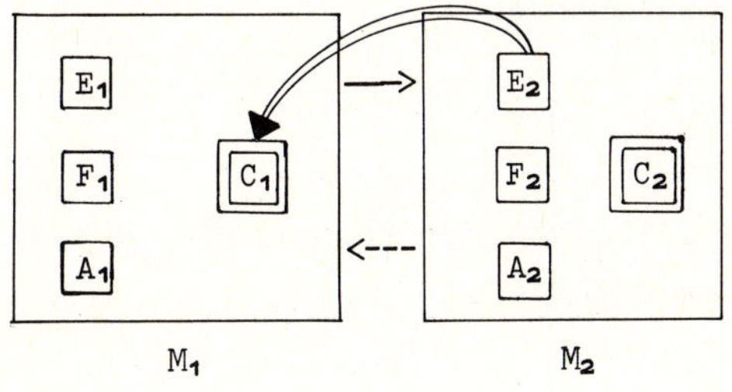

a) Verschränkung von M_1 mit M_2 an der Eingabeseite von M_2

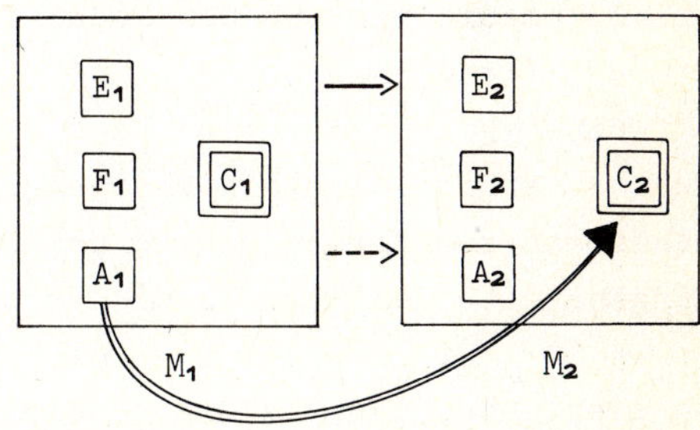

b) Verschränkung von M_1 mit M_2 an der Ausgabeseite von M_1

——> Informationsfluß
----> Aufrufbeziehung
===> Verschränkungsfunktion

Fig. 3 Verschränkung von Moduln

<u>Definition 8</u> (Eingabeseitige Verschränkbarkeit).
Seien M_1 und M_2 Moduln. M_1 heißt mit M_2 *an der Eingabeseite* von M_2 *verschränkbar*, falls es eine Abbildung

$$f : O_{E_2} \to O^*_{c_1} \text{, genannt } \textit{Verschränkungsfunktion}$$

mit folgender Eigenschaft gibt:

Sei $s \in S^o_{E_1}$, $as^E_{M_2}(m_1(s)) = e_1(p^1_1,p^2_1)e_2(p^1_2,p^2_2) \dots e_n(p^1_n,p^2_n)$ und $f(e_i) = o_{i1}\ o_{i2} \dots o_{ik_i}$,

Dann ist mit den Startgrößen $s_{11} = (s,s^o_{F_1},s^o_{A_1})$ und $p_{i1} = p^1_i$ für $1 \le i \le n$ folgendes definiert und es gilt

$$(s_{ij},p_{ij}) = \delta_{K_{M_1},O_{C_1}}(s_{ij-1},o_{ij-1},p_{ij-1}),$$
$$\text{für } 1 < j \le k_i \text{ und } 1 \le i \le n$$
$$(s_{i+1,1},p^2_i) = \delta_{K_{M_1},O_{c_1}}(s_{ik_i},o_{ik_i},p_{ik_i}),$$
$$\text{für } 1 \le i \le n.$$

Würde man also für eine Leseoperation e die Sequenz von Kontrolloperationen $f(e)$ aus M_1 einsetzen, so erhielte man den gleichen Effekt.

Beispiel 2 (Verschränkung von Scanner und Parser).
Der Scanner, der als Realisierung einer einseitig linearen Grammatik $(V^S_N,V^S_T,\pi^S,\gamma^S)$ mit endlicher Axiomenmenge γ^S aufgefaßt wird, werde durch folgenden Modul realisiert:

O_{E_S} = {read_char}, S_{E_S}: teilweise gelesene Zeichenfolge,
O_{A_S} = {write_symbol}, S_{A_S}: bereits ausgegebene Symbolfolge,
F_S ist für die Verschränkung irrelevant,
O_{c_S} = {scan}.

Die Grammatik geht in den Modul folgendermaßen ein:
$V^S_T = P_0(\text{read\_char})$,
$P_0(\text{write\_symbol}) = \{(z,w) \mid z \in \gamma,\ z \xrightarrow{*} w,\ w \in V^{S*}_T\}$,
aus π ergibt sich die Übergangsfunktion δ_{F_S} von F_S.

Wählt man zur Verschränkung des Scanners S mit dem Parser P an der Eingabeseite des Parsers die Verschränkungsfunktion

$$f : O_{E_P} \to O^*_{c_S} \text{ mit } f(\text{read\_symbol}) = \text{scan},$$

so sieht man, daß die angegebenen Moduln für Scanner und Parser verschränkbar sind.

Lemma 1
Sei M_1 mit M_2 an der Eingabeseite von M_2 verschränkbar und M_3 eingabeseitig äquivalent zu M_2. Dann ist M_1 auch mit M_3 an der Eingabeseite von M_3 verschränkbar.

Beweis: Ist f_{12} die Verschränkungsfunktion für M_1 und M_2, so definiere man die Verschränkungsfunktion f_{13} für M_1 und M_3 durch $f_{13} := f_{12}$.

Definition 9 (Eingabeseitige Verschränkung).
Sei M_1 mit M_2 an der Eingabeseite von M_2 verschränkbar und f sei eine Verschränkungsfunktion. Der Modul $V_E(M_1,M_2) := (E,F,A,C,m,\rho)$ heißt die *Verschränkung* von M_1 mit M_2 *an der Eingabeseite* von M_2, falls $E = K_{M_1,O_{c_1}}$, $F = F_2$, $A = A_2$, $C = C_2$, $m = m_2 \circ m_1$ und für $\rho : S_{EUFUA} \times O_c \times P_I \to W^+ \times P_O$ gelte: Sei $o \in O_c$, $p \in P_I$, $s \in S_{EUFUA}$, $s = ((s^1,s^2,s^3),s_2,s_3)$. Gibt es ein $s_1 \in S_{E_2}$, so daß
a) $\rho_2((s_1,s_2,s_3),o,p) = (w,p')$
b) $\exists s' \in S_{EUFUA} : s \xrightarrow[w']{} s'$ (zu w' siehe unten)
so ist $\rho(s,o,p) = (w',p')$ und undefiniert sonst.

Hierbei entstehe w' aus w durch Ersetzen eines jeden Auftretens eines $\tilde{o}(p_1,p_2)$ mit $\tilde{o} \in O_{E_2}$ durch $o_1(p_1',p_2')o_2(p_2',p_3') \ldots o_n(p_n',p_{n+1}')$, wobei $f(\tilde{o}) = o_1 o_2 \ldots o_n$, $p_1' = p_1$, $p_{n+1}' = p_2'$ und die übrigen p_i' durch b) eindeutig festgelegt werden.

Hierbei garantiert 3) in Def. 6, daß es zu vorgegebenem (s^1,s^2,s^3) höchstens ein solches (w',p'), unabhängig von der Wahl eines speziellen s_1 geben kann.

Definition 10 (Ausgabeseitige Verschränkbarkeit).
Ersetzt man in Def. 8 E_2 durch A_2 und vertauscht man E mit A und s mit $m_1(s)$, so erhält man die Def. für die *Verschränkbarkeit* von M_1 mit M_2 *an der Ausgabeseite* von M_2.

Beispiel 3 (Verschränkung von Parser und Attributbehandlung).
Sei der Parser P aus Bsp. 1 gegeben. Ferner seien den Nonterminals der CF-Grammatik semantische Attribute zugeordnet zusammen mit Vorschriften, wie ihre Werte lokal zu Produktionen aus π zu berechnen sind (5). Sei $\Sigma = \{\sigma : \prod_{i=1}^{n} D_{a_i} \to D_b\}$ eine endl. Menge von Attributberechnungsfunktionen, $\phi = \{\sigma(a_1, \ldots, a_n;b) \mid \sigma \in \Sigma\}$ die Menge der Aufrufe solcher Funktionen. Sei weiterhin $A(\pi) \subset \phi^*$ die oben erwähnte Menge von Berechnungsvorschriften. $A(\pi)$ teilt sich auf in $S(\pi)$ und $I(\pi)$, $A(\pi) = S(\pi) \cup I(\pi)$, jenachdem die Werte von inherited oder synthesized Attributen berechnet werden.

Der Modul AB (Attributbehandlung) wird dann definiert durch:
$O_{E_{AB}}$ = {read_prodnr}, $S_{E_{AB}}$: restliche Eingabefolge
A_{AB} irrelevant für die Verschränkung,
$O_{F_{AB}}$ ergibt sich aus Σ,
$O_{c_{AB}}$ = {inherit, synthesize} und
ρ(-,inherit,prodnr1) = φ read_prodnr(-,prodnr2) mit einem $\varphi \in I(\pi)$

$\rho(-,\text{synthesize},\text{prodnr1}) = \varphi'\text{read\_prodnr}(-,\text{prodnr2})$ mit einem $\varphi' \in (\pi)$

$$\left.\begin{array}{l}\delta_{c_{AB}}(-,\text{inherit},\text{prodnr1})\\ \delta_{c_{AB}}(-,\text{synthesize},\text{prodnr1})\end{array}\right\}=\begin{cases}(-,\text{inherit},\text{prodnr1}), & \text{falls prodnr1} > 0\\ (-,\text{synthesize},\text{prodnr1}), & \text{sonst}\end{cases}$$

Es lassen sich der LL(1)-Parser-Modul P und der Modul AB mit der Funktion

$$f : O_{A_P} \rightarrow O^*_{c_{AB}},$$
$$f(\text{write\_production}) = \text{inherit}$$
$$f(\text{write\_reduction}) = \text{synthesize}$$

verschränken, falls die Attributabhängigkeiten die Well-Formedness-Bedingungen aus (6) erfüllen. Diese stellen nämlich sicher, daß während der Verarbeitung einer Produktionsnummernfolge in jeder Realisierung einer inherit- oder synthesize-Operation alle Argumente lokal besetzt sind.

Analog zu Lemma 1 erhält man

Lemma 2

Es seien M_2 und M_3 ausgabeseitig äquivalent. Ist M_1 mit M_2 an der Ausgabeseite von M_2 verschränkbar, so gilt dies auch für die Verschränkbarkeit von M_1 mit M_3.

Die Definition der ausgabeseitigen Verschränkbarkeit erhält man mit Def. 10 analog zu Def. 9. Man erhält damit:

Lemma 3

Sei M_1 mit M_2 an der Eingabeseite von M_2 verschränkbar, M_3 mit M_2 an der Ausgabeseite von M_2 verschränkbar. Dann ist

a) die Verschränkung M' von M_1 und M_2 an der Eingabeseite von M_2 verschränkbar mit M_3 an der Ausgabeseite von M',

b) die Verschränkung M'' von M_3 mit M_2 an der Ausgabeseite von M_2 verschränkbar mit M_1 an der Eingabeseite von M''.

D.h. in Bezug auf die Verschränkbarkeit gilt eine gewisse Assoziativität.

3. ZUSAMMENFASSUNG UND AUSBLICK

> In der Verschränkung zeigt
> sich erst der Meister.
> (Frei nach Goethe)

Es wurde gezeigt, unter welchen Bedingungen Compiler-Moduln verschränkt arbeiten können, die in einer konzeptionell sequentiellen Compiler-Struktur beschrieben sind. Die gegebene Definition des Modul-Begriffs ist aber so allgemein, daß sie auch auf andere modular strukturierte Systeme zur Effizienzsteigerung anwendbar ist. Andererseits wird dadurch der Weg von der formalen Beschreibung einer Übersetzungsteilaufgabe und der Auswahl eines Algorithmus' zur Realisierung dieser Teilaufgabe bis zur Darstellung des realisierten Moduls in dem angegebenen formalen Modell etwas komplizierter. Zukünftige Arbeit wird zeigen, welche Einschränkungen nötig sind, um diesen Weg effektiv zu machen.

Es hat sich gezeigt, daß die Auswahl der zur Realisierung der Moduln verwandten Algorithmen entscheidend für die Verschränkbarkeit von Compiler-Moduln ist. Die in 2. definierten Äquivalenzbegriffe ergeben eine interessante Klassifizierung von Verfahren für die einzelnen Teilaufgaben bezüglich ihrer Austauschbarkeit.

In naheliegender Weise läßt sich der Begriff der "partiellen Verschränkbarkeit" definieren, der besagt, welcher Teil einer Übersetzungs-Teilaufgabe, die inhärent nicht in einem Lauf erledigt werden kann, mit anderen Moduln verschränkt ablaufen kann. Eine Verschränkung bzw. partielle Verschränkung aller Compiler-Moduln nach geeigneter Auswahl der Verfahren zur Realisierung in den Moduln ergibt dann einen Übersetzer mit minimaler Anzahl von Läufen für eine vorliegende Programmiersprache.

BIBLIOGRAPHIE:

(1) Bauer,F.L. und Eickel,J. (Editors): *Compiler construction, an advanced course*, Springer Lecture Notes in Computer Science, 21 (1974) (im folgenden abgekürzt mit AC)

(2) McKeeman,W.M., *Compiler Construction*, in AC, S. 1-36

(3) McKeeman,W.M. und DeRemer,F.L., *Feedback-free modularization of compilers*, 3. GI-Fachtagung über Programmiersprachen, Kiel (1974)

(4) DeRemer,F.L., *Transformational Grammars*, in AC, S. 121-145

(5) Knuth,D.E., *Semantics of context-free languages*, Math. Systems Theory 2, (1968)

(6) Koster,C.H.A., *Affix Grammars*, in Peck, J.E.L. (Ed.) ALGOL 68 implementation, North Holland (1971)

(7) Dahl,O.J., Dijkstra,E.W., Hoare,C.A.R., *Structured Programming*, Academic Press, London, 1972

L O G I S C H E   S Y S T E M E

FIRST ORDER LOGIC AS A TOOL TO SOLVE AND CLASSIFY PROBLEMS

D.Marini, P.A.Miglioli, M.Ornaghi

Gruppo di Elettronica e Cibernetica dell'Università di Milano

§0. Introduction

In the recent years formal logic (i.e. first order predicate calculus with one or more additional axioms and even the second order calculus) has been widely employed in Computer Science in order to formalize and solve problems in a reliable way: this approach is considered in a widespread literature and covers various kinds of questions such as Theorem Proving (2),(4),(5), Question Answering (6), (7), Problem Solving (8), (9) and Program Writing (10), (11) (for a more comprehensive discussion see Lee and Chang (12)). In this frame the possibility of looking at first order logic as a high level programming language has been proposed (3).

Following this point of view, we believe that two main attitudes, characterized according to different uses of formal systems, are to be distinguished.

1-In the first one, for any individual instance of a general problem, a specifical logical proof provides the solution, and the proof itself is seen as a computation of the solution. For example, we have not to solve in some general way the problem of finding the greatest common divisor of x and y, but we are always concerned with proofs of facts such as: "the greatest common divisor of 6 and 9 exists and is 3".

So, in the usual problem solving programs, the logical system may be seen as an "interpreter" which carries out single computations on the basis of the logical formulation of the problem. An impressive developement of this attitude is the resolution method used by Kowalski (3).

2-The second attitude is based on the following fact: from a logical proof of a suitable kind, a general algorithm to solve a whole class of individual instances of a given problem can be extracted.

Here the proof is always a general property and it is not equivalent to the execution of any particular computation related to the problem. On the other hand, in such a case we can construct (synthesize) a program (in a previously chosen programming language) which carries out, independently from the logical system, the computations corresponding to the individual instances of the problem, i.e. the solution is obtained by "compiling" a single logical proof into a program.

Of course if a problem can be solved according to the attitude 2, it can be solved according to the attitude 1 too. In solving a problem according to the attitude 2 we can achieve more efficiency and a deeper understanding of the overall cases, but such an approach may be unsuccessfull.

In our paper we try to precisely define what we mean by "logical solution of a problem": so a definition of the class of problems and the related class of the "logical algorithms "which solve problems" is given, in the frame of first order number theories. A second definition is then proposed in order to distinguish the "natural logical algorithms" (i.e. the logical algorithms which solve problems according to attitude 2) from the other ones, and an attempt is made in order to characterize the "natural problems": so the possibility of constructing a hyerarchy of problems is discussed in order to classify the problems solvable by natural algorithms according to some "degrees of unnaturalness".

§1. Basic definitions.

We make the following conventions:

= L_N will be the set of well formed formulas of both the Kleene's intuitionistic number theory T_{NI} and Kleene's classical number theory T_{NC} (see Kleene (1)).

= $\mathcal{N} = \langle N$, "equal to", "successor", "sum", "product" $\rangle$ will be the usual structure of the natural numbers, N being the set of all such numbers.

= The notation: $T_{NC} \vdash H$, $(T_{NI} \vdash H)$ will mean that the formula $H \in L_N$ is provable in T_{NC} (in T_{NI}). As it is known, if $T_{NI} \vdash H$ then $T_{NC} \vdash H$; the converse does not hold in general.

= The notation: $\mathcal{N} \models H$ will mean that the formula $H \in L_N$ is true (valid) on the structure $\mathcal{N}$.

We will accept the following result: both T_{NC} and T_{NI} admit as a model the structure $\mathcal{N}$, i.e.: if $T_{NC} \vdash H$ $(T_{NI} \vdash H)$ then $\mathcal{N} \models H$. Such a result, indeed, can be easily proved (see (1)); however it cannot be obtained by elementary (finitistic) methods, by a well known corollary of Goedel's incompleteness theorem.

= In order to indicate that the formula $H \in L_N$ contains free <u>exactly</u> the variables $x_1, \ldots, x_n$, we'll write $H(x_1, \ldots, x_n)$. In order to indicate that the formula $H \in L_N$ contains free <u>at least</u> $x_1, \ldots, x_n$, we'll write $H\langle x_1, \ldots, x_n \rangle$.

= The notation: $H \equiv K$ will mean that the formula H is the same formula as K; this convention holds for the formulas of L_N as well as for the formulas of the problem language $\mathcal{P}$, defined below.

= The symbols: $x, y, z, w, x_1, \ldots, x_n, y_1, \ldots, y_n, z_1, \ldots, z_n, w_1, \ldots, w_n$ will represent variables ranging over N; the symbols $\bar{x}, \bar{y}, \bar{z}, \bar{w}, \bar{x}_i, \bar{y}_i, \bar{z}_i, \bar{w}_i$, will denote natural numbers, whereas the symbols $\tilde{x}, \tilde{y}, \tilde{z}, \tilde{w}, \tilde{x}_i, \tilde{y}_i, \tilde{z}_i, \tilde{w}_i$, will be the corresponding constants of L_N (numerals).

Now starting from L_N, we define the problem-language $\mathcal{P}$.

<u>Def.1.</u> $\mathcal{P} = \{[\exists z^* \varphi(x_1, \ldots, x_n, z)] / \varphi(x_1, \ldots, x_n, z) \in L_N,\ n > 0\}$

<u>Remark.</u> The formulas of $\mathcal{P}$ do not belong to L_N: as a matter of fact,

they are enclosed between square brackets. Moreover, every formula of $\wp$ contains a "starred" variable following an $\exists$ quantifier.

Before defining the interpretation of $\wp$ the following definitions are in order.

Def.2. By an n-relation ($n > 0$) we mean any subset of $N^n \times N$, i.e. any set of couples $\langle\langle \bar{x}_1,\ldots,\bar{x}_n\rangle, \bar{z}\rangle$, where $\langle \bar{x}_1,\ldots,\bar{x}_n\rangle$ is an n-tuple of natural numbers. We will denote by $\langle \bar{x}_1,\ldots,\bar{x}_n\rangle [r] \bar{z}$ the fact that the couple $\langle\langle \bar{x}_1,\ldots,\bar{x}_n\rangle, \bar{z}\rangle$ belongs to the n-relation r.

Def.3. The domain of the n-relation r is the set of n-tuples $D_r = \{\langle \bar{x}_1,\ldots,\bar{x}_n\rangle / \langle \bar{x}_1,\ldots,\bar{x}_n\rangle [r] \bar{z}$ for same $\bar{z} \in N\}$.

Now we can define the interpretation map $\mathcal{I}_\wp$ of $\wp$.

Def.4. Let $P \equiv [\exists z^* \varphi(x_1,\ldots,x_n,z)]$ be any formula of $\wp$, then $\mathcal{I}_\wp(P)$ is the n-relation r_P, with domain D_P so defined:

1- $D_P = \{\langle \bar{x}_1,\ldots,\bar{x}_n\rangle / \mathcal{N} \models \exists z\, \varphi(\tilde{x}_1,\ldots,\tilde{x}_n,z)\}$;

2- if $\langle \bar{x}_1,\ldots,\bar{x}_n\rangle \in D_P$ then $\langle \bar{x}_1,\ldots,\bar{x}_n\rangle [r] \bar{z}$ iff $\mathcal{N} \models \varphi(\tilde{x}_1,\ldots,\tilde{x}_n,\tilde{z})$.

Def.5. A problem on $\mathcal{N}$ will be any couple $\langle P, \mathcal{I}_\wp(P)\rangle$, where $P \in \wp$.

A first obvious characterization of the logical solutions of problems is given by the following definitions.

Def.6. Let $P \equiv [\exists z^* \varphi(x_1,\ldots,x_n,z)]$ and let $\langle \bar{x}_1,\ldots,\bar{x}_n\rangle \in D_P$, D_P being the domain of the n-relation $\mathcal{I}_\wp(P)$, be given: we say that the problem $\langle P, \mathcal{I}_\wp(P)\rangle$ is logically solvable with respect to $\langle \bar{x}_1,\ldots,\bar{x}_n\rangle$ iff there is $\bar{z} \in N$ such that $T_{NC} \vdash \varphi(\tilde{x}_1,\ldots,\tilde{x}_n,\tilde{z})$; moreover any proof that: $T_{NC} \vdash \varphi(\tilde{x}_1,\ldots,\tilde{x}_n,\tilde{z})$ is said to be a logical solution of $\langle P, \mathcal{I}_\wp(P)\rangle$ with respect to $\langle \bar{x}_1,\ldots,\bar{x}_n\rangle$.

Def.7. A problem $\langle P, \mathcal{I}_\wp(P)\rangle$ is logically solvable iff for every $\langle \bar{x}_1,\ldots,\bar{x}_n\rangle$ belonging to the domain of $\mathcal{I}_\wp(P)$, the problem is logically solvable with respect to $\langle \bar{x}_1,\ldots,\bar{x}_n\rangle$. A problem which is not logically solvable will be said to be incompletely solvable.

Remark. We may look at the whole theory T_{NC} as a universal non deterministic logical algorithm, which (logically or incompletely) solves any problem $\langle P, \mathcal{I}_\wp(P)\rangle$; frm this point of view, any logical solution of $\langle P, \mathcal{I}_\wp(P)\rangle$ with respect to $\langle \bar{x}_1,\ldots,\bar{x}_n\rangle$ is an execution sequence of the algorithm for $\langle P, \mathcal{I}_\wp(P)\rangle$, with input $\langle \bar{x}_1,\ldots,\bar{x}_n\rangle$. Of course for any given problem $\langle P, \mathcal{I}_\wp(P)\rangle$, one can extract from the non-deterministic universal algorithm T_{NC} a deterministic non universal one which provides a logical solution of the problem for every $\langle \bar{x}_1,\ldots,\bar{x}_n\rangle$

with respect to which the problem is logically solvable. An enumeration of all the logical solutions of the problem is an example of such a deterministic algorithm.

§2. A calculus with Gentzen's sequents.

In order to define a class of logical algorithms (which we call " natural") based on logical proofs of formulas of L_N containing free variables, we shall consider proofs carried out in a calculus with Gentzen's sequents. Such a calculus is given by the following rules, where "$\mathfrak{M}$" and "$\mathfrak{N}$" denote any finite set of formulas of L_N , $\emptyset$ denotes the empty set of formulas of L_N , and H, K, Θ are any formula of L_N .

Rules for the propositional calculus.

Basic rules:

1.B $\dfrac{H \in \mathfrak{M}}{\mathfrak{M} \vdash H}$ 2.B $\dfrac{\mathfrak{M} \vdash H}{\mathfrak{M} \cup \mathfrak{N} \vdash H}$ 3.B $\dfrac{\mathfrak{M} \vdash H;\ \mathfrak{N} \cup \{H\} \vdash K}{\mathfrak{M} \cup \mathfrak{N} \vdash K}$

Introduction rules:

I$\neg$ $\{H, \neg H\} \vdash K$

I$\wedge$ $\{H, K\} \vdash K \wedge H$

I$\vee$ $\{H\} \vdash H \vee K$; $\{K\} \vdash H \vee K$

I$\rightarrow$ $\dfrac{\mathfrak{M} \cup \{H\} \vdash K}{\mathfrak{M} \vdash H \rightarrow K}$

Elimination rules:

E$\neg$ weak: $\{H \rightarrow K;\ H \rightarrow \neg K\} \vdash \neg H$; strong: $\{\neg\neg H\} \vdash H$

E$\wedge$ $\{H \wedge K\} \vdash H$; $\{H \wedge K\} \vdash K$

E$\vee$ $\dfrac{\mathfrak{M} \cup \{H\} \vdash \Theta;\ \mathfrak{N} \cup \{K\} \vdash \Theta}{\mathfrak{M} \cup \mathfrak{N} \cup \{H \vee K\} \vdash \Theta}$

E$\rightarrow$ $\{H \rightarrow K;\ H\} \vdash K$

Rules for the predicate calculus.

I$\forall$ $\dfrac{\mathfrak{M} \vdash H\langle x\rangle}{\mathfrak{M} \vdash \forall x\, H\langle x\rangle}$

E$\forall$ $\{\forall x\, H\langle x\rangle\} \vdash H\langle \tau\rangle$

I$\exists$ $\{H\langle \tau\rangle\} \vdash \exists x\, H\langle x\rangle$

E$\exists$ $\dfrac{\mathfrak{M} \cup \{H\langle x\rangle\} \vdash K}{\mathfrak{M} \cup \{\exists x\, H\langle x\rangle\} \vdash K}$

Remark. In the application of E$\forall$ and I$\exists$ the term τ must be free for x in H (see Kleene (1)); in the application of I $\forall$, x must not occurr free in the formulas of $\mathcal{M}$; in the application of E $\exists$, x must not occurr free in the formulas of $\mathcal{M}$ and in K.

Rules for the identity calculus.

ID1 $\emptyset \vdash \tau = \tau$ for any term τ

ID2 $\{\tau_1 = \tau_2, H\langle\tau_1\rangle\} \vdash H\langle\tau_2\rangle$

Rules for number theory.

Successor rules:

S1 $\emptyset \vdash \neg\, s(x) = 0$ S2 $\{s(x) = s(y)\} \vdash x = y$

Sum rules:

SM1 $\emptyset \vdash x + 0 = x$ SM2 $\emptyset \vdash x + s(y) = s(x + y)$

Product rules:

P1 $\emptyset \vdash x \cdot 0 = 0$ P2 $\emptyset \vdash x \cdot s(y) = x \cdot y + x$

Induction rule:

IND
$$\frac{\mathcal{M} \vdash H\langle 0\rangle ;\ \mathcal{N} \cup \{H\langle w\rangle\} \vdash H\langle s(w)\rangle}{\mathcal{M} \cup \mathcal{N} \vdash H\langle x\rangle}$$

Remark. We require that the variables w and x do not occurr free in the formulas of $\mathcal{M}$ and $\mathcal{N}$. We assume moreover, that w is a different variable from x; x and w will be respectively said to be the main and the auxiliary variable in the application of the IND rule.

Remarks. We say that $H \in L_N$ is derivable from the set of assumptions $\mathcal{M}$ (and we denote this fact by $\mathcal{M} \vdash H$) iff $\mathcal{M} \vdash H$ is the last sequent of a derivation sequence in our calculus. We omit the obvious definition of derivation sequence.

We say that H is derivable in our calculus iff $\emptyset \vdash H$.

In order to put into evidence that $\mathcal{M} \vdash H$ is proved without using the strong E $\neg$ rule we'll write $\mathcal{M} \overset{int}{\vdash} H$.

The following two facts can be easily proved:

1- $T_{NC} \vdash H$ iff $\emptyset \vdash H$;

2- $T_{NI} \vdash H$ iff $\emptyset \overset{int}{\vdash} H$.

§3. Natural logical algorithms.

In order to show a special class of logical algorithms and the related problems, we make the following conventions.

= $\mathcal{D}\langle x_1, \ldots, x_n\rangle$ will be any legal derivation sequence (i.e. any derivation sequence carried out by correctly applying the rules of the Gentzen's calculus defined in the previous §2.) such that:there is some $H\langle x_1, \ldots, x_n\rangle$

$\in L_N$ $(n > 0)$ which is on the right hand side of some sequent of $\mathcal{D}\langle x_1,\dots,x_n\rangle$; moreover, the variables $x_1,\dots,x_n$ are not auxiliary in any application of the IND rule. We will call such a $\mathcal{D}\langle x_1,\dots,x_n\rangle$ an open derivation.

= We say that the open derivation $\mathcal{D}\langle x_1,\dots,x_n\rangle$ is normalized iff:

1- any two applications of the IND rule have different auxiliary variables and different main variables;

2- no variable which is auxiliary in an application of the IND rule is the main variable of some other application of the IND rule.

= Let $\mathcal{S}$ be any set of sequents (legal or not) and let $\langle z_1,\dots,z_k\rangle$ be any k-tuple of variables $(k > 0)$, each of them occurring free in some formula on the right hand side or on the left hand side of some sequent of $\mathcal{S}$: for every $\langle \bar{z}_1,\dots,\bar{z}_k\rangle \in N^k$, we denote by $\sigma^{z_1,\dots,z_k}_{\bar{z}_1,\dots,\bar{z}_k}\mathcal{S}$ the set of sequents obtained by simultaneously substituting all the occurrences of $z_1,\dots,z_k$ in $\mathcal{S}$ respectively by $\bar{z}_1,\dots,\bar{z}_k$.

Now we are ready to explain what we mean by "expansion of the normalized open derivation $\mathcal{D}\langle x_1,\dots,x_n\rangle$ induced by $\langle\bar{x}_1,\dots,\bar{x}_n\rangle \in N^n$ ".

Let $\mathcal{D}\langle x_1,\dots,x_n\rangle$ be any normalized open derivation and let $\langle y_1,\dots,y_m\rangle$ $(m \geq 0)$ be, in some order, a set of free variables occurring in some formula of $\mathcal{D}\langle x_1,\dots,x_n\rangle$ such that: for every i $(1 \leq i \leq m)$, y_i is different from $x_1,\dots,x_n$ and y_i is not auxiliary in any application of the IND rule; let (according to the order of $\langle x_1,\dots,x_n,y_1,\dots,y_m\rangle$ and with $j,r \geq 0$) $\langle x_{i1},\dots,x_{ij},y_{k1},\dots,y_{kr}\rangle$ be the set of all the variables among $x_1,\dots,x_n,y_1,\dots,y_m$ which are the main variables of some application of the IND rule, and let $\langle x'_{i1},\dots,x'_{ij},y'_{k1},\dots,y'_{kr}\rangle$ be the corresponding set of auxiliary variables; finally, let $\langle\bar{x}_1,\dots,\bar{x}_n\rangle \in N^n$ and $\langle\bar{y}_1,\dots,\bar{y}_m\rangle \in N^m$: we define the expansion of $\mathcal{D}\langle x_1,\dots,x_n\rangle$ induced by $\langle\bar{x}_1,\dots,\bar{x}_n\rangle$ with respect to $\langle\bar{y}_1,\dots,\bar{y}_m\rangle$ by the following steps:

I) Set COLL:= $\emptyset$ (COLL means "collection").

II) Set PRUN := $\sigma^{x_1,\dots,x_n,y_1,\dots,y_m}_{\bar{x}_1,\dots,\bar{x}_n,\bar{y}_1,\dots,\bar{y}_m}$ $\mathcal{D}\langle x_1,\dots,x_n\rangle$. (PRUN means pruned).

III) Set COLL := COLL $\cup$ COLL', where COLL' is the set of all the closed formulas H such that $\emptyset \vdash H \in$ PRUN.

IV) $\mathcal{M} \vdash K$ belongs to the pruned set PRUN' iff one of the following conditions is satisfied:

1- $\mathcal{M} \cup \{H\} \vdash K \in$ PRUN and $H \in$ COLL;

2- $\mathcal{M}' \cup \{H(w_1,\dots,w_p)\} \vdash K' \in$ PRUN and $H(\tau_1,\dots,\tau_p) \in$ COLL and

$\mathcal{M}\{K\} = \text{SUBST}\,{}^{w_1,\dots,w_p}_{\tau_1,\dots,\tau_p}\, \mathcal{M}' \cup \{K'\}$, where $\text{SUBST}\,{}^{w_1,\dots,w_p}_{\tau_1,\dots,\tau_p}\mathcal{M}'\{K'\}$ indicates the set of formulas obtained by simultaneously substituting in the formulas of $\mathcal{M}'$ and K' the variables $w_1,\dots,w_p$ (if they occurr free) respectively by the terms $\tau_1,\dots,\tau_p$.

Set PRUN := PRUN'.

V) Repeat steps III and IV until COLL cannot be furtherly pruned.

VI) If all the constants $\bar{x}_{i1},\dots,\bar{x}_{ij}, \bar{y}_{k1},\dots,\bar{y}_{kr}$ are equal to 0, then STOP; otherwise GO TO step VII.

VII) Set $\langle \bar{x}'_{i1},\dots,\bar{x}'_{ij},\bar{y}'_{k1},\dots,\bar{y}'_{kr}\rangle := \langle 0,0,\dots,0\rangle$.

VIII) Set PRUN :=

$$\sigma^{x'_{i1},\dots,x'_{ij},y'_{k1},\dots,y'_{kr}}_{\bar{x}'_{i1},\dots,\bar{x}'_{ij},\bar{y}'_{k1},\dots,\bar{y}'_{kr}} \quad \sigma^{x_1,\dots,x_n,y_1,\dots,y_m}_{\bar{x}_1,\dots,\bar{x}_n,\bar{y}_1,\dots,\bar{y}_m} \quad \mathcal{D}\langle x_1,\dots,x_n\rangle$$

IX) Repeat steps III and IV until COLL cannot be furtherly enlarged.

X) For every $\bar{x}'_{is}, \bar{y}'_{kl}$ $(1 \leq s \leq j;\ 1 \leq l \leq r)$:

if a) $x'_{is} + 1 < x_{is}$ then set $\bar{x}'_{is} := \bar{x}'_{is} + 1$;

if b) $y'_{il} + 1 < y_{il}$ then set $\bar{y}'_{il} := \bar{y}'_{il} + 1$.

If for no $\bar{x}'_{is}$ condition a) is verified and for no $\bar{y}'_{il}$ condition b) is verified , then STOP; otherwise GO TO step VIII.

One can show that the procedure explained in the above steps always terminates; the final COLL is said to be the <u>expansion of $\mathcal{D}\langle x_1,\dots,x_n\rangle$ induced by $\langle \bar{x}_1,\dots,\bar{x}_n\rangle$ with respect to $\langle \bar{y}_1,\dots,\bar{y}_m\rangle$</u> (if m = 0 , then COLL is said to be the expansion of $\mathcal{D}\langle x_1,\dots,x_n\rangle$ induced by $\langle \bar{x}_1,\dots,\bar{x}_n\rangle$).

Now we can explain what we mean by " the normalized open derivation $\mathcal{D}\langle x_1,\dots,x_n\rangle$ naturally solves the problem $\langle P, \mathcal{T}_{\mathcal{P}}(P)\rangle$ ".

<u>Def.8.</u> Let $\langle P, \mathcal{T}_{\mathcal{P}}(P)\rangle$ be a problem, where

$$P \equiv [\exists z^* \exists y_1 \dots \exists y_m \varphi(x_1,\dots,x_n,y_1,\dots,y_m,z)] \quad (m \geq 0)$$

and $\varphi \not\equiv \exists v \varphi'$ for every variable v and every $\varphi' \in L_N$; let D_P be the domain of $\mathcal{T}_{\mathcal{P}}(P)$ and let $\mathcal{D}\langle x_1,\dots,x_n\rangle$ be a normalized open derivation; we say that $\mathcal{D}\langle x_1,\dots,x_n\rangle$ <u>naturally solves $\langle P, \mathcal{T}_{\mathcal{P}}(P)\rangle$</u> iff the following conditions are satisfied:

1- There is a formula $\mathcal{F}(x_1,\dots,x_n,v_1,\dots,v_i,z) \in L_N$ such that:

$\mathcal{F} \equiv \exists w_1 \dots \exists w_h\ \varphi(x_1,\dots,x_n,w_1,\dots,w_h,v_1,\dots,v_i,z)$, where $\langle w_1,\dots,w_h\rangle$ is any subset (in some order) of $\{y_1,\dots,y_m\}$ and $\langle v_1,\dots,v_i\rangle$ is (in some order) the set of the remaining variables of $\{y_1,\dots,y_m\}$ (eventually, h=0 or i = 0).

2- Either:

2'- for every $\langle \bar{x}_1,\dots,\bar{x}_n\rangle \in D_P$,

$\mathcal{F}(\tilde{x}_1,\ldots,\tilde{x}_n,\tau_1(\tilde{x}_1,\ldots,\tilde{x}_n),\ldots,\tau_i(\tilde{x}_1,\ldots,\tilde{x}_n),\tau(\tilde{x}_1,\ldots,\tilde{x}_n))$
belongs to the expansion of $\mathcal{B}\langle x_1,\ldots,x_n\rangle$ induced by $\langle \bar{x}_1,\ldots,\bar{x}_n\rangle$; or:

2" for every $\langle \bar{x}_1,\ldots,\bar{x}_n\rangle \in D_P$, there is $\langle \bar{z},\bar{v}_1,\ldots,\bar{v}_i\rangle \in N^{i+1}$ such that $\mathcal{F}(\tilde{x}_1,\ldots,\tilde{x}_n,\tilde{v}_1,\ldots,\tilde{v}_i,\tilde{z})$ belongs to the expansion of $\mathcal{B}\langle x_1,\ldots,x_n\rangle$ induced by $\langle \bar{x}_1,\ldots,\bar{x}_n\rangle$ with respect to $\langle \bar{z},\bar{v}_1,\ldots,\bar{v}_i\rangle$.

<u>Def.9.</u> A problem $\langle P, \mathcal{TP}(P)\rangle$ is said to be <u>a natural problem</u> iff there is a normalized open derivation which naturally solves it.

Of course, every natural problem is logically solvable; the converse proposition does not hold, as it is stated in the following theorem.

<u>Theorem 1.</u> There is a problem $\langle P, \mathcal{TP}(P)\rangle$ such that:

1- $P \equiv [\exists z^* \neg \exists w\, \varphi(x,w,z)]$;
2- $\langle P, \mathcal{TP}(P)\rangle$ is logically solvable;
3- $\langle P, \mathcal{TP}(P)\rangle$ is not a natural problem.

<u>Outline of the proof.</u>

One can choose a recursive class $\mathcal{C}$ of formulas $\varphi(x,w,z)$ which satisfies the following properties:

I) for every recursively enumerable predicate $p(x,z)$ there is a formula $\varphi_p(x,w,z) \in \mathcal{C}$ such that $T_{NC} \vdash \exists w\, \varphi_p(\tilde{x},w,\tilde{z})$ iff $\mathcal{N} \models \exists w\, \varphi_p(\tilde{x},w,\tilde{z})$ iff $p(\bar{x},\bar{z})$ is true;

II) for every general recursive predicate $\bar{p}(x,z)$ there is a formula $\varphi_{\bar{p}}(x,w,z) \in \mathcal{C}$ such that if $\bar{p}(\bar{x},\bar{z})$ is true then $T_{NC} \vdash \exists w\, \varphi_{\bar{p}}(\tilde{x},w,\tilde{z})$ and if $\bar{p}(\bar{x},\bar{z})$ is false then $T_{NC} \vdash \neg \exists w\, \varphi_{\bar{p}}(\tilde{x},w,\tilde{z})$. One can show:

a- the class $\mathcal{C}'$ of all the formulas $\varphi(x,w,z) \in \mathcal{C}$, such that $\mathcal{N} \models \neg\exists w\, \varphi(\tilde{x},w,\tilde{z})$ iff $T_{NC} \vdash \neg \exists w\, \varphi(\tilde{x},w,\tilde{z})$, cannot be the complementary of a recursively enumerable set ;

b- the class of all the normalized open derivations which do not naturally solve any given problem $\langle [\exists z^* \neg \exists w\, \varphi(x,w,z)], \mathcal{TP}([\exists z^* \neg \exists w\, \varphi(x,w,z)])\rangle$ where $\varphi(x,w,z) \in \mathcal{C}$, is recursively enumerable: hence the class of all the normalized open derivations which naturally solve a problem: $\langle [\exists z^* \neg \exists w\, \varphi(x,w,z)], \mathcal{TP}(\exists z^* \neg \exists w\, \varphi(x,w,z)])\rangle$ where $\varphi(x,w,z) \in \mathcal{C}$, is the complementary of a recursively enumerable set.

If every problem $\langle [\exists z^* \neg \exists w\, \varphi(x,w,z)], \mathcal{TP}([\exists z^* \neg \exists w\, \varphi(x,w,z)])\rangle$ with $\varphi(x,w,z) \in \mathcal{C}'$ were a natural problem, then, by b- , $\mathcal{C}'$ would be the complementary of a recursively enumerable set; this fact contradicts a-.

<u>Remark.</u> In the proof of Theorem 1. one can replace "$T_{NC} \vdash$ .." by "$T_{NI} \vdash$ .."; hence there is a logically solvable non natural problem $\langle P, \mathcal{TP}(P)\rangle$ such that $P \equiv [\exists z^* \neg \exists w\, \varphi(x,w,z)]$ and :

$$\mathcal{N} \models \exists z \neg \exists w\, \varphi(x,w,z) \text{ iff } T_{NI} \vdash \exists z \neg \exists w\, \varphi(x,w,z).$$

§4. Some classes of problems.

We have not yet shown that the class of the natural problems is a reasonable "large class"; in order to do so, we define the two following recursively enumerable classes of formulas (see (13) and expecially (14)).

Def.10. A formula $\varphi(x_1,\dots,x_n) \in L_N$ is said to be i.w.c. (intuitionistically well constructed) iff one of the following properties is satisfied:

a- $T_{NI} \vdash \varphi(x_1,\dots,x_n) \vee \neg\varphi(x_1,\dots,x_n)$;

b- $\varphi(x_1,\dots,x_n) \equiv \exists y\, \varphi_1(x_1,\dots,x_n,y)$ and $\varphi_1(x_1,\dots,x_n,y)$ is i.w.c.

c- there is $\bar{\varphi}(x_1,\dots,x_n) \in L_N$ such that:

c1- $\bar{\varphi}(x_1,\dots,x_n)$ is i.w.c. and:

c2- $T_{NI} \vdash \bar{\varphi}(x_1,\dots,x_n) \rightarrow \varphi(x_1,\dots,x_n)$ and:

c3- $T_{NC} \vdash \varphi(x_1,\dots,x_n) \rightarrow \bar{\varphi}(x_1,\dots,x_n)$.

We state without proof the following theorem (for a class of natural algorithms related to the i.w.c. ,formulas, see (15) and the definition of φ-dischargeable set).

Theorem 2. Every problem $\langle P, \mathcal{T}_{\wp}(P)\rangle$ such that $P \equiv [\exists z^* \varphi(x_1,\dots,x_n,z)]$ and $\exists z\, \varphi(x_1,\dots,x_n,z)$ is i.w.c. is a natural problem.

Theorem 2. may be seen as a soundness theorem for our definition of "natural problem"; as a matter of fact, the following facts hold.

= For every partial recursive function $f(x_1,\dots,x_n)$ with domain D_f there is an i.w.c. formula $\exists z\, \varphi_f(x_1,\dots,x_n,z)$ such that:

1- $D_f = \{\langle \bar{x}_1,\dots,\bar{x}_n\rangle / \mathcal{N} \models \exists z\, \varphi_f(\tilde{x}_1,\dots,\tilde{x}_n,z)\} = \{\langle \bar{x}_1,\dots,\bar{x}_n\rangle / T_{NI} \vdash \exists z\, \varphi_f(\tilde{x}_1,\dots,\tilde{x}_n,z)\}$;

2- if $\langle \bar{x}_1,\dots,\bar{x}_n\rangle \in D_f$ and $\bar{z} = f(\bar{x}_1,\dots,\bar{x}_n)$, then $T_{NI} \vdash \varphi_f(\tilde{x}_1,\dots,\tilde{x}_n,\tilde{z})$

= The class of the i.w.c. formulas is closed under conjunction, disjunction and universal bounded quantification. In (14) many subclasses of the i.w.c. formulas are discussed, which could be used in order to classify various level of "naturalness": here we omit the discussion for sake of brevity.

Def.11. $\varphi(x_1,\dots,x_n) \in L_N$ is said to be constructively meaningful (c.m.) iff one of the following conditions is satisfied:

1- $\varphi(x_1,\dots,x_n)$ is i.w.c.;

2- $\varphi(x_1,\dots,x_n) \equiv \exists y\, \varphi_1(x_1,\dots,x_n,y)$ and:

2a- there is an i.w.c. formula $\bar{\varphi}(x_1,\dots,x_n,y)$ such that:

$$T_{NC} \vdash \bar{\varphi}(x_1,\dots,x_n,y) \leftrightarrow \varphi_1(x_1,\dots,x_n,y).$$

We state without proof the following theorem.

Theorem 3. Every problem $\langle P, \mathcal{T}_{\wp}(P)\rangle$ such that $P \equiv [\exists z^* \psi(x_1,\dots,x_n,z)]$ and $\exists z\, \psi(x_1,\dots,x_n,z)$ is c.m., is a natural problem.

Of course, if $\psi(x_1,\ldots,x_n)$ is c.m., then $\mathcal{N} \models \psi(\tilde{x}_1,\ldots,\tilde{x}_n)$ iff $T_{NC} \vdash \psi(\tilde{x}_1,\ldots,\tilde{x}_n)$; on the other hand, there are c.m. formulas $\psi(x_1,\ldots,x_n)$ such that, for some $\langle \bar{x}_1,\ldots,\bar{x}_n \rangle$, $T_{NC} \vdash \psi(\tilde{x}_1,\ldots,\tilde{x}_n)$ but $T_{NI} \nvdash \psi(\tilde{x}_1,\ldots,\tilde{x}_n)$

An interesting fact is that the c.m. formulas are closed under universal bounded quantification. Other properties of the c.m. formulas are discussed in (14). Without entering into details, the c.m. formulas are "less constructively characterized" then the i.w.c. ones: therefore, we propose to put the related problems on a higher degree of unnaturalness.

Now we open the following questions:

1) Does the class of the natural problems coincide with the class of the c.m. formulas?

2) If the question 1) has a negative answer, is the class of the natural problems recursively enumerable?

Of course the possibility of giving a satisfactory classification of the natural problems is not independent from the possibility of answering the above questions.

REFERENCES

(1) Kleene S.C. - INTRODUCTION TO METAMATHEMATICS - Amsterdam, 1967

(2) Kowalski R., Hayes P.J. - SEMANTICAL TREE IN AUTOMATIC THEOREM PROVING in: Machine Intelligence vol. 4, New York, 1969

(3) Kowalski R. - PREDICATE LOGIC AS A PROGRAMMING LANGUAGE - Proc. of IFIP, 1974

(4) Robinson J.A. - A MACHINE ORIENTED LOGIC BASED ON THE RESOLUTION PRINCIPLE Journal of the ACM,vol.12, 1965

(5) Meltzer B. - THEOREM PROVING FOR COMPUTERS: SOME RESULTS ON RESOLUTION AND RENAMING - Computer J., 8, 1966

(6) Black F. - A DEDUCTIVE QUESTION ANSWERING SYSTEM - in: Semantic Information Processing, Minsky ed., Cambridge, 1964

(7) Green C. - THEOREM PROVING BY RESOLUTION AS A BASIS FOR QUESTION ANSWERING SYSTEM in: Machine Intelligence, vol. 4, New York, 1969

(8) Nilsson N.J. - PROBLEM SOLVING METHODS IN ARTIFICIAL INTELLIGENCE - New York, 1971

(9) Green C. - THE APPLICATION OF THEOREM PROVING TO PROBLEM SOLVING - Proc. Ist. Intern. Joint Conf. on Artificial Intelligence, 1969

(10) Manna Z., Waldinger R.J. - TOWARDS AUTOMATIC PROGRAM SYNTHESIS - in: Lecture Notes on Mathematics, Springer, 1971

(11) Lee R.C.T., Chang C.L., Waldinger R.J. - AN IMPROVED PROGRAM SYNTHESIZING ALGORITHM AND ITS CORRECTNESS - Com. ACM, 4, 1974

(12) Chang C.L., Lee R.C.T. - SYMBOLIC LOGIC AND MECHANICAL THEOREM PROVING - New York 1973

(13) Degli Antoni G., Miglioli P.A., Ornaghi M. - THE SYNTHESIS OF PROGRAMS IN AN INTUITIONISTIC FRAME - Report of Gruppo di Elettronica e Cibernetica (enlarged version of: Top down approach to the synthesis of programs" - Colloque sur la Programmation Paris, 1974

(14) Miglioli P.A. - NOTE SUI LINGUAGGI DI PROGRAMMAZIONE E SULLE MAPPE DI SINTESI - Atti del Convegno di Informatica Teorica, Mantova,1974 (An english version is available).

(15) Degli Antoni G., Miglioli P.A., Ornaghi M. - THE SYNTHESIS OF PROGRAMS AS AN APPROACH TO THE CONSTRUCTION OF RELIABLE PROGRAMS - Proc. of the Int. Conf. on Proving and Improving Programs, Arc et Senans, 1975

ON EVALUATING RECURSION

Peter Raulefs
Institut für Informatik I
Universität Karlsruhe
Postfach 6380
D-7500 Karlsruhe 1, B.R.D.

Abstract: Outermost and innermost interpreters, employing what is usually less precisely called call-by-name and call-by-value evaluation, are shown to be equivalent in the sense that both can mutually simulate each other. Under a correctness criterion which is independent of any other evaluation rule, outermost interpreters implement recursion correctly but innermost interpreters do not.

1. Introduction

Implementation techniques for evaluating recursive procedures employ strategies usually referred to as "computation rules" ([MANNA-VUILLEMIN 72], [MANNA-CADIOU 72]). Computation rules have been termed "correct" or "implementing recursion correctly" iff under such a rule any recursive procedure p computes the least fixed-point of a functional associated with p. In [MANNA-VUILLEMIN 72] and [VUILLEMIN 73] it is claimed that call-by-name evaluation is correct but call-by-value is not. [DE ROEVER 74] and [DE BAKKER 75] have pointed out that this result is incorrect because the call-by-value rule does also lead to least fixed-points if fixed-points are determined in the same way in the underlying formal system.

Closer inspection reveals that previous definitions of those computation rules lack precision, leading to uncertainties when investigating their relationship in detail. We define outermost and innermost interpreters, making more precise what is usually called call-by-name and call-by-value evaluation. Then, the following results are obtained:

(1) There is indeed a close relationship between outermost and innermost interpreters: both types of interpreters can mutually simulate each other, so that either kind of evaluation can be interpreted by means of the other one.

(2) We give a correctness criterion for recursion evaluation strategies based upon the existence of normal forms in an extended λ-calculus which, independently of any other evaluation rule,

relates directly to the least fixed-points of functionals associated with recursive procedures. W.r.t. this criterion, outermost interpreters do implement recursion correctly but innermost interpreters do not.

Mutual simulation between outermost and innermost interpreters is shown using the continuation technique ([FISCHER 72], [STRACHEY-WADSWORTH 74]) in the framework of the overtyped λ-calculus (Oλ-calculus) [RAULEFS 75-1, 75-2]. In the Oλ-calculus, finite types are completely retained as far as possible so that our results can be straightforwardly applied to existing programming languages.

In Section 2, some concepts and notations being used are briefly indicated. Outermost and innermost interpreters are defined in Section 3, and mutual simulations are presented in Section 4. Correctness results are contained in Section 5.

2. Basic Concepts and Notations

The overtyped λ-calculus (Oλ-calculus) being used throughout the paper is briefly reviewed in this section.

2.1. The type system of the Oλ-calculus is obtained from the type system of an "ordinary", i.e. finitely typed λ-calculus by adding a type ∞ and types such as $(\infty \to \alpha)$, $(\alpha \to \infty)$ $(\alpha \neq \infty)$, but not $(\infty \to \infty)$.

2.2. In the Oλ-calculus, Scott-models of λ-calculi are transferred back into the syntactical mechanism of an extended λ-calculus. The transfer function symbols Θ_α^β (for any types α and β) are interpreted in standare structures as transfer functions continuously imbedding the domain of type-α-objects into the domain of type-β-objects. Θ-conversion rules allow meaning preserving syntactical translations of terms into terms of different types.

2.3. If $s_{(\alpha\to\beta)}$ and t_γ are terms then $s_{(\alpha\to\beta)}:t_\gamma$ is a combination-term and $s_{(\alpha\to\beta)}::t_\gamma$ is a combination-term only if $\alpha = \gamma$. Conversion rules take care that for $\alpha \neq \gamma$ $s_{(\alpha\to\gamma)}$ is "automatically" converted into a term of a type fitting its context without loosing its original meaning. The result of such conversions is called a Θ-normal form.

2.4. Notation:

If t is a term of type α, t is also denoted by t_α.
TERM is the set of all Oλ-calculus terms.
$\{x \leftarrow r\}_f s$ denotes the term obtained from s by consistently replacing

all free occurrences of x in s by r (where x is a variable symbol, r,s ∈ TERM, and x and r have the same type).

≡ denotes syntactical identity of terms.

→ denotes the transitive and reflexive conversion relation of the Oλ-calculus.

= denotes the equality relation of the Oλ-calculus (note: from s → t we can infer s = t where s,t ∈ TERM).

3. Oλ-Calculus Interpreters

Interpreters of λ-calculi are algorithms performing conversions upon terms until terms being accepted as "values" have been obtained:

Def.: Let VAL with VAL ⊂ TERM qualify a set of values. An algorithm computing a function eval: TERM → TERM is called a VAL-interpreter of the Oλ-calculus iff [VAL 1] ∀r,s ∈ TERM:r ≡ eval{s} => r ∈ VAL;

[VAL 2] ∀t ∈ VAL:eval{t} ≡ t;

[VAL 3] ∀r,s ∈ TERM:r ≡ eval{s} => s → r.

In the sequel, we will informally confuse algorithm and computed function and denote an interpreter computing eval by eval, too.

We wish to model a situation common to programming languages having procedure-like constructs: Procedures are taken as subprograms not to be evaluated any further; when a procedure is being applied to an argument object, the argument may or may not be evaluated. In this simplification we need not interpret procedures in terms of closures obtaining their actual values under an environment being established at execution-time. However, all results reported in this paper are orthogonal to such considerations and straightforwardly carry over to more complicated mechanisms.

Procedural objects are modelled by abstraction-terms of λ-calculi.

Def.: VT := {t|t ∈ TERM and t is either an abstraction-term or an atomic term}.

A VAL-interpreter with VAL = VT is called a value-term (VT-) interpreter.

The next definition specifies the VT-interpreters to be considered in this paper:

Def.: A VT-interpreter eval s.t.

[COMB 1] ∀s,t ∈ TERM: s is no abstraction-term

$\Rightarrow$ eval{s:t} = eval{eval{s}:eval{t}} and

[COMB 2] $\forall u \in V \cup C : \forall t \in$ TERM:eval{u:t} = u:eval{t}

is called

(a) an <u>outermost interpreter</u> iff

[APPL A] $\forall t \in$ TERM. $t \equiv \lambda x.r:s$:eval{t} = eval{$\{x \leftarrow s\}_f r'$};

(b) an <u>innermost interpreter</u> iff

[APPL I] $\forall t \in$ TERM.$t \equiv \lambda x.r:s$:eval{t} = eval{$\{x \leftarrow$ eval{s}$\}_f r'$},

where r' stands for an α-variant of r s.t. bound variables in r' do not have free occurrences in s.

<u>Notation</u>: An innermost (outermost) interpreter eval is denoted by $eval_I$ ($eval_O$).

For the following technical lemmas, $eval_O$ ($eval_I$) denotes an outermost (innermost) VT-interpreter of the $O\lambda$-calculus.

<u>*3-1.</u> $\forall s,t \in$ TERM:

(1) $eval_O\{eval_I\{s\}\} = eval_I\{s\}$

(2) $eval_I\{eval_O\{s\}\} = eval_O\{s\}$

<u>*3-2.</u> $\forall \alpha \in T : \forall t_\alpha \in$ TERM:

$eval\{\Theta_\alpha^\beta[t_\alpha]\} = eval\{\Theta_\alpha^\beta[eval\{t_\alpha\}]\}$,

where eval $\in \{eval_O, eval_I\}$.

<u>*3-3.</u> $\forall \alpha \in T : \forall z_\infty \in V : \forall t_\alpha \in$ TERM:

$$\lambda z_\infty . z_\infty : t_\alpha \rightarrow \Theta_\alpha^\infty[t_\alpha].$$

<u>Notation</u>: $ID_\infty := \lambda z_\infty . z_\infty$.

4. Simulations

In this section, we show how to simulate outermost and innermost interpreters by each other. The simulations realize the following idea:

1. We define two effective translations O,I:TERM $\rightarrow$ TERM mapping any term an abstraction-term where a "continuation-variable" c_∞ is being abstracted upon.

2. We show that two innermost resp. outermost VT-interpreters $eval_I$ and $eval_O$ can simulate each other in the following sense: For any term t,

   (1) $eval_O\{O[t]:ID_\infty = eval_I\{t\}$ and

   (2) $eval_I\{I[t]:ID_\infty = eval_O\{t\}$.

The translations O and I are constructed in such a way that, using the continuations-technique, just the desired order of evaluation of subterms is enforced.

4.1. Simulating Outermost by Innermost Interpreters

Def.: Let O:TERM → TERM be a total function s.t.

[O1] $\forall\alpha \in T:\forall u_\alpha \in C \cup V: \mathcal{O}[u_\alpha] := \lambda c_\infty.\Theta_\infty^\alpha[c_\infty:u_\alpha];$

[O2] $\forall\alpha,\beta \in T:\forall x_\alpha \in V:\forall s_\beta \in \text{TERM}:$

$$O[\lambda x_\alpha.s_\beta] := \lambda c_\infty.\Theta_\infty^{(\alpha\to\beta)}[c_\infty:(\lambda x_\alpha.(\mathcal{O}[s_\beta]:c_\infty))],$$

where $\Theta_\infty^{(\alpha\to\beta)}$ is omitted if $\alpha = \beta = \infty$.

[O3] $\forall\alpha,\beta \in T:\forall s_{(\alpha\to\beta)},t_\alpha \in \text{TERM}:$

$$\mathcal{O}[s_{(\alpha\to\beta)}:t_\alpha] := \lambda c_\infty.\Theta_\infty^\beta[(c_\infty:(O[s_{(\alpha\to\beta)}]:c_\infty)):(O[t_\alpha]:c_\infty)]$$

$\forall\alpha \in T:\forall s_\infty,t_\alpha \in \text{TERM}:$

$$\mathcal{O}[s_\infty:t_\alpha] := \lambda c_\infty.[(c_\infty:(O[s_\infty]:c_\infty)):(O[t_\alpha]:c_\infty)]$$

[O4] $\forall\alpha,\beta \in T:\forall r_\alpha,s_\beta \in \text{TERM}.\ r_\alpha::s_\beta \notin \text{TERM}:$

$$\mathcal{O}[\Theta_\alpha^\beta[r_\alpha]] := \lambda c_\infty.\Theta_\infty^\beta[c_\infty:\Theta_\alpha^\beta[O[r_\alpha]:c_\infty]]$$

$$\mathcal{O}[r_\alpha:s_\beta] := \Theta[\Theta_\alpha^\gamma[r_\alpha]:s_\beta]$$

with $\gamma \in T$ so that $\Theta_\alpha^\gamma[r_\alpha]::s_\beta \in \text{TERM}$.

c_∞ is a variable symbol not occuring in r,s, and t; c_∞ is called continuation variable.

Remark: This definition defines O uniquely up to α-conversions.

*4-1. [Simulation Theorem "eval_I by eval_O"]

If eval_O and eval_I are arbitrary outermost resp. innermost VT-interpreters then

$$\forall t \in \text{TERM}:\text{eval}_O\{\mathcal{O}[t]:ID_\infty\} = \text{eval}_I\{t\}.$$

Proof: By induction on the term structure of t. We omit all other cases except
$t \equiv \lambda x_\alpha.r_\beta:s_\alpha$ where $(\alpha,\beta) \neq (\infty,\infty)$:

Inductive assumption: $\mathrm{eval}_O\{O[r]:ID_\infty\} = \mathrm{eval}_I\{r\}$ and

$\mathrm{eval}_O\{O[s]:ID_\infty\} = \mathrm{eval}_I\{s\}$.

=> $\mathrm{eval}_O\{I[t]:ID_\infty\}$

$= \mathrm{eval}_O\{\Theta_\infty^\beta[(ID_\infty:(\Theta_\infty^{(\alpha\to\beta)}[ID_\infty:(\lambda x_\alpha.(O[r_\beta]:ID_\infty))]):$

$(O[t_\alpha]:ID_\infty)]\}$

$= \mathrm{eval}_O\{\{x_\alpha \leftarrow \mathrm{eval}_I\{t_\alpha\}\}_f(O[r'_\beta]:ID_\infty)\}$

$= \mathrm{eval}_I\{\lambda x_\alpha.r_\beta:t_\alpha\}$ by [APPL I] and [VAL 2].

4.2. Simulating Innermost by Outermost Interpreters

Def.: Let I:TERM → TERM be a total function s.t.

[I1] $\forall\alpha \in T:\forall u_\alpha \in V \cup C:I[u_\alpha] := \lambda c_\infty.\Theta_\infty^\alpha[c_\infty:u_\alpha]$

[I2] $\forall\alpha,\beta \in T:\forall x_\alpha \in V:\forall s_\beta \in$ TERM:

$I[\lambda x_\alpha.s_\beta] := \lambda c_\infty.\Theta_\infty^{(\alpha\to\beta)}[c_\infty:(\lambda x_\alpha.(I[s_\beta]:c_\infty))]$

(for $\alpha = \beta = \infty$: replace $(\alpha \to \beta)$ by ∞)

[I3] $\forall\alpha,\beta \in T:\forall s_{(\alpha\to\beta)},t_\alpha \in$ TERM:

$I[s_{(\alpha\to\beta)}:t_\alpha] := \lambda c_\infty.[(\hat{I}[s_{(\alpha\to\beta)}]:c_\infty):I[t_\alpha]]$

(for $\alpha = \beta = \infty$: replace $(\alpha \to \beta)$ by ∞)

[I4] $\forall\alpha,\beta \in T:\forall r_\alpha \in$ TERM:

$I[\Theta_\alpha^\beta[r_\alpha]] := \lambda c_\infty.[c_\infty:\Theta_\alpha^\beta[I[r_\alpha]:c_\infty]]$

[I5] $\forall\alpha,\beta \in T:\forall r_\alpha,s_\beta \in \mathrm{TERM}.r_\alpha::s_\beta \notin$ TERM:

$I[r_\alpha:s_\beta] := I[\Theta_\alpha^\gamma[r_\alpha]:s_\beta]$

with $\gamma \in T$ so that $\Theta_\alpha^\gamma[r_\alpha]::s_\beta \in$ TERM.

Here, $\hat{I}$:TERM $\rightarrow$ TERM is a function s.t.

[$\hat{I}$1] $\forall\alpha,\beta \in T:\forall u_{(\alpha\rightarrow\beta)} \in V \cup C$:

$$\hat{I}[u_{(\alpha\rightarrow\beta)}] := \lambda c_{\infty}.\lambda d_{(\infty\rightarrow\alpha)}.[\Theta_{\infty}^{(\alpha\rightarrow\beta)}[c_{\infty}:u_{(\alpha\rightarrow\beta)}]:(d_{(\infty\rightarrow\alpha)}:c_{\infty})]$$

[$\hat{I}$2] $\forall\alpha,\beta \in T:\forall x_{\alpha} \in V:\forall s_{\beta} \in$ TERM:

$$\hat{I}[\lambda x_{\alpha}.r_{\beta}] := \lambda c_{\infty}.[\lambda\bar{x}_{(\infty\rightarrow\alpha)}.\{x_{\alpha} \leftarrow \bar{x}_{(\infty\rightarrow\alpha)}:c_{\infty}\}_{f}(I[r_{\beta}]:c_{\infty})]$$

where $\bar{x}_{(\infty\rightarrow\alpha)} \in \forall-(var(I[r_{\beta}] \cup \{c_{\infty}\})$

[$\hat{I}$3] $\forall\alpha,\beta \in T.\beta = (\beta_1 \rightarrow \beta_2):\forall s_{(\alpha\rightarrow\beta)},t_{\alpha} \in$ TERM:

$$\hat{I}[s_{(\alpha\rightarrow\beta)}:t_{\alpha}] := \lambda c_{\infty}.\lambda d_{(\infty\rightarrow\beta_1)}.[\Theta_{\infty}^{\beta}[c_{\infty}:(I[s_{(\alpha\rightarrow\beta)}:t_{\alpha}]:c_{\infty})]: (d_{(\infty\rightarrow\beta_1)}:c_{\infty})]$$

where $d_{(\infty\rightarrow\beta_1)} \in V-(fv(s) \cup fv(t))$

[$\hat{I}$4] $\forall\alpha,\beta \in T.\beta = (\beta_1 \rightarrow \beta_2):\forall r_{\alpha} \in$ TERM:

$$\hat{I}[\Theta_{\alpha}^{\beta}[r_{\alpha}]] := \lambda c_{\infty}.\lambda d_{(\infty\rightarrow\beta_1)}.(\Theta_{\infty}^{\beta}[c_{\infty}:I[\Theta_{\alpha}^{\beta}[r_{\alpha}]]]: (d_{(\infty\rightarrow\beta_1)}:c_{\infty}))$$

where $d_{(\infty\rightarrow\beta_1)} \in V-fv(r_{\alpha})$

[$\hat{I}$5] $\forall\alpha,\beta \in T:\forall r_{\alpha},\beta_{\beta} \in \text{TERM}.r_{\alpha}::s_{\beta} \notin$ TERM:

$$\hat{I}[r_{\alpha}:s_{\beta}] := \hat{I}[\Theta_{\alpha}^{\gamma}[r_{\alpha}]:s_{\beta}]$$

where $\gamma \in T$ so that $\Theta_{\alpha}^{\gamma}[r_{\alpha}]::s_{\beta} \in$ TERM.

c_{∞} is a variable not occurring in any of the surrounding subterms. c and d are called continuation variables.

<u>Remark</u>: $\hat{I}$ need not be total on TERM since for defining I,$\hat{I}$ is only applied to left subterms of combinations.

*4-2. [Simulation Theorem "$eval_O$ by $eval_I$"]

If $eval_O$ and $eval_I$ are any outermost resp. innermost VT-interpreters then

$\forall t \in TERM: eval_I\{I[t]:ID_\infty\} = eval_O\{t\}$.

Proof: Similarly to showing *4-1.

4.3. Remarks

4.3.1. The specific evaluation strategy characteristic for outermost resp. innermost VT-interpreters make precise what is usually referred to as "call-by-name"-resp. "call-by-value"-evaluation.

4.3.2. Taking the set TERM of all terms in the Oλ-calculus, we can set up two formal systems C_O and C_I so that the valid formulas in C_O resp. C_I are exactly given by

(a) $\forall s,t \in TERM: \vdash_O s \to t: \iff t = eval_O\{s\}$, and

(b) $\forall s,t \in TERM: \vdash_I s \to t: \iff t = eval_I\{s\}$.

We can use the Simulation Theorems to interpret either calculus by means of the other one:

Let $\bar{O},\bar{I}$:TERM → TERM be total functions so that

$\forall t \in TERM: \bar{O}[t] := O[t]:ID_\infty$ and $\bar{I}[t] := I[t]:ID_\infty$. Then,

$\vdash_O s \to t \Rightarrow \vdash_I \bar{O}[s] \to t$, and

$\vdash_I s \to t \Rightarrow \vdash_O \bar{I}[s] \to t$.

This is equivalent to saying that the following diagrams commute:

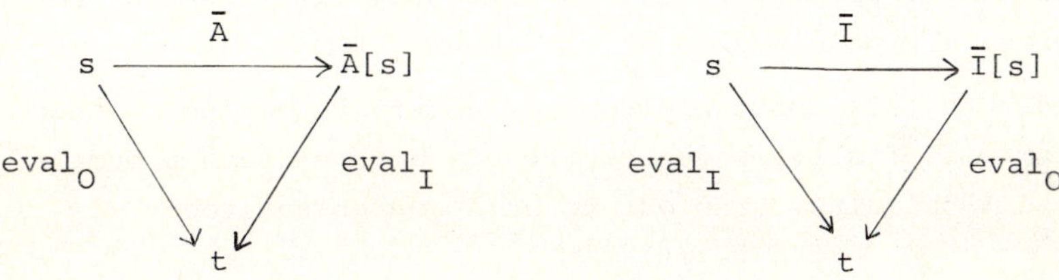

In this sense, outermost and innermost calculi are equivalent.

4.3.3. Evidently, continuations being used to define the translating functions O and I in a uniform way are required to be of type ∞. So, without using an overtyped calculus, these simulations can only be carried out in a type-free calculus ignoring any type-distinctions, whereas an overtyped calculus allows retaining finite types as far as possible. The semantics of procedural programming languages can be formalized by taking abstract objects denoted by terms of an overtyped λ-calculus to be the meaning of programs. Then, individual programs not involving infinite types can be translated by translating functions O' and I', being versions of O and I slightly revised for that specific program that do only involve finite continuations.

5. Correctness of Recursion Implementation Strategies

In earlier papers (e.g. [MANNA-VUILLEMIN 72], [DE BAKKER 75] et al.), correctness of recursion evaluation strategies has been defined in the following way:

Assume the semantics of a programming language P is described by assigning any program p a term t_p of a formal system $\mathfrak{F}$ so that t_p denotes the meaning of p. Any recursive procedure proc is associated a term t_{proc} denoting a functional F_{proc} s.t. the meaning of proc is the fixed-point of F_{proc} which is the least fixed-point determined from t_{proc} in $\mathfrak{F}$.

Hence, the meaning of recursive procedures somewhat arbitrarily depends on the evaluation strategy being employed in the formal system used to describe the semantics of the programming language.

Actually, this arbitrariness can be straightforwardly removed: Keeping in mind that the functional F_{proc} is a member of an abstract mathematical domain D, we want the meaning of proc to be the least fixed-point f_{proc} of F_{proc} in D. Then, we define a definitional interpreter I for P to implement recursion correctly iff, for any recursive procedure proc, I[proc] evaluates the least fixed-point f_{proc} of F_{proc} in D. In order to talk about elements of abstract domains we need a formal system s.t. its terms denote the elements of such a domain. Again, the overtyped λ-calculus turns out to be a convenient tool.

If f is a function of some domain and $t_f \in$ TERM a term denoting f, then a normal form of $Y{:}t_f$ denotes the least fixed-point of f, where $Y \equiv \lambda z_\infty.[(\lambda x_\infty.z_\infty{:}(x_\infty{:}x_\infty)){:}(\lambda x_\infty.z_\infty{:}(x_\infty{:}x_\infty))]$ denotes the least fixed-point operator. Hence we require an interpreter implementing recursion correctly to evaluate $Y{:}t_f$ to a normal form. Since we are only considering VT-interpreters that do not "penetrate" λ-abstractions, we define VT-normal forms accordingly:

Def.: A term t is in VT-normal form (VT-nf) iff there is no β-reducible subterm of t which is not within the scope of a λ-abstraction.

Def.: A VT-interpreter eval implements recursion correctly iff $\forall t \in$ TERM: if Y:t has a VT-nf n_t then eval{Y:t} = n_t.

*5-1. Any outermost VT-interpreter implements recursion correctly.
Proof: Follows from the Standardization Theorem of [CURRY-FEYS 74].

*5-2. Any innermost VT-interpreter does not implement recursion correctly.

Proof: Consider $t \equiv \lambda x.y:(\Delta:\Delta)$, $\Delta = \lambda z.(z:z)$.

Considering "mixed" strategies, we obtain the following result:

Def.: An interpreter eval is called uniform iff
$\forall s,s',t,t' \in$ TERM: if s and s' are homologuous subobjects of t and t' then s and s' are homologuous subobjects of eval{t} and eval{t'} (if at all).

*5-3. A uniform VT-interpreter implements recursion correctly iff it is an outermost VT-interpreter.

References

[DE BAKKER 75] J.W. de Bakker. Least Fixed Points Revisited. Proc. Symp. on λ-Calculus and Computer Science Theory, CNR Rome, March 1975.

[CADIOU 72] J.M. Cadiou. Recursive definitions of partial functions and their computations. Ph.D.-thesis. Computer Science Dept., Stanford University. Memo AIM-163/CS-266-72 (1972).

[CADIOU-MANNA 72] J.M. Cadiou and Z. Manna. Recursive definitions of partial functions and their computations. Proc. ACM Conf. on Proving Assertions about Programs, Las Cruces, 1972.

[CURRY-FEYS 74] H.B. Curry, R. Feys, and W. Craig. Combinatory Logic, vol. 1, Norht-Holland Publ. Co., 3rd printing 1974.

[FISCHER 72] M.J. Fischer. Lambda calculus schemata. Proc. ACM Conf. on Proving Assertions about Programs, Las Cruces, 1972.

[MANNA-VUILLEMIN 72] Z. Manna and J. Vuillemin. Fixpoint approach to the theory of computation. CACM: 15 (1972) 528-536

[RAULEFS 75-1] P. Raulefs. The overtyped lambda-calculus. Tech. Report No. 2/75, Institut für Informatik I, Univ. Karlsruhe, Feb. 1975.

[RAULEFS 75-2] P. Raulefs. Standard models of the overtyped lambda-calculus. Tech. Report No. 3/75, Institut für Informatik I, Univ. Karlsruhe, March 1975.

[DE ROEVER 74] W.P. de Roever. Recursion and parameter mechanisms: an axiomatic approach. In Proc. 2nd Coll. on Automata, Languages, and Programming, Saarbrücken 1974. Springer Lecture Notes in Computer Science, vol. 14 (1973) 34-65.

[STRACHEY-WADSWORTH 74] C. Strachey, and C.P. Wadsworth. Continuations A mathematical semantics for handling full jumps. Oxford Univ. Computing Lab. Tech. Monograph PRG-11 (1974).

[VUILLEMIN 73] J. Vuillemin. Correct and optimal implementation of recursion in a simple programming language. In Proc. Fifth Annual ACM Symposium on Theory of Computing, Austin, 1973.

ANALOGY CATEGORIES, VIRTUAL MACHINES, AND STRUCTURED PROGRAMMING

B.R. Gaines
Man-Machine Systems Laboratory,
Dept. of Electrical Engineering Science,
University of Essex, Colchester, U.K.

Abstract This paper arises from a number of studies of machine/problem relationships, software development techniques, language and machine design. It develops a category-theoretic framework for the analysis of the relationships between programmer, virtual machine, and problem that are inherent in discussions of "ease of programming", "good programming techniques", "structured programming", and so on. The concept of "analogy" is introduced as an explicatum of the comprehensibility of the relationship between two systems. Analogy is given a formal definition in terms of a partially ordered structure of analogy categories whose minimal element is a "truth" or "proof" category. The theory is constructive and analogy relationships are computable between defined systems, or classes of system. Thus the structures developed may be used to study the relationships between programmer, problem, and virtual machine in practical situations.

1. Introduction

There has long been a folk-lore of computing comprising moralistic fables (ESPOL and the Cactus Stack), mysterious creatures (the "good" programmer) and dark rites ("structured programming"), all concerned with value judgements about machines, problems and programmers, and their interrelationships. Like all real folk-lore this wealth of material cannot be dismissed - it provides the only constructive approaches to many problems central to computer systems engineering. And yet is is difficult to incorporate it in computer science because:

(a) it is evaluative rather than descriptive - not, "technique A exists", but, "technique A is better than technique B";

(b) as essential human element is often involved - not, "modular programs run better", but "modular programming techniques encourage programmers to produce better results".

These sources of difficulty, both involving subjective elements, have tended to undermine attempts to take a scientific approach to software development, or virtual machine design, and to make the results of studies in these areas to consist of isolated techniques or authoritarian dogma.

One effect of these problems has been to emphasize research on software production techniques that minimize human involvement, such as automatic program verification [1] which evaluates only in terms of 'correctness', or non-imperative, assertional languages [2] and theorem-proving [3] where programming is reduced to problem-description. However, the rigour of approach possible in these areas comes only because they avoid, rather than resolve, the problems stated above. The concept of program-proving is one component of "structured programming" but it does not contribute in itself to the actual process of structuring the problem to be suitable for algorithmic solution on a particular virtual machine. We cannot avoid the human component in terms such as "good programming techniques", "good machine design", and so on - terms which we all understand as going way beyond the sheer physical evaluation of correctness, speed, cost, etc.

It is the contention of this paper that both the problems stated above can be overcome and that a rigorous mathematical foundation can be established for the analysis and development of program development techniques, virtual machine design, and so on. The formulation proposed in this paper has the advantage of being constructive and leading to evaluations that can be computed in practical situations. The previously formalized concept of program verification plays a key role as a pivot for a far wider formalization of problem/programmer/machine relationships, in which both imperative and assertional languages appear as natural elements.

The basis for the formulation is the concept of an analogy relation as an explicatum of the comprehensibility of the relationship between two systems. The use of category theory enables the analogy relation to be formally defined independently of any particular structures for the two systems, and hence avoids the pre-supposition of theories of human cognitive skills, program structures, or the representation of problems. The application of the theory requires the relevant categories to be defined (in terms of automata [4,5], Petri nets [6], or lattices of flow diagrams [7,8], etc.), but the basic theory itself is independent of changes in our techniques for system representation. It turns out that the possible analogy relations between two systems form a natural and significant partial order (in fact a semi-lattice) and are finite in number when the two systems are themselves finite. It is these two properties, coupled with their psychological significance, which make analogy relations a practical explicatum of many of the concepts of structured programming.

The next section of this abstract is concerned with presenting the problems discussed in terms of a three-part relationship between programmer, problem and machine. Section 3 is a formal presentation and discussion of a category-theoretic formulation of analogy relations. The final section is concerned with how the results obtained may be applied (this paper presents work in progress and it is expected that the actual paper and presentation will contain more exemplars than can be given at present).

2. Machines, Problems and Programmers

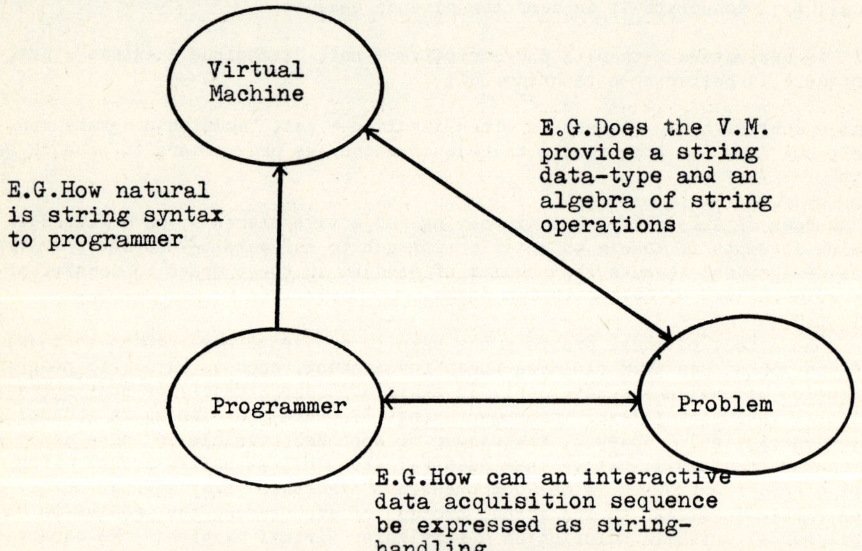

Figure 1 The Three-Part Relationship Between Virtual Machine, Programmer and Problem (with examples)

The obvious relationship to analyse in studying ease of programming is that between virtual machine and problem. However, this leaves the human component implicit in the evaluation, and a better basis for analysis is that of Fig. 1 which shows the full three-part relationship between virtual machine, problem, and programmer. Introducing the programmer explicitly and emphasizing the symmetry of the three separate relationships is important in enabling us to distinguish, for example, between something being "easier for the programmer" because: (a) it contributes to making the virtual machine intrinsically easier to use and understand; (b) it contributes to structuring the problem in a more comprehensible form; (c) it makes for a simple relation between problem and virtual machine which it is easy to express as a program. These possibilities are readily confounded - languages are both problem-orientated and programmer-orientated in their facilities and either aspect may make a contribution to ease of programming. Published discussions of structured programming [9] move freely between these three possibilities, commenting on language facilities which make for readable programs (the machine/programmer relationship), the structured fragmentation of problems for ease of understanding (the problem/programmer relationship), program verification (the problem/machine relationship), and so on.

Fig. 2 shows how the basic triangle of Fig. 1 iterates naturally to portray the tree of virtual machines [10,11] found on most systems. The usual hierarchy of the machines themselves is apparent, but its supplementation by the explicit incorporation of the programmer/machine relationships places new emphasis on the decoupling action of a virtual machine structure - the problem of the programmer at one level is the virtual machine of the next lower level, and there are no direct linkages between levels. One obvious question to ask in terms of Fig. 2 is whether a programmer/problem pair is being linked in at the appropriate node in the hierarchy, e.g. if, for some reason, the fluid dynamicist shown in Fig. 2 was tackling problems requiring high-speed bit manipulation, or list-processing, he might be better off linked to VM_{n+2} (intermediate language) or VM_{n+3} (LISP), respectively. That is, it raises the question of the VM node that has <u>greatest analogy to the problem structure</u>. However, on informing our errant programmer of these preferred alternatives, we are roundly informed that he finds the intermediate language too vast to remember and the LISP syntax too weird for words - FORTRAN is to him a natural language and he is sticking to it. That is, there is another question as to the VM node that has <u>greatest analogy to the programmer's (current) cognitive structure</u>!

The term "analogy" used in the preceding discussion has obvious colloquial connotations, but unless the meaning of the term can be defined more precisely, preferably operationally and quantitatively, the arguments must remain at their usual informal level. I first attempted to develop a rigorous explicatum for the concept when working on programmable digital differential analysers (DDA's) and attempting to classify problems in terms of the appropriate computing techniques [12]. In solving differential equations it is clear that the DDA has not only advantages in speed but also in ease of use. The psychological advantage arises because it is an <u>analog</u> computer whose structure closely resembles that of the differential equations it solves. The important psychological relationship between analogy and ease of use is explored in Ref. 1 where a tentative formulation in terms of category theory is proposed.

Although developed in a framework where it is fairly obviously appropriate, once abstracted this concept of analogy proved capable of wider extension to language and machine analysis and design. For example, two minicomputer designs provided a contrast between the earlier machine aimed at high packing density of programs (a major technical objective in microcomputers where store costs dominate) and the later machine aimed at ease of program development. The stark contrast between the requirement for detailed hand-coding and impossibility of compilation of the former, and the natural relationship to algebraic language of the latter, placed analogy in the role of another technical factor that could be traded against, for example, program packing density. There was a strong incentive to quantify "analogy" in such a way that these trade-offs could be clearly expressed. A possible quantification, based on the tentative category-theoretic concepts of Ref. 1 but now worked out in detail, is given in the following section. It turns out to be surprisingly straightforward and capable of direct application.

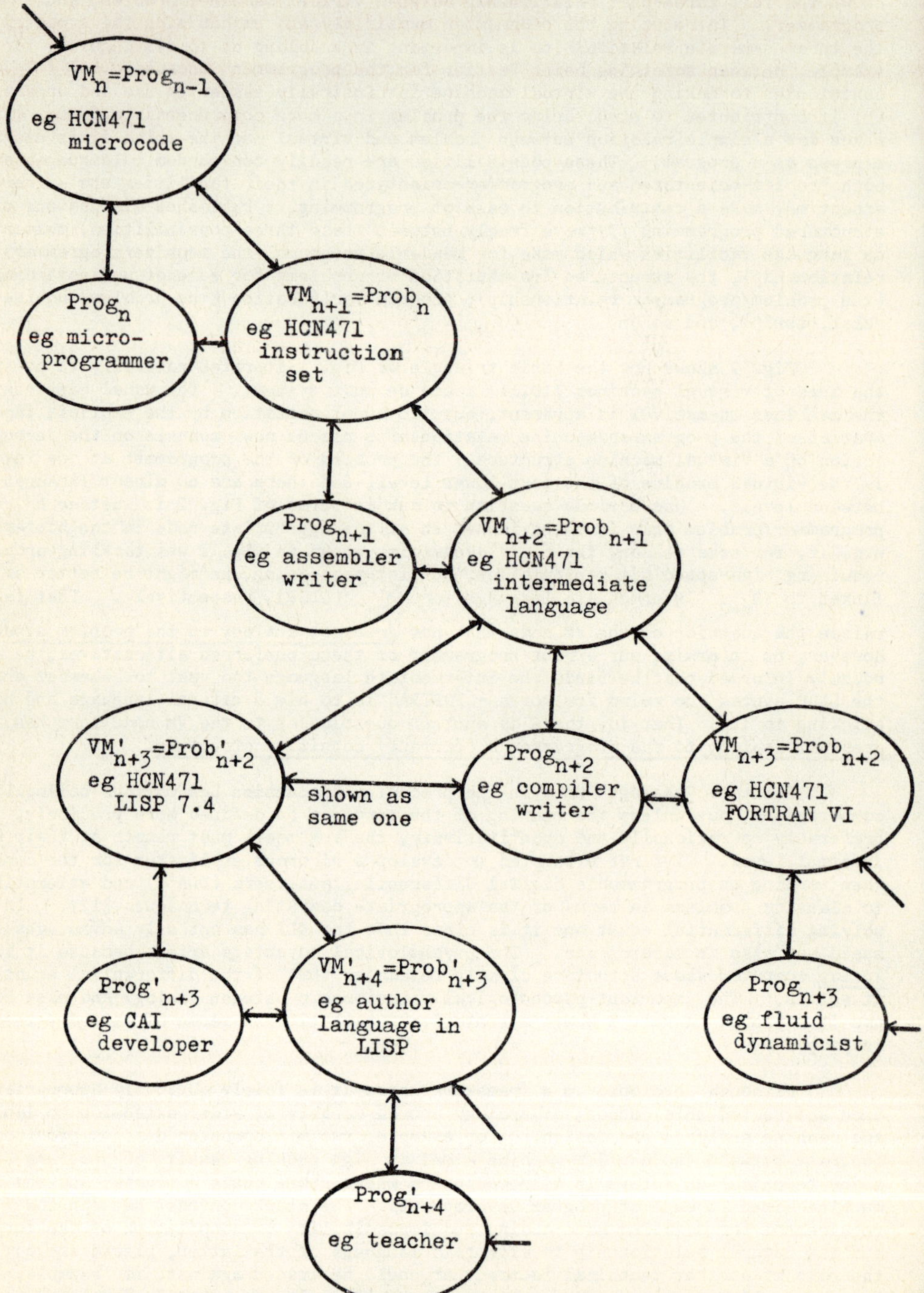

Figure 2 The Hierarchy of Virtual Machines and Programmers

3. A Category-Theoretic Formulation of Analogy

If we had tried to formulate the concept of an analogy relation a decade ago we would have been forced to frame it in terms of particular algebraic or topological structures. For the machine, a finite automaton structure would have been obvious. For the programmer or problem, however, any single structure would have imposed severe restrictions on the generality of the results and left them open to criticisms which applied only to the specific structures chosen to model human cognitive processes, or problem specifications, and not to the notion of analogy itself.

A category-theoretic framework for a theory of analogy avoids these problems. By representing the machine, programmer, and problem as arbitrary categories, the way is left open for any particular structure to be postulated for any one of them, and for the accepted structures to change with our states of knowledge and technology without affecting the fundamental concept of analogy. In addition, even if the basic structures we use remain unaltered, the use of category theory enables us to cope with changes in emphasis and significance - we may wish to examine the analogy between a particular problem and a particular program, or between a class of problems and a class of programs - we may wish to specify either a particular value or a particular function as a result to be verified. A category can be highly specific, e.g. a single discrete set, or highly general, e.g. a class of algebras, and it can express constraints upon both objects and functions.

This leads naturally into our first postulate:

Postulate I A system can be represented by a category.

This is, perhaps, immediately acceptable for virtual machines, acceptable on trust for problems, but dubious for programmers! The first two cases are adequate for many important results, and if programmer is replaced by, 'cognitive model of programmer', then the third case becomes more reasonable. Goguen's papers on category theory applied to the semantics of computation [8,13], system structure and behaviour [14,15], and human and artificial cognitive processes [16], present the case for this postulate far better than any arguments here.

The next question is how may we compare two systems (categories) for an analogy between them ? To get some idea of what is involved it is useful to have some informal specific category in mind, say that of automata [14,15]. The notion of isomorphism, or any kind of morphism, between the categories is not useful because in general we expect each to have structure not reflected in the other - an analogy is a partial correspondence - one automaton may transit many states during one transition in the other, and vice versa, but some states of each can be put into mutual correspondence. Since we cannot map directly from one system to the other we introduce a "correspondence" category that maps onto each, and ensure that these mappings are non-trivial by requiring them to be faithful functors. A faithful functor has important structure correspondence properties in that it carries commutative diagrams in one category into commutative diagrams in the other, in both directions.

Despite this restriction however our structure, like all partial correspondence concepts, is as yet very weak and allows for many trivial "correspondence categories". We strengthen it by introducing a key concept, that of a "truth" category, which is a correspondence category with the minimal structure sufficient to express the essence of one of the other two categories. For example, suppose one of our categories is essentially a description of a process for calculating tax due, and our other category (which we shall call the "model") is essentailly a computer program to perform this calculation. Then the truth category might represent a simple input/output map of data in and results out, i.e. we are not interested in how the original calculation was done and do not want this to be reflected in the program - all we want are correct final results for given data.

Note that the redundancy in the problem specification will probably be not only in structure but also in the domains of data - the domains in the truth category will tend to be smaller than the implied domains in the problem specification (and the actual domains in the computer program). The truth category is the minimal structure that we wish to reflect from the problem category through the truth category into the modal category, and vice versa. It clearly forms the basis for program verification and may be termed a "proof" category when the main categories are a problem and a program.

Postulate II A truth category having a faithful functor to each of a category and its model can adequately represent all that we mean by a "correct", or "significant", or "adequate", or "true", analogy.

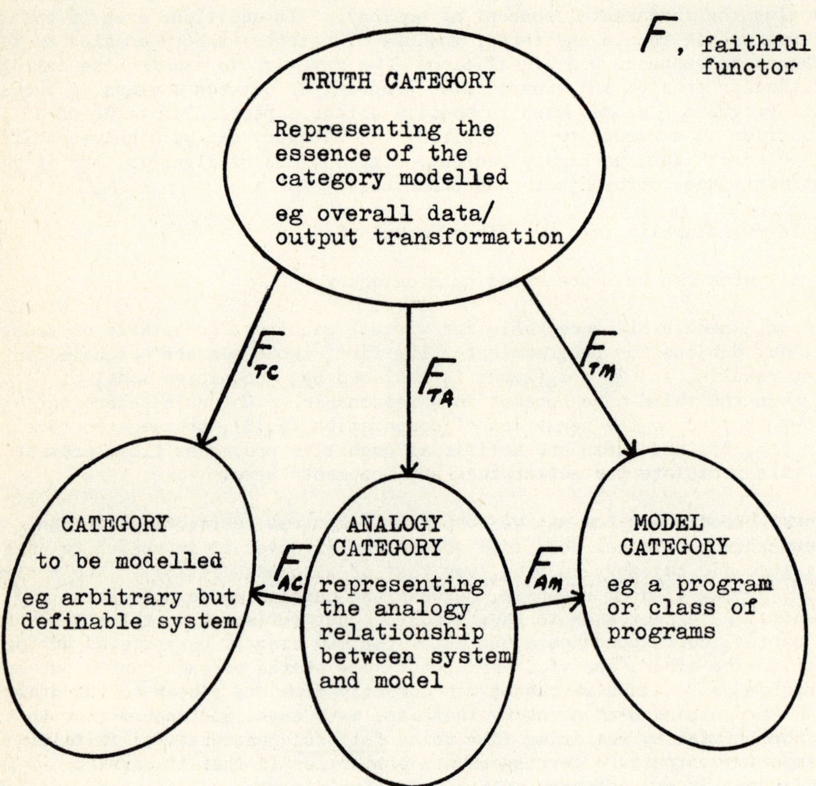

Figure 3 Diagram Defining the Analogy Category Between a System and its Model

We now have sufficient structure to formulate the concept of an "analogy category", or just "analogy". It is a correspondence category that makes the diagram of Fig. 3 commute, i.e. the faithful functors from the truth category factor through the analogy category. Hence the functors from the analogy category reflect all properties reflected by the truth category, together with certain others that the category and its model have in common but which go beyond those strictly required by the truth category. It is of course just these other properties which make the difference between the analogy for addition, say, offered by a universal Turing machine and that offered by a digital computer - at truth level the Turing machine is everything that the computer can be.

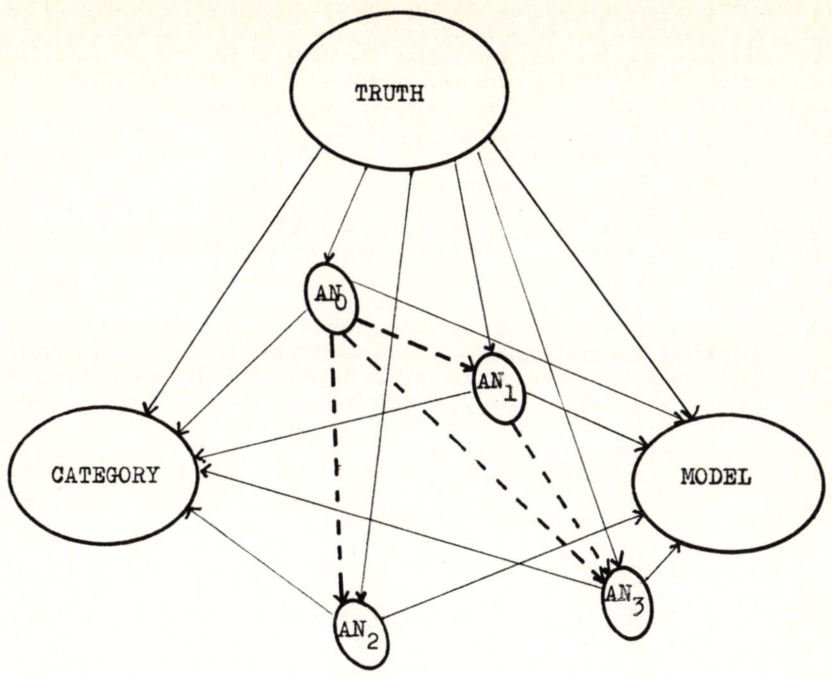

Figure 4 A Semi-Lattice of Analogies

The arrows are faithful functors: ——→ necessary

- - - → possible

There can clearly be many analogy categories for a given category/truth/model (CTM) triple, but the direction and faithfulness of the functors guarantee that the analogy categories are "smaller" than either the category or its model. Fig. 4 shows a set of four analogies, AN_0, AN_1, AN_2 and AN_3. Each necessarily has the prescribed triple of arrows connecting it to the CTM triple. However, there may also be faithful functors between the analogies themselves, and these define an important relation between analogies. Because the existence of faithful functors is reflexive, asymmetric and transitive, the relation induced is a partial order, and we shall write:

$$AN_n \geq AN_m \iff F: AN_m \xrightarrow{\text{faithful}} AN_n$$

where AN_n and AN_m are analogy categories. The relation is in fact somewhat stronger since we can show that least upper bounds, if they exist, are unique, and greatest lower bounds always exist and are unique (truth is a universal lower bound), and hence analogies form a lower semi-lattice.

It is this semi-lattice structure that forms the richest component of our formulation of analogy - it gives a rigorous explicatum to the concept of one structure being more analogous than another and it ensures that if two analogies cannot be compared directly there is a unique common analogy (their glb) which expresses their maximum mutual relationship.

Postulate III The semi-lattice ordering of analogy categories adequately represents what we mean by one analogy being "more comprehensive", "closer", or "more detailed", than another.

The role of the truth category may now be seen as a constraint ensuring the relevance of an analogy (our correspondence categories might be called "analogies" and our analogy categories "relevant analogies") - truth is the minimal element of an analogy. The non-existence of a maximal element (making the semi-lattice into a lattice) corresponds to the possibility of forming different analogies between the same parts of a structure. One should not be tempted to call them "false" analogies because these may be ruled out by appropriate choice of the truth category. The possibility of two analogies not being encompassed by another (having no common upper bound, or even no upper bounds at all) corresponds to the possibility of two people having "different points of view" - you may form an analogy which helps you, and I may form a very different one that suits me, but providing they are both adequate for the task in hand (have the truth, at least, in common) the present theory does not attempt to judge between them - i.e. it leaves ample scope for debates on style, salubrious habits, and so on. If, however, these styles and habits become incorporated into the truth category then the theory does provide the necessary legalistic tools to enforce them. It is also able to comment that X's style implies Y's (i.e. forces X to do all that Y does plus some other mannerisms), or that Z's structured programming techniques encompass those of both X and Y.

Other useful concepts may be expressed in terms of analogy categories and Figs. 3 and 4. If we require the model to be an "emulator" then essentially we require it to reflect all the structure in the system emulated and the functor from the truth category to the modelled category becomes an isomorphism. The diagram of Fig. 3 then collapses to a triangle in which a faithful functor from the category to its model factors through the analogy. Milner [17] gives some interesting examples of "simulation" between programs within an algebraic framework that represents one concrete form of the abstract categories discussed here. The development of assertional programming languages may be seen as an attempt to make the model category isomorphic to the modelled category. The semi-lattice then becomes a lattice with the maximal element being isomorphic to them both. Fig. 1 may also be expanded with more model categories and we may consider analogy categories that are common to two or more models, i.e. the common features of different models. This sets up a further partial order on analogies that is compatible with that already defined and hence extends it.

Diagrams of possible relationships, such as those of Figs. 1 and 2, may now be seen as imbeddable in a whole web of analogy relations which express all the differing bases on which one may wish to compare the various structures. The rigour and practical utility of this web of relations is a function only of the extent to which we are prepared to define the items in the boxes in such diagrams - a not unexpected result! However, it is worth noting that virtually any attempts at formal definition are utilizable, from weak constraints to highly specific structures - the approach developed in this paper enables the mutual relationships implied by various definitions to be explored.

4. Conclusions

The concepts developed in this paper are global in nature rather than specific to particular aspects of the theory of computation or programming (technology or psychology). They do not conflict with or supersede the many current studies of the mathematical structure of programming itself, of virtual machines, of system analysis, or programmer psychology, and so on. Rather they provide tools for relating these diverse studies not only within their own frame of reference, but also globally in terms of the compatibility and conflict between prescriptions based on differing terms of reference and points of view. The term "structured programming" has come to mean a great many things to a great many people, and in its very diversity lies the danger that the momentum generated will be dissipated in a range of dogmas from different "schools". The formalism of "analogy categories" developed in this paper enables the essential cohesion of the various approaches to be expressed both rigorously and meaningfully on a basis of secure mathematical foundations.

5. References

1. Elspas, B., Levitt, K.N., Waldinger, R.J. and Waksmann, A., "An assessment of techniques for proving program correctness", ACM Comp. Surveys, Vol. 4, pp. 97-147, June 1972.
2. Foster, J.M. and Elcock, E.W., "Absys 1: an incremental compiler for assertions; an introduction", in Meltzer, B. and Michie, D., Machine Intelligence 4, pp. 423-429, Edinburgh: University Press 1969.
3. Chang, C.L. and Lee, C.T.L., Symbolic Logic and Mechanical Theorem Proving, New York: Academic Press 1973.
4. Arbib, M.A. and Manes, E.G., "Foundations of system theory", Automatica, Vol. 10, pp. 285-302, 1974.
5. Bobrow, L.S. and Arbib, M.A., Discrete mathematics, Ch. 9, Philadelphia: Saunders, 1974.
6. Holt, A.W., "Introduction to occurrence systems", in Jacks, E.L. (ed.) Associative Information Techniques, New York: Elsevier, 1968.
7. Scott, D., "The lattice of flow diagrams", in Dold, A. and Eckmann, B. (eds) Symposium on the semantics of algorithmic languages, pp. 311-366, Berlin: Springer, 1971.
8. Goguen, J.A., "Semantics of computation", in Proc. 1st Int. Symp. on Category Theory Applied to Computation and Control, Massachusetts, February 1974.
9. Dahl, O.J., Dijkstra, E.W. and Hoare, C.A.R., Structured Programming, New York: Academic Press, 1972.
10. Goldberg, R.P., "Survey of virtual machine research", Computer, Vol. 7, pp. 34-35, June 1974.
11. Popek, G.J. and Goldberg, R.P., "Formal requirements for virtualizable third generation architectures", Comm. ACM, Vol. 17, pp. 412-421, July 1974.
12. Gaines, B.R., "Varieties of computer - their applications and interrelationships", IFAC Symposium, Budapest, April 1968.
13. Goguen, J.A., "System theory concepts in computer science", Proc. 6th Hawaii Int. Conf. on System Sciences, pp. 77-80, 1973.
14. Goguen, J.A., "Systems and minimal realization", Proc. IEEE Conf. on Decision and Control, pp. 42-46, 1971.
15. Goguen, J.A., "Realization is universal", Math. Syst. Theory, Vol. 6, pp. 359-374, 1973.
16. Goguen, J.A., "Concept representation in natural and artificial languages: axioms, extensions, and applications for fuzzy sets", Int. J. Man-Machine Studies, Vol. 6, pp. 513-561, September 1974.
17. Milner, R., "An algebraic definition of simulation between programs", Proc. 2nd Int. Joint Conf. on Artificial Intelligence, London: British Computer Society, pp. 481-489, 1971.

B E T R I E B S Y S T E M E II

KRITISCHER VERGLEICH VON ALGORITHMEN FÜR EIN SCHEDULING-PROBLEM

K. Ecker
Gesellschaft für Mathematik
und Datenverarbeitung
5205 St. Augustin/BRD

Abstract. In this paper we are concerned with algorithms producing schedules for processes which consist of a finite set of tasks and a precedence relation between them. For executing tasks a system of m identical processors is available. We are interested in algorithms producing non preemptive schedules which are nearly time-optimal. For some well-known algorithms the lengths of their schedules are compared with the lengths of time-minimal schedules. A new algorithm which produces considerably better schedules is presented and discussed.

1. EINLEITUNG

1.1. Bei dem Bestreben, Rechenanlagen mit größerer Leistungsfähigkeit zu bauen, werden immer häufiger Konzeptionen benützt, die mehrere identische Prozessoren in Rechenanlagen vorsehen. Dies führt zu Maschinen, wie z.B. Burroughs ILLIAC IV, CDC STAR, oder der Carnegie-Mellon University Multi-Mini-Computer, die eine simultane Ausführung mehrerer Rechenschritte ermöglichen. Bei der Organisation derartiger Maschinen treten allerdings Schwierigkeiten wie Mutual Exclusion, Deadlocks, oder beim Datenmanagement auf. Das Problem besteht darin, einen Schedule für die Menge der Rechenschritte unter Beachtung der genannten Schwierigkeiten so festzulegen, daß überdies eine vorgegebene Kostenfunktion optimiert wird.

Wir betrachten eine vereinfachte Form dieses Scheduling-Problems. Sei eine Menge E von Aufgaben (Tasks) gegeben, sowie eine partielle Ordnung $<$ auf E, die Bedingungen für die Reihenfolge der Ausführung der Tasks festlegt; E sei endlich. Das System $(E;<)$ heißt Task-Graph, und wir schreiben $G = (E,K)$ anstelle von $(E;<)$. Dabei ist K, die Kantenmenge von G, bestimmt durch $K = \{(a,b) | a,b \in E, a<b\}$. Die Ausführung der Tasks (Knoten von G) soll unter folgenden Nebenbedingungen erfolgen:

Es stehen $m \geq 2$ identische Prozessoren zur Verfügung;
während des Ablaufs ist jede Task einem der Prozessoren zur Ausführung zuzuordnen;
jeder Prozessor kann zu jedem Zeitpunkt höchstens eine Task ausführen;
die Tasks sollen ohne Unterbrechung ausgeführt werden.

Es ist ein Schedule für die Ausführung der Tasks von G zu ermitteln derart, daß der gesamte Zeitaufwand minimal ist. Insbesondere interessiert man sich für Algorithmen, die derartige Schedules erzeugen.

Nun ist nicht bekannt, ob für dieses Problem effiziente Algorithmen existieren, d. h. solche Algorithmen, deren Zeitkomplexität polynomial von der Anzahl der Knoten abhängt [7]; daher führten die Untersuchungen im wesentlichen in zwei Richtungen:

(i) Betrachtungen unter speziellen Voraussetzungen wurden durchgeführt (z. B. m=2 Prozessoren, spezielle Task-Graphen, gleiche Ausführungszeiten für alle Tasks) [2].

(ii) Ein steigendes Interesse besteht an Algorithmen, die zwar nicht immer einen optimalen Schedule erzeugen, sondern einen in dieser Hinsicht nicht zu schlechten (sub-optimale Schedules); diese Algorithmen sollen dafür aber schnell auszuführen sein [vgl. z. B. 5, 6].

Obwohl mehrere effiziente Algorithmen bekannt sind, die unter speziellen Bedingungen optimale Schedules erzeugen, weiß man i. a. noch sehr wenig über die Qualität dieser Algorithmen bei Anwendung auf allgemeinere Graphen. In dieser Arbeit beschäftigen wir uns mit einigen solchen Algorithmen und vergleichen deren Resultate mit bestmöglichen, d. h. zeitminimalen Schedules. Die folgenden Betrachtungen werden unter der vereinfachenden Annahme gleicher Ausführungszeiten aller Tasks durchgeführt. Diese Voraussetzung ist zwar sehr einschränkend und meist nicht mehr realistisch. Eine eingehendere Untersuchung dieses speziellen Problems erweist sich dennoch als sinnvoll; denn einerseits ist selbst dann noch nicht bekannt, ob effiziente Algorithmen existieren; andererseits lassen sich hier entwickelte Techniken und oftmals auch gewonnene Ergebnisse auf den allgemeineren Fall beliebiger, aber bekannter Ausführungszeiten übertragen.

1.2. Sei A ein Scheduling-Algorithmus; dann sei $t_{A,m}(G)$ (auch: $t_A(G)$) die zeitliche Länge des von A für den Task-Graphen G erzeugten Schedules für m Prozessoren. Sei $t_{O,m}(G)$ (auch: $t_O(G)$) die Länge eines zeitminimalen Schedules. Mit $\mathcal{S}_A$ wird ein von A erzeugter Schedule bezeichnet. $\mathcal{S}_O$ bezeichne einen zeitoptimalen Schedule. Das Verhältnis

$$r_m(A,G) = t_{A,m}(G)/t_{O,m}(G)$$

ist ein Maß für die Anwendbarkeit von A auf den Graphen G. Der Wert

$$R_m(A,n) = \max\{r_m(A,G) \mid G \text{ enthält höchstens } n \text{ Tasks}\}$$

ermöglicht einen Vergleich von A mit Algorithmen für zeitminimale Schedules. Vgl. [5].

2. EINIGE SPEZIELLE ALGORITHMEN

2.1. Im folgenden werden vier Algorithmen A_1, A_2, A_3, A_4 besprochen. Ihnen liegt folgendes Prinzip zugrunde: Bei Anwendung auf einen Task-Graphen G wird jeder Task von G ein Gewicht zugeordnet; dieses Gewicht ist nicht notwendig eine reelle Zahl. Auf der Menge der Gewichte wird eine Ordnungsrelation $<$ erklärt, und diese liefert ein Prioritätskriterium für die Ausführung der Tasks: Jeder Algorithmus erzeugt eine Prioritätsliste, die Bedingungen für die Reihenfolge angibt, in der die Tasks von G abgearbeitet werden. D. h., wenn Prozessoren für die Ausführung neuer Tasks frei werden, so werden unmittelbar und ohne zusätzliche Wartezeit - unter Beachtung der Abhängigkeiten im Task-Graphen - Tasks mit höherer Priorität vorrangig den Prozessoren zugeordnet (Listen-Scheduling; vgl. [2]).

Bekanntlich erfüllt jeder Algorithmus, dem dieses Prinzip zugrunde liegt, die Ungleichung

$$R_m(A,n) \leq \frac{2m-1}{m} \qquad (m \text{ Prozessoren})$$

[in 2 ist dieses Ergebnis für den allgemeineren Fall beliebiger, aber bekannter Ausführungszeiten nachgewiesen]. Insbesondere gilt dies auch für einen Algorithmus, der keine Prioritäten berechnet, dessen Prioritätsliste also leer ist, und es ist dann

$$R_m(A,n) = \frac{2m-1}{m} \qquad \text{für } n \geq m^2.$$

2.2. Mit A_1 sei der folgende, von HU [4] angegebene Algorithmus bezeichnet: Die Gewichtsfunktion $\lambda: G \longrightarrow \mathbb{N}^0$ $(=\{0,1,\dots\})$ ordne jedem Knoten seinen Level zu, das ist die Länge des längsten Weges zu einem der Endknoten. CHEN und LIU [1] haben gezeigt, daß

$$r_m(A_1,G) < 4/3 \qquad \text{für } m=2 \text{ Prozessoren und}$$

$$r_m(A_1,G) \leq 3/2 \qquad \text{für } m=3 \text{ Prozessoren}$$

gilt. Außerdem sind auch zu jedem $m>3$ Graphen G mit der Eigenschaft

$$r_m(A_1,G) = \frac{2m}{m+1}$$

bekannt. Es wird vermutet, daß $2m/(m+1)$ bereits eine obere Schranke für alle $r_m(A_1,G)$ ist.

2.3. Bei vielen Graphen erhält man einen kürzeren Schedule, wenn Knoten mit einer größeren Anzahl an unmittelbaren Nachfolgern mit einer höheren Priorität versehen werden. Wir betrachten daher als nächstes einen Algorithmus A_2, der diese Anzahl berücksichtigt: A_2 ist definiert durch eine Gewichtsfunktion $\nu\colon G \longrightarrow \mathbb{N}^0$, die jedem Knoten a die Anzahl jener Nachfolger zuordnet, die von a aus nur mit Kantenzügen der Länge 1 erreicht werden können.

<u>Satz</u>. Es gilt: $\forall m \in \mathbb{N}\ \forall \varepsilon \in (0,1]\ \exists\, n \in \mathbb{N}\quad R_m(A_2,n) \in [\frac{2m-1}{m} - \varepsilon, \frac{2m-1}{m})$.

Beweis. Sei $\varepsilon \in (0,1]$ und sei $r > 2/\varepsilon$ eine natürliche Zahl. Sei G der Graph $G_1 \cup G_2$, wobei G_1 eine Kette der Länge mr und $G_2 = (E_1 \cup \ldots \cup E_r, K)$, $|E_1| = \ldots = |E_r| = m(m-1)$, und $K = \bigcup_{i=1}^{r-1} E_i \times E_{i+1}$. Ein optimaler Schedule für G hat die Länge $t_0(G) = mr$. A_2 kann ungünstigstenfalls einen Schedule der Länge $t_{A_2}(G) = (r-1)(m-1)+mr$ erzeugen. Dann ist

$$r_m(A_2,G) = \frac{2m-1}{m} - \frac{m-1}{mr} > \frac{2m-1}{m} - \varepsilon. \qquad \blacksquare$$

2.4. Der im obigen Beweis angegebene Graph ist zwar für A_2 besonders ungünstig; dagegen erzeugt A_1 einen optimalen Schedule. Diese vermuteten gegensätzlichen Eigenschaften von A_1 und A_2 legen es nahe, Kombinationen dieser beiden Algorithmen zu betrachten. Dazu werden sowohl Level als auch Anzahl der unmittelbaren Nachfolger berücksichtigt: Jedem Knoten wird das Zahlenpaar $\gamma(a) = (\lambda(a),\nu(a))$ als Gewicht zugeordnet. Wählt man als Ordnungsrelation in $\{\gamma(a) \mid a \in G\}$ einfach

$$\gamma(a_1) < \gamma(a_2) \iff$$

$$\gamma(a_1) \neq \gamma(a_2) \text{ und } [\ \lambda(a_1) \leq \lambda(a_2),\ \nu(a_1) \leq \nu(a_2)\ ],$$

so erhält man einen Algorithmus A_3, der in vielen Fällen bessere Ergebnisse liefert als A_1 oder A_2; jedoch kann A_3 auch sehr ungünstig sein: Es gibt für jedes $m \geq 2$ Graphen mit $r_m(A_3,G) = 2m/(m+1)$.

<u>Beispiel</u>: Sei $m=3$, und sei G ein Graph mit der Darstellung Fig. 2-1. A_3 liefert für die Startknoten kein Prioritätskriterium; im ungünstigsten Fall kann A_3 daher einen Schedule mit $t_{A_3}(G) = 6$ erzeugen, und es ist $r_3(A_3,G) = 3/2$.

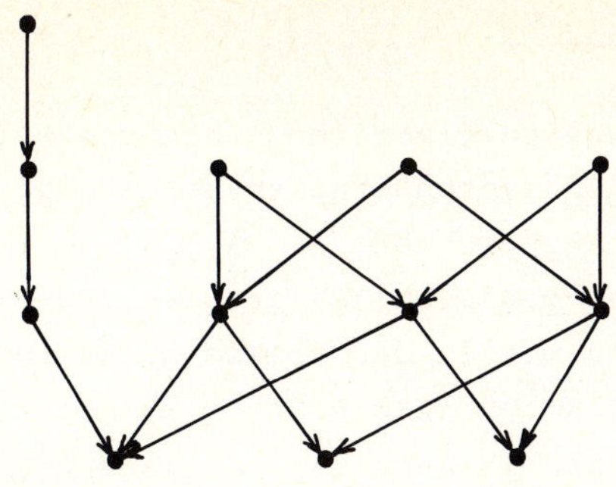

Fig. 2-1

2.5. Eine andere Möglichkeit der Definition einer Ordnungsrelation auf $\{(\lambda(a),\nu(a)) \mid a \in G\}$ ist die folgende:

$$(\lambda(a_1),\nu(a_1)) < (\lambda(a_2),\nu(a_2)) \iff$$

$$\lambda(a_1) < \lambda(a_2) \quad \text{oder} \quad [\ \lambda(a_1) = \lambda(a_2) \quad \text{und} \quad \nu(a_1) < \nu(a_2)\ ].$$

Der zugehörige Algorithmus sei A_4. Dieser Algorithmus hat ähnliche Eigenschaften wie die vorigen: Es konnte zwar bis jetzt noch kein Graph mit $r_m(A_4,G) = 2m/(m+1)$ gefunden werden, aber es gibt Graphen mit $r_m(A_4,G) = 2(m+1)/(m+3)$.

<u>Beispiel</u>: Sei $m=3$. Für den Graphen mit der Darstellung Fig. 2-2 gilt $r_3(A_4,G) = 4/3$.

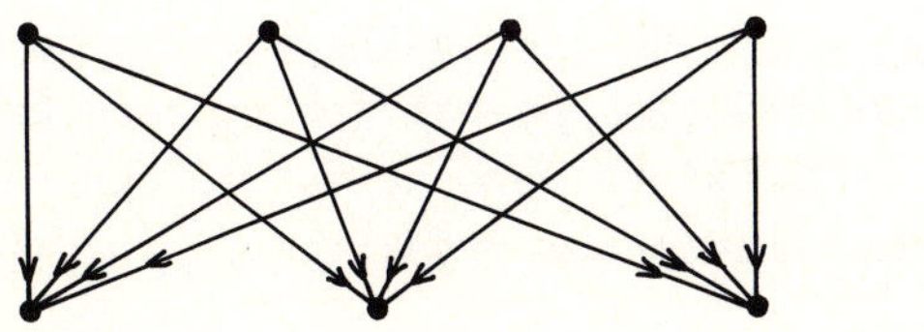

Fig. 2-2

2.6. <u>Bemerkung</u>. Die Schedules der Algorithmen A_i, $i \in \{1,\ldots,4\}$, sind nicht immer so gut, wie es wünschenswert wäre. Wenn man das Verhältnis $R_m(A_i,n)$ als Maß für die Güte benützt, so sind vor allem bei größerer Prozessorenzahl die A_i-Schedules unter Umständen sehr weit von optimalen Schedules entfernt, da $r_m(A_i,G)$ bei hinreichend großer Prozessorenzahl m der Grenze 2 beliebig nahe kommen kann. In dieser Hinsicht zeigen A_1, ..., A_4 kein besseres Verhalten als ein Listenscheduling mit leerer Liste. Daher besteht auch weiterhin die Frage nach anderen effizienten Algorithmen, die ein in dieser Hinsicht besseres Verhalten zeigen.

3. TIEFENBESCHRÄNKTE ALGORITHMEN

3.1. In diesem Abschnitt werden Algorithmen betrachtet, die beim Erzeugen des Schedules nicht den gesamten Graphen berücksichtigen, wie dies bei den Level-orientierten Algorithmen A_1, A_3, A_4 der Fall war, sondern zu jedem Zeitpunkt nur einen gewissen Teilgraphen. Derartige Betrachtungen können sinnvoll sein, da man in der Praxis zu Beginn des Prozessablaufs oft noch nicht den gesamten Task-Graphen kennt; z. B. kann dessen Struktur auch erst während des Ablaufs festgelegt werden, wie etwa bei Computerprogrammen mit bedingten Verzweigungen. Es erscheint also häufig vernünftig, einen Schedule nur für einen Teil des Graphen zu ermitteln, und in dem Maße, wie Tasks bearbeitet werden, weitere Knoten des Graphen bei der Erstellung des Schedules zu berücksichtigen.

Wir betrachten hierzu ein Modell, in dem stets nur Knoten bis zu einer bestimmten Tiefe berücksichtigt werden, d. h. nur solche Knoten, die von den temporären Startknoten aus durch Kantenzüge beschränkter Länge erreicht werden können. Dementsprechend nennen wir einen Algorithmus <u>tiefenbeschränkt</u>, falls ein $k \in \mathbb{N}$ existiert, und der Algorithmus berücksichtigt zu jedem Zeitpunkt nur jenen Teilgraphen T mit der Eigenschaft:

(i) Die Startknoten von T sind gleich den temporären Startknoten,

(ii) T hat die Höhe k.

Dabei hat ein Graph die <u>Höhe</u> h, falls in G Kantenzüge höchstens der Länge $h-1$ auftreten.

Ein Algorithmus heiße <u>k-optimal</u>, falls er auf jedem Graphen der Höhe k einen zeitoptimalen Schedule erzeugt. Selbstverständlich kann jeder k-optimale Algorithmus so modifiziert werden, daß er auf beliebige Task-Graphen anwendbar und dabei k-tiefenbeschränkt ist.

3.2. Seien S_k $(k \in \mathbb{N})$ k-optimale und k-tiefenbeschränkte Algorithmen. Speziell S_1 gibt keinerlei Bedingungen für die Reihenfolge der Tasks an. Daher ist $R_m(S_1,n) = (2m-1)/m$ für $n \geq m^2$.

<u>Satz</u>. Sei S_k k-optimal und k-tiefenbeschränkt für $k \geq 2$. Dann gilt:

$\forall m \in \mathbb{N}$ $\forall \varepsilon \in (0,1]$ $\exists n \in \mathbb{N}$

$$R_m(S_k,n) \in \left[\frac{2m-1}{m} - \varepsilon, \frac{2m-1}{m}\right).$$

Beweis. Sei $\varepsilon \in (0,1]$. Wir betrachten den im Beweis zu Satz 2.3 angegebenen Graphen G mit $r > k/\varepsilon$. G besitzt ungünstigstenfalls einen

S_k-Schedule der Länge $t_{S_k}(G) = (r-k-1)(m-1)+mr$. Damit folgt

$$r_m(S_k,G) = \frac{2m-1}{m} - \frac{(k-1)(m-1)}{mr} > \frac{2m-1}{m} - \varepsilon. \qquad \blacksquare$$

Wie man sieht, erzeugt S_k für spezielle Graphen sehr schlechte Schedules. Man kann aber durch eine geeignete Kombination von S_k mit dem Level-Algorithmus A_1 einen neuen Algorithmus konstruieren, der bessere Schedules liefert in dem Sinne, daß das Verhältnis R_m nicht beliebig nahe an die Grenze 2 herankommt. Ein solcher Algorithmus ist natürlich nur dann von Interesse, wenn er effizient ist, denn es sind nicht effiziente Algorithmen bekannt, die zeitoptimale Schedules erzeugen. In Abschnitt 4 wird ein Algorithmus mit den geforderten Eigenschaften betrachtet.

3.3. Zu jeder Menge Γ_k von Task-Graphen der Höhe $h \leq k$ kann ein Algorithmus angegeben werden, der auf Γ_k effizient ist und der für jeden Graphen $G \in \Gamma_k$ einen zeitminimalen Schedule erzeugt. Wir beschränken uns nun auf $k=2$ und geben einen 2-optimalen effizienten Algorithmus $\bar{S}_2$ an.

Sei $G = (E,K)$ von der Höhe 2, und sei die Eckenmenge E in disjunkte Mengen L_1, L_2 zerlegt:

$$L_2 = \{a \mid \exists\, b,\ (a,b) \in K\}, \quad L_1 = E - L_2.$$

Im Falle $|L_2| \equiv 0(m)$ erhält man einen optimalen Schedule für G, indem zuerst die Knoten von L_2 und dann die Knoten von L_1 den Prozessoren zugeordnet werden. Im Falle $|L_2| \equiv r(m)$, $0<r<m$, hängt die Optimalität des Schedules davon ab, welche r Knoten bei der Bearbeitung der Knoten von L_2 zuletzt genommen werden. Der folgende Algorithmus arbeitet dementsprechend in der Weise, daß (i) r Knoten $a_1,\ldots,a_r$ aus L_2 ausgewählt werden, und (ii) festgestellt wird, ob in L_1 $m-r$ von $a_1,\ldots,a_r$ unabhängige Knoten existieren; wenn (ii) nicht erfüllt ist, so werden r neue Knoten in L_2 gewählt.

3.4. <u>Algorithmus $\bar{S}_2$.</u>

(1) $r := \left(\frac{|L_2|}{m} - \left\lfloor\frac{|L_2|}{m}\right\rfloor\right) \cdot m$

($r \in \mathbb{N} \cup \{0\}$, $0<r<m-1$; $\lfloor p \rfloor$ (p reell) bedeute die größte ganze Zahl, die p nicht übersteigt).

Wenn $r=0$ ist, setze $P:=\emptyset$ und gehe nach (4).
Setze $\alpha:=m$; wähle r Knoten $a_1,\ldots,a_r$ aus L_2 und setze $P:=\{a_1,\ldots,a_r\}$.

(2) Ordne die Knoten von $L_2 - \{a_1,\ldots,a_r\}$ den Prozessoren in einer beliebigen Reihenfolge zu. Ordne die Knoten $a_1, \ldots, a_r$ und - sofern möglich - weitere Knoten aus L_1 zu (maximal $m-r$). Wenn in diesem letzten Schritt alle Prozessoren besetzt werden können, so setze $P:=\{a_1,\ldots,a_r\}$ und gehe nach (4). Wenn nicht alle Prozessoren besetzt werden können und wenn weniger als α Prozessoren frei geblieben sind, so ersetze α durch diese Zahl und setze $P:=\{a_1,\ldots,a_r\}$.

(3) Wenn alle $\binom{L_2}{r}$ r-tupel von Knoten aus L_2 durchlaufen sind, so gehe nach (4). Andernfalls wähle ein neues r-tupel $a_1,\ldots,a_r$ aus L_2 und gehe nach (2).

(4) Bilde folgenden Schedule:
   (i) Ordne die Knoten von L_2-P in beliebiger Reihenfolge den Prozessoren zu.
   (ii) Ordne die Knoten von P zu und weitere Knoten aus L_1 (so viele wie möglich, maximal $m-r$).
   (iii) Ordne die restlichen Knoten von L_1 zu.

STOP

3.5. <u>Komplexität von $\bar{S}_2$</u>. G habe n Knoten. Wegen $|L_2| \leq n-1$ und $r \leq m-1$ durchläuft $\bar{S}_2$ die Schrittfolge (2), (3) höchstens $\binom{n-1}{m-1}$ mal; d. h. $\bar{S}_2$ ist von der Zeitkomplexität $\binom{n-1}{m-1} = O(n^{m-1})$.

4. ALGORITHMUS H_2

4.1. Sei $G = (E,K)$ ein Task-Graph; E_1 sei die Menge aller Startknoten von G und E_1^i die Menge aller Startknoten mit dem Level i. D. h.: $E_1 = E_1^h \cup E_1^{h-1} \cup \ldots \cup E_1^1$, falls h der größte auftretende Level ist. Setze $E_1^{h+1}:=\emptyset$, $E_1^0:=\emptyset$.

Sei H_2 der folgende Algorithmus:

(2) l:= Höhe von G'; wenn $l \le 2$, so gehe nach (8). $k:=k+1$.

(3) Sei E_1 die Menge der Startknoten von G'. Wenn $|E_1|<m$ ist, so ordne die Elemente von E_1 den Prozessoren zu; setze $F_k:=E_1$, ersetze G' durch $G'-E_1$ und gehe nach (2). Andernfalls gehe nach (4).

(4) Bestimme $i \le l$ so, daß

$$\left|\bigcup_{j=i}^{l} E_1^j\right| \ge m \quad \text{und} \quad \left|\bigcup_{j=i-1}^{l} E_1^j\right| < m.$$

(5) Setze $F_k := \bigcup_{j=i}^{l} E_1^i$.

Setze $F_k' := \{a \mid \exists\, b \in F_k \quad (b,a) \in K, \quad (b,a) \notin K^2 \cup K^3 \cup \ldots\}$.

(6) Wende Algorithmus $\bar{S}_2$ (3.4) auf $F_k \cup F_k'$ an; ordne m Knoten aus F_k, die vermöge $\bar{S}_2$ ausgewählt werden, den Prozessoren zu (Knoten $a_1,\ldots,a_m$).

(7) Ersetze G' durch $G'-\{a_1,\ldots,a_m\}$. Gehe nach (2).

(8) Wende $\bar{S}_2$ auf G' an, bis alle Knoten bearbeitet sind:

(i) $k:=k+1$;

$$F_k := \begin{cases} E_1^2, \text{ falls } |E_1| \ge m \\ E_1^2 \cup E_1^1 \text{ sonst.} \end{cases}$$

(ii) $\bar{S}_2$ bestimmt Knoten $a_1,\ldots,a_{m'}$ $(m' \le m)$ von G'; ersetze E' durch $E'-\{a_1,\ldots,a_{m'}\}$; wenn $E'=\emptyset$, so gehe nach (i).

STOP

<u>Bemerkung</u>. Im Algorithmus H_2 werden der Reihe nach Knotenmengen $F_1, F_2,\ldots,F_k$ berechnet. Da diese Mengen später noch benötigt werden, wurden diese durch Indizierung festgehalten.

4.2. <u>Beispiel</u>. Sei G der Graph mit der Darstellung Fig. 4-1. Sei $m=3$. Die folgende Tabelle gibt die von H_2 berechneten Mengen E_1, F_i, F_i', sowie einen Schedule wieder.

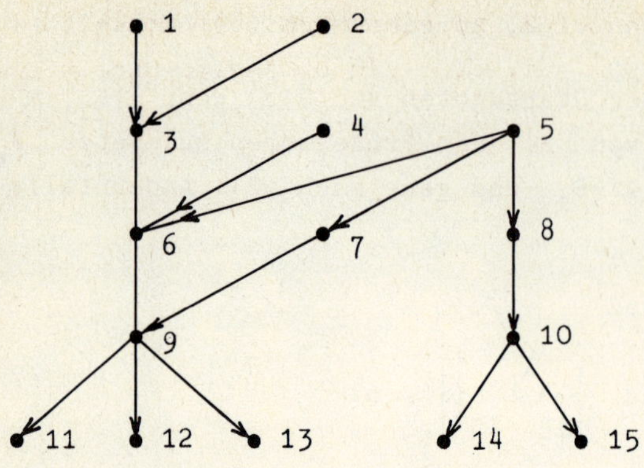

Fig. 4-1

Tabelle:

i	E_1	F_i	F'_i	Schedule
1	1,2,4,5	1,2,4,5	3,7,8	1,2,5
2	3,4,7,8	3,4,7,8	6,10	3,4,8
3	6,7,10	6,7,10	9,14,15	6,7,10
4	9,14,15	9,14,15	-	9,14,15
5	11,12,13	11,12,13	-	11,12,13

4.3. Komplexität von H_2. G habe n Knoten. Schritt (2), Schritt (3) und die Schrittfolge (4), (5) sind jeweils höchstens von der Komplexität $O(n^2)$, und die Schrittfolge (6), (7), (8) hat die Komplexität $O(n^{m-1})$. Die Schritte (2) bis (7) werden höchstens n-2 mal durchlaufen, zum Schluß erfolgt die Schrittfolge (2), (8); jeder Durchlauf benötigt $O(n^{m-1})$ Rechenschritte, so daß man insgesamt $(n-1)O(n^{m-1}) = O(n^m)$ Rechenschritte benötigt. H_2 ist daher effizient.

4.4. Wir wollen uns zum Abschluß der Frage zuwenden, wie gut die von H_2 erzeugten Schedules im Vergleich zu zeitoptimalen Schedules sind. Es zeigt sich, daß $R_m(H_2,n)$ nicht das von den anderen Algorithmen her bekannte ungünstige Grenzverhalten $(\lim_{m\to\infty} R_m = 2)$ aufweist.

Aufgrund des folgenden Lemmas können wir uns bei der Bestimmung von $r_m(H_2,G)$ auf solche Graphen G beschränken, für die ein lückenfreier Schedule existiert.

Lemma. Sei A ein Algorithmus, und es gelte $r_m(A,\bar{G})\leq\rho_m$ für alle Graphen $\bar{G}$ mit der Eigenschaft: Es gibt einen Schedule, bei dem zu jedem Zeitpunkt des Ablaufs alle m Prozessoren beschäftigt sind. Dann gilt für alle Graphen G: $r_m(A,G)\leq\rho_m$.

Beweis. Sei G ein Task-Graph mit n Knoten, und sei $mt_0(G)>n$. Dann gibt es in jedem optimalen Schedule Zeitpunkte, bei denen nicht alle m Prozessoren beschäftigt sind. Sei $\mathcal{S}_0$ ein optimaler Schedule für G; bezeichne $\mathcal{S}_0(t)$ die Menge der zum Zeitpunkt $t \in \{1,\dots,t_0(G)\}$ in $\mathcal{S}_0$ auftretenden Knoten. Wir erweitern nun G zu einem Graphen $\bar{G} = (\bar{E},\bar{K})$ mit $t_0(\bar{G}) = t_0(G)$ und $|\bar{E}| = mt_0(G)$; dann existiert zu $\bar{G}$ ein lückenfreier Schedule. Sei $t \in \{1,\dots,t_0(G)\}$ derart, daß $|\mathcal{S}_0(t)| = m_t < m$ ist. Wir wählen ein $a \in \mathcal{S}_0(t)$, ersetzen a durch $m-m_t+1$ unabhängige Knoten $a, a^{(1)}, \dots, a^{(m-m_t)}$, und führen zusätzlich Kanten in folgender Weise ein: Für alle $b \in E$ mit $(b,a) \in K$ sei $(b,a) \in \bar{K}$ und $(b,a^{(i)}) \in \bar{K}$, $i = 1, \dots, m-m_t$; analog: Für alle $b \in E$ mit $(a,b) \in K$ sei $(a,b) \in \bar{K}$ und $(a^{(i)},b) \in \bar{K}$, $i = 1, \dots, m-m_t$. Dies wird für alle Zeitpunkte aus $\{1,\dots,t_0(G)\}$, zu denen Prozessoren leer stehen, der Reihe nach durchgeführt.

Nun wird mittels des Algorithmus A ein Schedule $\mathcal{S}_A$ für $\bar{G}$ konstruiert; für $\bar{G}$ gilt: $r_m(A,\bar{G}) \le \rho_m$. Läßt man schließlich in diesem Schedule die vorhin hinzugefügten Knoten wieder weg, so erhält man einen Schedule für G, dessen Länge nach oben durch $t_A(\bar{G})$ beschränkt ist. Wegen $t_0(G) = t_0(\bar{G})$ folgt $r_m(A,G) \le r_m(A,\bar{G}) \le \rho_m$. ■

4.5. Satz. Für alle m und für alle Taskgraphen G gilt:

$$r_m(H_2,G) < \frac{3}{2}.$$

Beweisskizze. Sei G ein Taskgraph, für den ein lückenfreier Schedule existiert. Wir wenden nun den Algorithmus H_2 an; Ausgangspunkt für die weiteren Betrachtungen sind die dabei konstruierten Mengen F_i (4.1). Es treten genau $k := t_{H_2}(G)$ derartige Mengen auf, nämlich für jeden Zeitpunkt eine. Sei $l_i := \max\{\lambda(a) \mid a \in F_i\}$, $i=1,\dots,k$. Die Folge $(l_i)_{i\in\{1,\dots,k\}}$ ist monoton abnehmend, und es gilt: $l_i \le l_{i+1}+1$. Man hat mehrere Fälle je nach der Eigenschaft der Folge der l_i zu betrachten; z. B. gilt im Falle $l_1 > l_2 > \dots > l_k$: $\mathcal{S}_{H_2}$ ist optimal. Wenn in der Folge Gleichheitszeichen auftreten, etwa $l_r = l_{r+1}$, so enthält $\mathcal{S}_{H_2}$ zum Zeitpunkt r genau m Knoten. Falls $l_r = l_{r+1} > l_{r+2}$ vorliegt, so können zum Zeitpunkt $r+1$ bis zu $m-1$ Lücken auftreten. Durch elementare Überlegungen und unter Berücksichtigung der Tatsache, daß nach Voraussetzung für den zugrundeliegenden Graphen ein lückenfreier Schedule existiert, kann gezeigt werden, daß im H_2-Schedule von G die Dichte der Lücken nicht zu groß sein darf, und es gilt: $t_{H_2}(G) < 3t_0(G)/2$. Zusammen mit Lemma 4.4 folgt dann die Behauptung. ■

LITERATUR

1 Chen, N.F. and C.L. Liu: On a class of scheduling algorithms for multiprocessing computing systems, Proceedings of the Sagamore Computer Conference on Parallel Processing 1974. Lecture Notes in Computer Science 24, 1-16 (1975).

2 Coffman, E.G.,Jr., and P.J. Denning: Operating systems theory, Prentice-Hall, Inc., Englewood Cliffs, N.J., 1973.

3 Coffman, E.G.,Jr., and R.L. Graham: Optimal scheduling for two-processor systems, Acta Informatica 1, 200-213 (1972).

4 Hu, T.C.: Parallel sequencing and assembly line problems, Opns. Res. 9, 841-848 (1961).

5 Johnson, D.S,: Approximation algorithms for combinatorial problems, Proceedings of the 5th Annual Symposium on Theory of Complexity, Austin, Texas, 38-49 (1973).

6 Krone, M.: Heuristic programming applied to scheduling problems, Ph.D. thesis, Dept. of Electrical Engineering, Princeton Univ., Princeton, N.J. (1970).

7 Ullman, J.D.: NP-complete scheduling problems, Journal of Computer and System Sciences 10, 384-393 (1975).

PERFORMANCES OF "LEAST REFERENCE PROBABILITY" PAGING ALGORITHM UNDER LOCALITY IN PROGRAM BEHAVIOR

Trần-Quốc-Tê
Institut d'Informatique
Facultés universitaires N.-D. de la Paix
Namur - Belgium

ABSTRACT

For programs exhibing a locality trend in their page reference behavior, Least Reference Probability (LRP) paging algorithm, which replaces the page the least likely to be required at next time, is shown to be (nearly) optimal via two original probabilistic models. A simple "non parametric" test for model validation is also presented.

INTRODUCTION

A non-lookahead demand paging algorithm is essentially a forecasting principle : as the paging process progresses, page reference patterns are recorded and recurrently used to predict future ones. This prediction cas be done via some stochastic model of program behavior, i.e. a set of assumptions about the page requests process.

Given a model, we need now a replacement rule for facing situations in which reference is made to a page not in memory while the later is full. Since the objective is to avoid these page fault occurrences as much as possible, the two following rules seem you very "natural", at first sight :

- the "longest expected time until next reference" (LET) rule, and
- the "least reference probability" (LRP) rule.

Under LET, the page to replace from memory is the one whose mean recurrence delay is the longest. This "informal principle of optimality" [D1] is generally a good heuristic ; its optimality has been shown in the deterministic case (Belady algorithm [B1], [M1]) as well as for the independent reference model (A_o algorithm [A1]) and the LRU stack model whose reference probabilities (r.p.) decrease with stack distance (LRU algorithm [M1], [S1]).

Under LRP the page to replace is the one with the smallest r.p., i.e. the least likely to be referenced at next time. Although LRP is a very short term, even "immediate", optimisation principle, there are several reasons justifying its consideration :

- first, LRP is simple : given a model ; LRP is straighforward, while LET, for example, requires extra computations of mean recurrence delays ; moreover, explicit knowledge of the r.p.'s is not necessary, one only needs the instantanous rankings of pages according to their r.p.'s, i.e. a ranking model (section I).
- general models (including the two previous probabilistic structures) for which LRP = LET are presented : the sufficient ranking model with independent ranks (section III.3) and the $\mathcal{L}(\underline{a})$ model (section III.4), the later defining an auto-regressive process which is a transposition of the exponential smoothing forecasting scheme to our page prediction problem.
- for reference strings exhibing a locality trend, LRP is near optimal since, operating on a core capacity of m pages, it gives a page fault rate less than the best algorithm operating on m-1.
- LRP is optimal for $\mathcal{L}(\underline{a})$.

Beside these considerations, the key problem in algorithm design is obviously the choice of a model which fits the reference string under paging, condition sine qua non for a replacement rule (e.g. LET or LRP) to give acceptable performances. In section II, a (counter-) measure of this fitness, the mean observed rank, can lead to a general test for model validation.

CHAPTER I

MODELS FOR LOCALITY. DEFINITIONS AND EXAMPLES

I.1. Preliminary definitions and notations

is the set of program pages. The number of pages in X is $|X| = n$.

The page required at time t ($t=1, 1, \ldots$) is denoted by R_t, and the reference string up to is $\Omega_t = R_1 \ldots R_t$.

A ranking of X is a bijection $b : X \rightarrow N = \{1, \ldots, n,\}$.

B is the set of all rankings of X.

A couple (t, ω_{t-1}), $t=1, 2, \ldots$, $\omega_{t-1} \in X^{t-1}$ is a control state, and Q denotes the control states space.

Definition 1

A ranking model is a application :

(1) $m_\rho : Q \rightarrow B : (t, \omega_{t-1}) \rightarrow \rho_t(.|\omega_{t-1})$.

For $x \in X$, $\rho_t(x\ \omega_{t-1})$ is the rank of x at t, given the past patterns ω_{t-1}.

Definition 2

m_ρ is true the page request process $\Omega = R_1 \ldots R_t \ldots$ if

$\forall (t, \omega_{t-1}) \in Q, \forall i,j \nrightarrow n \geqslant i \geqslant j \geqslant 1$:

(2) $\Pr[\rho_t(R_t|\Omega_{t-1}) = i \mid \Omega_{t-1} = \omega_{t-1}] \leqslant \Pr[\rho_t(R_t|\Omega_{t-1}) = j \mid \Omega_{t-1} = \omega_{t-1}]$.

Remark

Assume that, $\forall (t, \omega_{t-1}) \in Q$, $Vx \in X$, we have a rule to compute quantities $p_t(x|\omega_{t-1})$, which we call the page reference "predictions" at t given ω_{t-1}. This "explicit" model induces a ranking model, not necessary unique, by requiring :

(3) $p_t(x|\omega_{t-1}) > p_t(y|\omega_{t-1}) \Rightarrow \rho_t(x|\omega_{t-1}) < \rho_t(y|\omega_{t-1})$.

For such models, when non unicity occurs, i.e. :

$p_{t+1}(x|\omega_{t-1}.r_t) = p_{t+1}(y|\omega_{t-1}.r_t)$, we shall adopt a "stationnary" tie-break rule :

(4) $\rho_{t+1}(x|\omega_{t-1}.r_t) < \rho_{t+1}(y|\omega_{t-1}.r_t) \Leftrightarrow \rho_t(x|\omega_{t-1}) < \rho_t(y|\omega_{t-1})$, given an initial rank $\rho_1(.)$.

Obviously, if the explicit model is true, i.e. if :
$\forall(t, \omega_{t-1}) \in Q$, $\forall x \in X$:

(5) $p_t(x|\omega_{t-1}) = \Pr[R_r = x|\Omega_{t-1} = \omega_{t-1}]$,
then any induced ranking model is also true.

I.2. Models for locality

Rather than a random scattering of page requests over X, one generally observes a "clustering of page requests in time so that the probability of reusing a page in the immediate future is high for pages used in the immediate past" [T1]. Hence, the effect of a reference is to increase the r.p. of the referenced page, and to decrease the r.p.'s of the other ones ; this leads to consideration of models such that, $\forall(t, \omega_{t-1}) \in Q$, $\forall r_t \in$:

$$p_{t+1}(r_t|\omega_{t-1}.r_t) \geqslant p_t(r_t|\omega_{t-1}),$$
$$p_{t+1}(x|\omega_{t-1}.r_t) \leqslant p_t(x|\omega_{t-1}), \forall x \neq r_t.$$

Since the second inequality implies the first one, we have the

Definition 3

An explicit model is a locality model (LM) if $\forall\ (t, \omega_{t-1}) \in Q$, $\forall r_t \in X$:

(6) $x \in\ , x \neq r_t \Rightarrow p_{t+1}(x|\omega_{t-1}.r_t) \leqslant p_t(x|\omega_{t-1})$.

A natural extension of this definition to ranking models leads to the

Definition 4

A ranking model is a locality ranking model (LRM) if $\forall(t, \omega_{t-1}) \in Q$, $\forall r_t \in X$:

(7) $x \in\ , x \neq r_t \Rightarrow \rho_{t+1}(x|\omega_{t-1}.r_t) \geqslant \rho_t(x|\omega_{t-1})$.

Example 1

LRU ranking models [M1], such that $\forall(t, \omega_{t-1}) \in Q$, $\forall r_t \in X$:

(8) $\rho_{t+1}(r_t|\omega_{t-1}.r_t) = 1.$

(9) $\rho_{t+1}(x|\omega_{t-1}.r_t) = \begin{cases} \rho_t(x|\omega_{t-1}) + 1, & \text{for } x \ni \rho_t(x|\omega_{t-1}) < \rho_t(r_t|\omega_{t-1}) \\ \rho_t(x|\omega_{t-1}), & \text{for } x \ni \rho_t(x|\omega_{t-1}) > \rho_t(r_t|\omega_{t-1}) \end{cases}$

are LRM.

Example 2

$\forall(t, \omega_{t-1}) \in Q, \forall x \in X$:

(10) $p_t(x|\omega_{t-1})$ = relative frequency of occurrence of x in ω_{t-1}, define a LM which induces a LRM.

Example 3

A more sophisticated probabilistic structure, which will be discussed further in III.3, is the following explicit model, which we call $\mathcal{L}(\underline{a})$.

Let $\underline{a} = a_t$; t=1, 2, ... be a sequence such that $\forall t : a_t \in [0,1]$, and $[p_o(x)]_{x\in}$ an initial probability vector.

Subsequent page reference predictions are recurrently given by :

$$(11) \quad p_{t+1}(x|\omega_{t-1}.r_t) = (1-a_t)p_t(x|\omega_{t-1}) + \begin{cases} o & \text{if } x \neq r_t \\ a_t & \text{if } x = r_t \end{cases}$$

This explicit model is merely an adaptation of the classical exponential smoothing method in forecasting theory to our page prediction problem. Such a model, which obviously satisfies Def3, can represent a wide variety of locality behaviors ranging from the independent Reference Model ($a_t = o, \forall_t$), to the "LFU" model of Example 2 ($a_t = t^{-1}$) or a LRU-like model ($a_t \geqslant 1/2$) ; the a_t's can be interpreted as instantanous degrees of locality.

Beside LRM, other kinds of ranking models we shall discuss later are quasi-stationnary ones and sufficient ones.

I.3. Quasi-stationnary ranking models

In [A1], Aho et al consider stationnary ranking models, for which page rankings remain invariant in time. Obviously, such models don't reflect locality.

For a LRM, successive rankings are allowed to change ; however some stationnarity remains, i.e. LRM's satisfy the

Definition 5

A ranking model is quasi-stationnary if $\forall(t, \omega_{t-1}) \in Q, \forall x \neq r_t \neq y$.

$$(12) \quad \rho_t(x|\omega_{t-1}) < \rho_t(y|\omega_{t-1}) \Rightarrow \rho_{t+1}(x|\omega_{t-1}.r_t) < \rho_{t+1}(y|\omega_{t-1}.r_t).$$

The reader should also verify that

Proposition 1

A ranking model is a LRM if it is quasi-stationnary and :

$\forall(t, \omega_{t-1}) \in Q$,

(13) $\forall r_t \in X : \rho_{t+1}(r_t | \omega_{t-1}.r_t) \leqslant \rho_t(r_t | \omega_{t-1})$.

I.4. Sufficient ranking models

Consider for example the LRU ranking model of 1.2, Example 1. Obviously, according to (8), (9), given

- the ranking of X at t, $\rho_t(| \omega_{t-1})$, and
- the rank of the referenced page $\rho_t(r_t | \omega_{t-1})$

one can deduce the ranking at t+1. Such a ranking model is called sufficient.

Definition 6

A ranking model is sufficient if $\forall(t, \omega_{t-1}) \in Q$, $\forall r_t \in X$:

(14) $\rho_{t+1}(.| \omega_{t-1}.r_t) = a_k \circ \rho_t(.| \omega_{t-1})$

where a_k is a permutation of 1, ..., n depending only on

(15) $k = \rho_t(r_t | \omega_{t-1})$.

The "LFU" model of 1.2, Example 2 is not sufficient.

CHAPTER II

A NON-PARAMETRIC TEST FOR MODEL VALIDATION

Except for some simplest models such as the independent reference model or the "LRU" stack model, almost no test is known about more complex probabilistic structures.

In our problem of analysis of LRP performance, we only need a test for ranking model validation. The philosophy of the test is very simple : according to Definitions 1 and 2, if a ranking model m_ρ is true for a page request process, then, at any time and given any past pattern, the rank of the referenced page is expected to be small (more precisely less than (n+1)/2, n being the total number of pages), so are the mean observed ranks :

(16) $\bar{\rho}_T = \frac{1}{T} \sum_{t=1}^{T} \rho_t(R_t | \Omega_{t-1}),$

which are a (counter-) measure of the fitness of m_ρ to Ω_T.
Hence, a simple procedure for ranking model validation can consist to consider a model as false whenever $\bar{\rho}_T$ exceeds $\frac{n+1}{2}$ for some T. Theorem 2 will show that the error of first kind, i.e. the probability of rejecting a true model decreases to zero as T tends to infinity.

Lemma 1

Let $p = [p_i]$ a probability distribution over $N = \{1, \ldots, n\}$, i.e. : $\forall i : p_i \geq o$ and $\sum_i p_i = \sum_{i \in N} p_i = 1$. If

(17) $p_1 \geq \ldots \geq p_i \geq p_{i+1} \geq \ldots \geq p_n \geq o$, then

(18) $\sum_{i>k} p_i \leq \sum_{i>k} u_i, \forall k,$

where $u = [u_i]$ is the uniform distribution over N :

(19) $u_i = \begin{cases} 1/n & \text{for } i \in N \\ o & \text{for } i \notin N. \end{cases}$

Proof

Since for $k \geq n$: $\sum_{i>k} p_i = \sum_{i>k} u_i = o$, and for $k \leq o$: $\sum_{i>k} p_i = \sum_{i>k} u_i = 1$, it suffices to prove that, $\forall k = 1, \ldots, n-1$: $\sum_{i>k} p_i \leq \sum_{i>k} u_i = \frac{n-k}{n}$.

Assume the converse is true, i.e.

$\exists\, k=1, \ldots, n-1 \ni \sum_{i>k} p_i > \frac{n-k}{n}$.

By (17) : $\frac{1}{n} < \max_{i>k} p_i = p_{k+1} \leq p_j, \forall j \leq k.$

Hence :

$\sum_{j \leqslant k} p_j \geqslant \frac{k}{n}$, and $\sum_{i \; N} p_i = \sum_{i>k} p_i + \sum_{j \leqslant k} p_i > \frac{n-k}{n} + \frac{k}{n} = 1$,

which is a absurd ⊠

Theorem 1

$\forall m_\rho$, if m_ρ is true then, $\forall k$, $\forall T$:

(20) $\alpha' = \Pr[\sum_{t-1}^{T} \rho_t(R_t | \Omega_{t-1}) > k] \leqslant U_k^{\star T}$,

(21) where $U_k^{\star o} = \begin{matrix} 1 < & \text{for } k & o \\ o \geqslant & \text{for } k & o \end{matrix}$,

(22) $U_k^{\star T} = \sum_\ell U_\ell^{\star T-1} \; u_{k-\ell}$, $\forall T > o$.

(Note that $U_k^{\star T}$ is the probability for the sum V_T of T independent random varables uniformly distributed over N to exceed k).

Proof

Note first that :

$$' = \sum_{\omega_{t-1}} \ldots \sum_{=r_1} \ldots \sum_{r_{T-1}} {}_{X^{T-1}} \Pr[\Omega_{T-1} = \omega_{T-1}] . \Pr[\rho_T(R_T | \Omega_{T-1}) >$$

$$k - \sum_{t=1}^{T-1} \rho_t(r_t | \omega_{t-1}) | \Omega_{T-1} = \omega_{T-1}]$$

Since m_ρ is true, by Lemma 1, we obtain a majoration of α' by letting

$\Pr[\rho_T(R_T | \Omega_{T-1}) = \ell | \Omega_{T-1}] = \omega_{T-1}] = u_\ell$, $\forall \ell$, $\forall \omega_{t-1}$,

i.e. by considering $\rho_T(R_T | \Omega_{T-1})$ as uniformly distributed over N and independent of $R_1, \ldots, R_{T-1}$.

(20) is obvious for T=0. Assume it is true for T-1 (⩾o). For T, α' can also be written as :

$$\alpha' = \sum_\ell \Pr[\sum_{t=1}^{T-1} \rho_t(R_t | \Omega_{t-1}) > \ell] . \Pr[\rho_T(R_T | \Omega_{T-1}) = k - \ell | \sum_{t=1}^{T-1} \rho_t (R_t | \Omega_{t-1}) > \ell]$$

$$\leqslant \sum_\ell \Pr[\sum_{t=1}^{T-1} \rho_t(R_t | \Omega_{t-1}) > \ell] \; u_{k-} \quad \text{(by the preceding remark)}$$

$$\leqslant \sum_\ell U_\ell^{\star T-1} \; u_{k-\ell} \quad \text{(by induction)}$$

$= U_k^{\star T}$ ⊠. A corollary of Theorem 1 is now :

Theorem 2

$\forall m_\rho$, if m_ρ is true then, $\forall \epsilon > o$, $\forall T$:

(23) $a = \Pr [\bar{\rho}_T - \frac{n+1}{2} \quad \epsilon] \leqslant \frac{1}{T} . \frac{\sigma^2}{\epsilon^2}$,

(24) where $\sigma^2 = \frac{1}{n} \sum_{i=1}^{n} (i - \frac{n+1}{2})^2$.

Proof

$$a = \Pr [\sum_{t=1}^{T} \rho_t (R_t | \Omega_{t-1}) > T \frac{n+1}{2} + T\epsilon] \leqslant \Pr [V_T > T \frac{n+1}{2} + T\epsilon],$$

where, by theorem 1, V_T denotes the sum of T independent random variables uniformly distributed over N,

$= \Pr [V_T - E(V_T) > T\epsilon] \leqslant \sigma^2/T\epsilon^2$,

by arguments analogous to those leading to Markov-Tch bitchev inequality ☒.

Remarks

1) Given $(\frac{\sigma}{\epsilon})^2$ and large T, a closer upper bound for a can be derived from Levy-Lindeberg central-limit theorem :

(25) $\Pr [V_T - E(V_T) > T\epsilon] \simeq 1 - F_G (\frac{\epsilon}{\sigma} \sqrt{T})$

where F_G is the gaussian distribution function.

2) The test presented in this section can provide a first clear in program modelization. However, the fact that a model, such as the LRU ranking model for example,

- leads to $\bar{\rho}_T < \frac{n+1}{2}$ doesn't imply that there doesn't exist a better one,
- leads to $\bar{\rho}_T > \frac{n+1}{2}$ doesn't infirm program locality : a weaker-locality model such as the "LFU" one may give a better fitness.

CHAPTER III

PERFORMANCE ANALYSIS OF LRP

III.1. The cost function

Recall briefly that, if m denotes the core capacity, a paging algorithm processing a reference string $\Omega = R_1, \ldots R_t \ldots$ is a decision rule A generating a sequence of memory states $S_t(m,A)$, $S_t(m,A) \in X$, $\forall$ t=1, 2, ..., such that :

(26) $\forall t \geqslant o : |S_t(m,A)| \leqslant m,$

(27) $\forall t > o : R_t \in S_t(m,A).$

we shall assume for convenience that :

(28) $S_o(m,A) = \emptyset.$

A is non lookahead if, $\forall t > o$, $S_t(m,A)$ is function of Ω_{t-1} only. The cost of an algorithm is taken as the number of page loads required over some time period. If A "starts" at time t-1 with a memory state σ, let :

(29) $C_{[t,T]}(\sigma, m, A) = |S_t(m,A) - \sigma| + \sum_{\tau=t+1}^{T} |S_\tau(m,A) - S_{\tau-1}(m,A)|.$

With this cost function, then, when looking for optimal algorithm i.e. those which minimizes :

(30) $\gamma_{[t,T]}(\sigma, m, A|\omega_{t-1}) = E\{C_{[t,T]}(\sigma, m, A)|\Omega_{t-1} = \omega_{t-1}\},$

one can restrict his investigations to demand paging ones [M1], [A1] :

(31) $S_t(m,A) = \begin{cases} S_{t-1}(m,A) & \text{if } R_t \in S_{t-1}(m,A) \\ S_{t-1}(m,A) + R_t & \text{if } R_t \notin S_{t-1}(m,A) \text{ and } |S_{t-1}(m,A)| < m \\ S_{t-1}(m,A) + R_t - y_t & \text{if } R_t \notin S_{t-1}(m,A) \text{ and } |S_{t-1}(m,A)| = m, \end{cases}$

where y_t is some page in $S_{t-1}(m,A)$.

In the next sections, we shall investigate properties of LRP algorithm for two probabilistic structures : the $\pounds(a)$ model, and the sufficient ranking model with independent ranks (SRMIR).

Definition 7

Given m_ρ, LRP is the demand paging algorithm for which the page y_t of (31) is the one with the largest rank :

(32) $\rho_{t+1}(y_t|\Omega_t) = \max_{x \in S_{t-1}(m,A)} \rho_{t+1}(x|\Omega_t).$

If m_ρ derives from some explicit model, then y_t is the page with the smallest "prediction", provided a stationnary tie-break rule. Before attacking these models, let us first show that LRP provides a good heuristic for locality ranking models (Def.4), provided they are true.

III.2. Sub-optimality of LRP for LRM

Theorem 3

If m_ρ is a LRM, then $\forall t \geqslant 1$, $\forall x \in X$, $\forall m = 1, 2, \ldots$

$$\left.\begin{array}{l} x \in \bigcup_{\tau=1}^{t-1} R_\tau \\ \rho_t(x \mid \Omega_{t-1}) < m \end{array}\right\} \Rightarrow x \in S_{t-1}(m, \text{LRP}) \tag{33}$$

Note that this deterministic implication holds whether m_ρ is true or not.

Proof

(33) is obvious at t-1, since $\bigcup_{\tau=1}^{0} R_\tau = S_0(m, \text{LRP}) = \emptyset$. By induction, assuming (33) true, we must prove that, if :

$$x \in \bigcup_{\tau=1}^{t} R_\tau \quad \text{and } \rho_{t+1}(x \mid \Omega_t) < m \tag{34}$$

then $x \in S_t(m, \text{LRP})$.

Two cases are to consider :

- 1.- $x \in S_{t-1}(m, \text{LRP})$
  - 1.1.- if no replacement is required at t, then $x \in S_t(m, \text{LRP})$ too.
  - 1.2.- if a replacement is required, then, the replaced page y_t is defined by (32) ;
    $\Rightarrow \rho_{t+1}(y_t \mid \Omega_t) \geqslant m$ (since $S_{t-1}(m,A)| = m$)
    $\Rightarrow y_t \neq x$ (since $\rho_{t+1}(x \mid \Omega_t) < m$, by (34))
    $\Rightarrow x \in S_t(m, \text{LRP})$.
- 2.- $x \notin S_{t-1}(m, \text{LRP})$. By induction (33), 2 subcases are to consider :
  - 2.1.- $x \notin \bigcup_{\tau=1}^{t-1} R_\tau \Rightarrow x = R_t$ (since $x \in \bigcup_{\tau=1}^{t} R_\tau$)
    $\Rightarrow x \in S_t(m, \text{LRP})$
  - 2.2.- $\rho_t(x \mid \Omega_{t-1}) \geqslant m \Rightarrow \rho_t(x \mid \Omega_{t-1}) > \rho_{t+1}(x \mid \Omega_t)$
    $\Rightarrow x = R_t$, from the locality assumption(7)
    $\Rightarrow x \in S_t(m, \text{LRP})$. ⊠

Let I [A] denote the boolean variable which takes the value 1 if event A occurs. Since LRP is demand paging :

(35) $C_{[t,T]}(\sigma, m, LRP) = \sum_{\tau=t}^{T} I[R_\tau \notin S_{\tau-1}(m, LRP)]$,

with $S_{t-1}(m, LRP) = \sigma$.

From theorem 3, $\forall\sigma$:

(36) $C_{[t,T]}(\sigma, m, LRP) \leqslant \sum_{\tau=t} I[\rho_\tau(R_\tau | \Omega_{\tau-1}) \geqslant m \text{ or } R_\tau \notin \bigcup_{\tau'=1}^{\tau-1} R_{\tau'}]$.

If furthermore $\bigcup_{\tau=1}^{t-1} R_\tau = X$, then :

(37) $C_{[t,T]}(\sigma, m, LRP) \leqslant \sum_{\tau=t}^{T} I[\rho_\tau(R_\tau | \Omega_{\tau-1}) \geqslant m]$.

This leads to :

<u>Theorem 4</u>

If m_ρ is true, then, $\forall m$

$\forall t \ni \bigcup_{\tau=1}^{t-1} R_\tau = X$, $\forall T \geqslant t$, $\forall\sigma = S_{t-1}(m, LRP)$:

(38) $E\{C_{[t,T]}(\sigma, m, LRP)\} \leqslant \min_{\sigma'} \min_{A} E\{C_{[t,T]}(\sigma', m-1, A)\}$.

<u>Proof</u>

The r.h.s. of (38) is :

r.h.s. $= \min_{\sigma'} \min_{\star} \sum_{\tau=t}^{T} Pr[R_\tau \notin S_{\tau-1}(m-1, A)]$

where the constraint ☆ means that A is demand paging ;

$\geqslant \min_{\star'} \sum_{\tau=t}^{T} Pr[R_\tau \notin S'_{\tau-1}(m-1)]$

where ☆' means that the S' must satisfy only the capacity constraint (25) : $|S'_{t-1}(m-1)| \leqslant m-1$;

$= \sum_{\tau=t}^{T} Pr[\rho_\tau(R_\tau | \Omega_{\tau-1}) \geqslant m]$, since m_ρ is true

$= \sum_{\tau=t}^{T} E\{I[\rho_\tau(R_\tau | \Omega_{\tau-1}) \geqslant m]\}$

$\geqslant E\{C_{[t,T]}(\sigma, m, LRP)\}$, by (37) ⊠

This theorem shows that, despite its simplicity, LRP gives a good heuristic, since, operating on a core memory of m pages, it gives better results than the best algorithm operating with m-1 pages.

III.3. The SRMIR

The model considered in this section satisfies the hypothesis :

H.1. It is a sufficient ranking model.

H.2. The ranks of referenced pages are serially independent :

$\forall\ (t, \omega_{t-1}), \forall i : \Pr\ [\rho_t(R_t|\Omega_{t-1}) = i|\Omega_{t-1} = \omega_{t-1}] = \pi_i > 0.$

With the notations of Def.6, and by Proposition 1, this model is a locality ranking model if

H.3. $\forall j > i, \forall k \neq i, j : a_k(j) > a_k(i)$

H.4. $\forall k \quad : a_k(k) \leqslant k.$

We first prove that LRP algorithm is identical to LET for a more general model, before giving an expression for the page fault rate.

Lemma 2

A sufficient locality ranking model (satisfying thus H.1., H.3. and H.4.) satisfies also H.1., H.3. and :

H.4.' : $\forall j > i : a_i(j) \geqslant a_j(i)$.

Proof

For $j > i$, H.3. and H.4. imply $a_i(j) = j$ and $a_j(i) \leqslant i+1$, hence H.4.' ⊠

Theorem 5

For a model satisfying H.1., H.2., H.3., H.4.', the mean recurrence delay of a page is non decreasing with its "actual" rank, provided :

H.5. : $\forall i = 2, \ldots, n : \pi_i \geqslant \pi_{i-1}$.

Proof

By definition, if t_o denote the 'actual' time :
recurrence time (R.T.) of page $x > \tau \Leftrightarrow \forall t = t_o+1, \ldots, t_o+\tau : R_t \neq x$.

Let $T(i) = E\ [\text{r.t. of } x|\rho_{t_o+1}(x|\Omega_{t_o}) = i]$.

Since $T(i) = \sum_{\tau=o}^{\infty} G_\tau(i)$, where

$G_\tau(i) = \Pr\ [\text{r.t. of } x > \tau|\rho_{t_o+1}(x|\ \Omega_{t_o}) = i]$, it suffices to prove that :

(39) $\forall j > i, \forall \tau : G_\tau(j) \geq G_\tau(i)$

(39) is obvious for $\tau = o$: $G_o(j) = 1$; assume it is true for $\tau-1$; for $\tau(\geq 1)$:

$$G_\tau(j) - G_\tau(i) = \sum_{k \neq i,j} \pi_k\{G_{\tau-1}(a_k(j)) - G_{\tau-1}(a_k(i))\} + \pi_i G_{\tau-1}(a_i(j))$$

$$-\pi_j G_{\tau-1}(a_j(i)).$$

By H.3., for $k \neq i$, j, $a_k(j) > a_k(i)$, and the terms in brackets non negative, by induction. The last two terms give also a non negative result since :

- by H.4.' : $a_i(j) \geq a_j(i)$, and by induction : $G_{\tau-1}(a_i(j)) \geq G_{\tau-1}(a_j(i))$;

- $\pi_i \geq \pi_j$, by H.5. ⊠

A corollary of this is that LRP=LET not only for models such as the Independent Reference Model or the LRU Stack Model with r.p. decreasing with stack distance, but also for non locality models such as an 'MRU Stack model' satisfying H.1., H.2., H.3., H.5. and

$\forall k : a_k(k) = n$,

since the last condition, together with H.3., imply H.4.'. We haven't been able to prove optimality of LRP alg. for SRMIR structures more general than the Ind. Ref. Model (A_o alg.) or the previous LRU Stack model (LRU alg.). Optimality of MRU alg. for the MRU Stack model, tedious to prove and presenting no pratical interest, is not presented.

We turn out to give a close form for the page fault rates under LRP for models satisfying $\{H_i$; i=1, 2, 3, 4$\}$, for which Theorem 3 is applicable.

Theorem 6

For models satisfying H.1., H.2., H.3., H.4., the page fault rates :

(40) $\delta(m) \stackrel{def}{=} \lim_{t\to\infty} \Pr [R_t \notin S_{t-1}(m, \text{LRP})]$

are given by :

(41) $\delta(m) = \sum_{i=m}^{n} \pi_i (1-a_i(m))$

where

(42) $a_m(m) = \sum_{k\geq m \ni a_k(k) \leq m} \pi_k \Big/ \sum_{k \geq m} \pi_k$,

(43) $a_i(m) = \sum_{k\geq m \ni \alpha_k(k)=i} \pi_k / \sum_{k\geq m} \pi_k$, for $i = m+1, \ldots, n$.

Proof : Let $a_i(m)$ be the asymptotic probability for a page of rank i to be in core :

$a_i(m) = \lim_{t\to\infty} \Pr[\rho_t^{-1}(i) \in S_{t-1}(m, \text{LRP})]$. Obviously : $\delta(m) = \sum_{i=1}^{m} \pi_i(1-a_i(m))$

Since $\pi_i > 0$, $\forall i$: $\lim_{t\to\infty} \Pr[\bigcup_{\tau=1}^{t} R_\tau = X] = 1$, and, by theorem 3 : $a_i(m) = 1$,

$\forall i < m$, hence (40), (41). From the locality assumption , we have :

$a_m(m) = \sum_{k\geq m \ni \alpha_k(k)\leq m} \pi_k + a_m(m) \sum_{k<m} \pi_k$.

(assume pages ranked 1, ..., m-1 are in core at time t, then t-1, page ranked m is in core if :

- either reference is made to a page ranked k ($\geq$m) such that $\alpha_k(k) \leq m$
- or page ranked m is previously in memory at t, and reference is made to a page ranked 1, ..., m-1).

And by an analogous argument, for $i>m$: $a_i(m) = \sum_{k\geq m \ni \alpha_k(k)=i} \pi_k + a_i(m) \sum_{k<m} \pi_k$.

The last two equations are equivalent to (42) and (43) ☒

Remarks

H.5. needs not to be satisfied ; if H5 is, then LRP is sub-optimal (theorem 4).

For the Ind. Ref. Model, $\alpha_k(k) = k$, $\forall k$; hence $\forall i \geq m$: $a_i(m) = \pi_i / \sum_{k\geq m} \pi_k$.

(Cfr. [A1]). If $\alpha_k(k) < m$, $\forall k$,then $a_m(m) = 1$ and $a_i(m) = 0$, $\forall i > m$; hence

$\delta(m) = \sum_{k>m} \pi_k$, and we have the page fault rate of the LRU-Stack Model under LRU.

III.4. The $\mathcal{L}(\alpha)$ model

Recall that given :

(44) $\underline{\alpha} = \{\alpha_t \in [0, 1], \forall t = 1, 2, \ldots\}$, and an initial prediction vector

(45) $p_1 = \{p_1(x), x \in X \ni \forall x : p_1(x) \geq 0, \text{ and } \sum_{x\in X} p_1(x) = 1\}$ subsequent predictions are given by :

(46) $p_{t+1}(x|\omega_{t-1}.r_t) = \beta_t p_t(x|\omega_{t-1}) + \alpha_t \delta_{r_t,x}$, where

(47) $\beta_t = 1-\alpha_t$, and

(48) $\delta_{r_t,x} = 1$ if $x = r_t$, or 0 if $x \neq r_t$.

We shall assume the model true, so that $\forall x$, $\forall(t, \omega_{t-1})$:

(49) $\Pr[R_t = x | \Omega_{t-1} = \omega_{t-1}] = p_t(x|\omega_{t-1})$.

First, theorem 7 shows identity between LRP and LET ; theorem 8 gives an exponential upper bound for the page fault rates under LRP (=LET) for the time-stationnary case: $\alpha_t = \alpha = c^{st}$, $\forall t$; theorem 9 establishes optimality of LRP.

Theorem 7 : For the $\mathcal{L}(\underline{\alpha})$ model, the mean recurrence delay of a page is non increasing with its actual prediction, provided the model is true.

Proof : For simplicity we consider the time-stationnary case, the following arguments can be extended easily to non time-stationnary ones.

If t_o denote the "actual" time, let : $G_\tau(\pi) = \Pr[\text{r.t. of } x > \tau | p_{t_o+1}(x|\Omega_{to}) = \pi]$

(if $\underline{a}$ is non time-stationnary, then the last probability is a function of t_o too).

As for theorem 5, it suffices to prove that the G's are non increasing with π, i.e:

$$(50) \quad \forall \tau \geq o, \forall \pi \in [o, 1] : G'_\tau(\pi) = \frac{d}{d\pi} G_\tau(\pi) \leq o.$$

(50) is obvious for $\tau = o$; assume it is true up to $\tau - 1$; since

$G_\tau(\pi) = G_{\tau-1}(\pi) \quad (1-\beta^{\tau-1}\pi)$, by (46), where $\beta = 1-a$, we have

$G'_\tau(\pi) = G'_{\tau-1}(\pi) \quad (1-\beta^{\tau-1}\pi) - G_{\tau-1}(\pi)\,\beta^{\tau-1} \leq o$, by induction ⊠.

Proposition 2

$\pounds(\underline{a})$ is page partition invariant : consider a partition $\Sigma = \{\sigma_1, \ldots, \sigma_p\}$ of X,

and let : $q_t(\sigma|\omega_{t-1}) = \Pr[R_t \in \sigma|\omega_{t-1}] = \sum_{x\in\sigma} \Pr[R_t = x|\omega_{t-1}]$

From (46), (47), (48) : $q_{t+1}(\sigma|\omega_{t-1}.r_t) = \beta\ {}_tq_t(\sigma|\omega_{t-1}) + a\ {}_t\delta_{r_t,\sigma}$

where $\delta_{r_t,\sigma} = 1$ if $r_t \in \sigma$, or o if $r_t \notin \sigma$.

Hence the "new" reference process $\Omega' = R'_1 \ldots R'_t \ldots$, where $R'_t = \sigma_j$ if $R_t \in \sigma_j$, is also $(\underline{a})$, with the same $\underline{a}$ as Ω, the original one.

Proposition 3

LRP is a priority list algorithm, hence a stack alg. [M1], i.e. having the inclusion property : $\forall m > o : S_t(m, \text{LRP}) \supset S_t(m-1, \text{LRP})$. Assume $\Omega_t = \omega_t$, $R_t \notin S_{t-1}(m,\text{LRP})$ and $|S_{t-1}(m,\text{LRP}| = m$; then the page $y_t(m)$ to replace from $S_t(m, \text{LRP})$ satisfies [M1] : $p_{t+1}(y_t(m)|\omega_t) = \min\{p_{t+1}(y_t(m-1)|\omega_t)\}$, $p_{t+1}(s_t(m)|\omega_t) \leq p_{t+1}(s_t(m)|\omega_t)$, a fortiori, where $s_t(m) = S_t(m), \text{LRP}) - S_t(m-1, \text{LRP})$.

Theorem 8 : For the time-stationnary $(\underline{a})$ model, $\forall m$, $\forall p_1$:

$$(51) \quad \delta(m) = \lim_t \Pr\ R_t \notin S_{t-1}(m, \text{LRP}) \leq \beta^m.$$

Proof : (51) is obvious for m = 1, since, by (46),

$\Pr[R_t \in S_{t-1}(1, \text{LRP})] = \Pr[R_t = R_{t-1}] \geq a$. Assume it is true for m - 1. Let :

$\delta_t(m) = \Pr[R_t \notin S_{t-1}(m, \text{LRP})]$, and $\delta'_t(m) = 1 - \delta_t(m) = \sum_{\omega_{t-1}} \Pr[\Omega_{t-1}=\omega_{t-1}].\delta'_t(m|\omega_{t-1})$,

where : $\delta'_t(m|\omega_{t-1} = \Pr[R_t \in S_{t-1}(m, \text{LRP})|\Omega_{t-1} = \omega_{t-1}] = q_t(S_{t-1}(m, \text{LRP})|\omega_{t-1})$.

Conditional on a past pattern ω_{t-1},

- either $R_t = r_t \in S_{t-1}(m, \text{LRP})$, an event of probability $\delta'_t(m|\omega_{t-1})$, in which case :

  $\delta'_{t+1}(m|\omega_{t-1}.r_t) = \beta\delta'_t(m|\omega_{t-1}) + a$, by Prop. 2,

- or $R_t = r_f \notin S_{t-1}(m, \text{LRP})$, an event of probability $1-\delta'_t(m|\omega_{t-1}$, and the faulting page replaces page $y_t(m)$ in core :

$\delta'_{t+1}(m|\omega_{t-1}.r_t) \geq a + q_{t+1}(S_{t-1}(m, \text{LRP})|\omega_{t-1}.r_t) - p_{t+1}(y_t(m)|\omega_{t-1}.r_t)$, since the

r.p. at t+1 of r_t exceeds a, by (46). On the other hand, by Prop.3 :
$p_{t+1}(y_t(m)|\omega_{t-1}.r_t) = \beta p_t(s_t(m)|\omega_{t-1}) = \beta\ \{\delta'_t(m|\omega_{t-1}) - \delta'_t(m-1|\omega_{t-1})\}$.
Hence, $Pr\ [R_{t+1} \in S_t(m,LRP)|\Omega_{t-1} = \omega_{t-1}] = \sum_{r_t \in X} p_t(r_t|\omega_{t-1})\delta_{t+1}(m|\omega_{t-1}.r_t) \geq$

$\delta'_t(m|\omega_{t-1})\ [\beta\delta'_t(m|\omega_{t-1}) + a] + [1-\delta'_t(m|\omega_{t-1})]\ [a + \beta\delta_t(m-1|\omega_{t-1})] \geq a+\beta\delta'_t(m-1|\omega_{t-1})$
(since $\delta'_t(m|\omega_{t-1}) \geq \delta'_t(m-1|\omega_{t-1})$, from the inclusion property).

Removal of the condition $\Omega_{t-1} = \omega_{t-1}$ leads to : $\delta'_{t-1}(m) \geq a + \beta\delta'_t(m-i)$ and, letting $t\to\infty$: $\delta(m) = 1 - \lim_{t\to\infty} \delta'_t(m) \leq \beta\delta(m-1) \leq \beta^m$, by induction ⊠.

<u>Remark</u>

If we approcimate the fault rates by their upper bound given by Theorem 8, then
- for fixed m, smaller $\delta(m)$ is obtained for strong locality (a large, i.e. β small).
- for fixed β, $\delta(m)$ decreases exponentially with m. Assume that, at the word level, word reference process is $\pounds(\underline{a})$, then, for any page size, the page reference process is also $\pounds(\underline{a})$, by Prop.2. On the other hand, since memory size (in words)=number of core pages x page size (in words), the page fault rate increases exponentially with page size, for fixed memory size.

We now establish optimality of LRP for this model. With the notations of (30), for fixed m and T, let :

(52) $\gamma_t(\sigma, A|\omega_{t-1}) = \gamma_{[t, T]}(\sigma, m, A|\omega_{t-1})$,

(53) $\tilde{\gamma}_t(\sigma|\omega_{t-1}) = \min_A \gamma_t(\sigma, A|\omega_{t-1})$.

According to the principle of optimality and optimality of demand paging, for $|\sigma| = m$, the $\tilde{\gamma}$'s must satisfy : $\tilde{\gamma}_t(\sigma|\omega_{t-1}) = \sum_{r\in\sigma} p_t(r|\omega_{t-1})\ \tilde{\gamma}_{t+1}(\sigma|\omega_{t-1}.r)$

(54) $+\sum_{r\notin\sigma} p_t(r|\omega_{t-1})\ \ \{1 + \min_{y_r\in\sigma}\ \tilde{\gamma}_{t+1}(\sigma + r + y_r|\omega_{t-1}.r)\}$,

$\tilde{\gamma}_T(\sigma|\omega_{T-1}) = \sum_{r\notin\sigma} p_t(r|\omega_{t-1})$.

For simplicity, we give a sketch of proof of optimality of LRP for the time stationnary case. Lemmas 5 and 6 have been established by Aho et al [Al], while lemmas 7 and 8, particular the $\pounds(\underline{a})$ model, can easily be verified by induction.

These lemmas apply to arbitrary t, T($\geq$t), m, $\sigma \subset X(|\sigma| = m)$, $\omega_{t-1} = r_1 \ldots r_{t-1}, r_{t-1} \notin \sigma$.

<u>Lemma 4</u> : For any model, we allways have :

(55) $\Delta\tilde{\gamma} \stackrel{def}{=} \tilde{\gamma}_t(\sigma + r_{t-1} - y|\omega_{t-1}) - \tilde{\gamma}_t(\sigma + r_{t-1} - y'|\omega_{t-1}) \geq -1, \quad \forall y, y' \in \sigma$.

<u>Lemma 5</u> : A sufficient condition for LRP to be optimal is :

(56) $\Delta\tilde{\gamma} \geq o$, for any $y \in \sigma$, provided

(57) $p_t(y'|\omega_{t-1}) = \min_{x\in\sigma} p_t(x|\omega_{t-1}), \ y' \in \sigma$.

<u>Lemma 6</u> : For the time-stationnary case, $\forall y, y' \in \sigma$, if condition (56) hold for

T, T-1, ..., t+1 and if :

(58) $p_t(y'|\omega_{t-1}) = \min\limits_{\sigma+r_{t-1}} p_t(x|\omega_{t-1})$, and

(59) $p_t(y|\omega_{t-1}) = \min\limits_{\sigma+r_{t-1}-y'} p_t(x|\omega_{t-1})$, then

(60) $\Delta\tilde{\gamma} = a.\varphi_t(b)$, where :

(61) $a = p_t(y|\omega_{t-1}) - p_t(y'|\omega_{t-1}) \geqslant o$,

(62) $b = q_t(\sigma+r_{t-1}-y-y'|\omega_{t-1})$,

(63) φ_t recurrently defined by : $\varphi_T(b) = 1, \forall b$

$$\varphi_t(b) = \beta\rho_{t+1}(\alpha + \beta b) + 1,$$

is a non negative function of b, so that ;

(64) $\left.\begin{array}{l} a + b = a' + b' \\ a' \geqslant a \end{array}\right\} \Rightarrow a' \;_t(b') \geqslant a\,\varphi_t(b)$.

<u>Lemma 7</u> : If only (58) holds, and (56) is true for T, T-1, ..., t+1, then

(65) $\Delta\tilde{\gamma} \geqslant a\varphi_t(b)$.

<u>Theorem 9</u> : LRP is optimal provided (44) - (49).

<u>Proof</u> : (for the case $\alpha_t = \alpha$, $\forall t$). It suffices to prove (56) true. (56) is obvious if (58) holds, by Lemmas 6 and 7, with y' satisfying (57). The remaining case to consider is : $p_t(r_{t-1}|\omega_{t-1}) = \min\limits_{\sigma+r_{t-1}} p_t(x|\omega_{t-1})$. (56) is obvious for T, in which case $\Delta\tilde{\gamma} = a \geqslant o$. Assume it is true for T, ..., t+1. For t :

$$\begin{aligned}\Delta\tilde{\gamma} = & \sum_{r\in\sigma+r_{t-1}-y-y'} p_t(r|\omega_{t-1}) \{\tilde{\gamma}_{t+1}(\sigma+r_{t-1}-y|\omega_{t-1}.r) - \tilde{\gamma}_{t+1}(\sigma+r_{t-1}-y|\omega_{t-1}.r)\} \\ & + \sum_{r\notin\sigma+r_{t-1}} p_t(r|\omega_{r-1}) \{\tilde{\gamma}_{t+1}(\sigma+r-y|\omega_{t-1}.r) - \tilde{\gamma}_{t+1}(\sigma+r-y'|\omega_{t-1}.r)\} \\ & + p_t(y|\omega_{t-1}) \{1+\tilde{\gamma}_{t+1}(\sigma|\omega_{t-1}.y) - \tilde{\gamma}_{t+1}(\sigma+r_{t-1}-y'|\omega_{t-1}.y)\} \\ & + p_t(y'|\omega_{t-1}) \{\tilde{\gamma}_{t+1}(\sigma+r_{t-1}-y|\omega_{t-1}.y') - 1-\tilde{\gamma}_{t+1}(\sigma|\omega_{t-1}.y')\}\end{aligned}$$

By induction, terms corresponding to the case $R_t = r \neq y, y'$, are non negative since $p_{t+1}(y'|\omega_{t-1}.r) = \beta p_t(y'|\omega_{t-1}) = \min\limits_{x\in\sigma} p_{t+1}(x|\omega_{t-1}.r)$. The last two terms give : $\ell.t.t. = a-p_t(y|\omega_{t-1})\delta_y+p_t(y'|\omega_{t-1})\delta_{y'}$, where $\delta_y = \tilde{\gamma}_{t+1}(\sigma+r_{t+1}-y'|\omega_{t-1}.y)-\tilde{\gamma}_{t+1}(\sigma|\omega_{t-1}.y) = c\varphi_{t+1}(d)$, with $c = p_{t+1}(y'|\omega_{t-1}.y)-p_{t+1}(r_{t-1}|\omega_{t-1}.y) = \beta\{p_t(y'|\omega_{t-1})-p_t(r_{t-1}|\omega_{t-1})\}$, $d = q_{t+1}(\ -y'|\omega_{t-1}.y) = \alpha+\beta q_t(\sigma-y'|\omega_{t-1})$, by Lemma 6, and : $\delta_{y'} = \tilde{\gamma}_{t+1}(\sigma+r_{t-1}-y|\omega_{t-1}.y') - \tilde{\gamma}_{t+1}(\sigma|\omega_{t-1}.y') \geqslant c'\varphi_{t+1}(d')$, with $c' = \beta\{p_t(y|\omega_{t-1}) - p_t(r_{t-1}|\omega_{t-1})\}$, $d' - \alpha+\beta q_t(\sigma-y|\omega_{t-1})$, by Lemma 7. By (64) : $\delta_{y'} \geqslant \delta_y$, hence $\ell.t.t. = a(1-\delta_y) \geqslant o$, by Lemma 4 ⊠.

IV. Concluding remarks

This work presents a little step towards the understanding of the relationships that exist between

- the behavior of the reference string under paging, and
- the principles of an "acceptable" replacement algorithm.

In the context of programs exhibing a locality tendancy, LRP, despite its conceptual simplicity, is rather good, as one can intuitively anticipate : pages in core, being those used at least once in the past, or those not replaced because they had large r.p., remain, by the locality and the quasi-stationnarity assumptions, the ones having the largest r.p., i.e. those precisely we must keep in core in order to avoid future page fault occurrences.

Since the works of Denning, locality is the kind of program behavior the most widely investigated, both experimentally and theorically. A cause of locality, pointed out by Denning, is "periodicity", for, when a program enters a looping phase, it concentrates, de facto, its references. A more thorough study of periodicity could lead to interesting loops detecting algorithms (ATLAS).

Finally, a major critical one can made about the structure of this "classical" storage allocation problem is that the page fault rate is not a realistic cost as the delay in response time can be.

A more realistic meta-model should include, for example, drum seek times [G1], or allow overlapping between CPU and DRUM so that prepaging (move pages anticipatively when DRUM is idle)can be better.

REFERENCES

[A1] Aho, A.V., Denning, P.J., and Ullman J.D., *"Principles of optimal page replacements"* J. ACM 18,1 (Jan. 1971), 80-93.

[B1] Belady, L.A., *"A Study of Replacement Algorithms for Virtual Storage Computers"* IBM Sys. J. 5,2 (1966), 78-101.

[C1] Coffman, E.G. Jr, and Denning, P.J.,*"Operating Systems Theory"* Prentice-Hall, 1973

[D1] Denning, P.J., *"Virtual Memory"* Comp . Surveys 2,3 (sept. 1970), 153-189.

[G1] Gelenbe, E., Lenfant, J. and Potier D., *"Analyse d'un algorithme de gestion simultanée mémoire centrale - Disque de pagination"*, Acta Informatica, Vol. 3, Fasc. 4 (1974).

[M1] Mattson, R.L., Gecsei, J., Slutz, D.R., and Traiger, I.L., *"Evaluation techniques for storage hierarchies"*, IBM Sys. J. 9,2 (1970), 78-117.

[S1] Schemer, J.E. and Shippey, B, *"Statistical analysis of paged and segmented computer systems"*, IEEE Tr. Comp. EC-15, 6 (Dec. 1966), 855-863.

[T1] Thorington, J.M. and Irwin, J.D., *"An adaptative replacement algorithm for paged-memory systems"* IEEE Tr. Comp. C-21, 10 (Oct. 1972), 1053-1061.

THE LOGIC OF PROTECTION

L. Kohout[*†]
[†]University College Hospital
Medical School,
University of London, U.K.

B.R. Gaines[*]
[*]Man-Machine Systems Laboratory,
Dept. of Electrical Engineering Science,
University of Essex, Colchester, U.K.

Abstract This paper presents a brief exposition of the role of various mathematical techniques in the development and utilization of resource protection structures for computers. The first section is concerned with the semantics of the problem - the distinction between protection problems in general and those whose complexity necessitates deeper theoretical treatment. The second section considers the roles of algebraic, topological, and modal/multi-valued logic, techniques in the analysis of protection. Finally we give an analysis of a current protection model to illustrate the problems and techniques.

1. The Problem of Protection

1.1 Introduction

The protection of the security of potentially shared resources, both information and activities, has become a problem of major interest in computer science and engineering. Fundamentally the problem is not different from those of personal, commercial and government security in the pre-computer era - the differences are quantitative ones of monitoring electronic activities whose speed, magnitude and inaccessibility far exceed the human transactions they mimic. Technically, aspects of security peculiar to computer-based systems may be seen to arise with the early time-sharing systems such as CTSS and MAC [1] which broke away from batch-processing of naturally isolated jobs and allowed users to share not only basic resources like storage and processing power but also to access joint data bases and processes for mutual interaction in real time. It was the announcement of the MULTICS [2] project in 1964, particularly the discussion of its aims and objectives in a group of 6 papers at the 1965 FJCC, that awoke the computer community at large to the new technical problems, as well as the new potentialities, of systems accessed simultaneously by multiple, competing and collaborating, users. Even at this early stage the social implications of such systems were discussed [3] and these have become a matter of increasing public concern in recent years [4,5].

Thus protection has arisen as an important and distinct problem in its own right. It is closely associated with many of the technical problems of operating systems, e.g. ensuring the correct functioning of co-operating sequential processes [6], but these may be seen as prerequisites to the implementation of protection rather than central to the problem itself. Equally the availability of adequate protection structures is itself a prerequisite to the full exploitation of techniques of modular [7] or structured [8] programming. Perhaps the neatest way to make the distinction is to note that the natural logics of protection are not the Boolean algebras so basic to computers, but rather the modal logics [9,10] of possibility and necessity (alethic), permission and obligation (deontic) - for example, we typically wish to know whether it is possible for a process which is permitted to access a data structure, but obliged to obey certain synchronization disciplines in changing it, to avoid these, or whether they are necessarily obeyed (hardware enforced). Ensuring that the disciplines are available (e.g. through semaphore mechanisms) and using them to ensure a formal and enforceable match to the problem structure (e.g. a hierarchy of processes) are not strictly part of the problem of protection itself. The central problem is that of the logic of protection, its consistency and its implications in particular implementations. This would be a comparatively straightforward problem were it not for the extremely dynamic nature of the environment in which the logic operates.

1.2 Motivation and Structure of Paper

This paper presents a brief exposition of the role of various mathematical techniques in the development and utilization of resource protection structures for computers. On the one hand we are concerned to present the problem as a new systems area, similar in status to such areas as identification, stability and control, and worthy of the attention of theorists. On the other hand we are concerned to investigate the nature and magnitude of practical requirements for, the current implementations of, protection structures to ensure that theoretical developments have a proper and useful semantics.

The studies reported arose from our experience in the design of a descriptor-organized minicomputer [11,12] in which the full power of hardware-enforced ring crossing processes may be invoked by procedure calls in high-level languages [13]. We became aware of the potential for essentially simple protection mechanisms to lead to complex dynamic problems that defied human intuition, and were led to investigate the applicability of logical [14] and topological [15] models of the phenomena involved. We found there to be a conflict between the essential simplicity of use of protection mechanisms in most current systems, and the theoretical complexity that could arise. The resolution is probably that the use of the capabilities of computers to administrate large organizations in a totally integrated fashion [16] is rare as yet. Most users of computer utilities still use them for economic reasons only and require a null-relationship of total confinement with other users.

The place of more complex analyses of protection is discussed in the following section. The middle section is concerned with the interplay between algebraic, topological and logical techniques in this problem area, and serves to introduce the final section which presents an example of their relative roles in relation to a model of protection based on that of Graham and Denning [17]. It is inappropriate in this paper to attempt to survey the many contributions to the protection literature, and we refer the reader to truly excellent recent survey of Popek [18] which lists some 84 references.

2. The Semantics of Protection Structures

2.1 Is There a Problem ?

Before any theorist moves in with an armoury of mathematical techniques it behoves him to ensure that the enemy actually exists and that he is not finally solely engaged in grappling with his own terminological obscurity. Any computer manager will confirm that his installation has a security problem. However his anecdotal reports are more likely to demonstrate human errors, software bugs and design faults, rather than any deep and elaborate failures. His problem is still security in the negative sense of containment, and the hardware mechanisms of most commonly used machines are designed with this in mind.

Even MULTICS, with its objectives of supporting collaborative user communities, is based on a simple linear order of protection rings of monotonically decreasing capability which it is simple to express logically. It allows users to share, or not to share, major data objects but does not realistically support more subtle interactions between them. The wide use of computer systems with far less complex protection facilities than MULTICS is evidence that a substantial part of the user community can get by without such subtlety for their current activities. This does not prevent them being adversely affected when manufacturers attempt to incorporate it, unsuccessfully, in their operating systems, but it indicates that we have to search with care for the positive requirements.

2.2 Capabilities and the Graham and Denning Model

A key paper in expressing these positive requirements and mechanisms for their satisfaction is that by Lampson [19] who introduces the term capability for the access right that a process may possess to an object, a generalized resource. Capabilities are themselves protected objects which may be created and passed between objects only according to prescribed rules. Graham and Denning [17] make explicit appropriate rules for the manipulation of capabilities in a second key paper. It is important to note that although these papers have abstracted the protection problem with a high degree of generality, the exemplary semantics given is still very simple (in terms of capabilities to read and write into files) and many basic problems are deliberately excluded (for example, access to data being dependent on its value). The concluding paragraph of [17, p.428] is particularly important in summarizing the state of the art.

Hardware realizations of capability-based protection structures are being developed [20] and at least one commercial machine is now in production [21]. The Graham and Denning model clearly merits investigation and extension in its own right [22]. However, the semantics provided by current protection hardware and even advanced operating systems is probably inadequate to justify such an investigation and certainly inadequate to assess the results. We can find a far richer semantics in the problems of large data-bases and information systems.

2.3 Data-Bases and Data-Interrupts

A key paper on data-base protection is that by Conway, Maxwell and Morgan [23] who consider security requirements in practical information systems such as personnel records. Here the units which must be protected are far smaller than those previously considered, being individual fields in a single record rather than complete files of information. Equally importantly the rights to access certain fields may be dependent on the data stored in these or other fields of the record. Thus a typical protection predicate might be: "an assistant manager may read the personnel records except medical history of employees in his division with salaries of less than $30,000". This level of detail coupled with the size of the data-base provides far richer and more complex examples of protection predicates than does that on operating systems.

What these examples lack, however, is the dynamic complexity of operating systems in which the protected objects are not only passive data items but also active processes which themselves initiate further activities and accesses to protected items. This may be introduced into the data-base problem by considering a suggestion of Morgan [24] of "an interrupt based organisation for management information systems" in which a predicate on the values of data items may be used to invoke a process. For example, an inventory control system might have processes attached to variables indicating stock levels that automatically re-order items if the stock falls below a prescribed level. Zelkowitz [25] has suggested a hardware implementation of this mechanism on the IBM360 and it is feasible with any tagged [26] or descriptor-based [11] machine in which the tags are retained in file structures.

Examples of data-interrupts in use are currently probably found only in such "artificial intelligence" languages as CONNIVER [27]. However, the use of "data-base-driven" processes is very much in line with concepts of modular programming [7] since they allow an activity dependent upon the value of a variable to be implemented as a single independent module rather than incorporated as conditional calls in every routine that may update that variable. They have a natural place in languages such as POP2 [28] and EL1 [29] which allow an "updater", or type-coercion routine, to be associated with an individual variable. Their availability is particularly attractive in quite simple transaction-processing systems where on-line users access the same data-base, e.g. dealing systems [30], since all activities naturally centre around, and are driven by, the state of the data-base. Whilst the hardware necessary to implement the data-interrupt is comparatively new, we have reported elsewhere [31] the practical success of commercial and medical transaction-processing systems based on the interpretation of a high-level language on a minicomputer, and are currently extending the facilities to include data-interrupts, a simple extension to an interpretive language.

2.4 Summary

Thus a combination of the finely detailed, data-dependent protection requirements of data-base systems together with the dynamic protection requirements of data-interrupt driven systems provides a far richer semantics for models of protection than does the conventional "operating-system" requirements, and one that is both generated by current needs and is feasible in many applications with current hardware/ software technology. The potential of such systems is well beyond our current intuitive conceptions of what computer systems can do. The possibility of adding arbitrary distinct processes, "unknown" to one another but mutually interacting through changes in state of a common data base, allows a far more natural development of a system, based on mimicing the activities of individuals in an organisation. Equally such a system may grow rapidly beyond the comprehension of its designers since the addition of a new activity may invoke a host of natural side-effects which have no referents whatsoever in the new activity itself. The problem of ensuring adequate security whilst at the same time taking full advantage of the mutual collaboration possible will become acute.

3. The Mathematics of Protection

3.1 The Roles of Different Formal Models

The natural representation of a protection structure relating processes to capabilities, adopted for example in both our key references [17,23], is that of a matrix expressing the (algebraic) relation between them. Such relations, expressed as matrices, can also model the dynamics of protection, the permission to pass a capability to another process, etc. The overall model obtained is naturally automata-theoretic with its analytic basis being clearly algebraic.

The algebraic model itself has a direct application to questions about procedures to follow in attaining certain aims. "How do I write into file A", is answered by enumerating trajectories of communication through processes which do not violate the protection. There may be none (not allowed), a unique solution or many possibilities with different properties. This corresponds to a control problem in the state space of the protection automaton.

However, many of the major questions of security are not of this nature but relate more to global properties of reachability, "can any of these processes access this information", "is this process contained in this domain". Such questions are naturally ones of closure [15] and best treated within a topological framework. They may be seen as stability problems in the state space of the protection automaton.

The actual closure spaces generated by any particular protection structure should reflect the intentions of users in setting it up. There are direct formal relations between such spaces and modal logics [32,33] so that the semantics of the model may be expressed in a communicable form. It is easier to understand, "it is desirable to do X and it is permissible to do Y but the system will not allow you to do Z", or, more globally, "the protection system of the HCN471 will not allow the user to follow this desirable practice and is dependent upon him obeying these rules", rather than "$X \in S_a(U)$, $Z \in S - S_c(U)$", or, "the HCN471 has no compatible closure relation".

In practice although both topological and modal logic techniques and vocabularies are useful, any real protection structure will be finite and users will tend to superimpose on it a readily understood structure of nested protection domains. The many-valued logics thus generated may be formally regarded as finite approximations to modal logics [32], and are an alternative natural expression of hierarchical, ordered structures (e.g. protection rings).

From a category-theoretic point of view [34,35,36] these distinctions are purely ones of terminology and perhaps the ultimate abstraction of protection structures should be expressed categorically. However, although the old lines of demarcation no longer exist, the old terminologies are still evocative and what is clumsily expressed in one may become quite elegant and transparent in another. Thus, in summary, we see the appropriate use of mathematical tools in the study of protection to be:

Algebraic formulation of protection axioms → topological formulation of closure properties → modal logics of resultant spaces → multi-valued logic representation in finite matrices.

3.2 The Graham and Denning Model

As noted in section 2.2 the best developed formal model of protection is that presented in [17], and we have based our analysis in the following section upon this. Briefly, Graham and Denning distinguished "subjects" which are active entities (a process and domain of access to resources) and "objects" which are essentially resources to which access must be controlled - a "subject" is also an "object". They represent a protection structure as a matrix of subjects against objects giving the access rights of each subject to the objects (including other subjects), together with a set of rules for changing the matrix (e.g. by adding or deleting subjects and objects).

The elements in the matrix form "capabilities" (an access right by a subject to an object) and the dynamics of the model arise to a large extent because capabilities can be passed from subject to subject. It is possible to treat the right to pass a capability (the "copy flag" in [17]) itself as a capability and such generality is desirable for theoretical compactness. However, in explaining the model it is useful to separate out the protection matrix from its dynamics and we introduce a pass as the right to pass a capability, and a permit as the right to give this right - further recursive extension is unnecessary to the example.

One extension we have not made in our analysis is to consider relationships and interactions between capabilities. In management information systems it is unlikely that the capabilities would be themselves simple, unitary actions. Rather they would reflect the fine structure of possible actions so that a major action, such as writing into a record, would be possible only to the possessor of multiple capabilities. Equally the act of so doing is likely to be necessarily accompanied by other acts, e.g. associated with transaction monitoring. This implies that there will be rather more complex relationship between capabilities and actions than is assumed in any current model, but the extension to allow for this is straightforward. The only remark we make for the moment is that the algebraic structure of interaction between capabilities must be positive (in the sense of [37, p.125]), i.e. one capability cannot cancel another out. This is implicit in the literature, but it is tempting in extending the models to add "anti-capabilities" (for example to allow a user of a subsystem to ensure that it is "memoryless" by removing its access to certain channels of communication). Non-positive capabilities make nonsense of the use of closures, and do not seem to have a proper place in the semantics of protection.

Two further concepts are necessary which are relevant to the use of Graham and Dennings model rather than its structure. Some ("privileged") subjects will have capabilities that would show up as dangerous in any analysis but which they will not use. We introduce an intention matrix that specifies what ones will be used. This enables the closures computed to reflect relationships of trust between subjects. In analysing his protection a user would adjust an intention matrix to specify his own use of capabilities (assuming other users have malicious intentions) and a trust matrix to prevent non-significant paths for protection failure being continually drawn to his attention, but both may be represented in the model as a single matrix.

4. One Formal Model of Protection

4.1 A Concrete Example

The terminology of the following sections would be opaque without some concrete examples. Unfortunately examples tend to be either trivial or too lengthy in description. The following artificial situation has been generated to serve as a basis for illustrating each technique discussed.

Start of example The company X runs a network of data processing systems. The basic flow of information is shown in Fig. 1: the system x can directly inspect x1 and x2, and indirectly inspect x3 and x4 or x5 via x1 and x2, respectively. In addition to this fixed hierarchical flow, the systems can exchange information within the network according to certain dynamic relations.

The type of problem we shall study is that there is exchange of information with similar systems operated by competitors: x5 with y5 of company Y and x4 with z5 of company Z. Y and Z must not obtain the information in x, x1 or x2 at the same time, although each part of the information on its own, or combinations at different times (say more than t a part) are harmless. The information flow is fully defined by a sequence of action, pass and permission relations. Computationally these might be represented as (sparse) matrices but for this text we shall work with the relations.

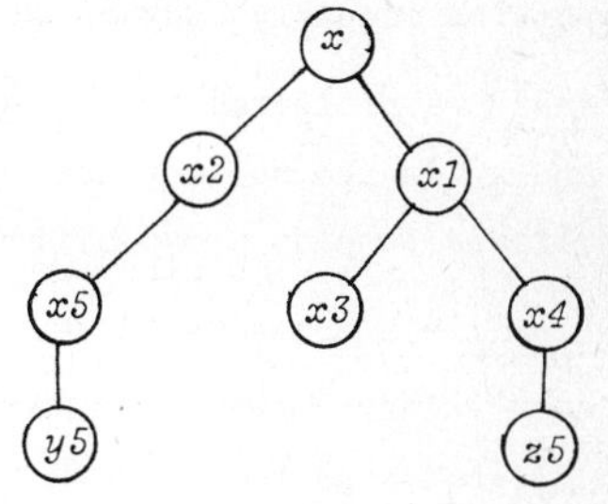

Figure 1 Data-Processing Network

4.2 Terminology and Definitions

In our terminology, we shall stress the dynamical character of protection.

Participants - abstract elements of a protection structure, which can be either subjects or objects. The set of all participants will be denoted by $X = \{x_1, x_2, \ldots\ldots, x_n\}$.

An object - a participant, manipulation of which must be controlled.

Subject - an active participant whose manipulation of objects must be controlled.

A participant x_j can simultaneously be a subject with respect to the object x_i and an object with respect to the subject x_k.

Action - certain precisely specified behaviour of participants. A subject acts on an object, and an object is manipulated by a subject. (Examples of action: read, write, seek, execute, etc.).

Activity - a sequence of actions with some unambiguously specified purpose.

Aim - an a priori specified (required) result of a sequence of actions, which form a particular activity. Note that a specific action can enter as a component into the formation of two or several distinct activities.

Aim controllable by a group of subjects X_t - an aim which can be achieved by a sequence of actions exclusively performed by the group X_t.

Aim protectable by a group of subjects X_t - an aim which cannot be achieved by an activity outside X_t without the specific permission of the group X_t.

It is important to realise that a certain specific action can form two or more distinct activities, or can contribute to the fulfilling of two distinct aims. Hence there may exist two different and often contradictory requirements of the protection in a case where the same action is a component of two distinct activities.

Action matrix - for an action α_i is defined by a relation $R_{\alpha_i}(x_j,x_k)$ between participants from {X}.

Capability - a protected name, a pair $\langle\alpha_i,x_j\rangle$ where α_i is an action and x_j is an object. A subject x_k has the capability $\langle\alpha_i,x_j\rangle$ if it can perform the action α_i on the object x_j.

A subject can pass a capability it holds to another subject. This action must be properly controlled. For this purpose we shall introduce

Pass - a protected name, a pair $\langle\langle\alpha_i,x_j\rangle,x_k\rangle$ where $\langle\alpha_i,x_j\rangle$ specifies the capability and x_k is the subject holding the pass. A pass signifies that a subject x_k is allowed to pass a capability.

Permit - a protected name, a pair, $\langle\langle\alpha_i,x_j\rangle,x_k\rangle$ where $\langle\alpha_i,x_j\rangle$ specifies the capability to which the pass refers and x_k is the subject which holds the permit; $\langle\langle\alpha_i,x_j\rangle,x_k\rangle$ signifies that the subject x_k can give the permission to pass the capability $\langle\alpha_i,x_j\rangle$.

4.3 Algebraic Models

An abstract algebraic model used for the investigation of the dynamics of protection structures, is formed by relations expressing the mutual dependencies of subjects and objects as well as relationships of capabilities, passes and permits.

The set A of all actions α_i, which are elements of an activity Z_k is denoted by:

$$A(Z_k) = \{\alpha_1,\alpha_2, \ldots\ldots,\alpha_\omega\}$$

The structure of an action α_1 can be described by the triple of relations $R_{\alpha_i}, R_{\phi_i}, R_{\pi_i}$:

$$R_{\alpha_i} = R_{\alpha_i}(x_k,x_l) \qquad R_{\phi_i} = R_{\phi_i}(x_k,x_j,x_m) \qquad R_{\pi_i} = R_{\pi_i}(x_k,x_j,x_m)$$

The relation R_{α_i} defines the subject-object relationship and specifies the capabilities of a set of subjects $\{sub\} \subset \{X\}$ to perform the action α_i on the set of objects $\{ob\} \subset \{X\}$.

The ternary relation R_{ϕ_i} specifies which subject x_k can pass the capability $\langle\alpha_i,x_m\rangle$, $x_m \varepsilon \{ob\}$ to a subject x_j. The ternary relation R_{π_i} specifies which subject x_k can give permission to copy the pass $\langle\langle\alpha_i,x_m\rangle,x_j\rangle$, $x_m\varepsilon\{ob\}$, $x_j\varepsilon\{sub\}$.

Each ternary relation R_{ϕ_i}, R_{π_i} can be expressed as a set of binary relations:

$$R_{\phi_i}(sub_1, sub_2, ob_m) \equiv \{R_{\phi_i,ob_1}(sub_1, sub_2), R_{\phi_i,ob_2}(sub_1, sub_2), \ldots \ldots, R_{\phi_i,ob_\alpha}(sub_1, sub_2)\}$$

where $m = 1,2,3,\ldots\alpha$; sub_1, sub_2, ob_m ε {X}. Similar expressions hold for R_{π_i}.

The relations which have been so far described deal with permissions. However, it seems necessary to introduce structures which can describe the intentions of the participants, as well as the permissions. This can be exemplified by the following example. Let us consider the permission which is described by the transfer rule R1 of Graham and Denning. The rule R1 permits a subject to transfer any capability it holds to any other subject, provided the donor has the corresponding pass (which is realised in the scheme as a copy flag). Without the introduction of some further structures we can investigate only the case where the intention of each subject with the appropriate pass is to give capabilities to all subjects. This limit case describes only the minimal restrictions which are enforced by the permission rules but not the actual state of the protection system in the case that the participants do not reach the limits forced by the permission rules.

However, this is required by a user who would like to find out how he should pass his capabilities and avoid some unwanted side effects.

Now we shall introduce a formal definition of a model of protection structures. It will be shown later (section 5) that the model can be interpreted as a <u>hierarchy of sequential machines</u>.

<u>Definition</u>

A model $\mathcal{M}(Z_k)$ of an activity Z_k is composed of the set of triples:

$$\mathcal{M}(Z_k) = \left\langle R_{A(Z_k)}, \Phi_{Z_k}, \Psi_{Z_k} \right\rangle = \left\{ \left\langle R_{\alpha_i}, \Phi_i, \Psi_i \right\rangle \right\}_{i=0}^{i=\omega}$$

where α_i runs over the set $A(Z_k)$ of all actions, which are the elements of the activity Z_k; i.e. $A(Z_k) = \{\alpha_1, \alpha_2, \alpha_3, \ldots, \alpha_\omega\}$.

$\Phi_i = \left\langle R_{\phi_i}, R_{\pi_i} \right\rangle$ belongs to the <u>permission structure</u> Φ_{Z_k}.

$\Psi_i = \left\langle R_{\gamma_i}, R_{\sigma_i} \right\rangle$ belongs to the <u>intention structure</u>.

The relation R_{γ_i} defines the interrelations between the intended passes, and R_{σ_i} between the intended permits in a way which is analogical to the definitions for the permission structure Φ_i. The difference between Φ_i and Ψ_i is only in the semantics.

In general, changes in the structure can be made by actions ϕ_i which operate on Φ_{Z_k} and which change the $R_{A(Z_k)}$ or by actions ψ_i which operate on Ψ_{Z_k} and change Φ_{Z_k}.

A <u>trajectory</u> of $\mathcal{M}(Z_k)$ is an admissible sequence of actions $\alpha_i \alpha_j \psi_i \phi_r \alpha_k \ldots \alpha_j \psi_i \phi_r \ldots \alpha_k \ldots$.

The <u>dynamics of a participant</u> is the current state of the vector

$$\mathrm{Dyn}_{Z_k}(x_k) = \left\{ \left\langle \alpha_i(x_k), \phi_i(x_k), \pi_i(x_k), \gamma_i(x_k), \sigma_i(x_k) \right\rangle \right\}_{i=1}^{i=\omega}$$

Only certain sequences of actions are admissible. The admissibility of sequences must be specified by some additional rules which depend on the type of activity and on the character of actions.

Example Continued - *the set of all actions* $A(Z_k) = \{\alpha_1, \alpha_2, \phi_1, \pi_1\}$

α_1 ..... *inspect data* ϕ_1 ..... *pass the capability inspect data*

α_2 ..... *record data* π_1 ..... *permit to pass the capability inspect data*

capabilities are defined by the action relations:

R_{α_1} = {(x,x), (x,x1), (x,x2), (x1,x1), (x1,x3), (x1,x4), (x2,x2), (x2,x5), (x3,x3), (x4,x4), (x5,x3), (x5,x5)}

R_{α_2} = {(x2,x2), (x3,x3), (x3,x5), (x5,x5)}

passes are defined by $\{R_{\phi_{1,x}}, R_{\phi_{1,x1}}, R_{\phi_{1,x2}}\} \equiv R_{\phi_1}$ *where*

$R_{\phi_{1,x}}$ = {(x,x1)}; $R_{\phi_{1,x1}}$ = {(x,x3)}; $R_{\phi_{1,x2}}$ = {(x,x5)}

permit is defined by $R_{\pi_{1,x1}}$ = {(x3,x4)}

model of an activity $\mathcal{M}(Z_k) = \{R_{\alpha_1}, R_{\alpha_2}, \Phi_1, \Psi_1\}$ *where*

$\Phi_1 = \{ \langle R_{\alpha_{1,x}}, R_{\alpha_{1,x1}}, R_{\alpha_{1,x2}} \rangle, R_{\pi_{1,x1}} \} \equiv \{R\Phi_1, R\Pi_1\}$

$\Psi_1 = \mathbb{1}$ *(universal relation , i.e. every element is in relation to all others)*

The intention structure in this example is the universal relation, which means that the intention of the participants is to go to the limits which are permitted by the permission structure. (Note that only the passes and permits which are related in the permission as well as in the intention structure can be used - the disjunction of the structures).

The trajectory $\alpha_1\alpha_2\phi_1$ *is the sequence of the following actions:*

(inspect) (record) (modify the R_{α_1} *according to the pass relation* $R\Psi$*)*

Let us choose the initial dynamics of the participant x1

$Dyn_{Z_k}(x1) = \{ \alpha_1(x1), \Phi_1(x1), \pi_1(x1) \}$ *where the ranges of the relations are*

$\alpha_1(x1)$ = {x1,x3,x4} ; $\phi_1(x1)$ = {(x,x1),(x,x3)} ; $\pi_1(x1)$ = {(x3,x4)} ;

If the action ϕ_1 *is applied, it causes the following changes:*

$\alpha_1(x1)$ = {x,x1,x3,x4}

Now, if the action π_1 *is applied, then* $\phi_1(x)$ = {(x,x1),(x,x3),(x3,x4)}.

4.5 Rules for Composition of Actions

Rules for composition of actions entering into an activity Z_k cannot be

entirely arbitrary. The set of admissible sequences of actions is determined by the type of activity and by the objectives of protection. However, it should be noticed, that the rules of composition also depend on the characteristics of a protected system. Let us take as an example the action 'read'. The previously quoted statement of Graham and Denning " ... reading implies ... the ability to read and copy file ..." means that in the system they had in mind the capability 'read' is equal to the capability 'read/write' in certain activities. We can, of course, design a monitor which would allow us to introduce the capability 'read' without the above mentioned unwanted consequences. From this example we can make some fairly general conclusions, which have impact not only on the design of protection structures as such, but what is more important, on the design of the whole system. That is, elementary actions should be chosen in such a way as to limit the consequences of uncontrollable transitivity of actions.

Now we shall introduce an appropriate semantics into our model in order to be able to handle this problem. An action of one participant upon another is called a direct action if there is no other participant involved as a mediator. An indirect action is an action in which a participant achieves certain aims with respect to another participant through a third participant or through a chain of participants.

Let x_i perform an action α_k on x_j, defined by $R_{\alpha_k}(x_i,x_j)$. We shall abbreviate this by $(x_i \xrightarrow{\alpha_k} x_j)$. Then we can give the following reduction rules, where the symbol o means the composition of actions:

$$\frac{(x_i \xrightarrow{\alpha_r} x_j) \circ (x_j \xrightarrow{\alpha_r} x_k)}{(x_i \xrightarrow{\alpha_r'} x_k)}$$

a transitive action which composed gives an indirect action α_r'; note that the direct action $(x_i \xrightarrow{\alpha_r} x_k)$ is not always defined.

$$\frac{(x_i \xrightarrow{\alpha_r} x_j) \circ (x_j \xrightarrow{\alpha_r} x_k)}{(x_j \xrightarrow{\alpha_r} x_j) \vee (x_j \xrightarrow{\alpha_r} x_j)}$$

an intransitive action either $(x_i \xrightarrow{\alpha_r} x_j)$ or $(x_j \xrightarrow{\alpha_k} x_k)$ or both

More generally:

$$\frac{(x_i \xrightarrow{\alpha_r} x_j) \circ (x_j \xrightarrow{\alpha_s} x_k)}{(x_i \xrightarrow{\alpha_p} x_k)}$$

$$\frac{(x_i \xrightarrow{\alpha_r} x_j) \circ (x_j \xrightarrow{\alpha_s} x_k)}{(x_i \xrightarrow{\alpha_r} x_j) \vee (x_j \xrightarrow{\alpha_s} x_k)}$$

Again similar rules can be given for passes and permits.

The action α_1 (inspect data) is not transitive and a corresponding indirect action cannot be formed by a simple composition of two direct actions α_1. For example, taking the subjects x,x2,x5, we get:

$$\frac{(x \xrightarrow{\alpha_1} x2) \circ (x2 \xrightarrow{\alpha_1} x5)}{(x \xrightarrow{\alpha_1} x2) \vee (x2 \xrightarrow{\alpha_1} x5)}$$

The action α_2 (record data) has different properties. For example, if x3 *records data into x5, and x5 into x2 consequently, then x2 owns the data of x3 although x3 cannot write into x2. This is an example of the indirect action* α_2'. *Take the participants x2,x3,x5 and look at the reduction rules:*

$$\frac{(x3 \xrightarrow{\alpha_2} x5) \circ (x5 \xrightarrow{\alpha_2} x2)}{(x3 \xrightarrow{\alpha_2} x2)}$$

The indirect action α_1' *(inspect data of ...) can be formed by the composition of* α_1 *and* α_2. *For example, if x3 records its information into x5 and x2 inspects x5, then x2 is able to inspect indirectly x3. Let us look at some interesting cases: for the activity* $\alpha_2\alpha_1$ *we get:*

$$\frac{(x3 \xrightarrow{\alpha_2} x5) \circ (x2 \xrightarrow{\alpha_1} x5)}{(x2 \xrightarrow{\alpha_1'} x3)} \qquad \textit{(indirect } \alpha_1'\textit{)}$$

but for the activity $\alpha_1\alpha_2$:

$$\frac{(x2 \xrightarrow{\alpha_1} x5) \circ (x3 \xrightarrow{\alpha_2} x5)}{(x2 \xrightarrow{\alpha_1} x5) \vee (x3 \xrightarrow{\alpha_2} x5)} \qquad \textit{(no indirect action)}$$

Following is the result of the activity $\alpha_1\alpha_2\alpha_1$:

$$\frac{(x5 \xrightarrow{\alpha_1} x3) \circ (x5 \xrightarrow{\alpha_2} x5) \circ (x2 \xrightarrow{\alpha_1} x5)}{(x2 \xrightarrow{\alpha_1'} x3)} \qquad \textit{(indirect action)}$$

5. Hierarchical Structure of the Protection Model and its Description by Systems of Logic and Topology

The crucial feature of the model $\mathfrak{M}(Z_k)$ is the highly specific hierarchical interrelation of its composing structures which forms a hierarchy of sequential machines. This static hierarchical structure as well as the dynamics of the model can be expressed in modal or many-valued logics or by general topological structures which can be made mutually interchangeable. It is necessary to distinguish three qualitatively different actions in the sequence of admissible actions: firstly, actions of subjects on objects, as they are enabled by capabilities, secondly, actions of subjects on other subjects which amount to the passing of capabilities, and thirdly, actions of subjects on other subjects which permit the transfer of passes. Hence, three qualitatively distinct levels appear in the dynamics of the whole model, as well as in the dynamics of the individual participants. This becomes obvious if the last statement is re-interpreted in terms of abstract automata.

The relation between subjects and objects which is described by the R_α of the model, represents in these terms a finite-state automaton, acceptor, which accepts all admissible sequences of α-actions. The set of all participants represents states and the transitions are represented by individual actions on participants. Similar finite-automata describe the R_ϕ and R_γ components of the model (passes). If the R_ϕ and R_γ both accept an action, which means the passing of a capability, the structure of the R_α will be modified i.e. a new transition added into the R_α automaton. At the same time, if the automata corresponding to R_π and R_σ accept the same action, the permitted passes and intended passes will be modified (i.e.) new transition added into R_ϕ and R_γ automata respectively.

5.1 Topological Models

As we stated above (section 3.1), questions about behaviour of participants and about possible violations of protection can be formulated in terms of reachability and controllability in the state-space of a protection automaton. Reachability and controllability can be discussed in terms of generalised closures in extended topologies [15] which have been shown to be semantic models of some modal logics [32], [33]. The considerable advantage of the topological approach consists in the fact that the topological structure 'forgets' parts of the automata structure which are inessential to the dynamics of the behaviour of participants. We can look at the behaviour either of mutually suspicious groups of processes, or of several rival groups inside which the member participants cooperate etc.

We shall use some elements of the theory of generalised (extended) topology in the sequel, the basic definitions of which are given in [15] together with more details and an extensive annotated bibliography on the subject.

Closures in generalised topologies offer a tool for investigation of the dynamics of protection as well as of its limit case established for infinite strings of admissible actions.

The basic element of the topological model is the direct action (pass, permit) closure $\alpha_i(f_i,g_i,r_i,s_i)$ generated by the action α_i. It is defined as a mapping on the power set of all participants:

$$\alpha_i : \mathcal{P}(X) \rightarrow \mathcal{P}(X) \qquad \alpha_i(A) = \mathop{\mathcal{E}}_{x_j \varepsilon A} \alpha_i(x_j) = \mathop{\mathcal{E}}_{\alpha_i}(A) \qquad A \subset \{X\}$$

It represents the set of all participants (objects in this case) which can be acted on by the subset A of the set of all participants by a direct action α_i in a particular activity.

An important closure derived from the direct closure action closure is the AIOU-modification [15] of the given A-topology. For this (transitive) closure the important U-axiom $u(u(x_i)) = u(x_i)$ holds. In terms of control and automata theory it is the <u>region of reachability</u> i.e. the limit case of propagation of the effect of particular action or a set of actions. In modal terms, it defines the <u>possibility</u> of the existence of the effect of a selected action on the participants which are members of that closure.

Propagation of the effect of a set of actions which is given by a particular trajectory of $\mathcal{M}(Z_k)$ (i.e. by a selected admissible sequence of actions) can be investigated using iterations of the above defined closures. The k-th iteration will be given by

$$c_i^k(A) = c_i(c_i^{k-1}(A)) \qquad c_i \varepsilon (a_i, f_i, g_i, r_i, s_i); \qquad A \subset \{X\}$$

<u>Example Continued</u>

We shall examine the direct closure a for the action α_1. We have already shown that the action α_1 is not transitive. Hence, the closure a will also determine the limit case of propagation of a_1 action. We shall list the closures of all *singletons of the example*

$a(x) = \{x, x1, x2\}$ $a(x2) = \{x2, x5\}$ $a(x4) = \{x4\}$

$a(x1) = \{x1, x3, x4\}$ $a(x3) = \{x3\}$ $a(x5) = \{x3, x5\}$

$a(X)$ is the set of all participants whose files can be inspected by X. Now, let the trajectory of the system be $\alpha_1\alpha_1\alpha_1 \ldots \alpha_1\phi_1\pi_1$, that is the pass is presented and a permit is given in this sequence. This will cause the following change in the closures from above:

$a(x1) = \{x, x1, x2, x4\}$ $a(x4) = \{x1, x4\}$

$a(x3) = \{x1, x3\}$ $a(x5) = \{x1, x3, x5\}$

Let us designate $\alpha = \alpha_1\alpha_1\alpha_1 \ldots \alpha_1\phi_1\pi_1$ and $\alpha_3 = \alpha_1\alpha_2$ then for the trajectory $\alpha\alpha_3$ we shall list the closures for all participants:

$a(x) = \{x, x1, x2\}$ $a(x2) = \{x2, x5\}$ $a(x4) = \{x1, x4\}$

$a(x1) = \{x, x1, x3, x4\}$ $a(x3) = \{x1, x3\}$ $a(x5) = \{x2, x3, x5\}$

The effect of the new application of the action $_3$ (i.e. the resulting trajectory $\alpha\alpha_3\alpha_3$) is computed by the second iteration $a(a(x_i)) = a^2(x_i)$. It will change the following closures:

$a^2(x2) = \{x, x1, x2, x3, x5\}$ $a^2(x3) = \{x, x1, x2, x3\}$ $a^2(x\ ) = \{x, x1, x2, x5\}$

For the third iteration (the trajectory $\alpha\alpha_3\alpha_3\alpha_3$) we get the changes:

$a^3(x) = \{x, x1, x2, x3, x5\} = a^3(x5) = a^3(x2)$ $a^3(x3) = \{x1, x3\}$

$a^3(x1) = \{x, x1, x3, x4\}$ $a^3(x3) = \{x1, x3\}$

Further iterations (applying α_3) will not change the closure. We can see that we have computed the transitive closure (the U-modification of the original topology). This determines the worst case of the security in the system.

From this last computation it can be seen that the requirement on the security specified in the above has been violated so that the competitors can obtain the content of the data files of x,x1,x2 from x5 at once. Hence, the permission structure has to be modified. This can be achieved e.g. by the elimination of the link (x2,x2) in R_{α_2}.

Then $a^3\{x5\} = \{x1, x2, x3, x5\}$.

5.2 Modal Logics

Detailed examination of the meaning of individual closures points at an interesting connection with modalities. For example a closure in the AIOU-modification of a topology describing the α-structures determines explicitly the set of subjects, i.e. it determines what is <u>possible</u> in certain situations. Similarly, different kinds of <u>possibilities</u> correspond to closures in other parts of the algebraic model (in permission and intention structures). It is obvious that, although formally the same in different parts of the model, the closures will express different grades of possibility according to the part of the model in which they appear. Apart from <u>alethic</u> modalities, there appear <u>deontic</u> modalities of permission and obligation. The intention structures are clearly connected with aims of subjects and this leads to yet another type of modality. However, each type of modality is not without relation to other types of modality and for this reason mixed modalities have to be introduced.

The algebraic method of McKinsey and Tarski, further extended by Lemmon [32], [33], provides a formal link between general topologies and modal logics. This approach can be extended to mixed modalities using results of [38] on lattices of topologies and modifications of generalised topologies [39], [15].

6. Computer-Aided Design of Protection Structures

The simple example developed through the paper clearly demonstrates great complexity of the dynamics of protection structures. Our proposed mathematical models would be an academic exercise, devoid of the relevance to the real world protection and security problems, if they were not directly amenable to computer-aided design. As a matter of fact, our search for computer-aided methods for analysis and synthesis of protection structures, has (amongst other reasons) motivated our choice of mathematical techniques. We shall briefly outline some computational aspects of our mathematical techniques in the next lines.

6.1 A Metalanguage of Protection Structures and Theorem Provers

The ultimate aim is to design a machine theorem prover of statements about protection structure. Alethic modalities are sufficient for this purpose for we are not directly concerned with psychology of a designer. Semantic studies of logic suitable for expressing scientific, technological and legal problems, especially the recent development of a "Calculus of Problems" [40] indicate that a S4 modal system may be sufficient for the study of the foundations of protection structures. Recently, very powerful mechanical proof techniques for modal logics have been developed, which are directly programmable on computers [10, p.12].

6.2 Computation of Dynamics of Protection Structures

The algebraic model (cf. 4.3), which is formed by a hierarchy of sequential machines, presents usual computational problems of combinatorial character which are encountered in automata theory.

By forming closures on the protection automata, we select only the information which is pertinent to the given question, reducing enormously computational complexity. Dynamics of actions can be comprehensively researched using iterations and modifications [15] of relevant topological spaces. Opting for these methods we eliminate exhaustive search for the sake of lattice structures and of iterations in lattices of topologies.

In the case where it is better to represent closures indirectly as possibilities in some modal logics, the techniques referred to in 6.1 above can be used. They are valid for very general modal systems [10].

The mechanical proof techniques for modal and many-valued logics, which are of very recent origin, and therefore very little known and largely unused in computing, supplied the main motivation for our uses of powerful logics. Their importance can be highlighted by a quotation from Snyder [10, p.12]:

"Proving theorems within a given system of logic involves following a straightforward mechanical procedure. ... The high adventure of seeking clever strategies for deductive proofs, and the concomitant satisfaction of finding such proofs and being able to claim new theorems, are lost in the present set of formal systems. Instead, the adventure of doing logic ... lies in the development of a variety of systems of logic for a variety of tasks".

7. Conclusions

At the current state of the art the conclusions one may draw are still best summed up by Graham and Denning's final paragraph [17], *"Our preliminary work has indicated that the abstractions formed in the modelling process are useful in themselves, and that the model provides a framework in which to formulate precisely previously vague questions. We hope this discussion will motivate others to undertake additional research in this area. Much needs to be done".* The combination of interests represented at this conference seems peculiarly well suited to taking up this problem.

8. Acknowledgement

We are very grateful to Peter Facey of this Laboratory for many strenuous discussions on the topic of protection.

9. References

1. R.M. Fano, "The MAC system: a progress report", in M.A. Fass and W.D. Wilkinson (eds) Computer Augmentation of Human Reasoning, Washington: Spartan Books, pp. 131-150, 1965.
2. E.I. Organick, The Multics System, MIT Press, 1972.
3. E.E. David and R.M. Fano, "Some thoughts about the social implications of accessible computing", AFIPS FJCC, vol. 27, pp. 243-247, Washington: Spartan Books, 1965.
4. A. Westin, Privacy and Freedom, New York: Atheneum, 1968.
5. A. Miller, The Assault on Privacy, University of Michigan Press, 1971.
6. E.W. Djikstra, "Cooperating sequential processes", in F. Genuys (ed.) Programming Languages, London: Academic Press, 1968.
7. J.B. Dennis, "Modularity", in F.L. Bauer (ed.) Advanced Course in Software Engineering, Lecture Notes in Economics and Mathematical Systems, vol. 81, pp. 128-182, Berlin, Springer-Verlag, 1973.
8. O.J. Dahl, E.W. Djikstra and C.A.R. Hoare, Structured Programming, London: Academic Press, 1972.
9. G.E. Hughes and M.J. Creswell, An Introduction to Modal Logic, London: Methuen, 1968.
10. D.P. Synder, Modal Logic, New York: Van Nostrand, 1971.
11. B.R. Gaines, P.V. Facey, F.K. Williamson and J.A. Maine, "Design objectives for a descriptor-organised minicomputer", Proc. EUROCOMP 74, pp. 29-45, London: Online Ltd, May 1974.
12. F.K. Williamson, B.R. Gaines, J.A. Maine and P.V. Facey, "A high-level minicomputer", IFIP, Stockholm, August 1974.
13. B.R. Gaines, M. Haynes and D. Hill, "Integration of protection and procedures in a high-level minicomputer", IEE Conf., London, November 1974.
14. L. Kohout, "The Pinkava many-valued complete logic systems and their application to the design of many-valued switching circuits", Proc. Int. Symp. on Multiple-Valued Logic, IEEE, pp. 261-284, May 1974.
15. L. Kohout, "Generalized topologies: works of the Čech topological school and their relevance to general systems", Int. J. General Systems, vol. 2, Jan. 1975, to appear.
16. "The plan for information society", Final Report of the Computerization Committee of the Japan Computer Usage Development Institute, Tokyo, 1972.
17. G.S. Graham and P.J. Denning, "Protection - principles and practice", AFIPS SJCC, vol. 40, pp. 417-429, 1972.
18. G.J. Popek, "Protection structures", Computer, vol. 7, pp. 22-23, June 1974.
19. B.W. Lampson, "Dynamic protection structures", AFIPS FJCC, vol. 35, pp. 27-38, 1969.
20. R.M. Needham, "Protection systems and protection implementations", AFIPS FJCC, vol. 41, pp. 572-578, New Jersey: AFIPS Press 1972.
21. D.M. England, "Architectural features of system 250", INFOTECH State of Art Report on Operating Systems, 1972.
22. A.K. Jones, "Protection in programmed systems", Ph.D. thesis, Carnegie-Mellon University, 1973.

23. R.W. Conway, W.L. Maxwell and H.L. Morgan, "On the implementation of security measures in information systems", Comm. ACM, vol. 15, pp. 211-220, 1972.
24. H.L. Morgan, "An interrupt-based organization for management information systems", Comm. ACM, vol. 13, pp. 734-739, 1970.
25. M. Zelkowitz, "Interrupt driven programming", Comm. ACM, vol. 14, pp. 417-418, 1971.
26. E.A. Feustel, "On the advantages of tagged architecture", IEEE Trans. Comp., vol. C-22, pp. 644-656, 1973.
27. G.J. Sussman and D.W. McDermott, "From PLANNER to CONNIVER - a genetic approach", AFIPS FJCC, vol. 41, pp. 1171-1179, New Jersey: AFIPS Press, 1972.
28. R.M. Burstall, J.S. Collins and R.J. Popplestone, Programming in POP-2, Edinburgh University Press, 1971.
29. B. Wegbreit, "The treatment of data types in EL1", Comm. ACM, vol. 17, pp. 251-264, 1974.
30. B.R. Gaines, P.V. Facey and J. Sams, "An interactive, display-based system for gilt-edged security broking", Proc. EUROCOMP 74, pp. 155-169, London: Online Ltd, May 1974.
31. B.R. Gaines and P.V. Facey, "Some experience in interactive systems development and application", Proc. IEEE, June 1975, to appear.
32. E.J. Lemmon, "Algebraic semantics for modal logics I", J. Sym. Logic, vol. 31, pp. 46-65, June 1966.
33. E.J. Lemmon, "Algebraic semantics for modal logics II", J. Sym. Logic, vol. 31, pp. 191-218, June 1966.
34. S. MacLane, Categories for the working mathematician, New York: Springer, 1971.
35. J.A. Goguen, "Semantics of computation", in Proc. 1st Int. Symp. on Category Theory Applied to Computation and Control, Massachusetts, February 1974.
36. A.A. Arbib and E.G. Manes, "Foundations of system theory", Automatica, vol. 10, pp. 285-302, 1974.
37. A. Eilenberg, Automata, Languages and Machines, vol. A, New York: Academic Press, 1974.
38. E. Čech, Topological Spaces, Academia, Prague & J. Wiley, Interscience, New York, 1966.
39. K. Koutský and M. Sekanina, "Modifications of Topologies", In: General Topology and its Relation to Modern Analysis and Algebra 1, (Proceedings of the Symposium Prague 1961). Academic Press, New York & Academia, Prague, 1962.
40. P. Materna, "On problems (semantic study)", Rozpravy Československé Akademie Věd, vol. 80, sešit 8, pp. 1-62, 1970. (Published by Academia, Prague).

A U T O R E N V E R Z E I C H N I S

Ammeraal, L.; Stichting Mathematisch Centrum, 2e Boerhaavenstraat 49 Amsterdam 1oo5

Ashenhurst, R.L. Institute for Computer Research, The University of Chicago, Chicago, Illinois USA

Baar, E.; Center for the Promotion of Computer in Civil Engineering, University of Liege, Quai Banning 6 B - 4ooo Liege

Bauer, F.L. München,

Biller, Institut für Informatik, Universität Stuttgart, 7 Stuttgart 1, Herdweg 51 Mitautor: Glatthaar, W.;

Bode, Arndt; Forschungsgruppe CUU, Justus-Liebig Universität, 63 Giessen, Roonstraße 31

Brandwajn, Alexandre; IRIA-LABORIA, Domaine de Voluceau, Rocquencourt, F - 7815o - Le Chesnay, France

v.Braunmühl, Burchhard; Gesellschaft für Mathematik und Datenverarbeitung, 53 Bonn, Schloß Birlinghoven

Brückner, Ingrid; Institut für Angewandte Mathematik, Technische Universität Braunschweig, 33 Braunschweig, Pockelstr.14

Coy, Wolfgang; Technische Hochschule, 61 Darmstadt, Magdalenenstr.11

Daquin, C.; 5 Rue Jean Bart 75oo6 Paris Mitautor: Girault C.

Dreckmann, K.H.; Betriebsforschungsinstitut GmbH, 4 Düsseldorf, Sohnstraße 65

Ecker, K.; Gesellschaft für Mathematik und Datenverarbeitung, 52o5 St. Augustin

Erbe, R.; IBM - Deutschland GmbH, Niederlassung Heidelberg Tiergartenstr. 15 Mitautor Walch, G.;

Feldmann, Harry; Universität Hamburg, Regionales Rechenzentrum, 2ooo Hamburg 13, Rothenbaumchaussee 81

Flick, Thomas; Technische Universität Berlin, Informatik Forschungsgruppe Fachbereich 2o, 1 Berlin 1o, Einsteinufer 35-37 Mitautor: Liebig, H.;

Frasson, Claude; 592 av. de la Libération, o67oo St. Laurent du Var, France

Gaines, B.R.; University of Essex, Department of Electrical Engineering Science, Wivenhoe Park, Colchester CO4 3SO

Ganzinger, Harald; Institut für Informatik der Technischen Universität 8 München 2, Arcisstr. 21

Gebhardt, Friedrich; Gesellschaft für Mathematik und Datenverarbeitung Institut für DV im Rechtswesen, 52o5 St.Augustin - 1, Postfach 124o

Genrich,

Grzymala-Busse W.Jerzy; Institute of Control Engineering, Technical University of Poznan, 6o-965 Poznan, Poland

Görke, Winfried; Institut für Informatik IV, der Universität Karlsruhe 1, Zirkel 2 (bzw. Postfach 638o)

Härder, Theo; Technische Hochschule Darmstadt, 61 Darmstadt, Hochschulstraße 1

Hansen, R.; Institut für Informatik und praktische Mathematik der Christian-Albrechts-Universität, 23oo Kiel, Olshausenstraße 4o-6o
Mitautor: Hoffmann, E.-G., Simon, C.;

Hultsch, H.; Institut für Kernphysik der Universität Mainz, 65 Mainz, Postfach 398o

Innes, D.R.; The University of Liverpool, Branlow Hill and Crown Street, P.O. Box 147, Liverpool L 69 3 BX
Mitautor: Leong, S.H., Langfield, M.D., Alty J.L.;

Kammerer, Peter; Fakultät für Informatik, Universität Karlsruhe, 75 Karlsruhe 1

Koch, Wilfried; Technische Universität Berlin, 1 Berlin-Charlottenburg, Ernst Reuter-Platz 8
Mitautor: Oeters Christoph

Kohuot, L.; University College Hospital, Medical School, University of London, U.K.

Kühn, Paul; Institut für Nachrichtenvermittlung und Datenverarbeitung, Universität Stuttgart, 7 Stuttgart

Leilich, H.O.; Institut für Datenverarbeitungsanlagen, Technische Universität Braunschweig, 33 Braunschweig

Levi, Giorgio; Istituto di Elaboraziane della Informazione, Via S. Maria 46, 561oo Pisa, Italy

Lewi, J.; Katholieke Universiteit Leuven, Fakulteit Toegenpaste Wetenschappen, Afdeling Toegepaste Wiskunde en Programmatie, Celestijnenlaan 2oo B
B - 3o3o Heverlee (België)
Mitautor: De Vlaminck, Huens, J., Mertens, P.;

Lockemann, Peter C.; Universität Karlsruhe, Fakultät für Informatik 75 Karlsruhe

Maiocchi, M.; Universita Degli Studio di Milano, Istituto di Scienze Fisiche "Aldo Pontremoli" Gruppo Elettronica e Cibernetica, Milano/Italien
Mitautor: Polillo, Roberto;

Meister, Bernd; IBM - Forschungslaboratorium, Säumerstr. 4
CH - 88o3 Rüschlikon/Schweiz

De Michelis, G.; Gruppa di Elettronica e Cibernetica, Istituto di Fisica, Via Viotti 5, 2o133 Milano/Italy
Mitautor: Simone, Carla;

Marini, D.; Gruppo di Elettronica e Cibernetica, Via Viotti 5, 2o133 Milano/Italy
Mitautor: Miglioli, P.A.; Ornaghi, M.;

Moraga, Claudio; Universität Dortmund, Abteilung Informatik I, 46 Dortmund - 5o, Postfach 5o o5 oo

Nawrot, P.; Hochschule Linz, Lehrkanzel für Informatik (Software) A - 4o45 Linz-Auhof
Mitautor: Rechenberg, Peter;

Nielinger, J.; CUU - Forschungsgruppe, Fachhochschule Furtwangen, 7743 Furtwangen/Schw.

Nijessen, G.M.; Control Data, Europe INC, Avenue des Arts 46, 1o4o Brussels/Belgium

Opp, Manfred; Universität Hamburg, Institut für Informatik, 2 Hamburg 13, Schlüterstraße 66-72

Petersen, H.; Forschungsgruppe 15 (spezielle Anwendungen) des ÜRF Informatik, TH - Aaachen, 51 Aachen, Seffenter Weg 32
Mitautor: Vorstädt, Norbert;

Priese, Lutz; Universität Dortmund, Fachgebiet Systemtheorie & -technik, 46 Dortmund - 5o, Postfach 5o o5 oo

Raulefs, Peter; Institut für Informatik I, Universität Karlsruhe, 75 Karlsruhe 1, Postfach 638o

Rennert, Paul; Hochschule für Sozial- und Wirtschaftswissenschaften, Institut für Informatik, A - 4o45 Linz-Auhof

Richter, Lut; Universität Dortmund, Abteilung Informatik III, 46 Dortmund - 5o, Postfach 5o o5 oo

Riedemann, Eike,Hagen; Universität Dortmund, Abteilung Informatik I, 46 Dortmund - 5o, Postfach 5o o5 oo

Rozenberg, G.; Department of Mathematics Antwerp University, UIA Wilnijk, Belgium

Schlageter, Gunter; Universität Karlsruhe, 75 Karlsruhe, Kollegium am Schloß, Bau IV

Schmid, Hans-Albrecht; Department of Computer Science University of Toronto, Toronto, Canada
Mitautor, Best, Eike;

Stewen, L.; Philips Forschungslaboratorium Hamburg GmbH, 2 Hamburg 54, Vogt-Kölln-Str. 3o

Straßer, W.;	Heinrich-Hertz-Institut für Schwingungsforschung, 1oo Berlin-Charlottenburg, Einsteinufer 37
Thimm, D.;	Institut für Informationsverarbeitung, TU - Berlin 1ooo Berlin
Trân - Quôc - Tê;	Institute de Informatique Facultes universitaires N.-D de la Paix, Namur, Belgium
Wätjen, Dietmar;	Lehrstuhl C für Informatik, TU - Braunschweig, 33oo Braunschweig, Gaußstr. 28
Zuse, K.;	6418 Hünfeld, Im Haselgrund 21